CONTEMPORARY
BUSINESS
COMMUNICATION

CONTEMPORARY BUSINESS COMMUNICATION

Louis E. Boone

Ernest G. Cleverdon Chair of Business and Management
University of South Alabama

David L. Kurtz

R.A. and Vivian Young Chair of Business Administration
University of Arkansas

Judy R. Block

President, JRB Communications, Inc.

Prentice Hall, Englewood Cliffs, New Jersey 07632

Acquisitions editor: Donald J. Hull
Development editor: Ronald Librach
Editorial / production supervisor: Mary Cavaliere
Interior design: Suzanne Behnke
Cover design: Wendy Helft, Design W
Cover photo: Carl Baker Photography
Editor in chief: Joe Heider
Editor in chief, College Book Development: Ray Mullaney
Managing production editors: Joyce Turner, Kris Ann Cappelluti
Supplements editor: David Shea
Formatting manager: Mary Araneo
Page formatters: John A. Nestor, David Tay, Michael Bertrand, John Jordan

Interior artist: Warren Fischbach
Marketing managers: Carol Carter, Frank Lyman
Advertising manager: Lori Cowen
Photo researcher: Teri Stratford
Photo editor: Lorinda Morris-Nantz
Copy editor: Nancy Marcello
Permissions researcher: Mary Helen Fitzgerald
Editorial assistants: Andrea Cuperman,
    Renée Pelletier, Asha Rohra
Prepress buyer: Trudy Pisciotti
Manufacturing buyer: Herb Klein
Indexer: Maro Riofrancos

Photo credits follow index.

©1994 by Prentice-Hall, Inc.
A Paramount Communications Company
Englewood Cliffs, New Jersey 07632

Printed in the United States of America
10 9 8 7 6 5 4 3 2 1

ISBN 0-13-174731-2

Prentice Hall International (UK) Limited, London
Prentice Hall of Australia Pty. Limited, Sydney
Prentice Hall of Canada Inc., Toronto
Prentice Hall Hispanoamericano, S.A., Mexico
Prentice Hall of India Private Limited, New Delhi
Prentice Hall of Japan, Inc., Tokyo
Simon & Schuster Asia Pte. Ltd., Singapore
Editora Prentice Hall do Brasil, Ltda., Rio de Janeiro

To Dr. Gloria Payne
of Davis and Elkins College.

Our candidate as a role model for future
business communication instructors.

BRIEF CONTENTS

CONTENTS

PART II   WRITING BASICS

5 REVISING AND EDITING BUSINESS DOCUMENTS   135

PART III   ORGANIZATIONAL LETTERS AND MEMOS

6 WRITING DIRECT REQUESTS 173

7 WRITING GOOD-NEWS, GOODWILL, AND INFORMATIVE MESSAGES   203

8 WRITING BAD-NEWS AND NEGATIVE MESSAGES   235

PART IV   REPORT AND PROPOSAL WRITING

PART V   FORMS OF ORAL COMMUNICATION

PART VI   EMPLOYMENT COMMUNICATION

16   TARGETING YOUR CAREER: WRITING RÉSUMÉS AND COVER LETTERS   519

17   EFFECTIVE EMPLOYMENT INTERVIEWING   555

PART VII   COMMUNICATION CHALLENGES

18 *COMMUNICATING IN A GLOBAL MARKETPLACE*   595

19 *THE CHALLENGE OF DIVERSITY* 631

20 *MASTERING COMMUNICATION TECHNOLOGY* 667

APPENDIX I

APPENDIX II

APPENDIX III

A friend of ours was teaching her first undergraduate business class at a major university. Throughout the term, she asked her students to submit documents similar to those that they would write when they began their business careers. Although the students spent a great deal of time on the content of the assignments, they devoted little effort to the writing itself. The results were predictable: Little thought was given to design; ideas were poorly organized and ineffectively presented, papers were filled with grammatical and spelling errors.

When our friend graded these papers on the basis of both content and writing, her students expressed dismay. If they wanted to learn communication skills, they told her, they would have enrolled in a writing course. (The university did not require students to complete a course in business communication.) They took her course, they insisted, to learn business, not business communication.

What these students failed to realize is that, in business, content and effective communication go hand in hand. Poorly written documents will not get a fair reading. In fact, they face the risk of being misinterpreted, minimized, or even ignored by readers with little patience for sloppy, inaccurate work. Similarly, when oral communication is weak, the impact of an idea—even a good idea—is reduced. Former President Gerald Ford summed up the importance of effective communication this way: "If I went back to college again, I'd concentrate on two areas: learning to write and to speak before an audience. Nothing in life is more important than the ability to communicate effectively."

Like President Ford and our friend, we believe that clear communication is the basis for business success. As a result, a fundamental objective of *Contemporary Business Communication* is to link effective written and oral communication with the ability to find and keep a challenging, personally satisfying job in today's increasingly competitive business world.

To achieve this objective, *Contemporary Business Communication* focuses on the skills involved in effective written and oral communication. From opening objectives to end-of-chapter exercises, every chapter emphasizes the critical communication skills necessary for business success.

AN APPLICATIONS FOCUS

At its heart, *Contemporary Business Communication* is a practical guide to business communication. Communication instructors have stressed the need for a practical "how to" text emphasizing the applications of communication concepts. Our reviewers have pointed out the importance of current, real-world business examples and the greatest possible variety of student writing assignments for every chapter.

This advice was heeded. From opening vignettes to closing cases, dozens of examples from actual companies are interwoven into every chapter. Opening vignettes focus on communication issues at both small organizations and large companies such as Euro Disney, General Electric, Citibank, Allstate Insurance, and New York's World Trade Center. Students will be able to identify with end-of-chapter cases featuring such organizations as Whittle Communications, Eaton Corp., Springfield Remanufacturing Corp., Mellon Bank, Apple Computer, Nordstrom, Accountemps, and Rowan State College.

Special features highlighted throughout the text as *Practical Tips* include such topics as the following:

- Cellular Phone Etiquette
- Applying the KISS Principle to Business Writing
- The Pros and Cons of Boilerplate Language
- Developing and Delivering Team Presentations
- The Art of Choosing for Visual Aids
- Five Reasons for Poor Writing
- Avoiding Computer Viruses

The practical focus of *Contemporary Business Communication* is also emphasized in the twenty interviews included in the text. In each chapter, a business professional shares concrete communication guidelines intended to help students improve their written and oral communication skills. The interview subjects and their topics are:

- Chapter 1. James F. Orr III, CEO of Unum Corp., on communicating in a business organization
- Chapter 2. Psychologist Beatrice Harris on the communication process
- Chapter 3. Professor and author Lynn Quitman Troyka on planning business communication
- Chapter 4. Business writing consultant Sana Reynolds on organizing, composing, and designing business documents
- Chapter 5. Letitia Baldridge, nationally known expert on business etiquette, on the etiquette of business writing

- Chapter 6. Writing consultant and author Mary A. De Vries on writing direct requests
- Chapter 7. James Ruppel, director of customer relations for Southwest Airlines, on writing good-news, goodwill, and informative messages.
- Chapter 8. Writing consultant and professor William Buchholz on writing bad-news and negative messages.
- Chapter 9. Sales-writing consultant David Topus on writing persuasive messages
- Chapter 10. Research consultant Marydee Ojala on using online databases in business research
- Chapter 11. Author and consultant Gene Zelazny on using visual aids in business reports and proposals
- Chapter 12. Business communication consultant and professor Lawrence D. Brennan on organizing and writing short and long reports
- Chapter 13. Business communication consultant and author Ron Tepper on organizing and writing short and long proposals
- Chapter 14. Speech communication consultant Bert Decker on delivering speeches and oral presentations
- Chapter 15. Tessa Warschaw, negotiations expert and author, on negotiating during business meetings
- Chapter 16. Alan B. McNabb, director of the career development center at Indiana University on employment communication
- Chapter 17. G. Frederick Reinhardt III, international private banker, on interviewing for an overseas job
- Chapter 18. International communication consultant George Simons on communicating in a global marketplace
- Chapter 19. Diversity consultant Helen Turnbull on the challenge of diversity
- Chapter 20. Gary Foley, videoconferencing manager at Xerox Corp., on communicating during a videoconference

EXTENSIVE END-OF-CHAPTER EXERCISES

To reinforce critical communication concepts, every chapter concludes with an extensive series of exercises. Instructors using *Contemporary Business Communication* in their classes will be able to choose from the following:

- 200 Questions for Discussion and Review

- 300 Application Exercises
- 20 assignments on *Building Your Research Skills*
- 20 assignments on *Building Your Teamwork Skills*
- 20 assignments on *Communicating in a World of Diversity*
- 40 business cases

Every exercise is keyed to specific learning objectives listed at the beginning of the chapter.

These exercises emphasize timely concepts in business communication, including collaborative communication, research, and the communication challenges presented by internal and international diversity. The two case studies at the end of each chapter place students in the midst of actual business communication situations. Questions are included to link each situation to chapter content, and case-related assignments frequently require students to create letters, memos, and other business documents.

THE MOST COMPLETE COVERAGE IN CRUCIAL AREAS

Reviewers assisted the authors in identifying important topics that are covered inadequately or simply not included in other business communication texts. The result is extensive treatment of such subjects as:

- nonverbal communication
- collaborative writing
- computerized research
- listening
- proposal writing
- communication technologies
- players in the job-search process
- laws safeguarding employment communication
- communicating across national boundaries

Contemporary Business Communication is also a pathfinder in examining current topics. For example, no other business communication text examines sexual harassment and the impact of the corporate culture on communication.

A TEXT FOR THE TWENTY-FIRST CENTURY

If the twentieth century were represented as a twenty-four hour clock, Charles Lindbergh's successful flight across the Atlantic would have occurred at 6:30 a.m., World War II would have ended at 10:50 a.m., Neil Armstrong would have first set foot on the moon at 4:34 p.m., and the Soviet Union would have dissolved at 9:50 p.m. Now only about an hour remains before our twenty-four-hour clock tolls in the beginning of a new century—the century in which today's students will spend most of their working lives and a century for which texts and teachers must prepare these students.

A number of challenges face the workforce of the twenty-first century. They include the need to master communication technologies, the challenge of communicating in a global marketplace, ethical challenges, and the challenge of communicating with an increasingly diverse workforce. Each challenge is addressed thoroughly in *Contemporary Business Communication*. No other text devotes an entire chapter to the issue of diversity, and none treats international communication and communication technologies so completely.

The impact of technology on business communication is the subject of a separate chapter. Among the specific technologies examined are word processing, electronic mail, facsimile machines, voice mail, teleconferences and video-conferences. In addition, the chapter discusses the technologies of business travel, including cellular phones, pagers, and laptop and palmtop computers, as well as the phenomenon of telecommuting. Specific suggestions for using communication technologies are presented throughout the chapter.

Technology, however, is too pervasive a topic to be covered in a single chapter. Specific techniques for applying technology are explored throughout the texts.

Among the topics discussed are the following:

- Collaborative Writing with Computers
- Symbol Libraries
- Using a Computerized Dictionary
- Attending a Computerized Meeting
- Filing Your Résumé in an Electronic Database

A separate chapter, "Communicating in a Global Marketplace," focuses on both the different audiences that make up an increasingly international business environment and the link between culture and communication. It also examines the advantages of being multilingual and presents guidelines for successful cross-cultural communication. In addition, special focus boxes on "International Issues in Business Communication" feature such subjects as technology problems encountered while traveling abroad and how the French write direct requests.

It is no secret that ethical issues are frequently encountered in today's business environment. Communications-related issues highlighted in the text include such topics as:

- Job References, Ethics, and the Law
- When Studies Mislead
- Plagiarism: The World's Dumbest Crime
- When Reference Checks Go Too Far
- How Companies Eliminate Sexual Harassment
- E-Mail and the Issue of Privacy

An entire chapter is devoted to the impact of diversity on business communication. It examines the ways in which gender, age, physical challenges, and race and ethnicity affect communication patterns. Among the topics discussed in the chapter are the communication breakdowns inherent in sexual harassment and the increasing number of diversity-training programs in business and government organizations.

INTEGRATING PRINT AND VIDEO TECHNOLOGIES

College and university teaching is greatly affected by today's technological advances. In recent years, business communication instructors have requested integrated video materials that are directly linked to major text concepts. *Contemporary Business Communication* is the first text to respond thoroughly to these requests.

Accompanying the text is an outstanding series of videos from Communication Briefings, a firm renowned for the quality of its monthly newsletter and its video series. Included in the *Contemporary Business Communication* video series are the following:

- Listening: The Key to Productivity
- Mastering Memos
- Everyone's Public Relations Role
- Get More Done in Less Time
- Communicating with Customers
- Communicating with People on the Job
- Better Business Grammar
- Make the Phone Work for You

The eight Communication Briefings videos are available at no cost to teachers who use *Contemporary Business Communication* in their classes. In addition, an ABC News Video Library has been specially developed to present news features of immediate interest to students and teachers of business communication. An accompanying *Video Activity Guide* is included in the *Instructor's Resource Manual*.

EXTENSIVE LEARNING TOOLS WITHIN EACH CHAPTER

An objective of *Contemporary Business Communication* is to help students learn. A variety of techniques is used to reinforce learning, including chapter-opening business communication situations that set the stage for the material to follow; task-oriented chapter objectives; periodic progress checks; summary tables and figures; and a marginal glossary highlighting key concepts.

LIVELY, CONVERSATIONAL WRITING STYLE AND AN ATTRACTIVE, OPEN DESIGN

As a result of the extensive use of examples and illustrations and the "you" orientation, students will find this text easy to read. Marginal quotations add a business perspective, interest, and frequent humor. The attractive open design and careful use of color further enhance readability.

INSTRUCTIONAL RESOURCE PACKAGE

Contemporary Business Communication is a comprehensive teaching/learning package unparalleled in its completeness. Although the textbook is the most critical element in the package, it is only one part. Also included are the following supplementary teaching aids:

Instructor's Resource Manual

These instructional materials coordinate each of the following sections with every chapter.

- Annotated Learning Goals
- Key Terms
- Lecture Outline
- Guest Lecture
- Answers to:
  - Progress Checks
  - Review and Discussion Questions
  - Application Exercises
  - Building Your Research Skills
  - Building Your Teamwork Skills
  - Communicating in a World of Diversity
  - Case Questions and Applications

The *IRM* also includes the *ABC News Video*

Activity Guide designed by Anna Easton and Judy McClain, both of Indiana University.

ATLAS Test Bank (Academic Testing and Learning Analysis System)

Also prepared by Anna Easton and Judy McClain, under the direction of Dr. John Ory of the University of Illinois, the ATLAS Test Bank contains approximately 1600 questions: multiple-choice, completion, matching, true/false, short-answer, and discussion. The Test Bank is available both in printed format and in the IBM Test Manager.

Study Guide

Anna Easton and Judy McClain have also developed an excellent *Study Guide* that elaborates on each chapter in outline format. Features include a chapter overview, a Key Terms fill-in review, and true/false and multiple-choice review questions. All answers can also be found in the *SG*.

Full-Color Transparencies

Designed by Lewis B. Hershey of Hershey Consulting Services, striking graphic illustrations are available in both acetate and electronic formats. Teaching Notes are provided for each transparency.

ACKNOWLEDGMENTS

A number of people have made significant contributions to *Contemporary Business Communication*. Their insights, suggestions, and advice served to convert a manuscript into a finished product. We are extremely grateful to these friends and colleagues for their invaluable assistance with this project.

It is difficult to acknowledge sufficiently the contributions of our long-time friend and colleague Judy R. Block. Judy's many hours of efforts are reflected in every chapter of the text.

Contemporary Business Communication benefited greatly from the efforts of a number of dedicated business communication professionals who served as consultants and manuscript reviewers. We would especially like to thank the following:

Vanessa Arnold
University of Mississippi

Carol Barnum
Southern College of Technology

Susan Becker
Illinois Central College

Carl Bridges
Ohio State

William Buchholz
Bentley College

Dwight Bullard
Middle Tennessee State University

Gloria L. Campbell
Wartburg College

Jack Cole
University of Akron

James Conley
Eastern Michigan University

John Flemming
New Hampshire College

David H. Gigley
Ohio University-Chillicothe

Garth Hanson
Brigham Young University

Debbie Hasley
Bluefield State College

Geraldine Hynes
University of Missouri-St. Louis

Thomas Inman
Southwest Missouri State University

Marcia James
University of Wisconsin-Whitewater

Paul Killorin
Portland Community College

Gary Kohut
University of North Carolina-Charlotte

Suzanne Lambert
Broward Community College

Mary Leslie
Grossmont Community College

Stephen Lewis
Middle Tennessee State University

Terry Long
Ohio State University-Newark

Jeanette Martin
University of Mississippi

Rachel Mather
Adelphi University

Kenneth Mayer
Cleveland State University

Rita Mignacca
SUNY Brockport

Thomas Lee Means
Louisiana Technical College

Thomas M. Miles
West Virginia University

Wayne Moore
Indiana University of Pennsylvania

Glena Morse
Georgia College

Alexa North
Georgia State University

Binford Peeples
Memphis State

Devon Perry
Brigham Young University

Doris Phillips
University of Mississippi

Merton E. Powell
Ferris State University

Patricia Rice
Finger Lakes Community College

Elizabeth Robertson
Tennessee State University

Tim Saben
Portland Community College

Stephen Shirring
Butler County Community College

Herb Smith
Southern College of Technology

Frankie Sprague
Palm Beach Community College

Jacqueline Stowe
McMurry University

Roberta M. Supnick
Western Michigan University

Vincent Trofi
Providence College

Mary L. Tucker
Nicholls State University

Edward Wachter, Jr.
Point Park College

John L. Waltman
Eastern Michigan University

Stan Wayne
Southwest Missouri State College

Judy West
University of Tennessee-Chattanooga

Jerry L. Wood
Northern Montana College

Barry Woodcock
Tennessee Technological University

Dan Wunsch
Northern Illinois University

Donald K. Zahn
University of Wisconsin-Whitewater

Thanks are also due to the twenty communication professionals who agreed to be interviewed in the text. We would also like to thank corporate recruiter Deirdre Anderson for her help with the employment communication chapters; Diane La Mountain for her advice on diversity in the workplace; Lauren Goldbert Block for her reminiscences about teaching business communication to business students; Sana Reynolds for her advice on international and intracultural diversity; and Dr. Beatrice Harris for providing the sample proposal used in Chapter 13. We have been fortunate to work with Alice Fugate, our research associate, who dedicated many hours to *Contemporary Business Communication*. We would also like to thank our capable research associates, Ginger Honomichl, Jeanne Lowe, and Dianne Wilkens for their invaluable assistance.

Last, but not least, we would like to extend our most profound gratitude to the professionals at Prentice Hall, who not only recognized the need for *Contemporary Business Communication* but who made it a reality. We would like to acknowledge the important contributions of the following people: Joe Heider, Editor in Chief, Accounting and Information Systems; Don Hull, Senior Editor, A&IS, and his assistant, Andrea Cuperman; Ray Mullaney, Editor in Chief, College Book Development, and his assistant, Asha Rohra; Joyce Turner, Senior Managing Editor, Business and Economics Production; Kris Ann Cappelluti, Managing Editor, B&E Production, and her assistant, Renée Pelletier; Pat Wosczyk, Design Director, Suzanne Behnke, Designer, and artist Warren Fischbach; Carol Carter, Director of Marketing, Frank Lyman, Marketing Manager, and Lori Cowen, Advertising Manager, B&E; Assistant Editor David Shea; Mary Araneo, Manager, Electronic Production Services, and formatters John Nestor, David Tay, Michael Bertrand, and John Jordan; Lorinda Morris-Nantz, Manager, Photo Archives; photographic researcher Teri Stratford and permissions researcher Mary Helen Fitzgerald.

The production of the book was very ably supervised by Mary Cavaliere. Senior Development Editor Ron Librach was involved from the very beginning in every element of the book.

Louis E. Boone
David L. Kurtz

ABOUT THE AUTHORS

Louis E. Boone (B.S., M.S., Ph.D.) holds the Ernest G. Cleverdon Chair of Business and Management at the University of South Alabama. He formerly chaired the Division of Management and Marketing at the University of Tulsa. Dr. Boone has also taught in Australia, Greece, and the United Kingdom.

Dr. Boone's research on chief executive officers, conducted with coauthors David L. Kurtz and Patrick Fleenor of Seattle University, has resulted in the publication of *CEO: Who Gets to the Top in America* (Michigan State University Press). In addition, he is the author of *Quotable Business* (Random House) and has published in such journals as *Business Horizons, International Journal of Management, Journal of Business Strategy, Journal of Marketing, Journal of Retailing, American Demographics, Journal of Psychology*, and the *Journal of Business of the University of Chicago*. He is a recent recipient of the Phi Kappa Phi Outstanding Scholar Award from the University of South Alabama and is listed in *Who's Who in America*.

David L. Kurtz (B.A., M.B.A., Ph.D.) holds the R.A. and Vivian Young Chair of Business Administration at the University of Arkansas. He previously held the Thomas F. Gleed Chair in Business and Finance at Seattle University and served as the Ian Potter Distinguished Professor at Australia's Monash University.

With coauthor Louis E. Boone, Dr. Kurtz ranks among the leading communicators in business education. Over three million U.S. and Canadian students have begun their study of business administration by using *Contemporary Business* and *Contemporary Marketing* in their classes. Dr. Kurtz has also been involved in consulting and training activities in business and has been the president of a small corporation.

THE NEW YORK TIMES PROGRAM

The New York Times and Prentice Hall are sponsoring "Themes of the Times:" a program designed to enhance student access to current information of relevance in the classroom.

Through this program, the core subject matter provided in the text is supplemented by a collection of time-sensitive articles from one of the world's most distinguished newspapers, *The New York Times*. These articles demonstrate the vital, ongoing connections between what is learned in the classroom and what is happening in the world around us.

To enjoy the wealth of information of *The New York Times* daily, a reduced subscription rate is available in deliverable areas. For information, call toll-free: 1-800-631-1222.

Prentice Hall and *The New York Times* are proud to cosponsor "Themes of the Times." We hope it will make the reading of both textbooks and newspapers a more dynamic, involving process.

INTERNATIONALIZE YOUR EDUCATION

Join International Business Seminars on an Overseas Adventure

Earn College Credit   ■   Gain International Expertise
Interact with Top-level Executives   ■   Visit the World's Greatest Cities
MAY 30, 1994 — JUNE 23, 1994

VISIT ORGANIZATIONS SUCH AS: Procter & Gamble Italia, NATO, The European Parliament, Elektra Breganz, Philip Morris, Allianz Insurance, Deutsche Aerospace, Digital Equipment, Coca-Cola, G.E. International, Ernst & Young, Esso Italiana, Guccio Gucci, Targetti Lighting, University of Innsbruck, and British Bankers Association.

Prentice Hall International Business Scholarship 1994

Prentice Hall and International Business Seminars have joined forces to create a scholarship for students to study and travel in Europe in the summer of 1994. We believe that in today's global business environment, students should be exposed to as many different cultures as possible. Although many campuses reflect diversity in both their students and faculty, nothing can replace the educational value of learning about a continent, country, or city first hand.

Each professor may sponsor one student to apply for the scholarship. You can receive more information on the Prentice Hall Business Scholarship and/or additional travel programs with International Business Seminars by contacting your local Prentice Hall representative or International Business Seminars, P.O. Box 30279, Mesa, Arizona 85275, Telephone: (602) 830-0902; Fax: (602) 924-0527.

FUNDAMENTALS OF BUSINESS COMMUNICATION

1

Communicating in an Organization

CHAPTER OBJECTIVES

After studying this chapter, you should be able to:

1 Explain why an effective *internal communication system* is important to a business organization.

2 Identify the major audiences in a company's *external communication network.*

3 Describe the nature of the *formal communication channel,* including the *communication flows* that exist inside and outside the organization.

4 Explain the nature of the *informal communication channel* and how it operates inside and outside the organization.

5 Describe how *corporate culture* affects communication.

6 Outline the four *communication challenges* that influence the ways in which businesspeople communicate.

7 Understand how effective business communication is linked to personal career success.

*T*he ability to communicate is everything.

Lee Iacocca
Former CEO, Chrysler Corporation

WORKING OUT COMMUNICATIONS PROBLEMS AT GE

Business communication is not what it used to be. A case in point is the communication revolution now taking place at General Electric. To foster employee involvement and increase productivity, GE chairman John F. Welch, Jr., has mounted a frontal assault on the business-as-usual attitude. Convinced that a corporation is doomed without "speed, simplicity, and self-confidence," Welch is determined to remove the "boss element" from business. He believes that 21st-century managers will communicate according to a different set of rules. Instead of being centers of power as they plan, organize, implement, and control company activities, managers will empower employees through counseling aimed at helping people think for themselves. "We're going to win on our ideas," says Welch, "not by whips and chains."

A key element of Welch's plan is Work-Out, a forum for a free and open exchange of ideas that began in 1989. Each Work-Out brings together between 40 and 100 people—from executives to factory workers—to grapple with productivity problems.

Communication takes center stage as each Work-Out turns into a three-day talk-a-thon. On day one, participants gather together in a conference or hotel room and listen as "the boss" sets the agenda. Anything from eliminating unnecessary paperwork to designing more productive machines and procedures is up for discussion. Then the leader leaves—and real communication begins. Broken down into five or six teams and aided by an outside facilitator, employees spend the next day and a half analyzing the agenda. Complaints are voiced, solutions debated, and presentations prepared.

On the third day, the team leader returns, often accompanied by senior executives. Knowing nothing about the details of the team meetings, the leader takes a special seat at the front of the room and listens as team members present a battery of proposals. Work-Out rules require the leader to answer each proposal in one of three ways: by agreeing on the spot, by saying no, or by asking for more information (which must be supplied by a specified date). The intensity of the communication is equaled only by the number of proposals. Recalls Armand Lauzon, head of plant services at a GE factory in Lynn, Massachusetts, and the person on the spot at a recent Work-Out: "I was wringing wet within half an hour. They had 108 proposals, I had about a minute to say yes or no to each one, and I couldn't make eye contact with my boss without turning around, which would show everyone in the room that I was chicken."

No one in the room felt the need to apologize for Lauzon's discomfort. "When you've been told to shut up for 20 years, and someone tells you to speak up—you're going to let them have it," explains Vic Slepoy, a factory electrician. Proposal results, it would seem, speak for themselves: In a recent year, implemented proposals saved the plant more than $200,000.

Other Work-Outs have yielded similar success. For example, at NBC, a GE division, the operations and technical services department decided to eliminate forms that had added up to more than two million unnecessary pieces of paper a year. At a Louisville, Kentucky, plant that manufactures washers and dryers, a team found a way to reduce the heat and humidity that had made the working environment unbearable. At GE's plastics plant in Burkville, Alabama, the waste of a salable polycarbonate used in auto bumpers and milk bottles was reduced by 37 percent. And working with Montgomery Ward, a GE customer, GE reduced the time required to open new individual charge accounts from 30 minutes to 90 seconds by linking Ward's cash registers directly to its own mainframe computers.

Other results are less tangible but no less important. Work-Outs, for example, build trust in a labor force that has learned to mistrust. With 6,000 jobs eliminated since 1986, the Lynn, Massachusetts, aircraft engine plant now employs 8,000 people—many of whom have little faith in the company. "We had the feeling they were trying to phase us out," explains Slepoy. "Now at least [Work-Outs give us] an avenue to make a pitch for our jobs."

Work-Outs have been adopted—indeed embraced—by General Electric. In a recent year, more than one out of eight employees—some 40,000 people—had their voices heard. This new brand of business communication is about openness—about talking and listening, personal dignity and empowerment, improved productivity and jobs, competitiveness, and corporate survival.[1] If Work-Outs succeed, they will mark an important change in the way people communicate at GE. With every employee viewed as a vital link in the information chain, Work-Outs also promise to redefine business communication as practiced by a Fortune 500 giant.

CHAPTER OVERVIEW

No matter what kind of organization you work for—whether a large corporation like General Electric, McDonald's, or Polaroid, a small individually owned bakery or dry cleaner, or a nonprofit organization such as a hospital or college—effective communication is increasingly becoming a matter of survival. **Communication**, which can be defined as the meaningful exchange of information through messages, is really a composite of everything we do and say. While communication is vital in all human endeavors, it is particularly important in business. Companies like Mattel, UNUM Corp., and Union Pacific Railroad have moved communication to center stage. As you will see in the next section, the role of **business communication**—the communication required of an organization in both its internal and external environments—is complex and varied.

communication
Meaningful exchange of information through messages

business communication
Communication required of an organization in both its internal and external environments

THE ROLE OF COMMUNICATION IN BUSINESS ORGANIZATIONS

Effective communication—that is, effective writing, speaking, and listening skills—affects every aspect of business, from the creation of a business image and goodwill to the sale of goods and services, from effective customer service to efficient internal operations, from dealing with suppliers to dealing with government officials. Let's begin by examining the importance of communication from the point of view of two different audiences: the company's **internal audience**, which consists of its employees and owners; and its **external audience**, which includes the general public, customers, suppliers and other businesses, and government officials. For example, while company newsletters illustrate communication with internal audiences, press releases are targeted at external audiences. Examples of communications with specific audiences are shown in Figure 1.1. In discussing both audiences, our focus will be on *formal communication channels* approved by the management of the organization. Later in the chapter, we will examine the differences between formal and informal communication channels.

internal audience
A company's employees and owners

external audience
A company's customers and suppliers as well as the general public, other businesses, and government officials with whom it interacts

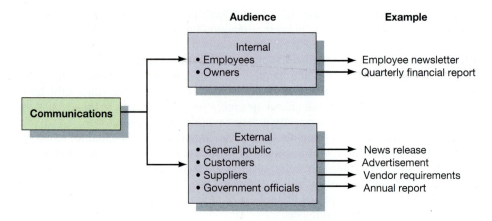

FIGURE 1.1   *Communications with Specific Audiences*

Communicating within a Company

internal communication
Communication through channels within an organization

Effective communication among employees is crucial to the success of all companies. **Internal communication** involves communicating back and forth *within* the organization through such written and oral channels as memos, reports, meetings, oral presentations, speeches, and person-to-person and telephone conversations. It involves communication up and down the organizational hierarchy. Communication takes place among co-workers as well as between superiors and subordinates. Through internal communication, business decisions are made, policies are set, and problems are analyzed and solved. Like General Electric, many companies are committed to improving their internal communication systems. For example:

- The 5,500 employees of the UNUM Corp. in Portland, Maine, use electronic mail to tell James F. Orr III, the company's chief executive officer, what they are thinking. Orr looks at these messages every night and often follows up the next day with personal phone calls.[2]

- At the Nelson Metal Products Corporation, a Grandville, Michigan, automotive supplier, workers have come together to solve the problem of too many defective parts. As a result of open communication and teamwork, the incidence of defective parts has been reduced from a staggering 2,500 parts per million to fewer than 10 per million.[3]

- For more than 15 years, top management at Hyatt Hotels has been surveying employees at its 106 hotels. By asking employees for such input as their opinions about management, managers develop "a general morale index," or GMI. Not surprisingly, the hotels with the highest GMI scores also have the highest sales, gross-operating profits, and customer-satisfaction ratings. In addition, senior managers meet regularly with groups of employees. Hyatt president Darryl Hartley-Leonard, who was initially skeptical about the value of these meetings, soon changed his mind. "I thought, 'Oh, no, people are just going to complain,'" reports Hartley-Leonard, but the program, he now admits, "has changed the whole organization."[4]

Using a variety of methods—including face-to-face conversation, formal meetings, speeches, phone calls, electronic mail, and questionnaires—these companies have linked success and profitability to effective internal communication. Similarly, when *Fortune* magazine asked 212 chief executive officers how their companies are attempting to improve communication and productivity, editors gathered the results shown in Table 1.1. Regular meetings were found to be the most popular method of making such improvements.

TABLE 1.1   *What CEOs Think About Improving Internal Communication*

Question	What has your company done in recent years that has most helped to improve communications and productivity?
Answer	Regular meetings with employees 41%
	Quality-improvement programs 20
	Incentive-based compensation programs (e.g., stock options, profit sharing)..17
	Internal newsletters/bulletins...16
	Team effort/employee involvement...11
	Informational videos 10
	Surveys/focus groups...9
	Delayering organization 7
	Training middle management (in human resources, etc.)..7
	Better communication between all layers of management 6
	Broadened participation in decision making...3
	Instituting grievance panels/hotlines...2
	Other 5

Total is more than 100 percent because of multiple responses.

Source: Anne B. Fisher, "CEOs Think That Morale Is Dandy," *Fortune,* November 18, 1991, p. 84.

An effective internal communication system is especially important in large companies where size and complexity are one and the same. Management authors Thomas J. Peters and Robert H. Waterman point out that while employee head count may go up arithmetically, demands on communications rise geometrically. As a result, many firms try to simplify their communication networks. Procter & Gamble, for example, now insists that memos be no longer than one page.[5]

Poor communication can also frustrate small companies. Each year, thousands of partnerships and small businesses break up because of communication problems. Although many breakups are unavoidable, others can be prevented through frequent meetings, open discussions, and written agreements. When trouble begins, it often takes the form of poor communication. "Partners begin to notice that it's harder to talk over problems," says Albert A. Murphy, a San Diego business consultant. "They begin withholding information from each other," and this tendency, according to Murphy and many of his colleagues, is often the beginning of the end.[6]

Communicating Outside a Company

A company's internal communication system is linked to its system of external communication. **External communication** refers to communication with a company's major audiences—the general public, customers, suppliers and other businesses, and government officials. Through external communication, businesses establish themselves in the marketplace and work with others to keep their operations functioning.

external communication
Communication with the major audiences in a company's external environment

COMMUNICATING WITH THE GENERAL PUBLIC   Companies communicate with the general public in an attempt to influence consumer decisions. Advertising, for example, creates an organizational image, provides information, and differentiates company products from similar products on the market.

COMMUNICATING WITH CUSTOMERS   Customers are the lifeblood of any organization, and companies communicate directly with customers through such activities as sales presentations, order fulfillment, and handling complaints. Customer communication may take the form of face-to-face conversations, telephone calls, meetings, letters, written proposals, and oral presentations.

PERSONAL SELLING   Sales presentations made to potential buyers may involve formal written proposals, oral presentations, meetings, and letters. For example, when Frank Pacetta took over as the district sales manager in Xerox's Cleveland office, improved communication became a top priority. To improve slumping performance, Pacetta required that sales representatives prepare proposals on weekends and evenings, report early for meetings, adopt the attitude that everything is negotiable, and dress like "a superior product." As a result of Pacetta's efforts to improve communication, the Cleveland district soared in one year from number eleven (the bottom of the barrel) to number one in the region and number four among Xerox's 65 national sales districts.[7]

order fulfillment
Process by which orders are received by company representatives to satisfy customer needs

ORDER FULFILLMENT   **Order fulfillment** is a process in which orders are received and handled by company representatives in order to satisfy customers' specific needs. Order fulfillment involves two-way communication between a company employee and a customer that may be handled in writing, in person, or over the phone. Any of the following activities may be involved: direct requests (orders) from the customer, requests for information and clarification from the company to the customer, requests for credit, refusals to grant credit, and notifications that goods are unavailable or that there will be a delay in delivery.

goodwill
Prestige, loyalty, and reputation acquired by a company beyond the value of its products

COMMITMENT TO CUSTOMER SERVICE   With each *customer interaction*, whether during sales communication, order fulfillment, or complaint handling, there is an opportunity to create **goodwill**—the prestige, loyalty, and reputation that a business acquires beyond the value of its products. **Customer service**—the act of ensuring that customers feel valued and that their needs are met—must be the foundation of your approach. Always consider yourself a company spokesperson and every letter and conversation a messenger of goodwill. "Cultivation of goodwill," explains L. A. Down, former president of the Illinois Central Railroad, "is not a departmental activity, but the work of the entire organization."[8] (We will discuss the principles of writing goodwill messages in Chapter 7.)

customer service
Act of ensuring that customers feel valued and that their needs are met

complaint
Message indicating a problem with a good or service or the perception of such a problem

HANDLING COMPLAINTS   When customers are not happy, they often say so in the form of complaints. **Complaints**, which may be written, oral, or both, are messages indicating that something is wrong with a good or service or that there is the perception of a problem. Complaints are handled by letter, through telephone conversations, or in personal meetings.

Complaints can be regarded as either annoyances or opportunities, and according to management authors Tom Peters and Nancy Austin, there are two corporate perspectives on complaints. "The first, the most typical," they observe, "views the complaint as a disease to be got over, with memory of the pain rapidly suppressed. The second views the complaint as a luscious, golden opportunity."[9]

service encounter
Interaction between a customer and a company representative

Handling customer complaints is especially important in companies that offer services instead of tangible goods. The success of these companies depends on the nature of the **service encounter**—the interaction that takes place between the customer and the company representative.[10] "You can't use the traditional manufacturing tools to measure [a service] or inspect it before you deliver it," explains James A. McEleny, a corporate quality-improvement executive at Chicago & North Western Transportation Co. "Our employees create it, and then it disappears." Stanley M. Cherkasky, president of a consulting company that specializes in quality, believes that the success of the service encounter depends on effective employee communication. "What management needs to understand," he explains, "is that it isn't in charge of customer satisfaction. It's the employee who talks [and writes] to the customer."

The same message has been heard at MBNA America, Inc., the country's fourth-largest bank-card issuer. At MBNA, service representatives talk or write to every customer who wants to cancel an MBNA Visa or MasterCard; they convince about half of those customers to retain their cards. As a result of this kind of service, MBNA's customers stay with the company twice as long as the industry average, use their credit cards more frequently, and have higher balances. "We can't point to any one thing that we do," says Vice-Chairman Bruce L. Hammonds. "But all the little things add up to a more loyal, more profitable customer base."[11]

I solemnly promise and declare that every customer that comes within ten feet of me, I will smile, look them in the eye, and greet them, so help me, Sam.

Employee pledge, Wal-Mart stores

("Sam" is Wal-Mart founder Sam Walton)

COMMUNICATING WITH SUPPLIERS AND OTHER BUSINESSES   Using letters, written proposals and reports, oral presentations, meetings, telephone calls, and informal conversations, businesses communicate with one another for a variety of reasons. One business, for example, may purchase goods or services from another company in order to produce its own products or to sell another company's products in its retail stores.

Each interaction provides the opportunity to cement a business relationship or in some way promote your company's best interests. The following are just some of the specific communication instruments used in business-to-business communication: letters placing orders, letters of complaint, adjustment letters, proposals for joint ventures, claim letters, and meetings to set up supplier relationships.

When communicating with suppliers and other businesses, clarity is essential—misunderstandings can be time-consuming and costly. To promote clarity, many companies establish procedures to communicate messages effectively. The placement of all orders, for example, may be handled according to a specified formula. Similarly, all complaint letters may receive the same level of investigation before adjustment letters are written. (As goodwill messages written in response to claims or complaints, adjustment letters are discussed in Chapter 7.)

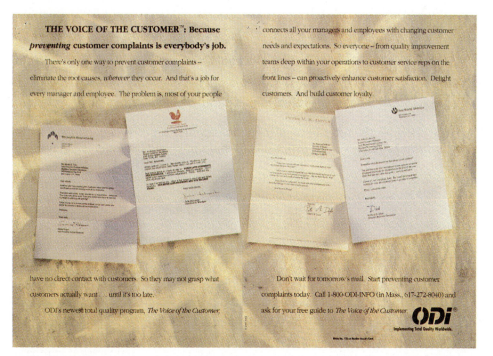

The "quality revolution" has had an important impact on the service encounter, especially in organizations that have recognized the service encounter as a companywide activity.

Source: © 1991 by ODI

The dangers of poor business-to-business communication are evident in the following story:

> In 1869, the Westinghouse Air Brake Company was organized to manufacture air brakes that functioned more quickly and safely than the hand brakes then in use. Although highly successful with his invention, George Westinghouse had trouble finding a sponsor for his idea in its early stages. Recognizing the invention's value to the rapidly growing railroad companies, he wrote to Cornelius Vanderbilt, president of the New York Central Railroad, detailing the advantages of the air brake. Vanderbilt returned his letter with a note scribbled on the bottom: "I have no time to waste on fools."
>
> Westinghouse was not discouraged and next contacted officials at the Pennsylvania Railroad. They were intrigued and gave him the funds he needed to continue working on his invention. The tests were successful and news of the breakthrough finally got back to Vanderbilt. He wrote a letter to Westinghouse, inviting him to meet with him. Westinghouse returned the letter with a note on the bottom: "I have no time to waste on fools. George Westinghouse."[12]

COMMUNICATING WITH GOVERNMENT   Business-to-government communication takes two basic forms:

1. Businesses sell trillions of dollars' worth of goods and services to federal, state, and local governments. For example, the federal government contracts with companies to purchase everything from military supplies to pencil sharpeners. Similarly, state and local governments purchase maintenance services, schoolbooks, office supplies, and uniforms for police and firefighters.

2. Businesses correspond with government about government regulations, tax payments, and reports. Drug companies like Upjohn and Abbott Laboratories, for example, must meet the requirements of the Food and Drug Administration. Interstate truckers like J. B. Hunt Transport are responsible to the Interstate Commerce Commission. And all companies, from General Dynamics to mom-and-pop operations, are subject to the rules and regulations of the Internal Revenue Service and the Social Security Administration.

request for proposals (RFP)
Detailed, formal government document requesting proposals and bids on a specific project

Governments have stringent communication requirements. For example, federal, state, and local governments inform private companies about opportunities to work with them by issuing invitations to bid on contracts. These invitations, known as **requests for proposals,** require interested companies to use the format and style required in government proposals (see Chapter 10). Meetings are similarly bureaucratic, and in order to get action, businesspeople must learn to identify contacts who can be of help.

Because government regulations are not always clear, companies often write letters asking for more information or questioning whether the company's interpretation of a regulation is correct. The complexity of tax regulations makes this kind of communication common with the IRS.

PROGRESS CHECK

1. In internal communication, who communicates?
2. How does the size of a company affect its internal communication?
3. Why is it important to handle customer complaints well?

FORMAL AND INFORMAL COMMUNICATION CHANNELS

Within the context of an organization's internal and external communication networks are formal and informal communication channels that define the *manner* in which messages are sent. **Communication channels** include such formal pathways as letters, reports, memos, proposals, speeches, and oral presentations and informal pathways like the office grapevine.

Formal and informal channels operate both within and outside the organization. While a memo, for example, is usually considered a formal internal message, a conversation around the water cooler is normally regarded as an informal internal message. Similarly, while a public relations press release is a formal way to communicate with outsiders, a casual phone conversation to a friend at another company is part of the informal external "grapevine."

Formal Channels

The **formal communication channel** includes communication that is sanctioned by company management—for example, when a regional sales manager reports directly to a vice president of sales and marketing. Formal communication channels follow a company's organizational structure. Often, this structure is laid out in an **organization chart**—a blueprint for the organization that indicates formal lines of communication. A model of a formal communication network is found in Figure 1.2.

COMMUNICATION FLOWS   The direction taken by communication within the formal channel is known as the **communication flow**. Communication can flow downward, upward, or horizontally. As Figure 1.3 shows, the type of message to be communicated is linked to the communication flow. Information, for example, generally flows upward while directives are generally communicated downward.

DOWNWARD COMMUNICATION   A message that flows from a superior to a subordinate is known as **downward communication**. The importance of this communication flow cannot be underestimated. Surveys have shown that most employees consider immediate supervisors to be their primary formal sources of information.[13]

communication channels
Formal and informal pathways that define the manner in which messages are sent within an organization's communication networks

formal communication channel
Communication sanctioned by company management

organization chart
Diagram indicating formal lines of communication and interrelationships among the positions, departments, and functions of an organiztion

communication flow
Direction taken by communication within a formal communication channel

downward communication
Message flowing from a superior to a subordinate level of an organization

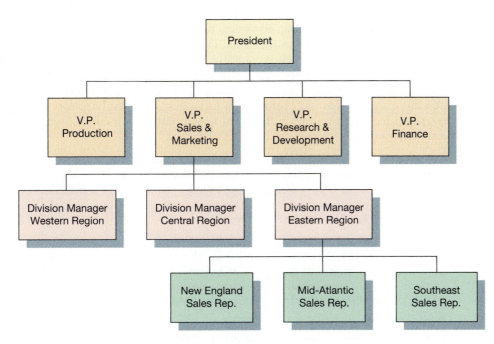

FIGURE 1.2   *Formal Communication Network*

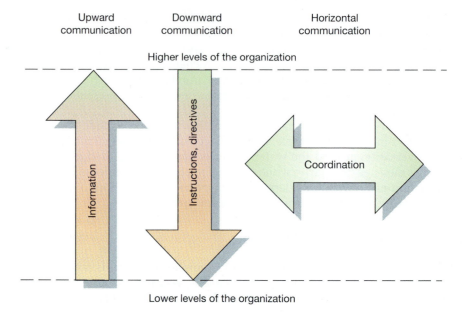

Upward communication   Downward communication   Horizontal communication

Higher levels of the organization

Information

Instructions, directives

Coordination

Lower levels of the organization

FIGURE 1.3   *Message Types and the Communication Flow*

Downward communication can be written or oral. For example, a manager's memo to his or her staff to delegate responsibilities on a new project is a written document; so is an employee-orientation handbook. Oral presentations also communicate messages to company subordinates through downward flow. For example, a regional sales manager may use a meeting to tell his or her salesforce of new restrictions on travel and entertainment budgets.

Downward communication can start in one form and be disseminated in another. This happened when former IBM chairman John F. Akers gave a stinging talk to some of the company's fast-rising managers about how IBM was losing its competitive edge. One of the managers at the meeting took detailed notes and distributed Akers's message via an electronic message system to everyone in the company. Within a short time, Akers's message had been received by all and the downward communication was complete.[14]

Downward communication, however, often becomes flawed as it passes from one organizational level to the next. This weakening of communication may result from a number of factors, ranging from lack of clarity on the part of the speaker or writer to poor listening or reading habits among receivers. Although the following humorous example involves the military, similar miscommunication problems are common in business. We simply follow on its downward path a communication flow that was initiated by a colonel who had issued the following directive to his executive officers:

> Tomorrow evening at approximately 20:00 hours Halley's Comet will be visible in this area, an event which occurs only once every 75 years. Have the men fall out in the battalion area in fatigues, and I will explain this rare phenomenon to them. In case of rain, we will not be able to see anything, so assemble the men in the theater and I will show them films of it.

■ AN EXECUTIVE OFFICER TO COMPANY COMMANDERS:

> By order of the Colonel, tomorrow at 20:00 hours, Halley's Comet will appear above the battalion area. If it rains, fall the men out in fatigues, then march to the theater where this rare phenomenon will take place, something which occurs only once every 75 years.

■ A COMPANY COMMANDER TO HIS LIEUTENANT:

> By order of the Colonel be in fatigues at 20:00 hours tomorrow evening, the phenomenal Halley's Comet will appear in the theater. In case of rain, in

the battalion area, the Colonel will give another order, something which occurs once every 75 years.

- THE LIEUTENANT TO HIS SERGEANT:

  Tomorrow at 20:00 hours, the Colonel will appear in the theater with Halley's Comet, something which happens every 75 years. If it rains, the Colonel will order the comet into the battalion area.

- THE SERGEANT TO HIS SQUAD:

  When it rains tomorrow at 20:00 hours, the phenomenal 75-year-old General Halley, accompanied by the Colonel, will drive his comet through the battalion area theater in fatigues.[15]

UPWARD COMMUNICATION   Communication that flows from a subordinate to a superior is known as **upward communication**. As we saw earlier in the chapter, this information flow is essential to organizational success. An increasing number of chief executive officers now realize that they are insulated from the workforce by various levels of management. Instead of reporting accurately to the CEO, middle managers may filter information and thus present a distorted final picture to top-level management. To combat this problem, W. Thomas Stephens, CEO of Manville Corporation, regularly sends letters to employees at their homes, thus eliminating problems that arise when middle managers neglect to distribute communications. Included in each letter is a stamped envelope addressed directly to Stephens to facilitate suggestions or criticisms of company operations. Since Stephens started the system, he has received—and personally answered—more than 500 letters.[16]

Upward communication is often more difficult than downward communication because of differences in *status*. The person initiating the communication has a lesser status than the person receiving it and may fear repercussions if he or she says or writes something perceived to be inappropriate. As a result, workers communicate with their superiors far less frequently than their superiors communicate with them. One study of managers, for example, found that only 15 percent of total communication time involved messages directed upward.[17]

HORIZONTAL COMMUNICATION   In **horizontal communication** (sometimes called **lateral communication**), people at the same organizational level communicate with one another. For example, the head of production in a clothing manufacturer may talk with the company's design chief about difficulties in manufacturing a particular kind of garment within budget. As companies grow larger and more complex, horizontal communication takes on increasing importance. In an insurance company, for example, the head of the underwriting department must work hand-in-hand with his or her counterparts in claims and sales.

Because horizontal communication involves people at the same organizational level, interactions are generally friendlier and less formal than those in other communication flows. However, problems can result when people perceive that they are competing for the same limited company resources.[18]

Horizontal communication has long been quite important to Japanese automakers. When a company like Toyota decides to develop a new car, the first step is to form a team that includes members from every department, including body engineering, interior design, purchasing, manufacturing, marketing, and finance. Team members all work in the same place and have constant communication as the development process proceeds.[19]

Figure 1.4 shows five common **communication networks**, each of which describes an interaction pattern involving upward, downward, and horizontal communication. Each network is made up of five members, each of whom is represented by a circle. In the *chain* formation, for example, information moves up and down but not horizontally. In the *wheel*, supervisors communicate with four subordinates who report back to higher management but not to each other. The *circle* network allows members to interact with members next to them but

upward communication
Message flowing from a subordinate to a superior level of an organization

horizontal or **lateral communication**
Message flowing from sender to receiver within the same organizational level

communication network
Interaction pattern involving upward, downward, and horizontal communication

INTERVIEW

James F. Orr III, Chairman and CEO, UNUM Corp.

Fortune magazine recently recognized James F. Orr III, CEO of UNUM Corp., as one of its "champions of communications." The honor was no surprise to employees of the Portland, Maine–based insurance company. Communication is part of UNUM's corporate creed. "We value communication," reads the company's statement of vision and values, including "communicating clearly, consistently and openly with everyone we deal with; building an environment which encourages open communication, participation, honesty and candor; and listening." We asked Orr to elaborate on the role played by open communication at UNUM, on the corporation's attempts to raise communication

competence to a higher level, and on his views on the link between effective communication and career success.

Question: What single communication skill is most important to business success?

Answer: The ability to listen as a member of a team. With the concepts of teamwork and collaboration becoming more important, we have to be able to listen—and learn—from business associates. Yet, listening is a lot more difficult than speaking.

Question: You have been quoted as saying that communication tends to break down most on lower- and middle-management levels. Why does this happen, and what kind of special problems do you see?

Answer: Our internal employee surveys and exit interviews with people leaving the company tell us that top-down communication at UNUM is quite good, but that bottom-up communication is not nearly as effective. That is, information

with no one else. The *all-channel* network is the only network in which free communication takes place among all group members. If the *Y* network is inverted, two subordinates are shown communicating with the same manager, with two more managerial levels shown above that. In this case, communication is limited primarily to workers and immediate supervisors.

collaboration
Process in which two or more people join together in a team to produce and deliver a message

Collaboration is a factor in many communication networks. **Collaboration** is the process in which two or more people join together in a team to produce and deliver oral or written presentations. As we will see in Chapter 10, collabo-

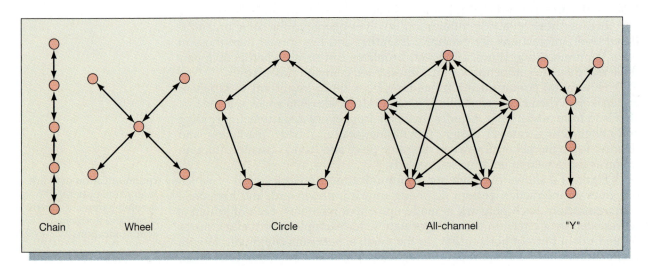

FIGURE 1.4   *Common Communication Networks*

doesn't filter up from subordinate to manager as well as it filters down from manager to subordinate. We believe this happens because communication up the line is threatening, particularly at lower- and middle-management levels. It involves suggesting improvements and criticizing managers and supervisors. That kind of communication is difficult to foster.

We have a number of programs that help encourage bottom-up communication, including team training and our version of the New England town meeting. Recently, for example, we gathered employees at our Toronto office and gave them the opportunity to ask questions of senior management. Many raised their hands; others preferred to remain anonymous and submitted questions in advance. Anonymity opened things up. People asked questions they would never ask an immediate supervisor. It was a very healthy situation.

Question: Are communication principles the same in good times and in bad times?

Answer: While the messages change, the basic communication philosophy should remain the same. For example, when we sold off one of our lines of business, we were forced to tell several hundred employees that they would have to find new jobs. Despite the nature of the message, we tried to be open and candid. We told everyone that they would know as much as we knew and that we would keep them fully informed.

Question: If you were to give college students one piece of advice about business communication, what would that advice be?

Answer: Take the time to do it right. Recognize how important communication skills are—from listening to speaking to writing. And start believing that effective communication will play a large part in your career success.

Source: Interview with James F. Orr III.

ration is an essential element in report and proposal writing and spans the planning, writing, and finalization stages.

COMMUNICATION FLOW OUTSIDE THE ORGANIZATION   The formal flow of communication to organizational outsiders is handled by the public relations department. **Public relations** is the communication that an organization conducts with its various *publics*, including, among others, stockholders and the general public. The broad goal of public relations is to build the organization's prestige and reputation. Written communication often takes the form of formal *press releases*—documents that send company announcements to the various media, including newspapers, magazines, television, and radio. Formal press conferences are meetings in which the message is communicated orally.

When Chemical Bank merged with Manufacturers Hanover Trust, announcements of the merger were made in a press conference and through press releases. These public relations messages dealt with issues that concerned different groups. For example, the announcements focused on the eventual consolidation and closing of bank branches—a subject of vital interest to the banking public. The announcements also explained that while the merger would result in the layoff of thousands of workers (an employee concern), a new, stronger financial institution would emerge—a fact that interested stockholders, customers, government officials, and employees alike.

public relations
Communication conducted by an organization with such publics as stockholders and the general public

Informal Communication Channels

Informal communication channels consist of communication patterns that are independent of the formal channels approved by management. These channels are often more efficient than formal channels. However, despite their power,

informal communication channel
Communication pattern independent of formal channels sanctioned by management

they often operate independent of management control. As the following examples show, informal communication channels can be both internal and external:

- At lunch, three co-workers from different departments talk about rumors of companywide layoffs.
- While exercising in the company fitness center, a marketing vice president mentions to an accounting supervisor that a new advertising campaign is being considered.
- During his weekly tennis match with a friend in a client company, a sales representative hears about a business opportunity.
- A rumor spreads that a popular food product manufactured by the company is contaminated by pesticides.

INFORMAL INTERNAL COMMUNICATION   Instead of learning about policy and personnel changes and new projects from supervisors and official company documents, employees sometimes gain information through unofficial, independent sources. These informal, internal communication channels are known as **grapevines**. According to one survey, although they much prefer formal information sources, employees frequently cite the grapevine as their most frequent source of information. The graph in Figure 1.5 details the results of this survey, itemizing the information sources cited most often by participating employees.

Keith Davis, a human relations expert who has studied informal communication patterns for more than thirty years, has characterized the grapevine according to its accuracy, speed, base of operations, confidentiality, and ties to formal communication:

- *Accuracy.* Grapevines pass on accurate information between 75 percent and 95 percent of the time. However, even though the failure rate is relatively low, small inaccuracies can garble an entire message.
- *Speed.* Communication travels through the grapevine at an extremely fast pace. While a message sent through formal channels may take days to reach its audience, messages sent through the grapevine can travel in hours. For one thing, grapevine messages tend to be oral and oral messages generally travel faster than written ones.
- *Base of operations.* Grapevine communication occurs primarily during working hours and at the work place.
- *Confidentiality.* Contrary to popular belief, confidential information is often protected as it passes through the grapevine.
- *Ties to formal communication.* The grapevine supplements formal communication. The two systems operate jointly.

Davis has also identified four distinct paths in which information travels through the grapevine (see Figure 1.6). In the *single-strand grapevine*, information travels in a straight line from Person A to Person B to Person C and so on. The farther the communication moves from its original source, the greater the chance of distortion. In the *gossip grapevine*, information comes from a single source—in this case, Person A. The *probability grapevine* is characterized by random communication: Person A passes information on a random basis to some people but not to others. Finally, in the *cluster grapevine*, Person A selectively communicates with some people but not with others, with only some of the grapevine participants passing the information on. According to Davis, the cluster is probably the most common form of the grapevine.[20]

Not surprisingly, the grapevine is threatening to managers who believe that it undermines their control. However, instead of attempting to destroy the grapevine (which may be impossible), many managers realize the importance of working with it to provide accurate information. This is especially true when rumors spread about anxiety-producing situations. A **rumor** is a story in general circulation that has not been confirmed by facts. In a corporate merger, for exam-

grapevine
Internal information channel conducting information through unofficial, independent sources

Good gossip is just what's going on. Bad gossip is stuff that is salacious, mean, bitchy—the kind most people really enjoy.

Liz Smith
Gossip columnist

rumor
Story about an organization which is in general circulation but which is unconfirmed by facts

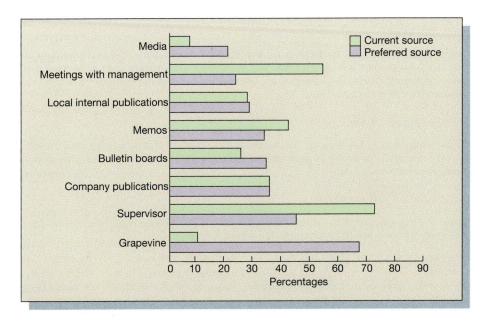

FIGURE 1.5   *Actual and Preferred Sources of Employee Information*
Employees were asked from which source do you *now get* the most useful
information about your company? From which source *would you prefer* to get
this information?
Source: 1991 Hay Research for Management Database

ple, rumors may spread about plant closings, layoffs, dismissals of top managers, and so on. "The more frightened people are by a rumor, the more likely
they are to repeat it," says psychologist Allan J. Kimmel, an expert on the anatomy of rumors. "People hope that they will repeat the rumor to someone who
will tell them they are wrong."[21]

Realizing the danger of unanswered rumors, managers may attempt to
deal with them through memos, meetings, and other formal communication
channels. They may also place someone in the informal communication
grapevine who can provide accurate information.

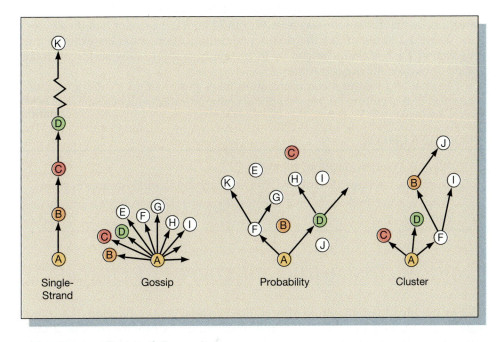

FIGURE 1.6   *Types of Grapevines*

Step 1: Be Alert

On first hearing a rumor, track the location and wording. Stay alert for further reports. If you hear ten or more, try to ask people who repeat it where they heard about it. Businesses targeted by rumors, for example, can request distributors, salesmen, and others in contact with the public to check with competitors to see if they share the problem.

Step 2: Evaluate the Rumor

See how damaging it is; for instance, a company can check whether it is slowing sales. Monitor whether it is damaging the morale of those who are its target. Try to determine how many people who hear the rumor believe it to be true.

Step 3: Plan a Counterattack

Assemble all facts about the forms of the rumor and where it has spread. Focus the counterattack in regions where it is most heavily concentrated. If it is local, treat it locally.

Step 4: Launch the Counterattack

Refute the rumor point by point, with solid evidence, backed by experts. Don't deny any more than is alleged in the rumor. Point out that the rumor is both untrue and unjust and that it is unfair to spread lies.

FIGURE 1.7   *How to Fight a Rumor*

Source: Reprinted from Daniel Goleman, "Anatomy of a Rumor: It Flies on Fear," *The New York Times,* June 4, 1991, p. C5.

INFORMAL EXTERNAL COMMUNICATION   Informal grapevines also operate outside the company and have the ability to affect company business. Rumors that spread through the general public can be particularly troublesome. For example, rumors have been told about children being kidnapped at Kmart; the involvement of Liz Claiborne and Procter & Gamble with Satanism; and Ku Klux Klan control of Tropical Fantasy, a soft drink marketed to minorities in northeastern cities. According to Frederick Koenig, a social psychologist who consults with organizations victimized by rumors, companies must use the four steps outlined in Figure 1.7 to put rumors to rest. Entenmann's, a New York baked-goods manufacturer, used this technique when it faced a rumor that the Rev. Sun Myung Moon's Unification Church owned the company. The company chairman held a news conference reviewing the history of the family-owned business and denying categorically that the rumor was true. Within 24 hours, the rumor had died.

Table 1.2 summarizes the distinct communication channels examined in this section. Each is characterized by its formality or informality and by its focus inside or outside the organization.

Formal and informal communication takes place within a *corporate culture.* The effect of this culture on organizational communication will be examined next.

PROGRESS CHECK

1. What is a communication channel?
2. Distinguish among downward, upward, and horizontal communication.
3. What are the four steps that a company can follow to fight a negative rumor?

COMMUNICATING WITHIN THE CORPORATE CULTURE

corporate culture
Patterns, traditions, and values that make one organization distinctly different from another

Just as the broad social culture affects interpersonal communication, the corporate culture affects organizational communication. **Corporate culture**, a term first coined by organizational consultants Terrence Deal and Allen Kennedy,

TABLE 1.2 *Communication Channels and Message Types*	
CHANNEL	TYPE OF BUSINESS MESSAGE
Formal, Internal	Memos, reports, meetings, written proposals, oral presentations, agendas, meeting minutes
Formal, External	Letters, written proposals, oral presentations, speeches, press releases, press conferences
Informal, Internal	Rumors spread through the grapevine
Informal, External	Rumors spread through the grapevine

refers to the patterns, traditions, and values that make one organization distinctly different from another.[22]

Corporate culture affects business writing in tangible ways. According to communication consultant Sana Reynolds, who helps firms improve employees' writing skills, the culture at Morgan Guarantee Trust discourages people from using the personal pronoun *I* and encourages instead references to "the writer" or "the undersigned." In addition, says Reynolds, the bank prides itself on its conservative image and, as a result, is still indenting letters instead of using full block format.[23] In the form of corporate vocabulary, oral language can also be affected. At Disney, for example, workers are "cast members" and customers "guests." At Wal-Mart, nonmanagerial employees are referred to as "associates."

Elements of a Corporate Culture

Deal and Kennedy define five distinct elements of a corporate culture: *business environment, values, heroes, rites and rituals,* and *cultural network.* As Table 1.3 shows, each element influences the ways in which information is communicated through organizational channels.

BUSINESS ENVIRONMENT   The *business environment* refers to the marketplace in which a company sells its goods or services. Included in the business environment are such factors as the nature of the company's products, its competition and customers, government regulation, and so on. IBM, for example, a company in a highly competitive industry, is defined by a strong sales culture which, in turn, provides the company with its communication focus.

VALUES   Values define both the company's philosophy for achieving success and the framework within which all employees conduct their day-to-day activities. For example, the values of Procter & Gamble focus on the consumer. "P&G

TABLE 1.3 *The Impact of Corporate Culture on Communication*	
ELEMENT	EXAMPLE OF IMPACT ON COMMUNICATION
Business Environment	Declines in air travel prompt announcements of special incentive programs.
Values	Company philosophy is reflected in the corporate mission statement.
Heroes	Interpersonal-communications style of managers may reflect that of the CEO.
Rites and Rituals	Everyone at Tyson Foods—even the CEO—wears brown work clothes.
Cultural Network	Microsoft CEO Bill Gates responds directly to computer queries from employees.

is a culture that glories in listening and listening well to consumers," explain Deal and Kennedy. "Furthermore, they have developed more ways to listen to consumers than anyone else," including polls and surveys, consumer hot lines, and test kitchens.

HEROES   Certain individuals represent tangible role models of the corporate culture. General Electric chairman John (Jack) Welch, whom we mentioned earlier, is one of these people. During the 1980s, Welch's aggressive communication style permeated General Electric. Once known as "Neutron Jack" for his skill at eliminating people while leaving buildings untouched, Welch has more recently come to believe that trust, respect, and openness between workers and managers is essential for success in the twenty-first century—a conviction that Welch expressed in GE's 1991 annual report. Coming from a cultural "hero," his views quickly defined a new, more cooperative management style for the organization.[24]

RITES AND RITUALS   The regular routines of company life, "rites" and "rituals" determine communication styles. For example, General Motors has a reputation for endless meetings and piles of paperwork. Instead of having desks on the factory floor, manufacturing executives, dressed in business suits, spend most of their time in offices and meeting rooms far removed from the assembly line. By contrast, Honda's top manufacturing executives dress in overalls, sit in rooms with as many as 40 engineers, and often work near assembly lines.[25]

CULTURAL NETWORK   The *cultural network* is the informal communication channel that transmits the messages of corporate culture. Deal and Kennedy use the following example to demonstrate the power of the cultural network:

> Consider how the cultural network operates at one company. The aggressive new CEO of this large company was concerned about lagging productivity. The company's markets had suddenly become very competitive and the company was losing share. No shrinking violet, the CEO launches a process that soon leads to a set of recommendations to reorganize the salesforce and institute a new set of sales incentives. These recommendations are written up and announced to the organization at large. Effective communication? Definitely not. The reason? Any such announcement and its distribution are only the beginning of the communication process. Here's what happens when the word arrives in a field office:
>
> The first people to see it are the secretaries. They receive their own copies and note with interest that their boss is getting a copy too. Each dutifully takes ten minutes to read the memo through. After all, they don't receive all that many memos directly from the CEO. So far so good.
>
> The first secretary finishes reading and waits for the others to finish as well.
>
> "What's this about?" they all want to know.
>
> "I have no idea," responds one. "Maybe the company is in trouble. Hmmm. I hope I'm not going to have to start looking for a job." For the next forty-five minutes not much work gets done as the pool of secretaries, working their end of the cultural network, debate whether or not the company is going under. The debate comes to a close when a woman who has been with the company for seventeen years and has seen it all before says, "It doesn't mean anything. Al sent out the same memo back in 1976 and nothing happened. Nothing."
>
> So ends round one. Score:
>
> Communication: 10 minutes reading time
>
> Cultural network: 45 minutes discussion time
>
> Round two begins when the boss arrives and picks up his mail. The secretaries are alert to see how he responds to the memo. He goes into his office, spends five minutes scanning the memo, and then reaches for the phone. The secretaries seem visibly relieved.

"Hello, Charlie. This is Bill. Did you see Henry's announcement? Old Fred lost out in that shuffle. I knew he had blown it when they left him off the speaker's list for the annual sales meeting." For the next half hour, the two friends talk about the politics of the reorganization, as well as how they will personally fare. They conclude that nothing will really change in the salesforce as a result of these moves since the salespeople in the field will still face the same conditions day-to-day in the marketplace.

End of round two. Running score:

Communication: 15 minutes total

Cultural network: 75 minutes total

The incident is not over, however. The CEO of this company understood how the cultural network worked and was suitably cynical about the direct effect of reorganization on the field salesforce's performance. He also thought he knew what the problem was; his salesforce had grown accustomed to taking orders without facing head-to-head competition. That's where his incentive plan came into play and the third round of communication began. This third round was designed to feed tangible examples directly to the salesforce through the cultural network.

To start this third round, the CEO first asked the field to send him weekly lists of competitive sales situations they were facing. Then each week he would allocate a day for work in the field on one of these accounts.... The CEO had started his career with another very competitive sales-oriented company. And, he was a first-class...[salesperson].... So soon, the cultural network was abuzz with stories like "Did you hear how Charlie knocked over that oil distributor's account in Omaha last Friday? We were almost out on our ears when he shows up and lands a ten-unit order. The account...[salesperson]...even got a $500 bonus payment out of the deal. They actually convinced the customer that our machine was twice as reliable as those Japanese models they were about to buy."

Score: The cultural network wins again—but this time because a manager knew how to use it. The stories about the CEO's exploits in the field were told over and over again in the company. They are still told today, years after the fact.[26]

COMMUNICATION CHALLENGES

Within the structure provided by corporate culture, communication is being forced to respond to challenges that are changing the very nature of communication. These challenges have the potential to affect every aspect of the corporate culture, including the business environment, values, heroes, rites and rituals, and the cultural network. The complexities of business communication will continue to grow during the final decade of the twentieth century. As Figure 1.8 shows, effective business communication must meet four distinct challenges:

- The challenge of *ethical communication*
- The challenge of communicating in a *global marketplace*
- The challenge of communicating with a *diverse work force*
- The challenge of *communication technology*

The Challenge of Ethical Communication

Ethics—the standards of conduct and moral judgment accepted by society— have a strong influence on business communication. Although ethics are first and foremost standards for the individual, they also apply to businesses as insti-

ethics
Standards of conduct and moral judgment accepted by society

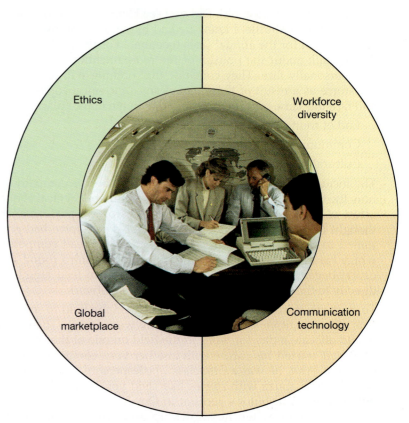

FIGURE 1.8   *Communication Challenges in Today's Environment*

tutions and to businesspeople as responsible agents. The ethics of business communication focuses on applying values to determine what is good and bad or right and wrong and raises questions about who is—or is not—harmed by specific business actions. Ethical considerations confront companies and individuals in numerous communication situations, including the following:

■ *Ethics influences what a candidate tells a prospective employer at a job interview and the questions that the employer asks the candidate in return.* For example, many job candidates lie on their résumés, and companies ask individuals discriminatory questions that the law expressly forbids.

■ *Ethics influences the information that a company reveals about goods and services and the information that it holds back.* For years, scientists at Dow Corning urged top management to conduct safety studies of its silicone gel breast implants, but those tests were never completed—a fact never revealed to women seeking implants. Realizing that he was involved in an ethical and moral crisis, A. H. Rathjen, a Dow Corning official in charge of developing a new implant, wrote a memorandum in 1976 that said in part: "We are engulfed in unqualified speculation. Nothing to date is truly quantitative. Is there something in the implant that migrates out of or off the mammary prosthesis? Yes or no! Does it continue for the life of the implant or is it limited or controlled for a period of time? What is it?"[27]

■ *Ethics influences how companies handle consumer complaints.* For example, after an automaker has received numerous customer complaints about cracking windshields, does the company begin a recall program or does it try to save money by telling people that no other incidents have been reported?

■ *Ethics influences the use of confidential information.* When information is communicated in confidence, ethical judgments determine the extent to which it

CURRENT ISSUES IN BUSINESS COMMUNICATION
Corporate Culture and Communication at Microsoft

The corporate culture of Microsoft, the $1.8-billion computer-software maker located in Redmond, Washington, is personified by founder William H. Gates III. Gates is the company hero; his values are shared by everyone who works for him, as are the rites and rituals that define his work life. Not surprisingly, Gates has also defined the company's communication style and cultural network. According to Jeff Raikes, a senior vice president who has worked for Microsoft for eleven years, "Bill" is the company. Like its founder, says Raikes, Microsoft is "high horsepower, high energy."

As a hero/role model, Gates sets an imposing pace. Although he is now the richest man in America, he works 15-hour days. He arrives at the office at 9:00 A.M. and usually stays past midnight. At home, he often spends another two hours writing memos on his home computer. Gates acknowledges that his behavior sets the tone for everyone who works for him; indeed, 60- to 80-hour weeks are standard. "I'm the biggest single influence in the corporate culture here," reports Gates.

Gates usually communicates with employees via electronic mail—a computer-based personal-message system. The communication is informal, and employees are encouraged to share ideas with anyone in the company—even if it means bypassing immediate supervisors.

When ideas are expressed, they often reflect a unique corporate language dubbed "Microspeak." For example, Gates himself once advised an interviewer that he populates his company by hiring "smart people that are pretty high *bandwidth*"—that is, intellectually talented. Here are just a few of the terms that Microsoft employees typically use in both speech and written communication:

- *flame mail*—electronic mail that is angry, sarcastic, or emotional
- *granularity*—fineness of detail
- *hardcore*—serious about and committed to work
- *nonlinear*—angry and out of control
- *random*—illogical

The nonverbal language of clothes is also important at Microsoft, though not in the way most businesspeople would expect. Shunning high fashion and expensive haircuts, Gates's own informal, somewhat rumpled look sets the standard. Not surprisingly, people who arrive at job interviews wearing expensive jewelry and fancy suits are usually perceived as mismatches.

The final product is a unique communication environment at Microsoft. Before marketing manager Richard I. Segal came to the company, he had worked for eight years at Aetna Life & Casualty, a company with a traditional corporate culture. Nothing there prepared him for Microsoft—and especially not for the sight of bathing suit–clad programmers discussing software bugs over a game of volleyball in the hallway. According to Segal, "Microsoft's biggest growth issue is getting people who have worked in a cubicle all their lives to function [and communicate] in this environment."

Source: Kathy Rebello and Evan I. Schwartz, "Microsoft: Bill Gates's Baby Is on Top of the World. Can It Stay There?", February 24, 1992, pp. 60–64 by permission of *Business Week.* © 1992.

---

is protected or revealed. A lapse in confidentiality can have serious business repercussions. For example, when a U. S. Navy consultant inadvertently left a confidential report containing information about a competitor's work at the Bath Iron Works, CEO William Haggett ordered a photocopy of the report. Although he realized soon after that he had made "an inappropriate business-ethics decision" and returned the report to the Navy, Haggett stepped down as CEO of the Maine shipbuilder—a position that he had held for eight years—because he failed to set a strong moral example.[28]

- *Ethics influences respect for individual privacy.* Lack of respect for individual privacy is an abuse of business ethics. For example, if a nurse in the company medical department reveals details of a worker's medical history, he or

ETHICS IN BUSINESS COMMUNICATION

Tracing Ethics at Procter & Gamble

Cincinnati-based Procter & Gamble admitted to invading the privacy of its workers when it turned to the Cincinnati police for help in tracing news leaks of confidential company information to *The Wall Street Journal*. In an attempt to find the source of the leaks, authorities searched the records of 803,000 telephone lines in the Cincinnati area. After the incident, an internal company survey revealed that many employees considered the search a "disgrace" and an "embarrassment." In a letter to employees admitting that the company had made a mistake, CEO Edwin L. Artzt had this to say: "We thought we were doing the right thing because we had a clear legal right to seek the assistance of the authorities to investigate potential damaging leaks of confidential company information.… [But] we created a problem that was larger than the one we were trying to solve."

When P&G launched its search into the records of every telephone user in southwestern Ohio, privacy rights collided with technology. Columbia University's Alan F. Westin, an authority on the issue of technology and privacy, points out that "when technology allows you to run millions of calls involving [hundreds of thousands of] telephone subscribers through a computer in order to identify who called a person, potentially to find out whether a crime was committed, you raise the question of whether technological capacity has gone over the line in terms of what is a reasonable search and seizure."

Although its recent experience highlights the ramifications of precisely this question, Procter & Gamble is not likely to loosen the flow of information to outside sources. While the company acknowledged that its actions crossed the line separating acceptable and unacceptable communication ethics, those who know the company speculate that the end result may be even tighter communication controls.

Sources: Timothy Egan, "Sometimes, the Disloyal Are Watched," *The New York Times*, October 27, 1991, Section 4, p. 16; Lisa I. Fried, "P&G's Search for Leaks Toughens Reporters' Jobs," *Folio: The Magazine for Magazine Management*, October 1, 1991, p. 37; "Procter & Gamble Says It Was Wrong to Have Phone Calls Traced," *The New York Times*, September 6, 1991, p. A18; James S. Hirsch and Alecia Swasy, "P&G's Directors Support Action on News Leaks," *The Wall Street Journal*, September 11, 1991, p. A4; and Randall Rothenberg, "Search for News Leak Spurs Ohio Phone Sweep," *The New York Times*, August 16, 1991, p. A10.

she has invaded the employee's privacy: Such details cannot be revealed without the employee's consent—even if a supervisor requests them.

- *Ethics influences how people respond to business pressures.* What happens, for example, when a manager pressures a subordinate to complete an assignment without allotting sufficient time? What happens if a project manager falsifies shipping dates on internal reports because of pressure from his or her boss to meet an earlier deadline (let's say that the boss's bonus depends on it)? What if an advertising copywriter plagiarizes ideas for a new campaign that the client wanted yesterday. The environment that creates this pressure comes from management—as does the potential solution. According to management consultant Barbara Ley Toffler, "Managers must make sure that subordinates have the ability, knowledge and resources to get the job done ethically. That means getting feedback from those who will be performing the work before targets are set, and then gearing those targets to the available resources. If a process takes four weeks with all operations at capacity, management must realize that a message to accomplish it in two weeks is likely to produce unethical behavior."[29]

Ask yourself how your action would look if it were reported tomorrow on the front page of the local newspaper.

Chester Burger
Public relations executive

IMPROVING THE ENVIRONMENT FOR ETHICAL COMMUNICATION   It is not just rhetoric to say that ethical communication is "good business." According to an Arizona State University study, corporations that have paid dividends for 100 years or more tend to be companies that place a high priority on ethics. In addition, a Deloitte Touche survey of corporate leaders, business school administrators, and members of Congress found that 63 percent of the respondents believed businesses with high ethical standards to be stronger competitors than those with relaxed standards.[30]

As a result, concerns for standards of both ethics and productivity have motivated many companies to establish internal ethics programs. Today, more than 15 percent of American companies with more than 50,000 employees have ethics offices empowered to examine reports of misconduct, and 37 percent of American companies with more than 100 employees offer ethics training. Since General Dynamics's program started in 1985, the office has received more than 30,000 employee contacts that have resulted in 1,419 sanctions, including 165 terminations, 58 cases requiring financial reimbursement, 26 demotions, and 10 cases referred to lawyers for civil action or criminal prosecution. Among the complaints regularly reported are falsified résumés.[31]

AN ETHICS CHECKLIST   An ethics checklist like the one in Table 1.4 will help you evaluate the moral integrity of your business-communication practices. As you can see, business communication ethics affects message purpose, research and selection of material, development of ideas, and use of language. The self-examination that goes into answering questions like those in Table 1.4 should be placed in a broader ethical context that involves communicating with others as you would like them to communicate with you. The ethical context should also involve a commitment to truth.

The Challenge of Communicating in a Global Marketplace

No longer a market unto itself, the United States is becoming part of an expanding global economy. This shift to a global marketplace is reflected in business revenues and profits. For example, while approximately one third of The Coca-Cola Company's unit sales are in the United States, two thirds are in Latin America, Europe, the Pacific, Africa, and Canada. More importantly, approximately 80 percent of the company's operating profits comes from international business.[32] Even markets that were once considered impenetrable by U.S. businesses are now cracking the trade door. When Toys 'R' Us opened a store just 40 miles outside of Tokyo, it became the first U.S.-owned discount store in Japan.

This shift to a global marketplace sets up the second communication challenge that we introduced in Figure 1.8—the challenge to understand cultural differences that affect communication patterns in different parts of the world. These differences will be examined in depth in Chapter 18.

The Challenge of Communicating with a Diverse Workforce

No longer is the U.S. workforce almost exclusively white and male. Indeed, demographic changes show that by the year 2000, women will account for more than 47 percent of the workforce, African Americans 12 percent, Hispanics 10 percent, and Asians 4 percent.[33] The challenge of increasing diversity is to develop new communication patterns that will enable men and women and people from different cultural backgrounds to understand each other and work together. In addition, with customers becoming increasingly diverse, business-people must learn new communication skills in order to maintain the same or a greater level of business activity. The challenge of diversity also means helping employees communicate with disabled and elderly co-workers and customers. The topic of communicating both in a diverse workforce and with diverse people outside the organization will be examined in more detail in Chapter 19.

The Challenge of Communication Technology

Communication technology—including such office necessities as word processors, fax machines, electronic mail, voice mail, and video conferences—has

First there is the law. It must be obeyed. But the law is the minimum. You must act ethically.

IBM employee guidelines

TABLE 1.4 *A Checklist for Ethical Communication*		
	YES	**NO**
Message Purpose		
If I accomplish my purpose, will it be in the best interest of my audience?	❑	❑
Am I targeting a small group who will benefit at the expense of a larger group?	❑	❑
Do hidden agendas affect my purpose?	❑	❑
Research Methods		
Did I conduct thorough research or cut corners because of pressure to complete the assignment?	❑	❑
Did I use recent, reliable, and unbiased sources?	❑	❑
Selection of Source Materials		
Did I choose sources that accurately represent the information available on my topic?	❑	❑
Did I reveal relevant information in documents and conversation or hold key details back to protect my interests?	❑	❑
Did I protect confidential information or ask permission before revealing confidential sources?	❑	❑
Development of Ideas		
Have I used sound logic and reasoning?	❑	❑
Did I rely too heavily on emotional appeals?	❑	❑
Have I avoided exaggerating or otherwise distorting information?	❑	❑
Language Usage		
Have I avoided jargon that would confuse my audience?	❑	❑
Are my references concrete and specific instead of ambiguous and abstract, since ambiguities and abstractions will also confuse the audience?	❑	❑

Source: Based on Judi Brownell and Michael Fitzgerald, "Teaching Ethics in Business Communication: The Effective/Ethical Balancing Scale," *The Bulletin of the Association for Business Communication*, September 1992, p. 18.

changed the ways in which businesspeople communicate. Communication today is immediate and allows people from different locations to communicate as if they were in the same office. The challenge of technology is knowing how to use it effectively in both written and oral communication and understanding how new technologies influence the messages that people are asked to send. The implications of communication technology will be examined in depth in Chapter 20.

The aspects of the business communication environment that we have examined throughout this chapter are also opportunities for personal career success. We will explore the link between effective communication and job success in the next section.

BUSINESS COMMUNICATION AND PERSONAL CAREER SUCCESS

In a recent survey of recruiters from companies with more than 50,000 employees, communication skills were cited as the single most important criterion in choosing managers. According to the survey, conducted by the University of Pittsburgh's Katz Business School, these skills include the ability to make effective written and oral presentations and the ability to work with others. Although these so-called "soft skills" do not involve sophisticated, theoretical knowledge, companies are convinced that they hold the key to job success.[34]

Analysts outside the business arena agree. In their "21st Century Report," Donald C. Hambrick and James W. Fredrickson, both professors at Columbia University's Graduate School of Business, asked respondents to name the three qualities that will be most in demand by top managers in the year 2000.

Respondents identified three characteristics—creativity, enthusiasm, and open-mindedness. Just as important, they added, is the ability to communicate these characteristics to different audiences.[35]

Yet, despite the growing importance of communication skills, many people still come to the workplace unable to compete. In a recent survey, 65 percent of human resources executives said that employee writing skills need improvement, 62 percent cited difficulties in interpersonal communication skills, and 59 percent cited poor customer-service skills.[36] To remedy this situation, companies now spend approximately $43 billion a year for employee education, with much of this money used to help workers in "writing clearly, reading better, being able to speak before audiences, and working harmoniously in groups." The Carnegie Foundation for the Advancement of Teaching believes that this figure is actually much higher.[37]

Another recent survey of 12,000 organizations with more than 100 employees showed that 81 percent provide communication training. A breakdown by training type and the percent of organizations offering each type is found in Figure 1.9. As you can see, between 43 percent and 64 percent of the corporations surveyed train employees in interpersonal communication, listening, conducting meetings, writing, public speaking and presentations, and negotiating skills.

As competitive pressures increase, people who come to the workplace unprepared to write and speak effectively are being either turned away or dismissed. For example, when the National Association of Manufacturers surveyed 4,000 companies, it found that 1 out of 3 regularly turn away job candidates because of poor writing and reading skills. According to business communication analyst Donald Walton, "Personnel managers agree almost unanimously that terminations result not from a lack of technical ability or industriousness, but most often from difficulties in relating to and dealing with people." Walton cites a Harvard University study showing that "for every dismissal based on a failure to do work properly, there were two [dismissals due to] personality factors. Poor communication is generally an integral part of this."[38]

> *To succeed in business, it is necessary to make others see things as you see them.*
>
> John H. Patterson
> Founder,
> National Cash Register Co.

PROGRESS CHECK

1. In what ways can corporate culture influence business writing?
2. Why is it important to develop good communication skills?

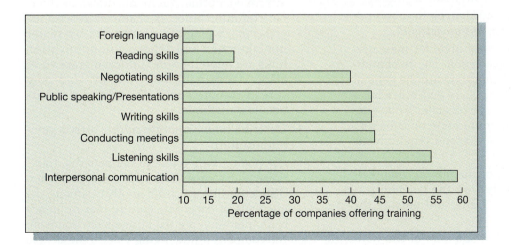

FIGURE 1.9   *Communication Training Offered by Large Organizations*

WHAT'S AHEAD

Contemporary Business Communication is designed to introduce you to the written and oral communication skills that will enable you to succeed in a business career. Part I of the text focuses on business communication fundamentals; the communication principles that you will learn here are the foundation for all that follows. Part II is devoted to the basics of written communication. Part III covers memos and letters, Part IV report and proposal writing, and Part V oral communication. Part VI deals with the practical aspects of employment communication. Part VII examines the challenges of communicating in a global marketplace, in a diverse environment, and through communication technology. We will begin in Chapter 2 with an examination of the communication process.

SUMMARY OF CHAPTER OBJECTIVES

1. **Explain why an effective *internal communication system* is important to a business organization.**

   Through a system of internal communication, messages are communicated up and down the organizational hierarchy and horizontally among co-workers. Through an effective internal communication system, policies are established and disseminated, business decisions are made, and problems are analyzed and solved. Internal communication tools include memos, reports, meetings, oral presentations, speeches, and face-to-face and telephone conversations.

2. **Identify the major audiences in a company's *external communication network*.**

   External communication involves messages sent outside the organization. The chief audiences for this communication are the general public, customers, suppliers and other businesses, and government officials. To be successful, external communication must be sensitive to the specific needs and requirements of each audience.

3. **Describe the nature of the *formal communication channel*, including the *communication flows* that exist inside and outside the organization.**

   Formal communication consists of the written and oral messages that are sanctioned by company management. The direction taken by communication—known as the *communi-*

   cation flow—can be downward, from a superior to a subordinate; upward, from a subordinate to a superior; or horizontal, between workers at the same organizational level. Formal communication outside the organization is often handled by the firm's public-relations department and may take the form of press releases and press conferences.

4. **Explain the nature of the *informal communication channel* and how it operates inside and outside the organization.**

   Informal communication is related to but separate from the formal channels approved by management. Informal internal communication is characterized by the *grapevine*, which is uncontrolled by senior management and whose communication links are often random. Informal grapevines also exist outside the company and may spread rumors about the company and its business methods.

5. **Describe how *corporate culture* affects communication.**

   Corporate culture refers to the patterns, traditions, and values that make one organization distinctly different from another. Among the elements of corporate culture that influence communication are the business environment, the company's underlying values, the people considered heroes, the rites and rituals that define the regular routines of company life, and the cultural network.

6. **Outline the four *communication challenges* that influence the ways in which business-people communicate.**

The challenge of ethical communication requires individuals to communicate according to the standards of conduct and moral judgment accepted by society. The challenge of communicating in a global marketplace is tied to the role of the United States as a global trading partner. The challenge of communicating with a diverse workforce is based on the changing demographic patterns of the U.S. workforce. Finally, the challenge of communication technology is linked to the need to adapt to the technologies that are changing the way business is conducted.

7. **Understand how effective business communication is linked to personal career success.**

Increasingly, managers are identifying the ability to communicate, both in writing and through effective speech, as the single most important criterion in choosing employees. People who do not have effective communication skills are being either turned away or dismissed when the nature of their problems becomes obvious.

*R*EVIEW AND DISCUSSION QUESTIONS

1. Explain the role of communication in business. (*Ch. Obj. 1*)
2. What is internal communication, and why is it important? (*Ch. Obj. 1*)
3. What are the major audiences that make up a firm's external communication network? (*Ch. Obj. 2*)
4. How might a company communicate with each of the audiences that you mentioned in your answer to QUESTION 3? (*Ch. Obj. 2*)
5. Distinguish between formal and informal communication channels. (*Ch. Obj. 3, 4*)
6. Describe the information flows that make up the formal communication channel. (*Ch. Obj. 3*)
7. What is the grapevine? Summarize its benefits and drawbacks for an organization. (*Ch. Obj. 4*)
8. What are the five elements that make up corporate culture? (*Ch. Obj. 5*)
9. Describe four major challenges faced by contemporary business communicators. (*Ch. Obj. 6*)
10. What is ethics? How might it affect business communication? (*Ch. Obj. 7*)

*A*PPLICATION EXERCISES

1. A friend in another town asks why you're taking a class in business communications. Write a letter explaining why it's important to develop good communication skills. (*Ch. Obj. 1*)
2. Write a description of the internal communication process at your office or workplace. (If you're not working presently, think of a job that you held in the past.) What are the most common channels that people use to communicate? Do they use different channels to communicate downward, upward, and horizontally? Do they use any of the methods shown in TABLE 1.1? (*Ch. Obj. 1*)
3. Now write a description of your employer's external communication channels. (Again, if you're not working at the moment, think of a job that you've had in the past.) How does your company deal with each of its various audiences? (*Ch. Obj. 2, 3*)
4. The CEO of your company, knowing that you're studying business communications, asks you to suggest any changes or improvements in the firm's internal and external communications. Write a memo in which you recommend several changes that you feel would help your employer be more effective. Be sure to explain why good communication is good for business. (*Ch. Obj. 1, 2, 3, 5*)
5. As a student, you are a customer of your school. Describe how the school communicates with its customers. What types of oral and written communication does it use? Do you feel that these forms of communication are effective in "selling" you on the school? How might the school improve its external communication system? Explain your answer. (*Ch. Obj. 2*)
6. In addition to its communications with you, your school is probably careful to communicate with the general public. Describe how the school's staff uses advertising and public relations to create an image, provide information, and distinguish your institution from others. (Written materials are probably available in the admissions or public relations

offices; you may wish to talk with a staff member in one of these offices. (*Ch. Obj. 2*)

7. Choose a formal internal communication network, involving five or more people, with which you're familiar. (It might be your office at work, a committee you belong to, or a school or social organization.) Diagram the usual pattern of interaction within this network. Does it correspond to one of the networks shown in FIGURE 1.4? If not, how does it differ? Does everyone in the network have equal access to information? If not, how could this pattern be improved? (*Ch. Obj. 3*)

8. Now think of a grapevine of five or more people in which you participate, whether at work or at school. Diagram the usual pattern of information flow within this network. Does it correspond to one of the grapevines shown in FIGURE 1.6? If not, how is it different? How much power does this grapevine have in the organization? (*Ch. Obj. 4*)

9. Think of a situation in which you were actually involved and in which you did not communicate as well as you would have liked. (This might be something that happened at work or at home; it might involve a stranger or someone you know well.) If you could go back and do things differently, how would you change the way you communicated on that occasion? Explain your answer. (*Ch. Obj. 1, 2*)

10. Think of an important event that took place at your job or school (maybe someone was hired or lost his or her job, maybe a new procedure was introduced, an office opened or closed). Write a brief description comparing the information that you received on that occasion from both formal and informal communication channels. Were the informal channels accurate? Were they faster than official channels? Did they convey more or less information than "approved" channels? Which did you trust more, and why? (*Ch. Obj. 3, 4*)

11. Find out what types of communication training are offered by a company in your community. Does the company offer its employees training in foreign languages, public speaking, negotiation, interpersonal communication, or any of the other skills shown in FIGURE 1.9? Does the company offer training in skills not included in this graph? Who generally receives this training? Management? Entry-level workers? Write a brief (one-page) description of the company's training programs. (*Ch. Obj. 1, 3*)

12. Write a description of the corporate culture at your present job or at a job that you've held in the past. Analyze the five major elements of its culture, and describe how each of these elements determines the company's goals, procedures, and external and internal communications. How does the corporate culture determine who gets hired and promoted? (*Ch. Obj. 5*)

13. Think for a moment of communication technologies with which you're familiar—personal computers? Electronic mail? Fax machines? Answering machines? What about "old" technologies such as telephones, television, and radio? How have these technologies changed the nature of your communication skills and practices? (For instance, how would you compare writing a paper by hand with writing it on a word processor? Writing a letter to a friend versus talking to him or her on the phone?) Write a brief essay in which you discuss the impact of these technologies on communication between people. (*Ch. Obj. 6*)

14. Many companies have adopted official policies regarding business ethics. Go to a library and read about the policies of three different companies. Take notes and then write a brief paper (one to two pages) that describes each firm's policy and ethics program. How does each company define ethical behavior? What procedures has it established to allow employees to report wrongdoing? Which program sounds best to you? Explain your answer. (*Ch. Obj. 6, 7*)

15. Does a company really have a responsibility to behave ethically? Some management theorists believe that a corporation's real responsibility is to its shareholders—that it owes its owners a profit. Others feel that a business has a certain amount of responsibility to society in general—that it owes it to society to behave ethically. What do you think? Write a brief essay in which you state your opinion and explain why you feel the way you do. (*Ch. Obj. 6, 7*)

*B*UILDING YOUR RESEARCH SKILLS

Set up a brief interview (approximately 15 to 30 minutes) with a member of your company's human-resources department. (If you're not presently working, you can choose someone from a firm in your community.) Meet with this person to discuss the ways in which the company handles internal communications. You might refer to the list of methods shown in TABLE 1.1 and ask the individual whether the company has had success with any of them.

Which of these methods were the most helpful in improving communication? Which were least helpful? Why? How would this staff member describe the firm's corporate culture, and how does that culture influence internal communication? Take notes on your conversation.

BUILDING YOUR TEAMWORK SKILLS

Your instructor will divide the class into small groups. Each group member should summarize the conversation that resulted from the previous exercise. Then, working as a group, draw up a list of conclusions. What do most companies seem to be doing to improve internal communication? Do the businesspeople with whom you talked agree with each other on common communication problems and solutions? What did you learn about the corporate cultures at these various firms?

Your instructor may wish to have one member of each group summarize your findings for the class.

COMMUNICATING IN A WORLD OF DIVERSITY

In a recent survey, *Fortune* magazine asked 201 chief executives at America's largest companies when they felt their company would be likely to hire a female CEO. Their responses were not encouraging. Only 2 percent thought the prospect "very likely" in the next 10 years; 63 percent thought it was "somewhat likely" in the next 20 years, and a hefty 82 percent found it "not very likely" or "not likely at all," at least during the next decade.

Why not? Many of the execs felt that it was because women "have not built up solid networks of connections and support." Nancy Hamlin, president of the consulting firm Hamlin Fox, notes that even in the best-intentioned companies, female managers are often left out of informal male get-togethers—lunches, games, sporting events, and the like. "Men don't do this on purpose," concludes Hamlin. "They just don't *think* about it."

Hazel O'Leary, who is now Administrator of the Environmental Protection Agency, remembers her stint as an executive vice president at Northern States Power in Minneapolis. "Without losing your own personality, it's important to be part of the prevailing corporate culture. At this company, it [was] golf. I resisted learning to play golf all my life, but I finally had to admit I was missing something that way." O'Leary reports that she bought a set of clubs and began taking golf lessons on weekends.

Relate the findings of the *Fortune* survey to the discussion in this chapter. What can women do to improve their communication with male co-workers?

Source: Anne Fisher, "When Will Women Get to the Top?" *Fortune*, September 21, 1992, pp. 44–56.

CASE 1.1

Autodesk: Who's in Charge Here?

"I realized this was a different place," recalls one manager, "when at my first staff meeting, I was licked by a dog."

Autodesk is indeed a "different" kind of company. If you've never heard of it, that's not surprising—even though it's the world's sixth-largest personal computer-software firm and even though the London Business School named it one of the world's most profitable companies during the 1980s. One reason why Autodesk is relatively unknown is its specialized niche. It makes software that allows inexpensive personal computers to produce powerful models for engineers, architects, and other professional designers.

The other reason is John Walker, the reclusive but talented programmer who founded the company in 1982. Walker doesn't like management: "I'm an engineer," he states categorically. "I'm a programmer, I'm a technologist. I have no interest in running a large U.S. public company, and I never have." Walker is also known for certain eccentricities. At one meeting, for example, he interrupted the description of an important new product to observe that "we are living on a small blue sphere in an endless black void."

Several years after starting the company, Walker handed official control of Autodesk to chief financial officer Alvar Green so that he could return to programming full-time. However, while CEO Green received some control, he received relatively little *power*. That remained largely with Walker and an elite group of programmers known collectively as "Core," many of whose members had helped Walker start the company or had worked on its most important projects. While you won't find Core on any Autodesk organization chart, its members wield a tremendous amount of power at the company. "The whole company," according to one consultant, "is a theocracy of hackers."

Core exercises its power through electronic mail (sending on-line messages through computer networks). Electronic mail is the preferred communication channel at Autodesk, where programmers have been known to attack co-workers and managers in violent, no-holds-barred electronic letters called "flame mail."

Not surprisingly, Green had trouble managing Core from the beginning. He'd been trained in finance and didn't even keep a computer on his desk—a fact that automatically cut him off from the vital electronic grapevine. Meanwhile, Autodesk's technical staff engaged in spirited informal debates over the future of the company. Notes one observer: "People met. They discussed things. Many flowers bloomed. But nobody harvested." A "tremendous schism," reports another, developed between Core members and the company's market-

ing personnel: While marketers wanted to bring out new products in response to customer demand, Core programmers often refused to work on new-product projects that they found boring. Marketing personnel, however, had no more success in dealing with Core than did nominal CEO Green: Opposing Core, reports a former employee, was seen as "attempting to butcher the sacred cow."

The end came for Green when Walker fired off the ultimate flame mail from his home in Switzerland: a 44-page electronic letter that attacked Green's handling of the company. Entitled "The Final Days," the letter accused Green of "taking [his] marching orders from the accounting rules rather than the real world." Walker wrote that he "was so appalled by what I heard at one management meeting that I vowed never to attend another management meeting and I never have."

Soon afterward, Green announced his resignation. Carol Bartz, former head of worldwide field operations for Sun Microsystems, replaced him. Whether Bartz will have better luck managing Core remains to be seen. On the subject of her unusual boss, she's tactful: "I admire John's amazing writing skills."

Questions and Applications

1. Describe the corporate culture at Autodesk.
2. How does Autodesk communicate internally?
3. Describe the communication mistakes that Alvar Green made.
4. Suppose that Carol Bartz has asked for your suggestions on the best ways to communicate with and manage Autodesk's staff. Write a memo in which you advise her.

Source: G. Pascal Zachary, "Tech Shop," *The Wall Street Journal*, May 28, 1992, pp. A1, A4. Reprinted by permission, © 1992, Dow Jones & Company, Inc. All rights reserved.

CASE 1.2

GE: What to Do When the Ethics Program Doesn't Work

At the beginning of this chapter, we read about General Electric's successful "Work-Out" program to improve communication and productivity among employees. Ironically, however, GE has had less success with its ethics program.

Not that the company's ethics program hasn't been well thought out. At GE's Philadelphia aerospace division, for instance, there are 160 interactive video terminals offering mandatory ethics courses for employees. Classes feature hypothetical work situations presented by actors, with cameo appearances from real-life GE managers. Training sessions promise employees that they can feel free to report unethical actions without waiting to collect too much evidence. GE management prides itself on making ethics training accessible to all employees; in fact, managers have been known to stop workers in hallways and quiz them about the company's ethics policies. And when workers do blow the whistle, GE says that they are not punished in any way. In addition to a toll-free phone number and special forms for reporting problems, the company has established the means by which workers can route anonymous notes to chairman John F. Welch, Jr.

Obviously, GE's ethics-compliance program is detailed and thorough. So why didn't long-time employee Chester Walsh take advantage of it?

Walsh spotted a $42-million scam involving a high-ranking GE official and a general in the Israeli army. Using fake bills for projects that GE never started, the two diverted U.S. aid to Israel into their personal bank accounts. However, instead of following the formal communication channels laid out in the GE ethics program, Walsh kept quiet: He spent several years gathering evidence about the ongoing crime before notifying the federal government and filing suit against GE for fraud.

Explains Walsh: "I did a lot of research to see what happened to people who went up the chain of command and reported wrongdoings. All I found was that they lost their jobs, their security; they lost everything." Several GE employees agree with Walsh's statement. Patricia Della Croce, formerly a government property administrator in a GE engine plant, claims that she was laid off after telling supervisors that some of her co-workers were unfairly billing the government. "I was told I wasn't a team player and was ostracized," says Della Croce. Salvatore Cimorelli says GE dismissed him after he complained to his boss about employees changing time vouchers and overcharging the government. A former vice president says GE fired him because he'd revealed that certain GE officials met with South African businessmen to fix industrial diamond prices.

In Walsh's case, he decided against going through formal channels when he found out that his boss was a good friend of the GE manager whom he suspected of fraud. To make things worse, another executive apparently involved in the scheme was Robert Brimelow—a member of the ethics-compliance board that's supposed to investigate shady deals like the one that Walsh had uncovered.

Since Walsh's action in exposing fraudulent activities, GE has fired more than 20 employees who, according to the company, should have known about the scheme and reported it. Many of those who were fired, however, charge that because GE puts such tremendous pressure on employees to meet sales goals, they are left with precious little time to scrutinize individual transactions. Moreover, some of those employees were reluctant to alienate Israel, whom they recognized as GE's second-largest defense customer after the United States. Says one such employee: "GE taught me how to go through the brick wall [to] support the customer, and that's what we were doing." Walsh agrees: "If you have ever worked at GE you know that every quarter you make a phenomenal effort to generate income."

Questions and Applications

1. Characterize GE's corporate culture.
2. Describe the company's ethics-compliance program.
3. John Welch is concerned that Chester Walsh didn't feel safe going through GE's formal communication channels to report fraud. He wonders if perhaps the company's culture was part of the reason. Suppose Welch asks you for suggestions to improve the company's corporate culture and ethics program. Write a memo in which you describe the current culture and ethics program, and make any recommendations that you feel might help prevent such problems in the future.

Source: Amal Kumar Naj, "Internal Suspicions," *The Wall Street Journal*, July 22, 1992, pp. A1, A4. Reprinted by permission, © 1992, Dow Jones & Company, Inc. All rights reserved.

2

The Communication Process

CHAPTER OBJECTIVES

After studying this chapter, you should be able to:

1 Describe the *transactional* nature of communication.

2 Explain why messages encounter *barriers* at different points in the communication process.

3 Explain the importance of *nonverbal communication* in the communication transaction.

4 Outline the stages of *listening*.

5 List ways to become an effective listener.

*T*he person who has the ability to make his or her point simply and
effectively, while clearly understanding what is being said by others,
will have the best chance of success in a society and business
environment as complex and multi-dimensional as ours.

Robert A. Beck
Former CEO, Prudential Insurance Company of America

WHEN ACTIONS SPEAK LOUDER THAN WORDS

The complexity of the communication process can be illustrated by outlandish but true stories of businesspeople getting manicures and shoeshines in the office while carrying on conversations. What do these grooming rituals communicate?

According to a New York publishing executive who was once interviewed for a job while her potential employer was having her nails done, the individual's behavior amounted to a nonverbal snub: "I figured if getting her nails done was just as important as hiring me, then I didn't care to work for her. It was insulting." Similarly, lawyer Debra Cafaro recalls working as a summer associate in a law firm and how she felt when one of the firm's partners shined his shoes during a meeting. "I found it hard to carry on a conversation while this man was on his knees, polishing like a slave," she remembers. "It was embarrassing."

Did the people who were engaged in personal grooming while they were supposed to be conducting business understand what they were *communicating*? Perhaps they did; if so, their actions may have been deliberate messages of control and power. If they did not, they may have been viewing their behavior only in terms of their own needs. "Most of us are so busy we can't spend an hour in a salon having our nails done," explains one businesswoman. "We don't think of it as an indulgence. It's a necessity." For better or worse, this woman has apparently never considered how her behavior may affect others.

Because behavior is such a powerful communicator, companies permitting shoeshines and manicures during office hours should be more concerned with the messages that they are sending to the people with whom they do business. An organization's attitude toward in-office personal grooming depends largely on the rules of the *corporate culture* that help define its communication context. In the fashion and beauty industries, for example, where good grooming is the corporate stock and trade, these rituals are accepted. In banking and finance, however—industries defined by conservative cultures—they are not.[1]

CHAPTER OVERVIEW

Although grooming rituals are not among the classic forms of communication examined in this book, a quick glance at them helps us to see that business communication is more than written and spoken language. As a composite of everything that we say and *do*, communication is a process by which information is exchanged through both verbal and nonverbal means. It involves constant inter-play among the sender of the message, the receiver of the message, and the message itself. It takes place through a specific channel and in a context that affects message reception, and it is dependent on feedback. In order to be effective, communication must also involve an audience—the individual or group to whom the message is sent.

COMMUNICATION: A TRANSACTIONAL PROCESS

Transactional communication is communication that involves two or more participants who act and react to one another and, in the process, create meaning. Effective transactional communication is tied to audience response as much as or more than it is tied to speaker intent. Throughout this text, therefore, we will use the term **audience** to refer to the receivers of verbal, nonverbal, and written messages. A message can be successful only when both the sender and the receiver—the audience—perceive it in the same way.

Consider the case of the Chemical Manufacturers Association, a trade group representing the makers of 95 percent of the chemicals manufactured in this country. In 1991, the organization confronted its failure to communicate the industry's contribution to economic growth. Despite the group's best efforts, chemical companies and their products continued to be perceived through the 1980s as threats to the environment and society. The public, for example, still remembered the disaster in Bhopal, India, that killed thousands and the polluting of New York's Love Canal that left hundreds homeless. Consequently, relatively little attention was being paid to industry products that created a safer, more productive environment. John W. Johnstone, Jr., chairman of both the association and the Connecticut-based Olin Corporation, summed up the industry's frustration over its communication failure: "We said [to our member companies], 'Look out, guys. We are going to end up in worse shape than the atomic industry if we don't do something.'" Ironically, recalls Johnstone, "we thought of ourselves as righteous and very successful" and were shocked at how the public perceived our message.[2]

Here and in all cases, audience *perception* is critical in effective communication. In addition, the consideration of your audience is just as important in formal written and oral communication as it is in everyday verbal and nonverbal language. It is the key ingredient in all successful business communication.

The interaction of the six elements that comprise all transactional communications—sender, message, channel, receiver, feedback, and context—are illustrated in Figure 2.1. Here you see that while the message flows from sender to audience, feedback from the audience gives the sender the opportunity to adjust the message. Every communication takes place through a specific channel and in a broader situational and cultural context.

transactional communication
Communication involving two or more participants who react to one another to create meaning

audience
Receivers of verbal, nonverbal, and written messages

We are talking at *each other instead of to each other. That is not communication; it is monologue.*

James D. Robinson III
CEO, American Express

FIGURE 2.1   *A Transactional Model of Communication*

INTERVIEW

Beatrice Harris, Psychological Consultant

Psychologist Beatrice Harris, partner in the psychological consulting firm of Harris, Rothenberg Inter-national, views companies as economic and psychological systems. While economics addresses marketplace and other external forces, psychology focuses on the factors that influence the way people communicate and work together.

Working with such major corporations as Primerica, Mobil Oil, Bankers Trust Company, and National Westminster Bank, Dr. Harris helps companies improve the psychological environment in which people function. In this interview, we asked Dr. Harris about important issues that affect the communication process.

Question: What characteristics do the best communicators share?

Answer: The best communicators are quite thoughtful; they know the purpose of every interchange and communicate it to others. They are also good listeners and are able to adjust their agenda based on what they hear.

Problems develop when people fail to stick to the point—or don't know what the point is. In addition, when they focus exclusively on the content of the message at the expense of what they want to happen on a relationship level, they miss an important communication opportunity. For example, while on one level you may begin a meeting hoping that your boss will approve a specific request, on another level you may also want to be perceived as a serious, hard-working employee.

Question: Is understanding the audience generally a high priority?

Answer: For most people, it is not. Most people don't understand their audience. As a result, they misinterpret what others say or write and react to the misinterpretation. Under stress, we have even less capacity to think in terms of other frames of reference.

Question: It is common for junior-level employees to draft memos and other documents for their supervisors. What problems do people face when writing documents for others?

---

communication barriers
Problems that arise during the communication transaction and raise the possibility of misunderstanding and confusion

Communication barriers are the problems that arise at every stage of the communication transaction and have the potential to create misunderstanding and confusion. Such problems may not only hinder communication but can actually alter meaning. Keep in mind, of course, the fact that barriers are inevitable because the communication transaction is never perfect. Often, for example, our attempts at communication express our own needs rather than the needs of our audience or the requirements of our situation. We may allow our emotions to take over or come to the interchange intellectually unprepared. As a business communicator, your goal is to minimize the frequency and seriousness of communication barriers.

ELEMENTS OF COMMUNICATION

We will look next at the specific transaction elements—sender, message, channel, receiver, feedback, and context—and the communication barriers that affect each element. As you will see, it is often difficult to examine one element apart from the others because they are so closely linked. At times during this discussion, therefore, we will refer to transaction elements as *stages* because we want to emphasize the view of communication as a transactional *process*.

senders
Participants in the transaction who communicate messages to an audience

Sender

Senders are the participants in the communication transaction who communicate messages to an audience. These messages are influenced by **sender credibil-**

Answer: Before drafting a document for another person, you have to understand what outcome he or she wants. This information allows you to visualize the reader. When you have worked for someone for a period of time, you know the players and understand what the communication is trying to accomplish. But new employees don't have this information and are often reluctant to ask for it. As a result, many early drafts fail. The best way to minimize the failures is to ask questions.

Question: Can people be taught to listen?

Answer: Psychologists learn listening skills all the time, and these skills can be learned by others as well. People can be trained to listen for such diverse messages as content, affective tone, and conflict. But learning takes persistence and motivation. People who are not motivated are wasting their time.

Question: Is communication more direct in some organizations than in others?

Answer: Some companies are so big that you can't generalize in that way; rather, communication styles vary by department and subgroup. In small companies, if the people at the top are open and indicate that disagreement is all right, that message usually filters down through the entire organization.

No matter the size of the organization, open communication is difficult for most of us. Humans have not achieved mastery in relation to each other, and we bring these flaws into the workplace. We have difficulty trusting each other even in intimate relationships. When we enter an environment filled with people we hardly know, we are less likely to be open.

Question: What can we do to improve communication?

Answer: First, we must realize that everyone brings different perceptions of the world, different value systems, and different ways of framing their priorities to every communication interchange. We must also realize the tendency to project our own meanings onto messages—to interpret things according to our own world view rather than the view of the person speaking or writing. Finally, we must acknowledge that improvement takes time—time to analyze what people are really saying.

Source: Interview with Beatrice Harris, Ph.D.

---

ity—that is, the extent to which the sender is perceived to be believable, ethical, trustworthy, competent, responsible, sincere, or authoritative. In other words, your personal reputation and that of your organization affect the way your audience reacts to what they read or hear.

There are three types of sender credibility, each of which affects successful communication at a different stage. **Initial credibility** refers to the receiver's judgment of the sender prior to hearing the sender speak or reading what he or she has written. **Derived credibility** is determined while the oral or written message is being communicated. **Terminal credibility** is the receiver's evaluation of the sender after the message has been delivered. Realizing the importance of all three forms of credibility, an increasing number of CEOs now travel to meet customers in person to close important deals. For example, CEO Paul Allaire of Xerox Corporation recently met with the chairman of a Southeast food company to win a $300,000 contract. Without saying a word, his presence delivered the message that the top executive of Xerox was willing to travel more than a thousand miles to win the account and to ensure that customer service was a top priority. As CEO, Allaire's initial credibility preceded him, and the credibility derived from the extra effort made to deliver his message helped close the deal. His presentation reinforced the perception that Xerox was willing and able to meet customers' needs: "We're the key contact to the customer," explains Allaire. "If at any time a customer is dissatisfied with anything, they'll feel comfortable picking up the phone and giving me a call."

In business communication, the sender's credibility is closely linked to his or her knowledge of the material, audience, and the context in which the mes-

sender credibility
Extent to which a sender is perceived as believable, competent, authoritative, and so on

initial credibility
Receiver's judgment of the sender prior to receiving the message

derived credibility
Receiver's judgment of the sender while the message is being communicated

terminal credibility
Receiver's judgment of the sender after the message has been delivered

sage is communicated. It is also linked to position and title, which communicate whether the sender has the *authority* to send the message and whether communication is taking place between the right people. Says Diane Sanchez, president and CEO of Miller, Heiman, Inc., a West Coast sales-management consulting firm: "Generals like to talk to generals, lieutenants to lieutenants."[3]

It is also important to keep in mind that everything about a person sends a message. Your personality, clothing, handshake, the quality of your stationery and the error-free copy of your letter, and the tone of your voice all communicate not only intention but also competency and sincerity.

BARRIERS TO EFFECTIVE SENDING   Many problems may arise at this stage of the communication transaction. While many of these problems involve poor preparation, others involve flawed personal communication styles.

FAILURE TO KNOW YOUR MATERIAL   People who have difficulty making their points may not have done their homework. They usually do not know enough about a subject to talk or write about it intelligently or do not organize and present the material in ways that others can readily understand. The result may be unfocused, disorganized writing or speech, generalizations when specifics are needed, and uncertainty that reduces credibility. Typically, your audience will respond to lack of preparation by "tuning out" your message—people simply stop reading or listening—or by dismissing what you say. In either case, the impact of the message is minimized, if indeed not lost. Robert A. Beck, former CEO of the Prudential Insurance Company, has long recognized the link between knowing his material and communicating with his audience. "Starting my Prudential career as an agent," he reports, "I understood quickly that although people may listen, they don't always hear. I had to make sure, therefore, that my presentations were clear, concise, and to the point."[4]

FAILURE TO KNOW YOUR AUDIENCE   Even with a thorough knowledge of the material and effective organization, your presentation may fail to meet audience needs. An audience, for example, will not understand your message if it is either too technical or simple, if it uses unexplained jargon, if it fails to focus on audience concerns, or if it is simply too long. Because businesspeople are bombarded with facts and figures, giving an audience too much to read or hear automatically decreases the chances of getting your point across.

When first impressions must be made across borders, potential barriers to successful communication are raised. Japanese businesspeople, for instance, reserve the use of first names for family and close friends. Your card should be given to the most important person first, and you should carefully read all cards extended to you.

Communication also fails when the sender lacks audience empathy. **Empathy** is the ability to experience the world from another person's perspective. It is an essential element in effective communication because it allows you to set aside your own opinions as you reach for common ground with your audience. An empathetic communicator may be able to predict how a person will respond to his or her message. Empathy may also enable you to frame your communication in ways that are more likely to be effective.

Because it acknowledges people's interests and concerns, empathy usually affects the starting point of the message. For example, Helen Shih, a New York Life Insurance agent, begins customer correspondence with the implicit acknowledgment that clients are worried about the financial stability of the insurance industry. Before several major insurers were taken over by regulators, explains Shih, "all that clients really wanted to see was a big return and a small premium. Now, you really have to tell them how strong the company is. And they don't just want an A-rated company; they want an A-plus."[5]

AN ABRASIVE PERSONAL STYLE   Personal styles can enhance or obstruct communication. An abrasive personality, for example, typically makes feedback difficult and an openness to change impossible. It can also create communication tension—when people do not like the way a speaker addresses them, their attention to what is said or written is often weakened. An abrasive style is often expressed in the *tone* of a message. Consider the differences between the following versions of a manager's communication to an employee:

VERSION 1   Evan, print 500 copies of the new advertising brochure right away. Then send them to the customers on this list.

VERSION 2   Evan, I think it's important for all our established customers to know about the promotion we're running next month. The information is in this new brochure. I would like you to handle distributing copies to customers and printing additional copies, if necessary.

While Version 1 issues orders, Version 2 explains the assignment. Such differences in tone can have an important influence on audience response.

An abrasive personality is as evident in writing as in conversation. A condescending, dismissive, paternalistic, angry, or negative tone comes through clearly on paper. Indeed, because they give the audience the opportunity to reread what has been said, written messages can create even bigger problems than spoken messages.

Self-monitoring, therefore, is essential. For example, if a message is ill-received even though its points are accurate, examine the way you relate to people. If the problem can be traced to your attitude or style of communication, you need to make adjustments.

MAKING A POOR FIRST IMPRESSION   First impressions count in business as well as personal affairs. Failure to look, act, or speak in a manner that is consistent with your appropriate role may be detrimental when meeting someone for the first time. Even a single unfortunate word in a memo can leave a negative impression about your intent. Capitalize on the power of first impressions by trying to anticipate negative reactions. Dress appropriately, shake hands firmly, speak well, and be organized. Before sending written messages, reread every letter, memo, and report from the perspective of the person who will receive it. Analyzing the likely response of your audience can help eliminate unfortunate mistakes.

Message

A **message** is the written, oral, or nonverbal communication that the sender transmits to an audience. Your words and tone, your method of organization,

empathy
Ability to experience the world from another person's perspective

message
Written, oral, or nonverbal communication transmitted by a sender to an audience

Much as sign language communicates messages to the deaf, these Boy Scout merit badges communicate messages through pictures. The written and spoken word comprise the most universal system of symbolic communication.

© 1993 Ka Yeung

the soundness of your argument and its emotional impact, what you choose to communicate and what you choose to leave out, and your style of presentation are part of every message.

Messages have both intellectual and emotional components. Through the use of reason and evidence, we seek to inform or convince. Through the use of emotional or motivational appeals, we seek to arouse feelings, change minds, and encourage action.

BARRIERS TO EFFECTIVE MESSAGES   Not surprisingly, messages which are poorly focused and organized, use inappropriate language and tone, or contain technical errors create communication problems. Spoken language that contains slang or that is punctuated by too many "you knows" or "ums" reduces the impact of the message. Similarly, sloppy letters, memos, and reports, as well as those that use unfamiliar or erratic formats, make communication difficult to understand. Part II of this text, WRITING BASICS, will examine effective written messages, while Part V, FORMS OF ORAL COMMUNICATION, will focus on public speaking, meetings, and other forms of oral communication.

Channel

Every message is transmitted through a **channel**—the medium through which the message sender and the message receiver communicate. As we saw earlier in this chapter, Paul Allaire of Xerox often chooses face-to-face verbal communication to close major deals. Other means of verbal communication include the telephone and videoconferencing.

Generally speaking, written messages are transmitted in one of three forms: *letter, memo,* or *report.* For example, instead of calling a meeting of network affiliates to announce that NBC was exploring the possibility of a one-hour daytime shopping show, NBC president Pierson G. Mapes wrote a memorandum. Mapes explained that NBC was considering this programming option as "an entry to the huge promotion budgets of corporate America as well as an entry directly to our viewers' homes. Granted," he added, "this is a different business than broadcasting and advertising, but in this era of change, why not?" He "warned" affiliates that it would "take some 'non-traditional' thinking to give it a real chance." By putting his thoughts in writing, Mapes had taken steps to ensure that his message was taken seriously. Indeed, word of the memo was reported in *The Wall Street Journal.*[6]

As we will see in Chapter 20, technology has spawned a host of new communication channels. Computers, for example, allow us to receive and send messages to business associates around the world over ordinary phone lines. Videoconferences are now a viable alternative to face-to-face meetings. Messages are transmitted by electronic mail, voice mail, and fax machines, and as a result, the *way* in which a message is sent is often part of the message itself. Faxing a message, for example, communicates its urgency. Similarly, traveling across the country to hold a face-to-face meeting emphasizes the importance of the interchange more than, say, holding a videoconference. As choices become more complex, therefore, choosing the right communication channel is becoming more important than ever.

CHANNEL BARRIERS   According to communication theorists, **noise** is anything that interferes with message transmission by distorting the message or otherwise changing its meaning. Physical noise may take the form of environmental sounds (a wailing siren, for example) that prevent one person from hearing another. In written communication, "physical" noise might be a poorly printed page or smudged paper. Other forms of noise that interfere with listening will be examined later in the chapter.

Receiver

Receivers are the audience to whom messages are directed. As a rule, receivers enter every communication transaction with a preconceived set of ideas and feelings that influence how they respond. The most successful communicators take these needs into account and use them as the starting point in their effort to inform or persuade.

All audiences are inherently "selfish" in the sense that they react to messages with the basic, self-centered question, "How will this help me?" A customer, for example, wants your letter to resolve his or her credit problem. A supervisor expects your report to contain recommendations for a new project. A coworker expects your return phone call to solve a computer glitch. To a large extent, these needs determine audience interest and response.

Let's look again at the memo circulated by NBC's Pierson Mapes. The tone of his message makes it clear that Mapes expected his home-shopping idea to meet some resistance—and indeed it did. "It won't [get us] ratings, the whole world knows that," argued one receiver of the message, John Spinola, the general manager of NBC's Boston affiliate. "It's a limited kind of appeal and those who want this already watch it on cable." Mapes, however, had considered this

channel
Medium through which message sender and audience communicate

noise
Anything that interferes with a message by distorting its meaning

receivers
Audience to whom a message is transmitted

Different types of noise can exist in a communication channel. Physical noise—the type described here—may involve the static on a cellular phone that prevents the listener from receiving the intended message. Another type of noise occurs when the wrong channel is chosen, yet another when the message is misinterpreted due to failure to match the receiver's frame of reference with that of the sender. This last type of noise occurs frequently and is extremely difficult to prevent.

OKI is a registered trademark of OKI Electric Industry Company, Limited. Copyright © 1982 by OKI America, Inc. All rights reserved.

objection before it was expressed. He wrote in his original memo that NBC was looking at a "daily, morning, live, interactive, electronic retailing and catalog program with celebrity guest stars, contests and games, consumer education and information. Think of *The Price Is Right*," he reminded his audience, "where your viewers could actually purchase quality products at low prices from the convenience of their own homes." Similarly, while trying to be positive and anticipate audience response, Mapes also realized the potential concern of network affiliates. He thus wrote that the project could not proceed "unless the vast majority of you think the opportunities outweigh the risks."

RECEIVER BARRIERS   When your audience has poor listening or reading skills, communication is compromised. Without an ability to understand and accept new ideas, a willingness to find interest in seemingly uninteresting messages, and a commitment to pay attention and overcome first impressions, your audience may turn away from the message before its value becomes clear. We will examine specific methods for improving listening skills later in the chapter.

Lack of empathy can also create problems for both audience and sender. For example, Catherine A. Gohn, a United Steelworkers union organizer, once found herself the victim of an audience's unwillingness to entertain her point of view. After spending a month trying to organize 200 office and technical workers in Trenton, New Jersey, Gohn left without success. "It's very frustrating," she recalled. "White-collar workers are their own worst enemies.... But I want them to know unions are for everybody, not just for that blue-collar worker over there." Gohn expects a certain amount of resistance when she begins her message. "I'm helping the union break stereotypes," she observes. "It's a matter of people recognizing themselves in me. They have to know unions are people like themselves or they won't join."[7]

An audience may also have trouble paying attention when more than one message is competing for its attention. Because conflicting messages reduce the attention that a receiver can give any single message, no message may be given its fair due. Finally, because communication is transactional, both audiences and communicators must make positive impressions. Should communicators get the impression that the audience is not responding to the message, they may simply stop trying. For example, if a manager repeatedly tells sales representatives to focus on dealer relations but continues to receive numerous dealer complaints, the manager may very well decide to fire the salespeople responsible for the problem rather than repeat the message for the entire salesforce.

Feedback

Feedback consists of messages which the audience sends back to the sender. Feedback may cause the sender either to alter the presentation of the message or to cancel it entirely. As we saw in Figure 2.1, feedback creates a circular rather than linear communication transaction that involves both sender and receiver. For example, verbal communication, whether a speech, a presentation, or an ordinary conversation, allows immediate feedback. Listeners tell the sender how they feel through interruptions and nonverbal signals ranging from frowns and yawns to smiles and applause. By contrast, feedback on written materials is delayed. The sender must wait for either written or oral response before deciding what to say next and how to say it.

Feedback also allows an audience to clarify messages. Through pointed fact-finding questions, for instance, receivers can ensure that their understanding of a message is correct. Messages like the following typically benefit from this sort of questioning:[8]

> *Message*: "Due to downsizing, all employees are expected to increase their productivity."
> *Fact-finding question*: "Does this mean that we are expected to shorten our lunch hour and take less vacation time?"
> *Message*: "Give that job as much time as it needs."
> *Fact-finding question*: "Does that mean that a month is okay?"

BARRIERS TO FEEDBACK   An atmosphere that discourages discussion may make it impossible for employees to provide feedback on what they read or hear. According to some observers, this type of atmosphere characterized some companies during the recent recession. Management in these companies moved all organizational decision making to upper levels, while making it clear that criticism was unwelcome. According to business consultant Orry Shackney, these companies also put "preventive measures" in place to discourage dissension. "Someone will be called in," he explains, "and told, 'You've had a lot of negative things to say; you're getting a reputation as a negative person. You don't want to be seen that way.'" The predictable happened: Fearing for their jobs, many people in these organizations stopped offering feedback—even on serious problems.[9]

In addition, feedback may be insufficient or delivered too late. It can focus on personalities rather than issues or on minor items rather than key points. For example, asking the company's human resources manager why she did not men-

feedback
Messages returned by the audience to the sender that may cause the sender to alter or cancel an original message

CURRENT ISSUES IN BUSINESS COMMUNICATION

Cubicle Communication

In approximately 70 percent of U.S. companies, offices lack walls. Many offices are made up instead of partitioned cubicles, or *workstations*, with low dividers and doorless openings. Although its defenders point to the efficiency of such an environment, critics contend that cubicles pose the potential for serious communication problems. For example, lack of privacy and the sense of being a face without a name present formidable challenges.

American companies began cubing their offices in the 1960s after a German management consulting firm developed a planning model called *burolandschaft*, or "office landscaping," to encourage an egalitarian work atmosphere. According to this plan, workers at different organizational levels from management to support staff would sit—and work—together as part of teams. Planners theorized that communication would be enhanced by the absence of such physical barriers as walls and doors. Not surprisingly, the concept attracted American companies eager to embrace any idea that would save them thousands, and sometimes millions, in real estate and construction costs.

Unfortunately, the people who work in cubicles often hate them: "Those damn closets," complains one secretary in voicing a common criticism. "They're so demeaning." According to a recent study conducted by a New Jersey–based design-consulting firm, four out of ten people who work in cubicles actively despise them. At one New York City bank included in the study, the employee turnover

tion the length of coffee breaks in her speech on productivity fails to provide meaningful feedback because it focuses on a relatively unimportant point. Similarly, after reading a product-development report, criticizing the writer's occasional use of trite expressions fails to provide appropriate help.

As you will see later in this chapter, feedback is often communicated nonverbally through facial expressions, gestures, and tone of voice. In fact, such nonverbal cues often send more powerful messages than words.

We can lick gravity, but sometimes the paperwork is overwhelming.

Wernher von Braun
Former director,
U.S. space program

Context

context
Every factor surrounding and affecting the transmission of a message

The communication **context** refers to the situation in which communication takes place and to every factor affecting its transmission. This context may include anything in the immediate environment and anything in the broader culture. The firm's operating environment, for example, may have an immediate effect on communication—a request for an activity report in the midst of a corporate merger will be treated differently than the same request made under more normal circumstances. Other immediate factors might include any of the following:

- The occasion that created the need for the message (such as a government agency's request for a proposal)
- Co-workers' attitudes toward one another (co-workers who dislike one another may have difficulty communicating)
- The number of people communicating the message (a meeting with seven people has different communication dynamics than a meeting between only two people)
- The amount of information competing for the receiver's attention (a man-

rate skyrocketed from 3 percent to 27 percent in a single year after the company shifted from private offices to cubicles. "During the exit interviews, people said they had lost their sense of territory, their sense of control," reports consultant Robert Engel, who conducted the study.

With so many people complaining about cubicles, numerous companies are thus returning to the tradition of private offices. Apple Computer, for example, has already torn down workstations to make room for 120 private offices in its Cupertino, California, complex. Apple's move was motivated by the loss of software designers to other companies that were willing to provide them with private offices.

Meanwhile, employees who remain cubicled use different techniques to overcome the communication problems built into their environment. In order to avoid broadcasting private conversations to everyone in the vicinity, they have learned to hunch over the phone and speak in a relatively low voice. To discourage casual conversation, some individuals place chairs in their cubicle doorways or open file cabinets to obstruct easy entry. One innovative manufacturer, Cubicle Cues, even developed a message board system to tell coworkers whether a cubicle "door" is open or closed. Sympathetic with employees required to work in the cubicle environment, companies like Disney and AT&T actually hand out cubicle-etiquette booklets. AT&T's booklet is aptly titled "Survival and Sanity in the Open Plan."

Dissatisfaction aside, cubicles are still being installed in offices across the country. According to Bud Klipa, a manager at workstation manufacturer Steelcase Inc., many companies are even going a step further and installing continuous kidney-shaped communal desks with dividers that are even lower than normal workstation walls. Klipa sees his company's commitment to such designs as part of a trend: "Everything we read about productivity," he explains, "said team-based communications-based offices [are] in the future."

Source: Elaine Underwood, "The Cubing of America," *Adweek's Marketing Week*, March 30, 1992, p. 24. © 1992 Adweek L.P. Used by permission

ager with three pressing projects on his desk may respond differently to a memo than a manager whose desk is clean)

The broader cultural context involves the corporate culture, community and national cultures, and the international cultures that now constitute both the marketplace for many U.S. goods and services and the workplace for many U.S. citizens. Cultural differences, for example, may be expressed in different working styles that influence the unwritten rules of communication. According to a recent study conducted by Hilton Hotels, for instance, people on the East Coast feel more pressure to work than those on the West Coast, who often have a relaxed attitude about getting work done. Thus, if you work in Los Angeles, leaving early on a Friday afternoon might be more acceptable than if you did the same thing in New York.[10]

CONTEXTUAL BARRIERS   One of the most serious contextual barriers to communication is **information overload**—the demands made on receivers by an ever-expanding number of messages from a variety of sources. Today, businesspeople must read letters, memos, reports and proposals, professional journals, newspapers, magazines, and books. Too much information and too little time leaves many with the sinking feeling that none of their messages has received the attention it deserves.

One victim of the information age, software engineer John Whiteside, once returned to his office after a three-week assignment for Digital Equipment Corp. to find 1,000 electronic messages waiting for him on his flashing computer screen. Whiteside's solution was to assign each incoming message a code identifying the sender. While messages from the company president got top priority, cafeteria announcements were placed in proper perspective. According to Harvard Business School professor John Kotter, the best way to deal with infor-

information overload
The demands made on receivers by an expanding number of messages from a growing variety of sources

TABLE 2.1 *Common Communication Barriers*	
ELEMENT IN THE TRANSACTION	COMMUNICATIONS BARRIERS
Sender	• Poor preparation • Poor audience analysis • Grating personal style • Bad first impression
Message	• Poor organization • Inappropriate language • Technical errors • Unfamiliar written format • Spoken language filled with nervous fillers
Channel	• Various forms of external noise
Receiver	• Poor listening or reading skills • Lack of empathy
Feedback	• Environment that discourages feedback • Insufficient feedback • Feedback that comes too late • Responses that focus on minor points
Context	• Information overload • Failure to understand cultural differences

mation overload is to define your purpose: "People really suffer when they're in an organization that has no sense of direction, where everything is relevant," observes Kotter. "It helps enormously if you can look at things and say, 'irrelevant, irrelevant, irrelevant—ah, relevant.'"[11]

Failing to understand how cultural differences affect communication styles can also lead to serious misunderstandings. Chapters 18 and 19 will examine how to overcome cultural barriers so that you can communicate effectively with diverse groups in this country and abroad. Table 2.1 summarizes some of the most common communication barriers that affect every stage of the communication transaction. Overcoming these barriers is an important step in improving communication.

CASE: THE TECHNOLOGY BARRIER   Ever since computers entered the daily business mainstream, countless stories have been told about computer-created havoc. Lack of communication is frequently cited, as is the confusion resulting from computer errors. According to *The Wall Street Journal*, for example, managers at the credit-reporting agency TRW Inc. found themselves in a predicament when the company inadvertently "turned the affluent village of Norwich, Vermont, into a town of deadbeats. Suddenly, for no apparent reason, all of Norwich's taxpayers were red-flagged as high credit risks in TRW's nationwide network of credit records. Within a week, Norwich was beset by an epidemic of personal-finance crises."

If his lips are silent, he chatters with his fingertips; betrayal oozes out of him at every pore.

Sigmund Freud
Founder of psychoanalysis

The fact that a simple credit-reporting error was the root of the problem did not ease the crisis for Norwich residents who found themselves unable to qualify for mortgages and forced to explain unaccepted credit cards. What they expected from TRW was immediate action and an acknowledgment that its mistake had turned people's lives upside down. What they got was a failure to empathize with the community's plight. According to *The Wall Street Journal*, a TRW spokesperson told the local newspaper that "no huge number, probably less than 3,000 people," were affected by the mistake. The acknowledgment, reports the *Journal*, was "small comfort to the town of 3,100."

In communicating the company's message, the TRW spokesperson had ignored the needs of town residents—that is, the company's audience. In fact, because TRW's reputation for mishandling consumer complaints had already preceded it, neither its message nor its messenger enjoyed any credibility. Moreover, the political climate reinforced the town's negative response. People all across the country had been dissatisfied with the credit-reporting industry for some time, and nationwide pressure was already being applied on Congress to pass corrective legislation.[12]

PROGRESS CHECK

1. Name the six elements that comprise all written and oral communication.
2. In which of these elements can we find communication barriers?
3. What is credibility, and why is it important for the sender to possess it?

HOW MESSAGES ARE SENT

As we have seen, messages in the communication transaction actively convey meaning both through written and spoken words and through nonverbal language. It is the purpose of this text to give you the skills you need to write and speak with authority and effectiveness. Chapters 3 through 13 examine the art of *written communication*: planning, organizing, and editing memos, letters, and reports. Chapters 14 and 15 focus on *oral communication*—delivering speeches and presentations, participating in meetings, and mastering the art of the brief telephone call and the face-to-face encounter. Chapters 16 and 17 put both communication forms into action as they examine the process of applying and interviewing for a job.

Although the primary focus of this book is verbal messages, we saw in the opening vignette of this chapter that nonverbal language can actually be more powerful than words. We will thus examine the nature of nonverbal language and its function in business communication.

Nonverbal Communication

In using oral communication, we actively send messages to one another both with and without words. **Nonverbal communication** is communication that takes place through *nonverbal cues*; through such forms of *nonvocal communication* as gestures, eye contact, facial expressions, touch, clothing, and personal space; and through the form of nonverbal vocal communication known as *paralanguage*. One value of such unspoken messages is the power to reveal feelings. Author Michael Lewis, for example, describes how the magnetic nonverbal communication of John Gutfreund, former chairman of Salomon Brothers, could reduce bond traders to quivering juveniles:

> He was the last person a nerve-racked trader wanted to see. Gutfreund liked to sneak up from behind and surprise you. This was fun for him but not for you. Busy on two phones at once trying to stem disaster, you had no time to turn and look. You didn't need to. You felt him. The area around you began to convulse like an epileptic ward. People were pretending to be frantically busy and at the same time staring intently at a spot directly above your head. You felt a chill in your bones that I imagine belongs to the same class of intelligence as the nervous twitch of a small furry animal at the silent approach of a grizzly bear. An alarm shrieked in your head: Gutfreund! Gutfreund! Gutfreund! Often as not, our chairman just hovered quietly for a bit, then left. You might never have seen him. The only trace I found of him on two of these occasions was a [cigar] ash on the floor beside my chair, left, I suppose, as a calling card.[13]

Perhaps more than most of his colleagues in the business community, Gutfreund apparently preferred to deliver a significant part of his message

nonverbal communication
Form of communication, including nonvocal and nonverbal vocal communication, taking place through such media as gesture, eye contact, clothing, and tone of voice

subtext
Unspoken language with the power to communicate meaning

through a **subtext** of nonverbal cues—that is, through unspoken language that has the power to communicate meaning.[14] Research attests to the power of subtext. In one study, for example, 93 percent of a message's emotional impact came from nonverbal signals such as hand motions.[15]

NONVERBAL CUES   Nonverbal cues have several functions. For one thing, they can repeat verbal messages. For example, in telling a supervisor that he or she cannot understand how a new machine works, a factory worker may punctuate the plea with open palms held at chest level—a common sign of helplessness. Nonverbal cues can also substitute for verbal messages. Shaking your head up and down while saying nothing is an accepted way of saying yes. They can regulate or control verbal interaction. Changing vocal tones in normal conversation, for instance, may provide other people with cues when to speak and when to listen. Finally, nonverbal cues may contradict verbal messages. Listening to a department head ramble on at a meeting, participants may feign interest while looking around the room or turning their bodies away from the speaker.

Even when we make a conscious effort to "say" nothing, nonverbal language may continue to send messages. For example, fiddling with papers or doodling during a meeting may be signs of disengagement, while folding your arms across your chest may communicate defensiveness. The fact that everyone "leaks" nonverbal cues means that an ever-changing source of uncensored data is always present, just waiting to be noticed and interpreted correctly.

As we have already indicated, nonverbal cues are especially powerful in communicating a wide range of feelings and attitudes. A discrepancy between a person's tone of voice and gestures may indicate that a lie is being told; poor eating habits may indicate a disregard for the sensibilities of others. Julius Fast, an authority on nonverbal communication, relates the following conversation with a prominent CEO who had once interpreted the effect of poor eating habits on a young colleague's otherwise polished image of competence:

> "I have this incredibly bright, well-educated guy who really has a grasp of the business," said the CEO. "Well, we had lunch with an important client and he ate like an animal, shoveling food into his mouth without the slightest regard for appearance!"
>
> "What do you mean by appearance?" I asked.
>
> "Why, the message he was sending to the client! In effect, he was saying, 'I don't know the rules for eating properly. How can I know the rules for interacting with people?'"[16]

Despite their power to communicate, however, nonverbal cues are easily misinterpreted, and conventional wisdom about the meaning of such cues is often questionable. For example, realizing that these cues are often culturally biased, officials responsible for upgrading the Washington-Moscow hotline decided not to use video and voice communication, relying instead on written messages. In a crisis, reasoned the experts, "we wouldn't want to leave room for mistaken interpretations or impressions that might be drawn from facial expressions or voice patterns."[17] (Chapter 18 offers a more detailed discussion of nonverbal communication from the cross-cultural perspective.)

nonvocal communication
Form of nonverbal communication including gesture, eye contact, facial expression, posture, touch, clothing, and the use of space

nonverbal vocal communication
Form of nonverbal vocal communication, including tone of voice and such voice qualities as loudness

NONVERBAL COMMUNICATION   Nonverbal cues fall into two broad categories. **Nonvocal communication** refers to gestures, eye contact, facial expressions, posture, touch, clothing, and the use of space; **nonverbal vocal communication** refers to tone of voice and such voice qualities as loudness and pitch.

GESTURES   Gestures can both complement and contradict other forms of communication. For example, imagine a businesswoman who is slightly dyslexic. Although she has no trouble reading, she often confuses right from left. On a car trip to a supplier's office, she acts as navigator, telling the driver where to turn and the direction to take. On two occasions calling for right turns, she verbally tells the driver to turn "left" while pointing right with her right hand. Aware of the woman's impairment, the driver turns right, understanding that her gesture, not her words, conveyed the intended message.

The gestures that you will see in everyday business communication include a wide range of hand and arm movements. When examined in context, they may have specific meanings:

- Baton-like pointing movements of the hands and arms punctuate words and may communicate control.
- Finger wagging is often a sign of disagreement.
- When hands are placed at chest level with palms held up, helplessness may be the message.
- Open palms with fingers pointing up, palms out, and hands moving forward emphasize the importance of the message.
- A hand or finger covering the mouth may indicate that the speaker is holding something back or is too embarrassed or reluctant to speak.
- Hands on the hips with thumbs back communicate toughness and a reluctance to back down.
- Counting off with your fingers may be a sign of clear thinking and logic.
- Arms crossed over the chest may indicate disagreement.

Although they can be used deliberately to communicate a subtext like honesty, self-confidence, straightforwardness, and control, most gestures are used unconsciously.

EYE CONTACT   When people look directly into each other's eyes, they are making eye contact. Although eyes are traditionally viewed as receivers of information, they can also transmit clear signals in social interactions. Indeed, eye contact can be the most powerful form of nonverbal communication. In business as in personal relationships, eye contact sends different messages:

- Purposefully looking at someone is a signal of recognition. Direct eye contact tells a job applicant that you are interested in learning more.
- Purposefully looking away from someone may be a sign of arrogance or anger. Refusing to look directly at a business partner whose mistakes have cost your company a new account may be an expression of disgust.
- Conversations often begin with both verbal messages and eye contact. Most people engage the other person's eyes when they begin to speak and look away as soon as the other person looks back.
- The length of time that eye contact is held has a message of its own. Eye contact with a stranger is instantaneous; more than a glance makes both parties uncomfortable. Maintaining eye contact with a person of the opposite sex can mean sexual interest—a message not appropriate in business. Extended eye contact between men who do not know each other is an implicit threat. By contrast, it is acceptable in public speaking to hold eye contact with audience members as a sign of involvement and engagement.

Eye contact is the most difficult of all facial features to fake. Even subtle changes in eye contact and expression have the power to communicate strong feelings of being interpreted correctly.

The power of eye contact as a form of communication was demonstrated in an important court trial during the 1980s. In a lawsuit between Pennzoil and Texaco in which Pennzoil claimed that Texaco had illegally interfered with its deal to buy Getty Oil, Pennzoil's lawyers instructed their witnesses to look directly at the jurors while testifying. By contrast, Texaco's lawyers told their witnesses to avoid eye contact and to be as serious as possible. When the trial ended, the jury awarded Pennzoil over $2.5 billion, the largest damage award in U.S. history. Although eye contact was certainly not the deciding factor in the jury's decision, apparently it did contribute to jurors' overall impression of Texaco's guilt. "Those Texaco witnesses," said one juror after the trial, "never looked at us once. They were arrogant and indifferent. How could we believe them?"[18] Of course, the belief that shifty eyes are lying eyes is not always accurate. Nevertheless, it is a belief that left a lasting mark on the jurors in one very expensive court case.

FACIAL EXPRESSIONS   Closely linked to eye contact, facial expressions—movements of the face that reflect attitudes and emotions—are often difficult to read. With the vast number of possible expressions, the speed at which they change, and the ability of most people to "mask" messages that they do not want to send, all but the most obvious expressions may be misinterpreted. Psychologists have identified six emotions that are expressed in the face in all parts of the world: happiness, sadness, anger, disgust, surprise, and fear.

POSTURE   Posture—the position of your body as you sit or stand—can communicate strong nonverbal cues. For example, Chemical Bank CEO Walter Shipley brought bank employees together in 1991 to announce that Chemical would merge with Manufacturers Hanover, another New York–based bank. As he spoke, everyone in the room understood the implications of the merger. Although the resulting bank would become the third largest in the country, at least 6,200 people would lose their jobs. As people listened, various forms of body posture indicated various feelings. Many audience members, for example, leaned forward with their legs drawn back in rapt interest. Others sat erect, appearing tense and concerned, while still others sat with their arms folded across their chests, their bodies communicating disagreement with the merger plans.

Thus, in business situations as in other aspects of interaction, body posture has the ability to communicate different messages:

- Turning your body away from a speaker may be a sign of noninvolvement. It can be interpreted as a snub.
- Boredom can be expressed by letting your head drop, leaning back, and supporting your head with your hand.
- Adopting an "open" sitting posture, with your head and body to one side and legs uncrossed, often communicates agreement.
- Walking rapidly with your hands moving freely at your side may communicate confidence and goal orientation.

Research has shown that *status* also affects body posture. When employees talk with supervisors, for example, their posture is often tense. The supervisor, on the other hand, may lean back in his or her chair in a relaxed pose.[19]

TOUCH   In business, the most important form of touch is the handshake—a "pressing of the flesh" that, if done properly, can indicate involvement and interest but, if done poorly, can indicate lack of interest and weakness. In a job interview, a strong handshake communicates self-confidence, a first impression that lasts.

Often, men and women have different handshake styles. For women, the business handshake is in fact a relatively recent development. Some women are still reluctant to shake hands firmly and tend to offer their fingers instead of the whole hand—a gesture that is sometimes interpreted as weakness and uncertainty. By contrast, some men shake hands with such vigor that they communicate an overeagerness and even aggressiveness. Learning a strong, effective handshake that is neither too long nor too short is an essential part of nonverbal business communication; the proper handshake is the stuff from which first impressions are made.

CLOTHING   For years, male employees at IBM wore dark suits and white shirts—clothing that communicated the seriousness and consistency required in the computer field. Similarly, when Frank Pacetta took over as the district sales

When Mickey Drexler, president of The Gap Inc., comes to work, he wears rumpled khaki pants with pleats, a wool sports coat, and soft leather shoes—clothing that is consistent with his position as head of a major fashion retailer.

manager of Xerox's Cleveland office, he demanded that shirt collars be so heavily starched that "you can skate on them." He also required that shoes be polished, that faces be clean-shaven, and that everyone look fit and trim (he asked several sales representatives to diet). According to Pacetta, his dress code reflected the look required in business (or at least *his* business).[20]

In the world of business, clothes act as a kind of uniform, telling everyone around you such things as your willingness to conform to organizational standards. Being neither overdressed nor underdressed—that is, by "looking the part" while combining individuality and personal flair—signals your acceptance of organizational rules. On the one hand, adhering too rigidly makes it hard for others to read you. On the other hand, observes management consultant Mark H. McCormack, men "who show up for business meetings wearing loafers with no socks, their shirts half unbuttoned, and gold chains visibly exposed can evoke disturbing generalities about their entire personalities." In general, says McCormack, your clothes should say nothing about you except that you are part of the group.[21]

In most business offices, accepted dress for men is a conservative suit, a shirt and tie, and dark socks and shoes. For women, conservative suits and dresses are appropriate. The more conservative the industry, the more sober the dress. For example, if you work for a bank or brokerage firm, your clothing options are limited. Every item of clothing must communicate stability and competence. By contrast, if you work in advertising, fashion, or architecture, less formal clothing is accepted. In such "creative" fields, a shirt and tie, jacket, and neat denim jeans for men and pantsuits for women are statements of relaxed control.[22]

PERSONAL SPACE   The physical distance between people who are engaged in communication is known as **personal space**. Customary usage of this space indicates a great deal about social relationships within a culture. As you can see from Figure 2.2, for example, most business conversations in the United States take place in a *social zone* that places individuals between four and twelve feet apart. Anything closer generally indicates an intimacy that is inappropriate for business. Note especially the differences in the relationships between verbal and nonverbal cues as the zone widens from *personal* to *public*.

It is important to remember that spatial relationships can also be manipu-

personal space
Physical space between people engaged in communication

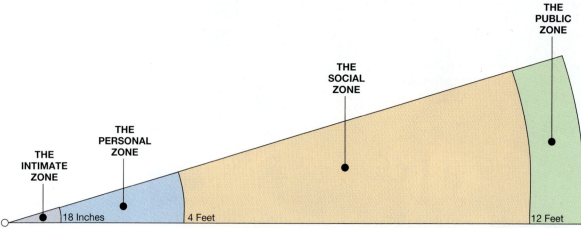

- In the **Intimate Zone,** within 18 inches of each other, good friends and family members engage in activities like comforting, lovers make love, and competitors in sports events wrestle and tackle. Not only can partners touch and hug each other, but they are aware of each other's body heat and body odor. If people whisper, they can be heard.

- In the **Personal Zone,** from 1.5 – 4 feet, less intense exchanges are allowed. Touch is more limited, and body heat and odor are unnoticeable (unless odor is strong). Speech becomes louder, and looking becomes more important than in the intimate zone: Not only is it easier to focus but you can also see more of the other person.

- In the **Social Zone,** from 4 – 12 feet, exchanges are more formal. Typical are those between business associates. They can touch at the closer end of the range, and then only if one or both leans toward the other. Visual cues become more important, and voices become louder.

- The **Public Zone,** 12 feet and more, is characteristic of brief standing exchanges, such as calling to a friend across a street, or formal exchanges between a speaker (perhaps teacher or minister) and an audience. Voices have to be loud, and it is impossible to see much detail of facial expressions.

FIGURE 2.2   *Personal Space and Social Interaction*

Source: Peter March, ed., *Eye to Eye: How People Interact,* Topsfield, MA: Salem House, 1988, p. 42.

lated to one person's advantage. For example, a supervisor who wants to intimidate an employee may stand in the employee's "personal zone" during the message transaction. Crafty salespeople know such strategies as positioning themselves deliberately close to susceptible customers.

The arrangement of space in an office can also be used either to ease communication or to increase control over it. For example, a desk that is positioned in such a way as to keep visitors at a distance acts as an emotional as well as a physical barrier. In a less intimidating arrangement, the visitor's chair is placed at the side of the desk, reducing the distance between people as they talk and thus eliminating the feeling that the person behind the desk is somehow "in charge" of the conversation.

paralanguage
Nonverbal vocal messages embodied in tone, emphasis, volume, pauses, and so on

PARALANGUAGE   Nonverbal vocal messages are known as **paralanguage**. Because of tone, emphasis, speed, pitch, volume, use of pauses, and *disfluencies* (such as "um" and "you know"), messages can be communicated with a wide variety of effects. In fact, emphasis and intonation often hold the key to meaning. For example, when you say, "I'm very nervous about this deal," you deliver a different message than when you say the same thing with the emphasis changed to "I'm *very* nervous about this deal" or "I'm very nervous about *this* deal."

Research has shown that paralanguage can communicate language even more strongly than the content of words and that when vocal qualities actually contradict words, the paralanguage will have more impact.[23] For example, *shouting* at a supplier while claiming that you are *not* angry at him for missing an important deadline lacks credibility: It contradicts the content of your message by communicating the opposite sentiment—namely, the intensity of your anger.

THE DIFFICULTY IN READING NONVERBAL COMMUNICATION   Despite the potential impact of nonverbal communication, studies have found that our ability to read and interpret nonverbal cues is more limited than we think. According to social psychologist Robert Gifford, "people read much into nonverbal cues that just isn't there, while missing much that is."[24] For example, while obvious traits such as gregariousness are relatively easy to read, more subtle traits are often misjudged. In a recent study, Gifford showed videotapes of job applicants to 18 experienced corporate recruiters. Although the recruiters were able to judge obvious social skills, they were poor judges of motivation, a key element of job success. The recruiters believed, for instance, that highly motivated candidates smiled, gestured, and talked more than candidates with low motivation. In truth, however, none of these nonverbal cues has any important relationship to motivation. The result, Gifford concludes, suggests strongly that "coming across well in your job interview is no guarantee of other traits that might matter in your day-to-day job performance. People are being hired for some of the wrong reasons." Other studies reveal additional problems in interpreting nonverbal cues:

- Although it is commonly believed that dominant people make greater eye contact than submissive people, the opposite is true.
- The following people are not as "cold" and "quarrelsome" as is commonly thought: people whose arms remain folded and whose hands and legs move very little during conversation, people who extend their legs toward their partners and wiggle their feet, people who make limited eye contact, and people who nod and seldom smile.
- "Shifty" eyes are not necessarily a clue to lying. On the contrary, liars have as much direct eye contact as people telling the truth. A more accurate measure of lying is *inconsistent nonverbal cues*—for example, differences between a person's tone of voice and gestures. Stumbling over words, repeated swallowing, and a climbing voice pitch can also indicate that a lie is being told. However, even these cues can be difficult to read.

Mark H. McCormack also points to certain problems in interpreting nonverbal cues. During tense negotiations, for example, McCormack has seen some people "lean into" the conversation and push aside papers in an unconscious act of total attention. Just as often, however, he has seen others lean back in their chairs and relax. "It's not that I don't think there's a message behind body language," he explains. "There usually is. But you have to resist hasty conclusions…or reading meaning where none exists. And you have to fold your insights into an overall context of more reliable observations."[25]

As we have seen, nonverbal cues come in many forms. Learning to use these cues to communicate messages can be as important to business success as the ability to write and speak effectively. Although nonverbal cues are more subtle than these other forms of communication, they often have greater impact.

PROGRESS CHECK

1. How often do we communicate nonverbally?
2. Name the two broad categories of nonverbal cues.

HOW MESSAGES ARE RECEIVED

Much as throwing and catching are equal and complementary parts of the game of baseball, reading and listening are complements to speaking and writing: The first two activities involve responses to an initial activity. In other words, the communication transaction would be incomplete without *readers* and *listeners* acting as message *receivers*.

You can see a lot by observing.

Yogi Berra
New York Yankee catcher

INTERNATIONAL ISSUES IN BUSINESS COMMUNICATION
Japan's View of American Literacy: Facing Some Facts

In the superheated trade environment shared by the United States and Japan, many U.S. business executives angrily cite unfair trade practices that have kept their goods out of Japanese markets, thus contributing to the U.S. trade deficit. Responding to this charge, one of Japan's most senior politicians blamed America's trade problems on the illiteracy of many American workers. According to Yoshio Sakurauchi, speaker of Japan's powerful lower house of Parliament, Americans "cannot even read. Managers," charged Sakurauchi, "cannot convey their orders in written form. Therefore, they get a high ratio of bad parts" and goods that are inferior when compared to those manufactured in Japan.

Is Sakurauchi's charge about the illiteracy of the American workforce correct? As we have seen, many American workers do indeed have poor reading skills. However, Sakurauchi's conclusion that nearly a third of American workers "cannot read" is based on a misunderstanding of what *illiteracy* really means. In reality, only about 5 percent of the U.S. population cannot *read*—a much smaller percentage, of course, than Sakurauchi suggests.

However, although this figure can be regarded as good news, the issue of literacy reaches beyond the basic ability to read and write, and American workers do not always perform well on tests of functional literacy. According to the U.S. Department of Education, there are three types of literacy—*prose, document,* and *quantitative*—and levels of achievement within each type. Statistics on people able to perform the literacy skills required by various tasks are available only for prose literacy. In addition, these percentages apply only to young adults, ages 21–25.

Prose literacy refers to the ability to understand and use information from such sources as newspaper and magazine articles and to write about what has been read. At its lowest level, a proficiency in prose literacy requires the ability to write a simple description of job duties. Using this measure, 96.1 percent of all Americans are "literate." At the highest level, however, prose literacy requires people to synthesize and restate the main argument in a lengthy newspaper editorial or similar source. According to this criterion, only 21.1 percent of young American adults are literate.

Document literacy refers to the knowledge and skills required to locate and use information from such documents as statistical tables, indexes, and pay stubs. The most basic form of document literacy requires a person to perform such rudimentary tasks as matching cents-off coupons to supermarket shopping lists. At the highest level, it requires the ability to use a complex train schedule to determine departure and arrival times.

Finally, *quantitative literacy* refers to the knowledge and skills needed to apply arithmetic concepts, including addition, subtraction, multiplication, and division. This skill ranges from the ability to add two entries in a customer order to the ability to use a percentage chart to determine appropriate sales-tax charges.

Thus, although Yoshio Sakurauchi's allegations do not necessarily reflect the facts, there is unquestionably some room for improvement in the literacy skills of American workers. The need is especially urgent in light of higher Japanese educational standards. According to Diane Ravitch, an assistant secretary in the U.S. Department of Education, the Japanese "workforce is, on a whole, better educated than ours."

Sources: Karen DeWitt, "U.S. Aide Rejects View from Japan on Illiteracy," *The New York Times,* January 21, 1992, p. D11; David E. Sanger, "A Top Japanese Politician Calls U.S. Workforce Lazy," *The New York Times,* January 21, 1992, p. D1.

Reading

With the information overload so typical in business today, people are being asked to read, absorb, and analyze more and more written materials, many of which are technical and complex in nature. At the same time, statistics tell the story of a literacy crisis that may limit the ability of U.S. companies to compete in the world market. Approximately 23 million people currently in the U.S. workforce read at or below an eighth-grade level. Eleven to 14 million more read at or below a fourth-grade level.

Over 90 percent of U.S. companies, ranging in size from 51 to 10,000 employees, employ workers who lack basic reading skills. According to a Conference Board survey of 1,600 manufacturers and service firms, "Most companies are concerned about illiteracy among their workers and expect the problem to get worse." Only 16 percent of the nation's largest manufacturing and service companies are satisfied that their workers have the literacy skills necessary to do the job.[26]

The ability to read, analyze, and absorb written information is critical to your success in business. By the year 2000, for example, only one in four jobs will fall into "low-skilled" categories like maintenance worker and supermarket bagger. The others will require not only well-developed reading skills but also an ability to research, organize, and prepare written materials. Of the small number of firms currently satisfied with workforce makeup, many report having to interview up to eight job applicants before they find one who is acceptable.

Effective reading requires the ability to focus attention on a topic, even in the midst of distractions. It requires the ability to analyze and evaluate information and to respond in an appropriate manner. It also requires *introspection*. The best readers understand that responses to written materials are tied to what we know and feel about the material and the writers.

Listening

Listening is the act of sensing, interpreting, evaluating, and reacting to what is said. In fact, listening is for most people the most used and least taught communication skill. As a result, many of us often do not "see" because we lack the skill to "observe." Not surprisingly, then, successful business leaders stress the importance of listening in effective communication. Consider the following examples:

- When he was developing the idea for a national newspaper, Al Neuharth, founder of *USA Today*, listened to what newspaper editors and readers thought of the competition: "I carried my vision of a national newspaper everywhere I went. But only inside my head," recalls Neuharth. "I listened more than I talked. The message I was hearing over and over was that newspaper people thought they were putting out better newspapers than newspaper readers thought they were reading."[27]
- Chicken king Frank Perdue is what management consultant Tom Peters calls an "engaged" listener—someone who becomes completely and actively involved with what he hears. He demonstrates his engagement by taking copious notes and by applying the ideas that he picks up to his own operations. At a West Coast seminar, for example, Peters observed Perdue at his note-taking best: "Perdue topped the rest of us put together," reports Peters. ". . .The next morning [he] was up at 3 a.m. discussing with his people on the East Coast the implementation of the stuff he'd heard the day before. A major new executive compensation plan [that] focused on quality...was among the big ideas Perdue took from the seminar—and implemented in short order."[28]

listening
Act of sensing, interpreting, evaluating, and reacting to what is being said

Listening is more than hearing. It's an active process that involves thought and an expenditure of energy.
Rand V. Araskog
CEO, ITT

THE IMPORTANCE OF LISTENING SKILLS   In business, effective listening can mean the difference between maintaining a customer's goodwill or losing it forever, between being able to work effectively with a fellow employee or making no headway, between keeping your job because you do what your supervisor wants or being fired because of poor performance. Despite the importance of listening, however, most people are poor listeners. Table 2.2 shows how Lyman Steil, a pioneer in listening research, ranks four communication skills according to when they are learned and the extent to which they are used and taught. According to Steil, although listening is both the first communication skill that we

TABLE 2.2	*A Ranking of Communication Skills*		
COMMUNICATION SKILLS	WHEN LEARNED	EXTENT USED	EXTENT TAUGHT
Listening	1st	45%	4th
Speaking	2nd	30	3rd
Reading	3rd	16	2nd
Writing	4th	9	1st

Source: Research reported in Philip R. Harris and Robert T. Moran, *Managing Cultural Differences: High Performance Strategies for a New World of Business*, 3rd ed. (Houston: Gulf, 1991), p. 36.

learn in life and the one that we use most often, it is also the skill to which we pay least attention.[29]

Perhaps listening is undervalued as a communication tool because it seems to come so easily—after all, we can do it without trying. Or can we? In reality, listening is more complex than we think. For example, although the average person talks at the rate of about 150 words per minute, the brain can actually handle about 400 words per minute—an overcapacity that can lead to inattention, misinterpretation, and boredom.[30] Table 2.3 lists ten common reasons for not listening. The first reason—"I want to talk first"—can cause serious communication problems. Imagine, for example, that instead of listening to the comments of other participants in a meeting, all you think about is making your own points. Your internal focus will probably prevent you from understanding the subtleties of what others are saying and the contributions that they are making.

In addition, research has shown that the information we *hear* often fails to coincide with the information we *comprehend*. According to listening researcher Ralph G. Nichols, immediately after listening we are likely to remember only half of what was said to us. Several days later, we may at best recall only a quarter of the content—and often nothing at all.[31]

To listen is an effort, and just to hear is no merit. A duck hears also.

Igor Stravinsky
Composer

sensation
Physiological process by which sound waves are transmitted from the ear to the brain

STAGES OF LISTENING   To better understand the complexity of the listening process, consider the fact that it is a process made up of four progressive stages: *sensation, interpretation, evaluation,* and *reaction*. These stages are shown in Figure 2.3.[32]

SENSATION   On its most basic level, listening involves **sensation**—the physiological process by which the ears hear sound waves and transmit them to the brain. Sensation is affected by the loudness of the speaker's voice.

TABLE 2.3	*Common Reasons for Not Listening*

WHAT YOU SAY TO YOURSELF...

I want to talk first.

I'm thinking about what I'm going to say.

I'm not interested in the subject.

That's too hard to understand.

I don't like you.

I don't like the way you talk.

I'm too upset, or worried, about other things.

I don't want to believe what I know you're about to tell me.

I'd rather give my attention to people or activities around me.

I'd rather daydream or doodle.

Source: Donald Walton, *Are You Communicating?* (New York: McGraw-Hill, 1989), p. 27.

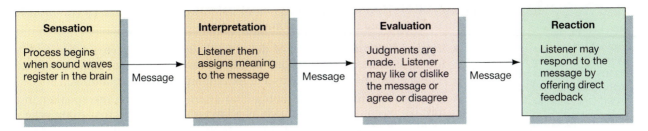

Sensation		Interpretation		Evaluation		Reaction
Process begins when sound waves register in the brain	Message →	Listener then assigns meaning to the message	Message →	Judgments are made. Listener may like or dislike the message or agree or disagree	Message →	Listener may respond to the message by offering direct feedback

FIGURE 2.3   *Four Stages of Listening*

Normal conversation usually takes place at about 60 decibels; lower sounds may never be heard. The environment, of course, also affects the sensory process of hearing. For example, when Herman Moore arrives at his job as a manufacturing manager at a Reynolds Metals Co. aluminum-rolling plant, his first job is to listen to the night superintendent's activity report. Naturally, Moore performs this task in the quiet of his office, not next to the factory's blasting furnaces or aluminum-rolling presses.[33]

According to communication theorists, however, only some "environmental noises" actually involve sounds and hearing. The din of competing sounds (a factory blast furnace, for example) is one form of noise, but so are perfume-filled rooms and an overheated buildings. Hunger, pressures at work, and personal problems are still others. All share a crucial characteristic. They are distractions that make the sensory process of listening difficult and sometimes impossible.

INTERPRETATION   The second listening stage involves **interpretation**—attributing *meaning* to a message. For example, when Herman Moore attends afternoon staff meetings, he listens to the frenzied jargon of plant employees struggling to solve problems: *"Change the two-J's...testing is holding up the MD301...No. 5 is down...I can't run it at 45 percent...we've got to hit that 80 million...we're running out of time here!"*[34] Although outsiders would be baffled by these "coded" messages, Moore's experience allows him to interpret them as part of a listening process that is among his job skills.

Among other factors, intellectual limitations have the power to skew interpretation, creating possible discrepancies between what a speaker says and what a listener perceives. Preconceived notions, a point of view that differs from the speaker's, the lack of certain knowledge, and the inability to deal with the complexity of a message—all of these can act as intellectual barriers to listening. Similarly, when speakers or their messages generate negative emotional responses, listening becomes more difficult. For example, a supervisor who is angry with a worker for losing an important memo may be less willing to listen to the employee's ideas about an unrelated project.

EVALUATION   **Evaluation** involves the decision to accept or reject, like or dislike, agree or disagree with a message. Part of this process involves deciding whether a new message is consistent with your personal values. When you are exposed to information that contradicts your value system, that information may place you in a state of conflict, or mental stress, known as **cognitive dissonance**.[35] In order to reduce this discomfort, you may reject the new idea, sometimes simply because it is different. Effective listening involves an understanding of this tendency to reject most messages that contradict your own value systems.

REACTION   As a stage of listening, **reaction** refers to the response generated by a message—a response that may take the form of direct feedback. Wilt Wagner, a Reynolds vice president and Herman Moore's boss, explains Moore's reaction style as the style of "a new breed. When he disagrees with me," Wagner admits, "I'm going to hear about it."[36] While this type of direct response minimizes misunderstanding, responses that do not include feedback may perpetuate communication problems.

interpretation
Listening stage during which meaning is placed on a message

evaluation
Listening stage involving the decision to accept or reject, like or dislike, agree or disagree with a message

cognitive dissonance
State of conflict arising from exposure to messages that contradict one's value system

reaction
Listening stage referring to the response generated by a message

FORMS OF LISTENING   Many types of listening behavior are as common in business as they are in personal communication.

cynical listening
Defensive listening that occurs when receivers fear that a message will take advantage of them

offensive listening
Listening that tries to catch the sender in a mistake or contradiction

polite listening
Mechanical listening characterized by inattention

active listening
Listening that requires involvement with the information of a message and empathy with the sender

- **Cynical listening** is a type of defensive listening that occurs when people fear that a message is intended to take advantage of them. This form of listening often characterizes divisive labor-management bargaining.

- **Offensive listening** is listening that attempts to catch the speaker in a mistake or contradiction, much as a lawyer does when cross-examining a witness. A supervisor, suspicious that an employee is faking a back problem, may take an offensive posture when listening to the worker describe his or her pain.

- **Polite listening** is a kind of mechanical listening characterized by inattention. The listener really wants the speaker to stop talking so that he or she can begin. Because polite listeners often rehearse their own lines instead of paying attention, polite listening usually accomplishes very little. Many job applicants are guilty of polite listening. Instead of actively listening to what the job recruiter is saying, they are planning what to say next. Conversations based on polite listening rarely move people from their original points of view.

- **Active listening**, on the other hand, is a form of listening that requires both sincere involvement with the information and empathy with the speaker's situation. It is the kind of listening practiced by Frank Perdue. In business, active listening is the basis for effective communication. Bob Crawford, founder and CEO of Brook Furniture Rental, a company with $50 million in estimated annual sales, regards active listening as his most powerful communication tool. "The secret of good human dynamics," Crawford contends, "is a balance between talking and listening. You need to absorb data before imparting information."[37]

BECOMING AN EFFECTIVE LISTENER   You can improve your listening skills in both formal and informal business situations by applying the following principles. Many of the same principles can also be used to improve reading.

LEARN THE ART—AND WISDOM—OF SILENCE   Silence not only gives someone else the opportunity to speak but gives you the opportunity to learn from another person's perspective. "Silence," explains Mark McCormack, "is a void, and people feel an overwhelming need to fill it. If someone has finished speaking and you don't play along by taking up your end of the dialogue, after only the slightest pause that person will automatically start to elaborate."[38]

BE AWARE OF "EMOTIONAL FILTERS"   Ask yourself whether you have strong opinions about the subject of the message or about the person to whom you are listening. Emotional reactions to words, people, or situations can cloud your thinking.

BE SLOW TO JUDGE   If your natural tendency is to interrupt and argue when you disagree with what you hear, you may lose the opportunity to learn and, perhaps, to change your opinions for the better. Realizing that we all come to listening situations with preconceived viewpoints will help you avoid judging alternative ideas too quickly. Keeping an open mind often means being aware of your prejudices and seeking out evidence to disprove your own point of view. For instance, the results of a new study revealing the increased productivity of home-based workers should come as good news to managers opposed to giving employees the option to work at home once a week. Of course, whether or not a given manager changes his or her mind should depend, among other things, on the scientific merit of the study and whether the facts are convincing.

My greatest strength as a consultant is to be ignorant and ask a few questions.

Peter F. Drucker
Business philosopher and management consultant

TURN LACK OF INTEREST INTO AVID INTEREST   What do you *do* during a business meeting that seems to have little to do with you? If you let your mind wander, you may miss an opportunity to discover and apply concepts or procedures seemingly unrelated to the immediate demands of your own job. Assume, for example, that you are head of maintenance for Hampton Inn, a nationwide hotel chain, when the chain announces that dissatisfied customers will receive full, unconditional refunds. You might well wonder why you were asked to attend meetings to discuss this new competitive strategy.[39] Instead of becoming an inactive listener, however, perhaps you will decide to think further about the impact of the new campaign on your job. Before long, you will probably have a host of job-related questions: Should hotel maintenance be improved? Should changes in maintenance be geared to customer complaints or should an internal monitoring system be developed? Are staff changes necessary? Such enlightened self-interest can mean the difference between effective and ineffective listening.

ASK QUESTIONS TO FOCUS YOUR LISTENING   "The only dumb question is the question not asked." This maxim is as true in business as it is in personal communication. When you do not understand a concept, word, or phrase, be direct and ask, "What does that mean?" In the end, these interruptions are time savers, not time wasters. Listening patiently without understanding accomplishes little.

When you are finished asking questions, use clarifying statements to make sure that you have understood the message correctly. For example, you can avoid miscommunication by following a question with a statement like "Then what you are telling me is that Citicorp is planning to give independent marketers like us access to the files on its 21 million credit-card customers." By restating the message, you reassure both yourself and the message sender that the communication transaction is performing its function.

FOCUS ON WHAT IS IMPORTANT   It is estimated that only one in four people listening to a formal speech actually grasps the speaker's main idea.[40] In normal business conversation as in public speaking, when poorly organized speakers intermingle unrelated facts with key points, it may be difficult to focus on critical issues. You can make listening easier by asking pointed questions, taking clear notes, being sensitive to repetition, and recognizing language transitions that focus attention on key concepts. For example, if during a short conversation a co-worker on a major project repeats three times her concern over meeting the project deadline, the repetition should emphasize the seriousness of the message. Similarly, if she uses transitional phrases like "I want to emphasize..." or "Let me stress..." she is also focusing special attention on her message.

Often, you can tell what is important by paying attention to the *way* people speak. Mark McCormack advises listeners to "pay attention to the adjectives and adverbs people choose, their intonation in responding to certain topics. If you listen to how people are saying something, you'll understand why they're saying it."[41]

BE AN ACTIVE LISTENER   To avoid becoming an inattentive listener, focus your "extra" listening time—the time available to you because listening is faster than speaking—on the speaker's message: Try to anticipate what will be said next, review and summarize the points already made, evaluate and question the presentation, and listen between the lines (remember that changes in volume, tone, and body language can be more important than words). *Active concentration* is the key to effective listening.[42]

Finally, bear in mind that active listening may involve note taking. Although you may choose a less prolific style than Frank Perdue, note taking forces activity and engagement.

DEVELOP PERSONAL LISTENING METHODS   For example, practice listening by thinking of yourself as a business consultant. Ask a co-worker or a subordinate to describe a problem, then focus on the specifics until you find out what is

CURRENT ISSUES IN BUSINESS COMMUNICATION

The Art of Listening to Customers

In every instance we found that the best-run companies stay as close to their customers as humanly possible.

Thomas J. Peters
American business writer

Solid customer relationships are the basis for a successful business. Building and maintaining these relationships requires mastering the art of listening to customer needs and complaints. On a corporate level, companies like Procter & Gamble and IBM have institutionalized customer-listening programs. P&G, for example, was the first consumer-goods company to encourage communication with customers by including a toll-free 800 phone number on all its packaging. Today, many of the calls that P&G receives contain the germs of important product-improvement ideas. Similarly, IBM developed its first computer by listening to and working with its largest customer—the U.S. Census Bureau.

Listening to customers is also an institution at Wal-Mart. When the company's founder, the late Sam Walton, made store visits, he made a point of standing in checkout lines and asking customers what they bought and why, what they thought of the service, and how Wal-Mart compared with its competition. Walton also listened to the advice of every store employee, from managers to baggers, because he believed that the people who did the work knew the most about it. Observing the practice of managers like Sam Walton has enabled business communication specialists to identify several principles common to all good customer listening. Here are some of the guidelines that they have proposed.

■ **Meet Customers on Their Own Territory, Not from behind Your Desk**

The unspoken message of this practice is that you care enough about what your

going wrong or what could be done better. As you listen, keep in mind that important facts may be buried beneath unrelated details. Repeat this type of "fact-finding listening" until you notice a marked improvement in your skill. Your goal is to get to the heart of the matter in as little time as possible.

In general, understanding the nature of the communication process will help you work more effectively. Instead of struggling against the barriers that are inevitable in the communication process, you should find yourself better able to focus your energies on your job duties and your job goals. Effective communication skills are important in all jobs—from entry-level trainee to chairman of the board.

PROGRESS CHECK

1. Why are effective communication skills vital to your success in business?
2. Everyone talks about how important listening is, but few people seem to be good at it. Why?
3. Chances are that you enjoy talking to some people more than others— they're just such good listeners. What makes someone a "good listener"?

WHAT'S AHEAD

Having explored the fundamentals of business communication, both in terms of organizational communication and the communication process, we will turn next to the first steps in communication practice. In Part II, we will examine several tasks that are basic to the creation of all effective business docu-

customers are saying to be part of their world. According to Brooks Furniture Rental president Bob Crawford, listening to customers in their home territory makes them feel as important as they really are. "In this impersonal society," Crawford believes, "people want a personal touch." Face-to-face meetings in a customer's office, factory, or distribution center also provide invaluable information that you may miss in a telephone conversation or in a meeting in your company conference room.

■ Listen with an "Open" Mindset

"Open" listening involves being *receptive* to whatever direction the conversation takes. For example, instead of coming to every meeting armed with a formal presentation, you might encourage your customers to talk about their operations and the way they use your good or service—

and then just listen. In naive listening, expect the unexpected.

■ Provide Fast Feedback and Action

Feedback and action are concrete proof of the intensity of listening. They are tangible signs of your commitment to customer service. For example, provide feedback by sending a letter summarizing a conversation or meeting—and then take action based on your findings. Immediate actions say loud and clear, "I heard what you said and I consider it important."

Sources: Faye Rice, "Champions of Communication," *Fortune*, June 3, 1991, p. 112; Donald Walton, *Are You Communicating?* (New York: McGraw-Hill, 1989), p. 24; Thomas J. Peters, *Thriving on Chaos: Handbook for a Management Revolution* (New York: Knopf, 1987), p. 149; and Thomas J. Peters and Robert H. Waterman, Jr., *In Search of Excellence: Lessons from America's Best-Run Companies* (New York: Harper & Row, 1982), pp. 193–95.

ments. Chapter 3 explores the fundamental issues in planning a document; Chapter 4 takes a closer look at the processes of organizing, composing, and designing documents; and Chapter 5 deals with the specifics of editing and revising documents.

SUMMARY OF CHAPTER OBJECTIVES

1. Describe the *transactional* nature of communication.

Transactional communication consists of six distinct elements: sender, message, channel, receiver, feedback, and context. Message senders—speakers or writers—communicate messages to receivers who take in the information, interpret, and evaluate it. At the heart of this transaction is the message itself, which is shared by the sender and receiver. When receivers transmit messages back to a speaker or writer, they provide feedback, which may result in message alteration. Messages are transmitted through different channels—for example, face-to-face verbal communication and written letters and memos. Message transmission is influenced by the communication context, which includes environmental and cultural forces.

2. Explain why messages encounter *barriers* at different points in the communication process.

Communication barriers are problems that arise at every stage of the communication transaction and may create misunderstanding and confusion. Communication barriers are created by senders who fail to know their material or audience, have abrasive personal styles, or make poor first impressions. The message itself can obstruct communication by being poorly organized or by using inappropriate language and tone. In its various forms, noise can obstruct the communication channel. Receivers who have poor listening or reading skills, lack *empathy* for the sender's message, or have various messages competing for their attention can also create communication barriers, and information overload can turn the context itself into a communication barrier. Finally, feedback can create barriers when it focuses on unimportant details rather than key points.

3. **Explain the importance of *nonverbal communication* in the communication transaction.**

   Nonverbal communication—which includes gestures, eye contact, facial expressions, posture, touch, clothing, personal space, and nonverbal vocal qualities—often reveals the subtext of communication. The function of nonverbal cues is to repeat, substitute for, regulate or control, or contradict verbal messages. Although nonverbal cues are especially powerful in communicating emotions, they are often misread.

4. **Outline the stages of *listening*.**

   In sensation, the first stage of listening, the ears pick up sound waves and transmit them to the brain. This transmission is often obstructed by various internal and external noises. In the second stage, interpretation, listeners attribute meaning to the message. In the third stage, evaluation, they make judgments about the message. The final stage, reaction, involves the listener's response to a message—a response that may take the form of direct feedback.

5. **List ways to become an effective listener.**

   Effective listeners are active listeners who become involved with both the information and the speaker. Effective listening requires a conscious effort to be silent when others speak, an awareness of emotional filters that cloud judgment, and a commitment to the careful formation of opinions. It also requires involvement with the information, an ability to focus on what is important, and a willingness to ask questions and to practice the art of listening.

REVIEW AND DISCUSSION QUESTIONS

1. Define *transactional communication*. Why do we call it *transactional*? *(Ch. Obj. 1)*

2. Summarize the goals of effective business communication. *(Ch. Obj. 1, 2)*

3. Discuss possible communication barriers that can affect each of the following: *(Ch. Obj. 2)*

   a. the sender   d. the receiver

   b. the message   e. feedback

   c. the channel   f. the context

4. Can we ever get rid of communication barriers entirely? Explain your answer. *(Ch. Obj. 2)*

5. What is nonverbal communication? What function(s) does it serve? *(Ch. Obj. 3)*

6. Distinguish between nonverbal communication and paralanguage. *(Ch. Obj. 3)*

7. What is listening? Explain its importance. *(Ch. Obj. 4)*

8. Describe the stages of the listening process. *(Ch. Obj. 4)*

9. What steps can you take to become a more effective listener? *(Ch. Obj. 5)*

10. Discuss the importance of good listening for building good customer relations. *(Ch. Obj. 5)*

APPLICATION EXERCISES

1. Think of a recent conversation that you didn't find satisfactory. Now, draw a diagram illustrating the elements of transactional communication. Identify each of the six elements involved in this conversation. For instance, what channel(s) did you use? What was the context? Analyze this particular communication transaction. Did a problem occur in any of the elements? If so, how did this problem affect your feelings about the transaction? *(Ch. Obj. 1)*

2. Keep a list for a day of the various sources from which you receive communications: written, oral, nonverbal, pictorial. Relate your list to the chapter's discussion of information overload. *(Ch. Obj. 1, 2)*

3. Suppose that you're a high-ranking communications expert for the U.S. government. You're aware that, in updating the Washington-Moscow hotline, both governments decided to rely on written messages rather than on video or voice communication. Now the President, knowing that you took a course in business communications, has asked you to report on the communication barriers that still exist, even with written

notes. Write a memo summarizing the risks resulting from these barriers. *(Ch. Obj. 2)*

4. Keep track for several days of people's eye contact when you talk to them. How is your eye contact affected when you know your audience well? How is the eye contact of others affected? How does eye contact influence your communication transactions with them? *(Ch. Obj. 2, 3)*

5. Several years ago, there was a best-selling book called *Dress for Success*. Do you think clothing can influence business success? Explain your answer. *(Ch. Obj. 2, 3)*

6. A publisher has contacted you with a hot idea for a new book: updating the old *Dress for Success* and applying its ideas to a variety of professions. Write a description of a "dress-for-success" look for each of the following jobs: banker, President of the United States, and rock musician. What would the members of these professions want to communicate via their clothing? *(Ch. Obj. 2, 3)*

7. Pay attention to your preconceived ideas and feelings while communicating with people for several days. What preconceptions do you have when starting a conversation with your best friend? With an instructor? With someone you don't know well? Do these preconceptions differ, and if so, how? When might your preconceptions act as communication barriers? Write a paragraph describing what you observe. *(Ch. Obj. 2, 4)*

8. Next time you're with a group of people, observe their nonverbal communication. How large is the personal space maintained by each person? Notice their gestures, eye contact, expressions, and postures. Can you tell which members of the group already know each other and which don't? If so, how? Write a summary of your observations. *(Ch. Obj. 3)*

9. The chapter notes that many of us are poor at interpreting nonverbal cues. Why? *(Ch. Obj. 3)*

10. Your friend Joe is getting ready to interview for his dream job. Understandably, he's a bit ner-

vous. What advice would you give Joe about his nonverbal cues during the interview? *(Ch. Obj. 3)*

11. While Joe knows that he really wants this job, he also has lots of questions about it. How can he use listening skills to learn more and make a good impression? *(Ch. Obj. 4, 5)*

12. The next time you listen to the radio, choose a song that's new to you and listen carefully to the words. After the song ends, write down as many of the lyrics as you can remember. How did you do? *(Ch. Obj. 4, 5)*

13. During the next week, pay attention to how people listen—or don't listen—to each other. Note examples of cynical, offensive, polite, and active listening. How did the type of listening affect the communication process in each case? *(Ch. Obj. 4, 5)*

14. Pair off with a partner (preferably someone whom you don't know well). One of you should speak for about two minutes on a topic while the partner simply listens. (The topic is up to you—perhaps something that you read this morning or a favorite hobby.) After you've finished, your partner should paraphrase what you've just said, being careful not to make judgments or express opinions. Analyze the interchange. Were you able to communicate effectively? Did your partner listen well? Now it's your partner's turn: He or she gets to talk for two minutes on any topic while you listen and then paraphrase. Again, check your communication skills. What did you learn from this exercise? *(Ch. Obj. 4, 5)*

15. Your instructor (or a volunteer from the class) will read aloud a brief article on a business topic. (The article should take no longer than three minutes to read.) Then, each person in the class should write a summary of the article's main points. Brave students can volunteer to read their reports aloud and have other students discuss any points on which their own reports differ. *(Ch. Obj. 4, 5)*

*B*UILDING YOUR RESEARCH SKILLS

Business communication textbooks (like this one) say that communication is an important business skill. Are they correct? Let's find out.

Go to the library and find two examples of business situations in which communication—or the lack of it—played a role. (Possible sources might include *The Wall Street Journal*, *Fortune*, *Business Week*, or your local newspaper. The com-

munication could be either written or oral, good news or bad.) Write a short report summarizing each situation and the role that communication played. Was the communication effective or ineffective? Could the people involved have communicated better? If so, what would you recommend?

Your instructor may wish to have you present your report to the class.

*B*UILDING YOUR TEAMWORK SKILLS

Begin by examining Case 2.1, entitled CAN THIS PARTNERSHIP BE SAVED?, at the end of this chapter. Then have the class divide into groups of four students each. Two students in each group will take the part of Cap Pannell, while the other two will take the role of Arthur Eisenberg. Each "Cap" pair will prepare an explanation of why Cap acted the way he did, present his views on what went wrong in the business, and make suggestions for what should be done about it. Meanwhile, each "Arthur" pair will do the same from Eisenberg's viewpoint. Finally, the two pairs will present their respective sides and discuss their options. (Remember to practice active listening!)

When all four of you have agreed on what Cap and Arthur should do, have one person from your group present your decision to the class. (Note: If there's an odd number of students in the class, one group could consist of three students, with the third serving as moderator. The moderator could practice active listening and offer clarifying statements to help Cap and Arthur state their positions.)

*C*OMMUNICATING IN A WORLD OF DIVERSITY

Effective communication is definitely a challenge. It's even more challenging when we try to communicate with people from other cultures. Just imagine, for example, what businesses go through when they try to design advertisements that will appeal to people in other countries.

Sometimes advertisers make the mistake of assuming that if it worked in the United States, it will work overseas. Here are three advertising concepts that failed in foreign countries. Can you explain why?

1. One company designed an extensive promotional campaign, involving radio, TV, and newspaper ads, to sell products in Haiti. The advertising staff felt that using a variety of advertising media would help them reach lots of potential customers.

2. Chevrolet poured millions of dollars into a campaign to promote one of its cars in Latin America. The model was the Nova.

3. A soft drink manufacturer succeeded in the United States by touting its beverages as "glacier fresh" and an "avalanche of taste." However, when the company used the same ads in Africa, it bombed.

Source: These examples are taken from Philip Cateora, *International Marketing* (Homewood, IL: Richard D. Irwin, 1990), pp. 482–88.

CASE 2.1

Can This Partnership Be Saved?

Sad but true: Poor communication can destroy a booming business. Let's look at one real-life example.

Arthur Eisenberg and Cap Pannell seemed to have the perfect partnership. Quiet Cap concentrated on design; outgoing Arthur won clients over. With Pannell's wife, Carol St. George, as head copywriter, they created a successful design firm called Eisenberg/Pannell/St. George. Sales began to soar; revenues rose 50 percent in two years, pushing the $2-million mark; a national magazine praised their work.

Behind the scenes, however, resentment was building between Arthur and Cap. One problem:

The two partners had never really discussed what each wanted from their business venture. How much profit did each of them want? What did they expect from each other? Workaholic Arthur admits that "this company is my life. I do not have anything else." Cap, on the other hand, had a wife and a new baby—and other priorities besides working constantly. When Cap refused to work all night long or to take business trips at a moment's notice, Arthur resented what he saw as a lack of commitment to the company. Arthur was furious when Cap and Carol brought baby Ben to work (even though, says Cap, they'd agreed that "we could have the baby at the office with us, with a nanny").

Did Arthur communicate his growing anger? Certainly—but not to Cap or Carol. Instead, he complained to other employees. Meanwhile, Cap and Carol resented Arthur's resentment and talked about it to each other—but not to Arthur. Recalls Cap, "We were coming home every day and saying, 'Gee, I can't believe he did that today.'" Adds Carol: "Early on, Arthur made noises about how difficult it was to have a married couple there. But I don't think it registered with us. That was kind of dumb on our part."

The crisis occurred when Cap and Carol returned from vacation. Three days later, Arthur asked them into his office and broke the news: "I'd like to discontinue the relationship." Stunned, Cap replied, "If you don't want me around, I don't want to be around." Cap and Carol left the office in silence and collected their belongings. "It was humiliating," remembers Cap. "We had to pack everything we had ourselves. Everybody was watching us, all the employees. He didn't offer us anything. I can't bring myself to think we were treated right." "As far as I'm concerned," charges Carol, "we were used and then discarded."

Cap and Arthur haven't spoken to each other since their partnership foundered. Cap, still bitter, says, "The business always did well. I don't even know the real reason we split up. I really cannot forgive him right now in my heart." For his part, Arthur insists, "If Cap and I were at a party, we'd shake hands and talk about old times.... I think Cap was as unhappy as I was. He probably wanted out of the situation, too.... I wish I knew what he felt."

Questions and Applications

1. Discuss the communication barriers that plagued Cap and Arthur's partnership.
2. Carol admits that Arthur's "noises" about the difficulty of working with a married couple hadn't "registered" with them. Why not?
3. Arthur says he wishes that he knew how Cap felt. What could Arthur have done?
4. As an employee at Eisenberg/Pannell/St. George, you're familiar with the tensions between Cap and Arthur. Arthur has asked you to write a report for the firm's advisory board explaining why Cap and Carol left. Write this report, keeping in mind that many of the board's members are longtime friends of Cap, Arthur, and Carol.
5. When asked why their partnership broke up, Arthur answers, "My problem is that I didn't research my partner enough." Cap says, "I guess I didn't realize that Arthur was just an opportunist." What do you think about their answers? Write a paragraph explaining why you think their business ended. What steps could they have taken, if any, to save it?

Source: Joshua Hyatt, "Reconcilable Differences," *Inc.*, April 1991, pp. 78–87. Reprinted with permission, *Inc.* magazine. Copyright © 1991 by Goldhirsch Group, inc., 38 Commercial Wharf, Boston, MA 02110.

CASE 2.2

Do It Now: Linda Wachner's Action Agenda at Warnaco

When she was eleven years old, Linda Joy Wachner lay flat on her back, imprisoned in a plaster cast from her head to her knees. Linda had severe scoliosis (curvature of the spine). Doctors warned her parents that she might never walk again.

Today, Wachner is not only walking, she's running—a major corporation, that is. As chief executive officer of clothing manufacturer Warnaco, she's the only female top exec of a Fortune 500 industrial company and America's most successful businesswoman. Ironically, she credits much of her success to her early health problems: "The focus I have today comes from when I was sick," she says. "When you want to walk again, you learn how to focus on that with all your might, and you don't stop until you do it."

Wachner's direct approach influences her communication style, which is an important factor in her success as a manager. For example, rather than relying on reports to see what customers want, she does her research firsthand by roaming stores around the country and chatting with salespeople. Reports one store owner: "Linda's strength is that she is constantly in touch with customers in the stores and her retailers." She's direct when collecting debts, too. When a company owes Warnaco money, its president is likely to get a call from Linda: "I tell them, 'I don't want to disturb you; however, I need the money because we can't continue shipping to you without it.'"

Back in the corporate office, communication plays a big role in Wachner's management style. Every Friday night, the seven heads of her divisions must fax her one-page memos summarizing any problems: "I just want to have an overview on Friday night," she explains, "so we can attack any problems on Monday morning." Another of her suggestions: Each of Warnaco's top execs carries a spiral notebook—with DO IT NOW embossed on the cover—in which they jot notes and ideas to be followed up later. Recalls one manager: "At one of the first meetings I attended, I sort of scratched my head trying to figure out why all these people had the same exact notebook. Then Linda told me about them. She doesn't check what's in them, but I think it is a sound way for everyone to keep on top of what has to be done."

Not everyone, of course, likes Wachner's approach. "She gets right to the point," says a for-mer boss, "and I think her frankness scares people." Adds another associate bluntly: "A lot of people have been run over by Linda. She will do anything, just anything, to get to the bottom line." A former employee, who resigned after eight months, believes "she's weak in managing people correctly."

But Linda Wachner feels the results speak for themselves. Since she took over Warnaco, she's cut the company's debt by 40 percent and doubled its cash flow. "Have I yelled at meetings?" she asks. "No question…. Look, I just want people to be good," she explains, "and I apply an enormous amount of pressure to get everybody moving this company in the right direction. I know I push very hard, but I don't push anyone harder than I push myself."

Questions and Applications

1. What steps does Wachner take to break down communication barriers?

2. What communication channels does she prefer?

3. List the advantages and disadvantages of her approach to communication.

4. Suppose that you head one of Warnaco's divisions and report directly to Linda Wachner. One Friday afternoon at 4:46, she calls you to say that, when visiting a Chicago mall, she heard comments from two salespeople about your line of menswear. It seems that some jeans are arriving in the store without buttonholes and customers are complaining. Linda asks you to look into the matter and fax her a report Monday morning. Write this report.

WRITING
BASICS

Planning
Business Documents

CHAPTER OBJECTIVES

After studying this chapter, you should be able to:

1 Identify the stages in the *writing process.*

2 Define the objectives of a document in terms of its *general purpose, specific purpose*, and *core idea.*

3 Describe the different types of *audiences* for business documents.

4 Identify and briefly explain alternative *audience-analysis techniques.*

5 Describe the role of *research* in document planning.

6 Explain the *prewriting techniques* of *brainstorming, mindmapping, freewriting*, and *asking the six questions of journalists.*

*P*lans are nothing; planning is everything.

Dwight D. Eisenhower
General, U.S. Army, and 34th President of the United States

YOUR AUDIENCE:
AN OWNER'S MANUAL

The *Harvard Business Review* tracks the interest level of the numerous articles that it publishes each year by counting the number of requests for reprints. Among the fifty top-selling reprints in the past three decades is an article entitled "What Do You Mean I Can't Write?" Written in 1964 by John Fielden, now a business professor at the University of Alabama, this article summarizes common business-writing problems and emphasizes lack of appropriate planning. "What good is it," asks Fielden,

if a message is excellent in all the other respects…[and] the content is faulty? Much disorganized writing results from insufficient preparation, from a failure to think through and isolate the purpose of the writing job. Most writers think as they write; in fact, most of us do not even know what it is we think until we have written it down.

Lack of planning, for example, is painfully obvious in the following recall notice—a letter from the Buick Division of General Motors—which demonstrates quite forcefully the consequences of failing to keep in mind both a document's purpose and its audience:

Dear Buick Owner:

This notice is sent to you in accordance with the requirements of the National Traffic and Motor Vehicle Safety Act.

Reason for Recall:

General Motors has determined that some 1988 LeSabres fail to conform to Federal Motor Vehicle Safety Standard No. 209 which covers seat belt assembly usage. The owner's manual information did not include instructions on the proper usage of the rear seat belt systems.

What We Will Do:

To correct this omission, new Owner's Manuals will be provided for each vehicle involved.

What You Should Do:

Please place the provided new Owner's Manual in your vehicle's glove box and discard the old manual or take it to your dealer for installation at no charge to you. Instructions for this service have been sent to your Buick dealer. The time to install the new Owner's Manual is approximately five (5) minutes.

Presentation of the provided Owner's Manual and this letter to your dealer will assist him in promptly making the necessary correction if you decide to seek the dealer's assistance.

Your Buick dealer is best equipped to obtain parts and provide service to ensure your vehicle is corrected as promptly as possible. However, if he does not remedy this condition on that date, or within five (5) days, we recommend you contact the Buick Customer Assistance Department....

After contacting your dealer and the Buick Home Office, if you are still not satisfied that we have done our best to remedy this condition without charge within a reasonable time, you may wish to write the Administrator, National Highway Safety Administration....[1]

Believe it or not, the *purpose* of this letter is simply to get Buick owners to replace the manuals that they received when they bought their cars. If the task is too difficult, says the letter, owners can bring their cars and manuals to local dealers, where mechanics will replace the manuals for them.

Whether this document leaves you laughing or insulted, you can be sure that neither was the intent of its author. The letter fails to achieve its purpose because it is written without the reader in mind—an error caused in large part by lack of basic planning. When audience feedback took the form of ridicule aimed at the world's leading car maker, technical writers at GM quickly realized a fundamental communication truth: Planning is the backbone of all effective writing.[2]

CHAPTER OVERVIEW

This chapter explains the role played in effective written communication by the *planning process*. We begin by placing planning in the context of the entire *writing process*—a process involving *research, organization, composition and design*, and *revision*. We will then analyze the planning process itself into four major steps: Identifying the *mission* of a document, defining its *objectives*, defining its *audience*, and implementing the plan. Finally, we will survey a variety of *prewriting strategies*—techniques for gathering and organizing ideas.

STAGES IN THE WRITING PROCESS

According to at least one popular handbook on business writing, "Successful writing on the job is not the product of inspiration, nor is it merely the spoken word transferred to paper—it is primarily the result of knowing how to structure ideas on paper."[3] We can begin by showing how effective structure reflects a series of carefully considered stages of preparation. Figure 3.1 divides the writing process into six distinct stages: *planning, research, organization, revision, composition and design*, and *revision*. We will begin by describing each of these stages in order to provide a clearer introduction to the activities involved in the writing process. Keep in mind, of course, that a *process* consists of integrated activities and not a series of separate steps.

PLANNING   In business writing, **planning** is the process by which document objectives are set, audience needs and responses assessed, and a course of action developed to accomplish the objectives. Although effective planning takes time, in the long run it is actually a time saver because it helps the writer *focus* on what is important. Much as a business organization needs plans in order to function effectively, a business document needs a strategy that sets the stage for effective communication.

planning
Process by which document objectives are set, audience needs and responses assessed, and a course of action developed to accomplish established objectives

RESEARCH   **Research** is an important part of the planning process. The amount of research needed for a written assignment depends on the nature of the document and the extent of the knowledge available about the topic. While minimal research is usually needed for simple memos or letters, longer, more complex documents often require extensive fact-finding research.

research
Systematic investigation of a subject in order to discover facts, opinions, or beliefs

FIGURE 3.1   *The Writing Process*

For example, a report analyzing sales by geographic region will be based on such factual information as actual sales for the time period being analyzed, sales for corresponding operating periods the previous year, and quotas set for the region at the beginning of the period. However, the report may also include the results of customer surveys containing suggestions for improving sales during a future period. Published reports of overall industry sales during the period may also reveal the need to adjust projected quotas in order to reflect changing conditions.

ORGANIZATION   Based on their communication objectives, the requirements of their audiences, and the limitations of their formats, writers make crucial decisions about **organization**. These decisions determine both the order in which your ideas are presented and the logical connections that exist among these ideas. Organizational decisions include determining an approach. In turn, the approach taken by a document can indicate the purpose of its organization. For example, is your purpose to identify a problem and propose a solution? Or do you wish to clarify a problem by showing a sequence of causes and effects? When you explain your approach, you offer your audience a guide to the organization of your document. (Chapter 4 identifies various approaches to written documents and explains how each can reflect the different purposes of different documents.)

COMPOSITION AND DESIGN   The process of **composition** involves following your organizational writing plan to produce a rough draft. During composition, decisions are made about such matters as tone, style, and level of formality. At this stage, you will probably begin developing an effective design for your document. **Design** is the process of placing information on a page so that it is easily accessible to readers. Various design elements that help improve presentations include the use of headings, underlining and capitalization, and bulleted lists. The design you choose should help to clarify your organization.

REVISION   The final stage in the writing process, **revision** involves specific steps that transform a rough draft into a finished document. These steps include checking the most fundamental aspects of effective written communication:

organization
Process of arranging information and connecting different ideas to produce a unified, coherent message

composition
Process of combining parts or elements into a coherent whole by following a writing plan to produce a rough draft and finally a finished draft

design
Process of planning, writing, illustrating, and structuring a document to make it inviting and easy to read

revision
Process of transforming a rough draft into a finished document by adding, deleting, replacing, and reorganizing words, sentences, and paragraphs

- Selecting the proper words, style, and tone to communicate your message.
- Checking for clarity and conciseness and removing all jargon.
- Eliminating all punctuation, grammatical, and spelling errors.
- Focusing on coherence through the use of effective transitions.

Naturally, you should also check for such errors of fact as incorrect statistics and for inappropriate phrasing (for example, the inadvertent use of sexist language).

The revision process has two phases. In the first stage, the writer examines the document and makes revisions. In the second stage, the criticisms of others are incorporated into the final product. For example, you may decide to submit your report to your immediate supervisor before handing it to the person who originally requested it. After reading the report, your supervisor may make suggestions for changes that you can then incorporate into your draft. Learning to use feedback to improve the quality and professionalism of your work is a crucial step in the writing process.

We will turn next to the concept of planning. As you will see, the planning process that guides business decision making can also be applied to decisions that you will make in business writing.

CAN YOUR ENTERPRISE KEEP UP WITH YOUR STRATEGIC VISION?

THE MOST COST-EFFECTIVE WAY TO IMPLEMENT STRATEGIC CHANGE.

Prepared by X/Open, The International, Not-For-Profit Organization For Open Systems.

R e-engineering your organization to meet the challenges of the 1990s is one of the most difficult tasks facing top executives. Open systems are proven to be the most flexible and cost-efficient way to enable strategic change. Without jeopardizing your current IS investment.

But in order to move safely to open systems, you need a standard you can count on. That's where X/Open™ comes in. We're an independent, not-for-profit consortium of end-users, and just about every major international system and software vendor. We don't sell products. We provide the information

and tools to ensure that open systems are truly open.

The X/Open brand means that a product has passed our stringent tests for conformance to open systems standards. And that the supplier guarantees future conformance. Insist on the X/Open brand, and your enterprise's capabilities will never have to lag behind your vision.

Our free brochure details the compelling business arguments for using open systems to implement strategic change. For a copy, call 1-800-568-OPEN in the U.S. and Canada, or +1-818-898-3886 internationally. It's required reading for the 1990s.

x/Open BASE XPG4

The World's Standard For Open Systems.

© 1992 X/Open Company Ltd. All rights reserved. X/Open and the X device are trademarks of X/Open Company Ltd. in the U.K. and other countries.

In the broadest sense, *strategy* refers to the way in which both organizations and individuals plan to act in and respond to their environments. The appeal to strategic advantage here, for example, refers to the highly interactive flow of information between an organization and its environment. Business writers think strategically when they understand their environment to include audiences who provide feedback and influence courses of action.

PRACTICAL TIPS

Attitudes and Writing

Your attitude toward writing itself will often affect your ability to communicate your objectives. Your responses to the follow- ing statements will reveal what your attitude toward writing actually is. Check the box that best applies.

	Agree	Don't Know	Disagree
1. Writing is difficult for me.	❏	❏	❏
2. Applying the rules of grammar is the most important measure of good writing.	❏	❏	❏
3. Since I wrote well in school, I can write well in business.	❏	❏	❏
4. Since I am a good speaker, I will surely be a good writer.	❏	❏	❏
5. Since I am sure I will know what everyone in my office is doing, I will not need to write that much.	❏	❏	❏
6. I expect that writing will be one of my least important job responsibilities.	❏	❏	❏

STRATEGIC AND TACTICAL PLANNING FOR WRITERS

strategic planning
Process by which managers determine the major objectives of an organization and choose courses of action to achieve those objectives

tactical planning
Process by which objectives are translated into specific, achievable plans

Business decision making typically involves two forms of planning. **Strategic planning** is the process by which managers determine the major objectives of an organization and choose courses of action to achieve those objectives. **Tactical planning** is the process by which objectives are translated into specific, achievable plans. IBM's decision at the end of 1992 to return to profitability by a major reorganization into divisions responsible for achieving individual sales and profit goals is an example of strategic planning. The decision to price new IBM personal computers to better compete with Compaq, Dell, Gateway, and other PC suppliers involves tactical planning.[4]

The management tool of strategic planning can guide business writers as they identify the purpose of a document, define its objectives, analyze its audience, and choose a course of action. Tactical planning for business writing begins with organizing, composing, and designing business documents and concludes with editing and revising.

Every business message can be viewed as the focal point for a series of decisions that must be made about alternative courses of action. Although the planning *process*, like the writing process, may be examined as a series of distinct steps that naturally follow one another, those steps are actually integrated—that is, interactive and overlapping. For example, brainstorming and audience analysis may be conducted before research, after research, or both. Throughout the planning process, then, experienced business writers move back and forth among various related activities. In this sense, each of the four stages summarized in Table 3.1 should be considered an ongoing process of planning and revising.

Now consider your responses in terms of the following comments:

Now consider your responses in terms of the following comments:

1. *Even experienced business writers often find writing difficult.* This is especially the case when writing involves translating technical information for a lay audience or when dealing with complex subjects. Try to overcome *writer's block*—the anticipation and anxiety that you feel when staring at a blank page.

2. *Although correct punctuation, grammar, and spelling are necessary elements in business writing, they are not sufficient to produce a well-written document.* The best writing is built on effective planning; thorough research; clear, logical organization; an open, easy-to-read format; a style and a tone that meet audience needs and writer intent; and a willingness to make revisions.

3. *Writing successfully in business is possible if you practice the art of audience analysis and adapt your writing to the unique requirements of your audience.*

4. *Being a good conversationalist does not necessarily mean that you will be a good writer.* Writing is less spontaneous than conversation. It requires careful planning, organization, and decisions about design, style, tone, and language. It is also a multistage process involving one or more drafts and revisions.

5. *Even in offices where there is a high degree of verbal communication, writing is a critical part of every workday.* Writing is the channel through which many of the most important business messages are sent. Therefore, the ability to write well influences career success.

6. *Almost every career—from accountant to engineer, from human resource manager to sales representative—requires an ability to communicate effectively in writing.* Accomplishments are worth very little unless they can be communicated to others.

Source: Based on Herman A. Estrin and Norbert Elliot, *Technical Writing in the Corporate World: Basic Strategies for Success* (Los Altos, CA: Crisp Publications, 1990), pp. 3–6.

IDENTIFYING THE MISSION OF YOUR DOCUMENT

The *mission statement* summarizes the fundamental purpose that distinguishes an organization from all others of its type. It is a general, enduring statement of company intent.[5] Ford Motor Co., for example, expresses its corporate mission this way:

> To improve continually our products and services to meet our customers' needs, allowing us to prosper as a business and to provide a reasonable return for our stockholders, the owners of our business.[6]

Much as a mission statement guides every business organization, the **mission** that governs a business document is the fundamental purpose for which the document was written. In its most basic sense, the mission of every document is communication—getting a message to an audience without misinterpretation or misunderstanding. Whether the document is a collection letter, a letter of reference, a memo

When you come to a fork in the road, take it.

Yogi Berra
Longtime New York
Yankee catcher

mission
Fundamental purpose for which a document is written

TABLE 3.1	*Stages in the Planning Process*
STAGE	PURPOSE
Identify your mission.	To focus on the goal of communication
Define your objectives.	To provide clear and specific direction for your writing effort
Define your audience.	To identify audience needs, knowledge, and interests
Implement your plan.	To research the core idea and revise it, if necessary, based on research findings; to gather ideas through prewriting strategies; and to select the most effective written communication

PRACTICAL TIPS

Five Reasons for Poor Writing

Although there are numerous reasons for poor writing, five of them occur most often. Fortunately, each problem has a solution.

1. *Thinking and planning that are unclear.* Without a plan, writing often lacks direction. In such instances, your ideas and point of view can be lost as the audience struggles to follow your train of thought. Effective planning, on the other hand, leads to clear organization.

    One widely used and highly effective method for planning a document is arranging information in outline form. Clarity is achieved because information is presented to the audience in a step-by-step fashion. In the same way, you can decide which visual aids are most likely to enhance the reader's understanding of your written material.

2. *Failing to write with your audience in mind.* Failure to analyze your audience can re-

sult in writing beneath or above the audience's level of knowledge. Your writing may also fail to address the interests and needs of your audience. An audience-centered approach tells readers what they want to know in a way that is useful to them. Some familiar examples of writer-centered rather than audience-centered or "reader-friendly" documents are computer manuals, Internal Revenue Service tax forms, and insurance policies.

3. *Writing to impress rather than communicate.* Flowery language, jargon, and long complex sentences obstruct rather than enhance communication and often disregard the reader's point of view. Keep in mind that nothing impresses readers more than clear, simple communication that tells them what they want to know. If, for example, you are providing information on a new design for

announcing a meeting, a sales forecast, a request for credit information, or a formal report, the audience must be able to understand the sender's primary purpose.

DEFINING YOUR DOCUMENT OBJECTIVES

Defining a document's *objectives* is the most critical step in the planning process. Without it, documents lack a reason for being. Objectives serve at least four functions:

- They provide a sense of direction as you gather information, analyze your audience, and begin to compose.

- They focus your efforts, allowing you to use your writing time effectively. With limited time available for any task, effective time management is crucial.

- They guide your writing decisions. As a step in your planning, stating your objectives will help you decide the best way to organize material, the right words to choose, the most effective tone and format, and when and how to send a document.

- They enable you to evaluate your progress as you write. Writing is a process that involves constant reevaluation, editing, and revision. Objectives provide the standard against which to measure your work.

There is nothing so useless as doing efficiently that which should not be done at all.

Peter Drucker
American business
philosopher and author

To be effective, objectives should focus on both the *content* of your message and the best *means* of communicating that message to a specific audience. Defining objectives requires limiting the scope of your topic by deciding what information to include and what to omit.

Consideration of the audience is often just as important as the information provided in your document. For example, a report detailing various improvements being made in the company might contain information that every depart-

your firm's product label, avoid the temptation to describe the colors as beautiful and eye-catching and the fact that the print reflects a contemporary style. It is much clearer to the reader to state simply that the red and white labels will stand out when placed beside competing product lines on retail-store shelves and that the print is large and can be easily read.

4. *Failing to consider design as a crucial part of communication.* Information overload is a fact of life in today's business world. Businesspeople are often too busy to wade through pages of details to get to the point of a letter, a memo, a report, or a proposal. To make the reader's job as easy as possible, plan and revise the *design* of your document as you plan and revise its content. Use headings, bulleted lists, indented paragraphs, and plenty of white space. By accen-

tuating important aspects of the document, you assist the reader in grasping your major points as easily as possible.

5. *Failing to revise and edit.* Few documents are right the first time around. They need fine-tuning and sometimes major revision to meet your objectives. A review of your document may alert you to the fact that one objective has been overemphasized to the detriment of others. This overemphasis may even adversely affect the document's main purpose. For example, although the document's purpose might pertain to the company as a whole, it is easy to let those objectives that directly affect your department become a major thrust of your presentation.

Source: Sherry Sweetnam, *The Executive Memo: A Guide to Persuasive Business Communications* (New York: John Wiley & Sons, 1986), pp. 9–11. © 1986 John Wiley & Sons. Reprinted by permission.

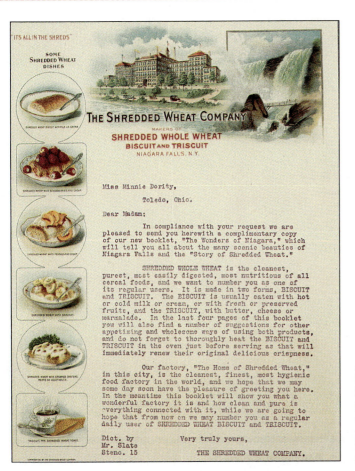

At the turn of the century, The Shredded Wheat Company of Niagara Falls, New York, conceived its mission as being fairly straightforward—namely, the marketing of shredded-wheat products. As this contemporary letterhead shows, corporate communications, while sometimes elaborate in design, directly reflected the company's understanding of both its mission and its audience.

ment could use. However, the report is likely to include sections that are applicable only to specific departments. In such instances, you may decide to convert these sections to appendixes or addenda that will be provided only to the relevant departments. The result would be a document that meets the overall objectives of the entire firm as well as the specific objectives of individual departments.

Objectives work best when they are clear in the writer's mind and can be incorporated with equal clarity in a document that readers will understand. Nevertheless, millions of business documents are written each year that leave readers asking, "What is this trying to accomplish?" As a summary of your objectives, your purpose, therefore, must always be clearly stated in the document itself. For example, the *objectives* of your document may be to achieve a 10-percent reduction in office expenditures and a 5-percent increase in sales; the *main purpose* can be stated as controlling costs and increasing sales. Defining a document's objectives, therefore, involves defining its *general purpose*, its *specific purpose*, and its *core idea*.

Define Your General Purpose

general purpose
Primary reason for which a document is written or an oral presentation is made; typically to inform, persuade, and/or initiate action

A document's **general purpose** is the primary reason that it is written. In this sense, *purpose* refers to the goals that you want to accomplish as a direct result of

---

OFFICES *BY AUSTIN*

1615 San Felipe Drive   Tucson, Arizona 85713
(603) 555-4358

February 15, 199X

Dear Ms. Alexander:

We appreciate your order for three business desks. Your choice of cherry wood is popular with many of our clients. Unfortunately, its popularity has surpassed the supply we currently have in our warehouse, so we are forced to delay shipment for about two weeks.

I will be in touch with you very shortly with a firm delivery date. I am sorry for any inconvenience this delay might have caused.

Sincerely,

John Austin

John Austin
President

FIGURE 3.2   *Writing to Inform*

your decision to communicate in writing. The three most common general purposes of written communication are *writing to inform, writing to persuade,* and *writing to initiate action.*

WRITING TO INFORM   To a large extent, business writing is informative writing. Examples include status reports on current projects, memos to set up meetings (and follow-ups that include the minutes of prior meetings), and letters telling customers that orders will be delayed or that credit has been granted. Figure 3.2 is a letter whose primary purpose is informative.

WRITING TO PERSUADE   Persuasive writing attempts to convince readers. Persuasive documents include proposals and suggestions for new procedures, products, or business; letters of recommendation; and sales brochures. In Figure 3.3, the memo supporting a proposal to increase the number of employees at Offices by Austin is an example of a persuasive document.

WRITING TO INITIATE ACTION   Many letters ask the reader to do something or to respond in a certain way. Examples include sales letters, requests for information or action, and job-application letters. Although action-oriented letters can also inform or persuade, their main purpose is to generate responses that have concrete results. The letter in Figure 3.4 is an action-oriented letter.

Knowledge is a process of piling up facts; wisdom lies in their simplification.
Martin H. Fisher
American author
and educator

FIGURE 3.3   *Writing to Persuade*

OFFICESBY AUSTIN

1615 San Felipe Drive   Tucson, Arizona 85713
(603) 555-4358

July 12, 199X

Dear Mr. Vanderburg:

I read your proposal and was impressed by its thorough coverage
of environmentally sound consumer products pointing out the
benefits of "green marketing." Although we are interested in
your recycling services, we need the following information to be
able to consider your company any further:

  • at least three references from long-term clients

  • a written cost estimate of your marketing proposal

  • and a time frame for completing the marketing campaign.

Please get back to me as soon as possible with these details so
we can proceed with our discussion.

Sincerely,

John Austin

John Austin
President

FIGURE 3.4   *Writing to Initiate Action*

Define Your Specific Purpose and Core Idea

specific purpose
Brief summary of the reason for which a document is written or an oral presentation is made

Think of the **specific purpose** of a document as a brief summary of your reason for writing it. Although it focuses on the message that you want your audience to receive, the message itself will be fully developed in your completed document. Here, for example, are two specific-purpose summaries, both audience-centered:

  • to inform all Ben & Jerry's employees that the company will help pay the cost of their children's college educations.
  • to persuade consumers to try Kodak's new line of single-use cameras.

core idea
One-sentence statement of the central message of a written or oral presentation; sometimes called the *thesis statement*

Developed out of the specific-purpose summary, the **core idea** (sometimes called the *thesis statement*) is the central message of the document. Ideally, it can be stated in a single sentence, and it is the point at which you state the message that you want to communicate to your reader. While your specific purpose, therefore, may be thought of as a note to yourself, stating your core idea is an important element in your message itself. The two specific-purpose summaries shown above can be used to create the following core-idea statements:

As an employee, you should be aware that Ben & Jerry's is now offering to help workers pay for their children's post-secondary education by contributing as much as $4,000 per child for school expenses and subsidizing the fees and interest payments on certain educational loans.

When you are on a vacation, consider using Kodak's new line of single-use cameras, including the Kodak Fun Saver Weekend 35mm camera, priced between $9 and $17.

In long reports and proposals, the core idea often appears in the form of a *purpose statement* that informs recipients why they received your document. The purpose statement can be as simple as the following sentences in a cover memo:

Attached are the regional crime reports for the six largest budget-priced motels. These data should help clarify the issues you raised last week.

Sometimes, however, more detail is necessary in telling your reader precisely what to expect:

Law enforcement agencies throughout the state are citing increased crime at low-budget motels. A rash of burglaries, rapes, and homicides have been reported, as well as drunkenness and car theft. It is the purpose of this report to examine the implications of this crime wave on higher-priced lodging chains, including our own. Among the key issues to be examined are implications for increased security and for marketing our chain to middle-class travelers who now use budget-priced lodging.

Some documents (for example, formal reports) may require an additional explanation in the form of an *executive summary*—a formal statement of the document's purpose, scope, methods, results, conclusions, and recommendations. Executive summaries will be examined in detail in Chapter 12.

Taken together, your specific purpose and core idea can show you at a glance whether your document is trying to accomplish too much. For example, the following summary of specific purpose fails to limit the scope of the memo:

To inform all Offices by Austin sales representatives that the next sales meeting will be held on March 18 in Phoenix and that pricing changes for such electronic office products as fax machines, telephone answering machines, and copiers will go into effect on April 1.

What is the problem? Combining these two important purposes into one document weakens the impact of both messages and probably guarantees that neither will get the attention it deserves.

At this stage of the writing process, therefore, consider your specific-purpose summary and core-idea statement as features of your first or working draft. After further considering your audience and researching your topic, you might decide to revise them.

PROGRESS CHECK

1. Define planning in the context of business writing.
2. Distinguish between strategic planning and tactical planning as they apply to business writing.
3. Give an example of a document's general purpose, specific purpose, and core idea.

DEFINING YOUR AUDIENCE

To do two things at once is to do neither.

Publilius Syrus
Latin writer of mimes

Although clearly stating your objectives typically answers many questions, it can raise others. For example:

- Is your stated purpose relevant to your audience?

- Is it too trivial? Too technical? Too detailed?
- Will your document stand alone or must it be reviewed with others?
- How do your readers usually respond to memos longer than one page?
- Is your document intended for one reader or for a number of readers?

audience analysis
Process by which business communicators analyze the needs and knowledge of their readers in order to improve the likelihood of communicating effectively through written documents

These and other questions can only be answered through careful **audience analysis:** the process by which business writers analyze the needs and knowledge of their readers in order to improve the likelihood of communicating effectively through written documents. Audience analysis is crucial in every aspect of business.

Consider, for example, the following informal sales presentation that hinges on a certain confusion about customers and audiences:

> A fisherman went into a sporting goods store to buy a lure. Happy to oblige, the sales clerk showed him a wide array of colored feathers, plastic insects, and other clever gadgets designed to attract the fish. Confused by the array and not sure whether any would really work, the fisherman inquired, "Do fish really like this sort of thing?" Without hesitating, the clerk responded, "I don't sell to fish."[7]

The moral of the story, of course, is clear: If your persuasive message has the specific purpose of selling fishing lures, the people who fish—not the fish—are your primary audience. However, the ramifications of the same story may be much more complex. Communication success depends on the ability to identify the *primary audience* as well as *secondary, initial,* or *multiple audiences* who will receive your document. In this section, we will define each of these types or levels of audience. We will also discuss *visualization* as a technique for analyzing audience needs and offer a model for understanding audience *motivation*.

Types of Audiences

primary audience
Reader for whom a document is directly intended and who will actually use its information

initial audience
First reader of a document

secondary audience
Readers, other than the primary reader, who will use the document in a variety of ways or who may be asked to comment on its content

multiple audiences
Primary, secondary, and/or initial audiences who receive, use, and may provide feedback regarding a document

It is common for business documents to have more than one audience. The reader for whom the document is directly intended and who will actually use the information is considered the **primary audience**. Although formal letters are typically addressed directly to the primary reader, such is not always the case with internal memos and reports. For example, your company's director of marketing research might ask you for a status report on the impact of a new advertising campaign in the Atlanta market. The first reader of your document is your **initial audience**—in this instance, the director of marketing research.

Although your report, therefore, would be written for this manager, your primary audience might be the vice president for corporate advertising, who intends to use the information in evaluating the company's advertising agency and its current ad campaign. Your audience also includes readers who will use your document in a variety of ways or who may be asked to comment on its content. Such readers comprise a **secondary audience**. After reviewing your report, for example, the vice president for corporate advertising (the primary audience) is likely to send a copy to the ad agency's account executive. In this case, then, your secondary audience is the agency that created the ad campaign.

In this illustration, your document has **multiple audiences**, which can include *one or more* primary, secondary, and initial audiences. Multiple audiences are common for many business documents. Among the different audiences who read corporate annual reports are workers, stockholders, customers, suppliers, government officials, the media, and the general public.[8] The requirements of each audience must be considered when drafting your document. For example, while your primary audience (the vice president for corporate advertising) might want a quick overview, your secondary audience (the ad agency) might require additional statistics on demographic groups in the Atlanta market.

Visualizing Your Audience

One effective technique for audience analysis is to *visualize* your primary audience. The visualization process is different depending on how well you already know that audience. In the simplest terms, audience visualization can be a process of developing a mental picture of either someone you know or someone you do not know.

VISUALIZE SOMEONE YOU KNOW   Many of the documents that you write are directed to people whom you know—for example, co-workers, steady customers, and suppliers. To help determine the best way to approach these people, business writing authority L. E. Frailey suggests that you start by studying your correspondence files. In the following example, Frailey focuses on a hypothetical dealer named Martin:

> The correspondence file reveals that Martin pays his bills promptly, that his relations with the sales department always have been friendly, that one of his sons went to Yale, that he was once mayor of his city. Gradually, the mental image of dealer Martin begins to form. His letters, too, are revealing. They indicate a sense of humor, a capacity for seeing both sides of a moot question, but also a well-defined stubbornness once Martin has declared his point of view. His letters frequently mention seeing a football game, playing golf, or something about his bowling average. It is plain he is the athletic type, at least he is keenly interested in sports.... If you sat at your desk one morning, with a letter from dealer Martin in your hand, wondering what to say because a situation has developed which may break the business relationship—if that were true, wouldn't you want to get from Martin's file all of the help it might give you?[9]

Because files help you apply what you already know about your audience to your current needs, they are often a good starting point for audience analysis. In order to tap your current knowledge of your audience, try asking yourself the following questions:

- How much does my reader know about the subject? Does he or she know a great deal or a modest amount? Should I assume no knowledge at all?
- Will my reader respond to my document with a biased point of view? Will preconceived ideas stand in the way of a fair hearing?
- How does my reader feel about me, my company, and the products we produce? Is he or she likely to be favorable or negative?
- Is my reader likely to be interested in what I have to say? (This question is especially important if you are introducing new goods or services.)
- What kind of response can I expect from my reader? Is he or she in a position to make a decision to purchase a product, provide a recommendation, or answer a credit question?
- What writing style does my reader prefer? (For example, past experience may tell you that a particular supervisor wants memos no longer than a page.)

VISUALIZE SOMEONE YOU DON'T KNOW   In most cases, your audience is at least partially unknown to you. By asking the following questions, you can begin your analysis by identifying both your audience and the information that you need about that audience:

- Does my reader know anything about me or my company? Do I have credibility or must I build it?
- Who is my reader in terms of his or her company, title, and functional area?
- Does my reader come from an area of the country or world that has a different communication style?

■ What can I learn about my reader from others? Do I know anyone who might know this reader?

Whether you are dealing with someone you know or someone you do not know, approach the reader in either case with the understanding that communication success is directly related to satisfying audience needs. To find out what your audience wants and how you can provide it, analyze the *motivation* involved. Motivational analysis is especially important when the general purpose is persuasion.

Motivational Analysis: Maslow's Hierarchy of Needs

hierarchy of needs
Grouping that arranges in hierarchical order the physical, safety, social, status, and self-actualization needs common to most humans

More than fifty years ago, psychologist Abraham Maslow explored human motivation by creating what is now known as Maslow's **hierarchy of needs**—a grouping that arranges in hierarchical order the physical, safety, social, status, and self-actualization needs common to most humans.[10] Maslow's description of motivation has become a useful management tool, and it can provide invaluable assistance to business writers.

As you can see in Figure 3.5, Maslow's classification system is based on the theory that people are motivated by five identifiable groups of needs:

■ *Physiological needs* for such basic necessities as food, water, oxygen, shelter, sleep, and sex
■ *Safety or security needs* for comfort, tranquility, and freedom from fear and financial worry
■ *Social needs* for acceptance, belonging, and friendship
■ *Ego or esteem needs* for recognition, prestige, leadership, and success
■ *Self-actualization needs* for self-fulfillment and the realization of one's potential

Maslow's needs-hierarchy concept is based on the belief that people generally respond best at the level on which they currently have some concern. In other words, someone who is striving to save enough money for the deposit on an apartment is not likely to be motivated by the desire for self-fulfillment. As soon as lower-level needs are met, the individual is free to seek the satisfaction of needs on the next level in the hierarchy. If a threat reappears at a lower level, however, the individual's attention returns to the more basic need.

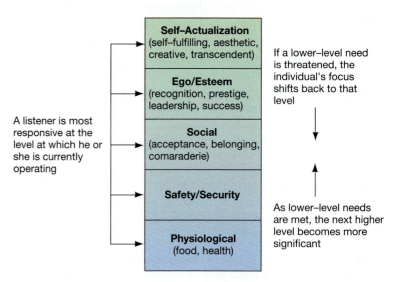

FIGURE 3.5   *Maslow's Hierarchy of Needs*

Source: Thomas Leech, *How to Prepare, State, and Deliver Winning Presentations,* New York: © 1982 AMACOM, a division of the American Management Association, p. 57. Reprinted with permission. All Rights Reserved.

IMPLICATIONS FOR BUSINESS WRITERS   Gear your writing to the level in the hierarchy that you believe reflects your reader's motivation. For example, if you have the task of writing a collection letter to a man who owes $1,500 on a department-store charge card, you might learn from his credit report that the bank is about to foreclose on his house due to nonpayment of his mortgage. In this case, a threat to cancel his retail credit privilege at your store is not likely to succeed. Because the individual is focusing on a more basic need for shelter, he is likely to use all available funds to repay past-due home mortgage payments. Only the serious threat of a lawsuit by your employer is likely to prompt him to address his charge-card debt at this time. However, if six months later the man has resolved his mortgage problem, he may be more receptive to repaying a department-store debt that reflects a safety and security need.

Similarly, when writing an evaluation of a subordinate's work, remember that the employee may be motivated to work more effectively if you focus on ego needs for recognition and success. Praise past performance and, when possible, link continued good work to such concrete results as promotions, raises, a more spacious office, or other tangible evidence of his or her success in the job.

Using Audience Analysis to Meet Audience Needs

The following suggestions will help focus your document on audience concerns. These suggestions make it clear that your audience's response to your message is as important as the message itself.[11]

CONSIDER THE READER'S KNOWLEDGE   Understanding the reader's knowledge of a subject involves knowing what other documents he or she has read. Assume, for example, that a superior has reviewed a consultant's report on alternate office space arrangements and has asked you to study the report and make recommendations. You need not repeat the consultant's suggestions in detail. What the manager wants is your opinion on the consultant's advice, not a rehashing of a report that he or she has already read. Similarly, if you produce a document as part of a collaborative effort, plan the document with the team's total contribution in mind. Avoid placing the reader in the position of reading the same information in multiple places.

CONSIDER THE READER'S QUESTIONS   To ensure that your focus is on the right issue and that you have sufficiently limited the scope of your coverage, try phrasing your summary of specific purpose in the form of a question that your reader might ask. For example, if your specific purpose for a memo is to persuade the company's art director to print a new brochure in color rather than black and white, you might phrase your summary of purpose as the question "Why should I print the new brochures in color?"

LEARN TO INTERPRET REQUESTS   Similarly, if you are writing in response to a request, turn the request into a question that must be answered in your written response. For example, if a superior writes you, "I need a memo on the distribution problem at the New Orleans plant," he or she is really asking, "What steps can I take to solve the problem at the New Orleans plant?" In answering your own rephrased question, you will provide a more satisfactory reply to the request.

CONSIDER THE READER'S POSITION   Ask yourself, for example, whether you are writing up the company hierarchy to a supervisor, down to a subordinate, or laterally to a co-worker. "In upward communication," explains communication consultant John Fielden, "tact is important. An argumentative or insulting tone will certainly reap trouble. The boss who writes down to subordinates should use diplomacy. Being overbearing or insulting limits a manager's effectiveness. And it is the foolish manager who tries to speak to subordinates as a representative of management or even of the entire company."[12]

CONSIDER THE READER'S MOTIVATION   Remind yourself your audience might not be motivated by the same details that motivate you. As communication consultants Marya W. Holcombe and Judith K. Stein explain:

> Suppose that you are a manager for a soft-drink bottling company. You fondly remember the soft drink of your childhood in Maine. You have developed an extract that closely resembles the original flavor, and you want to tell the president of the company about your idea. If you define your tasks as writing a memo to tell the CEO about your idea, the memo might begin: When camping in the Maine woods last summer I had a terrific idea.
>
> Many memos begin this way. They tell the reader how the writer came upon the idea, what work has been done, and if the reader is lucky, what the writer has found. The reader, on the other hand, has other needs. He or she is likely to be less interested in the genesis and development of the idea than in its value. Why should we produce this new drink? You might start the soft drink memo this way: Market research shows a strong consumer demand for products with flavors reminiscent of the "good old days."[13]

CONSIDER THE READER'S BIASES AND INTERESTS   Suppose you suggest to the managers of a pizza restaurant chain the idea of meatless pizzas. You might decide to focus on the appeal of these dishes to new restaurant customers. In this case, your memo could begin: "Increasing the number of items on the menu by offering a mixed-grill vegetarian with smoked mozzarella cheese pizza and a five-cheese and tomato pizza will attract health-conscious and vegetarian customers."

However, if one of the managers is most concerned about ensuring the success of two new outlets, the memo might begin: "Approximately 10,000 vegetarians live within a two-mile radius of both of the new restaurants in San José and Encino."

You should also remember that overly long or overly detailed memos and other documents are less likely to be read than those that are brief and to the point. Write with the reader's information needs in mind and keep written messages short, simple, and as easy to read as possible.

MEASURE YOUR LEVEL OF FORMALITY   Make the formality or informality of your writing style complement the style preferred by your reader. For example, a client who has done business with your company for 20 years might prefer a message that acknowledges a business rather than a personal relationship. In that case, you could use the company's name rather than *I* or *we*. Similarly, you might begin formal letters by writing: "International Life Insurance company stands behind every policy it writes." On the other hand, the following opening would be acceptable in an informal letter: "As an agent for International Life, I want to personally assure you that the company stands behind every policy."

GUARD AGAINST FALSE ASSUMPTIONS   Never forget that any of the following assumptions can result in miscommunication:

- *Gender*. Assuming that someone is a man or a woman based on an ambiguous first name; assuming certain stereotyped roles and responsibilities
- *Age*. Assuming knowledge and attitudes tied to certain age groups
- *Education*. Assuming that everyone reached the same position through the same educational route
- *Income*. Assuming that income has little effect on people's responses to goods and services
- *Occupation*. Assuming that people with similar titles in different organizations perform the same function or have the same income and authority level
- *Knowledge*. Assuming that everyone reads a document with the same level of knowledge about the subject

■ *Attitudes.* Assuming that everyone shares the same feelings about an idea, a person, or a product.

MAKE SURE YOU MAKE SENSE   Finally, ask yourself whether your document makes sense. The person who wrote the following letter from the Atlanta Internal Revenue Service's Taxpayer Assistance Section never applied the simple test of common sense. The letter was addressed to a dead man instead of to the widow who had filed her late husband's tax return:

> We are processing your gift tax return, Form 709, for calendar year 1990 and find we need more information. Please provide your date of death.... If we do not hear from you, your account may reflect incomplete or incorrect information.... If you have any questions about this letter...you may call the IRS telephone number listed in your local directory...but the office at the address shown on this letter is most familiar with your case.... We apologize for any inconvenience we may have caused you, and thank you for your cooperation.[14]

Getting the facts is the key to good decision making. Every mistake that I made...came because I didn't take the time. I didn't drive hard enough. I wasn't smart enough to get the facts.

Charles Knight
Chairman,
Emerson Electric

IMPLEMENTING A WRITING PLAN

Having satisfied yourself that you have sufficient knowledge about your audience, you are ready for step four of the planning process: developing specific methods for *implementing* a writing plan. These methods involve testing your core idea against your research, revising if necessary to reflect new information or points of view, and defining and redefining the specific ideas that will make up the body of your document.

Researching the Core Idea

Research involves gathering both primary and secondary information that either supports your position or forces revisions. **Primary sources**, such as U.S. census data or data from surveys, are sources containing new information, including statistics and other data. Primary sources also include interviews and surveys that you conduct yourself. **Secondary sources** are compilations of the ideas of others. For example, a *Wall Street Journal* article citing a study on injury rates for air-bag equipped cars is a secondary research source. The primary source is the original study.

Naturally, it is important to evaluate all your research sources in terms of accuracy and usefulness. Table 3.2 can be used as a checklist for evaluating sources.

primary source
Person or organization supplying firsthand information on a subject

secondary source
Person or organization compiling data and ideas supplied by others

TABLE 3.2   *Evaluating Primary and Secondary Sources*

PRIMARY SOURCES

1. Will the source have a vested interest in the result of the study?
2. Does the source have a reputation for accuracy?

SECONDARY SOURCES

1. Is the source objective? Are there any biases?
2. Is the source up-to-date?
3. Are statistical sources comparable? (It may be impossible to use two sets of statistical data to support your argument because they used different samples or different methods. Check for consistency before you try to incorporate different sources.)

It is a bad plan that admits of no modification.

Publilius Syrus
Latin writer of mimes

Source: Marya W. Holcombe and Judith K. Stein, *Writing for Decision Makers: Memos and Reports with a Competitive Edge* (Belmont, CA: Lifetime Learning Publications, 1981), p. 34.

Using Your Research to Reevaluate Your Core Idea

Before implementing your writing plan, you should test your core idea against your research findings. The following example demonstrates how such an "accuracy check" can be made. Assume that you are a marketing analyst working for a major credit-card company and believe that a vast untapped market of credit-card customers exists among students enrolled in the nation's colleges and universities. You decide to write a memo to your superior, suggesting that the company begin an aggressive marketing program directed toward this group. Your preliminary core idea states:

> The nation's 5.8 million full-time four-year college students are prime candidates for an aggressive credit-card marketing program, and I recommend that we begin such a program at once in order to tap the potential of this market.

In addition to stating your point of view, this statement of your core idea should define the scope of your research. Primary research in this case might mean surveying the spending habits of college students who are currently credit-card users. Secondary sources might include back issues of *Credit Card News*, a bimonthly trade newsletter that recently ran a series of articles on the student market. Perhaps you will also find a comprehensive review on the subject in a major newspaper such as *The New York Times* or national magazines like *Fortune*, *Forbes*, or *Business Week*.

Assume that your research not only confirms your suspicion that college students represent a large untapped market of potential credit-card users but also reveals that these individuals can be considered the market of the future. After all, the average non-student cardholder already owns seven cards. However, you also uncover a small but disturbing trend; namely, a high non-payment rate of credit-card debt among cardholders who are full-time college students. This discovery causes you to revise your core idea, which now reads:

> The nation's 5.8 million full-time four-year college students are prime candidates for an aggressive credit-card marketing program, and I recommend that we begin such a program at once, using such prescreening measures as detailed credit histories, income requirements, and parental signatures to eliminate obvious credit risks.[15]

Your research has now changed the focus of your core idea by emphasizing the need for applicant screening and stringent credit requirements.

Using Prewriting Strategies

prewriting strategies
Techniques for gathering and organizing ideas, including such processes as *brainstorming, mindmapping,* and *asking journalists' questions*

brainstorming
Creative problem-solving technique in which ideas are listed as they come to mind and which encourages unrestrained participation in group discussion

Although developing the specifics of a document is part of the planning phase, it is not only crucial in the organizing process but also sets the stage for a formal outline. (The formal stages of document organization are examined in Chapter 10.) This stage of idea development is the point at which you employ certain **prewriting strategies**: techniques for gathering and organizing ideas that involve such processes as *brainstorming, mindmapping, freewriting,* and *asking journalists' questions*. The goal of each prewriting technique is to begin putting your plan on paper.

BRAINSTORMING   **Brainstorming** is a planning technique in which you list ideas as they come to mind. Because it is difficult to be both creative and judgmental at the same time, no evaluation of ideas occurs until after the brainstorming session. Quantity is desired at this stage and a freewheeling method is encouraged—indeed, the stranger the idea, the better.[16]

Brainstorming is an unstructured writing tool that involves two distinct steps. First, the writer must create an uncensored list of words, phrases, and sentences that express topic-related points. Items are not organized (for example, listed by priority)—they are simply written down as they occur to you.

The second step is to organize the items on your list into patterns. Assume, for example, that you work for Puma, the athletic-shoe manufacturer, and have been assigned to analyze the high end of the sneaker market. After conducting research—but before writing—you decide to brainstorm. In Step 1, you come up with the following list:

- Nike Air is the market leader
- $5.5-billion tennis shoe market in United States
- what's hot today is gone tomorrow
- fickle teenage market
- Reebok Pump is now dated
- Reebok targeted 18- to 35-year-olds but younger kids bought the shoes
- unhappy customers
- Reebok's answer: the Double Pump
- customers wary of high-tech hype
- gimmicks are in
- too many offerings, too much confusion
- advantages of Puma's new Disc System sneaker
- problems of competing with Reebok and Nike
- limited advertising budget compared to Reebok and Nike
- problems with the pump

In Step 2, you group these topics into five categories:

1. *Nature of Industry*
   - gimmicks are in
   - $5.5-billion tennis shoe market in U.S.
   - what is hot today is gone tomorrow
2. *Customers*
   - fickle teenage market
   - Reebok targeted 18- to 35-year-olds but younger kids bought the shoes
3. *Competition*
   - Nike Air is the market leader
   - Reebok Pump now dated
   - problems with the pump
   - unhappy customers
   - Reebok's answer: the Double Pump
4. *Future Trends*
   - customers wary of high-tech hype
   - too many offerings, too much confusion
5. *Where Puma Stands*
   - advantages of Puma's new Disc System sneaker
   - problems of competing with Reebok and Nike
   - limited advertising budget compared to Reebok and Nike[17]

A primary benefit of brainstorming is the creativity that evolves from group sessions. In the preceding Puma example, you engaged in individual brainstorming to develop a list of ideas. This list can be submitted independently or to a group as part of a group brainstorming effort. The primary purpose of this technique is to present as many ideas as possible to solve a problem.

MINDMAPPING   A closely related prewriting technique, **mindmapping** (or **clustering**), is a visual technique for grouping information into categories. The nontraditional format of this technique allows many writers to associate ideas more easily and more freely.

Figure 3.6 is designed to apply the information gathered in our athletic-shoe market report to the following general guidelines for effective mindmapping. Like brainstorming, mindmapping is a technique for practicing the association of ideas; don't worry if your organization appears to be random.

mindmapping
or **(clustering)**
Visual technique for grouping information into categories

FIGURE 3.6   *Applying the Technique of Mindmapping*

1. Draw a circle in the center of an unlined piece of paper.
2. In the circle, write the topic of your document.
3. Draw lines from the center circle to outer circles, indicating the subdivisions of your topic.
4. Write the name of each subdivision in an outer circle.
5. Draw lines from your subdivision circles to outer "detail" circles.
6. Write details of each subdivision in each of these outer circles.

freewriting
Unstructured writing process that allows writers to express their thoughts without worrying about spelling, grammatical mistakes, or organizational problems

Recording thoughts in this way appears to be effective because our brains are less likely to operate in a linear fashion. Budget planners at Pacific Bell, for example, have used mindmapping in group sessions in which employees are asked to suspend traditional ways of thinking in order to focus on priorities.[18]

FREEWRITING   **Freewriting** is an unstructured writing process that allows you to express your thoughts without worrying about spelling, grammatical mistakes, or organizational problems. As in brainstorming and mindmapping, the primary goal of this *stream-of-consciousness* process is to begin putting your ideas on paper. The following section of our athletic-shoe market report reflects the typical result of a freewriting exercise, including the absence of complete sentences and the omission of such words as *the* and *in*:

> I want to talk about industry—and competition. Young kids who wear sneakers looking for something new. Reebok started it all with the Pump. But Pump is old hat. Also problems that turned customers off. "Several of my customers brought the pump back because soles fell off or because of flat-tire feeling in arch area," reported Gregory Hatch, asst. mgr. of Snyder's Shoe Store in D.C. "Consequently, Pump starting losing status symbol in eyes of my customers." Even though kids want something new, they've also overdosed on too much high-tech hype. Too many offerings, too much confusion.

As you can see, quotations and other research can be roughly woven into freewriting to help focus thinking. Again, note that the writer is not concerned about typographical errors or complete sentences.

ASKING JOURNALISTS' QUESTIONS   It is difficult to say where or when the six questions *Who? What? When? Where? Why?* and *How?* were first grouped together on paper. In contemporary journalism, they are referred to as **journalists' questions** because journalists use them as guidelines to focus their thinking in preparing stories. Because answering these six questions helps to analyze information from different perspectives, they can also be used to plan business documents. They can, for example, be applied as starting points for analyzing our athletic-shoe market report:

journalists' questions
Six questions (who, when, where, what, why, and how) coined by journalists for use as guidelines to structure their thinking in interviewing and preparing stories

Who?   Who buys our high-end sneakers? Who is the market leader?

What?   What is the nature of the industry today? What do customers want? What advantage does Puma's Disc System hold over the competition?

When?   When is Reebok introducing its new Double Pump?

Where?   Where is the market still growing?

Why?   Why are customers unhappy with the Reebok Pump? Why is the market so fickle? Why are customers wary of high-tech hype?

How?   How can Puma take advantage of market weakness? How can Puma compete with Nike and Reebok? How can we maximize our advertising budget?

In particular, journalists' questions can focus your writing on what *is* known and what is *not* known—both of which are critical in the planning stage.

PROGRESS CHECK

1. The chapter discusses using people's self-actualization needs to help motivate them. Suppose it's time for your annual evaluation at your job. Give examples of your own self-actualization needs that a writer could use in a memo to help motivate you.
2. Distinguish between primary and secondary research sources. Give an example of each.
3. What are the six *journalists' questions* that can help us gather and organize our ideas?

WHAT'S AHEAD

Effective planning provides the foundation for the writing process. This process—which includes organizing, composing, and designing business documents—is examined in Chapter 4. Chapter 5 explores the elements of word selection and style.

INTERVIEW

Lynn Quitman Troyka, Writing Authority

As a professor with a specialty in writing and as the author of the *Simon & Schuster Handbook for Writers*, Lynn Quitman Troyka has helped thousands of students discover the link between effective planning and effective writing. We asked Professor Troyka about the nature of the planning process and, more specifically, how individual writers can learn and practice the planning techniques that work best for them.

Question: How should writers begin to plan?

Answer: They can start by experimenting with different planning techniques. While some writers use mindmapping, freewriting, and other devices with great success, others have a hard time putting these techniques to good use. Instead, they discover what they want to say by talking with associates or friends. Or they plan as they write. In the end, there is no right way or wrong way to plan—only individual approaches to an extremely personal process.

Question: Is the nature of the process affected by what is being planned?

Answer: Different tasks require different types of planning. While I might freewrite a short business memo, I probably couldn't use this technique to plan a research report.

Question: Are there different levels of planning?

Answer: There are two kinds of planning—one relating to content, the other to presentation. Planning what you want to accomplish in terms of specific goals is the first part of the process. Superimposed on that is a plan of presentation—for example, what points you want to make first. Do you start with a compliment and then tell the reader what has to be done or vice versa? Decisions like this determine the way material is organized.

Question: Do all writers focus on the content of the message and the audience at the same time?

Answer: People learn in different ways, think in different ways, and conceptualize how they want to put thoughts on paper in different ways. While it is helpful for some people to think about the audience at the start, others have to focus on the message before the audience. If they mix the two, they may worry about what the reader will think and be unable to write. Although they ultimately revise the document with the audience in mind, they make these adjustments after they've written the message.

Question: Is incubation sometimes part of the planning process?

Answer: For many writers, incubation is absolutely necessary. When they brainstorm and nothing comes, they force themselves to think about a totally different topic or read a novel or even go to sleep. They allow their brain to rest, as it were, and to work on the problem subconsciously. The results can be amazing. Having said that, I should add that it is important to structure your incubation time by giving yourself a deadline. If an incubation period is open-ended, you run the risk of procrastinating instead of incubating.

Question: If you were to give business writers one piece of advice about planning, what would that advice be?

Answer: When a document is complete, take a few minutes and reflect on what you did during the planning stages that made it turn out well or poorly. Use your insights the next time you plan. As always with writing, be your own monitor—and judge—before anyone else sees your work.

Source: Interview with Lynn Quitman Troyka.

The following special feature, Business Writing in Action, will appear in each chapter in Part II, Writing Basics. Its purpose is to help you apply the concepts discussed in each chapter to a concrete business writing assignment. All aspects of document planning will be covered in these assignments.

BUSINESS WRITING IN ACTION

Planning a Business Memo to All Company Employees

THE ASSIGNMENT

As brand manager at IBM, you have been assigned to write a memo to all company employees. The purpose of the memo is to make every IBM employee a potential salesperson for the OS/2 personal-computer operating system—a system that competes against Windows 3.1, a Microsoft Corp. product.

THE METHOD

Step 1: DEFINE THE MISSION.
Communicate clearly.

Step 2: SET MEMO OBJECTIVES.
General Purpose: To persuade
Specific Purpose: To persuade all IBM employees to become spokespersons for the OS/2 personal-computer operating system
Core Idea: To achieve marketplace success with the OS/2 operating system, every IBM employee needs to act as a personal spokesperson for the product, spreading the word about its features and advantages to friends, family, and community members.

Step 3: ANALYZE THE AUDIENCE.
Audience Identification: All IBM employees
Identification Method: Question and answer
> **Question:** How much does the audience know about my subject?
> **Answer:** A great deal. The OS/2 operating system is critical to the success of IBM and every employee knows it. In addition, OS/2 will be advertised to the general public more than any other IBM product.
> **Question:** Are my readers likely to be interested in what I have to say?
> **Answer:** Yes. IBM is in a struggle against Microsoft's latest version of Windows. Everyone realizes that the success of OS/2 is crucial to the company.
> **Question:** What kind of response can I expect from the audience?
> **Answer:** Our goal is to encourage IBM employees to contact friends, relatives, and acquaintances to tell them about OS/2. IBM will supply every employee with brochures and a list of points to cover when talking about OS/2 to prospective customers.

Audience Motivation: To satisfy ego needs for prestige and success. To reinforce this need, incentives will be offered for the effort made by employees as spokespersons for OS/2. These incentives include honorary medals, IBM software and hardware, and cash.

Step 4: IMPLEMENT THE PLAN.
Conduct Research: Interview staff members to do the following.
1. Determine the most appropriate advertising campaign to support employee efforts.
2. Critique Microsoft's campaign for the latest version of Windows.
3. Compare the price of OS/2 to Windows.

Reevaluate the Core Idea Based on Research Findings: No change in core idea
Write Down Ideas: Use mindmapping
Select the Best Form of Written Communication: Memo to be sent through interoffice and electronic mail

To be continued in Chapters 4 and 5.

SUMMARY OF CHAPTER OBJECTIVES

1. **Identify the stages in the *writing process.***

   The writing process is made up of five distinct stages: planning, research, organization, composition and design, and revision. Planning involves setting document objectives, assessing audience needs and probable responses, and developing a course of action to accomplish objectives. Research, a planning tool, involves fact finding through the use of primary and secondary sources. Organization focuses on the way in which ideas are presented. Composition and design involve writing a rough draft in a manner that is accessible to readers. Revision focuses on proper word choice, clarity, conciseness, and the elimination of punctuation, grammatical, and spelling errors.

2. **Define the objectives of a document in terms of its *general purpose, specific purpose,* and *core idea.***

   Document objectives provide a sense of direction as information is gathered and the audience is analyzed. Objectives are defined in terms of the document's general purpose, specific purpose, and core idea. The general purpose—the overriding reason for which the document is written—may be to inform, to persuade, or to initiate action. The specific purpose briefly summarizes the reason for writing, while the core idea is a one-sentence statement of the document's thesis.

3. **Describe the different types of *audiences* for business documents.**

   Four distinct audiences may read a written document. The primary audience consists of the readers for whom the communication is intended and who will use that information in their own work. The initial audience is often the person who assigns the document, and that person is usually the first to read it. The sec-

ondary audience is made up of people who may use the document in different ways or who may be asked to comment on the ideas contained in it. Multiple audiences are composed of the different audiences who may read the document and for whom it is intended.

4. **Identify and briefly explain *alternative audience-analysis techniques.***

   Effective audience analysis involves visualizing readers by asking a series of questions about attitudes, knowledge, interest, and needs. It also includes checking correspondence files, rephrasing the specific purpose in the form of questions, focusing on details that will motivate readers, and avoiding incorrect assumptions about the audience. Finally, analyzing readers' motivations is an important step in focusing on their need.

5. **Describe the role of research in document planning.**

   Research, the first step in implementing a plan, tests the validity of the core idea and directs revision to reflect new information. Research sources can be either primary or secondary.

6. **Explain the *prewriting techniques* of brainstorming, mindmapping, freewriting, and *asking the six questions of journalists.***

   Prewriting strategies are techniques for gathering and organizing ideas before actually writing a document. Brainstorming refers to the process of listing ideas as they come to mind and then organizing them into patterns. Mindmapping is a visual technique for grouping information into categories. Freewriting involves a process of uncensored writing. Finally, by asking the six journalists' questions—*Who? What? When? Where? Why?,* and *How?*—you can analyze information from different perspectives.

REVIEW AND DISCUSSION QUESTIONS

1. Name the six stages of the writing process. *(Ch. Obj. 1)*
2. Explain the value of spending time on planning before you write. *(Ch. Obj. 1)*
3. Distinguish among a document's general purpose, specific purpose, and core idea. *(Ch. Obj. 2)*
4. Define the different types of audiences that a business writer must keep in mind. *(Ch. Obj. 3)*
5. Think of an audience that you know—for example, members of an organization to which you belong. Give examples of several questions that you could ask yourself to better focus a document addressed to that audi-

ence. What about questions you could ask yourself regarding an audience that you don't know? *(Ch. Obj. 3, 4)*

6. Draw a diagram illustrating Maslow's hierarchy of needs. Label each level of the hierarchy with a brief description of the needs involved. *(Ch. Obj. 4)*

7. Summarize alternative audience-analysis techniques that can help you focus a document more effectively on a projected audience. *(Ch. Obj. 4)*

8. Explain why research is important to writing good business documents. *(Ch. Obj. 5)*

9. Describe four prewriting strategies that can help you gather and organize ideas. *(Ch. Obj. 6)*

10. Summarize the advantages and disadvantages of written documents. *(Ch. Obj. 1, 3)*

APPLICATION EXERCISES

1. Refer to the chapter's discussion of informative writing. Now write an informative memo or letter (one to two paragraphs) that relates to a work project or situation in which you have been involved—perhaps on your present job or on a job that you've held in the past. The letter might be addressed to your boss, to a coworker, or to a customer. *(Ch. Obj. 2)*

2. Write a letter, a memo, or a report (one to two paragraphs) that is an example of writing to persuade. The subject of the document should be a work situation on your present job or on a job you've held in the past. *(Ch. Obj. 2)*

3. Write an action-oriented letter (one to two paragraphs) that asks your reader either to respond in a certain way or to take certain action. This letter may be a follow-up to your persuasive letter in EXERCISE 2. *(Ch. Obj. 2)*

4. Choose a letter, a memo, or a report written by someone else. Analyze the audience(s) for this communication. Who are the primary, initial, and secondary audiences? Does the document have multiple audiences? How successful do you feel the document is in communicating with its intended audience(s)? Explain your answer. *(Ch. Obj. 3, 4)*

5. As the director of the advertising department of a large company, you always try to give your staff enough time to plan documents before they write them. The firm's CEO, however, isn't so well informed, and one day he suggests that your staff speed up production by eliminating the planning phase of your communications. You decide to write a memo that will persuade him of the importance of planning. Write this memo, keeping your audience in mind. *(Ch. Obj. 1, 3)*

6. Ralph, an employee who reports to you, develops advertising and promotions for your firm. He seems uncomfortable working in teams or sitting through meetings, preferring to work alone. In fact, he's been known to shut himself up in his office for hours at a time—sometimes working straight through weekends—in order to perfect ideas and designs. While Ralph knows every artistic detail of the advertising campaign he's working on, he's vague about more concrete facts such as schedules and prices. For instance, you asked him one day what his current salary was and he couldn't remember.

Your boss asks you to write a memo to Ralph, praising him for his work and persuading him to undertake a new project. Write this memo, keeping your audience in mind. According to Maslow's hierarchy of needs, what sorts of needs are likely to motivate Ralph? *(Ch. Obj. 3, 4)*

7. Jason, another of your employees, enjoys working with people. He's a sociable type who tends to take over at meetings. He's also highly competitive—even on the company softball team, he plays to win. Jason likes to wear designer-label clothes and seems genuinely to enjoy it when coworkers ask his advice. *(Ch. Obj. 3, 4)*

Your boss has asked you to write a memo to Jason, complimenting his work performance and asking him to take on a time-consuming new project. Write this memo and gear it to Jason's motivational needs. *(Ch. Obj. 3, 4)*

8. Apply brainstorming and mindmapping to one of your own writing assignments. The assignment could be a document that you have to write for this class, for another class, for your job, or for a social organization. Try brainstorming, then mindmapping, to help you get started and to organize your thoughts. Do you find these prewriting techniques helpful? Explain your answer. *(Ch. Obj. 6)*

9. Now use the other prewriting techniques discussed in the chapter—freewriting and journalists' questions—to help you get started on another writing assignment. Which of the

four prewriting techniques seems most helpful? *(Ch. Obj. 6)*

10. Suppose that your boss has asked you to research and write a report giving your recommendations on whether the company should allow employees to smoke anywhere in the building and, if so, where and to what extent. Because this is a controversial topic, you know that your report will require careful research and planning.

    First, the research. Working outside of class, find three articles—from different sources—that deal with the issue of smoking in the workplace. After reading the articles, write a brief evaluation of the sources, following the evaluation guidelines given in the chapter. *(Ch. Obj. 2, 5)*

11. Having done your research, you now have a particular recommendation to make. Define your memo's objectives in terms of its general purpose, specific purpose, and core idea. *(Ch. Obj. 2)*

12. Next, analyze your audience (your boss) in order to plan your communication. You know, for example, that your boss is a nonsmoker who jogs regularly, avoids fatty foods, and subscribes to *Healthbeat* magazine. Using the nine suggestions for audience analysis in this chapter, analyze this audience. *(Ch. Obj. 3, 4)*

13. Choose one of the prewriting techniques dicussed in the chapter and use it to plan the report. Do this on paper rather than in your head. *(Ch. Obj. 6)*

14. Following the chapter suggestions on writing persuasive memos, write your report on whether smoking should be permitted in your workplace. *(Ch. Obj. 2, 3)*

15. Your boss liked your report so much that he's asked you to write a memo on the same topic to coworkers who smoke. Write this memo, keeping your audience in mind. *(Ch. Obj. 3, 4)*

*B*UILDING YOUR RESEARCH SKILLS

Your instructor will assign a topic. Working outside of class, each student should find and read three articles that relate to the topic assigned. Keep notes on what you read. Bring your notes to class and be prepared to summarize the major points of each article from your notes.

*B*UILDING YOUR TEAMWORK SKILLS

As a class, brainstorm ideas for writing a report on the topic that you researched for the assignment in Building Your Research Skills. Have a volunteer record ideas on the board as they are suggested. Be sure that everyone gets a chance to contribute.

When you have a lot of ideas written down, go on to the next step of organizing this list into patterns. Again, brainstorm as a class on the best way(s) to organize your ideas. Select a new volunteer to record your suggestions on the board.

Do you feel that having more people involved in brainstorming generates more ideas than if you had brainstormed all by yourself? Explain.

*C*OMMUNICATING IN A WORLD OF DIVERSITY

D. J. Hulet started out fifteen years ago as a salesperson for Pacific Bell in San Francisco. Although she's been promoted several times since then, D. J. is concerned that her career isn't progressing as fast as she would like.

Part of the problem may be her communication style. A male coworker, for example, says that "some people" at Bell see her as "very bright but too aggressive. In my opinion," adds the coworker, "there's no such thing as too aggressive. But you do have to learn how to approach people in a way that doesn't create enemies." D. J. thinks that her gender is the real issue. "I'm very candid, and I speak my mind," she says. "Other managers have told me, 'You know, if you did the same things you're doing and you were a guy, you'd be OK.'"

D. J. has asked you for advice on improving her communication skills. What would you tell her?

Source: Anne Fisher, "When Will Women Get to the Top?" *Fortune*, September 21, 1992, pp. 44–56.

Jefftown Video Plays to a Captive Audience

So you think you have trouble figuring out what your audience wants from you? It could be worse—you could have Joe Corpier's job. Joe is a convicted murderer. He's also the manager of a television station. Jefftown Video, to be precise: the official TV station of the Jefferson City (Missouri) Correctional Center.

As head of a station run by and for the prisoners, Joe faces some unusual challenges. For one thing, he has to gauge his audience reactions by what he calls the "noise system." Movie thrillers, for example, tend to score high on the noise system—a film called *I'm Dangerous Tonight* once silenced the entire prison for two hours. On the other hand, *Vincent and Theo*, a quiet film about the 19th-century artist Vincent Van Gogh and his brother, didn't do as well—in fact, it almost caused a riot. "Show another art film, and we'd probably get stabbed in the back," jokes a station employee who happens to be a convicted robber.

Another challenge is censorship. While violence and R ratings are OK, freedom isn't. "Escape movies aren't a good idea," notes one official at the institution. Granted, Jefftown did manage to screen Academy Award–winning *Silence of the Lambs* twice before officials realized that the villain escapes from jail after killing two guards. Corpier's review: "Won't be showing that movie anymore."

In addition to movies, Jefftown Video runs informational programs. One tape stars prison warden Michael Groose, who sternly passes on such advice as "Wet clothes cannot be hung to obstruct views into the cell." Groose has also found the station useful for combatting rumors. When he first came to Jefferson City, for example, he found that prisoners were worried about him. "They'd heard I was a Texas import," he recalls, explaining that some inmates assumed that he had been brought to Missouri to introduce some harsh new Texas-style rules. "I went on air to explain I was Missouri born and bred, and that defused it."

As more facilities across the country install satellite dishes and cable channels, TV has become so popular behind bars that it's threatening to turn hardened prisoners into couch potatoes. When given a choice between two privileges—receiving packages from home or having individual TV sets installed in their cells—inmates at half of New York state's prisons opted for the TVs. The vote was fine with prison officials because "care packages" from home had long been a major source of drugs and other contraband.

Finally, in-house TV may even give prisoners a chance to serve their country in unexpected ways. One popular show is *America's Most Wanted*, which presents unsolved real-life crimes and asks viewers for their help. Two of these mysteries have been solved by inmates who recognized the criminals. In one case, prisoners in Florida recognized a man wanted for bank robbery in Oklahoma as one Mark Austin Goodman—a fellow inmate doing time under another name. "During the segment about himself," reports a spokesperson for the program, "Goodman kept trying to change the channel, but the other inmates wouldn't let him."

Questions and Applications

1. Describe the challenges that Jefftown Video faces in addressing the needs and interests of its audience.
2. Describe the ways in which Jefftown meets these challenges.
3. While prisoners like having TV, people outside the prisons aren't so sure. "There are a lot of folks who feel it isn't much punishment to be locked up in a cell with 15 channels," says one city mayor. The Florida attorney general is trying to get satellite dishes and cable hookups removed from all prisons. "If satellite dishes are allowed today, what will be allowed in our correctional centers tomorrow? High-definition televisions? Cellular telephones?"
Do you feel that it's ethical for prisons to install multiple cable channels when many law-abiding citizens can't even afford cable? Or do you think that the advantages of TV in prison outweigh the disadvantages? Write a persuasive letter to the governor of your state in which you express your point of view.

Source: Kevin Helliker, "On TV Today: Tips from Our Warden and the Lunch Menu," *The Wall Street Journal*, July 9, 1992, pp. A1, A4. © 1992 Dow Jones & Company, Inc. Reprinted by permission. All rights reserved.

Technically Speaking at Microsoft

Traditionally, corporate America has motivated its employees by rewarding them with higher salaries and step-by-step promotions. Eventually, the ladder led to management positions in which the lucky promotees got to supervise and dictate to underlings who were doing the same jobs in which they'd started years before.

Many companies have discovered, however, that this traditional career path doesn't work for employees in technical jobs—engineers, computer programmers, and software and hardware designers, for instance. Although "techies" are certainly considered valuable members of their respective corporate teams, corporations don't always know how to motivate them—or even what to do with them.

For one thing, technical staffers do not seem to be motivated by the traditional workplace perks. When *Fortune* magazine interviewed three dozen engineers and programmers, reporters found that not one of them mentioned career advancement as an important goal. Many of them admitted that they didn't "really have a career plan."

What did motivate them, however, was technical challenge. They enjoyed wrestling with problems until they solved them, and the reward they valued most was the satisfaction of solving a puzzle and doing it well. One engineer described the feeling as "the existential pleasures of engineering." Nevertheless, few American companies offer high-ranking technical positions. To make more money, therefore, most engineers end up leaving the technical work they love—and in which they are quite productive—to become managers.

One company that does a good job of motivating technical staff is Microsoft, the world's largest maker of software for personal computers. Started two decades ago by a hotshot young programmer named Bill Gates, Microsoft nurtures its "techies" by offering parallel career tracks: Although programmers can become managers if they wish, they also have the option of becoming "technical leads"—project directors who don't have to supervise teammates or evaluate their progress. Neil Konzen, a 30-year-old software developer at Microsoft, tried the management career path and hated it: "I was doing a lot of managing, and it got to be a bummer after a while. I was getting away from the programming, the hands-on stuff that I like. So I moved back to the technical side." Thanks to the company's generous stock-option plan, techies like Konzen needn't suffer financially when they choose the lab over the boardroom.

In addition to a technical career path, Microsoft offers other motivators—for example, flexible schedules and an informal dress code. Programmers come to work at all hours, often wearing T-shirts, jeans, and sneakers. Konzen keeps two electric guitars in his office. In his spare time, he races Porsches and once showed co-workers how to make rocket fuel in an office kitchen. David Weise, one of Konzen's colleagues, keeps a cardboard skeleton in his office that he made from a kit. A typical work outfit for Weise includes a T-shirt lettered with the mathematical symbols for Maxwell's four laws of electromagnetics.

Another motivator for techies is the chance to interact. A few years ago, the petroleum giant Arco assembled a small team of engineers to develop a clean-burning gasoline that would be economical to produce. The group's best ideas surfaced during lively brainstorming sessions, as team members argued hotly in weekly meetings and spontaneous hallway conferences. "They got amazingly combative with each other at times," recalls Dan Townsend, the chemical engineer who headed the group. "It definitely wasn't a tea-and-cookies atmosphere." Between arguments, however, the team analyzed numerous gasoline blends and wrote a computer program that calculated the cost of producing them. In just two years, it had developed three low-emission fuels—two of which Arco already has on the market.

No matter how technical the job, however, good communication skills are always in demand. Chemist Helen Connon, who oversees the refrigerants lab at DuPont, feels that she owes her success at least partly to her ability to communicate. One day, she recalls, "One of the lab directors called me into his office and said, 'You're the new boss.' I guess they thought I had good people skills."

Questions and Applications

1. What factors motivate many employees with good technical skills? How do these motivators compare to the traditional motivators offered by many corporations?
2. Suppose that you've just been hired to supervise a team of programmers at Microsoft. Among other tasks, your job will involve writing memos, letters, and reports to your staff. Analyze and describe your audience.

3. Another manager at Microsoft comes to you, complaining about the problems he's having in supervising his team of programmers. "They don't do what I want them to do," he laments. "I really try to keep everyone informed. We hold regular weekly meetings in which I present the goals for the week, month, and year. I tell them all about the latest sales figures and the company's earnings. Last week I even gave them a report on how our stock is doing, but they just looked bored. I've asked them for regular weekly progress reports, but no one does them. Even though I keep my office door open all day, no one comes in to talk to me. I know I'm a good manager. On my last job, I supervised a team of thirty accountants, and we got along great. I just can't communicate with these guys."

You decide to write this manager a tactful memo to persuade him that programmer teams might need to be managed differently from other employees. Write a memo in which you explain effective ways to manage employees like those on this man's team.

4

Organizing, Composing, and Designing Business Documents

CHAPTER OBJECTIVES

After studying this chapter, you should be able to:

1 Describe the different *outline forms* used in organizing business documents.

2 Identify the three parts of a *business document* and describe their functions in communication.

3 List the alternative *patterns* for organizing material in the middle of a document.

4 Describe the four forms of *evidence* used in business documents.

5 Explain the elements of document *design* and their functions in a document.

*R*eading maketh a full man; conference a ready man; and writing
 an exact man.

Francis Bacon
English philosopher and Lord Chancellor

A LETTER FROM FORBES

While most business correspondence can benefit from attention to organization, composition, and design, some documents need more help than others. A recent case in point involves a letter written by *Forbes* executive Timothy Forbes regarding *Audacity*, a business-history magazine being launched by the Forbes family publishing empire.

Forbes was looking for articles to include in the new magazine. He had drafted a form letter and mailed individually typed versions to 100 well-known business journalists. However, though he had printed the letters on his raised letterhead and personally signed each letter, the recipients realized immediately that their letter was simply one piece in a large mailing.

Forbes felt that his mailing had been appropriate. After all, he perceived each letter as a "collegial and cordial invitation" for story ideas and finished manuscripts. In fact, he had requested that writers bring to *Audacity* ideas they had not been able to incorporate into regular assignments.

One immediate problem with Forbes' approach is that many publishers prohibit their employees from working for competitors. *Business Week* doesn't want *Business Week* writers developing stories for *Fortune*, and *Forbes* doesn't want its writers authoring stories for *The Wall Street Journal*.

Then there was the matter of the typical writer who had received a copy of Forbes' letter, was at the top of his or her profession, and tended to react negatively to being on the receiving end of a mass mailing. One recipient was Michael Schrage, a syndicated columnist for the *Los Angeles Times*. His response to the letter was to throw it away. "I recall getting [the letter]—and throwing it out," says Schrage. "I thought it was kind of bizarre. I thought it was another public relations solicitation."[1]

Like many writers, Timothy Forbes had encountered problems in composing his letter in a way that would communicate his message and meet the needs of his audience. Actually, he had gotten bogged down in the tactical aspects of planning. As we saw in Chapter 3, while strategic planning is about determining the major long-term objectives of an assignment, a department, or even an entire organization, tactical planning is about implementing short-term activities and allocating resources needed to achieve specific objectives. While strategic planning, then, is about vision, tactical planning concentrates on carrying out that vision.

Forbes' letter might have succeeded had he been able to convince his audience, through solid evidence, that his request was legitimate. For example, he might have reduced concerns about submitting an article to a competing publication by providing such evidence as a proposed table of contents for the magazine's first issue. This information would have supported the fact that *Audacity* was in fact conceived as a *noncompeting* business publication. This occasion also required a personal letter from one writer to one recipient. As we shall see in this chapter, both evidence and form are elements of tactical planning, as are organization and design.

CHAPTER OVERVIEW

This chapter focuses on the nuts and bolts of document writing—that is, the methods for implementing an idea in the form of a first-draft written document. We will begin by stressing the importance of organizing a document and using an outline to achieve the best results. We will also examine the composition process, including guidelines for opening and closing a document and strategies for choosing an organizational pattern and "building" the middle of a document through evidence. Finally, we will examine design—a critical factor that can mean the difference between a document that is read and one that is put aside.

ORGANIZING A DOCUMENT

To communicate, put your thoughts in order; give them a purpose; use them to persuade, to instruct, to discover....

William Safire
Newspaper columnist and former presidential speechwriter

In their classic handbook *The Elements of Style*, William Strunk, Jr., and E. B. White explain why effective organization is the underpinning of all written messages, including business documents:

> Writing, to be effective, must follow closely the thoughts of the writer, but not necessarily in the order in which those thoughts occur. This calls for a scheme.... The first principle of composition, therefore, is to foresee or determine the shape of what is to come and pursue that shape.[2]

In document writing, **organization** refers to the process of arranging information and connecting different ideas to produce a unified, coherent message. In this section, we will focus on the crucial link between organization and effective communication.

organization
Process of arranging information and connecting different ideas to produce a unified, coherent message

The Link between Organization and Communication

Because of the nature of your audience and the environment in which you are communicating, your business documents require clear organization. Readers must be able to see at a glance both *what* you are trying to accomplish and *how* it can be done. Moreover, with information overload a fact of business life today, every document must get to its point as quickly as possible while stating its purpose as clearly as possible. These goals can be met most efficiently by working according to an organizational plan.

A clearly organized document accomplishes the following objectives:

- It makes its purpose clear and helps the reader respond appropriately.
- It provides all needed information but no more.
- As in conversation, it introduces, discusses, and closes the topic.
- It guides the reader through the arrangement of ideas and logical connections to a precise conclusion.
- It can help to eliminate any misunderstanding that may result from its message.
- It reduces the risk that it will not be read. When reading requires too much work, people are likely to put a document aside.

Good organization, therefore, helps the writer as much as the reader. For one thing, having a clear picture—before you begin to write—of what you need to say and how to say it helps to eliminate the fear of facing a blank page. Like a carpenter, a writer is engaged in the craft of building a structure whose plans are already set. As a writer, your task is to find the right words and tone, not to formulate basic ideas or logical connections. Those tasks should have been accomplished in the planning and organization stages.

To appreciate the connection between effective organization and effective communication, read carefully the letter in Figure 4.1.

The recipient of this letter is likely to be confused about just what the writer is trying to accomplish. For example, although Mr. Dwyer requests a catalog, it is not clear whether he is *also* asking for replacement bicycle seats. Because the letter does not specifically request replacements, Ms. O'Neill cannot be sure. In addition, many of the details in the first two paragraphs are irrelevant. In order to respond to Mr. Dwyer's request, Ms. O'Neill does not really need to know about the background of Alabama Sports Resort, the success of its exercise facility, or its ongoing research into exercise bicycles. As a result, this letter is likely to raise more questions than answers about the letter's purpose. Because of such difficulties, a busy recipient may simply put aside a letter like this one. Now compare this letter with the revised version in Figure 4.2.

This version gets to the point quickly and eliminates irrelevant details. It also states clearly and precisely the action that the writer wants Summit Sports Equipment to take. In this revision of his original draft, the manager decides not to ask for a catalog because it diverts attention from his main request. He does

ALABAMA SPORTS RESORT

1250 Outlaw Road   Mobile, Alabama 39600

205-555-8672

August 27, 199X

Ms. Jenny O'Neill
Summit Sports Equipment
1374 Figaro
Dallas, TX 74911

Dear Ms. O'Neill:

Last year Alabama Sports Resort decided to build a state of the art exercise facility for guests. After completing most of the work, we contacted your firm because of your reputation for manufacturing the best exercise bicycles on the market, and we decided to buy ten bicycles for the facility. Needless to say, your equipment has been a great success. Many guests have told us that your bicycles gave them a wonderful workout.

It is interesting that they feel this way because we have continued to do market research on exercise bicycles and still feel that our original purchase decision was the right one.

There is one small problem, however. The bicycle seats are not comfortable. Many guests have complained that after ten minutes they have to stop riding.

With regular exercise a way of life to millions of Americans, your equipment has helped turn our facility into a huge success. Please send me your current catalog so that I can see your latest offerings.

Sincerely,

Robert Dwyer

Robert Dwyer
Manager

FIGURE 4.1   *Sample: A Poorly Organized Letter*

ALABAMA SPORTS RESORT

1250 Outlaw Road   Mobile, Alabama 39600

205-555-8672

August 27, 199X

Ms. Jenny O'Neill
Summit Sports Equipment
1374 Figaro
Dallas, TX 74911

Dear Ms. O'Neill:

On May 21, ten of your exercise bicycles arrived at Alabama
Sports Resort. The bicycles have functioned perfectly for three
months, and many guests have told us how much they enjoy the
workout.

However, many have also told us that the bicycle seats are
uncomfortable and that they have trouble sitting on them for
periods longer than ten minutes. To eliminate this problem, I
would like replacement seats for the ten bikes. If you need further information, please contact me.

Your equipment continues to be the finest on the market. I am
sure that once this minor problem is resolved our guests will
agree that your reputation for manufacturing exercise bicycles
of the highest quality is well deserved.

Sincerely,

Robert Dwyer

Robert Dwyer
Manager

FIGURE 4.2   *Sample: A Well-Organized Letter*

not want to give the impression that a catalog request and a request for actual service are comparable.

Using an Outline to Organize Ideas

Recall from Chapter 3 our discussion of brainstorming, mindmapping, freewriting, and other prewriting exercises. The purpose of such exercises is both to stimulate the free flow of ideas and to group ideas into preliminary categories. These exercises also form the basis for a cohesive outline, which can be the key to successful organization.

An outline acts as a "road map," guiding the writer from the introduction of a document through its conclusion. In particular, an outline helps to produce a logical pattern of connections among ideas *before* the document is actually written. In addition, because whole sections of an outline can be easily shifted, ideas can be rearranged to determine the most effective presentation. Finally, the outline reduces even the most complex material into digestible chunks. Deciding whether to use a *formal* or *informal outline* depends on both the needs and preferences of the writer and the requirements of the document.

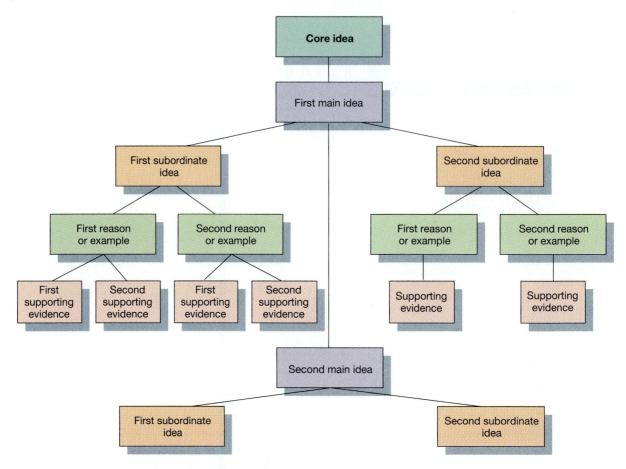

FIGURE 4.3   *Structure for a Formal Outline*

formal outline
Organizational device that shows the precise relationship among ideas by following prescribed rules concerning content and format

FORMAL OUTLINES   A **formal outline** follows prescribed rules concerning content and format in order to show the precise relationship among ideas. The form shown in Figure 4.3 is normally used in formal outlines. Notice that the core idea is placed at the top of the outline to guide the document's organization. Although this example illustrates the outline structure for a single main idea, more complex documents are likely to involve two or more main ideas. In that case, the structure shown in Figure 4.3 would be repeated for each main idea to be developed in the document. Once the outline is completed, the writer can easily revise it by shifting the order of main or subordinate ideas.

informal outline
More loosely connected organizational device that need not follow the strict structural rules of a formal outline

INFORMAL OUTLINES   An **informal outline** is a more loosely connected organizational device that need not follow the strict structural rules of a formal outline. Nevertheless, it lists main and subordinate ideas as well as supporting evidence. An example of an informal outline is shown in Table 4.1.

Despite their value, most businesspeople resist using informal outlines and rarely use formal outlines. Recognizing this resistance, communication consultant Sana Reynolds avoids the term *outline* in her workshops and encourages a more informal style of organizing. Instead of laboring with Roman numerals and indentations, she suggests inserting a word or phrase in the margin and then assigning a numerical value to each notation. This system both connects ideas and identifies them by priority. This informal plan is an effective way to organize short documents, including memos and letters.[3]

For longer documents, either formal or informal outlines can be equally effective. Although your outline should provide you with a *guideline*, you should plan to adjust it as your work proceeds. Remember that revision is inevitable during the drafting process.

TABLE 4.1	*Informal Outline for New Business Proposal*
OUTLINE	**SUPPORTING EVIDENCE**
Core Idea	Our inspection of the plants, trees, and grass surrounding your office complex shows the need for a comprehensive treatment program.
Results of Our April 4 Inspection	A. Pervasive crab grass B. Maple trees with leaf spot and powdery mildew diseases C. Poison ivy around tree trunks and stone walls

Recommendations	D. Annual program consisting of four components
	  1. Application of lime on lawn to correct soil PH balance
	  2. Application of insecticide to destroy insect eggs
	  3. Removal of poison ivy
	  4. Application of fertilizer to encourage root and foliage growth

Cost	$250 per treatment Ten percent discount available if cost of annual service is paid in advance

Outlines and Document Design

As ideas are organized into an outline, the writer should begin to think in terms of *document design*. Business writing consultant Edward P. Bailey, Jr., suggests using a model that contains *headings*, a critical design element.[4] Bailey then suggests organizing information into blocks of related material—main points and then specific details—of one or more paragraphs each. Because they help direct the reader's eye to units of information, headings can become part of the actual document.

The decision made during the early 1990s by top management of United Parcel Service (UPS) to move its corporate headquarters from Greenwich, Connecticut, to Atlanta provides a good illustration of how Bailey's model works. Table 4.2 shows how a memo to inform management of the measures necessary to relocate up to 900 UPS employees can be developed from blocks of materials related to both a core idea and major headings. In this example, the writer has first decided to phrase major headings in question form and then to answer each question with several sentences that provide related information.

COMPOSING A DOCUMENT

Like a newspaper article or an essay, a business document contains a beginning, a middle, and an end. Depending on the length and purpose of the document, these sections may be as short as a single sentence or as long as several pages. The process of composing a document consists of three distinct stages:

1. Creating the *opening, middle,* and *conclusion* of the document.
2. Deciding on a logical *pattern* in which to present the information.
3. Integrating *evidence* to support the core idea of the document.

Words fly, writings remain.
Latin proverb

Composing the Opening of a Document

Because letters, memos, and reports must capture and hold attention from the first word, the opening is as important as the message itself. Indeed, most people read business correspondence in much the same way they read a newspaper.

If you don't get the reader's attention in the first paragraph, the rest of your message is lost.
Public relations maxim

TABLE 4.2	*Document Model: Relocation of UPS Corporate Headquarters*
ELEMENT OF WRITING MODEL	**BLOCK OF RELATED MATERIAL**
Opening Statement or Core Idea	To inform management of the measures necessary to relocate up to 900 UPS employees from Greenwich to Atlanta.
Heading	**Who is affected by the move?**
Main point first, then details	All 900 employees working at our Greenwich headquarters are being offered positions in Atlanta. According to PHH Fantus, our relocation consultant, eight out of ten managers will probably make the move as well as 15 percent of the support staff. However, these are conservative estimates; actual percentages may be higher.
Heading	**How will UPS help employees sell their Connecticut homes?**
Main point first, then details	UPS is offering employees an arrangement in which they lose none of the money they invested in their primary residence. The company will cover any loss incurred in selling a home, including the cost of improvements. A loss is likely in many cases, since many employees moved into Fairfield County, Connecticut, during the mid-1980s at the height of a strong real estate market.
Heading	**How will UPS help employees relocate to Atlanta?**
Main point first, then details	UPS has hired a relocation consulting company to help employees evaluate real-estate opportunities in Atlanta. The company, which has opened offices in both Greenwich and Atlanta dedicated solely to UPS staff, is arranging two-day tours of Atlanta for employees and their spouses. In addition, individual counseling services will be available at both locations.

Source: The UPS relocation of corporate headquarters is described in George Judson, "Moving from Greenwich to Georgia with the Employees' Needs in Mind," *The New York Times*, December 15, 1991, p. 44.

They glance at the first paragraph and skim the rest. If the document doesn't grab their attention, they go on to something else.

The document writer's task, therefore, is much like that of the creator of a television commercial who realizes that the ad must attract and hold the viewer's attention within the first five seconds. After five seconds, the number of viewers always declines; it never goes up.

Except when you must convey bad news by letter, the first paragraph of your business documents should state your main point in a clear, succinct way. Readers want to know at the start what a document is about and why they should continue reading. If they fail to find that information in the opening paragraph, they may jump to the end or disregard the document entirely. As one communication specialist points out, "We simply don't put up with writing that asks us to slog through fact, fact, fact, logic, logic, logic to reach that 'perfect' bottom line. If the writer doesn't start with the bottom line, we—as readers—do. We make the bottom line the top line by skipping ahead. We take charge of the organization because the writer didn't."[5]

In both short and long documents, however, many writers tend to bury the main point, forcing the reader to work in order to locate it. For example, if a consultant prepares you a report analyzing the efficiency of your salesforce, you do not want to be required to read an analysis of his or her methods before learning

People don't read today; they flip.

John Lyons
Advertising writer

about the findings. You want to know immediately what the report has to say. Similarly, when too many words are used to make a point, the busy reader will lose patience. Finally, if you do not begin by focusing on the needs of your audience, you run the risk of reader inattention from the outset of your document. The following example of an opening paragraph is guaranteed to generate reader interest in a single sentence:

> Our company is considering leasing 15 luxury automobiles for use in Florida, Georgia, and Alabama and would like to discuss financial terms for 15 open-end, 24-month leases on Cadillacs.

This opening paragraph is effective because it goes immediately to the bottom line and avoids long, unduly complex sentences. If your message is important and does not require a buffer, you should be prepared to reveal your main point in the opening paragraph of your document.

PROGRESS CHECK

1. Describe *organization* as it applies to business writing.
2. This chapter argues that the opening of a document is just as important as the message itself. Why do you think this is true?

Organizing the Middle of a Document

The middle of a business document contains its major points and supporting evidence. As we will see later in the chapter, *evidence* may take the form of facts, statistics, examples, or expert opinion. Supporting evidence, however, must also be organized into carefully designed *patterns* that support specific premises. One of the first steps in organizing the middle of your document is to select the most appropriate method for developing your material.

Depending on both the nature of your material and the needs of your audience, you can choose from a variety of organizational patterns. Bear in mind, however, that your core idea will usually dictate your organizational pattern. For example, if your purpose is to explain a series of events or a step-by-step process, a chronological pattern of development might be required. If your purpose is to examine certain events, their causes, and their outcomes, you will probably choose a cause-and-effect pattern of development.[6]

We will begin by describing two pairs of general categories into which organizational patterns may fall: *deductive* and *inductive patterns* and *direct* and *indirect patterns*. We will then analyze each of the four most common patterns of document development: *problem/solution, cause and effect, climactic order*, and *chronological*.

DEDUCTIVE VERSUS INDUCTIVE PATTERNS   Most effective business documents move from a *general* idea to a series of *specific* ideas, thereby providing the most important information first and then supporting it with details. This **deductive organizational pattern** is the most common approach used in contemporary business writing. The deductive approach requires that information be presented in the following manner:

deductive organizational pattern
Writing approach in which discussion moves from a *general* idea to a series of *specific* ideas

- Answers before explanations
- Requests before reasons
- Summaries before details
- Conclusions before discussions
- General statements before specifics[7]

Using the deductive approach, for example, you might propose that a new women's specialty clothing store would be a financial success in the world's largest retail mall—Mall of America in Bloomington, Minnesota. You would then proceed to list the reasons supporting your argument. These are likely to include the tremendous publicity following the mall's opening; the tens of thousands of shoppers attracted to the mall on a daily basis; and the presence of numerous major department stores that attract shoppers who, once in the mall, are also expected to shop at smaller retail outlets, including the one you are proposing.

inductive organizational pattern
Writing approach in which discussion begins with a *specific* idea and moves step by step to a *general* topic

By contrast, when a discussion begins with a specific idea and moves step by step to a general topic, it follows an **inductive organizational pattern**. This approach assumes that a general or broadly meaningful pattern can be described on the basis of specific facts or observations. For example, you might argue *against* the idea of opening the proposed outlet in Mall of America by pointing out specific observations, such as the potential competition posed by five other recently opened stores, comparatively high lease terms, and the need to make substantial personnel, inventory, and promotional outlays to be competitive. Using an inductive pattern, you could thus argue that these facts suggest a general pattern that lessens the likelihood of success for a new store in this location.

Define the problem before you pursue a solution.

John Williams
CEO, Spence Corp.

Remember, however, that an inductive pattern is based on a *sampling* of the facts rather than on every possible detail mentioned. If you do not consider a sufficient number of facts, your conclusion may be flawed. Perhaps the five recently opened stores offer goods that may be priced too high for your likely customer base; perhaps a specialty store might appeal to the changing demographics of the Twin Cities area. Inductive conclusions must be analyzed carefully in relation to both the quantity and quality of supporting evidence.

DIRECT VERSUS INDIRECT PATTERNS   Selecting an organizational pattern also depends on whether a *direct* or *indirect approach* is more appropriate for your message. Like the deductive pattern, the **direct organizational pattern** organizes material so that the main point is presented at the beginning of the message. Documents using direct patterns make the message as clear and straightforward as possible. A direct pattern is effective in direct requests, informative messages, positive correspondence, and persuasive messages.

direct organizational pattern
Writing approach that presents the main point in the beginning part of the message

indirect organizational pattern
Writing approach that presents the main point in the latter part of the message

By contrast, an **indirect organizational pattern**, much like the inductive organizational pattern, prefers to hold back the main point until later in the message: The writer's purpose may be to prepare the reader to accept information favorably or to use supporting information as the best means of persuading the reader. The indirect pattern is often used to convey bad news or when persuasion is an important goal of the message.

Part III of this text, ORGANIZATIONAL LETTERS AND MEMOS, examines specific circumstances calling for the choice of direct or indirect approaches in correspondence. You will see, for example, why some persuasive messages use the direct approach and others do not and how your decision to use one or the other is often a matter of your relationship with your reader.

problem/solution pattern
Writing approach that focuses first on a particular problem and then on possible solutions

PROBLEM/SOLUTION PATTERN   In the **problem/solution pattern** of development, the discussion opens with a particular problem or problems and works toward a solution. The opening statement identifies the problem and the following statements introduce the main idea of the solution by limiting or clarifying the opening statement. This approach is most useful, of course, when you want to persuade someone that you can remedy a difficult situation. You can use a series of steps to illustrate the specific details of your solution. Consider the presentation of problem and solution in the memo in Figure 4.4.

cause-and-effect pattern
Writing approach that focuses on events or consequences and the reasons for them

CAUSE-AND-EFFECT PATTERN   Some issues lend themselves naturally to a development pattern that focuses on events or consequences and the reasons for them. The **cause-and-effect pattern** is typically used, for example, to explain a problem and how it has affected an organization; it can also be used to identify events and activities that resulted in opportunities or advantages. For example, if the purpose of a message is to inform a customer that an important delivery deadline will not be met, the message might read: "A wildcat strike at our Chicago plant resulted in a two-week shutdown of the entire plant. As a result, we cannot meet our promised shipment date."

Cause-and-effect analysis must show clear relationships (typically a chronological order of events) and repetitious patterns (every time *A* occurred, *B* also occurred). In addition, if you select the cause-and-effect development pattern for your document, you must take definite steps to avoid oversimplification. Loss of credibility is likely if the reader can detect immediately that several factors in addition to the one(s) mentioned in your document could have caused the problem or event on which you have chosen to focus.

CLIMACTIC-ORDER PATTERN   As a rule, when you are dealing with controversial issues, the material with which the reader is most likely to agree should be presented first. A pattern based on **climactic order** helps enlist the reader's support for the rest of the document even if what you say next is even more controversial. "If the reader agrees with the first argument," say communication consultants Marya W. Holcombe and Judith K. Stein, "you will have established credibility, increasing the likelihood that the rest of your assertions will be viewed positively."[8]

climactic-order pattern
Writing approach that presents the material with which the reader is most likely to agree first

**ONE
AMERICA
BANK**

MEMORANDUM

TO: Merger Reorganization Committee Members
FROM: Joe Locklear, Committee Chair
DATE: November 27, 199X
SUBJECT: Retail branch duplication

Because of the recent merger between BankAmerica Corp. and Security Pacific Bank, considerable duplication in retail branch systems exists. In an attempt to reduce the remaining number of branches to a manageable and appropriate number, I suggest taking the following measures:

• Analyze each neighborhood for duplication of services.

• Close branches where appropriate.

• Transfer the strongest personnel to the remaining branches.

• Launch an extensive advertising and public relations campaign focusing on improved service at remaining branches.

Please let me know if you have any additional suggestions or considerations on this subject.

FIGURE 4.4   *Problem/Solution Memo*

CHRONOLOGICAL PATTERN   Sometimes it is important to describe a series of events chronologically, either in the order in which they occurred or in reverse sequence. **Chronological patterns** are especially useful in setting out the sequence for a new project or setting the agenda for a conference or meeting. A chronological pattern may also be effective in a message designed to detail a series of steps in a sequence or process. For example, a letter to a new customer might indicate the steps involved in placing orders, requesting service calls, or clarifying billing questions.

chronological pattern
Writing approach used to describe a series of events chronologically, either in the order in which they occurred or in reverse sequence

INTEGRATING EVIDENCE IN THE MIDDLE OF A DOCUMENT

evidence
Details that communicate information and support the core idea of a document

Documents must offer **evidence**: details that communicate information and support the core idea of the document. In order to persuade readers that a particular position is sound, supporting evidence must meet certain criteria. Evidence that meets the following standards is considered not only effective in its ability to persuade but also ethical in its application:

1. Evidence should be sufficient and representative. Your goal is to persuade readers that your point of view applies to an overview of the actual situation, not to an isolated case.
2. Evidence should be relevant to the core idea of your document. It should be used to support or illustrate a point made in the document and should be directly related to your subject matter.
3. Evidence should be accurate. Not only should your sources be reliable, but you must correctly interpret the evidence that you draw from those sources. Misrepresentations and distortions will produce a document that is inherently flawed.[9]

In written communication, evidence generally takes one or more of four forms: *facts, statistics, examples*, and *expert opinion*.

Using Factual Evidence

In the context of business communication, the role of facts is to accomplish one or more of the following:

■ To clarify why a situation exists in its present form
■ To specify what is being done to change or remedy a situation
■ To explain why a decision has been made

When you have mastered the numbers, you will in fact no longer be reading numbers, any more than you read words when reading books. You will be reading meanings.

Harold Geneen
Former Chairman of the Board, ITT Corp.

In the early 1990s, top management at AT&T decided that something had to be done about the growing number of complaints received from credit-card applicants. These prospective long-distance telephone customers of the communications giant reported increasing irritation at the number of errors contained in their credit reports. Internal AT&T memos urging the decision to take action undoubtedly included such *factual* evidence as the number of complaints received, the extent to which such complaints had changed over time, and the nature of these complaints, with particular emphasis on reports of errors in credit reporting. Armed with these facts, AT&T's top management formally requested that the nation's major credit-reporting agencies simplify their procedures when soliciting AT&T credit-card applicants and decided to establish toll-free telephone numbers for applicants to use in resolving problems. The facts that were assembled in response to the original memos were convincing, and both of AT&T's requests were quickly implemented.[10]

Facts can also focus on how something is done. Instructions fall into this category. For example, when a letter is sent to a customer outlining steps for

General business publications like *Fortune* have long been a source of secondary research information—that is, information collected for various business-related purposes and adaptable to the specific needs of researchers. Not surprisingly, services like *Fortune Business Reports* constitute a natural extension of the company's offerings.

Source: *Fortune Business Reports.*

repairing defective merchandise, it contains a factual explanation. To be effective, facts must accomplish the following goals: (1) They must clarify the main point; (2) they must define all new terms and concepts; and (3) they must present evidence supporting the main point.

As usual, the best explanations are brief and geared to the needs of the audience. They should supply just the amount of detail needed by readers and no more. For example, in the AT&T memos referred to above, there was little need to explain in detail the operation of the 800-numbers to be established by credit bureaus, the number of employees who would be assigned to answer the calls, and the projected complaint-response times. However, these issues were appropriately included in correspondence between AT&T and major credit-reporting agencies.

Factual explanations are also strengthened by specific, concrete language. Instead of responding to a customer complaint with a form letter, for example, it is much more effective to use a direct, factual explanation of the steps being taken to solve the problem. If possible, it is also wise to indicate when the problem will be resolved.

Using Statistical Evidence

statistics
Mathematical expressions that describe findings in an objective, uniform way and provide standards for determining whether those findings are valid measurements or chance occurrences.

Numerical evidence is presented as **statistics**—mathematical expressions that describe findings in an objective, uniform way and provide standards for determining whether those findings are valid measurements or chance occurrences. Among the statistical concepts commonly referred to in business writing are the following:

- *Mode, median* and *mean* measure the central tendency for a group of numbers. For example, a document might state that the mean, or average, starting salary for computer programmers is $24,000. The median, or midpoint, is the middle number in an array of numbers from the smallest to the largest. The mode is the most frequently appearing number in an array of numbers.

- *Correlation* refers to the statistical relationships between different variables. For example, a company recruiter might report, "We have found a high correlation between grade-point average and on-the-job success. As a result, we try to hire people with at least a *B* average in their major."

- *Sampling* is a method used for surveys of relatively small numbers of people and applying your finding to a larger population. For example, a marketing memo might state, "Based on our findings from a sample of 400 consumers in Des Moines, Milwaukee, and Cleveland, we believe that a market exists for a new line of low-fat, reduced-calorie ice cream."

Because the focus of business communication is the clear presentation of information, we will emphasize a few practical guidelines for using statistics as evidence in persuasive messages.

PROVIDE A CONTEXT FOR NUMBERS   Numbers often mean very little when presented out of context. However, they take on great meaning when compared to other numbers and related facts. For example, instead of simply pointing to a 17-percent companywide gain in sales, place that figure in context—say, of industrywide sales. What would it mean if industrywide sales had increased only 12 percent? Comparisons paint pictures for your reader, and your message will persuade when you emphasize the difference in these two numbers.

ROUND OFF NUMBERS   Numbers also have more impact when they are placed in formats that people can remember. For example, a marketing report issued by a company thinking of expanding operations into San Antonio might cite population figures as "approximately 1.3 million" rather than the exact number (1,346,370). Similarly, fractions such as 41.867 are better remembered as "almost 42 percent" or "about two out of five."

INCLUDE SOURCES   Statistics are credible when attributed to specific sources. Attribution gives your readers confidence in the accuracy of your numbers. However, because statistical studies are constantly revised to provide up-to-date information, it is important to remember that the most current sources lend the most credibility to your document. Finally, by listing sources, you assist interested readers who are seeking more information on a given topic.

Torture the data long enough and they will confess to anything.

Anonymous

LIMIT THE USE OF STATISTICS   Readers have a tendency to skip words—and even entire sections of a document—when too many numbers are presented at once. Numbers, therefore, make their greatest impact when used selectively—that is, when used to focus on a specific point. Because visual aids present statistical information effectively, one way to exercise selectivity is to emphasize statistics through charts and graphs.

Using Examples

Examples—descriptive stories and specific cases—make information both real and memorable. Even when you are writing to someone with a keen interest in your subject, examples can bring your point home more effectively than even a well-reasoned argument. Using an example, of course, is an inductive strategy. One story is by definition a small sample, and your story will be meaningful only if it is supported by the general reliability of your evidence.

Examples may be as short as a phrase or several paragraphs long. The following guidelines can help you improve your effectiveness when using examples:

1. Examples should reinforce your point, not come before it. Examples play *supporting* roles. Even if your story is extremely interesting, busy executives want to know the point of your message first.

examples
Descriptive stories and specific cases that make information real and memorable

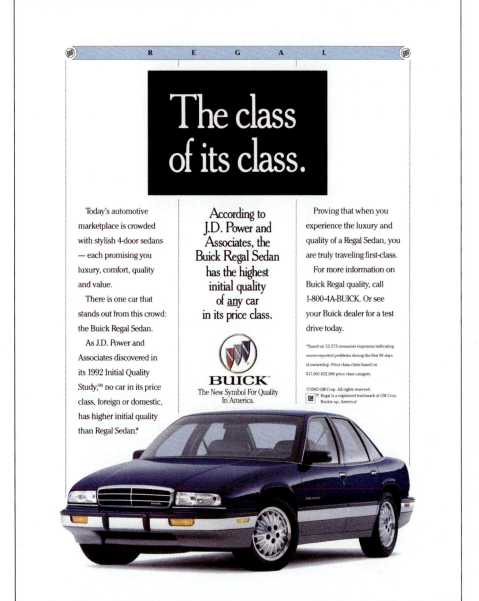

In the automotive industry, J.D. Power & Associates is widely regarded—or at least treated—as an expert primary resource on customer satisfaction. Relying largely on questionnaires mailed to car owners, Power issues about 200 reports each year. The company's biggest customers are automakers, who often adopt the results of its customer-satifaction surveys and other highly publicized studies for their marketing campaigns. Power's willingness to share its findings with such "secondary sources" as advertisers and the media has been the source of long-standing criticism from its own competitors.

Source: Featured with permission from Buick Motor Division.

PRACTICAL TIPS

Using Copyrighted Material

When researching and gathering evidence for business documents, you will encounter copyrighted materials, including books, periodicals, tapes, unpublished manuscripts, illustrations, photographs, computer programs, and other original materials. Copyrighted materials are considered the property of the individuals who authored them or the persons or firms who legally hold the copyrights to them.

Copyrighted materials are protected by both federal law and international treaty, which specify the conditions under which these materials may be cited. Among the provisions of federal copyright law are:

■ *The ability to register the work with the United States Copyright Office in Washington, D.C. Copyright protection is issued for the life of the author plus 50 years. If a corporation or* business registers a copyright, protection lasts between 75 and 100 years.

■ *Notification.* Prior to 1989, copyrighted materials had to inform the public of their status through official copyright notices. This notice included the copyright holder's name, the copyright symbol © the word "Copyright" (or the abbreviation "copr"), and the year in which the material was copyrighted for the first time. Although works created since 1989 are no longer required to include this notice, many still do in order to alert the public to the material's legal status.

■ *Limitations.* Among items not subject to copyright protection are ideas and news.

Although copyright law gives authors substantial rights to protect their works and receive compensation for their efforts, these

---

2. Examples should include only the details necessary to state your case. The amount of detail that you use should be determined more by audience needs than by the nature of the example itself.

3. Choose examples that accurately reflect the broader situation. The purpose of an example is to illustrate a point *further*; it should, therefore, be consistent with a point that can also be made by more direct means.

People, including managers, do not live by pie charts alone—or by bar graphs or three-inch statistical appendices to 300-page reports. People live, reason, and are moved by symbols and stories.

Tom Peters
Business writer

Using Expert Opinion

The opinion of a recognized authority or an expert often provides effective support for an argument. Who can be considered an expert? In general, an expert is someone who is more familiar with primary sources than you are. Expert testimony can be gathered from both primary sources (experts themselves) and secondary sources (the media that report on expert opinion). For example, while conducting interviews takes you directly to expert opinion through primary sources, quoting from business journals and books, newspapers, magazines, and government reports gives you access to expert opinion through secondary sources. Both avenues to expert opinion can be helpful in supporting the points that you want to make.

The following guidelines should help you in selecting expert opinions:

1. Be certain that the person you are quoting is a recognized expert. For example, does the name of your primary source appear in other secondary sources?

2. Be certain that your experts are reliable. Are they really familiar with primary source material? Are they being objective? Do they base their opinions on up-to-date information?

3. Avoid distorting testimony. Make every effort to quote sources accurately and in the proper context.

rights are not absolute. They are limited by the doctrine of *fair use*, which gives other writers a limited right to use brief sections of copyrighted material without asking for permission. For example, although quoting a single sentence from a journal article is considered fair use, quoting an entire page is not.

To determine what is fair use and what is not, the law examines various factors. Among these are whether the quoted material will be used for commercial or educational purposes, the proportion of the citation in relation to the size of the copyrighted document, and the effect of usage on the potential market for the copyrighted work. The intent of the law is to ensure that copyright owners are not deprived of income when others benefit from the use of their material.

Fair use, however, does not eliminate the need to cite sources. Footnotes should always be used when quoting directly from another work or paraphrasing a work's unique conclusions or research. Failure to use footnotes, especially when quoting directly, may result in the serious act of plagiarism, the topic of an Ethics in Business Communication feature in Chapter 12.

When citing substantial amounts of copyrighted material, you must obtain permission from the copyright owner. Some copyright owners permit the use of their material only if a fee is paid. Failure to obtain permission or pay the fee is considered copyright infringement and is subject to legal action.

Sources: Copyright protection is discussed in Henry R. Cheeseman, *Business Law: The Legal, Ethical, and International Environment* (Englewood Cliffs, NJ: Prentice Hall, 1992), pp. 117–23; and William C. Paxson, *The Business Writing Handbook* (New York: Bantam Books, 1981), pp. 247–51.

PROGRESS CHECK

1. Distinguish between deductive and inductive organizational patterns.
2. List three standards that evidence should meet in order to be both effective and ethical.

COMPOSING THE CONCLUSION OF A DOCUMENT

The conclusion of a business document serves three important functions. First, it provides a *summary* of the critical points made in the document. Second, it communicates *closure* by placing the discussion in a broader context. Finally, it clarifies *action to be taken.*

SUMMARIZING CRITICAL POINTS   Summaries are usually necessary in documents longer than two pages. The main points of shorter documents are usually easy to find, especially if they are visually highlighted with headings and bullets. However, in long letters, memos, reports, and proposals, a summary is an important way of reinforcing your core idea. Remember: Your summary is your last opportunity to communicate a message that you needed to write in order to express that core idea.

COMMUNICATING CLOSURE   When the body of your document has focused on a particular problem, you can add emphasis by stating how that problem relates to the same problem on a larger scale. For example, consider a memo in which you recommend establishing a companywide safety program. As an indication that such a program will be beneficial to your company, you can conclude by mentioning the success of similar programs in companies across the nation.

PRACTICAL TIPS

Composing Prototypes

Prototypes are model documents that can be used repeatedly. They are commonly created for activity reports, sales reports, and credit-information requests. They can be used as parts of documents. For example, if your company typically includes background information on company products, services, and key personnel in its documents, sections can be written in advance and filed for future use. *Form letters* are common prototypes.

Word-processing programs enable business writers to create, store, retrieve, and personalize prototypes of business correspondence. Rather than retyping frequently used letters, writers can easily store and personalize numerous documents on computers.

Not surprisingly, prototypes save an enormous amount of time and money. Communication consultant Sana Reynolds explains how to determine when to use prototypes:

I try to encourage people to ask themselves, "Will I ever have to write this again?" If they answer yes, I suggest they design a prototype and stick it in their files. For example, if you have to write an activity report every three months, create a basic prototype to use repeatedly. Having a prototype will eliminate the need to rewrite the document every time.

You won't have to struggle with how you are going to begin, what to say, and how to motivate the reader. By restricting your phrasing options, you minimize writing difficulty.

Keep in mind, however, that although a prototype can store the nuts and bolts of a document, it is not personalized for your reader. Additions and changes are often needed to meet audience and situational needs. As a result, it is important to review prototypes on a regular basis—as often as two or three times a year—to make sure that they still meet audience needs and incorporate updated information.

One of the critical issues in using prototypes is to review them to ensure that messages are appropriate for the various situations for which they are intended. It is important to read through each paragraph every time the prototype is used, selecting only those paragraphs that apply to the situation at hand. Before computers became common in office procedures, some business writers would actually send form letters with irrelevant paragraphs marked out. Today, few veteran message senders would disagree that, at least in this case, technology has spelled progress.

Sources: Interview with Sana Reynolds, November 6, 1991; Jeffrey L. Seglin, *The AMA Handbook of Business Letters* (New York: Amacom, 1989), pp. 43–44.

CLARIFYING ACTION TO BE TAKEN   Many reports, memos, and letters ask the reader to take action. By "action," you may mean adopting a recommendation, pursuing the next step in a project, or simply hiring an employee. Your conclusion allows you to emphasize once again that a reply is required or that action should be taken.

DESIGNING A DOCUMENT

design
Process of planning, writing, illustrating, and structuring a document to make it inviting and easy to read

Because design often determines whether a document will actually be read, it is as crucial to the success of a document as any element that we have discussed so far. In this chapter, **design** refers to techniques for making business documents inviting and easy to read. We will first survey the goals of document-design techniques and then discuss some of the most important elements of document design.

Goals of Document Design

Most of us have received one of those sweepstakes letters that announce at least 500 different ways to win millions of dollars—most of which require tearing out various colored stamps and searching for the appropriate places to attach them. Perhaps you have noticed that while some paragraphs are single-spaced and indented, others are double-spaced with important words typed in bold print or underlined. Handwritten notes may appear in the margins, sometimes in colored ink. Some announcements even feature highlight stars to bring certain points to your attention. Although business documents are typically devoted to much different kinds of information, they use many of the same design elements to achieve their objectives.

USING DESIGN ELEMENTS EFFECTIVELY   Design decisions are particularly important when a document has more than one audience. Because different readers use information in different ways, a well-organized and effectively

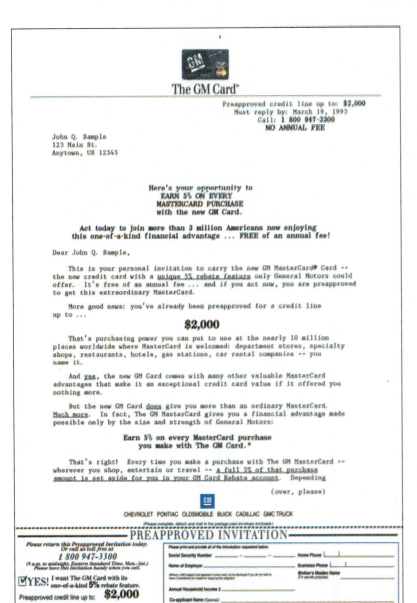

As will see in Chapter 9, effective design is an extremely important element in making a persuasive appeal. Here, the design not only helps to generate a sense of excitement about the offer being made but encourages the reader to focus on the product and its benefits. The design of this letter makes effective use of headlines, boldface type, and underlining, and its most obvious feature is its "Preapproved Invitation"—the postage-paid response form that facilitates reader response.

Source: GM. Reprinted with permission.

designed document makes information readily accessible to everyone who receives it.

Integrating design elements into computer-stored documents also aids in retrieval. When the document is accessed, the computer can be told to *search* for particular design elements such as bullets, underlines, and capitals. It also allows the computer operator to scroll through the document rapidly and spot various design elements.

As we describe various design elements, keep in mind that document design seeks to satisfy the following objectives:

- To clarify organization through the use of visual cues
- To help the writer compose a document in an organized manner
- To encourage people to read a document instead of setting it aside
- To make specific blocks of information accessible and easy to find
- To focus attention on certain parts of a document
- To give the reader an overview of document content
- To arrange every element so that the eye moves progressively from one section to the next
- To make information useful to both primary and secondary readers[11]

A document that pays little attention to design is guaranteed to be less effective than one that displays a clear sense of the document's objectives by establishing a relationship between design and readability. The two documents in Figure 4.5 illustrate how a document can be revised and redesigned to increase effectiveness. Document 1 (Fig. 4.5A) is a letter that was submitted during an actual business writing workshop. Document 2 (Fig. 4.5B) is a corrected

---

ARKANSAS TRIAL CONSULTANTS
723 Rock River Road   Little Rock, Arkansas 72799
(501) 555-2413

July 15, 199X

Ms. Katherine Fitzhugh
5619 Allendale
Little Rock, AR 72777

Dear Ms. Fitzhugh:

I was surprised and happy to hear the news of the birth of the baby. I know it was a little sooner than expected, but I was glad to hear you both are well.

I have enclosed the required documentation pertaining to your maternity leave. I will explain each of the pieces of documentation. The Pre-Leave Checklist outlines the company's policy concerning your leave, each item check pertains to you. Please review this form and sign the bottom indicating you have reviewed it and return it to me in the enclosed envelope. The Flex Family Status Change Form and the Dependent Form must be completed if you plan to cover the baby under your plan within 30 days of the birth of the baby. Within 60 days of the birth of the baby a copy of the birth certificate must be sent to the company. Both the forms and the copy of the birth certificate must be sent to:

         Mr. Alex Gardner
         Arkansas Trial Consultants
         723 Rock River Road
         Little Rock, AR 72799

The Return to Work Guidelines Form notes that before you return to work you must see your doctor and obtain a note stating that you can return on the return date designated. You are to bring this note with you when you return to work and go directly to the medical department before reporting to your work area.
                                        (More)_

ARKANSAS TRIAL CONSULTANTS

(Page 2)

You will be paid during your maternity leave for 8 weeks through September 4, 199X, plus an additional 6 days for vacation earned before you went out on maternity leave. When your salary ends, you will be billed by the company for your benefits coverage, payments must be made within 14 days of the receipt of the bill. In addition during the period of your leave that you are not receiving a salary you are not eligible for long-term disability benefits. This coverage will resume when you return to the company. You will also be receiving from the Medical Department the State Disability Forms that your doctor is to complete and return to the Medical Department at 723 Rock River Road. When your salary continuation ends you may be eligible for State Disability benefits, based on the information provided by your doctor.

When your salary ends your eligibility for the Savings Plan also will end. I have enclosed the Entry Form which is to be completed when you return to work in order to re-enroll you in the Plan. If you have a Savings Plan loan you are to contact me as soon as possible so that I may arrange repayment of the loan when your salary continuation ends.

I have also enclosed the Leave of Absence Form signed by your manager, for your files.

Please review all enclosed information, and call me if further explanation is needed.

Sincerely,

Mary Ellen Simms

Mary Ellen Simms
Human Resources Director

FIGURE 4.5A   *Revising Documents for Effective Design: Document 1*

and revised version of the same letter. We will refer to these two documents throughout the following discussion.[12]

While Document 1 discourages reading, the use of attached instructions indicated in Document 2 as an enclosure makes it easy for the reader to focus attention on distinct units of information. In addition, while Document 1 is confusing, Document 2 is well organized. The improved organization is a direct result of the design itself.

Design Elements

Five design elements are examined in this section: *short paragraphs, headings, underlining*, and *capitalization*, and *bulleted lists*. As we shall see, each has specific functions, and all of these elements can contribute to effective written communication.[13]

SHORT PARAGRAPHS   In today's sophisticated visual environment, it is a mistake to design a document with too much verbage. The layout of a document with wall-to-wall words shouts, *DON'T READ ME!* Document 1, for example,

This report, by its very length, defends itself against the risk of being read.

Winston Churchill
British prime minister
and author

ARKANSAS TRIAL CONSULTANTS
723 Rock River Road   Little Rock, Arkansas 72799
(501) 555-2413

July 15, 199X

Ms. Katherine Fitzhugh
5619 Allendale
Little Rock, AR 72777

Dear Ms. Fitzhugh:

I was surprised and happy to hear the news of the birth of your baby. I know it was a little sooner than expected, but I was glad to hear you both are well.

The enclosed documents are required for maternity leave:

- Pre-Leave Checklist
- Flex Family Status Change Form and Dependent Form
- Return to Work Guidelines Form
- Savings Plan Entry Form
- Leave of Absence Form

Each form is explained with instructions on how you should complete it. These explanations are followed by details on salary and benefits.

Please review all enclosed information and call me if you need further explanation. Again, congratulations on the birth of your baby. We look forward to welcoming you back to work after your leave.

Sincerely,

Mary Ellen Simms

Mary Ellen Simms•Human Resources Director

encl: instructions and forms

FIGURE 4.5B   *Revising Documents for Effective Design: Document 2*

contains too many long paragraphs, and part of the job of redesigning it is to reduce paragraph length.

Try to begin your document with a short paragraph that expresses your core idea or main purpose. The thrust of your message will be communicated immediately and your reader will have less trouble understanding your reason for writing it. Note that in Document 2, however, the writer starts with well-wishes because the baby's birth is directly related to the subject of the letter.

headings
Visual markers that indicate the parts of a document and give clues to its organization

HEADINGS   Visual markers that indicate the parts of your document and give clues to its organization are called **headings**. Headings make documents easy to use by drawing the reader's eye to distinct sections. Even short letters and memos benefit from the use of headings.

primary headings
Visual markers indicating major organizational sections in a document

Headings both describe information and break it down into manageable units, thereby highlighting its content and focus. Both primary and secondary headings are likely to be used in the instructions for Document 2. **Primary headings** indicate major organizational sections. Primary headings are centered and, to further emphasize their importance, printed in CAPS. The primary headings that might be used in these instructions are:

INSTRUCTIONS FOR COMPLETING REQUIRED FORMS
SALARY AND BENEFITS INFORMATION

secondary headings
Titles used to organize information into subsections within the context of primary headings

Secondary headings organize information into subsections within the context of primary headings. They are typically placed flush against the left margin and underlined, with the first letter of major words capitalized. The secondary headings likely to be included with the instruction that accompany Document 2 in Figure 4.6B are:

Pre-Leave Checklist
Flex Family Status Change Form and Dependent Form
Return to Work Guidelines Form
Savings Plan Entry Form
Leave of Absence Form

Longer reports often use third- and fourth-level headings to subdivide sections further.

The following suggestions are designed to help you use headings to enhance the visual impact of a document.

1. Use a consistent style for the placement and design of headings. Your goal is to design headings that indicate careful organization and the subordination of sections. Because conflicting styles create confusion, simplicity is the best policy. Remember that the risk of confusion increases with increased experimentation in computer type sizes and fonts.

2. Use descriptive headings that create expectations. Instead of using headings like "Problem" and "Solution," *name* the problem or solution. For example, by giving the topic a name, headings like "Design Flaws in Model FXW" and "Model FXW Recall and Redesign" can explain the problem more specifically, indicate a solution, or both.

UNDERLINING AND CAPITALIZATION   Information can also be emphasized through the selective use of underlining and capitalization. These design elements direct the reader's attention to items that the writer chooses to emphasize. In Document 2, for example, the phrase "within 30 days" is underlined for emphasis. Underlining and capitalizing, however, should be used sparingly. Because underlining suggests that particular information merits top priority and close attention, underline only critical phrases and sentences.

Many businesspeople consider writing to be the most difficult part of their job. Even if they do only a limited amount of writing, they struggle with every word and sentence. Often, the problem lies not in poor writing skills, but in poor writing habits that undermine confidence and quality. Here are some suggestions for breaking these habits and producing more effective material:

- *Become self-motivated.* Motivation comes from knowing that there is a job to be done and a deadline for submission. It also comes from understanding the document's business purpose. For example, realizing that a report is needed before an important decision can be made or that a proposal is the key ingredient in acquiring a new account is powerful motivation for most writers. Waiting for inspiration to strike or for the "right mood" is a way of avoiding the task.

- *Learn to work despite distractions.* Almost no one who works in an office writes for an entire day without interruption. On the contrary, phone calls, face-to-face meetings, and other pressing work interfere with the writing process. Learning to overcome these distractions requires discipline, focus, and a commitment to getting the job done.

- *Set daily writing goals.* This resolution means putting yourself on a production schedule. For example, if you are writing a 50-page report that is due at the end of next week, your goal may be to write ten pages a day.

- *Set an artificial deadline.* To make sure that your work is done on time, set yourself an early deadline. By scheduling completion a few days before the actual deadline, you will have breathing room in case of unexpected problems or interruptions.

- *Learn to work around unexpected delays.* Writers do not work in a vacuum. On the contrary, they depend on such input as the contributions of co-workers, the availability of research materials, and approvals from senior executives. When a delay occurs in one part of a writing project, learn to put that section aside and work on other, unrelated materials. Because many long reports and proposals have distinct sections, this practice is usually easy to adapt to.

- *Develop an effective pace.* Take regular breaks to pace your writing and avoid pushing yourself to the point that you are no longer effective. Trying to do too much because a deadline is approaching is usually counterproductive.

Creating an atmosphere in which effective writing is possible involves taking personal responsibility for getting the work done effectively and on time. The only things at risk are bad habits that interfere with productivity.

BULLETED LISTS   **Bullets** are visual cues that indicate critical information by highlighting items contained in lists. They are symbols such as an asterisk (*) or a dash (—) to the left of the items to be highlighted. Many computer programs can create solid circles (•) or squares (■) as bullets. Because business writing often contains lists, bullets can be a particularly effective design element. While Document 1, for example, contains no bullets, the cover letter in Document 2 uses a bulleted list to provide a preview of the enclosed forms. This technique lets the reader know in advance what to expect.

From the reader's perspective, bullets transform imposing blocks of unrelenting typeface into more inviting units of information. By highlighting information, bullets make it easier for readers to find specific details within the text of a document. They are particularly valuable, for example, in communicating sets of instructions.

bullets
Visual cues such as asterisks and dashes that indicate critical information by highlighting items contained in lists

BUSINESS WRITING IN ACTION

Organizing, Composing, and Designing a Business Memo

THE ASSIGNMENT

This assignment picks up where it left off at the end of Chapter 3. You are now ready to organize, compose, and design a persuasive memo to the entire staff of IBM about the OS/2 personal-computer operating system. The purpose of your memo is to enlist the help of all employees in selling this product in an extremely competitive marketplace.

THE METHOD

Step 1: ORGANIZE THE MEMO USING AN INFORMAL OUTLINE.

Core Idea: With the introduction of the OS/2 operating system, IBM needs every employee to act as a personal spokesperson for the product, spreading the word about its features and advantages to friends, family, and community members.

- Every employee is a product spokesperson who spreads the word by talking with relatives, friends, and acquaintances
- Need to convince personal-computer users to purchase OS/2 instead of Microsoft's Windows 3.1
- Need to stop Microsoft's momentum as the leading manufacturer of computer operating software

What we want employees to do:
- Talk about product to everyone they know in order to convince them to purchase OS/2
- Use brochures to help explain the advantages of OS/2 over Windows 3.1
- What employees will receive for effort:
- Incentives such as medals, software, hardware, and cash
- Pricing and promotions:
- OS/2 list price $195
- Owners of earlier versions of OS/2 get free software
- Additional discounts up to $146
- Individual efforts backed by huge advertising campaign

Step 2: COMPOSE A FIRST DRAFT GUIDED BY YOUR OUTLINE.

IBM is reintroducing the OS/2 personal-computer operating system to the market. To make the product a success, IBM needs the help of every employee. To help sell as many OS/2 units as possible, we want you to communicate the merits of this new product to people you know—relatives, friends, and acquaintances—even your family dentist.

IBM is asking for help because of the tough competitive environment. As you know, Microsoft Corp. is now the leading manufacturer of operating software for computers. Microsoft's Windows has already sold more than 10 million units, and its latest version—Windows 3.1—has momentum on its side.

Employees are an integral part of an extensive companywide campaign to promote OS/2. Because we believe that our entire workforce is our best salesforce, we will provide everyone with materials—including brochures—explaining the features of OS/2. The purpose of the brochures is to describe the many advantages of OS/2 over Windows 3.1. In return for your efforts, we have arranged a series of incentives ranging from medals to IBM software, hardware, and cash. We are also promoting the product through a special pricing strategy. Those with earlier versions of OS/2 receive the new program free. For others, substantial discounts slash as much as $146 off the $195 list price. Finally, we will back the efforts of employees with a nationwide advertising campaign.

Step 3: **DESIGN THE DOCUMENT.**

THE REINTRODUCTION OF OS/2

IBM is introducing the OS/2 personal-computer operating system to the market. To make the product a success, IBM needs the help of every employee.

To help sell as many OS/2 units as possible, we want you to communicate the merits of this new product to people you know—that includes relatives, friends, acquaintances, and even your family dentist.

OS/2 Competitors

IBM is asking for help because of the tough competitive environment. As you know, Microsoft Corp. is now the leading manufacturer of operating software for computers. Microsoft's Windows has already sold more than 10 million units, and its latest version—Windows 3.1—has momentum on its side.

COMPANYWIDE PROMOTIONAL STRATEGY

A three-pronged strategy will be used to promote OS/2:

- Employees will act as product spokespersons
- Product prices will be discounted
- Nationwide advertising campaign will begin.

Employees as Product Spokespersons

Employees are an integral part of an extensive companywide campaign to promote OS/2. Because we believe that our employees are our best salespeople, we will provide everyone with materials—including brochures—explaining the features of OS/2. The purpose of the brochures is to describe the many advantages of OS/2 over Windows 3.1. In return for your efforts, we have arranged a series of incentives ranging from medals to IBM software, hardware, and cash.

Deep-Discount Pricing

We are promoting the product through a special pricing strategy:
- Owners of earlier versions of OS/2 receive the new program free
- Substantial discounts slash as much as $146 off the $195 list price

Nationwide Advertising Campaign

Tens of millions of dollars will be spent to promote the OS/2 in a nationwide advertising campaign.

This document is now a first draft that, by definition, is subject to change. We will complete this exercise in Chapter 5, where we will see how attention to language, tone, and intent will change this draft in some dramatic ways. Also involved will be a rethinking of whether the draft has achieved its intended purpose or whether reorganization and substantial rewriting are necessary.

To be continued in Chapter 5.

PROGRESS CHECK

1. When would you include a summary in a document?
2. What two guidelines can enhance the visual impact of headings?

WHAT'S AHEAD

As we will see in Chapter 5, once your draft is complete, you can begin to fine tune your document through editing and revising. Having organized, composed, and designed your document, you have in your hands at this point a completed first draft. By its very nature, however, a first draft is subject to rethinking, refinement, and revision. Chapter 5 will explore the revision process as it examines word selection, style, and tone of voice. It will also examine how to offer and respond to constructive criticism.

SUMMARY OF CHAPTER OBJECTIVES

1. **Describe the different *outline forms* used in organizing business documents.**

   An outline guides document writing from the introduction through the conclusion. It enables the writer to make logical connections among ideas before actually composing and to rearrange ideas when necessary. It also provides a way of coping with a large amount of information by dividing it into small sections. A formal outline follows prescribed rules concerning content and format in order to show the precise relationship among ideas. An informal outline is a more loosely connected organizational device that need not follow the strict structural rules of a formal outline.

2. **Identify the *three parts of a business document* and describe their functions in communication.**

   The opening of a business document must capture and hold the reader's attention and communicate the purpose of the document in a clear, succinct way. The middle contains the document's main points and supporting evidence. The conclusion summarizes the document's message, communicates closure, and clarifies action to be taken.

3. **List the alternative *patterns* for organizing material in the middle of a document.**

   The organization patterns that shape a document determine how directly its message will be presented as well as the way in which its ideas are linked together. Business docu-

   ments can be organized in terms of two general categories that can be described as either *deductive versus inductive* or *direct versus indirect*. Within this framework, documents can follow a number of different organizational patterns, including problem/solution, cause and effect, chronological, and climactic order. The core idea of a message generally determines the choice of an organizational pattern.

4. **Describe the four forms of *evidence* used in business documents.**

   The four forms of evidence are facts, statistics, examples, and expert opinion. Facts are statements that clarify a situation by adding informative details. They clarify your main point, define all new terms and concepts, and demonstrate that you can support your point of view. Statistics, a form of numerical evidence, are mathematical expressions that describe findings in an objective, uniform way and provide a standard to determine the validity of the results. Examples are descriptive stories and specific cases that make abstract information real and memorable. Expert opinion—the testimony of a recognized authority—adds weight to your position.

5. **Explain the elements of *document design* and their functions in a document.**

   Important document-design elements include short paragraphs, headings, underlining and capitalization, and bulleted lists. These elements clarify organization, aid in the composition process, encourage reading, make information, make information accessible, focus attention on certain information, give the reader an overview of the content, and make information usable by primary and secondary readers.

REVIEW AND DISCUSSION QUESTIONS

1. Why is it important for business documents to be well-organized? *(Ch. Obj. 1)*

2. Why is it useful to organize a document in outline form before writing? *(Ch. Obj. 1)*

3. Distinguish between formal and informal outlines. *(Ch. Obj. 1)*

4. Identify the three major sections of a business document. *(Ch. Obj. 2)*

5. What primary function(s) are served by each of the sections referred to in QUESTION 4? *(Ch. Obj. 2)*

6. Identify the patterns that can be used to organize information in the middle of a document. *(Ch. Obj. 3)*

7. What are the four forms of evidence used in business documents? *(Ch. Obj 4)*

8. What guidelines should be followed in choosing expert opinions to use as evidence? *(Ch. Obj. 4)*

9. Identify and briefly explain each of the major elements of document design. *(Ch. Obj.5)*

10. What are the objectives of effective document design? *(Ch. Obj. 5)*

APPLICATION EXERCISES

1. Choose a topic that interests you and which you would like to discuss in a letter to a friend or family member. The topic could relate to a hobby, a class in which you are currently enrolled, or a recent incident. Organize your ideas for this letter by writing a one-page formal outline. Include supporting evidence and/or examples with your outline. *(Ch. Obj. 1, 3)*

2. Write a one-page letter, report, or memo based on the formal outline assigned in EXERCISE 1. Did you find it helpful to organize your ideas in an outline first? *(Ch. Obj. 1, 3)*

3. Choose another topic that would also be a good subject for a letter. Organize your thoughts for this letter by writing an informal outline. Include supporting evidence and/or examples with your outline. *(Ch. Obj. 1, 3)*

4. Now write another letter, report, or memo following the informal outline that you created for EXERCISE 3. Which did you find more Helpful, the informal or the formal outline? Explain your answer. *(Ch. Obj. 1, 3)*

5. Write a memo or letter that defines the deductive organizational pattern and explains why it is the most frequently used pattern in business documents. What are the advantages of this approach? Organize your document in a deductive pattern; be sure to include an opening, a middle, and a conclusion. *(Ch. Obj. 3)*

6. Write a letter to a friend describing an experience that you have had, either recently or in the past. Organize your letter chronologically. *(Ch. Obj. 3)*

7. Think of a job that you would love to have. Now write a letter, addressed to the person who would hire you, explaining why you would be perfect for the position. Include an opening, a middle, and a conclusion, and design your letter to be as effective and readable as possible. Use evidence to support your point—for instance, examples of your experience, achievements, and accomplishments. What organizational pattern would you want to use for this letter? *(Ch. Obj. 2, 3, 4, 5)*

8. A well-known business book was published several years ago with the thought-provoking title *How to Lie with Statistics*. Is it possible to create a false impression by misusing statistics? Explain your answer. In both your own writing and your reading of other people's documents, what should you watch for to make sure that statistics present an accurate picture? *(Ch. Obj. 4)*

9. Your boss has asked you to write a concise, one-page memo on the importance of good design in business documents. Write this memo and include an opening, a middle, and a conclusion. Design it to convey maximum visual impact. What organizational pattern would you recommend for this document? *(Ch. Obj. 2, 3, 5)*

10. Write a report describing the layout of your school's campus or major buildings. Use a geographical organization pattern, and design your document to be as clear as possible. *(Ch. Obj. 3, 5)*

11. Write a memo discussing some type of problem at your school or workplace and describing its effects (that is, why is it a problem). Organize your document in a cause-and-effect pattern; use the design elements described in the chapter to make it more effective. *(Ch. Obj. 3, 5)*

12. Write a memo summarizing the problem that you discussed in EXERCISE 11 and then present a solution. Organize your memo in a problem/solution pattern and design it to be as readable as possible. *(Ch. Obj. 3, 5)*

13. Suppose the following memo, written by Jack Bunch of Quick Calculators, were to appear on your desk:

> As you know, we've expanded our overseas shipments to England and Germany lately. This requires additional shipments of 5,000 units to each country. Demand seems to be rising there. We could start shipping to China as well. Demand is rising for our calculators in the U.S., too. Sales are up 25,000 units over last year in the U.S. Right now, we're selling about 50,000 units a year in the U.S. alone. Our current supplier, Englewood Electronics, doesn't seem able to meet this increased demand. This past year, Englewood has been late five times in its shipments to us. This in turn makes us late in getting our calculators to customers. I understand that changes in management at Englewood have made it harder for the company to meet its schedules, and things will probably get worse before they get better. I'd recommend that we think about locating another supplier. I'm sending this memo to all employees just to keep everyone informed, but would the employees who are in the shipping department please get back to me as soon as possible with your suggestions for another supplier? Thanks.

a. Is this an effective memo? Explain your answer.

b. If your answer is no, design a new memo that you believe will be more effective. Outline your new memo so that it is organized according to the problem/solution pattern; in order to turn your outline into blocks of information with headings, use the model suggested in the chapter by consultant Edward Bailey, Jr. *(Ch. Obj. 1, 3, 5)*

14. Compose the memo that you designed for EXERCISE 13. Organize it in the problem/solution organizational pattern, and use design elements to clarify your message. *(Ch. Obj. 3, 5)*

15. Suppose that all the employees in Quick Calculators' shipping department are good friends with the staff of Englewood Electronics. After all, they have been doing business together for years, and they enjoy socializing together. Although Jack Bunch still feels strongly that Quick Calculators needs to find another supplier, he knows that he must be very tactful in presenting his case. Rewrite the memo that you composed for EXERCISE 14, organizing it in the climactic-order pattern. *(Ch. Obj. 3, 4, 5)*

BUILDING YOUR RESEARCH SKILLS

Pair off with a classmate. As a two-person team, choose a business topic that you both would like to research. Then, working independently outside class, read three articles that deal with the topic that you have chosen. Analyze each article to determine whether it follows the guidelines in this chapter for clear, effective writing. Does it seem well-organized? Do its ideas flow logically? What type of organizational pattern does each article use? What type(s) of evidence does each use to support its points? Are the designs easy to read and follow?

Take notes on your analyses and be prepared to explain why each article is effective (or why not).

BUILDING YOUR TEAMWORK SKILLS

Meet with your partner from the previous exercise. Go over your respective articles and analyses. Determine whether you can explain clearly to your partner why you think each article is effective or ineffective. Does your partner agree with your conclusions? Do you agree with his or hers? Explain your answer.

COMMUNICATING IN A WORLD OF DIVERSITY

While reading one day, you come across the following facts:

- The Pentagon recently released its first major study of sexual harassment in the U.S. military.
- Studies of sexual harassment in the private sector show that 30 percent to 40 percent of women say they have been harassed at work.
- In the private sector, 14 percent to 15 percent of men say they have experienced sexual harassment at work.
- The Pentagon's study revealed that over one-third of women in the Armed Forces have experienced some form of direct sexual harassment (touching, pressure for sexual favors, or rape).
- In the Pentagon study, about two-thirds of the women surveyed said that they had been sexually harassed, either directly or in more subtle ways (for example, catcalls, leering, and teasing).
- Experts say that sexual harassment often declines in a profession when it is entered by more women.

- In the Pentagon study, 17 percent of the men surveyed said that they had been sexually harassed in some way.
- The military has long claimed that women have been integrated smoothly into the Armed Forces.
- Says the assistant secretary of defense for force management and personnel: "The results are sobering. These numbers are clearly too high....The policy is clear: Sexual harassment will not be tolerated."
- Jehn plans to conduct another survey in two to three years to measure the military's progress.

Using this information, write a memo suggesting that the military begin an immediate program of training and support services to reduce its rate of sexual harassment. Address the memo to the Joint Chiefs of Staff. Assume for the purposes of this question that the Joint Chiefs are a conservative group who are likely to require considerable convincing before they would agree to your proposal.

Source: Susan Webb, "Women in Armed Forces Face Frequent Sexual Harassment," *Personnel*, March 1991, p. 15.

CASE 4.1

Dealing with Too Much of a Good Thing

William Anderson likes the environment as much as anyone. But he's not feeling too friendly toward the government's efforts to save the earth.

So far, Anderson has spent two years and more than $100,000 on what seems like a simple task: disposing of five small underground gas and oil tanks. The tanks are buried in the lot behind Anderson's Dreisbach Buick dealership outside Pontiac, Michigan.

Certainly, underground storage tanks can pose an environmental threat. Gas, oil, and chemicals can leak from broken tanks, polluting water supplies and endangering residents' health. In 1988, the federal

government passed a law aimed at eliminating faulty underground tanks. Anderson is only one of many small-business owners who are affected—some might say hurt—by this law. As it happens, Anderson's tanks aren't polluting anything. But to escape various liability risks, he and other car dealers and service-station operators want to replace their old tanks with new ones. In the process, however, many such businesspeople, like William Anderson, have encountered a confusing maze of regulatory rules and a mountain of mandated paperwork.

Like many states, Michigan has set up a trust fund designed to pay for all but $10,000 of the business owners' costs for removing storage tanks like those on William Anderson's property. To be eligible for reimbursement, however, Anderson must follow a strict timetable of procedures—each of which costs money. Among his expenses:

- $500 to register the tanks with the state
- $375 to buy a required surety bond
- $1,100 to test the tanks' contents before digging them up
- $25,000 to dig up the tanks
- $73,000 to fill in the holes

To top it off, Anderson has already paid $12,000 to an environmental consultant to guide him through each step of the process.

So far, Anderson hasn't received any money back from the state. Michigan has already identified over 7,000 problem tanks, almost 3,000 of which, like Anderson's, qualify for reimbursement. "We had no idea of the scope of the problem," says Amy Carter, acting coordinator of Michigan's tank-removal program. "We're backed up, and we admit it. When you have 1,000 reports on your desk, and it takes a day and a half to read one, you have panic."

Not surprisingly, Anderson's problems aren't over yet. True, the troublesome tanks have been removed, cut up, and sold for scrap metal, and the oily dirt in his car lot has been hauled to a landfill. But Anderson's consultant now informs him that the state will next order him to begin Phase II: sinking four to ten shallow wells around the old tank storage area to determine whether water is contaminated and, if so, how far the problem extends. This procedure will require hiring a drill rig, monitoring the area, and capturing any pollut-ed water to remove the oil. "A nice Phase II investigation with a report," says Anderson's consultant, "…we're talking $25,000."

Says William Anderson: "Ours is just one small business, and we're trying very hard to be a good citizen and comply with environmental regulations. If it wasn't tragic, it'd be comical."

Questions and Assignments

1. As head of the chamber of commerce in Pontiac, Michigan, you feel that Anderson's plight is typical of many small-business owners who are hampered by too much bureaucracy. You decide to write a memo to the federal Environmental Protection Agency, suggesting that it reevaluate its rules on the disposal of underground storage tanks. Write an outline of your memo. What organizational pattern should the memo follow?
2. Follow suggestions in this chapter for transforming your outline into a series of headings, with each heading followed by a main point and supporting evidence.
3. Based on the outline and headings that you created for ASSIGNMENT 2, write your memo to the EPA. Design it to be clearly readable and effective.

Source: Eugene Carlson, "Small Firms Spend Much Time, Money Complying with Environmental Rules," *The Wall Street Journal*, June 15, 1992, pp. B1, B7. © 1992 Dow Jones & Company Inc. Reprinted by permission. All rights reserved.

CASE 4.2

Springfield Remanufacturing Corp.: The Income Statement as an Open Letter

In 1982, Jack Stack worked at a small factory in Springfield, Missouri, owned by International Harvester Corp., the predecessor of Navistar Corp. By 1983, the little factory had become an independent firm called Springfield Remanufacturing Corp. (SRC), and Jack was its president.

This state of affairs, however, was not quite as impressive as it sounds. Fighting for its corporate survival, former parent International Harvester had been forced to sell off its operations as fast as it could just to stay in business. In desperation, Harvester had offered to sell SRC to Stack and eleven other managers. The prospective buyers agreed, primarily because they were afraid that if someone else bought the company, they all would lose their jobs. When they bought SRC, Stack and his partners had acquired a company loaded with debt; during their first year, they lost $60,488.

As Stack recalls, however, "It's amazing what you can come up with when you have no money, zero outside resources, and 119 people all depending on you for their jobs, their homes, and their prospects of dinner for the foreseeable future." What Stack had come up with was "The Great Game of Business."

As Stack sees it, there are really only two critical factors in business success: making money and generating cash. He was convinced that if he could just teach all SRC employees to understand and work toward those goals, the company would succeed. And the best way to teach people to understand business, according to Stack, is getting them to understand financial statements.

At SRC, therefore, employees now start by looking at the company income statement. At company meetings, for example, Stack uses the statement to show the cause-and-effect of business decisions and to help employees follow the "action" of the game that they are all playing. He highlights those categories in which SRC spends the most money, further breaking down categories into controllable elements. For instance, a sales organization can break down "expenses" into such controllable elements as travel, entertainment, and meals. Stack then shows employees how changes in the income statement lead to changes in the balance sheet. According to Stack's rules of the game, while the income statement illustrates the game's action, the balance sheet is the true scorecard that shows a firm how it's doing.

At SRC, costs are thus broken down and examined in detail. Production costs are itemized as material, labor, and overhead. Office supplies are closely monitored, even down to the amount spent each month on receptionists' note pads. The company constantly measures how long it takes to perform certain tasks, how much materials cost, and how fast

each employee is working. It posts sales figures daily: who is buying, what they are buying, how they buy it. While many companies would make this information available only to managers, it is distributed among SRC employees regardless of rank. All supervisors then meet once a week with their staffs to go over updated financial statements and discuss how SRC is doing in relation to its annual goals.

Is SRC's system working? Apparently. The company went from a $60,000 loss in 1983 to pretax earnings of $2.7 million four years later. By 1991, it boasted annual sales of almost $70 million, and its workforce had grown from 119 to 650. Best of all, says Stack, the company has been able to provide job security for its employees: "We never laid off a single person," he reports, "not even when we lost a contract representing 40 percent of our business for a whole year."

Questions and Assignments

1. As a writer for *Business Week*, you are convinced that Stack's Great Game of Business approach could benefit many companies. You decide to write a report describing how the Game works, what it can do for employees and employers, and how it has succeeded at SRC. Write an outline for this memo.
2. Organize your outline into blocks of headings with related material. Be sure to lay out clearly all the steps that a manager in another firm would follow in order to implement Stack's approach.
3. Write the memo, and design it to be clearly readable and striking. Include lots of evidence to convince more traditional managers that this unusual approach can work.

Source: Jack Stack, "The Great Game of Business," *Inc.*, June 1992, pp. 52-66.

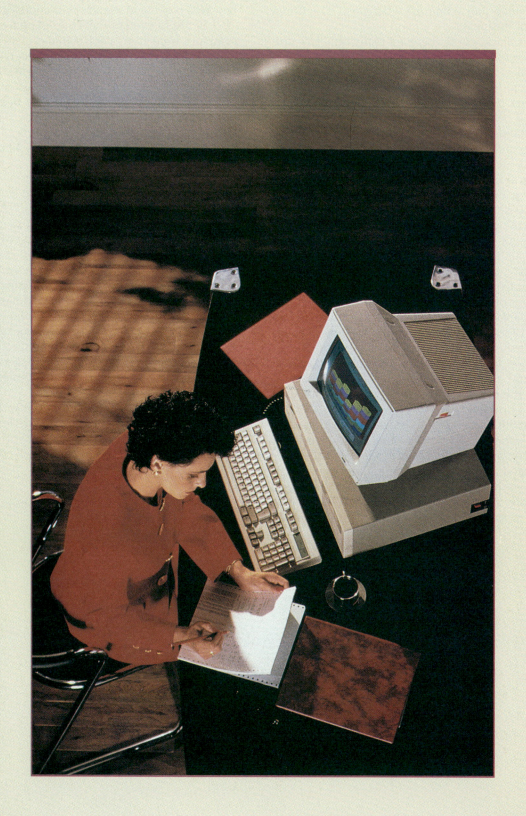

Revising and Editing Business Documents

After studying this chapter, you should be able to:

1 Explain the importance of *revising* business documents.

2 Describe the characteristics of clear, conversational language and identify the qualities of concise, concrete, and correct language.

3 Explain the importance of *persuasive* and *constructive language* in business documents.

4 Outline strategies for constructing *effective sentences* and *paragraphs.*

5 Discuss the relationship between *style* and *writing strategy.*

6 Explain the characteristics of *nondiscriminatory writing.*

7 Identify ways to evaluate a *final draft.*

To improve is to change; to be perfect is to change often.

Winston Churchill
British statesman

THE COMMUNICATION CONTEST

Perhaps nothing typifies the trials of business writing and reading better than an organization's *proxy statement*—the report that a public company issues prior to its annual stockholders' meeting. Proxy statements tell stockholders what will happen at the meeting and usually include such details as executive compensation—the total amount that top executives earn from such sources as salaries, bonuses, stocks and stock options, and deferred compensation plans. All too often, however, proxy statements are impossible to understand.

To demonstrate how hard it is to make sense out of the typical proxy statement, a recent meeting of the Council of Institutional Investors, a nonprofit group that represents 70 percent of the country's largest pension funds, sponsored a proxy-reading contest. In attendance were more than 200 investment experts, many of whom had earned doctorates in economics and mathematics. Only 27 of them agreed to enter the contest.

Contestants were asked to determine how much three top executives had earned during the previous year. Under scrutiny were former General Motors Corp. CEO Robert C. Stempel; Martin S. Davis, CEO of Paramount Communications; and Roberto C. Goizueta, CEO of Coca-Cola. As the following examples demonstrate, the problems faced by contestants stemmed in large part from poor writing.

- The General Motors proxy statement disclosed that Stempel had been paid an "annual average" of $115,000 as part of a five-year incentive plan. What the proxy statement did not explain was that in order to calculate the value of this incentive plan, contestants had to multiply $115,000 by 5 to arrive at a figure of $575,000—a considerably higher number for readers to consider.

- Although Davis earned $3.4 million as the head of Paramount, guesses ranged from $2 million to $4.2 million. Estimates were often wrong because information was scattered in various locations throughout the proxy statement. Absent were summary tables or a listing of previous earnings for comparison purposes.

- Wide disparity also occurred in calculating Goizueta's earnings as head of Coca-Cola. Although his total compensation equaled $63.5 million, estimates were as low as $4.1 million. To estimate the value of Goizueta's compensation correctly, contestants needed to know the value of his restricted stock. But many of the expert participants could not find this figure, partially because it had been placed several pages later in the document and partially because the information did not catch their attention (the number had been written out rather than shown numerically).

Not surprisingly, the growing tendency of business writing to lend itself to confusion has led to complaints inside business itself. "The current system," suggests Sarah Teslik, executive director of the Council of Institutional Investors, "does not allow even sophisticated investors to make good ball-park guesses." "You need a Ph.D. to understand it," adds Gray Davis, comptroller of the state of California. Not so, replies New York City Finance Commissioner Carol O'Cleireacain: "I am a Ph.D. and I can't figure it out."

Perhaps the last word on the daunting task faced by our contestants came from Raymond J. Sweeney, a lawyer representing the sheet metal workers' pension fund who shuddered at the mere thought of entering the contest. As Sweeney tells it, his union had decided two years earlier to take an active part in the annual meetings of companies in which its pension funds were invested. "I was assigned to [read all the proxies]," reports Sweeney. "I thought, 'I can read and write, I can understand this.' But after billing my clients for six hours and getting nowhere, I gave up."[1]

CHAPTER OVERVIEW

The manner in which proxy statements are so often written is a symptom of a larger problem common to many business documents—the problem of failing to revise information so that readers can understand critical concepts without undue struggle. The result is usually a document that boasts unintelligible jargon instead of conversational English and prefers the long-winded to the short and simple—a document, in other words, that confuses rather than clarifies.

Although the corporate proxy typifies the kinds of problems that can result when information is not presented in a clear, concise way, dozens of other examples can be found. The Internal Revenue Service, for example, has been soundly ridiculed for providing incomprehensible directions for preparation of tax forms. Insurance policies and legal documents are also notorious for lengthy, complex wording that seems to be hiding rather than expressing something.

The purpose of this chapter is to demonstrate the connection between effective communication and *word selection* and *style*—the two operations that occur during document revision. This chapter examines the revision process as part of the overall writing strategy. We will suggest criteria for judging the quality of a draft, choosing appropriate language, and constructing effective sentences and paragraphs. We will discuss the concept of writing style and make use of numerous examples to show how the best writers adapt style to the needs of their documents. We will also provide some practical tools for evaluating your final drafts and take a close look at the revision process.

REVISING A BUSINESS DOCUMENT

Although some people use the terms *revising* and *editing* interchangeably, they are distinct processes. **Revising** refers to the processes of adding, deleting, replacing, and reorganizing words, sentences, and paragraphs to produce an unedited final draft. **Editing** involves correcting mistakes in grammar, spelling, and punctuation and producing a document that reflects a consistent style for elements such as numbers, abbreviations, and capitalization.[2]

While editing, therefore, focuses on technical correctness, revising is a process of evaluating and assessing your meaning and your effectiveness in communicating it. Appendix II in this text is a detailed guide to help you edit your draft in order to polish your presentation. This chapter focuses on the art of revising your draft on every level, from communicating your core idea to choosing your words.

revising
Process of transforming a rough draft into a finished document by adding, deleting, replacing and reorganizing words, sentences, and paragraphs

editing
Correcting mistakes in grammar, spelling, and punctuation and producing a document consistent in style for such elements as numbers, abbreviations, and capitalization

INTERNATIONAL ISSUES IN BUSINESS COMMUNICATION

Comparing American and French Business Correspondence

The way business documents are written in the United States is not necessarily the way they are written in other countries. In fact, if you analyze documents from different parts of the world, you will find marked differences in format, organization, and writing style. To evaluate these differences, Illinois State University professor Iris I. Varner studied typical business correspondence from the United States and France. She analyzed format, the style used to begin and end letters, and basic writing principles. Her findings demonstrate a strong link between culture and communication.

Correspondence, for example, exhibited important formatting differences. While Americans generally use the block format in business letters, the French prefer to indent paragraphs. In the United States, the date always precedes the inside address, while in France the writer has the option of adding the date after the inside address. French writers place the inside address on the right-hand side of the page—a practice never followed in the United States. While the U.S. Zip code follows the name of the state, in France the postal code precedes the name of the city.

Salutations also differ. The French are more formal than their American counterparts. Even when people know each other very well, they rarely use first names in official correspondence. The first sample letter in

Anne Carpenter Exports
6751 Whispering Pines
Chicago, Illinois 29145
312-555-1144

October 30, 199X

Mr. Michael Mason
President
Midwest Credit
15904 Airport Blvd.
Chicago, IL 29326

Dear Mr. Mason:

American Salutation Format

Is revision necessary to produce an acceptable final draft? Absolutely, says William Zinsser, author of *Writing with a Word Processor*. Writing, he emphasizes,

> is not some sort of divine act that can only be performed by people of artistic bent, though obviously a gift for words is helpful. Writing is the logical arrangement of thought.

> To clarify what we write, it is important to constantly ask, "Have I said what I wanted to say?" Usually we haven't. Even for a professional writer very few sentences come out right the first time, or even the second or third time.[3]

this box illustrates the format used in the United States, while the second shows the format used by the French.

Beginnings and endings of letters also vary. In France, letters begin and end with formal, sometimes flowery prose. Americans, on the other hand, like to be courteous but get to the point. Interestingly, gender issues do not seem as important in French business writing as they are in the United States. For example, when the sex of the recipient is not known, the French consistently use the male salutation. In addition, French letters of request usually close by thanking the reader in advance in language that most Americans would find too formal.

As might be expected, American and French businesspeople use words and sentences in different ways. For example, Americans tend to use more concrete language than the French and typically follow a general principle with an example. After presenting the principle, the French tend to be more theoretical and, therefore, typically write longer letters.

Source: Iris I. Varner, "A Comparison of American and French Business Correspondence," *Journal of Business Communication*, Fall 1988, pp. 55–65.

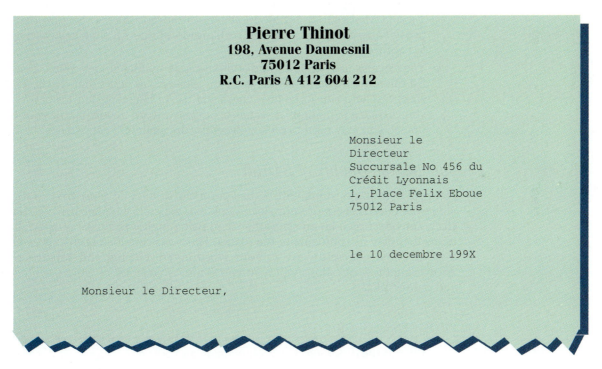

Pierre Thinot
198, Avenue Daumesnil
75012 Paris
R.C. Paris A 412 604 212

```
                              Monsieur le
                              Directeur
                              Succursale No 456 du
                              Crédit Lyonnais
                              1, Place Felix Eboue
                              75012 Paris


                              le 10 decembre 199X

      Monsieur le Directeur,
```

French Salutation Format

Certainly, the importance of writing that is lively, concise, and direct cannot be overemphasized. Perhaps even more important, however, is knowing how to word the simplest of statements so that the reader is drawn to your perspective and responds to your message. For example, a memo to employees regarding cost control could get the job done by stating simply that certain measures are being taken to improve the company's profitability and competitiveness. Although there would be no confusion as to what the company is doing, the same memo would probably be more effective if it were written with the *reader's* perspective in mind: Of what benefit is this to me? As we will see in this chapter, the "you" attitude often plays a significant part in the writing of memos, letters, reports, and other documents.

The Art of Revision

How well we communicate is determined not by how well we say things but by how well we are understood.

Andrew S. Grove
CEO, Intel Corp.

The literal meaning of the word *revision* is "to see again." Even the most accomplished writers rarely get a draft right on the first try. As a result, much of the process of writing is actually *rewriting*. When revising a document, then, the writer understands that revision is not only necessary but also desirable. Many revised documents, therefore, differ markedly from their first drafts. Here are some preliminary and very general suggestions for turning first drafts into final documents that satisfy the needs of the reader, the material, and the situation.[4]

- Effective revision requires a critical reading of the document to determine whether it accomplishes its intended purpose and meets the reader's needs. It is often advisable to put the document aside for a period of time so that you can look at it again with fresh eyes. Of course, waiting a few hours or even a few days is ideal, but deadlines and work pressures usually make this impossible.

- Reading a draft aloud can ensure that the sound and tone of your language are appropriate. Ernest Hemingway, for example, read his novel *The Old Man and the Sea* aloud several hundred times to be sure that his prose reflected the all-important sounds of speech that he was trying to capture.[5]

- You can also use checklists and style sheets as writing guides. While a checklist can remind you to include such key elements as tables and charts, a style sheet can help you focus on a consistent use of language and format. When you change a paragraph, a sentence, or even a word in one part of your document, you may need to review the entire document for consistency.

Judging the Quality of a Draft

Naturally, your revisions will be based on the quality of your first draft. To judge the effectiveness of your document, ask yourself whether it is written in clear, conversational language, rather than using highly technical or specialized terms that may be confusing to the reader. Has your core idea been expressed in a concise and concrete way? Is your wording convincing and constructive? Answering these questions will help you evaluate your use of words, sentences, and paragraphs.

PROGRESS CHECK

1. What is the difference between revising and editing?
2. Do all writers have to revise their work?

CHOOSING EFFECTIVE LANGUAGE

Words are, of course, the most powerful drug used by mankind.

Rudyard Kipling
English poet and novelist

Words are the building blocks of communication. They convey information through both literal meaning and tone, each of which affects the way a message is received and each of which influences a message in different ways.

Unfortunately, words are often used ineffectively. Instead of clarifying, they confuse; instead of motivating, they dull the senses. Consider the frustration of Thomas Sobol, commissioner of the New York State Education Department. More than 10,000 letters are sent out with his signature each year, and thousands of

In other words, word choices can either create vivid images and lasting impressions or result in little impact at all. The effect of words can depend on striking the successful tone. Because English, for example, has about 900,000 words, advertisers usually strive for the kind of precision and economy that is made possible by such a large vocabulary. By the same token, English is quite flexible, accomodating the kind of variety in word choice that makes it possible to say the same thing—roughly—in either a formal or informal tone or somewhere in between.

additional letters, memos, and reports—all requiring responses—are addressed to his attention. Sobol found himself overwhelmed by messages such as these:

- Careful implementation of this policy is needed in order to avoid the pitfall of goal displacement.
- Existing variance procedures should be examined with regard to their potential for extension to circumstances not currently within their scope.
- This office is in receipt of your correspondence.

Sobol's solution: He ordered 250 of his highest-ranking department officials—many of whom held doctorates in education—to attend writing classes.[6]

In the following sections, we will examine some basic considerations in choosing effective language. To be effective in business communication, language should be *familiar, conversational, concise, specific and concrete, correct, persuasive,* and *constructive.*

In language it is simply required that it conveys the meaning.

Confucius
Chinese philosopher and teacher

Familiar Language

Consider the following memo excerpt and pity the poor manager who must read material like this dozens of times a day:

Our research and storage workload consists primarily of those records which have expired their "In Office" retention periods, therefore, our temporary disruption of service would not have the same direct impact to the customer as would a department that is dealing with customers on a daily one-to-one basis.

A first rule of thumb, then, is that words should be clear and simple enough for readers to understand your message. Simple words echo the language of everyday speech—they are familiar rather than obscure. As we pointed out earlier, it is more effective to avoid writing in an "elevated manner"—that is, to avoid complicated phrases and technical words or terms that are not used by the average person in daily conversation. Even the memo above can be restored to familiar language when simplified as a short sentence:

Both the research and storage workloads are in-house and so do not affect customer sales.

PITFALLS OF OBSCURE LANGUAGE   Obscure language has the power to confuse rather than clarify communication; it challenges readers to prove their intelligence rather than respond to information. It is a challenge that few readers enjoy. Because it has little in common with the reader's own English, obscure language makes basic person-to-person communication more difficult. Below, for example, are two columns of word choices. The first column features commonly used obscure words and phrases; the second column lists correspondingly simple words and phrases—replacement choices for clearer writing. Now look at Figure 5.1: Compare the word choices on the left with those on the right. The revised paragraphs in Figure 5.1 illustrate how replacing the italicized obscure language with simple words from the list on the right makes each statement easier to read and understand.

OBSCURE LANGUAGE	SIMPLE WORDS
utilize	use
deliberate	think about
concur	agree
transpire	happen
deem	consider
party	person/specific name
the undersigned	I/me
disburse/remunerate	pay
facilitate	aid/help
incumbent upon	must

BUSINESS JARGON   Consider the use of language in each of the following business contexts:

- A credit company refers your overdue car payment to the "fulfillment office" instead of the collection or billing department.
- A bank says "nonperforming assets" when it means "bad debts."
- Instead of referring to companywide "layoffs," an employer announces "workforce adjustments," "downsizing," and "negative employee retention."[7]

In each case, word choice is characterized by **jargon**—the vocabulary peculiar to a specific group, trade, or profession and used by its members to describe their activities. A sort of private language, jargon can also take the form of unexplained abbreviations and acronyms that leave outsiders puzzled. Does *AMA*, for

Ineffective Paragraph Using Obscure Language	Effective Paragraph Using Simple Words
We have *utilized* this list of words so that you can *deliberate* the reading difficulty created by their use. We feel certain that you will *concur* and *deem* revision necessary in order to *facilitate* understanding.	We have *used* this list of words so you can *think about* the reading difficulty created by their use. We feel certain that you will *agree* and *consider* revision necessary to *aid* understanding.

FIGURE 5.1   *From Obscure Language to Simple Wording*

example, refer to the American *Management* Association, the American *Marketing* Association, or the American *Medical* Association? Is a *PC* a *personal computer*, a *professional corporation*, or a reference to being *politically correct*?

Jargon may be useful when the writer is certain that readers understand it. However, because a select group of colleagues may be the only people who understand the jargon of a business or profession, it is important to use plain English when corresponding with people outside those contexts. For example, a recruiter for a large corporation might tell job applicants that the company simply is not hiring rather than try to explain that it is downsizing to increase a return on equity that is below the industry average.

Conversational Language

Closely related to obscure language is language that fails to reflect *conversational language*—that is, familiar word choices and patterns of speech. Inappropriate, nonconversational language is usually impersonal, stilted, overly formal, and often silly. Unfortunately, nonconversational business writing is common in letters, memos, and reports—documents which, after all, are intended for readers who are more familiar and comfortable with conversational language. Table 5.1 lists several phrases that appear frequently in business writing and compares them with conversational equivalents that allow the writer to say the same thing more clearly and more succinctly.

The following suggestions are designed to help eliminate obscure, nonconversational language from first drafts and to produce reader-friendly documents:

■ Try to picture the reader of your document; try to imagine an actual conversation with your reader.

A great many people think that polysyllables are a sign of intelligence.

Barbara Walters
Television reporter
and commentator

TABLE 5.1   *Conversational Phrases in Business Writing*

INSTEAD OF...	SAY...
I wish to acknowledge the receipt of your payment	Thank you for your recent payment.
As per our recent conversation,	As we agreed when we spoke,
Contents duly noted,	I read your comments,
We are mailing the specifications under separate cover.	We are sending the specifications by over night mail.
We regret to inform you that we are in error.	We apologize for our mistake.

- Read your document out loud. Jargon and other forms of obscure language should become obvious and can be replaced with conversational language.
- Ask yourself if you are more comfortable with such personal pronouns as *I, we,* and *you* or if you prefer referring to yourself as "the undersigned."
- Wherever necessary, appropriate, or even possible, simplify, clarify, and shorten your message.

Concise Language

In 1656, the French scientist Blaise Pascal added the following postscript to a twenty-page letter: "I hope you will pardon me for writing such a long letter, but I did not have time to write you a shorter one." An apparent contradiction, perhaps, but this statement actually explains why so many writers are overly wordy: A short, uncluttered document takes more time and thought than one littered with repetition and unnecessary verbiage. Nevertheless, many business writers tend to equate quantity with quality. They apparently believe that they will be perceived as more productive if a document takes four pages instead of four paragraphs. Perhaps they also associate length with professionalism, fearing that short documents indicate that they have nothing to say. Tightening prose is one of the main tasks of revision.

WORDINESS   Given the premium on time in most business organizations, it is not surprising that people have little patience with unnecessary words that hinder rather than enhance communication. *Wordiness* is the choice of vocabulary and sentence structure that require you to get to your point indirectly. Wordy expressions, for example, are often redundant, sometimes combining two or more words that mean the same thing and sometimes using passive constructions that require three or four words instead of one or two. When unnecessary words are removed and passive constructions revised, statements become more concise—shorter and easier to read. The difference between *wordy* and *concise* is clear in the following pair of sentences:

Wordy: The bill that was introduced in Congress was favored by members of the majority party.

Concise: Majority members in Congress favored the bill.

Table 5.2 lists several commonly used wordy and redundant expressions that can be revised to be more concise.

TABLE 5.2 *Revising for Conciseness*	
WORDY EXPRESSION	**REVISED VERSION**
at this point in time	today
at a later date	later
the question as to whether	whether
the reason why is that	because
call your attention to the fact that	remind you
during the course of our meeting	in our meeting
REDUNDANT EXPRESSION	**REVISED VERSION**
enter into	enter
new beginner	beginner
past experience	experience
4:30 p.m. in the afternoon	4:30 p.m.
assemble together	assemble
endorse on the back	endorse

REVISING FOR CONCISENESS   To bring conciseness to your writing, it is important to communicate your message in the fewest number of words. Readers typically do not have time to delve into lengthy documents to find out what you have to say. Although just about anything can be said in a variety of ways, the best way usually involves the fewest—and, of course, the best—words. Because first drafts are often wordy, it is important to revise a document with conciseness as one of your primary goals.

Be especially careful about using empty qualifiers—words and phrases that pad sentences without adding meaning. Evaluate every word and expression by asking yourself if it is necessary. Can your thought be expressed more concisely without loss of meaning? Consider the following sentence, which uses two of the worst offenders among empty phrases:

> *As a matter of fact*, statistics show that *in the case of* the baby-boom genera-tion, Americans know more about world events than their parents did.

Revising for conciseness reveals the following message:

> Statistics show that American baby boomers know more about world events than their parents did.

Specific, Concrete Language

Imagine words and phrases placed along a continuum running from the most abstract to the most concrete. At the abstract end, you might find a word like *cir-cumstantiate*; closer to the concrete end, words like *support* and *prove* are more like-ly to appear. In business writing, concrete words are almost always the most effec-tive because they provide the specific details that people need in their work. They are also easier to remember. Concrete terms have the following characteristics:

Care should be taken, not that the reader may *under-stand, but that he* must *understand.*

Quintilian
Roman rhetoric teacher

- They describe by painting word pictures.
- They quantify ideas. Words that tell readers exactly *how many* or *what per-centage* are usually more effective than words that give vague suggestions.
- They minimize misunderstandings and mistakes.

Even seemingly innocent words like *assistance, topic, issue* and *matter* can be vague and, depending upon your purposes, require further explanation. For example, the sentence "Please let me know if I can be of assistance in this mat-ter" is courteous and probably acceptable in closing most letters. However, if the purpose of your document is to offer real help, you might want to be more spe-cific—for example, "I will be happy to help by forwarding your question about our fall prices to Mr. Jacobsen in the marketing department." Note that in this case, the added words constitute precise information.

Correct Language

Correct language communicates exactly what you want to say in exactly the way you want to say it. Correct language is thus precise in three senses: (1) It is accu-rate, and (2) it avoids exaggeration by practicing *moderation*. Finally, it also avoids miscommunication by following rules of grammar, spelling, and punctu-ation that are understood by both writer and reader.

ACCURACY   Inaccurate, imprecise language threatens not only misinterpreta-tion but costly errors as well. For example, writing in a memo that you "suggest" a change is far different than writing that you "recommend" a change. If your purpose is to *recommend*, say so through precisely chosen words.

Accuracy, of course, requires correct word usage. If you write, for instance, that you are a "disinterested observer," do you mean that you are "uninvolved" or "unbiased"? If you want to say that you are not *involved*, the correct term is *uninterested; disinterested* means *impartial*.

PRACTICAL TIPS

Applying the KISS Principle

You may have encountered the military acronym KISS—"Keep It Simple, Stupid." The principle here is as basic as the phrasing is blunt: Short, clearly worded messages tend to result in clear, effective communication. Many analysts are fond of pointing out that the Gettysburg Address consists of 271 words, the Lord's Prayer 71, and the Ten Commandments 297; the marriage vow has two. During the World War II Battle of the Bulge, U.S. General Anthony McAuliffe needed only one word to respond to a surrender ultimatum: "Nuts!"

In the widely reprinted business ad reproduced here, United Technologies Corp. protests the use of obscure language in business writing.

Among other things, this ad reminds us that much of the language that we share most comfortably has long been pared down to the essentials— "Walk. Don't walk." Much of our shared phrasing is derived from common experiences, activities, or knowledge. "Strike three" is not usually meant literally but we know that something is now over. Although we have developed complicated ways of saying things ("enter into a meaningful romantic involvement"), we usually translate them back into something that gets to the point ("fall in love"). In short, because we accept the principle that "basic events require simple language" in life, there is no reason we cannot accept it in business communication as well.

Keep It Simple

Strike three.
Get your hand off my knee.
You're overdrawn.
Your horse won.
Yes.
No.
You have the account.
Walk.
Don't walk.
Mother's dead.
Basic events
require simple language.
Idiosyncratically euphuistic
eccentricities are the
promulgators of
triturable obfuscation.
What did you do last night?
Enter into a meaningful
romantic involvement
or
fall in love?
What did you have for
breakfast this morning?
The upper part of a hog's
hind leg with two oval
bodies encased in a shell
laid by a female bird
or
ham and eggs?
David Belasco, the great
American theatrical producer,
once said, "If you can't
write your idea on the
back of my calling
card,
you don't have a clear idea."

© United Technologies Corporation 1979

A message as published in the *Wall Street Journal* by United Technologies Corporation, Hartford, Connecticut 06101

MODERATION   Obviously, strengthening the accuracy of your word choice will depend in large part on exercising your vocabulary. Practicing moderation in your judgment also helps. *Overgeneralization*, for example, not only leads to careless word choice but also suggests careless thinking. For instance, you might conclude a report by recommending that your department buy Lotus 1-2-3 because it is "the best value in business spreadsheet programs." Your conclusion *may* be true—but only with qualification. If you surveyed only three software programs, then Lotus may the "best value" among the programs in the *class* that you examined. Moreover, because *best value* in a product can refer to *lowest-priced, most flexible*, or a number of other criteria, that term also requires qualification.

"Absolute certainty," warns writing consultant John Tarrant, "even when justified, can damage credibility."[8] Qualifiers make statements more believable. Even though we live in an age of inflated claims, exaggeration can destroy a writer's credibility. According to communication authority Roy W. Poe, "Even when you can justify the use of such terms as *most, greatest, largest percentage, overwhelming majority*, and *fewest*, it is usually better to give specific data when you can."[9]

An effective method of avoiding exaggeration is to be as specific as possible. Refer to actual numbers, examples, and cases, and draw reasonable conclusions. The following statement, for instance, suffers from unnecessary exaggeration: "The vast increase in minorities and immigrants will make them the most important market segment in the next century." If you revised this statement to reflect a more moderate judgment, you could say: "Because 40 percent of the under-30 population will consist of minorities, they will become a core market by the year 2000." Again, note that because it is balanced with specific language, such potential jargon as "the under-30 population" and "core market" contribute to a more precise statement.

GRAMMAR, SPELLING, AND PUNCTUATION   You can spend hours drafting and revising a document, choosing the best words to suit the exact meaning that you want to convey. However, your efforts will be undermined by errors in spelling and grammar. Indeed, in a recent poll conducted by the executive search firm Robert Half International, 98 percent of executives from 200 large firms reported that grammar and spelling are important factors in reviewing job applicants.[10] Although Appendix II in this text focuses on the basics of grammar, it is important at this point to state that business writing is unacceptable when it contains errors in grammar, spelling, or punctuation.

Despite the importance of grammar and spelling, however, mistakes remain common. In fact, mistakes can have serious repercussions. For example, a punctuation error in a 1916 banking law resulted recently in a federal appeals court decision to deny the national banks the right to sell insurance in small towns.[11] As you can see in the photograph of the picketing auto worker in Figure 5.3, mistakes can, at the very least, create negative impressions. What is your impression of the worker who wrote the sign? Do you think his error helps or hurts his case?

Finally, grammatical and spelling errors can also be embarrassing. A business language group called Grammar for Smart People has received about 15,000 inquiries about hundreds of matters since it began operation. Of these, 15 percent have misspelled the word *grammar*. The word was also misspelled by the group's accountant on its federal tax return.[12]

Persuasive Language

Words can either enliven writing or reduce credibility. When language is being used in an effort to persuade, the writer's success or failure may depend upon whether the language used conveys power or weakness. When words are too weak to carry the burden of persuasion, writing consultant Patricia H. Westheimer calls them "hidden dissuaders."[13] We will consider strong, persuasive language from two perspectives: strong verb choice and assertive phrasing.

FIGURE 5.3   *Making the Erroneous Impression*
This sign is being carried by a Ford assembly-plant worker as he pickets a Toyota dealership near Detroit. He is angered by criticism in high Japanese circles of the education and industriousness of U.S. workers. How does his sign support or undermine his position?

STRONG VERBS   In each of the following pairs of sentences, a weak first sentence has been improved by revising it with a stronger verb. Main verbs and verb phrases are italicized.

> *Weak:* I *want to give you the authorization* to hire temporary help.
>
> *Strong:* I *authorize* you to hire temporary help.

> *Weak:* This rule *will have an adverse effect on* new employees.
>
> *Strong:* This rule *adversely affects* new employees.

> *Weak:* The plant's hiring policy *is in violation of* federal laws.
>
> *Strong:* The plant's hiring policy *violates* federal laws.

In each case, the revised sentence features a main verb that is stronger because it expresses *action* on the part of the subject. The most effective verbs move the reader along in a direct action-oriented way. As you can see, verbs that communicate action also strengthen a message because they are simpler and more direct (and have the added advantage of reducing sentence length). By contrast, "state-of-being" verbs—or "to be" verbs—are more static and passive. A sentence is also less effective when it depends on helping verbs. The noun form of a verb (frequently ending in *-tion*) also weakens a sentence.

ASSERTIVE PHRASING   What would you say about an individual whose letters and memos consistently relied on such phrases as "If you could possibly," "If I could trouble you," "I'm sorry to interrupt you," and "I know how busy you must be"? Some words and phrases lack persuasiveness because they seem too deferential—that is, they suggest that the writer prefers to yield rather than assert opinion or judgment. By implication, then, these words and phrases may tell readers that the writer is in a relatively weak position of power. By eliminating telltale weak phrases, you can communicate greater self-assurance and reflect more accurately the power relationship between you and your reader.

Constructive Language

Because it encourages readers to take action that you support, a positive attitude can be one of your most important communication tools. You can communicate a positive attitude by avoiding certain words and phrasing and by focusing your message on constructive action—on what to *do* rather than on what *not* to do.

AVOIDING NEGATIVISM   Perhaps the first step in communicating a positive approach is to avoid communicating a negative approach. Work to avoid words that encourage negative responses. Some words, such as *blame, wrong, poor, insist, failure,* and *unreasonable,* can even cause readers to get angry or defensive—especially when preceded by the pronouns *you* and *your.*

Words like these not only communicate a variety of negative emotions but also suggest unequal positions of power. At their worst, they even embarrass recipients and will almost certainly discourage cooperation. Your goal should be to communicate diplomatically and to establish a partnership between writer and reader based on the mutual need to act toward some goal.

TAKING A POSITIVE APPROACH   Encouraging your reader to take mutually beneficial action also involves a positive approach that focuses on what you *can* rather than *cannot* do. There are times, of course, when every businessperson must communicate negative or unpleasant information. By taking a positive approach, however, you can present this information in ways that will encourage readers to respond in a productive manner.

Table 5.3 summarizes our seven criteria for choosing the most effective language for business and most other forms of writing.

TABLE 5.3 *Criteria for Choosing Effective Language*	
CHOOSE LANGUAGE THAT IS...	HOW TO DO IT
Familiar	Use simple, direct language; avoid business jargon and other language that obscures meaning.
Conversational	Make your language reflect familiar word choices and patterns of speech.
Concise	Use as few words as possible to make each point; replace wordy phrases and passive constructions with language that makes points directly; use qualifiers with care.
Specific and concrete	Use words that provide specific details, balance general and abstract phrasing with language that offers precise information.
Correct	Use precise language to be accurate and avoid miscommunication; be moderate in your judgments, avoiding overgeneralization and exaggeration; use correct grammar, spelling, and punctuation.
Persuasive	Choose words that convey enough confidence to persuade readers; rely on strong verbs and assertive phrasing.
Constructive	Avoid words likely to encourage negative responses and misrepresent positions of power; communicate a positive approach to working relationships.

PROGRESS CHECK

1. Why is it important to be concise and clear in business writing?
2. Cover the right-hand column of Table 5.3. Based on what you have just read, try to describe each category of effective language.

CONSTRUCTING EFFECTIVE SENTENCES

Like effective language, effective sentences reflect familiar patterns of speech. Appendix II provides an in-depth coverage of sentence construction and grammar. Our focus here is on active versus passive voice in sentence structure, with an emphasis on the effective use of the active voice. In this section, we will highlight three of the most important strategies for constructing effective sentences in a variety of business documents: use of the *active voice*, *brevity and variety*, and *concreteness*.

The Active Voice

active voice
Writing style in which the subject of a sentence performs the action

passive voice
Writing style in which the subject of a sentence is acted upon

In the **active voice**, the subject of the sentence performs its action. When you read a sentence in the active voice, you know who is responsible for the action:

The manager scheduled a meeting.

In the **passive voice**, the subject of the sentence is acted *upon*. In many cases, you can identify the person or thing doing the acting because it is the object of the preposition *by*:

A meeting *was scheduled by the manager.*

In other cases, it is not clear who is taking the action because the subject is not identified:

A meeting *was scheduled.*

The passive voice focuses on events and situations rather than on people taking action. It therefore lacks the vitality of the active voice and typically has a bureaucratic tone. It also uses more words and can be quite vague (sometimes intentionally so). Here are two examples:

- The product *was determined* to be inadequate.
  (Determined by whom? Perhaps the writer does not want to say.)
- A commitment *has been made* to finish the project by the end of the month.
  (Who will finish the project? The sentence does not say, even though the issue is critical.)

Note, however, the use of the passive voice in the following sentence:

A new voice mail system *will be installed* by next week.

Here, the passive voice is appropriate because the installer is less important than what is being installed. There are a few other instances in which the passive voice is acceptable—and some in which it can be more effective than the active. For example, while the active voice is a voice of direct action, the passive voice may be appropriate for diplomacy. You may want to use it, for instance, when making direct requests to superiors or to someone outside your company. Similarly, the passive voice may be appropriate when you are delivering a message on someone else's authority. For example, you can use the passive voice to forward a request or an order without implying that you are exercising responsibility that is not yours. We will discuss the applications of active and passive voice as stylistic strategies in a later section of this chapter.

Brevity and Variety

Short sentences of between 16 and 20 words command attention because they are easy to read and understand. However, many business writers find themselves composing lengthy sentences in the effort to unify related thoughts in sentence units. Although the theory is sound, practice usually demands shorter sentences for greater readability. As you will see later in the chapter, transitional words like *however, therefore, in addition,* and *for example* help to connect ideas while reducing sentence length.

Sentence length also increases when language is indirect and when the writer introduces unnecessary detail. On the other hand, although it is generally advisable to limit sentence length, too many short sentences can also be a problem. They are typically choppy and difficult to read because they *disconnect* related ideas. On the whole, therefore, sentence *variety* is the best way to give a conversational tone to written messages. Variety adds color to writing as it mimics the rhythm of speech. Here, for example, are two versions of an excerpt that could have appeared in the annual report of a company called MediCorp. The first draft fails to show what the writer wants to emphasize and suggests that he or she has not thought through the relationship between major and minor points:

> MediCorp is driving growth in many ways. One way is turning changes in the business environment into opportunities. For example, MediCorp has capitalized on changes in the hospital-supply market. This market has undergone many recent changes because of the need to control health care costs. We adjusted very early to these changes by both government and private employers. Our medical-surgical business, therefore, has grown twice as fast as the industry average. Profitability has thus increased.

In the revised version, the writer has used a variety of sentence structures to emphasize the relationships among important ideas:

> Seeking different ways to drive growth, MediCorp is finding ways to turn changes in the business environment into opportunities. For example, we have capitalized on the recent changes in the hospital-supply market, adjusting very early to the needs of both government and private employers to control health care costs. Growth in our medical-surgical business has doubled the industry average, with profitability increasing accordingly.

Concreteness

Like words, sentences can be either abstract or concrete. In general, abstractions are appropriate when the audience does not require further explanation. However, if you think your readers may not completely understand the abstract version, specific details should be given.

Brief stories are also effective in describing or illustrating your point. For example, if you are writing to advise a department head on recently approved sexual-harassment guidelines, you may choose to include the story of a recent incident. When a story is used, however, it should be short and clearly connected to the purpose of the memo. Never tell a story—even a good one—just to tell it.

Concrete writing is also effective in the close of a document. Even though this approach usually adds several words to the document, it is a good strategy for reinforcing your message at a critical point. It is an especially effective way to close persuasive messages.

CONSTRUCTING EFFECTIVE PARAGRAPHS

Think of the paragraph as the basic unit of composition—the unit in which ideas are grouped to communicate your message. In business writing, the most effective paragraphs follow several important guidelines:

- They are short.
- They include topic sentences.
- They use transitional expressions to connect ideas.

The memo shown in Figure 5.4 illustrates the successful application of these guidelines.

Short Paragraphs

Because few businesspeople have the time or patience to wade through "fat" paragraphs, the shorter you can make a paragraph the better. As you can see in Figure 5.5, the eye is drawn naturally to short paragraphs—paragraphs that are thus more likely to be read, understood, and remembered.

To keep paragraphs as short as possible, limit each paragraph to a single idea. The best points for paragraph breaks can be identified by determining where one thought ends and another begins. For example, consider a page-long memorandum written in one paragraph. Now envision the same memorandum written in four or five brief paragraphs. Obviously, breaking the paragraph into

memo

THOMPSON POWER MACHINERY
7641 Shoreway Avenue Cleveland, OH 44116
(216) 555-7161

TO: Division Managers
FROM: Antoine DuBois
SUBJECT: Division Managers Meeting
DATE: June 14, 199X

A meeting of all division managers will be held at 2 p.m., July 17, 199X, in the Hendersen Conference Room.

The purpose of the meeting is to explain the employee health benefits under the new HMO plan. A representative from the HMO will be there to answer questions.

To disseminate the information, division managers will appoint a spokesperson for each department to attend informative briefings. These briefings will be held daily during the week of July 24-28.

FIGURE 5.4   *Sample Memo: Effective Paragraphing*

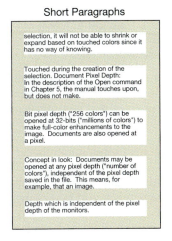

Long Paragraphs

> The following information is not documented in the manual. You can print this document using the Print command in the TeachText File menu.
> Shrinking and Expanding selections with the Lasso: When the point becomes the current tool while a selection is active, but the Lasso was not used to create the current selection, any options checked in the point's menu will not immediately take effect.
>
> Selection in Superselect Mode and then switching back into Paint Mode, the point will be automatically chosen as the current tool. However, the point will not automatically shrink or expand, even if shrink or expand is selected. If you want the selection to shrink past Background color or expand to Background color, you must explicitly (re)select the appropriate options.
>
> Current tool. In addition, if you did not use the point to create the current

Short Paragraphs

> selection, it will not be able to shrink or expand based on touched colors since it has no way of knowing.
>
> Touched during the creation of the selection. Document Pixel Depth: In the description of the Open command in Chapter 5, the manual touches upon, but does not make.
>
> Bit pixel depth ("256 colors") can be opened at 32-bits ("millions of colors") to make full-color enhancements to the image. Documents are also opened at a pixel.
>
> Concept in look: Documents may be opened at any pixel depth ("number of colors"), independent of the pixel depth saved in the file. This means, for example, that an image.
>
> Depth which is independent of the pixel depth of the monitors.

FIGURE 5.5   *Paragraphing for Visual Appeal*

smaller sections, each devoted to a single idea, makes the memo easier to read and understand. Revising the single, long paragraph into sections helps the reader to focus on the issues.

The Topic Sentence

A **topic sentence** states the purpose of a paragraph. It is usually the first sentence in a paragraph, and it is crucial in business writing because it "announces" what the paragraph will say. Here is a first-draft paragraph drawn from our Business Writing in Action exercise in Chapter 4. Note the function of the first sentence as a topic sentence:

> <u>Employees are part of an extensive companywide campaign to promote OS/2.</u> Because we believe that our employees are our best salespeople, we will provide everyone with materials—including brochures—explaining the features of OS/2. The purpose of the brochures is to describe the many advantages of OS/2 over Windows 3.1. In return for your efforts, we have arranged a series of incentives ranging from medals to IBM software, hardware, and cash.

topic sentence
Sentence that states the purpose of a paragraph

The preceding paragraph concerned the competitive environment of OS/2, and the following paragraph dealt with IBM's planned pricing strategy. This paragraph, however, focuses on the topic announced in its topic sentence: the company's plans—namely, the distribution of support materials and the offer of incentives—to enlist employees as "salespeople" for OS/2 software.

The topic sentence also gives readers the option of reading a paragraph in detail or simply scanning it for relevant information. Rather than read every word of every paragraph, people tend to select those paragraphs that satisfy immediate needs. In setting the stage for what follows, the topic sentence "previews" the paragraph for its usefulness to the reader.

Transitions

Transitions are words and phrases that connect ideas to produce coherent paragraphs. Transitional expressions build bridges, both from one sentence to another and from one paragraph to another. Readers need this help as they make their way through the unfamiliar territory of a document. The following excerpt illustrates the important role played by transitions in clarifying the sequence in which the reader is asked to follow the writer's ideas:

transition
Word, phrase, or sentence used to connect ideas and produce coherent paragraphs

> An increase in reported accidents in the plant during the last quarter has led management to focus heavily on safety. Specifically, in April alone, 13 acci-

dents occurred and 5 safety hazards were reported on the shop floor. As a result, 372 work hours were lost at a cost of $7,564. Consequently, every person must be made aware of the importance of safety on the job. The first step will be training meetings held once a week in every office of every department.

Table 5.4 identifies many of the most common transitional expressions. At the left is the idea relationship that each expression signals to the reader; at the right are the words and phrases that communicate that relationship.

CHOOSING AN APPROPRIATE STYLE FOR A DOCUMENT

In conversation, it is fairly easy to gauge someone's communication tone or style: Tone of voice, eye contact, and body language send signals that are often as important as the message itself. However, because these cues are absent from written documents, we must look elsewhere for indications of style. In its most basic sense, the **style** of a written document refers to the *way* something is said rather than *what* is said. It is a reflection of the writer's attitude—the decision to be formal or informal, apologetic or forceful, personal or impersonal, controversial or conservative. The effectiveness of a writing style is determined by the way in which the reader responds.

According to management communication professor John S. Fielden, every written document must meet the unique needs of both your situation and that of the person to whom you are writing. *Style*, according to Fielden, "is that choice of words, sentences, and paragraph format which, by virtue of being appropriate to the situation and to the power positions of both writer and reader, produces the desired reaction and result."[14]

In this section, we will survey several stylistic *strategies*—approaches to document writing that reflect the writer's sensitivity to both situation and audience. We will also discuss the importance of the *"you" approach* as a key to effective reader-centered writing. Finally, we will observe some important principles in *nondiscriminatory writing*.

Style and Writing Strategy

Fielden's definition actually requires that you develop many writing styles instead of one. Each style must adjust to different situations and different audi-

style
Distinctive method of expressing thought in writing or speech; refers to the *way* something is said or written rather than *what* is said or written

TABLE 5.4	*Transitional Expressions*
RELATIONSHIP	WORDS THAT SIGNAL THE RELATIONSHIP
Additionally	Further, furthermore, besides, too, moreover, and, also, in addition, next, then, equally important, finally
Example	For instance, thus, specifically, namely, as an illustration, for example
Contrast	But, yet, however, nevertheless. conversely, on the other hand, on the contrary, still, at the same time, nonetheless
Comparison	Similarly, likewise, in the same way, in comparison, in like manner
Concession	Of course, to be sure, certainly, naturally, granted
Result	Therefore, thus, consequently, so, accordingly, due to this
Summary	As a result, hence, in short, in brief, in summary, in conclusion, finally, on the whole, therefore
Time Sequence	First, next, then, finally, afterward, before, soon, later, during, meanwhile, subsequently, immediately, eventually, in the future, currently
Place	In the front, foremost, in the background, at the side, adjacent, nearby, in the distance, here, there

Source: Lynn Quitman Troyka, *Simon & Schuster Handbook for Writers*, 2nd ed. (Englewood Cliffs, NJ: Prentice Hall, 1990), p. 96.

ences.[15] In general, business writers can be called upon to find the appropriate style for messages required by the following situations:

- Conveying routine information and making direct requests
- Communicating good news and conveying goodwill
- Communicating bad news
- Attempting to persuade

The need to adjust your writing style to your situation also depends on whether the message is intended for a superior, a coworker, or a subordinate. "This is where the politics of writing comes in," says writing consultant Sherry Sweetnam. "You are not going to make demands of your manager, nor are you going to grovel with your subordinates. With a superior, you will probably be diplomatic and tactful. With subordinates, you will probably be more direct and forceful."[16] In general, the person with the greatest power is the one who will determine your communication strategy. If your manager is formal, then you, too, should be formal, even if you normally write in a friendly, open way. The same advice applies to communication with customers and other outsiders with clout: Let them determine the style of your correspondence.

Communicating effectively with different people thus begins with understanding style as an aspect of strategy. Recognizing that situations and people determine your writing style is the first step in developing your strategy. The second step is developing specific techniques for carrying out your strategy. In this section, we will examine techniques for situations that call for the following strategies: being *forceful, passive, personal, impersonal,* or *persuasive.*[17]

BEING FORCEFUL   A forceful writing style is typically used to add emphasis. For example, a memo to company employees regarding safety rules and regulations may warn of life-threatening situations if the rules are not followed. In this situation, it becomes essential to write forcefully.

Forceful writing is defined by several characteristics. It is usually direct in its approach and positive in its tone. Because the active voice always enhances directness, it is typically used when writing forcefully. Seldom are weak words like *perhaps, possibly,* and *might* used to express a point forcefully. Forceful writing also avoids dependent and subordinate clauses that lengthen messages and weaken emphasis.

BEING PASSIVE   When you are writing to individuals in higher positions or communicating negative information, a passive writing style may be the best choice. Passive writing, however, is not a strategy for saying less than you would like. It is a strategy for communicating information that may require some diplomacy on the writer's part. Nor is it a strategy for shifting responsibility. It is a strategy for communicating the level of authority from which you are writing the document. Passive writing also allows the writer to hedge on taking a firm stance when such a position is not warranted either by the situation or by the writer's position of authority. For example, words like *possibly* and *maybe* help to tell superiors or customers something that they might not want to hear. Careful choice of passive language also allows the writer to avoid giving a direct order when such a stance is not appropriate.

BEING PERSONAL   A personal writing style is typically used to convey good news or to persuade the reader to take some action. Moreover, a personal writing style is always conversational in tone, and short sentences are more conversational than longer ones. Generally, this strategy makes use of contractions, personal pronouns, first names, and personal references that make the reader feel that the document has been specially written for him or her.

Personal writing also relies on the active voice, whether to place the writer at the center of the action or to motivate the reader to action. The personal strategy may include direct questions asking the reader about the subject of the document. A good example of a personal writing style is shown in Figure 5.6.

BEING IMPERSONAL   An impersonal strategy is almost always used to convey bad news. Unlike personal writing, this strategy removes the writer from the center of action by using such techniques as the passive voice. Because the writer wants to maintain distance and a level of formality, personal pronouns and first names are generally avoided in impersonal letters. Writing bad-news and negative messages is the subject of Chapter 8.

BEING PERSUASIVE   The goal of many documents—for example, sales letters—is persuasion. The persuasive approach is characterized by descriptive adjectives and adverbs and creates interest through lively and vigorous writing. Persuasive writing is examined in detail in Chapter 9.

The "You" Attitude

The best business writing incorporates the **"you" attitude**—a writing style that focuses on the reader rather than the writer. This focus is conveyed through the

---

The most important words in
the English language:
5 most important words:
I am proud of you!
4 most important words:
What is your opinion?
3 most important words:
If you please.
2 most important words:
Thank you.
1 most important word: You.
                    Anonymous

"you" attitude
Writing style that focuses on the reader rather than the writer

---

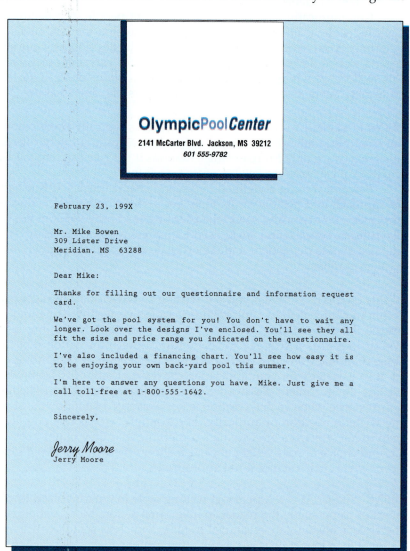

FIGURE 5.6   *Sample: Effective Personal Style in a Letter*

use of the simple word *you* and can be achieved by gearing your writing to audience needs. With the exception of bad-news letters, reader-centered writing should be practiced in almost all letter writing. Figure 5.7 illustrates how an *I* letter can be revised to create a *you* letter.

The "you" attitude derives from the process of *audience analysis* we examined in Chapter 3. To develop a reader-centered style, you must ask yourself questions like the following:

- What does the reader need from me?
- What can I say to motivate the reader to respond favorably?
- What issues interest the reader?
- What is the reader's perspective or position?

As communication consultant Jeffrey L. Seglin points out, your reader

must be convinced that what you are trying to get him or her to do or react to is of some personal value. If you are responding to someone about the lack of job openings…, you don't want to scare off a potential employee by sending a cold form letter. Nothing overly elaborate is necessary, of course, but a cordial negative response to a potential employee now may pay off in the future when your [company] does need someone with his or her expertise.[18]

The failure to focus on the reader, however, is common. For example, sales-communications consultant David Topus believes that overusing the word *I* and failing to explain how a good or service will help the *customer* causes many sales letters to fail. According to Topus, if you simply write that your company has six distribution centers throughout the country, the client may ask, "So what?" But if you add, "So we can get our product to you faster," clients will better understand how your distribution system can help *them*.[19] The "you" attitude also cre-

```
Dear Mr. Hodges:

I am writing to provide information I have regarding Claim 57-
423. I believe that I have included all pertinent forms and
instructions. I am unable to continue processing this claim
without the enclosed forms being completed.

I will be happy to answer questions or discuss this claim with
you.

Sincerely,
```

(A) "I" Letter

```
Dear Mr. Hodges:

In response to your Claim 57-423, I have enclosed information
that you will find helpful in completing the necessary forms,
which are also enclosed. As soon as you have completed the forms
and returned them to me, I will be able to continue processing
your claim.

Should you have any questions or if you would like to discuss
this claim further, please give me a call.

Sincerely,
```

(B) "You" Letter

FIGURE 5.7   *Converting an "I" Letter into a "You" Letter*

INTERVIEW

Letitia Baldrige, Arbiter of Manners and Business Etiquette

Perhaps no one knows more about the power of business letters to establish and cement personal relationships than Letitia Baldrige, nationally known expert on business etiquette and author of *Letitia Baldrige's Complete Guide to Executive Manners*. Ms. Baldrige was Jacqueline Kennedy's chief of staff during the Kennedy administration and currently conducts seminars on etiquette for such major corporations as Westinghouse, Pittsburgh Plate Glass, and Xerox. In this interview, we asked Ms. Baldrige about the importance of etiquette in business letters.

Question: Should business letters be strictly business, or is there a place for the human touch?

Answer: We have to put humanity back into communication. Letters that mention a person's family or health as well as business create relationships that last. It is very hard to create these relationships when communicating via cryptic, abbreviated E-mail messages.

People who receive personal letters sit back and smile at the fact that you remembered their spouse or dog or child. And often, they resolve to take action. For example, as a result of your letter, they may decide to visit your company's booth at an industry fair, even though they had no intention of making the visit in the first place. A personal letter may not make the deal happen, but it makes the deal possible.

ates goodwill—an intangible but priceless quality at the heart of every successful business relationship. In effect, this approach reminds readers that you care enough about their concerns to focus your communication on them.

Nondiscriminatory Writing

connotation
Implied meaning of a word or phrase

Communicate unto the other guy that which you would want him to communicate unto you if your positions were reversed.

Motto of
Aaron Goldman
CEO, The Macke Company

A reader-centered writing style is sensitive to the **connotations** or implied meanings of words. Because certain language contributes to stereotyping, this sensitivity can be especially acute when you are communicating with women and minorities. It is thus important to develop a writing style that is nondiscriminatory in its consideration of others' sensitivity to language.

The norm in nondiscriminatory business writing is to let the preferences of others guide your language choices. For example, it is typical to address women as *Ms.* rather than *Mrs.* or *Miss* unless they specifically request that you do so. If you do not know the sex of your correspondent, several different salutations can be used. For example, it is quite acceptable to use "Dear Sir/Madam" or to address the individual by position title—"Dear Director" or "Dear Customer Service Representative." Many companies commonly address form letters to individuals according to good or service—for example, "Dear Cellular Phone User" or "Dear GE Appliance Owner." To avoid this problem, use a simplified letter format, which does not include a salutation (see Appendix I).

It is difficult to overemphasize the need to avoid terms that perpetuate stereotypes or that devalue others. It is more appropriate, for example, to say, *administrative assistant* than *girl Friday*, and *physically challenged* is a better choice than *crippled* or *disabled*. Similarly, nondiscriminatory writing avoids terms which imply that only men perform certain jobs. No longer does the U.S. Post Office, for instance, refer to employees as *mailmen*, but rather calls them *mail car-*

Question: Why is it so important to write letters rather than use the phone?

Answer: Writing puts the message on record. It is read and reread by the participants, and it is read by other people as well. It may be passed around to other members of the entire organization or to family members if it is a letter of condolence or praise. Personal letters also reflect positively on the writer. Someone who took the time and trouble to write a thoughtfully composed letter is perceived well.

Question: Does proper etiquette require a quick response?

Answer: Etiquette requires that you answer mail quickly—within a week or two—although increasingly this is not done. People aren't even bothering to answer invitations that include an R.S.V.P. They simply show up at the event without a reply. This behavior is thoughtless and inconsiderate, but in the last few years, it has picked up at an accelerated rate.

Question: Are companies encouraging proper etiquette in business correspondence?

Answer: They're encouraging good manners and etiquette is part of it. Companies are realizing that they can't afford to lose customers because young executives are needlessly abusing relationships with customers. Often, these executives don't even realize that they are doing anything wrong. That is what is so sad.

Question: If you were to give young people a single piece of advice on the etiquette of business communication, what would you say?

Answer: Write letters as an antidote to technological overkill. Don't delay or forget them. Don't write them so many weeks late that they've lost their impact. *Do it now.*

Source: Telephone interview with Letitia Baldrige.

---

riers. *Chairman* has been broadened to *chairperson* (or simply *chair*), and *manhours* are now referred to as *employee hours* or *work hours*.

The general use of masculine and feminine pronouns such as *his* and *her* is also quite limited in today's business world. They are used only when they refer to a specific male or female or when *both* are used, as in *"his or her* work." The *his/her* combination is annoying to many readers, however. In most cases, the writer can eliminate this awkward phrasing by converting the sentence from singular to plural and replacing the *his or her* pronoun with *their*.

EVALUATING A FINAL DRAFT

With editing completed and revisions in place, the evaluation of your final draft can begin. As we observed earlier, this process involves evaluating your document against a checklist that reviews the elements of effective style. It also involves carefully *proofreading* your document.

Evaluating Style

The checklist in Figure 5.8 is designed to help you to critique the effectiveness of your document by using the revision suggestions covered in this chapter. Every *no* response means that more revision is needed in a particular area.

Proofread EVERYTHING, dummy!

Thomas "Wayne" Brazell,
U.S. Army
Material Command

Proofreading the Document

The last opportunity to evaluate your document is the proofreading stage. **Proofreading** involves checking for obvious errors or inconsistencies in content, grammar, spelling, and punctuation. Although proofreading is a necessary task,

proofreading
Process of checking for obvious errors or inconsistencies in content, grammar, and spelling

YES	NO	
❏	❏	Has unnecessary business jargon been eliminated?
❏	❏	Is the document written in clear, easy-to-read language?
❏	❏	Is the language conversational?
❏	❏	Is the wording specific and concrete?
❏	❏	Do the words communicate the precise meaning intended?
❏	❏	Have blanket statements and exaggerated claims been eliminated?
❏	❏	Is the document grammatically correct?
❏	❏	Are strong verbs used to communicate the message?
❏	❏	Is the approach positive and constructive?
❏	❏	Are sentences short and varied?
❏	❏	Do the sentences communicate specific information?
❏	❏	Are the paragraphs short?
❏	❏	Does each paragraph include a topic sentence?
❏	❏	Are transitions used to connect ideas?
❏	❏	Does the style of the document reflect the reader's needs and the situation?
❏	❏	Is the "you" attitude employed in the writing style?
❏	❏	Is the document sensitive to diversity issues?
❏	❏	Are all sexist references eliminated?

FIGURE 5.8   *Final Draft Checklist*

it is often overlooked. Communication consultant Sana Reynolds considers the problem to be a failure to see proofreading as time well spent: "I have seen documents," she reports, "that are incomprehensible. They have spelling and typographical errors and include sentence fragments. They make absolutely no sense. When I mention this as gently as I can, I hear, 'I meant to go back and play with it some more, but I never got the time.' I am convinced that making the time is the real issue."[20]

Examples of embarrassing results that can occur when the proofreading stage is skipped frequently appear in the newspaper and on signs posted at retail establishments. One such sign spotted on an interstate highway read, "Eat at Stuckey's and Get Gas." Another eye-catching headline appeared in a church magazine: "Do you know what Hell is really like? Come to our service at 7 P.M. Thursday and hear our new organist." The following ads appeared in the classified section of a major metropolitan newspaper. Apparently the authors had no time to proofread them.

Wanted: Experienced Truck Driver. Willing to Travel on Short Notice. Acme Gunpowder Company 742–2688.	**For Sale**: German Shepherd. AKC Registered. Will eat most anything. Especially fond of children.	**For Sale:** 1984 Cadillac Hearse. Body in good condition.

BUSINESS WRITING IN ACTION
Revising a Draft to Produce a Final Copy

THE ASSIGNMENT

You are now ready to complete the assignment started in Chapter 3 and continued in Chapter 4. As you recall, you have been assigned to write a persuasive memo to the entire staff of IBM, requesting help in promoting and selling the OS/2 personal computer operating system.

THE METHOD

Step 1: Analyze the first draft that you wrote in Chapter 4, paying attention to all the writing basics that you have learned up to this point. Ask yourself whether your draft uses effective words, sentences, and paragraphs; whether it is organized and designed effectively; and whether your writing style is appropriate. Below is the original version along with revision suggestions. As you can see, the memo will require substantial change.

Rewrite title so that it tells readers why they are receiving this memo.

This paragraph focuses too much on IBM. Revise to reflect "you" attitude.

Add motivating heading, "you" attitude. Answer question readers are sure to ask—"What should we say?"

This paragraph is unnecessary. Focus instead on the concept of becoming a spokesperson for OS/2.

Uninteresting heading. Rewrite all headings to make sure readers take notice.

Talk about pricing, advertising, but avoid details that follow. Instead, put information in context of becoming an OS/2 spokesperson.

This information comes too late. Talk about it earlier.

Rewards are too important to bury at the bottom of a paragraph. Use a separate heading to highlight this information.

Rework this information so that it focuses on the reader. As it is, readers might ask, "What does this have to do with me?"

THE REINTRODUCTION OF OS/2

IBM is introducing the OS/2 personal computer operating system to the market. To make the product a success, IBM needs the help of every employee.

To help sell as many OS/2 units as possible, we want you to communicate the merits of this new product to people you know—that includes relatives, friends, acquaintances, and even your family dentist.

OS/2 Competitors

IBM is asking for help because of the tough competitive environment. Right now, Microsoft Corp. is the leading manufacturer of operating software for computers. Microsoft's Windows has already sold more than 10 million units, and its latest version—Windows 3.1—has momentum on its side.

COMPANYWIDE PROMOTIONAL STRATEGY

A three-pronged strategy will be used to promote OS/2:

- Employees will act as product spokespersons.
- Product pricing will be discounted.
- Nationwide advertising campaign will begin.

Employees as Product Spokespersons

Employees are part of an extensive companywide campaign to promote OS/2. Because we believe that our employees are our best salespeople, we will provide everyone with materials—including brochures—explaining the features of OS/2. The purpose of the brochures is to describe the many advantages of OS/2 over Windows 3.1. In return for your efforts, we have arranged a series of incentives ranging from medals to IBM software, hardware, and cash.

Deep-Discount Pricing

We are promoting the product through a special pricing strategy:

- Owners of earlier versions of OS/2 receive the new program free.

(Continued)

BUSINESS WRITING IN ACTION

Revising a Draft to Produce a Final Copy (Continued)

- Substantial discounts slash as much as $146 off the $195 list price.

The end? Memo should tell readers what to do next. It might be a good idea to enclose a response coupon.

<u>Nationwide Advertising Campaign</u>

Tens of millions of dollars will be spent to promote OS/2 in a nationwide advertising campaign.

Step 2: Using this first-draft analysis as the basis of your revision, you produce the following final draft:

WHY OS/2 NEEDS YOUR HELP

In reintroducing OS/2, we at IBM have established ourselves as a leading contender in the computer operating system market. But we cannot take the lead without your help—and the help of all company employees.

<u>How You Can Make a Difference</u>

In the computer-software business, we have learned that word of mouth is one of our most powerful weapons. That is why we want you to tell everyone you know—your relatives, friends, acquaintances, even your family dentist—about the OS/2 operating system.

Tell them that:

- The product has been improved dramatically since its initial introduction five years ago.
- The price has been slashed as an introductory promotional special.
- OS/2 looks and works better than its leading competitor, Microsoft's Windows 3.1.

<u>How IBM Will Help You Become an OS/2 Spokesperson</u>

Help will come in three different ways:

- We will provide you with brochures, handouts, and other materials to help you make the strongest possible case.

You can take several steps to ensure that your document is correct regarding spelling and punctuation. Popular word processing software packages include spell-checks that can be used as a preliminary step, but you should not get into the habit of relying on these too heavily. The computer, for example, cannot tell if you meant to use a particular word; only a person can decide if word choices and sentences are logical and sensible. To ensure that you are correct, logical, and sensible, you should print out your document and read it carefully.

Depending on the length of your document, the proofreading process may require several readings. For example, the first reading might focus on spelling; a second on facts, figures, and numbers; and a third entirely on content. After you make a change, it is a good idea to proofread the entire sentence or paragraph. Finally, proofread the envelope or mailing label to ensure that it, too, is correct.

- We will implement a special introductory pricing strategy that will slash as much as $146 off the $195 list price. Users of the earlier version of OS/2 will receive the program free of charge.
- We will spend millions of dollars to promote OS/2—an advertising budget unequaled by any other current IBM product.

The Rewards

Your efforts are so important to the success of OS/2 that we have created an incentive program that will reward you with:

- Medals
- IBM software
- IBM hardware
- Cash

These rewards are linked to the success you have in convincing people to try OS/2.

How Can I Help?

That is the question I hope you are asking right now. To find out more about becoming an OS/2 spokesperson, complete the coupon below and return it to me as soon as possible.

- -

I would be interested in learning how I can become an OS/2 spokesperson. Please contact me as soon as possible with information and brochures.

Signature   _____

Title   _____

Department   _____

Extension   _____

PROGRESS CHECK

1. Name three important guidelines for writing a good paragraph.
2. What is a topic sentence? Explain its importance.
3. What are transitions, and why are they helpful? Give an example.
4. Explain the importance of nondiscriminatory business writing.

WHAT'S AHEAD

This chapter completes Part II of *Contemporary Business Communication*. So far, we have focused on communication fundamentals, the challenges that you face as you write and speak, and the basic skills that you need to write effectively. Our next step is to apply this wealth of information to specific written documents.

Part III begins this process by examining the letters, memos, and other short documents that you will encounter when you join a business organization. Each chapter in this part explains how specific documents are written and, more importantly, how to focus on the needs of your situation and audience to produce documents that meet your specific goals.

SUMMARY OF CHAPTER OBJECTIVES

1. **Explain the importance of *revising* business documents.**

   Revision—the process of adding, deleting, replacing, and reorganizing words, sentences, and paragraphs—moves your document from first to final draft. Revisions are necessary because it is rare to produce an acceptable document the first time around. The revision process requires that you keep an open mind, be a critical reader, and take a disciplined approach.

2. **Describe the characteristics of clear, conversational language and identify the qualities of concise, concrete, and correct language.**

   Clear language uses simple English to communicate in the most direct way. Business jargon—the technical terminology used by members of a group—is acceptable only when the writer is sure the readers understand it. Conversational language reflects the sounds of everyday speech.

   Concise writing eliminates extra words and phrases. It makes each point as economically as possible. Concrete language includes words and phrases that provide specific details. It quantifies ideas and minimizes misunderstandings and mistakes. Correct words communicate ideas in a precise way. They are accurate, avoid overgeneralizations and exaggerations, and follow the accepted rules of grammar, spelling, and punctuation.

3. **Explain the importance of *persuasive* and *constructive language* in business documents.**

   Persuasive language enlivens writing by communicating self-confidence and power. It relies on strong verbs and eliminates weak phrasing. Constructive language takes a positive approach: It avoids words likely to create negative responses and emphasizes what to do rather than what not to do.

4. **Outline strategies for constructing *effective sentences* and *paragraphs*.**

   Effective sentences use the active voice unless there is a strategic reason not to. The passive voice is appropriate when you are trying to be diplomatic. In addition, effective sentences are short—generally consisting of between 16 and 20 words—and focus on single ideas rather than multiple ideas. Finally, effective sentences are concrete when they provide the specific details that readers need in order to understand a message.

   The most effective paragraphs have three characteristics. They are short: Because short paragraphs are more likely to be read, you should limit each paragraph to a single idea. Effective paragraphs also include a topic sentence that states the purpose of the paragraphs. Finally, effective paragraphs use transitions to connect ideas.

5. **Discuss the relationship between *style* and *writing strategy*.**

   The best business writers learn to vary writing style according to different situations. Style is influenced by requirements like the following: conveying routine information or making direct requests, communicating good news and conveying goodwill, communicating bad news, and communicating persuasive messages. The need to adjust your writing is also influenced by your audience—for example, whether you are writing to a manager, a peer, or a subordinate.

   In general, the most effective business writing reflects a "you" attitude—one that focuses on the reader rather than the writer.

The "you" attitude reflects a reader-centered approach.

6. **Explain the characteristics of *nondiscriminatory writing*.**

   Nondiscriminatory writing takes into account the language preferences of readers. In addition, it avoids terms that perpetuate stereotypes at the expense of another individual or group.

7. **Identify ways to evaluate a *final draft*.**

   A checklist helps to evaluate written documents by focusing on words, sentences, paragraphs, and issues of style. Proofreading is also part of the evaluation process: Check for obvious errors or inconsistencies in content, grammar, spelling, and punctuation.

REVIEW AND DISCUSSION QUESTIONS

1. Why is it important to allow sufficient time to revise your writing? *(Ch. Obj. 1)*

2. How can you judge the effectiveness of a document? *(Ch. Obj. 2, 3)*

3. Explain why it is risky to use obscure language in important business documents. *(Ch. Obj. 2, 3)*

4. Summarize several tips that can help you make your writing more conversational. *(Ch. Obj. 2, 3, 4)*

5. Cover the revised version (right-hand column) in TABLE 5.2. Challenge yourself to come up with your own revised versions of each expression listed in the left-hand column. Can you think of other common but wordy expressions that can be similarly revised? *(Ch. Obj 2, 3, 4)*

6. Distinguish between passive and active voice. Give an example of each. *(Ch. Obj. 2, 4)*

7. Define *style* as it applies to writing. What makes an effective writing style? *(Ch. Obj. 5)*

8. What is the "you" attitude and why is it important? *(Ch. Obj. 4, 5)*

9. What do we mean by "nondiscriminatory" business writing? *(Ch. Obj. 6)*

10. Why is proofreading important? *(Ch. Obj. 7)*

APPLICATION EXERCISES

1. Find an old document you have written, perhaps a class assignment or a work memo. Reread your document and analyze it according to what you learned in this chapter. Can you think of ways to improve it—to make it more concise, readable, direct? Revise it, using the guidelines in this chapter. What changes do you find yourself making, if any? *(Ch. Obj. 1, 2, 4)*

2. Bring an article or a book to class that deals with a topic with which you are familiar. Make sure that the item has been written for someone in that field, not for the general public. Pair off with a classmate who is also unfamiliar with that field and whose own article deals with a topic about which you don't know very much. Read each other's selection, noting examples of jargon, obscure language, and unfamiliar abbreviations and acronyms. Does the jargon seem necessary? Does it make it harder for you to understand what the writer means? Can you and your classmate summarize the main points of each other's selection without using jargon? *(Ch. Obj. 2, 3)*

3. Are there ever times when it might actually be best to write in vague, impersonal terms? What business situations, if any, can you think of that might require such a tone? *(Ch. Obj. 5)*

4. For someone who may be replacing you while you are on vacation, write a description of your current job or a job that you have held in the past. Write two versions of this description—one for an employee who already works for the same company and another for a temporary employee brought in from outside just to fill your job. How do the two descriptions differ? To what extent can you use jargon and other insider language in each? Based on your descriptions, would each person know what to do? *(Ch. Obj. 2, 3, 4)*

5. Could you improve on the following sentences? If so, revise each one. *(Ch. Obj. 2, 3, 4, 7)*

   a. It is to be hoped that we can be of service to you in the future.

   b. This test is to be administered to all new employees, irregardless of the new positions.

c. If we follow these new procedures, it would avoid duplication of effort and also facilitate communication among employees.

d. We hope the information in this chapter will aid you in monitoring the length of your sentences and, if necessary, making the length shorter.

e. As a first step, the number of potential customers versus non-customers should be identified.

6. Revise each of the following two-sentence statements in order to make them more effective. *(Ch. Obj. 4)*

a. We do not know the best way to proceed on this matter. We will ask the employees for their opinion.

b. Bureaucracy, Inc., has many subsidiaries that operate independently. Maverick, Inc., is a subsidiary that has its own chief executive officer.

c. Timmy got mad and threw his milk around the room. His father had to clean it up.

d. I've been exercising regularly. I feel stronger.

e. You're taking a class in business communications. You are writing the answer to these questions.

7. Rewrite each of the following sentences in the active voice: *(Ch. Obj. 2, 4)*

a. It is greatly feared by employees that many of them will lose their jobs after the merger.

b. The new board of directors was approved by the stockholders of the corporation on January 15.

c. All of the relevant information should be examined before making a decision.

d. It was felt by the committee that the best choice for chairperson would be Margarita.

e. Your expense report should be submitted to the accounting office by Friday.

f. When he walked onto the stage, the speaker was greeted with a loud burst of applause.

8. Revise the following paragraph, following the chapter's guidelines for transitions, active voice, and nondiscriminatory writing. Does the paragraph have a topic sentence and, if so, it is in the right place? *(Ch. Obj. 4, 6, 7)*

> Any secretary can lubricate an office chair if she tries. All office furniture is designed by us to be easily lubricated when necessary. Most adjustable chairs have nylon hub tubes that hold spindle rods. Lubricate these spindle rods occasionally. Loosen the set screw in the adjustable bell. Lift the chair from the base so the entire spindle rod is accessible. Apply the lubricant to the spindle rod and the nylon washer. Use the lubricant sparingly to avoid dripping. Replace the chair and tighten the set screw. The secretary can fix her chair and still have plenty of time to see what her boss wants when he calls.

To complete Exercises 9 through 13, use the following information:

- Smokers also run a 20 percent to 60 percent greater chance of dying from heart disease or a stroke.
- Every pack of cigarettes could be labeled: "The price of smoking this pack of cigarettes is $3\frac{1}{2}$ hours of your life."
- Cancer kills about 25 percent of all people who die in the U.S. each year.
- One third of all people who die of cancer have lung cancer.
- Ninety-six percent of lung cancer victims smoked cigarettes.
- In the U.S., death rates from lung cancer are now almost the same for men and women.
- Until the 1960s, lung cancer was relatively rare among American women.
- Many American women didn't smoke cigarettes until after World War II, when changing social customs made it more acceptable for women to smoke.
- The more cigarettes you smoke, the greater your risk of contracting lung cancer.
- If you smoke two or more packs of cigarettes a day, your risk of getting lung cancer is 40 times greater than if you don't smoke at all.

9. Suppose that, as the no-nonsense CEO of Bureaucracy, Inc., you have read the above statistics and decided to ban all cigarette smoking in the company building. Write a memo to your employees announcing the new policy and explaining the reason for it. What style do you feel would be most effective here? Feel free to use any of the previous information that you think would make a more effective memo. *(Ch. Obj. 3, 4, 5)*

10. Having introduced this new policy to your own employees, you now want to spread the word to other companies as well. Write a letter or memo to a good friend who happens to be CEO of another firm, Management Pyramid, Inc. Use a personal writing style to convince your friend to institute the same policy at his or her company. *(Ch. Obj. 3, 4, 5)*

11. Now imagine that you are a file clerk in Bureaucracy, Inc. You have read these statistics about smoking and decided to write a memo to the CEO in which you will suggest a no-smoking policy for your entire office building. What writing style would you use? Write this memo. *(Ch. Obj. 3, 4, 5)*

12. A government employee has been assigned the task of summarizing in a report the latest data on the link between cancer, heart disease, and smoking. Write this report, using the impersonal style. *(Ch. Obj. 3, 4, 5)*

13. A sales representative for a company that markets nicotine patches has been asked to write a sales letter to smokers who might be potential customers. Nicotine patches are supposed to reduce smokers' desire to smoke. Write this letter in a persuasive style that will create good will, focus on your readers' concerns, and convince them to try your product. *(Ch. Obj. 3, 4, 5)*

14. Suppose that you are the manager of the well-known Wild 'n' Wooly Resort. Loretta James, director of the state chapter of the United Way, sends you this letter:

> Dear _____:
>
> The United Way will hold its annual staff meeting on August 17–18 this year. We would like to use your resort for this two-day meeting, which will include about 70 staff members. We would need to use your meeting hall from 8 A.M. to 4 P.M. each day. We would require an overhead projector, a flip chart, and a podium with microphone for speakers who will address our group.
>
> Since some of our staff members will stay at your resort for two days or more, and

> since we will be paying for meals in your dining room, we would like to use your meeting room free of charge. I'm sure the exposure that your facilities will gain during these two days will more than pay for the facilities in your meeting hall.
>
> Please let me know by January 15 if we can use your resort for this meeting. Thank you.
>
> Sincerely,
>
> Loretta James

Naturally, you would like Ms. James and her well-respected charitable organization to use your facilities. However, you have a longstanding policy of charging $300 per day to any group that uses the meeting room. Because it costs you money to air-condition the room, light it, clean it, and provide audio-visual equipment, you can't afford to let people use it for free. If other charities learned that you let this one use it at no charge, they would want to do the same. Write Ms. James a persuasive letter in which you convince her to use your resort even though you have no choice but to charge her group the usual $300 fee for the meeting room. *(Ch. Obj. 3, 4, 5, 6)*

15. Read over your responses to EXERCISES 1, 4, and 9 through 14. Now critique them against the final-draft checklist shown in FIGURE 5.8. How do they compare? If you answer no to any of the checklist items, take another look at your writing. Revise your answers further until you can say yes to every item on the checklist. *(Ch. Obj. 4, 7)*

*B*UILDING YOUR RESEARCH SKILLS

Choose a topic that interests you—perhaps a hobby, a subject you deal with at work, or a topic in your major at college. Go to the library and find two articles that deal with some aspect of this topic. Write a one-page report (typed, double-spaced) based on these sources and bring it with you to class.

*B*UILDING YOUR TEAMWORK SKILLS

Your instructor will divide the class into small groups to read and evaluate each other's reports from the previous exercise. Each group should work on one report at a time, first reading it and then working as a team to suggest ways for revising it. Follow the guidelines in this chapter to analyze the wording of each report, to clarify it, and to make it more concise if necessary. Be very careful to be tactful and constructive in your comments—remember, your turn is coming! All team members should feel free to speak up if they feel someone is being too hard on a writer.

COMMUNICATING IN A WORLD OF DIVERSITY

As an admissions officer for the business school of a large university, you have noticed that the number of women enrolling in your Masters in Business Administration (M.B.A.) program has fallen 10 percent over the last three years. You do some research and learn the following facts:

- According to many college officials, the percentage of women enrolling in M.B.A. programs has fallen 25 percent or more in recent years.

- At the University of California–Los Angeles, women represented 40 percent of the entering M.B.A. class in 1985 but only 30 percent in 1992. Female enrollment in the University of Chicago M.B.A. program has fallen from 27 percent in 1990 to 23 percent in 1992; at Indiana University from 31 percent in 1989 to 23 percent in 1992; and at Washington University from 31 percent in 1988 to 25 percent in 1992.

- According to Joseph Pica, director of the M.B.A. program at Indiana University, "We're all taken aback." Adds Eric Mokover, head of the M.B.A. program at the University of California–Los Angeles, "Frankly, we're at a loss to explain it."

- Possible explanations: women are starting to question the value of getting an M.B.A.; women worry about getting stopped by "glass ceilings" in companies that may not promote them beyond a certain level; a lack of female business professors may mean a lack of role models; some women perceive conflicts between business careers and family needs.

- Possible solutions: conducting focus groups with female students, alumni, professors, and M.B.A. applicants; doing special mailings to convince more women to apply after they have requested information; hiring more female business school faculty; actively recruiting more women students.

Write a memo to the Dean of the Business School in which you discuss this trend and recommend several actions. You want to persuade him to budget funds for further research.

Source: Gilbert Fuchsberg, "Female Enrollment Falls in Many Top M.B.A. Programs," *The Wall Street Journal*, September 25, 1992, pp. B1, B6.

CASE 5.1

Helping Those Who Help Themselves

Would you lend money to Dorothy Wallace? Separated from her husband, Dorothy must support herself and her two teenagers on welfare. She hasn't held a steady job since 1984. She admits that her credit rating has been "ruined by accounts I messed up."

But thanks to the Women's Self-Employment Project, Dorothy has turned into a good credit risk.

The Women's Self-Employment Project (WSEP) was founded in 1986 to help low-income women who were interested in self-employment as a way out of poverty. Its funds come mainly from contributions and loans by foundations and corporations. Dorothy Wallace borrowed $800 from the Project to set up her own business selling perfumes door-to-door in downtown Chicago offices.

Although Dorothy owes the Project $33.22 every two weeks, she is careful to make $40 payments in order to reduce interest charges. Lately, she has started to talk about opening her own office and working her way off welfare.

Over the past three years, the Women's Self-Employment Project has loaned about $60,000 to sixty women, all of whom would be considered bad risks by any bank. Moreover, although WSEP didn't even check credit histories, the group hasn't suffered a single default on any loan. (As a comparison, the American Bankers Association reports that, for the American population as a whole, the delinquency rate is around 3 percent on credit cards and 3.75 percent on personal bank loans.)

What's WSEP's secret? Peer pressure. Borrowers like Dorothy Wallace must participate in "borrowing circles" of five women who meet twice a month. The five members choose the first two of their circle to get loans. These first two borrowers must then stay current on their repayments, and all five circle members must attend meetings regularly before the third loan can be made. "Peer support and peer pressure," explains WSEP director Connie Evans, "really serve as a good way to lower your risk."

The other members of Dorothy Wallace's borrowing group also hope to start their own businesses. One borrowed $600 for materials to make jewelry that she sells. A retired bank clerk borrowed $700 to buy a sewing machine; she sells hand-sewn lingerie and linens. Another circle member, who borrowed $500, peddles fruit and customer gift baskets in local parks. A woman with four children of her own and four foster children plans to learn to read and obtain a day-care license.

Naturally, all of these women appreciate the financial support. The emotional support of their groups, however, is often far more important. Indeed, the women in Dorothy Wallace's borrowing circle have nicknamed their group, "Too Blessed." As Dorothy says, "They gave me a chance to start all over again."

Questions and Assignments

1. Describe the Women's Self-Employment Project and its loan programs.
2. Why has WSEP had such good results getting its loans repaid?
3. Suppose that you're a fund-raiser for WSEP. Write a letter to the board of directors of a large corporation in which you persuade them to provide financial support to the WSEP loan program.

Source: David Wessel, "Small Victories," *The Wall Street Journal*, June 23, 1992, pp. A1, A6.

CASE 5.2

In-Flight Takes Off at Digital Technology

In-Flight Phone Corporation doesn't want you to get any peace during plane flights. The company, based in Oak Brook, Illinois, plans to introduce lots of new gadgets to your airplane seat. It's already started installing advanced digital-telephone systems, including video screens and ground-data links, in planes owned by corporate customers like USAir, which is currently outfitting its fleet of new Boeing 757s.

Every passenger will have a handset stored in the armrest and a 4.5-by-6-inch screen mounted in the seat ahead—just above the tray table. As you take your seat, you will see your name and "WELCOME ABOARD" printed on your screen. Next come the news and weather, followed by a menu with instructions (in four languages) for using a credit card to make phone calls from your seat. Thanks to new digital technology, sound quality on calls will be much better than on present air-phone systems. And, for the first time, you will also be able to receive phone calls at 30,000 feet. Incoming calls will be silently announced on your screen so they don't disturb dozing passengers.

If you need to communicate while in flight, you will be able to transmit computer or telefax data from your seat. Passengers carrying laptop computers can simply plug them in and go to work; those without can type out messages on the system's built-in keypad and send them to planet Earth. The In-Flight system will make every airplane seat a work, shopping, and entertainment center, giving passengers access to computerized catalogs, Nintendo games, and electronic mail from the office.

Market analysts predict huge growth in the market for in-flight digital-communications systems. Airline passenger volume, for example, is expected to rise from the current 452 million to nearly 800 million by 1999. Meanwhile, the number of U.S. commercial planes carrying telephones—currently around 1,700—is expected to double by 1995. According to United Airlines spokesman Joe Hopkins, on-board telephone service has already "evolved from a unique feature to an everyday necessity. We now hear complaints when it's *not* available." Adds David Shipley, an assistant vice president at USAir: "It's a communications and profit center for us all. If you want to compete with the majors, you'd better have digital phones."

Questions and Assignments

1. Describe the technical features of In-Flight's new telephone system.
2. Suppose that you are head of sales training at In-Flight. You want to train In-Flight representatives to emphasize the customer-service benefits offered by the company's new technology. Being careful to adopt the "you" attitude, write a memo that tells company reps how to sell customers on what your system's features can do for them.

Source: Bruce Van Voorst, "The Office Goes Airborne," *Time*, June 8, 1992, p. 72.

ORGANIZATIONAL LETTERS AND MEMOS

6

Writing Direct Requests

CHAPTER OBJECTIVES

After studying this chapter, you should be able to:

1 Explain how *letters* differ from *memos*.

2 Explain the functions of the opening, middle, and close of a *direct request*.

3 Explain how to write *requests for information*.

4 List the characteristics of *letters placing orders*.

5 Distinguish between *credit applications* and *inquiries about creditworthiness*.

6 Identify the elements of an effective *claim letter*.

7 Describe two types of request letters associated with *personal references*.

8 List the essential details included in an *invitation*.

9 Describe how the relationship between the writer and reader affects *internal request memos*.

The difficulty is not to write, but to write what you mean, not to affect your reader, but to affect him precisely as you wish.

Robert Louis Stevenson
Scottish author

A BRIEF TREND IN DIRECT REQUESTS

Kevork K. Kalayjian was mad as hell and wasn't going to take it anymore. As controller of Bouley (pronounced *boo-LAY*), one of the trendiest French restaurants in New York, Kalayjian was fuming over sloppy vendor letters. Math errors were common, and worse yet, perforated computer strips were still attached to many letters. "[We] spend a lot of time cleaning paper," Kalayjian complained. "When you get paper with the [strips] still on it, you can't fit it in a folder. It makes life difficult for everybody."

Determined to upgrade what he considered unacceptably low standards, Kalayjian composed a letter to inform vendors of his plans for dealing with such problems. Letters or invoices with perforated strips still attached, he announced, would incur "productivity charges" of $1 per page; each arithmetic mistake would cost $5, and pricing problems would result in $50 fines.

Moreover, Kalayjian went on to trace the need for such penalties to a growing trend among American workers toward laziness. "We don't know about you," his letter stated, "but we've had enough of everybody taking a shot at American Productivity.... Well! We're not going to stand by while the Japanese and others make fun of American Worker Productivity. We are going to do something about it."

The response to the policy announced in Kalayjian's letter was predictable: Vendors were insulted and made it clear that they wouldn't take it either. "Has New York's No. 1–rated restaurant sunk to new depths?" asked one vendor out loud. "Is business so bad for Bouley that they must nickel and dime their suppliers and insult our American laziness?"

Realizing that Kalayjian's letter had done more harm than good, owner David Bouley was forced to institute a damage-control campaign. Characterizing his controller's letter as a "joke," Bouley followed with a letter of his own disavowing any knowledge of productivity penalties and fines for human error. Moreover, he denied any advance knowledge of the controller's letter, concluding that he "would never have allowed such a letter to be sent." The upshot of this little correspondence saga, observed *The Wall Street Journal*, was the spectacle of an exclusive New York restaurant eating its own words.[1]

CHAPTER OVERVIEW

In its most basic sense, Kervork Kalayjian's letter delivered a *direct request*: In effect, it asked, "Can you please take more care in your correspondence so that we at Bouley do not have to spend time correcting your errors and tearing your computer strips?" As written, however, the message failed as a direct request.

Besides neglecting to take into account potential reader reaction, it was anything but direct. Instead of asking vendors to be more businesslike, the letter confused the issue by veering off on the "productivity crisis" that plagued U.S. workers.

This chapter explains how to craft an effective direct request by beginning with a statement of purpose, adding necessary details, and ending with a courteous close that communicates goodwill. As you will see, the most effective direct requests use an organizational pattern that places key points up front. We will examine different kinds of direct requests, such as requests for information, orders, credit-information requests, claims, requests for personal references, and invitations. We will also discuss the unique requirements of requests made in memo form. We will begin by discussing the direct request in terms of its audience and then analyze the differences between messages written in letter form and memo form.

THE AUDIENCE

Direct requests are written to people both outside and inside the business organization. The four most important potential audiences for these requests include *customers, suppliers and other businesses, government agencies*, and *employees* (both current and potential). As you recall from Chapter 1, these four audience groups are the same for all the different types of business correspondence examined in this text.

Audience Groups

As we observed in Chapter 1, an organization's external communication helps it to establish itself in the marketplace and to maintain smooth operations in its work with other organizations and individuals. In addressing different groups as external audiences, direct requests perform very common—and often very specific—functions in establishing relationships. When you are preparing direct-request documents, therefore, it helps to think in terms of the specific requirements of each of these audience groups.

CUSTOMERS   Requests to customers have two equally important purposes. They ask for something and they attempt to maintain goodwill. Three rules of thumb thus apply in writing direct-request letters to customers. First, the last letter a customer receives is generally the one that he or she remembers best. If it is negative—if, for example, it uses the wrong tone or is filled with grammatical errors—it may affect the quantity and quality of future business transactions.

Second, as we observed in Chapter 5, customer correspondence should avoid obscure or otherwise unintelligible business jargon. Finally, remember that the "you" attitude in writing reminds the customer that his or her interests come first.

SUPPLIERS AND OTHER BUSINESSES   Business-to-business requests are quite common. Whether you are inquiring about credit terms or asking for office-rental information, be careful to keep requests direct. Vague requests only confuse. Therefore, adopt such policies as describing merchandise in the supplier's language and include dates, account numbers, and part numbers from invoices and bills of lading. Be as specific as possible about what you want to accomplish.

GOVERNMENT AGENCIES   Government bureaus and agencies play a major role in the life of every firm. Both profit-seeking and nonprofit organizations commonly request information from federal, state, and local governments on taxes, workplace safety, zoning, and other issues. Because you are dealing with a bureaucracy, your letters must be direct, simple, clear, and restrained.

Tax expert and computer-software developer Andrew Tobias recently received a letter from the Internal Revenue Service telling him that, due to a mistake on Schedule E of his tax return, he owed the government money. Tobias, of course, wanted to know what the error was, and he also wanted to complain in no uncertain terms. Ultimately, he reconsidered: "I tore up [my first letter] and sent, instead, a meek request that they identify my error. Call it a sixth sense I have for dealing with a bureaucracy."[2]

EMPLOYEES AND POTENTIAL EMPLOYEES   Requesting information or action from employees is typically done through office memos or electronic mail. These requests may involve anything from wanting to know the status of a project to requesting attendance at a meeting. Direct requests are also sent to and about potential employees. For example, a manager interviewing a potential job candidate may request information on the candidate's job history or educational background.

Because dealing with prospective employees can present legal problems, letters and memos must be precise. Experts suggest a cautious approach. Focus on facts, not opinions, and show all statements with contractual implications to an attorney. In addition, readers are likely to respond more favorably if you use an objective rather than adversarial tone. For example, if you are requesting more information about a candidate's job history, avoid an accusatory tone even if you suspect that the candidate doctored the facts.[3]

Some of the most important differences between letters and memos can be explained by the different audiences to which they are directed, and we will explore these audience differences in the next section. We will discuss other specific differences between letters and memos in the context of direct requests, but we can apply the basic differences in audiences to all types of correspondence.

Letters and Memos: Audience and Purpose

Because letters and memos are written to different audiences, they differ in fundamental ways. These differences are reflected on several levels of purpose, content, and style, including *distribution, possible benefits, language,* and *level of detail.*

DISTRIBUTION   While a letter is usually sent to a single person outside the organization—a customer, a supplier, a government official—memos are generally distributed within a company. Indeed, the purpose of memos is to maintain a flow of information among people at various organizational levels. Because they may be routed to managers, co-workers, and subordinates, memos are also more likely to have multiple audiences.

POSSIBLE BENEFITS   Just as every letter has the potential to create goodwill for a company and its products, every memo has the potential to improve an individual's status within the company. For example, businesspeople who use memos to communicate effectively on critical issues make positive contact with individuals who can contribute to their success within the organization.

LANGUAGE   Whether addressed to co-workers, subordinates, or managers, memos often use less formal language than business letters: After all, people who work for the same company, often in the same building or even the same department, tend to be less concerned about formality with one another than with outsiders. However, this is not always the case, especially when a subordinate is writing to someone at a higher organizational level. In general, let your relationship with the reader guide your decision regarding formality.

In addition, because most people in a company speak the same business language, memos are often filled with jargon—esoteric shorthand language appropriate only to those in the know. Used in letters to customers, however, jargon risks alienating readers.

LEVEL OF DETAIL   People in your own company are more likely to be familiar with the subject of your communication than outsiders. As a result, less detail may be needed in a memo than in a letter. Whether writing a memo or letter,

TABLE 6.1	*Comparing Letters and Memos*	
	LETTERS	**MEMOS**
Distribution	Usually sent to a single person outside the organization	Generally distributed within a company
Possible Benefits	Potential to create good will	Potential to improve an individual's status within the company
Language	High degree of formality generally required	Generally less formal than letters when addressed to business colleagues; may also contain more jargon
Level of Detail	Cannot assume shared experiences or knowledge and must be detailed enough for an outsider	Familiarity of co-workers with projects may make many details unnecessary

you should analyze your audience to find out how much your reader understands. If background is needed, provide it, and use language appropriate to the knowledge and sophistication of the reader.[4]

These differences between letters and memos are highlighted in Table 6.1. They will become more apparent as you study different types of correspondence. We will begin by examining the art of writing an effective direct request.

WRITING DIRECT REQUESTS

A **direct request** is a straightforward written message that asks another individual for information, merchandise, or assistance. Direct requests are made in both letters and memos and are used to obtain information, order merchandise, gain credit information, file claims, obtain personal references, and extend invitations. The most effective direct requests use the following organizational pattern: They start with the purpose, add specific details, and end with a courteous close that leaves the reader with positive feelings.

direct request
Straightforward written message that asks another individual for information, merchandise, or assistance

Opening a Direct Request

A direct request is most effective when it gives readers crucial information in the opening paragraph. Business-writing authorities John S. Fielden and Ronald E. Dulek characterize the best approach as "bottom-line" writing: Within the first few sentences, readers should be informed of the reason that you are writing to them as opposed to someone else, the purpose of your request, and the action that you want them to take.[5]

This approach is designed to save your readers' time. Instead of forcing people to read an entire document, you can state your purpose in your opening paragraph—as does the writer of the letter in Figure 6.1.

The finest eloquence is that which gets things done.

David Lloyd George
British prime minister

Middle of a Direct Request

The middle of the request provides the additional details that the reader needs in order to take action. When a request is simple, it can be stated in full in the opening paragraph. Nothing more need be said and the writer can move directly from the opening to the close.

However, when additional information is necessary, the reader's needs should determine what to include and the order in which to provide the information. In the letter in Figure 6.2, for example, the second paragraph tells the reader specifically what the writer wants.

If you get all the facts, your judgment can be right; if you don't get all the facts, it can't be right.

Bernard M. Baruch
American financier

ALLEN AND FROST INTERNATIONAL
300 North Crescent Drive
Beverly Hills, CA 90210
213-555-8345

October 22, 199X

Mr. William O'Brian, Vice President
National Society of Business Consultants
One Franklin Plaza
Philadelphia, PA 19101

Dear Mr. O'Brian:

Thank you for the opportunity to speak at your annual meeting.
Although my arrangements are in order, I have several meeting-
related questions:

- Will I meet you before my presentation?
- May I see the meeting room in advance?
- May I check the audio-visual equipment I ordered to make
  sure it is in good working order?

Please get back to me by November 15 about these details.

It is an honor to address the National Society of Business
Consultants. I look forward to it and to my visit to Chicago.

Sincerely,

Joan Frost

Joan Frost
President

FIGURE 6.1   *Direct-Request: Opening*

Gear the middle of your letter or memo to the knowledge and sophistication of your audience. Use language that the reader will understand and avoid business jargon that clouds your request. Use a tone appropriate to the person to whom you are writing. For example, a forceful tone might be appropriate if you are requesting action or information from a subordinate. But when writing to a customer, a tone that is both objective and personal might be better. One of the best ways to ensure that your document supplies all the needed details is to put yourself in the position of the reader and then ask yourself whether the letter is complete and understandable.

Closing a Direct Request

Close your document by focusing once more on the action that you want the reader to take. Be as specific as possible. For example, instead of saying, "Please send

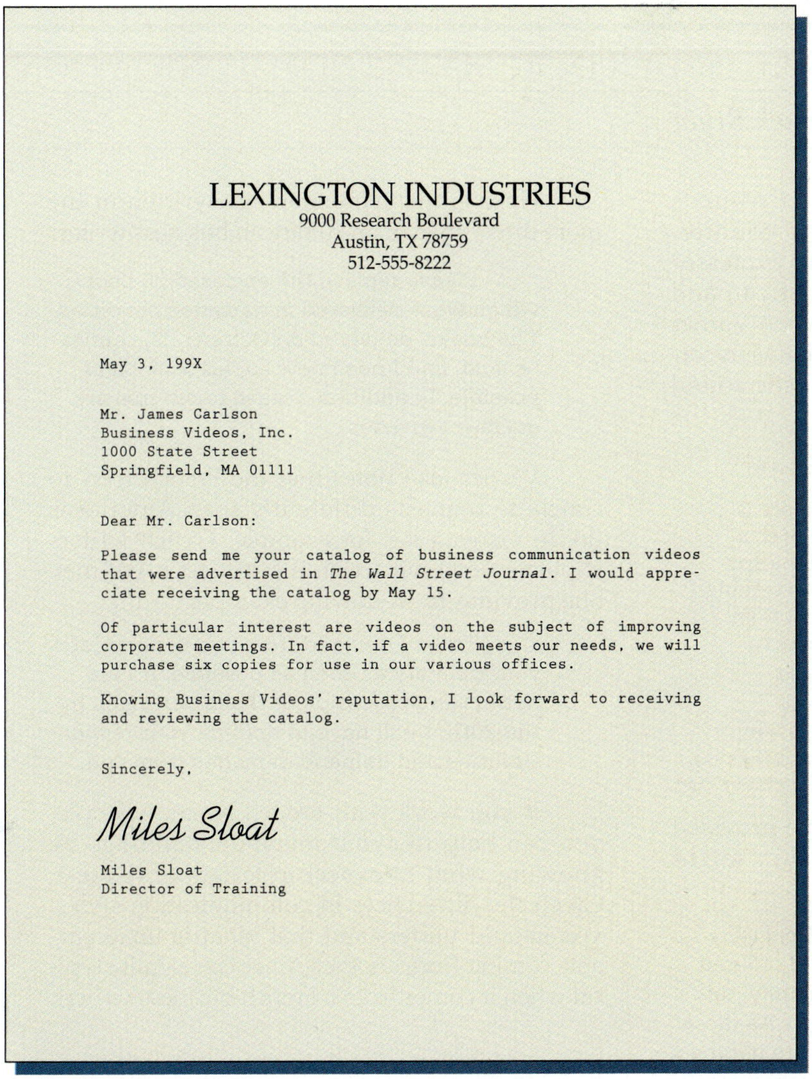

LEXINGTON INDUSTRIES
9000 Research Boulevard
Austin, TX 78759
512-555-8222

May 3, 199X

Mr. James Carlson
Business Videos, Inc.
1000 State Street
Springfield, MA 01111

Dear Mr. Carlson:

Please send me your catalog of business communication videos that were advertised in *The Wall Street Journal*. I would appreciate receiving the catalog by May 15.

Of particular interest are videos on the subject of improving corporate meetings. In fact, if a video meets our needs, we will purchase six copies for use in our various offices.

Knowing Business Videos' reputation, I look forward to receiving and reviewing the catalog.

Sincerely,

Miles Sloat

Miles Sloat
Director of Training

FIGURE 6.2   *Direct-Request: Middle*

me the information in the near future," write, "Please send me the information about my December 12–December 24 reservation no later than November 12."

The close of many business letters is also designed to communicate goodwill. It tells the reader that you value his or her product, service, or contribution. The closing of the letter in Figure 6.2, for example, accomplished both goals—restating its request and communicating goodwill:

> Knowing Business Videos' reputation, I look forward to receiving and reviewing the catalog.

Positive language also helps to motivate readers to comply with your request. If you know the person to whom you are writing, a personal comment is appropriate. For example:

> Please send me the information on the Model 4567 facsimile machine. By the time we see each other at the convention in two weeks, I'll be ready to place an order.

Memos, on the other hand, typically do not use the same type of close and often come to an abrupt end after the details of the request have been given.

INTERNATIONAL ISSUES IN BUSINESS COMMUNICATION
Direct Requests, French Style

French businesspeople write direct requests differently than their American counterparts, says Illinois State University professor Iris I. Varner, who compared American and French business correspondence. When Varner compared the phrasing of routine claims in correspondence from both countries, she found these differences:

FRANCE	UNITED STATES
■ The problem and its consequences are stated first to provide background information	■ The sequence is reversed, with a request for a specific action coming first (the bottom-line approach)
■ With the stage set, the writer then requests a specific action to solve the problem	■ The request is followed by reasons why the action is needed.

Consider the following example provided by Varner. A French business writer might phrase a claim letter as follows:

> The Transports du Centre Co. just delivered to me the 20 books that I ordered from you on October 28. Unfortunately, the package came in very bad shape…. As these books, all more or less damaged, are improper for selling, I return them to you, at your cost, and pray you to replace them urgently.

Here is the same message written in the more direct style of an American business writer:

> Please replace the enclosed 20 books, which were delivered in damaged condition. The books, delivered on October 28, cannot be sold, and I need new copies as soon as possible. In addition, please reimburse my mailing expenses.

Varner also notes that the French tend to conclude requests differently than Americans do. In many cases, for example, French writers stipulate potential action if a request is not met. She provides the following example:

> Thus, I demand from you to complete your delivery as soon as possible. If I am not in the possession of these perfumes by the 20th, I will have to enforce your responsibilities and demand damages from you.

If you work with French businesspeople, you can help to avoid misunderstandings by knowing what to expect in letters of request. Given the differences in communication styles, you should understand that what is unacceptable coming from another American is quite typical when it comes from a French business writer.

Source: Iris I. Varner, "A Comparison of American and French Business Correspondence," *Journal of Business Communication*, Fall 1988, pp. 55–65.

Writing Effective Requests

The following suggestions are designed to help you in writing effective direct requests. These suggestions also apply to other documents that take a direct approach.[6]

- *State your purpose in full*. When you have more than one purpose in writing a document, make all of your goals clear in your opening paragraph. It is a mistake to begin by stating one purpose and then "hiding" the others somewhere in the middle of your document. Your reader may assume either that you are asking for only one thing or that you attach more importance to your first request.
- *Provide information in the proper place*. Even when you are convinced that readers need background information, state your direct request at the beginning of the document and then provide details as you proceed. The following example from Fielden and Dulek demonstrates what can happen when you ignore this approach:

> Suppose your company plans to raise prices on October 1. You want to urge your most important customers to place their orders before

that date. But you do not know for certain whether they want to buy or not. You are afraid to bottom-line your purpose and begin your letter with, "Please get your order in before September 30." You are afraid of appearing too pushy....

In situations like this, most writers start rehearsing the history of price changes in the recent past, leading up to the fact that there is going to be a price change on October 1. Only then do they feel safe enough to tell the readers that they had better get their orders in before September 30.[7]

Fielden and Dulek disagree with this strategy. The result, they contend, is likely to be frustrated readers who do not understand why you are bombarding them with information and who, as a result, may pay little attention. They recommend that instead of beating around the bush, you state your purpose in the opening paragraph and explain later.

- *Seek the action-oriented response.* Focus on the actions that you want the reader to take in response to your request. This approach, of course, may be easier in some cases than in others. For example, while you may have no problem making a direct request to a subordinate, it may be more difficult to be as direct with someone at a higher organizational level. However, even when dealing with managers, the direct approach is often the most effective.

- *Seek the useful response.* Try to maximize your odds of getting a useful response by anticipating the details that your reader will need. Here, for example, is a simple but vague request that might be made to a business writing consultant:

  > Please send me information about your business writing services so that I can determine whether they fit our business needs.

  You are much more likely, however, to get the information that you actually *need* by phrasing your request as follows:

  > The consumer-products division of our company is interested in hiring a business writing consultant to work with a group of 20 customer-service representatives, and we would like to learn more about your services. The consultant we hire will provide two one-hour workshops that focus on handling difficult complaint situations.

  While the first version provides very little practical information, the second helps the reader by *informing* him or her of your needs.

- *Strike the proper tone.* Remember that being direct is not necessarily the same thing as being overbearing: A nonintimidating request can still get your message across. For example, instead of saying, "Call me immediately after you have reviewed this proposal," it may be better to say, "I am eager to hear what you think about this proposal." Gear your tone to your purpose and to your analysis of how the reader will respond.

- *Reflect your authority to make your request.* Requests are part of everyday business life, and your documents should reflect your position of power in relation to your recipient. For example, don't apologize for your request even if it involves a great deal of work; unnecessary apologies lessen your perceived power.

- *Edit to delete minor points.* Focus on your specific purpose by weeding out unimportant or extraneous points from the middle of your letter. For example, comments about unrelated events occurring in the company should not be included.

- *Design your request for clarity.* Use an effective layout to focus your reader's attention on your request. For example, use bulleted lists and sur-

INTERVIEW

Mary A. De Vries, Publishing Consultant and Expert on Word Usage

Although direct requests are among the most commonly written documents in business organizations, they are often poorly written. We asked editorial and publishing consultant Mary A. De Vries for her advice on improving the effectiveness of these documents. De Vries has authored more than thirty books as well as professional articles on word usage and written and spoken communication.

Question: Even though direct requests are relatively simple and straightforward, is it important to plan in advance what you want to accomplish?

Answer: Always. Plan what you want to say, how you want the reader to respond, and how you can help the reader provide what you want. For example, would it help to enclose a questionnaire? An outline of your project? A checklist for giving quick answers?

Question: When writing a direct request, how important is it to try to maintain the reader's goodwill? Can a clipped, unfriendly request defeat your purpose?

Answer: It's very important. If you were the reader, would you want to expend extra effort on someone who sounded unfriendly and unappreciative? Remember the old cliché about catching more flies with honey than with vinegar.

Question: What are some of the most serious mistakes writers make when they compose direct requests?

Answer: Most writers are too vague and don't provide specific examples of what they want. They don't focus on the specific request until the second or third paragraph. They don't plan their remarks, so they often aren't stated in a logical order. They are either too abrupt and demanding or too timid and apologetic about bothering the reader. They fail to give a date by which they need the response. They neglect to enclose a stamped, self-addressed envelope. They don't explain how they are going to use the information they need. They sound cold, unfriendly, and unappreciative.

Question: Since claim letters are written when something goes wrong, there is often a tendency to write these letters in anger. Do you recommend a cooling-off period before these letters are written?

Answer: Definitely. Hostility only aggravates a situation. If something needs rectifying, you must sound reasonable and fair if you want to

round the specifics of your request with white space. Underlining key points also adds emphasis.

We will turn next to the major types of direct requests typically required in business today: *requests for information, orders, credit-information requests, claims, requests for personal references,* and *invitations.* We will focus first on letters to company outsiders and then on internal company memos.

PROGRESS CHECK

1. Name four distinct audiences that would receive direct requests from businesspeople.
2. List the major types of direct requests used in business.

REQUESTING GENERAL INFORMATION

With information as much a business commodity as any tangible product, letters requesting information are becoming an increasingly common feature of commerce. As an important service commodity for many businesses, information itself must be packaged and made available to customers, suppliers and other businesses, and government agencies. Moreover, information supply requires

motivate the reader to be willing to correct the problem.

Question: Are people less willing to give job references today than years ago because of the possibility of being sued? Are requests for references often ignored?

Answer: Companies have different policies regarding job references, and some won't provide them for legal or other reasons or will provide only basic information such as term employed and job title. But requests for references aren't simply filed in the wastebasket, and you shouldn't hesitate to ask for one unless the company has a stated policy of not providing them.

Question: When writing a direct request in the form of a memo, how important is it to adjust the language and style of the request to your internal audience? That is, should the language and style differ depending upon whether the letter is being written to a subordinate, a co-worker, or a manager? What kinds of changes do you recommend?

Answer: It's very important to tailor a message to the audience. It doesn't matter if it's a memo or a letter or whether the message is going inside or outside the company. For example,

address superiors with a title, and don't call them by their first names unless asked to do so. Use courteous, straightforward language with superiors and avoid the casual remarks or personal comments that you might use with a peer. Although you might *instruct* a subordinate to do something, you would *ask* a superior.

Question: If you were to give business communication students one piece of advice about writing effective direct requests, what would that advice be?

Answer: Be specific. Don't say, "Please send me any information you have on widgets." Think what that covers—How to build them? Where they're sold? Sales volume per state, region, and country? What type of consumer buys them? Which companies offer competitive products? It could take reams of paper and months or years of work collecting all of the information available on widgets. The reader either has to give a very general response or write back and ask you to be more specific.

Source: Interview with Mary A. De Vries.

two-way communication. Organizations not only supply information to individuals and other organizations with whom they do business but gather and collect information from them.

In this section, we will focus on the flow of general information required by an organization from sources in its business environment. We will thus treat customers, suppliers and other businesses, and government agencies as audiences to whom requests for general information must be directed. General information often takes the form of brochures and booklets and other items which are normally sent free of charge and which are not part of any formal order.

You don't just wait for information to come to you.
Robert H. Waterman
Management consultant
and writer

Requests to Customers

There are many reasons to request information from customers. For example, you may need information about an account or about a customer's current needs. Or your information request could be part of a companywide customer survey. In each case, however, customer requests have the same twofold goal: to gather information while maintaining goodwill.

Suppose, for example, that you are required to make a request for which the customer receives no immediate payback. It will be your job to forge the link between the request and improved customer service. The letter in Figure 6.3 is a good example of how this sometimes delicate task can be performed. Note in particular the presentation of the request in the opening and closing paragraphs.

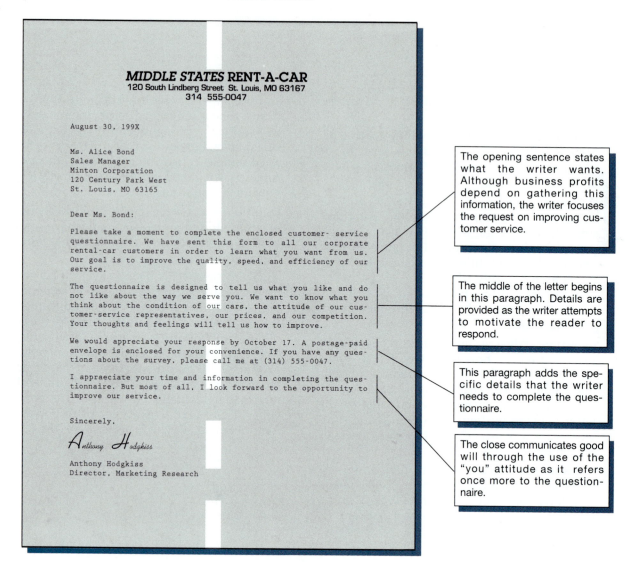

FIGURE 6.3   *Sample Request to a Customer*

Requests to Suppliers and Other Businesses

Information requests to suppliers and other businesses are usually short and to the point. Although goodwill is critical, you need to spend relatively little time motivating the recipient to comply with your request. You can assume that the recipient will answer as a matter of good business practice. Figure 6.4 is a sample of a short information request sent from one business to another. Note the tone in which the writer refers to the business relationship.

Requests to Government Agencies

For the most part, businesses communicate with government bodies through a bewildering array of forms. In fact, agencies like the Internal Revenue Service, the Social Security Administration, and state bureaus of unemployment insurance generate thousands of forms to be completed by large and small businesses.

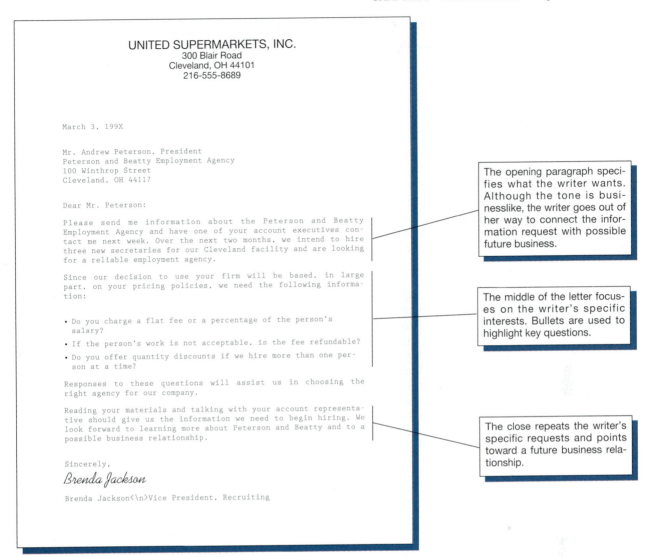

UNITED SUPERMARKETS, INC.
300 Blair Road
Cleveland, OH 44101
216-555-8689

March 3, 199X

Mr. Andrew Peterson, President
Peterson and Beatty Employment Agency
100 Winthrop Street
Cleveland, OH 44117

Dear Mr. Peterson:

Please send me information about the Peterson and Beatty Employment Agency and have one of your account executives contact me next week. Over the next two months, we intend to hire three new secretaries for our Cleveland facility and are looking for a reliable employment agency.

> The opening paragraph specifies what the writer wants. Although the tone is businesslike, the writer goes out of her way to connect the information request with possible future business.

Since our decision to use your firm will be based, in large part, on your pricing policies, we need the following information:

- Do you charge a flat fee or a percentage of the person's salary?
- If the person's work is not acceptable, is the fee refundable?
- Do you offer quantity discounts if we hire more than one person at a time?

> The middle of the letter focuses on the writer's specific interests. Bullets are used to highlight key questions.

Responses to these questions will assist us in choosing the right agency for our company.

Reading your materials and talking with your account representative should give us the information we need to begin hiring. We look forward to learning more about Peterson and Beatty and to a possible business relationship.

> The close repeats the writer's specific requests and points toward a future business relationship.

Sincerely,

Brenda Jackson

Brenda Jackson\n>Vice President, Recruiting

FIGURE 6.4   *Sample Request to a Supplier*

PLACING ORDERS

Because they generate income and profits, **orders**—written directions commissioning purchases—are the lifeblood of a business. When a company receives an order, it begins what is often a multipart process. For example, the process could include a credit check, applying the appropriate credit to a sales representative's commission account, entering the sale in the company's accounting ledgers, and shipping goods for delivery.

To avoid confusion or error, use order forms whenever available. When ordering by letter, include the following details:

- Name of the item being ordered (use the manufacturer's terminology, not your own)
- All relevant numbers pertaining to the item, including catalog number, style number, model number, and so on
- A description of the item, including (where applicable) size, weight, color, material, finish, and any additional features
- The number of items in the order (when large quantities are ordered, you

order
Direct request asking a seller to ship specified goods to the sender

may have to specify quantity in terms of dozens, cases, or other bulk-quantity measurements)

- Unit price
- Any applicable discounts that apply to the purchase
- Applicable sales tax
- Total price
- Method of order (among the options are check, C.O.D., and charge account; if you use a charge, be sure to include your account number)
- Preferred date for merchandise delivery
- Preferred method of shipment (options include shipment via parcel post, United Parcel Service, or overnight delivery)
- Name of the individual to whom the item is being delivered (this may be someone other than the person placing the order)
- Delivery address (which may differ from the billing address)
- Authorized signature

Although business-to-business goodwill is important, you need not explain what you plan to do with your purchase. There is no need to say, for example, "I am purchasing a new Canon PC-6RE photocopier because I am expanding my accounting business from part- to full-time and need a machine that can handle the greater workload." Orders, observes business communication authority Andrea B. Geffner, "are routine and handled in quantity. As long as you are a paying customer, your impetus for buying does not interest the seller."[8]

Explanations, however, can be helpful if you lack a catalog or model number or are trying to describe the purpose to which the item will be put. For example, if you are ordering a staple gun from a office-supply company without a catalog, the following statement of purpose will help the company identify the model you need:

The staple gun will be used to bind booklets containing at least 60 pages. Please supply a stapler that will do the job.

REQUESTING CREDIT INFORMATION

credit
Arrangement whereby a business sells goods or services to another business or individual in exchange for the promise to repay the money

Companies purchasing goods and services pay for them with either cash or credit. In a **credit** arrangement, a business sells goods or services to another business or individual in exchange for the promise to repay the money. Repayment schedules are specified in advance, with unpaid balances subject to interest charges.

Whereas many consumers use third-party commercial credit cards issued by creditors like American Express and Visa, businesses issue credit to one another at the time orders are placed. These credit accounts are crucial to attracting and maintaining business clients. In fact, they are so prevalent in business today that in many companies, outstanding credit purchases (products shipped but not yet paid for) make up between fifteen and twenty cents out of every dollar of assets. Companies issue business-to-business credit primarily in order to increase sales.

Because credit purchases are so important to business success, companies conduct the credit-granting process very carefully. As a result, a series of letters relating to the process is often necessary. These letters fall into five categories: (1) credit applications, (2) inquiries about creditworthiness, (3) responses about creditworthiness, (4) letters granting credit, and (5) letters refusing credit. Because *credit applications* and *inquiries about creditworthiness* involve direct requests, we will examine them here. We will examine the remaining categories of credit-related correspondence in subsequent chapters.

Credit Applications

When consumers apply for credit, they must complete application forms that provide credit-granting companies with the information needed for credit decisions. By contrast, when a business applies for credit, the application is often made by letter and may actually accompany the first order that the company places.

To increase your company's chances of gaining credit, application letters must be as specific as possible. Include any information that will attest to your company's financial stability—for example, the names and addresses of business credit accounts, bank references, and a copy of your firm's latest financial statement. Although the credit-granting company may check further with such credit-reporting agencies as Dun & Bradstreet and Retail Credit Company, your written application will contain information that is invaluable in speeding the process. Consider the credit application letter in Figure 6.5. In particular, note the ways in which the writer carefully integrates detailed information; note, too, the means by which he tries to encourage a positive response.

Inquiries about Creditworthiness

Once a company receives a credit request, it tries to determine whether the applicant is *creditworthy*. In part, this process includes written inquiries to the references provided on the credit application. The goal of the inquiry is to gather information that will help the company make a wise credit decision.

Retail merchants must frequently check the credit references of individuals who apply for store credit. In doing so, they can send letters to applicants' employers, requesting verification of position, salary, employment record, and length of employment. If you are called upon to write such an inquiry, be sure your request is simple to answer. For example, consider such formats as fill-in-the-blank. Not only is it more likely to be answered but your response will probably be faster.

FILING CLAIM LETTERS

Like all other human endeavors, business transactions are plagued by Murphy's Law—"Whatever can go wrong, will go wrong." As a result, claims and adjustments are a necessary part of business life. A **claim** is a notice from a customer that there is something wrong with a good or service. The most effective claim is a notice sent to the company in letter form. An **adjustment**—the company's response to the claim—is also made in writing. Because claims are letters of request, they will be examined in this chapter. We will look at adjustment letters in Chapters 7 and 8.

claim
Notice from a customer of a problem with a good or service

adjustment
Company's response to a claim

Among the problems that cause business customers to write claim letters are billing errors resulting in overcharges; bills for undelivered merchandise; delivery of damaged or defective merchandise; deliveries containing unordered or incorrect merchandise; missed delivery dates; and improperly credited merchandise exchanges. Because claim letters are often occasioned by mistakes, many people tend to write them in the heat of anger. Writers who succumb to anger, however, forget that their purpose is to get results, not to rant and rave. Even if right is entirely on your side, an abusive letter will rarely achieve positive results and can even delay a solution to your problem.

Like all direct requests, claim letters should start by telling the reader what you want and why you are writing. You should then explain the problem and describe all the details that the reader will need to assess the situation. Among the details that you may have to provide are order or invoice numbers; delivery dates (or dates promised); methods of shipment or locations where services were rendered; and descriptions of the items in question (model and style numbers, and so on). It is also a good idea to attach copies of sales slips or invoices.

PARK AVENUE AUTO SUPPLY CENTER
4 Long Lots Road
Alexandria, VA 22301
703-555-8820

June 5, 199X

Mr. Nicholas Holliday
Credit Manager
Overhill Auto Wholesalers
Alexandria, VA 22304

Dear Mr. Holliday:

As the owner of Park Avenue Auto Supply Center, I would like to order the tires, taillights, and hubcaps listed on the enclosed purchase order. At the same time, I would like to open a credit account with your company.

Although we have been in business for only six months, you will find that already we have established a strong credit rating. Among the companies with which we have an excellent credit standing are:

- Acme Automotive
  400 Albermare Avenue
  Alexandria, VA 22304
  (contact in accounts receivable—Don Adams)
- Alexandria Auto Radio Supply Center
  3224 Smith Street
  Alexandria, VA 22304
  (contact in accounts receivable—Stephanie Mason)

Since opening, we have used the American Eastern Bank in Alexandria. Seth Overfeld, the branch manager, is familiar with our account and credit standing. You can reach him at 1111 Empire Boulevard, Alexandria, VA 22304.

I look forward to establishing an account with Overhill Auto Wholesalers as soon as possible, since I anticipate frequent purchases. Please let me know if there are any additional questions I can answer about our firm's credit standing.

Sincerely,

Jonathan Baron

Jonathan Baron

> The letter has two purposes, both stated in the opening paragraph. Instead of cluttering the letter with a list of items being ordered, the writer decides to include a separate purchase order. This decision allows the letter to focus on the credit request.

> This paragraph provides specific credit references, including company names, addresses, and contacts.

> This paragraph adds additional details by giving a bank reference.

> The closing paragraph makes it clear that the writer is open to further questions. The reference to additional business is intended to encourage the recipient to make a positive credit decision.

FIGURE 6.5   *Sample Credit Application Letter*

Finally, your letter should suggest a solution. For example, tell the company that you want a replacement or an adjustment to your bill. At the same time, make every attempt to end your letter on a positive, forward-looking note, expressing confidence that the company will settle your problem fairly. In the sample claim letter in Figure 6.6, note the writer's focus on a clear presentation of both the problem and a possible solution.

When services rather than tangible goods are involved, claims may be more difficult to handle. For example, if you are unhappy with an office-cleaning service, you have nothing tangible to return, nor can you point to a missed delivery. In these cases, make your case in a logical, reasonable way, explaining the nature of the problem and how you would like it resolved. Provide as much detail as you would if your claim involved merchandise.

PROGRESS CHECK

1. What are orders, and why are they so important in business?
2. What is credit, and why is it so important to business?
3. Distinguish between a claim and an adjustment.

October 1, 199X

Mr. Enrico Rosario
Better Jeans, Inc.
206 East 32nd Street
New York, NY 10001

Dear Mr. Rosario:

On September 30, I received a shipment of 100 pairs of women's jeans, sizes 2-16 (see attached invoice). Although I specified that only 4 items were to be size 2, the delivery contained 32 pairs of size 2 jeans. I am returning 28 pairs of jeans for an immediate adjustment.

Please send me the following replacement pairs. These items were requested but not received in the original order:

  8 pairs size 8
10 pairs size 10
  5 pairs size 12
  5 pairs size 14

If any of these items are not in stock, please credit my account for the amount. Since my needs are specific, do not ship any merchandise except the items I have specified.

As you know, we are in the height of the fall selling season and your merchandise is an important part of my business. Many of my customers come to my store because they always know they will find a ready supply of jeans. Therefore, I would appreciate the replacements sent by overnight mail with any additional shipping costs handled by you.

Sincerely,

Virginia Harding
Virginia Harding
Buyer, Women's Sportswear

> The opening paragraph states the problem and requests a resolution. A copy of the invoice provides the background information that the supplier needs to assess the problem.

> This paragraph tells the reader how to resolve the claim. Notice that the writer does not express anger or threaten to stop doing business with the company unless her demands are met, nor does she place blame. Rather, her approach is positive.

> The close focuses on re-establishing positive feelings as it expresses urgency in receiving the replacements.

FIGURE 6.6   *Sample Claim Letter*

PERSONAL REFERENCES

As a job seeker, you will probably ask someone who knows you for a **personal reference**—a recommendation stating that you are qualified to perform the duties of the job for which you are applying, attesting to your character, or both. On the other hand, as a manager considering a job candidate's application, you may request information from the individuals or organizations identified as references by the candidate.

personal reference
Recommendation stating that an applicant is qualified to perform the duties of the job for which he or she is applying, attesting to the applicant's character, or both

Requesting a Personal Reference

Effective personal references can mean the difference between getting a job and remaining unemployed. With so much at stake, job candidates should make special efforts to line up positive, effective references—a process that often starts with a letter. The letter has two primary purposes: (1) to ask an individual whether he or she is willing to give you a letter of recommendation, to be contacted by prospective employers at a later date, or both; and (2) to describe the position that you are seeking and explain how this person's knowledge of your background might help get you the job. Consider the sample request letter in Figure 6.7, in which the writer asks a former co-worker if he can use him as a reference on a job application. As you can see, the request takes a direct approach.

Although many requests for personal references are made in person or by phone, many are also written. Written requests are common when people haven't seen each other in several years. A subordinate might also feel more comfortable writing to a former boss, especially if their relationship was formal. Many written requests are followed by phone conversations.

In the letter in Figure 6.7, the writer has asked for the recipient's cooperation in the event that he should be contacted by a prospective employer. Alternately, the writer could ask for a letter of recommendation that can be given directly to a prospective employer, perhaps during an interview. Your request should be specific in pointing to particular facts that could be included in the reference letter. Because you know your own background better than anyone else, offer examples of abilities and job successes to which your reference can attest. We will analyze effective recommendation letters in more detail in Chapter 7.

Among the people typically enlisted as references are former employers and managers, college professors, clients, and other professional colleagues, including both peers and subordinates. In any case, says outplacement specialist Peter J. Leets, the people you select as references should be able to sell your skills to others: "Make sure those you select can vouch for you as someone who will contribute added value. They should have the desire…to sell your skills, personal qualities and professional attributes."[9]

The writer states the request in the context of his job search.

This paragraph describes the position that the writer wants as it reminds the reader about the writer's accomplishments.

Here the writer attempts to motivate the recipient by stressing the importance of his cooperation. The "you" attitude emerges as the writer focuses on the recipient rather than himself.

The initial request is restated. The writer concludes the letter by explaining the urgency of his request.

JARED WELLS
40 Red Coat Road
Rockville, MD 20852
410-555-3390

July 9, 199X

Mr. John Peters, Vice President
Hoffman-La Roche Inc.
340 Kingsland Street
Nutley, NJ 07110

Dear John:

I am looking for a new position with a pharmaceutical company as a product detailer and would like to use your name as a reference. It would help my job search immeasurably if potential employers could call you to inquire about my performance during the three years we worked together.

The position I am seeking is similar to the one we both held at Upjohn. I hope you will agree that I am at my best when dealing directly with doctors, explaining the benefits and uses of different pharmaceutical products. As you recall, in 1993, I was the top performer in our district for the year.

Since you and I shared so much professionally, your recommendation would give my job search a tremendous boost. It is my hope that you will hear from sales managers who are interested enough in me as a potential candidate to contact my references.

Please let me know if I can use your name as a reference. Although you can reach me at my current job for another month, I plan to begin my search in the next week.

Cordially,

Jared Wells

Jared Wells

FIGURE 6.7   *Sample Request for a Personal Reference*

Requesting Information about Job Candidates

On the other side of the employment fence is the potential employer who wants to learn as much about a job candidate as possible before making a job offer. The employer's search for information typically begins when the candidate hands the employer a list of references. The list contains the names, titles, organizations, addresses, and phone numbers of people who have agreed to talk to the employer about the candidate's background. The candidate's application should also contain a one- or two-sentence statement describing the professional relationship between the candidate and the individual providing the reference.

Many people telephone candidates' references instead of writing to them. Whether verbal or written, however, your request is a direct request for information. Written requests should be short, explaining the position to which the applicant is applying and requesting verification of employment and performance information. In the sample personal-reference request in Figure 6.8, the writer carefully combines specific and open-ended requests for information.

EXTENDING INVITATIONS

Invitations are requests for business associates, potential customers, or personal acquaintances to attend business or social events such as receptions and open

invitation
Request for business associates, potential customers, or personal acquaintances to attend a business or social event

The opening paragraph states the reason for the letter. The job applicant is identified in the first sentence so that the rest of the letter makes sense.

The middle of the letter lists the specific information that the writer needs. An open-ended request is then added to elicit additional information.

In this paragraph, the writer acknowledges that it is a mistake to ask the former employer to verify the job applicant's information. You are more likely to get an honest, accurate account if you compare two separate versions.

The close indicates when the response is needed and thanks the person for providing the reference.

BELLEVUE MARKETING CONSULTANTS
27 Bellevue Avenue
New Orleans, LA 70112
504-555-5044

October 10, 199X

Ms. Cecilia Antonia
Account Manager
Nettles Marketing Group
200 West Virginia Avenue
Reno, NV 98501

Dear Ms. Antonia:

Richard Magrath has applied for the position of office manager in our five-person marketing research firm. Mr. Magrath listed you as a reference, and I am writing for information about his work history.

Please provide the following information about Mr. Magrath's experience with your firm:

• job title and responsibilities
• dates of employment
• performance rating
• reason for leaving

Please add any information that might be important for us to know as we evaluate his candidacy. You can be assured that everything you communicate will be kept confidential.

Since we are currently evaluating several candidates, we need your response by next week. Your cooperation is appreciated.

Sincerely yours,

Pricilla Peterson

Pricilla Peterson
Vice President

FIGURE 6.8   *Sample Follow-Up Request for a Personal Reference*

ETHICAL ISSUES IN BUSINESS COMMUNICATION

Job References, Ethics, and the Law

Asking for a job reference is no longer a simple matter. Ethical and legal considerations have complicated what was once a straightforward, information-gathering process for both companies and individuals.

In fact, during the past decade, many companies stopped giving meaningful job references. Instead, they provided the equivalent of the former employee's name, rank, and serial number—and no more. Afraid of slander and libel suits, many companies often supplied references that included only two pieces of information—the former employee's job title and his or her dates of employment. Job performance was never mentioned, and even praise was discouraged for fear that if praise were tempered by a slightly negative comment, the company could wind up in court. As a result, honest written references became nearly impossible to find. People tended to tell the truth, whether in person or over the phone, only when they knew their words could not be traced.

This tendency—to tell the truth without committing it to writing—is also motivated by the risk of involvement in *negligent-hiring* lawsuits. These lawsuits, which usually pit one company against another, follow patterns like the following: Company A is charged with wrongfully hiring someone who has harmed someone else in the company's employ; Company A then sues Company B—the worker's former employer—for withholding critical information that may have permitted Company A to avoid the incident. Company B, for example, may have withheld information about a former employee's prison record or a history of alcoholism, sexual harassment, or drug abuse. Company A thus contends that, had it known this information, it would not have hired the employee in the first place. An anonymous manufacturing executive explains: "When it comes to alcoholism, sexual harassment, drug dependency, anything that can cause really serious problems, I'll find a way to send up a red flag. The repercussions can just be too great—for the new employer, for its customers, and other employees—and for us."

After years of stopping short of the truth, many businesspeople, like this executive, are motivated by a renewed sense of ethics. When it comes to references, many are now determined to do unto others as they would want others to do unto them. For example, when Gregory M. Jenks, an operations manager for an electrical-parts manufacturer in Elmsford, New York, was stung by a dishonest reference that withheld a candidate's police record, he vowed never to withhold important reference information from anyone who asked for it. On one occasion, then, when he received a reference request about a former employee, he felt obliged to mention that the man could not leave his personal problems at home. "I really believe that people are entitled to know if they are about to hire someone unsuitable," says Jenks.

In addition, many businesspeople now realize that withholding information allows dishonest job seekers to say nearly anything on their résumés without fear of being discovered. Thus, with genuine references having gone the way of doubtful references, many con artists have gone on to bigger and better jobs while honest job seekers have suffered.

In an effort to rectify this situation, companies like New Jersey–based Engelhard Corporation, a manufacturer of specialty chemicals and precious metals, has modified its no-reference rule. For the first time in years, executives are now permitted to write letters of recommendation for employees who request them—as long as the letter is not written on company stationary. Explains Margaret M. Contessa, Engelhard's director of human resources: "It is our hope that by making it clear that the executives are acting as individuals, not official representatives of the corporation, we can assist the employee as well as minimize our own exposure and risk."

Source: Claudia H. Deutsch, "Psst! References Are Sneaking Back, for Real," *The New York Times*, December 2, 1990, p. F25.

houses. Although invitations are designed to communicate specific information, they are also intended to communicate goodwill through sincerity and openness.

Every invitation should accomplish three things: (1) request the recipient's attendance at a specific event; (2) explain why the gathering is being held; and (3) provide all the details that the recipient needs in order to attend, including date, time, and location. Many invitations also ask for a response, often by a specific date.

Some events require formal invitations, which are written in the third person and are often engraved or printed. Invitations for many events are more personal and individualized.

DIRECT REQUESTS IN COMPANY MEMOS

There are many reasons to request internal information or action in writing rather than in conversation. You want someone to attend an important meeting; you need work completed by a certain date; you want a schedule change; you need a new assistant and must request one through formal channels; you want a new office chair or desk. When requesting something in a business

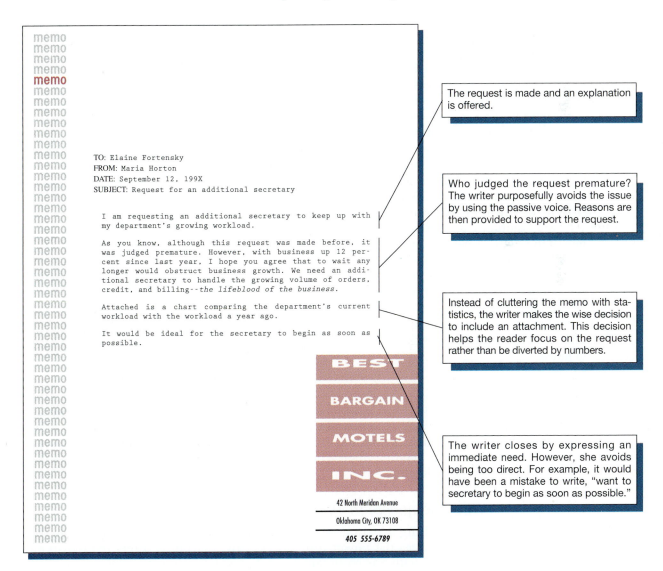

FIGURE 6.9   *Sample Direct-Request Memo to a Manager*

CURRENT ISSUES IN BUSINESS COMMUNICATION

Why Computers Can't Write

Recently, newspaper columnist Russell Baker applied his nationally syndicated wit to the subject of the relationship between poor letter writing and computer technology. In Baker's opinion, word processors make graceless writing all too easy. Here are some of his observations:

After using my powerful word processor to write a letter . . . , I printed it on my state-of-the-art laser printer. What a professional look it had! It didn't look like a letter at all. It looked like a piece of junk mail.

Every day brings a dozen documents that look exactly like this letter. Every day they flutter into my trash can unread. One knows their messages too well:

An astounding new shampoo is available. An officeholder praises his own achievements. A sales pitch disguised as a lottery advises the recipient to steel himself for the arrival of an armored truck full of dollars. A friend of the President says a contribution of $10,000 is imperative in this critical year though $25 will not be sneered at.

My beautifully printed letter showed me caught in the American comedy about the silliness of progress. Just look at this letter: Writing it required several thousand dollars' worth of electronic machinery, not to mention a supply of electricity provided by vast corporations whose hot wiry tentacles stretched across thousands of miles.

With all these resources, what emerged? A letter that looked so like junk mail that [the recipient] would probably toss it away unread.

What's more, it was a poorly written letter—not a graceful phrase in it, too much stiffness in the prose joints, and twice as long as it needed to be.

Such gassiness is characteristic of writing done on computers. Computers make the physical toil of writing so negligible that the writer can write on forever, and often does, as I am currently doing at this very particular and precious point in time, a.k.a. now....

My second-rate letter with the junk-mail look is a typical child of progress. With a goose quill, Thomas Jefferson could have written a letter at a fraction of the cost. It would have looked like the work of a human being, and it would have been a better letter than mine.

It would have been better not only because Jefferson had the more interesting mind but also because writing with goose feathers is such messy work that a writer has to put his mind in order before starting. With a computer, he merely flips a switch, then lets his brain mosey around in the fog on the chance it may bump into an idea....

Source: Russell Baker, "Ruled by Tools," *The New York Times*, May 12, 1992, p. A23. Copyright © 1992 by The New York Times Company. Reprinted by permission.

organization, you must focus on your relationship with the reader. Although this is obviously important in all communication, it is especially important within business organizations because your tone and approach can vary widely depending upon whether you are writing to a manager, a co-worker, or subordinate.

Direct Requests to Managers

When asking a manager for information or action, choose a tone that acknowledges the power differences between you. A direct request to any individual with greater organizational power should never make demands or give orders. In the sample memo in Figure 6.9, note the way in which the writer avoids being too direct and adopts the passive voice in conveying negative information.

Direct Requests to Co-workers

Memos asking co-workers for information or action are usually personal and direct. The sample memo in Figure 6.10 is effective in striking a conversational tone, both through word choice (personal and informal) and sentence construction (short).

Direct Requests to Subordinates

In this situation, you are in a more powerful position than the person who will read your memo. This power difference enables you to make your request in a polite but firm way.

PROGRESS CHECK

1. In a work setting, why would you make a direct request in writing rather than in conversation?
2. Explain why it is important to choose wisely when asking someone to give you a personal reference.

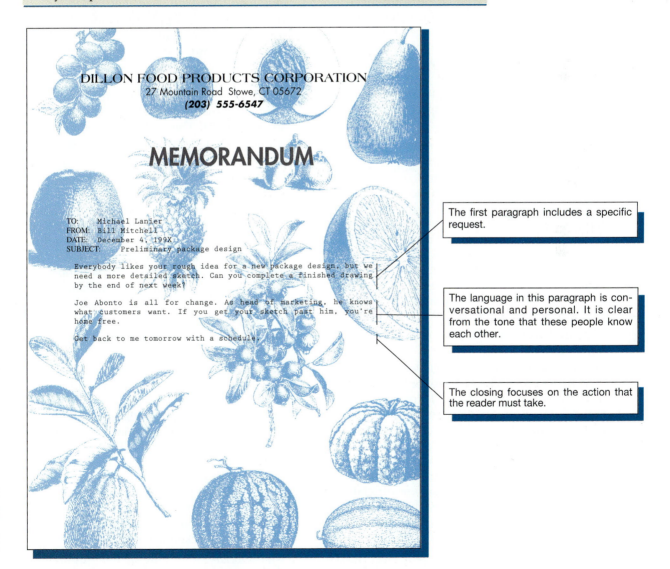

DILLON FOOD PRODUCTS CORPORATION
27 Mountain Road Stowe, CT 05672
(203) 555-6547

MEMORANDUM

TO: Michael Lanier
FROM: Bill Mitchell
DATE: December 4, 199X
SUBJECT: Preliminary package design

Everybody likes your rough idea for a new package design, but we need a more detailed sketch. Can you complete a finished drawing by the end of next week?

Joe Abonto is all for change. As head of marketing, he knows what customers want. If you get your sketch past him, you're home free.

Get back to me tomorrow with a schedule.

> The first paragraph includes a specific request.

> The language in this paragraph is conversational and personal. It is clear from the tone that these people know each other.

> The closing focuses on the action that the reader must take.

FIGURE 6.10   *Sample Direct-Request Memo to a Coworker*

WHAT'S AHEAD

As we have seen, the most effective direct requests use the bottom-line approach, delivering the message in the first paragraph. The same approach is used to write good-news, goodwill, and informative messages, which is the subject of Chapter 7.

*S*UMMARY OF CHAPTER OBJECTIVES

1. **Explain how *letters* differ from *memos*.**

   Letters and memos differ in four fundamental ways. First, while letters are usually distributed to individuals outside the organization, memos often have larger audiences within a company. Second, while letters have the potential both to create goodwill outside the company and to increase sales, memos can boost your status with co-workers. Third, memos are often less formal than letters to outsiders. Finally, depending upon the situation, letters are usually more specific and less detailed than memos.

2. **Explain the functions of the opening, middle, and close of a *direct request*.**

   The opening of a direct request should tell your reader why you are writing to him or her as opposed to someone else; it should also explain both the purpose of your request and the action that you want the reader to take. The middle of the request provides any additional details that the reader will need to fulfill your request. The close focuses again on the needed action. In letters and many memos, the close also communicates goodwill.

3. **Explain how to write *requests for information*.**

   Direct requests for information follow the standard direct approach, with the request stated in the opening paragraph. Informational requests to customers should be "you"-centered and should always focus on maintaining goodwill. Requests to suppliers and other businesses should spend little time motivating recipients. Rather, they should be short and to the point. Requests to government officials should be as specific as possible.

4. **List the characteristics of *letters placing orders*.**

   Letters placing orders should include the details found on standard order forms. The letter should be designed to make your order

easy to read. Focus on the information needed to place the order rather than on explaining why you are placing it.

5. **Distinguish between *credit applications* and *inquiries about creditworthiness*.**

   When businesses apply for credit, the application is typically in letter form. The letter should include any information that will attest to the company's financial stability and should be organized as a direct request. By contrast, inquiries about creditworthiness are written by the company that is being asked to extend credit. The goal of the inquiry is to gather information that will help the company make a wise credit decision.

6. **Identify the elements of an effective *claim letter*.**

   Claim letters are notifications that something is wrong with a good or service. Effective claim letters focus on requesting an adjustment and describing the details that the reader needs in order to assess the situation. The letter should also suggest a solution, such as replacing a defective item or adjusting an erroneous bill.

7. **Describe two types of request letters associated with *personal references*.**

   Personal references are recommendations stating that a job applicant is qualified to perform the duties of a job, attesting to the applicant's character, or both. Job applicants often request personal-reference letters from former business associates and professors. The request letter asks the individual whether he or she would write a letter of recommendation or be willing to be contacted by prospective employers. The letter also describes the type of position being sought and explains how the recipient's knowledge of your background can help.

   On the other side of the employment fence, reference requests are made by potential employers who want to learn about a candidate's background before making a hiring decision.

8. **List the essential details included in an** *invitation.*

   Every invitation should request the reader's attendance at a specific event, explain why the gathering is being held, and provide all the necessary details, including the date, time, and location.

9. **Describe how the relationship between the writer and reader affects** *internal request memos.*

   When requesting information or action from managers, avoid giving orders and use the passive voice to convey negative information. Memos asking co-workers for information or action can be conversational. When writing to subordinates, be polite but firm.

REVIEW AND DISCUSSION QUESTIONS

1. Distinguish between letters and memos. (*Ch. Obj. 1*)
2. What are the functions of the opening, middle, and close of a direct request? (*Ch. Obj. 2*)
3. Summarize the chapter's suggestions for writing effective direct requests for information. (*Ch. Obj. 3*)
4. What features contribute to an effective letter placing an order? (*Ch. Obj. 4*)
5. Summarize the chapter's tips for writing effective credit applications versus effective inquiries about creditworthiness. (*Ch. Obj. 5*)
6. Describe an effective claim letter. (*Ch. Obj. 6*)
7. How would you go about writing an effective letter requesting a personal reference? (*Ch. Obj. 7*)
8. Describe the elements of an effective letter requesting information about a job candidate. (*Ch. Obj. 7*)
9. What information should be included in an invitation? (*Ch. Obj. 8*)
10. Compare the different tones and approaches that you would use in writing to a manager, a co-worker, or a subordinate. (*Ch. Obj. 9*)

APPLICATION EXERCISES

1. Which would be the better way to communicate—letter or memo—in each of the following situations? (*Ch. Obj. 1*):

   a. A shipping manager politely asks a new customer to supply further information.
   b. A shipping manager sends a message to all other managers at a company to tell them about a new computer system.
   c. A shipping manager sends a message to all of the firm's customers to give instructions and provide details about how to use the new computer system.
   d. The president of a university sends a message to all of the school's professors, administrators, and students, asking them to stop trampling the grass in the school's quadrangle.

2. Martha Brown, manager of DePaul Memorial Hospital, is writing a letter to General Television, Inc., on April 22. Place each the following facts in the appropriate part of her letter—opening, middle, or close. (*Ch. Obj. 2*)

   - DePaul has received seven tuners, all labeled TR-555-2, for the model TV-23 color receiver.
   - DePaul has been billed three times for tuners that it did not receive.
   - Ms. Brown ordered nine TV tuners from General Television with the tuner part number of TR-222-5.
   - When the wrong tuners arrived, she returned them immediately to General Television.
   - She would like General Television to send the correct tuners as soon as possible.
   - She tried twice to call General Television's manager; both times, she was put on hold and then the connection was cut off.
   - If General Television cannot fill her order, she would like to cancel it.
   - The original order was scheduled to arrive March 9.
   - The nine TV tuners that Ms. Brown ordered are for the model TV-20 color receiver.
   - She hopes that the customer relations manag-

er for General Television will address this problem promptly.

3. Use the information in Exercise 2 to write a claim letter to General Television. (*Ch. Obj. 6*)

4. Find a catalog that sells products or equipment with which you are familiar, such as computer supplies, stereo components, jewelry, or clothing. Using the information that you find in the catalog, write a letter placing an order from the catalog. (*Ch. Obj. 4*)

5. Assume that you receive the product from the catalog company and there's something wrong with it—maybe it's the wrong size or color or perhaps it's been damaged in some way. Write a claim letter in which you explain the problem and request a replacement. (*Ch. Obj. 6*)

>6. Write a letter in which you ask the catalog company in Exercises 4 and 5 for some type of information—perhaps you'd like to know more about a product in the catalog or you'd like to ask if the firm carries other brands or sizes. (*Ch. Obj. 3*)

7. Write a letter to Marshall Loeb, managing editor of *Fortune* magazine, in which you request a reprint of an article on mainland China. Although you don't remember the exact title of the article, you do recall that it discussed business development and entrepreneurship in China and included a chart on China's major exports and commodities. The article appeared sometime during September or October of 1992. You don't know how much a reprint will cost, but you'll be glad to send a check once the magazine has told you the price. Address the letter to the Time & Life Building, Rockefeller Center, New York, NY 10020–1393. (*Ch. Obj. 3*)

8. It turns out that the *Fortune* article was entitled, "China Really Is on the Move" and appeared on pages 114–23 of the October 5, 1992, issue. The author was Brenton Schlender. Write a letter ordering five reprints of the article at $3.00 each and note that you have enclosed a check for the total. (*Ch. Obj. 4*)

9. Write a letter to a friend or former co-worker whom you haven't seen in a while. Ask this person to write a personal reference recommending you for a job that you would like to have. (*Ch. Obj. 7*)

10. Now suppose that the employer for the job in Exercise 9 writes to your friend to ask for further information about you. Taking the role of your prospective employer, write this letter. (*Ch. Obj. 7*)

11. Write a letter to a store or company in which you request credit. (*Ch. Obj. 5*)

12. As a member of the International Marketing Division at Smallco Sweats, a maker of athletic clothing, you feel it's important to begin a new marketing campaign in South America. You decide to schedule an important meeting to brainstorm ideas and discuss ways to expand Smallco's markets there. The meeting is set for Thursday, October 22, at 8 A.M. in the Walnut Boardroom. You will invite three co-workers: Craig Culden (from the Advertising Department); Cindy Sanders (Accounting); and Barbara Wadsworth (Sales). Craig has good ideas for creating promotional campaigns, Cindy knows the budget that's available, and Barbara knows how to motivate the firm's sales representatives. You know all of these co-workers quite well and frequently get together for lunch.

Write a memo inviting Barbara to this meeting. (*Ch. Obj. 8, 9*)

13. In addition to Barbara, Cindy, and Craig, you would like to have your boss, Ramon Esteverria, attend the meeting. Esteverria comes from Peru. Before joining Smallco, he was director of international marketing for a competing firm, where he headed a successful marketing campaign in Argentina. You feel that his experience and cultural insights would be valuable. You're not sure he can make the meeting because he travels a great deal, but you want to write a persuasive memo that both invites him to the meeting and expresses how helpful his presence would be. Write this memo. (*Ch. Obj. 8, 9*)

14. You would also like Martin Bozeman, a market researcher who reports to you, to come to the meeting. Before the meeting, you want him to run the latest computer printouts showing sales statistics from Smallco's outlets in South America and then write a brief report summarizing these statistics. Write a memo to Martin. (*Ch. Obj. 8, 9*)

15. You've asked Martin Bozeman to write a letter to the chamber of commerce in Lima, Peru, to get more information about the business climate there. Among other items, you want to learn more about how the Peruvian government taxes companies, more about any tax advantages it might give to foreign-based companies, whether there are any special restrictions on clothing manufacturers, and what sorts of restrictions Peru places on imports and exports. You also want to know whether a representative of the Lima Chamber of Commerce

would be able to meet with you during April. Write this letter. (Assume for this exercise that the chamber of commerce employees read English well and are comfortable with an American-style approach to writing direct requests.) (*Ch. Obj. 3*)

BUILDING YOUR RESEARCH SKILLS

Choose a company or product about which you would like to gather more information. Go to the library and look up whatever you would need in order to write a letter to that company: name and job title of the right person to receive your letter, address, a description of what you're looking for, and so on. Write a letter requesting information from that person and company. Type or write the letter so that it's clearly readable and bring it with you to class.

BUILDING YOUR TEAMWORK SKILLS

Your instructor will divide the class into small groups. As a group, take turns reading the letters that each member wrote for the previous exercise. Critique the letters, using the guidelines you studied in this chapter. Working as a team, revise each letter to make it as effective as possible. Be sure to be tactful and to give positive feedback as well as negative!

COMMUNICATING IN A WORLD OF DIVERSITY

Wang Jia Ying loves fashion—so much so that she left her waitressing job and started her own business in a small town near Shanghai, China. At first, her only employees were herself, her husband, and two retired tailors. Today, her company, ZhiMeiNai, employs fifty people to produce Western-style wedding gowns and formal wear for Chinese movie studios. Last year, the firm's revenues were about $150,000, with profits of $37,000.

ZhiMeiNai pays its employees an average of $1,100 to $1,555 a year—triple the national average salary in China. "We are completely self-made people," says Wang. "We had nothing at first and knew nothing about business except what we had read. All I knew was that designing clothes is fun."

Wang Jia Ying wants to buy a heavy-duty sewing machine that will allow her to expand her business by using a wider variety of fabrics. The machine that she would like to buy is made by a U.S. company, and she wants to write to the company to ask for $10,000 in credit. Wang knows that she isn't totally fluent in English, and so she asks you to write a letter that she can sign.

Write the letter.

Source: Brenton Schlender, "China Really Is on the Move," *Fortune*, October 5, 1992, pp. 114–23. © 1992 Time Inc. All rights reserved.

CASE 6.1

The Safer Tire from Bridgestone

Up to now, having a tire blow while driving on the highway has been highly dangerous. A car with a flat tire is hard to steer and can careen out of control. But tire makers are planning to change that situation soon. Bridgestone, for example, is introducing new high-performance tires that will run on stiff sidewalls if they lose air pressure. Bridgestone's Expedia S-01 will be fitted on new Chevrolet Corvettes and will also be available as an after-market add-on for any Corvette of the model year 1988 or later.

Bridgestone claims that its Expedia S-01 can travel 50 miles at 55 miles per hour without air. The company's innovative tire system has three elements: strong sidewalls, a unidirectional rim that keeps the flattened tire in place, and a low-pressure warning system that alerts drivers to the problem. Tires can be repaired after a flat, but Bridgestone won't guarantee a second airless run. Instead, the company offers generous trade-in allowances and overnight delivery of replacement tires.

The entire system—tires, wheels, and sensor—will cost about $5,000.

Questions and Assignments

1. Describe the innovative features of the Expedia S-01.
2. Suppose that you own a luxury-car dealership called Upscale Roadsters. Write a letter ordering 12 Expedia S-01s to be fitted, after-market, on three Corvettes that you currently have in stock. In addition, you want to order four new Corvettes with the Expedia S-01s already installed.
3. A customer buys a new Corvette from Upscale Roadsters. While driving one day, she gets a flat tire. The Expedia's sidewall cracks on one side, making the car difficult to steer. Fortunately, she isn't driving fast and is able to stop the car safely. She is, however, decidedly unhappy about the cracked sidewall. She writes a claim letter to Upscale in which she requests a free replacement tire. Write this letter.

Source: "Running on Empty," *Automobile Magazine*, November 1992, p. 11.

Lending on Character at South Shore Bank

South Shore Bank specializes in making loans that few other banks would want to touch. Many of these loans help minority business owners in inner-city neighborhoods. One such business owner is Vivian Wilson, who, ironically, had to get a loan due to too much success.

At first, Wilson was ecstatic when her firm, the Star Security & Detective Agency, won a $1-million bid to provide security guards to the city of Chicago. Her mood changed as soon as she realized how long it took the city to pay its bills. She had to dip into her own savings to pay her staff, and the bank where she'd had an account for decades refused to lend her any money. By the time she came to South Shore, she was within two weeks of running out of cash.

In situations like this, most banks would demand significant collateral, a detailed credit history, and audited cash-flow statements. David Shryock, South Shore's vice president for commercial lending, relied on character. Shryock knew that Wilson's father had started the Star Agency in 1923 and passed it on to his daughter; Vivian's own daughter, a Chicago police officer, helped run the company. "We had confidence she could make the city payment system work," explains Shryock. Within two weeks, he had arranged a $250,000 line of credit for Wilson, and the Star Agency was prospering again.

South Shore continues to work closely with Vivian Wilson, keeping the Star Agency's accounts and receiving copies of all its bills. The bank's relationship with the Star Agency is typical of its personalized lending style: It chooses good risks and follows their progress closely. Unlike many banks, says one South Shore official, "We spend…a lot more time…working with the borrower one-on-one."

Questions and Assignments

1. Compare South Shore Bank's approach to granting credit to that of most banks.
2. Imagine that you are Vivian Wilson. Write a letter to David Shryock requesting a $250,000 line of credit for the Star Agency. Explain why you need credit and mention any facts that you feel will increase your chances of getting the loan.

3. Assume that you are David Shryock and you have just received Vivian Wilson's letter. You're curious to learn more about Vivian, her daughter, and their business. Write a letter to the commissioner of the Chicago Police Department in which you inquire about the creditworthiness and general history of the Wilson family. (Assume that Vivian's daughter reports to the commissioner.)

Source: David Wessel, "Small Victories," *The Wall Street Journal*, June 23, 1992, pp. A1, A16.

7

Writing Good-News, Goodwill, and Informative Messages

CHAPTER OBJECTIVES

After studying this chapter, you should be able to:

1 Describe the use of the *direct approach* in good-news letters.

2 Explain the importance of expressing *goodwill* in *inquiry responses*.

3 Identify five specific types of *good-news letters*.

4 List the characteristics of an effective *goodwill message*.

5 Apply the direct approach to writing *informative letters*.

6 Explain the requirements for writing effective *good-news and informative memos*.

What is a Customer?

A Customer is the most important person ever in this office…in person or by mail.

A Customer is not dependent on us…we are dependent on him.

A Customer is not an interruption of our work…he is the purpose of it. We are not doing a favor by serving him…he is doing us a favor by giving us the opportunity to do so.

A Customer is not someone to argue or match wits with. Nobody ever won an argument with a customer.

A Customer is a person who brings us his wants.

It is our job to handle them profitably to him and ourselves.

Sign posted at the headquarters of L.L. Bean
Freeport, Maine

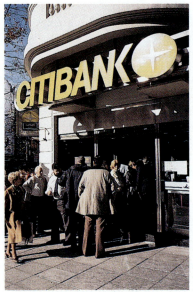

GOOD NEWS FROM CITIBANK

Along with many other banks, New York–based Citibank found itself on the receiving end of negative publicity about its credit-card interest rates. Although interest rates on bank accounts and certificates of deposit were lower than they had been in years, Citibank MasterCard and Visa accounts were still charging 19.8 percent on unpaid balances—a rate that most consumers considered excessive.

Angry consumers blasted Citibank and its competitors for maintaining such high rates. Determined to get even as well as mad, thousands of customers switched to banks that charged less. Citibank's response to consumer dissatisfaction came in the form of a letter in which the bank informed its best customers of interest rate reductions. Because it is in many ways a model for communicating good news effectively, let's consider this letter in some detail.

Citibank's letter is effective for a number of reasons. For one thing, it presents its good news first. In fact, the writer chooses the unconventional but effective approach of spelling out the news even before the salutation. To further emphasize its importance, this single sentence is printed in boldface type. The opening paragraph then uses a direct approach both to repeat the key message and to communicate goodwill. To add further emphasis, the sentence "You have earned Premier Member status with a new lower interest rate" is italicized. In part, then, the paragraph is effective because it is written from the reader's perspective.

The second paragraph presents the important details of Citibank's offer, mentioning for the first time the lower 15.9-percent interest rate. To ensure that it will be noticed immediately, the writer puts the most important information (the new interest rate and the continuation of the interest-free grace period) in boldface type. Rather than cluttering the letter with legal technicalities that reduce its impact, Citibank places these details on the back of the letter.

The next two paragraphs continue to communicate good news. Although some of it is old news (for example, "unsurpassed free benefits"), repeating this information emphasizes the card's overall value. The important new benefit—the special-edition card for premier members—is announced first and italicized. The final paragraph thanks the reader while emphasizing goodwill and customer service.

CHAPTER OVERVIEW

Many people, or course, would no doubt argue that in an environment in which their savings accounts yield less than 4 percent, a 15.9-percent credit-card interest rate is nothing for consumers to get excited about. The theme of the Citibank letter, however, is the good news that Citibank is lowering its rates, and the strength of its presentation comes from the way in which this letter puts its energy into announcing its good news. The important elements of this letter are easy to identify: the direct approach, the clearly focused message of goodwill, the adoption of the "you" attitude, and an effective layout. As we will see throughout this chapter, these elements are equally important in all forms of good-news correspondence.

In this chapter, we will examine a variety of business correspondence that takes the direct approach to delivering a message, including *order acknowledgments, letters of credit, adjustment letters, and positive personnel letters*. In addition, we will review various forms of goodwill messages, including *thank-you messages, responses to invitations, letters of congratulations, letters of condolence, and greetings*. This chapter will also examine *informative letters* which follow the same direct organizational pattern. Finally, we will focus on the unique requirements of communicating good news and information in *memo* form.

We will begin by describing an approach for writing good-news correspondence. Because this approach is based on a direct organizational plan, it has a great deal in common with the model organizational plan for direct requests. We will conclude this section by explaining why positive letters to customers should always be considered *customer-service letters*.

THE DIRECT APPROACH TO GOOD NEWS

Most of us want to hear good news right away, and presenting good news first has a number of advantages. For example, when you know that a message offers you something positive, you are more likely to read the entire letter and, more importantly, to pay close attention to the details. The direct approach also makes the purpose of the letter unmistakable. Stating your purpose first puts busy readers on your side; unconsciously, they may actually thank you for not wasting their time. These advantages typically make the direct approach the best choice in the following types of correspondence: order acknowledgments; letters of credit such as positive credit references and letters granting credit; adjustment letters; personnel-related letters such as letters of recommendation and employment-related letters, and in social correspondence that communicates goodwill.

The following rules of thumb will help you organize information according to the direct approach:

- Give your good news and, when appropriate, state what specific steps are being taken.
- Explain the details of the news. Refer specifically to any enclosures.
- Close with an expression of goodwill that may also summarize and prompt the reader to take action.

As you will see later in this chapter, communicating goodwill is a crucial part of any good-news message and is often part of the close. Your closing, however, may have other objectives. For example, you may need your closing to tell your reader what will happen next, to ask your reader for input, or to point to future action, either by asking questions or making suggestions. Table 7.1 summarizes these possible functions and gives an example for each.

TABLE 7.1	*Functions of the Letter Closing*

FUNCTION	EXAMPLE
• Tell the reader what will happen next.	Now that we have succeeded in improving our internal mail-delivery system, you can expect incoming mail to remain in the mail room no longer than one hour before being delivered.
• Ask the reader for input.	As I have explained, we can settle your claim in either of two ways. Please let me know which option you prefer.
• Point to future action by asking a question.	Now that your credit line with us has been increased to $100,000, can we talk about how we can better serve your company's needs?
• Point to future action through a suggestion.	We are all pleased that you have agreed to write this book. We are ready to begin planning the project as soon as we can arrange a meeting. Let me suggest that you consider submitting the manuscript electronically because computers can cut months off the schedule. I will be glad to discuss this with you when we meet.

EXPRESSING GOODWILL IN RESPONSE TO INQUIRIES

Many good-news and informative letters are responses to inquiries. Both businesses and individual customers send letters ordering merchandise, requesting credit, asking for information, making claims, issuing invitations, and so on. Instead of perceiving such requests as tedious demands on your time (or even nuisances), consider them opportunities to cement relationships and, ultimately, to generate sales.

In a speech to fellow business colleagues, W. G. Werner, manager of public relations at Procter & Gamble, once emphasized the importance of the goodwill approach to handling inquiries. Because most of the customers who write P&G are homemakers, Werner's comments were addressed to women. "A letter to the company," he began,

> is a personal act of the writer. When we are confronted with a pile of mail, this fact is easy to forget. Business correspondence, through the years, not only in its traditional stilted phraseology, but also too often in its very physical handling, has been considered a mechanical process…—almost a nuisance—instead of a most important channel for building friendship and goodwill.
>
> When a woman takes up her pen to write a letter, she is entering into quite a different and unique relationship—a personal relationship—with the company. Suddenly she has stopped being one of the mass market; she is a human being writing to some rather mysterious entity which she knows only as a "company" or a "corporation." Whether she is expressing appreciation for the way a product serves her, writing a complaint, seeking help, or offering an idea, she hopes that she is writing to another human being like herself.
>
> The way in which her letter is handled may determine whether she is a friend for life, a disappointed and embittered antagonist, or a confirmed cynic concerning "cold-blooded corporations."[1]

Goodwill can, of course, be communicated in many ways—in the tone and language of a letter, in the speed with which a company responds to an inquiry, even in the condition of the response when it arrives. Although paying attention to such seemingly small details seems to make good business sense, many writers fail to do so. As an experiment, business writer Paul Vincent wrote to fifty companies whose ads invited inquiries. Within ten days, he had received only eight responses; nine responses took between twenty-one and thirty days; twenty-nine responses took more than a month. Four letters were never answered. Not only did most of the responses arrive late, but Vincent's name was also misspelled a dozen times on the return envelopes; six envelopes arrived with postage due; the contents of four envelopes were in bad condition; and two envelopes were empty.[2]

On the other hand, many companies fully realize the importance of handling inquiries properly. One such company gave the following instructions to the department responsible for dealing with customer requests:

1. Answer all inquiries the same day they are received. Strike while the iron is hot! Give inquiries the right of way over all other correspondence.

2. Size up the needs of the prospect and answer his or her inquiry in terms of the advantage of our product to *him* or *her*.

3. Don't make the reader wait for information while you refer him or her to "local representatives" or "branch offices." Answer the reader's questions first—and let your local agents follow it up.

4. Allow a reasonable amount of time for an order or a reply to come in, and then follow it up with another letter. Keep on writing at regular intervals as long as the percentage of returns from similar follow-ups makes it profitable.[3]

As you can see, time is regarded as a critical factor in handling customer inquiries. The best advice is to answer every inquiry as soon as possible. In the event of a delay, send a short note acknowledging the inquiry and explaining when you will answer. When an inquiry is better answered by someone in a different department or someone with special expertise, forward it as soon as possible. If you yourself are asked to handle this type of inquiry, it may be necessary to explain the situation to the reader. In your opening paragraph, for example, explain why you are writing rather than the person to whom the inquiry was originally addressed.

In the following sections, we will examine five specific types of good-news and goodwill correspondence: *order acknowledgments, letters of credit, adjustment letters, positive personnel letters,* and *social correspondence.* All are inquiry responses.

ORDER ACKNOWLEDGMENTS

Orders are not generally acknowledged by letter. Because most orders are routine, customers expect to receive merchandise without the formal letter of explanation known as an **order acknowledgment**. There are, however, two exceptions to this rule. Letters are often sent to accompany orders from new customers and very large orders from old customers. In these cases, order acknowledgments give the writer the opportunity to suggest future sales and to introduce other goods or services. When used in this way, order acknowledgments are also considered business-promotion letters.

Every order acknowledgment should contain the following specific information: the order date and invoice number; the date on which the order will be shipped and the method of shipment; a statement thanking the customer for the order; and a goodwill message that focuses on helping the customer with future goods or services. Figure 7.1 is a sample order acknowledgment. Note the care that the writer must take in order to organize a variety of different types of information.

order acknowldgment
Formal letter of explanation concerning receipt of an order for merchandise

LETTERS OF CREDIT

Two types of credit letters communicate good news: letters that provide positive credit references and letters granting credit. Such communication is important to businesses and customers alike—the granting of credit to responsible applicants is the backbone of U.S. business.

Credit is a system whereby a person who can't pay gets another person who can't pay to guarantee that he can pay.

Charles Dickens
English novelist

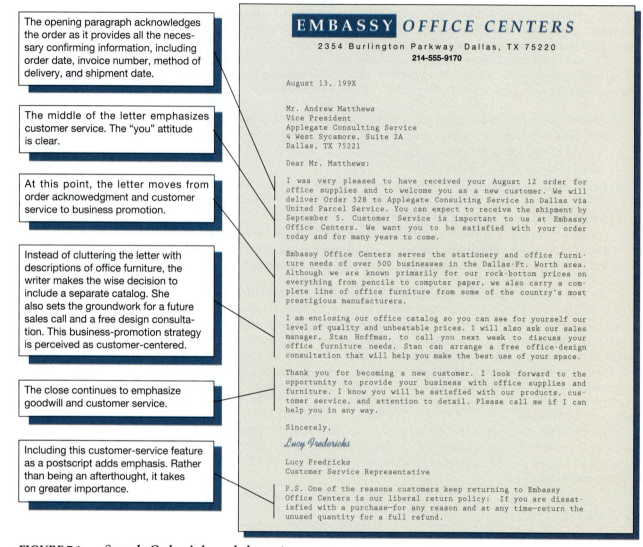

The opening paragraph acknowledges the order as it provides all the necessary confirming information, including order date, invoice number, method of delivery, and shipment date.

The middle of the letter emphasizes customer service. The "you" attitude is clear.

At this point, the letter moves from order acknowledgment and customer service to business promotion.

Instead of cluttering the letter with descriptions of office furniture, the writer makes the wise decision to include a separate catalog. She also sets the groundwork for a future sales call and a free design consultation. This business-promotion strategy is perceived as customer-centered.

The close continues to emphasize goodwill and customer service.

Including this customer-service feature as a postscript adds emphasis. Rather than being an afterthought, it takes on greater importance.

EMBASSY *OFFICE CENTERS*

2354 Burlington Parkway Dallas, TX 75220
214-555-9170

August 13, 199X

Mr. Andrew Matthews
Vice President
Applegate Consulting Service
4 West Sycamore, Suite 2A
Dallas, TX 75221

Dear Mr. Matthews:

I was very pleased to have received your August 12 order for office supplies and to welcome you as a new customer. We will deliver Order 528 to Applegate Consulting Service in Dallas via United Parcel Service. You can expect to receive the shipment by September 5. Customer Service is important to us at Embassy Office Centers. We want you to be satisfied with your order today and for many years to come.

Embassy Office Centers serves the stationery and office furniture needs of over 500 businesses in the Dallas-Ft. Worth area. Although we are known primarily for our rock-bottom prices on everything from pencils to computer paper, we also carry a complete line of office furniture from some of the country's most prestigious manufacturers.

I am enclosing our office catalog so you can see for yourself our level of quality and unbeatable prices. I will also ask our sales manager, Stan Hoffman, to call you next week to discuss your office furniture needs. Stan can arrange a free office-design consultation that will help you make the best use of your space.

Thank you for becoming a new customer. I look forward to the opportunity to provide your business with office supplies and furniture. I know you will be satisfied with our products, customer service, and attention to detail. Please call me if I can help you in any way.

Sincerely,

Lucy Fredericks

Lucy Fredricks
Customer Service Representative

P.S. One of the reasons customers keep returning to Embassy Office Centers is our liberal return policy: If you are dissatisfied with a purchase—for any reason and at any time—return the unused quantity for a full refund.

FIGURE 7.1   *Sample Order Acknowledgment*

Positive Credit References

credit reference
Good-news letter in which one company attests to the financial well-being of another

Like a doctor's diagnosis of health or illness, a **credit reference** is a letter that entrusts one company with the most confidential information about another company's financial well-being. If you are asked to supply such a reference, remember that the recipient may be looking for reasons to deny credit. As a result, positive credit references must be carefully worded to avoid any suggestion of financial trouble. They should also stick to the facts—speculation can place writers in the middle of a lawsuit.

Because credit references are stamps of approval attesting to the financial health of other individuals or firms, do not give them lightly. State your reference in terms of facts and place it only in the context of specific dealings with an organization or individual. Avoid general impressions or broad statements of confidence in the company's financial health.

As we observed in Chapter 6, many credit inquiries request that information be supplied either on the inquiry letter itself or on a separate form. However, letters are often necessary. Figure 7.2 is an example of a credit-reference letter. Note the writer's handling of factual details throughout the middle of the letter.

AMERICAN EASTERN BANK
1111 Empire Boulevard
Alexandria, VA 22304
(703) 555-1214

June 15, 199X

Mr. Nicholas Holliday
Credit Manager
Overhill Auto Wholesalers
3000 Mason Boulevard
Alexandria, VA 22304

Dear Mr. Holliday:

I am glad to give you the credit information you requested on Jonathan Baron, owner of Park Avenue Auto Supply Center in Alexandria. Although this company began only six months ago, it has met all its financial obligations with American Eastern Bank. In addition, Mr. Baron has an excellent personal credit history with our bank.

Currently, Mr. Baron has a $20,000 business loan from this bank. He has made regular monthly payments on this loan. Park Avenue Auto Supply Center has no other outstanding business debt with the American Eastern Bank.

Mr. Baron also has maintained a personal checking and money-market account with us for the past five years. He has always maintained adequate balances to meet his checking needs and has never overdrawn his account.

Based on our experience, Park Avenue Auto Supply Center and Jonathan Baron have demonstrated a history of creditworthiness. It has been a pleasure working with this company.

I hope this information is helpful, and I trust that it will remain confidential.

Sincerely,

Seth Overfeld

Seth Overfeld
Branch Manager

> The letter opens by identifying the subject of the letter and stating the good news.

> Here, the letter supplies concrete facts about the company's dealings with the bank.

> This paragraph provides information about the subject's personal financial dealings with the bank. In both cases, the writer focuses on facts rather than speculation or opinion.

> The recommendation, which concludes the middle of the letter, avoids general statements. Rather, it focuses on the bank's experience with Park Avenue Auto Supply Center and Jonathan Baron.

> The close stresses the confidential nature of this information.

FIGURE 7.2   *Sample Credit Reference*

Letters Granting Credit

When a company decides to issue credit, it usually sends a letter to inform the customer of its decision. This letter has four equally important functions:

1. To state that credit has been approved
2. To summarize the specific terms of the credit agreement
3. To establish goodwill by welcoming the customer as a new business client
4. To encourage future sales

Tone is also critical in letters granting credit. According to business communication authorities Robert L. Shurter and Donald J. Leonard, a letter granting credit

> may be compared in its general tone to a note of welcome to a friend who has just arrived in the writer's city; it should welcome him or her and express the hope that the "visit" will be enjoyable and that he or she will take advantage of the many facilities the "city" offers. The general tone of welcome, of interest in the customer's welfare, and of willingness to serve is invaluable at the beginning of what the creditor hopes will be a long and pleasant business relationship.[4]

I have discovered the philosopher's stone that turns everything into gold: It is "pay as you go."

*John Randolph
American statesman*

Letters granting credit, therefore, should be as positive as possible. For example, try to eliminate negative statements that might suggest the failure of the credit relationship. What strategies does the letter in Figure 7.3 use to strike its positive tone?

GOOD-NEWS ADJUSTMENT LETTERS

adjustment letter
Good-news letter written in response to a claim letter to inform the customer how a company intends to handle a specific problem

Written in response to a claim letter, an **adjustment letter** informs the customer how you intend to handle a specific problem. More than anything else, adjustment letters are opportunities to build goodwill by repairing past damage and restoring confidence in a future business relationship.

In writing an adjustment letter, you are often dealing with someone who is annoyed or angry. Even if you concede an error, therefore, the tone of your letter must be conciliatory and your words precise. Handle this situation by responding throughout in a positive manner that shows that you respect the customer's position. For example, instead of rehashing the details of the problem, focus instead on how your company will correct it in order to satisfy the customer.

If your company is at fault, admit the error. Avoid alibis or excuses when you know you are wrong. At the same time, however, do not make your compa-

The opening paragraph provides the good news that credit has been granted. It also extends a goodwill welcome to the customer.

Because the original credit request is tied to an order, the first detail that the writer mentions is the order information.

The middle of the letter explains the credit terms. This explanation avoids any mention of such negatives as failure to comply with the agreement.

At this point, the letter focuses on business promotion and customer service. It communicates the "you" attitude.

Business promotion continues. However, the focus always remains on customer service.

The close emphasizes goodwill as it encourages future sales.

OVERHILL AUTO WHOLESALERS
3000 Mason Boulevard
Alexandria, VA 22304
(703) 555-6994

July 1, 199X

Mr. Jonathan Baron
Park Avenue Auto Supply Center
4 Long Lots Road
Alexandria, VA 22304

Dear Mr. Baron:

I am pleased to inform you that your credit account with Overhill Auto Wholesalers has been approved. I am delighted to welcome you as a new credit customer.

Your first order for tires, tail lights, and hubcaps, issued on purchase order 268, in the amount of $2,130.43, will be shipped on July 23.

Starting today, your company has a $5,000 credit line with Overhill Auto Wholesalers. Monthly statements, mailed on the fifteenth of each month, include a ten-day grace period. All outstanding balances are subject to an interest charge of 1 percent per month.

Please keep us in mind for all of your auto supply needs. We carry a complete line of automotive products for both foreign and domestic cars.

When you need a part for an emergency repair, we can have it to you the next day.

I have asked Sales Representative Vincent Gower to handle your account. He will call you on Friday to arrange a meeting. He is anxious to tell you more about our goods and services, including point-of-purchase promotional displays. I am also enclosing our latest catalog, which shows our complete merchandise line.

We at Overhill Auto Wholesalers look forward to serving your company for many years. Our greatest satisfaction is to form a working relationship with young companies and watch them grow and prosper.

Sincerely,

Nicholas Holliday

Nicholas Holliday
Credit Manager

FIGURE 7.3   *Sample Letter Granting Credit*

PRACTICAL TIPS
The "You" Attitude

There is nothing more basic than focusing on the interests and needs of your readers. However, making the reader the center of attention does much more than satisfy an academic exercise; as business communication authority Barbara Lau demonstrates in the following example, it also gets results.

To update its address file, an insurance company sent this message to half of its customers:

Since we haven't written you in some time, please help us bring our records up to date by filling in and returning the other half of this card.

Meanwhile, the other half of the company's customers received a revised message that focused on the reader:

So that your dividend checks, premium notices, and other messages of importance may reach you promptly, please fill out and return the other half of this card.

Not surprisingly, while only 3 percent of the company's policyholders bothered to answer the first card, 90 percent of those who received the second card answered within a week. The source of the difference: the *"you" attitude.*

The "you" attitude is relatively simple to master: It means shifting your point of view from "I" the writer to "you" the reader. Each of the five sentences below is written from the "I" perspective and could be revised to focus on the reader:

1. We are pleased to announce…
2. We are glad you have chosen our firm.
3. We cannot reinstate your service until your bill has been paid.
4. We expect all employees to request their vacation schedule by March 1.
5. We are happy to approve your credit application.

Revised in the interest of reader-friendliness, these sentences now communicate a significantly different attitude:

1. You will be glad to learn that…
2. Thank you for giving us the opportunity to serve you.
3. Your service will be reinstated within one day after you pay your bill.
4. Your deadline for scheduling vacation time is March 1.
5. Congratulations for qualifying for our "preferred customer" line of credit.

Is there any time when the "you" attitude is *not* effective? Perhaps when you must inform a reader that he or she has made a mistake. In these cases, rely on the passive voice. For example, instead of writing, "You failed to send us a check this month," write, "No payment was received."

Source: Barbara Lau, "Adding Instant Readership Appeal to Your Business Correspondence," *NRECA Management Quarterly,* Summer 1989, pp. 13–15.

ny look foolish or incompetent in the process. Saying something like "This mistake has plagued our production process for the past two years" will cause the buyer to lose complete confidence in your firm. Although it is acceptable to apologize for the mistake once, offering more than one apology indicates unnecessary weakness.

Try to focus on the way your language will affect the reader. If the customer feels that an adjustment is being made condescendingly or that you are agreeing to terms only grudgingly, you may be creating further resentment. In addition, remember that business customers making claims do not consider themselves "complainants." They regard themselves as people seeking fair treatment. Therefore, instead of referring to the problem as a *complaint*, call it an *error* or use the more neutral term *misunderstanding.* Similarly, avoid language which implies that you are questioning the customer's truthfulness. Writing "I received your letter *claiming* that four dishes arrived damaged" is inflammatory. Say instead, "I appreciate knowing about the problem in the shipment of dishes."

Say nothing to minimize the importance of a customer's claim. If it is important to the customer, it should be important to you. Customers also appreciate genuine expressions of sympathy—for example, "I'm sure this error caused inconvenience and delay. We're working to get the problem solved as soon as possible." Sympathy helps customers to feel that you are on their side in your desire to resolve the problem.

Finally, the wording of an adjustment letter should take into account both company policy and legal issues. Do not make promises that your company cannot or will not back, and avoid language that can be used against your company in court. Admitting, for example, that a product is "defective" is tantamount to admitting liability.[5]

There are two types of positive adjustment letters: letters that grant the requested adjustment and letters that offer a compromise solution. We will examine each type of letter in detail but point out first that both types use the following pattern to communicate good-news messages:

- Communicate the good news at the start of the letter. Explain that you are granting the adjustment. If necessary, apologize for the problem.
- While communicating goodwill and a commitment to customer service, explain the nature of the problem and how you intend to solve it.
- Conclude by promoting company products or services as you continue to rebuild goodwill. Express appreciation for the customer's continued business.

Letters Granting Adjustment

Depending on the responsibility for correcting a problem, letters granting an adjustment fall into two categories: letters written when the *company* is at fault and letters written when the *customer* is at fault. Naturally, some adjustment letters are offers of compromise. Although all three use a good-news approach, the intent of each letter is somewhat different.

WHEN THE COMPANY IS AT FAULT   Every company, of course, enjoys receiving letters of praise from satisfied customers. As a rule, however, companies are subject to human and other forms of error and therefore make mistakes. They deliver wrong or damaged merchandise, miss crucial delivery dates, or provide unsatisfactory service. When the customers on the receiving end of these problems submit claims, they deserve immediate attention and a fair solution. When the company is at fault, the most important challenge is to reestablish goodwill: You want the customer to return.

Consider the case of Patti Trantow of Morgan Hill, California. Several years ago, she was sitting in an aisle seat on a United Airlines flight when the overhead storage bin opened. A laptop computer fell from the bin and struck her on the head, causing intense pain and raising a bump the size of a goose egg. "I didn't sleep for four days," reports Trantow. When she complained to United, she received a check for $500 and a travel voucher. The situation was hardly unique—United Airlines alone received 118 similar complaints in that year.

The sample adjustment letter in Figure 7.4 could have been written by an airline to an injured passenger like Patti Trantow. Notice the attitude that the writer adopts as he attempts to reestablish goodwill. Note, too, the combination of conciliatory tone and specific details for addressing the problem.[6]

WHEN THE CUSTOMER IS AT FAULT   In front of a large supermarket in Norwalk, Connecticut, there is a giant boulder that reads:

Rule 1: The customer is always right.

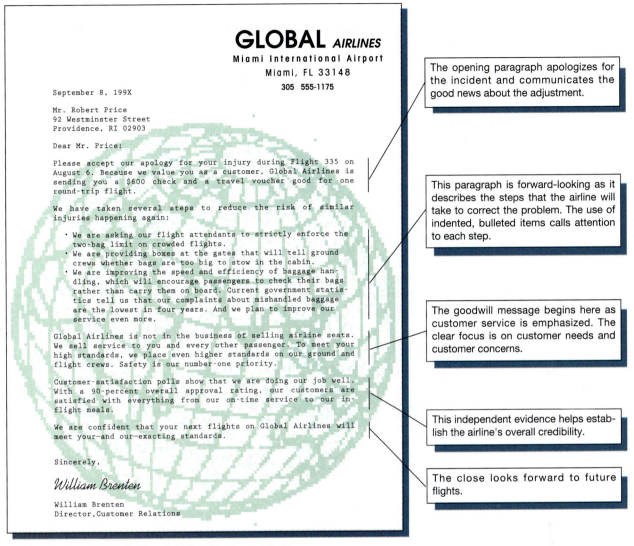

GLOBAL AIRLINES
Miami International Airport
Miami, FL 33148
305 555-1175

September 8, 199X

Mr. Robert Price
92 Westminster Street
Providence, RI 02903

Dear Mr. Price:

Please accept our apology for your injury during Flight 335 on August 6. Because we value you as a customer, Global Airlines is sending you a $600 check and a travel voucher good for one round-trip flight.

We have taken several steps to reduce the risk of similar injuries happening again:

- We are asking our flight attendants to strictly enforce the two-bag limit on crowded flights.
- We are providing boxes at the gates that will tell ground crews whether bags are too big to stow in the cabin.
- We are improving the speed and efficiency of baggage handling, which will encourage passengers to check their bags rather than carry them on board. Current government statistics tell us that our complaints about mishandled baggage are the lowest in four years. And we plan to improve our service even more.

Global Airlines is not in the business of selling airline seats. We sell service to you and every other passenger. To meet your high standards, we place even higher standards on our ground and flight crews. Safety is our number-one priority.

Customer-satisfaction polls show that we are doing our job well. With a 90-percent overall approval rating, our customers are satisfied with everything from our on-time service to our inflight meals.

We are confident that your next flights on Global Airlines will meet your—and our—exacting standards.

Sincerely,

William Brenten

William Brenten
Director, Customer Relations

The opening paragraph apologizes for the incident and communicates the good news about the adjustment.

This paragraph is forward-looking as it describes the steps that the airline will take to correct the problem. The use of indented, bulleted items calls attention to each step.

The goodwill message begins here as customer service is emphasized. The clear focus is on customer needs and customer concerns.

This independent evidence helps establish the airline's overall credibility.

The close looks forward to future flights.

FIGURE 7.4 *Sample Goodwill Adjustment Letter*

Rule 2: If the customer is ever wrong, go back and reread rule number 1.

The philosophy behind this policy is that customer loyalty is essential to business success. Firms like this bend over backward to give the customer the benefit of the doubt in the event of a problem. To keep customers happy, customer-service manager Helen Telesco gives complaining customers what they want even when she is sure that complaints are unfounded: "I'll refund money," says Telesco, "even if I'm sure someone is returning an item we don't even sell. My job is easy. I just say yes." The store's founder liked to affirm his company's policy by recounting the following incident. "A woman comes in after Thanksgiving with a turkey she claims was dry. We sold 30,000 turkeys—was there one dry one? You know she cooked it too long, but you give her another $20 turkey. At the end of the year, she's spent $5,000—what the hell is one $20 turkey?"[7]

If you work for a company that embraces this attitude, you may find yourself in the position of agreeing to customer requests even when you are sure that a customer is at fault. In these cases, you may choose —after saying yes—to explain to the customer what he or she did to cause the problem. Tone is crucial in these instances—sounding self-righteous or condescending will turn customers away just as quickly as refusing a request.

WHEN COMPROMISE IS NECESSARY   When neither the customer nor the company is entirely at fault, compromise may be the best solution. This is especially true when you expect that giving the customer the same merchandise or the same service a second time will cause the same problem. In these cases, an adjustment letter acts as a kind of counteroffer by suggesting a fair and equitable compromise. It is a good-news letter because you are offering a solution of equal or greater value that you believe will benefit the customer. Business communication authority L. E. Frailey uses the following example to make the point. "A restaurant wanted 75 pounds of chicken parts. A meat supply house had 30 whole chickens ready for immediate delivery. The compromise was actually in the customer's favor, and comments about extra meat, bones for stock, etc., further warmed the customer's feelings toward the company."[8] Of course, customers must accept your judgment and, in the end, the decision is theirs. In some cases, you may decide to offer the customer a choice of the same merchandise, alternative merchandise, or a full refund. Consider the example in Figure 7.5, in which the writer must use the middle of the letter to explain the details of his solution in a tone that encourages continued goodwill.

PROGRESS CHECK

1. Why is it wise to present good news first in a letter?
2. Why do we say "the customer is always right"?
3. In which situations do companies generally send order acknowledgments to customers? What purpose(s) do order acknowledgments serve?
4. Why are adjustment letters an opportunity to build goodwill?

POSITIVE PERSONNEL LETTERS

The hardest thing is writing a recommendation for someone we know.

Frank McKinney
(Kin) Hubbard
American humorist

As a businessperson, you may be called upon to write a variety of personnel-related correspondence, including *letters of recommendation* and other positive *employment-related letters*. Personnel letters play a crucial role in hiring the best people and in starting the employment relationship in a positive direction.

Letters of Recommendation

letter of recommendation Good-news personnel letter which speaks positively about a candidate's background and performance and which may tie the candidate's knowledge, skills, and abilities to a specific job objective

Among a job candidate's most valuable assets are well-written letters of recommendation. When candidates can present positive recommendation letters, they help employers do what they will try to do anyway—check each candidate's background. **Letters of recommendation** are reference letters that speak positively about a candidate's background and performance and may tie the candidate's knowledge, skills, and abilities to a specific job objective (see Chapter 16). If you can attest to a job candidate's background and accomplishments, you may be approached for a written recommendation. Former employers, co-workers, and even subordinates are in positions to write effective recommendation letters.

Every letter should start with an introductory paragraph that names the job candidate and recommends that person for employment. In doing so, the paragraph should state the candidate's full name, the position for which he or she is applying, and the relationship between the candidate and the writer.

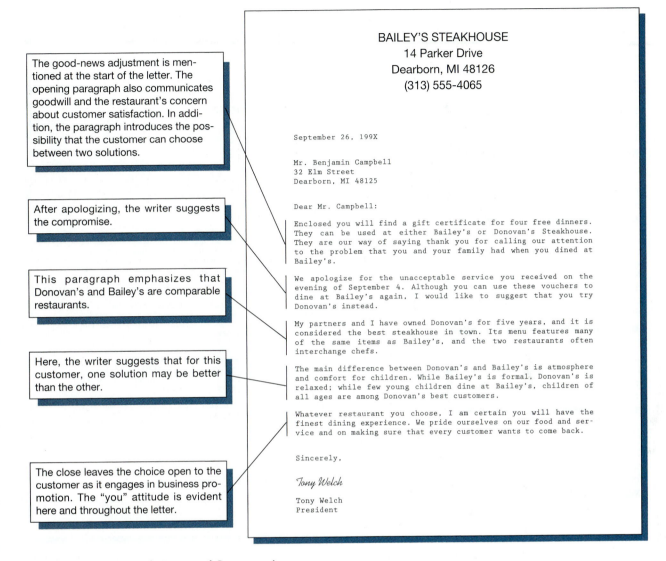

The good-news adjustment is mentioned at the start of the letter. The opening paragraph also communicates goodwill and the restaurant's concern about customer satisfaction. In addition, the paragraph introduces the possibility that the customer can choose between two solutions.

After apologizing, the writer suggests the compromise.

This paragraph emphasizes that Donovan's and Bailey's are comparable restaurants.

Here, the writer suggests that for this customer, one solution may be better than the other.

The close leaves the choice open to the customer as it engages in business promotion. The "you" attitude is evident here and throughout the letter.

BAILEY'S STEAKHOUSE
14 Parker Drive
Dearborn, MI 48126
(313) 555-4065

September 26, 199X

Mr. Benjamin Campbell
32 Elm Street
Dearborn, MI 48125

Dear Mr. Campbell:

Enclosed you will find a gift certificate for four free dinners. They can be used at either Bailey's or Donovan's Steakhouse. They are our way of saying thank you for calling our attention to the problem that you and your family had when you dined at Bailey's.

We apologize for the unacceptable service you received on the evening of September 4. Although you can use these vouchers to dine at Bailey's again, I would like to suggest that you try Donovan's instead.

My partners and I have owned Donovan's for five years, and it is considered the best steakhouse in town. Its menu features many of the same items as Bailey's, and the two restaurants often interchange chefs.

The main difference between Donovan's and Bailey's is atmosphere and comfort for children. While Bailey's is formal, Donovan's is relaxed; while few young children dine at Bailey's, children of all ages are among Donovan's best customers.

Whatever restaurant you choose, I am certain you will have the finest dining experience. We pride ourselves on our food and service and on making sure that every customer wants to come back.

Sincerely,

Tony Welch

Tony Welch
President

FIGURE 7.5   *Sample Letter of Compromise*

The letter should continue with a *value paragraph*—a paragraph describing the candidate's background and outstanding characteristics and explaining why he or she is qualified for the job. Short examples can be an effective way to communicate this information. Finally, a complementary close repeats the recommendation and opens the door for future contact.

Be truthful as you describe the candidate's background. Not only are embellishments unfair to prospective employers, but they have been known to involve writers in lawsuits. Stick to the facts as you discuss the candidate's knowledge, skills, and personal characteristics and place the discussion in the context of his or her job history and job objective. If you cannot write a positive recommendation, avoid writing one at all—the letter may create legal problems for you and your company.

A recommendation, of course, need not say everything—indeed, there are things that you *should* not have to say and things that you may not *want* to say. For example, you need not mention why a candidate left your company or discuss unimportant work problems.

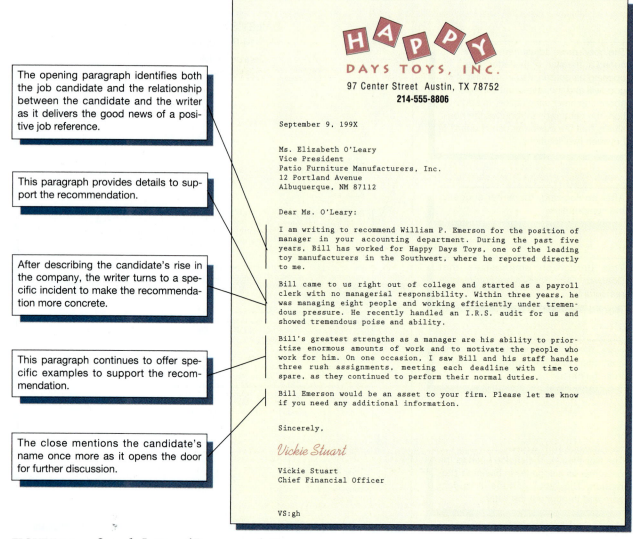

The opening paragraph identifies both the job candidate and the relationship between the candidate and the writer as it delivers the good news of a positive job reference.

This paragraph provides details to support the recommendation.

After describing the candidate's rise in the company, the writer turns to a specific incident to make the recommendation more concrete.

This paragraph continues to offer specific examples to support the recommendation.

The close mentions the candidate's name once more as it opens the door for further discussion.

HAPPY

DAYS TOYS, INC.

97 Center Street Austin, TX 78752
214-555-8806

September 9, 199X

Ms. Elizabeth O'Leary
Vice President
Patio Furniture Manufacturers, Inc.
12 Portland Avenue
Albuquerque, NM 87112

Dear Ms. O'Leary:

I am writing to recommend William P. Emerson for the position of manager in your accounting department. During the past five years, Bill has worked for Happy Days Toys, one of the leading toy manufacturers in the Southwest, where he reported directly to me.

Bill came to us right out of college and started as a payroll clerk with no managerial responsibility. Within three years, he was managing eight people and working efficiently under tremendous pressure. He recently handled an I.R.S. audit for us and showed tremendous poise and ability.

Bill's greatest strengths as a manager are his ability to prioritize enormous amounts of work and to motivate the people who work for him. On one occasion, I saw Bill and his staff handle three rush assignments, meeting each deadline with time to spare, as they continued to perform their normal duties.

Bill Emerson would be an asset to your firm. Please let me know if you need any additional information.

Sincerely,

Vickie Stuart

Vickie Stuart
Chief Financial Officer

VS:gh

FIGURE 7.6   *Sample Letter of Recommendation*

Letters of recommendation may either state the candidate's background in a general way or target the candidate's background to a specific job. When a candidate requests a letter that can be submitted at various job interviews, the letter will be more general than one written at the request of a specific employer. Consider the sample letter in Figure 7.6, in which the writer's task is to apply specific details about the candidate to a prospective employer's specific needs.

Employment-Related Letters

Hiring employees involves writing positive employment-related letters. **Employment-related letters** present job offers, acknowledge candidates' applications, invite applicants for interviews, and discuss additional details after an offer has been accepted.

Because employment-related letters often have potential legal ramifications, learn company policy before putting anything in writing. This is especially important in job-offer letters. In many companies, these letters come only from the human-resources department, which is charged with having a knowledge of the law. Remember that statements made in job offers can generally be considered legally binding promises. Therefore, include only those

employment-related letters
good-news letters presenting job offers, acknowledging candidate's applications, inviting applicants for interviews, or discussing additional details after an offer has been accepted

facts necessary to communicate your offer. State the offer, the title of the position, starting salary, and the date to report to work. Moreover, in a business environment where change is constant, avoid statements that are in fact speculation—for example, "Within three years, you can expect to be promoted to a manager" or "Although you are starting at a salary of $30,000, within two years you can expect to earn $45,000." Finally, if the ultimate hiring decision depends on such factors as background checks, medical examinations, or drug testing, be cautious about stating categorically that the candidate has been awarded the job.

GOODWILL MESSAGES

The most precious thing a man can have Is the goodwill of others. It is something as fragile as an orchid And as beautiful; As precious as gold nugget— And as hard to find; As powerful as a great turbine— And as hard to build; As wonderful as youth— And as hard to keep.

Anonymous

Goodwill messages are messages written to create or maintain bonds of friendship or understanding—personal, professional, or both—between writer and recipient. Goodwill messages are usually written from one individual to another rather than from one company representative to another. However, although the exchange of personal messages generally relegates business to a secondary role in the relationship, goodwill messages maintain links, both direct and indirect, with future business activities. According to writing consultant L. E. Frailey, the difference between regularly issued letters and goodwill messages

goodwill message Message written to create a bond of friendship or understanding—personal, professional, or both—between writer and recipient

> is not so much in spirit as in purpose. The regular letters accomplish a double job—they sell, they collect, they adjust, *and* they win goodwill. But the winning of goodwill is the *only* job performed by [goodwill letters]. They can be ignored, and the routines of the business will continue. For some they may be "unnecessary," but you can be sure it is a mistake not to use them.[9]

How would you feel if you received a letter from a supplier congratulating you on a promotion or on the birth of a new baby? Similarly, imagine how a customer would feel if you sent a birthday greeting or a letter of condolence on the death of a parent. In a strict business sense, these messages are not expected or necessary, but they are sure to leave a residue of good feelings toward you and your company.

Goodwill messages fall into five categories: *thank-you messages, responses to invitations, letters of congratulations, letters of condolence and sympathy*, and *greetings*. To be effective, these messages must be personal and sincere and should never be form letters. They are generally brief and use a direct organizational approach.

Thank-You Messages

Many situations in business that have nothing directly to do with business transactions create opportunities to express appreciation. For example, it is appropriate to thank someone for a recommendation, for agreeing to an interview, for spending an hour on the phone explaining information, for making a presentation at a meeting, for providing emergency service above and beyond the call of duty, or for cutting through government red tape. Because notes of thanks are personal messages, they can be either handwritten or typed.

Say thank you to the individual who helped you and, when appropriate, consider sending a copy to the person's supervisor. For example, a mid-level manager might work with a Social Security Administration representative to solve a complex benefits-eligibility problem involving a member of her department. When the problem is solved, the manager might very well send a

INTERVIEW

Jim Ruppel, Director of Customer Relations at Southwest Airlines

Dallas-based Southwest Airlines is known for its determination to keep customers happy—an attitude that comes from the top. CEO Herbert Kelleher believes in "dignifying" the customer and uses responses to customers' letters to communicate his message. About a thousand customers write to Southwest each week, and most receive detailed, individualized replies (a seven-page response is not uncommon). Forty-five employees spend more than 1,500 person-hours a week answering these letters, which include requests for information, complaints, and letters of praise. We asked Jim Ruppel, director of customer relations at Southwest, about the approach that he and his staff take to the company's correspondence.

Question: Does Southwest Airlines have an overriding philosophy that guides its responses to customers' letters?

Answer: We take an individualized approach. We take the time to investigate every letter so that customers feel they are at the center of our attention. We want every customer to continue flying Southwest, and we see letters as opportunities to cement goodwill, even when dealing with complaints.

Customers are one of the best sources of feedback we know. If we started with the attitude that everything were perfect, we would never look for new solutions—and we certainly wouldn't find any help in the thousands of letters we receive each year. But because we begin with the conviction that we can improve, we realize that customers—the people who actually use our service—can help us remain competitive.

Question: Do you ever rely on form letters?

Answer: Only for routine matters. For example, we use form letters when passengers forget to give the gate agent their frequent-flyer card and write to us for frequent-flyer credit. In a case like this, consumers don't expect an individual-

note of thanks to both the representative and his supervisor. These notes often become part of a worker's permanent personnel file and may affect future raises and promotions.

Responses to Invitations

Businesspeople are often invited to different functions, such as conferences and meetings. Whether an invitation is made in writing, in person, or over the phone, a written response may be appropriate. Responses to invitations are considered letters of appreciation because they thank someone for a specific offer. In accepting an invitation, express goodwill by making your response forward-looking and positive.

Letters of Congratulations

There are many reasons to offer congratulations in business—a promotion, an award for professional excellence or community involvement, a graduate degree awarded after years of night school, a store opening, a new hard-won account. Every letter of congratulations should begin with well wishes and end with a further expression of goodwill. Specific details contribute a sincere, personal tone. Letters of congratulations can be as short as a paragraph or as long as a page.

Word your congratulations according to your relationship with the recipient. For example, when the relationship is not personal or the recipient is in a

ized response—but they do expect a timely response. We try to answer every letter within two to three weeks.

Question: Are you always successful?

Answer: That's our goal, but responses sometimes take as long as six weeks. Southwest is a 24-hour-a-day, seven-day-a-week operation. People have Wednesdays and Thursdays off; flight attendants and pilots can have nine days off in a row. So it may take time to get information from employees in order to answer a letter. Although it's faster to use form letters in non-routine cases, we won't do it.

Question: Do you have a special way of dealing with angry complaint letters?

Answer: I try to keep my composure at all times. If I get emotionally upset, I won't be able to help the customer solve the problem. What also helps is the willingness to admit errors if we make them. Of course, we're not shy about telling customers when we're right.

Question: Is it sometimes difficult to understand what customers want because of their poor writing skills?

Answer: In some cases, we spend a lot of time trying to understand what the customer is saying. When we aren't sure or don't have enough information, we write back asking for more details.

Question: Southwest seems to go one step further than most companies in attempting to create goodwill. You send birthday cards to frequent flyers and always capitalize the word "customer" in correspondence and ads. What kind of responses have you gotten from these goodwill gestures?

Answer: We get warm letters from many customers thanking us for the birthday cards; everyone likes to be remembered. Employees feel wonderful about the program, too. They appreciate working for a company that cares enough about its customers to do something like this.

Sources: Telephone interview with Jim Ruppel; background information from Richard S. Teitelbaum, "Southwest Airlines: Where Service Flies Right," *Fortune*, August 24, 1992, pp. 115–116.

higher position than you, choose a formal, reserved style. However, when the reader is a professional colleague, it is acceptable to be warm and companionable. Similarly, when you know the recipient well or have a higher professional status, feel free to engage in a light and friendly tone.[10]

Letters of Condolence and Sympathy

A **letter of condolence** is sent when a business associate or an associate's family member dies. Because letters of condolence arrive during periods of great loss, they should express sorrow and respect in a simple, direct way.

Many people have trouble finding the right words to express their feelings; others fear that contact at such a time may be an intrusion. As a result, many messages of condolence are never sent; many others are sent in the form of commercial cards. To express feelings that give comfort to the bereaved, ask yourself what words you would appreciate if you were in that person's position. Then ask yourself what you would say if you were offering condolences face to face. While you should avoid discussing the details of a person's death or allusions to your own religious beliefs, it is appropriate to offer tangible help if you are actually willing to give it.

Use the direct approach in a letter of condolence. The writer of the letter in Figure 7.7 starts with an expression of sympathy and then adds a personal touch by recalling an incident that impressed him about the character of the deceased. Finally, he expresses goodwill and extends an offer to help.

letter of condolence
Goodwill message sent when a business associate or an associate's family member dies

```
                    KARL SOLOMON ENTERPRISES
                         42 Biltmore Boulevard
                         Los Angeles, CA 90044
                           (213) 555-1977



       August 11, 199X


       Mr. Ted Davenport
       35 Abbey Lane
       Los Angeles, CA 90058


       Dear Ted:

       I was saddened and shocked by the terrible news of Alice's
       death. Please accept my deepest sympathy in your time of grief.

       When Alice and I worked together last year, her enthusiasm was
       infectious. She approached even the most mundane tasks as a
       challenge. I remember when her secretary was ill the day before
       our project deadline and no temporary help was available; she
       sat down at her computer and pecked away until the report was
       finished. It took hours, but at the end she was proud of her
       accomplishment, not resentful or angry.

       Please call me if there is anything I can do to help. Maybe
       later, I can tell you more about the Alice I knew.


       Sincerely,

       Karl Solomon

       Karl Solomon
```

Figure 7.7   *Sample Letter of Condolence*

letter of sympathy
Goodwill message conveying personal concern on such occasions as illness, accident, or other misfortune

Letters of sympathy convey personal concern on such occasions as illness, accident, or other misfortune. They may be written, for example, when someone is in the hospital or has undergone some traumatic experience, such as the loss of home or business to a fire. Letters of sympathy follow the same general pattern as condolence letters, except that it is appropriate to conclude with some expression of hope for the future—for example, "Although the fire destroyed your Cleveland plant, I am certain that you and your staff will be able to rebuild and overcome the loss. The fire destroyed a building; it did not consume your spirit or ability to make things happen."

Greetings

Although businesspeople commonly exchange greetings at Christmas, greetings may be extended on other occasions as well. As a supplier of menus and other materials, for example, the owner of a small printing company may send greetings to a local restauranteur on the yearly anniversary of his or her business.

greeting
Goodwill message commemorating either holidays or special events

Greetings, then, are messages that can commemorate either holidays or special events. They are sometimes sentimental and may thank individuals for their business during the year. While many businesspeople choose commercial cards to extend wishes on holidays and special events, the best greetings are personal letters and notes.

PROGRESS CHECK

1. Why are personnel letters important?
2. What business situations might call for a thank-you letter?

INFORMATIVE LETTERS

If you don't give people information, they'll make up something to fill the void.
Carla O'Dell
President, O'Dell
& Associates

Like good-news letters, letters whose primary function is to supply information use a direct organizational approach. On the surface, however, because these letters are less compelling than good-news messages, you may have to work much harder to capture the reader's attention. And indeed, with every contemporary businessperson surrounded by too much information, your contribution to the supply may very well seem unimportant or irrelevant if you do not take effective steps to prove otherwise.

The following plan for informative letters recognizes that before you can accomplish anything else, you must convince the reader *in the first few sentences* that your information deserves attention.

- Open your document with a statement of purpose. Show your reader why your information is important by listing its specific benefits.
- Incorporate details in the middle of your document by relating them to your reader's needs.
- Close by emphasizing how your information is designed to help your reader. Focus as well on communicating goodwill and on laying the foundations for future action. In long documents, a summary may also be necessary.

Whatever the immediate reason for writing a given letter, all informative writing shares certain characteristics, the most important of which is the need for *clarity*. Be certain that your reader understands the background and context of your message. Use precise, jargon-free language and present your points in clear, logical order. The following additional suggestions are designed to improve informative letters:

- Give priority to your information in terms of its importance to your reader. In other words, let the order of information be determined by *your reader's needs*.
- Let your reader's need to know determine whether you include details or leave them out. You may decide, for example, to present merchandise pricing in very general terms when you write to a business owner but to describe prices in greater detail when you write to the company's purchasing agent.
- Even if you are sure that your reader will ultimately need some background information to understand it fully, state the *purpose* of your message in your opening paragraph. Reserve needed clarification for the middle of your letter.
- Be as concise as possible by relegating relatively unimportant information to attachments.
- Help your reader follow a lengthy or complex presentation by including helpful written signposts—for example, transaction tags like *first,...second,...third,...as a result,...on the contrary.*

- When introducing particularly complex material, consider inserting a short "preview" paragraph—that is, a paragraph that tells your reader precisely how you plan to handle the material. In other words, tell the reader what you will do before you do it.
- Design your document so that your most important points stand out. Use bulleted lists surrounded by plenty of white space.

Informative writing may be motivated by any of the following occasions: a written or verbal request, an event requiring explanation, the need to set forth or explain company policy, the need to confirm a phone or face-to-face conversation, documents that must be transmitted from one business office to another, and the need to acknowledge information or materials.

Request Responses

Start your reply by thanking the reader for his or her interest in your company. Then state the type of information that you plan to present. The middle of your letter should be devoted to the specific facts required to answer the inquiry. Close your letter by telling the reader that you will be glad to answer any more questions that he or she might have. (Do this, of course, only if you are committed to future help.)

As you answer the request, try to place yourself in the reader's position. For example, if someone is interested in your company's line of luggage, would it help to include more information than was specifically requested? Instead of just sending a price list, consider explaining the quality difference between your luggage and competitors' products. This approach can be a valuable business-promotion tool.

Announcements of Company Activity

There are as many reasons to write letters about events, personnel, and company policies as there are companies—for example, merger announcements and letters announcing quantity discounts and changes in billing procedures. An informative letter may be written to the Internal Revenue Service changing the name and location of your business. Letters may inform customers that a new sales representative has been assigned to accounts in their region.

Informative letters about events and policy also provide the opportunity to promote business at the same time that you communicate information. Consider the letter in Figure 7.8, which informs a customer of a personnel change. Note how the middle of the letter balances information about a new sales representative with information about the company's continued service commitment to its customers.

Follow-Up Letters

follow-up letter
Informative letter written to ensure that everyone's version of the verbal points made at a meeting is the same

Many informative letters confirm previous telephone or face-to-face conversations. **Follow-up letters** reiterate verbal points to ensure that everyone's version of the information is the same. Some follow-up letters simply state basic facts—for example, confirming the time, place, and purpose of a meeting. Others are more complex—say, written statements to clarify verbal agreements or set terms for a working relationship. The purpose of all follow-up letters is to forestall misunderstanding.

Bear in mind that follow-up letters pass on information as *you* remember it—which may or may not be the same way *others* remember it. The writer of the follow-up letter in Figure 7.9, therefore, assures his reader that he understands *his* version to be precisely that. Note that he is careful to leave the door open to further discussion.

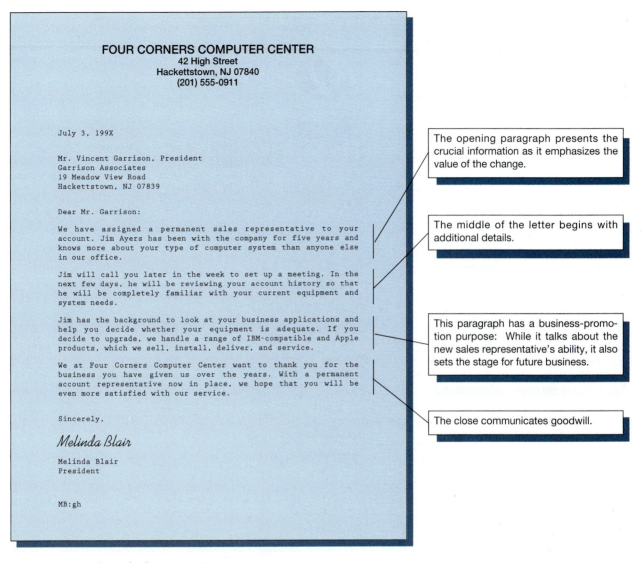

FOUR CORNERS COMPUTER CENTER
42 High Street
Hackettstown, NJ 07840
(201) 555-0911

July 3, 199X

Mr. Vincent Garrison, President
Garrison Associates
19 Meadow View Road
Hackettstown, NJ 07839

Dear Mr. Garrison:

We have assigned a permanent sales representative to your account. Jim Ayers has been with the company for five years and knows more about your type of computer system than anyone else in our office.

Jim will call you later in the week to set up a meeting. In the next few days, he will be reviewing your account history so that he will be completely familiar with your current equipment and system needs.

Jim has the background to look at your business applications and help you decide whether your equipment is adequate. If you decide to upgrade, we handle a range of IBM-compatible and Apple products, which we sell, install, deliver, and service.

We at Four Corners Computer Center want to thank you for the business you have given us over the years. With a permanent account representative now in place, we hope that you will be even more satisfied with our service.

Sincerely,

Melinda Blair

Melinda Blair
President

MB:gh

> The opening paragraph presents the crucial information as it emphasizes the value of the change.

> The middle of the letter begins with additional details.

> This paragraph has a business-promotion purpose: While it talks about the new sales representative's ability, it also sets the stage for future business.

> The close communicates goodwill.

FIGURE 7.8 *Sample Company Announcement*

Transmittal Letters

Transmittal letters, also known as **cover letters**, accompany materials sent from one person to another. They are important because they provide written records that the materials have indeed been sent.

Transmittal letters accompany shipments of materials ranging from literary manuscripts and blank checks to in-store promotional displays and auto parts. Although most transmittal letters accompany materials sent by mail, they can also accompany materials that are transmitted personally from one individual to another. Transmittal letters that are part of formal business reports will be examined in detail in Chapter 12.

Transmittal letters come in two forms. The brief version identifies and/or describes the item being sent and states the reason for its delivery. The longer version adds explanatory details and may raise questions. Both versions close with expressions of goodwill.

transmittal letter (or cover letter)
Informative letter accompanying materials sent from one person to another and providing written records that the materials have indeed been sent

Using a direct approach, the letter opens by summarizing the main point.

The middle of the letter relates important details. The phrase "as I recall" tells the reader that the writer is not certain of this information.

The letter closes with a goodwill ending and a view to the future.

FIGURE 7.9   *Sample Follow-Up Letter*

Acknowledgments

acknowledgement
Informative letter telling the reader that information or materials have been received

Acknowledgments inform readers that information or materials have been received. Although an acknowledgment is often primarily a matter of courtesy, note that the writer of the letter in Figure 7.10 also takes the opportunity to point toward future action between her business and her reader's business.

GOOD-NEWS AND INFORMATIVE MEMOS

Like letters, good-news and informative memos should follow a direct organizational plan. Present your purpose in the opening paragraph, follow with essential details, and, if necessary, close with a summary statement or a request for action.

The Purpose of Good-News and Informative Memos

Among the most common good-news memos are messages of congratulations and hiring and promotion announcements. Informative memos fall into a number of different categories, including *transmittal memos*, which introduce enclosed materials or longer documents; *delegating memos*, which provide the details of

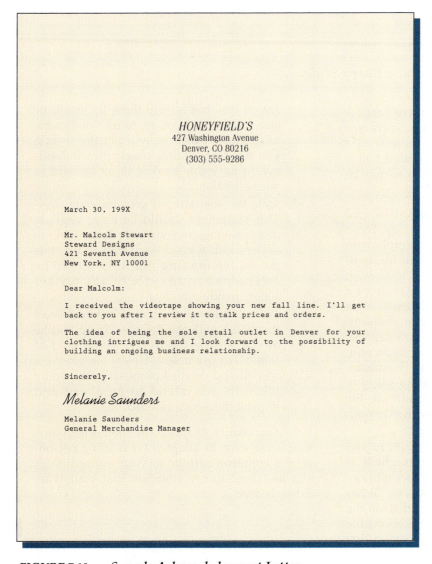

HONEYFIELD'S
427 Washington Avenue
Denver, CO 80216
(303) 555-9286

March 30, 199X

Mr. Malcolm Stewart
Steward Designs
421 Seventh Avenue
New York, NY 10001

Dear Malcolm:

I received the videotape showing your new fall line. I'll get
back to you after I review it to talk prices and orders.

The idea of being the sole retail outlet in Denver for your
clothing intrigues me and I look forward to the possibility of
building an ongoing business relationship.

Sincerely,

Melanie Saunders

Melanie Saunders
General Merchandise Manager

FIGURE 7.10   *Sample Acknowledgement Letter*

assignments; *instructions*, which explain how something works or describe the
steps in a process; and *policy announcements*.

Style and Length

Critical to the success of good-news and informative memos is a sensitivity to
the issues of style and length.

STYLE   As we have seen, in writing direct requests and negative and persuasive messages, it is wise to adopt a style that is appropriate to the position of
your reader. Style, however is less crucial in positive correspondence. Because
colleagues at all levels—managers, co-workers, and subordinates—welcome
positive messages for the same reasons, there is little need to distinguish among
readers in the style of good-news and informative memos.

Style, then, is less important than the message itself. According to one team of
communication consultants, "If someone is told, Yes, you got the raise, the recipient of the message doesn't really pay much attention to the style in which the good-
news is conveyed."[11] Similarly, tone is also fairly consistent in informative memos.
Whether your memo is being written up, down, or horizontally in the organization,
be straightforward and forceful to communicate the details of your message.

PRACTICAL TIPS

Business Memos, Dave Barry Style

Nothing is sacred to humorist Dave Barry— not even the business memo. Here are Barry's suggestions for writing memos that leave a lasting impression. Keep in mind that if you take Barry's advice too literally, you may be forced to rewrite your résumé.

1. *Always start by saying that you have received something and are enclosing something.* These can be the same thing. For example, you could say: "I have received your memo of the 14th, and am enclosing it." Or they can be two different things: "I have received a letter from my mother, and am enclosing a photograph of the largest known domestically grown sugar beet." As you can see, these things need have nothing to do with each other, or with the point of the memorandum. They are in your memo solely to honor an ancient business tradition, the Tradition of Receiving and Enclosing, which would be a shame to lose.

2. *State that something has been brought to your attention.* Never state who brought it. It can be virtually any random fact whatsoever. For example, you might say: "It has been brought to my attention that on the 17th of February, Accounts Receivable notified Collections of a prior past-due balance of $5,878.23 in the account of Whelk, Stoat, and Mandible, Inc." Ideally, your reader will have nothing to do with

any of this, but he will think he *should*, or else why would you go to all this trouble to tell him? Also, he will get the feeling you must be a fairly plugged-in individual, to have this kind of thing brought to your attention.

3. *State that something is your understanding.* This statement should be firm, vaguely disapproving, and virtually impossible to understand. A good standard one is: "It is my understanding that this was to be ascertained in advance of any further action, pending review."

4. *End with a strong closing line.* It should leave the reader with the definite feeling that he or she is expected to take some kind of action. For example: "Unless we receive a specific and detailed proposal from you by the 14th, we intend to go ahead and implant the device in Meredith."

The beauty of this basic memo format is that is can even be adapted for sending personalized communications to your subordinates ("It has come to my attention that your wife, Edna, is dead").

Source: Reprinted from *Claw Your Way to the Top: How to Become the Head of a Major Corporation in Roughly a Week,* © 1986 by Dave Barry. Permission granted by Rodale Press, Inc., Emmaus, PA 18098.

LENGTH   However, the need to focus on the most important information and eliminate extraneous details is crucial in informative memos. A good way to gauge the right amount of information is to analyze the use to which your reader is going to put your information. For example, if you are writing a memo to your manager describing how you plan to delegate responsibility on a project, find out whether he or she wants a detailed account or simply a short overview of your plan. Analyze the amount of time and effort that will be required of both you and your reader. While the first memo may take ten pages or more, the latter may require only several paragraphs.

PROGRESS CHECK

1. In writing an informative letter, what determines the way you present the information?
2. Summarize the chapter's tips for writing clear, logical informative letters and memos.

WHAT'S AHEAD

Although direct requests and good-news, goodwill, and informative messages all rely on some form of the direct organizational approach, this approach is generally ineffective for communicating bad news or critical messages. Chapter 8 will examine the best way to present unpleasant or difficult messages. As you will see, communication in these circumstances is usually more effective when the writer adopts an indirect organizational plan.

SUMMARY OF CHAPTER OBJECTIVES

1. **Describe the use of the *direct approach* in good-news letters.**

   Good-news letters should start by telling the reader the purpose of the document, including the good news. The middle of the letter should explain essential details, and the closing should express goodwill. The closing may also suggest future action, ask the reader for comments, raise questions, or offer suggestions.

2. **Explain the importance of expressing *goodwill* in *inquiry responses*.**

   Expressions of goodwill give writers the opportunity to build personal business relationships with their readers—relationships that may ultimately result in increased sales. Language and tone communicate goodwill, as does the speed with which an inquiry receives a response.

3. **Identify five specific types of *good-news letters*.**

   Good-news correspondence falls into four categories. Order acknowledgments are letters of explanation that may accompany orders from new customers or very large orders from old customers. Credit-related letters include positive credit references and letters granting credit. In good-news adjustment letters, the writer may either grant adjustment of a customer's claim or suggest a compromise solution. Finally, good-news personnel letters include letters of recommendation and such employment-related let-

ters as job offers. Common forms of social correspondence include such goodwill messages as thank-you letters, responses to invitations, and letters of congratulations.

4. **List the characteristics of an effective *goodwill message*.**

   A goodwill message attempts to establish or maintain a personal relationship between writer and recipient. No attempt is made at business promotion. Among the most common goodwill messages are thank-you messages, responses to invitations, letters of congratulation, condolence and sympathy letters, and greetings.

5. **Apply the direct approach to writing *informative letters*.**

   Like good news, information is best communicated through a direct approach. Start with a statement of purpose and include reasons why the information is important to the reader. In the middle of the document, flesh out the information as you continue relating it to the reader's needs. Depending upon the document, the closing may include a statement of goodwill, a summary, or steps for future action.

6. **Explain the requirements for writing effective *good-news* and *informative memos*.**

   Good-news and informative memos also follow a direct organizational plan. Because everyone welcomes positive messages, there is no need to change the style of the message according to the audience. Memo length should be geared to the reader's needs.

DISCUSSION AND REVIEW QUESTIONS

1. Summarize the general pattern for organizing an effective good-news letter. (*Ch. Obj. 1*)

2. Why is it important to express goodwill when responding to inquiries? (*Ch. Obj. 2*)

3. Name the types of good-news correspondence. (*Ch. Obj. 3*)

4. Identify the function of the letter closing. (*Ch. Obj. 1*)

5. Compare and contrast credit references and letters granting credit. (*Ch. Obj. 3*)

6. What is an adjustment letter? How should such letters be written? (*Ch. Obj. 3*)

7. Discuss letters of recommendation. What considerations are involved in writing such letters? (*Ch. Obj. 3*)

8. What characteristics make an effective goodwill message? (*Ch. Obj. 4*)

9. Describe a three-point plan for writing an effective informative letter. (*Ch. Obj. 5*)

10. What characteristics make for effective good-news and informative memos? (*Ch. Obj. 6*)

APPLICATION EXERCISES

1. Cover the right-hand column in TABLE 7.1. Now write your own example for each of the functions listed. Be sure to make your own examples different from the ones in the table. (*Ch. Obj. 1, 5*)

2. La Tanya Johnson buys a pair of jeans from The Clothes Closet, a small boutique. After taking the jeans home, she decides that she wants to exchange them for another pair of a different color. The next day, however, she's called out of town on an emergency business trip. When La Tanya returns, she takes the jeans back to The Clothes Closet and asks the salesclerk if she can exchange them. The clerk explains that the boutique has a two-week deadline for exchanges; thanks to her trip, La Tanya is three days past the limit. La Tanya points out that she's been a faithful customer at the shop, but to no avail. Finally, she storms out of The Clothes Closet, goes home, and writes an angry letter.

   As the boutique manager, you're the one who receives the letter. Write an adjustment letter in which you try to resolve the problem and keep La Tanya as a customer. (*Ch. Obj. 3*)

3. After the incident with La Tanya Johnson, you decide, as manager of The Clothes Closet, that it would be a good idea for the store to change its policy on returns and exchanges. However, the store's owner, Liz Smith, is worried that a more liberal policy could cost the store too much money. Write an informative memo telling Liz about your experience with La Tanya (who, thanks to your excellent letter, has remained a loyal customer). Relate your memo to Liz's concerns. (*Ch. Obj. 6*)

4. Liz is so impressed by your memo that she agrees to your new policy suggestion. You decide to write a letter to regular customers of The Clothes Closet to tell them about the new policy and its advantages for them. (You also figure that this would be a prime opportunity for a goodwill message and an announcement of

an upcoming sale.) Write the letter. (*Ch. Obj. 5*)

5. Six months later, La Tanya Johnson discovers that a blouse which she bought at The Clothes Closet has shrunk two sizes. She phones you to request a new one. While talking on the phone, you discover that she washed the blouse in hot water even though the label in the garment clearly states, "Hand wash in cold water." What do you do? (*Ch. Obj. 2, 3*)

6. Smallco Sweats, a small firm that makes athletic clothing, often gets letters inquiring about its products—sizes and styles available, where customers can buy them, prices, and so on. As a longtime Smallco staff member, you realize that the company has no standardized policy for responding to such inquiries. You decide that it would be a good idea to write a brief "how-to" manual that explains the importance of handling customer inquiries and describes how to write good responses. Write this manual as an informative memo to Smallco's staff. (*Ch. Obj. 2, 6*)

7. Josefina Lombardo manages the public-relations department at a large company. Part of her job involves coordinating slide shows and oral presentations given by various company employees to the general public. The slides and other visual aids are created by the firm's in-house graphics department.

   Each presentation may be long and complex, requiring as many as 200 slides and various illustrations. Josefina, therefore, is not surprised to learn that the artists in the graphics department keep typed lists of illustrations as they are developed for each presentation. Often, however, these lists are thrown away when the illustrations have been finished. Meanwhile, the public-relations staff has been creating its own detailed lists for each presentation as it receives finished slides and illustrations. Public relations' lists are all typewritten rather than computerized.

   After being used for presentations, the

illustrations are returned to the graphics department, where they're stored. Thus, when public relations wants to reuse them for future presentations, graphics staffers must hunt for the materials. Obviously, this is a time-consuming (and boring!) chore, largely because no one keeps a master list of the illustrations on file.

Josefina realizes that both departments would save time and effort by creating a master list that both can use. She discusses her idea with Ana Delgado, the graphics director, who reports to Josefina. Ana agrees and suggests ways to streamline the process. They decide that the staffs of the two departments will meet to determine which facts about each illustration should be included on the new master list. They agree that graphics employees will then create the lists on the company's computer system, which will assign a tracking number to each illustration. In the future, employees of both departments

should be able to locate illustrations more easily by using the assigned number.

Josefina gets back to her office and decides to write Ana a follow-up memo confirming their conversation. Write this letter. (*Ch. Obj. 6*)

8. Ana gets Josefina's memo and agrees with what it says. She volunteers to write an informative letter to her staff in the graphics department which will describe the new policy, explain how it works, and summarize its advantages for them. Write this letter. (*Ch. Obj. 5*)

9. Suppose that one day the memo below lands on your desk.

The rest of Ms. Malapro's six-page memo discusses the dangers of wordy, unclear corporate memos. She concludes by referring staff members to a 160-page style manual entitled *Keep It Brief*.

MEMORANDUM

TO: All Staff Members of Worde, Incorporated
FROM: Denise Malapro
Vice President for Internal Communications
DATE: August 29, 1992
SUBJECT: Long memos

The ability to develop effective internal communications is a crucial skill that we all should practice consistently. Concise, effective memos have always been a priority here at Worde. Indeed, I can safely say that our corporation has always been know for the quality of its sentence construction, since, as you would no doubt agree, overly long and complex sentences can confuse people and disguise meanings, leading to misunderstanding on the part of the reader and, certainly, frustration on the part of the writer, since his or her meaning has been misconstrued, whether partially or totally, to the point of almost complete obfuscation.

In a recent conversation with my staff, I learned that over 50 percent of our internal memos are more than five pages in length. Furthermore many of us use words that the average person just wouldn't use in normal conversation. This is simply heinous! This is why I am announcing a new companywide policy. From now on, we will write only short, effective memos that get to the point quickly. It is time to be more aggressive about length control.

a. Does Ms. Malapro's memo follow the chapter's guidelines for writing effective informative memos?

b If not, rewrite the memo to make it more effective. (*Ch. Obj. 6*)

To complete EXERCISES 10 and 11, pair off with a classmate.

10. Each of you should think of a job that interests you. Now write a letter of reference for each other, addressed to individuals who might be able to hire you for those positions. Critique each other's letters and (tactfully) suggest any improvements that can be made. (*Ch. Obj. 1, 3*)

11. Congratulations! You both got your jobs. Each of you can now write a letter to your partner from the person who hired him or her to inform the candidate of the company's decision. The letter offers the position and mentions the new title, salary, and the date on which work begins. (*Ch. Obj. 1, 3*)

12. Now that you have your dream job, it's time to extend your credit.

a. Write a positive credit reference for yourself; address the letter to a company other than your employer.

b. Write yourself a letter from this company, informing you of its decision to issue you credit. Follow the chapter guidelines for writing credit-related letters. (*Ch. Obj. 1, 3*)

13. Things are going so well that you are promoted from the position you obtained in EXERCISE 11. Write the good-news memo that announces your promotion and your new title and summarizes your new responsibilities. (You can also brag a bit about your past performance, if you wish!) (*Ch. Obj. 4, 6*)

14. Refer to the chapter's discussion of the five categories of goodwill messages. Now think about real-life situations for which you could write goodwill messages. These situations might arise from a current or former job, a social group to which you belong, or a class. For instance, did a co-worker recently have a baby? Did someone you know win an award, get married, or invite you to a social event? Write five goodwill messages—one for each category—that address these real-life situations. (*Ch. Obj. 3, 4*)

15. Downsize, Inc., is restructuring. The facts are as follows:

OLD ORGANIZATION

- Ten major divisions
- Offices located in five countries
- Corporate officers included:
  John Reynolds, president; Jim Zaloukis, vice president for finance; Robert Bouse, vice president for operations; Janice Cameron, vice president for engineering; Jesse Rollover, vice president for marketing
- Corporate headquarters located in New York City; finance division in Houston; operations division in Los Angeles; marketing division in Seattle; engineering division in Garden City, Kansas

NEW ORGANIZATION

- Four major divisions
- Offices located in ten countries
- Corporate officers include:
  Janice Cameron, president; Gustav Hansen, vice president for operations; Juan Velasquez, vice president for engineering; Martha Zeloff, vice president for marketing
- Corporate headquarters and all other divisions now located in Greenville, South Carolina

Janice Cameron, the new president, has asked you to write an informative letter to all of the firm's employees to explain the new organization. Janice, who took a business communication class in college, understands the importance of effective communication. She asks that instead of merely listing the above facts, you to restate them in a narrative form. Close the letter with an expression of goodwill and thank employees for their continuing contributions to the company. (*Ch. Obj. 5*)

*B*UILDING YOUR RESEARCH SKILLS

Do most letter writers in real-life organizations follow the guidelines given in this chapter? Let's find out.

Collect three examples of good-news, goodwill, and informative messages. Although these examples can come from any of the categories dis-

cussed in this chapter, choose three from three different categories. These messages can come from businesses, nonprofit organizations, social groups, your school, or various publications. Analyze each message to see how effective it is. Does it follow the guidelines for communicating its message effectively? If it does a good job, explain why it's effective. If it doesn't, how could it be improved?

Take written notes and be prepared to explain why you think each example is good or bad.

BUILDING YOUR TEAMWORK SKILLS

Your instructor will divide the class into small teams. Each group will meet to discuss the examples that students found for the previous Research Skills exercise. As a group, discuss each example of writing and decide whether or not it's effective. If it is effective, explain why; if it's not, show how it can be improved. Choose "best" and "worst" examples and have one member take notes on the group's suggestions for improving the ineffective message.

Appoint a spokesperson for your team. Your spokesperson will present the group's best and worst messages to the class, along with suggestions for improving the ineffective message. See if the class can come up with additional ideas for improving it.

COMMUNICATING IN A WORLD OF DIVERSITY

A major food retailer had a big problem: Its sales were slipping. The company tried a variety of approaches to boost sales—coupons, in-store promotions, more ads—but nothing seemed to work. In desperation, it did some market research to figure out why people weren't buying. The research turned up a fact that surprised the stores' managers. More than 50 percent of its customers were Hispanic. However, the only Spanish in company outlets appeared on signs reading, "Todos los rateros de tienda serán demandados en juicio bajo las leyes del estado!" ("All shoplifters will be pros-ecuted to the fullest extent of the law!")

Why do you think the chain's stores weren't attracting more Hispanic customers? What steps would you recommend to help the company communicate more effectively with potential Hispanic customers? Write an informative memo to store managers in which you summarize the market-research findings.

Source: Gary Berman, "The Hispanic Market: Getting Down to Cases," *Sales & Marketing Management*, October 1991, pp. 65–74.

CASE 7.1

Team Spirit at Eaton Corp.

At Eaton Corporation, the morning quiz is underway.

Ten employees sit around a boardroom table. A supervisor asks, "What were our sales yesterday?"

A worker scans a computer printout and replies, "$625,275."

"And in the month?" asks the manager.

"$6,172,666," says another worker.

The quiz continues: What was the cost of materials and supplies used the day before? What was the cost of labor, shipping, and utilities?

Meanwhile, out on the shop floor another employee demonstrates to the plant manager a new technique for making welding electrodes that could save the plant $5,126 annually. This marks the 193rd time this year that employees have come up with ideas for improving the plant's operations. Clearly, workers at Eaton aren't just taking tests; they're also doing their homework.

Eaton's business—making gears, engine valves, truck axles, and circuit breakers—may not be glamorous, but its progress is breathtaking.

Last year, Eaton lost $12 million; in its first quarter this year, it netted $33 million. The company's productivity (output per hour worked) has risen 3 percent every year during the past decade—compared to 1.9 percent for all U.S. manufacturers. Employees' suggestions have helped the firm save $1.4 million—and earned workers $44,000 in credits toward purchases at the factory store.

How does Eaton do it? Managers attribute much of the company's success to its improved communication with workers. Show employees how the firm's success benefits them, say supervisors, and they'll find creative ways to help. Hence the daily morning quizzes in which managers and workers assess the plant's progress on a continuing basis. In the company cafeteria, a TV monitor compares the daily performance of each shift and department to its cost and performance goals. Attention to the common cause, says metal fabricator Ricky Rigg, "gives you a sense of direction, and makes you appreciate what you do more." Adds machinist Rodney Romine: "If the company can't make money, you can't expect to have a job very long."

Eaton has also found that communication improves when employees work in teams. Boasting such names as "The Hoods" and "The Worms," worker-led groups constantly look for production bottlenecks and areas where costs can be cut. Sometimes, the search pays off in ways that nobody expected. For example, "Scrap Attack," a team of eight forge-press operators, had long been trying to reduce the plant's scrap-metal waste by 50 percent. Along the way, team members noticed that the dies used to forge gears on one press consistently lasted 25 percent longer than any of the other dies employed to perform the same task. Why? "Nobody knew," recalls team leader Anthony Ourada, "but we got to thinking about it." Eventually, the group discovered that one press operator preheated the dies before using them—a practice that extended their life. Now—at a cost savings of $50,000 a year—every press operator in the plant preheats dies.

Another worker team responsible for maintaining plant machinery decided that machines broke down too much. The workers approached their boss with an offer: "You're buying all this

on the outside. We can do it for you better." At costs of $80,000 and $250,000, respectively, the team proceeded to build two new machines to replace equipment for which outside vendors had charged Eaton $350,000 and $250,000. The new machines have taken over the most boring tasks in the department and freed workers to handle more challenging jobs. Moreover, the department's output doubled in one year, and the team plans to double it again in another year. "It's nice to start out with a concept and see it through," says Romine, "especially when it gets rid of monotonous work. We're more or less our own bosses."

Office clerk Luci Donaldson sums up the Eaton attitude: "Our opinions matter here. What we say counts—and it's not just to appease us."

Questions and Assignments

1. How does Eaton promote good communication with its employees?
2. Your boss at Eaton asks you to prepare an informative report to describe for the company's board of directors the plant's new system and its benefits. Write this report, keeping your audience in mind and addressing its needs and concerns.
3. Eaton's approach requires workers who are comfortable working in teams and who enjoy constantly looking for ways to improve their work. As the plant's head of human resources, you're in charge of hiring new employees. You decide to create an informative memo, addressed to job applicants, that describes the plant's method of operation, how it affects workers' jobs, and the benefits that employees gain from such a system. Write this memo; again, gear your writing to the needs and concerns of your audience.

Source: Thomas O'Boyle, "Working Together," *The Wall Street Journal*, June 5, 1992, pp. A1, A5. Reprinted by permission of *The Wall Street Journal*, © 1992 Dow Jones & Company, Inc. All rights reserved worldwide.

And Now—Whittle Communications
Brings You M.D. TV

Ordering drugs by TV? Why not? The process could soon become a reality if a new system, a joint venture of Whittle Communications and the Dutch firm Philips Electronics, passes its initial tests.

Currently, drug manufacturers market their wares to doctors through huge networks of sales representatives. The reps visit physicians in their offices and at hospitals, bringing information and samples of various medicines and products. This approach, while effective, is also expensive. Face-to-face sales calls aren't cheap. Drug companies must pay reps' salaries and expenses in addition to footing the bill for all the free samples that reps typically give away.

Whittle Communication's new venture could revolutionize drug marketing. When doctors sign up for the service, their offices will be equipped with satellite dishes, videocassette recorders, and TV monitors. The company will then broadcast daily fifteen- minute summaries of medical news. Whittle predicts that its "M.D. TV" could become an important tool for keeping physicians up-to-date on daily developments in the drug industry, including new products, drug recalls, side effects, and the latest research. The system would also be interactive, allowing doctors to order drug samples, ask for scientific reports on specific drugs, and request additional information on news items shown on the Whittle network—all electronically.

Because it will provide them with an advertising outlet, drug companies are also eying the medical-news network with great anticipation. Major drug manufacturers like Bristol-Myers Squibb, Merck, and Johnson & Johnson have already agreed to advertise during a planned trial period. These companies hope that the new system will ultimately help them reduce their costly in-person sales calls. "It is a new way to sell," explains one health-care marketer, "and an intelligent way to deliver information."

Questions and Assignments

1. Explain how Whittle's M.D. TV could change the nature of drug marketing to health-care professionals.
2. The system's broadcasts would include informative reports on new drugs and other medical developments. Suppose that a Whittle staff member were assigned to write one of these reports. It's the first time he's written anything like this, and he comes to you for advice on how to organize the report. What advice would you offer? Do you think that the medium involved—doctors will be reading this message on a TV screen—should affect how this message is written? Explain your answer.
3. Whittle decides to send an informative letter to physicians to tell them about its new service, describe its advantages, and ask them to participate in the "test run" of the system. Write this letter.

Source: Patrick Reilly, "Whittle, Philips Plan Interactive M.D. TV," *The Wall Street Journal*, June 26, 1992, p. B1. Reprinted by permission of *The Wall Street Journal,* © 1992 Dow Jones & Company, Inc. All rights reserved worldwide.

8

Writing Bad-News
and Negative Messages

CHAPTER OBJECTIVES

After studying this chapter, you should be able to:

1 Explain the *indirect* and *direct plans* for organizing bad-news messages.

2 Describe different circumstances for writing bad-news letters involving *orders.*

3 Distinguish between *credit refusals* to businesses and credit refusals to individual consumers.

4 Identify the most effective way to refuse a *claim.*

5 Explain why tact is necessary when declining *requests,* including *invitations.*

6 Describe circumstances under which bad-news messages are sent to *job applicants* and why an indirect approach is appropriate.

7 Identify circumstances under which *unfavorable policies* and *crisis information* are conveyed.

8 List the special requirements for sending *bad-news memos* to subordinates, superiors, and coworkers.

The worse the news, the more effort should go into communicating it.

Andrew S. Grove
CEO, Intel Corporation

INSURING GOODWILL AT ALLSTATE

With more than 485,000 auto-insurance policies, the Allstate Insurance Company insures more automobiles in New Jersey than any other company. This giant insurer also provides an additional 250,000 New Jersey residents with policies on their homes, apartments, boats, and other property. New Jersey consumers, therefore, were shocked when Allstate announced in 1991 that it was leaving the state.

Despite the company's level of business activity in the state, Allstate faced some serious problems in New Jersey. For example, although Allstate's property-insurance profits were impressive, its auto-insurance business was a disaster. New Jersey's stringent auto regulations had resulted in a $450-million loss over a twenty-year period, with a $72-million loss the year before the company decided to leave. Unable to convince the state to grant substantial rate increases for problem drivers, Allstate made the difficult decision to close down its auto-insurance business. In addition, because New Jersey state law requires all property insurers to write auto-insurance policies as well, Allstate's decision to forego auto insurance forced the company to abandon the state completely.

The company's dilemma, however, did not end here: Not only did Allstate have to inform policyholders of its decisions, but state law required the company to find alternate insurance for all of its 430,000 policyholders. Management, therefore, had to reassure policyholders that they would not receive termination notices and suddenly be forced to scramble for other coverage. Allstate understood that the process of finding alternative insurance for 430,000 policyholders could take as long as five years. "There is no need for panic," explained company attorney Richard Levenfeld. "This is going to be a slow and responsible process. Customers need take no immediate action."

Allstate sent a letter to all New Jersey policyholders informing them of the company's bad news. In doing so, however, Allstate buffered its bad-news announcement with the reassurance that its departure would be gradual. Among other devices, the letter emphasized in boldface type that "coverage is not immediately affected" by the company's withdrawal plan.

Despite its negative message, then, the tone and content of the company's announcement were reassuring. "Please rest assured," Allstate advised policyholders, "that your current insurance protection is still valid and will be for quite some time to come. We will give you at least one-year notice prior to the expiration of your policy, followed by an additional notice prior to any nonrenewal action." The letter closed by giving a telephone number that policyholders could call with further questions.[1]

CHAPTER OVERVIEW

It is never easy, of course, to tell people something they do not want to hear. In business as well as personal affairs, the act of spreading bad news can create as much discomfort for the writer as the news itself creates for the recipient.

Moreover, the stakes are often quite high in business. When business writers bungle bad-news messages, they risk losing the goodwill of valued customers, suppliers, and other business colleagues.

Allstate understood this dilemma when it wrote New Jersey policyholders to inform them of its decision to leave the state. Although at the time the company believed that it would no longer do business in New Jersey, the conduct of its relations with its customers there would certainly affect the perceptions and opinions of policyholders and potential customers in other states. Had Allstate treated its New Jersey policyholders shabbily—say, offering them little or no help in navigating the insurance maze in search of another company—policyholders elsewhere might well have assumed that, under similar circumstances, the company would do the same to them. In addition, the company realized that if it could reach a rate-hike agreement with the state, it could conceivably continue doing business in New Jersey—which is exactly what happened a year after the bad-news letter was written.

This chapter will help you to communicate bad news effectively by analyzing specific types of bad-news messages: messages involving orders, credit, claims, requests, invitations, and personnel issues. It will also examine methods for communicating negative information (such as price increases) and for sending bad news and other negative information in memo form. We begin by focusing on the key to successful communication—the use of a carefully considered organizational plan. We will look at the organization of bad-news messages according to *indirect* and *direct plans*, and we will evaluate the importance of *tone* in maintaining or salvaging goodwill.

ORGANIZING BAD-NEWS MESSAGES

In general, a bad-news or negative message can be organized according to either an indirect or a direct organizational plan. The appropriate plan is determined by the nature of the information, the requirements of the situation, and the sender's relationship to the recipient.

Using an Indirect Plan

Saying no is difficult for many reasons. No one, for example, likes to disappoint or anger an associate, especially when a continuing business relationship is involved. In such a situation, you are faced with a dilemma. On the one hand, you have a good reason for saying no, while on the other, you want to do everything you can to soften the blow.

This dilemma can often be resolved by constructing your message according to an **indirect organizational plan**—a method of organizing documents by *delaying* bad news rather than announcing it immediately. This plan calls for both an opening paragraph that serves as a *buffer* and a preliminary *explanation* before the bad news is announced. It also calls for a *closing* that tries to maintain or repair goodwill. As you will also see, appropriate language and tone are critical to the success of any bad-news message.

indirect organizational plan
Method of organizing documents by *delaying* bad news rather than announcing it immediately

BUFFERS   Imagine having to tell a subordinate in a face-to-face meeting that he or she will not get a raise this year or to tell a customer that a merchandise damage claim is unfounded. Are you likely to blurt out the news immediately upon meeting the person? Or will you try to ease the blow with a neutral opening remark? If you are sensitive to the individual's feelings—and if you recognize the link between personal sensitivity and the success of future business relations—you will begin with a buffer. It makes sense to follow the same approach in written correspondence.

A **buffer** is a protective barrier that helps cushion the shock of bad news. In business correspondence, a buffer generally appears in the first paragraph of a letter or memo and serves as the backdrop for the bad news. Although the bad news follows, the buffer eases the reader into it, thereby making it less likely that the mes-

buffer
Protective barrier that helps cushion the shock of bad news

| **TABLE 8.1** | *Types of Bad-News Buffers* | |

BUFFER	FUNCTION	EXAMPLE
Appreciation	Thanks the reader for his or her contribution, thoughts, claim, credit application, job application, or inquiry	Thank you for contacting Maytag about a marketing position. I always appreciate hearing from qualified college graduates who are eager to join our company.
Agreement	Refers to an area of common ground shared by the reader and the writer	Having worked together in the marketing department for five years, it is clear that we agree on the importance of point-of-purchase advertising.
General Principle	Starts with a statement that defines company business practices	It is our policy at Barney's to track the purchases of regular customers on computer and to send these customers handwritten notes when we think they might be ready for another purchase.
Chronology of Past Communications	Retraces what has happened to reach this point	When you and I spoke on January 2, we agreed that I would take another look at your credit application in light of the two errors in your credit file.
Compliment	Praises the reader's actions or contributions	No matter the objective, your efforts have always focused on what we need to accomplish, and now is no exception. You have given me a well thought-out and timely proposal.

sage will generate a defensive—or even angry—reaction. (A word of warning: Although buffers attempt to establish common ground, they should not mislead the reader into thinking that a positive response follows.)

Among the most frequently used buffers are expressions of *appreciation*, *agreement*, and *general principle*. A chronology of *past communications* and *compliments* can also be helpful. Although the temptation to add a sales message may be strong, a buffer is the wrong place to give in to that temptation. Table 8.1 explains the function of each type of buffer and includes examples.

Buffers are often necessary when dealing with customers and job applicants or when writing to someone at a higher organizational level. In such cases, they help to distance the writer from information that cannot always be positive. They are always necessary when politics demands sensitivity to people and situations. For example, if a friend of a senior vice president writes to you for a job, it would be a mistake to turn him down without attempting to soften the blow. Finally, combined with an overall conciliatory tone, buffers are especially important when the person to whom you are writing is already angry with you or your company.

diplomacy
Art of handling affairs in a tactful way to avoid arousing hostility

DIPLOMACY   When you use a buffer to introduce a bad-news message, you acknowledge the importance of diplomacy in handling difficult situations. **Diplomacy**—the art of handling affairs in a tactful way to avoid arousing hostility—is just as important in business as it is in relations among nations. The key to diplomacy is the understanding that people often need help in adjusting to bad or unpleasant information and that being direct in conveying such information may be the worst possible approach.

Words that carry strong negative connotations contradict the purpose of a buffer. You can thus provide your reader with help in adjusting to bad news by avoiding unduly negative terms in your opening paragraph—your language here sets the tone for your entire document. Table 8.2 contains examples of negative words, including words that begin with negative prefixes like *un-*, *non-*, and *im-*. According to business-communication authorities Ray E. Barfield and Sylvia S. Titus,

TABLE 8.2	*Negative Words to Avoid in a Buffer*	
loss	cannot	nonnegotiable
difficult	never	impossible
forced	unable	unacceptable
emergency	unreasonable	impractical
no	unimportant	unwise
not	unfortunately	unwilling

these words are "early warning signals [that are] counterproductive to your aim of having the reader take in your whole explanation, not just the opening lines."[2]

THE EXPLANATION   Continue using the indirect pattern by citing the reasons that require you to say no. When you begin by presenting these reasons, you set the stage for the announcement of your bad news. Your goal, of course, is to present your reasons so that your reader understands why you made a particular decision. You may, for example, explain how time limits, inventory, employment opportunities, or other resources justify what you can and cannot do.

To be effective, use language the reader can understand and avoid technical jargon. Choose positive language to describe the reasons for your decision; avoid sarcasm even if the reader has been an unending source of trouble. Finally, remember that it is petty and shortsighted to try to score points at the expense of your reader. For example, even if you are convinced that the reader is completely wrong in making his or her claim, avoid communicating the sense that you take any satisfaction in detailing the reader's wrongheadedness.

In fact, direct accusations of any kind are counterproductive. Eliminate expressions like *you claim, your error,* and *you mistakenly did*—that is, phrasing that casts doubt on the reader's actions or motives. In addition, consider using the passive voice or other means of softening the harshness that seems to accompany "personal" criticism. For example, instead of saying,

> Our analysis shows that you chipped your diamond ring, perhaps while gardening or washing pots and pans,

rephrase your explanation by using the passive voice and nonaccusatory language that removes blame—for example:

> Your diamond has been scratched, perhaps as the result of some inadvertent abrasive activity.

You might further depersonalize your explanation by eliminating the pronouns *you* and *your*:

> Although diamonds are extremely hard stones, they can be scratched, even during everyday wear.

Sometimes one explanation may be all you need to clarify or justify your decision. However, if your explanation requires more than one item, present them in the order that you believe most important to your reader. As a general rule, tell people only what they need to know; if one explanation is sufficient, you need say no more. For example, it may be sufficient to tell a customer that a part is out of stock but unnecessary to add details about a warehousing problem. In some cases, confidentiality will limit what you say and how you say it. Telling a job applicant why someone was previously fired from the position may breech employer/employee confidentiality and can create potential legal problems.

However, although it is often wise to limit your explanation, it is also a mistake to base your explanation on "company policy." As a rule, your reader has a right to know the *particular* reason for your decision, and citing company policy is just not enough.

A diplomat is a person who can tell you to go to hell in such a way that you actually look forward to the trip.

Caskie Stinnett
Humorist

These products are to be used for enhancing coffee and tea. Carolco cannot assume the cost of subsidizing your morning cereal. Quite frankly, we've all become rather spoiled by these services. It all takes a toll on the company from a financial perspective.

From an interoffice memo to employees of financially strapped Carolco Pictures Inc., which halved its supply of milk and cream to office coffee drinkers

THE BAD NEWS   Communicate the bad news next. Remember that stating *bad news* is not the same thing as being *negative*. You are basically telling the reader about a partial delivery, a credit refusal, or a claim that cannot be satisfied, and in order to minimize—and possibly eliminate—misunderstandings, it is important to state this news clearly and unequivocally. Depending on the situation, however, the best approach may be to subordinate your bad news to some positive information, perhaps using the passive voice. Although an apology generally weakens a writer's position, it may be necessary to apologize if your company is involved in wrongdoing or has made a serious mistake.

More than any other section in your document, your bad-news announcement should avoid negative language and tone, both of which jeopardize goodwill. Words and phrases like *wrong, reject, unqualified, poor credit risk, carelessness, can't believe,* and *a failure to read instructions* can be perceived as overly harsh and may antagonize your reader. Instead, try such strategies as complex sentences that help to soften the news. For example:

> Although a hiring freeze is in place for the next six months, I have every hope that at the end of that period we will be hiring someone with your talents.

Another technique is rephrasing the bad news so that it has a positive dimension. For example, instead of writing,

> Since the fountain pen shows clear signs of damage, *we can only give you* a $50 credit toward the purchase of a new pen,

rephrase the sentence in the following way:

> Since the pen no longer works, *we are pleased to give you* a $50 credit toward the purchase of a new pen.

In addition, do not make your reader guess what you are saying by burying your bad news in an unlikely place. Even though it is difficult to tell people what they do not want to hear, do not hide your point among generalizations or side issues.

Finally, if possible, try not to end your bad-news paragraph with a refusal. If there are any alternatives, suggest them here. For example, although it might not be possible to refund someone's money, you may be able to offer a discount or a special service like free delivery or gift wrapping on a future purchase. "Your reasonable counteroffer," explain Barfield and Titus, "will show...that you understand [your reader's] needs and will work within your capacity to meet them."[3] In other words, despite having a legitimate reason for conveying bad news, you are also sending the clear message that you want to help.

THE CLOSING PARAGRAPH   The purpose of the closing paragraph is to refocus on a continuing, positive business relationship. Although it is a mistake to conclude a bad-news message with an actual sales presentation, you may take the opportunity for promoting goodwill in the business relationship.

First, try to maintain goodwill by not repeating the bad news or referring to it more than once in any way. Avoid words and phrases like *mistake, problem,* or *unfortunate situation,* and do not apologize for having to say no.

In addition, make sure that your close is consistent with the content of your document. For example, it would be a mistake to refuse a request and then close by saying, "Please call me if I can help you in the future." Suggest future contacts only if you are certain you want them. For instance, encouraging job applicants to contact you again may create conditions for further disappointment. Instead, simply reassure applicants that you will keep them in mind if suitable openings arise. Similarly, do not invite readers to tell you what they think of your response. If you close by saying, "Please let me know what you think of this solution," you may be inviting an unpleasant reply.

You may also find it helpful to acknowledge the impact of your bad news by being sympathetic to the reader's situation. You can say, for example, "While you may have hoped for a different decision, I am sure you will do everything you can to continue building the reputation of your department." This approach often requires that you help the reader put bad news in perspective. For example, reminding a client that this is the first delivery problem in a five-year business relationship will help underscore the reliability of your service.

Because an indirect message takes the time to explain bad news in a diplomatic way, it is usually longer than a direct message. Indeed, the more important the message, the longer it may be. For example, if one of your best customers complains about defective merchandise, you may decide that a three-page explanation is warranted. Although you may not be able to grant a requested adjustment, your explanation can clarify the reasons for your decision. Figure 8.1 presents a sample indirect bad-news letter and identifies each of its major components. In particular, note the comparative amount of space devoted to each section of the letter.

Using a Direct Plan

Often, bad-news memos use a direct organizational plan by starting with a statement of the news. This plan is most often used to communicate bad news to subordinates. Policy memos announcing bad news also use a direct approach. For

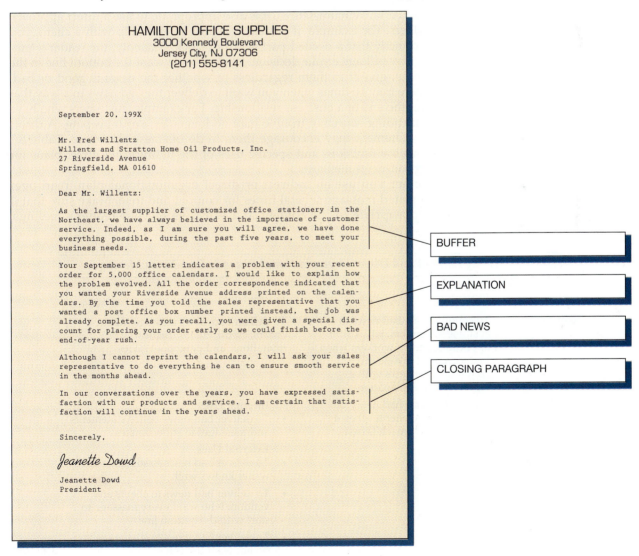

FIGURE 8.1   *Components of an Indirect Bad-News Letter*

example, if management is announcing a reduction of vacation time from five to four weeks, the opening paragraph of the memo might state:

> Starting May 1, annual vacation time will be reduced from five to four weeks.

Even in this context, however, it is possible to soften bad news and avoid the suggestion that blame should be placed with a specific management source. The passive voice, for example, can be used to avoid pinpointing a source of criticism. Instead of telling a subordinate, "You made a mistake in your budget projections," a manager may indicate the broader implications of the criticism by writing, "A mistake has been made in your budget projections."

As we saw in Chapter 5, the passive voice avoids using the personal pronoun *you*. For example, if a manager writes,

> Your plan shows that you have not thought out the consequences of eliminating all regional sales managers,

he or she may suggest that the problem exists on some "personal" level between writer and reader. The problem can be more accurately characterized as an organizational issue if the memo reads instead:

> Eliminating all regional sales managers may not prove feasible.

Under certain circumstances, it is also appropriate to use a direct approach with outsiders. For example, if you have a close relationship with a client, you can state directly that a needed part is out of stock. Secondly, the reader's temperament may influence your decision. When people want the bottom line in the first sentence, give it to them regardless of whether the news is good or bad. Finally, there may be times when you want to deliver the bad news in a way that encourages the end of a business relationship. For example, customers who have been an unending source of trouble may no longer be worth keeping. A direct bad-news statement may encourage them to do business elsewhere. Table 8.3 summarizes the functions and specific uses of the indirect and direct plans for delivering bad-news messages.

Whether you use an indirect or direct organizational plan, read over your completed message several times for content and tone. Make sure that it is both appropriate to the content and sensitive to your reader's feelings.

TABLE 8.3   *Using Indirect and Direct Organizational Plans in Bad-News Messages*

Type	Function	When Used
Indirect	To communicate bad news to customers, vendors, job applicants, and co-workers when there is a need to ease the reader into the news with a buffer and an explanation	To deliver bad-news messages about orders, credit, claims, requests, invitations, and personnel issues
Direct	To communicate bad news to co-workers and clients when a bottom-line approach is best	**Internal Uses** • To deliver bad-news policy statements and messages to subordinates **External Uses** • To deliver bad news to someone the writer knows well • To deliver bad news to clients and vendors who want every message to start with the bottom line • To deliver bad news to customers you do not want to keep

Some bad-news messages—for example, recall form letters—can be composed according to a formula. However, because most bad-news messages are written without the benefit of a formula, writers must decide what to say and how to say it. Naturally, most decisions begin with understanding the type of message to be sent.

PROGRESS CHECK

1. Why is it important to be careful in composing bad-news messages?
2. Name the basic components of an indirect bad-news message.
3. Summarize some tips for writing the bad-news portion of an indirect message.

TYPES OF BAD-NEWS MESSAGES

Bad-news business messages fall into six categories. Defined by the subjects that they address, they include messages about *orders, credit, claims, requests, invitations*, and *job applications* (see Figure 8.2).

All of these messages involve *external* communication—they are messages sent to customers, suppliers, professional colleagues in other companies, and job applicants. Later in this chapter, we will also look at the communication of bad

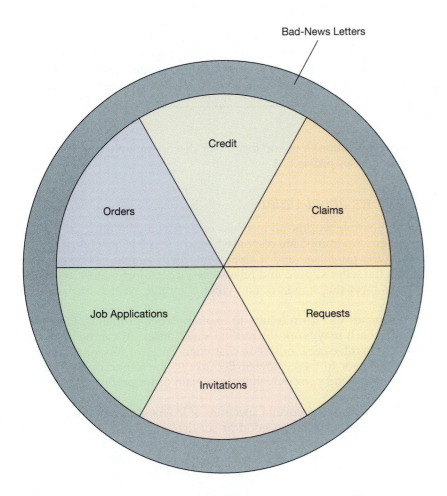

FIGURE 8.2 *Bad-News Messages*

INTERVIEW

William Buchholz, Consultant and Professor of Business Communications

According to William Buchholz, professor of business communications at Bentley College in Waltham, Massachusetts, and a corporate communication consultant, it is a mistake to think that an indirect approach fits all bad-news message situations. Rather, Buchholz believes that every situation must be judged individually and with an eye toward subtle factors that affect how the message is written and received. He explains his thoughts in the following interview.

Question: What is the most serious mistake writers make in bad-news letters and memos?

Answer: Many writers pay too much attention to formulas that stress the indirect approach and not enough attention to the subtleties that define the bad-news situation. They fail to consider the audience and such intangible factors as the corporate culture, their own personality, and the personality of the reader. As a result, an indirect approach is chosen when a direct approach would be more effective—or vice versa. In many cases, a direct negative approach is exactly what you need because it is more efficient.

Question: What kind of strategy do you suggest when a writer is faced with a bad-news situation?

Answer: I advise people to write the "inside" of the letter first—what it is they are refusing, why they are refusing it, and what they can offer instead. With an indirect approach, I suggest writing the buffer last. This gives you the best chance of choosing the right buffer. Sometimes, a buffer can look forward to a reason or even a counterproposal. Or the counterproposal may be part of the buffer. Starting from the inside-out discourages you from writ-

news *within* an organization in memo form. Our discussion here begins with an examination of bad-news orders.

Writing Bad News about Orders

In the best of all possible worlds, all business orders would be filled on the day sellers receive them. An immediate response has two tangible benefits. It speeds up payments by the purchaser and it creates goodwill among customers who are pleased with the seller's speed and reliable service. Unfortunately, businesses cannot always meet this standard, and when they fail, written explanations are needed.

Many companies use form letters to explain order problems. However, although this approach may work for routine small orders, it can be a mistake when the problem involves new or steady customers, large orders, or orders that are especially important to the customer. Because of the importance of orders, many businesses thus send personal letters to explain order problems and maintain goodwill.

Bad-news order messages cover a spectrum of letters. At worst, they may be needed to inform customers that a good or service will no longer be offered because it has been discontinued; at best, they may be needed only to explain short delivery delays. Order-related problems also include partial deliveries, substitute deliveries, and delivery delays due to unclear orders or orders containing mistakes.

DISCONTINUED ITEMS AND SERVICES   There are many reasons why firms discontinue goods or services: Demand may be limited, an item may be too expensive

ing a misleading buffer, one that is too long, or one that delays the information.

Question: What role does diplomacy play in communicating bad-news messages?

Answer: Writers have to weigh what's at stake when they write a bad-news message, and they must be sensitive to the consequences of their actions. For example, if I make the conscious decision to offend the reader because I no longer want to do business with him, I'm not throwing diplomacy out the door. If I'm direct, negative, and abrupt, I'm doing exactly what I want to do to achieve my objective. However, if I take the same approach with a *valued* client, I've made a serious mistake. In other words, you have to think through the consequences of what you are saying and ask yourself whether you can afford what is likely to happen.

Question: Are careful language choices more critical in bad-news than good-news messages? For example, can negative or harsh words have a more potent effect when the message is bad?

Answer: I think so. But sometimes that's the exact effect you want to achieve. If you want a customer with a poor payment history to stop asking for credit, then fill your letter with phrases like *poor credit risk*. Use strong words and shut the door.

Question: If you were to give students one piece of advice about writing effective bad-news messages, what would that advice be?

Answer: To start at the end and work toward the front. Assess the consequences before you decide on the approach, on the degree of diplomacy, on whether to use the active or passive voice. Even the nuances of language and tone can be gauged fairly accurately if you think ahead to what the results of your actions might be. Starting with the consequences puts the entire message in perspective.

Source: Interview with William Buchholz.

to produce, greater sales opportunities may exist in other areas, or government regulations may have limited the market and increased costs. Whatever the reason, the goal of the seller's message is simultaneously to encourage customers to purchase other items or services and to empathize with the buyer's disappointment. Figure 8.3 is a sample letter showing how these goals may be accomplished. The writer's explanation is specific but straightforward, and in her bad-news paragraph, she is tactful in suggesting a solution to the customer's problem.

BACK ORDERS AND PARTIAL DELIVERIES   A small company that cannot fill an order immediately will inform the customer of **back orders**—orders that the company promises to ship at some later date, which may or may not be specified. When an order involves more than one item, the company often sends those items that are in stock while back-ordering the rest. This practice is known as **partial delivery**.

Most large companies, however, do not face this problem. Computerized ordering systems can connect them directly with their suppliers in order to maintain adequate inventories. For example, Dillard's, a nationwide retailer headquartered in Little Rock, Arkansas, avoids back orders through a supplier connection known as an **electronic data interchange**, or **EDI**. Electronic data interchange refers to the ability to transmit information about orders and other communications via computer linkups maintained by various companies in the supply chain. For example, clothing maker Levi Strauss does not wait to receive orders before replenishing retailers' inventories. Using its "LeviLink" computer system, the company's goal is a "quick response" that eliminates the need for back or partial deliveries.[4]

When back-order and partial-order letters are needed, however, they should be written with the assumption that your customers are willing to wait

back order
Order that the company promises to ship at some later date, which may or may not be specified

partial delivery
Seller's decision to deliver in-stock items while back-ordering all others

electronic data interchange (EDI)
Ability to transmit information about orders and other communications via computer linkups maintained by various companies in a supply chain

The buffer expresses appreciation for the order. Although it avoids a sales pitch, it emphasizes the value of the existing business relationship.

The explanation begins with background information about the company. It then explains why the order for helium tanks cannot be filled.

This paragraph communicates the bad news as it refers specifically to the customer's order. Although the writer suggests a way to purchase the tanks, she avoids naming a specific company. In general, avoid suggesting direct competitors—your customer may never return to you.

The close focuses on goodwill and business promotion. The writer extends an olive branch with her offer.

EASTERN TRADING COMPANY
12 Valencia Drive San Francisco, CA 94110
(415) 555-7222

March 22, 199X

Ms. Karen Bellamy
Pacific Party Supplies
87 Plainview Road
San Diego, CA 92131

Dear Ms. Bellamy:

Thank you for ordering your company's party supplies from the Eastern Trading Company. It has been a pleasure serving you this year as your business has grown. We hope that the quality of our merchandise and fast, efficient service have contributed to your business success.

As you know, the Eastern Trading Company offers party-supply stores like yours a complete line of toys, giftware, novelties, carnival supplies, balloons, and accessories. We are a full-service wholesaler. However, a rise in shipping costs has made it impractical for us to continue selling helium tanks along with our balloons.

Therefore, I am returning your March 15 order for three helium tanks. May I suggest that you contact a local wholesaler whose primary business is to deliver and refill helium tanks.

The Eastern Trading Company continues to offer the most competitive prices for more than 300 varieties of mylar and latex balloons as well as thousands of other party supplies. Although our mail-order service guarantees shipment within 14 days, I am going to expedite your next order so that you receive it within a week.

Sincerely,

Penelope Pines

Penelope Pines
Manager

FIGURE 8.3   *Bad-News Letter about a Discontinued Item*

for your merchandise. (This assumption, of course, may not hold when the delay is inordinately long or when your customer has placed a rush order.) The sample partial-delivery letter in Figure 8.4 focuses on the value of the purchase to the customer while explaining the delay. Note, too, how the writer uses his explanation to communicate good news about his company's product.

SUBSTITUTE-DELIVERY LETTERS   Letters that inform customers that a new item can be sent in place of an item that is either temporarily out of stock or permanently out of inventory are known as **substitute-delivery letters**. The substitution, of course, should have features similar to those of the original item, and although prices obviously vary from product to product, original and substitute items should also be comparably priced. When writing a substitute-delivery letter, do not assume that your customer will agree with your suggestion. Give your customer both the option to accept or reject your offer and to get back to you either by phone or return mail.

In writing a substitute-delivery letter, your primary responsibility is to promote the features of the suggested substitute item without giving the impression that your sole purpose is to salvage a sale at any cost. Most importantly, customers should feel that you are trying to help them meet specific needs. Consider the sample substitute-delivery letter in Figure 8.5. The bad news is pre-

substitute-delivery letter Letter informing a customer that one item can be sent in place of another that is either temporarily out of stock or permanently out of inventory

MATTRESS KING, INC.
872 Broadway
New York, NY 10027
(212) 555-1108

January 27, 199X

Ms. Barbara Colletti
27 Ocean Terrace
Staten Island, NY 10301

Dear Ms. Colletti:

We received your order for a Serta Distinction queen-size mattress and box spring and for a Simmons Propedic twin-size mattress. You have made excellent bedding choices that will last for many years.

We can ship the Serta mattress set as soon as we make delivery arrangements. Please call our toll-free customer service line to arrange a delivery date. For your convenience, we can deliver the mattresses in the evening or on weekends as well as during the regular workweek.

The Simmons Propedic mattress is normally one of our best-selling products, and it has become even more popular during this special sale. Demand has been so great that we are temporarily out of stock.

Because we expect a shipment from the manufacturer by the end of next week, you can be sure that the mattress will be in your home within a very short time. I will contact you as soon as the mattress is in our warehouse to arrange a delivery date.

Because retail sales and service are such an important part of our business, we recently conducted a customer service survey to find out why we have so many repeat customers. We learned that our customers are convinced that we carry the best merchandise at the best prices and that we stand behind every sale.

Your order is no exception. Within a very short time, you will have your new Simmons Propedic mattress--a superior product purchased at the lowest price in town.

Sincerely,

Matthew Zeller

Matthew Zeller
Customer Service Representative

> The buffer acknowledges the order and compliments the customer on making excellent choices.

> The explanation begins with the good news that part of the order is ready to be delivered. The writer emphasizes the company's flexible delivery policy without mentioning the back order.

> The explanation now turns to the back-ordered item. The popularity of the mattress is stressed before the writer informs the customer about the delivery problem.

> The writer takes a positive approach to the bad news as he promises excellent service.

> This paragraph begins the close. It attempts to salvage goodwill by pointing to the results of a customer-satisfaction survey. In effect, the writer is telling the customer that other customers are satisfied with the service and that the delay should not change the customer's mind

> The final paragraph refers once more to the delayed delivery and ends on a positive business-promotion note.

FIGURE 8.4   *Sample Letter Explaining Partial Delivery*

sented as indirectly as possible without obscuring the message, and the writer devotes considerable attention to the service encounter.

LETTERS TO CLARIFY ORDERS   When original orders are received, they are not always clear or complete. Follow-up letters may thus be needed to clarify the customer's needs. For example, you may have to ask for more information or for an explanation of certain details. Make it clear that the purpose of your letter is not to delay the order but to ensure that the customer will receive exactly what he or she needs.

Your request for clarification should be as specific as possible. If necessary, photocopy the customer's original order and circle confusing items. If a careless mistake has been made, do not criticize the customer or suggest that your time is being wasted. Focus instead on the fact that clarifying information will expedite the order, and emphasize your desire to help in any way you can.

Writing Bad News about Credit

Many business writers confess that letters refusing credit are the most difficult of all bad-news letters to write. In addition to saying no, such letters must also try

The buffer compliments the reader for his choice and puts him in a larger group of satisfied customers and critics.

This paragraph sets the stage for the bad news that the Lilehauser tape is no longer available. Notice how the explanation avoids negative images.

The reader learns that a substitution is necessary, but no time is spent dwelling on the bad news. The toll-free phone number is designed to help the reader make the switch. The offer to send back the money at the end of the month tells the customer that the decision is his and that strong-arm sales tactics will not be used. However, the decision to hold the money for a short period is based on the belief that the customer may be reluctant to send the money twice.

The close focuses on the value of the substituted merchandise.

LISTENING TAPES, INC.
22 Court Street
Brooklyn, NY 11201
(718) 555-2794

June 22, 199X

Mr. Mitchell Steinberg
12 Barry Street
Kansas City, MO 64111

Dear Mr. Steinberg:

Your order is typical of thousands we receive each year. Lovers of Charles Dickens are thrilled to have the master's novels on audiotape. The critics agree, saying that our Dickens series provides hours of listening pleasure.

Your order included a request for the Charles Dickens series of 10 tapes, read by Anthony Lilehauser. Although these tapes have been a staple in our library for more than 10 years, several months ago we published a new series read by British actor Laurence Bauer. These readings have received universal critical acclaim.

I would like to suggest sending you the new series because we no longer sell the Lilehauser readings. The Bauer tapes sell for the same price and are currently in stock. If you agree to this substitution, please call me, toll-free, at 1 (800) 555-5555. Meanwhile, I will hold your $395.00 payment--the full cost of the Lilehauser tapes--until the end of the month. If we do not hear from you by then, a full refund will be issued.

As one critic said, "Laurence Bauer understands the soul of Charles Dickens better than any contemporary actor. To understand his soul is to deliver a memorable performance." This performance will be yours as soon as you pick up the phone.

Yours truly,

Mila Monroe

Mila Monroe
Order Fulfillment Manager

FIGURE 8.5   *Sample Substitute Delivery Letter*

Life was a lot simpler when what we honored was father and mother rather than all major credit cards.

Robert Orben
American writer

to encourage the applicant to continue doing business on a cash basis. Methods for accomplishing this twofold task depend both on the applicant's status as a business or individual consumer and on the specific reasons for the refusal.[5]

REFUSING CREDIT TO BUSINESSES   When a business client is refused credit, the refusal usually results from information offered by the applicant—from what the applicant has told the supplier about its finances rather than what third parties have told the supplier. This distinction is important. While the first situation involves such objective factors as undercapitalization, heavy debt, or a poor business location, the second situation often involves a poor track record in paying bills. In addition, refusing on the basis of the applicant's own information does not question the applicant's character or business skills in the same way as refusing on the basis of information supplied by disgruntled creditors.

Knowing that most credit refusals to businesses stem from the applicant's own information simplifies matters as you begin to write a credit-refusal letter. You can state your case in a fairly straightforward way while still trying to convince the reader to do business on a cash basis. To encourage future business, you can also offer various incentives, including discounts for cash, the elimination of credit-related interest charges, and such options as making repeated, small cash purchases (which gives the customer the advantage of access to the most up-to-date merchandise) and building a reputation of on- time payment (which may permit you to grant future credit). The applicant, of course, may already be aware of these advantages, but mentioning them in your letter allows you to frame a positive, hopeful response. The letter in Figure 8.6 puts this approach into action by turning a difficult refusal into a business opportunity. Note, too, the tone of the letter—the positive phrasing and the adoption of the "you" attitude.

REFUSING CREDIT TO CONSUMERS   Consumer credit is a multibillion-dollar industry in the United States. Department stores like Macy's and specialty retailers like Home Depot and Firestone Tire offer customers store credit accounts in addition to accepting such international charge cards as MasterCard, Visa, and American Express. When card-issuing companies refuse personal credit, they base their decisions not only on information received from individual applicants but on information provided by third parties. Credit-refusal letters thus vary according to the source of negative information.

Variety Beauty Supplies
149 Calhoun Drive   Omaha, NE 68124
(402) 555-8606

May 9, 199X

Ms. Amy Waller, President
Waller Beauty Salon
27 Fontina Road
Omaha, NE 68101

Dear Ms. Waller:

After receiving your application for credit, I contacted the four businesses you listed as credit references. All had positive comments about their credit experiences with your company.

The credit information you provided on your application helped us analyze your current debt situation. Although your company's profits have increased substantially over the past year, we feel that your current debt is still too high to justify taking on additional monthly payments. In our opinion, additional debt could hamper your ability to remain competitive.

Because of this, I would like to suggest that we begin our relationship on a cash basis and reevaluate the situation in six months. During that period, you will be eligible for a 3-percent cash discount on every purchase. To help your cash flow, may I suggest placing smaller orders on a regular basis that will maintain adequate inventories without adding any unnecessary financial burden.

Your business with us over the next six months will give us some of the information we need to reevaluate your credit application. I look forward at that time to being able to establish a line of credit.

Sincerely yours,

Barry Simons

Barry Simons
Credit Manager

> The buffer provides the good news about positive credit references.

> This paragraph explains the refusal. It focuses on the health of the applicant's company rather than on the creditor's fear of taking on a bad credit risk. The writer is careful to use phrases such as *we feel* and *in our opinion*, which communicate the subjective nature of the evaluation.

> The bad news that credit has been refused is given in the first sentence. Rather than stating the refusal in negative terms, the writer focuses on the opportunities that paying in cash provides. The "you" attitude is reflected here and in the entire letter.

> The letter closes on an optimistic note.

FIGURE 8.6   *Credit-Refusal Letter to a Business Customer*

REFUSALS BASED ON INFORMATION FROM APPLICANTS When individuals apply for credit in retail stores, they complete credit applications requesting such information as current income and monthly debt. Just as businesses may deny credit to companies that are overextended, retailers will likely deny credit to individual applicants with shaky financial records. Therefore, a writer responding to a consumer application that fails to meet minimum credit standards is in much the same position as the writer who must deny credit because of information contained in a business application. Although you must deny credit, you can also hold out the hope that the individual's financial situation may change.

In general, follow the same pattern that we laid out for the refusal of business credit. Although cash discounts seldom apply to individuals, you can offer other incentives—for example, a layaway plan. While no applicant enjoys being turned down, your goal is to increase the likelihood that he or she will become a cash customer.

REFUSALS BASED ON INFORMATION FROM THIRD PARTIES When negative information about the applicant is supplied by a credit bureau or a credit reference, a different kind of refusal situation exists. In this case, you are dealing with an applicant who has not met certain financial obligations. For example, a credit report may show a history of late payments or court judgments for unpaid bills. Because this information usually reflects the applicant's character and financial behavior, a letter of refusal must take a more cautious approach. In particular, because repeating a litany of unpaid bills will only make the applicant angry and will accomplish little of benefit to your company, your letter should deal in generalities rather than specifics.

According to the provisions of the Fair Credit Reporting Act (FCRA), if credit is denied because of information issued by a credit-reporting agency, the firm refusing credit must supply the name and address of the agency along with the refusal. This stipulation allows the applicant to request a copy of the credit statement and to correct any mistakes that may have been made. This law does not apply to information received from a third party such as a credit reference listed on the application.

During periods of economic recession or personal financial upheaval caused by unemployment, illness, or divorce, many individuals encounter credit problems. However, because individual situations often improve, many individuals who fail to qualify for credit today may be valued customers tomorrow. Even when denying credit, therefore, treat these potential customers politely and in a businesslike manner. Although you can offer very little in the way of a tangible business relationship, your attitude may sow the seeds for future business interaction.

Refusing a Claim

Claim refusals often place business writers in the midst of emotionally charged situations. Customers who may have been angry when they first made their claims now learn that they will not get the adjustments they sought. Your biggest challenge is to soften the blow and salvage goodwill.

Self-control is crucial even if you have just received a scathing, accusation-filled letter; it becomes even harder when the customer is at fault. Although giving the customer a piece of your mind may make you feel better for the moment, you will regret it later. Harsh words guarantee only that your customer is lost forever.

Although there are people who try to cheat businesses with false claims, it is a mistake to approach every claim with the attitude that you are dealing with a cheater. Instead, start with the assumption that the claim resulted either from something that the customer did not understand or from an honest mistake.

CURRENT ISSUES IN BUSINESS COMMUNICATION

The Fair Credit Reporting Act

Businesspeople involved in writing credit letters must be familiar with the provisions of the Fair Credit Reporting Act (FCRA) of 1970. The FCRA protects consumers who are subject to credit reports from unfair or unethical practices. *Credit reports*—official compilations of a person's credit history—are distributed to businesses for a variety of reasons. For example, companies that offer consumer credit cards, loans, mortgages, or insurance, as well as companies evaluating individuals for employment, have access to credit reports.

Among the specific information included on credit reports are bank, credit-card, and retail-store transactions. The report lists businesses that provide the consumer with credit and includes the details of a person's payment history. Late payments are noted, as are more serious problems like court judgments or bankruptcies.

The FCRA requires companies to inform consumers if they are denying credit or insurance or charging higher fees because of credit-report information. The company is also required to disclose the name and address of the credit agency issuing the negative report. The consumer then has sixty days to request, in writing, a copy of the report. The nation's three largest credit bureaus are TRW Inc., the Trans Union Corporation, and Equifax Inc.

If the consumer finds what he or she believes to be a mistake, the credit bureau is required to investigate the problem. Substantiated errors must be deleted from the applicant's file. If no error is found, the consumer can dispute or explain a negative item

by filing a short written statement (100 words or less) describing his or her version of the problem. This statement then becomes a permanent part of the individual's credit report. For example, an individual may attribute several late payments to a period of joblessness or a divorce.

Negative information on credit reports has a limited life. In most cases, bankruptcies can be reported for only 10 years; lawsuits, judgments, tax liens, accounts in collection, and accounts considered bad debts remain on file for seven years.

All these provisions are designed to protect the consumer while providing businesses with the information they need to make credit decisions. Unfortunately, the credit-reporting business has been criticized lately for a number of problems—providing incorrect information, failing to correct errors, and failing to provide corrected versions to companies that have received incorrect reports. In addition, credit bureaus have a history of confusing the files of people with the same or similar names. Under pressure from Congress and dissatisfied consumers, TRW has agreed to provide one free credit report per year to any consumer who asks for it—a service that formerly cost up to $20.

Sources: Henry R. Cheeseman, *Business Law: The Legal, Ethical, and International Environment* (Englewood Cliffs, NJ: Prentice Hall, 1992), pp. 1038–39; Peter Kerr, "Big Credit Bureau to Let Consumers See Reports Free," *The New York Times*, October 15, 1991, pp. A1, D9; and Michael W. Miller, "TRW to Give Credit Reports Free of Charge," *The Wall Street Journal*, October 15, 1991, p. B1.

Try to communicate sympathy with the customer's request and a desire to be fair. Even when you are forced to say no, customers should believe that they have been treated fairly. And remember that nothing upsets customers more than to be told that a refusal is based on "company policy." Every claimant has a right to know the *specific* reason for a refusal. These principles are applied in the claim refusal in Figure 8.7, which skillfully subordinates the writer's bad news to her detailed explanation of her company's decision.

Refusing a Request

Businesspeople often receive letters asking for information they cannot share, favors they cannot grant, or materials they cannot send. These letters require tactful refusals. Your goal is to maintain goodwill while you say no.

The buffer thanks the reader for his letter and refers to something mentioned in the letter to establish goodwill.

The problem is important enough for the writer to provide a detailed explanation of the effects of acid rain. The goal is to show why environmental problems, rather than poor products or workmanship, were responsible for the marred finish.

The bad news is stated as a subordinate clause in a sentence that offers positive information.

This paragraph highlights industry efforts to solve the problem.

To close, the writer refers once more to the reader's original letter, which expressed satisfaction with other aspects of the car. The last sentence conveys a broad, companywide commitment to customer satisfaction.

November 1, 199X

Mr. Elliott Waldron
270 Milton Drive
Grand Rapids, MI 49503

Dear Mr. Waldron:

Thank you for your October 22 letter. It raised an important issue that deserves a careful and thorough response. Because you describe yourself as committed to purchasing American cars, I want to do everything I can to keep your commitment strong.

Your letter noted that the high-gloss finish on your new car has blotches that cannot be washed away. This was confirmed by Bart Covington, the service manager at your local dealer. Our researchers tell us that this marring is the result of acid raid and other pollutants. Acid rain is created when factories and power plants spew sulfur dioxide and nitrogen dioxide into the air. When these compounds are in the atmosphere, they turn into sulfuric acid and nitric acid, which fall to the earth as rain or snow. When acid raid hits your car's surface, the sun evaporates the moisture, leaving the acid to mar the finish. The effect is particularly noticeable on cars with dark metallic finishes.

Although repainting your car is not covered under the warranty, I would like to offer the best advice the auto industry has. Wash your car after every rain and keep it garaged, especially during the first six months when the paint is still hardening.

Rest assured that we are doing everything we can to develop tougher clear-coat finishes that are more resistant to the effects of acid raid.

I am glad that your car has met all your other expectations for safety, performance, and comfort. As a company, we are committed to manufacturing the finest automobiles on the road.

Sincerely,

Julia Hagerty

Julia Hagerty
Customer Service Manager

AMERICAN AUTOMOBILES, INC.
37 Transportation Drive Detroit, MI 48235
(313) 555-5119

FIGURE 8.7   *Sample Claim-Refusal Letter*

Refusing a request is especially difficult when the person involved is an important customer or a business associate with whom you have a close relationship. In these cases, it is important to develop a strategy that will accomplish your goal without offending the individual who has made the request.

Be as positive as possible. For example, if two separate items are requested and you can supply only one, say so in your opening paragraph. If you can offer an alternative, suggest it first. Instead of saying, "We cannot send you a tape of the May 6 interview," say, "Although we cannot send you a tape of the May 6 interview, transcripts are available for $6."

Empathy is also critical, especially when the request is important to the reader. As always, expressing genuine sympathy and concern will help maintain goodwill. If you feel the need to apologize, do it once and move on. Keep in mind that a reasonable explanation is the most effective apology.

Refusing an Invitation

Invitations are often a formal part of business life. An invitation to speak at a meeting, attend a fund-raising dinner, or write an article for a business publication should be handled like any other important business request. When you must refuse the invitation, a tactful strategy is needed.

Tact is especially important when the person extending the invitation has a higher position—an important client, for example—or when the invitation puts you in a difficult position. In these situations, an impersonal approach that uses the passive voice to avoid a direct refusal may be the best choice.

Writing Bad News to Job Applicants

Even experienced businesspeople often have trouble rejecting job applicants. Realizing both how difficult it is to find a job and how rejections affect a person's self-confidence, they hesitate to write letters telling applicants that their companies can offer no immediate opportunities. When they finally do write, they often make the mistake of doing it too quickly, failing to encourage the applicant or soften the rejection.

These letters fail to communicate goodwill—an essential ingredient of most bad-news messages addressed to applicants. Goodwill is important because the company's ability to attract a continuing supply of qualified job seekers is at stake. If a company gets a reputation as uncaring or overly harsh, the quantity and quality of its applicant pool may be seriously reduced.

Saying no to job applicants may be necessary when you receive unsolicited résumés, when you decide not to interview an applicant whose résumé you did seek, and when you must follow up after a disappointing job interview.

Even when you have either no interest in hiring an applicant or no future job opportunities to offer, you can still subordinate your bad news to a positive message of good luck. You can conclude, for example, by saying, "Although the position for which you are applying has been filled, I wish you the best of luck in building a career."

Two additional types of employment-related bad-news messages need a word of warning—letters of reference and termination letters. In short, don't write them if you are at all concerned about legal ramifications. If you cannot write a positive letter of reference, exercise one of two options: Either provide minimal information in the form of the individual's job title and dates of employment or don't write anything. Quite simply, the legal environment surrounding reference letters is too delicate for employers and managers to criticize former employees in writing. One executive we know routinely tears up reference requests if he cannot answer positively. If you are called upon to write a letter of termination, follow the guidelines set forth by your company's human-resources department. Promises in such letters—for example, about the continuation of benefits—can be considered legally binding in certain circumstances.

PROGRESS CHECK

1. Name the six major categories into which bad-news messages fall.
2. Many business writers feel that messages refusing credit are among the most difficult to write. Why?
3. How can you maintain goodwill when you have to refuse someone's request?

Communicating Unfavorable Policies and Crisis Information

Negative information consists, in part, of policy and product decisions that are perceived as unfavorable to a specific audience. For example, when both Hertz and Avis announced major price increases for rental cars in New York City, their customers perceived the announcement as bad news. Similarly, when American

Express announced a tightened credit policy for its Optima Card, the new policy was interpreted as bad news for both current and prospective card holders. When policy changes are made, letters are usually sent to specific audiences of interested parties. To maintain goodwill, these letters must not only explain the changes that are being made but also stress the positive things that the company is doing as well.

When conveyed during a crisis, negative information should usually face the crisis directly. Sometimes, for example, an apology must be offered. For example, when the Consumer Affairs departments of California and New Jersey charged Sears Roebuck & Company with systematically overcharging for automotive repairs, the company's first response was to deny any fraud and turn the matter over to its lawyers. Within a short time, however, Sears realized that this response was beginning to erode consumer confidence. The company thus ran a series of newspaper advertisements, in the form of letters from company chairman Edward A. Brennan, intended to counteract this erosion of trust. These letters took a direct approach, beginning in one case as follows:

> You may have heard recent allegations that some Sears Auto Centers in California and New Jersey have sold customers parts and services they didn't need. We take such charges very seriously, because they strike at the core of our company—our reputation for trust and integrity.[6]

Although Sears did not offer a direct apology, at least one letter contained an implicit admission that a problem existed:

> With over two million automotive customers serviced last year in California alone, mistakes may have occurred. However, Sears wants you to know that we would never intentionally violate the trust customers have shown in our company for 105 years.[7]

Notice how the first sentence—in admitting the problem for which it implicitly apologizes—uses the passive voice, while the second sentence returns to the active voice to pledge that the incidents in question were not intentional.

A company's effectiveness in responding to a crisis is often measured by the way it communicates negative information. Johnson & Johnson, for example, received high marks in its handling of the Tylenol poisoning problem in 1983. Exxon, on the other hand, suffered a public-relations nightmare after trying to minimize the impact of the 1989 Exxon *Valdez* oil spill in Alaska. Depending on the way it is handled, a crisis can improve or erode a company's credibility. While Johnson & Johnson saw its reputation improve, Exxon lost credibility.

WRITING BAD-NEWS AND NEGATIVE MEMOS

The organization of bad-news memos depends on whether the message is being written to subordinates, higher-level management, or co-workers—that is, on whether your communication is downward, upward, or horizontal. Your organizational plan will change according to your need to be sensitive to differences in power and office politics.[8]

Sending Negative Messages to Subordinates

In each of the following cases, when senior managers at several large U.S. corporations felt the need to send bad-news memos to subordinates, internal communications found their way into newspapers and magazines.

- William Gates III, founder and chairman of Microsoft Corporation, wrote a scathing memo to his top executives in which he admitted that some of his worst fears were coming true: "Our nightmare—IBM

When Exxon mishandled its public relations response after the 1989 Exxon *Valdez* oil spill in Alaska's Prince William Sound, *Fortune* magazine compiled a list of actions that companies could take to prevent bad-news delivery from becoming full-scale crisis management. Among other things, editors suggested that companies respond immediately, become news sources rather than news stories, and release their own bad news before the press does it for them. They also recommended that managers consider (and, if necessary, research) their audiences, including the public as well as the press.

'attacking' us in system software, Novell 'defeating' us in networking, and more agile, customer-oriented applications competitors getting their Windows act together—is a reality."

Gates also complained about the quality of Microsoft's customer service: "The number of customers who get a bad impression," he speculated, "...must be in the millions world-wide."[9]

- Jeffrey Katzenberg, chairman of Walt Disney Studios, wrote a 28-page memo on the need to control spiraling costs and improve the quality of the company product. The studio, he declared, should "concentrate on what happens in the big room where the lights dim and the magic is supposed to happen."[10]

- Before Pan American World Airways went out of business, it endured a period of great uncertainty that affected every employee. Concerned about the effects of stress, Pan Am's vice president of flight operations issued a memo acknowledging the problem. In part, it said: "Stress stemming from Pan Am's current situation affects all levels of the organization.... Flight crews internalize stress...but it's there. Accept that mistakes...yours too...are more likely now than before."[11]

Despite content differences, these messages share one important characteristic: They communicate bad news in a direct way. This common denominator is not surprising: Many organizations want their communications to be direct whenever possible. These examples are also consistent with advice that we offered in Chapter 4—that is, to use a *direct pattern* when framing negative messages to subordinates.

Being direct is not the same thing as being unkind. As in all bad-news messages, you should criticize an act or a product, not a person. Where appropriate, leave the door open for change.

Sending Negative Messages to Managers

By contrast, negative messages intended for readers in positions of greater organizational power usually benefit from an indirect plan. Use a buffer to soften the news and a passive, impersonal colorless style. If you are asked, for example, to critique a proposal that your manager is about to deliver to an important client, it would be a mistake to make the following statement:

> Your opening is weak. Unless you get the client involved in the first paragraph, you might as well throw the rest of the proposal away.

You should probably phrase your comments like this:

> Although the detail provided in the middle of the document is convincing, a less numbers-oriented approach could be considered in the first paragraph.

Here, the passive voice allows the writer to avoid a direct, negative statement. Similarly, the *impersonal* style avoids an inappropriate level of familiarity. The opinion is offered without drawing attention to the *person* offering it.

Sending Negative Messages to Co-Workers

Occasionally, co-workers may ask each other for constructive criticism on projects or other aspects of their work. Such requests can be made when you are engaged in joint projects or when you are asked for an opinion about work in which you are not personally involved. In both cases, you are taking on the role of a superior—at least temporarily.

The operative word in the description of this situation is *temporarily*. After your opinion is given, you and your co-worker will be equals once more. As a result, even though you may be writing from a superior position, it may be a mistake to be too direct or forceful. It is often wiser to be indirect and diplomatic when conveying negative messages to co-workers. Base your organizational and stylistic decisions on both the situation and the personality of the recipient.

Table 8.4 summarizes the various organizational plans for writing office memos to different audiences. It also gives examples of the circumstances under which each memo might be written.

PROGRESS CHECK

1. How should a company communicate negative information during a crisis?
2. Why is it smart to be diplomatic and indirect when giving a negative message to a co-worker?

TABLE 8.4	**Organizing Bad-News Memos**	
AUDIENCE	ORGANIZATIONAL PLAN	THIS MESSAGE COULD BE SENT WHEN...
Superiors	Indirect	You cannot meet a deadline
Subordinates	Direct	You are disappointed with a subordinate's work
Co-workers	Sometimes direct, sometimes indirect	A co-worker asks you to critique his or her contribution to a joint project

WHAT'S AHEAD

While this chapter focused on writing effective bad-news messages, Chapter 9 will examine the art of writing persuasive messages. Specifically, we will look at the nature of persuasion and how it is used in the form of sales letters. We will also examine the role of persuasion in collecting past-due bills.

SUMMARY OF CHAPTER OBJECTIVES

1. **Explain the *indirect* and *direct plans* for organizing bad-news messages**.

   The indirect plan for organizing bad-news messages allows the writer to delay the bad news rather than communicate it immediately. The opening paragraph of the message acts as a buffer as it eases the reader into the news. Explanations follow to tell the reader why you must say no. The bad news is communicated next, followed by a closing paragraph that promotes goodwill. The direct plan opens with the bad news and does not attempt to soften it in any way.

2. **Describe different circumstances for writing bad-news letters involving *orders***.

   Businesspeople write bad news about orders for a variety of reasons. Among the most common are discontinuations of goods or services; delivery delays (known as *back orders*) and partial deliveries; requests to substitute different items for those that are temporarily out of stock or permanently out of inventory; and problems with the original orders that make order fulfillment impossible.

3. **Distinguish between *credit refusals* to businesses and credit refusals to individual consumers**.

   At different times, businesses must refuse to extend credit, whether to other businesses or to individual customers. When a business is involved, the refusal is usually the result of what the applicant has told the creditor about its finances rather than what third parties have told the creditor. By contrast, refusals to individual customers often reflect negative information supplied by such third parties as credit bureaus.

4. **Identify the most effective way to refuse a *claim***.

   The most effective claim refusals avoid emotions while communicating specific reasons for refusing a requested adjustment. The writer's goal is to make customers feel that they have been treated fairly. Citing company policy will probably get the reader upset. Every claimant has a right to know the *specific* reason for a refusal.

5. **Explain why tact is necessary when declining *requests*, including *invitations***.

   Tact is especially necessary when an important customer or business associate is involved. Tact is based on carefully considered strategy. Be positive and, when possible, suggest alternatives. When dealing with someone in a higher position, consider using the passive voice.

6. **Describe circumstances under which bad-news messages are sent to *job applicants* and why an indirect approach is appropriate**.

   Businesspeople may have to say no to job applicants when they receive unsolicited résumés, when they decide not to interview an applicant whose résumé they did seek, and when they must follow up after a job interview has failed to produce satisfactory results. Rejection letters should communicate goodwill by using various techniques to ease the blow.

7. **Identify circumstances under which *unfavorable policies* and *crisis information* are conveyed**.

   Companies communicate negative information when they announce policy changes (such as price increases) that will be perceived as unfavorable to a specific audience. Negative information may also be conveyed during a crisis and may include an apology for mistakes or errors in judgment.

8. **List the special requirements for sending** *bad-news memos* **to subordinates, superiors, and co-workers.**

Bad-news memos sent to subordinates usually take a direct, bottom-line approach. By contrast, negative messages intended for readers in positions of greater organizational power generally benefit from an indirect approach. Although you are usually in a superior role when you send messages to co-workers, this role is temporary. Therefore, it is often wise to be indirect and diplomatic rather than direct and forceful.

REVIEW AND DISCUSSION QUESTIONS

1. Distinguish between the indirect and direct plans for organizing bad-news messages. (*Ch. Obj. 1*)

2. When would you use an indirect approach to present bad news? When would you use a direct approach? (*Ch. Obj. 1*)

3. When might you write a bad-news letter about an order? (*Ch. Obj. 2*)

4. Distinguish between credit refusals to companies and credit refusals to individual consumers. Which are easier to write, and why? (*Ch. Obj. 3*)

5. Summarize some key guidelines for refusing a customer's claim. (*Ch. Obj. 4*)

6. Why is it so important to be tactful when refusing requests? (*Ch. Obj. 5*)

7. When might you write bad-news messages to job applicants? (*Ch. Obj. 6*)

8. What are the legal issues involved in writing negative reference letters and termination letters? (*Ch. Obj. 6*)

9. When might you write a bad-news message describing a crisis or an unfavorable policy? (*Ch. Obj. 7*)

10. Summarize the guidelines for conveying bad news to subordinates, superiors, and coworkers. (*Ch. Obj. 8*)

APPLICATION EXERCISES

1. Cover the right-hand column in TABLE 8.1. Create your own example for each type of buffer listed. (*Ch. Obj. 1*)

2. The chapter notes that diplomacy is just as important in business as it is in international politics. Do you agree or disagree? Why? Write a brief essay in which you present your point of view and explain why you feel the way you do. (*Ch. Obj. 1, 5, 7*)

3. Which approach would you use—direct or indirect—to convey bad news in each of the following situations? (*Ch. Obj. 1–3, 6, 8*)

   a. A supplier with whom you've been working for five years delivers the wrong part.

   b. You're forced to tell a qualified job applicant that you can't offer him a position due to a hiring freeze.

   c. As CEO, you decide to send a memo to all employees in which you emphasize the importance of turning off all copy machines and personal computers before individuals leave each evening.

   d. You have to turn down a new customer's request for credit because he's been in business for only five months.

4. In an earlier chapter we recommended using passive voice only sparingly. In this chapter, why do we suggest that it can be both appropriate and effective? (*Ch. Obj. 1*)

5. Ralph Martin has ordered a new wood-burning stove, the SomewhatWarm model, from Tickemeyer Stove Company. Unfortunately, Tickemeyer has discontinued the line due to lack of demand, although it still makes five other wood-burning models. These models are the Heat-o-lator, the CozyWarm, the ReallyWarm, the Snug-n-Elegant, and the SummersDay. Tickemeyer has a catalog of its products and a toll-free number customers can call to order stoves. Suppose that you're head of sales at Tickemeyer; write a letter to Ralph in which you explain the situation. Will you use a direct or indirect approach? (*Ch. Obj. 1, 2*)

6. You do such a good job with your letter to Ralph Martin that he not only requests a catalog but also orders a stove. Unfortunately, his order is not very clear. He asks for the Snug-n-Warm model but gives the model number as 2511-Z. There is no Snug-n-Warm stove, and none of your

stoves has this model number; the CozyWarm is Model # 2511-C, the ReallyWarm is 2511-D, and the Snug-n-Elegant is 2511-S. Write a letter to Ralph explaining the problems with his order and asking for clarification. (*Ch. Obj. 2*)

7. Ralph Martin replies, specifying that he wants to order a Snug-n-Elegant stove, Model # 2511-S. The price is $1,500. He also asks if he can open a charge account with your company and pay for the stove on credit. Tickemeyer does offer credit to qualified customers, but when Martin's credit application is processed, you learn from the Equifax credit bureau that he has a poor credit rating. Apparently he has several outstanding student loans that he hasn't repaid. Now you face the task of refusing credit to Martin while persuading him to go ahead and buy the stove. Tickemeyer has a layaway plan that would allow Martin to make monthly payments toward any purchase. Write this letter to Martin. (*Ch. Obj. 3*)

8. Martin settles for the layaway plan and finally takes delivery of his new stove after six months. However, three months after it's installed, he calls you, angrily claiming that his stove "isn't working right." It seems that waxy deposits are building up on the interior of the stove and coating the inside of the glass door. Martin also claims that the stove isn't putting out as much heat as it did when it was new. In talking with him, you discover that he routinely starts fires in the stove by using a fire-starter log made of pressed-wood byproducts and other flammable substances. You recognize the problem. Because they contain waxes and resins that coat interior walls and clog heating vents, fire-starter logs should not be burned in your stoves. When the stove was delivered, Martin also received a brochure that contained instructions and warned users about substances that would damage their stoves.

    Martin claims, nonetheless, that the company owes him a new stove. Write him a letter in which you explain the situation and refuse this request. (*Ch. Obj. 4*)

9. Pretty Penny Corporation offers a budget plan to its cellular-phone customers. They pay 10 cents per minute for phone use during peak hours and 1 cent per minute during off-peak hours. Peak hours begin at 7 A.M. and end at 8 P.M., Monday through Friday. Pretty Penny has signed up numerous customers under this plan. After six months, management has reviewed the bills and made a discovery. Many customers are using their phones between 8 P.M. and 9 P.M., when it's not too late to call people but late enough to avoid peak-hour rates. CEO Joe Penny decides to institute a new policy. From now on, off-peak time will begin at 9 P.M. rather than 8 P.M. Because he doesn't like to write bad-news letters, Penny delegates the task to his customer service manager. Write this letter to Penny's customers informing them of the company's new policy. (*Ch. Obj. 1, 7*)

10. *The Wall Street Journal* has asked you to write an article on business communication for an upcoming issue. You would love to, of course, but unfortunately you're extremely busy, preparing for an international conference in Geneva and opening a new import business to the Near East. Even more important, you have to study for a test that's coming up in your business communications class. Write a letter in which you refuse the *Journal*'s request while explaining that you remain quite interested in writing this piece or another at some later date. (*Ch. Obj. 5*)

11. As the human-resources manager of your company, you've interviewed two applicants for the same position. It's a difficult decision because you were impressed by both candidates. You decide to offer the job to Alicia because her work experience more nearly matches the requirements of the job. However, you want to send a tactful letter to the other applicant, Juan. While Juan didn't have quite the right experience for this job, you were impressed with his energy and motivation. There are no other openings at the company right now, but you may want to hire him for another position in the future. Write a letter explaining to Juan that he didn't get the job. (*Ch. Obj. 6*)

12. A sales manager finds out that one of the salespeople she hired had lied on his résumé. He had given himself a fancier job title and a longer tenure in his previous position than he'd really had; he also claimed to have done graduate study that he had not done. The sales manager confronts her subordinate with her findings; he apologizes for any "misunderstanding" but says that she must have "misread" his résumé. After thinking it over and discussing the matter with the human-resources department, the sales manager decides to fire the salesperson. Write a memo that gives him the bad news and explains why the action is being taken. (*Ch. Obj. 6, 8*)

13. In the decade after its founding in 1982, Autodesk, which makes design software for personal computers, had a string of successful years. In the early 1990s, however, sales slowed and profits fell. The company's stock fell 22 percent in a single day. No one was more upset over the company's failing performance than Autodesk's founder, John Walker, who blamed it on CEO Alvar Green. Walker had appointed Green, the firm's former finance officer, to succeed him but now felt that Green was keeping the firm's profit margins too high instead of investing in new products and marketing. Because Walker prefers to communicate through electronic mail, he wrote a 44-page electronic memo to Green in which he said that it pained him to "watch Autodesk squander everything I've been working 16 hours a day for since 1982." Walker accused Green of "taking [his] marching orders from the accounting rules rather than the real world." He also said he was "so appalled by what I heard at one management meeting that I vowed never to attend another management meeting and I never have."[12]

Do you feel Walker went about conveying bad news to Green in the right way? Explain your answer. (*Ch. Obj. 7, 8*)

14. If you feel that John Walker's memo could stand improvement, write your own. Your version of the memo should express Walker's concern about Autodesk, thank Green for his contributions to the company, and suggest that it might be best for the firm if someone else replaced Green as CEO. (*Ch. Obj. 7, 8*)

15. Northeast Research Company has been located in Connecticut since the firm was founded 25 years ago. Most of its employees are Connecticut natives with relatives living nearby. Thus, the company's CEO knew that it would be a big change for employees when he decided to relocate Northeast to Greenville, South Carolina. Business costs are lower in South Carolina, as is the cost of living; the CEO suspects that employees will be pleasantly surprised at housing prices after living in New England. This, plus the milder weather, are selling points that may help reassure employees about moving. Even though Northeast is relocating, it is not planning to lay off anybody—everyone who wants to move will have a job.

The CEO asks you to write a memo to all employees that announces the relocation in as positive a manner as possible. (*Ch. Obj. 7, 8*)

BUILDING YOUR RESEARCH SKILLS

Go to a library and find an article describing a situation in which a business had to give bad news to somebody. This situation could cover a wide range of activities: laying off employees, relocating corporate headquarters, explaining a bad year to the board of directors, dealing with an environmental disaster—to name just a few possibilities.

Bring the article (or a photocopy) to class. Be prepared to discuss it.

BUILDING YOUR TEAMWORK SKILLS

Your instructor will divide the class into small groups. Each member of the group should get a chance to present his or her article to the others and to answer their questions about it. Working as a group, create a memo that effectively presents the bad news which each company had to convey. Which situations call for a direct approach? Which call for an indirect approach? Can you think of something positive to say in each memo to help buffer the news? Have a volunteer in each group write down each memo as you compose it.

Your instructor may wish to have you read your memos to the class and explain the situations involved.

COMMUNICATING IN A WORLD OF DIVERSITY

Fashion and France—a no-lose combination, right?

Not for Galeries Lafayette, a French retailer that has had a hard time transplanting its stores in the United States.

At home, Galeries Lafayette is an upscale,

highly profitable enterprise. But its American boutique, located in New York's Trump Tower, has been less successful. It has lost almost $8 million over the past two years.

Why? Analysts suggest two reasons. First, they suspect that Galeries Lafayette's expensive clothing (for example, dresses averaging $1,000 each) simply hasn't appealed to value-conscious consumers. Second, observers have also suggested that, ironically, perhaps Galeries Lafayette has just not been sufficiently French. "We wanted a modern image of France, not Versailles and the Eiffel Tower," explains Stephane Constans-Gavarry, the company's vice president for international development. But the result was a store that looked like lots of other American retailers; one consultant said it "could be in a suburban mall in Topeka."

Galeries Lafayette isn't giving up yet. To lure bargain hunters, the New York store will start carrying three new private-label lines of clothing that sell for 30 percent less than the store's usual inventory of designer duds. To lure Francophiles, it will also make a bigger fuss about its French pedigree. For starters, it will sport miniature Eiffel Towers in its windows.

Suppose that you're the manager of Galeries Lafayette's New York store. Write a memo to your boss in which you break the bad news that the store is losing money and present your ideas for reversing the trend.

Source: Stewart Toy with Morton Sosland and Wendy Zellner, "Getting from *Rouge* to *Noir*," *Business Week*, July 13, 1992, p. 35.

CASE 8.1

Taking Bad News with the Good at Pro Fasteners, Inc.

Pro Fasteners, Inc., is actually a success story. The small (fifty-five employees) California-based company, which distributes industrial hardware and components to the electronics industry, is popular with both customers and vendors. "They're the best," says one purchasing agent. "They're way out ahead of the curve."

But even successful companies have problems. For Pro Fastener, both its success and its problems emerged when founder and president Steve Braccini decided to make over the firm. Impressed by theories of total-quality management, Braccini traded in the firm's typical "pyramid" structure for an organization that empowered employees to make more decisions and take on more responsibility. He set up an employee committee called the Continuous Improvement Council (CIC) to oversee employee work teams and improve quality levels. Then he hired a new general manager, Robert Landau, to oversee general operations and thus free up his time for planning the company's growth and finding new customers.

At first, things seemed to go smoothly. Employees took classes in subjects like responsibility management, Landau hired more salespeople to handle a growing number of orders, and Braccini planned the firm's expansion into another division in Austin, Texas. But then, progress stalled. Flexing its collective muscle, the CIC asked department managers to step off work teams so that their CIC members could manage them instead. Managers resented the proposal because they still retained responsibility for implementing CIC's suggestions; some managers also felt that their authority was being undermined. Many of Pro's longtime employees resented Landau, the new manager, because they felt he was too cold and distant; they preferred the old "family" feeling that they had had when the company was smaller and run directly by Braccini.

Morale sank companywide—and so did earnings. By the early 1990s, Braccini was spending $200,000 on training (more than $4,000 per employee), and profits had dropped by 50 percent.

Reluctantly, Braccini looked for ways to cut costs. For example, although Pro had always bought health insurance for both employees and their dependents, Braccini decided that the company could afford coverage only for workers. If employees wanted to cover their families, premiums would have to be deducted from their paychecks.

We're happy to report that Pro Fasteners has weathered these storms and appears to be healthy and growing. However, these incidents show that, no matter how successful a company is, situations will still arise that require people to convey bad news of one sort or another.

Questions and Applications

1. Summarize the crises, policy changes, and other developments at Pro Fasteners that might necessitate writing bad-news messages.
2. Suppose that you're a member of the Continuous Improvement Council. Even though you like your manager, Pat Robbins, you agree with the other Council members that Pro would benefit if the firm's managers no longer participated on work teams. You feel that this change would encourage employees to support Pro's quality movement by making them more responsible for their own work and the team's accomplishments. You also feel it will give everyone valuable practice in teamwork. Write a memo to Pat in which you suggest this policy change.
3. Steve Braccini has asked you to write a memo to employees, explaining the firm's new health-insurance policy and the reasons for the changes. Write this memo.

Source: John Case, "Quality with Tears," *Inc.*, June 1992, pp. 83–95. Reprinted with permission. Copyright © 1992 by Goldhirsh Group, Inc., 38 Commercial Wharf, Boston, MA 02110.

CASE 8.2

Morgan Stanley: Deciding When to Invest in Bad News

In this chapter, we've talked about the problems that both individuals and companies face in communicating bad news. Investment bank Morgan Stanley seems to have a different problem: This firm didn't communicate bad news often enough.

Like all investment firms, Morgan has two branches, each with its own goal. One branch competes with other banks to sell stocks for corporate clients; this is a highly competitive field in which firms do their best to encourage demand for those stocks among investors. The other branch provides research and advises investors on which stocks to buy and sell.

Lately, some Morgan employees claim that these two lines of business have come to constitute a conflict of interest. After all, how can you sell stocks if your own analysts are advising investors not to buy? "We sit on opposite sides of the table, like a law firm representing both sides of a divorce," admits a former Morgan chemical-industry analyst. "When corporate finance and research clash, it's a real problem."

Several Morgan analysts claim that Morgan bankers have pressured them to change negative research reports on the stocks of Morgan clients. To encourage its analysts to cooperate with its bankers, Morgan management recommended that a bigger part of analysts' pay be tied to how much they contributed to investment-banking transactions. Morgan analysts did not appreciate the pressure. "We were held accountable to corporate finance—playing the game the way corporate finance dictated," complains a former food-retailing analyst. "We shouldn't have been put through the wringer to do our job professionally."

Consider the internal war fought by Morgan over Safeway. When the supermarket chain went public, Morgan won the chance to sell some of its stock. Its corporate-finance group, headed by Robert

Matschullat, recommended that Safeway price its stock between $19 and $22 a share. But Morgan analyst Stacy Dutton felt the stock was actually worth only $10 to $13 a share—almost 50 percent less. Thus, while one branch at Morgan was trying to sell Safeway stock at $19 to $22, one of the firm's analysts was advising clients that it was overpriced.

Dutton arranged a meeting with Matschullat to discuss the disagreement. When she began, says Dutton, Matschullat reminded her that her pay would be tied to her help with investment-banking deals. Dutton says she was stunned: "I was coming to him with a strictly objective quantifiable issue, and he wasn't interested at all in the substance of my work. He wasn't interested in debating the merits of one valuation versus another. He was strictly interested if I was going to help him get the deal done."

Other analysts agree with Dutton's story. A few years ago, Morgan Stanley was trying to win part of Occidental Petroleum's stock-underwriting business. When one Morgan analyst concluded that Occidental's stock was overpriced, angry Occidental execs complained to Morgan. The bank quickly removed the offending analyst from the account. When another analyst wasn't sufficiently optimistic about a client's prospects, Morgan shift-ed him to another division.

Morgan chairman Richard Fisher feels that his firm knows how to handle a common industry-wide problem: "I guarantee you the tension between investment bankers and research exists at every firm," he argues, "but Morgan Stanley deals with it as well as anyone."

Questions and Applications

1. What situation produces the "tension" between investment bankers and research analysts at Morgan Stanley?
2. Summarize the ethical dilemma faced by Morgan Stanley and its staff.
3. Chairman Richard Fisher asks you to draft a memo to Morgan's staff in which you present the bad news that there are conflicts between the company's two branches. Your main point, he stipulates, is to be that the firm's research has never been compromised and that these conflicts have been isolated incidents and not companywide. Write this memo.

Source: Michael Siconolfi, "Under Pressure," *The Wall Street Journal*, July 14, 1992, pp. A1, A4.

Writing Persuasive Messages

CHAPTER OBJECTIVES

After studying this chapter, you should be able to:

1 Explain the concept of *persuasion* and the four *persuasive goals*.

2 Identify and contrast the three major *persuasive appeals*.

3 Identify and describe the three types of *sales letters*.

4 Apply the *AIDA concept* to the organization of a sales letter.

5 List the four types of *collection letters* and explain the purpose of each.

6 Explain when to use a direct approach in *persuasive memos* and when to be indirect.

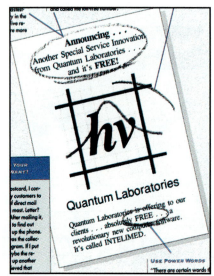

QUANTUM LABS SENDS POSTCARDS TO PROSPECTS

Quantum Laboratories, a clinical lab based in Renton, Washington, was recently faced with the challenge of selling its newly developed Intelimed, a computer system designed primarily for the automation of medical offices. Michael Lillig, vice president of sales and marketing, was assigned the task of persuading customers to purchase the office-automation system. Because Quantum specializes in laboratory systems rather than office systems, Lillig needed a cost-effective marketing approach that would attract the greatest number of potential buyers in the new market. He also needed a sales presentation that could not be ignored.

Lillig considered face-to-face sales calls but decided against them because, at an estimated average cost of $250 per call, they were too expensive for initial sales efforts. After attending a direct-response seminar, Lillig became convinced that a direct-mail campaign was the appropriate way to begin what he realized would be a long process before final purchase decisions were made. His campaign would begin with postcards sent to the firm's prime prospects—the managers of 750 physicians' offices. In part, direct mail was attractive because it was so inexpensive: For just $500, Quantum could purchase the appropriate mailing list and print and mail the postcards.

Why would Lillig decide to put such important information on a postcard instead of, say, in a letter or even a four-color brochure? After speaking with a group of potential customers, Lillig realized that in order for his message to succeed, he had to deliver it in the least amount of time. "For busy doctors and nurses, a postcard is very time efficient," he explains. "I had 30 seconds of a prospect's time to give him or her a good reason to call us. Under those conditions, you have to figure out the one thing that makes your product different from everything else on the market—and sell it."

When he sat down to write his copy, Lillig focused on communicating the dual benefits offered by Intelimed—saving money and reducing work. As you can see in Figure 9.1, the headlines, words, and format that Lillig designed into his postcard are all critical to the success of his message. Included with his postcard are Lillig's own comments about his content and format choices.

The postcard had an immediate impact. "The phone started ringing two or three times a day, for a solid week," recalls Lillig, who eventually came up with seventeen serious prospects. Within six months, he had signed six contracts, worth about $300,000 a year, and was working on eleven more.

Although the total response rate to the postcard was only 4 percent, Quantum's return on its original $500 investment was an astounding 60,000 percent—a figure that might still double if more potential contracts are signed. Michael Lillig's direct-mail project helped Quantum's annual sales grow by more than 50 percent, to $2.5 million, in 1991. It also convinced Lillig that a persuasive well-written sales card or letter can be worth its weight in gold.[1]

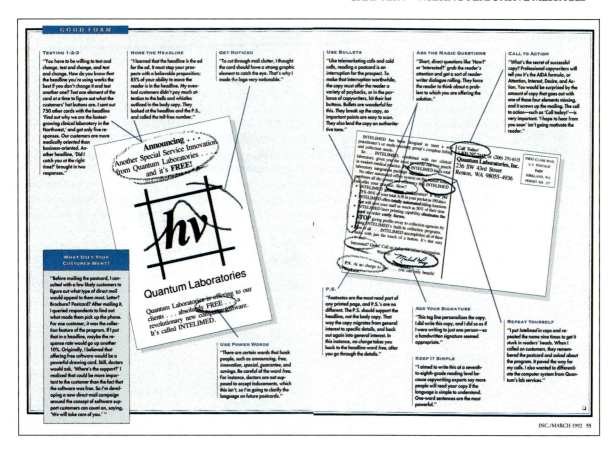

FIGURE 9.1   *A Persuasive Message from Quantum Laboratories*

CHAPTER OVERVIEW

As the center of Quantum's direct-mail campaign, Michael Lillig's postcard is a model of effective persuasion. It uses many of the elements of a persuasive message: a free offer in the headline, strong graphics, power words, bullets, questions that involve the reader, simple language, deliberate repetition, a call to action, a personal signature, and a postscript. Quantum's postcard sets the stage for the topic of this chapter—writing persuasive business messages. Of course, many persuasive business messages, including sales letters and collection letters, are aimed at customers. Others try to convince colleagues or peers to take action.

Persuasive messages make use of a variety of formats. The head of a construction firm, for example, may write a letter to a potential client who plans to build a neighborhood shopping center in a local suburb. Like most of the messages discussed in this part of *Contemporary Business Communication*, this letter would be a piece of one-to-one correspondence. In other cases, the persuasive message may be communicated in a mass mailing sent to a list of persons. Michael Lillig's direct-mail project is a good example of this approach. Finally, persuasive messages may involve mass mailings in which each letter or postcard is personalized: Special word-processing programs can actually insert the names of recipients and make each message appear to be an individualized letter.

Even though purpose and audience may vary, all successful persuasive messages involve appeals to *reasoning*, *credibility*, and *emotion*. We will begin by defining *persuasion* in terms of specific goals and purposes for written documents. We will then examine the nature of *persuasive appeals* in more detail before applying some key principles to *sales letters*, *collection letters*, and *persuasive memos*.

Words are, of course, the most powerful drug used by mankind.

Rudyard Kipling
English author

persuasion
Process of influencing or changing attitudes, beliefs, values, or behaviors

WHAT IS PERSUASION?

Each month our mailboxes at home and at work seem to contain a growing number of persuasive messages. A political candidate wanting our vote, a non-profit organization requesting donations, a business firm trying to market its goods or services, an office co-worker who wants a proposal approved—all these are examples of the many types of persuasive messages. **Persuasion** is the process of influencing or changing attitudes, beliefs, values, or behaviors. It is, of course, a key element in sales contacts that try to convince prospects to purchase company products. Persuasion is also crucial in collecting past-due accounts from customers who have failed to pay outstanding debts. Finally, as business-people make recommendations and requests that either support, modify, or reject a current situation, persuasion is vital in stimulating various activities both within and outside an organization.

We will begin by describing the broad goals of persuasive messages and then discuss the more specific purposes that business communicators identify in order to focus more clearly on those goals.

Persuasive Goals

Every persuasive message attempts to achieve one of four broad goals: *adoption, continuance, discontinuance,* and *deterrence.* The first step in composing a persuasive message is to define what you want your reader to do in terms of one of these four basic goals. You are then in a better position to clarify the specific purpose of your document.

message of adoption
Document that seek to persuade readers to *start* doing something

ADOPTION   **Messages of adoption** try to persuade readers to *start* doing something. Adoption is the essence of most sales letters. For example, American Express sends letters to prospective cardholders urging them to apply for various cards. Omaha Steaks International relies heavily on persuasive letters to promote its line of gourmet meats. JCPenney cardholders, catalog recipients, and other people on company mailing lists receive invitations to storewide sales extravaganzas.

message of continuance
Persuasive message that urges the continuation of a behavior

CONTINUANCE   **Messages of continuance** urge the continuation of a behavior. Continuance is the basis for selling any ongoing service. For example, magazines like *Newsweek* and *Time* send letters to current subscribers trying to convince them to renew subscriptions. Near the end of service periods, professionals from veterinarians to exterminators send letters encouraging customers to renew contracts. Banks encourage active customers to make home-improvement, vacation, and other loans.

Because both businesses and nonprofit organizations know the importance of loyal subscribers, customers, and donors, they work doubly hard to retain them. Messages of continuance are thus sent frequently and in large numbers, and senders face the challenge of ensuring that their messages reach recipients by penetrating high volumes of "noise." For example, as part of a $100-million marketing campaign designed to introduce the new Impreza, Subaru Executive Vice President Chuck Worrell sent 900,000 letters to current Subaru owners. His objective was to entice them into Subaru showrooms with offers of a $500 rebate on a new Impreza. Worrell's persuasive letter-writing campaign was based on his belief that current Subaru owners are more likely to be well-informed about the auto's merits and are strong prospects to purchase another Subaru.[2]

Similarly, to increase the likelihood that its message would break through the noise levels created by competing messages of continuance, the subscription department of the humor magazine *National Lampoon* sent current subscribers the novel mailing shown in Figure 9.2. Not surprisingly, the magazine's tongue-in-cheek "ransom note" stood out from the other mailings in the typical sub-scriber's mailbox. It was read, and it prompted thousands of subscription

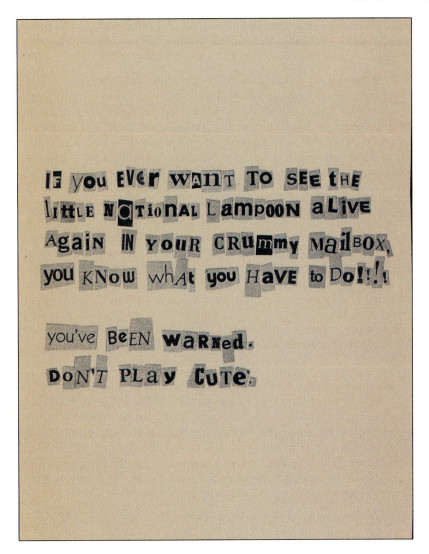

FIGURE 9.2   *A Persuasive Message from* **National Lampoon**

renewals by readers who appreciated an unorthodox approach to an issue as basic as a subscription renewal.

DISCONTINUANCE   Collection letters frequently use persuasive messages to encourage credit customers to make payment on delinquent accounts. In effect, they are asking customers to stop avoiding payment. Messages that ask for such behavior changes are referred to as **messages of discontinuance**. Discontinuance is a common theme in office memos that try to persuade colleagues to cease a given activity—say, to halt opposition to an existing policy or procedure or to join together in modifying it so that existing problems will be minimized.

message of discontinuance
Persuasive message that asks for a behavior change

Messages of discontinuance are also used in persuasive letters—for example, when its competitors have succeeded in attracting a firm's customers. Thus, in the midst of the long-distance telephone wars involving AT&T, MCI, and Sprint, AT&T offered former customers a special bonus of $200 if they returned to AT&T as their long-distance provider.

Similarly, Chuck Worrell's Subaru Impreza mailing can be considered a discontinuance message. In addition to contacting Subaru owners about the new Impreza, Worrell's campaign was aimed at owners of competing brands with which the new model was expected to compete—for example, the Honda Civic and the Toyota Corolla. Subaru's direct attack on the competition included a mailing of 600,000 letters, each arguing that the new Impreza was a better buy.

To entice owners of competing cars into local Subaru showrooms, the letter offered a premium of a Columbia Sportswear parka to consumers who test-drove the Impreza.[3]

DETERRENCE   **Messages of deterrence** try to prevent an action from taking place. They might be used, for example, when an important client is considering moving his or her account to a different company. A deterrence letter might be written to convince the client that the move is a mistake. Similarly, if a marketing executive objects to the proposed location of a new retail store, the counterproposal is most likely to be effective if it includes one or more alternative sites, together with documentation showing the superiority of the new location over the original.

Specific Persuasive Purposes

Once you have determined the broad goal of your message, you can then define the specific purposes that will accomplish your overall objective. As you recall from Chapter 3, a statement of specific purpose is most effective when it specifies a goal in a way that appeals to a clearly defined audience. In other words, you are more likely to accomplish your goal if you know your audience and can visualize it before you begin writing. Direct-mail marketer Daniel S. Kennedy uses his own writing experience to explain why it is important to address the priorities of the reader rather than those of the writer:

> I was asked to write a corporate fund-raising letter for the Arthritis Foundation's annual telethon in Phoenix. In examining samples of letters other nonprofit organizations sent to corporate donors, I noticed that they all had this failing in common: They talked at great length about their own priorities—what they needed the money for, how it would be used, how funds were low, etc.—but they hardly addressed the donor's priorities at all. So I visualized myself as the business owner or executive being banged at by all these worthy charities' pleas and asked myself, "If I were to give, what would be important to me?" I came up with this list:
>
> 1. What benefit to me or my company justifies the cost?
> 2. Who else had picked this drive to contribute to? How can I validate my judgment?
> 3. How would I get the money to give? What budget would it come out of? What other expense would have to be reduced to afford this new one?
>
> With this in mind, I wrote the letter....[4]

Knowing your reader, therefore, is the key to focusing a broad persuasive goal on a specific persuasive purpose. Although your persuasive purpose must be kept in mind (say, marketing a product or collecting a debt), your document will be effective if you frame the purpose from the perspective of the reader and in terms that the reader will appreciate.

Your purpose in writing a sales letter, for example, is not to tell readers about a wonderful product, but rather to persuade them that it will help *them* in specific ways. The purpose of a collection letter is not to express anger at the customer's nonpayment, but rather to persuade the credit purchaser to send money. The purpose of a memo urging the adoption of a proposal is to show how your recommendations will benefit the *other people* in the company who will be responding to the proposal—how *they* will improve the efficiency of a department, simplify a task, increase sales, or reduce costs. In each case, you should be answering the question that is uppermost in the reader's mind: "How will this help me?"

As we suggested in Chapter 5, the most powerful persuasive word in the English language is *you*. This word underscores the benefits of a message to the individual recipient in the most direct, personal way.

Sell solutions, not just products.

Klaus M. Leisinger
Department director,
Ciba-Geigy, Ltd.

PERSUASIVE APPEALS

Effectively used, persuasive techniques work simultaneously on three levels. Persuasive messages appeal to the reader's sense of *reasoning*, establish the *credibility* of the document, and evoke an *emotional response* from the reader.

Persuading through Reasoning

Persuasive documents try to convince readers to accept a particular point of view through the logical presentation of evidence. They thus involve the act of **reasoning**—using available evidence to reach a conclusion.

> **reasoning**
> Process of using available evidence to reach a conclusion

Reasoning involves presenting different forms of "evidence"—non-numerical facts, statistics, examples and anecdotes, expert opinion, and analogies—that have a direct bearing on the document's specific persuasive purpose. As we saw in Chapter 4, for example, the use of logical organizational patterns, such as chronological, spatial, cause-and-effect, or problem-solution, improves the chances that the reader will accept a document's point of view. Organizational patterns are persuasive, in other words, because they show how a point of view lends itself to logical development. In Figure 9.3, therefore, the magazine *Eating Well* makes effective use of the problem-solution pattern as it tries to persuade people to subscribe.

> *The right to be heard does not automatically include the right to be taken seriously. To be taken seriously depends entirely upon what is being said.*
>
> *Hubert H. Humphrey
> Former Vice President
> of the United States*

To decide which logical pattern will be most effective for a given document, you can identify and then try to answer questions that the reader is likely to raise after reading it. For example, someone who is reading a sales letter for a European tour will probably want to know exactly *where* the tour will go and *when*. Thus, if you were a travel agent composing such a sales letter, you might use a chronological approach to describe the trip's itinerary.

Persuading through Credibility

The ability to persuade is directly affected by the credibility of the document. **Credibility** is the degree to which a statement, a person, and/or a company is perceived to be ethical, believable, trustworthy, competent, responsible, and sincere. As we saw in Chapter 2, three types of credibility influence whether messages succeed or fail. *Initial credibility*—what the reader already knows—is particularly important in sales letters. For example, a special sales-promotion letter for Motorola cellular phones from the company's regional office will prompt many people to respond positively to the firm's international reputation for quality. Similarly, a letter signed by Motorola's CEO is likely to command more respect and attention than the same letter signed by a lower-ranking executive.

> **credibility**
> Degree to which a statement, a person, and/or a company is perceived to be ethical, believable, trustworthy, competent, responsible, and sincere

By contrast, *derived credibility*—credibility created during the message—is influenced by the logic of the presentation, the strength of the evidence, the emotional appeal, and even the way the information is arranged on the page. Even if you are marketing a product that is relatively unknown to potential customers, the strength (or weakness) of your presentation can convince readers to investigate further and eventually make a decision to purchase (or not purchase) your product.

Finally, *terminal credibility*—credibility created when readers evaluate the writer, company, and product after reading the message—is the sum total of all previous reactions. For example, while the reader's response to a sales letter from Sears Auto Centers might be affected by allegations that individual Sears outlets were overbilling some customers (initial credibility), the reader may also be influenced by the persuasiveness of the offer itself (derived credibility). After considering these factors, the reader may accept or reject the offer; in either case, the decision is a measure of the company's terminal credibility.

ENHANCING CREDIBILITY WITHIN A DOCUMENT   Although you cannot control exactly how others will perceive a message, you can use various techniques to influence how people perceive the document that you actually write. For

Dear Reader:

Consider this advice:

- "Limit the use of shrimp to no more than one serving per week . . ."
  – American Heart Association

- "Shrimp is no worse than chicken, and that is not counting the (beneficial) fish oils in it . . ."
  – The New York Times

- "Shrimp contains 2 to 3 times as much cholesterol as other fish. Accordingly, it would be safer not to eat any shrimp . . ."
  – Healthwise Newsletter

Remember when eating well was so simple?

The days when we could savor a juicy shrimp without thinking twice about <u>cholesterol</u> . . . when we could tuck into a prime steak and not worry about <u>growth hormones</u> . . . the times when an apple a day wasn't clouded with concerns about <u>pesticides</u> . . . the good old days when all the <u>salt</u> in chicken soup meant nothing to us . . . the innocent times when we popped seemingly harmless red candies that owed their bright color to a <u>carcinogenic</u> dye . . .

If you love good food –– and if you are dismayed by all the bad news and conflicting advice about nutrition –– welcome to EATING WELL, The Magazine of Food & Health.

Discover an entirely new kind of food magazine, an intelligent ally in these times of unprecedented change in the ways we eat and think about food. With EATING WELL you will:

- <u>Have the facts:</u> Make better decisions about your own eating habits –– using the very latest findings and candid advice from leading researchers, nutritionists and physicians. Hear the inside story without bunk, fluff or misinformation.

- <u>Cook lighter:</u> Every issue will bring you a wealth of tempting new recipes. Full-flavored recipes. Nutritious recipes. Recipes that call for realistic ingredients. Recipes that work. Recipes that look as good as they taste –– use EATING WELL's dazzling photography to guide the way.

  You'll discover the techniques of cooking with less fat, less salt, less sugar –– and in the process learn how to

FIGURE 9.3   *A Persuasive Message from* **Eating Well**

example, the language that you choose for the headline and body of your message can be a powerful persuasive tool. Michael Lillig of Quantum Laboratories realized this fact after creating two mailings with unsuccessful headlines. When he wrote, "Find out why we are the fastest-growing clinical laboratory in the Northwest," he received only five responses. He got only two responses to a mailing sent with the headline "Did I catch you at the right time?" Finally, the headline "Announcing…another special service innovation from Quantum Laboratories…and it's FREE!" brought in twenty-eight inquiries.[5]

Your credibility is also enhanced when your document focuses on customer benefits instead of dwelling on features of the product, proposal, or idea. For example, if you are trying to convince your manager to support your recommendations to restructure the department's computerized-data system, you are more likely to gain that support by focusing on how the enhanced system will increase productivity rather than on the bells and whistles of the latest software.

ETHICAL ISSUES IN BUSINESS COMMUNICATION

Logical Fallacies

You can try *too* hard to be persuasive. For example, the desire to make a sale, collect a bad debt, or convince a manager to take action has led more than one writer down the path of the *logical fallacy*—a flaw in the writer's reasoning that can have the effect of manipulating the reader's response. Based on their impact on the reasoning process, logical fallacies fall into distinct groups. Among the fallacies that affect persuasion are *post hoc, ergo propter hoc*; red herrings; bandwagoning; card stacking; and citing false or irrelevant authorities.

The Latin phrase *post hoc, ergo propter hoc* means "after this, therefore on account of this." It is used in logical-fallacy arguments in which a cause-and-effect sequence is assumed where one may not exist. Suppose, for example, that a sales letter states: "After the installation of a new inventory system, our sales doubled in the last quarter." While the new inventory system may or may not have been a factor in doubling sales, various other factors (an improving economy, new product introductions, price changes, improved customer service) might also have contributed to the sales increase. There is no inherent cause-and-effect relationship between the new system and the increase in sales.

A *red herring* is a technique for diverting attention from the central issue or from an important issue by introducing largely (and even totally) unrelated points. The effect of the red herring is to distract the reader, usually from an issue or problem. For example, Kellogg promotes its cornflakes with the one-liner "Taste them again for the first time." Unlike competitors who emphasize nutritional and health benefits, Kellogg avoids this topic—and competitive disadvantage—by focusing instead on the taste of its cereal. The approach is not necessarily dishonest, but the decision to avoid the issue of nutritional benefit amounts to a recognition of its probable importance.

The writer who uses *bandwagoning* urges the reader to agree with his or her position because everyone else does. The implication is that the approval of others should be enough to earn the reader's agreement. Bandwagoning, for example, would be at work in an interoffice memo that concludes by saying, "I know you will support this proposal because Hank, Andy, and Ellen have already given me the go-ahead." You may hold Hank, Andy, and Ellen in the highest regard, but your feelings about your co-workers should have nothing to do with your response to the message.

Card stacking is another ethically questionable approach in which the writer fails to deal with conflicting facts that may contradict his or her position. Although most people naturally emphasize certain facts over others, stacking the cards occurs when the writer deliberately omits crucial facts that have the potential to weaken his or her position. For example, if a production assistant is trying to persuade a manager to choose a new supplier on the basis of excellent service, failing to mention the supplier's high prices would be considered card stacking.

When you cite the opinions of people who have no expertise in a field, you are *citing false or irrelevant authorities*. While it is no doubt valid for professional athlete Bo Jackson to be cited as an authority on exercise equipment, his opinion is obviously much less credible in the selection of a computer-system supplier.

Fallacies that create doubts can cause readers to question the integrity of an entire presentation. When you resort—or succumb—to fallacies, you run the risk of weakening an argument that might have won the day on its own merits. Moreover, by avoiding the use of fallacies—and by treading lightly when manipulating the facts for a more effective presentation of your point of view—you give readers credit for more, rather than less, intelligence.

Sources: Logical fallacies are discussed in Lynn Quitman Troyka, *Simon & Schuster Handbook for Writers*, 2nd ed. (Englewood Cliffs, NJ: Prentice Hall, 1990), pp. 153–56; Jo Sprague and Douglas Stuart, *The Speaker's Handbook*, 2nd ed. (San Diego: Harcourt Brace Jovanovich, 1988), p. 325; and Roy W. Poe, *The McGraw-Hill Guide to Effective Business Reports* (New York: McGraw-Hill, 1982), pp. 49–50.

Your document, therefore, might read, "With this change, the department will be able to retrieve information at twice the speed and half the cost."

Although the same document may include brief descriptions of the new system's features, your emphasis should be on the way these features will help the reader solve a problem. In this instance, you want to be careful to focus on your reader instead of the product you support; therefore, you want to distinguish between reader-oriented benefits and product-oriented features. Thus, you could include with your document a list like the one in Table 9.1.

testimonial
Words of praise for a firm, for its products, or for an idea generated by someone whose name or reputation the reader respects

Finally, your level of credibility can often be raised through the use of **testimonials**—words of praise for a firm or its products or an idea attributable to someone whose name or reputation the reader respects. Many sales letters begin with testimonials intended to establish immediate credibility. For example, a testimonial lead-in paragraph might read as follows:

> Peggy Carpenter, human resources manager at MMM International, is a satisfied customer of BusinessTemps and endorses our service. In her words, "Thanks to the services of BusinessTemps employment agency, we were able to replace absent secretaries on a moment's notice with qualified temporary help."

Persuading with Emotion

In many situations, emotions remain the most powerful persuasive factor. Where logical arguments sometimes fail, emotions often have the power to motivate people to respond and act. Not surprisingly, then, understanding which emotions to tap and which to avoid is one of the most important tasks of a persuasive writer.

One way to determine the most effective emotional appeal is to analyze readers according to the needs hierarchy discussed in Chapter 3. For example, if *security needs* are most important to your reader, your message should be phrased quite differently than if your reader were most concerned with *belongingness (social) needs*. AT&T's "Reach Out and Touch Someone" theme focuses on belongingness needs, while Alka Seltzer's "Will it be there when you need it?" campaign focuses on safety needs. The U.S. Army slogan "Be All You Can Be" is an appeal to self-actualization needs. GM's "Isn't it time you owned a Cadillac?" campaign focuses on esteem needs, and Campbell Soup's "Soup Is Good Food" appeals to physiological needs.

Reader analysis also involves using language that is likely to evoke the responses you seek. Because words like *free, new, announcing,* and *special* tend to be power words, they are frequently used to enhance persuasiveness.

Emotional appeals, of course, are quite common in all kinds of communications. For example, an advertisement for commemorative coins celebrating the United Nations victory in the Persian Gulf is likely to include words and phrases that trigger patriotic feelings: "Remember the brave men and women of Desert Storm." Emotional appeals can also focus on multiple emotions—hope, pleasure, pride, honor, courage, respect and responsibility—at the same time. For example, in a memo urging the consolidation of two departments and the elimination of fifteen jobs, a writer may focus on both the *courage* that it takes to make such a difficult decision and the *responsibility* needed to move the company forward.

TABLE 9.1	*How to Derive Benefits from Features*
FEATURES OF A NEW DRESS	BENEFITS
Material: wool blend and polyester	The material doesn't wrinkle--that means no ironing.
Color: blue plaid	The color doesn't show dirt--that means fewer trips to the cleaners.
Size: 8 petite	It is a perfect fit that needs no alterations.

In some cases, emotional appeals are chosen to arouse negative feelings like fear or anxiety. An exterminating service, for instance, may stress the extent to which carpenter ants can damage a house and emphasize the fact that home-owners should invest in prevention rather than repairs. A life-insurance sales letter may appeal to a parent's fear of dying and leaving young children insufficient funds to satisfy their basic needs. Many last-resort collection letters include messages intended to draw attention to the debtor's fears of legal action.

Concrete examples also add emotional power to a message. In a letter to potential subscribers, for example, *Eating Well* magazine focused on both the reader's interest and concerns in this brief description of a typical article:

> Join investigative reporter Bryan Bashin in a California produce warehouse filled with imported fruits and vegetables from Latin America. Discover why this deceptively fresh-looking bounty is actually depleted of vitamins and laced with pesticides banned in North America. Learn how to shop for truly fresh, uncontaminated vegetables and fruit.

The same letter also makes a concrete appeal to the reader's sense of pleasure:

> Share an unforgettable dinner at the Moosewood Restaurant in Ithaca, New York. Sample the Spicy Caribbean Fish, the Greek Potatoes, the Zesty Szechuan Noodles, and the Russian Chocolate Torte. Meet the chefs and come away with a selection of their favorite recipes.[6]

The following section shows how persuasion can be used to create more effective sales letters. Basically, every persuasive message is a sales presentation—an attempt to sell an idea, a good, or a service to individuals who may not recognize its value.

PROGRESS CHECK

1. What is the most powerful persuasive word in English? Why?
2. What is credibility? How does it affect the persuasiveness of a document?

Don't forget that [your good or service] is not differentiated until the customer understands the difference.

Tom Peters
Business writer

SALES LETTERS

The current cost of an average face-to-face industrial sales call is $224; the average consumer-goods sales call now costs $196, the average service-industry sales call $165. Not surprisingly, therefore, an increasing number of businesses are turning to **sales letters** as a relatively inexpensive alternative for both locating prospective accounts and increasing sales to current customers.[7]

Types of Sales Letters

Sales letters are directed at both individuals and business accounts, including manufacturers, retailers, and wholesalers, as well as government agencies and other nonprofit organizations. Today, sales letters are increasing in popularity as businesspeople apply them in three distinct ways: as *direct-mail messages*, as *retail-sales announcements*, and as *inquiry solicitations*. We will describe each of these functions and then examine more closely some general strategies for creating them.

sales letter
Written communication channel used for locating prospective accounts or increasing sales to current customers

DIRECT-MAIL MESSAGES   On any given day, both businesspeople and consumers receive mail promoting goods, services, and causes ranging from office computer systems to appeals to help save the rain forest. Mail-order retailers now produce 14 billion pieces of mail a year in the form of letters, postcards, folders, booklets, and catalogs. Approximately 18 percent of total advertising is spent on direct marketing. Why? Because it works.

She doesn't want to touch it. She doesn't want to smell it. She doesn't want to hear it. Lord love her. She's a mail order freak.

Jim Fishel
Direct-mail specialist

Direct-mail sales letters allow businesses to send personalized sales presentations to groups specially selected from mailing lists of target-market customers—customers to whose specific needs and preferences a firm markets its goods or services. In addition to personalization, direct mail offers the advantages of selectivity, intensive coverage, speed, format flexibility, and completeness of information. For example, direct mailers can select recipients by several methods, including segmentation by ZIP codes, occupations, or prior purchases. Direct mail affords intensive coverage because a high percentage of offices or homes can be reached with a single mailing. Mailings can also be presented in a number of different formats and can include exactly as much detail as is necessary.

The direct-mail letter attempts to complete a sale without benefit of either follow-up presentation by a salesperson or customer inspection of the product. The customer is urged to make a purchase primarily on the basis of a sales presentation and product credibility in the marketplace.

RETAIL SALES ANNOUNCEMENTS   Retailers commonly use sales letters to announce such events as storewide specialized sales. A department store, for example, may use a sales letter to alert customers to price reductions on mattresses. The children's clothing retailer Trader Kids often uses a combination of letters and discount coupons to encourage regular customers to visit stores and view newly arriving merchandise. Retail sales letters are designed to answer the key questions that customers will have about an event. For example, they explain when and why it is being held and describe the items on sale, including such information as comparative prices.

INQUIRY SOLICITATIONS   Almost everyone has seen a letter or postcard announcing that the recipient is a winner—a commonly used method of getting the reader's *attention*. To claim prizes, however, readers must fill out and return prepaid responses or call telephone numbers to set up appointments for sales presentations about joining organizations or purchasing products. By initiating the inquiry through the offer of a prize, the writer is ensured of an *interested* target market. The reader is then contacted again by phone, in person, or by additional letters in an effort to turn interest into *desire* by pointing out special features and/or benefits. Then, to increase the possibility that the customer will take *action*, a coupon or discount certificate is often given.

When we turn to the discussion of organizing sales letters, we will examine in greater detail the fundamental goal of the typical sales letter: namely, to move the reader through the four steps of attention, interest, desire, and action (the AIDA concept) and then to close the sale. Here, however, we need to remind ourselves that such lofty goals are unrealistic in situations characterized by highly complex products—for example, new communications equipment—whose purchases are frequently made after months of evaluation by different specialists in an organization. In such cases, writers try to narrow their objectives: They try to generate an inquiry from the person receiving the message. Representatives of the sender will then follow up by phone, in face-to-face meetings, and/or through additional letters.

The nature of the follow-up—whether it will be followed by a personal sales call or be allowed to stand on its own—is often determined by the level of detail in the letter itself. Because a large percentage of direct mail is allowed to stand on its own, much of it requires a great deal of detail. By contrast, the goal of a letter soliciting inquiries is to set the stage for the information that will be provided in a face-to-face sales call.

Developing a Sales Letter Strategy

Despite the frequent use of sales letters, their success remains mixed because so many people consider them "junk mail." In fact, a one-percent response rate is often considered a success. To give yourself a chance of making the sale, therefore, it is critical that you capture and hold your reader's attention. You should begin by defining exactly what your letter is trying to accomplish. Careful planning is the basis of a successful sales strategy. Before writing the first draft of a sales letter, clearly specify what you seek to accomplish in terms of your *sales goals*, your *audience*, and your *product*.

SALES GOALS   The first step in preparing a sales letter is to define its purpose. For example, are you trying to make a sale, encourage an inquiry, prompt a store visit, or promote goodwill? Once your purpose has been clarified, you might record it as a *purpose statement*. For example, the purpose of a sales letter from Merrill Lynch regarding a new municipal-bond offering might be to produce customer inquiries. Account executives from the firm can then supply detailed information, including a printed prospectus, to clients expressing an interest in the offering. Before organizing a sales letter, however, you must focus on both your audience and your product.

AUDIENCE   Sales letters are mailed to a variety of individuals and organizations. In most instances, however, the first people who receive such letters are the firm's regular customers. After all, holders of store credit cards, charge customers, and others who have made previous purchases represent good prospects for sales letters.

So numerous are the potential prospects who can be reached by mail that over the past two decades, commercial mailing-list brokers have emerged to match writers of sales letters with the names and addresses of individuals and organizations whose characteristics pinpoint them as prospects for a firm's goods and services. To rent these lists, firms pay list brokers specified amounts per thousand names and addresses. More than 175,000 customers, for example, have obtained lists from Nebraska-based American Business Information. The company publishes a catalog of business lists with more than 9 million names, a consumer-lists catalog with more than 84 million names, and other lists ranging from car owners by make/model to millionaires and students to real-estate agents. For instance, to secure the names and addresses of more than 30,000 stock-brokerage executives, a firm pays $71 per thousand names. This fee permits the mailer to make a one-time mailing to individuals and organizations on the list.

The key advantage of such detailed lists is that they provide you with an audience with shared characteristics. When the people whom you are writing share common attributes, you can personalize your message and thus increase the likelihood that they will respond.

PRODUCT   All successful sales strategies depend on a thorough knowledge of the product and, more importantly, on understanding why people are likely to buy it. Because benefits create a product-customer connection, it is thus critical to stress benefits over features.

For example, a successful sales-letter strategy was used in a follow-up letter sent by Jaguar Cars, Inc., to potential customers in 1992. The sales goal of the letter was to encourage readers to visit Jaguar dealers to test-drive cars. The letter's audience was a preselected group of high-income consumers who could afford the $50,000-plus price tag for these luxury automobiles. By focusing on the so-called "Dream Guarantee"—and the benefits that it provided—the letter directly addressed consumers' concerns about Jaguar's history of mechanical problems and expensive repairs. Such product information assured consumers that Jaguar had achieved a level of manufacturing excellence sufficient to warrant consumer trust—after all, the company was willing to offer a 30-day money-back guarantee to back its quality pledge.

ORGANIZING A SALES LETTER

For the typical consumer, purchasing a good or service is often a process of problem solving. First, the product gains the attention of the customer through its ability to solve a problem. Attention is followed by interest in the proposed

Last year our customers bought over one million quarter-inch drill bits and none of them wanted to buy the product. They all wanted quarter-inch holes.

Anonymous

AIDA concept
Principle that an individual goes through four steps—*attention, interest, desire,* and *action*—before making a purchase decision

solution and then by a desire to apply the solution to the problem at hand. Finally, the consumer takes action by actually purchasing the product or subscribing to the service. As a description of the four steps that an individual takes before making a purchase decision, this model is known as the **AIDA concept**.

A successful sales letter must take a prospective customer through each of these four steps. First, it must gain the *attention* of the reader, and then it must arouse *interest*. Next, the letter should try to stimulate *desire* by convincing the reader to accept an idea or to purchase a good or service. Finally, it should convince the reader to take *action*, usually in the form of a purchase. An indirect approach is typically the most effective approach to these objectives.

Gaining Attention

attention
In the AIDA concept, first step in capturing and holding an audience so it will continue to read a document or listen to an oral presentation

Many persuasive documents are unsolicited. They have never been requested and may even be considered nuisances by those who receive them. Knowing that a potential customer is not eager to receive your message means that the opening of your message is crucial. You must find a way to capture and hold **attention** so that your recipient will continue to read your letter.

There are a number of ways to gain a reader's attention. You can use provocative headlines, ask questions, provide testimonials from credible sources, relate startling incidents or statistics, make readers feel unique or special, and identify needs. In each case, your goal is the same—to pique interest so that your reader wants to learn more. Table 9.2 gives examples of each of these techniques.

Regardless of your strategy, you are always looking for a way to draw readers into your message. For example, a recent subscription letter from a major business publication began by referring to a best-selling book, *The One-Minute Manager*, with an attention-grabbing headline. The letter then proceeded to pique interest by spelling out precisely the reason why the phrase *one-minute manager* should be of interest to the magazine's readers:

> THE ONE-MINUTE WHAT?
>
> I think we're being insulted. The professional practice of management is as challenging and complex as the practices of medicine and law.[8]

TABLE 9.2	*Techniques for Gaining Attention*
TECHNIQUE	EXAMPLE
Using Provocative Headlines	YOU WILL NEVER MISS AN IMPORTANT CALL AGAIN!
Asking Questions	When is the last time someone offered you a deal you couldn't refuse?
Providing Testimonials from Credible Sources	Matthew would not have been conceived without the laser surgery I received at Bridgehaven Hospital, said May Fenton as she cradled her six-month old son in her arms. Nearly two years ago, Mrs. Fenton had been treated at Bridgehaven for endometriosis—a condition that prevents thousands of women from having children.
Beginning the Letter with a Startling Incident or Statistic	We are defoliating our planet earth. Each year another 1,000 plants become extinct.
Making the Reader Feel Unique or Special	Managing your personal finances wisely has its rewards. You've been selected for Approved Membership for our Gold Card.
Identifying a Need	With the ups and downs of business, you need a weekly publication that will help you navigate the choppy seas.

Because headlines are such an important component of the typical sales letter, we will begin by looking more closely at the different ways in which they can be used. We will also examine the important connection between headlines and opening paragraphs.

CREATING EFFECTIVE HEADLINES   Many successful sales letters use eye-catching headlines that elicit immediate responses. Direct-marketing expert Daniel S. Kennedy explains why:

> What your headline says and how it says it are absolutely critical. You might compare it to a door-to-door salesperson wedging a foot in the door, buying just enough time to deliver one or two sentences that will melt resistance, create interest, and elevate his status from annoying pest to welcome guest. You've got just about the same length of time, the same opportunity.[9]

Headlines may be placed either above the salutation or between the salutation and the middle of the letter. They are often set apart visually by italic or boldface type or by a type size larger than the rest of the letter. It may also be helpful to think of headlines as falling into categories according to the message with which they attempt to gain your attention. Four such categories, plus an example of each, are listed in Table 9.3.

CREATING AN OPENING PARAGRAPH   Naturally, an effective headline should encourage the reader to examine the letter's opening paragraph. Wherever they may be placed in the letter, the best "opening" paragraphs focus simultaneously on the sales purpose and the reader's interests. For example:

> The time to stop burglars from robbing you blind is before they get into your home.

Or:

> Being a salesperson means you're rarely at your desk to answer important phone calls. The best solution—a full-time secretary—is too costly. Other solutions, like answering machines and voice mail, turn many calls into hangups.
>
>   THERE IS AN ALTERNATIVE.

Attention getters must also be both accurate and ethical as they create interest. Recently, for example, former U.S. Marine Major (and now political columnist) Oliver North crossed this sometimes sensitive line. North had sent a direct-mail fund-raising letter of behalf of the Freedom Alliance—an organization he supports. He had captured his readers' attention by comparing himself with retired General Norman Schwarzkopf, hero of Desert Storm: "We both served in Vietnam," wrote North. "We both were wounded. And we both came home to vicious leftist protests and condemnation." When Schwarzkopf learned of the letter, he insisted that the reference to himself be removed.[10]

Although North presented accurate facts—both he and Schwarzkopf had been wounded in Vietnam—his letter became inaccurate when it implied that

TABLE 9.3	*Strategies for Effective Headlines*	
HEADLINE	EXAMPLE	WHY IS IT EFFECTIVE?
"How to..."	How to Live Like a King!	Information is being offered.
"Are you..."	Are You Caught in a Dead-End Job?	The question challenges the reader and provokes interest.
"If you are... you can..."	If You Are 50 or Over, You Can Join AARP.	The statement targets the reader specifically.
"Warning!"	Warning! Smoking can kill you!	The announcement focuses on the solution to the reader's problem.

INTERVIEW

David Topus, Sales Communication Consultant

David Topus, president of David Topus & Associates, a sales communication consulting firm in Longmont, Colorado, helps businesspeople learn to write results-oriented sales letters. Topus, who conducts sales-writing workshops throughout the country for such major corporations as General Electric Capital, 3M, and Roadway Express, explains his approach to persuasive writing in the following interview.

Question: What role do letters play in the sales process?

Answer: When buying decisions get made, more often than not decision makers have paper in their hands. Unlike face-to-face and phone communication, the written message has a lasting value. A letter can help get you an appointment or presell your position before

a meeting. It can follow up a face-to-face or telephone conversation. It can reinforce a reason to buy. It can accompany research that you want the reader to see while considering your product.

Sending a letter before a meeting can create anticipation for the meeting. For example, you might write, "When we get together next Wednesday you'll have a chance to find out about the most advanced accounting software on the market—a package that will increase performance while making key information available to your entire staff." A letter like this can put a salesperson in a good position before the meeting begins.

Question: Should letters stress benefits rather than features?

Answer: They should stress solutions to specific problems or show how your products and services help the prospect accomplish his or her business goals. For example, the marketing letter for my workshop begins by telling the reader that "getting a meaningful and memorable message through to customers and prospects is one of the biggest challenges facing salespeople." It sets up the problem so that later in the letter, I can propose a solution. Starting with how I am going to train salespeople to communicate more effectively would have been too much about me and not enough about the prospect.

Question: Do sales letters tend to overuse the word *I*?

both men held the same opinion about the reception that they received upon returning. Ethical issues arose when North associated himself and his cause with Schwarzkopf without the latter's permission.

Creating Interest

interest
Second step in the AIDA concept; implies that the message has tapped a need in the reader, either to solve a problem or to satisfy a desire

Capturing attention is not necessarily the same thing as creating **interest**. *Interest* implies that the message has tapped a need in the reader—for example, a need to solve a problem or satisfy a desire. Interest is created in basically two ways: by presenting claims that emphasize benefits over features and by making emotional as well as logical appeals.

Advertising tries not only to gain attention but also to maintain interest until a complete message has been presented. Because people tend to scan and browse information in letters and advertisements, maintaining interest is more difficult than attracting attention. A particular brand of bar soap might appeal to one person as a deodorant soap and to another as a complexion bar. Thus, pre-

Answer: Many salespeople tend to put too much of their egos into the process and ignore the customer's concerns. I've seen letters that start like this: "I'm glad we had the chance to speak on the phone today about your company's software package." The emotional state of the salesperson is irrelevant, and how glad he is doesn't matter to the customer. It is better to start by saying, "In your efforts to improve productivity within your department, you need a software package that offers multiple user capabilities along with ease of installation." Write to the *customer's* point of view; address *his* needs and problems.

Question: In addition to *I*, what other words weaken a letter?

Answer: *Me, my, mine, our* (as in "*our* company"). Salespeople also overuse the word *hope*. They say things like, "I *hope* this information is useful to you." You have to ask yourself from whose perspective "hope" is being raised and, more importantly, what a customer will do with this statement. The information that you send will either be useful or irrelevant, and hoping won't make a difference.

Believe is another word that can weaken a letter. Writing "I *believe* this is a terrific software package for your company" can leave the reader scratching his head. Of course, you *believe* it! You're the sales rep. Words like *believe, hope,* and *feel* reduce the power of your letter. Instead of communicating statements of fact, they communicate opinions.

For example, it is better to write, "By doing business with our company now, your firm can take advantage of recent product upgrades at last year's prices" than to write "I feel the time is right for your company to do business with us." Similarly, instead of writing, "I hope we can talk again soon," write, "The next time we talk, you'll hear about a new approach that will give you an even greater advantage in the market."

Question: How do you draw the reader into a sales letter?

Answer: By making statements about the customer's problem in a way that gets the customer's head nodding in agreement. Often, you'll be writing statements that are universally true. For example, my sales letter says, "Getting a meaningful and memorable message through to customers…is one of the biggest challenges facing salespeople. Product and market knowledge alone is no longer enough; salespeople must sharpen their communication skills to succeed.…" In making this statement, I'm establishing rapport by focusing on the reader's needs. I'm also demonstrating that I know the customer's world. In itself, that will take you a long way toward building credibility and value as a provider of soutions rather than just a salesperson looking for a quick sale.

Source: Interview with David Topus.

senting *all* the benefits of your idea, good, or service increases the likelihood of appealing to a larger audience. Similarly, some people enjoy eating health foods while others eat health foods as a logical way to maintain good health. Consequently, it is important to provide both pleasurable and logical reasons for purchasing a product so that more members of your audience become interested enough to desire your product.

Translating Interest into Desire

While interest is largely an intellectual response, **desire** is basically an emotional reaction that propels people to action. Desire and motivation are thus closely connected. For example, once we make the decision that we want a new drill press to improve factory efficiency (the desire stage), we are often motivated to make the purchase (the action stage).

Although motivation varies from person to person, there are certain basic human needs that, if satisfied, can support positive responses. For example, to

desire
Third step in the AIDA concept; implies that a document can prompt an emotional reaction that propels people to action

encourage recipients to take action in the form of purchases, sales letters are quite likely to use one or more of the twenty-five reasons for spending money listed in Table 9.4. Note the correspondence between many of these reasons and various forms of motivation (for example, curiosity and safety). Similarly, collection letters focus on the credit purchaser's desire to protect his or her personal reputation, avoid trouble, act responsibly, and save money (in legal expenses and interest charges). Persuasive memos may tap into both personal and professional desires—for example, desire for business success, cost reduction, or the ability to simplify a task.

To move the reader from the interest to the desire stage, the persuasive letter writer must present specific facts. During the attention and interest stages, claims are generally sufficient to capture your reader's attention. At this stage, however, mere claims must be supported. Your support is most likely to take the form of facts and statistics organized in a logical, easy-to-understand presentation. For example, the advertisement for the Gold MasterCard in Figure 9.4 tries to spur initial interest by dissociating the brand from the usual imagery used by gold card marketers. Rather, it focuses on claims about the superior usefulness of Gold MasterCard: its worldwide acceptance, higher credit limit, and other benefits provided at no additional cost.

The strategy in this ad is based on marketing research—a specialized field that has emerged over the past half-century in an attempt to understand human motivation and predict purchase behavior. Marketing research can be gathered by specialists in your firm or purchased from independent suppliers. Like most business communicators, you will have access to marketing research, and you will find it an extremely important tool in creating persuasive messages. If such information is unavailable to help you target your audience, you will probably find it necessary to mail several versions of the same letter to identify the format that generates the best response.

For example, if your product is an office-cleaning service, focusing on the need for the service may be the wrong approach—most businesspeople already agree that a clean office is important. A more effective approach might be to stress reliability, price, and job responsibilities. Offering subscribers a money-back guarantee, therefore, may produce better results.

The real issue is value, not price.

Robert T. Lindgren
Cross & Trecker Corp.

DISCUSSING PRICE   Discussing the benefits of the product sets the stage for discussing price. In many instances, such discussion is both easy and productive—when, for example, your company offers a better price than any of its competitors. In this case, you may want to herald the price in a headline and emphasize it several times in your letter. But when price is not a marketing advantage,

TABLE 9.4 *Why People Spend Money*	
To make money	To gratify curiosity
To save money	To protect family
To save time	To be in style
To avoid effort	For beautiful possessions
For comfort	To satisfy appetite
For cleanliness	To emulate others
For health	For safety in buying
To escape physical pain	To avoid criticism
For praise	To be individual
To be popular	To protect reputation
To attract the opposite sex	To take advantage of
To conserve possessions	opportunities
For enjoyment	To avoid trouble

Source: Direct Mail Advertising Association

It's About Time Someone Took

The *Plastic* Out Of Credit Cards.

In the real world, gold cards aren't status symbols.

 They're tools. And none is more

useful than Gold MasterCard. You

see, no card is more accepted on

the planet. It gives you a credit

line of at least $5000, and you

can use it to get local currency all over the world, so

it's a smart thing to have. Really. *Gold MasterCard.*

It's more than a gold card. It's smart money.

©1993 MasterCard International Incorporated

FIGURE 9.4   *A Persuasive Message from MasterCard*
Source: Courtesy of MasterCard International, Inc.

your letter should try to minimize its impact. The following techniques are widely used to draw the reader's attention away from noncompetitive prices.[11]

- *Compare apples and oranges.* Let's say that your product is reproduction antique furniture that sells at about the same price as that of several competitors. Featuring the price in your sales letter, then, would offer little advantage. The customer is much more likely to respond if you point out that your $150 chair is virtually undistinguishable from an actual antique chair costing $1500.
- *Sell bulk.* You can make items seem more substantial by describing them in terms of their component parts. This technique urges people to focus on aspects of the product that they might not have considered valuable enough to influence their decision. For example, if you are selling a refer-

ence book, you can list the number of topics covered, the number of illustrations, or even the number of words in the book.

- *Focus on the costs involved in developing the product.* Talk about how much time and money your company spent perfecting your product before bringing it to market. Such information makes the selling price understandable and helps people appreciate the item's real value.
- *Bury the price.* Instead of stating that an item costs $100, some letters conceal the total purchase price by stating it in terms of small monthly installments. For example, you can lessen the impact of the cost of a small household appliance in the following manner:

> You can have this highly popular cappuccino maker in your home for just five monthly installments of $20, charged to your credit account.

When people feel that they are receiving fair value, they are more likely to respond to your offer. It is important, therefore, that a product's price be linked to its benefits. Language can remind people of value—and even create it—through the use of phrases like *special offer*, *unique opportunity*, *sensational savings*, and *a small investment for a lifetime of security*.

Encouraging the Reader to Take Action

action
Final step in the AIDA concept; implies that readers must be convinced to take specific steps to purchase the product

The **action** step is the most critical step in all sales letters. Readers must be convinced not only to take specific steps to purchase the product but to act quickly. Experienced sales professionals realize that unless most readers respond immediately, they are unlikely to respond at all. Among the many techniques for producing action, we will focus on three of the most common and effective: identifying the specific action you want the reader to take; offering special terms and inducements; and making it easy to respond.

IDENTIFYING SPECIFIC ACTION   It is important to give readers clear purchase instructions in the form of commands or action statements. A typical sales letter might thus tell the reader: "To take advantage of this special offer, call NOW!" In addition, sales and promotion letters typically reinforce the message by repeating action statements.

inducement
Gift or other consideration that encourages readers to take immediate action

USING INDUCEMENTS   **Inducements** are gifts or other considerations that encourage readers to take immediate action. Inducements are considered *positive* when they give readers something they want, *negative* when readers must take action in order to avoid unpleasant consequences. For example, while premiums, sweepstakes, contests, and discounts are all positive inducements, deadlines and the threat of limited availability ("This offer ends Saturday, November 30, 199X, and will not be repeated") represent negative inducements. Depending on your design and strategy, you can announce inducements at the end of your letter or organize the entire letter around inducements as your major theme.

POSITIVE INDUCEMENTS   One common form of positive inducement is the offer of *discounts* to readers who take immediate action. Besides offering a better price value, discounts encourage readers to respond quickly. Subscriptions and new products are often promoted in this way. For example, immediately before the release of the video version of *Aladdin*, Walt Disney Co. offered customers a discount for early purchase.

Items given free or at reduced cost with the purchase of another product are known as *premiums*. They typically have some relationship with the purchased item. For example, cosmetic companies frequently offer other items from their own product lines as premiums for "any $25 purchase." A car wash might offer an air freshener with a full-service wash, and many magazine and journal subscriptions offer books as premiums for subscribing. To attract customers and introduce new goods and services, many organizations sponsor *sweepstakes* and *contests*. These inducements give people the incentive to respond immediately by extending the likelihood of winning.

NEGATIVE INDUCEMENTS   Two common negative inducements are deadlines and limited availability. The use of deadlines is effective in reminding readers that they have limited time to purchase an item at a quoted price or to receive a premium. Deadlines are particularly effective when combined with other strategies such as premiums. Some products—say, rare Roman coins, time-share condominiums, or the four remaining models on a car dealer's showroom floor—lend themselves to limited-availability offers. The reminder that a product is available only in limited numbers also serves as a powerful inducement for prompt action.

FACILITATING READER RESPONSE   The typical sales letter is just one part of the persuasive message. Included with most sales letters are pre-addressed postage-paid response cards, order forms, and envelopes requiring readers to take one or more of the following actions: mail checks; list credit card names, numbers, and expiration dates; or simply check appropriate response boxes, sign, and return. Many sales letters also rely on toll-free telephone numbers that readers can call at any time for immediate service. Obviously, these enclosures and instructions are designed to make it as easy as possible for customers to respond.

The letter in Figure 9.5 applies the AIDA concept to a sample sales letter. Notice how all the elements—attention, interest, desire, and action—are designed to encourage a prompt and positive response.[12]

Sales letters, of course, are not the only type of persuasive letter used in contemporary business communication. For example, when payment from a credit purchaser has not been received by a predetermined date, the creditor firm will issue persuasive requests for payment in the form of collection letters. Claims and requests for adjustments to an account can also be categorized as persuasive letters; however, these are generated from the customer rather than the company.

PROGRESS CHECK

1. Why are more businesses opting for sales letters over face-to-face sales calls?
2. Why is it important to use an eye-catching headline on a sales letter?
3. Name several techniques that are often used to downplay price when it's not a marketing advantage.
4. What inducements might a sales letter include to encourage readers to respond immediately? Do you tend to respond when you receive letters with these inducements?

COLLECTION LETTERS

Because a sale is not completed until the money has been collected, many companies create their own debt-collection programs intended to ensure that they will be repaid in full for all credit sales. In general, companies will refer past-due accounts to commercial collection agencies only as a last resort. They adhere to this policy for two reasons. They wish to maintain goodwill, and they receive only a fraction of any funds recovered by collection agencies. In fact, after uncollected debts and agency fees are deducted, a company can expect to receive only 12 cents of every dollar owed.[13]

Nevertheless, many companies are heavily involved in credit sales, and many have learned to handle the collection process. Success stories abound. For example, Albany Ladder, a $23-million construction-equipment and supply firm headquartered in Albany, New York, issues credit to home-improvement con-

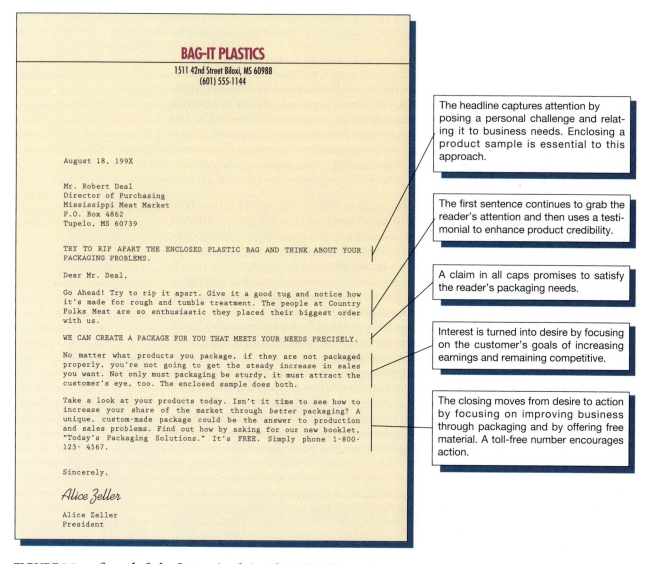

FIGURE 9.5   *Sample Sales Letter Applying the AIDA Concept*

tractors and tradespeople with no proven credit history, yet is forced to write off an amazingly small one percent of sales as bad debts.[14] Helen Chen, president of Joyce Chen Inc., a Waltham, Massachusetts, cookware manufacturer, takes a proactive stance in extending credit to her customers. She makes credit terms clear before the sale and follows up immediately after if payment is delayed. "You can talk all you like," advises Chen, "but when it comes down to brass tacks, you've got to have it written or it doesn't mean a thing."[15]

collection letter
Written correspondence seeking to persuade a debtor to pay an outstanding debt while encouraging continued business

Basically, **collection letters** have a dual purpose. They try to persuade debtors to pay the money they owe while encouraging continued business. The purpose of a collection letter is to convince credit purchasers that the credit-granting firm is willing to work with them if they are willing to fulfill their financial obligations. The typical writer of collection letters starts with the assumption that most credit purchasers want to repay their debts and that, with a little finesse, persuasion, and time, the firm will be able to collect all or most of what it is owed.

We will begin by examining the important question of *tone* in the effective collection letter and then describe the documents comprising the *collection series*.

The Importance of Tone

The successful writer of collection letters focuses on three descriptive adjectives. Letters should be *persuasive* rather than threatening, *constructive* rather than accusatory, *empathetic* rather than cold. Jim Ullery, customer financial-services manager at Albany Ladder, is convinced that empathy is critical. "Collectors fail to remember that when we make the decision to give customers money, we're buying into it. We really become a cosigner. So now my role in collection is to help."[16]

A helping attitude, then, is in the creditor's best interest. If you are able to maintain the customer's goodwill during the collection process, you increase the likelihood that you will collect an outstanding debt. Moreover, you will be working to satisfy your secondary goal—to encourage future business should the customer's financial situation improve.

Help for both parties comes in the form of a positive, respectful tone that avoids anger, bullying, sarcasm, or threats. Word choice, therefore, is critical. Negative words and phrases send a message that the problem cannot be resolved. As we shall see, words like *irresponsible, embarrassment*, and *dishonorable*, have a place only in so-called last-resort collection letters.

When the collection appeal is linked to the possibility of future purchases by the delinquent credit customer, the need for a positive, helpful tone becomes especially clear. Frequently, these letters emphasize the benefits of resolving the situation as soon as possible because further sales cannot be made or credit granted on an overdue balance.

The tone of a collection letter depends on many factors, including the length of time the account has been delinquent; the number of letters that have already been sent; the perception of the debtor as a good, fair, or poor credit risk; the individual's or company's business dealings; and the general state of the economy. For example, if a delinquent account is nevertheless considered a good credit risk, the collection letter will be less aggressive than if the debtor is perceived as a poor risk.

As we will see in the next section, no single letter is applicable to all credit-collection situations. On the contrary, firms that rely heavily on credit sales realize that they need a series of letters to handle different delinquency situations.

Collection Series Letters

The letters in the **collection series** can be categorized according to the four types of persuasive appeals used to collect outstanding debts: *reminder letters, inquiry letters, aggressive collection notices*, and *last-resort letters*, which threaten legal action. Every letter in the collection series should state three pieces of information: the amount owed, the length of time the bill has been overdue, and the specific action the customer should take to remedy the situation.

REMINDER LETTERS   The collection process begins automatically in the case of bank-card holders, retail credit-card holders, and other people who are expected to repay suppliers of services (lawn or pool care and legal services, among others). If no payment is received following an end-of-month billing, the next month's billing typically includes a reminder of the unpaid bill and a late-payment fee, typically calculated at a rate of one and one-half percent per month. Such late-payment fees have been agreed to in writing by both parties, either at the time of card issuance or at the beginning of the relationship between the client and the service supplier.

Other agreements involve continuing contact between seller and credit purchaser, and many of these are made with the expectation of future business relationships between the two. In this case, the collection process is likely to begin on a much more informal note. The initial contact typically begins when a bill is more

collection series
Written correspondence categorized according to the four types of increasingly persuasive appeals used to collect outstanding debts: *reminders, inquiries, aggressive notices,* and *last-resort letters*

reminder letter
Written correspondence informing a customer that payment has not been received

inquiry letter
Written correspondence seeking to determine if a problem exists that is preventing a customer from making required payment; typically, the third step after a statement and reminder letter

aggressive collection notice
Written correspondence in the form of a firm request that attempts to convince a debtor to pay a bill

last-resort letter
Written correspondence expressing a reluctance to begin legal action but a determination to do so if a delinquent customer does not pay within a stated time limit

than a month overdue. After sending out a monthly statement informing the customer of the outstanding debt, most companies wait a few weeks for a reply. If none comes, a second statement is sent, perhaps marked "Past Due," or a short **reminder letter** is included with the statement to inform the customer that payment has not been received. Seldom is there a direct request for money—usually just a reminder that the account is overdue.

Although many companies use form letters for their reminders and other early collection letters, it is important to personalize these letters by including the customer's name and the specific amount owed. Instead of writing to a title, use the name of the person who appears on the bill. At Albany Ladder, Jim Ullery makes a practice of always writing to the company owner or CEO: "It's his cash, it's his reputation and, more often than not with us, it's his personal guarantee. I want it clear I'm talking to *him*."[17]

INQUIRY LETTERS   If a combination statement and gentle reminder do not work, the next step is to determine if a problem exists that is preventing the customer from making the required payment. Your tone in the **inquiry letter** should be friendly and conciliatory as you question the customer about whether he or she has forgotten to pay or whether there is something you can do to help ease the situation. For example, you might suggest that the customer call you to work out a payment plan. Above all, communicate the message that you are certain the customer intends to pay and stress future business. A sample collection-inquiry letter is shown in Figure 9.6.

AGGRESSIVE COLLECTION NOTICES   The next letter, the **aggressive collection notice**, is firmer and more insistent in attempting to convince the debtor to pay the bill. Indeed, the writer of the aggressive notice is likely to draft several versions before selecting the letter with the appeal that best matches a particular situation. Starting with the assumption that your method of persuasion must be stronger than in your previous communications, try the following appeals to find one that works:

- *Fairness.* An appeal to fairness emphasizes that the customer is already using your company's goods and services and that it is only fair that you receive payment in return.

- *Sympathy.* When you appeal to sympathy, you make the point that payment is crucial to your own operations and that late payments put you, the creditor, in a difficult position. This approach is intended to place the customer in the position of helping the supplier who was willing to extend credit.

- *Self-interest.* This appeal emphasizes the consequences of continued nonpayment. Future credit problems are mentioned as the writer threatens to notify the delinquent customer's credit bureau and thus jeopardize other lines of credit.

LAST-RESORT LETTERS   If your aggressive collection notice does not produce a telephone call, letter, or check from your delinquent account, you must assume that the past-due customer will pay only if threatened with one or more unpleasant actions. These include turning nonpayment information over to a credit bureau, starting legal action, and referring the account to a collection agency. The **last-resort letter** informs the customer that unless the money is received by a specific date, your company will begin taking action.

The tone of the last-resort letter should express a reluctance to take these actions but a determination to do so if the customer does not pay within a stated time limit—usually no more than ten days. To reinforce the seriousness of your message, have a senior executive sign the letter and consider sending it by certified mail, return receipt requested. The letter that Jim Ullery sends to his customers as Albany Ladder's last resort is shown in Figure 9.7. Ullery mails this letter if no payment has been received sixty days after the sale. Within a month after receiving the letter, 25 percent of Ullery's recipients pay

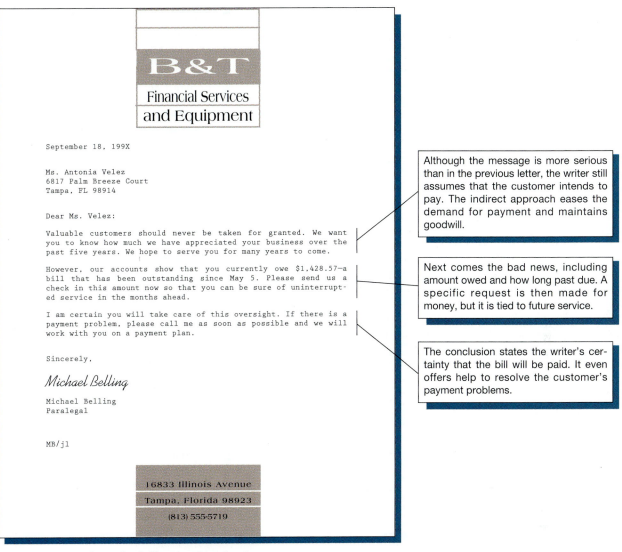

FIGURE 9.6   *Sample Collection Inquiry Letter*

in full, 30 percent negotiate a repayment plan, and 35 percent ultimately pay after more coaxing in the form of actions threatened by the letter; 10 percent never pay.[18]

While collection and sales letters are written to customers, persuasive memos are written from one business associate to another. The final section of this chapter examines how this difference—as well as other differences between persuasive letters and memos—changes the way in which the persuasive message is crafted.

WRITING PERSUASIVE MEMOS

A **persuasive memo** cannot be written in the same tone or manner as a sales letter. Persuading professional colleagues, whether inside or outside a business organization, rarely involves the typical format of a sales letter. Using the AIDA concept to sell your ideas may be viewed by the memo's recipients as manipulative and is usually a mistake. Generally, it is best to be direct when writing persuasive memos and letters.

As in all forms of persuasive communication, it is important to arrange information in a logical, convincing order and to use evidence to support your

persuasive memo
Document seeking to change the recipient's attitudes, beliefs, values, or behaviors

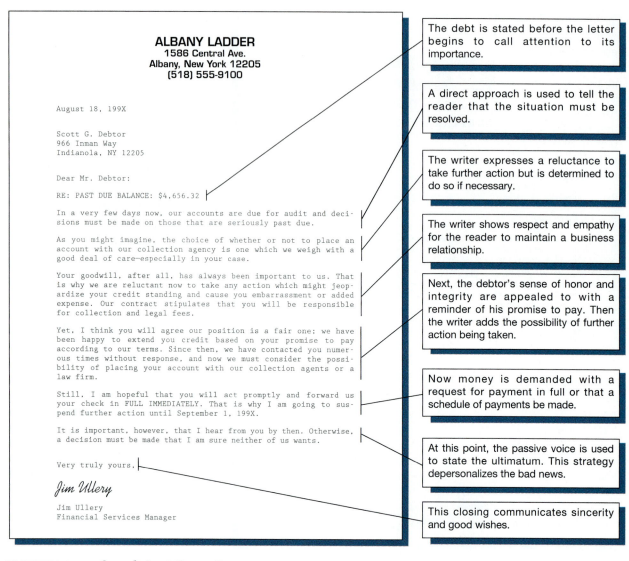

FIGURE 9.7   *Sample Last-Resort Letter*

ideas. Using a direct approach also prompts the reader to take specific action. Telling the reader, for example, to initial a memo so that a project can begin makes compliance easy.

Certain circumstances, however, make an indirect approach more effective, and we will offer some advice on using the indirect approach in persuasive memos. Assume that you are attempting to persuade a reader with whom you do not have a close relationship to take action that is in your mutual best interest. In this instance, an indirect approach may increase the likelihood of success by reducing the appearance of being pushy.

In addition, an indirect approach is essential when trying to persuade a high-ranking manager to do something that he or she does not want to do. In certain instances, this approach may also be necessary to encourage subordinates to take action. "We doubt that [a direct approach] would be effective in a letter where a boss asks you to double your Community Fund pledge," suggest business-communication authors John S. Fielden and Ronald E. Dulek.[19]

SELECTING AN APPROPRIATE WRITING STYLE   In addition to the type of information being communicated, the most effective persuasive writing style for a memo takes into account the relationship between the writer and the reader. In general, when writing a negative persuasive message to a subordinate, choose a forceful writing style that uses words like *urge, recommend*, and *expect*. Under these circumstances, it is also generally advisable to be impersonal by avoiding direct references to either the reader or the writer. Minimize the use of *I* and *you* and aim for a tone similar to that of a policy statement.

When the situation is reversed and a first-level supervisor is writing to a superior, a passive style is advisable—one that avoids making forceful demands. For example, instead of writing, "I want you to do this," it is more effective to say, "It would help the department a great deal if this were done." Similarly, an impersonal approach is appropriate for a negative message written to a superior.

PROGRESS CHECK

1. What are collection letters?
2. What three items of information should be included in every letter in a collection series?

WHAT'S AHEAD

This chapter completes Part III, "Organizational Letters and Memos." In addition to letters and memos, business writing also involves reports. Part IV of *Contemporary Business Communication* will focus on report and proposal writing by analyzing the nature of business reports. We will begin Chapter 10 with a discussion of the types and uses of business reports and proposals. We will also examine the development and writing of reports and proposals, the creation of visual aids, and the preparation of the final document.

*S*UMMARY OF CHAPTER OBJECTIVES

1. **Explain the concept of *persuasion* and the four *persuasive goals*.**

   Persuasion is the process of influencing or changing attitudes, beliefs, values, or behaviors. It is a key element in sales letters, collection letters, and appeals for action within an organization. Persuasive goals define the nature of the change that the message seeks. Messages of *adoption* try to persuade readers to initiate action. Messages of *continuance* urge that a specific behavior be continued, whereas messages of *discontinuance* urge that a behavior be stopped. Finally, messages of *deterrence* attempt to prevent an action from taking place.

2. **Identify and contrast the three major *persuasive appeals*.**

   The three major persuasive appeals are reasoning, credibility, and emotion. When a business document appeals to reason, it tries to guide the reader to a conclusion by presenting its message in a logical way. The way in which material is organized helps build the writer's case. The chronological, spatial, cause-and-effect, and problem-solution patterns are frequently used in making appeals to reason. Persuasive appeals also involve issues of credibility—how readers perceive the writer, company, and message. Document credibility is influenced by language choice, a focus on benefits rather than features, and the use of testimonials praising the company, product, or idea. Often the most powerful persuasive appeal is the appeal to emotion. This appeal can focus on such positive emotions as hope, pleasure, and pride or on such negative emotions as fear and anxiety.

3. **Identify and describe the three types of** *sales letters.*

Sales letters represent a relatively inexpensive alternate channel for both locating prospective accounts and increasing sales to current customers. The three basic types are direct-mail messages, retail-sales announcements, and inquiry solicitations. Direct-mail sales letters offer the advantages of personalization, selectivity, intensive coverage, speed, format flexibility, and completeness of information. Retail-sales letters announce such events as special sales and should answer customers' key questions about an event—for example, when and why the sale is being held and a description of the items on sale, including comparative price information. Letters seeking inquiries are used to generate an inquiry from the person receiving the message. Representatives of the firm sending the inquiry letter will then follow up by phone, in face-to-face meetings, and/or by additional letters.

4. **Apply the** *AIDA concept* **to the organization of a sales letter.**

Most sales letters are organized according to a persuasive plan known by its initials—*AIDA*, for attention-interest-desire-action. The letter opens with an attention getter that attempts to convince the audience to continue to read. Among the most commonly used attention getters are provocative headlines, questions, testimonials, and startling facts and statistics. Attention getters continue in the opening paragraph. Sales letters then attempt to create interest by tapping a need in the reader, often through the presentation of specific claims. These claims stress benefits and involve logical and emotional appeals. Desire, the next

stage of the sales letter, is created through the presentation of evidence to support claims about its benefits. In turn, evidence motivates action. Finally, every sales letter attempts to convince readers to take specific steps to purchase a product and to do so quickly. Three techniques to produce action are to identify the specific action, use inducements, and make it easy to respond. Inducements to buy include premiums, sweepstakes and contests, discounts for immediate action, limited quantities, and deadlines.

5. **List the four types of** *collection letters* **and explain the purpose of each.**

Collection letters are persuasive letters that attempt to collect outstanding debts while simultaneously maintaining goodwill. The first letter in the collection series is a reminder. Reminders have a positive tone while gently informing the customer that the debt has not been paid. The next letter in the series, the inquiry, questions whether there is a problem preventing the customer from paying. The tone of this letter is friendly and conciliatory. Aggressive collection notices are sent next. These notices use various appeals to insist that the bill be paid. Finally, last-resort collection letters threaten unpleasant actions if the debt is not paid within a specific time. These actions include turning the debt over to a collection agency and taking legal action. Last-resort letters should communicate the writer's reluctance to take these actions while affirming his or her determination to do so.

6. **Explain when to use a direct approach in** *persuasive memos* **and when to be indirect.**

In general, persuasive memos are more direct than sales letters. However, certain circumstances make the indirect approach best. These include trying to persuade a reader with whom you do not have a close relationship to do something in his or her best interest. This approach is also used to persuade people in higher organizational positions to do something that they do not want to do.

REVIEW AND DISCUSSION QUESTIONS

1. What is persuasion? *(Ch. Obj. 1)*
2. The chapter notes that every persuasive message attempts to achieve one of four major persuasive goals. Describe the differences among these goals. *(Ch. Obj. 1)*
3. Distinguish among the three major persuasive appeals. *(Ch. Obj. 2)*
4. Distinguish among initial, derived, and terminal credibility. *(Ch. Obj. 2)*
5. What are the three major types of sales letters? *(Ch. Obj. 3)*
6. Explain the AIDA concept. Why is it important in organizing a sales letter? *(Ch. Obj. 4)*

7. Name several techniques that can help motivate readers to take immediate action after they have read a persuasive document. (*Ch. Obj. 4*)

8. Name the four types of collection letters. (*Ch. Obj. 5*)

9. Compare the approaches that a writer might

use in each of the four types of collection letters. (*Ch. Obj. 5*)

10. When would you use a direct approach in a persuasive memo to a business colleague? When would you want to be indirect? (*Ch. Obj. 6*)

*A*PPLICATION EXERCISES

1. Write a persuasive letter in which you convince a skeptical friend that it's important to be able to write persuasively in business. (*Ch. Obj. 1*)

2. Suppose that you've decided to write a persuasive memo to your boss, either on your current job or on a job that you've held in the past. You want to persuade him or her that you deserve a promotion. Which of the four persuasive goals are you trying to achieve in this memo? (*Ch. Obj. 1*)

3. Define the specific purposes that will accomplish the goal for your memo that you identified in your response to EXERCISE 2. Now write a brief description of your audience—that is, your boss. What are his or her priorities and concerns? How can you persuade your boss that your promotion will also benefit the company? (*Ch. Obj. 1*)

4. Using your notes from EXERCISE 3, list the statements that you could make in this memo that would help you to establish credibility, appeal to your boss's sense of reasoning, and produce the response you want. (*Ch. Obj. 2*)

5. Finally, using your statements for EXERCISE 4, write your memo to your boss. Be prepared to explain why you chose an indirect or direct approach. (*Ch. Obj. 1, 2, 6*)

6. Every persuasive message attempts to achieve one of four major goals. Cite examples of messages which you have received recently and which tried to meet these goals. Were these messages effective? Why or why not? What changes would you suggest to help the writer(s) improve their persuasive skills? (*Ch. Obj. 1–4, 6*)

7. Write a memo in which you persuade the president of your school to alter a rule or procedure that you feel needs changing. Be prepared to explain why you chose a direct or indirect approach. (*Ch. Obj. 1, 2, 6*)

8. Write a memo to your fellow students in which you persuade them to accept your

point of view on a certain issue. Possible topics include driving within the legal speed limit, the importance of doing homework regularly, or the benefits of studying a foreign language. Be sure to appeal to your readers' sense of reasoning and work to create a credible document. (*Ch. Obj. 1, 2*)

9. Think of a good or service that you would like to sell. Now create two lists—one describing the features of this item, the other detailing the benefits that these features provide to customers. (*Ch. Obj. 2, 3*)

10. Apply the AIDA concept to think through the steps that a customer would go through before buying the item or service that you described for EXERCISE 9. What arguments might you use in a sales letter to take the customer through each of these steps? (*Ch. Obj. 3, 4*)

11. Based on your notes for EXERCISE 10, write a sales letter to potential customers for the item or service that you have selected. (*Ch. Obj. 2–4*)

12. Suppose that Bob Rowse, a personnel manager at an electronics firm, has bought the product or service that you described in EXERCISE 11. He bought it on a six-month installment plan that calls for him to make equal payments every month. Bob made the first two payments on time but has since fallen behind on his payment schedule. Your company has sent him two invoices, and he's now two months late with his third payment. You decide that it's time to write a collection letter. You don't know why Bob is late on his payments, but you do know that his company is in trouble and has had to lay off 100 employees. Write an effective collection letter to Bob. (*Ch. Obj. 5*)

13. Larry Laggard has also bought the good or service that you described in EXERCISE 11. Larry has been late before in paying his bills, and this time is No exception. He is now three months late with his first installment payment on this item, and you have already sent him both a reminder letter and an inquiry letter. Write Larry an aggressive col-

lection notice. How will this letter differ from the one that you wrote to Bob Rowse in EXERCISE 12? (*Ch. Obj. 5*)

14. In political advertisements, candidates sometimes resort to name-calling, mudslinging, and, in general, making negative allegations and generalizations about their opponents. Why do

you think they take this approach? How do such advertisements affect you when you watch them? Explain your answer. (*Ch. Obj. 1, 2*)

15. Cover the right-hand column in TABLE 9.2. Test your persuasive skills by creating your own examples for each technique listed. (*Ch. Obj. 4*)

*B*UILDING YOUR RESEARCH SKILLS

We all are constantly bombarded by persuasive messages of some type—advertisements, memos, letters, newspaper and magazine articles, books, even popular songs and movies. Collect four examples of persuasive messages that you have received recently—one for each of the four persuasive goals discussed in the chapter. Analyze each message to

determine its effectiveness. If you find it effective, explain why it works. Does it use the AIDA concept? Does it mention benefits as well as features? On the other hand, if the message fails to persuade you, why is it ineffective? Write a brief analysis of each message to present to the class.

*B*UILDING YOUR TEAMWORK SKILLS

Your instructor will divide the class into small teams. Meet with your team to discuss the four messages that each of you analyzed in the Research Skills exercise. Do the other members of your team agree with your analysis of each message? Do they have any explanations for effective

or ineffective messages that you did not consider? As a group, discuss recommendations for improving the ineffective messages.

Your instructor may wish to have each group present the best and worst persuasive messages to the class.

*C*OMMUNICATING IN A WORLD OF DIVERSITY

Suppose that you're a new member of the American Medical Association. While doing research for a paper, you discover the following facts:

- Female doctors in private practice earn median incomes that are 34 percent less than those of male colleagues.
- This income disparity exists even in specialties with many female physicians. Women's median incomes are 27 percent less than those of men in family practice; 29 percent less in internal medicine; 34 percent less in pediatrics. This information comes from a recent survey of 17,000 group-practice doctors commissioned by the Medical Group Management Association of Denver.
- Only one of the 126 medical schools in the United States has a female dean.
- Eighty-one percent of female medical students say that they were the targets of sexist insults in school, mostly from male medical students. Over 50 percent of female students say that they were targets of sexual advances, often from the same male students.

- Many female physicians complain that male colleagues exclude them from informal consultations and formal conferences about patients.
- One doctor, Rose Kumar, began work as a staff physician at the Kaiser Permanente Medical Center in Sacramento, California. Her first performance review rated her as "outstanding." A year later, after she had asked her boss to investigate discrimination against women at the hospital, she received an "unsatisfactory" evaluation and was told to find another job.

    Write a persuasive memo to the president of the American Medical Association. You want to convince the president—who happens to be male and rather conservative—to let you start a committee to study these issues further.

Source: Meredith Wadman, "Often Belittled by Their Male Colleagues, Women Doctors Also Find Pay Disparity," *The Wall Street Journal*, November 25, 1992, pp. B1, B6. Reprinted by permission of *The Wall Street Journal*, © 1992 Dow Jones & Company, Inc. All rights reserved worldwide.

The High-Tech Touch in Greeting Cards

Hallmark has a new product called Touch-Screen Greetings. Using a color laser printer, Touch-Screen prints cards on blank card stock and allows customers to create their own greeting cards. Currently, customers can choose from 120 cards, but Hallmark plans to program the system to handle 500 cards within a year.

Touch-Screen kiosks are located inside Hallmark stores. As the system's name suggests, customers start the program by touching the computer screen. They can then choose to give commands by touching the screen, by using a keyboard, by filling in blanks, or by writing out messages themselves. If their desired changes require more words than the options available by filling in blanks, they must rewrite an entire card. All in all, while the system is fairly easy to use, it is occasionally inflexible. For instance, people who decide to create cards by touching the screen must deal with letters arranged in alphabetical order—an obstacle that can slow down the typing process considerably.

Moreover, at $3.50 each, a Touch-Screen card costs twice what customers might pay for a "regular" card. The target audience includes younger people and men. Interestingly, while only 10 percent of regular greeting-card buyers are men, sales so far show 20 percent of Touch-Screen customers to be male.

Competing products include CreataCard from American Greetings, which uses a plotter pen to create line drawings and messages. These products, however, look less sophisticated than those produced by Hallmark's color laser printer. Greeting-card software is also available for home computers, but it requires expensive printers in order to produce high-quality cards.

Questions and Applications

1. Describe the target market for Touch-Screen Greetings.
2. Explain how the AIDA concept can be applied to a sales campaign for Touch-Screen Greetings.
3. Write a sales letter for Touch-Screen addressed to a typical member of Hallmark's target market.

Source: Joan Rigdon, "Old-Fashioned Sentiments Go High-Tech," *The Wall Street Journal*, November 9, 1992, pp. B1, B8. Reprinted by Permission of *The Wall Street Journal*, © 1992 Dow Jones & Company, Inc. All rights reserved worldwide.

Greetings from a Small-Business Creditor

Ariane Smythe likes the Hallmark Touch-Screen system. In fact, she likes it so much that she used it to create 30 cards in one sitting. For Ariane, Touch-Screen is a great product. Unfortunately, Hallmark markets Touch-Screen for profit, and Ariane's local Hallmark store has billed her for her 30 personalized cards. Ariane is late in paying.

Suppose that you are the owner of Ariane's local Hallmark store. Because you own a small business, you can't afford to have many people late in paying their bills. You would like to keep Ariane as a customer, and you are willing to waive a late-payment fee if she will pay within ten days.

Questions and Assignments

1. Write a reminder letter to Ariane about her debt.

2. After four weeks, there has been no response from Ariane. Write a collection-inquiry letter.

3. After another month, you still haven't heard from Ariane. Things are getting more serious. Write an aggressive collection notice. Ask her to respond within two weeks.

4. Ariane has not responded by the two-week deadline. It's time for you to write a last-resort collection letter.

REPORT AND PROPOSAL WRITING

Planning and Researching Business Reports and Proposals

CHAPTER OBJECTIVES

After studying this chapter, you should be able to:

1 Identify the characteristics of business *reports* and *proposals.*

2 List the seven steps in the report and proposal writing process.

3 Describe the characteristics of *collaborative writing.*

4 List three questions that are used in evaluating *primary* and *secondary research.*

5 Explain how *measures of central tendency* and *correlation* are used to organize statistical data.

6 Identify the four major types of *secondary business research.*

7 Explain how business researchers use *online databases* to secure needed information.

8 Compare the two major sources of *primary data research.*

Writing is an exploration. You start from nothing and learn as you go.

E. L. Doctorow
American novelist

STRIKING GOLD IN ETHNIC FOOD

In recent years, a large number of major U.S. corporations have decided to reduce business risk through diversification. Tobacco products giant R. J. Reynolds became RJR Nabisco by purchasing the packaged-goods maker of such household brands as Oreo, Life Savers, Planters, Ritz crackers, and Grey Poupon. PepsiCo has expanded beyond its soft-drink origins by acquiring the Taco Bell and Pizza Hut fast-food chains. Faced with a declining market for canned-milk products, executives at Pet, Inc., have taken advantage of the growing popularity of Mexican food by launching the Old El Paso line of salsa and related products.

But both strategies for diversifying— acquiring existing companies and introducing new products—typically involve millions of dollars in investments. Not surprisingly, such decisions are usually made only after considerable research has been conducted and top management has studied extensive reports analyzing the opportunities and risks present in such ventures.

During the past two decades, General Mills has been particularly successful in moving from such products as Hamburger Helper into the fast-growing casual dining segment of the restaurant industry. Beginning with the Red Lobster chain, the company created an atmosphere of informal dress, moderate prices, and family dining. The concept also proved successful when General Mills ventured into the ethnic food field with its popular Olive Garden chain of Italian restaurants. By the mid-1990s, the number of Olive Garden restaurants had passed the 500 mark, with annual sales of more than $1 billion.

General Mills managers then posed a major question for their market researchers: Could Olive Garden's success be repeated with a Chinese food menu? Certainly, Chinese restaurants have high-profit potential. For one thing, points out Michael Bartlett, editor in chief of *Restaurants & Institutions*, "Chinese has lots of noodles in it. The rice is inexpensive, and it can be heaped in many ways to give the impression of abundance."

The task of thoroughly researching every aspect of this market was given to Terry Cheng, a Chinese-American chef with a background in food biology. To find out which foods were most familiar to American diners, Cheng began by gathering menus from Chinese restaurants across the United States. From those menus, Cheng developed six test menus. The menus were then tried out on consumers in taste tests. Questionnaires were used to elicit information about specific menu items that were highly ranked. To secure customer feedback in a real-life setting, frequently mentioned favorites like moo goo gai pan, fried rice, egg foo young, and spareribs were tested on the menu at General Mills' prototype China Coast restaurant in Orlando, Florida.

Cheng quickly recognized the importance of making certain that what people *said* matched their actual food ordering *behavior* in the restaurant. For example, although questionnaire responses revealed a preference for healthy, low-sodium, low-calorie entrees, most customers ordered foods highest in fat, sugar, salt, and sauces. Although they stated a strong desire for authentic Chinese foods, most diners chose old Americanized favorites from the menu.

Cheng's research generated a proposal to apply the Olive Garden pattern in entering the Chinese-restaurant market. If the decision proves to be a success, American diners may soon enjoy even more options for ethnic-food dining within a few years. Greek and Middle Eastern cuisines could be next.[1]

CHAPTER OVERVIEW

Market research is an essential component of many business reports and proposals, and it is always crucial that research findings be interpreted correctly. Had General Mills, for example, added menu items in keeping with respondents' stated desires for "authentic" Chinese food, China Coast diners would no doubt have been disappointed. As Terry Cheng points out, American diners and Chinese-food preparers can understand "authentic" in very different ways. "Chinese people," she explains, "talk about authentic Chinese food and they're talking about chicken feet, jellyfish, and bird's nest soup."[2]

In this chapter, then, we will discuss the most effective ways to convert research findings into information for use in business reports and proposals. Indeed, as we shall see, reports play a crucial role in communicating information in profit-seeking businesses, nonprofit organizations, and government agencies. For example, reports are often used to solicit business from outside the organization. In addition, they are frequently used inside organizations to suggest new programs and approaches for internal change. In general, reports and proposals affect a company's relationships with its business clients, suppliers, government agencies, company employees, and the general public.

This chapter is the first of four chapters on business reports and proposals. Here, we will focus on planning and research as two key steps in writing effective documents. We will also stress the fact that gathering and reporting information is fundamental to the success of all reports and proposals. In fact, many documents are called upon to synthesize so much information that they are doomed to failure unless they are carefully organized and written with a clear sense of purpose.

This chapter also examines information sources and methods of gathering information in the form of *primary* and *secondary research*, as well as appropriate methods of arranging and interpreting information. Because report writing is often a group effort, the chapter also examines the benefits and potential problems involved in *collaborative writing*.

We begin by examining the nature of *reports* and the ways in which they are used in business. This chapter also discusses the nature of business *proposals*—what they are and how they function.

WHAT ARE BUSINESS REPORTS?

As we shall see, business reports take many different forms. Not surprisingly, however, they also share several important characteristics. While the content of a document determines whether or not it is technically a *report*, its basic characteristics determine the fundamental importance or purpose of any document. Defined by its basic characteristics, a **business report** is a compilation of organized information on a specific topic that is provided to one or more people inside or outside an organization who will use it for a specific business purpose. The cornerstone of an effective business report is the presentation of *verifiable*

business report
Compilation of organized information gathered on a specific topic and delivered to specific users

data—facts. "No matter how far reports go into interpretation and analysis," explains one team of business communication experts, "they begin by presenting and summarizing facts.... Reports share the journalist's interest in the fundamentals of who, what, when, where, why, and how."[3]

Characteristics of Business Reports

Although the purpose of all reports and proposals is to inform and/or persuade, we can distinguish them according to seven basic characteristics: *length, degree of formality, distribution, frequency of submission, format, use of visual aids*, and *method of assignment*. Each of these characteristics is briefly described in Table 10.1, which also provides a preliminary distinction between types of reports that we will describe as *formal* and *informal*.

LENGTH   Of these seven characteristics, length is probably the most obvious. Short reports are typically one or two pages in length and can be in either letter or memo form. Although they may not fit the common concept of a "report," such memo-type documents can be classified as reports because of their content—they present information to specific individuals for specific purposes. Long reports, meanwhile, may require dozens—and sometimes hundreds—of pages of information in order to focus on and analyze complex issues and problems.

DEGREE OF FORMALITY   Business reports can also be formal or informal. **Formal reports** are typically long and follow prescribed organizational patterns determined by the importance and complexity of the subject matter. Certain identifiable parts, such as title pages, tables of contents, and executive summaries, also characterize formal reports. They usually entail extensive research and almost always feature impersonal language.

Informal reports are typically written in shorter time frames to present findings derived from smaller research bases. They tend to be shorter than the typical formal report and generally feature a relatively relaxed, personal style.

DISTRIBUTION   A third distinguishing characteristic of written reports and proposals is the extent of their circulation, or distribution, to other individuals within the organization, outside it, or both. **Internal reports** can be directed to

formal report
Relatively long document based on extensive research and organized according to a prescribed system

informal report
Relatively short document typically written over a short period and based on a comparatively small research base

internal report
Report distributed to individuals within the organization

TABLE 10.1	*Characteristics of Business Reports*	
CHARACTERISTIC	FORMAL REPORTS	INFORMAL REPORTS
Length	Long	Short
Degree of Formality	Impersonal language More highly structured with identifiable parts	Personal writing style Less structured
Distribution	May be circulated outside the organization and to superiors, subordinates, and coworkers within the organization	Less likely to be circulated outside the organization
Frequency	Can be specialized, one-time reports or periodic reports	Can be specialized, one-time reports or periodic reports
Format	Can be form reports or narrative reports	Can be form reports or narrative reports
Visual Aids	Extensive use of visual aids	Less likely use of visual aids
Assignment	Can be initiated externally, self-initiated, or assigned to a department or individual by another manager	Can be initiated externally, self-initiated, or assigned to a department or individual by another manager

the top hierarchy of the organization, to subordinates, or to persons at comparable levels of authority and responsibility. A report sent to senior management, for example, might focus on the results of a meeting with an important client. A comparative analysis of productivity among various departments might be the subject of a report sent to a subordinate in one of those departments. A report sent to a colleague at the same level in the corporate hierarchy might discuss the status of an ongoing project.

External reports are circulated to interested parties outside the organization. Suppliers, customers, consultants, creditors, and government officials are only a few of the outside parties likely to receive these reports. By their very nature, informal reports are less likely to be distributed to persons outside the organization.

FREQUENCY OF SUBMISSION   A fourth characteristic of reports involves the frequency with which they are issued. **One-time** or **singular reports** deal with specific issues and are designed to aid management in making specific decisions. For example, an informal survey assessing user satisfaction with different brands of long-distance telephone carriers might be the basis of a one-time report to a manager who must decide whether to award the firm's long-distance business to AT&T, MCI, or Sprint.

Other activities require the distribution of **periodic reports**. Some reports—for example, a comparative analysis of this year's retail sales with last year's—may be issued every day. Other periodic reports are issued weekly, monthly, quarterly, semiannually, or annually. Corporations, whose ownership shares are held by thousands of individuals and institutions like mutual funds, insurance companies, and pension funds, are required by law to supply these owners with both quarterly financial reports and more extensive annual reports detailing company plans, financial data, and significant business developments. Even marketing research–based reports may be revised periodically. For example, PepsiCo marketers, fond of competing with rival Coca-Cola by means of consumer taste tests, repeat such tests periodically and release new reports containing the latest findings.

FORMAT   Many reports follow specific formats that can be completed by simply filling in the blanks on standardized forms. Because they focus on specific information, **form reports** discourage narrative. For example, an inventory-control report form for a local manufacturer might request information on three categories of inventory: raw materials, work in progress, and finished goods on hand and available for sale. Another section of the form might address a particular inventory-related problem that has arisen since the last report.

By contrast, the format of a **narrative report** is largely determined by what the writer decides to say and *how* he or she chooses to say it. In some companies, for instance, the person assigned to write a benefits-analysis report might choose to use a figure or table to summarize and compare the health-insurance benefits offered by several competing companies. Elsewhere, the person assigned this task may simply choose to integrate this comparison in the narrative of the report.

USE OF VISUAL AIDS   A sixth distinguishing characteristic of business reports is the extent to which they use visual aids. Longer formal documents—say, reports presenting quantitative findings from company operations or research studies—are likely to make extensive use of visual aids. Short informal reports may use none. Visual aids (which we will discuss in detail in Chapter 11) range from simple tables, charts, and graphs to more complex computer-generated graphics. They can be extremely effective in long, formal reports to summarize, compare, or emphasize important information.

METHOD OF ASSIGNMENT   Finally, business reports can be classified according to the way they are assigned. Some reports, for instance, are initiated externally while others may be assigned on a periodic basis to a particular individual or department within the company. For example, the firm's sales manager might ask the director of marketing research to analyze demand for a proposed

external report
Report distributed to interested parties outside the organization

singular report
One-time report designed to deal with specific issues and to aid in making specific decisions

periodic report
Report distributed according to an established schedule, such as weekly, quarterly, or annually

form report
Document, such as an inventory-control report, following a specific format and focusing on specific information

narrative report
Report whose format is largely determined by what the writer decides to say and how he or she chooses to say it

Written reports stifle creativity.

Ross Perot
Founder,
Electronic Data Systems

PRACTICAL TIPS

To Report or Not to Report

No one wants to read business reports unless they are absolutely necessary. We also don't want to be bothered with duplicate information or more information than we need. Knowing when a report is unnecessary, therefore, can be as critical to business communication as knowing when one is needed. Several guidelines can be used if you want either to shorten a document or to determine whether you need to write one at all.

Ask yourself whether it is possible to consolidate some of the information contained in a report to produce a shorter document. This is often possible in periodic reports, such as status reports, where information has been presented in the same way for a long period of time. As you plan a document, try to avoid the mind set that longer is better. As you will see in Chapter 12, depending on your purpose, short reports can be as effective as long reports to communicate critical information. Similarly, ask yourself whether periodic reports are written too frequently and whether you can reduce the number of times they are submitted each year. For example, monthly reports may really be needed only once a quarter.

It is also possible to consolidate similar reports and, in the process, save an enormous amount of preparation and writing time. For example, instead of writing three separate budget reports for three separate departments, consider creating a single document that provides each department with the information that it needs.

Finally, consider replacing a report with a face-to-face meeting. Michael C. Thomsett, an authority on business reports, observes that in large, highly departmentalized companies,

> the tendency to produce a large number of reports can actually reduce the level of communication. You already know how little contact you have with a department on another floor, for example. The reports you send back and forth might be unnecessary if you simply met once each month to address the underlying issues. The time required for the meeting might be much less than the time you're now spending in preparing and sending out a report—and the meeting would have better results.

Write every report only after you consider the issues of length, the possibility of combining it with other reports, and the possibility of replacing it with an oral report in a face-to-face meeting. Because each recipient knows that your reports have survived your personal screening procedures, this practice should increase the impact of your reports on your readers. Given the time and effort involved in creating an effective business report, you should launch such a project only after you have determined that there is no better way to distribute requested information.

Source: Quotation from Michael C. Thomsett, *The Little Black Book of Business Reports* (New York: Amacom, 1988), pp. 97–104.

---

new product in certain regions or territories. Still other reports fall within a company's standard operating procedure. Form reports, such as a bank's quarterly loan analysis, fit into this category. Finally, reports may be self-initiated. A compensation manager, for example, may discover that one group of workers is underpaid compared to workers holding similar positions in comparable companies. He or she might decide to analyze the situation in a report to the human resources manager.

Types of Business Reports

In recent years, various bids submitted to government agencies by the giant garbage and trash hauler Waste Management, Inc., have prompted several different types of reports from those agencies. For example, when Waste Management bid on the contract to handle garbage in San Diego County, the county district attorney issued a 260-page *expert report* detailing "a combination of environmental and antitrust violations and public corruption cases which must be viewed with considerable concern." Environmental concerns also played a major role in the firm's application for a hazardous-waste disposal permit in Indiana. There, state officials requested that Waste Management prepare and submit an *informational report* detailing past environmental violations before they would consider the application. Finally, Seattle officials, satisfied with Waste Management's proposal to handle its trash and garbage disposal, issued a *recommendation report* supporting the company's proposal.[4]

As you can readily see from the experience of Waste Management, Inc., reports, like letters, can be classified according to purpose. As Table 10.2 shows, a business report falls into one or more of five major categories: *information, study, expert, status,* and *recommendation.* Although the breakdown here describes these categories separately, remember that many reports include overlapping elements. A status report, for example, may also present new information. Similarly, although recommendation reports can be considered a separate category, a recommendation section is found in many different types of reports (for example, expert and study reports).

PROGRESS CHECK

1. What are business reports and why are they important?
2. Distinguish between formal and informal reports.

TABLE 10.2   *Types of Reports*

TYPE	PURPOSE	EXAMPLE
Information	Presents, explains, and interprets historical and new information	New marketing opportunities in Eastern Europe
Study	Focuses on a problem and alternative solutions; includes analyses and recommendations	Analysis of reasons why factory productivity declined during the last twelve months
Expert	Interprets and evaluates information and suggests solutions from an expert's perspective	Analysis of different benefits provided by two companies that have recently merged
Status	Provides updates of a current situation, plan, or project and recommends solutions to potential problems	Summary of a major product-development project
Recommendation	Suggests a new procedure or policy, changing responsibilities, or different budget allocations to improve productivity or profits	Recommendation that the sales department be reorganized to give greater authority to the nine regional sales managers

Source: Adapted from Michael C. Thomsett, The Little Black Book of Business Reports (New York: Amacom, 1988), p. 7.

WHAT ARE BUSINESS PROPOSALS?

proposals
Document presenting ideas and plans for consideration by others who may accept them and agree to invest funds in their development

Proposals are documents that set forth ideas and plans in the hope that readers will accept them and agree to fund their development. Indeed, the key difference between reports and proposals is that proposals, if accepted, usually require financial investment on the part of their recipients. Like reports, proposals can be either formal or informal, short or long. When compared to the various types of reports, proposals are most similar to recommendation reports. In this section, we will describe some of the most important types of proposals and then offer some guidelines for evaluating both reports and proposals.

Types of Business Proposals

Proposals can be written for both internal and external audiences. Three types exist: *internal proposals, sales proposals*, and *proposals to government agencies in response to official requests*.

internal proposal
Persuasive document that attempts to convince top management to spend money on specific projects intended to change or improve the organization

INTERNAL PROPOSALS   **Internal proposals** are persuasive documents that attempt to convince top management to spend money on specific projects that will change or improve the organization. For example, a post-merger proposal might suggest ways to integrate the two companies' accounting and mail-handling departments. Another internal proposal might suggest opening a new distribution facility to serve a growing market better.

sales proposal (or private-industry proposal)
Persuasive document seeking to convince potential buyers to purchase a firm's goods or services

SALES PROPOSALS   By contrast, **sales proposals** (also known as **private-industry proposals**) seek to sell a company's goods or services to potential buyers. For example, an outplacement firm may try to sell its services to a corporation's director of human resources. Similarly, the owner of a trucking company may propose a more efficient delivery service to a large retail chain.

request for proposal (RFP)
Detailed, formal government document requesting proposals and bids on a specific project

RESPONSE PROPOSALS   Sales proposals are sometimes submitted to government agencies at the federal, state, or local level in response to **requests for proposals (RFPs)**—detailed, formal documents that request proposals and bids on government projects from universities and other nonprofit organizations as well as from firms in the private sector. RFPs include projects as diverse as an order for uniforms by the U.S. Navy, an order for highway repairs by a state department of transportation, or an order for custodial services by a local school district. To ensure equal opportunity in responding, the same RFP is widely distributed throughout an industry.

Evaluating Reports and Proposals

All reports and proposals can be evaluated according to such factors as *usefulness, organization, readability*, and *persuasiveness*. In determining usefulness, you ask how well the document meets its stated purpose and whether the information is accessible to the reader. The test of effective organization is whether the presentation is clear and easy to follow. A readable document includes language that is free of jargon and includes devices such as headings and visual aids that enhance understanding.

Persuasiveness is an especially important factor in evaluating business reports and proposals that contain recommendations. Much like persuasive oral presentations, persuasive reports and proposals should be supported by evidence and logical arguments. Meeting these criteria requires careful planning and an understanding of the multistep process involved in writing reports and proposals. That process is the subject of the next section.

STEPS IN THE WRITING PROCESS

Formal reports and proposals can take months of work hours, involve teams of workers, and often result in documents hundreds of pages long. Undertaking a project of this magnitude without a writing plan inevitably leads to failure. Simplicity and clarity are essential in all reports and proposals, but especially so in complex, lengthy documents. These objectives were apparently ignored in a report recently issued by the City of New York that listed 60,000 separate indicators to be used in measuring the performance of city agencies. The result was a document so massive and complex that it was impossible to understand. According to the city's former deputy commissioner, two indicators—"one measuring services from the citizen's perspective, another measuring the productivity of city workers"—could have replaced all the others to produce an equally effective but much simpler document.[5]

Achieving simplicity and clarity involves a systematic approach to each of the steps in the writing process. As Figure 10.1 shows, seven distinct steps lead from problem identification through finalization and submission of the document: *defining the audience and purpose; creating a work plan; collecting and evaluating data; developing the outline; writing the first draft; revising the document;* and *finalizing and submitting the document.*

We will begin by describing each of these steps in terms of the writer's basic objectives and activities. In describing Step 2, the creation of a work plan, we will explore in some detail the nature of collaborative writing. We emphasize, however, that the major function of a report or proposal is the effective presentation of data. For that reason, Step 3—collecting and evaluating data—is perhaps the most important of these seven steps. Although we will thus describe data collection and evaluation as a stage in this seven-step process, we will begin the next major section of this chapter—the process of conducting research—by examining more fully the important tasks of organizing and interpreting data.

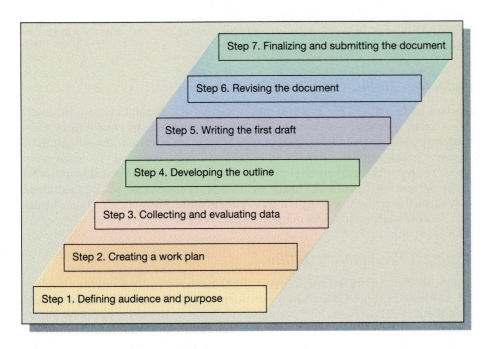

FIGURE 10.1   *Steps in the Writing Process*

DEFINING THE AUDIENCE AND PURPOSE

I can't write without a reader. It's precisely like a kiss— you can't do it alone.

John Cheever
American novelist

As we have seen throughout this text, keeping the audience in mind is an important aspect of every communication because the receiver must understand the information being presented. Similarly, in preparing reports and proposals, you must both match the document with its audience and define the precise purpose of your document. You can address both requirements by asking yourself a single question: "How will the information contained in this document be used by its audience?" The specific content of your document will depend on the information needed by the reader to make a decision or evaluate a situation.

Neglecting to identify both your audience and your purpose, therefore, can lead not only to false starts on your part but also to project failures for the team with which you are working. Imagine, for example, that your manager asks you to prepare a report that not only evaluates the pros and cons of several sites for a new retail outlet but also recommends a specific location. Obviously, your report would be incomplete without a recommendation. Just as obviously, you would not omit the recommendation if you understood the needs of your manager.

At this stage in your project, you will find it helpful to perform three operations: stating your specific purpose, conducting an informal investigation of your problem, and creating a preliminary outline. At the conclusion of this stage, you should be ready to create your work plan.

Stating Your Specific Purpose

As we saw in Chapter 3, the planning process for all documents should begin with a clear *statement of purpose*. This simple statement should serve as a compass to guide you during the writing process.

Sometimes, of course, you will require clarification of your reader's needs before you can define the specific purpose of your document. To learn exactly what information is needed, you may have to question the person who gave you the assignment. For example, does your manager want a complete analysis of competing stores in each area, a recommendation to buy or lease the property, an analysis of possible leases for proposed store sites, or a demographic analysis of potential customers in each area? Because each of these investigations can take literally weeks of work, it is critical to know *at the start* what your reader needs and wants.

Conducting an Informal Investigation

Once you have defined the broad boundaries of your document, you are ready to move from a general overview to a microscopic analysis of your writing task. In order to identify specific issues, you can begin an informal investigation. If necessary, speak with the person who assigned the document. To learn what approaches have been taken to similar projects in the past, check departmental records for similar documents. Talk with co-workers, suppliers, or customers involved in the project. Finally, to gain background knowledge, consult published sources such as business magazines and books.

Creating a Preliminary Outline

Having completed your informal investigation, you are ready to create a preliminary working outline. Guided by your purpose statement, this outline should divide the general problem into parts that can be investigated separately. Figure 10.2 first states a specific purpose for your report on retail sites and then shows how a brief working outline might segment your work into relatively small, manageable portions. Although the outline will be developed more fully later in the writing process, you will find that it is crucial in the development of your *work plan*—a document that enables you to complete your report on schedule.

CREATING A WORK PLAN

Because of their complexity and the amount of time they take to complete, most long reports and proposals need a **work plan**—a document that defines how the work will be done, who will do it, and when each phase of the project will be completed. Creating a work plan is the second step in the writing process, a step in which tasks are linked to deadlines. Dividing your report into specific tasks linked to interim deadlines has the advantage of making the entire project seem less formidable. This approach is similar to that typically used by the author of a book. While it is difficult to conceive of writing an entire book, it is a manageable task to envision, plan, outline, and then develop twenty individual chapters.

To create a work plan, the writer must first decide on both the amount and types of research needed to complete the report. In the case of the outline in Figure 10.2, the writer might decide to obtain data about costs and collect information about the competitive retailing environment by interviewing a variety of people. It may also be necessary to review recent census data for population characteristics in each area and to contact local newspapers and chambers of commerce for statistics on general economic conditions. If sufficient time and resources are available, the writer may decide to implement a collaborative work plan and involve other people in the writing process.

Collaborative Planning and Writing

Long, formal reports are routinely drafted by writing teams who engage in **collaborative writing**—the process whereby a group of people works together to produce finished reports and proposals. According to a recent study, nine out of ten business professionals have had experience with collaborative writing. Another study suggests that collaboration is in fact the standard in the writing of formal reports and proposals.[6]

The word *collaboration*, of course, inspires immediate real-life associations of two or more people working together: retailing pioneers Richard W. Sears and Alvah C. Roebuck; San Francisco Forty Niners quarterback Steve Young and wide receiver Jerry Rice; musical composer Richard Rogers and lyricist Oscar Hammerstein II; and Beatles band members John Lennon, Paul McCartney, George Harrison, and Ringo Starr. In business, collaboration can take place at

work plan
Document specifying work to be accomplished, the individuals to perform it, and completion deadlines for each phase of the project

Writing is manual labor of the mind: a job, like laying pipe.
John Gregory Dunne
American novelist

collaborative writing
Process of creating finished reports and proposals by groups of individuals working together

---

Specific Purpose

To identify for senior management the possible sites for a new retail outlet, including the advantages and disadvantages of each site, and to recommend a specific site.

Working Outline

I. Identify at least three possible retail sites, including Des Moines, Omaha, and Tulsa
II. For each site, discuss:
    A. Real estate costs for purchasing or leasing the property
    B. Competing stores
    C. Demographic characteristics of potential customers
    D. Economic conditions in the community
III. Compare the advantages and disadvantages of each location
IV. Recommend a specific location

FIGURE 10.2 *Specific Purpose and Outline*

any of the stages during the document-development process, including planning, writing, editing, and/or finalization.

PLANNING AND TEAMWORK   Collaborative writing is becoming so prevalent because it has many benefits. For example, when the required document is long and complex and the deadline short, it may be impossible for a single individual to complete it on schedule. Dealing with a team also makes available a wider range of expertise. For example, team members on a marketing proposal for a new state-of-the-art fax machine might include marketing-research analysts, engineers, designers, advertising account executives, creative directors, and accountants. Collaboration is also important when the document must reflect a consensus among key decision makers. Having everyone contribute means that everyone assumes "ownership" of writing decisions along the way.

You can never over-coordinate.

Cle Cox
American Airlines training manager

SHARING PERSPECTIVES   Research is just one aspect of the planning stage during which collaboration can improve the team's work. During this stage, researchers must develop a strategy for conducting research and presenting their findings. In planning a marketing proposal, for example, teams of workers may find it necessary to hold one or more meetings to develop a strategy for differentiating the products of their firm from competing brands. The meeting process itself will expedite the research for focusing the group's task: "This process," stresses business-communication professor Terry R. Bacon,

> is usually a complex endeavor in which the participating individuals must not only share information and perspectives but also negotiate their understanding of the issues. In short, their task is to arrive at consensus on the best…posture for this audience—the customer—and situation.[7]

ASKING QUESTIONS AND RAISING ISSUES   Planning, then, begins with dialogue among team members, both in joint meetings and in one-on-one discussions. One way to transform individual contributions into a cohesive team effort is to ask a series of questions like those in Figure 10.3. Questions like these can help determine crucial issues regarding content, purpose, audience, organization and development, design, and document synthesis.

ASSIGNING RESPONSIBILITY   One of the most important parts of the planning stage is the assignment of specific areas of responsibility. This step involves dividing the team's task into various components and deciding which person or group is likely to be the most effective in completing each assignment. In our site-selection illustration, for instance, the work could be divided on the basis of the individual sites. One person would be responsible for evaluating Des Moines, another Omaha, and a third Tulsa. Another approach might be to segment the work according to function. For example, a marketing analyst might be given the responsibility for analyzing census data, an attorney might be chosen to examine lease provisions, and a real-estate specialist assigned the task of examining purchasing opportunities.

LEADING AND COORDINATING   At this stage, effective oral-communication skills are especially important for the project leader, who must coordinate the work of every member of the team. The first task of the team leader is to ensure that everyone understands the role that his or her contribution will play in the entire project. Otherwise, contributors may lack commitment to the work and may ignore deadlines. The team leader must help every contributor perceive the overall picture.

MONITORING CONTRIBUTIONS   Once team members have collected data in their assigned areas, they can begin developing a first draft. Much of this work is accomplished independently. To help keep track of everyone's contributions, however, team leaders typically ask for progress reports at regular intervals. A *status worksheet* like the one in Figure 10.4 can check and record the

WRITING CHECKLIST

Content Questions

- What more can we say about ____?
- What additional information might we include?
- Have you considered including [excluding] ____?
- Don't you think we should include [exclude] ____?

Purpose/Key Point Questions

- What do you see as our main point [purpose]?
- What did you mean by ____? Could you clarify the point about ____?
- I can't quite see why you've decided to ____. Could you explain why?
- I see a conflict between ____ and ____. How will we deal with it?

Audience Questions

- Who is our intended audience? Why is this the appropriate audience?
- What does the reader expect to read [learn, do]?
- How will our reader react to ____? Connect ____ to ____?
- What problems [conflicts, inconsistencies, gaps] might our reader see?

Questions Relating to Conventions of Organization and Development

- How can we *explain* ____?
- How will we *organize* [develop, explain] this?
- What *support* [or evidence] could we use? What *examples* could we use?
- How does this [convention] let us deal with ____?

Questions Relating to Conventions of Design

- Have you considered using ____? How do you think it would work?
- Couldn't we also try ____?
- How does this [convention] let us deal with ____?
- Why do you like ____ better than ____ as a way to present this information?

Synthesis/Consolidation Questions

- How does ____ relate to [develop, clarify] ____?
- Given our purpose and audience, should we use ____ [convention]?
- Is there a conflict between using ____ and ____?
- Why do you think ____ is a good way to explain our key point to this audience?

FIGURE 10.3 *Checklist for Collaborators*

progress of manuscript submissions at different project phases. This tool is especially helpful in planning and monitoring interdependent contributions that are phased in over time.

SCHEDULING TEAMWORK   A constant challenge in writing reports and proposals is establishing and following a working schedule. Typically, long documents are defined in terms of completion dates for various phases that are scheduled to meet the overall project-deadline date. Scheduling is especially important to the success of collaborative writing teams. The writing schedule shown in Figure 10.5 illustrates how interim, overlapping dates are set for each department involved in a project. This schedule allows the team to work smoothly between August 1 and August 22. With the first draft due by August 22, the team leader still has ten days to finalize the report, which is due on September 1.

EDITING AND FINALIZING COLLABORATIVE INPUT   Once the independent work is complete, the team members usually meet again as a group to review,

How does a project get to be a year behind schedule? One day at a time.

*Fred Brooks
IBM Corp.
systems designer*

```
                    MANUSCRIPT SUBMISSION SCHEDULE


        Chapter      1st Draft Due      2nd Draft Due      Chapter to
                                                           Production


           1            9/1/94            10/15/94          10/20/94
           2            9/1/94            10/15/94          10/20/94
           3            9/23/94           10/28/94          11/3/94
           4            9/30/94           10/28/94          11/6/94
           5            10/6/94           11/11/94          11/17/94
           6            10/12/94          11/11/94          11/20/94
           7            10/16/94          11/23/94          11/27/94
           8            10/22/94          11/23/94          12/2/94
           9            10/29/94          12/7/94           12/11/94
          10            11/4/94           12/7/94           12/16/94
          11            11/10/94          12/21/94          12/24/94
          12            11/16/94          12/21/94          1/4/95
          13            11/20/94          1/4/95            1/6/95
          14            11/26/94          1/4/95            1/8/95
          15            12/3/94           1/18/95           1/20/95
          16            12/9/94           1/18/95           1/22/95
          17            12/15/94          1/18/95           1/27/95
          18            12/21/94          1/25/95           1/29/95
          19            12/29/94          1/25/95           2/1/95
          20            1/6/95            1/25/95           2/1/95


        Note: Colored areas indicate completed work.
```

FIGURE 10.4   *Status Worksheet*

revise, and finalize their document. After resolving content and organizational questions, one person is usually assigned the task of editing and finalizing the entire document and giving it a consistent voice. This step helps to avoid the problems that arise when a document is written by a number of people with different writing styles and organizational approaches.

Keep in mind that, like any other formal meetings, collaborative writing meetings involve interpersonal dynamics. Getting people motivated and working together smoothly may be the most difficult challenge. Chapter 15 provides specific suggestions for establishing and maintaining a cohesive, productive working environment for group projects.

COLLECTING AND EVALUATING DATA

With the work plan in place, the third step in the writing process is to identify sources and gather data. Research is the foundation of all successful reports and proposals. By incorporating facts, statistics, expert testimony, and examples, documents inform and persuade. The result of the information explosion of the 1990s is a proliferation of information sources both inside and outside

APPLYING TECHNOLOGY

Collaborative Writing with Computers

With collaborative writing becoming an increasingly popular technique in business organizations, it is not surprising that computer software is now available to assist in the process. Collaborative-writing software includes word-processing systems, computer-conferencing systems, and group-authoring systems.

Word processing systems like WordPerfect and Microsoft Word enable group members to enter comments right on text pages produced by another member of the team. These same programs also have strikeout and redlining features that use strikethroughs and underlines to identify text that is either to be deleted or inserted. After receiving comments and editing suggestions from other group members, the lead writer can then review the original text along with proposed changes, accepting or rejecting suggestions as necessary.

Computer-assisted conferencing systems, such as Action Technology's *The Coordinator,* help manage collaborative writing projects by allowing participants to place each message in one of seven categories: a question, an offer, a request, a promise, a what-if speculation, a simple note, or information. The system allows these messages to be answered via electronic mail. It also issues receipts and files all correspondence so that it can be found at a later time.

Group-authoring systems, also known as *groupware,* let participants make comments on document drafts. All comments then become part of an official "edit trail." For example, Computer Associates' *ForComment* software allows participants to review documents, make online comments, see each other's comments, and clarify questions or problems. The dialogue function enables participants to respond to comments and raise questions electronically, thus reducing the need for time-consuming face-to-face meetings. In the following illustration, reviewers' comments accompany the part of the document to which they refer and include reviewers' names and the date and time at which each comment was made.

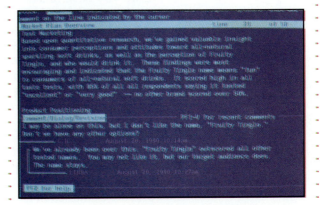

These and other software programs have the potential to make collaborative writing easier, faster, and more efficient. Learn as much as you can about these programs to choose the one best suited to the type of collaborative writing you do.

Sources: Annette Easton, George Easton, Marie Flatley, and John Penrose, "Supporting Group Writing with Computer Software," *The Bulletin of the Association for Business Communication,* 53:2 (June 1990), 34–37; 1992 promotional material from Computer Associates International Inc., *CA-ForComment: Document Review Software.*

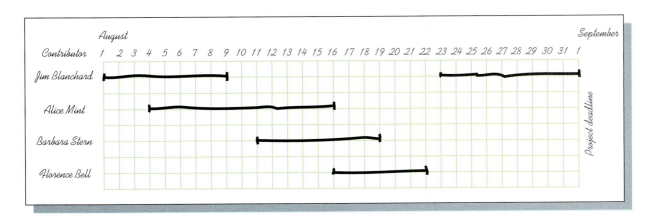

FIGURE 10.5   *Writing Schedule*

the organization. Coupled with the limited time that defines most writing projects, it is more critical than ever to develop search strategies that lead quickly to usable sources.

The second half of this chapter focuses on the various sources of research used in report and proposal writing as well as methods for taking effective research notes. Among the primary information sources are personal interviews, surveys, and observation. Secondary sources include company records, library research, government publications, and private business publications. We will begin that section of the chapter by discussing some basic considerations in the collection and evaluation of data.

DEVELOPING THE OUTLINE

Once you have finished evaluating your collected data, you are ready to begin the fourth step in the writing process: developing an outline to use when writing your report or proposal. Using either the formal or informal outline forms suggested in Chapter 4, you can now begin to stitch together the different threads of your data into a coherent whole. Begin by deciding on a specific *organizational plan*—for example, problem/solution, cause and effect, geographical, or chronological. At this point, you should also focus on document design. Your outline should contain all the prescribed elements you will need, such as an executive summary and a table of contents. These elements will help you create a format that will present the data effectively. At this stage, you should also decide upon the number and types of visual aids you will need. Inserting them in your outline at this point lets you know in advance how many visual aids your document will ultimately contain and where they will be placed. Visual aids are examined in greater detail in the next chapter.

Finally, your research findings should be keyed to the outline of your report or proposal. By linking the two, you will know exactly where every source will be used when you begin to write your first draft. To ensure that your data play an important role at this stage, try arranging the index cards or computer printouts to match the subjects treated in your outline; refer to them routinely as you begin to write.

WRITING THE FIRST DRAFT

With an outline in place, you can proceed to the fifth step in the writing process: preparing the first draft of your report or proposal. Remember that even when you are preparing a long document, the writing process involves working with small, manageable sections of material until your entire outline has been filled in. Also bear in mind that your focus may shift as your writing progresses, especially if you are working on a long document. It is thus important to keep the specific purpose of your document in mind as you write. At this point, your primary goal is to complete all the elements of your outline. Refinements and adjustments can be made during the revision stage.

REVISING THE DOCUMENT

Document revision, the sixth step in the writing process, is an important step in the preparation of both short and long documents. Although revising both long and short documents involves the same skills, converting the first draft of a long document into a finished report or proposal is a more demanding task because you are dealing with dozens—and sometimes hundreds—of pages.

Start the revision process by evaluating whether your draft has satisfied the document's specific purpose. You can do this on both the macro and micro levels. You can, for example, ask yourself questions like the following:

- Is your presentation effective as a whole?
- Do the specific sections of your document relate to your purpose?
- Is your logic coherent and clear?
- Is your evidence convincing enough to support your recommendations and conclusions?
- Do your visual aids add impact?

You can then evaluate individual paragraphs and sentences on the same basis.

Next move to the issue of clarity. Evaluate clarity by asking yourself two related questions:

- Precisely what is your document intended to accomplish?
- What do your readers know about your topic?

Do not use your own knowledge as a basis for criticism. After several weeks of doing nothing but writing your report, you are an expert, not a typical reader. Be especially careful, therefore, about making assumptions regarding your readers' level of knowledge about your topic. As you study your draft, ask yourself if you have left any gaps in your research. If you discover any, try to eliminate them by locating and presenting additional information.

Finally, revise your draft on the basis of language, style, and format. Chapters 4 and 5 described the elements to consider in the revision process. Chapters 12 and 13 will examine these elements in the context of long proposals and reports.

OBTAINING FEEDBACK   Important reports and proposals are often submitted to a committee or colleagues for review before finalization. A marketing researcher, for example, might submit a sales report to an immediate supervisor before submitting it to the director of sales. Feedback can result in small wording changes or major revisions to entire sections.

FINALIZING AND SUBMITTING THE DOCUMENT

After you have incorporated feedback and revisions, your last document can be prepared. At this last step in the writing process, it is important that technical errors are detected. Proofreading is thus critical in creating effective as well as professional-looking documents. Graphics, headings, labels, and captions for visual aids all should be clearly presented.

At this stage, copies of your final document will be printed for distribution. Depending on the report, photocopies are generally acceptable; however, many legal documents, as well as those with numerous figures, tables, and graphs should be printed rather than photocopied.

In the next section, we will examine the methods used in conducting effective research. Although the specific tools may change with advances in technology and may range from library research to personal interviews, the research strategy remains the same.

PROGRESS CHECK

1. What are proposals? What role do they play in business?
2. Why is it important to have a clear idea of your audience and purpose before you start writing?
3. When finalizing a long report, it is tempting to finish quickly. Why is it important to be just as careful with this step as with the previous steps?

CONDUCTING PRIMARY AND SECONDARY RESEARCH

*Every man has a right
to his opinion, but no
man has a right to be
wrong in his facts.*

*Bernard M. Baruch
American businessman
and statesman*

When writing business reports and proposals, one of the most important factors is knowing where to find data and, once you find them, how to evaluate them. This section examines the ways in which *primary and secondary research sources* are used in collecting data and presenting them in business writing. We will then offer some guidelines for taking effective *research notes*.

Evaluating Research

Not all research is created equally. Although the data collected by your firm or obtained from previously published sources may be perfectly sound, they must also be appropriate for the document you are preparing. To evaluate both primary and secondary research, you must ask the following questions:

- Is it valid?
- Is it reliable?
- Is it current?

validity
Extent to which a research study accurately measures what it was intended to measure

reliability
Extent to which data collected in a research study is consistent, stable, and free from systematic sources of error

VALIDITY AND RELIABILITY   One of your first tasks is to evaluate your data in order to find out how useful they will be to you. Research findings are typically evaluated on the bases of validity and reliability. **Validity** is the extent to which a research study accurately measures what it was intended to measure. For example, a study that relies on data from polygraph tests may not be valid because the accuracy of these tests is questionable.

Reliability means that the collected data are consistent and stable and free from systematic sources of error. Weighing shipments of goods on a bathroom-type spring scale, for example, is unreliable if the weights vary according to the positioning of the shipment on the scale.

A continuing concern of writers who rely on published sources of data is that reported findings may no longer be accurate by the time they are gathered for use in a subsequent document. What, for example, could you do with the data derived from a ten-year-old economic analysis of Central Florida? Because of the major changes that have occurred in the Orlando area as a result of the growth of such international tourist attractions as Disney World, Epcot Center, and Universal Studios, the data would be virtually useless. In short, data sources should be as current as possible. If the data that you need have not been recently collected and published, be prepared to invest the time and money required to collect data that you can use.

Evaluating Data

Do not be surprised when your reward for a successful research project turns out to be stacks of undigested data. Turning these data into usable information is one of the most important steps in the writing process—one that requires organization and interpretation.

ORGANIZING DATA   Evaluation depends on organizing data so that relationships, trends, and recurring themes become clear. Organization begins when you group materials according to the topics in your preliminary outline. For example, if you are writing a report analyzing union contracts in the auto industry, you may decide to group research findings by domestic auto makers (General Motors, Ford, and Chrysler) on the one hand and imports such as Volvo, Mitsubishi, Saab, and Hyundai on the other. Next, you may choose to divide your list of contracts further by specific contract provisions—say, wages, pension funds, health insurance, and other employee benefits. When note cards are used in the research process, they can be separated according to various subject files. When a computer is used and your document is quite long, separate computer files can be used to organize data by subjects.

Many sources, both primary and secondary, include **statistics**—information presented in numerical form that helps researchers describe findings in an objective, uniform way. In their simplest form, statistics are nothing more than individual numbers with little meaning. However, when they are analyzed to discover such representative relationships as *central tendencies* and *correlations*, they become important research instruments.

MEASURES OF CENTRAL TENDENCY   Statistical researchers use standard *measures* to represent an entire group of data. For example, a study of 200 people might be used to represent an entire group of 10,000. One useful method for summarizing a large number of observations is the **measure of central tendency**. This measure produces a single representative score that can be viewed as the *typical* score for the group, event, or object being studied. Central tendency can be calculated with three different measures: the *mean*, the *median*, and the *mode*.

The **arithmetic mean** (or **average**) is the sum of all the numbers in a group divided by the number of items in that group. The **median** is the midpoint in a group of numbers that are arranged in numerical order. The **mode** is the number in the group that occurs most frequently.

Each of these measures has its limitations. Although the mean is the most commonly used measure of central tendency, it is subject to distortions when extremely low or high numbers appear. For example, consider the data shown in Table 10.3. Six of seven businesses in Columbus, Ohio, have approximately the same number of employees on their payrolls (37 to 40). However, one huge company has a payroll of 1,000 employees. Thus, when the mean number of employees for *all* seven firms is calculated, the large employer distorts the average. As you can also see, however, calculations of the median and the mode provide much more useful approximations of the *typical* number of employees in these seven companies.

As in Table 10.3, the median is often used to represent statistics when the presence of one or more atypical numbers would distort "average" figures if the mean were utilized. "Average" income figures, for example, would be distorted by the presence of a few millionaires. The mode, meanwhile, might be useful to a travel agency in planning package-vacation tours for the upcoming season. By knowing last year's most popular vacation area—the location that appears most frequently in its records—the firm should be better able to meet the demands of its clients.

CORRELATION ANALYSIS   While the mean, median, and mode are useful in summarizing data, the report writer also needs methods for determining *variables* in order to predict such events as sales. For example, what is the relationship between sales and television advertising? Will relocation to a shopping cen-

statistics
Numerical data gathered and presented to help describe research findings in an objective, uniform way

measure of central tendency
Method for producing a single representative score that can be viewed as a typical score for a group, object, or event under study

arithmetic mean
(or **average**)
Measure of central tendency calculated by adding the sum of all researched observations and dividing by the number of observations

median
Midpoint score in the distribution of quantified observations arranged in numerical order

mode
Most frequently occurring number in a series of quantified observations

---

TABLE 10.3	*Calculating Measures of Central Tendency*

NUMBER OF EMPLOYEES IN SEVEN COLUMBUS, OHIO, COMPANIES

COMPANY	NUMBER OF EMPLOYEES
1	40
2	39
3	37
4	36
5	1000
6	38
7	40
Total	1230

Mean = 75.7 employees
Median = 39 employees
Mode = 40 employees

ter result in more customer traffic than a freestanding store? Will contracting out maintenance, repair, and custodial services to specialized providers adversely affect the morale of company employees?

correlation analysis
Statistical technique used to measure the positive, negative, or nonexistent relationship between two or more variables

Answers to important questions like these may be found by using a technique called **correlation analysis**—a statistical technique used to measure the relationship between two or more variables. For example, if a firm finds that sales increase when television advertising is increased, this correspondence would indicate positive correlation. On the other hand, research by a cable-television company might find that people who regularly attend movies are less likely to be cable TV subscribers than those who only rarely go to movies. The correlation between these two variables would be negative. Other studies may indicate zero, or no, correlation between such variables as standardized IQ scores and an individual's height.

Figure 10.6 illustrates the different types of correlation. Is this correlation between the age of your car and its value positive or negative? How about the correlation between your carrot consumption and your night vision.

Although correlations express relationships, they do not necessarily express *cause and effect*. Indeed, because additional factors may also be involved, it is dangerous to draw cause-and-effect conclusions from mere correlations. For example, concluding that your company's sales increased *as a result of* increased advertising may ignore the role of several other factors—say, a new national sales manager, an improved product, or the bankruptcy of a major competitor.

There is a profound difference between information and meaning.
Warren G. Bennis
American educator

INTERPRETING DATA   Once you begin to interpret your data, your focus moves from organizing to analyzing. Still using your document's specific purpose as your compass, you must now evaluate all of your data in terms of your premise. Do your data support your premise? Do they provide strong support or moderate support? Should you modify your premise?

As you analyze your collected data, try to identify logical patterns or draw logical conclusions that will help to structure your report or proposal. Because they will be the basis of your outline, you should consider the virtues and drawbacks of these patterns as you proceed during the research stage. Finally, remember that your data will have an extremely important influence on the specific conclusions and recommendations that you will make. **Conclusions** are the logical results of the evidence presented in your report or proposal. **Recommendations** are specific actions that you suggest when you have interpreted the information compiled in your document.

conclusions
Logical results of evidence presented in a report or proposal

recommendations
Specific actions suggested as a result of conclusions presented in a report or proposal

Determining Positive, Negative, or Zero Correlation			
	CORRELATION		
EXAMPLE	(+) POSITIVE	(-) NEGATIVE	(0) ZERO
1. Age of automobile and its value	☐	☐	☐
2. Unemployment levels and new home sales	☐	☐	☐
3. Carrot consumption and quality of night vision	☐	☐	☐
4. Percentage of body fat and likelihood of finishing among the first ten runners in the Boston Marathon	☐	☐	☐
5. Years of formal education and annual income	☐	☐	☐
6. Amount of smoking and incidence of lung cancer	☐	☐	☐

ANSWERS: 1. negative 2. negative 3. zero 4. negative 5. positive 6. positive

FIGURE 10.6   *Correlation Sampler*

Developing a Search Strategy

Knowing how to locate needed data is as important as knowing what data you need. Success in securing data results from developing a **search strategy**—a systematic method for locating research sources. The most effective search strategies move from general to specific sources in a step-by-step fashion.

As you can see in Figure 10.7, one model of the search strategy starts when you state your specific purpose in the form of a problem; it includes both primary and secondary sources of data. **Primary data** are collected specifically for use in preparing the report or proposal. Interviews, surveys, and observations can be used to obtain primary data. By contrast, **secondary data** have been previously published in company, trade-association, and industry publications; government reports; and books and articles in newspapers, magazines, and journals. Secondary information has already been analyzed, evaluated, and organized into an accessible form. Whether primary or secondary, data can be obtained from sources within your organization or from outside sources.

Internal and External Sources of Information

Internal data are generated within your organization. Various company records can be used to generate invaluable data for your report or proposal. These data may range from sales reports, consultants' evaluations, and wage and salary reviews to analyses of potential markets, performance appraisals, and information contained in correspondence files. Information on quality levels of materials purchased and the rejection rate of products produced by the firm can be supplied by the quality-control department. Even customer-complaint letters can serve as information input.

A tremendous amount of useful information is also available from accounting records. Here data can be obtained on changes in accounts receivables; cash on hand; comparisons of sales by territory, customer, product line, or salesperson; inventory levels; outstanding loans; and profitability of particular divisions or product lines. Because this type of data is collected on a regular basis, it can be secured quickly and at very low cost.

Securing the internal documents that you need typically requires the coop-

Information may be accumulated in files, but it must be retrieved to be of use in decision making.

Kenneth J. Arrow
American economist

search strategy
Systematic method for locating research sources

primary data
Data collected specifically for use in preparing a report or proposal

secondary data
Data that has been previously analyzed, evaluated, organized, and published

internal data
Data generated within an organization

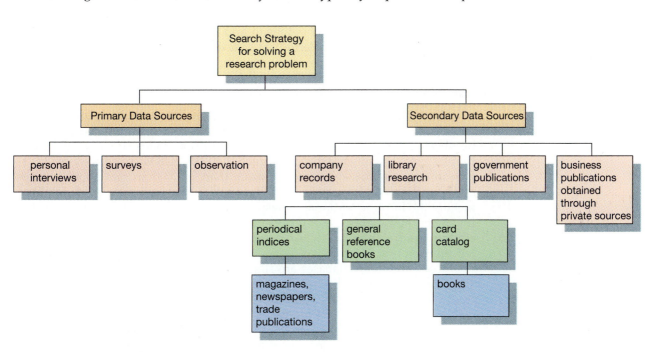

FIGURE 10.7   *Search Strategy*

eration of co-workers in charge of their preparation. In most cases, simply explaining your writing purpose will be sufficient to obtain needed materials.

Much of the information needed for complex reports and proposals will come from **external data**. These represent data generated outside the firm and will be of two types: *primary* or *secondary*. As a rule, researchers seek out secondary data before committing the time and money necessary to collect primary data.

external data
Data, primary or secondary, generated by sources outside an organization

Collecting External Secondary Data

Although you can find much secondary data inside your organization, even more is available from external sources. In fact, so much data are available at little or no cost that business writers must be able to locate precisely what they need without being overwhelmed.

Four major sources of secondary data exist: *libraries, government publications, private business sources,* and *online databases.*

CONDUCTING LIBRARY RESEARCH   Libraries are not only for college students and the general public; they are also used by business writers searching for historical, financial, or other statistical data. Even in major cities served by public libraries with extensive collections, many large companies and organizations maintain their own in-house libraries to serve the research needs of employees at their own and related companies. For example, the American Council of Life Insurance library in Washington, DC, contains materials that are either directly or indirectly related to the life-insurance industry. Knowing how to use library facilities is vital to the success of any major research project.

With the mammoth number of resources available at most libraries, you should conduct your library research systematically, moving from general to more specific sources. To get an overview of your research assignment, it is helpful to consult general reference books like encyclopedias, almanacs, and fact books. For example, almanacs like *The World Almanac and Book of Facts* and yearbooks like the *United Nations Statistical Yearbook* compile data on events that occurred during the past year. The researcher should next turn to more specialized reference books, such as directories of companies in a particular industry or associations and organizations in a specific area. Specialized reference sources are available in most major fields.

Because business reports must often deal with current information, many researchers turn to *periodical indexes* to find relevant magazine, newspaper, and trade-publication articles. Periodical indexes are found in the form of bound books and, increasingly, in computerized databases. Bound-book indexes include the *Readers' Guide to Periodical Literature*, the *Business Periodicals Index*, and *The Wall Street Journal Index*.

USING A COMPUTERIZED DATABASE   Each item in a computer database includes the article title, authors, journal information (volume, date, and page numbers), key terms and concepts, classification codes (for dividing broad topical areas), and an article abstract. ABI/INFORM, produced by H. W. Wilson Co., contains references to more than 200,000 articles about business and management from nearly 700 journals. Other computerized databases include the Infotrac National Newspapers Index, which contains references to five major newspapers, and the Applied Sciences & Technology Index, which contains more than 200,000 references to technical journal articles from 335 publications.

Computerized databases are stored on laser disks known as *CD-ROM*, an acronym for *compact disc read only memory*. These databases actually allow researchers to read and print information on the disk itself without changing the disk in any way. CD-ROM increasingly is changing the nature of research for current periodicals and is also being used to transform books into electronic form. Sony, for example, produces a single compact disk that can store up to 250,000 pages of text.[8]

USING A LIBRARY CARD CATALOG   Technology has advanced far beyond the days of actual library card catalogs. Originally, a library's complete inventory was printed on cards filed alphabetically in drawers in large cabinets. Today, most libraries have converted their card catalogs to computerized systems that save space and provide quick accessibility to information from various locations. However, the organization of the information remains the same. Library card catalogs are generally divided into three categories: authors' names, book titles, and subjects. Entries are listed alphabetically in each category.

Despite the introduction of time-saving computerized systems, so much information is becoming accessible and library research is becoming so complex that many cost-conscious firms are assigning research tasks to nonprofit libraries that charge on a per-use basis. For many people and businesses, such services save valuable time and money. For example, Archer Daniels Midland Co. of Decatur, Illinois, uses the research services of the University of Illinois. Consultant Mark Finegan of Nobelsville, Indiana, uses professional library research to uncover information on client projects. For instance, Finegan recently paid $200 for librarians to compile a list of all the state's private golf courses.[9]

CONSULTING GOVERNMENT PUBLICATIONS   The federal government is one of the richest sources of business and economic information. Perhaps the most important information source is the Census of the Population, conducted every ten years by the U.S. Department of Commerce. The most current census is available both in bound volumes and on computers in most libraries. Other Department of Commerce publications record industry information on agriculture, housing, and minerals.

The *Statistical Abstract of the United States* is published annually and includes various public and private statistical data on such topics as politics, economics, industry, and science. This 1,400-page book costs $20 and may be purchased from the Superintendent of Documents, U.S. Government Printing Office, Washington, DC 20502. Among the thousands of statistics included in the *Abstract*, you could uncover items like the following:

- Fifty-nine percent of U.S. households have cable television; seventy-two percent own at least one VCR.
- The price of a 1-megabit DRAM computer chip fell from $162.50 in 1985 to $6.33 in 1990.
- The three leading metropolitan areas in retail sales per household are St. Cloud, Minnesota, $36,640; Portland, Maine, $32,650; and Honolulu, Hawaii, $32,340; the national average is $19,488.
- There are 763,000 mobile homes among the housing units in Florida, the most for any state.[10]

Other useful government publications include the *County and City Data Book*, which provides information every three years on counties and cities with more than 25,000 residents. Information on general business indicators, domestic trade, finance, and transportation is updated monthly in the *Survey of Current Business*. While these and many other publications are compiled by the U.S. government, state and local governments also publish information on such business-related areas as real estate, home building, retailing, and manufacturing.

OBTAINING INFORMATION FROM PRIVATE SOURCES   Business researchers can also turn to private information sources. For example, one invaluable source for marketers is *Sales & Marketing Management*'s annual "Survey of Buying Power," which calculates the buying power found in specific counties, cities, and states. Among other information, the extensive amount of quickly accessible data available from this source includes the most recent data available on population characteristics, household buying income, and retail sales in cities and counties across the country. In addition, trade associations like the American Petroleum Institute and the American Hotel and Motel Association provide a variety of printed materials on industry-related topics.

INTERVIEW

Marydee Ojala, Information Consultant for Business and Industry

When Marydee Ojala talks, businesspeople listen. They listen because she brings relevant, timely, and accurate business and financial information gleaned from online databases. Ojala's company in Park City, Utah, specializes in using online-database technology to ferret out vital facts for reports, proposals, and other business purposes. We asked Ojala about the nature of online research and how it will evolve in the years ahead.

Question: How do online databases benefit researchers?

Answer: You can retrieve information much faster in an electronic environment than you can by scanning print indexes or looking through copies of old publications. Online databases also give you everything you need in one place. If you conduct manual research with printed indexes, you have to search through a number of years of an index for a complete picture. An electronic search lets you search all the years at the same time. Finally, online research is cost-effective. You have access to an incredible amount of information without having to subscribe to different indexes or publications. This means that you don't have to pay for every single printed source of potential information. You can focus on the information you need without having to buy it up front.

Question: How do researchers gain access to online databases?

Answer: Many large companies have information centers that conduct the search. For example, if you're doing research for a report, you start by calling in the information request. A specialist then chooses the databases, conducts the search, and may even write an executive summary of what he or she found. In other companies, researchers log onto the system with a special password and conduct the online search themselves.

---

online database
Computerized information retrieval system operated by commercial suppliers and made available to business users for a service fee

Telecommunications enables companies to move information rather than people.

Erik K. Clemons
American Educator

USING ONLINE DATABASES   A true revolution in data retrieval is found in **online databases**—computerized information-retrieval systems operated by commercial companies and made available to business users for service fees. Online databases include complete articles and books, not just citations. Among the major business-related online databases are the Dow Jones News/Retrieval, Nexis, and Dialog.[11]

To establish a telecommunications link between a personal computer and the online database, a modem is used, which allows information to be sent across telephone lines. Special telecommunications software is installed to control the modem. Various factors affect the cost of an online search, including the length of the search, the time of day the search is conducted, the speed of the modem, and the fee charged by the company providing the online service. Advances in technology have produced faster modems, decreasing the overall time per search by about 50 percent in the past two decades. However, an explosion in the number and size of databases has kept search costs high. Today, nearly 7,700 databases, operated by a thousand different vendors worldwide, contain 4.6 billion records. In total, some 34.5 million searches are conducted every year.[12]

Collecting Primary Data

The wise business writer exhausts all possible sources of secondary data before deciding to invest the time and money required to conduct primary research. There will be times, however, when the data you need are not available from secondary sources. In some instances, available data may be obsolete. In other cases, the needed classifications of data may not be available. Because the secondary data were originally collected for a specific purpose, they may not exist in a form that is suitable for your particular report or pro-

Still other companies use a tape-lease system in which they buy one or two databases directly and make them available on a local area computer network. Although the tape-lease system makes information more accessible (there are no charges for the online search), you generally can't get the breadth of information available from an online service like Dialog, which accesses over 400 databases.

Question: What trends do you see in the online-database industry?

Answer: I see easier access and pricing changes. In the opinion of many people, the current pricing system doesn't work. Online information is generally priced by the amount of search time plus a fee for the information you pull out of the computer. This system was developed over 25 years ago, and it's not optimal. But no one has found a better way yet. They're still looking. The online industry believes that people need information, but it operates in an environment in which people are reluctant to pay for information because it's supposed to be free. What people don't realize is that even free public libraries are supported by tax dollars.

Question: As we move into the twenty-first century, how important will online-search skills be?

Answer: They will be critical. People who have been in the online industry can tell you horror stories about business failures that were the direct results of poor research. For example, a Kansas City firm named a new product without bothering to check if the name belonged to anyone else. It turned out to be another company's trademark. The most elementary online search would have revealed the problem.

The bottom line is that in business you have to do your homework with solid research. If there are gaps, you may not keep your job very long.

Source: Interview with Marydee Ojala.

posal. In each of these cases, you may have to collect primary data to secure the information you need.

As we saw earlier, primary data consist of data collected for the first time for use in solving a particular business problem. Most primary data are collected by one of two methods: *observation* or *surveys*.

OBSERVATION METHOD   **Observational studies** are conducted by actually viewing—either by visual observation or through mechanical devices—the actions of a respondent. For example, a researcher seeking information about the use of the company cafeteria may observe such things as the number of people eating there, the types of meal combinations selected by different groups, and the number of people who take their food back to their offices. Quality-control departments often use the observation method in checking for defective products. Traffic counts may be used to determine the best location for a new fast-food restaurant. Television ratings are usually measured by the Nielsen Audimeter, which, when attached to a television set, records the times when the set is turned on and the channel being viewed.

> **observational study**
> Method of collecting primary data by actually viewing the actions of respondents

Skillful researchers begin the observation process with a clear idea of what they want to learn. For example, the researcher evaluating the company cafeteria may use a checklist containing the following questions:

- What kinds of foods are people eating? Do the choices appear to vary by age, sex, or departments in which the people work?
- How much of the cafeteria traffic represents repeat business? Do the frequent users of the cafeteria appear to be similar in age? Are they more likely to be men or women?
- Do the same people come back several times a day?
- Are people eating in the cafeteria or returning with their food to their offices?

surveys
Method of collecting primary data in which respondents' knowledge, attitudes, and opinions are assessed through interviews and questionnaires

sample
Group selected as representative of a larger, statiscally significant group

random sample (or probablility sample)
Sample chosen so that each member of a population has an equal chance of being selected

SURVEY METHOD   When primary data cannot be obtained by an observer, either human or mechanical, the researcher must ask questions. For example, when information is needed about *attitudes* or *opinions*, the survey method can be used. **Surveys** are primary data-collection methods used to gather data about the knowledge, attitudes, and opinions of respondents.

It is interesting to note that although surveys are common in North America, Western Europe, and Japan, they are a new phenomenon in countries like Hungary, Poland, and the newly formed republics of the former Soviet Union. In an attempt to learn more about 350 million Eastern bloc consumers, many Western businesses, including Gillette and Eastman Kodak, are currently using surveys to research consumer tastes in this huge new market.

SAMPLING   Survey information is rarely gathered from every possible source. Instead, the researcher selects a representative group called a **sample**. For example, instead of trying to gauge customer satisfaction by questioning every Volvo owner in the United States, marketers at Volvo may decide to contact a representative sample of 3,000 Volvo purchasers.

If the sample is chosen so that every member of the relevant population has an equal chance of being selected, it is called a **random sample** (or **probability sample**). For example, a quality-control check of every fiftieth unit on an assembly line may give production-control engineers a representative sample of the overall quality of the work done on the line. Similarly, a random selection of student names from the campus directory should provide a probability sample of students at your college. Three types of surveys exist: telephone surveys, mail surveys, and surveys obtained through personal interviews.

TELEPHONE SURVEYS   When researchers want to gather information quickly and inexpensively, they turn to the telephone. In fact, more than half of all primary marketing research in the United States is conducted by phone. New technologies, such as Computer Assisted Telephone Interviewing (CATI), are improving the speed and efficiency of telephone interviewing. Using CATI, interviewers read questions from a computer screen. After each answer is recorded, the next question automatically appears. While this is going on, computer tabulations are being made. The system is so fast that 1,000 interviews can be conducted in a single day and the data interpreted in a matter of hours.[13]

Despite the popularity of telephone interviewing, however, it has several important limitations. Subjects contacted by phone are generally reluctant to reveal personal information like income level and marital status. In addition, because questionnaires must be short and simple, the amount of obtainable information from telephone interviews is limited. Because visual contact is impossible, questions that rely on objects, pictures, or product demonstrations cannot be asked. Finally, researchers looking for a representative sample of an entire population may find themselves stymied by the omission of households without phones or with unpublished numbers. Unpublished phone numbers now equal more than a quarter of all phones nationwide and more than half the phones in Los Angeles.[14]

MAIL SURVEYS   Mail surveys allow researchers to conduct national studies at reasonable costs. They also offer several other advantages for the researcher. Because results are anonymous, respondents may be more willing to answer personal and economic questions. Mail surveys also give respondents some flexibility. They can answer questionnaires at convenient times rather than at times chosen by telephone interviewers.

Despite these advantages, mail surveys may be flawed because of differences in the characteristics of those who respond and those who do not. Depending on the respondents' interest in the subject and the skill of the person who prepares the questionnaire and cover letter, response rates for mail surveys are usually between 10 percent and 50 percent. For example, people generally respond to mail surveys when they feel strongly about an issue—either positively or negatively. Often, these people do not constitute a representative sample of the entire group. To minimize discrepancies, researchers sometimes mail respondents a second questionnaire to secure additional responses. Mail surveys are most often used in marketing research but can also be used for other research projects, such as anonymous employee-attitude surveys.

PERSONAL INTERVIEWING   The personal interview is the most expensive and most time-consuming survey method. It depends on trained interviewers who must travel to meet with respondents. But it is also a highly effective means of obtaining detailed information. Interviewing encourages the development of a personal relationship between interviewer and respondents and allows the interviewer to explain confusing or difficult questions. Combined with the obtainability of detailed information, the flexibility of this method often more than offsets time and cost limitations.

Once the firm has decided to collect primary data through observation or surveys, it has the option of collecting data through its own in-house research department or contracting the research assignment to specialized business-research organizations. The latter is an appropriate choice when specialized know-how is required, special equipment is used, or objectivity is crucial. For example, even though auto makers have large marketing-research departments, they still use independent research firms like J. D. Power and Associates to conduct new-car buyer-satisfaction surveys.

As one would expect, problems arise in efforts to interpret the responses to all kinds of surveys conducted in foreign countries. Susan Hooper, Eastern Europe marketing director for Pepsi Cola International, knew something was wrong when she looked at the results of a survey showing that drugstores sold soft drinks in Hungary. "Drugstores don't exist" in Hungary, explains Hooper. "The information was forced into a structure" developed in the West.[15]

QUESTIONNAIRE DESIGN   **Questionnaires** are scientifically designed lists of questions used to gather data. Well-developed questionnaires are essential tools in the research process. Whether your data are obtained through telephone, mail, or personal-interview surveys, the questionnaire itself will play a major role in the quality and quantity of information that you collect. If the questionnaire is too long, incomplete, or confusing, respondents may be unwilling to spend time trying to decipher its meaning.

questionnaire
Scientifically designed list of questions used to gather primary data

The following guidelines should be kept in mind when designing a questionnaire. First, every question should be linked to your research objective; questions unrelated to your topic should be eliminated. Second, because it will be necessary to tabulate the responses, questions should be designed with this need in mind. Although essay questions may yield interesting results, reading and then categorizing 400 essay-type answers is far more difficult than tabulating the results of 400 multiple-choice questions.

Finally, the questionnaire should be user-friendly to both interviewer and respondents. Anything less is self-defeating. A user-friendly questionnaire begins by explaining the purpose of the study and describing the prospective respondents. This twofold task can be accomplished in a cover letter or in a brief introduction. Generally, cover letters are used when surveys are sent outside the company, while explanatory statements are reserved for internal distribution. Your explanation should include a deadline for returning the questionnaire and should express appreciation for the respondent's cooperation.

Survey questions can be categorized as *opening* and *substantive questions*. As you write specific questions, focus on the time that it will take to answer the entire questionnaire. The greatest number of survey responses are obtained when respondents can complete the task in no more than five to ten minutes.

OPENING QUESTIONS   The typical questionnaire begins with questions that are not difficult or overly personal. They are designed to stimulate the interest of the respondent to continue the interview. For example, demographic questions that focus on such personal factors as marital status, income level, and educational background are typically asked at the end of the interview. If these questions are asked at the beginning of the interview, the respondent may refuse to answer them, and the interview may be terminated. When they are asked at the end of the interview, most of the important questions will have already been answered.

SUBSTANTIVE QUESTIONS   Substantive questions can be divided into three basic types: *fixed-alternative, scale,* and *open-ended questions.* While fixed-alternative and scale questions are answered with check marks or numbers, open-ended questions allow respondents to say whatever is on their mind.

Fixed-alternative questions limit responses to one or more choices from a list of possible responses. Multiple-choice questions fall into this category, as do questions that ask for a simple yes or no response. Questions can also be in list form so that respondents can choose from or rank items according to certain criteria such as preference or use. These questions yield standardized responses and are easy to tabulate. However, they force people to choose among the responses listed and do not indicate the intensity of a response.

Scale questions are a specialized type of fixed-alternative question that structure responses along a continuum. In the Likert Scale, for example, respondents are asked to respond along a continuum like the following:

Strongly Disagree	Disagree	No Opinion	Agree	Strongly Agree
-2	-1	0	+1	+2

Other scales ask respondents to rate answers on a scale of 1 to 5, 1 being the least important and 5 the most important.

Open-ended questions allow respondents to formulate their own answers. Table 10.4 includes examples of the various types of questions used in survey questionnaires.

CONDUCTING INTERVIEWS   Because of the high cost and the amount of time involved, one of the most important steps in the interviewing process is deciding whom to interview. The answer is usually straightforward: The person most likely to provide information is the person to interview. For example, if you are writing about the need for a more sophisticated office-security system, a likely interview subject is the company's director of security. If, on the other hand, you are writing about the design of the security system, the best candidate is probably a design engineer.

After choosing a subject, you can formally request an interview by telephone or letter. In your initial contact, explain who you are, the topic of the interview, the projected use to which the information will be put, and the specific type of information you need. After setting a time and place for the interview, prepare a list of questions that you want to ask. However, do not limit yourself to these questions. Think of them as the foundation for your questioning, not the entire structure. Depending upon the responses, you may find it necessary to inquire further about a particular subject or issue.

STAGES OF AN INTERVIEW   At the start of the interview, repeat what you hope to accomplish and ask a question that focuses on your most important point. Then listen as the subject starts talking. Except for questions, minimize your interruptions. Keep in mind that you are not there to impress anyone with how much you know, but to learn from an expert. As you listen, you will find that certain answers prompt additional questions. Inevitably, however, you will also find that the subject has moved off the track. When this happens, ask specific, direct questions that refocus the interview.

In general, make each question short and to the point. If you need any help—for example, understanding unfamiliar concepts or properly spelling a name—ask for clarification. At the close of the interview, review your list of

TABLE 10.4	*Types of Survey Questions*

MULTIPLE CHOICE QUESTIONS	Fixed alternative questions that allow the repondent to choose one or more answers
	Example: what health insurance options does your company offer? (Check all that apply.)
	❑ traditional reimbursement plan ❑ health maintenance organization ❑ preferred provider organization ❑ other _____
YES/NO QUESTIONS	Fixed alternative questions that allow the respondents a choice between two answers
	Example: Do you use a personal computer in your daily work?
	❑ yes ❑ no
LIST QUESTIONS	Fixed alternative questions that allow the respondent to choose among a list of answers
	Example: Which of the following have you attended in the last year? (Check all that apply.)
	❑ motion picture ❑ play ❑ concert ❑ ballet ❑ opera ❑ lecture
RANKED-LIST QUESTIONS	Fixed-alternative questions that ask the respondents to rank a list of answers
	Example: Rank the following items in order of national importance, 1 representingt the most important and 5 the least important.
	❑ education ❑ foreign affairs ❑ employment ❑ inflation ❑ poverty
SCALE QUESTIONS	Fixed alternative questions that allow the respondents to scale each answer along a continuum
	Example: After using Heven's Air Freshener in your home for a few days, please complete each statement below, indicating whether you agree, have no opinion, or disagree.

	AGREE	NO OPINION	DISAGREE
1. Heven's Air Freshener eliminates odors.	❑	❑	❑
2. I like not having an air freshener fragrance in the air.	❑	❑	❑
3. I like the hideaway dispenser.	❑	❑	❑
4. The suggested retail price of $1.29 is reasonable.	❑	❑	❑

OPEN-ENDED QUESTIONS	Allow respondents to express opinions in their own words
	Example: What changes would you like to make in the advertising and promotion of political candidates? Explain your reasons.
DEMOGRAPHIC QUESTIONS	Focus on factors such as the respondent's age, marital status, race, occupation, income, religion, political party, or educational background.
	Example: What is your annual income?
	❑ $10,000–$24,999
	❑ $25,000–$49,999
	❑ $50,000–$74,999
	❑ $75,000 and over

questions for any that have not been covered. You may also want to ask for leads to other experts in related fields. Finally, ask the interviewee for written materials on the subject that might help you in your work. Because follow-up interviews may be difficult or impossible to arrange, it is important to take accurate and complete notes or use a tape recorder to gather information.

TYPES OF INTERVIEW QUESTIONS   Every interview question should be tied to a specific informational goal and asked in such a way as to yield the most and best results. Questions that are too long or too complex are frequently difficult to answer because they usually involve more than one subject, explanation, or point of view. Remember that the wording of a question directly affects the usefulness of the answer and should be an overriding concern when preparing interview questions. Interview questions can be either open-ended or closed-ended.

Whereas *closed-ended questions* limit responses to a specific discussion, *open-ended questions* give the interview subject flexibility to respond in different ways. For example, "What do you think of the new union contract?" is an open-ended question, while "What measures are being taken to improve productivity under the new union contract?" is closed-ended. In addition, open-ended questions that begin with *how* or *why* invite respondents to explain the reasons for their answers. They are intended to produce anecdotes, examples, and in-depth answers.

By contrast, closed-ended questions encourage brief, specific answers. They should be used—not overused—to define the details of a story. However, if you are too direct, you may make subjects feel as if they are being interrogated. Closed-ended questions typically ask for specific information, add clarification, probe further into details, or offer a specific set of answers to choose from.

Closed-ended questions that ask for specific information are critical when you are trying to learn basic facts, figures, dates, times, or locations. Because it is difficult to avoid answering closed-ended questions, they reduce vagueness and ambiguity. In much the same way, questions that clarify the topic of discussion also avoid vague answers and misunderstandings. For example, often an interviewer will simply ask, "What do you mean by that?" Probing questions are another type of closed-ended questions that are designed to encourage greater depth in their responses. These questions are particularly useful when the person being interviewed doesn't provide the information you need.

Leading questions are designed to lead the interviewee to a single response. Careful wording, of course, is needed to prevent the interview from becoming biased or slanted. For example, consider the following question: "Were you as excited as everyone else with last month's sales figures and, specifically, Joe Hall's performance?" The phrase *as excited as everyone else* will probably lead the interviewee to agree with the interviewer and apparently everyone else.

Multiple-choice questions give the respondent a limited choice of answers. Opinions or explanations are eliminated in this type of questioning. For example, a human resource manager might be asked a multiple-choice question like "Which of the following do you believe is your company's most pressing employee-relations problem: sexual harassment, limited opportunities for promotions, or relatively low wages as compared with other firms in the state?"

Taking Effective Research Notes

Effective note taking is essential in any research project—especially if you are working with a variety of different sources. Taking good notes is important for several reasons. In addition to providing all the publication details necessary for use in the source notes that will appear at the end of your formal report, research notes provide a mechanism for organizing your information. In addition, carefully written source notes help prevent **plagiarism**—the act of using someone else's words or unique approach without crediting the source.

Writing each note on a separate index card provides flexibility. You can organize the cards in different ways as you build the outline of your report. Therefore, you might collect twenty different index cards from the same book, each card dealing with a different aspect of the topic.

plagiarism
Act of using someone else's words or unique approach without crediting the source

At the top of each card, write all the information that you will need in your footnotes or endnotes (the formatting of source notes is examined in Appendix I). Each card should include the name of the person interviewed or, in the case of secondary sources, the author's full name, the article title, the publication in which the article appeared, the date of publication, and the page numbers where the information is located. If you are using the same source more than once, only the title and page numbers need be written at the top of subsequent cards. Under this information, paraphrase, summarize, or quote the material taken from the source.

Many researchers write all the information they need on source cards and have little reason to look at the sources themselves as they write. Others use note cards in conjunction with copies of the actual sources. Copies can be either actual books and articles or photocopies of relevant pages. Using copies, of course, means that you do not need to write as much on each card—the sources themselves will provide all the vital information. This does not mean, however, that cards are unnecessary. Although annotations necessarily abbreviate blocks of information, they can be extremely helpful when you are constructing your outline. Thus, if you have a copy of the source, your source card need only contain minimal information—perhaps a thumbnail reference to a main point in your outline. When you are dealing with photocopies, you will find that underlining critical points and writing marginal notes helps you focus on the important parts without having to reread your entire source.

PROGRESS CHECK

1. Distinguish between primary and secondary data and name two examples of each.
2. Have you ever been contacted to participate in a telephone survey or mail survey? If so, were you willing to answer questions? How did you feel about the experience? Compare your reactions to the chapter's discussion of the advantages and disadvantages of these research methods.
3. Why is it important to take complete research notes?

WHAT'S AHEAD

More than any other business documents, reports and proposals rely on visual aids for clear and effective presentation. Chapter 11 examines the effective use of visual aids in reports and proposals, while Chapters 12 and 13 show how these tools are incorporated into short and long.

SUMMARY OF CHAPTER OBJECTIVES

1. **Identify the characteristics of business *reports* and *proposals*.**

   Business reports are compilations of organized information on specific topics. A report is provided to one or more people inside or outside an organization who will use it for a specific business purpose. Reports differ in length, formality, circulation, distribution, frequency of submission, format, use of visual aids, and method of assignment. Depending on what they are trying to accomplish, reports fall into six major categories:

information, survey, study, expert, status, and recommendation.

Proposals are documents that set forth ideas and plans for consideration in the hope that readers will accept them and agree to spend money on their development. The three types of proposals are internal, sales (or private-industry), and response proposals.

2. **List the seven steps in the report- and proposal-writing process.**

Because report and proposal writing is so complex, the preparation of these documents follows a multistage process. The process begins by defining the audience and purpose to be served by the document. Creating a working plan is the second step, followed by collecting and evaluating resources and data, developing a writing outline, writing the first draft, revising, and finalizing and submitting the document.

3. **Describe the characteristics of** *collaborative writing.*

Collaborative writing is the process of working together with one or more people to produce finished reports and proposals. Collaboration involves developing a strategy for researching and presenting your information. Crucial issues are examined, including content, purpose, audience, organization and development, and design. Collaborative planning also involves assigning specific areas of responsibility. During the writing phase, much of the work is accomplished independently. Progress reports and status worksheets are often used to check the progress of the various contributors. Schedules are critical, especially when writing long documents.

4. **List three questions that are used in evaluating** *primary* **and** *secondary research.*

With so much information available, it is important to evaluate the worth of every research source. The following questions guide this evaluation: Is the research valid? Is it reliable? Is it current?

5. **Explain how** *measures of central tendency* **and** *correlations* **are used to organize statistical data.**

The central tendency is a single, representative score that can be viewed as a group's typical score. The arithmetic mean, median, and mode all are measures of central tendency. Correlations are statistics that link one set of results with another set of results. Although correlations express relationships, they do not imply cause and effect.

6. **Identify the four major types of** *secondary business research.*

Libraries are used to conduct in-depth research on a variety of subjects. Moving from general to specific sources, research-ers may consult general library references like encyclopedias; periodical indexes to find relevant articles in magazines, newspapers, and trade publications; and the library card catalog for books. Government publications, including those published by the U.S. Census Bureau, are also invaluable information sources. Private information sources, including industry trade associations and specific publications, provide helpful data. Finally, online databases are computerized information-retrieval systems operated by private commercial organizations and made available for service fees.

7. **Explain how business researchers use** *online databases* **to secure needed information.**

Online databases, such as Dow Jones News/Retrieval, Nexis, and Dialog, are computerized information-retrieval systems operated by commercial companies and sold to computer users for service fees. These systems, which give researchers immediate access to thousands of sources, require the use of a personal computer, a modem, a phone line, and telecommunications software.

8. **Compare the two major sources of** *primary data research.*

The two major sources of primary research are direct observation and surveys. Observational studies involve the actual viewing of respondents, often through mechanical devices. For example, Nielsen television ratings are the result of observational studies. Surveys are conducted by telephone, by mail, and in face-to-face meetings (interviews). To be effective, survey questions must be carefully designed to elicit specific information. Among the types or questions asked on a survey are fixed-alternative questions, scale questions, and open-ended questions. Interviewing allows business writers to gather information from experts. Effective interviews involve understanding the interview stages and knowing how to formulate effective questions, including open-ended and closed-ended questions.

REVIEW AND DISCUSSION QUESTIONS

1. Describe the important characteristics of business reports and proposals. (*Ch. Obj. 1*)
2. What are the six major categories of business reports? (*Ch. Obj. 1*)
3. Identify the seven steps involved in the report- and proposal-writing process. (*Ch. Obj. 2*)
4. What is collaborative writing? Describe its benefits. (*Ch. Obj. 3*)
5. Explain the basic strategy for evaluating primary and secondary research. (*Ch. Obj. 4*)
6. How can we use measures of central tendency and correlation analysis to organize statistical information? (*Ch. Obj. 5*)
7. What are the four major sources of secondary business research? (*Ch. Obj. 6*)
8. Explain how an on-line database can be a valuable research tool. (*Ch. Obj. 7*)
9. Distinguish between the two major methods for collecting primary data. (*Ch. Obj. 8*)

APPLICATION EXERCISES

1. Test yourself on the differences between formal and informal reports. Cover the two right-hand columns in Table 10.1 and supply the information from memory. (*Ch. Obj. 1*)
2. Write a short, informal report about your business communication class. Address it to a fellow student who is interested in taking the class. Explain what the class covers and what you are learning from it. (*Ch. Obj. 1*)
3. Suppose your boss asks you to write an internal proposal in which your task is to persuade a higher-ranking person in the organization to allot money to a specific project or charity that you feel is important. The proposal could relate to your present job, a job that you have held in the past, or to your activities at school.

   First, research your topic. Use a variety of research sources; collect primary, secondary, internal, and external data. Try to use both the specific sources mentioned in this chapter and other sources as well. (A librarian might suggest additional possibilities.) Include measures of central tendency and correlation analysis if appropriate. Take notes on your research and keep track of the sources that you consult. (*Ch. Obj. 4, 5, 6, 8*)
4. Write the internal proposal that you researched in EXERCISE 4. Follow the chapter guidelines in evaluating your document for usefulness, organization, readability, and persuasiveness. (*Ch. Obj. 1, 2*)
5. Plan and research a sales proposal in which you try to sell a good or service. Your proposal might relate either to your present or former job or to a product or service that interests you. Use a variety of research sources involving primary, secondary, internal, and external data. Include measures of central tendency and correlation analysis if appropriate. Take notes on your research and keep track of the sources that you consult. (*Ch. Obj. 4, 5, 6, 8*)
6. Write the sales proposal that you researched in EXERCISE 5. Follow the chapter's guidelines in evaluating your document for usefulness, organization, readability, and persuasiveness. (*Ch. Obj. 1, 2*)
7. Using an online database such as Nexis or Dow Jones News/Retrieval Service, research one of the topics that you wrote about in EXERCISE 4 or 6. Consult a librarian for information on other databases that are available in your community. Write a brief report in which you compare your online research process with the earlier research. Did you find the online approach more efficient, less efficient, or about the same? What do you like or dislike about the online service? Does it affect your ability to do research and, if so, how? (*Ch. Obj. 7*)
8. Test yourself on the major categories of reports. How many types of reports are there, and what is the purpose of each? Give an example of each type. (*Ch. Obj. 1*)
9. Calculate the arithmetic mean, median, and mode for the following series of numbers: 247, 20, 21, 556, 20, 557, and 755. Summarize any limitations of these measures. (*Ch. Obj. 5*)
10. Suppose that your boss asks you to write a brief report summarizing the methods for collecting primary data. Write this report, and include discussions of the advantages and disadvantages of each method. (*Ch. Obj. 4, 8*)

11. Choose a topic about which you would like to learn more. Business-related possibilities include advertising/marketing strategies for a particular product or service, trends in computer software or hardware, and environmental issues confronting companies in a particular industry. Now choose someone with whom you could conduct a personal interview about that topic. For instance, you might interview a marketing manager about marketing strategies at his or her firm. After scheduling the interview, develop a list of questions that you might ask this individual. Include a good mix of open-ended and closed-ended questions. *(Ch. Obj. 8)*

12. Conduct the interview that you scheduled for EXERCISE 11. Follow the chapter guidelines for conducting an effective interview. Take careful notes or use a tape recorder. Ask your interviewee to suggest any additional research sources that you might consult for more information. Write a brief report (one page) summarizing the most important information that you gathered from your interview. *(Ch. Obj. 8)*

13. Choose a collaborative writing partner, and select a business-related topic on which you both agree to write a report. Work together to create a brief written work plan that defines your purpose and audience, summarizes your planned procedure for writing your report, and lists the research sources that you plan to use. Do the necessary research; you may wish to divide up the work by having each partner "specialize" in certain sources or topics. Be sure to take notes and to keep track of your sources. *(Ch. Obj. 2, 3, 8)*

14. Working with your partner, evaluate the data that you researched for EXERCISE 13. Write an outline that organizes the data that you collected into a form that you can use to create a report. *(Ch. Obj. 2, 3, 4, 5)*

15. Working with your partner, write a first draft based on the outline that you created for EXERCISE 14. Then revise the report to make sure that it is clear and convincing. Include footnotes as needed. *(Ch. Obj. 2, 3)*

*B*UILDING YOUR RESEARCH SKILLS

Your instructor will divide the class into small groups. Meet with your team members and choose a business-related topic on which you all agree to write. Compile a list of primary and secondary research sources, and assign several sources and aspects of the topic to each team member. Consult your particular sources, taking careful notes and keeping track of any footnotes.

*B*UILDING YOUR TEAMWORK SKILLS

Bring your notes from the previous exercise to class and meet with your team members to construct a report based on your group's research. The group may wish to develop a brief outline before writing its report. Assign one team member to write down a first draft as the group collaborates to develop the report. The group should then work together to revise this first draft into a final version.

*C*OMMUNICATING IN A WORLD OF DIVERSITY

Suppose that during your research, you encounter the following facts:

- In 1947, almost 75 percent of all first-generation Australians were born in Great Britain or Ireland. By 1989, only 33 percent of all first-generation Australians came from those countries.

- By the early 1990s, eight of the top ten source countries of new immigrants to Australia were located in Asia.

- At present, while only 4 percent of Australian citizens are of Asian origin, the government expects 25 percent of the population to be Asian-Australian within 50 years.

- Trade between Australia and Asia has grown steadily since the 1970s.

- Australian schools are introducing students to Asian cultures and languages at an earlier age. In the state of Victoria, for example, four of the eight "priority languages" taught in primary schools are Asian (Japanese, Mandarin, Indonesian, and Vietnamese). The Asia Education Foundation has begun a three-year program to introduce Asian themes into Australian curricula. "Two years ago," says Foundation manager Jenny McGregor, "the Australian community did not recognize that Australia was part of Asia, or that it lived anywhere near Asia. Our job is to change that utterly.... [The goal is] to make a future generation more prepared for managing the economic ties."

■ Exports to Asia are growing. Telecom, Australia's telephone company, has started a joint venture with the electronics firm AWA to install a new phone system in Vietnam. AWA's exports to Asia are responsible for a quarter of the firm's $172

million in sales revenue. Says AWA manager John Dougall: "Going back five years, we had almost zero exports.... We don't think of Australia and Asia anymore. We think of Jakarta just as we think about Perth.... We're here in Asia. We're in the same time zone, so if something goes wrong we can pick up the phone and ring them."

■ One Australian politician has proposed a plan that would link the fifteen separate nations of the Asia Pacific Economic Cooperation group into an integrated economic market.

Write a report in which you incorporate these facts. In what type of report would you probably incorporate these data? What would be a likely purpose for such a report? A likely audience?

Source: Susan Lawrence, "Reaching Out to Asia," *U.S. News & World Report*, March 1, 1993, pp. 57–49.

CASE 10.1

Responding to the Environment at Shaw Industries

Suppose that you want to write a report for your boss that illustrates how important it is for a company to stay flexible and respond to changes in its markets. You decide that your report will be more effective if you include an example of a firm that profited by following your projected advice. You thus conduct some research, which yields the following data about Shaw Industries, a carpet maker based in Georgia:

■ In 1980, Shaw Industries had less than 5 percent of U.S. market share in carpets. Today, it produces one-third of all carpeting sold in the United States and controls 42 percent of the residential market.

■ Ten years ago, Robert E. Shaw, director of Shaw Industries, faced a wrenching change in the industry. Carpets were turning into a

commodity product. Customers were starting to buy them according to price rather than brand. "For years," says Michael Berns, head of E.T.C. Carpet Mills, "the business fought being treated as a commodity. Bob Shaw gave in and started acting on the fact that things were changing."

■ Shaw introduced changes to cut costs. These changes included installing a communications system that allowed Shaw Industries to bypass wholesalers and take orders directly from 37,000 retailers; making carpet yarn from inexpensive nylon filament rather than more expensive wool; negotiating lower prices from suppliers for fiber and backing materials.

■ Another change was to invest in new equipment. Shaw estimates that his firm now invests as much in capital equipment as the rest of the carpeting industry combined. Tufting, for example, is the important process of sewing long loops of fiber onto backing material to create a thick pile, and new equipment at Shaw includes machines that can tuft 20,000 yards of carpet a day—several times more than many competing companies can produce.

■ One industry analyst estimates that Shaw Industries pays 10 percent less for supplies than its competitors do.

■ Increasing competition among carpet makers has forced many carpet makers out of business. Today, for example, there are 170 carpet mills—compared with 370 ten years ago.

■ Ironically, this increased competition may bring the carpet industry full-circle, making it a brand-name business once again. As it becomes dominated by just a few companies, these firms will probably begin advertising their respective strengths to consumers. Robert Shaw is convinced that "down the road, brand recognition will be important."

Questions and Applications

Write a report in which you discuss the importance of responding to changes in the marketplace.

Source: Brian O'Reilly, "Know When to Embrace Change," *Fortune*, February 22, 1993, p. 90.

CASE 10.2

Inc. *Magazine Polls Readers for Some Faxes*

Inc. magazine, which targets owners of small businesses, runs a regular feature called "FaxPoll." Each month, the magazine's staff selects a different business-related issue and develops a questionnaire that respondents can fax or mail back to the magazine's offices. Results are tabulated and printed in later issues.

The *Inc.* FaxPoll is reproduced on the next page. Readers were asked whether business is obligated to "give something back" to society.

Questions and Applications

1. Analyze the effectiveness of this questionnaire. Does it follow the chapter guidelines for effective questionnaire design? Is it user-friendly? Can you find examples of the three basic types of substantive questions (fixed-alternative, scale, and open-ended)?

2. Faxing is an increasingly popular way to send out and return questionnaires. For the editors of *Inc.*, what do you think are the advantages and limitations of this data-collection method?

Source: "The *Inc.* FaxPoll: Is Social Responsibility a Crock?" *Inc.*, February 1993, p. 15. Reprinted with permission, *Inc.* magazine. Copyright © 1993 by Goldhirsh Group, Inc., 38 Commercial Wharf, Boston, MA 02110.

IS SOCIAL RESPONSIBILITY A CROCK?

Business owners these days talk a lot about "giving something back," about being socially responsible. What exactly does that mean to you? Do you think you have a corporate obligation to society beyond being successful, generating jobs, paying taxes, and obeying the law?

1. WHAT IS YOUR REACTION TO THE IDEA THAT, BEYOND BEING SUCCESSFUL AS BUSINESSES, "GOOD" COMPANIES HAVE AN OBLIGATION TO "GIVE BACK TO SOCIETY"?

☐ I agree. Business can't be separated from other forms of social interaction. Social responsibility *is* good business.
☐ It's a good idea for companies that have the resources, but it's not an obligation.
☐ It's hype and posturing, just a passing business fad.
☐ Other _____

2. WHAT *SPECIFIC* ACTIONS OR PROGRAMS DOES YOUR COMPANY UNDERTAKE THAT YOU CONSIDER TO BE SOCIALLY RESPONSIBLE (FOR EXAMPLE, CONTRIBUTIONS TO CHARITIES, COMMUNITY-OUTREACH PROGRAMS, ENVIRONMENTALLY FRIENDLY POLICIES, AND SO ON)?

1. _____
2. _____
3. _____

3. WOULD YOU CONTINUE THEM EVEN IF YOU FOUND OUT THEY WERE CUTTING INTO YOUR PROFITS?

☐ Yes   ☐ I would probably discontinue some of them.   ☐ No

4. IN ADDITION TO REACHING OUT TO THE COMMUNITY AS A COMPANY, DO YOU ENCOURAGE OR REQUIRE ANY SOCIAL OUTREACH ON THE PART OF YOUR EMPLOYEES?

☐ No, what they do is their business.   ☐ Yes, I strongly encourage them to reach out.
☐ Yes, I require them to reach out.   Please describe. _____

5. IF PRESIDENT CLINTON FOLLOWS THROUGH ON CAMPAIGN PROMISES TO CREATE NEW SOCIAL PROGRAMS AND BEEF UP EXISTING ONES WITH GOVERNMENT FUNDING, DO YOU THINK THE NEED FOR BUSINESSES TO REACH OUT WILL:

☐ Increase   ☐ Decrease   ☐ Stay the same   Why? _____

6. DESCRIBE YOUR BUSINESS. ☐ Service company ☐ Manufacturer ☐ Retailer/wholesaler ☐ Distributor ☐ Other _____

7. WHAT IS YOUR POSITION WITHIN THE COMPANY?

☐ Founder/owner ☐ Department head/supervisor ☐ President/CEO ☐ Employee ☐ Top manager ☐ Other

8. BESIDES YOURSELF, HOW MANY PEOPLE DOES YOUR COMPANY EMPLOY?

☐ None ☐ 1–5 ☐ 6–10 ☐ 11–20 ☐ 21–100 ☐ 101–500 ☐ More than 500

9. WHAT REVENUES DID YOUR COMPANY HAVE FOR ITS MOST RECENT FISCAL YEAR?

☐ Less than $500,000 ☐ $1 million–$2.9 million ☐ $10 million–$49.9 million
☐ $500,000–$999,999 ☐ $3 million–$9.9 million ☐ $50 million or more

10. OTHER COMMENTS (USE ADDITIONAL SHEETS IF NECESSARY): _____

_____
_____

OPTIONAL:
Name _____   Phone number _____

FAX TO 800-231-1886

Or mail to the *Inc.* FaxPoll™, *Inc.* magazine, 38 Commercial Wharf, Boston, MA 02110. Please respond by February 22, 1993.

THE INC. FAXPOLL IS SPONSORED BY XEROX

ILLUSTRATION: ERIC PALMA

RESULTS OF THE NOVEMBER FAXPOLL:

ARE SMALL COMPANIES BETTER?

Turn the page for the answer. . . .

11

Using Visual Aids in Business Reports and Proposals

CHAPTER OBJECTIVES

After studying this chapter, you should be able to:

1 Describe the function of *visual aids* in reports and proposals.

2 Explain the importance of linking each visual aid to its specific message.

3 List the characteristics of *tables*.

4 List the different kinds of comparisons that can be made by *charts*.

5 Contrast *pie charts, bar charts, column charts,* and *line charts* and explain the advantages of each.

6 Explain the uses in business documents of *organization charts, flow charts, drawings* and *photographs,* and *maps*.

7 Describe the mechanics of constructing visual aids.

8 Explain methods for integrating visual aids into the text.

9 Describe the role of *presentation-graphics software* in the creation of visual aids.

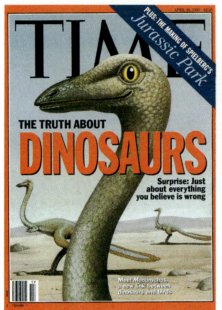

A NEW LOOK FOR TIME

Like many contemporary industries, the newsmagazine business went through difficult times in the early 1990s. With advertising revenues down and competition intense, profitable operations become increasingly difficult to maintain. In addition, magazines like *Time, Newsweek, U.S. News & World Report,* and others faced another challenge: defining the mission of the newsmagazine in an era of instant communication. According to former *Time* managing editor Henry Muller, timeliness and newsworthiness had become more synonymous than ever: "Five years ago," said Muller, "two-thirds of the magazine was still driven by last week's news. Now two-thirds of the magazine is original."

To remain competitive and honor their mandate to provide both breaking news and probing articles, Muller and other *Time* executives also recognized that design changes had to accompany the magazine's redirection in content and focus. As a result, *Time* underwent its most radical redesign since it was first published in 1923. The goal was to create an architectural framework for its print journalism that would make the magazine's news and feature content more reader-friendly.

The new design made its debut in the April 20, 1992, issue. Although the red border that had long defined *Time*'s cover was still intact, the rest of the magazine had a new look. In order to make content more accessible, *Time* was reorganized into three new sections: an eight-page section of news items up front; longer, more in-depth articles in the middle section; and a final section focusing on cultural reviews. In addition, a new typeface made the magazine easier to read and a larger cover logo promoted instant recognition. Finally, the new design allowed the magazine's editors to use larger and more dramatic photographs.

Although creating a new look was important, so was ensuring that readers would still recognize *Time* as the newsmagazine they had turned to for almost seven decades. With so much at stake, the design team spent months preparing changes. First, the new design was tested on 250 people in 30 focus-group interviews, each of which included 8 to 10 people whom marketers had identified as typical *Time* readers. Only when the design staff was confident that "look" enhanced content were mockups of redesigned pages presented to top management for approval.

Executives at *Time* spent hundreds of thousands of dollars and considerable effort to create a new look that would both distinguish the magazine from its competitors and communicate a message to an audience of newsmagazine readers. Was the effort to link content and design worth it? Undoubtedly, yes. With television covering news items almost instantaneously and cable television offering access to news channels twenty-four hours a day, it is critical to the success of any written work—especially to newsmagazines and newspapers—to deliver effective visual presentations.

With the average adult watching more than thirty hours of television every week, success in the world of print journalism is now measured by what looks good as well as what reads well. According to Robert W. Pittman, creator of the MTV cable network, the reason for the new rules of the game is clear: TV babies—the generation who grew up with television—perceive visual images better than previous generations. This generation, says Pittman, "can 'read' a picture...at a glance."[1]

CHAPTER OVERVIEW

For *Time* magazine, of course, its design is part of its brand franchise—its distinctive appeal as a product that enjoys a high rate of consumer acceptance. Although "design" can mean much more than mere visual appeal, it is a mistake to assume that readers apply entirely different design standards to business materials than to publications like *Time*. Granted, an effective visual presentation is not as critical in business reports and proposals as it is in mass-media publications. Nevertheless, when we read business documents, we apply certain standards of visual excellence which owe a good deal to the standards of design excellence that we observe on newsstands. As a result, our judgment of professional business documents derives in large part from the application of our standards of effective visual presentation.

The growing number of home computers has given many people the ability to create their own graphic designs. For that reason, too, people typically expect more from professionally designed business documents. Many software packages on the market today incorporate visual aids in their programs. For example, personal financial-management software usually allows budgets to be displayed in the form of pie charts, bar charts, or tables. Several time-management software packages use a calendar-style format for scheduling appointments and entering notations on specific dates. Such graphics software is considered a valuable component in the creation of business documents and has become accepted, if not expected, in many reports and proposals.

The quality of visual presentations is a function of *design* and *layout*—topics that we examined in Chapter 4. That quality also depends on a writer's use of *visual aids*. This chapter examines how visual aids—in the form of tables, charts, diagrams, and other illustrations—can help communicate messages. Specifically, it focuses on the variety of charts that are available in every business writer's arsenal: pie, bar, column, line and flow charts; as well as tables, maps, and other illustrations. This chapter will also present guidelines for conceiving and creating more effective visuals. Because visual aids are an increasingly popular feature of computer software programs, we close with an examination of *computer graphics*.

HOW VISUAL AIDS FUNCTION IN REPORTS AND PROPOSALS

Imagine that you are given a class assignment on demographics and asked to present data on the ethnic background of the U.S. population. By referring to the most recent edition of *The World Almanac*, you are able to locate Census Bureau statistics revealing that 177 million Americans are categorized as White-non-Hispanic. You find that African-Americans account for another 30 million and persons of Hispanic descent a total of 22 million. Two other smaller population segments are the nation's 7 million Asians and Pacific Islanders and 2 million American Indians, Eskimos, and Aleuts.

Although you are satisfied that this information is accurate, you want to present it in a more dramatic fashion than a simple narrative description. Your decision is to use the visual aid shown in Figure 11.1. This illustration, formally called a *pictorial chart*, communicates to the reader at a glance the relative size of the ethnic backgrounds of the American population.

Visual aids such as these relieve the monotony of long narrative passages in a document. At the same time, however, they perform more important tasks—for example, highlighting statistical relationships. A chart can show trends, movements, distributions, and cycles that may not be readily apparent in a completely narrative presentation. In addition, visuals can help readers make sense of difficult concepts. By restating information in different and often lively ways, they encourage meaningful comparisons between pieces of information that may have little appeal to the imagination when presented in dry narrative form.

During the data-gathering process discussed in Chapter 10, it frequently becomes self-evident that a visual aid will enhance reader understanding due to the quantity or complexity of data involved. Although data presented in narrative form may allow for a more detailed discussion, the use of accompanying visual aids further enhances understanding and accessibility.

visual aids
Tables, charts, and illustrations used to present data in visually appealing and understandable ways

Visual aids—the tables, charts, and illustrations used in reports and proposals—provide a means for presenting data in ways that make it both visually appealing and understandable. Visual aids are also frequently used to shorten text. A summary table or chart can present statistics more concisely—and more clearly—than words arranged in paragraph form.

The bar chart in Figure 11.2 shows the results of a *Wall Street Journal* survey on brand loyalty. Each bar indicates the percentage of respondents who plan to make a repeat purchase of a given brand. Not only is the presentation more concise than listing and explaining each category within a written text, but the information is also easier to understand and remember. More importantly, the reasons for compiling the data in the first place should be clearer. Realizing, for example, that brand loyalty for cigarettes is almost three times as great as brand loyalty for athletic shoes could certainly be an important first step in comparing different marketing strategies for the two products.

Linking Visual Aids to the Message

Every visual aid must have a message. Just as business writing cannot succeed without a clear statement of purpose, visual aids are either ineffective or unnec-

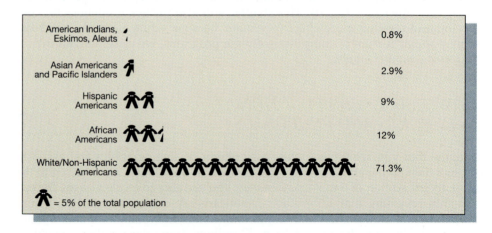

FIGURE 11.1   *Pictorial Chart: Ethnic Backgrounds of the U.S. Population*

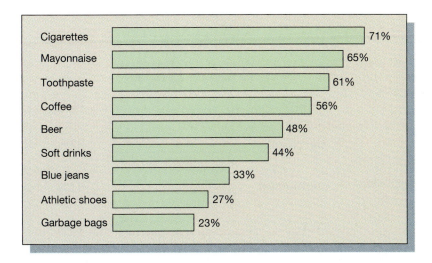

FIGURE 11.2   *Sample Bar Chart: Percentage of Brand-Loyal Users*

essary unless they are helping to clarify or amplify a specific purpose and message. The process of focusing your message may have begun with data collection. Perhaps you started by rounding off some numbers on your notepad computer or by arranging a complex array of data on a sophisticated spreadsheet. In either case, knowing precisely what you want your visual to communicate enables you to decide on the most appropriate visual aid. "It is not the data—be they dollars, percentages, liters, yen, etc.—that determine the chart," says Gene Zelazny, director of visual communication for McKinsey & Company. "It is not the measure—be it profits, return on investment, compensation, etc.—that determines the chart. Rather it is *your* message, what you want to show, the specific point you want to make."[2]

Let's say, for example, that as an employee of Northwest Airlines, you are asked to write a report comparing Northwest's on-time performance with that of its major competitors during the previous year. You would almost certainly want to highlight the fact that Northwest has the best on-time record in the industry. You could present your data in a number of ways—in a list embedded in the text of your report, in a formal table set apart from the text with a title and a source note, or in a bar chart. Each alternative is illustrated in Figure 11.3. Although both the in-text listing and the formal table represent the information accurately, the bar chart not only supplies the same specific data but provides a quick visual comparison among the top five competitors.

As you can also see, the bar chart requires less word-reading to understand the message contained in the data—namely: *Although Northwest ranked first among the five U.S. passenger air carriers, the difference between first and last place is less than ten percentage points.*

PROVIDING DIRECTION IN YOUR TITLE   Look once again at the bar chart in Figure 11.2. In the context of a document whose purpose was merely to report on the findings of a *Wall Street Journal* survey, that chart might simply have been titled "Brand-Loyal Users." The title would say essentially what the chart itself says: The users of some products are more brand-loyal than the users of other products.

But what if the title chosen for the chart had been something like "Cigarettes Pass the Loyalty Test—Blue Jeans Fade"? Obviously, the context would not be simply a report on some survey findings. It would probably be a document whose purpose is to *interpret* those findings. *Why* is it interesting or important that cigarettes enjoy much greater brand loyalty than blue jeans?

When you have mastered the numbers, you will in fact no longer be reading numbers, any more than you read words when reading books. You will be reading meanings.

Harold Geneen
Chairman, IT&T Corp.

In-Text	Bar Chart
In a comparison of five major U.S. airlines, the percentage of on-time flights during the past year were: Northwest, 86%; American 83%; Continental, 81%; TWA, 79%; United, 78%.	**Percentage of On-Time Flights for Major U.S. Air Carriers**

Formal Table

Percentage of On-Time Flights for Major U.S. Air Carriers

Air Carrier	Percentage
Northwest	86
American	83
Continental	81
TWA	79
United	78

Bar Chart

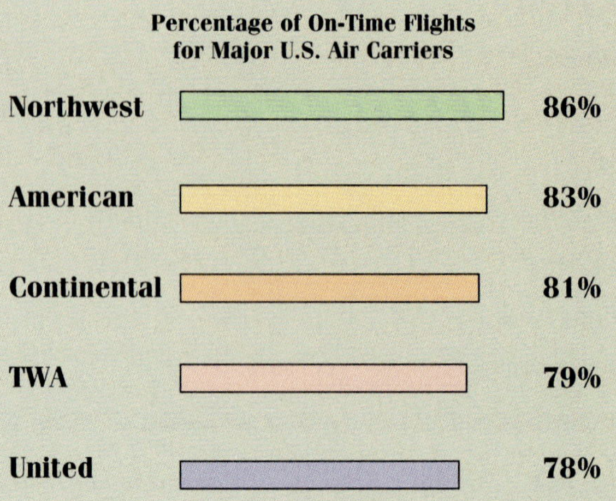

Percentage of On-Time Flights for Major U.S. Air Carriers

- Northwest 86%
- American 83%
- Continental 81%
- TWA 79%
- United 78%

FIGURE 11.3   *Alternative Methods of Presenting Data*

report visual
Visual designed and presented to let its data convey the necessary information

presentation visual
Visual designed to support a message and requiring a directive title and interpretation by the writer or speaker

Our two different titles reflect the difference between report and presentation visuals. While **report visuals** let the facts speak for themselves, **presentation visuals** *interpret* data. When you choose to support your message with a presentation visual, you must tell your reader *why* a table or chart is important. Providing such information is the primary purpose of your title. The best titles, then, are directive titles: simple, clear statements that focus on a relationship between facts that you want to emphasize and about which you have something to say. Directive titles deliver specific, focused messages. The table below pairs a list of directive headings with a list of unfocused nondirective titles.

DIRECTIVE TITLES	NONDIRECTIVE TITLES
Factory Productivity Soars	Factory Productivity
Current Inventory Level Declines 30 Percent	Current Inventory
Employee Benefits Rising Faster than Inflation	Employee Benefits
Southwest Sales 20 Percent Higher than Northwes	Sales by Region

The differences between report and presentation visuals reflect the basic differences in the purposes that visual aids can be made to serve. Different types of visual aids, however, do not serve the same purposes. Determining which visual aid will best support your message requires an understanding of the specific nature of different types of visuals—in particular, tables and charts. We will begin this examination by focusing on the function and use of tables in business reports and proposals.

table
Systematic arrangement of data and/or words in rows and columns to provide readers with a fixed reference and a method of comparison

USING TABLES IN REPORTS AND PROPOSALS

Tables are systematic arrangements of data and/or words in rows and columns that provide readers with a fixed reference and a method of comparison. They can consolidate large quantities of information in a relatively small space without losing detail. For example, specific (and often complex) numerical information can be shown in tables with more exactness than in charts. Two types of tables—data tables and word tables—are illustrated in Table 11.1.

Word tables are used extensively in reports and proposals. They make it easier for readers to understand and evaluate material by allowing the writer to consolidate often complex information in one place. Instructional materials are frequently listed in word tables. For example, a company safety officer might write a report on workplace safety with a table listing various symptoms, remedies, and techniques for administering first aid; a human-resources manager might write a report with a table listing the various positions in the firm, job descriptions for each position, and salary ranges.

A table can also be classified as either a **spot table**, which runs into the text without title or number, or a **reference table**, which has a title and number but need not appear immediately following the text reference. While spot tables are used for incidental information, reference tables ordinarily contain data that the writer wants highlighted. In this chapter, the two-column list of directive and nondirective titles above is a spot table; Table 11.1 is a reference table.

Despite their value in consolidating information, however, tables have several limitations. Although they imply relationships—say, growth or decline dur-

spot table
Unnumbered, untitled table included in the text of a document; ordinarily contains incidental data

reference table
Table with title and number that usually does not appear immediately following the text reference; ordinarily contains highlighted data

---

TABLE 11.1   *Sample Data and Word Tables*

A. Data Table

COMPARING RATES OF MAJOR CREDIT-CARD ISSUERS

ISSUER*	LOWEST RATE	HIGHEST RATE	ANNUAL FEE**
Citicorp	15.9%	19.8%	$20
Sears Discover	18.0	19.8	15
Chase	16.4	19.8	20
Bank of America	16.9	19.8	18
MBNA America	15.5	19.8	20

*Issuers listed in order of market share.
**Fees do not apply to gold cards.

B. Word Table

COMPARING DIFFERENT TYPES OF MORTGAGE AGREEMENTS

TYPE	DESCRIPTION	CONSIDERATIONS
Fixed rate	Fixed interest rate; usually long-term; equal monthly payments of principal and interest until debt is paid in full.	Offers stability and long-term tax advantages; interest rates may be higher than other types of financing; new fixed rates are rarely assumable.
Adjustable rate	Interest rate changes over life of the loan; possible changes in monthly payments, loan term, and/or principal; some plans have rate or interest caps	Starting interest rate is slightly below market, but payments can increase sharply and frequently if index increases; payment caps prevent wide fluctuations in payment but may cause negative amortization; rate caps limit the total amount that the debt can expand
Balloon	Monthly payments basedon fixed interest rate; usually short-term; payments may cover interest only with principal due in full at term end	Offers low monthly payments but possibly no equity until loan is fully paid; when due, loan must be paid or refinanced; refinancing poses high risk if rates climb

Sources: Credit-card rates provided by the issuers. Mortgage descriptions from the Federal Trade Commission, *The Mortgage Money Guide* (Washington, DC: Government Printing Office, n.d.)

If you can't measure it, you can't manage it.
If you don't measure it, it won't happen.

Anonymous

ing a specific period—these relationships are not always clear, and misinterpretations are possible. An ambiguous title or one that does not identify the purpose of a visual aid often creates further confusion and possible misinterpretation. To be effective, it is important for a title to identify the subject and purpose of the data, thereby increasing reader understanding.

PROGRESS CHECK

1. What do we mean by the term *visual aids?*
2. What purpose(s) do titles serve in visual aids?

USING CHARTS IN REPORTS AND PROPOSALS

chart (or graph)
Diagram that presents numerical data in visual form to show trends, movements, distributions, and cycles

When you wish to illustrate your point in more dramatic fashion than through in-text description or a table, you may decide to use one of several types of charts. **Charts**, also known as **graphs**, are diagrams that present numerical data in visual form in order to show trends, movements, distributions, and cycles. Because charts are usually less detailed than tables, they are sometimes accompanied by tables providing exact data. The most common and useful forms of charts are *pie, bar, column, line,* and *flow charts.* All charts highlight comparisons, and before we describe different chart forms, it is important to understand the different types of comparisons that they make.

Types of Chart Comparisons

Business reports and proposals typically use charts to make four basic types of comparisons: *component, item, time-series,* and *frequency-distribution comparisons.*[3] The message communicated by a chart is defined by the kind of comparison that it highlights.

component comparison
Data-presentation technique in which the size of each item is shown as a percentage of a total

COMPONENT COMPARISON   In a **component comparison**, the size of each item in the chart is shown as a percentage of their total. For example, each of the following statements indicates that a component comparison is being made:

- Two sales districts accounted for nearly three-quarters of total corporate sales.
- Generic clothing bleaches hold less than 10 percent of market share.

Such topics as market share by company, budget allocations among divisions, and employee population by income also invite component comparisons.

item comparison
Data-presentation technique in which relative rankings of individuals, geographic areas, products, production facilities, or other variables are examined to determine whether they are the same or more or less than one another

ITEM COMPARISON   An **item comparison** examines relative rankings—individuals, geographic areas, products, production facilities, or a whole host of other variables—in order to determine whether those variables are the same or more than or less than one another. This comparison analyzes items at a single point in time. For example, the following statements indicate item comparisons:

- Employee satisfaction in all four departments is about *equal.*
- Productivity at the Wisconsin plant is significantly *less than* at the virtually identical Michigan plant.

The variables being compared here are different levels of employee satisfaction and productivity, respectively. In general, terms like *equal, larger than, smaller than,* and *less than* indicate that an item comparison is being made.

TIME-SERIES COMPARISON   A **time-series comparison** measures the changes in items over time. This comparison is useful for tracking trends over a specific time period, usually weeks, months, quarters, or years. The following statements indicate that a time-series comparison is being made:

- Mortgage-interest rates have declined over the past four months.
- Company exports have risen dramatically since last May, when the dollar started losing value on world markets.

Terms like *increase, decrease, fluctuate, grow, decline, rise*, and *remain constant* indicate the working of a time-series comparison.

FREQUENCY-DISTRIBUTION COMPARISON   A **frequency-distribution comparison** shows how many items fall into a series of defined, progressive numerical ranges. For example, income distributions are often categorized as numerical ranges—less than $20,000, $20,000 to $29,999, $30,000 to $39,999, and so on. A frequency distribution, therefore, could be used to divide a company's total number of wage earners into progressively higher income brackets. Terms like *range, concentration, frequency*, and *distribution* characterize frequency-distribution comparisons.

time-series comparison
Data-presentation technique that shows how items change over a specific time period. usually weeks, months, quarters, or years

frequency-distribution comparison
Data-presentation technique showing how many items fall into defined, progressive, numerical ranges

TYPES OF CHARTS

When constructing visual aids, one of your primary goals is to define and develop a strong relationship between specific comparisons and the type of chart that you intend to use. Four basic types of comparative charts—*pie, bar, column*, and *line charts*—are illustrated in Figure 11.4. In some cases, you will find one type of chart clearly superior to your other alternatives. Component comparisons, for example,

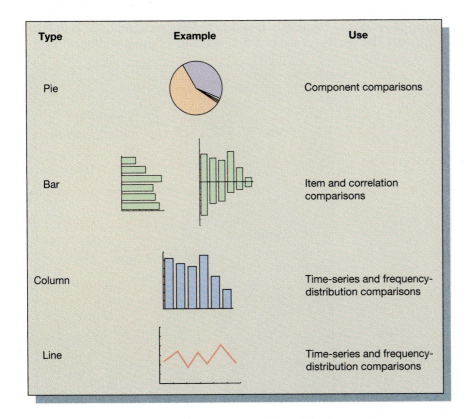

FIGURE 11.4   *Effective Chart Forms and Specific Comparisons*

are best made with pie charts. In other instances, however, you may face more than one option in choosing an effective means of providing your reader with a summary illustration of important materials. As we shall see, for example, in showing age groupings of federal employees (a frequency-distribution comparison), you could use either a column chart or a line chart with equal effectiveness.

In this section, we will describe each of the major types of charts by focusing on the kind of relationship that each expresses best. We will also describe some specialized charts that have been developed to describe business relationships or to aid in describing certain business activities.

Pie Charts

pie chart
Diagram presenting data as wedge-shaped sections of a circle; used for component comparisons, with the entire circle representing 100 percent of a given whole and each wedge a portion of the whole

Among the most common and easy-to-understand visual aids is the **pie chart**—a graph that presents data as wedge-shaped sections of a circle. Pie charts are typically used for component comparisons, with the entire circle representing 100 percent of a given whole and each wedge a portion of the whole.

The strength of the pie chart in showing portions of an overall whole is illustrated in Figure 11.5, which shows how Nike, Inc., the largest company in the athletic-shoe market, allocates its advertising budget among the various media. The fact that magazine advertisements and local, network, cable, and syndicated television ads account for the overwhelming share of the firm's promotional budget is vividly illustrated. If you had simply been informed that Nike spends almost one-half million dollars annually on radio ads and another one-quarter million dollars each on newspaper and outdoor ads (billboards, transit advertising, etc.), you might consider the expenditures more significant than they are. The pie chart in Figure 11.5, however, shows that each of these media represents less than 1.5 percent of Nike's total advertising budget.

Bar Charts

bar chart
Diagram consisting of horizontal bars of varying lengths, each representing different items for comparison

A second type of visual aid frequently found in reports and proposals is the bar chart or bar graph. **Bar charts** consist of horizontal bars of equal width and vary-

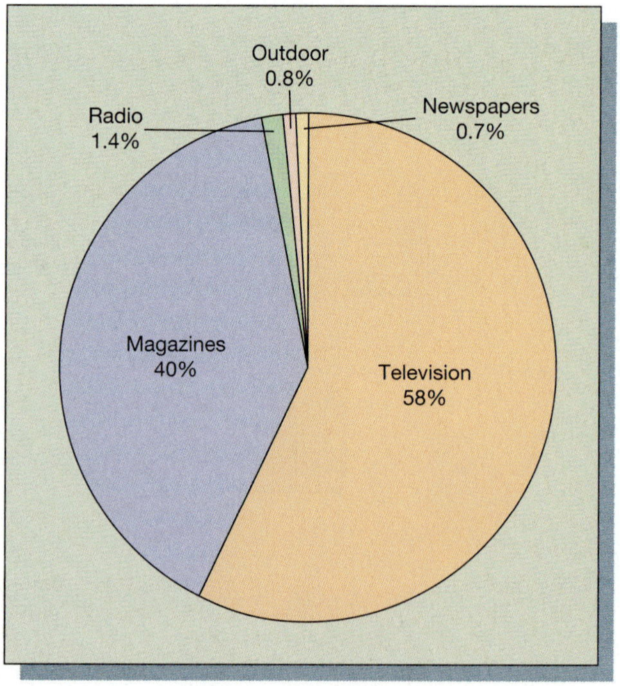

FIGURE 11.5   *Sample Pie Chart: Dividing the Nike Advertising Market*

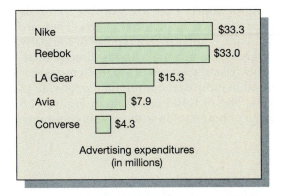

FIGURE 11.6   *Sample Bar Chart: Total Media Expenditures of Major Athletic-Shoe Makers*

ing lengths, each representing a different item for comparison. They are best used for analyzing how items compare *with one another* rather than as single components of a whole. The bar chart in Figure 11.6 compares total annual media spending by five major athletic-shoe manufacturers.

Depending on their use, bar charts can be subdivided into three categories. A **grouped bar chart** compares various parts of the same item—for example, labor costs with and without employee benefits included.

The **subdivided bar chart** divides each bar into components of the same item. For example, a bar chart reporting the number of female employees in your firm might be divided into three sections. The entire length of the bar may represent all female employees; the first subsection may represent full-time employees; the second subsection might represent part-time employees, and the third subsection temporary employees. You could go a step further and emphasize a point by comparing this bar to a similar bar for male employees.

Finally, the **bilateral bar chart** starts from a central point and shows positive and/or negative deviations from that point. It may be used, for example, to highlight a comparison of company territories with net losses and gains in sales. Each of these three types of bar charts is illustrated in Figure 11.7.

grouped bar chart
Diagram comparing various parts of the same item

subdivided bar chart
Diagram dividing each bar of a figure or chart into components of a single item

bilateral bar chart
Diagram starting from a central point to show positive or negative deviations from that point

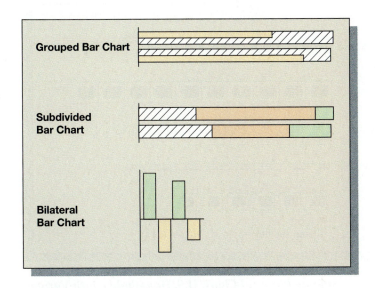

FIGURE 11.7   *Specialized Bar Charts*

pictorial chart
Bar or column chart using graphic symbols instead of horizontal or vertical lines

PICTORIAL CHARTS   Bar and column charts that use graphic symbols instead of horizontal or vertical lines are known as **pictorial charts**. They are used most often in documents aimed at wide audiences—in reports to company shareholders, for example. The effectiveness of a pictorial chart is directly related to the appropriateness of its symbols. Using pictures of small factories, for instance, is a good way to show the trend in industrial output but a poor way to depict a company's employment trend. The pictorial bar chart in Figure 11.8 uses symbols to represent the percentage of households with various communication media.

Column Charts

column (or vertical-bar) chart
Diagram consisting of vertical bars of different heights, each height representing a different quantity

Although quite similar to bar charts, **column (or vertical-bar) charts** are most effective for time-series comparisons that indicate changes taking place over a period of time. They are also useful in frequency-distribution comparisons, in which they highlight a series of items that are part of a progressive numerical distribution.

Column charts consist of vertical bars of different heights, with each height representing a different quantity. In a time-series comparison, for example, the height of each bar measures the value of the data for a given period of time. Figure 11.9 is a column chart showing the allocation of advertising expenditures by Nike. Compare the impact of the data in this chart with the emphasis in the pie chart in Figure 11.5.

grouped column chart
Diagram consisting of grouped or overlapping columns that compare two different items at a given time and demonstrate how the relationship between those items changes over time

subdivided column chart
diagram showing how the individual parts of a whole change over time

SPECIALIZED COLUMN CHARTS   Two specialized column charts are shown in Figure 11.10. The **grouped column chart** consists of grouped or overlapping columns that can perform two functions at once: They can compare two different items at a given time and demonstrate how the relationship between these items has changed over time. For example, while one bar in a series (say, the red bars in Figure 11.10A) may show advertising expenditures, a second bar (the blue bars) may show company profits. A **subdivided column chart** shows how the individual parts of one whole unit have changed over time. For example, a financial analyst may create a subdivided column chart to show how a company's current and long-term liabilities have changed over two successive ten-year periods (Fig. 11.10B).

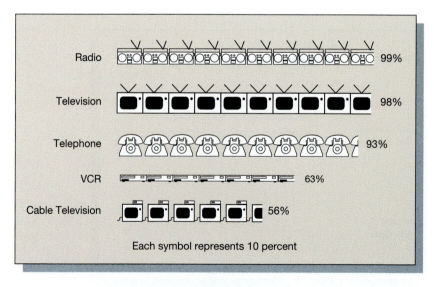

FIGURE 11.8   *Sample Pictorial Chart: U.S. Households with Various Communication Media*

APPLYING TECHNOLOGY

Symbol Libraries

Special presentation-graphics software such as Harvard Presentation Graphics and Princeton Graphics provide a variety of symbols and images for use in pictorial charts. Called *symbol libraries*, these software packages can supply writers with different symbols for hundreds of subjects almost instantly.

Freelance Plus, a symbol library in the bestselling Lotus spreadsheet software package, allows thousands of images to be enlarged or reduced, rotated, colored or shaded, or customized in other ways. Presentation-graphics software also enables you to emphasize the meaning and impact of nonpictorial charts by supplementing them with appropriate background symbols. For example, in a chart analyzing home-construction trends, overlaying the trend line on a symbol

of a house under construction would reinforce the content. Representative symbols can also be placed near titles and used as borders for charts.

Pictorial symbols are also frequently used to enhance maps. In promoting tourism, for example, state maps typically use symbols to highlight events, activities, or facilities available in different areas of the state. California's Department of Tourism might use a tent to indicate camping in the northern part of the state, a wine bottle for the Napa Valley area, a cable car for San Francisco, a movie camera for Hollywood, and a surfboard for the beaches of southern California. An agricultural-products map could use different animals and crops to indicate the primary products of different regions of a state or nation.

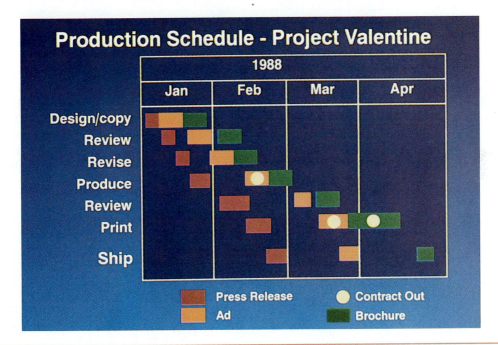

Line Charts

The line chart is the most frequently used visual aid in business reports and proposals. Used to show both frequency distributions and trends over time, **line charts** are graphs that show the relationship between numbers on a combination horizontal and vertical axis. The points plotted along these two axes are connected to form a continuous *trend line*. Both horizontal and vertical *axes* are reference lines that determine the exact position of the data being charted. While the horizontal axis often shows a span of time, the vertical axis may represent a variety of measurements, including dollars, units, or percentages.

line chart
Diagram showing the relationship between numbers on the intersection of horizontal and vertical axes

If two lines on a graph cross, it must be important.

*Ernest F. Cooke
American educator*

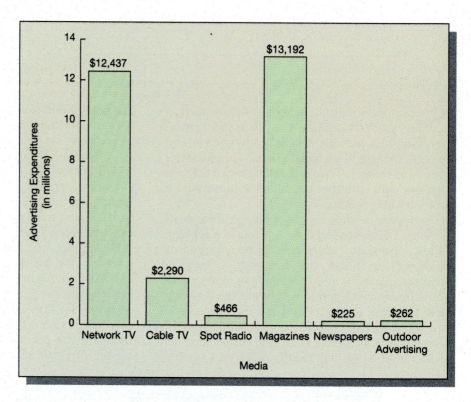

FIGURE 11.9   *Sample Column Chart: Nike Advertising Dollars*

grouped line chart
Line chart that makes comparisons between two or more items

surface chart
Line chart that is shaded between the baseline and trend lines

When the comparison involves two or more items, the chart is called a **grouped line chart**. Naturally, it is important to ensure that distinct trend lines are easily distinguishable. In another variation, **surface charts**, the surface of the chart between the trend line and the baseline is shaded. The effect is to emphasize the trend by making it visually prominent. Figure 11.11 shows a grouped line chart of media expenditures for three leading U.S. sportswear marketers.

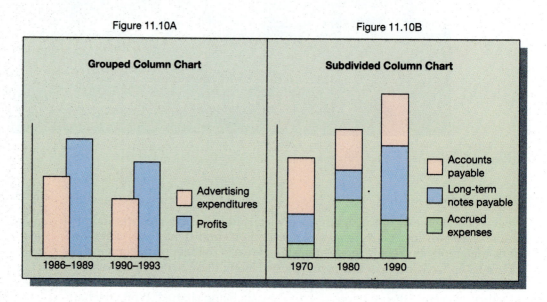

FIGURE 11.10   *Specialized Column Charts*

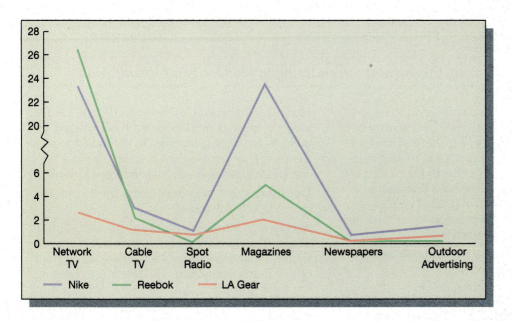

FIGURE 11.11   *Sample Grouped Line Chart: Media Spending by Major Athletic-Shoe Makers*

Flow Charts

Diagrams that describe the stages in a process are known as **flow charts**. By making procedures visible, flow charts give readers the opportunity both to identify the distinct steps in a particular process and to see how and when all the steps fit together. Flow charts begin with the initial step in a procedure and end when the procedure is complete. They can be used to describe any number of processes, ranging from how to build a house to how a bill becomes a law.

flow chart
Diagram describing the stages in a process

PROGRESS CHECK

1. What are the functions of the various types of bar charts?
2. Contrast the two basic types of column charts.
3. Describe two subcategories of line charts.

OTHER TYPES OF VISUAL AIDS

Although tables and charts are the most common illustrations used in reports and proposals, many documents use other forms of visual aids. The most useful of these graphic aids are *maps, drawings,* and *photographs.*

Maps

Maps highlight statistical comparisons of various geographical regions. For example, a map can compare the potential market for a new product in all fifty states or in a smaller geographic region, such as the Midwest or Southwest. Statistical maps are valuable only if the quantitative differences that they represent are clear. Therefore, color, shading, or cross-hatching, coordinated with an explanatory legend, is typically used to differentiate regions on maps.

INTERVIEW

Gene Zelazny, Consultant Specializing in the Design of Visual Aids

For the past thirty years, Gene Zalazny, Director of Visual Communications for Mc Kinsey & Company, has helped his colleagues in the firm and members of top management choose and use charts for presentations, reports, and other business documents. In this interview, we asked Zelazny, who is also the author of *Say It With Charts*, to give us his perspective on the art of the chart.

Question: What common elements do the most successful charts share?

Answer: The best charts demonstrate relationships more clearly and more quickly than information in tabular form. They have a message title—a brief sentence that focuses attention on the point you want to emphasize. They are attractive and legible. The fact that charts are decorative or help to break the monotony of a presentation or a page of text is incidental and never justifies using them.

Question: How do you decide when a chart is needed?

Answer: Your message makes the decision for you. If your message is simple—for example, company revenues have doubled—showing a chart with two columns, one twice the height of the other, is not necessary and risks insulting the intelligence of your audience. But if the message is com-

plex— for instance, you need to tell the reader how the mix of market share has changed by quarters for eight companies in the industry over the past five years—then a chart showing the changes will be more effective than words alone.

Question: What are some of the most common chart-making mistakes?

Answer: The most common offense is poor design: The chart is too cluttered or complex to be legible. Aside from this obvious shortcoming, two other mistakes stand out. The first is not choosing the right chart *form* for the point you want to make—say, using pie charts to show changes over time when a line chart would work better. The second is confusing complexity for information. Take a look at the first chart below. What you see is the chart in its early stages of development—many components, data down to two dec-

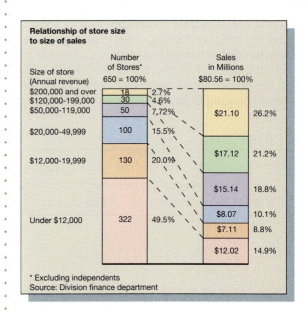

Drawings and Photographs

Custom drawings let you focus on the structure and function of products and equipment. Because you actually create what you want the reader to see, you can omit all extraneous information—something that a photograph cannot do. Computers are frequently used in business today to create sophisticated drawings and diagrams.

It is important both to tie each drawing to your overall purpose and to keep your reader's needs in mind. For example, in a report describing how to correct a manufacturing problem in an automobile braking system, one or more drawings would be needed to show the interrelationship among the system's internal parts.

imal points, footnotes, and so on. The second chart shows what the chart should look like to get its point across clearly and quickly.

Question: Can charts suffer from poor audience analysis?

Answer: I'd turn that question around. After all, it's not the chart that suffers—it doesn't care. It's the audience. The final test of a chart is not what goes into it but what the reader gets out of it. Failure to analyze your audience can result in charts that fail to communicate, no matter how well designed they are. Some people simply do not respond well to charts; either they have difficulty reading graphic representations or they are more comfortable with information in tabular form. Leave it be.

Question: Should charts be explained in the text?

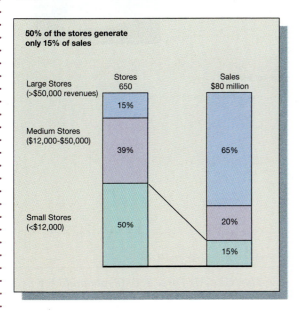

Answer: Yes. Too often we assume that the chart should speak for itself. Not so. A chart is a visual aid in the sense that it is an aid to the text and not a substitute for words. As such, it is there for the reader to refer to while the text explains how to read the chart and what point it is demonstrating. The same thing happens in a visual presentation. The chart is on the screen for the audience to look at while the presenter explains it orally.

Question: How has computer technology changed chart making? Have the sophisticated approaches that are now possible in presentation-graphics software made simple hand drawings out-of-date?

Answer: In my career, I have seen the rise of visual-aids people and I am now witnessing their fall; today, they are computer operators who create finished charts in the time it takes me to do one rough sketch. Remarkable. I find it fascinating that I can walk into our production department and not find a pencil on anyone's desk. Come to think of it, I can't find a desk; they're now called *workstations*. And it's all for the good. After all, we've drawn enough pie charts to know how thick to make the outline and where to position the chart on the page. Let's face it: Today, computers are to visual aids what pocket calculators became to multiplication tables.

Question: If you had one piece of advice about chart making, what would it be?

Answer: Remember that *less is more than enough.* Use fewer charts and put less on them. The philosophy that *more is never enough* simply doesn't apply to charts.

Source: Interview with Gene Zelazny.

Sometimes, relationships can be emphasized when drawings are shown in sequence. Figure 11.12, for example, consists of five separate drawings, including one three-part graphic, showing the components of Nike's Air Force 180 basketball sneaker. The drawings help the reader see each individual component of the shoe's construction, enhancing the reader's perception of quality and pointing out the benefits of the multistep construction.

As the saying goes, a picture is worth a thousand words, and photograph represent another popular category of visual aids in reports and proposals. A photograph can be the closest thing to reality in presenting facts. Photos are an effective way to bring the reader closer to the idea, person, or product. As an ele-

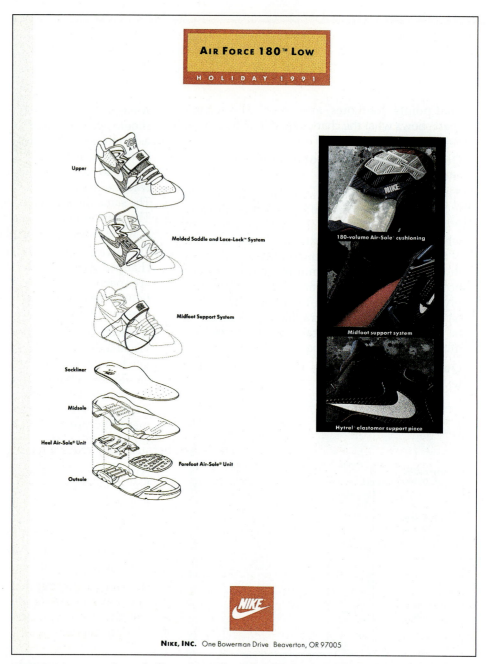

FIGURE 11.12   *Sample Drawing: The Nike Air Force 180, Inside and Out*

ment of design, photographs enhance not only the appearance of a document but also the credibility of the information in a report or proposal. They are also used to increase reader interest and retention. Most corporate annual reports include photos of people, production facilities, and products. Advertising agencies typically use photographs in their proposals. Photographs show the surface appearance of an object but cannot depict internal workings or small details.

DESIGNING EFFECTIVE VISUAL AIDS

To be effective, visual aids must look professional. Above all, your document must be characterized by *simplicity*, *clarity*, and *consistency* of design in the appearance of its visual aids. Several factors affect these qualities in the design of visual aids: size; titles and numbers; captions, labels, and legends; footnotes; color, shading, and cross-hatching; borders and rules; grid lines and tick marks; and source acknowledgments. These are the *mechanics* of design—the factors that determine the final appearance of a visual aid.

Simplicity of Design and Content

The best tables and charts have simple, consistent, clear designs that help the reader focus on specifics. Keep in mind that your readers may not have your level of expertise on your subject and may be overwhelmed by visuals that try to accomplish too much. For example, large amounts of data in a visual aid typically result in a crowded, overly complicated appearance. In such cases, you may want to divide your data into two or more visual aids. In general, every visual aid should tell a single story—that is, highlight one important relationship.

A simple design focuses on content over form. When design interferes with the reader's understanding of the relationship being illustrated, it fails as a communication tool. Simple tables and charts contain no unnecessary data. Figures are rounded off, and the level of detail stops when the accumulation of information ceases to be useful. Let's say, for example, that you want to illustrate an employment-growth trend at your company over the past year. Will it be necessary to show the employment of workers in various job categories at the plant? Probably not: This information is irrelevant to your main point that *companywide* employment has increased. One way to eliminate excess detail is to select your illustration title first; you can then measure the complexity of your topic against the more modest claims of your title.

CONSISTENCY: SIZE   In general, the size of a figure should be directly related to its importance and complexity. The more important the figure, the larger it should be. Similarly, complex figures require greater space because they require more detailed explanation. Incidental figures should take only a small portion of a page. Finally, the sizing of visual aids should be internally consistent. Decisions about sizing should be made according to guidelines that take your whole document into account. Two tables of equal importance should be of basically equal size.

CONSISTENCY: TITLES AND NUMBERS   Consistency is important in the presentation of visual aids, and a key way to ensure consistency is to develop a pattern for titles and numbers. For one thing, your pattern will be reflected in your reference system. There are, for example, two ways to refer to tables and charts. You can label each item as an "Exhibit" and number them *sequentially* as they appear in the document; or you can separate "tables" and "figures" and number *each in order*. In this sense, a **figure** is any visual aid other than a table, including charts, maps, drawings, photographs, and other illustrations.

figure
Any visual aid, other than tables, including charts, maps, drawings, photographs, and other illustrations

Your narrative should refer to table and chart numbers rather than to the pages or relative positions in which an item appears. For example, the reference "as shown in Table 4" for a numbered visual aid is better than "as shown in the table below." Remember that when your final pages are laid out, each visual aid will be placed as close as possible to the reference in your narrative—that is, as soon as page space permits. The reference to "below," therefore, may be highly variable, ranging from immediately following to the next available space a page and a half later.

CLARITY: CAPTIONS, LABELS, AND LEGENDS   In many cases, visual aids require, in addition to titles, explanatory captions. A **caption** is a brief explanatory or descriptive narrative that should support the title as it focuses on the visual's most important point. The caption is usually placed at the bottom of the visual aid and limited to no more than a sentence or two. Often, a phrase is sufficient. If your caption has nothing to add to your title, clarification probably isn't necessary.

caption
Brief narrative that supports the title and focuses on the most important point of a visual aid

labels
Headings and subheadings that define the parts of a visual aid, including all identification of items being compared

legend
Marginal explanation of symbols used in a chart

footnote
Mechanism for explaining specific details in a visual aid

Labels consist of all the headings and subheadings that define the parts of the exhibit, including all identifications of the items being compared. For ease of reading, these should be written horizontally, as in the line chart in Figure 11.11. A common exception is the labeling for the vertical axis of a chart, which is often inserted at a right angle to the text. **Legends** are marginal explanations of chart symbols that contribute to a cleaner appearance than the separate labeling of various elements. Legends, then, are best suited to charts displaying more than one set of data.

SPECIFICITY: FOOTNOTES   While captions add information that applies to an entire item, **footnotes** provide a mechanism for explaining specific details. For example, you might want to explain an unusually low pattern in electricity usage during the summer months by footnoting the fact that it was the coolest summer on record.

When a visual aid has only one or two footnotes, asterisks (*) or double asterisks (**) are sufficient to indicate that additional information can be found in the footnote. When footnotes are more numerous, you should use lower-case letters (*a, b, c…*) instead of asterisks. Place the lower-case letter next to the detail you want to highlight; at the bottom of the figure or table, write the letter again, followed by the footnote explanation.

If you find that your visual aid calls for numerous footnotes, you may need to simplify it. Perhaps you could divide the information between two or more visual aids or add more in-depth explanation in your text. Some business writing experts discourage the inclusion of footnotes or other explanations except in rare cases. It is usually possible to say what you need to say about an item in a title and a brief caption; if further explanation is still needed, you can put it in your text.

PRECISENESS: OTHER VISUAL TOOLS   In addition to these generally applicable tools for design simplicity, consistency, and clarity, writers can take advantage of numerous other design elements. Most of those described in the following section are quite common, and each can contribute to both the appearance and preciseness of your visual aids.

COLOR, SHADING, AND CROSS-HATCHING   Some visual aids cannot be understood without the use of color, shading, or cross-hatching to distinguish their elements. Often a necessity rather than a luxury, these techniques highlight and differentiate selected elements by forming visual groupings. Use the color wheel in Figure 14.3 to choose the most effective color combinations for your visual aids. Once you have chosen a basic color scheme—white lettering on a black background, for example—use it consistently throughout your document.

When color is either unavailable or inappropriate, you can distinguish different elements with shading and/or cross-hatching. The specialized bar charts in Figure 11.7, for example, feature shading and cross-hatching instead of coloring. Similarly, a line chart can differentiate each line by using bold, thin, and interrupted lines as well as colored lines.

border
Any line that surrounds a visual aid to separate it from surrounding text

rule
Internal line that separates the various elements of a chart or table

grid lines
Series of horizontal and vertical lines crossing at 90-degree angles to establish specific values in an illustration

BORDERS AND RULES   Clarity can also be greatly improved through the consistent use of borders and rules. **Borders** are the lines that surround visual aids and separate them from the surrounding text; **rules** are the internal lines that separate the various elements of an exhibit. For example, horizontal rules are often placed below the title and between the column headings and the body of a table. Similarly, vertical rules are often used to separate columns in a table. In general, writers have considerable discretion in deciding how to use these elements. When decisions are made, they should be used consistently throughout the document.

GRID LINES AND TICK MARKS   In some charts, a series of solid horizontal and vertical lines, known as **grid lines**, cross one another at 90-degree angles to establish specific values. Other charts designate the same numerical intervals with short broken lines known as *tick marks.* Because it is easy to follow solid lines back to their sources on the horizontal and vertical axes, a chart with grid lines is usually emphasizing *exact values.* (The line charts in this chapter's Ethics in Business Communications box feature grid lines.) Tick marks, on the other hand, are typically used to show *general trends.* Keep in mind that in some charts, such as line charts, too many grid lines make it difficult to distinguish more important trend lines.

SOURCE ACKNOWLEDGMENTS   When the material in your exhibit is taken from another document, you must cite that document in a source note at the bottom of your own visual aid. Simply write the word *Source* followed by a colon and then provide the attribution. Many of the tables and figures in this text provide examples of the format used in listing source notes.

Constructing Specific Types of Visual Aids

Specific visual aids have special construction guidelines. Just as your choice of a type of visual aid depends primarily on the nature of the information being presented, your design must also be appropriate for the type of visual aid you have chosen. Certain guidelines are available to help you in creating each of the visual aids that we have discussed so far, including tables, pie, bar, column, and line charts; and drawings.

TABLES   Tables are most effective when they are easiest to read, and they are easiest to read when they follow a consistent format. Figure 11.13 illustrates the parts of a table and their typical arrangement on the page. Below the table title are column titles, which are also known as *captions.* In some cases, tables are divided into several sections that require subcaptions. The captions running

Stub Head	Caption		Caption	
	Subcaption	Subcaption	Subcaption	Subcaption
Stub	XXXX	XXXX	XXXX	XXXX
Stub	XXXX	XXXX[a]	XXXX	XXXX
Stub	XXXX	XXXX	XXXX	XXXX
Stub	XXXX	XXXX	XXXX	XXXX
Stub	XXXX	XXXX	XXXX	XXXX
Total	XXXX	XXXX	XXXX[b]	XXXX

TABLE NO.

TITLE OF TABLE

[a]Footnote
[b]Footnote
Source:

FIGURE 11.13   *The Parts and Arrangement of a Table*

along the horizontal rows are known as *stubs*. When column *totals* are included, they usually appear immediately following the last horizontal row.

PIE CHARTS   As we saw earlier in this chapter, pie charts must be simple and easy to read. To emphasize clarity, experts suggest that a pie chart contain no more than six to ten components. Each component's share should be accurately represented as a part of the 360 degrees in the circle.

The pieces of a pie chart should start at the top of the figure, with the pieces or sections arranged in order according to size or importance. Labels should be written horizontally and, whenever possible, *within* the appropriate section of the pie. If the label will not fit inside the pie section, it can be placed outside the pie with a rule drawn from section to label. This technique is used in the pie chart in Figure 11.5.

BAR AND COLUMN CHARTS   As illustrated in Figure 11.6, the title of each bar (*Nike, Reebok...Converse*) should appear either as a stub to the left of the bar or on top of the bar. When (as in Fig. 11.2) bar charts are labeled with individual values (*71%, 65%...23%*), no further clarification is necessary. However, when the values of bars must be identified, a scale can be added either at the top or the bottom of the chart. In Figure 11.9, for example, the value of each column is identified in dollars (*$12,437; $2,290...$262*); if those labels were removed, it would be necessary to identify the value of the numbers in the stubs (*0 to 14*) in a scale.

Follow the same basic rules to construct a pictorial chart. When you choose the chart's symbol, make sure it is self-explanatory and that each symbol represents a single unit. Include a legend at the bottom of the table to explain the value of each unit. For example, each symbol of a worker in an employment-related table might equal 1,000 workers. Rather than increasing the size of each symbol, you indicate increased quantities by adding symbols and portions of symbols to extend each bar or column.

When a chart contains several data sets, it is important to use consistent colors or patterns to connect sets referring to the same category. For example, if a column chart shows a company's profits and losses over a two-year period, all the profit columns should use one color (black) and all the loss columns should be another single color (red). The same principle holds for charts which, like the grouped and subdivided bar charts in Figure 11.7, use cross-hatching or shading. It is also important to avoid patterns that clash, especially in simple black-and-white charts; different shades of gray are often more effective.

Color, shading, and cross-hatching can also be used to distinguish actual data from projected data, different items being compared at a given point, and the components on a subdivided column.

LINE CHARTS   Line charts are relatively easy to prepare. In general, begin the vertical axis with zero, even if the values being measured are much higher. When plotting begins at a higher value, insert a break in the vertical axis to reduce the height of the line. Let's suppose, for example, that a chart should be expressed in increments of 10; the meaningful data, however, begins at 5,000 units. To indicate the appropriate increment of 10, you would begin the left axis with 0, then 10, 20, 30; you would then insert a break in the line and continue at 5,000, 5,010, 5,020, and so on. Note the break in the vertical axis of the line chart in Figure 11.11.

There is one important exception to beginning the vertical axis with zero—charts that include negative values. In this case, the vertical axis begins with a negative number and continues into positive numbers to the top of the axis; zero falls somewhere in the middle, with the chart balanced above and below as evenly as the data allow.

Because the purpose of a line chart is to indicate a trend, it is important that the trend line be emphasized. In a single-line chart, emphasize the trend with a thick line or a bold color. Try to limit multiple-line charts to no more than three or four lines; differentiate each line with a different color or pattern, such as dots versus dashes or bold lines versus fine lines. Dashed or dotted lines are also frequently used to show projections or estimates.

DRAWINGS AND OTHER ILLUSTRATIONS   With the increasing use of computers in business, more and more drawings, diagrams, and other graphics are being computer-generated. Computer-aided design systems for creating such visual aids are especially popular in fields like architecture and engineering. The following guidelines are designed to help you get effective results whether you are drawing an illustration by hand or generating it with a computer.[4]

- Create your drawing from the point of view of the person who will read your document.
- Keep all parts in their correct proportions unless you state that a specific part is enlarged.
- Show a subsystem in relation to the larger system of which it is a part.
- Arrange a sequence of drawings from left to right or top to bottom.
- Clearly label all parts. Place the labels on the parts themselves; if the parts are too small, use letter or number symbols with an accompanying key.

Because visual aids do not stand alone but rather as part of a narrative, the way they are integrated into the text is critical. In the next section, we will examine some of the more effective methods for integrating these two aspects of your presentation.

INTEGRATING VISUAL AIDS INTO THE TEXT

Communication is enhanced by a smooth flow between your text (what you say) and your visual aids (what you illustrate). That flow is made possible by *integration*—text references that both explain the visual aids and announce their physical location in relation to the text.

In most cases, visual aids supplement written text. They support written material not merely by emphasizing key points but by allowing the message to communicate through two channels—text and illustration. Once you have designed your visual aids to support the message of your text, you must be sure to "interweave" your text and your illustrations. This interweaving is accomplished not only by finding the best place to add each illustration but also by explicitly linking your visuals to your narrative. For example, even though a chart may be referred to in a number of different places, it is up to you to choose the best place to insert it. The best place is where the chart best helps communicate your message.

Text references should be smooth and complete. Use phrases like "The monthly overhead, *as illustrated in Figure 9*, includes…" or *"According to the data in Table 3*, sales.…" The initial reference should be followed by a discussion of the data presented there, especially its significance to the reader. Usually, your text does not need to explain everything in your visual. It is never effective, however, to say merely that a figure or table has been included without providing some explanatory text.

In most reports and proposals, tables and charts are placed as close as possible to initial text references—but always *after* the first text reference. While small visual aids can appear on a page with continuing text material, a larger figure may take an entire page. If the discussion of a figure or table is longer than one page, the visual is usually inserted after the first reference to it in the discussion.

In some cases, tables and figures are compiled in appendixes. Although this practice is usually cumbersome, it is useful in some documents, such as reports designed to provide overviews of complex material. For example, a short summary report may include an appendix with detailed tables. While the sum-

ETHICS IN BUSINESS COMMUNICATION
Misleading Charts

There are three kinds of lies: lies, damned lies, and statistics.

Benjamin Disraeli
English prime minister and novelist

Although charts enable you to depict statistical data in ways that highlight important relationships, they also provide the opportunity to mislead. Whether intentionally or not, writers sometimes distort the relationships depicted in various types of charts. As a result, readers often come away with distorted versions of the truth.

Line charts are especially vulnerable to distortion. When improperly drawn, they can exaggerate growth or minimize problems. For example, although the charts in the following illustration (a) are based on the same data, the trend line in the chart on the right suggests a more rapid growth than the one on the left. The distortion occurs because even though the value of both is the period 1986 to 1994, the horizontal scale on the right is *collapsed* in comparison to the scale on the left.

The distortion is even more apparent in illustration (b). While the line in the first graph shows a steep increase due to the compression of years on the horizontal axis, the line in the second graph is more gradual and accurate. Although this illustration is intentionally simplified, it is fairly easy to predict the false impression that the first line chart might give. It would support a writer's argument that the increase in expenditures has been significant (out of control?) even if a more moderate interpretation should find them more modest (well within projected limits?).

Charts can also mislead if they are incomplete or if the proportions between the vertical and horizontal axes are changed. The following illustration (c) shows a series of three charts, each of which indicates a 7-percent upward trend in national income over a year. While the chart on the left shows accurate

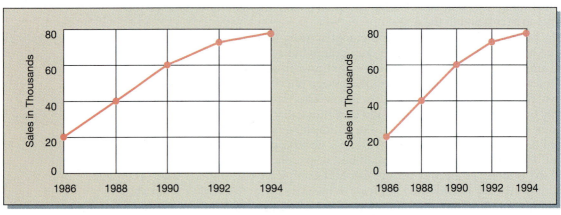

(a)

mary provides an adequate overview, the appendix is available for the reader who wants more in-depth information. Sometimes, the information contained in a visual aid is included to supplement the text rather than develop it directly. For example, a report dealing with government regulations of the mutual-fund market might contain a table comparing the features of 100 competing mutual funds. While not directly related to the writer's topic, the information would nevertheless be interesting to his or her readers. Such material may be placed in an appendix.

In an increasing number of business organizations, visual aids are created on computers with the use of presentation-graphics software. We will take a closer look at these programs in the next section.

information, the other two charts distort the same data. On the second chart, prosperity is understated because the bottom of the vertical axis (the value of the data from 0 to 10) is missing. The third chart contradicts the data presented in whole numbers simply by extending the vertical scale to include decimal values for the very same data.

Source: Charts excerpted from Darrell Huff, *How to Lie with Statistics* (New York: W. W. Norton, 1954), pp. 165–66, 278.

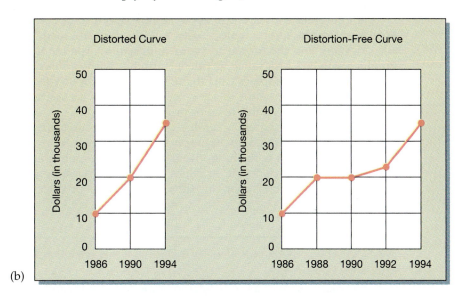

(b)

(c)

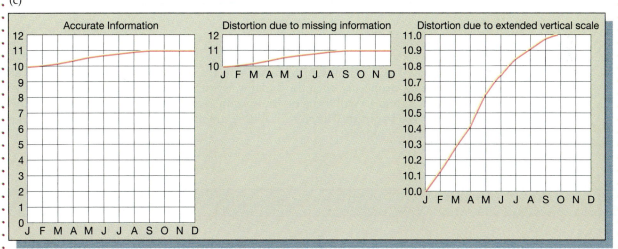

PRESENTATION GRAPHICS

Only a few decades ago, business writers had to produce charts and tables by hand. The job either took hours of painstaking effort or forced writers to send graphics to artists, either inside or outside the office. Waiting for these materials to be produced typically added days or even weeks to a schedule and additional costs to the project.

presentation-graphics software
Special computer programs used to create such visual aids as bar charts, line charts, pie charts, tables, drawings, and other graphic features by using data already in the computer

Any sufficiently advanced technology is indistinguishable from magic.

Arthur C. Clarke
Science fiction writer
and scientist

The creation of **presentation-graphics software**—computer programs for creating a variety of visual aids—now allows report and proposal writers to produce their own visual aids. Among the leading graphics programs are Harvard Graphics, developed by Software Publishing Company, and Freelance Graphics, produced by Lotus Development Corporation.

Presentation-graphics visuals, including charts, tables, drawings, and even three-dimensional diagrams, can be adapted for use in slides and overhead transparencies in either black and white or color. With presentation graphics, writers can pull data from spreadsheets and databases, arrange data in charts or tables, and add appropriate labels to communicate their messages. In a matter of seconds, a writer can produce a finished product that is accurate, visually attractive, and perfectly proportioned.

All graphics software leads you step by step through the creation process. Freelance Graphics, for example, uses a fill-in-the-blank page format to handle size, location, and the format for your information. The requirements for using graphics-software programs include a computer with sufficient memory to handle the software; a graphics card that enables the computer to process drawings and charts; a color monitor to see color variations; a mouse; and a high-quality printer, usually one capable of color printing.

In Chapter 13, we will examine desktop-publishing programs that enable you to create professional-quality reports and proposals from your own office—including documents containing visual aids. Desktop-publishing programs usually work in conjunction with graphics and word-processing programs. As you will see, this innovation is changing the way businesses produce printed materials.

PROGRESS CHECK

1. Describe some factors that lend simple, clear, effective design to visual aids.
2. How large should a figure be in relation to the surrounding text?

WHAT'S AHEAD

Chapters 10 and 11 have introduced you to critical functions common to all reports and proposals, including planning, researching, and using visual aids. Chapters 12 and 13 will focus on the specific requirements of short and long documents. We begin in Chapter 12 with guidelines for organizing and writing short and long reports.

SUMMARY OF CHAPTER OBJECTIVES

1. **Describe the function of *visual aids* in reports and proposals.**

   Charts and tables present data in a visual format that breaks the monotony of long narrative documents and helps shorten the text. In addition, visuals help readers make sense of difficult concepts and form meaningful comparisons.

2. **Explain the importance of linking each visual aid to its specific message.**

   To be effective, a visual aid must be linked to a specific purpose and message. This message is often communicated through the chart or table title. The title choice depends on whether the visual aid presents or reports data. While presentation visuals interpret data, report visuals let the facts speak for themselves.

3. **List the characteristics of *tables*.**

   Tables are systematic arrangements of data in rows and columns that provide readers with both a ready reference and a method of comparison. Composed of numbers, words, or a combination of both, tables can consolidate large quantities of information in a relatively small space without any loss of detail.

4. **List the different kinds of comparisons that can be made by *charts*.**

   Charts make four basic types of comparisons. In component comparisons, charts show the size of each part as a percentage of the total. In item comparisons, they analyze relative rankings to determine whether variables are the same or more than or less than one another. In time-series comparisons, charts measure how items change over time. Finally, in frequency-distribution comparisons, they show how many items fall into a series of defined, progressive numerical ranges.

5. **Contrast *pie charts, bar charts, column charts*, and *line charts* and explain the advantages of each.**

   Used for component comparisons, pie charts are graphs that present data as wedge-shaped sections of a circle that represents 100 percent of a given whole. Bar charts are graphs consisting of horizontal bars of equal width and varying lengths; each length represents a different quantity. Bar charts are best used for item comparisons. Column charts, which feature vertical rather than horizontal bars, are best used for time-series and frequency-distribution comparisons. Line charts show the relationship of numbers that intersect on horizontal and vertical axes and are used for time-series and frequency-distribution comparisons.

6. **Explain the uses in business documents of each of the following: *organization charts, flow charts*, and *drawings* and *photographs*, and *maps*.**

   Reports and proposals also use other types of visual aids besides bar charts and tables. Organization charts illustrate the interrelationship between the positions, departments, and functions of an organization. Flow charts describe the stages in a process. Gantt charts are graphic representations of production schedules. Drawings and photographs are illustrations that focus on the structure and function of products and equipment. Finally, maps show statistical comparisons in terms of geographic regions.

7. **Describe the mechanics of constructing visual aids.**

   Effective visual aids have simple, consistent, clear designs that focus on content over form. In general, the size of a figure is directly related to its importance and complexity. Titles and numbers identify each visual, while captions, labels, legends, and footnotes clarify information.

   Color, shading, and cross-hatching distinguish the elements of a chart. These techniques highlight selected elements and form visual groupings. By helping visually to define the parameters of a chart, borders, rules, grid lines, and tick marks make charts easier to read. Finally, source acknowledgments, which are usually placed at the bottom of a chart, tell readers where the data came from.

8. **Explain methods for integrating visual aids into the text.**

   Communication stems from the smooth integration of tables and charts in the text. Integration refers both to text references that explain the visuals and to the physical location of the visuals in relation to the text. A discussion of its main findings and significance to the reader should follow the initial reference to a table or chart. In most cases, tables and charts are placed as close to the initial text references as possible.

9. **Describe the role of *presentation-graphics software* in the creation of visual aids.**

   Presentation-graphics software enables writers to create charts and tables, add drawings, and select page layout and design. These programs permit you to pull data from spreadsheets and databases, arrange data in charts or tables, and add appropriate labels to communicate a message. The finished product is produced in a matter of seconds.

Review and Discussion Questions

1. Why is it important to give your reports an effective visual presentation? (*Ch. Obj. 1*)
2. What purpose(s) do visual aids serve in business documents? (*Ch. Obj. 1*)
3. Why is it important to link each visual aid to a message? (*Ch. Obj. 2*)
4. What are the characteristics of a good title? (*Ch. Obj. 2*)

5. What are the various types of comparisons that can be made by charts? (*Ch. Obj. 4*)

6. Describe the advantages of each of the following: pie charts, bar charts, column charts, line charts. (*Ch. Obj. 5*)

7. Summarize the functions of the following visual aids in business documents: organization charts, flow charts, drawings and photographs, maps. (*Ch. Obj. 6*)

8. Describe the mechanics of designing effective visual aids. (*Ch. Obj. 7*)

9. Explain how visual aids can be integrated effectively into a document. (*Ch. Obj. 8*)

10. How can presentation-graphics software help you create visual aids? (*Ch. Obj. 9*)

*A*PPLICATION EXERCISES

1. This chapter notes that every visual aid must have a message. Explain this statement. (*Ch. Obj. 1, 2*)

2. When is it advisable to present information in a table? What are the disadvantages, if any, of using tables? (*Ch. Obj. 3*)

3. Using sources outside class, find four charts used to enhance printed material. Each chart should illustrate one of the four basic types of comparison discussed in the chapter. For each chart, write a brief description of the kinds of data presented. Evaluate the effectiveness of each chart. Does it convey its message well? Why or why not? (*Ch. Obj. 4, 5*)

4. Test yourself on your ability to choose the best type of chart to make comparisons. Cover the center and right-hand columns of FIGURE 11.4. Sketch your own example of each type of chart and summarize the comparisons that each type can illustrate effectively. (*Ch. Obj. 4, 5*)

5. Research and design a visual aid that illustrates how your school or employer allocates its advertising budget among various media. Which type of visual aid did you decide to use? Why? (*Ch. Obj. 5, 7*)

6. Research and design a visual aid that compares your school's or employer's current advertising-budget allocation with the budget allocations for each of the last two years. Follow the chapter's guidelines for effective design. Which type of visual aid did you choose to illustrate this information? Why? (*Ch. Obj. 5, 7*)

7. Research and create an organization chart illustrating the interrelationships among various positions/functions at your employer or school. Follow the chapter's guidelines for effective design. (*Ch. Obj. 6, 7*)

8. Research and create a flow chart that illustrates a process at your workplace or school. Identify each stage of the process and show the beginning and end. (*Ch. Obj. 6, 7*)

9. Your school's public-relations staff has asked you to compile some brief guidelines for designing effective tables, pie charts, bar and column charts, and line charts. Write these guidelines. (*Ch. Obj. 7*)

10. The public-relations staff liked your guidelines for charts, and the director now wants you to write guidelines for designing and using drawings and other illustrations in business documents. Write these guidelines. (*Ch. Obj. 6, 7*)

11. The public-relations director is back again. This time she asks you to write guidelines for the best way(s) to integrate visual aids into a narrative. Write these guidelines. (*Ch. Obj. 8*)

12. Using presentation-graphics software, recreate some of the charts pictured in this chapter, such as FIGURES 11.2, 11.3, and 11.11. Experiment with different chart types. Include clear labels and legends. Print your charts and hand them in to your instructor. (*Ch. Obj. 5, 7, 9*)

13. How have various types of bonds performed for investors over the last few years? Using the following data, create a visual aid that compares the yield of these bonds over time. Then write a brief summary of what can be learned by studying this visual aid. (*Ch. Obj. 5, 7*)

Approximate Yields of Treasury Bonds

December 1987	8.8 percent
December 1988	8.2
December 1990	8.5
December 1991	7.2
December 1992	7.4

Approximate Yields of Municipal Bonds

December 1987	8.2 percent
December 1988	7.8
December 1989	7.2
December 1990	7.1
December 1991	6.8
December 1992	6.3

Approximate Yields of Money Funds

December 1987	6.3 percent
December 1988	8.1
December 1989	7.9
December 1990	6.9
December 1991	4.8
December 1992	2.8

14. You have been asked to give a report on the personal-computer software market. Here are the market shares of the top software manufacturers:

    Borland, 6.6 percent   Microsoft, 30 percent

    Lotus, 10.9 percent   WordPerfect, 7 percent

    Novell, 8.4 percent

    95 separate companies with collective shares of 37.1 percent

    Create a visual aid summarizing this information. Is there a market leader? (*Ch. Obj. 5, 7*)

15. Your school's placement office has asked you to prepare a report entitled "Where the Jobs Will Be." Your research yields the following statistics:

    > Between now and the year 2005, the following industries will offer more jobs than they do now. Doctors' offices will add 1,290,000 more jobs by 2005; private hospitals will add 1,058,000 new jobs; and nursing will add 762,000 new jobs. Public schools will add 1,320,000 new jobs; construction will add 923,000 new jobs; computer services will add 710,000 new jobs; restaurants and bars will add 2,147,000 new jobs; retailers will add 2,974,000 new jobs, and wholesalers will add 1,005,000 new jobs.

    Prepare a visual aid comparing the number of new jobs to be added in each of these industries between now and 2005. What can you learn from the information presented in this visual aid? (*Ch. Obj. 5, 7*)

BUILDING YOUR RESEARCH SKILLS

Using sources outside class, find two articles on topics related to business—one article that you feel is well illustrated and one that you feel is poorly done. Write an analysis of the visual presentation of each article. Explain why you feel the visual aids are better in one article than the other. How could the visual presentation be improved in the poorly illustrated article? Bring your written analysis, plus the two articles, to class.

BUILDING YOUR TEAMWORK SKILLS

Your instructor will divide the class into small groups. Meet with your team to discuss the two articles that you analyzed in the previous exercise. Work together to think of more ways to improve the visual presentation of each team member's articles. Your instructor may want to have a representative from your team present the "best" and "worst" articles from your group to the class.

COMMUNICATING IN A WORLD OF DIVERSITY

Your company is considering opening an office in Japan and your boss has asked you to find out how the Japanese stock market is doing. You do some research and find the following data:

In one recent year, the Nikkei (Japanese stock-market index) showed these approximate values:

January: 101	February: 100	March: 110
April: 105	May: 108	June: 106
July: 94	August: 97	September: 90
October: 100	November: 108	December: 98

During the same year, the Dow Jones Industrial Average (the U.S. stock-market index) showed these approximate values:

January: 84	February: 87	March: 94
April: 93	May: 94	June: 98
July: 95	August: 97	September: 98
October: 97	November: 98	December: 94

The following year, the Nikkei showed these approximate values:

January: 103	February: 99	March: 93
April: 84	May: 74	June: 81
July: 71	August: 70	September: 82
October: 85	November: 77	December: 79

January: 103	February: 104	March: 105
April: 104	May: 108	June: 110
July: 106	August: 109	September: 106
October: 105	November: 104	December: 106

During the same year, the Dow Jones showed these approximate values:

Prepare a visual aid that compares the performance of the Nikkei and the Dow Jones indexes for these two years.

CASE 11.1

Picturing the Investment Landscape

Your boss has asked you for advice on the best ways to invest the corporation's assets during the next decade. As part of your research, you discover statistics showing the annual growth rate of different types of investments over the past three decades.

During the 1960s, for instance, average annual growth rates were as follows:

- Small-company stocks, 15.5 percent
- 20-year government bonds, 1.4 percent
- 20-year corporate bonds, 1.7 percent
- Treasury bills, 3.9 percent
- Residential real estate, 7.5 percent

During this decade the annual inflation rate averaged 2.5 percent.

During the 1970s, average annual growth rates were as follows:

- Small-company stocks, 11.5 percent
- 20-year government bonds, 5.5 percent
- 20-year corporate bonds, 6.2 percent
- Treasury bills, 6.3 percent
- Residential real estate, 12.9 percent

During this decade, the annual inflation rate averaged 7.4 percent.

During the 1980s, average annual growth rates were as follows:

- Small-company stocks, 15.8 percent

- 20-year government bonds, 12.6 percent
- 20-year corporate bonds, 13 percent
- Treasury bills, 8.9 percent
- Residential real estate, 11.5 percent

During this decade, the annual inflation rate averaged 5.1 percent.

During the 1990s, annual growth rates have so far averaged as follows:

- Small-company stocks, 7 percent
- 20-year government bonds, 11.9 percent
- 20-year corporate bonds, 12.5 percent
- Treasury bills, 5.9 percent
- Residential real estate, 5.0 percent

During this period, the annual inflation rate averaged 4.2 percent.

Questions and Applications

1. Write a report in which you give your opinion on the best long-term investment(s) for your firm.
2. Include a visual aid in which you chart annual growth rates for various investments from the 1960s to the present.

Source: Louis Richman, "How to Protect Your Financial Future," *Fortune*, January 24, 1993, pp. 58–60.

Picturing a New-Product Opportunity

"Most of the products in the frozen-breakfast category that are growing and successful right now involve the toaster," says Marc Schwinner, general manager of frozen-breakfast business at Quaker Oats. "In evaluating new products, it is certainly an important factor to take into account." Ellen Perl, head of the breakfast team at rival Pillsbury agrees: "The toaster is very big right now. We are going to ride it."

The numbers support food-industry executives like Schwinner and Perl. Sales of frozen waffles, for example, grew 15 percent during one recent year. Sales of frozen bagels, Pop Tarts, and other toaster pastries are also growing. Not surprisingly, sales of toasters are also up by 16 percent.

Currently, the following products are big sellers in the frozen-breakfast market: Eggo frozen waffles (annual sales of $340.2 million, up 18.7 percent from the previous year); Downyflake frozen waffles ($88.8 million, up 31.6 percent over the past year); Lender's frozen bagels ($163.3 million, up 4.6 percent over the previous year); Kellogg's Pop Tarts ($305 million, up 6.4 percent over the previous year); private-label toaster pastries ($45 million, up 41.7 percent over the previous year);

and Pillsbury Toaster Strudel ($50.7 million, up 16.6 percent over the previous year).

Some marketers see this renewed interest in the humble toaster as a reaction against high-tech gadgets. "The toaster," suggests market researcher Ann Clurman, "is an interesting counterpoint to the microwave and all of the technology in the kitchen. It doesn't yell at you. . . . It's like, put up the lace curtains and get out the toaster. It is a wonderfully evocative image."

Questions and Applications

1. As director of new products for your company, you feel that the firm should develop a new line of frozen-breakfast foods that can be cooked in the family toaster. Write a report in which you suggest this idea and explain how it could benefit the company.

2. Include at least two visual aids to support the arguments in your report.

Source: Eben Shapiro, "Food Shoppers Warm to Toaster Cuisine," *The Wall Street Journal*, December 29, 1992, p. B1.

12

Organizing and Writing
Short and Long Reports

CHAPTER OBJECTIVES

After studying this chapter, you should be able to:

1 Identify six differences between *short* and *long reports*.

2 List the elements contained in short *progress* and *trip reports*.

3 Identify the elements contained in the *front matter* of a long report.

4 Explain the role of the *executive summary* in a long report.

5 List the functions of the *introduction* in a long report.

6 Describe the types of *structural guideposts* that can be used to create *internal connections* in the body of long reports.

7 Explain how *summaries, conclusions*, and *recommendations* are used to close long reports.

8 List the elements contained in the *back matter* of a long report.

9 Explain the use of direct and indirect organizational patterns in long reports.

WHY REPORTS MAKE RECOMMENDATIONS

The mid-1980s were years of concern for almost everyone responsible for security at major government and commercial buildings in New York City. A series of bombings in and around the city had left the general public shaken and had led to growing demands for increased security. Few organizations had greater responsibility for security measures than did the New York Port Authority, the agency in charge of the towering 110-story twin skyscrapers of the World Trade Center. On a typical day, more than 100,000 workers and visitors pack the two landmark buildings that rise above the skyline of lower Manhattan.

In 1985, a special task force composed of both police and civilian anti-terrorist experts was appointed to study security procedures at the World Trade Center. The group was commissioned to prepare a short report with specific recommendations for minimizing the possibility of a terrorist attack. After several months of study, the task force submitted a report with 170 specific recommendations to Stephen Berger, who was then the Port Authority's executive director. Among the group's recommendations were the following:

- The center's parking garage is vulnerable to bomb attack and should be closed to the public.

- The backup command center should be removed from underground levels, away from primary systems, and located behind airline counters on the first level.

- In case Consolidated Edison generators should ever be disabled, an alternative source of power, separate from main Con Ed generators, should be brought in from New Jersey.

- Glass throughout the buildings should be reinforced with Mylar coating.

- Contingency and evacuation plans must be drawn up, and increased lighting should be installed throughout the buildings, including battery-supported lighting for stairwells.

- Emergency-exit stairs should be repaired or otherwise improved.

- New methods of venting smoke produced by possible fires should be devised.

Although the report's recommendations were reviewed by Port Authority officials, most of them were rejected. The suggestion to restrict parking, for example, was bypassed as impractical. After all, concluded one Trade Center representative, the need for public parking was indisputable in a location with "hundreds of tenants having thousands of business interactions each day, and with restaurants, shops, and hotels." Battery-supported lighting in the stairwells was considered a good idea, but currently available systems were considered unreliable and required high maintenance.

Interest in the eight-year-old report was renewed shortly after the morning of February 26, 1993, when a huge bomb ripped through the underground parking garage of the World Trade Center. The explosion, one of the most dramatic terrorist attacks in U.S. history, claimed six lives, caused more than 1,000 injuries, and forced thousands of people to walk down almost 100 floors of dark emergency-exit stairways.[1]

CHAPTER OVERVIEW

Although relatively few business reports deal with life-and-death issues like those raised in the World Trade Center antiterrorism report, they do represent a critical communication tool, not only for compiling and evaluating information but for aiding management in recommending and taking action. As we saw in Chapter 10, business reports may be long and formal or they may be short and informal. They may be directed at key decision makers within a company, or they may focus on issues involving customers, suppliers, or government agencies. Finally, a report may be released periodically or issued on a one-time basis.

Although reports are as individual as their topics and their writers, there are certain characteristics that many short reports share. Similarly, most long reports follow specified formats. As we describe the formal report, we will introduce a model outline that identifies the sections contained in a typical report. Using this outline, we will examine the specific elements included in the *front matter, body,* and *back matter* of a report. Focusing on sample documents to show how various elements take shape, we will also analyze specific *structural guideposts* that help writers create coherent documents. Finally, we will examine the use of *direct* and *indirect organizational styles* in long reports. We begin with a discussion of short reports and how they differ from longer documents.

SHORT BUSINESS REPORTS

The most common type of written report in most business organizations is the short report. Short reports may focus on a variety of issues, including employee productivity, inventory, meetings, and project-progress checks.

Regardless of their type or length, all business reports share one important characteristic. They take readers on a journey that starts with a statement of purpose and ends with a summary of conclusions and recommendations. As you will see, the location of these elements in a given report depends on whether you choose a direct or indirect organizational approach.

Although all reports tell a story, some do it in fewer words than others. Interestingly, the purpose and audience of a report often have a greater influence on its length than its topic. Business-communication professors Ray E. Barfield and Sylvia S. Titus use the following example to make this point:

This is the short and long of it.
William Shakespeare

> If an employee has a fender bender in a company truck, a supervisor files a brief accident report, insurance claims are settled, and the matter is soon relegated to the files. On the other hand, a large organization's Director of Transportation, seeing an alarming three-year trend in accident frequency, will ask for a comprehensive report to assess fleet reliability and maintenance needs, employee driver training, and insurance cost containment. The short accident report will pass through only two or three employees' hands, but the lengthy investigative report will be printed (perhaps in dozens of bound copies) and circulated to all interested parties.[2]

In such a case, then, although both reports deal with insurance matters, the long report has not only a broader purpose but also a larger audience than the short document.

Short and long reports also differ in a number of other ways. Generally, short reports do not require elaborate front or back matter. They spend little time introducing the topic in the body, and they get to the point immediately; they are usually more personal and require fewer writing devices to aid comprehension.[3] In addition, short reports often follow prescribed outlines or use printed forms.

FRONT AND BACK MATTER   Most short reports do not include covers, title pages, letters of transmittal, tables of contents, or lists of illustrations. Similarly, appendixes, bibliographies, and indexes are rare in short reports. Geared toward simplicity, many short reports are written in letter or memo form.

INTRODUCTORY MATTER   In general, short reports spend little time introducing the topic or providing background information in the body. The writer assumes that everyone reading the document will be familiar with its background. Because most short reports are addressed to relatively few readers, this assumption is usually valid.

Before beginning a short report, then, you should analyze your audience to decide whether introductory materials are necessary. If your topic is discussed often or can be considered common knowledge among your readers, a single introductory sentence may be sufficient. Progress and trip reports usually fall into this category. However, if your report will be read by a fairly large number of people (many of whom may be unfamiliar with the topic), or if it is likely to be kept on file for an extended period, a more detailed introduction may be necessary. (Investigative reports usually fall into this category.)

CONCLUSIONS AND RECOMMENDATIONS   The goal of most short reports is to get to the point immediately. Thus, they typically begin with *report summaries*, which may include *general* conclusions and recommendations and which may also describe the logical steps that led the writer to make them. The *specific* details that support the initial summary accompany the conclusions and recommendations made at the end of the report. Material is developed in a logical, analytical way, starting with the introduction, moving to the body of the report, and ending with conclusions and recommendations.

LANGUAGE   Short reports tend to use more personal language than long reports, including such personal pronouns as *I, we,* and *you.* In addition, first names, contractions, and personal references add a familiar tone. This should not be surprising—after all, writers and readers of short reports are likely to know each other and topics are often routine.

Ultimately, the reader's position and preferences will determine whether a personal or impersonal writing style is appropriate in the short report. For example, unless top management sets a more relaxed tone, mid-level managers writing to the CEO or other senior-level executives should use an impersonal style. When the reader is a stranger, the best advice is to err on the side of caution. Use impersonal language until you learn more about the reader's preferences.

WRITING DEVICES TO AID COMPREHENSION   Because they contain relatively few pages, short reports generally do not require the use of formal writing devices to aid comprehension. These devices, which are common in long reports, include internal summaries and previews placed at key points in the document. We will examine these devices later in the chapter when we describe the long report.

Although short reports must be clearly organized, the connections between sentences and paragraphs can usually be made with simple transitions. Ideas can be sufficiently connected with phrases like *As the previous paragraph demonstrated...* or *Based on this information....*

PRESCRIBED OUTLINES OR FORMS   As we saw in Chapter 10, many reports, especially short reports like progress and trip reports, are submitted periodically. To save time, many writers thus use standard outlines. Past reports, for example, may serve as models for current and future reports written on the same topics.

The outline provides a flexible guide for structuring and organizing a report. However, it is important to consider the outline as merely a guide—your situation may very well require adding, deleting, or rearranging information that appeared in previous documents. The advantage of using an outline to write short periodic reports is the structure it provides.

Periodic reports may also be written on preprinted forms. Form reports are typically used for routine matters because they save time for the person who must complete them. They also organize numerical information so that data are easily tabulated. In general, these reports should be completed in full sentences rather than phrases. In addition, responses should be limited to requested information. (Chapter 10 covers form reports in more detail and provides examples.)

Table 12.1 summarizes the six basic differences between short and long reports.

COMMONLY USED SHORT REPORTS

As we saw in Chapter 10, business reports fall into six major categories summarized in Table 10.2: information, survey, study, expert, status, and recommendation. Within these categories we will look more closely at some specific types of reports, including *progress, trip, investigative,* and *trouble reports,* all of which are frequently written in short form.[4]

Progress Reports

No business can afford to leave important project details to chance. Progress reports, then, are among the most common business reports. **Progress reports** provide status information, including updates, on current work.

Progress reports serve many purposes and are written for both internal and external use. For example, in order to summarize what has been done and what remains to be done, an automotive subcontractor developing a new

progress report
Short report providing status information on current work, including what has happened on a project since the previous report

TABLE 12.1	*Characteristics of Short and Long Reports*

SHORT REPORTS	LONG REPORTS
No front or back materials	Cover, title page, letter of transmittal, table of contents, list of illustrations, and forward
Short introduction	Lengthy introduction that describes the report's purpose and scope, organizational plan, and research methods
Bottom-line orientation	Indirect or direct organizational approach
Personal writing style	Impersonal writing style
Few devices to connect materials	Heavy use of internal previews and summaries, transitions, headings, and summary tables and charts to connect report elements
May use a prescribed outline or form	Written from scratch

INTERVIEW

Lawrence D. Brennan, Consultant and Professor of Business Communications

Lawrence D. Brennan, professor emeritus of business communication at New York University, spent many years consulting with major corporations about business writing. Much of his work involved teaching executives how to write more effective business documents, including reports. We asked Professor Brennan for his views on effective report writing and on the report writing process.

Question: Why are business reports written?

Answer: The best reports give readers the answers they need to complete a job. They're usable documents.

The best reports are well-displayed. They make it easy for readers to move from left to right, from the top of the page to the bottom of the page, with very little need to reread material.

The best reports have a rhetorical and display structure that arranges thoughts in a logical, psychologically effective order.

Finally, the best reports are written by people who know their jobs inside-out. Indeed, they know ten times more about the job than they can possibly put on paper. Anything you do to

improve your knowledge of your work will also improve your ability to write a report.

Question: What misconceptions surround the report-writing process?

Answer: The four most serious misconceptions are (a) that reports don't count—

only job performance counts; (b) that jargon makes reports sound official; (c) that electronic devices will soon replace human report writers; and (d) that business writing and literary writing are the same. This last misconception, unfortunately, is often held by otherwise talented people. They lose track of their purpose and attempt to invest their writing with stylistic flourishes.

Question: What role does collaboration play in report writing?

Answer: Collaboration, or team play, is inevitable in the development of important business documents. But a group cannot sit around a table and phrase the document into shape. The group can create an overall design for the report during a conference and capture that design in a dummy. But individual members of the group must independently draft the sections of the report.

Question: What are report conferences?

Answer: A report conference is a meeting of concerned collaborators working on a project headed by a knowledgeable leader. At a first conference, collaborators discuss the report purpose, concept, design, and needed contents. They agree upon a dummy and accept responsibility for phrasing assigned sections within constraints of the dummy. The sections that each one phrases addresses his or her areas of expertise—say, accounting, finance, or marketing. They may meet at interim conferences, but the final report is synthesized at a closing conference when all the copy has been drafted. The group leader, often with an editor, integrates the draft and tightens consistency of viewpoint and style.

Source: Interview with Lawrence D. Brennan.

---

type of seat belt might submit progress reports throughout the life of the project. Similarly, a specialist in employee-benefits design may submit regular progress reports to the director of human resources concerning the work being done on a companywide pension plan. Because they are timely and current, progress reports help managers allocate equipment and personnel, adjust schedules, revise budgets, and spot potential problems.

ORGANIZING PROGRESS REPORTS   The outline shown in Table 12.2 can be used as a guideline for organizing the information in a progress report to tell the reader what has been done and what remains to be done. A budget analysis may also be included in any of the final four sections. Keep in mind that this and other model outlines presented in this chapter are only guides; your final draft may differ widely in content and form. Figure 12.1 is a sample short progress report in memo form.

TABLE 12.2   *Model Outline: Progress Report*

SECTION	DESCRIPTION
Summary	Describes the stage of the project covered in the report, progress that has been made to date, and the future forecast; conclusions and recommendations are also highlighted
Work Completed	Focuses on the items completed since the last report as well as any associated problems and solutions
Work in Progress	Lists work currently being completed; problems are highlighted, as are proposed solutions
Work to be Completed	Focuses on what remains to be done, including any foreseeable problems and proposed solutions
Forecast	Forecasts progress to be made between this report and the next scheduled report
Conclusions and Recommendations	Focuses on the details of the conclusions and recommendations; may, for example, analyze changes needed to maintain the project's progress, including scheduling, personnel, materials, technology, and funding changes; report concludes with appraisal of the entire project

6000 Bandini Boulevard
Los Angeles, CA 90040

213 555-6791

TO: Nicholoas Demy, Marketing Manager
FROM: Thomas G. Niver, Director of Product Development
DATE: July 19, 199X
SUBJ: Progress in Meeting California's New Standards for
Controlling Lawn Mower and Chain Saw Emissions

Lawn Master is currently on schedule in meeting California's standards for lowering hydrocarbon emissions from lawn mowers and chain saws. As you know, California's regulations—the strictest in the nation—are gradually being phased in and will take effect in 1999. Our work is focusing on developing rechargeable machines and redesigning our gasoline engines to reduce emissions.

Work in Progress

We are currently exploring several possibilities to reduce the gasoline-engine emissions from Lawn Master mowers and saws. They include:

■ redesigning of combustion chambers to overhead rather than side valves.

■ Design of engines to operate on a leaner fuel-air mixture.

■ Development of a safe, efficient catalytic converter for use in gas-powered mowers and saws.

Forecast

The test program and user survey for the electric mower will be complete in September. I will provide you with a survey report by October 15. Because the development of the improved gas mower is on schedule, I should have more information about the three redesign issues within a month.

FIGURE 12.1   *Sample Progress Report*

Trip Reports

trip report
Short report that summarizes the events of a business trip

A second commonly used short report is the trip (or travel) report. Usually written to direct supervisors, **trip reports** summarize the events of a business trip. More than listing of itineraries and expenses, however, these reports often highlight what the writer accomplished on the trip. Using a direct approach, effective trip reports tell the reader at the start where you went, why you went there, and what you did with your time. According to the classification system described in Table 10.2, trip reports would be included in the *information* and *status* categories.

ORGANIZING TRIP REPORTS Although the temptation is strong to organize trip reports chronologically, most business writers prefer the following model outline. Figure 12.2 is a sample trip report based on this model.

- *Summary.* Include the locations that you visited, the reason for your trip, the dates of your trip, who accompanied you, and a brief evaluation of the trip. Your evaluation should mention trip-related conclusions and recommendations.
- *Details.* Moving from a broad overview to a more specific discussion, review the details of your trip. To meet the needs of busy readers, arrange details in order of importance.

POWER PRINTING
201 Van Dyke Avenue Warren, MI 48090
313 555-1106

TO: Alice Madera
FROM: William Reilly
DATE: November 1, 199X
SUBJ: Trip to Deborah Gordon Public Relations, Inc., Chicago

On October 28 and 29, Joan Deaver and I visited Deborah Gordon, President of Deborah Gordon Public Relations, Inc., in Chicago. The purpose of the trip was to learn how to make Power Printing's nationwide franchise system more visible in the marketplace.

The visit was informative and productive. Joan and I came away with concrete strategies that medium-size businesses like ours can use to create corporate visibility and generate specific client leads. Among the strategies that I recommend is increased employee involvement in community activities.

<u>Suggested Strategies</u>

Gordon suggested two related approaches for heightening Power Printing's visibility in the community:

- Community involvement. She recommended that all sales representatives be required to join at least one outside group, such as a charity or business association.
- Regular follow-up. She also suggested that employees follow up at least one new business contact each week through lunch and office meetings.

<u>Conclusions and Recommendations</u>

The suggestion to increase community involvement has the potential to increase visibility and sales. I particularly like the idea of sponsoring a local event, such as a community 10K charity run. Not only should we encourage employees to take part in the run, but we can also provide T-shirts for all participants with our company name and logo. I recommend that we consider doing this in April for the annual spring run held downtown. The approximate cost for our sponsorship and involvement would be $2,000.

FIGURE 12.2 ***Sample Trip Report***

- *Conclusions and recommendations.* In the final section, specific details regarding the trip are provided. They are based on information gathered in the text.
- *Closing.* The document closes by examining the need for future visits to the same site.

Investigative Reports

Let's say that you have been asked to evaluate seven different laser printers to determine which printer will best meet your company's needs. How will you present your findings? Or suppose your company is about to merge with another firm. How would you analyze such duplicated systems as accounting, management information, and benefits in order to decide which system would best serve the needs of your new company? Each of these tasks might require an investigative report.

Investigative reports examine and analyze the details of a particular topic and then present conclusions and recommendations based on that analysis. Depending upon their topic and scope, investigative reports may be short or long. In short documents, it is usually preferable to use a direct approach and organize your material according to the specific needs of your topic. Based on the classification system established in Table 10.2, investigative reports are study reports.

investigative report
Short report that examines and analyzes details of a particular topic and presents conclusions and recommendations based on that analysis

Trouble Reports

When a problem affects a company's day-to-day operations, a trouble report may be called for. In addition to determining the cause of problems, **trouble reports** try to present recommendations for solving them and preventing recurrences. For example, a trouble report may focus on a rash of worker injuries or on the failure of a computer system.

Using the direct approach, trouble reports usually begin with summaries to highlight conclusions and recommendations. Details follow in the next section, where the reader learns what happened, when, where, and how, and who was involved. The report concludes with details of the conclusions and recommendations. Based on the classification system established in Table 10.2, trouble reports would be categorized as study documents.

trouble report
Short report that attempts to determine the cause of a problem and presents recommendations for solving it and preventing its recurrence

PROGRESS CHECK

1. Explain the importance of reports in business.
2. Suppose that you're writing a report for someone whom you don't know personally. Would you use a personal or impersonal writing style? Explain your answer.

LONG BUSINESS REPORTS

Although short reports are straightforward and relatively simple to write, they are not always appropriate to the needs of the topic, situation, or audience. When a short report will not accomplish your objectives, a longer formal report may be necessary.

Formal reports are usually linked to major projects—the development of new products, a companywide structural reorganization, a study of competitive products or methods. The decision to write a formal report usually means several things:

- The complexity of the subject requires in-depth analysis.
- The document requires extensive research that may be time-consuming and costly.

ETHICS IN BUSINESS COMMUNICATION

Plagiarism: The World's Dumbest Crime

Let's not beat around the bush: Plagiarism is theft. It is the act of stealing the ideas or words of another writer without crediting the source and, where appropriate, asking for permission. Although it is also against the law, plagiarism remains common wherever words are written—in business, politics, academia, journalism, and government. Plagiarism is also a problem in public speaking.

Recently, journalist Gregg Easterbrook uncovered nearly three pages of his own words in a book authored by Richard Pascale, a Stanford University business-school lecturer. Easterbrook had written these words four years before Pascale's book was published. Compare two sentences taken from each version:

■ **Easterbrook Version,** from an article in a 1986 issue of *The Washington Monthly*:

> On a very dark day in 1980, Donald Petersen, newly chosen president of Ford Motors, visited the company design studios. Ford was in the process of losing $2.2 billion, the largest single-year loss in U.S. history.

■ **Pascale Version,** from his 1990 book, *Managing on the Edge*:

> On a dark day in 1980, Donald Petersen, the newly chosen President of Ford Motor Company, visited the company's Detroit design studio. That year, Ford would lose $2.2 billion, the largest loss in a single year in U.S. corporate history.

Knowing how to avoid plagiarism like this is as crucial as knowing the rules of grammar. Here are some guidelines that will help you avoid the problem.

1. Develop the habit of documenting the ideas and words that you obtain from other sources. When citing the exact words of a source, set off the citation in quotation marks and use a footnote for documentation.

2. Develop effective note-taking habits and be very careful in your use of quotation marks. Plagiarism often occurs when, during the research stage, sources are copied verbatim without quotation marks.

3. You are still responsible for *documenting* your sources even if you rephrase someone else's thoughts in your own words and with your own sentence structure (the essence of paraphrasing and summarizing).

4. Finally, learn when documentation is *not* necessary. First, personal ideas and knowledge require no documentation. Footnotes, for example, are not needed if you are presenting an *original* new-product marketing strategy. Second, "common knowledge"—information known and readily available to most people—is not subject to plagiarism. Thus, when writing a report on a major corporation, there is no need to document the source that gave you the name of the CEO or the location of corporate headquarters.

Plagiarism is a breach of ethics as well as a theft of property. It is also "the world's dumbest crime," says Gregg Easterbrook. "If you are caught, there is absolutely nothing you can say in your own defense."

Sources: James Atlas, "When an Original Idea Sounds Really Familiar," *The New York Times*, July 28, 1991, p. E2; Gregg Easterbrook, "The Sincerest Flattery," *Newsweek*, July 29, 1991, pp. 45–46; and Lynn Quitman Troyka, *Simon & Schuster Handbook for Writers*, 2nd ed. (Englewood Cliffs, NJ: Prentice Hall, 1990), pp. 580–83.

■ The report will be read by various primary and secondary audiences.

■ The document may influence major decisions.

■ The document may become part of an official record that is referred to over time.

Because of the complexity of long report topics and the typical length of the resulting documents, the formal report requires a more prescribed structure than the short report. This structure is characterized by the presence of front and back matter in addition to the body of the report. It is also defined by the use of internal structural devices that connect the elements of the report body itself. We will examine each of the elements of the long report in the next section.

ELEMENTS OF A MODEL REPORT

When experienced business readers pick up a formal report, they expect to see certain elements arranged in a given order. Indeed, many companies and business organizations give employees writing manuals that detail the "house style" for long reports, including the elements to be used and the order in which they should appear. If you receive such a manual, use it as your model. If no manual is provided, use the elements presented here as your composition guide. All the elements that you are likely to find in a formal report are listed in Figure 12.3. While some of these elements are mandatory, such as a table of contents and an executive summary, others are optional and reflect the special needs of your document. For example, a title-fly sheet and glossary are not always necessary.

Dividing these elements into three main categories—*front matter, body,* and *back matter*—we will describe each in some detail and clarify with examples wherever necessary.

FIGURE 12.3 *Elements of a Formal Report*

Front Matter

front matter
Parts of a formal report that are included before the body

It is a foolish thing to make a long prologue and to be short in the story itself.

2 Maccabees 2:32

The parts of a formal report that appear before the body are known as the **front matter**. This material describes the document's purpose and gives readers an overview of the information that they will find in it. It also provides a "road map" for locating specific report sections, figures, and other important information. Because both reports and proposals use many identical front-matter elements, samples of these elements are included both here and in Chapter 13.

COVER   Report covers include the following information:

- Title and subtitle
- Name, title, and address of the company or person to whom the report is being sent; this block of information is often preceded by the words *Submitted to* or *Prepared for.*
- Author's name, title, company or department, and address; this information may be preceded by the phrase *Submitted by* or *Prepared by.*

To give reports a professional appearance, covers are often printed on heavy-duty stock and may include company logos.

title fly
Optional opening page of a formal report that includes only the report title

title page
Front-matter page of a formal report that usually includes the title, the name of the intended recipient, the author's name, and the submission date

TITLE FLY AND TITLE PAGE   Some reports open with a page that includes only the report title. This page, which is optional even in the most formal documents, is commonly referred to as the **title fly**. By contrast, the **title page**—which is usually the first page that readers see when they open a report—may include any or all of the following elements:

- Title and subtitle
- Name, title, and address of the person or group for whom the report is intended; once again, precede this information with *Submitted to* or *Prepared for.*
- Author's name, title, company or department, address, phone and fax numbers; preface this information with *Submitted by* or *Prepared by.*
- Date of submission

As the first front-matter page, the title page, although unnumbered, is considered *page i.* Begin *numbering* the front matter on the next page with *page ii.*

The title, of course, is the most important element on both the cover and the title page. After all, it tells readers what your report is all about. Because of its importance, your title should be chosen carefully and should indicate your document's purpose and scope. For example, this title–subtitle combination

<u>Shifting to a Just-in-Time Inventory System
at Wayside Industrial Park</u>
Cost-Containment Implications to the Year 2000

is better than the neutral and uninformative

<u>Just-in-Time Inventory System</u>

Avoid prefacing your title with phrases like *Report on....* Your reader already knows that he or she is about to read a report.

letter of transmittal (or cover letter)
Front-matter page that officially conveys the report to the reader, identifying the specific report being sent, the person to whom it is directed, and the reason for sending it.

LETTER OF TRANSMITTAL   The **letter of transmittal** (or **cover letter**) officially conveys the report to the reader. Transmittal letters often begin with simple, direct statements. For example:

> Here is the report on productivity changes you asked me to complete by December 3.

Note, however, that this statement not only transmits the report but also refers to the authorization under which the document was written. The transmittal letter identifies the specific report being sent, the person to whom it is directed, and the reason for sending it. This letter thus provides a permanent document-delivery record for both writer and reader. Transmittal memos serve the same purpose in internal reports.

The next item in the transmittal letter is usually a brief statement of the report's purpose. This statement helps the reader focus on the reason for which the report was written. For example:

> As you recall, you asked me to assess how eliminating secretarial support for assistant vice presidents would affect productivity.

Because a formal report will include an executive summary, the transmittal letter need not provide a detailed summary of conclusions and recommendations. Rather, it should orient readers in a general way to the discussion that follows.

The amount of information included in the transmittal letter depends in part on whether the report contains good news or bad news. If it contains good news for the reader, the writer will typically include a short summary of the report's findings and recommendations. Use a direct organizational approach to convey this information: Start with the main idea in the form of a summary statement. If the news is negative, you may choose to provide few details at this early stage.

Transmittal letters are often written in informal, conversational language. They may also use personal pronouns such as *I* and *you* and personal references. These qualities also make transmittal letters the ideal place to acknowledge the work of others who contributed to the report. Finally, transmittal letters generally close with goodwill messages. You can choose, for example, to thank your reader for the opportunity to complete the assignment and express your willingness to conduct follow-up research.

Even though your transmittal letter will not be mailed, it should include, where appropriate, the elements of an official letter or memo: inside address, salutation, close, and signature. It is considered *page ii* of the report, but because it is a letter, the page number is often omitted.

PREFACE When a report is written for more than one reader, a preface may be more appropriate than a transmittal letter. Although the preface usually does not include transmittal information ("Enclosed are eight copies of the marketing report"), it does provide a *descriptive narrative* about the document's organization. This narrative may then be followed by a tabulated description in the table of contents. Like the transmittal letter, the preface may also focus on the uses to which the report may be put. It is also the point at which the author may thank those who contributed to the document.

TABLE OF CONTENTS The **table of contents** is a list of the report's primary and secondary headings. Taken from the document outline, these headings provide readers with an overview of the material that follows. The table of contents is like a skeletal system revealing the report's overall *structure*. It reflects the outline of the report by citing material contained in the body, front-matter material that follows the contents page, and back-matter material, including appendixes and other end-of-report sections.

table of contents
Front-matter list of a report's primary and secondary headings to provide readers with an overview of the material that follows

In general, the complexity of your table of contents will be directly related to the length of your report. While the table of contents in shorter documents may cite only primary-level headings, the contents page in longer documents may also include secondary- and third-level headings. Page numbers are usually placed next to each heading, to which they are typically connected by spaced periods known as *leaders*.

LIST OF ILLUSTRATIONS The **list of illustrations**—the figures and tables that are included in the document—appears on a separate page immediately following the table of contents or on the contents page itself. As we saw in Chapter 11, figures and tables can be grouped together as "Exhibits" or listed separately as "Figures" and "Tables." The first format requires one illustration list, the second two lists. Regardless of the system you use, your list should include the title and page number of every illustration.

list of illustrations
Front-matter list of the figures and tables included in a document

forward
Introductory statement written by a person who did not author the report to provide a context for the report by discussing its background information or broad, general applications

FORWARD   In some reports, a forward concludes the front matter. A **forward** is an introductory statement written by someone who did not author the report. The purpose of the forward is to provide a context for the report by discussing background information or broad, general implications.

The Report Body

The heart of the report is found in the report body. Included in the body are an *executive summary, introduction, text discussion, closing sections*, and *references*.

executive summary
Synopsis in the body of a report that condenses it into relatively few pages

EXECUTIVE SUMMARY   Busy executives are often unwilling to take time to read an entire document without first getting an overview of what it says. This overview is provided in the **executive summary**—a synopsis that condenses the report into relatively few pages. Executive summaries are intended for readers who need digested versions of the information contained in reports. Although most readers will continue reading, some will stop after the executive summary, and the typical reader will refer back to it for key points. Because of its crucial role, the executive summary is one of the most important elements of a formal report.

descriptive summary
Synopsis that acts as an expanded table of contents to tell the reader what to expect and that states the purpose and scope of a report

Executive summaries can be descriptive or informative. **Descriptive summaries** are synopses that act like expanded tables of contents that tell the reader what to expect in the pages that follow. Rather than presenting information, they state what the report is intended to accomplish in terms of its purpose and scope. The **scope** of the report refers to any limitations that define its coverage, including limitations of time and geography. The methodology used to collect data contained in the report may also be mentioned.

scope
Any limitations, such as time and geography, that define a document's coverage

An **informative summary** is an abbreviated version of the report that includes conclusions and recommendations as well as descriptions of purpose, scope, and methods. The examples of descriptive and informative summaries in Figure 12.4 will help clarify their differences. Notice that the informative summary shown in Figure 12.4B is longer because it includes substantive details.

informative summary
Abbreviated version of a report that includes conclusions and recommendations as well as descriptions of purpose, scope and methods

The executive summary presents material in the same order as the report itself. When the report uses a direct approach, the executive summary presents conclusions and recommendations before explanations or methods. When the report is indirect, conclusions and recommendations close the executive summary, just as they do the report. Style and tone should also be the same. Your objective here is to prepare readers for what will follow. Because your executive summary is generally read before your text discussion, it is important to avoid unexplained jargon and abbreviations, even if they are defined at a later point. In addition, your summary should not refer to figures and tables that follow later in the document. Finally, although it is considered a part of the report body, the executive summary should not contain exhibits or footnotes.

You should, however, include headings that will help the reader organize your material. In addition, use transitional words and phrases such as *therefore* and *in addition* that make smooth, logical connections between ideas. As the first section in the body of the report, pagination of the executive report begins with the Arabic number 1.

The typical executive summary is about one-tenth the length of the report body. A one hundred-page report, therefore, would include an executive summary of about ten pages. Some business communicators recommend that executive summaries simply list main points and be limited to one page. In order to make the material easy to read, bulleted and numbered lists should be used in this format.[5]

Finally, although the executive summary is the first element in the report body, it should be written last. Writing a summary requires that you extract the core idea or thesis of your report by reviewing each section of the full

This report contains information on the growth of videoconferencing as an alternative to face-to-face business meetings. Included is information on the cost of establishing a dedicated videoconferencing center and the per-hour cost. The report will also examine the pros and cons of videoconferencing, including the difficulty that participants have communicating.

This report recommends establishing video-conferencing centers at Avery Corporation's Seattle headquarters as well as at the St. Louis, Tampa, and Milwaukee manufacturing sites.

Breakthoughs in technology have created high-quality, practical video conferences, and per-minute costs are as low as a cellular phone call. A New York-to-San Francisco videoconference can cost as little as $30 an hour.

Currently, three companies are the major manufacturers of videoconferencing systems: Compression Labs of San Jose, California; the Picturetel Corp. of Peabody, Massachusettes; and the Videotelecom Corp. of Austin, Texas. The systems offered by these companies range in price from $20,000 to $85,000, with the best-selling models priced in the $30,000 to $40,000 range.

Videoconferencing allows participants in diverse locations to meet with each other at any time without being away from their home offices. As a result, it produces enormous productivity gains. However, despite its advantages, videoconferencing has drawbacks, including a slight delay in signal reception that makes participants appear as if they are swimming underwater. It is not a perfect substitute for face-to-face meetings.

(A) Descriptive Summary   *(B) Informative Summary*

FIGURE 12.4   *Comparing Descriptive and Informative Executive Summaries*

report. Your next step is to distill this information into a shortened form. Depending on the length of the report, a given section may require no more than a sentence in the executive summary; for other sections, several paragraphs or pages may be needed.

INTRODUCTION   An **introduction** acts as a preamble to your entire report, providing your readers with enough information to grasp the significance of the pages that follow. Experienced writers report that effective introductions often begin with attention-getters. Although reports are serious business documents, the people who read them must be convinced that the subject holds interest. One of the most effective ways to gain your reader's confidence, both in your subject and in your treatment of it, is to use an opening sentence or paragraph that captures attention. For example, if you have developed a solution to a chronic problem, that solution should be stated in your opening sentence.

More importantly, introductions have a number of basic functions, the first of which is to clarify the subject.[6] Definitions and background information may be necessary to help readers understand the subject. For example, it may be important to explore the historical background of a problem, focusing on how other solutions have failed. Stating the importance of the issue is one way of clarifying the nature of both your subject and your report.

A second function of the introduction is to state the purpose of your report. Just as the topic sentence tells readers what to expect in the paragraph, the *purpose statement* focuses on the purpose and goals of the report. For example, the introduction may state either that your material provides an overview of existing programs or that it presents a new approach to a problem. Not surprisingly, pur-

introduction
Preamble in the body of a report intended to gain reader's attention by providing them with the information they need to evaluate the report itself

pose statements are often problem-centered: That is, they state goals in terms of the need to remedy a problem situation.

A third function of the introduction is to define the scope of your report. Scope is closely linked to purpose. When you state the scope of the report, you tell readers how broad your coverage will be. For example, will your proposal for adjusting inventory to seasonal patterns of demand apply to worldwide operations or just to the Southwest Division?

Introductions perform a fourth function by describing your plan for developing your subject. Here the introduction sets the stage for your organizational approach—that is, the *way* your material will be presented and developed in the body of your document. For example, the introduction may tell readers that your report will take a chronological approach or will examine its material from the perspective of cause and effect. Introducing the issue of development at this point also helps readers evaluate the means by which your report reaches its conclusions and recommendations.

A fifth function of your introduction is to clarify your research methods. For example, if you conducted a nationwide survey to judge responses to a new-product idea, your introduction would briefly describe the survey as the source of your research data.

Finally, the introduction sets the style of the report. The structure of sentences and paragraphs and the use of personal or impersonal language tells the reader what to expect on the pages that follow.

Perhaps because it serves such an important function, many people consider the introduction the most challenging part of the report to write. While many writers draft the introduction after the rest of the report is complete, because time pressure is usually greatest at this point, the introduction may receive insufficient attention. A more effective approach is to draft an introduction at the start of the report and then continually review and revise it as your report progresses. When the report is complete, your introduction can be refined until it is in final form.

PROGRESS CHECK

1. Are all of the elements in the front matter of a long report mandatory? If not, which elements can be considered optional?
2. Suppose that you've written a report that is twenty pages long. About how long should your executive summary be?
3. The chapter notes that introductions are often the most difficult portion of a report to write. Why?

TEXT DISCUSSION   All the elements that we have examined so far prepare the reader for the substance of the report contained in the text discussion. This is the discussion in which you record your ideas according to the logical plan developed in your report outline. As you recall from Chapter 4, data may be arranged according to a number of development plans, including deductive, inductive, problem/solution, cause-and-effect, climactic-order, and chronological. Choose the plan that allows you to cover the subject in a logical, ordered sequence that readers will understand.

Although most formal reports close with separate sections devoted to conclusions and recommendations, separate sections of major reports may also include interim conclusions and recommendations tied to the discussions in those sections. The sample report in Figure 12.6 uses this technique.

INTERNAL CONNECTIONS: STRUCTURAL GUIDEPOSTS   Because your discussion may be dozens—even hundreds—of pages long, readers need help in following your ideas with the same logic that you used to organize them in the first place. Remember that even if your document is logically organized and clearly written, your readers may still be overwhelmed by the sheer volume of information. This problem places a special requirement on report writers. In order to highlight important connections, writers must provide **structural guideposts** that help the readers move smoothly from one part of the discussion to another. These guideposts take such forms as *internal previews* and *summaries*; words, phrases, and sentences that act as *transitions*; *headings*; and *summary tables and charts*.

Internal Previews and Summaries. An **internal preview** appears at the beginning of a section to preview the material covered in the section. An internal preview may be stated in a simple sentence: "This section will cover points A, B, and C." The section then continues, as promised, with a full discussion of points A, B, and C. At other times, a more extensive preview is necessary. For example:

> Deciding whether to equip all J. B. Hunt trucks with on-board computers depends on a number of factors, each of which will be examined in the next section of this report. The analysis focuses on increased fleet efficiency resulting from on-board computers in relationship to increased costs.

> Efficiency will be examined first. Specifically, the opening section will discuss the application of this technology to long-haul trucking. The following section will examine the cost of IBM on-board computers for the 6,000 trucks in the J. B. Hunt fleet.

In both cases, the internal preview helps readers to establish key expectations for what they will read in the remainder of the section.

By contrast, the **internal summary** appears at the *close* of a section, where it reiterates key points and links them both to other report sections and to the report's specific purpose. In effect, internal summaries tell readers what they have just read and clarify the relationships among different pieces of information in the report.

An internal summary usually appears at the end of a lengthy section, often setting the stage for a new direction in the discussion. Indeed, the last sentence in an internal summary may be forward-looking. For example:

> Now that the implications of opening manufacturing facilities in France and Germany have been examined, the next section of the report will focus on the output of Brunswick Corporation's manufacturing facilities in the United States.

In deciding where to place internal previews and summaries, examine your writing outline carefully. Internal summaries should be located at key points in the report, generally where primary-level headings appear. Use them immediately before and after these headings.

Transitions. The use of connections is also desirable *within* report sections. They take the form of transitional words and phrases, especially those that compare and summarize items. Comparison transitions include *similarly*, *in the same way*, and *likewise*; summary transitions include *as a result*, *hence*, and *in conclusion*. These and other transitions were examined in more detail in Chapter 5. By contrast, *transitional sentences* connect thoughts that have been completed to those that are about to begin. As a rule, they link ideas within a section rather than ideas across different sections. The intent of all transitional devices is to present clear relationships among ideas as well as smooth, coherent writing.

Headings. Primary-, secondary-, and third-level headings also serve as connectors in lengthy reports. In effect, headings are abbreviated previews of the material to follow. They enable readers to pick out key sections at a glance and to see how these sections relate to sections immediately preceding and following. In effect, a series of headings establishes a *hierarchy* of material. As we saw in Chapter 4, readers know that material prefaced by secondary- or tertiary-level headings fall within the framework of the primary-level heading that began the section.

---

internal preview
Sentences and paragraphs that appear at the beginning of text-discussion sections to introduce the material that will be covered in them

internal summary
In documents, sentences and paragraphs that appear at the close of text-discussion sections to restate key points and to link them both to other report sections and to the report's specific purpose

Every person seems to have a limited capacity to assimilate information, and if it is presented to him too rapidly and without adequate repetition, this capacity will be exceeded and communication will break down.

R. Duncan Luce
Professor, University
of Pennsylvania

APPLYING TECHNOLOGY

Desktop Publishing

Nowhere is business desktop publishing more common than in the production of reports and proposals. *Desktop publishing* is the process by which camera-ready copy is designed and created on a microcomputer. Using a desktop-publishing system, including the appropriate computer hardware, software, and a laser printer, a document can be produced with a layout and graphics presentation that resembles professional typesetting.

Desktop publishing has three major functions: It allows you to change the appearance of the characters on the page, add graphics, and design pages in final form.

Changing Characters

Starting with the text you created on your word-processing software, desktop-publishing software lets you choose from a variety of type styles, including plain, **bold**, *italic*, outline, shadow, and condensed type.

You can also choose from a variety of fonts—characters that share the same design, style, and size. For example, you can select specific fonts to enhance different text elements such as headings and tables.

Desktop publishing also allows you to position your text attractively along the left or right margins by reducing or increasing the space between characters. Text may be posi-

tioned in four different ways: aligned left, aligned right, centered, and justified.

Aligned Left

This is a sample of text aligned left. This is a sample of text aligned left. This is a sample of text aligned left. This is a sample of text aligned left. This is a sample of text aligned left.

Aligned Right

This is a sample of text aligned right. This is a sample of text aligned right. This is a sample of text aligned right. This is a sample of text aligned right. This is a sample of text aligned right.

Aligned Center

This is a sample of text aligned center. This is a sample of text aligned center. This is a sample of text aligned center. This is a sample of text aligned center. This is a sample of text aligned center.

Justified

This is a sample of text justified. This is a sample of text justified. This is a sample of text justified. This is a sample of text justified. This is a sample of text justified.

Adding Graphics

Desktop-publishing programs also allow you to add nontypographical artwork and display type.

Summary Tables and Charts. As summary devices, tables and charts are also important connective tools. They condense various pieces of information from different sections of your report and display them in one location. For example, in a report on the use of cellular phones by sales representatives, the writer may choose to include a summary table that lists the features of various brands. Tables and charts are also useful methods of reinforcing text comparisons.

CLOSING SECTIONS   The close of your report may include a *summary* and sections offering *conclusions* and *recommendations*. While some reports feature all three sections, others may combine these components in a single section. Remember that although your closing sections may offer slightly different perspectives on your findings, they should not introduce new material. On the contrary, every statement made in these sections should be justified by facts already presented.

SUMMARY   Informational reports—those that present facts but not interpretations—usually conclude with final summaries. The **summary** condenses the most important information from the report, often recapping the internal summaries from the conclusions of various sections. Summarized information should be presented in the order in which it appears in the report.

summary
Closing section of a report that condenses its most important information

Nontypographical artwork includes graphic illustrations created right on the page or imported into the desktop publisher from a graphics-presentation program. You can also use predrawn images called electronic *clip art. Display type* refers to type that has been enhanced to include a design element. Four of the most commonly used enhancement devices are shown here:

Drop Cap

> As brand manager of IBM, you have been assigned to write a memo to company employees. The purpose of the memo

Drop Shadow

> Define the Mission

Reverse Type

> Implement the Plan

Display Type

Setting Objectives

Laying Out Pages

In the page-layout stage, you create a *format* for your document. During this process, you define your margins, choose the number of your columns and define column widths, set your page size, and create your white space. Once your format is set, graphic elements and type are added to your design. The result is a series of master page layouts and designs that are used throughout the document. After each page is finalized and locked into place, a laser printer produces finished, camera-ready copy.

Information Processing, 3rd ed. (Englewood Cliffs, NJ: Prentice Hall, 1991), pp. 373–88; Larry Long and Nancy Long, *Computers*, 3rd ed. (Englewood Cliffs, NJ: Prentice Hall, 1993), pp. 412–15; and W. E. Wang and Joe Kraynak, *The First Book of Personal Computing* (Carmel, IN: SAMS, 1990), pp. 139–52.

CONCLUSIONS   **Conclusions** are the logical result of the evidence presented in the report. Indeed, they grow out of this evidence and are judgments derived through a logical chain of reasoning. In effect, your conclusions answer the question that is uppermost in your reader's mind: *What does all this mean?*

In order to be effective, conclusions must be linked to the purpose and methods of your report, as stated in your introduction. For example, if your introduction told the reader that your purpose was to examine the feasibility and cost of installing robots on an assembly line, your conclusion should not focus on the relationship between robots and employee morale. Although this issue may have been mentioned in your report, it is certainly not the problem you promised to explore in your introduction.

The following guidelines should be used in writing effective conclusions:

- Assume that your conclusions will be read independently of the rest of your document. Briefly restate your purpose and methods and avoid unexplained jargon and abbreviations.
- Organize your results according to the order in which they are presented in the body of your report. Using this strategy means that you will usually present your most important conclusions first.

conclusions
Logical result of the evidence presented in a report or proposal

recommendations
Specific actions suggested
as a result of conclusions
presented in a report or
proposal

references
In a report or proposal, the
section in the document
body that lists material
from other sources actually cited in the text

back matter
Supplemental information
included in the parts of the
report that follow the
report body

bibliography
Back-matter list identifying all references used in
researching a report or
proposal

appendix
Back matter that supple-
ments material presented
in the text of a report or
proposal

glossary
Alphabetized back-matter
list, accompanied by definitions, of words and phrases used in a report

- Organize your conclusions with the same care that you brought to the body of your report.

RECOMMENDATIONS   Following your conclusions, **recommendations** are the specific actions that you suggest as a result of the information that you have presented. For example, if your report presents options, you should select the one that you think will prove most effective.

Your recommendations, of course, should be financially realistic and appropriate to the problem. Although recommendations are sometimes diffi-cult to make, your reader will expect to find them in your report. If you hon-estly feel that you cannot recommend any action, say so. Be prepared, howev-er, to supply your reader with an explanation for your position. If the problem requires further study before recommendations can be made, your recommen-dations should include specific plans for pursuing the problem.

Finally, you should remember two things about the nature of recommen-dations. First, they must flow logically from the findings of your report. When considering recommendations, many readers will carefully reexamine the spe-cific evidence presented in the report to determine the extent to which it sup-ports your recommended course of action. Second, recommendations are by definition advisory. They tell readers what they *should* do. The final decision to act is made by the person for whom the report is written—your plant man-ager or supervisor, a customer, a client, or a government official.

REFERENCES   When your report cites material from other sources, these sources are likely to be listed in a **references** section included at the end of the report body. This section, which may be labeled *References, Notes,* or *Footnotes,* lists sources according to a consistent documentation style. Various styles are examined in detail in Appendix I. Long reports may include references at the end of each section.

Back Matter

Supplemental information is included in the **back matter**—the parts of the report that follow the report body. Depending on the nature and length of your report, your back matter may include a *bibliography, appendixes,* a *glossary,* and an *index.* Each ele-ment should start a new page and should be labeled with its appropriate title.

BIBLIOGRAPHY   A **bibliography** is a list of references used in researching the report. While the reference list refers to work actually cited in your text, the bibliog-raphy identifies *all* works consulted, regardless of whether you specifically cited them. Naturally, if your reference list contains all the sources that you used, a sepa-rate bibliography is unnecessary. The bibliography is usually an alphabetized list.

APPENDIXES   An **appendix** is back matter that supplements material present-ed in your text. Appendixes may be placed at the end of the report either because they are tangential to your purpose or because they are too long or detailed to be included in the body. Among the types of material included in appendixes are questionnaires, statistical analyses, technical support, and the texts of legal statutes and interviews.

Although you may include as many appendixes as you need, each appen-dix should be limited to one type of supplemental material. When only one appendix is used, simply label it *Appendix.* Label multiple appendixes *Appendix A, Appendix B,* and so on.

GLOSSARY   When your report includes unfamiliar or technical words or phrases, a glossary may be necessary. A **glossary** is an alphabetized list of words and phrases accompanied by definitions. Remember that glossary definitions are meant to supplement rather than replace definitions that appear when you first introduce terms in your text. Each glossary entry should begin a new line and be followed immediately with a definition written in traditional dictionary style.

INDEX   Finally, a major report may also include an **index**—an alphabetized list of report topics that includes the page on which each topic appears. Many writers find indexes unnecessary when the table of contents also lists topics and pages. However, this alphabetical listing of key words and topics is especially useful in the case of long, complex reports.

index
Alphabetized back-matter list of report topics that includes references to the pages on which each topic appears

ORGANIZING REPORT FINDINGS

Report information can be presented in either direct or indirect order. The *indirect order*, in which conclusions and recommendations are presented at the end of the report, was described earlier in the model outline. Using the so-called *building-block format*, the report opens with an introduction, moves to a discussion of report findings, and ends with conclusions and recommendations based on these findings. The advantage of this format is that it enables the writer to develop an argument systematically, using a series of logical steps.

Despite this advantage, the indirect organizational approach is also withholding critical information until the end of the document. Understandably, this approach is not a favorite among busy readers who want conclusions and recommendations presented first. These readers prefer a direct organizational approach that can be characterized as an inverted pyramid. The report begins with an introduction and moves immediately to conclusions and recommendations. A detailed discussion follows. Figure 12.5 illustrates how the order of information differs in direct and indirect organizational approaches.

The direct approach is risky, and when your findings are controversial, readers must be *convinced* that your conclusions are correct. However, because your supporting information appears *after* the statement of your conclusions, readers may be reluctant to accept unsupported conclusions. In addition, if your conclusions are complicated or limited, the direct approach is likely to be less effective than the indirect approach.

As business becomes more complex, markets become more diverse, and information overload becomes a fact of life, an increasing number of companies are asking employees to use the direct approach in business reports. When you use this approach, keep in mind that because the reader has not yet encountered your supporting data, your explanations must be thorough and complete.

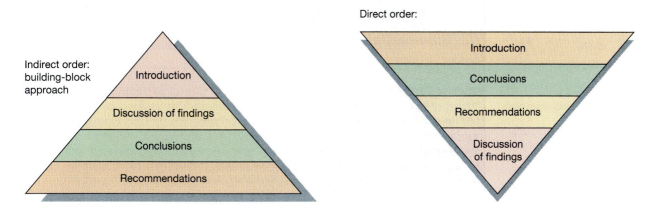

FIGURE 12.5   *Organizing Findings: Alternative Approaches*

A SAMPLE LONG REPORT

After a school bus accident resulted in the death of an elementary-school student, residents of a small Connecticut suburb formed a school bus safety advisory committee charged with recommending ways to improve the school-bus transportation system. On that committee were members of the private company that operated and maintained the town's fleet of school buses as well as teachers, parents, police officials, and other town representatives.

After months of work, the committee produced a fifty-two-page report, parts of which are reproduced as Figure 12.6. Included in the sample are the transmittal memo, executive summary, introduction, and details from the text. The report was submitted by the town's superintendent of schools to the board of education.

In part, this document was selected as an extended illustration because it demonstrates the relationships among diverse groups—businesspeople, government officials, and community members—who have gotten together to work on the solution to a joint problem. Through a collaborative effort, the twenty-five-person committee produced a business document that would ultimately result in the implementation of a paid school bus monitor system. Interestingly, although businesspeople helped write the report, the document was submitted by a government official (the superintendent of schools) to a government body (the board of education). In the real world, businesspeople play many different roles, including advisors to government officials.[7]

As you read the report, keep in mind that although it follows our model outline in some ways, it deviates in others. Like all effective business documents, it is oriented first toward the needs of the subject and audience and only then toward the requirements of the report form.

A third party, the superintendent of schools, presented the report. This is not uncommon in highly bureaucratic organizations such as school systems.

The message is written in a traditional memo format.

The memo begins by identifying the report and defining its purpose and scope.

Unlike many transmittal letters and memos, it uses an impersonal writing style, including third-person references. This style is maintained throughout the report.

The report's role in the bureaucracy is explained next.

The inclusion of this explanation in the transmittal memo enables readers to understand how the report will be used in the decision-making process.

TRANSMITTAL MEMO

TO: BOARD OF EDUCATION MEMBERS
FROM: SUPERINTENDENT OF SCHOOLS
SUBJ: REPORT OF THE BUS SAFETY COMMITTEE
DATE: JUNE 16, 1994

Attached is the report of the School Bus Safety Advisory Committee. The committee was appointed as an advisory group to the superintendent following the tragic death of one of our students in December.

The committee was charged with reviewing all components of the town's school bus safety procedures, bus scheduling and its impact on safety, pupil training, the board of education's transportation policies, and parental responsibility for teaching and reinforcing bus safety. A key charge focused on the merits of a bus-monitor program, and as a result of the committee's preliminary recommendations, a voluntary program was put into effect this spring.

PROCEDURES

The committee report does not constitute a formal recommendation to the Board of Education. Advisory committees such as this make recommendations to the superintendent, and I have been kept informed as the committee's work progressed. Following tonight's committee presentation, I and my administrative staff will study the recommendations carefully, considering them in the context of feasibility, probable effectiveness, impact on other aspects of the school program, legal implications, and cost. Our review of the report may raise

FIGURE 12.6 *Selections from a Sample Report*

FIGURE 12.6 *Selections from a Sample Report (continued)*

further questions about some of or about the recommendations themselves. Based upon this review, I will make preliminary recommendations to the Board of Education regarding implementation of some or all of the committee's recommendations, timing of implementations, and avenues for funding those with cost implications.

The recommendations will then be considered by the Board of Education at a public meeting. Final recommendations for Board action will be developed following this session.

The transmittal memo closes by acknowledging the contributions of committee members and by looking, with hope, to the future.

ACKNOWLEDGMENTS

The committee has been working for five months, meeting frequently and doing extensive research. Members have done a real service to the school system, and the administration and Board of Education acknowledge the time and effort that went into producing their thorough report. We thank all the members for their service.

There is no doubt that our safety program will improve as the result of the work of this outstanding group.

This is an example of an informative executive summary. The summary follows the order of material presented in the report as it highlights and explains the recommendations that appear at the end of each section. Subheadings correspond to report recommendations.

EXECUTIVE SUMMARY

Getting students to school and home safely and on time is similar to mounting a small-scale military operation daily on community streets. Each day, 32 buses and vans transport an average of 2,500 students on 61 arrival routes and 74 dismissal routes. They travel about 1,350 miles a day, or 245,700 miles every school year.

About 50 employees of the bus company operate and maintain the fleet of 26 Thomas Built diesel-powered buses and seven 16-passenger vans. The locally owned bus company has held the school contract for 22 years. Although operated and maintained by this private company, the vehicles are owned by the town.

Bus safety became an overriding issue for this community after an elementary-school child was killed getting off a bus in December 1993. After this incident, the Bus Safety Committee was formed, and this report is the result of the committee's efforts. To improve the safety of the town's school-bus transportation system, the committee submits the following recommendations.

This paragraph provides a transition to the summary of specific recommendations. An internal preview sets the stage for the material that comes next.

Begin a Full-Scale Paid School Bus-Monitor Program at the Elementary School

Committee members agree unanimously that one of the most effective safety improvements that the town could make is a full-scale paid elementary school bus-monitor program. The committee recommends that the Superintendent and Board of Education endorse a full-scale paid monitor program and develop a plan and timetable for its implementation.

Hire a Permanent Safety Coordinator to Improve Driver Performance

The position of safety coordinator should be made permanent. This person should monitor, support, and evaluate the job performance of bus drivers and monitors and participate in bus driver and monitor training.

Improve Communication among Drivers, Administrators, and Parents and Standardize School Bus Disciplinary Procedures

All drivers should use the bus conduct report form to report student safety violations. All school administrators should follow the same guidelines for complaints about student behavior and enforce guidelines uniformly.

Tighten Procedures for Complaints about Drivers

All complaints about drivers should be directed to the Board's transportation coordinator. The coordinator should keep records of complaints and bring them to the attention of the bus company.

Make Elementary Bus Stops Safer and All Students Eligible to Ride Buses

All kindergarten through eighth-grade students should be assigned to buses. This will discourage walkers, who are at a greater risk than riders of becoming involved in accidents. With fewer walkers, school-crossing guards can be eliminated, and crossing-guard funds can be channeled into other bus-safety programs.

Revise Opening and Closing Times

The opening and closing times between middle and elementary levels should be increased by 10 minutes to reduce the need for drivers to hurry through their runs.

Make School Loading and Unloading Zones Safer

A professional traffic engineer should be engaged to study the traffic patterns at school grounds and make recommendations for improved safety. Communication with parents should be improved regarding parking, waiting, and drop-off/pick-up procedures.

Appoint a Permanent School Bus Safety Advisory Committee

A permanent School Bus Safety Advisory Committee should be appointed to review procedures, technologies, and equipment, including seatbelts. The committee would make continuing recommendations for improvement.

Improve Student Education Program, Including Standardized Bus Evacuation Drills

Schools should develop and standardize a continuous student-education program about bus safety. Bus and van evacuation drills should be an integral part of the program.

Improve Public Education Regarding Traffic Regulations and School Buses

The schools, in cooperation with the police department, should improve the public's awareness of school bus traffic safety.

The cost to implement the recommendations proposed by the committee is between $67,000 and $81,000.

INTRODUCTION

The introduction begins with an explanation of why the report was written.

The superintendent of schools appointed the School Bus Safety Advisory Committee in January 1994 following the tragic death of a student in a school bus accident in December 1993.

The charge of this committee was to review school bus safety to ensure that the town and bus company are operating school buses as safely as possible and to restore the credibility of our transportation program. The superintendent's charge also focused on the specific question of whether the town should begin a school bus-monitor program.

Here the document's scope is specified.

Our review was intensive and extensive. It paid particular attention to:

- safety of loading zones
- safety of school areas
- student education

FIGURE 12.6   Selections from a Sample Report (continued)

FIGURE 12.6 *Selections from a Sample Report (continued)*

In the process of conducting this research, the committee examined findings of national and state groups.

- driver supervision
- safety of bus equipment
- scheduling of bus runs

To achieve its goals, the committee broke into three subcommittees covering feasibility of monitors, bus equipment and driver training, and student and parent education. As part of its research, the committee held a public hearing and interviewed drivers and parents.

In general, the committee found the town school bus-transportation system to be good. Bus equipment exceeds state and federal requirements. Driver training has been strengthened in recent years, and all drivers have passed new state licensing regulations introduced this spring.

However, we found room for improvement. Although a student-education program is in place, it can be standardized further and enhanced. We also concluded that a monitor program would strengthen the safety of elementary-school bus riders.

In making our recommendations, the committee focused on enhancing the safety of students. The superintendent's charge did, however, include a request to consider the economic impact of a paid monitor program. Thus, the report includes estimated costs.

The remainder of this report will focus on the specific recommendations made by the three subcommittees to improve the school bus system. The costs associated with the recommendations will then be analyzed and ideas for implementation explored. It is our earnest hope that the Superintendent and Board of Education endorse our recommendations and implement them without delay.

REPORT OF THE MONITOR SUBCOMMITTEE: BEGIN A FULL-SCALE PAID SCHOOL BUS MONITOR PROGRAM AT THE ELEMENTARY LEVEL.

Both state and national statistics clearly show that the most dangerous part of a school bus ride occurs when children enter or leave the bus, in the area commonly referred to as the loading zone. The National Highway Traffic Safety Administration reports that an average of 37 students are killed each year in loading-zone accidents. As Table 1 shows, this number represents more than 75 percent of all fatalities related to school bus accidents.

Children under the age of nine are particularly susceptible to loading-zone accidents. As Figure 1 shows, more than half of all fatalities involve children between five and six years of age.

TABLE 1
Children Killed in School Bus Accidents During Five-Year Period

CATEGORIES	AVERAGE DEATHS PER YEAR	CATEGORIES	AVERAGE DEATHS PER YEAR
School Bus Passengers		Pedestrians at Loading Zones	
Type 1 School Bus	9.6	Struck by Type 1 School Bus	24.0
Struck by Other Vehicles Used as School Buses	2.4	Struck by Other Vehicle Used as a School Bus	1.8
		Struck by Other Vehicle	11.6
TOTAL PASSENGER DEATHS	12.0	TOTAL PEDESTRIAN DEATHS	37.4

Source: National Highway Traffic Safety Administration

Margin notes:

Bullets help to highlight this information.

Here the introduction explains how the committee accomplished its goals. This information is crucial because the discussion that follows the introduction is organized according to the findings of each of the three subcommittees.

General conclusions—both positive and negative—come next.

The scope of the report is further defined in the context of report recommendations.

The final paragraph of the introduction is an internal preview describing what the reader can expect in the pages that follow.

All primary-level headings in the report are centered and capitalized. This heading includes a title and subtitle.

Research data begin the report and establish its credibility. A table is used to illustrate an important point. The text reference to the table explains its importance. Notice that the position of the table is close to the text reference to it.

Both figures and tables are used in the report. Each follows its own numbering system.

FIGURE 1 **Age Distribution of Children Fatally Injured by School Buses**
Source: National Highway Traffic Safety Administration

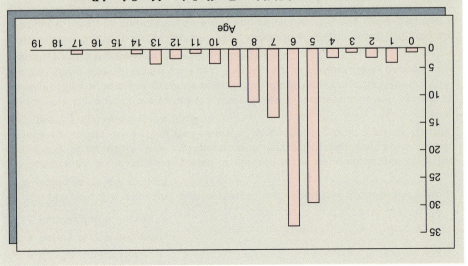

In Connecticut, these figures are even more dramatic. Over the past 20 years, all bus-related fatalities have occurred outside the bus. Since 1972, 20 Connecticut children have died in school bus accidents. One was struck by a motorist passing the bus illegally; 19 were struck by the school bus. Fifteen of the victims—75 percent—were under the age of nine; all of the children were under the age of 13. A report compiled by the Connecticut School Transportation Safety Commission indicates that 14 of these fatalities, fully 70 percent, might reasonably have been prevented if well-trained safety monitors were riding the buses. . .

Loading-zone safety can be improved by a staff of paid bus monitors or volunteer monitors. The report will examine the details of these alternatives next.

Programs Involving Paid Monitors

The use of adults as paid school bus monitors is not a new idea. A number of communities, including Boston, Greeley, Colorado, and North Haven, Connecticut, began using paid monitors in the 1970s. In many instances, the monitors were hired initially to deal with disciplinary problems. Some communities hired them primarily to assist on vehicles carrying special-education students. Still others began their programs as a direct result of a school bus accident. Rhode Island is the only state to mandate the statewide use of monitors. It began its program in 1986. In recent months, while a number of communities have scaled back or eliminated monitor programs for fiscal reasons, others have launched studies to start programs. As far as this committee can determine, no school bus loading-zone fatality has occurred in any community with a paid monitor program.

In Connecticut, North Haven and Glastonbury are the only communities with some form of paid monitor program. The report will examine these programs along with the program in Rhode Island. Each of these programs was initiated as a direct result of a bus-related fatality.

North Haven's Monitor Program

In North Haven, monitors trained in procedures to ensure safe boarding and exiting are used on elementary bus trips to and from school. They act as crossing guards when children cross the street and assist the driver in keeping order on the bus. The city and Board of Education continue to support the use of paid

FIGURE 12.6 *Selections from a Sample Report (continued)*

These data are presented according to a geographic organizational pattern.

National data are presented first followed by data for the state of Connecticut.

This paragraph presents another internal preview.

This secondary-level heading appears flush against the left margin, is underlined and uses upper- and lower-case letters.

This internal preview is carried through in the tertiary level headings that follow.

The headings refer to the programs in North Haven, Glastonbury, and Rhode Island.

monitors after 15 years, believing that it has been responsible for the accident-free record during that time.

The January 1993 report of the Connecticut School Transportation Safety Commission said,

"The primary difficulty North Haven has with its program is finding enough monitors."

Rhode Island's Monitor Program

Rhode Island began its monitor program following a year in which three young children were killed in loading-zone accidents. The Rhode Island legislature mandated paid monitors on all elementary buses in the state's eight cities and 31 towns. Some communities include middle school as well.

Monitor training covers procedures in crossing, pupil loading and unloading, behavior management, and emergencies. The monitor's duties are ensuring that pupils cross the street safely and that the loading zone is clear before the driver pulls away.

After five years, some Rhode Island school districts continue to have difficulty maintaining a full monitor staff. Few districts have full staffing at all times and most districts must use variances of emergency procedures allowed under state guidelines. Nevertheless, the latest data indicate that 85 percent of all elementary bus runs were covered by a monitor. See Appendix A for a detailed discussion of the monitor program in Middletown, Rhode Island.

Volunteer Monitors

The committee examined ways to offer the services of monitors without cost. Unfortunately, we did not find any research dealing with specific plans or programs involving volunteer monitors. The committee, therefore, decided to develop, implement, and evaluate its own volunteer-monitor plan at the elementary-school level.

The plan called for a two-phase approach. In the first phase, volunteer monitors were to ride one time each week for six weeks on dismissal runs. One hundred and fifteen volunteers were needed to staff fully all afternoon elementary-school bus runs. Parents of elementary school students formed the basis of the volunteer group, and all received training.

The committee evaluated the first phase through a questionnaire and interviews with parents and bus drivers. It concluded that enough additional volunteers could not be obtained for the second phase and canceled plans to expand the program. At the same time, the committee decided to continue with phase one—afternoon dismissal runs—until the end of the school year.

Availability of Volunteers

Seventy parents signed up and served as volunteer monitors during phase one. After signing up, a few dropped out but replacements were found. Approximately 60 percent of the afternoon buses had volunteer monitors ride on them during this phase.

During the last week in April, the committee sent a questionnaire to all elementary-school parents to determine their interest and availability for phase two. . . . A copy of the questionnaire is included in Appendix B. The survey showed:

- 25 of 70 phase-one volunteer monitors would continue during the second phase
- 31 parents agreed to volunteer during phase two
- three community members expressed interest in volunteering; a few senior citizens expressed interest but could not handle the constant up-and-down movement that is required.

Margin annotations:

Here, a direct quotation is used as evidence.

The third-level heading uses upper- and lower-case letters that are centered on the line.

The geographic organization-al pattern continues as exist-ing programs are examined by location.

Instead of cluttering the body of the report with the specifics of the Middletown program, the information is placed in an appendix. Three separate appendixes are mentioned in the sections of the report shown here.

The discussion of the volun-teer monitor program is orga-nized chronologically accord-ing to the program's two phas-es. Different sections of the report use different organiza-tional approaches, including a chronological and a geo-graphical approach.

The research base for the report includes a question-naire, a copy of which is included in the appendix. A bulleted list highlights key sur-vey findings.

FIGURE 12.6   Selections from a Sample Report (continued)

The total number of volunteers for phase two (59) was less than the number who participated in the first phase (70).

Conclusions

Before knowing how the initial volunteer monitor program worked, the committee considered how best to staff a volunteer monitor program over a full school year. In what seemed the best way to minimize a volunteer's commitment, the committee assumed that a monitor would ride once a week for nine weeks. This would require 460 volunteers to staff fully an afternoon program (PM dismissal) and 920 volunteers to staff fully a total plan a total AM and PM dismissals).

Based on our limited experience, neither goal seemed achievable. The coordination required for a program involving so many volunteers also seemed beyond the community's resources. Therefore, the committee concluded that a safety-monitor program that relies solely on volunteers cannot be successful because of the limited availability of volunteer monitors and the amount of required coordination.

Recommendations

The committee recommends unanimously that paid safety monitors ride on all elementary school buses.

The committee endorses the findings of the Connecticut School Transportation Safety Commission that using monitors is the single most effective way to improve school bus safety at the elementary level. The committee struggled with the best way to implement such a program—whether to do it in stages or all at once. A majority recommends every effort be made to begin full implementation by September 1994.

Although time is short, other communities have begun their programs in similar time frames. Rhode Island did it in 35 days, and our town can benefit greatly by that experience.

If it is not possible to have all monitors in place by September, the committee recommends that temporary procedures be developed until positions are filled. These may include use of interim monitors from a list of available substitutes. Such substitutes could be recruited initially from the corps of volunteer monitors used between April and June 1994. . . .

COSTS ASSOCIATED WITH RECOMMENDATIONS

Among the recommendations proposed by the committee, the following have direct cost implications. The figures presented represent costs during the 1994–95 school year.

RECOMMENDATION	COST
Paid Monitor Program: Elementary Buses	$53,000–$67,000

These costs are based on information obtained from other communities using the monitor system. The lower figure is based on an hourly wage for monitors ($8.50) while the higher figure is based on a payment per run ($8.00). This budget allocation would fund 23 monitors for the entire school year.

Hire Safety Coordinator on a Permanent Basis	$7,000

This person would monitor, support, and evaluate the job performance of bus drivers and paid monitors. The coordinator would report to both the bus com-

FIGURE 12.6   Selections from a Sample Report (continued)

The report includes conclusions at the end of each major section.

Recommendations are also tied to each major report section. The end of the report focuses on costs associated with all the recommendations and implementation of suggestions.

Like many reports, a break-down of budget projections is included. Explanations accompany each projection.

pany and the school system, and the cost of this position would be shared equally by the two groups. The amount shown represents the school system's portion of the safety coordinator's salary.

Hire Professional Traffic Engineer $7,000

The committee has significant concerns regarding the congestion and traffic patterns at each elementary and middle school. The committee sees the engineer working with the school administration and the police department in examining and developing the safest traffic configuration at each school. This project will require funding for two years.

	Average Cost
Total Cost for All Recommendations	$67,000–$81,000 $74,000

IMPLEMENTING THE RECOMMENDATIONS

Recommendations are the focus of the last primary heading in the report.

The committee has examined how its recommendations might be implemented and presents ideas to consider. Recognizing that the Superintendent of Schools may revise these suggestions, the committee views the following thoughts as a starting point in the implementation process.

The framework for our suggestions is built on the following key ideas:

A bulleted list highlights three critical points.

- The school system and the bus company must work cooperatively in addressing the recommendations. Key personnel within the school system and bus company must be identified and provided with the responsibility to implement specific recommendations.
- Within the school system, the Superintendent of Schools, business manager, assistant superintendent of schools for curriculum, and transportation coordinator must take an active role in implementing specific recommendations.
- Job descriptions and responsibilities for the newly created positions of safety coordinator and bus monitor must be developed carefully.

This short paragraph contains another internal preview.

Following are specific details for implementing the committee's recommendations. Included are suggested time frames for each recommendation.

Paid Bus Safety Monitors: Elementary Schools

The committee suggests that the school business manager, working with the bus company, be responsible for implementing this recommendation. The business manager should:

- **Write a job description** focusing on safe boarding and exiting from the bus, crossing students to the other side of the street, and assisting the driver in keeping order on the bus. This job description, developed by the committee for volunteer monitors, is shown in Appendix C and can be used as a reference.
- **Establish payment rates and qualifications** for the monitor position, as well as procedures for advertising, hiring, training, and supervision of monitors.
- **Develop training procedures and schedules** for paid safety monitors. The committee sees the training provided in two to three sessions involving classroom and actual time on the school bus. Training can be provided by the bus company.

TIME FRAME: July–August 1994

Tighten Procedures for Complaints about Drivers

Each school principal should inform parents that all complaints about bus drivers should be reported to the board's transportation coordinator. The transportation coordinator will keep a record of all complaints and bring them to the attention of the bus company. The bus company will investigate all complaints

FIGURE 12.6 *Selections from a Sample Report (continued)*

WHAT'S AHEAD

As this chapter shows, both long and short reports require careful planning, organization, and writing. As you will see in Chapter 13, the same skills are needed to write effective business proposals.

PROGRESS CHECK

1. What do we mean by creating "internal connections" in a long report? Why is this important?
2. List three guidelines for writing an effective conclusion to a long report.

---

and contact the safety coordinator when appropriate. The bus company will notify the transportation coordinator of the disposition of all complaints, and the transportation coordinator will provide the business manager with a status report on a monthly basis.

TIME FRAME: September 1994–June 1995

Review and Update Driver's Manual

The business manager, working with the bus company and transportation coordinator, will review and update the driver's manual on an annual basis each summer. The bus company will distribute and review the contents with drivers in early September. The business manager will distribute copies of the manual to each principal on an annual basis.

TIME FRAME: July 1994

Prepare an Accident Plan

The business manager, working with the bus company, nursing supervisor, and police department, should develop an accident plan to establish procedures that will be used following a school bus accident or other school-related emergency. This plan will then be presented to the Board of Education, bus drivers, school personnel, and parents.

TIME FRAME: September–December 1994

Appoint a Permanent School Bus Safety Advisory Committee

The present committee has spent nearly four months dealing with a very complex topic. We have studied certain issues in great detail. However, other areas need further review and study. Among these are:

- the use of seatbelts on school buses
- the use of coach-type or seatbelt equipped school buses for student trips on interstate highways
- new technologies related directly to school bus safety
- additional safety measures on school vans. The committee recognizes that the vans purchased in 1991 meet all state and federal safety regulations. But because they are frequently used to transport special-education or mobility-impaired students, further study is needed to determine if any other safety measures are required. The Connecticut School Transportation Safety Commission has made a number of recommendations that merit consideration.

FIGURE 12.6   *Selections from a Sample Report (continued)*

SUMMARY OF CHAPTER OBJECTIVES

1. **Identify six differences between *short* and *long reports*.**

   Although both short and long reports tell a story, they differ in six important ways. Short reports typically do not include front or back matter and have short, rather than extended, introductions. Most short reports get immediately to the point and, unlike long reports, are personal and use fewer devices to aid comprehension. Finally, short reports sometimes follow a prescribed outline and may even use printed fill-in-the-blank forms.

2. **List the elements contained in short *progress* and *trip reports*.**

   Progress reports—documents that provide status information on current work—often begin with summaries and then focus on work completed, work in progress, and work yet to be done. They may also include work forecasts, conclusions, and recommendations. Trip reports—documents that summarize the events of business trips—often start with summaries that highlight conclusions and recommendations which emerged from the trip. Details follow, then conclusions and recommendations are spelled out. Trip reports often close by examining the need for future visits to the same site.

3. **Identify the elements contained in the *front matter* of a long report.**

   The front matter of a long report typically includes a cover, a title fly, a title page, a letter of transmittal, a table of contents, a list of illustrations, and a forward. These elements describe the document's purpose and provide a road map for locating specific report parts.

4. **Explain the role of the *executive summary* in a long report.**

   The first feature usually found in the report body, the executive summary is a digested version of the information contained in the report. It plays a crucial role because many busy executives read only the summary. Executive summaries can be descriptive or informative. Descriptive summaries are report synopses that state what the report is intended to accomplish in terms of its purpose and scope. An informative summary is an abbreviated version of the report that contains substantive details.

5. **List the functions of the *introduction* in a long report.**

   The introduction to a long report clarifies the subject and states the report's purpose and scope. In addition, it may describe the plan for developing the subject and clarify research methods. The introduction also sets the style of the report and may begin with an attention-getter.

6. **Describe the types of *structural guideposts* that can be used to create *internal connections* in the body of long reports.**

   Because of their length and complexity, formal reports need structural guideposts that move the reader from one part of the discussion to another. Among the most commonly used guideposts are internal previews—sentences and paragraphs that appear at the beginning of sections and preview the material to come; internal summaries are sentences and paragraphs that appear at the close of sections and reiterate key points. Transitional words and phrases help to make connections within report sections. Headings and summary tables and charts are also important connective tools.

7. **Explain how *summaries, conclusions,* and *recommendations* are used to close long reports.**

   The summary highlights the most important information from the report. Conclusions, which embody the logical results of the evidence presented in the report, tell readers what report findings mean. Finally, recommendations are the specific actions that the writer advises as a result of the information presented in his or her report.

8. **List the elements contained in the *back matter* of a long report.**

   The back matter of a long report may include a bibliography, appendixes, a glossary, and an index. This material supplements the information presented in the body of the report.

9. **Explain the use of the direct and indirect organizational patterns in long reports.**

   Long reports may be organized using direct or indirect approaches. Developed according to an indirect order, arguments are presented systematically. The report opens with an introduction, moves to a discussion of report findings, and ends with conclusions and recommendations. Using a direct organizational approach, the report begins with an introduction, moves to conclusions and recommendations, and then provides supporting details.

REVIEW AND DISCUSSION QUESTIONS

1. Name six ways in which short and long reports differ. (*Ch. Obj. 1*)

2. Summarize the elements contained in short progress and trip reports. (*Ch. Obj. 2*)

3. This chapter gives five reasons why you might decide to write a long, formal report rather than a short one. What are these reasons? (*Ch. Obj. 1, 3*)

4. What elements are typically found in the front matter of a long report? (*Ch. Obj. 3*)

5. Explain the importance of an executive summary in a long report. (*Ch. Obj. 4*)

6. Summarize the function(s) of an introduction to a long report. (*Ch. Obj. 5*)

7. Describe ways to create internal connections within the body of a long report. (*Ch. Obj. 6*)

8. Distinguish among the functions of summaries, conclusions, and recommendations. (*Ch. Obj. 7*)

9. What components make up the back matter of a long report? (*Ch. Obj. 8*)

10. Describe the differences between the direct and indirect organizational patterns in long reports. (*Ch. Obj. 9*)

APPLICATION EXERCISES

1. For each of the following business situations, would you choose to write a short report or a long one? (*Ch. Obj. 1*)

   a. A co-worker asks for a quick update on your latest project.

   b. An important customer—one whom you do not know well—requests more information about a complex group of products.

   c. You take this important customer to lunch and discuss your report from (b) above. The customer asks you to write a follow-up explanation of one point in the report that he did not understand.

   d. Your boss wants a summary of your discussion during the lunch in (c) above.

2. Using the model outline discussed in this chapter, write a short progress report that summarizes the status of a project in which you are involved. This project could be related to your job, to your classes, or to a social group or hobby. (*Ch. Obj. 2*)

3. Using the model outline presented in this chapter, write a trip report that discusses a trip that you have made. Your subject could be a business trip, a vacation, or a trip that you made somewhere within your community. (*Ch. Obj. 2*)

4. Write a short trouble report that discusses a problem that you have encountered at work or school. This problem might be a faulty piece of equipment, a procedure that doesn't seem to work well, or a negative trend of some type. Use a direct approach and make recommendations on how to resolve the problem you have identified. (*Ch. Obj. 1, 2*)

5. Write a short investigative report that summarizes your research and recommendations on a particular topic. Possible topics include buying a new piece of equipment for your job; buying a car, a stereo, a computer, or a bicycle; comparing the merits and drawbacks of several stores; choosing a dormitory or apartment to live in. (*Ch. Obj. 1, 2*)

6. By surveying several typical business documents, find examples of each of the *structural guideposts* discussed in this chapter as means of creating internal connections within a document. Your examples can come from the same document or from separate reports. (*Ch. Obj. 6*)

7. Each of the following business situations requires a written report. In each case, which would be most effective—a direct or an indirect organizational pattern? (*Ch. Obj. 9*)

   a. Your boss must meet tomorrow with journalists to discuss a high-profile project. She asks you to prepare a report that she can read tonight that will brief her on the major issues involved in the project.

   b. You have suggested hiring ten new employees in a particular division of your firm. Your boss is skeptical and asks for a report proving that the additional workers are needed.

   c. For five years, your company has offered the same rates to its longtime customers. Now, however, costs are rising and you've decided that you simply must raise your rates—albeit modestly—in order to remain profitable. How would you present this suggestion to customers?

   d. You have been assigned to a committee that is assessing alternative sites for a new office. The committee chairperson asks you for your recommendations.

EXERCISES 8 through 15 deal with writing a long report. If possible, write on a topic related to your present job or to a job you have held in the past. Other possible business-related topics include the role of ethics programs in American companies; the use of diversity training in U.S. firms; the experience of a specific company in dealing with environmental problems and issues; or important trends in a particular field or job that interests you.

8. Write the text discussion of a long report on the topic of your choice. Your instructor will specify the length. Organize your report in the most effective pattern—direct or indirect. Keep track of your references and be sure to use structural guideposts to create internal connections. (*Ch. Obj. 6, 9*)

9. Write the summary, conclusions, and recommendations sections for your report. Set off each section with a separate heading. (*Ch. Obj. 7*)

10. Create a list of references and a bibliography for the report that you have developed in response to EXERCISE 8. In addition, briefly describe two topics that might be appropriate as appendixes to this report. (*Ch. Obj. 8*)

11. Write an introduction to the report that you began in responding to EXERCISE 8. (*Ch. Obj. 5*)

12. Write an informative executive summary for the report that you began in EXERCISE 8. Make this summary about one-tenth the length of the report body, including headings. (*Ch. Obj. 4*)

13. Create an appropriate cover and title page for the report begun in EXERCISE 8. (*Ch. Obj. 3*)

14. Write a letter of transmittal to convey your long report to the reader. (*Ch. Obj. 3*)

15. Develop a table of contents and a list of possible illustrations for your long report. (*Ch. Obj 3*)

BUILDING YOUR RESEARCH SKILLS

Research and write a short report (length to be determined by your instructor) on a business-related topic of your choice. Base your report on sources other than your text and class materials. Include an introduction and conclusion and, if appropriate, your recommendations. Present your completed report to the class.

BUILDING YOUR TEAMWORK SKILLS

Pair off with another student in your class. Read and critique each other's reports from the previous exercise. Pay particular attention to the effectiveness of introductions, conclusions, and recommendations. Are there appropriate transitions and internal connections? Does the report express a clear idea? Try to give each other constructive suggestions for improving your reports.

COMMUNICATING IN A WORLD OF DIVERSITY

Your boss has asked you to create a short report on Europe's most profitable companies. You do some research and find that *Business Week* rates the firms in the table at right as the top ten in terms of their annual increase in market value during one recent year.

You also discover the following statistics:

- In one year, Britain added sixteen firms to *Business Week*'s list of the Top Global 1000 companies—more than any other European nation.

- During the same year, Britain added $162 billion to its total market capitalization—an increase of 26 percent over the previous year.

- The most prosperous British firms tend to be consumer and drug companies that sell to widespread global markets.

- Return on equity for investors during the same year averaged 17.7 percent for Britain, 12.8 percent for Germany, 12.9 percent for France, 11.9 percent for Switzerland, and 35 percent for the Netherlands.

COMPANY	COUNTRY	MARKET VALUE (IN BILLIONS)	INCREASE IN MARKET VALUE (IN BILLIONS)
Glaxo Holdings	Britain	$42.6	$12.6
Wellcome	Britain	15.3	6.9
Guinness	Britain	21.4	6.6
Grand Metropolitan	Britain	19.3	6.2
BTR	Britain	17.2	5.7
Roche Holding	Switzerland	20.8	5.6
Marks & Spencer	Britain	17.0	5.4
J. Sainsbury	Britain	15.2	5.1
Ciba-Geigy	Switzerland	14.2	4.3
Total Française Petroles	France	9.2	4.3

Write a short report in which you summarize the data shown here.

Source: Richard Melcher, "Britain's Rather Good Show," *Business Week*, July 13, 1992, pp. 50–52.

How to Drive Sales When the Consumer Downshifts

American marketers are have identified a new trend in consumer behavior—"downshifting." *Downshifting* means that consumers are doing more comparison shopping; they look not only for quality but also for bargains.

One downshifter is accountant Melba Turner, who says that when she and her husband "turned 30, we faced the reality that our resources [were] limited.... If I see something I like, I usually think about it for at least 24 hours before I buy, and I only buy when the price is right.... I've learned," says Turner, "that you can always get it cheaper if you are patient." Another downshifter is Anne McBride, a vice president of MacAndrews & Forbes Holdings, who has started buying her clothes at Kmart. "I used to pay $1,000 for one suit," she says. "Now I get three by top designers for $500." Still another is hotel concierge Jim Moore, who buys many of his clothes at thrift shops because "I'm not buying into department store markups anymore."

Naturally, marketers in almost every industry are scrambling to find ways to reach downshifters. One avenue is private-label brands, which usually sell for 5 percent to 50 percent less than brand items. In the last four years, for example, private-label sales in grocery stores has risen from 16.4 percent to 18.2 percent of sales. Private-label sales are growing at more than twice the rate of those for name brands.

Marketers are also are trying to reach downshifters by affiliating themselves with discount stores. For example, American Express, which has traditionally cultivated an upscale image, has persuaded Kmart to take its credit cards. Kmart also finds itself an appealing outlet for more name brands like Elizabeth Arden cosmetics.

Downshifters also shop in factory outlet malls, warehouse clubs, and so-called "category killers"—stores that dominate certain retailing sectors. Category killers like Toys 'R' Us and Home Depot buy in quantity and can operate on markups of only half to two-thirds the cost of traditional department stores. As a result, they can sell name brands for less.

One businessperson who is profiting from the downshift trend is Elysa Lazar, who publishes *The S&B Report*, a monthly newsletter highlighting sales in New York City. Demand for her newsletter has grown almost 25 percent in the last two years, and she now has 10,000 subscribers. "Consumers hate to waste money these days," says Lazar, "and why should they when they can get anything they could possibly want off-price?"

Questions and Applications

1. What types of organizations are most likely to feel the effects of consumer downshifting?

2. How would you characterize the various motivations of consumers who are downshifting?

3. Write a report in which you discuss the trend of downshifting and how it is affecting American consumers and businesses.

Source: Raye Rice, "What Intelligent Consumers Want," *Fortune*, December 28, 1992, pp. 57–60.

A Report on How to Make Things WORK

As chairperson of the charitable donations committee at your company, you're looking for a solid, tax-deductible project in which to invest some of the firm's earnings. A co-worker suggests a not-for-profit organization called Workers of Rural Kentucky (WORK). You do some research and collect the following information:

- WORK makes loans to low-income residents in rural Kentucky. Many of these loans help residents start their own small businesses.

- WORK is one of about 200 programs in 41 states that encourage self-employment as a way to help people living on welfare to become self-sufficient.

- A recent study of self-employment concluded that although it is too soon to evaluate the economic impact of such programs, they do improve the self-confidence, self-esteem, and abilities of those who participate.

- The director of WORK is Stella Marshall, who is herself an example of how the program can change lives. Six years ago, Marshall was depressed and suicidal because of poverty and a failing marriage. Says Marshall today: "It was the WORK group that kept me alive and saved my life." Development workers taught her bookkeeping, marketing, and computers. Today, she tracks WORK's budget on computer spreadsheets.

- One WORK-financed business is the Owsley Cleaning Service, founded by Pam Thornton. Thornton, who was unemployed and almost illiterate, taught herself to strip tile floors and operate a heavy-duty floor buffer. She also learned how to drive a car and began taking classes in reading, writing, and mathematics at a nearby school. Ultimately, she repaid her WORK loan in one year (two years ahead of schedule) and is planning to open a plant nursery as a second business. Reports Thornton: "If it hadn't been for the WORK group telling me that you can do a lot…I would never have tried anything. I'd still be in a little shack doing nothing."

- Another beneficiary is Teresa Bowles. She bought silk-screen equipment, learned how to print letters and pictures on bags, jackets, and shirts, and opened a T-shirt shop. Business is so good that she's struggling to keep up with orders.

- Each applicant for a WORK loan must submit a business proposal, including a cash-flow projection and a marketing plan. WORK meets twice a month to monitor the progress of the businesses that it finances. At each meeting, business owners must report their revenues and expenses, as well as any ongoing problems. The support group offers both personal and professional advice.

- The WORK group operates on a tight budget and sometimes can't pay all its bills. When that happens, director Stella Marshall doesn't pay herself. "Some nights," she admits, "I can't sleep worrying that all of this is going to fall through the floor."

- Teresa Bowles declares that "if this group falls apart tomorrow, what we've all learned here won't be forgotten. It's the greatest thing that's ever happened to all of us."

Assignment

Write a report in which you discuss the benefits of your company investing in Workers of Rural Kentucky.

Source: Timothy O'Brien, "Pride of Ownership," *The Wall Street Journal*, January 22, 1993, pp. A1, A5.

13

Organizing and Writing Short and Long Proposals

CHAPTER OBJECTIVES

After studying this chapter, you should be able to:

1 Explain how *logic* and *reasoning, emotion,* and *credibility* communicate the *purpose* of proposals.

2 Identify the special characteristics of proposals.

3 Describe the elements included in the *front matter* of a model proposal.

4 Describe the elements contained in the *body* of a model proposal.

5 Explain how *appendixes* are used in proposals.

6 Explain the importance of effective language and style in proposals.

7 Identify the important features of successful *internal proposals.*

8 Identify the important features of successful *sales proposals.*

Executives who get there and stay suggest solutions when they present the problems.

Malcolm Forbes
American business publisher

WINNING BUSINESS WITH TOUGH PROPOSALS

Imagine that you're a marketing consultant who earns your living by convincing company executives that you can help them sell their products. Now suppose that you have the opportunity to work with a mid-sized company, with $6 million in annual sales, that sells collectibles. Although this company prospered during years of high inflation, profits dropped when inflation declined. No longer needing a hedge against rising prices, consumers looked for other investments. Seeing opportunity during one of these downturns, you launch a full-scale campaign to convince the company that your ideas can boost sales.

Step one in your marketing plan is to call the company president. After convincing the president's secretary that you have something important to say, you spend the next thirty minutes giving the president free advice on how he might improve lagging sales. Your presentation is specific because you realize that vague, superficial promises almost never make sales. Rather, you give the president information that *you* know *he* can use.

One of your key selling points is to suggest marketing the company's products through a network of retail stores located in malls that cater to upper-income shoppers. You also suggest that each collectible be sold with a document that attests to its authenticity and value. The company's goal, you emphasize, is to convince shoppers that collectibles are long-term investments that are likely to increase in value.

When the conversation ends, the president is impressed with your ideas. He is not, however, convinced—a situation that forces you to follow up with a lengthy proposal letter in step two in your marketing plan. Your persistence is impressive. For a period of three months, you send a new proposal about every two weeks.

Each letter contains new ideas that could help make money for the firm. With each proposal, you aim for yet another angle that will increase sales for your prospective client. In one letter, for example, you suggest sending a direct-mail color brochure with photos, pricing, and retail-sales information to upper-income consumers. In another letter, you suggest including in the brochure testimonials from noted authorities on collectibles. Your proposals finally pay off when the president of the client firm invites you to company headquarters to sign a lucrative consulting contract.[1]

CHAPTER OVERVIEW

As you can see in this example, written proposals are designed to sell ideas—as well as goods and services—to prospective clients. In many cases, of course, verbal communication will set the stage for sales, but deals are sealed by written documents. As we will see in this chapter, proposals are also used for a wide range of projects, from suggesting internal changes in company operations to seeking government contracts. However, despite differences in audiences, specific purposes, and final forms, all proposals share a common thread: They focus on audience needs as they attempt to convince readers that the proposal writer can solve a pressing problem, improve sales, decrease costs, or otherwise increase profits.

This chapter will introduce you to the art of writing long and short proposals by focusing on the special characteristics of proposals. We will describe the elements common to many proposals and point to the key roles of *language* and *style*. Finally, we will analyze successful *sales* and *internal proposals* in both short and long forms. We will begin by taking a closer look at the *purpose* of proposals.

THE PURPOSE OF PROPOSALS

As we saw in Chapter 10, **proposals** are nothing more or less than sales tools that try to convince readers that you and your organization can solve a particular problem or meet a specific need. Every proposal must communicate the same twofold message: an economically feasible solution to a specific problem and the conviction that the writer is in the best position to implement that solution. A successful proposal must thus demonstrate a complete understanding of a good or service, the requirements of a market, the needs of a client, and the strengths and weaknesses of the competition. Internal proposals should put the same sales effort into convincing top management to make organizational changes. In other words, proposals are persuasive documents.

proposal
Document presenting ideas and plans for consideration by others who may accept them and agree to invest funds in their development

Persuasive Appeals

Proposals persuade through appeals to *reasoning, emotional needs* and *self-interest*, and *credibility*. The most effective proposals combine all three appeals, but it is important to remember that your appeal must be supported by a strong focus on your readers' needs.

Problems are only opportunities in work clothes.

*Henry J. Kaiser
American industrialist*

PERSUADING THROUGH FACT   Successful proposals are both specific and concrete as they try to anticipate the kinds of questions that readers might ask. They should contain an abundance of facts and figures, including all necessary budget information, and they must organize data in an understandable and convincing way. Schedules and deadlines should also be addressed. Claims and inferences should be substantiated, and as writing consultant William C. Paxson emphasizes, every proposal must have a factual base. "Facts," says Paxson, "constitute the sales pitch in a winning proposal, not emotional statements or superlative expressions. Proposals succeed on logic, not rhetoric."[2]

The effective proposal, then, requires a well thought-out organizational plan that develops data in a logical way. At their heart, most proposals rely on a problem/solution approach, which defines the nature of the client's problems or needs and suggests mechanisms for improvement. For example, a communications consultant asked to evaluate the writing skills of a company's salesforce may identify a weakness in sales-letter writing (the problem). He or she may then propose a series of workshops to improve this vital communication skill (the solution).

As you plan your proposal, let the concerns of your prospective client guide your thinking about what to say and how to say it. For example, if your client is particularly concerned about budget requirements, build your proposal around the demonstration that your solution is financially responsible. In fact, proposals written around single themes are among the most convincing, in part because of their simplicity.

INTERVIEW

Ron Tepper, Authority on Writing Effective Business Proposals

We asked Ron Tepper, a marketing consultant based in Costa Mesa, California, for his thoughts on writing successful proposals. Throughout the interview, Tepper, the author of *How to Write Winning Proposals for Your Company or Client*, points to a mix of thorough research and salesmanship.

Question: What do clients look for when evaluating proposals?

Answer: They look for proposals that are need-based. They expect you to find out what *they* need—what *their* problems are—before you propose a solution. Your company's capability doesn't mean anything unless you pin these needs down.

Question: How do proposal writers identify needs?

Answer: By talking with the client and doing research. You have to find out what the company is doing, how it's operating, and what its problems are. The head of a company may tell you, for example, "We need a better accounting system, one that processes receivables faster." So then you have to discuss the situation with people in the accounting department to find out exactly what's being done.

It's important to be flexible, especially at the early stages of the research process. You'll get into trouble by starting with a preconceived idea of what's wrong or by taking as gospel the needs that the client identifies. The client may tell you, for example, that slow, inefficient procedures are responsible for the accounting problem. When you get in there, however, you may discover that these procedures are not the culprit at all. Maybe it's a software problem, maybe the head of the department doesn't release any work unless he sees it first. A variety of things can cause the problem, so your research should never be dogmatic.

Question: How important is selling your solution?

Answer: When you present your ideas, you *have* to sell them. You have to convince the client that your solution is right and that you're the right person to handle the problem. Selling a solution is particularly important when times are tough.

APPEALING TO EMOTIONAL NEEDS AND SELF-INTEREST   The goal of a proposal, however, is not merely to present a solution. The successful proposal presents a solution that appeals to the reader's emotional needs and self-interest. After reviewing a proposal, the prospective client should be convinced that its suggestions will take the form of tangible benefits.

To decide which emotional appeal will work best, you might recall Abraham Maslow's hierarchy of needs from Chapter 3. You can, for example, ask yourself whether the primary needs of the reader can best be described as physiological, safety and security, social, esteem and status, or self-actualization needs. For instance, depending on the emotional needs of a prospective client—say, the sales manager of a consumer-goods company—an automobile company's proposal concerning the lease of twenty automobiles for the firm's sales staff could stress either status or safety. If you are addressing a manager who is focused on status, you can appeal to both his pocketbook and his concern for status by stressing that you can provide top-of-the-line cars at the same price for which other dealers offer less prestigious models. On the other hand, if your client is more concerned about vehicle safety, you could focus not only on the safety features of your cars (antilock breaks, airbags, and so forth) but also on your company's special 800 phone number for emergency road service. In both cases, your emotional appeal centered on tangible benefits and not simply on your intuition about your client's psychological makeup.

Companies don't want to spend money if they can help it, and you have to show them that your ideas will improve the bottom line.

Question: What are the most common mistakes made by inexperienced proposal writers?

Answer: Lack of research is the biggest mistake. Not knowing the players—the people who will make the final decision—is another. Sloppy writing also turns clients off. You have to write in plain, grammatically correct English. Typographical errors are deadly. They show that you're careless. The client feels that if your document is filled with typos, you'll probably make mistakes on the project, too.

Question: Many proposals are written by teams of people. Can this strategy create problems?

Answer: Not if there's a consistent approach and language throughout the document. While many people can do the research and contribute ideas, one person has to do the actual writing.

Question: Have proposal-writing requirements changed in recent years?

Answer: Three things have happened since companies began cutting their staffs. First, they're more tight-fisted with their funds than ever before. Second, they're more business ori-ented; they don't require consultants trying to get business to wine-and-dine them as much as they did in the '80s. Third, the door for consultants is wide open. Downsizing has trimmed staffs to the point that many departments are now undermanned. These companies are more likely to consider consultants today than they were before.

Question: Are small companies and large corporations judged according to the same standards when submitting proposals?

Answer: The company that's done its homework, that knows the client's needs best, has the greatest advantage regardless of size. I've seen small companies grab big contracts when they've done a better job of focusing on the client's needs. A while back, I was trying to get business from a company that was also being pitched by four other firms. My company got the business because we listened to how the president identified the problem. None of our competitors picked up on it, even though they had been doing business with this company for years. In this case, listening got us the job.

Source: Interview with Ron Tepper.

SELLING YOUR CREDIBILITY   As you sell your solution, you also sell your personal and business credibility. Indeed, creating a positive organizational image is one of your most important goals when you submit a proposal. Professors John Schell and John Stratton advise proposal writers to "include your firm's successful past record; parade the credentials and honors or key personnel; attach a financial statement that proves your firm's solvency; append important managerial documentation that illustrates sound business practices. Do whatever you must to prove your company's strength, resolve, skill, and reliability."[3] Your credibility can also be established by the professionalism with which your proposal is prepared and presented. Naturally, a well-written document is more likely to be taken seriously than one with organizational, formatting, writing, and other technical problems.

SPECIAL CHARACTERISTICS OF PROPOSALS

As sales tools, proposals have special characteristics that distinguish them from other documents. Proposals gain their distinctive quality from four main characteristics. Differences in audience, for example, define a proposal as *internal* or *external*. Differences in the situation that prompts it define a proposal as *solicited* or *unsolicited*. Proposals are also distinguished by preparation methods and the manner in which they are evaluated.

internal proposal
Proposal issued to suggest some change within an organization

external proposal
Proposal issued outside an organization to prospective clients in government or private industry

solicited proposal
Proposal submitted in response to a formal or informal request

unsolicited proposal
Proposal that has not been invited by the potential customer who receives it

INTERNAL AND EXTERNAL PROPOSALS   The audience for whom a proposal is written determines whether it is an internal or external document. **Internal proposals** are issued to suggest some form of change within an organization; **external proposals** are issued to prospective clients in government and private industry. When they deal with relatively minor issues, internal proposals are usually written in memo form. A bookkeeper, for example, may propose ways to eliminate unnecessary steps in a billing procedure. On the other end of the spectrum, internal proposals that suggest major organizational changes as a result of extensive research and months of work will be lengthy and formal. For example, the strategic-planning office of a major defense contractor may issue an internal proposal to suggest changes in company operations because of Department of Defense cutbacks.

Even short external proposals are usually written in letter form. Many small businesses use short proposals to address the problems of prospective clients. For example, a window manufacturer trying to persuade a homeowner to install insulated storm windows may send a letter to describe the benefits and costs of the work and the reputation of the company and product. In such a case, the letter can be considered a proposal. As we will see later in the chapter, many long internal and external proposals share similar elements.

SOLICITED AND UNSOLICITED PROPOSALS   A **solicited proposal** is a response to a formal or informal request. An insurance agent, for example, might be approached by a prospective client and asked to propose a comprehensive disability and health-insurance plan for the client's thirty-person company. More formal solicitations are issued by government agencies and large corporations in the form of *requests for proposals* (*RFPs*) (see Chapter 10).

Regardless of formality, solicited proposals put you in the position of satisfying a need identified by the firm to whom you are writing. At the same time, however, they also give you the advantage of knowing a great deal about that need before you begin. In addition, they provide some degree of certainty that the money is available to pay for the project if your proposal is accepted.

Unsolicited proposals, on the other hand, have not been invited by the potential customer. Indeed, unsolicited proposals may offer something with which customers are unfamiliar, for which they have no need, or for which they cannot pay. Not surprisingly, unsolicited proposals present the greatest persuasive challenge.

METHOD OF PREPARATION   Like formal reports, formal proposals are often written in collaborative teams that may include members from the various departments that will work on the project if the proposal is accepted. It is not unusual, for example, for twenty or more people to work on a lengthy proposal at the same time. When each completes his or her individual contribution, the material is submitted to the project manager for coordination, review, editing, and finalization. (We discussed collaboration as an increasingly common method of preparing proposals and reports in Chapter 10.)

EVALUATION   Unlike most other business documents that are considered on an informal basis, proposals are generally evaluated according to predetermined standards. These standards focus on the capacity of your company to solve a client's problem, your financial requirements, and your qualifications to do the job. Moreover, these factors are not evaluated simply on their own merit. They are also viewed in comparison with the statements submitted by other organizations competing for the same business. To make the best impression, creativity, clarity, accuracy, and consistency are essential qualities in written proposals.

With the special nature of proposals in mind, we will now focus on the features of a model proposal. Later in the chapter, we will apply these features to internal and sales proposals. Many of the same techniques can also be used to answer RFPs.

THE ELEMENTS OF A MODEL PROPOSAL

Proposals can be as short as a single page or run to hundreds of pages that include prefatory sections and appendixes in addition to the proposal body. In general, the longer the proposal, and the more sections it includes, the more *formal* it is.

Although short proposals generally present relatively simple ideas, such is not always the case. Depending on the business being conducted and the relationship between writer and client, multimillion-dollar deals have been proposed on a single page. In most cases, however, the long proposal is the document of choice when a complex deal must be presented.

In this section, we will examine the specific parts of a model proposal as they are identified in Table 13.1. As the table shows, although the front matter and appendixes are found only in long documents, the elements contained in the proposal body are common to both long and short forms. As you review this model, keep in mind that many proposals do not include all these elements.

Prefatory Section

Certain parts of the proposal precede the body and prepare readers for what follows. Depending on audience expectations and client specifications, a long proposal may include a *cover*, a *title fly* and a *title page*, a *letter of transmittal*, a *table of contents*, and a *list of illustrations*. Depending on the instructions contained in the RFP, you may also be asked to include a copy of the RFP. (Because many front-matter elements are the same for reports and proposals, a number of these elements are described both in this chapter and in Chapter 12.)

When transmittal letters are included with solicited proposals, they are generally short and to the point. The opening paragraph explains that a proposal is being sent and states the reason for its transmission. For example, it might say simply:

> Here is the marketing proposal that we spoke about for your company's paint-products division.

The second paragraph might then summarize the nature of the proposal while pointing to sections that will hold special interest to the reader. This paragraph may also explain why the writer and/or the writer's organization is espe-

TABLE 13.1	*Elements of Long and Short Proposals*
ELEMENTS OF LONG PROPOSALS	ELEMENTS OF SHORT PROPOSALS
FRONT MATTER	
Cover	
Title Fly	
Title Page	
Letter of Transmittal	
Table of Contents	
List of Illustrations	
Copy of RFP	
PROPOSAL BODY	PROPOSAL BODY
Introduction	Introduction
Technical Plan	Technical Plan
Management Plan	Management Plan
Organizational Qualifications	Organizational Qualifications
Costs	Costs
Conclusion	Conclusion
Appendixes	

cially qualified for the work. Finally, many transmittal letters close by expressing the hope that the proposal will meet the reader's needs and extending an offer of additional assistance.

The letter that transmits an unsolicited proposal has a different purpose. This letter contains a persuasive message that tries to convince the reader that the proposal deserves attention. The letter must also summarize the proposal and the writer's qualifications for handling the prospective client's problem.

In general, the transmittal letter is less formal than the proposal itself. Transmittal letters use conversational English and rely on such personal pronouns as *I, we*, and *you* to refer to proposal participants and readers.

The Proposal Body

Although all proposals communicate essentially the same type of information, the *way* that information is conveyed varies considerably—a situation that gives writers a certain amount of creative flexibility. As a sign of this flexibility, proposal parts do not feature the relatively standard labels found in most formal reports. For example, while reports generally include sections labeled "Summary," "Conclusions," and "Recommendations," proposal terminology varies according to the preferences of the writer. The most common exceptions are proposals that respond to RFPs and those for which the prospective client suggests a specific format.

Experienced writers have identified at least one criterion for the effective organization of a proposal: You must find a way to organize your proposal as an effective persuasive tool. In general, the best proposals begin by establishing need, provide increasingly greater depth of information as the reader moves further into the proposal, and leave cost until the end.[4] Many proposals thus include the following elements: an *introduction*; a *technical plan* or *work statement*; a *management plan*; a *statement of organizational qualifications*; a *cost analysis*; and *conclusions*.[5]

INTRODUCTION   The introduction is the first part of your actual proposal that most prospective clients read. It contains your summary of the problem and your proposed solution. Because you are trying to "sell" your ideas by creating interest in the detailed solution that will follow, your introduction is a crucial marketing tool.

The introduction tries to convince prospects that it is worth their time to read the complete document. Many writers thus use attention-getters that argue for the superiority of their solutions over those of competitors. For example, if you propose an innovative solution, at least part of your introduction should focus on how standard techniques (which will probably be proposed by competitors) will fall short in this case. Your introduction may also highlight your company's credentials. Because of its importance, professionals recommend that your introduction be written only after the rest of your proposal is complete.

As you summarize the content of your proposal, focus on the benefits that clients will enjoy if they agree to do business. Be as specific and as concrete as possible in stressing benefits from increased productivity and profits, decreased absenteeism and injury, and so on. Compare your per-unit costs and success rates with those of your competition—for example:

> While Acme's widgets cost $1.20 a unit and are 80-percent effective, our comparable product is significantly less expensive at $1.02 a unit and has a 91-percent success rate as proven by extensive factory testing.

Your goal is to show—in no more than a paragraph or two—the efficiency and effectiveness of your solution.

In defining the scope and organization of your proposal, the final section of your introduction tells the reader what to expect in the pages that follow. Avoid the tendency to merely repeat the table of contents. Rather, focus the reader's attention on your document's overall organization and key sections.

Finally, the length of your introduction will be directly proportional to the length of your proposal. While a paragraph or two may be all that is needed to summarize a short proposal, five to ten pages may be necessary for a 150-page technical document.

TECHNICAL PLAN   The **technical plan**, also known as the **work statement**, is a detailed description of the work that you will complete if your proposal is accepted. Technical plans are specific and concrete and often include visual aids to illustrate their descriptions of procedures and projected goals. Although the contents of technical plans vary from proposal to proposal, they often include the following elements:

- *Statement of the problem.* This statement focuses on the purposes of the proposal. It states the prospective client's specific need for your company's products. In effect, this statement tells your readers that you understand the nature and scope of *their* problem. At this point, it may also help to define the project in terms of its major and minor tasks.

  If the proposal is in response to an RFP, avoid repeating the language of the RFP. Instead, rephrase and change the language to show that you have thoroughly analyzed the prospective client's needs.

- *Technical description.* Here, you describe the steps that you will take to achieve the proposal's specific objectives. As appropriate, include the following categories of information: the methods, equipment, and materials that you will use to complete the task; specifications for all products produced; the types of data that will be collected; the results that can be expected at each stage of a multistage project; and quality-control techniques. Use a series of subheadings to organize this information.

- *Facilities description.* This section describes the facilities and equipment needed to implement your proposal. These may include facilities and equipment that the company currently has or will obtain if your proposal is accepted.

- *Exceptions.* When you cannot give readers everything they want or expect, it is important to say so in your technical plan. You should always be clear about what the proposal will—and will not—accomplish.

Finally, the technical plan often describes the specific steps in the proposed project, in the order in which they will be taken. It may also describe solutions that have been rejected and the reasons for their rejection, especially if these options are likely to be introduced by competitors.

MANAGEMENT PLAN   The **management plan** describes your organization's plans for managing the project after it is awarded. Among the elements in the management plan is usually a *functional analysis,* in which you would describe your company's plans for dealing with all the functions entailed by the project—for example, subcontracting and accounting. Flow charts and schedules should be used to describe the timing and sequence of project phases.

ORGANIZATIONAL FUNCTION   Finally, your management plan should use your company's standard organization chart to indicate those people in your organization who will participate in the project. Next, describe the specific roles they will play. In addition, make it clear whether a special group is being formed to implement the project and show how this group will work with the rest of your company. For example, special groups are often formed by advertising agencies that win large consumer accounts and by aircraft manufacturers seeking Defense Department contracts.

ORGANIZATIONAL QUALIFICATIONS   This section addresses the capability of your organization and its people to complete the task for which it is bidding. The following elements are often included in this section:

technical plan (or **work statement**)
Part of the body of the proposal that describes in detail the work that will be completed

management plan
Component of a proposal that describes plans for managing a proposed change after it is approved

PRACTICAL TIPS

The Pros and Cons of Boilerplate Language

Must every word of every proposal be written fresh, or is it sometimes acceptable to use boilerplate language? *Boilerplate* refers to language that is taken verbatim from other company documents. Because the documents from which material is taken are company property, the borrowed language is not plagiarized. Boilerplate language usually involves résumés, corporate history and accomplishments, legal issues, description of facilities, and various policies and rules.

Boilerplate is used for two very practical reasons. First, lifting sections from previous documents saves time, especially if the useful sections are lengthy or technical. It also allows the writer to focus on problem solving rather than on spending time reworking such noncreative but essential elements as the firm's qualifications or individual résumés.

On the other hand, the pitfalls of boilerplating are equally obvious. When it is clear, for example, that a business proposal has not been customized, readers may question the amount of time and energy that has been devoted to their unique problems—and will be devoted if the proposal is accepted. The last thing you want potential clients to feel is that the proposal they are reading is the same document that every other client reads; no one wants to be part of a crowd, especially when spending money.

Ironically, boilerplating can also lessen your competitive edge. Using recycled language has the tendency to make thinking old and stale. Boilerplate can also place you in the position of ignoring recent accomplishments in the client's industry and omitting facts that can work in your favor. For example, if a description of your firm's accomplishments was written six months ago, it will not mention work you just completed—even if this work is relevant to the proposal. In general, never rely on old facts. Review recent accomplishments before writing and add any that will strengthen your presentation.

Knowing when to use boilerplate language and when to start fresh is a judgment call. As a general rule, use boilerplate to save time but always customize your language. For example, instead of simply picking up résumés from previous proposals, rewrite each one to reflect the unique requirements of the current project. Your goal is to show why each person is qualified for the project. To avoid its pitfalls, many seasoned writers restrict boilerplate to no more than 25 percent of a document.

Sources: William C. Paxson, *Write It Now: A Timesaving Guide to Writing Better* (Reading, MA: Addison-Wesley, 1985), p. 75; and Ron Tepper, *How to Write Winning Proposals for Your Company or Client* (New York: John Wiley, 1990), pp. 236–37.

- *Company background.* Emphasize the experience that qualifies your company to complete the assignment. The section should list other related contracts as well as the general background and work of your company.
- *Personnel qualifications.* Focus on the backgrounds of the individuals who will take part in the project. Whether you devote a short paragraph or an entire résumé to each individual, your descriptions should focus on the match between available skills and project needs.
- *Administrative functions.* Cover such necessary details as employee safety and health measures, equal-opportunity and affirmative-action procedures, and security standards. These details are especially crucial when responding to government RFPs. At this point, you may also refer to specific administrative documents. Do not, however, include them in your narrative. When administrative documents are submitted, you can usually place them in appendixes.

COST ANALYSIS   The specific costs involved in a project are generally listed next. Include costs for material, equipment, and labor. In some cases, you may want to show how these costs were estimated and the methods that you will use to minimize cost overruns. If the project will continue for several years, consider such factors as the effects of inflation.

CONCLUSIONS   Conclude with a persuasive statement that tries once more to convince your reader to accept the terms of your proposal. Emphasize the point that the company which you represent is better qualified to do the job than its competition and that your proposed solution is the reader's best choice.

Appendixes

Include in an appendix any material that is either too specific to be included in the body of the proposal or tangential to the persuasive development of your argument. For example, if your client wants to see that your company has adequate insurance coverage in case of injury, include a copy of your certificate of worker's compensation insurance. Other supporting materials might include labor–management agreements, the specific provisions of your company's affirmative-action plan, additional drawings and illustrations, lengthy mathematical calculations, contracts, résumés, and client lists.

Proposals containing all these elements may still fail because of inappropriate language or tone. In the next section, we will thus examine the ways in which proper language and tone contribute to successful documents.

PROGRESS CHECK

1. What function(s) do proposals serve in business?
2. Distinguish between internal and external proposals.
3. Should a proposal be short or long? Explain your answer.
4. Why is a good introduction important to a proposal?

THE LANGUAGE AND STYLE OF PROPOSALS

The most effective proposals depend on specific facts and details. They are written with an eye on simplicity and clarity, in a forceful style, and on an appropriate level of formality. As we review each of these characteristics, remember that your style and language should always be geared to the needs of your reader.

The short words are best, and the old words are the best of all.

*Alistair Cooke
British historian*

Let Specifics Tell the Story

Proposal writing is factual writing. Proposals persuade not through the force of overblown language but through the creativity of the solutions and the clarity of the ideas that they put forth. Language that relies more on accumulated adjectives than on hard facts may very well persuade readers that you can talk about a job better than you can analyze and perform it.

Nor will you persuade many readers if you develop the content of your proposal around a series of impressive but unsubstantiated generalizations. For example, it should be convincing to express confidence in your ability to solve a problem that is similar to one you have solved in the past. Ironically, however, the effect will be the opposite if you fail to provide the specific details that will generate confidence in your ability. Indeed, failure to detail the nature of your past successes may create doubt where none existed before. In short, instead of bolstering your position, generalizations often cause readers to ask, "Where are the specifics?" When readers ask that question, they are probably questioning your credibility. A more effective method, then, is to point to past successes and creative solutions and let them tell the story—the whole story.

At the same time, however, feel free to express confidence in the tone of your proposal. A "can-do" attitude helps convince readers that you and your company have the qualifications that you claim to have. "There is a big difference," says business-proposal authority Ron Tepper, "in 'we will' and 'we have' versus 'we will try.' Clients go for outside help because they want the expertise. They do not want someone to try, they want someone to 'do.' "[6]

Aim for Clarity

Effective proposal writing is also clear writing. In large part, clarity results from the use of simple, nontechnical language (even when the subject matter is technical). Clear writing means that you have avoided jargon, defined key terms, and explained abbreviations so that every reader—even those with nontechnical backgrounds—can understand the message of your proposal. Writing above the reader's level of understanding is a sure route to failure, especially when nontechnical readers decide key funding issues.

If the nature of your material requires the use of technical terminology (as, for example, responses to RFPs often do), you may be required to submit a separate document to describe and explain the technology for a select group of technical readers, such as engineers and scientists. In other cases, explain as you proceed.

Choose a Forceful Style

Because proposals are persuasive documents, it is important to write forcefully. "Forceful" language is *direct* language that has a positive, forward-looking tone. Avoid qualifying words like *maybe, possibly*, and *perhaps*—they will only minimize the impact of your message. When communicating a selling point, it is especially important to use simple sentences that are not bogged down with dependent or subordinate clauses.

However, because internal proposals are directed *up* the organizational hierarchy—that is, submitted by a lower-ranking to a higher-ranking individual—a less forceful, more passive style is often preferable. Among the features of this style are the indirect approach, the appropriate use of the passive voice, and the use of carefully chosen qualifiers. These features help to avoid the perception of a "hard-sell" approach.

Use Appropriate Formality

In general, let your level of formality be determined by your reader—that is, by your relationship with your reader and the requirements that he or she sets down for the project. Choose an informal style when you know the reader well and when he or she is comfortable with the choice. By contrast, if you are dealing with someone you have never met, a higher level of formality is advisable.

Long proposals are usually formal. To increase your level of formality, use impersonal language and a third-person narrative. Except in your transmittal letter, avoid first- and second-person references, including *I, we*, and *you*. Because brief proposals, in both letter and memo form, are generally less formal, first- and second-person references are generally more acceptable.

With the elements of language and style in mind, it is time to examine some specific internal and sales proposals. As you will see when you study these documents, proposals vary in length, organization, and formality. Often they do not include all the model elements that we categorized in Table 13.1. Table 13.2 focuses on the function of business proposals by listing examples of various types, including answers to RFPs.

WRITING AN INTERNAL PROPOSAL

Internal proposals suggest changes or improvements within an organization. Among other things, such changes might involve new-product ideas; proposals for research and development; suggestions for the reorganization of depart-

APPLYING TECHNOLOGY
Using a Computerized Dictionary

Although computerized spell checkers can eliminate embarrassing spelling mistakes from business proposals, they can make business writers look...well, less literate than they had hoped. They do this by putting the stamp of approval on words that are correctly *spelled* but incorrectly *used*. The following poem, which was circulated at Coastal Corp. in Houston, Texas, shows how spell checkers can fail:

> I have a spelling checker.
> It comes with my PC.
> It plainly marks four my revue,
> Mistake I cannot see.
> I've run this poem threw it,
> I'm sure your please too no.
> It's letter perfect in it's weigh,
> My checker tolled me sew.

Although using a dictionary solves usage problems, few writers are willing to thumb through one for every questionable word. As an alternative, electronic dictionaries can be installed on your computer's hard disk or on a compact-disk-player attachment. These dictionaries are faster and have more functions than dictionaries in book form.

Among the electronic dictionaries that are available are the 116,000-word *American Heritage Electronic Dictionary*, the 180,000-word *Random House Webster's Electronic Dictionary*, and the 616,000-word *Oxford English Dictionary*. Moreover, because they are electronic, these dictionaries have features not found in standard volumes. For one thing, an electronic dictionary can supply words that you do not know. Say, for example, that you do not know—or cannot remember—the name of a male duck. If you simply type *male* and *duck*, the computer will tell you that the correct term is *drake*.

Despite their advantages, however, there is still resistance to using electronic reference tools. Critics point to the fact that they are relatively expensive compared to hard-cover versions, and that they take up considerable space on a computer's hard drive. The latter objection has eased somewhat as the space on standard hard drives has increased and as computer-software developers have learned the art of data compression. The result is a happy marriage: Hard drives with more space for information and software that takes less of it.

Those who try electronic dictionaries quickly become hooked on them as they check meanings and spellings in seconds. It is an especially important tool if your job involves regular writing. T. R. Runnels, deputy director of the South Carolina Department of Archives and History, writes letters, memos, and other documents all day and considers an electronic dictionary an indispensable tool. "It's aggravating at best and costly at worst to stop and use a dictionary," he says, especially because "there are many things...spell checkers won't do."

Source: William M. Bulkeley, "PC Dictionaries, Full of Features, Win More Users," *The Wall Street Journal*, August 4, 1992, pp. B1, B5.

ments; and requests for new machinery and plants. Internal proposals are generally submitted by lower-ranking individuals to managers with the authority to approve their plans.

TABLE 13.2	*Types of Proposals*
DOCUMENT	EXAMPLE
Short internal proposal	Request to change billing procedure on business credit accounts
Long internal proposal	Plan to change method used to calculate benefits in company pension plan
Short sales proposal	Bid on a landscaping job for a private residence
Long sales proposal	Bid to install new telephone system for a Fortune 500 company
Answer to RFP	Request to be considered for a highway repaving contract

Because every internal proposal asks management to spend money, it must justify the expenditure in terms of the bottom line. Proposals may thus address questions like the following:

- Will the idea save money? How much and when will the savings occur?
- How will this change give us an advantage over the competition?
- Will this procedure reduce costs? Increase productivity? Increase sales?

Because the senders and receivers of internal proposals usually know each other, there is generally no need to mention the qualifications of either the departments or people involved in the plan. An exception is the proposal for something out of the ordinary—something for which management might not expect you to possess the capability. For example, if your department deals with planning and implementing personnel benefits, suggesting that you also handle employee compensation would require the department to prove some expertise in this area.

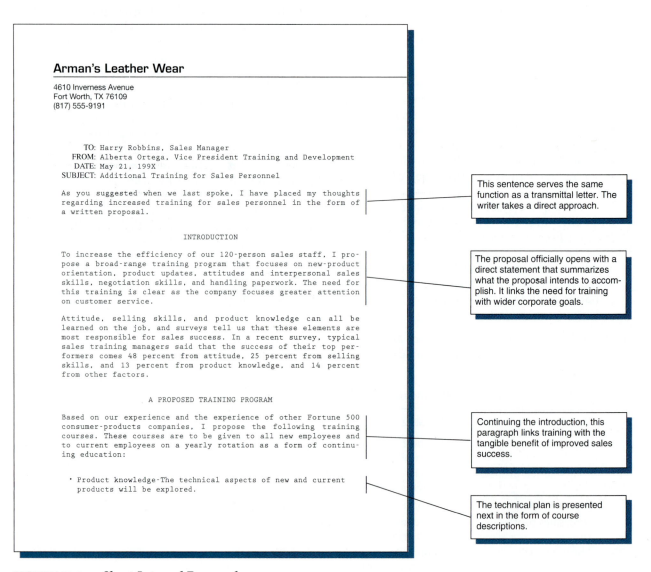

FIGURE 13.1   Short Internal Proposal

A Short Internal Proposal

Short proposals are written in memo form. Length is determined by a number of factors, including the limited scope of the subject or management's wish to keep circulating documents to a manageable length. Figure 13.1 is a short internal proposal submitted by a training specialist who wants to increase training time for sales representatives.[7] Although you will not find such terms as *technical plan* and *management plan*, you will see that the corresponding concepts are addressed.

An Extended Internal Proposal

Naturally, more complex ideas require more extended proposals. An extended proposal is typically submitted along with a transmittal memorandum that is part of the proposal. The proposal in Figure 13.2 was submitted by the medical director of a major corporation to the head of the company's human-resources department.

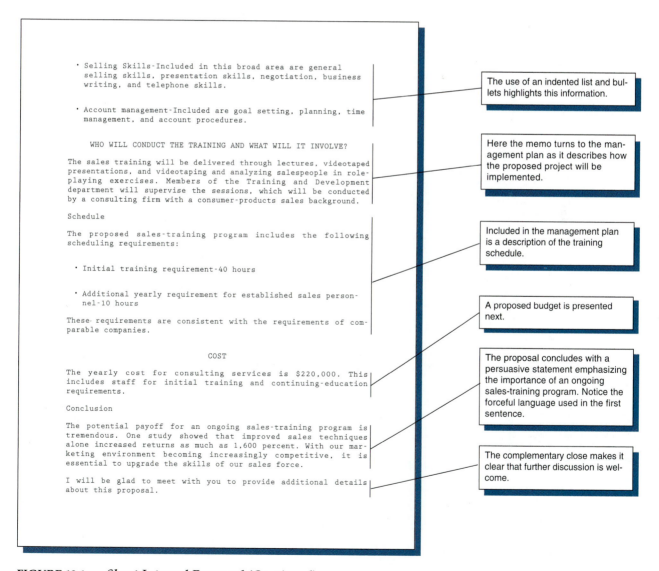

FIGURE 13.1 *Short Internal Proposal (Continued)*

This is the proposal cover. The title and subtitle are printed in uppercase letters. Boldface type or underlining can also be used to empha-size the title's importance.

HEALTH IMPROVEMENT PLAN:
A PILOT STUDY OF COMPANY RETIREES

The person to whom the pro-posal is directed is listed next. Included are the per-son's title and department. It is not necessary to include the company name since it is an internal proposal.

Prepared for
Allan Alderman
Vice President, Human Resources

This is followed by the name and title of the pro-posal writer.

Prepared by
Francis H. Blair, M.D.
Medical Director

The date is listed at the bot-tom of the cover.

June 22, 199X

This transmittal memoran-dum appears on the first page of the proposal.

Appleton Securities, Inc.

2374 Arnold Avenue
New Orleans, LA 70112
(504) 555-7889

MEMORANDUM

TO: Allan Alderman
      Vice President, Human Resources
FROM: Francis H. Blair, M.D.
      Medical Director
DATE: January 2, 199X
SUBJECT: Pilot Program—Health Improvement Program

FIGURE 13.2   *Sample Long Internal Proposal*

Enclosed is a proposal for a pilot project that will test the impact and effectiveness of a health-improvement plan on the health status and medical-claims experience of a select group of retirees from Appleton Securities. A successful pilot project has important cost-saving implications for the entire organization.

With your approval, the pilot program will begin on March 1 and continue for one year. Health-risk data will be collected at the start, at six months, and at 12 months. The impact of the program on medical claims will be measured after 9 and 12 months.

I look forward to your response to this proposal. Please let me know if I can supply any additional data.

> The opening paragraph explains the proposal's purpose and links it to the tangible benefit of the companywide savings. Because the proposal is written from a lower-ranking to a higher-ranking person, its style is somewhat passive. The last sentence, for example, avoids the hard sell.

> The memo focuses on important scheduling information.

> The complementary close opens the door to further communication.

-2-

INTRODUCTION

The plan proposed on the following pages is a personal, confidential health-enhancement program designed to help individuals monitor and change personal health risks and use medical-care services effectively. These factors have a direct impact on the amount of money the corporation spends each year on medical-insurance benefits.

> The introduction begins with a summary of the proposed program.

In recent years, we have seen company health-care costs skyrocket 300 percent. Although some factors are beyond our control, helping current and former employees control such health risks as high blood pressure, smoking, and high cholesterol and make smart choices when seeking medical advice will reduce substantially medical costs to the company and individual employee.

> This paragraph focuses on the benefits to the corporation if the proposed plan is adopted.

The program is administered by mail and consists of sequential health-risk questionnaires, feedback letters, a consumer guide to medical care, and other educational resources.

> Additional summary information is provided.

The pilot project proposed on the following pages is structured to compare participants with a control group of nonparticipants. The population studied in the pilot consists of company retirees. The results we obtain will determine whether to spread the project to the entire population of insured company employees.

> The summary ends by focusing on the purpose of a pilot study.

FIGURE 13.2   *Sample Long Internal Proposal (Continued)*

-3-

GOALS AND OBJECTIVES

The goal of the health-improvement program is to provide motivation and resources for retirees to enhance their health and to use the medical-care system to best advantage. Specific objectives include:

- the reduction of unnecessary outpatient visits
- the expediting of necessary outpatient visits
- motivating and monitoring health-behavior changes

The goal of the pilot program is to measure the impact and outcomes of the program, test the implementation and administration of the program, and determine how receptive retirees are to providing medical information and modifying behaviors based on the program's suggested advice.

PILOT DESIGN

Approximately 100 retirees enrolled in Appleton's medical plan during the past two years. These retirees will be randomly placed into three study groups.

Group 1-"Full Program"

Participants will receive the full health-improvement program intervention consisting of

-4-

health-risk-assessment questionnaires at six-month intervals; corresponding feedback letters and reports, a medical care consumer's guidebook; and quarterly health newsletters.

Group 2-"Questionnaire Only"

Participants will receive and complete health-risk-assessment questionnaires at six-month intervals. However, they will not receive feedback or other program materials. This group will provide comparative data on health-risk behaviors.

This section is part of the technical plan as it focuses on the purposes of the proposal.

A more specific technical description begins here as methods for studying the population are examined.

Headings and consistent indentation patterns make the material inviting and easy to read.

FIGURE 13.2 *Sample Long Internal Proposal (Continued)*

Group 3-"Claims Only"

Retirees in this group will serve as control subjects for claims comparison only. They will not
receive any communications or program information.

Participants in groups 1 and 2 will receive letters from the Vice President of Human Resources and
the Medical Director explaining the project. These
letters are contained in Appendix 1.

> Instead of cluttering the body of the proposal with letters that are tangential to the main point, the writer decides to include them in an appendix.

PILOT EVALUATION

The data received on questionnaires from Groups 1
and 2 will be compared to the experience of the non-
participant control group in three major areas:

- Health-risk behaviors
- Days of hospitalization

-5-

- Outpatient visits

The medical-claims experience of all three groups
will be compared for the year preceding the program and
the 12 months following program intervention.

Timeline for Pilot Program

> The timeline is part of the management plan as it describes the sequence of the project phases.

March 1	Announcement letter from the Vice President of Human Resources to Group 1 and 2 retirees
March 15	Questionnaire package and cover letter from Medical Director to Group 1 and 2 retirees
March 15-31	Special phone line available for retiree inquiries
April	Health-risk-feedback letters to Group 1 respondents
May	Group health-risk report to company
September	Second health-risk-questionnaire cycle for Groups 1 and 2
November	Comparative data analyzed for six-month health-risk changes

FIGURE 13.2   *Sample Long Internal Proposal (Continued)*

-6-

February   Gather claims data for Groups 1, 2, and 3
             for analysis

March   Third and final health-risk questionnaire

May   Final analyses of health-risk and claims
             data, including changes in the data that
             resulted from intervention.

Costs and Potential Savings

    The pilot program proposed here would cost the
company approximately $160,000 over a 14-month period.
This figure breaks down into the following components:

- Consultants' fees $100,000
- On-staff program specialist
  (salary and benefits) $32,000
- Overhead (including office $28,000
  space, mailing expenses,
  secretarial services)

    Based on the experience of our medical-cost con-
tainment consultant, potential savings to the company
in medical-insurance payments could equal more than
twice that amount.

CONCLUSION

If the pilot proves successful, the company may be in

-7-

a position to implement it on a broader scale. Involved
in this second stage would be active as well as retired
employees. A third stage might involve employees' families. As the program expands, so would potential savings to the company in the form of lowered health-care
costs.
The first step is approving this pilot project. This
will set into motion the timeline I just described.

The proposal turns next to a discussion of costs as it breaks down the total cost into its component parts.

The discussion concludes by focusing on how possible benefits far outweigh costs.

The conclusion expands the discussion of the pilot to a broader framework as it focuses once more on benefits to the reader.

The last paragraph in the body of the proposal contains a call to action.

FIGURE 13.2   *Sample Long Internal Proposal (Continued)*

APPENDIX

Appleton Securities, Inc.

2344 Arnold Avenue
New Orleans, LA 70112
(504) 555-7889

March 1, 199X

Dear Appleton Securities Retiree:

All of us—you and the company—are very concerned about
health care. To address this concern at Appleton, we
are piloting a program that promotes good health and
has the potential to lower health care costs.

The program is designed to help participants improve
their health and become better informed about using
medical-care services. It is offered at no cost to you
and is not connected in any way with your health-
insurance coverage or pension.

In approximately two weeks you will receive a
brochure, which describes the program as well as a
simple confidential questionnaire. To enroll, complete
the questionnaire and return it promptly to us using
the postage-paid return envelope. Any information you
provide is completely confidential. Over the course of
the year you will receive additional material designed
to help you maintain your health.

If this trial program proves successful, Appleton
Securities may be in a position to implement it on a
broader scale. Therefore, this program is not only of
personal value to you, but provides information that
can make a difference to all of us. Early next year, we
will be sharing the results of our first year with you.

Our hope is that this program can help you lead a
healthier, more vital life.

Sincerely,

Allan Alderman
Vice President of Human Resources

> These letters are placed in
> an appendix. Including
> them in the body of the pro-
> posal would distract from
> the proposal's purpose.

Appleton Securities, Inc.

2344 Arnold Avenue
New Orleans, LA 70112
(504) 555-7889

March 15, 199X

Dear Appleton Retiree:

You recently received a letter from Appleton
announcing a health-improvement program. Enclosed
is a brochure describing the program and a
"Personal Vitality Questionnaire" with a return
envelope.

You are invited to participate in this health-

FIGURE 13.2   *Sample Long Internal Proposal (Continued)*

improvement program at no cost to you. Take the first
step by carefully completing the enclosed questionnaire and returning it promptly in the prepaid return
envelope.

Let me emphasize that all information you provide is
completely confidential. Group data summarizing the
experience of thousands of retirees will help us
determine the usefulness of this program.

To measure the effectiveness of this pilot study, we
have randomly assigned retirees to three groups. You
have been selected to be in Group 1 or 2. Group 1 will
receive questionnaires and educational materials, Group
2 will receive questionnaires only. Group 3 will be a
control group.

(more)

(Page 2)

If you have any questions, you may send written
inquires to:

Appleton Securities Medical Department
2344 Arnold Avenue, 2nd Floor
New Orleans, LA 70112

In addition, a Medical Department representative is
available to answer your questions from March 15-31 at
(504) 555-5555.

Sincerely,

Francis H. Blair, M.D.

FIGURE 13.2   *Sample Long Internal Proposal (Continued)*

WRITING A SALES PROPOSAL

Designed to convince prospective customers that a company has what it takes to complete a project successfully, the best sales proposals focus on solving problems rather than selling goods or services. Developing solutions may require considerable time. As a rule, you will have to investigate your prospective client's needs and identify the client's competition.

For example, when a major soft-drink company asked marketing executive Don Kracke to submit a proposal for handling the licensing of its trademarked name, Kracke's first step was to find out as much as he could about the company and its industry. He read trade newspapers and talked to key parties, including personnel inside the company and current licensees who paid the soda company royalties on the sale of such items as cups, glasses, and T-shirts. As a result of his efforts, Kracke was able to identify a major problem in the company's current licensing arrangement and develop a solution. His research told him that licensees felt that they were receiving very little in return for their royalties, and he was able to convince the manufacturer that this perception had to change if future licensing deals were to succeed.[8]

The length of sales proposals is usually determined by the complexity of the plan and by the amount of detail the writer feels obliged to provide. For example, while some writers may take a short approach to bidding on an office-equipment service contract, others may map out a detailed strategy for servicing each machine. In general, the more complex the proposed deal, the longer the document. Obviously, for example, a document proposing a new telephone network for a multinational corporation is likely to be lengthy. At the same time, however, even a proposal for a multimillion-dollar deal can be short if it is a straightforward business financing proposal.

If you think you can, you can. And if you think you can't, you're right.

*Mary Kay Ash
Chairman, Mary Kay
Cosmetics, Inc.*

Writing a Short Sales Proposal

A short sales proposal can accompany a transmittal letter or be written in letter form. If no separate transmittal letter is included, your proposal can begin with a statement that clarifies its purpose and scope. Your introduction can then describe why your proposed approach is particularly well-suited to meeting a particular need or solving a particular problem. It may also introduce your company's credentials.

The body of your proposal letter should provide the details of your technical plan, including a description of the goods and services that you are offering and any procedures that are part of your plan. The body should refer to certain aspects of your management plan, including time schedules and costs.

The conclusion of your proposal letter may try to reinforce a positive perception of your company and ideas. You might, for example, list any advantages that your company has over your competition. The proposal can close with a statement that expresses your anticipation at the prospect of working closely with the prospective client.

Remember that because there is no set formula for proposal writing, these are only general guidelines. Unlike formal reports, many proposals permit flexibility in format and style. The sample proposal in Figure 13.3 shows how these guidelines can take shape in an actual document. Although this proposal is relatively short, the tone and language are formal. As you can see, there is no section on organizational qualifications—the reader and writer have had a long- standing business relationship. However, frequent references are made to the company's expertise and ability to do the job.

DRB Capital, Inc.

4 Embassy Boulevard • Burbank, CA 91520 •

(213) 555-1456

June 15, 199X

Ms. Caroline Teller
Vice President, Business Development
Anderson, Peters, Stern Associates
1437 Avenue P
P.O. Box 817
Chicago, IL 60633

Dear Ms. Teller:

I am pleased to have this opportunity to follow up
on our recent discussions and present you with a
proposal for DRB Capital, Inc., to act as the exclusive financial advisor in connection with the purchase by Anderson, Peters, Stern Associates (APS) of
a furniture manufacturer with at least $100 million
in annual sales. I believe that DRB is uniquely
qualified to serve as financial advisor to APS by
virtue of its experience in advising companies that
have acquired companies in the furniture-manufacturing industry.

In this proposal, I have outlined several areas that
I believe are important for the contemplated transaction. I will begin with a review of my understanding
of APS's strategic objectives. In the next section,
the activities associated with the acquisition program are outlined and discussed. The proposal concludes by defining the role that DRB would play in
the transaction.

Ms. Caroline Teller
June 15, 199X
page 2

REVIEW OF THE ACQUISITION

As we discussed, APS is currently interested in purchasing a furniture manufacturer with at least $100 million
in annual sales. Ideally, the company will be located in
the furniture-manufacturing region of North Carolina.

ACQUISITION PROGRAM OUTLINE AND ASSOCIATED ACTIVITIES

Based on this understanding, DRB has developed a seven-
step purchasing program, which focuses on refining APS's
objectives, collecting and screening opportunities, and,
finally, selecting, negotiating, and closing an acquisi-

The introductory paragraph summarizes the proposal and establishes DRB's credibility as a qualified investment advisor. The style is forceful as the writer attempts to persuade. Although first- and second-person references are used occasionally throughout the proposal, the third person is more common and sets a formal tone.

This paragraph describes the organization of the proposal. This overview helps the reader make the transition to the specific details of the proposed deal.

This paragraph sets the stage for the technical plan by restating the writer's assumptions about the deal. This technique ensures that both parties are in complete agreement.

The technical plan begins here as the proposal describes the project stages and includes a schedule for each stage. Included are DRB's specific duties at each stage. The sentence that refers to DRB's experience adds to company credibility.

FIGURE 13.3   *Sample Short Sales Proposal*

tion. In each of the areas, the advisory group at DRB will provide its experience on major issues affecting the transaction. The acquisition program's total duration is expected to be approximately seven months.

Initial Meeting

As part of the effort, APS, with DRB's assistance, will review its specific objectives and criteria. These will include:

- desired purchase price
- company size
- composition of company assets
- market position
- products
- new-product potential
- geographic location
- financial structure
- upside potential as a result of APS ownership and potential management
- competition

> Key issues are highlighted through the effective use of headings and indented lists.

Ms. Caroline Teller
June 15, 199X
page 3

The initial meeting will consist of a review of APS's purchasing and management experience with furniture-manufacturing companies. In addition, a group composed of DRB and APS members will be identified, a schedule established, and responsibilities assigned. The completion of these activities will take approximately ten days.

Screen List and Information Collection

The group will identify categories to define potential acquisition targets. These categories will coincide with APS's objectives and preferences. Categories include:

- owners and ownership structure
- company size
- current market share
- current labor/management agreements
- land and factory facilities
- location
- company history
- potential upside (e.g., expansion)

> This paragraph focuses on the amount of research necessary in data collection. Statements like this help justify the fees to be charged.

Much of this information will be collected through direct contact. In the past, DRB has found that attractive opportunities are not necessarily present in the market at any given time, but must be created through extensive research and negotiation. The team will make site visits and verify information. These activities will take approximately four weeks.

FIGURE 13.3 *Sample Short Sales Proposal (Continued)*

Ms. Caroline Teller
June 15, 199X
page 4

Candidate Selection

From the information collected, the group will summarize the results and recommend potential candidates for acquisition. These recommendations will be based on analysis of the firms in regard to both the economics and strategic objectives outlined earlier.

As part of this analysis, DRB will prepare cash-flow analyses. The group will work closely with APS to make sure that our analyses reflect you expectations. These activities will take approximately six weeks.

Initial Negotiations

DRB will assist in developing the strategy to approach potential sellers. We will jointly develop a term sheet, outlining the target purchase price and acquisition structure. DRB will identify major issues and work with you to negotiate these points. It is our recommendation that several potential sellers be contacted during this activity in order to maximize the potential seller competition.

Confirmation Process

As part of the purchase process, it will be necessary to confirm the original assumptions. DRB will assist APS in the information-collection and review process, as requested. DRB will perform economic analyses to support APS's purchase price as well as to verify risk items identified during the candidate-selection stage.

Final Selection

Based on the results of these various analyses, a final acquisition selection will be made by APS with the assistance of DRB. the time required from initial

> Formal language is used in this section of the proposal. Third-person references are favored over the first and second person.

Ms. Caroline Teller
June 15, 199X
page 5

negotiations to final selection will be approximately seven weeks.

Closing Process

Once final selection has been made, the advisory team at DRB would participate in the negotiations and assist in improving upon the terms of the final proposal before and during closing. Throughout this period, group members will be available to advise on all aspects of the negotiation. These activities may take six to eight weeks.

FIGURE 13.3   *Sample Short Sales Proposal (Continued)*

DRB'S ROLE AND FEES

DRB Capital, Inc. would be pleased to act as your advisor. In that regard, we would work with Anderson, Peters, Stern Associates in all stages of the acquisition, from conducting initial marketing research to closing the transaction. As this proposal has explained, our services include assisting APS in establishing acquisition criteria, identifying companies, and negotiating closing terms. DRB would prepare an economic analysis of potential acquisition companies, contact sellers, and assist APS as your advisor in the acquisition. Finally, we would be available to actively work with and advise APS as the transaction develops over time, drawing on our professional experience as an advisor in major acquisitions of this kind.

DRB proposes the following fee structure for the services rendered during this transaction:
- a monthly retainer
- a success fee based on APS's total investment

> The subject of fees is introduced in the context of DRB's role in the deal. This places the company's financial requirements in perspective.

Ms. Caroline Teller
June 15, 199X
page 6

- reimbursement of reasonable expenses incurred in performing the services described in this proposal

I look forward to working with you and hope that this letter will serve as a basis for this undertaking. I will be in touch with you shortly. If in the interim you have any questions or comments, please call me.

Sincerely,

Peter Langley

Peter Langley
Chief Executive Officer

> The proposal closes with statements that look forward to a future business relationship.

FIGURE 13.3   *Sample Short Sales Proposal (Continued)*

Writing a Long Sales Proposal

A long sales proposal may contain all or most of the elements that we discussed earlier in this chapter, including a cover, a title fly and title page, a letter of transmittal, a table of contents, a list of illustrations, an executive summary, a detailed proposal body, and appendixes. The sample proposal in Figure 13.4 includes parts of a lengthy proposal from Harris, Rothenberg International (HRI), a consulting firm that provides psychological services to major corporations. This proposal is for an employee-assistance program (EAP) to help individual employees manage personal problems that can interfere with on-the-job performance. The proposal is submitted to a hypothetical financial institution, XYZ Bank. Shown in the excerpt in Figure 13.4 are the table of contents, the introduction, a partial description of the organization's qualifications, a description of the EAP program being offered, and an introduction to the section on program costs.[9]

This table of contents is organized in the form of a traditional outline with Roman numerals, upper-case letters, and numbers. These outline markers are also used in the proposal itself. Notice the importance that appendixes play in this proposal. Tangential materials are placed in appendixes so that the proposal can focus on the selling of services.

This introduction has several purposes. It makes clear in the first sentence that the document to follow is a sales tool and that HRI is eager to win the business. It also summarizes the key advantages of an HRI employee-assistance program. Finally, the introduction tells the reader how the proposal that follows is organized. This technique is helpful in long proposals.

2

INTRODUCTION

Harris, Rothenberg International (HRI) wants very much to be XYZ Bank's provider of choice for its national employee-assistance program (EAP). We believe that our high quality and expertise will be a good match for XYZ's business and culture. One of the goals of the proposal is to make clear the experience of HRI professionals not only in the EAP field but also in the financial-services business. This will be spelled out in Part II.

Harris, Rothenberg International delivers integrated EAP services nationwide and this HRI will do for XYZ efficiently and professionally. The quality in delivery will be the highest quality XYZ wants and deserves. This will be the focus of Part III.

XYZ has moved to its leadership position through sound financial management. HRI will deliver

FIGURE 13.4   Sample Long Sales Proposal

a quality EAP at a cost modest for the service and
sensitive to XYZ's fiscal parameters. The cost will be
reviewed in Part IV.

At the conclusion of your reading of HRI's proposal for an employee-assistance program, we hope you
will agree that HRI should be your choice.

6

HARRIS, ROTHENBERG INTERNATIONAL
HIGHEST QUALITY PROVIDER

Getting Bigger With Quality

Harris, Rothenberg International is not new on the
block. We have been delivering employee-assistance-program services to businesses since 1982. The partners
made a decision at the time of HRI's creation to hold
its growth to a rate that would ensure HRI's position
as a quality provider.

> Because of the importance of qualifications in choosing a psychological consulting firm, HRI's proposal begins by establishing its credibility to deliver EAP services.

HRI grew by word of mouth. As you can see by our
partial client list (Appendix A), businesses talk to
each other, especially when they deliver the same services. As a result, over the years, HRI has been providing services to many financial-service businesses
and law firms. They came to us. Some turned to us after
disappointing experiences with other providers. HRI, in
contrast, has never lost a client. . .

> It then establishes the firm's expertise in the financial-services and legal industries. Instead of including a long client list, the reader is referred to an appendix.

The Highest Quality People

HRI has a lot of grey hair. In our business, a
seasoned professional is more effective. That was also
part of HRI's strategic plan, going after professionals
who have been working for years in the EAP field, who
understand the world of business as well as how people's psychologies impact their behavior at work.

> The description of qualifications moves from the firm as a whole to its individual people. This part of the proposal describes the experience and credentials of HRI staff.

HRI's people have managed employee-assistance programs on site for different companies or have worked
for the competition. Our people began their careers
elsewhere and then came to us with considerable experience. HRI's professional staff are highly skilled
senior practitioners and program administrators whose
many years of diverse business experience bring the
greatest depth and range to your EAP. Partners and
staff of HRI are therapists who are either licensed
psychiatrists, psychologists, or certified social workers. Many hold doctoral-level degrees in their respective fields.

> Instead of including résumés, this section focuses on staff qualifications and how these qualifications enable HRI to perform effectively.

HRI maintains a multicultural workforce with language capability in Spanish and French.

> The complexity of work-force diversity makes this statement important.

FIGURE 13.4   *Sample Long Sales Proposal (Continued)*

8

Because HRI is an international organization providing psychological services worldwide, the proposal also focuses on the process of selecting affiliate professionals. This subject has special interest to multinational corporations.

Worldwide Affiliates. The quality of HRI extends to its associates and affiliates worldwide. This is important because so many of XYZ's population are distributed among may sites...The process of selecting an affiliate initiates the ongoing attention to quality.

An appendix is used once again to present tangential material. Including these details here would sidetrack the reader.

Affiliates are referred to us by experienced professionals in our own network. A prospective affiliate sends us his or her résumé, copy of licensure, and malpractice insurance. If he or she has the requisite credentials, license, expertise and experience, and extensive interview is held...The affiliate is assessed, in depth, on clinical expertise, i.e., ability to diagnose, knowledge of short-term treatment approaches; intervention skills; knowledge of EAP work; and familiarity and relationships with community resources. A contract is then set up with the affiliate wherein he or she is paid on a fee-for-service basis (see Appendix C). The fee paid to the Affiliate is one consistent with the high level of expertise that we mandate.

17

HARRIS, ROTHENBERG INTERNATIONAL
DELIVERS THE HIGHEST QUALITY SERVICE

EAP Program

    HRI offers assessment and referral, short-term treatment (when indicated) and follow-up for all EAP clients.
    Keeping in mind that HRI services are always specifically tailored to the unique needs of the client organization, the following describe the overall components and strategies for a full-service EAP.

This section includes the technical plan, or work statement, as it describes the specific services that HRI will complete if the proposal is accepted. The plan moves from overall strategies to services to individual employees.

- Full-Service Assessment and Referral Model
  - Comprehensive employee-assistance-program development to include assistance in drafting policies, procedures, and publicity material.

FIGURE 13.4   *Sample Long Sales Proposal (Continued)*

- Assistance in the development of written information for all employees, including brochures and business cards.
- Orientation meetings with key managers and supervisors.
- Management training for all supervisory personnel with focus, content, and method jointly determined by Harris, Rothenberg International and the client firm. . .
- Annual and quarterly statistics and reports on program usage and information regarding corporate climate. . .

■ Employees/dependents who are referred or who find their own way to the Employee Assistance Program can expect a variety of services to be available. These include:

- As many counseling sessions as required to make proper assessment and referral for a variety of personal, family, career or marital problems.
- Short-term treatment where indicated.

18

- Referral of those employees who need longer-term professional care to appropriately qualified and competent practitioners.
- Referral of those employees needing in-patient treatment for substance abuse and for psychiatric problems.
- Referral of employees with special needs, i.e., legal, financial, career, addictions, and family problems to appropriate private or public service agencies. . .Over the years HRI has maintained a high success rate in returning a significant majority of impaired employees to their jobs...

FIGURE 13.4   *Sample Long Sales Proposal (Continued)*

23

A Walk Through the Process

It may be helpful to walk through one possible process. The actual events will be determined jointly by XYZ and HRI...

When an employee contacts the EAP, he or she will speak directly with a professional counselor. The system operates 24 hours a day, seven days a week. Our phones are initially answered by our receptionists during business hours or by a bonded medical answering service during evenings, weekends, and holidays. Such calls are immediately turned over to a professional counselor...

A brief discussion of the presenting problem and an orientation to the EAP take place during the initial phone contact. Employees are offered an appointment with a counselor within a 24-hour period. Emergencies, of course, receive immediate attention...

After the counselor completes the assessment process with the employee, he or she carefully considers the nature of the problem, the diagnosis, treatment plan, and the client's insurance coverage. This information serves as the basis for determining the best referral source.

When an employee comes to the EAP for the first visit, he or she is given HRI's Statement and Policy of Confidentiality (see Appendix K)...

One of the first steps that the account manager will take is to familiarize him or herself with the health-insurance policies and benefits of XYZ Bank. The account manager then sees to it that all associates and affiliates are familiar with the policies. Whenever a referral is made, the counselor always takes the individual's health-insurance coverage into consideration. We are dedicated to informing the individual of the most cost-effective form of treatment. In this way, we are also able to monitor insurance plans...

> This section describes the specific steps that will be taken to achieve the proposal's objectives. Details and procedures are introduced here that have not been addressed before.

24

We structure our relationships with providers so that there is collaboration in developing treatment plans. We review this treatment plan with the providers periodically to ensure that the treatment is proceeding as originally designed. We strive to ensure that the overall objectives are obtained. This constitutes the gatekeeping process of the EAP. . . .

The EAP counselor maintains ongoing contact with each employee who is referred and the referral source at one month intervals. The purpose of follow-up is to ensure that the employee has received the required services in accordance with his/her treatment plan. Follow-ups will stop when we are sure that the employee has received the appropriate services and is functioning successfully on the job.

FIGURE 13.4   *Sample Long Sales Proposal (Continued)*

28

THE COST

Having an EAP Saves Money

Employees bring their problems to work and that affects how they work. An employee in a major company experiences a great deal of stress in today's business climate. Add to that the fact that one in five employees has significant personal problems and that in half of these situations, productivity is negatively affected.

- Alcoholism and drug abuse exist in the workplace as never before. Direct and indirect costs to American business as a result of substance abuse were 80.7 billion dollars according to the National Institute of Alcohol and Alcohol Abuse report to Congress in April, 1987. These data, however, were collected prior to 1983. Experts are convinced that the costs have since escalated significantly.
- One out of four Americans suffers from a mental-health problem, e.g., depression, anxiety. When left unattended, such problems will not only cause employees' productivity to decline progressively, but will also have an expanding negative impact on co-workers and supervisors.
- Nearly half of all couples currently married will at some point undergo marital discord resulting in separation or divorce. Workers affected by this problem will experience difficulties in concentrating, executing routine responsibilities, and maintaining stable business relationships.

> The proposal spends several pages introducing how much the services will cost. The section begins with the key concept that spending money on an EAP actually saves money.

> A thorough research base is evident here as the proposal cites statistics on substance abuse, mental illness, and marital discord, all of which affect performance at work.

29

- One out of ten Americans who drinks alcohol develops the disease of alcoholism. Persons suffering from this disease have an accident rate three times higher, a suicide rate fifty times higher, a life expectancy fifteen years shorter, and an average decline in productivity of more than 25 percent compared to the general public...

HRI clients have recognized that it makes good business sense to help their employees resolve their personal problems as quickly as possible. They are accomplishing this by sponsoring employee-assistance programs. . .These companies have clearly seen the cost/benefit advantages of an EAP. They also report that many employees use the EAP when they feel their personal problems will result in deteriorating job performance. As a result, the company and the employees are simultaneously helped.

> Following this section is a description of the various costs for an EAP program.

FIGURE 13.4   *Sample Long Sales Proposal (Continued)*

Compared to the shorter proposal in Figure 13.3, this proposal has a relatively informal tone. Note, however, that it should be considered a formal document because it features such elements as a cover, a table of contents, and various appendixes. The tone is set in the opening sentence of Section II, which reminds the reader that "Harris, Rothenberg International is not new on the block." Several paragraphs later, the proposal observes that "HRI has a lot of gray hair." At another point, the proposal asks, "Does HRI understand your business?" and answers its own question: "Absolutely!" This informal tone helps make the proposal reader-friendly. In addition, the proposal itself—especially the introduction—speaks in a highly personal tone of voice:

> At the conclusion of your reading of HRI's proposal for an employee assistance program, we hope you will agree that HRI should be your choice.

It is clear that in this document, one person is speaking directly and personally to another.

PROGRESS CHECK

1. The chapter advises proposal writers to aim for clarity. What features characterize a clearly written proposal?
2. Why is it important to use a forceful style in writing proposals?

WHAT'S AHEAD

Chapter 13 concludes Part IV on report and proposal writing. Part V of *Contemporary Business Communication* moves the discussion from written to oral communication. Specifically, Chapter 14 will focus on "Delivering Speeches and Oral Presentations." As we will see, oral communication, like written communication, is more an art than a science.

SUMMARY OF CHAPTER OBJECTIVES

1. **Explain how *logic* and *reasoning, emotion,* and *credibility* communicate the *purpose* of proposals.**

   As sales tools, proposals communicate through appeals to reasoning, emotion and self-interest, and credibility. Appeals to reason rely on an organized presentation of facts and figures that make the document specific and concrete. Emotional appeals mold this information so that proposed solutions are perceived as tangible benefits that will help the reader. The appeal to credibility helps to sell you and your company's ability to do the job.

2. **Identify the special characteristics of proposals.**

   In part, proposals are defined by whether they are internal or external, solicited or unsolicited, by their method of preparation, and by the manner in which they are evaluated. An internal proposal is submitted within an organization to bring about change; external proposals are sent to both private and government clients. Whereas solicited proposals respond to formal or informal requests, unsolicited proposals have not been invited. Many proposals, internal and external, solicited and unsolicited, are written in collaborative teams.

3. **Describe the elements included in the *front matter* of a model proposal.**

   The front matter of a model proposal may contain the following elements: a cover, a title fly and title page, a letter of transmittal, a table of contents, a list of illustrations, and a copy of an RFP. Many or all of these elements are included in most long proposals. By contrast, short proposals, whether written in letter or memo form, normally do not include these prefatory materials.

4. **Describe the elements contained in the *body* of a model proposal.**

   The introduction contains the writer's synopsis of the problem and the proposed solution. It may also highlight the credentials of the writer's company and define the scope and organization of the proposal that follows. Next, the technical plan often includes a detailed description of the work that the writer's company will complete if the proposal is accepted. The management plan describes how the writer's organization intends to manage the project. Included are a functional analysis, flow charts and schedules, and a description of participants. Organizational qualifications may also be included to describe the qualifications of the company and the individuals who will work on the project if it is awarded. This section is often followed by a description of costs, including budget estimates. The body ends with a conclusion, which is a persuasive statement that attempts once more to sell the proposal's main ideas.

5. **Explain how *appendixes* are used in proposals.**

   Appendixes help reduce potential clutter in the proposal body. Appendixes include materials that are either too specific to be included in the proposal body or tangential to the proposal's main purpose. Among the items that can be shifted to an appendix are résumés, contracts, client lists, and additional drawings.

6. **Explain the importance of effective language and style in proposals.**

   The most effective proposals rely on specifics rather than generalizations; they use simple, clear language, a forceful style, and an appropriate level of formality. In general, successful proposal writers gear their language and style to the needs of their readers.

7. **Identify the important features of successful *internal proposals*.**

   Internal proposals are typically written from lower-ranking to higher-ranking individuals within an organization. To be successful, these proposals must emphasize the ways in which suggested changes will improve the bottom line. While short internal proposals are often written in memo form, long proposals may include many or all of the elements of a model proposal.

8. **Identify the important features of successful *sales proposals*.**

   The most effective sales proposals focus on solutions as they demonstrate the writer's grasp of the prospective client's problem or need and the writer's ability to handle it. Short sales proposals, written in letter form, include an effective introduction, details of the technical and management plans, budgets, and a strong conclusion. Long sales proposals contain all or some of the prefatory elements of a model proposal.

REVIEW AND DISCUSSION QUESTIONS

1. What are proposals? (*Ch. Obj. 1*)
2. How might you make appeals to logic, reasoning, emotion, and credibility in writing an effective proposal? (*Ch. Obj. 1*)
3. Identify the four special characteristics of proposals. (*Ch. Obj. 2*)
4. Which do you think would present a greater challenge—writing a solicited proposal or an unsolicited proposal? Why? (*Ch. Obj. 2*)
5. What elements comprise the front matter of a long proposal? (*Ch. Obj. 3*)
6. What are the components of a proposal body? (*Ch. Obj. 4*)
7. When might you include appendixes with a proposal? (*Ch. Obj. 5*)
8. Describe some guidelines for the effective use of language and style in proposal writing. (*Ch. Obj. 6*)
9. What characteristics contribute to successful internal proposals? (*Ch. Obj. 7*)
10. What are the characteristics of a good sales proposal? (*Ch. Obj. 8*)

APPLICATION EXERCISES

1. Why is it important to be able to write an effective proposal? (*Ch. Obj. 1, 6*)

2. Suppose that your boss (at your present or former job) has asked you to write an external proposal to sell a skeptical businessperson on a product offered by your company. Describe some specific ways in which you could appeal to logic, emotion, and credibility in order to make your proposal more effective. (*Ch. Obj. 1*)

3. Write the technical plan (work statement) for the proposal that you planned in EXERCISE 2. What visual aids, if any, might be helpful? (*Ch. Obj. 4, 6, 8*)

4. Write the management plan to accompany the technical plan that you wrote for EXERCISE 3. (*Ch. Obj. 4, 6, 8*)

5. Write the organizational qualifications section to accompany the management plan that you developed for EXERCISE 4. (*Ch. Obj. 4, 6, 8*)

6. Write the costs section to accompany the organizational qualifications section that you wrote for EXERCISE 5. (*Ch. Obj. 4, 6, 8*)

7. Write a persuasive conclusion to the proposal you created for EXERCISES 2–6. (*Ch. Obj. 4, 6, 8*)

8. Finally, write an effective introduction for the sales proposal that you prepared for EXERCISES 2–7. Convince your readers that your solution is the best one for their purposes. (*Ch. Obj. 1, 4, 6, 8*)

9. Your boss likes your sales proposal but asks you to add additional information in an appendix. Describe the information that the client might find useful in this appendix. (*Ch. Obj. 5*)

10. Write the front matter that might accompany the proposal that you crafted for EXERCISES 2–9. What front-matter elements would be most appropriate? (*Ch. Obj. 3*)

11. Think of a problem that exists at your present or a former workplace. Now prepare to write an internal proposal, addressed to your boss or other appropriate readers, in which you would suggest a solution. How could you appeal to logic, emotion, and credibility to make your proposal more effective? Be specific. (*Ch. Obj. 1, 7*)

12. Write a short internal proposal based on your answer to EXERCISE 9. Be sure to address your audience's concerns and show how and why your solution would be effective. (*Ch. Obj. 4, 7*)

13. Cover the right-hand column in TABLE 13.2. Test yourself by supplying your own examples for each type of proposal listed in the table. (*Ch. Obj. 2, 7, 8*)

14. Think of a need for training at your present or a former job. For example, perhaps you feel that the staff would benefit from a business communication class. Write a short internal proposal, addressed to your boss, in which you suggest this additional training and convince him or her that it's important. (*Ch. Obj. 6, 7*)

15. The admissions office at your school has asked you to write a sales proposal for prospective students. Write this proposal designed to persuade prospective students to attend your school. (*Ch. Obj. 6, 8*)

BUILDING YOUR RESEARCH SKILLS

Interview a businessperson whose job calls for him or her to write proposals frequently. This individual might be someone in sales at a local company or even someone at your school who writes proposals for projects or funding. Ask this professional for tips on writing effective proposals. What style guidelines and research sources does this person favor? What usually works and what usually doesn't? Write a report on your interview in which you summarize the major points of your conversation.

BUILDING YOUR TEAMWORK SKILLS

Your instructor will divide the class into small groups. Each group will choose an issue at your school that you feel could be solved. Working as a group, write a short proposal, addressed to the school's president, in which you describe your solution and explain why it would improve matters. Select one group member to coordinate and write out the group's proposal as you create it.

Your instructor may wish to have your group present its proposal to the class.

COMMUNICATING IN A WORLD OF DIVERSITY

During your reading one day, you encounter the following statistics:

- In 1985, the U.S. workforce had the following composition: 47 percent U.S.-born white males; 36 percent U.S.-born white females; 5 percent U.S.-born nonwhite males; 5 percent U.S.-born nonwhite females; 4 percent immigrant males; 3 percent immigrant females.

- By the year 2000, the American workforce is expected to be composed as follows: 15 percent U.S.-born white males; 42 percent U.S.-born white females; 7 percent U.S.-born nonwhite males; 13 percent U.S.-born nonwhite females; 13 percent immigrant males; 10 percent immigrant females.

- Hispanics will account for about 23 percent of new entrants into the workforce. Meanwhile, the segment of the labor force made up of other races, such as Asians, Pacific Islanders, and native Americans, will increase by 70 percent.

- These trends are also apparent among school-age children, from whose ranks will come new entry-level workers. In certain areas of the country, so-called "minority groups" form a large percentage of students. These groups make up 40 percent of public-school enrollment in New York State. In California, Caucasian students are the minority (42 percent).

Imagine that you're the vice president for human resources at a large American corporation. You feel that the firm needs to become more active in recruiting, hiring, and retaining so-called "minority" employees. Write a short proposal addressed to the CEO in which you discuss the importance of starting such a program.

CASE 13.1

McKinsey & Co. Preaches the Joy of Going Horizontal

McKinsey & Co., a well-respected business-consulting firm, has some new advice for its clients on how to organize: Try horizontal.

McKinsey principal Douglas Smith notes that vertical (hierarchical) organizations are traditional in corporate America. In such firms, organizational issues tend to revolve around the question "Do we centralize or decentralize—and where do we stick international?" Companies have tried different approaches, but Smith contends that whatever the approach, virtually all of these organizations and reorganizations "mattered only to the top people in the company. Below them you found the same functional, vertical organization. For the 90 percent of the people who serve customers and make the product,"

claims Smith, "all that changed was the boss's name."

By contrast, so-called "horizontal" organizations group workers into self-managed teams with the authority to solve customers' problems as they arise and to change work procedures as needed. "The people who do the work," observes one consultant, "should have in their hands the means to change to suit the customer." Some companies that have switched from hierarchy to self-management have seen 40-percent increases in productivity.

Kodak is one company that has experienced these changes firsthand. In 1989, for example, its black-and-white film division was running 15 percent over budget, took up to 42 days to fill an order, was late in filling them one third of the time, and scored worst in the company's morale surveys. Then, the division reorganized, forming work teams in which employees mostly manage themselves. A twenty-five-member employee team watches over the division's performance and measures important customer-satisfaction guidelines such as on-time delivery. The result? Now the black-and-white group is running 15 percent under budget and has cut its response time on orders in half; it is late in filling orders only one time out of twenty, and employee morale has soared. With reorganization, explains one Kodak veteran, "you find where you're wasting time, doing things twice. And because we own our entire process, we can change it."

Questions and Applications

1. Distinguish between the "vertical" and "horizontal" approaches to organizing a company.
2. Suppose that you've just joined the staff at McKinsey & Co. Your boss asks you to write a sales proposal geared to prospective corporate clients, in which you persuade them to sign up for McKinsey's latest series of seminars, "The Horizontal Workplace." Write this proposal.

Sources: Sami Abbasi and Kenneth Hollman, "Managing Cultural Diversity: The Challenge of the '90s," *Records Management Quarterly*, July 1991, pp. 24–32; and Thomas Stewart, "The Search for the Organization of Tomorrow," *Fortune*, May 18, 1992, pp. 92–98.

CASE 13.2

Apple Computer Commits to Talking Heads

There are 2 million conference rooms in America, but only about 10,000 of them are wired for videoconferences. One company that has found videoconferencing technology especially useful is Apple Computer.

Apple began experimenting with video meetings when it started doing a lot of its business abroad. Videoconference manager Peter Kavanagh explains the situation this way: "When you ask someone, 'How'd you like to go to Paris on Friday for a meeting?' they say, 'Yeah, great!' But when you say, 'How'd you like to go every other week for the next six months?' it gets old very fast." Videoconferencing at Apple continued to grow during the Persian Gulf War, when engineers stayed home due to fears of terrorism. The company now has ten video meeting rooms in the United States, three in Europe, and two in Japan.

Naturally, videoconferencing is a big investment. In four years, Apple has spent about $6 million on equipment, transmission, and staffing. But Kavanagh estimates that the company's commitment to high-tech encounters has also saved $28 million in travel costs during the same period. "The technology is not very cheap," he admits, "but it's very, very cost-effective."

According to Kavanagh, videoconferencing also boasts several additional advantages. For one

thing, it means better meetings because more people can attend without adding to the cost. Videoconferencing also eliminates the need for more subsequent travel when new issues and questions surface. Overall, Apple has found that the new technology speeds up decision making and allows it to develop and market new products more quickly.

Questions and Applications

1. What benefits has Apple gained from videoconferencing?
2. Suppose that you're working for a company that competes against Apple. You decide that your firm could benefit from more videoconferencing, and you want to write an internal proposal that will convince your company's president to make this investment. Describe specific ways in which you could appeal to logic, emotion, and credibility in order to make your proposal more effective.
3. Write a short internal proposal in which you persuade your employer to buy a videoconferencing system.

Source: Andrew Kupfer, "Prime Time for Videoconferences," *Fortune*, December 28, 1992, pp. 90–95.

FORMS OF ORAL COMMUNICATION

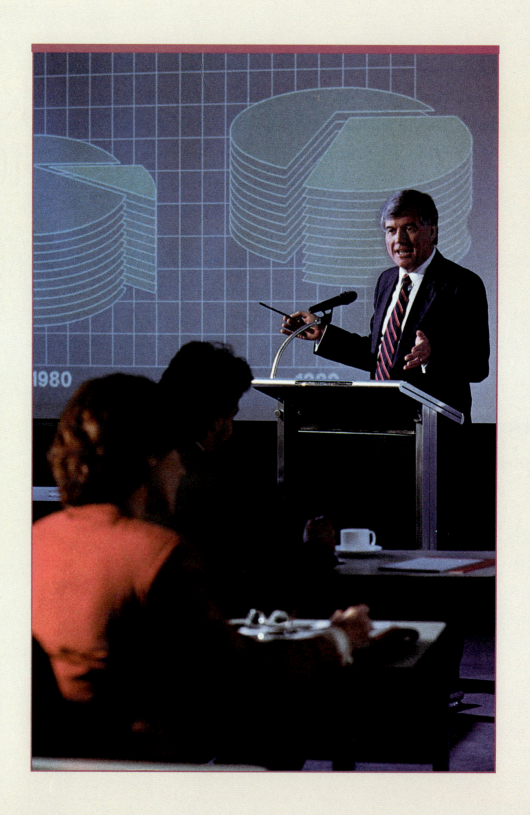

14

Delivering Speeches and Oral Presentations

CHAPTER OBJECTIVES

After studying this chapter, you should be able to:

1 Identify the characteristics of a *speech* and an *oral presentation*.

2 Define the concepts of *general purpose, specific purpose*, and *core idea*.

3 Identify the characteristics of effective *audience analysis* for a speech or an oral presentation.

4 Describe the purposes and characteristics of an effective *introduction, body*, and *conclusion* for a speech or an oral presentation.

5 Describe three special requirements of *oral communication*.

6 Identify the characteristics of a *planning outline* and *speaking notes*.

7 Describe the different types of *visual aids* used in speeches and oral presentations and identify elements of effective visual-aid design.

8 Describe four types of *oral delivery*.

9 Analyze techniques for handling *audience questions*.

445

MAKING IMPRESSIONS

The stakes were high—$10 million for the advertising agency that landed the $70-million Subaru account. Originally, thirty-five agencies were in the running. Then there were twelve, and finally six. Only the surviving half dozen were invited to make presentations—a process that meant conducting market research, creating an advertising campaign and a media plan, and responding in writing to a lengthy questionnaire. A week after the paperwork had been submitted, each agency was allowed three hours to make an oral presentation to Subaru executives. On the basis of both written and oral work, Subaru would pick a winner.

The first agency to present, Warwick Baker & Fiore, concluded that Subaru should focus on the "character" of its cars rather than their "content." Subaru gives consumers "the wherewithal, the freedom, the peace of mind, to do what they want to do," began Bob Fiore, the agency's creative director, who opened the presentation. "What kinds of cars are those?" Pausing for dramatic effect, he looked around at his listeners. "Cars that *can*!" he boomed.

Using three easels in the center of the room, Fiore moved storyboards covered with copy and art in and out of view. "Why," he asked the assembled executives, "would Ken Schaeffer drive 100 miles into the desert, braving potholes, 110-degree heat, and his wife's nagging, just to show his kids a rarely seen mesa?" As Fiore spoke, he unveiled an ad depicting a deserted road leading to nowhere. "Because he *can*," said Fiore, answering his own question with the tagline of his proposed campaign. Continuing to work his strategically placed easels, Fiore revealed another ad showing a snow-covered city street. "Why would Phil Mockler take his family out for pizza on a night like this?" Fiore asked pointedly. "Because he *can*!"

The second agency to make a presentation, DCA, proposed the slogan "The perfect car for the imperfect world"—a theme echoed on storyboards for dozens of print ads and on the mockup for a TV commercial. Using spliced footage from its warehouse of existing television commercials, DCA had created a television ad whose music and color gave emotional power to its proposed campaign.

Wieden & Kennedy, the third agency to present, positioned Subaru as the "mainstream alternative"—the Levi's jeans of the automobile world. "The theme is the truth," announced copywriter Jerry Cronin. "To get rid of the fluff and myth about cars. The reason you should buy it is the way it's built. What the machine is." Hence, the slogan proposed by Wieden & Kennedy: "Subaru. What to drive."

Wieden & Kennedy won the Subaru contract despite a disorganized, unpolished presentation. No one, for example, knew where to sit (someone had neglected to assign conference-room seats), and a noisy slide projector made

446

hearing difficult. In addition, Christopher Riley, Wieden's director of planning, presented an "unconventional" appearance with a ponytail halfway down his back. Agency co-founder Dan Wieden had in fact apologized for the impression that his group made: "We don't do presentations a lot," Wieden said with a loud, nervous laugh.

What Wieden & Kennedy *did* do was combine a reputation that few could ignore with an idea that worked. With Nike's "Just Do It" campaign already notched in its corporate belt, Wieden & Kennedy made a disorganized but powerful impression on decision makers at Subaru.[1]

CHAPTER OVERVIEW

The story of Wieden & Kennedy's success in landing the Subaru advertising account contains elements common to many stories about oral presentations: the competitive atmosphere; the reliance on both oral and written presentations; the deployment of multimedia visual aids and staging devices to complement language; voice quality, eye contact, and the dramatic pause; the inevitable problems associated with inexperience; machines that malfunction; unconventional hairstyles; the right idea at the right time coupled with a positive reputation that adds credibility—all these are elements that will reappear throughout your career as a business speaker. These and other issues are discussed in this chapter to emphasize the increasing importance of public speaking in the business world.

WHAT IS A SPEECH? WHAT IS AN ORAL PRESENTATION?

A common tool in business communication, a **speech** is a highly structured form of address in which a speaker addresses an audience gathered to hear a message. Most feedback comes after the speech is over, although nonverbal feedback can occur at any time.

By contrast, **oral presentations** are almost always extemporaneous, are very often delivered with the help of visual aids, and are frequently participative. As you will see later in the chapter, *extemporaneous presentations* are delivered using only notes and visual aids to guide the performance. Although many formal speeches also include visual support, visual aids are integral to most oral presentations. Similarly, audience participation often takes the form of comments and questions that can punctuate the oral presentation at any point. Because it indicates involvement and interest, such give-and-take is both expected and welcome.

Oral presentations play important roles in both a company's internal and external communication systems. Internally, for example, they are used to present budget requests and sell programs. A redesigned benefits package, for instance, will probably be presented to top management through an oral presentation.

As an important part of a company's external communications, oral presentations are used as tools to win and keep new clients. As you can see from our story about Wieden & Kennedy and the Subaru account, when advertising executives submit advertising plans, they are making presentations. When a small business owner presents a company's credentials as a subcontractor to a major corporation, he or she is making a presentation. When engineers from large corporations like General Dynamics submit proposals for government contracts, they are making presentations. As our opening story also demonstrates, presentations often combine oral and written material. In many cases, for example, companies bidding for new contracts must first submit detailed written proposals that must then be summarized in often lengthy oral presentations.

speech
Highly structured form of address in which a speaker addresses an audience gathered to hear a message

oral presentation
Extemporaneous speeches, frequently participative and delivered using only notes and visual aids to guide the speaker's performance

A talk is a voyage with a purpose, and it must be charted. The man who starts out going nowhere, generally gets there.

*Dale Carnegie
American writer
and speaker*

FROM GENERAL PURPOSE TO CORE IDEA

In all forms of formal communication, both written and oral, it is essential to focus on your purpose and message. You can accomplish this task in preparing both speeches and oral presentations by following a careful step-by-step process of identifying your *general purpose*, defining your *specific purpose*, and clarifying your *core idea*. Although this process leads you to a *written* statement of the main point that you hope to communicate to your audience, your goal is not to craft words that your audience will hear. Rather, it is to *plan* the message of your speech or oral presentation, just as you plan the message of written documents.

Identifying Your General Purpose

general purpose
Primary reason for which a document is written or an oral presentation is made; typically to inform, persuade, and/or initiate action

Despite the differences between formal speeches and oral presentations, the oral communication skills that characterize both forms of public address are the same. They also share common **general purposes**—that is, the speaker's overriding reasons for communicating with an audience. The general purpose of a formal speech or an oral presentation may be to inform or persuade an audience. A third general purpose—meeting the needs of a special occasion—is unique to public speaking.

informative speech or **presentation**
Address that describes, demonstrates, or explains information

INFORMATIVE SPEECHES AND PRESENTATIONS   During his years at Random House, Donald Klopfer always told groups of new employees about how he and Benett Cerf had founded the publishing company as he recounted its history of great authors and even greater literature. Klopfer's message, then, presented information as a means of transmitting the corporate culture. An essential part of business training, informative addresses are used to teach such varied functions as word processing or the operation of a new product-scanning system for controlling inventory. **Informative speeches** and **presentations** describe, demonstrate, or explain information, and the best informative speeches and presentations share the following characteristics:

- *They are accurate.* When you communicate facts, accuracy is essential.
- *They are clear.* Information must be communicated in a way that listeners can understand.
- *They are meaningful.* They must answer the question that every listener asks: "How will this help me?"
- *They are memorable.* Information not remembered has little value.

In addition, informative presentations are often interactive: That is, audiences frequently attempt to understand or clarify details through questions and comments.

persuasive speech or **presentation**
Address in which a speaker tries to convince an audience to accept a point of view and/or take specific action

PERSUASIVE SPEECHES AND PRESENTATIONS   In **persuasive speeches** and **presentations**, speakers try to convince audiences to accept their points of view and, often, to take specific actions. For example, when George V. Grune, CEO of the Reader's Digest Association, delivered a major speech to the Magazine Publishing Congress, his purpose was persuasion:

> The time has come to return to the practice of setting prices for our pages based on their value to advertisers and a reasonable return to publishers. Then we should work as hard as we can to sell that value to our clients. If we don't, the value of magazines will eventually diminish to the point that magazines won't be of value to anyone. And frankly, I fear that only magazines with very deep pockets will survive.[2]

Sales presentations have a persuasive purpose, as do presentations promoting new programs and policies. For example, in trying to convince her company's human-resources department to adopt a "wellness" approach to employee health, a corporate medical director will use a persuasive presentation to argue her case. To persuade the company to budget money for promoting employee health, she can use statistics and charts to point out the relationship between exercise, good eating habits, smoking cessation, and stress reduction on the one hand, and increased productivity and reduced absenteeism on the other. As we saw in Chapter 9, persuasion is measured in terms of changes in attitude and action, and persuasive presentations generally appeal both to reason and emotion in order to motivate change on both levels.

SPEECHES FOR SPECIAL OCCASIONS   **Special-occasion speeches** are speeches of presentation, acceptance, or commemoration. Businesspeople, for example, are often involved in award-ceremony presentations. They may be asked to introduce speakers, present eulogies or toasts, or deliver keynote or commencement addresses. An effective special-occasion speech meets the specific needs of the occasion and is usually sincere and to the point. As a special-occasion speaker, you speak for yourself and your company. In the truest sense of the word, you are a company "spokesperson."

special-occasion speech
Speech of presentation, acceptance, or commemoration

Defining Your Specific Purpose

Within the context of these three general purposes, speakers must define the specific purpose of a speech or presentation. In oral communication, the **specific purpose** is a statement—in the form of a clear, unambiguous sentence—of what speakers want to accomplish when they address the audience. For example:

specific purpose
Brief summary of the reason for which a document is written or an oral presentation is made

- Persuade managers at Burger King's corporate headquarters to offer reduced-calorie, low-fat menu items in conjunction with Weight Watchers International.

- Inform the production department of alternative compact-disc packaging designs that are more acceptable to environmentalists.

- Deliver a commencement address at Central Michigan University on business ethics.

Fixing your objective is like identifying the North Star— you sight your compass on it and then use it as the means of getting back on the track when you tend to stray.

*Marshall E. Dimock
American author*

The specific-purpose statement focuses on both the speaker's message and the audience. That is, it identifies both the specific nature of the message and the group to whom the speaker is communicating.

Clarifying Your Core Idea

A natural extension of the specific purpose, the **core idea** of a speech or presentation is a one-sentence statement of the main idea that you want to communicate to your audience. Every core idea should define what speech-communication experts Gerald Phillips and Jerome Zolten call the "residual message—the idea that breaks through the resistance, that stays in the listener's mind when everything else is forgotten."[3]

core idea
One-sentence statement of the central message of a written or oral presentation

Here is the core idea for each of the previous specific-purpose statements:

- Changing consumer tastes and an awareness of the health risks in consuming too much fat leads me to recommend that Weight Watchers meals be test-marketed in one or more key Burger King restaurants.

- Environmentally acceptable compact-disc packaging designs include the eco-pak, the laserfile, and the inch pack, all of which have the advantage of reducing cardboard waste.

- Every business decision you make must be guided by a basic sense of ethics that allows you to differentiate between what is right and what is wrong, between what helps your co-workers and customers and what hurts them.

Because the core-idea statement is not part of your actual presentation, specific terms need not be defined. During the course of your presentation, however, you will define terms according to the needs of your audience.

INTERNATIONAL ISSUES IN BUSINESS COMMUNICATION

Addressing International Audiences

International business presentations are more common today than ever before. With business taking place all over the globe, it is almost as likely for Americans to be involved in presentations in Paris and Tokyo as in Des Moines and Phoenix. Unfortunately, Americans who approach international presentations in the same way they do presentations delivered at home may be in for a rude awakening. If they are perceived as ill-prepared, boorish, and rude, they may doom their presentations—and prospective deals—to failure.

What are the most common mistakes that Americans make in presentations to international audiences? Here are several—and suggestions for correcting them:

- *Projecting Informality.* The same informal presentations that receive the highest marks in the United States may be considered unprofessional in places like Germany and Japan. Businesspeople in these countries feel slighted when a presentation appears unrehearsed. They may also question why flip charts are completed during the presentation rather than in advance. While this common practice is geared toward increasing involvement among U.S. audiences, it is often perceived abroad as reflecting lack of preparation among many audiences. In the minds of many non-Americans, anything short of a fully rehearsed, scripted talk shows a lack of respect.

- *Overcomplicating the Message.* International presentations in English should be simple enough to be understood by non-American listeners. Colloquial expressions, jargon, slang, and acronyms should be avoided and pacing should allow for translation.

- *Obstructing the Message with the Medium.* Although colorful slides, flip charts, and audio-visual presentations may be appreciated in the United States, they are perceived as "razzle dazzle" in the Arab world and other business cultures. For these listeners, entertainment value detracts from the business message.

AUDIENCE ANALYSIS

audience analysis
Process by which business communicators analyze the needs and knowledge of their listeners in order to improve the likelihood of communicating effectively through oral presentations

To improve communications, work not on the utterer, but the recipient.

Peter F. Drucker
American business
philosopher

Audience analysis is the process whereby speakers try to understand who the members of their audiences are and what those audiences know and feel about them and their topics. As we saw in Chapter 3, audience analysis plays a crucial role in all business communication. Because audience analysis gives speakers tools to link their specific purposes to audience interests and needs, it is at the heart of any successful speech or oral presentation. This chapter focuses on the types of analysis that are necessary in preparing speeches and oral presentations.

Understanding the Target Group

As a speaker, the audience is your reason for being. Satisfying this target group thus requires asking yourself certain key questions:

- *What does my audience know about me?* This question goes to the heart of speaker credibility: Will my position and reputation affect audience response?

- *What does my audience know about my organization?* Motorola's reputation for quality and service, for example, precedes a Motorola sales representative when he or she makes a client presentation.

- *How much does the audience know about my topic?* Experts in compact-disc packaging, for example, are familiar with eco-paks, laserfiles, and inch packs. A general audience, even within the music industry, will require explanations.

- *How much interest does the audience have in my topic?* Interest is often tied to how strongly listeners believe that the subject of the speech or presentation will help them.

- *How does the audience feel about my topic?* Your audience may be comprised of supporters and/or noncommitted or hostile groups.

- *Rushing the Race.* Presenters who begin too abruptly or who try to push things along are making a serious mistake in many business cultures. In the Middle East, Asia, and Latin America, for example, listeners expect relationships to build before business begins. Moreover, trying to close the deal too quickly may cause it to fall apart.

- *Unbalancing the Relationship.* In Japan and other Asian countries where status means so much, it may be a mistake to have a relatively young executive address senior management. A sixty-two-year-old senior official in a Japanese company expects presenters to have similar status and age.

- *Failing to Orient Interpreters.* Interpreters cannot do their jobs effectively unless they know what to expect. Thus, it is wise to spend time before your meeting to review the essence of your remarks (as well as any supporting visual aids and handouts).

- *Failing to Consider Nonverbal Cues.* Virtually all forms of nonverbal message, including facial expressions, hand movements, and clothing, have specific culture-based meanings. If you are unaware of these meanings your chances of offending someone are much higher.

Finally successfully navigating the waters that surround an international presentation means following this cardinal rule:

Know your audience.

Although this rule is essential to the success of every presentation, it is absolutely critical here. Your audience brings with it an added dimension of complexity in the form of cultural and language differences that determine how everything you say and do will be perceived.

Sources: Lennie Copeland and Lewis Griggs, *Going International: How to Make Friends and Deal Effectively in the Global Marketplace* (New York: Random House, 1985), pp. 116–17; and Thomas Leech, *How to Prepare, Stage, and Deliver Winning Presentations* (New York: Amacom, 1982), pp. 348–59.

- *How does the audience feel about me?* Command of your subject, delivery, appearance, and point of view all influence the attitude of your audience.

- *What is the context for my presentation?* When presenting a business proposal, find out who else is competing for the business. When delivering a speech, ask if you are the first speaker or the last, the one right before lunch or the one at the end of a conference. This information will help you predict audience response and adjust your information, delivery, and approach to make the best presentation.

- *What is the audience capable of doing?* Find out the power of your listeners to close the deal. If they are not key decision makers, learn what role they may play in influencing the deal.

THE DIVERSE AUDIENCE   Although you can assume that some audiences have roughly the same level of interest and knowledge in you, your company, and your topic, many audiences are diverse, with wide variations in information, attitudes, and responsibilities. To address such a diverse group, start by believing that the response of each person in the room may be crucial to your objective. Consultant Jim Elms explains:

Suppose I had an audience of 80 people and am sure that ten [people] in the front row have 99 percent of the power and that the others are there because it's something to do.… The guys in the back row may have more to do with it than you think. They can tell [a manager] your proposal is all [wrong] technically and that he shouldn't have anything to do with it. Especially when you give them [visuals] they can't read and [they've almost decided] to give the business to your competitor. All they needed was some reason to quit listening—and you gave it to them. If those guys in the back row come in and say the presentation by XYZ Company (your competitor) was satisfactory, but they haven't the foggiest idea what those guys from ABC Company (yours) were talking about, you've sure had an ineffective presentation.[4]

When the needs of audience members differ greatly, arrange for the large group audience to be broken up into smaller subgroups with separate presentations given to each. For example, one group may deal with technical issues, another with budgetary constraints, a third with production or design issues. When it is not possible to separate the group, keep everyone's interests in mind as you decide what to include and what to omit, focusing always on the best way to communicate your core idea.

Tools for Doing Your Homework

One successful retailer in the Northeast reports that before he delivers a speech to a corporate audience, he does his homework:

> I start by sending out a questionnaire that asks the goals and objectives of the meeting and the challenges facing the company. I also like to learn as much as I can about the audience—the age of the people attending, how many males, how many females, their educational backgrounds, jobs, and so on. I ask for reactions to other recent speakers as well as for annual reports, newsletters, internal memos, even training videos.[5]

Among the most common—and most useful—tools for researching an audience are the questionnaire and the interview. Less formal but often just as effective is careful observation.

QUESTIONNAIRES   To a speaker trying to learn the needs of an audience, a questionnaire can be an invaluable planning tool. With the right questions, you can learn how much your audience knows or cares about your topic, the job titles and responsibilities of your listeners, the environment in which your presentation will be delivered, the impressions that people have of you and your company, and the goals that different people hope to meet as a result of the event.

INTERVIEWS AND OBSERVATION   You can also gather this information through interviews or observation. Before a major presentation or speech, for example, it is helpful to talk to members of your potential audience in order to find out what information they need from you. Follow the advice offered by management consultant Tom Peters to be a "naive" listener: Listen with an open mind and you will hear ideas that will benefit your speech or presentation.[6]

The information that you gather through questionnaires and other research tools should lead to a clear idea of your audience's needs and of the ways in which you can help your listeners. "Every presentation," says Ron Hoff, a leading business speaker in advertising and marketing,

> begins in this way. The audience *needs* something—usually *help*. (Ask a seasoned [salesperson] what he wants to get out of a presentation and invariably he will say, "Just give me *one* idea, that's all I ask, something I can use tomorrow.")
>
> By coming to your presentation, by simply showing up, your audience is expressing a need for help, counsel, wisdom, inspiration—maybe even something that can change its life. Not its collective life—its personal, individual lives.
>
> If truth be told, the audience arrives on the scene with the ardent hope that the presenter knows something that it does not know.[7]

For example, an audience of sales representatives might listen to a speaker describing a recent consumer-attitude survey in the hope of learning how to target their own potential customers better.

THE MAJOR PARTS OF SPEECHES AND ORAL PRESENTATIONS

Like written documents, speeches and oral presentations have beginnings, middles, and ends. In this section, we will describe some specific techniques for shaping a speech or an oral presentation with an effective *introduction, body,* and *conclusion.*

The Introduction

In the first minute to ninety seconds—the time it takes to make a first impression—listeners decide whether a speech or presentation has any value, whether the speaker is credible, and whether they should pay attention. If you make a bad impression during your introduction, you will probably spend the rest of your time trying to regain the good graces of your audience.

Following are some suggested techniques for introducing your subject effectively. Bear in mind that despite its importance, an introduction should take no more than 10 percent of your entire speaking time.

ESTABLISH YOUR CREDIBILITY   Through your words and delivery, you must convince your audience that you are qualified to speak. Although speakers are typically introduced before they begin, making a low-keyed statement about your expertise enhances credibility. Here is how T. Boone Pickens, general partner in Mesa Limited Partnership, established his credibility when he spoke before the Japan Society:

> I've been asked to talk about my recent experiences in Japan.... As a geologist and an oil and gas producer, I've done business in the United States, Canada, the United Kingdom, Australia, and Africa.
>
> In the past few years, I've given hundreds of speeches where I've talked about the importance of free trade and the critical need for competition in the global economy.[8]

Although everyone in the audience could identify T. Boone Pickens, Pickens nevertheless began by establishing his credibility as an expert on free trade and global economics.

CAPTURE ATTENTION   The main purpose of your introduction is to capture the attention of your audience and make them want to hear more. Whether you choose *humor*, a *startling statement*, an *anecdote, rhetorical questions*, a *quotation*, or a *demonstration*, there must be a clear link between your introduction and the subject of your speech. An unrelated joke or a story with little or no connection to your core idea will reduce credibility.

The need to capture the audience's attention is actually a novel idea to many business speakers, especially speakers who deliver routine presentations to the same audience. Instead of opening with an attention getter, they often proceed as if business as usual means putting people to sleep. Consider the impact of these two opening statements:

Version 1

My subject today is the introduction of Weight Watchers meals to Burger King Restaurants. I would like to talk about test-marketing the idea in one Florida restaurant.

Version 2

When does offering less mean getting more? Think in terms of calories and you'll have the answer. Offer consumers meals like this with fewer than 300 calories [the presenter holds up a Weight Watchers meal] and count the customers we attract—even those who never ate at Burger King before. I recommend test-marketing the Burger King/Weight Watchers combination in one of our Florida restaurants.

By asking a question and holding up a prop, the speaker in Version 2 succeeded in capturing audience attention. The speaker in Version 1 promised nothing more than a routine presentation.

HUMOR   Humor is one of the most effective ways to capture audience attention because it establishes an immediate bond between the speaker and the audience. According to Melvin Helitzer, a journalism professor at Ohio University and an expert in humor, the humorous introduction "signals your listeners that you are not about to deliver a long, boring speech without some attempt at entertainment. A joke at the start says, 'I'm confident. I've got a smile on my face. I want you all to relax and enjoy yourself as you also learn something from my remarks.'"[9]

Elias Kusulas, Director of Administrative Services for the management-consulting firm A. T. Kearney, Inc., once opened his remarks to an audience of real estate brokers as follows:

> Thank you for giving me the opportunity to participate in your sales conference this morning. I've dealt with real estate brokers for years, but I've never seen so many of you in one place at one time. It reminds me of my recent trip to California. As I was checking into the hotel, the desk clerk asked me for some identification, and she suggested I show her my real estate license. I looked at her in surprise and asked, "Don't you mean you want to see my driver's license?" She replied, "No, not everybody has a driver's license."
>
> I'm sure many of you have heard…and probably told that old joke about the proliferation of real estate brokers. In a way it's symptomatic of the problems that face your industry as you enter the 1990s.
>
> There are too many brokers, too few deals, and too much product.[10]

Humor, of course, can also be used effectively in the body and conclusion of your presentation.

THE STARTLING STATEMENT   Say the unexpected: Surprising your audience is a good way to capture and hold its attention. For example, if you are delivering a presentation on CD-package design, you might start with a startling statistic. Every year some 250 million CDs are sold. And every year this business produces an estimated 23 million pounds of garbage—the discarded outer boxes of CD packages.

Similarly, George C. Dillon, a director of the Manville Corporation, once began a speech on business ethics with the unexpected. In view of Manville's bankruptcy as a result of over $1 billion in asbestos liability claims, even his topic choice is surprising:

> When it comes to shining examples of morality in business, I suspect it's rather unlikely that many of you think instantly of Manville. In the annual *Fortune Magazine* poll of America's Most Admired Companies, Manville finished in the cellar, among the least admired companies, for five consecutive years…. We don't know yet if the future can redeem the past, but that, clearly, is Manville's ethical legacy. And that is why it is appropriate that my topic is ethics.[11]

Finally, a cautionary note. There is a difference between the effective startling statement and the offensive shock tactic. Pounding the lectern for no reason but to gain attention, using profanity, or telling offensive jokes reduces credibility.

anecdote
Short entertaining account of some event

ANECDOTES   Few of us can resist an **anecdote**—a short entertaining account of some event—especially if it has personal meaning. Company manager and author Harvey B. Mackay started his commencement address at Pennsylvania State University with the following anecdote:

> On the day I graduated the world was very different from today. So different, in fact, that I wasn't sure what would be on the minds of people graduating in 1991. That's why I decided to do a little market research. I already knew my market niche. That's you. But I wanted to design a product, a speech, that would fit, using a process I call niche picking.
>
> So I called up my student advisor, Warren Chaiken, and asked him to arrange for me to spend some time on campus. Then I got myself this wig and these horn-rimmed glasses and disguised as Warren's "Uncle Ron" from Chicago, I was ready to go.

I learned quite a bit being back on campus. It was the height of the recruiting season, and the topic on everybody's mind was jobs, jobs, jobs. "Hey," I thought to myself, "this sounds just like when I graduated." And the more I listened, the more I realized we aren't really very different. You want to find a good job, just like I did. You're also concerned about making an impact and finding balance in the world. In other words, you're wondering what it will take to succeed in life.[12]

This story succeeds because it leads naturally to Mackay's main idea—that finding a job is every graduate's worry.

Similarly, a presentation on safety to a group of long-distance truckers can start with a story of how a serious injury was prevented because the driver was wearing a seat belt. Even hypothetical examples make the point.

RHETORICAL QUESTIONS A **rhetorical question** excites involvement in a subject without requiring an actual answer. For example, when speakers ask listeners questions like the following during the course of their remarks, they are asking rhetorical questions:

rhetorical question
Question designed to produce receiver involvement in a subject without requiring an answer

- "What do you think it will take to meet government environmental requirements?"
- "Should we build an on-site child-care facility?"
- "Do our ads target baby boomers at the expense of the elderly?"

In a sense, then, rhetorical questions create involvement by encouraging listeners to question themselves and thus be better prepared to examine certain answers. Generally, speakers pose rhetorical questions because they intend to propose their own answers to them.

QUOTATIONS Quoting someone who is well-known or who is an authority on your subject can add credibility to your speech or presentation. Here John Cady, president of the National Food Processors Association, invoked the words of Mark Twain to open a speech on a crisis of public confidence in the food industry. "Mark Twain," Cady began, "had a rule about food. 'Eat what you like,' he said, 'and let the food fight it out inside.'" Cady then moved quickly from the humorous quote to his main idea:

These days the idea of some seems to be to fight it out with our food and its producers to keep it from ever getting inside....

Let me suggest that the first step to restoring public confidence in our food supply is for us in the industry to recognize that these special interest groups would not be so prominent if the public were not receptive to their message. Dealing with those public attitudes is the challenge for us.[13]

Similarly, a quote from the CEO or another high company official adds authority to an in-house presentation. For example, starting a presentation on sexual harassment with a statement from the CEO makes it clear that sexual harassment will not be tolerated.

DEMONSTRATIONS Ask Burger King executives to taste-test Weight Watchers' meals. Bring in prototypes of new compact-disc packaging. Demonstrate how a defective five-cent part can cause a $100 tool to fail. Demonstrations like these are attention grabbers and lead naturally into the body of your speech or presentation.

PREVIEW YOUR MAIN POINTS Your introduction should also preview things to come. In no more than a sentence or two, your preview can provide the reasons why your audience should continue listening.

A speech on the history of television by media critic Newton N. Minow illustrates the use of an effective preview. It was Minow, in a speech thirty years earlier, who had referred to television as a "vast wasteland." He thus began his 1991 address on a humorous note and then a short statement of things to come. "After finishing that speech...to the National Association of Broadcasters (NAB) thirty years ago," recalls Minow,

> I remained near the podium talking with LeRoy Collins, a former governor of Florida who was serving as NAB president. A man from the audience approached us and said to me, "I didn't particularly like your speech."
>
> A few moments later the same man returned with, "The more I thought about it, your speech was really awful."
>
> A few minutes later he was back a third time to say, "Mr. Minow, that was the worst speech I ever heard in my whole life!"
>
> Governor Collins gently put his arm around me and said, "Don't let him upset you, Newt. That man has no mind of his own. He just repeats everything he hears...."
>
> It is not my intent today to cover every part of that speech, but rather to use its anniversary to examine, with thirty years' perspective, what television has been doing to our society and what television can do for our society.[14]

Never promise more than you can perform.

Publius Syrus
Latin writer of mimes

Previews that promise too much may, of course, set up false expectations that ultimately result in lost credibility. Similarly, too much detail in the preview obliges you to spend much of the body of your speech repeating yourself rather than saying something new. Like Minow, tell your audience what to expect in general but relevant terms and then proceed to the body of your message.

The Body

The body of a speech or oral presentation uses common organizational patterns to present main points and supporting materials. These patterns—including *problem/solution, cause and effect, climactic order, and chronological order*—are examined in Chapter 4. Choose an organizational plan that suits your purpose, the nature of your material, and, most importantly, the needs of your audience. Because listeners have no chance to "rehear" points once they have been made, avoid saying too much; as a rule, limit yourself to between two and five main points.

It is within the context of these main points that you present your *evidence*—the material, drawn from firsthand observation, outside sources, or both, that supports your opinion or position. You may support your specific purpose and main points through such evidence as factual information, statistics, brief or extended examples, narratives that involve the audience in a story, testimony and quotations, or analogies. As you move from point to point, your goal is to lead listeners to accept a particular point of view or to understand the information that you are presenting.

Always remember that listeners have a limited ability to absorb spoken information. Don't overload people with too many details—they will forget at least some of them. Choose your supporting materials carefully and develop them so that they are easily and clearly interpreted. Make your points concrete. For example, instead of talking in general about a storewide shoplifting problem, talk about the theft of forty pairs of shoes, ten suits, and fifty sweaters in a month's time.

Some speakers make the mistake of spending too much time introducing and concluding their presentations and too little time developing their main points. The body is the heart of your speech or presentation and should receive the most speaking time. Within the constraints of time, you can handle main points in three ways. Our assumption, of course, is that there is a direct relationship between the time you spend on a point and its importance in your presentation.

1. Start with *your strongest point first*. If, for example, you are developing three main points in a speech whose body is fifteen minutes long, you can allot eight minutes to the first, five minutes to the second, and two minutes to the third.

2. In a *progressive pattern*, power builds as you move from point to point. For example, the first point may take two minutes, the second five minutes, and the third eight minutes.

3. Finally, all of your points can be treated equally, with each one receiving five minutes of time.

The Conclusion

The conclusion of a speech or an oral presentation, like the conclusion of a written document, serves four important functions. It summarizes your message, it extends your message to a broader context, it personalizes your message, and it calls for specific future action. The same techniques used to introduce a speech or presentation—anecdotes, humor, quotations, rhetorical questions, startling statements, demonstrations—can conclude it as well. Like the introduction, the conclusion should take about 10 percent of your presentation time.

As you think about your conclusion, keep in mind that these are the last words your listeners will hear and that it is important to leave them with a lasting impression. Remember, too, that your listeners need a signal that your speech is over. Simply stopping at the conclusion of your last point is abrupt and may leave the audience with the impression that you did not spend as much effort concluding your remarks as developing them.

Use your conclusion to communicate *closure*—the sense that your remarks are completed, not merely finished. Your conclusion, then, is not the place at which to make yet another point. All your points should have been introduced and developed prior to the conclusion. Finally, even if you are disappointed in your performance, don't conclude by apologizing for your failure.

SUMMARIZE YOUR MAIN POINTS   Follow the advice of Winston Churchill, who once said, "If you have an important point to make, don't try to be subtle or clever. Use a pile driver. Hit the point once. Then come back and hit it again. Then hit it a third time—a tremendous whack." Think of your summary as your last opportunity to "nail" your message—in effect, to tell people what you have already told them.

Restatement—recasting rather than just *repeating* your point—is absolutely necessary to get your point across. For example, a presentation recommending the initiation of an employee-assistance program to aid troubled workers might conclude like this:

> With stress a fact of life for almost all of us, an employee-assistance program can help us all function better. In summary, it promises to:
> - deal with drug and alcohol problems;
> - help employees cope with crises at home like illness and divorce;
> - intercede when workers do not get along; and
> - deal with emotionally disturbed workers.
>
> I recommend that we begin this program in the next quarter and that we begin right away to search for the best employee-assistance consulting firm. Our employees deserve it and so do our stockholders.

If you are forced to abbreviate your speech or presentation, your summary may be even more critical. Even when details or visual aids are omitted, your summary can still make your point. According to one expert on public speaking, the formula becomes in this case "Tell 'em, in brief, what you would have told 'em in full if you hadn't run out of time."[15]

EXTEND YOUR MESSAGE TO A BROADER CONTEXT   Use your conclusion to look ahead—to tie your ideas to a broader framework of goals and ideas. In the following excerpt, for example, Linda Winikow, a vice president of Orange and Rockland Utilities, Inc., uses her conclusion to broaden her thoughts on cultural diversity in the workplace:

> Now, as much as I enjoy singing Orange and Rockland's praise, let me close my talk not with what we're doing, but rather what remains unfinished.
>
> I began my talk by saying that cultural diversity—as complex as it is and as threatening as some find it—is the thing that can make American business even greater. Our challenge is to manage diversity—to put that great force to work for us.
>
> That's no small challenge, but I'm convinced that it's one that we can achieve.[16]

In an oral presentation, the broader context may include a summary of conclusions or recommendations.

PERSONALIZE YOUR MESSAGE   At the conclusion of your speech or presentation, reemphasize your focus on your listeners' needs—that is where their real motivation lies. Listeners who perceive themselves as the focus of your final remarks are more likely to receive your entire message in personal terms. For example, an employee-relations executive might conclude by explaining how sexual harassment affects everyone in the workplace.

Notice that in his commencement address on career success, Harvey Mackay uses an effective concluding story to personalize his remarks:

> Being rich isn't about money. Being rich is a state of mind.... One of the best examples of what I'm talking about comes from an experience I had with my mentor, Curt Carlson. He's the wealthiest man in Minnesota....
>
> It happened the day Minnesota was hit with the worst blizzard in fifty years. Minneapolis-St. Paul International Airport, which is used to dealing with the worst of the worst in weather, was closed for the first time in years. I had to go to a meeting in New York that day, and Curt had generously offered me a ride in his jet. Our prospects of getting out of town seemed exceedingly slim.
>
> Finally, although the storm continued to pummel us, the airport inexplicably provided a short grace period and opened a runway for small craft only....
>
> As we were taxiing down the runway to take off, Curt turned to me and said gleefully, "Look, Harvey, no tracks in the snow!"
>
> Curt Carlson, seventy years old at the time, rich beyond anyone's wildest dreams, could still sparkle with excitement about being first.
>
> From my standpoint, that what it's all about....
>
> • Never stop learning
>
> • Believe in yourself, even when no one else does
>
> • Find a way to make a difference, and...
>
> • Then go out and make your own tracks in the snow.[17]

MAKE A CALL TO ACTION   Asking your listeners to do something is a task best left to the end of your message. Many persuasive speeches and sales presentations conclude with appeals that urge action, such as George V. Grune's concluding remarks on the challenges to the magazine industry:

> I think we should be thankful we have a great organization like the MPA leading the charge. The MPA is *our* organization and its record of accomplishment is *our* record of accomplishment. The MPA has been our most potent catalyst for constructive change.
>
> If you belong to companies or organizations that are not MPA members, I urge you to encourage them to join. We must put aside our partisan interests and work together to support our industry—*your industry*.
>
> To those of you who are MPA members, I urge you to get actively involved. We need your contributions, your suggestions and your help.
>
> Let's leave here today rededicated to that mission—and above all, believing in the power of magazines.
>
> Why let a few challenges get in the way. Let's tackle them one by one. And let's do it together.[18]

In concluding a presentation, you may also talk about the steps that come next. For example, talk about responsibilities or tasks that must be accomplished and the people responsible for them. Leave your audience with a mission and a sense of energy.

Table 14.1 summarizes the various purposes of the introduction, body, and conclusion in a speech or an oral presentation. It also lists techniques for accomplishing these purposes.

TABLE 14.1	*Purpose and Technique in the Formal Presentation*	
ELEMENT	PURPOSE	TECHNIQUES
Introduction	Establish credibility	Refer to your personal background
	Capture attention	Use humor Tell a story Ask rhetorical questions Use quotations Demonstrate
	Preview main points	Briefly tell your audience what is to come
Body	Present main points	Rely on common organizational patterns
	Present supporting material	Use facts, statistics, examples, narratives, testimony and quotations
Conclusion	Summarize main points	Use repetition
	Extend message to broader context	Form conclusions and recommendations
	Personalize message	Focus your message on the needs of your audience
	Call to action	Focus on the future and what must be done

PROGRESS CHECK

1. Describe some business situations in which you might give a speech or an oral presentation.
2. List four characteristics that make effective informative speeches and presentations.
3. List some tips for capturing an audience's attention during the introduction to a speech.
4. Fill in the blanks:

   In the body of a presentation, limit yourself to between _____ and ____ main points.

THE SPECIAL REQUIREMENTS OF ORAL COMMUNICATION

In Chapter 5, we analyzed elements of word selection and style for written communication. Although oral communication shares most of these characteristics, differences naturally emerge when words are spoken. Among these differences are the need for *repetition, verbal signposts*, and *word pictures*.

Repetition

Recall Winston Churchill's emphasis on the importance of *repetition*—the reminder that saying something once may not be enough to communicate meaning. Repeating key points not only gives your listeners time to understand your message but communicates the value that you place on a thought. The second time around, your message clearly begins with the appeal to "PAY ATTENTION."

Repeating key thoughts at strategic places, then, is not the same thing as amassing synonyms or trying out a variety of sentence constructions on the same idea. Tight, concise language is as important in speaking as it is in writing. Below are two hypothetical presentations made by a sales manager from Ralston Purina to A&P buyers, urging the grocery chain to introduce a new line of natural pet foods:

> Version 1
>
> I am here to tell you about our new line of pet foods, which we have named Nature's Course, that every one of your nutritionally oriented customers will want. These pet foods are targeted at people who do everything they can to avoid fat and a wide range of additives and artificial colorings in their own diets. Foods like these, manufactured for years by small companies like Natural Life and Nature's Recipe, lack the marketing strength of the Ralston Purina name. They are sold through veterinarians' offices, health-food stores, and pet-supply boutiques. It is my proposal that natural pet foods should go mainstream and appear on A&P's shelves.
>
> Version 2
>
> People who care about their own nutrition are beginning to care what their pets eat. For years, small companies like Natural Life and Nature's Recipe have marketed low-fat pet foods with few additives and artificial colorings through veterinarians' offices, health-food stores, and pet-supply boutiques. We propose to place Nature's Course, our own line of natural pet foods—with the marketing appeal of the Ralston Purina name—on A&P's shelves.

Version 2 communicates the same message using only 66 percent of the word total required by Version 1.

Verbal Signposts

verbal signpost
Brief statement that gives listeners "clues" to the organization and structure of a speech

transition
Word, phrase, or sentence used to connect ideas and produce coherent paragraphs

Verbal signposts are brief statements that give listeners "clues" to the organization and structure of a speech. Verbal signposts include *transitions, internal previews*, and *internal summaries*.

TRANSITIONS   The words, phrases, and sentences that connect ideas are called **transitions**. Here are several examples:

- The *second* restriction on expense-account spending that I would like to discuss...
- *On the contrary*, inflation has not been a significant factor in increased expense-account spending.
- *To conclude*, we can reduce the amount of reimbursable out-of-pocket spending on sales calls without affecting our relationship with customers.
- *What does all this mean?*

The italicized words act like verbal flags as they show the relationship between ideas. For example, the transition tag *second* tells listeners that you will state the second point in a series of restrictions; *on the contrary* indicates a contrasting point of view; *to conclude* indicates the end of a presentation; the rhetorical question *What does all this mean?* signals a move from one part of a presentation (information) to another (interpretation). Here are some other common transitional words and phrases:

In other words,	Finally,
Therefore,	However,
On the one hand,	On the other hand,
In addition,	Nevertheless,
For this reason,	Specifically,

Verbal transitions fall into four categories. First, they *show the relationship* between a new idea and a previous idea:

> *On the other hand*, small-appliance sales were strong in the last quarter.

They *enumerate*:

> *First*, the IRS is telling us that our lunch room subsidy may be a taxable benefit to employees.

They *repeat or restate* key words or phrases:

> *These opportunities* are important enough for us to take action.

And they *communicate emphasis*:

> The opportunity open to us in the over-65 market *cannot be overemphasized*.

INTERNAL PREVIEWS   Transitions that tell listeners what you intend to say before you say it are called **internal previews**. These verbal signposts are especially important if the point that you are introducing is long and complex. In helping your audience to anticipate your remarks, they also prepare the listener to follow their development. For example, the speaker's opinion about a topic is announced in the following preview:

> In the next few minutes, I will focus on how the environmental movement is changing the way that customers respond to our products.

Similarly, the following preview prepares listeners for a sequence of major ideas:

> First, I am going to talk about why our line of natural pet foods is superior to competing brands. Second, I will examine our marketing approach. And finally, I will look at possible distribution problems.

INTERNAL SUMMARIES   Unlike the summary delivered at the end of a speech or presentation, **internal summaries** occur at key points within a message. Their purpose is to *restate and emphasize* what you have just said and to *connect* internal elements. For example:

> In review, Velcro balls and mitts are the toy of the season, with sales exceeding expectations. However, as I have shown, sales have been limited by the manufacturer's inability to ship the quantities we need.

Internal previews and internal summaries may also act as transitions to connect the major points within your speech or presentation.

internal preview
Verbal signpost that tells listeners what the speaker intends to say before he or she says it

internal summary
In oral communication, verbal signpost occurring at a key point within a speech, restating and emphasizing what was just stated, and connecting internal elements

Word Pictures

When you paint "word pictures" and tie your points to them, your audience is more likely to remember your message. "People remember stories and their morals a lot better than they remember written policies," advises David Armstrong, vice president of Armstrong International, Inc., and an authority on corporate storytelling. Thus, when one successful grocery retailer delivers a presentation on customer service to his employees, he often uses this story about tuna fish sandwiches:

> I unwrap one of our tuna sandwiches, and this package of mayonnaise rolls out. I figure, the sandwich has enough mayo already. So I call Bill Hollis, my deli manager, and tell him, get rid of the extra mayo, it's expensive.
>
> So next week, I open a sandwich, the Hellman's pops out again. I call Bill again, and he says, you gotta talk to Mary Ekstrand, she makes the sandwiches. I call Mary, who says, "Sorry, the customers want the extra mayo, so I'm packing it again." You know my reaction? Bravo, Mary!

Had this manager talked for an hour about the principles of customer service and worker empowerment, few employees would have left the presentation with the same understanding afforded by this simple story. "Making employees giggle with a story," he says, "is a better way to teach them something than reciting a list of rules."[19]

OUTLINING ORAL PRESENTATIONS

As you will see later in the chapter, extemporaneous speaking is the most effective delivery form for speeches and the only acceptable form for business presentations. Two outline forms that are commonly used to prepare extemporaneous presentations can also be useful in preparing other forms of presentations: the *planning outline* and *speaking notes*.

The Planning Outline

planning outline
Full-content outline that includes every part of a speech or presentation—introduction, body (including main points and supporting materials, internal previews, and summaries), and conclusion

The **planning outline** is a full-content outline that includes every part of a speech or presentation—the introduction, the body (including main points and supporting materials, internal previews, and summaries), and the conclusion. It also includes statements of your specific purpose and core idea. The traditional outline form that we examined in Chapter 4 enables you to see the connections among ideas as quickly and clearly as possible.

The planning outline also helps you think in terms of language choices. Because it is composed of full sentences rather than words or phrases, it lets you judge how your speech or presentation will sound. The example in Figure

---

THE STATES INSIST ON CLEANER AIR

Specific Purpose

To inform top management that stricter rules on car emissions are coming from the states, not the federal government.

Core Idea

State governments, which seem to want clean air more than the Environmental Protection Agency, are following California's lead and establishing standards stricter than the federal government requires.

Introduction

When is the last time you heard states volunteering for stricter regulation--especially in the area of environmental protection? The impossible seems to be happening as eleven eastern states and the District of Columbia are telling oil companies and auto makers that the provisions of the federal Clean Air Act of 1990 are simply not strong enough.

Preview Statement

Because our business of producing gasoline is so closely connected with clean-air standards, I will examine the reasons behind this fundamental change in state-government attitudes and what it means to our corporation. I will start by looking at the history of the current Clean Air Act.

    I. The Clean Air Act of 1990 was preceded by the Clean Air Acts of 1970 and 1977.

        A. The states enforced the earlier federal acts only when threatened with sanctions, such as the loss of federal road-construction funds.

        B. The oil companies didn't willingly cooperate either, often refusing to acknowledge that they could play a role in cleaning the air.

Transition

So why have the states changed their minds?

    II. States later began to realize the power of environmentalist sentiments. They also realized that if they wanted clean air, they would have to regulate the oil companies themselves.

        A. Maine, New Hampshire, Vermont, Massachusetts, Rhode Island, New York, and New Jersey decided in 1989 to require cleaner gasoline within their borders.

        B. These states, along with Virginia, Maryland, Delaware, Pennsylvania, and the District of Columbia, are now threatening to adopt California's car-emissions standards--the strictest in the nation.

Internal Summary

As you can see, the states are taking seriously their responsibility to clean the air. What do these changes mean?

    III. The implications are varied

        A. Instead of lobbying Washington, we have to lobby fifty state capitals, where decisions are being made.

        B. Some of our competitors are already reformulating their gasoline products for cleaner air.

            1. Arco has reformulated its entire product line--a move that we may have to counter.

            2. Their motivation is to preclude the introduction of gasoline alternatives.

        C. Other companies are trying different approaches including Unocal which is putting its energy and money into buying and crushing old cars that pollute the environment. The company has already spent over $6 million to destroy more than 7,400 polluters.

Transition

Now that we have examined the history of clean-air regulation, the role currently taken by state governments, and the implications to our industry, it is time to look ahead.

Conclusion

The political climate is clear: the states want clean air and it can be good business to give it to them. A story I heard recently will give you an inkling of how much we can do to take positive action. The exhaust emissions from many of the old clunkers that Unocal bought are literally hundreds of times dirtier than emissions from new cars. In one case, the unburned hydrocarbons in the exhaust could have acted as fuel for a new car.

In the short run, embracing even the strictest clean-air standards will reduce demand. In the long run, the market is large enough to do this without being hurt. And in the process, we'll make it possible for all of us to breathe easier.

FIGURE 14.1 *Sample Planning Outline*

Source: Information from Matthew L. Wald, "When the E.P.A. Isn't Mean Enough about Cleaner Air," *The New York Times*, October 13, 1991, p. F25.

14.1 is a planning outline for a presentation on clean-air standards that might have been delivered by an environmental regulatory manager at a major oil company. In particular, note the points at which the speaker feels it necessary to detail his remarks: These are the points at which he or she wants either to be specific or to show the connection among ideas.

Speaking Notes

An abbreviated key-word outline designed to guide a speaker's actual *delivery* is known as **speaking notes**. Unlike the planning outline, speaking notes are short and to the point. Complex sentences have been reduced to key words, phrases, and simple sentences; transitions, internal previews, and summaries appear in an abbreviated form.

speaking notes
Abbreviated key-word outline designed to guide a speaker's actual delivery

The advantage of speaking notes is that although they provide structure, they allow you to deliver your speech or presentation extemporaneously and, in the process, to maintain contact with your audience. Remember that there is an important difference between *extemporaneous* speaking and *impromptu* speaking. Whereas *impromptu* means without preparation—offhand—*extemporaneous* means that although you have prepared your *content* in the form of speaking notes, you will let the manner of your *delivery* be determined by the particular occasion.

In preparing speaking notes, follow the same outline form that you used in your planning outline. You want to see at a glance the structure of your speech or presentation. Write legibly and large because you will be glancing at your notes for guidance as you speak.

The previous planning outline is presented in the form of speaking notes in Figure 14.2. Notice that neither the specific purpose nor the core idea is included because these points are never put directly into words.

In the margin of your speaking notes, you may want to include instructions for improving your delivery. For example, at a key point you might write, "SLOW DOWN" or "LOOK AT AUDIENCE." You can also indicate the exact spot where

---

The States Insist on Cleaner Air

Introduction
The impossible happens: States ask for more stringent clean-air standards.
Preview
Why? What does it mean to us? Look at history behind the current Clean Air Act.
   I. 1990 Clean Air Act preceded by acts in 1970 and 1977.
      A. State resistance to earlier acts
      B. Poor cooperation from oil companies.
Transition
Why the change?
   II. Political climate and environmental sentiments.
      A. 1989 action of New England states
      B. California's emission standards now standard for these and other states.
Internal Summary
Clean air is serious to states.
   III. Implications of change
      A. Decentralized political lobbying
      B. Reformulate gasoline
         1. Arco's example
         2. Reason: to stop alternative fuels.
      C. Different approaches, including Unocal and its old clunkers
Transition
Looking ahead
Conclusion
Clean air/good business link. End with story of emissions mess from Unocal's clunkers.

FIGURE 14.2 Sample Speaking Notes

Source: Information from Matthew L. Wald, "When the E.P.A. Isn't Mean Enough about Cleaner Air," *The New York Times*, October 13, 1991, p. F25.

you want to introduce a visual aid—"SHOW MAP HERE" or "TRANSPARENCY #2 GOES HERE." As we will see in the next section, visual aids can also be used not merely to complement your presentation but also to *organize* it.

VISUAL AIDS

Visual aids may be the only notes you need during a speech or presentation. Business speakers often structure their presentations around series of slides that provide both visual appeal and content, interest, and clarity. Experienced speakers have added a number of interesting options to the use of visual aids in written documents. We will begin by taking a closer look at the types of visual aids available to speakers and then offer some guidelines for both designing and using them.

Types of Visual Aids

Business speakers have a broader selection of visual aids than those available to writers. Freed from the constraints of paper—for example, limitations of size and space—speakers can think in terms of such media as *objects* and *models*; *flip charts, chalk* and *writing boards,* and *posters; handouts; overhead transparencies; slides,* and *videos.*

OBJECTS AND MODELS   If you were presenting the prototype for a new hammer, your best visual aid would of course be the hammer itself. If you were involved in the manufacture of a new commercial jet, a scaled-down model would help you demonstrate its unique characteristics. On the one hand, as objects and models are passed around the room, they encourage active, hands-on interaction. On the other hand, you may find yourself competing with your own visual aids for audience attention.

FLIP CHARTS, CHALK AND WRITING BOARDS, AND POSTERS   These media are effective in presenting information to small interactive groups. Flip charts are the most common way to display visuals in a business presentation, allowing you to show a sequence of graphic information with the turn of a page. Because flip charts can be prepared in advance, your presentation can also be neat and exact. In addition, advance preparation eliminates the need either to turn your back as you speak or to pause while you draw or write.

In certain situations, however, you may actually prefer to write as you speak. When used in this manner, aids like flip charts and posters are excellent group-interaction tools. In a problem-solving situation, for example, you can record key ideas as they are contributed. For an informative presentation, you can list your most important points in the order in which you want to make them. Visuals mounted on posterboard can also be prepared before you arrive. If you choose this medium, be sure that an easel is available in the presentation room.

HANDOUTS   In order to refer to them as they speak, many speakers hand out printed materials like agendas, reports, letters, and other documents and such visual aids as graphs, charts, and tables. Handouts are especially useful in small working groups because they encourage active interaction. However, they can distract the audience by pulling attention away from you. Many speakers thus save their handouts until the end of the presentation.

OVERHEAD TRANSPARENCIES   Overhead transparencies allow an image to be projected without darkening the room and without losing touch with the audience. They are easy to use and are widely employed in many business settings. They are also flexible, allowing you to add or highlight a concept while it is being shown.

High-quality transparencies can be produced in-house on photocopy machines that handle transparent film. Using a sophisticated system like Kodak

The technology for computer output devices offers a variety of tools to assist in delivering speeches and oral presentations. For example, in addition to desktop film recorders for creating high-resolution images on film, there are screen image projectors that can project graphic images onto large screens in much the same way that television programs are projected onto large TV screens.

Datashow or Polaroid's 35mm Slide Printer, you can actually create full-color computer graphics that are transferred from the computer onto the projection screen.

SLIDES   Both color and black-and-white slides can add a professional touch to a presentation. Slides can be used to display any type of two-dimensional visual aid, including photographs, maps, lists, tables, and graphs.

Today's remote-control slide projectors allow you to change slides without stationing yourself next to the machine. You can stand in front of the room where the audience can pay attention to you as you point out important details on the slide. Unlike transparencies, however, slides require a darkened room and may make audience contact difficult. They also require that the projection equipment be in good working order. Projection bulbs, for example, burn out, and some experienced speakers have been known to carry spares in their briefcases. Although production costs for slides and overhead transparencies are about equal, slides take more time to produce.

VIDEOS   Videos are an integral part of many business presentations. Advertising agencies use videos to screen new commercials for clients. A video may be part of a marketing presentation for an in-store security package. A fashion designer may use a video to display his latest creations on live models.

Video has the advantage of easy recording and instant playback—a feature especially valuable when you must record activities in the midst of a presentation. A visual image in the middle of a cassette is also easy to locate. Because most videos are shown on small television screens, they are most effective for small audiences. Well in advance of your speech or presentation, check to be sure that a VCR is available and in good working order. Table 14.2 compares the features of some of the visual aids that we have examined in this section.

Designing Visual Aids

Following are some design guidelines for effective visual presentations. Because visual aids are used to give graphic dimension to presentations, design is critical to their successful use.

SIMPLICITY   Visuals that try to communicate too much run the risk of overload. Communicate your message in a simple, direct way by limiting each visual to a single point. If you want to pursue a series of related ideas or facts, use a series of visuals. If something must be written out, use key words, not sentences, and eliminate all unnecessary detail. Most illustrations drawn from other sources—for example, books and articles—cannot be used without extensive revision.

SIZE   Use print large enough for everyone in the room to read. If necessary, bring your visuals to the presentation room in advance and read them from the back of the room. If you squint, your writing is too small. Also use plenty of white space to reduce clutter.

TABLE 14.2   *Using Visual Aids in Formal Presentations*

FORMAT	AUDIENCE	ADVANTAGES	DISADVANTAGES
Flip charts, chalk and writing boards	Small	• Help to organize/summarize • High flexibility; low human error • Informal	• Low-impact
Overhead transparencies	Medium/large	• Portable • No technician needed • High flexibility	• Can be distracting • Complex charts and graphs are ineffective
Slides	Medium/large	• Flexible/Modular • Minimum equipment needs • Type serves as outline • Graphs show relationships • Charts save time conceptually	• Do not show motion • Lights must be dimmed
Video cassettes	Small/medium	• High-impact • Instant replay • Flexible • Easy assembly • Supports other AV formats • Provides change of pace	• Requires equipment • Availability

a.

b.

c.

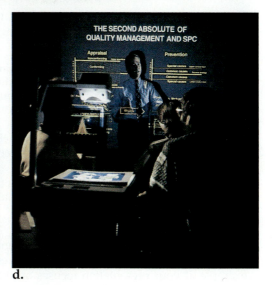

d.

Visual aids are quite effective in both clarifying a speaker's message and bolstering its impact. The technology for projecting graphics—two-dimensional aids used to illustrate or underscore visually a point being made orally—runs the gamut from such simple devices as flip charts (a) and writing boards (b) to more elaborate media machinery, like overhead slide projectors (c) and transparency projectors (d). Perhaps most importantly, using visual aids forces speakers to become more physically involved in their deliveries and thus communicate a sense of energy and commitment.

When producing transparencies, use the guidelines in Table 14.3 to determine size.[20]

COLOR   When used correctly, color can make visuals not only more attractive but also easier to read. Orange lettering on a dark blue background, for example, increases legibility. By the same token, carelessly chosen colors can make visuals more difficult to read.

If you examine the color wheel in Figure 14.3, for instance, you can see that orange lettering against a red background is extremely difficult to read because the contrast between the two colors is so low. The pairing of colors that are adjacent to one another on the color chart, therefore, may produce subtle, harmonious effects but little contrast. Not surprisingly, white images on dark backgrounds provide the greatest contrast, followed by images in yellow, orange, green, red, blue, and violet. Black images show up best on light backgrounds, followed by images in red, orange, green, blue, violet, and yellow.

In addition to using colors for the strongest contrasts, you can select colors for their so-called "temperatures." While "warm" colors like red and orange highlight visual presentations because they "advance" toward the audience, "cool" colors like blue and green, which tend to "recede," make excellent backgrounds.

PRACTICAL TIPS

Using Color to Enhance Visual Aids

Color is one of your most powerful presentation tools. Effectively used, for example, it can encourage your audience to focus on specific points in a specific order. It can also link related presentation elements and explain processes through color motion.

USING COLOR TO EMPHASIZE OR DE-EMPHASIZE INFORMATION

There are a number of ways to highlight or de-emphasize specific concepts by manipulating color on a visual aid:

- Use a bright color to highlight important words in a visual containing a key sentence or paragraph. Of course, this color should also contrast with the background color on the rest of the visual.
- Use the same technique to highlight a chart element that is discussed or emphasized during your presentation.
- Use a dark color to de-emphasize data that disagree with the point that you are making.

USING COLOR TO CREATE DISTINCTIVE THEMES

One of the best ways to link repeated elements in a presentation is by developing color themes. For example, if your presentation focuses on the performance of four sales districts, choose a "signature" color for each district and use it throughout your presentation consistently when referring to each district in your charts. The North could be light blue, the South yellow, the East green, and the West orange. In a pie chart comparing the percentage of total sales coming from each district, each pie segment would bear the appropriate signature color. This technique creates consistency and increases readability.

In a long presentation involving several speakers, you may decide to use different background colors to distinguish each speaker's visual aids.

USING COLOR MOTION TO EXPLAIN A SEQUENCE OR STEPS IN A PROCEDURE

Use "moving highlights" to help explain a confusing process depicted on a chart. In this technique, a segment on the chart is highlighted with a bright, contrasting color as the speaker focuses on that segment. At the same time, the rest of the chart is toned down and may appear in a lighter shade of the background color. As the speaker moves to the next element in the chart, that element is highlighted and the rest fades into the background. As you can see in the figure below, the sequential highlighting is repeated until all the elements are explained. Many speakers who use this technique begin with a visual that shows all the elements highlighted—for example, all the elements on an organizational chart. As each element is highlighted in sequence, the entire chart remains in view.

These and other techniques can do much to improve the clarity of your message. They also add a professional quality not only to your visual aids, but also to your entire presentation.

Source: Michael Talman, *Understanding Presentation Graphics* (San Francisco: SYBEX, 1992), pp. 116–20. Reprinted by permission of SYBEX Inc. © 1992 SYBEX Inc. All rights reserved.

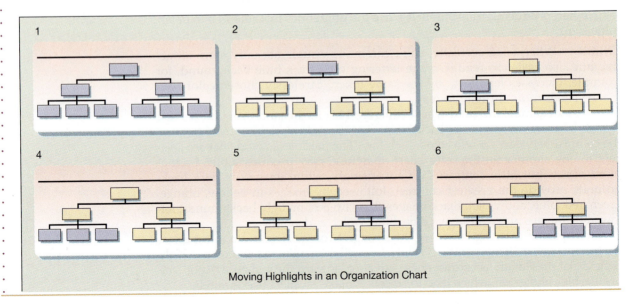

Moving Highlights in an Organization Chart

TABLE 14.3	*Guidelines For Determining Visual-Aid Letter Size*	
SITUATION/SETTING	SUGGESTED MINIMUM LETTER SIZES (ALL CAPITALS)	
Informal, Small conference room 10-20 attendees	Typeface: Hand Lettering:	14 point 3/16 (0.19) inch
Medium-size conference room 21-50 attendees	Titles: Body:	20 point (about 5/16 inch) 16 point (about 5/16 inch)
Large auditorium more than 50 attendees	Titles: Body:	24 point 18 point

Source: Adapted from Thomas Leech, *How to Prepare, Stage and Deliver Winning Presentations,* (New York: AMACOM, 1982), p. 166.

DESIGN FOR CONSISTENCY   Develop a consistent format and style for your visual presentation. For example, unless you have a good reason, avoid mixing color with black-and-white slides. Use the same style and size of lettering and the same palette of colors on every visual.

Guidelines for Using Visual Aids

Depending on how they are used, of course, visual aids can enhance or detract from a speech or an oral presentation. The following guidelines will help you select and design effective visual aids.

■ *Choose the right visual aid.* Limit your visuals to important points. Your choices should be determined by the purpose of your speech, the size of

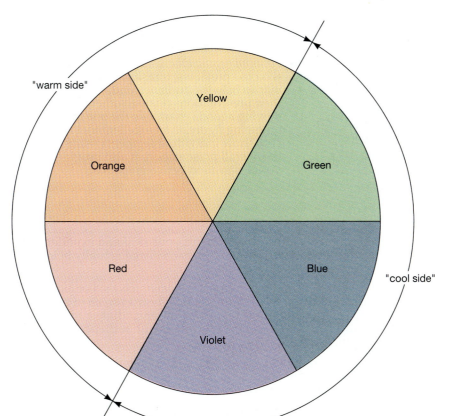

FIGURE 14.3   *The Color Wheel*

Opposites give the strongest contrast, whereas adjacent colors blend. The "warm" side advances toward the audience; the "cool" side retreats.

PRACTICAL TIPS

Developing and Delivering Team Presentations

Oral presentations are often developed and delivered by teams of presenters. This is especially common if the presentation requires the input of people with different forms of expertise. For example, individuals from marketing, accounting, and human resources all may be involved in an internal team presentation regarding the redeployment of staff members for a new account.

The best team presentations function like well-oiled machines. Each segment supports the presentation's overall purpose and is linked to but does not repeat the functions of the other segments. In addition, performances are coordinated as each person acts according to a carefully crafted plan intended to maintain the focus of the final presentation.

The most successful team presentations involve three stages: *predesign, design,* and *delivery.* The techniques used in each stage are intended to shape the team into a unified whole.

PREDESIGN

Careful planning is crucial in team presentations, and special attention must be paid to defining the overriding theme of the presentation. Unless everyone knows in advance exactly what the team is trying to accomplish and focuses on that purpose as they would the North Star in a darkened sky, wrong decisions are inevitable from that point on.

The predesign stage also involves identifying channels of communication and the person who will lead the team's effort. It is the leader's responsibility to coordinate individual segments and to ensure that everyone knows what every-

one else is doing. Among the leader's tasks are dividing the presentation into distinct segments and assigning speakers for each.

DESIGN

During the design stage, general themes are translated into concrete, specific presentation plans. To coordinate the presentations of all group members, it is often helpful to develop storyboards for each speaker that define what he or she will cover, the visuals that will be used, and the time needed to complete the presentation. Completed storyboards may be prominently displayed—for example, taped to a wall—so that every presenter can see exactly what will be said at each point in the presentation. This information minimizes duplication.

Visuals are also created during the design stage. To produce a coordinated, cohesive effect, visuals should all have the same type and art style.

DELIVERY

If the predesign and design stages are successful, the team will be prepared to make an effective delivery. Here are some of the factors that contribute to a successful delivery:

- *Strict adherence to time.* Speakers who fail to watch the clock take time allotted to others.
- *Focus on organizational clarity.* Speakers who use previews, transitions, and summaries help the audience understand how their presentations relate to others. The moving agenda chart, like the one in the following figure, is an excellent tool to show how individual segments relate to the overall presentation. It also provides a visual transition between speakers.

your audience, the needs of the occasion, and your skill and experience in using the medium. Ask yourself whether each visual actually belongs in your presentation or could be eliminated.

- *Remember that your audience wants to see you, not your visuals.* For example, beginning your presentation with slides projected on a screen in a darkened room will prevent you from establishing an immediate audience connection. Ending with a visual will encourage your audience to remember the visual instead of you.

- *Don't repeat the content of the visual when you comment on it.* Although you must resist describing every detail, you should *explain* to your audience what it is seeing—for example:

This slide shows how workforce reduction has reduced company overhead in the last three years.

- *An effective team leader.* It is the role of the leader to introduce speakers, provide transitions from one speaker to another, and make sure that the group maintains its focus throughout the entire presentation.
- *Mutual team support.* Because a team is only as successful as its weakest member, all team members must support one another. Team support can be demonstrated in many ways—for example, deferring to another team member's expertise, being flexible so that you can coordinate your segment with the last-minute changes of other members.

Although team presentations are undoubtedly more complex than single-person presentations, they can be successful if they are carefully planned and executed. Achieving your goal takes a commitment of time and energy as well as an understanding of the unique characteristics of team presentation and the increasing importance of these presentations in business organizations.

Source: Reprinted, with permission of the publisher, from *How to Prepare, Stage and Deliver Winning Presentations* © 1982 Thomas Leech. Published by AMACOM, a division of the American Management Association. All rights reserved.

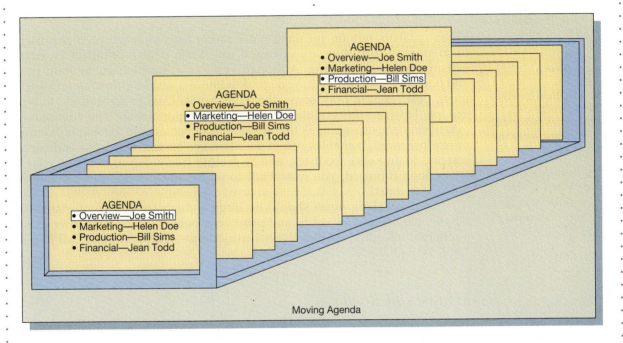

Moving Agenda

- Stop after your main point and allow the audience to scan the information projected on the visual. In addition, because you will force your audience to choose between you and your visual if you speak "on top" of it, pause for several seconds after displaying a visual aid.
- *Avoid turning your back on your audience.* Maintain eye contact throughout your speech, even when displaying a visual.
- *Work on your timing.* Never display a visual before talking about it; remove it when you have finished the thought.
- *Rehearse.* Integrate your visual and oral presentations before your actual performance. Rehearsal is especially important if you use more than one medium. Moving from a flip chart to a slide projector to a VCR requires familiarity with the equipment (and a back-up plan if something goes wrong).

PROGRESS CHECK

1. What do we mean by *verbal signposts*? Why are they useful?
2. What design guidelines help create an effective visual design?
3. Summarize the guidelines for using visual aids.

DELIVERY

delivery
Method of giving any form of speech or oral presentation, including voice quality and body language

The will to win is important, but the will to prepare is vital.

Joe Paterno
Football coach

Delivery refers not only to your method of speaking but to your voice quality and body language. In this section, we will discuss the four basic methods of delivery—*extemporaneous speaking, manuscript reading, memorization,* and *impromptu speaking.* We will then examine the ways in which voice quality and nonverbal language influence what people hear and how receptive they are to your message. Finally, we will offer some advice on overcoming *speech tension* ("stage fright").

Extemporaneous Speaking

extemporaneous speaking
Delivery method in which the speaker relies on speaking notes rather than on a complete manuscript or memorization

All the great speakers were bad speakers at first.

Ralph Waldo Emerson
American essayist and poet

When speakers rely on speaking notes rather than on a complete manuscript or memorization, they are engaged in a form of presentation known as **extemporaneous speaking**. Although you know both what you want to say and how you want to say it, you speak without a *detailed* prepared text—at the most, you prepare only some speaking notes. Oral presentations to small groups, for example, are almost always extemporaneous. The advantage of extemporaneous speaking is that it sounds conversational instead of "canned" or overprepared. It enables you to maintain eye contact with your audience, to respond to audience feedback, and to gesture freely. For example, if your listeners look confused, you may want to pause and provide more detail than you had planned.

Your speaking notes should be large enough to read comfortably. Use 5-by-8-inch lined index cards, and print your notes in bold, clear letters. Using a different ink color, write delivery instructions—"REPEAT FOR EMPHASIS," "ASK FOR QUESTIONS"—in the margins.

Manuscript Reading

manuscript reading
Delivery method in which the speaker reads to an audience from a detailed prepared text

When speakers read from *detailed* prepared texts, they are engaged in **manuscript reading**. For example, when White House press secretary David Gergen delivers a statement on Administration policy, he is likely to read from a manuscript. Although his presentation no doubt lacks spontaneity, he has good reason to choose this delivery method. With a good deal at stake, he obviously cannot afford to misstate the President's position. Business speakers may also have good reasons to read prepared texts. When the message is politically sensitive or highly technical, for example, reading can prevent serious errors.

In manuscript reading, the natural tendency of the speaker is to focus on the manuscript first and audience second—a situation that makes feedback difficult. Gestures are limited because the speaker typically holds the manuscript or lectern instead of moving freely about the room and using hand movements to emphasize key points. To counter such problems, rehearse your presentation with your audience in mind. Learn it well enough so that you can glance regularly at your listeners. Practice varying your rate of speech and the quality of your voice.

Finally, recall the fate of the late Soviet leader Leonid Brezhnev, who once read the same page of a nationally televised speech twice without realizing what he had done. Prepare your manuscript so that you can find your place after looking around the room. Use large boldfaced type, wide margins, and triple spacing.[21]

Teleprompters—electronic devices for rolling prepared texts—enable speakers to appear to be speaking extemporaneously while actually reading detailed scripts. These machines provide enormous flexibility when used properly. However, they require practice and, for peace of mind, a full script on the lectern in case of malfunction.

Memorization

Under certain circumstances, memorization—learning your remarks by heart—can give you confidence and poise. When delivering a toast at a retirement party or accepting an award from a professional association, memorizing your comments is an acceptable delivery form. Memorization is quite effective for short announcements or for introducing speakers. In most other situations, however, memorization is a mistake. You run the risk not only of sounding wooden and overrehearsed but also of forgetting your script, especially if you are nervous.

It usually takes me more than three weeks to prepare a good impromptu speech.
Mark Twain (Samuel Langhorne Clemens) American author and lecturer

Impromptu Speaking

When remarks are delivered without advance preparation, speakers are engaged in **impromptu speaking**. Impromptu speaking is common in business meetings where participants are often asked to speak about such subjects as current projects or department functions.

When called on to make impromptu remarks, focus on the needs of your audience as you make short, clear points. Limit your remarks to a specific purpose and resist the temptation to say too much. Keep in mind that although your audience may not expect a formal presentation, it does expect intelligent, cogent comments.

impromptu speaking
Delivery method in which the speaker makes remarks without advance preparation

TIME YOUR PRESENTATION   If you promise a twenty-minute presentation, don't ramble on for an hour. In today's no-nonsense business world, you may find your audience walking out in front of your eyes.

Always be prepared to cut your remarks short if an unexpected interruption pulls people away. It's not personal, it's just business, and flexibility is a hallmark of good public speaking.

I do not object to people looking at their watches when I am speaking. But I strongly object when they start shaking them to make sure they are still going.
Lord William Norman Birkett British lawyer and judge

Voice Quality and Nonverbal Language

The quality of your voice and the way you move during a speech or presentation are also elements of your delivery These elements make important and lasting impressions, as do several other forms of nonverbal language.

VOICE QUALITY   **Voice quality** (sometimes called *paralanguage*) refers to a variety of voice elements, including *loudness, pitch, rate, pauses, articulation,* and *pronunciation*. Improving these elements improves your entire performance.

voice quality
(or *paralanguage*)
Distinctive nature of a variety of voice elements, including loudness, pitch, rate, pauses, articulation, and pronunciation

LOUDNESS   Your audience must be able to hear you. In order to speak loudly but without shouting, project your voice from the diaphragm—the flat respiratory muscle in your chest wall—not from the vocal folds. With a little practice, you will find that you can give your voice appropriate "intensity" without shouting.

PITCH   *Pitch* refers to how high or low your voice sounds. Because speaking in a monotone can make listening difficult, try varying the pitch of your voice as you emphasize key words or phrases.

RATE   Here, too, the key is variety. Varying your rate of speech can also make your delivery more interesting. Slow down to emphasize important points; speed up when recounting familiar material.

PAUSES   When used effectively, pauses add emphasis, power, and effective timing. They can influence the impact of a dramatic story, a joke, a series of rhetorical questions, a quotation, even a visual aid. Plan your pauses in advance for maximum impact.

Remember, however, that unplanned vocalized pauses are verbal annoyances. The *umms, ers, you knows,* and *ahs* of everyday spoken speech can cost you attention and credibility. To perfect your timing and eliminate vocalized pauses, rehearse your presentation with a tape recorder. Some experienced speakers have found that jotting reminders in the margins of their speaking notes—something like "DON'T SAY 'YOU KNOW'"—can help eliminate verbal habits.

ARTICULATION AND PRONUNCIATION   The clarity and distinctiveness of vocal sounds is determined by a process known as **articulation; pronunciation** refers to the formation of the proper sounds to create words. Saying *dint* instead of *didn't* is an articulation mistake; saying *hunnert* instead of *hundred* is usually an error in pronunciation. Both types of error can reduce credibility. Many experienced speakers recommend using a tape recorder to listen to your voice and identify undesirable speech habits. Many articulation and pronunciation mistakes are childhood habits, and changing them may require considerable practice.

articulation
Process of determining the clarity and distinctiveness of vocal sounds

pronunciation
Formation of the proper sounds to create words

NONVERBAL LANGUAGE   As we saw in Chapter 2, communication takes place nonverbally as well as verbally. Nonverbal communication is especially important in public speaking because it conveys an overall impression of your competence and credibility. "You have to reach people emotionally, not mechanically, if you want to cause change," argues Bert Decker, founder of Decker Communications, a San Francisco company that trains public speakers. According to Decker, you undercut your message through such visual cues as poor posture and darting eyes.[22]

Business Week reporter Dick Janssen, who took Decker's course, has described what he learned about the importance of nonverbal cues:

> Decker reminds us of things our mothers probably taught us, plus some finishing touches. Like not slouching. We learn to stand with our knees flexed, tilting slightly forward, a nuance of body language meant to serve us as well at a cocktail party as on the speaker's platform. Instead of averting our eyes from one amorphous glob of an audience, we learn to seek eye contact with an individual—for three to six seconds, max, that is. We find we do gain encouragement from this fleeting but intimate human contact. Then we move on to nurture rapport with another listener.[23]

OTHER FORMS OF NONVERBAL LANGUAGE   We will conclude this section with some advice on improving your use of important forms of nonverbal language that can affect audience response—*eye contact, gestures,* and *movement.*

EYE CONTACT   As you speak, look at people across the room but avoid the tendency to dart your eyes back and forth or to look above their heads. Choose people who are smiling or who appear receptive to your message. Speakers who make eye contact with their listeners are perceived as more open and confident than speakers who keep their eyes buried in their notes. Eye contact also communicates that you are eager for feedback.

GESTURES   Gestures, both voluntary and involuntary, play an important part in every speech and presentation. Displaying a chart and pointing to it, using your fingers to count critical points, clenching a fist to emphasize a point—all these gestures are natural outgrowths of your message. They add support by communicating involvement and self-confidence. By contrast, gestures that appear forced call attention to themselves by suggesting speaker discomfort.

MOVEMENT   Natural, relaxed movements also communicate self-confidence. Instead of holding on to the lectern for dear life, it is more effective to cross the room and point to visual aids, circulate in the audience, then walk back to the lectern. Movements tell your audience, "I'm involved. You are, too."

Depending on the skill with which they are used, many of the gestures that speakers make have both positive and negative connotations. The hand in the pocket, for example, can make a speaker seem either appropriately informal or excessively casual. The gesture might also seem quite unnatural—and actually be distracting—if the speaker seems unaware of it. Public speaking experts also caution against such body language as the "parade rest" stance (standing stiffly with hands behind the back) and the "fig leaf" stance (standing with your hands drooping down in front of you). In general, it is sound advice to practice gestures that emphasize, repeat, or complement your verbal message.

A NOTE ABOUT CLOTHING   Finally, also remember that before you speak your first word, your clothes communicate whether or not you are part of the group in the room. For example, although business consultants working with advertising agencies can wear sports clothes during presentations, they should dress differently for presentations to clients in the banking industry.

Overcoming Speech Tension

Speech tension (more commonly known as "stage fright") is the body's "fight-or-flight" reaction to the stress of delivering an oral presentation or otherwise performing before an audience. Sensing "danger," the heart rate zooms, the palms sweat, the mouth becomes dry, hands and knees shake, and breathing becomes labored. As we all know, these symptoms can be immobilizing. They can turn a presentation into a demonstration of collapsed nerves.

All over the country, therefore, businesspeople are taking courses to overcome speech tension and sharpen their deliveries. For one-on-one instruction costing up to $3,000 a day, companies like Speakeasy in Atlanta, Decker Communications in San Francisco, Communispond in New York, and Dale Carnegie & Associates nationwide are teaching people to be comfortable, effective speakers. These courses are necessary because most people fear public speaking more than death (one public-opinion poll actually found this preference to be literal). According to a *New York Times* headline, many of us consider speaking before an audience the "public equivalent of a root canal."[24]

speech tension
(or *stage fright*)The body's "fight-or-flight" reaction to the stress of delivering an oral presentation or otherwise performing before an audience

Not surprisingly, then, communication experts have devoted a good deal of study to the subject of public speaking and nervous tension. Here are some of their findings.

- *Almost everyone gets nervous.* The growing business of expensive public-speaking courses proves this point. Even people whose jobs require them to speak publicly may suffer from speech tension. Bert Decker puts nervous tension into perspective. "I've trained over 32,000 people and there isn't anyone who comes here who really wants to be here."[25]

- *Tension can work for you.* That extra flow of adrenalin can actually heighten your performance and improve your delivery.

- *Your tension is not obvious.* In most cases, your audience cannot detect how nervous you are.

- *Visualization works.* Visualize your own success as a speaker. Veteran business speaker Ron Hoff suggests that as you rehearse by listening to your voice, "let the words sink into your consciousness, and see yourself up on the platform in that room. The verbal and the nonverbal begin to blend together, reinforcing each other. Also, you're minimizing the possibility of surprise. You hear what you sound like. You visualize what you look like. And you're familiar with the environment—so what's to worry about? Relax. Glide."[26]

- *Breathe deeply and drink some water.* In the seconds before you begin speaking, breathe slowly several times; deep breathing will relax your entire body. If your mouth is parched, drink some water (and be sure to have a glass available during your presentation).

- *Use gestures and movements.* Gestures and movements are natural outlets for nervous tension.

- *Use visual aids.* When you are actively involved with your visual aids, your nervous tension will seem less evident, both to you and to your audience.

- *Look at people.* People want to see you succeed, not fail. They also want to learn something from you—they want to come away with something they can use. Look people straight in the eye for enormous positive feedback.

- *Don't let a mistake shake your confidence.* Don't aim for perfection—it's not possible. If something goes wrong, just keep on going. Chances are that your audience will not even know what happened.

- *Be prepared.* Know your material; know your audience; know the reason for your presentation. Organize your thoughts into speaking notes. Memorize your first sentence. Then put it all together in practice. The more you prepare, the less anxious you will be.

- *Rehearse in front of a mirror;* use a tape recorder or a video camera. If the presentation is important enough, ask a friend or colleague to sit in on a practice session. Have a dress rehearsal with all your visual aids. If possible, practice in the actual presentation room.

HOW TO HANDLE AUDIENCE QUESTIONS

Most business presentations include question-and-answer periods. Depending on the type of presentation, questions may arise at any point or only at the end. According to Sarah Weddington, the lawyer who argued the landmark abortion case *Roe v. Wade* before the Supreme Court, handling questions can be an artform. "I remember watching President Reagan handle hostile questions during the Iran-Contra scandal," she recalls. "In response to a question about whether he thought Oliver North was still a hero, the President answered that you could not take away from North the medals he had won in Vietnam. He sidestepped the question in an extremely effective way, which is a technique all speakers need to learn."[27]

In a formal speech, questions begin when the speaker asks for them. If no hands are raised, you may say something like, "I must have answered all your questions during my talk. Thank you for your attention." When hands are raised,

INTERVIEW

Bert Decker, Consultant in Public Speaking

To the thousands of business executives who have taken his communication course, Bert Decker, Founder and Chairman of the San Francisco-based Decker Communications, Inc. has the single-mindedness of a drill sergeant offset by the empathy of one who's been through it himself. Decker sees his mission as helping executives face one of their biggest fears: public speaking." We asked Decker for his thoughts on effective and ineffective speaking and on ways in which all business speakers can improve their skills.

Question: How would you define a successful speech or oral presentation?

Answer: The best speeches reach the emotions as well as the intellect of the listeners. They are delivered by speakers who move their audiences to action even if the "action" involves nothing more than grasping the information that the speaker is trying to convey. The best way to reach the emotions is through an impassioned, energized delivery—through vocal tone, gestures, excitement, enthusiasm, and eye communication. Eye communication is especially important.

Question: How important is eye communication when you're addressing a large audience?

Answer: Very important. Ironically, when you make eye contact with a few people in a large

auditorium, several hundred of those people think you're looking directly at *them*. The benefits are enormous. This kind of personal connection comes from looking at someone for three to five seconds, not fleeting moments.

Question: What are the hardest mistakes for speakers to correct?

Answer: Poor eye contact and the lack of animated energy—the energy that you have when you gesture and move, when you're excited and passionate. Many speakers tend to inhibit this energy when they're in front of a group. These mistakes are the hardest to correct because people don't know what they're doing unless they see themselves on videotape.

Question: Does videotape analysis help reduce speech tension?

Answer: Watching yourself on videotape will help you channel your energy in the right direction rather than having it come out in unfocused spurts. I always tell speakers that their goal is not to get rid of the butterflies, but to get the butterflies to fly in formation. Before every speech, you feel the same emotions as an athlete preparing for a race. Because you want to perform at your peak and because there's a lot riding on it, your emotions are heightened.

Question: Many speakers rely heavily on visual aids. Is this a good idea?

Answer: Visual aids are excellent reinforcement tools—except when they're abused. Executives who present slide after slide in darkened rooms put people to sleep. I recommend overheads because they give you greater control and because they don't encourage a written script.

Question: If you were going to give business students one piece of advice about public speaking, what would that advice be?

Answer: Just do it. Emerson once said: "Do the thing that you fear and death of fear is certain." The skill to do comes from *doing*.

Source: Interview with Bert Decker.

be sure to take questions from every part of the room, including the back (watch a presidential news conference to see this technique in action). When your presentation is in a large room or an auditorium, repeat each question so that everyone can hear (rephrasing also gives you time to think).

Knowing your audience can also help you to anticipate questions. According to Ron Hoff, "People ask questions about the issues of greatest concern to them—their positions in the organization, the problems affecting them that day. Sales managers ask about sales promotions. Corporate communications directors ask about images. Human-resources managers ask about recruitment methods. And everybody asks about costs. If you've done your homework, you'll be able to anticipate at least 70 percent of the questions you actually get."[28] Practice answering anticipated questions with a tape recorder and listen critically to the effectiveness of your response.

However, although you will be able to anticipate many questions, there will be others that you cannot answer. Say so in a direct way. But also tell the questioner that you will try to find the answer and respond as soon as possible. Of course, there may also be questions that you do not want to answer, just as Ronald Reagan did not want to say whether he thought Oliver North was a hero. Use finesse or hand off the question to a colleague. Sometimes you can maintain your credibility by saying something like, "Since public relations is Ann's area, I'll turn that question over to her."

Try to turn hostile questions to your advantage by remaining calm and recasting questions in a less confrontational style. For example, if someone asks, "How could you have approved those garish colors on the toothpaste box?" repeat the question in a less inflammatory way: "I've been asked about the colors on the product packaging. Our research shows that...."

Finally, always be conscious of the individual who is asking a question. Is it the CEO or a low-level employee? As you might expect, you may get the toughest questions from top managers who are looking for both broad implications and specific data. In order to handle such questions, you must be prepared and be able to think on your feet. Try to refer difficult questions to your previous remarks, but assure the questioner that you are ready to adjust your response when you obtain more of the facts.

PROGRESS CHECK

1. Why is it important to pay attention to your voice quality and nonverbal language during a presentation?
2. Summarize tips for overcoming stage fright.

WHAT'S AHEAD

As forms of oral communication, speeches and oral presentations can largely be characterized by predictable or formal modes of speaker-audience interaction. In Chapter 15, we will examine a number of more common, often daily, interchanges in which both group and one-on-one exchanges are generally participative encounters that are determined by the nature and requirements of the particular interchange itself.

SUMMARY OF CHAPTER OBJECTIVES

1. **Identify the characteristics of a** *speech* **and an** *oral presentation.*

Speakers delivering formal public speeches address audiences that give no verbal feedback until after the speech is over. By contrast, oral presentations are characterized by an interchange between speaker and audience that may occur at any point during or after the presentation. Oral presentations also rely heavily on visual aids and are almost always extemporaneous.

2. **Define the concepts of** *general purpose, specific purpose,* **and** *core idea.*

The general purpose of a speech or oral presentation defines the overriding reason for making the communication. These reasons include information, persuasion, and meeting the needs of a special occasion. The specific purpose states as precisely as possible what a speaker hopes to accomplish when he or she addresses an audience. The core idea is a one-sentence statement of the main idea, summarizing what you want your audience to remember after your speech or presentation is over.

3. **Identify the characteristics of effective *audience analysis* for a speech or an oral presentation.**

   Effective audience analysis requires an understanding of what your audience knows and feels about you and your topic. Questionnaires, interviews, and observation are often used to gather this information. The goal of audience analysis is a clear picture of what the audience needs from a speech or presentation.

4. **Describe the purposes and characteristics of an effective *introduction, body,* and *conclusion* for a speech or an oral presentation.**

   The introduction establishes the speaker's credibility; captures attention by means of humor, startling statements, anecdotes, rhetorical questions, quotations, and demonstrations; and previews the main points. The body presents the speaker's main points and supporting material. The conclusion summarizes the speaker's message, extends the message to a broader context, personalizes the message, and, when appropriate, makes a call for future action.

5. **Describe three special requirements of *oral communication.***

   Oral communication requires the repetition of key ideas to aid audience recall. It also requires verbal signposts—in the form of transitions, internal previews, and internal summaries—that signal the organization and structure of a speech or presentation. Finally, it requires word pictures, which are stories linked to the speaker's main points.

6. **Identify the characteristics of a *planning outline* and *speaking notes.***

   The planning outline is used in the preparation of a speech or an oral presentation. It is a full-content outline that includes what you plan to say in the introduction, the body, and the conclusion as well as statements of your specific purpose and core ideas. Speaking notes, which are used in the actual delivery of a speech or an oral presentation, are key-word outlines based on the planning outline.

7. **Describe the different types of *visual aids* used in speeches and oral presentations and identify the elements of effective visual-aid design.**

   Among the visual aids commonly used in speeches and oral presentations are objects and models; flip charts, chalk and writing boards, and posters; handouts; overhead transparencies; slides; and video clips. Visual aids are most effective when they have a simple design, when they are large enough for everyone to read, when they use color effectively, and when they are consistently designed.

8. **Describe four types of *oral delivery.***

   In extemporaneous speaking, speaking notes guide your presentation as you speak without a prepared text. In manuscript reading, remarks are read from a prepared manuscript with little or no opportunity for spontaneity. In memorization, remarks are learned by heart; in impromptu speaking, they are delivered without advance preparation.

9. **Analyze techniques for handling *audience questions.***

   Start by anticipating the questions that might be raised. If you cannot answer a question, say so in a direct way. Learn to finesse questions that you do not want to answer. Handle hostile questions by rephrasing them so they are less confrontational.

REVIEW AND DISCUSSION QUESTIONS

1. Distinguish between speeches and oral presentations. (*Ch. Obj. 1*)
2. Explain what we mean by the terms *general purpose, specific purpose,* and *core idea* in speeches and oral presentations. (*Ch. Obj. 2*)
3. Explain the importance of audience analysis. (*Ch. Obj. 3*)
4. List several questions that you can ask yourself to help in analyzing an audience. (*Ch. Obj. 3*)
5. Name the three basic components of an oral presentation. What are the functions of each? (*Ch. Obj. 4*)
6. What are the three special requirements of oral communication? (*Ch. Obj. 5*)
7. Distinguish between a planning outline and speaking notes. (*Ch. Obj. 6*)
8. As a business speaker, what types of visual aids are available to you? (*Ch. Obj. 7*)
9. What are the four different methods of delivering oral presentations? (*Ch. Obj. 8*)
10. Summarize some basic techniques for handling audience questions. (*Ch. Obj. 9*)

APPLICATION EXERCISES

1. Write a script for an oral presentation in which you discuss the importance of good communication skills, both oral and written, in business. You might include examples of businesspeople whose good communication skills you have seen in action. (*Ch. Obj. 1*)

2. Imagine that someone whom you admire has been invited to receive an award from your school. You've been asked to give a speech in which you introduce this person, describe why the award is being presented, and explain why you admire the recipient. Write down the general purpose, the specific purpose, and the core idea of your presentation. (*Ch. Obj. 2*)

3. Prepare a short (three- to five-minute) special-occasion speech based on your preparation for EXERCISE 2. Your instructor may ask you to deliver this speech to the class. (*Ch. Obj. 1, 5, 8*)

4. Choose a product you enjoy. Plan a five-minute oral presentation in which you persuade your audience (the class) to buy that product. For example, you could sell your favorite performer's latest CD or a great stereo system. Or you could sell advertising time on your favorite TV show by showing your audience how the show does a good job of reaching its target audience.

   Write an outline that lists the three major sections (introduction, body, and conclusion) of your talk. Under each heading, briefly describe how you might accomplish the functions of that section. For instance, how might you establish your credibility and capture your audience's attention during your introduction? (*Ch. Obj. 4, 6*)

5. Prepare and give the presentation that you planned in EXERCISE 4. Use visual aids; you might even want to bring in an example of the product to demonstrate. Give your audience time to ask questions at the end. (*Ch. Obj. 1, 7, 8, 9*)

6. You have been asked to give a presentation to all thirty-two employees of a small company. Included in the audience will be the firm's president, the human-resources staff, the accounting staff, clerical workers, salespeople, advertising copywriters—the entire spectrum of organization members. Describe the challenges involved in giving such a presentation. Write a plan for analyzing your audience and defining its needs. (*Ch. Obj. 3*)

7. Prepare and give an informative presentation to the class on your job or a favorite hobby. If you wish, you may use visual aids. Make the presentation interactive by allowing the audience to ask questions throughout your talk rather than just at the end. (*Ch. Obj. 4*)

8. Attend a speech or an oral presentation. Write an evaluation (approximately two pages) of the speaker's performance. Did the speaker follow the guidelines suggested in this chapter? Did the speech contain an effective introduction, body, and conclusion? Did the speaker use visual aids and handle audience questions effectively? If you feel the speaker could have done a better job, state why you feel that way and suggest specific improvements. (*Ch. Obj. 1, 4, 7, 9*)

9. Research several major business publications for information and forecasts about the U.S. economy for the upcoming year. (Possible sources include *The Wall Street Journal*, *Fortune*, and *Business Week*; a reference librarian can suggest others.) Prepare a script for a summary oral report. Your audience is the president of the company at which you're presently working or one for which you have worked in the past. What types of visual aids would make this presentation more effective? (*Ch. Obj. 3, 6, 7, 8*)

10. Cover the "Audience," "Advantages," and "Disadvantages" columns in Table 14.2. Test yourself on the merits, drawbacks, and ideal audience for each of the formats listed. (*Ch. Obj. 7*)

11. Research and prepare an oral report that discusses the job outlook for students graduating from college this year. What are the "hot" jobs? What are the growing areas of the country and the economy? What qualifications do employers look for? Discuss and compare the outlook for at least three different college majors. What types of visual aids would make your talk more interesting? (*Ch. Obj. 3, 7*)

12. Research and prepare an oral report that advises your classmates on how to conduct an effective job search. Include such topics as researching employers, conducting informational interviews, designing good résumés, performing well in job interviews, and following up after job interviews. What types of visual aids would be good for this presentation? (*Ch. Obj. 3, 7*)

13. Think of some procedure or operation at your school that you feel could be improved. (Registration? Housing assignments? The library? The cafeteria? Curricula? Parking? Dormitories?) Prepare the script for an oral

presentation to the school's administrators in which you explain both why this item needs improvement and how you would improve it. Make your plan practical and convincing. Your instructor will determine the length of your presentation and may ask you to give your talk to the class. (*Ch. Obj. 3, 4*)

14. Choose a piece of legislation that has a big impact on business (possibilities: the Civil Rights Act of 1991; tax laws; environmental regulations; the Fair Credit Reporting Act). Write the script for an oral presentation that discusses the provisions of this law and the ways it affects business and consumers. Be sure to present all sides of the issue along with the appropriate evidence. Include effective visual aids. Your instructor will determine the length of your presentation and may ask you to give your talk to the class. (*Ch. Obj. 3, 7*)

15. What type of oral delivery would you use in each of the following situations? (*Ch. Obj. 8*)

    a. You prepare an oral report on different types of accounting software currently on the market and present the report to a committee of seven people.

    b. You accept an award from the local chapter of the American Marketing Association with a short speech of thanks.

    c. You present a highly detailed technical report on your firm's computer system.

    d. At a staff meeting, your boss unexpectedly asks you for a brief status report on your latest project.

*B*UILDING YOUR RESEARCH SKILLS

Go to a library and research a business-related topic that interests you. Your research should include reading at least three articles or chapters from books, not including this textbook. Prepare a short (three- to five-minute) oral presentation summarizing your research. Be sure to include an introduction, a body, and a conclusion.

*B*UILDING YOUR TEAMWORK SKILLS

Your instructor will divide the class into pairs or small groups. Each member of the group should take turns presenting his or her talk to the others. After each presentation, the group should critique the presentation and make constructive suggestions for improvement. For instance, was the introduction effective? If not, how could it be improved? Remember to state your criticism tactfully; after all, your turn is coming up.

*C*OMMUNICATING IN A WORLD OF DIVERSITY

The Americans with Disabilities Act of 1990 requires businesses to be accessible to physically challenged people. It also prohibits discrimination against them.

Research and prepare a script for a three- to five-minute talk that discusses the steps that companies can take to meet the needs of physically challenged customers and employees. Discuss the ways in which the Act might affect recruitment, hiring, and training practices. You could also discuss changes in physical facilities (parking lots, building layouts) that would be required by the law.

The Benchmark in Borrowing at Mellon Bank

A recent *Fortune* article called it a way "to steal the best ideas around." *Benchmarking*, said the magazine, is the "art of finding out, in a perfectly legal and aboveboard way, how others do something better than you do so you can imitate—and perhaps improve upon—their techniques." Firms like Toyota, AT&T, IBM, Mellon Bank, Xerox, and Milliken use it as a standard tool for improving productivity and quality. In some quarters, it's referred to as "borrowing," as in the cheerful admission of textile maker Milliken & Co. "We borrow shamelessly," reports the company's CEO.

Mellon Bank, for instance, targeted its procedures for handling credit-card billing disputes as an area in need of benchmarking. Mellon appointed a team of eight employees from different departments, including four who ordinarily handled such disputes, and gave them the authority to change the process. Meeting once a week, the team benchmarked seven other companies, including several credit-card firms, an airline, and a competing bank. By visiting three of its benchmark companies and talking to representatives from the others on the phone, the team picked up several ideas about improving the bank's credit-card service.

One ongoing service problem was locating documents when customers registered complaints. Because clerks had to search numerous possible sites, this step alone often took three to four days. At other companies, better software enabled clerks to view all relevant documents at once on a computer terminal. Benchmark companies also maintained "help desks" staffed by experienced employees who could tell customers the exact status of their complaints.

Mellon adopted these improvements and several others. The result in 1992 was a drastic fall in complaints outstanding from 5,200 in December to 2,200 in June. Borrowed procedures also reduced the amount of time necessary to resolve complaints from an average of forty-five to twenty-five days.

Questions and Applications

1. What is *benchmarking*?
2. Plan and research an oral presentation on benchmarking; your audience will be the president of the company for which you work (or one for which you have worked in the past). Research the benchmarking procedures of various firms, learning what they've gained from the strategy and what they've determined to be the best ways to use it. (Be sure to consult other sources in addition to this textbook and the *Fortune* article cited here.) Develop specific suggestions for how your employer could apply benchmarking. What procedures/ problems would you target first? Draft a general purpose, a specific purpose, and a core idea for this presentation.
3. Write a script for your presentation. Be sure to tell your audience what benchmarking is and how it can benefit a company. What visual aids would be effective for this talk?

Source: Jeremy Main, "How to Steal the Best Ideas Around," *Fortune*, October 19, 1992, pp. 102–6.

Nordstrom Takes a Hard Look at the Corporate Culture

With sixty-eight upscale stores located nationwide, Nordstrom is one of the country's leading retailers. By 1992, however, Nordstrom management knew that it had a problem.

Several minority employees at the company's downtown Seattle store had filed discrimination complaints with the Equal Employment Opportunity Commission. Four former African-American employees had filed a $113-million discrimination lawsuit against Nordstrom, claiming that they had been fired on the basis of race. One of the plaintiffs was Jim Nicholson, former manager of the downtown Seattle store, who was fired after accusing the company of ignoring federal affirmative-action policies. In addition, black residents in the Seattle area had complained that Nordstrom security guards followed them around while they were shopping. One former employee referred to Nordstrom as a "racist company that's got the idea they can destroy people's lives."

Nordstrom management hired Tom Nesby as an outside consultant to analyze the firm's corporate culture. Nesby interviewed hundreds of store employees, asking them to describe Nordstrom, the shoppers to whom it caters, and the personal characteristics of employees who were likely to be promoted at company outlets. Nesby's conclusion: the "Nordstrom look" referred to a woman who was young, blonde, and fair-skinned, with a slim, athletic build and a middle- to upper-class background. Above all, she projected an image of sorority-girl enthusiasm.

When Nesby presented his findings to a group of top executives, the entire room fell silent. Some problems at company stores fell into perspective. For example, although Nordstrom had wanted to promote more minority employees, it couldn't seem to attract and retain qualified candidates. The chain had tried to attract more minority customers but had met with little success. "The Nordstrom look," observed Nesby, "didn't include people of color. It sent a subliminal message that if you were a person of color, you wouldn't fit."

Marilyn Gist, a professor at the University of Washington, agrees. Thumbing through Nordstrom catalogs, she found that most of the models were white; even the rare minority models tended to have light skin and conform to what Gist calls a "European standard of beauty.... I was basically left with the impression," says Gist, "that this company was not comfortable with a diverse society."

Questions and Applications

1. Describe the "Nordstrom look."
2. Imagine that you're Tom Nesby and that Nordstrom management has asked you to present an oral report to summarize your findings on the "Nordstrom look." Nordstrom wants to know why this perception has become a problem for the company; management wants you to suggest solutions. Start by researching the practices by which other companies have encouraged cultural diversity among employees and customers. Then write your general purpose, specific purpose, and core idea for your presentation.
3. Write a script for this oral report. What visual aids would be helpful in your presentation?

Source: "Diversity in Style—Nordstrom is Fashioning a New Look That Includes People of Color." *The Seattle Times*, January 19, 1992, E-1.

Communicating at Formal Meetings, by Telephone, and during Informal Conversations

CHAPTER OBJECTIVES

After studying this chapter, you should be able to:

1 List the responsibilities of a *meeting leader*.

2 Classify *formal meetings* according to seven general purposes.

3 Describe a *simple agenda* and a *formal agenda*.

4 Identify the responsibilities of a *meeting participant*.

5 Explain the purpose and content of *meeting minutes*.

6 Describe the *mechanics of a meeting* and their influence on a meeting's outcome.

7 Explain the steps in the *negotiating process*.

8 List ways to improve *informal business conversations*.

9 Describe methods for improving *telephone communication*.

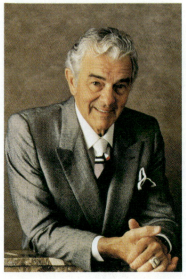

AL NEUHARTH CALLS A MEETING OF THE MINDS

Making something happen in business typically means calling a meeting. A case in point: the creation of *USA Today*, the country's only full-color national newspaper.

When Al Neuharth, CEO of the Gannett newspaper chain, conceived of the idea for *USA Today*, he held a series of meetings to build a companywide consensus. He began by calling together the Office of the Chief Executive, a group composed of Gannett's top decision makers: John E. Heselden, president of the newspaper division; John C. Quinn, Gannett's chief news executive; and Douglas H. McCorkindale, chief financial and legal officer. As their meetings unfolded, it became clear that while McCorkindale wanted to analyze the year that was ending, Neuharth had other plans.

"Let's talk about next year and the future," he argued. "Our business is changing.... If we want to stay in front, we've got to be building more—either on what we already have or some new ventures from the ground up. We need to spend some money and time on research. Figure out how to harness the satellite to help us deliver and sell more of what we have or can produce.... Maybe a national newspaper."

"How much money?" McCorkindale asked.

"I'm only thinking of a million or so for research next year," Neuharth replied. A million dollars was a relatively small sum for a media giant like Gannett, and Neuharth's tone was low-keyed.

McCorkindale didn't quibble with the amount, but he wanted to know more. "How will the money be spent? Who will you hire? What will you explore?"

"Doug, I'll figure out how to spend it," answered Neuharth with authority. "You figure out how to budget it."

When the meeting ended, Neuharth speculated about the impact that he had made on each participant. McCorkindale, he thought, was ready to say yes, believing that if the scheme were crazy, there was still time to kill it. Heselden was also ready but cautious. Quinn, Neuharth's staunchest ally, was solidly behind the plan.

Meeting number two took place a month later. This time, the participants were Gannett's Board of Directors. With profits up more than 19 percent from the previous year, the Board was in a good mood and receptive to a new project. Yet Neuharth had planned a cautious strategy to get the Board's support. He waited until the last item on the agenda, "Other Business," to reveal his plan.

"We're going to establish a task force of a few of our brightest young executives," Neuharth began. "They'll study what's new in newspapers and television. And especially whether we can harness the satellite to deliver more news to more people in more ways. We've set aside about a million dollars for the [research-

and-development] work. Hopefully, before the year is out, we'll have some interesting possibilities to kick around with you."

Although Neuharth's plans were monumental, his approach was understated. During the early stage of his plan, he didn't want to tell the Board any more than he had to. Nor did he want to ask the Board to act before he himself was ready.

Two years later, Neuharth was ready. On December 15, 1981, the Gannett Board voted to launch *USA Today*. Although it would be another year before the paper actually hit the newsstands, Neuharth believed that an early signoff on the project signaled a commitment from the Board, even during the costly startup period. "No matter how cruel the criticism or how red the ink got in those early years," Neuharth recalls, the early signoff meant that the Board was "determined to stay with 'their' project until it succeeded."[1]

Using the mechanism of the company meeting, Al Neuharth had built an increasingly broad foundation for his revolutionary idea for a national newspaper. Knowing both the personalities and agendas of meeting participants and the psychology of group behavior, he had introduced information when he thought it appropriate and held it back when he thought it wise. Most of all, he knew how to make business meetings work for him—how to lead a group to the end that he desired. Using a combination of planning, strategy, and an understanding of human nature, he had articulated his vision while maintaining a clear leadership hold.

CHAPTER OVERVIEW

Although few people in or out of business are as accomplished at meeting strategy as Al Neuharth, we can all do a great deal to get the most out of every meeting we attend. This chapter provides insight into the art of effective oral communication during *formal business meetings*. It also focuses on improving communication during *informal meetings* that may take place either over the phone or in face-to-face business encounters.

FORMAL BUSINESS MEETINGS

Depending on your company and position, you may spend between 25 percent and 40 percent of your time in formal meetings—or more.[2] At Xerox, managers meet about 70 percent of the time. It is not surprising, then, that a recent survey of 2,000 business leaders found that considerably more time is now spent in meetings than five years ago.[3] **Formal meetings** are meetings that involve a leader and participants, are prearranged, and have specific stated goals.

Formal meetings may be internal or external. While **internal meetings** involve only company personnel, **external meetings** also include outsiders. For example, when the Oral-B Laboratories unit of Gillette Co. wanted to increase consumer demand for toothbrushes, managers no doubt held internal marketing meetings to evaluate different ideas. After the company had devised the Indicator brush (a toothbrush with a patch of blue bristles that fade to white when a replacement is needed), additional internal meetings were undoubtedly held to price the product and determine a marketing plan. External meetings with advertisers and retailers were then called to plan strategies for introducing the product to consumers.

All meetings, of course, take time—time to prepare, time to meet, time to pursue agreed-upon tasks. According to George David Kieffer, an authority on business meetings, "When someone in your office asks if you're available for a half-hour meeting this afternoon, don't be fooled. In all likelihood you will be allocating at least two hours of your time and forgoing far more than one-half hour doing something else.... Every meeting leverages your time, so you must make sure you leverage it wisely."[4]

formal meeting
Prearranged meetings with stated goals and involving a leader and participants

internal meeting
Formal meeting that involves only personnel within an organization

external meeting
Formal meeting that involves outsiders as well as company personnel

A Word About Staying Focused.

If there's one thing we've learned in the past hundred years, it's this: You'll never reach your goal if you take your eye off the ball.

Which is why we stick to these fundamentals: Listen. Concentrate on the client's needs. Zero in on the best plan of action. Then, follow through as promised. No excuses. No missed deadlines.

No wonder we're one of America's top accounting, tax and consulting firms. We're Deloitte & Touche. A world-class organization that never loses sight of our clients' needs.

Deloitte & Touche

Accounting, Tax and Consulting Services

We Listen. We Deliver.

Deloitte Touche Tohmatsu International

In recent years, the so-called "Big Six" accounting firms, including Deloitte & Touche, have actually made the effective external meeting and professional communication with clients a hallmark of industry-wide quality control. For example, programs at Coopers & Lybrand and Arthur Andersen require auditors to be especially responsive to clients' information about various environments in which they perform, and Price Waterhouse gives Client Service Awards to auditors who are especially attuned to clients' accounting procedures and long-term goals.

One way to ensure that meeting time is well spent is to decide whether a meeting is really necessary. Before scheduling a meeting, ask yourself whether the work can be accomplished without it, whether an informational memo will suffice, or whether the same result can be achieved by calling two or three people on the phone. Bennett Cerf, co-founder of Random House, was famous for leaving the room every time a meeting was called—he believed that working alone was the only way to get things done in a creative and personal field like publishing.[5] Although there are good reasons to call meetings—even in publishing—Cerf's point is well-taken: If you can accomplish something on your own, don't call a meeting.

When you do call or attend a meeting, remember that the way you communicate in group sessions tells others how competent you are. During every meeting you attend, whether as a leader or a participant, others judge your communication and "people" skills. They also judge your knowledge and ability to solve problems while working as part of a team. Most importantly, they judge your ability to get the job done—to work with people who have diverse opinions but who are trying to reach the same goal. "Any time you're in a meeting," says former Norton Simon Industries CEO Harold M. Williams, "you're sending a message about who you are, what your abilities are, and what league you belong in. Whether I'm dealing with employees or international business associates, I am always evaluating the people at the table with a view to future responsibilities and relationships."[6]

Meetings are a kind of theater where managers observe and evaluate the performance and progress of key players. Even in the most ordinary meeting (a weekly staff meeting, for example), what you say and how you say it demonstrate whether you are ready for more responsibility—or less.

No one person can accomplish much if they don't work with others.
Daniel Levinson
Chief Justice, U.S. Merit
Systems Protection Board

Although there are many good reasons to have meetings, there are also many bad ones. Meetings can be substitutes for work, arenas for gossip, or mechanisms for avoiding personal responsibility or demonstrating power. Nevertheless, the potential benefits are enormous. Bringing together people with diverse abilities and opinions can achieve amazing results.

The communication that takes place within meetings can be defined by each individual's role as *leader* or *participant*. In this section, we will thus discuss the nature of these roles in some detail. We will also describe the role played by *meeting minutes* and the nature and function of *meeting mechanics*.

Leading a Meeting

Leading a meeting involves the ability and responsibility to communicate in a variety of ways. While many of the following leadership responsibilities apply to all meetings, some apply only in special situations.

DEFINING AND LIMITING TASKS   Much as you define a general purpose for written documents, speeches, and oral presentations, you must define the function of the meetings that you chair. Believing that group activities will somehow find their own focus may well be your first—and biggest—mistake. It is the leader's responsibility to make sure that each participant understands the purpose of a meeting. "I'm stunned," says television producer David Corvo, "by the number of people who don't know what kind of meeting they're in. One of the best examples is when the boss convenes a meeting to convey a decision that has already been reached, and a staff member persists in debating the decision. The time for that is past! You're in the wrong meeting. This meeting is informational and delegatory. By continuing to question the decision, you are only showing your own poor judgment and insensibility to the boss's purpose and needs."[7]

Being an effective meeting leader also means recognizing what the group can and cannot do. For example, entry-level managers do not develop company policy because it is not within their province. Similarly, corporate directors generally do not gather information—this job usually is done at a lower organizational level.

Task definition also requires task limitation. Because trying to do too much almost always ensures failure, it is critical to limit the purpose of a meeting. Each of the following types of meetings has different basic goals. Although two or more of these goals can be combined under certain conditions, it is generally wise to call separate meetings when goals get too broad or prove incompatible.

TO GIVE OR EXCHANGE INFORMATION   In **informational meetings**, information is delivered to participants by means of oral reports. Reports are most effective when they clarify written information that participants have already received rather than present information for the first time.

informational meeting
Formal meeting in which information is delivered to participants by means of oral reports

TO DEVELOP NEW IDEAS   In **brainstorming sessions**, new ideas are suggested in an open, nonauthoritarian atmosphere. For example, to develop innovative child-care solutions for their employees, forty companies, including IBM, Exxon, Amoco, Tenneco, and Johnson & Johnson, recently held a brainstorming session in Greenwich, Connecticut.[8]

brainstorming session
Group process of generating new ideas in an open nonjudgmental, nonauthoritarian atmosphere

decision-making meeting
Formal meeting called to debate issues and make decisions

delegating meeting
Formal meeting in which specific tasks are assigned to individuals or groups who are then responsible for their completion

My definition of a leader…is a man who can persuade people to do what they don't want to do, or do what they are too lazy to do, and like it.

Harry S. Truman
Thirty-third President of the United States

collaborative meeting
Formal meeting in which participants work together to prepare memos, letters, or reports or to develop projects

persuasive meeting
Formal meeting involving presentations designed to achieve group concensus or support for a course of action

inspirational meeting
Formal meeting that attempts to build enthusiam toward the company and its products, encourage teamwork, or generally improve organizational morale or interaction

No one's a leader if there are no followers.

Malcolm Forbes
American publisher

TO MAKE DECISIONS   **Decision-making meetings** bring people and companies together to debate issues and make decisions, often by taking votes. Before building a $2-million child-care center in Charlotte, North Carolina, for example, IBM, American Express, Allstate, and Duke Power held decision-making meetings to finalize the deal.[9] Decision-making meetings are usually held to reconcile conflicting views and generally should not be used to gather information. In most cases, information should be collected as advance preparation for the decision-making stage.

TO DELEGATE WORK OR AUTHORITY   Even when job responsibilities have already been assigned (perhaps over the phone or by memo), a delegating meeting may be necessary to clarify specific details. In **delegating meetings**, specific tasks are assigned to individuals or groups who are then responsible for their completion. For example, meetings were undoubtedly called when Hardee's purchased 648 Roy Rogers restaurants from Marriott Corp. in 1990 and converted outlets in Washington, DC, and Baltimore to the Hardee's name. When business dropped significantly after what was literally an overnight name switch, the company wanted to know why. While one or more people may have been assigned the job of investigating the decline, others may have been delegated the responsibility for developing a different conversion plan in other locations.

Meetings to delegate are often followed by informational and decision-making meetings. Hardee's solution to its problem—easing consumers into the conversion by using both the Hardee's and Roy Rogers names—was probably the result of decision-making meetings in which managers debated the solutions proposed by managers who had been delegated to formulate a strategy.[10]

TO COLLABORATE   In **collaborative meetings**, participants work together to prepare memos, letters, or reports or to develop projects. Collaborative efforts, however, usually succeed only when participants work together as teams. Efforts may be doomed if group members have trouble completing joint assignments.

TO PERSUADE   **Persuasive meetings** involve oral presentations designed to achieve group consensus or support for a course of action. Purchasers and office managers, for example, may hold persuasive meetings to discuss and debate the merits of several competing office-equipment suppliers.

TO INSPIRE AND BUILD ENTHUSIASM   **Inspirational meetings** attempt to build enthusiasm toward the company and its products, encourage teamwork, or generally improve organizational morale or interaction. Inspiration, argues Mary Kay Ash, founder and chairman of Mary Kay Cosmetics, is the heart of her company's many sales meetings:

> The most important weekly events in our organization are the sales directors' unit sales meetings. Monday morning is the best time for these meetings, because it marks a 'new beginning….' In addition to being informative, these meetings provide both inspiration and motivation. Even if the last week's sales were poor, here's a new week to start fresh. We often say, 'If you had a bad week, *you* need the sales meeting; if you had a good week, the sales meeting needs *you*!' When a consultant leaves a sales meeting full of enthusiasm, she has an entire week to let that enthusiasm work for her.[11]

CHOOSING PARTICIPANTS   With your broad purpose in mind, you are ready to choose the participants for your meeting. Group communication works best when everyone in attendance has a reason for being there and can contribute to the discussion. For example, when more than one person has the same expertise or point of view, it may be wise to simplify communication by choosing only one. For the best results, limit the group to no more than ten to twelve people. A meeting half that size makes communication even easier. As AFL-CIO president Lane Kirkland once said, "the usefulness of any meeting is inversely proportional to the size of the group."[12]

Corporate culture may also affect who may and may not be invited to a meeting. In formal, highly stratified companies, meetings are usually attended

At Mary Kay Cosmetics, Mary Kay Ash regards the inspirational sales meeting as a direct reflection of corporate culture. She is "proud," she declares, "to be associated with … the finest sales organization in the world," and the motivational attitude is borne out in the company's expression of formal values—in management attitude and behavior, not simply in mission and policy statements. Successful salespeople are rewarded with lavish gifts, and although Mary Kay sales directors can earn substantially more than their counterparts at Avon, they are expected to motivate subordinates by supporting them in their field work.

by people from the same organizational level. For example, all seven attendees at a planning meeting might be vice presidents. In less structured companies, there is often less emphasis on seniority and position, with participants more likely to span the entire organization.

SETTING MEETING TIMES   Meetings are often defined by how long they take as well as by what they accomplish. Show your awareness of time by establishing as soon as possible times when a meeting will begin and end, and sending this information to participants in memo form. This practice encourages punctuality and pressures people to close meetings on time. Placing time limitations on specific agenda items may also help focus the discussion.

Most meetings last too long—a tendency that made Thomas Theobold, CEO of Continental Illinois Corporation, declare that his company meetings would improve communication by starting "about halfway through." For one thing, the longer the meeting, the greater the likelihood of environmental and internal distractions. When participants are called away for phone calls or begin focusing on other things ("I can't wait for this to be over so I can finish my marketing report"), real communication is over.

The best way to shorten a meeting is to remember why the meeting was called in the first place. Alan Miller, COO of the Original New York Selzer Co., often stops presenters after about two minutes and asks, "How are you going to increase the market share of this company?" A question like this forces participants to focus on meeting goals.[13]

CREATING AN AGENDA   An **agenda** is a written document that defines the meeting by telling participants why it was called and what it should accomplish. By urging or requiring people both to prepare in advance for a specific type of discussion and to focus on that discussion while the meeting is underway, the agenda exerts a powerful force both before and during the meeting. In a sense, the agenda is the leader's promise to the participants that the meeting will deal with specific issues. Regardless of the size or length of a meeting, an agenda is needed. Generally speaking, agendas may be *simple* or *formal*.

SIMPLE AGENDAS   Typically used for short meetings with few participants, **simple agendas** are written documents that outline meeting goals without describing the sequence of meeting events. Say, for example, that you and two

agenda
Written document that defines a meeting by telling participants why it was called and what it should accomplish

simple agenda
Agenda that outlines meeting goals without describing the sequence of meeting events

other members of your department are assigned the task of investigating child-care options for company employees. As the group leader, you call a half-hour meeting to delegate responsibility and set a schedule. You announce the meeting in a memo, along with the date, time, and place. Although the meeting is short, the project is important, so you also include an agenda like the one in Figure 15.1.

formal agenda
Agenda that schedules the order of meeting business and the approximate time allotted to each scheduled item

FORMAL AGENDAS   When you call a larger meeting, a formal agenda is probably required. **Formal agendas** are written documents that schedule the order of business and the approximate time allotted to each agenda item. When you distribute a memo to call the meeting, place the formal agenda on a separate sheet and send it to participants several days in advance to give everyone time to prepare. Figure 15.2 is a sample formal agenda for a book-planning meeting.

In a meeting that involves various presentations, talk with each presenter in advance to find out how much time he or she will need. The final agenda should reflect input from everyone participating in the meeting.

CONVENING THE MEETING   Because convening the meeting is your first act of control in front of the group, you should do it with direction and purpose. Open the meeting by restating the specific tasks you hope to accomplish. Although this information is part of your agenda, repetition will focus group attention. Your

---

ARROWHEAD PRESS

5800 Cornfield Lane
Bridgeport, CT 06443   (203) 555-5169

MEMORANDUM

To: Ann Hagerty and Juan Hernandez
From: Ariane Alexander
Date: January 15, 1994
Subject: Meeting to delegate responsibility for child-
           care project

Let's have our first meeting on January 22, at 3:00 P.M. in my office.

   Agenda:

■ Delegating responsibilities
■ Setting a schedule to meet management's February 7 deadline
■ Setting dates for future meetings

Call me if you have a time conflict.

FIGURE 15.1   *Simple Agenda*

ARROWHEAD PRESS

5800 Cornfield Lane
Bridgeport, CT 06443   (203) 555-5169

Meeting Agenda

Meeting purpose: To introduce new authors to the book
                    planning process
Participants: Lucy Reinhardt, Michael Narad. Lanny
                    Fox, Andrew Scarella, Nathan
                    Arington, Beth Schnapp. Emily
                    Gopstein, and Barabara Willis
Date and time: October 15, 1994, 9:00 A.M.-4:00 P.M.
Place: Board Room

Order of Business

1. 8:55 Introductions. General comments

2. 9:00-10:00 Table of Contents, chapter organiza-
    tion, review of competition

    10:00-10:15 Break

3. 10:15-11:15 Unique content ideas. design ideas,
    pedagogical elements

4. 11:15-12:15 Book development process. Writing
    procedure, number of drafts, review plan

    12:30-1:45 Lunch

5. 2:00-2:30 Production. Manuscript turnover/sched-
    ules, design and pedagogical elements pertaining
    to production

6. 2:30-3:30 Marketing/sales. In-stock data, market-
    ing/advertising ideas

7. 3:30-4:00 Book supplements

FIGURE 15.2   *Formal Agenda*

statement should be positive and forward-looking even if problems are anticipated. (Never start by apologizing for previous mistakes or blaming others for problems.) Convening the meeting on time shows determination to get the job done.

Let's suppose in the next few sections that you are the leader of a decision-
making meeting called to explore the possibility of a reserved-ticket policy for a
chain of movie theaters.

FOCUSING THE GROUP'S PROGRESS   Use your agenda to focus the direction
to be taken by the meeting. Problems arise when participants fail to stay on the
topic—when attention drifts to peripheral issues or personal concerns. For example, if one of your participants starts voicing personal concerns or experiences, it
may be necessary to say something like, "Nick, I'd really like to hear about that
restaurant—after the meeting. Right now, let's talk about...." Be polite and
friendly but determined to keep the group on track. Take the same tack if a participant leads the group down an unrelated business path.

Participants who ramble waste precious meeting time. Instead of making
statements in concise, focused ways, some people talk around a subject, never
quite getting to the point. When you encounter ramblers, summarize what you
think they have said and, if necessary, pose a question designed to point them in
a specific direction. For example:

John, you've been telling us about Loews Theaters' early experience with advance movie ticketing in New York. With only 6 percent of all purchases made in advance, the system seems shaky at best. What does Loews project for the future?[14]

If the question is focused and direct, the answer should be, too:

My sources tell me that Loews is working on the assumption that when word gets out about the service, one out of four people will reserve their movie tickets in advance.

Summaries can also be used to move the group forward. An effective group leader thus looks for signs of confusion—puzzled looks, questions asking for clarification, signs of drifting attention. Whenever necessary, the leader can interject a summary, restating what the group has accomplished, what is now being discussed, and where the discussion is heading.

ENCOURAGING ACTIVE PARTICIPATION   In many groups, a few people seem to dominate the conversation while others rarely say a word. A group leader typically tries to balance these contributions—to encourage ceaseless talkers to say less and quiet types to say more. Without intervention, the meeting could become a platform for one person's point of view and a true consensus might never be achieved.

Participants who say little can be encouraged to participate by means of specific direct questions. For example:

Anita, you are our computer expert. Will adding a reserve-seat policy tax our existing computer system? Will we have to upgrade?

Often, when people start talking about an area they know well, confidence and competence come to the fore. Although participation cannot be forced, you can make sure that the climate is positive and opportunities abundant.

Handling an overzealous contributor may be more difficult. Start with the direct approach:

Dan, as you can see on the agenda, we have a lot to cover in two hours. I can only give you five more minutes to discuss these survey results.

If this approach fails, redirect the discussion to another person. If necessary, interrupt the person and say something like:

Your survey points to the need to communicate our policy shift to consumers. Deborah, can you fill us in on the advertising plan?

When the lion fawns upon the lamb, the lamb will never cease to follow him.

William Shakespeare

SETTING THE TONE   As the leader, you set the tone for the meeting through your fairness, work ethic, and control. The following strategies usually contribute to successful meetings.

RECOGNIZING EVERYONE'S CONTRIBUTION   Not surprisingly, participants who feel that their contributions are valuable and well received will contribute more and better work. Even if a proposal is questionable, therefore, focus on its positive aspects and lead the group forward. For example, you might say something like:

Jean, your idea of using a service like MovieFone, which provides free hardware and software to theaters for advance credit-card purchases, is a good one. But I can't get past the $1 fee they charge for every ticket. How much are people willing to pay for a movie? Andy, what does your research tell you about pricing?

MAINTAINING HIGH STANDARDS   Don't accept slipshod work or opinions that masquerade as facts. You may have to confront participants whose statements lack support:

Andy, what you've just given us is the story of one woman who said she wouldn't pay extra to call ahead and charge her tickets on her MasterCard. What I'm looking for are broader research results. Have you conducted any surveys?

When too many participants are unprepared with the information that the group needs, a postponement may be necessary.

MAINTAINING ORDER   Follow your agenda as the discussion moves through the various meeting stages. At the conclusion of each item, summarize points of agreement and disagreement, including any actions that will be taken. These internal summaries improve communication and make it likely that everyone will leave the meeting with the same message.

Maintaining order also involves silencing whisperers. Allow only one person to speak at a time and discourage private conversations.

HANDLING DIFFICULT PEOPLE   Unfortunately, handling difficult people may be the single greatest challenge faced by any meeting leader. Because you do not often get to handpick participants, sooner or later you will find yourself face-to-face with an **obstructionist**—someone whose personality or hidden agenda threatens group success. According to various observers of business-meeting behavior, obstructionists tend to be *blamers, boilers,* or *know-it-alls.* The following suggestions are designed to help you control situations involving these difficult people.

BLAMERS   Criticizing ideas and even making personal attacks, **blamers** are participants who focus on problems rather than solutions. To counter this aggressive behavior, try sitting next to a blamer at a meeting and make him or her part of the group's "inner circle." When a blamer makes cutting remarks, resist the temptation to strike back. Wait a few seconds and then try responding in a positive, conciliatory way.

Former Transportation Secretary and White House Chief of Staff Samuel K. Skinner once found himself engaged in settlement negotiations with Exxon chairman Lawrence G. Rawl over the damage done in the 1989 *Exxon Valdez* oil spill. Frustrated by the lack of credit given to Exxon for its $2-billion cleanup effort along the Alaskan coast, Rawl lashed out at negotiators, saying that he was sick and tired of the abuse. Everyone was silent, except Skinner. "Look Larry," he said. "Let's not relive it. If we do, we'll never get past it."[15] Bear in mind, however, that dealing with blamers may not be as easy as it seems in the hands of a skilled negotiator like Sam Skinner. It often requires a planned strategy with rehearsed questions and language.

BOILERS   **Boilers** are group participants who typically respond with anger when they do not get their way. Justified or not, these outbursts can destroy a meeting. Whether the anger is directed at you or someone else, your job as meeting leader is to depersonalize the attack. Business-negotiation experts Juliet Nierenberg and Irene S. Ross believe that self-control is a key element in handling anger: "You can protect your self-esteem," they advise,

> by reminding yourself that the tantrum is a matter of style, and doesn't indicate a particular antagonism toward you. [The person] probably persists because explosions always get results for him, and so he is not likely to change. Your problem is to stand up to him without upping the ante. Adopt good eye contact and a firm stance. Calmly allow him to wind down before you speak, and then deal in unemotional facts on a corrective basis. [Say something like], "What would you like me to do to correct the error?"[16]

Remember that anger can be a method of manipulation—boilers may rant and rave until someone gives in. Resist the temptation, therefore, to restore peace at a high price by promising boilers—or anyone who has become angry—that you will discuss the problem later when tempers have cooled. When you refuse to make on-the-spot concessions, you rob them of their control and initiative.

obstructionist
Meeting participant whose personality or hidden agenda threatens group success

blamers
Meeting participants who focus on problems rather than solutions

boilers
Meeting participants who typically respond with anger when they do not get their way

know-it-alls
Meeting participants who
try to control meetings,
often by leading partici-
pants in directions that
they prefer regardless of
group goals

KNOW-IT-ALLS   Believing they have all the answers before the meeting begins, **know-it-alls** are participants who try to control meetings, often by leading participants in directions that they prefer regardless of group goals. Deal with know-it-alls by establishing in advance equal speaking time for everyone in the room; you can also try to make allies of know-it-alls before the meeting begins.

HELPING TO IMPROVE DECISION MAKING   When participants are reluctant to make decisions, the leader must try to move them forward. For example, you might start by asking a probing question:

Does anyone need more information about how the reserve-seat system works?

Very often, those who persist in making requests for further information— or in otherwise going over ground that you have already covered—are also preventing a decision. When the information is available, the leader can summarize it as succinctly as possible:

Now that the volume-pricing issue has been clarified, we can make a decision.

When the information is not readily available, you may have to postpone the decision for another meeting. If allowed to go on too long, requests for additional information or debating time can cripple a group. If you sense that this is happening, force a decision.

The opposite problem occurs when the group makes a decision before the leader feels it is ready. In such cases, with perhaps one aggressive faction stampeding the whole group toward a premature vote, you might find facts to be less important than emotions. Some experts recommend delaying tactics to postpone action. For example:

*The first EDSer [Electronic
Data Systems employee] to
see a snake kills it. At GM
[General Motors], the first
thing you do is organize a
committee on snakes. Then
you bring in a consultant
who knows a lot about
snakes. Third thing you do is
talk about it for a year.*

*Ross Perot
American entrepreneur
and presidential candidate*

I've listened carefully to all the information, but I still have some questions. Bill, tell me again why you think moviegoers are ready for a reserve-seat plan.

You can also tell the group quite bluntly that you think a decision is premature:

We need more cost information before we can take a vote. I know this is an attractive plan, but we have to justify it to the CEO. Let's get more solid data and meet again next week.

Even if the group does not agree with you, your hesitation will probably delay a decision by generating further discussion.

ENDING THE MEETING   At the end of the meeting, summarize what happened and move the group ahead to future action. Your summary should review the discussion so that everyone understands how the group progressed from thought to action. Items needing further consideration should also be summarized, assignments and deadlines for future work reviewed, and the time and place for the next meeting set. Your goal is for every participant to leave the meeting understanding what is expected.

Table 15.1 summarizes the responsibilities of meeting leaders. It also focuses on some of the common failures that result from the lack of sufficient leadership control.

PROGRESS CHECK

1. Why is it important to make a good impression at meetings?
2. What is an agenda? What purpose does it serve?

Participating in a Meeting

Let's suppose that the head of your company's human resources department has asked you to participate in a meeting to explore cost-saving options in employee benefits. Although you are not running the meeting, you are a group member

TABLE 15.1 *Responsibilities and Common Failures of Meeting Leaders*	
RESPONSIBILITIES	FAILURES
Define the task	Trying to accomplish too much
Choose participants	Including too many people; choosing the wrong people
Define the meeting time	Allowing meetings to last too long
Create an agenda	Being poorly focused and producing a disorganized agenda
Convene the meeting	Starting too late; failing to restate goals
Focus the group's progress	Permitting the discussion to stray from the topic
Encourage active participation	Allowing some people to dominate the meeting and others to say nothing
Set the meeting's tone	Failing to make participants feel valued; allowing slipshod work; permitting disorganization
Handle difficult people	Losing control
Help improve decision making	Failing to reach a decision; making a premature decision
End the meeting	Permitting participants to leave the meeting room unclear as to what is expected of them and what will happen next

because of your expertise on medical insurance and your reputation for active involvement in the human-resources activities of the company.

BEING AN ACTIVE PARTICIPANT   Active participation means that each person is a "part owner" of the meeting. The leader's goal is the group's goal—even when there are different points of view. Joining the leader in being responsible for success requires participants to look forward, not backward, and to channel group energy into accomplishing the task.

This type of participation requires *involvement*—a process that begins before you enter the meeting room. For example, when you receive an agenda telling you that new information about your benefits program will be presented, you can make a list of questions that you would like to ask:

- Are insurance deductibles increasing?
- Will premiums rise?
- Are we going with the same insurance carrier?
- How will our retirees be affected by these changes?

If you learn that the meeting has been called to make a decision, you should come prepared to support your point of view. Perhaps you have access to data showing that reimbursement for such preventive medical care as mammograms and vaccinations saves money as well as lives.

Taking part ownership, therefore, does not mean agreeing with everything that is said by your "partners"—even the managing partners. In fact, with the high cost of meetings today, few managers want to be "yes'd." They feel that if they must bear the expense of a meeting, they should accomplish something that could not be accomplished without the give and take of a meeting. Don Gevertz, chairman of the board and CEO of the Foothill Group, a financial-services company, wishes that

> more of my employees would maintain a greater sense of what we're trying to accomplish in the meetings we have. I'm trying to maintain an objective, but I'm not perfect. I wish they would take as much responsibility for keeping us on track as I have to. If they did, we'd get more done a lot

Don't let your vision get diluted, but don't be afraid of teamwork.

James B. Patterson
CEO,
J. Walter Thompson, USA

PRACTICAL TIPS

Avoiding Groupthink

Psychologist Irving Janis developed his theory of *groupthink* after studying the decision by President John F. Kennedy to launch the Bay of Pigs invasion of Cuba in 1961—an invasion in which 1,400 Cuban exiles tried unsuccessfully to defeat 200,000 Cuban soldiers. According to Janis, all groups have the tendency to take positions they believe their leaders want to hear—even when these positions are flawed or poorly conceived. The group thus tends to move toward uniformity by ignoring or failing to evaluate key information properly, by dismissing warnings that their actions are mistakes, by relying on stereotypes, by rejecting doubts and counterarguments, and by impugning the motives and loyalty of those who raise objections to a proposed course of action.

Does groupthink operate in business? Management consultant Mark H. McCormack thinks so, and he also believes that all group decisions are flawed because of it. "Something happens to people's skepticism when they're gathered in a room with the stated goal of achieving consensus," explains McCormack. "They become too agreeable. They're intimidated by the boss and take positions they think the boss wants to hear. They're reluctant to challenge their allies. After a while, with everyone echoing the same opinion, a group euphoria…takes over. This surreal euphoria often leads people to conclusions that fly in the face of reality."

Janis believes, however, that it is possible to counteract groupthink by taking preventive measures:

- As a meeting leader, surround yourself with people who are not likely to "yes" you; as a participant, define your role in terms of meeting group objectives, not pleasing your manager.
- Be an impartial leader when the meeting

faster. Instead, they put the whole burden on me. They're more interested in saying what they think I want to hear at a given moment than achieving the goal—our goal—for the meeting.[17]

MAKING AN IMPACT   The following suggestions are designed to improve your value as a group participant. They not only reflect an appreciation of organizational and interpersonal skills but also call upon common sense.

1. *Take a position but be willing to change it.* Groups work best when participants are open to new information and different points of view. If you change your mind, explain why—others who share your view may be convinced if they understand the reasons behind the new position.

2. *Be brief, simple, and organized.* Speak in a direct, clear way so that others will want to listen. Clarity increases when you connect your comments to what has already been said. For example: "I agree with Jim that our health-insurance costs are more than we can afford, but I'm not sure passing the total increase on to our employees is the right decision."

3. *Engage in discussion, not argument.* While discussion involves an exchange of ideas, argument often results from heated emotional reactions that leave reason behind. Arguments often start when participants put their ideas ahead of group objectives and refuse to listen to differing points of view. Worse, they become defensive, suggesting that every expression of disagreement is a personal attack. Even when you believe that the group is making a costly error, remain calm as you state your point of view. The moment you begin shouting is the moment you lose credibility. It is also the moment the group stops functioning.

4. *Avoid personal attacks.* Mutual respect is the key to group functioning. When one person says something like, "Only a fool would make that

begins. Leaders who refuse to advocate positions are less likely to encourage groupthink than those who state strong opinions.

■ As a leader, encourage participants both to evaluate their own thinking critically and to air objections and doubts.

■ As a leader, assign one or more members the role of devil's advocate to challenge group thinking.

■ Hold a "second-chance" meeting after a decision has been made to give everyone the opportunity to air residual doubts.

Indeed, studies of group behavior at various organizations reveal that groupthink does not have to be the rule. In their landmark book *In Search of Excellence*, for example, Thomas J. Peters and Robert H. Waterman, Jr., explain what they saw at Exxon and Citibank—companies which, according to these authors, are largely unencumbered by groupthink. "The difference between their behavior and that of their competitors," say Peters and Waterman, "is nothing short of astonishing." After a presentation, they report, "the questions are unabashed; the flow is free; everyone is involved. Nobody hesitates to cut off the chairman, the president, a board member. And how that contrasts with the behavior of most companies we encounter! Senior people...can't seem to do anything other than watch presentations and then politely comment on the contents."

Sources: Irving L. Janis, *Victims of Groupthink: A Psychological Study of Foreign Policy Decisions and Fiascoes* (Boston: Houghton Mifflin, 1972); Mark H. McCormack, *What They Still Don't Teach You at Harvard Business School* (New York: Bantam Books, 1989) pp. 76–77; and Thomas J. Peters and Robert H. Waterman, Jr., *In Search of Excellence: Lessons from America's Best-Run Companies* (New York: Harper & Row, 1982), p. 219.

statement" it becomes impossible for two or more people to work together. When you disagree, criticize the idea, not the person, and try to make your criticism palatable. Being too negative will make it impossible for the group to move forward. Consider the following two statements. Although they both express the same sentiment, the first is inflammatory, the second productive:

> If you had bothered to prepare for this meeting, you would have realized how costly our current medical insurance plan is. It's stupid to suggest continuing with this dinosaur.

> Yes, I agree that our medical plan has worked so far. But our costs have skyrocketed and our needs are changing. Our benefits have to change, too.

Resist the temptation to blame others for mistakes or problems. Pointing a finger only gets people angry and obstructs group goals.

5. *Engage in fair play.* Don't dominate the discussion. Give everyone the opportunity to speak. Ironically, participants who try to seize control undermine their own positions when their behavior is perceived as inconsistent with group goals.

6. *Use nonverbal language to your advantage.* Make eye contact when you begin speaking, speak slowly and calmly even when you are excited, and make sure that your posture communicates authority and confidence. Just as important is paying attention to the nonverbal cues of others—they may tell you what people are really thinking (see Chapter 2 for a more complete discussion of nonverbal communication).

Table 15.2 summarizes the responsibilities and failures of meeting participants.

TABLE 15.2 *Responsibilities and Common Failures of Meeting Participants*	
BE AN ACTIVE PARTICIPANT	FAILING TO REGARD THE GOALS OF THE MEETING AS PERSONAL GOALS
State your position	Remaining uninvolved; choosing not to share your views with the group
Be organized	Rambling from topic to topic; speaking for too long
Be willing to discuss ideas	Arguing with people who disagree
Focus on the topic	Engaging in personal attacks
Engage in fair play	Dominating the discussion and otherwise acting unfairly

Meeting Minutes

meeting minutes
Written record of what occured at a meeting

Meeting minutes are a written record of what occurred at a meeting. They review group activities (the positions of individual members are recorded), measure productivity (the number of decisions that were made is noted), highlight participation (group members with the greatest influence are cited), and summarize the proceedings (a single, cohesive report adds strength to the group's conclusions).

Minutes are written by either the leader or the secretary of the group and distributed to participants and others who request them. The most effective minutes are brief but thorough summaries. They begin with the date, time, and place of the meeting. Depending on the nature of your meeting, the body of the minutes can use the following outline:[18]

Call to order
State where and when the meeting was held and give the name of the meeting leader.

Attendees
List the names and titles of everyone in attendance.

Those absent
List the names of people who were absent.

Previous minutes
State whether minutes from the previous meeting were read, whether any amendments were made and accepted, and whether the minutes were approved.

Agenda and opening
State that the meeting leader reviewed the agenda and made an opening statement that included the following facts (list the facts).

Discussion: Presentation
State the nature of the opening presentation and identify the participant who delivered it.

Discussion: Questions
List the people who asked questions and the nature of their questions.

Discussion: Responses
Relate how these questions were answered.

Discussion: Facts
Describe the discussion that followed the presentation, including the names of those involved and their positions on the issues.

Record of vote
State that the meeting moved to a vote. List those voting in favor and those voting against. Include also any recommendations for different action.

Decision
State how the matter was decided.

APPLYING TECHNOLOGY

Attending a Computerized Meeting

In many companies, there is no greater way to waste time than to attend formal meetings. To make meetings more productive and reduce the number of unstructured, long-winded monologues, some companies are turning to computerized meetings, which involve sophisticated computer software and specially equipped meeting rooms. Instead of speaking, participants make their voices heard through strokes on their keypads. Although some oral discussion may take place, most of the work occurs on the computer screen.

Let's say that you are attending a computerized meeting that has been called to generate new ideas. The meeting begins with everyone brainstorming via computer for the first half hour. Then participants transmit their ideas anonymously to a big screen in front of the meeting room for others to see. Those who have used this technique claim that productivity skyrockets. According to Lynn Reed, vice president for technology at J. P. Morgan & Co., which recently built its own computerized meeting room, "We'll have 10 to 12 managers generating 60 to 100 ideas in half an hour."

Participants then categorize and rank projected ideas in order to come up with a manageable list. Special computer software helps them narrow down their choices by means of a voting system. The result, claims Bruce Ezell, business- development manager at Dell Computer Corporation in Austin, Texas, is a highly productive, focused meeting. "Naming a new product," recalls Ezell, "we got 75 names. We were able to narrow it to 10 names in 45 minutes. On problems where people like to discuss and discuss and discuss, this gives a way to quickly list and prioritize."

Computerized meetings are also effective forums for sharing criticism. For example, each department head at Phoenix-based Greyhound Financial Corp. orally presents annual plans to other department heads, who then type their comments and criticisms into the computer. At the end of the meeting, the presenter leaves with a printout of every casual remark and every piece of constructive criticism. Feedback is immediate. Computerized meetings are also used for group editing of reports and proposals. The process can be extremely fast as participants rewrite sections and choose the best options.

Among the software used in computerized meetings are VisionQuest from Collaborative Technologies Corp., TeamFocus by IBM, and OptionFinder by Optional Technologies. The goal of these software packages is to facilitate an efficient collaborative effort.

Despite its potential, computerized meetings are still a new frontier for many companies; so far, only about two hundred fully equipped meeting rooms have been installed throughout the country. In part, slow growth may be due to the cost—about $200,000 per room. It may also be tied to the reluctance of managers to redefine meeting communication and move from the oral to the written word.

Source: "William M. Bulkeley, "'Computerizing' Dull Meetings Is Touted as an Antidote to the Mouth That Bored," *The Wall Street Journal*, January 28, 1992, pp. B1, B2. Reprinted by permission of *The Wall Street Journal*, © 1992 Dow Jones & Company, Inc. All rights reserved worldwide.

Call for unanimity

    If one was made, describe the call for a unanimous decision.

Record of agreement/disagreement

    State either that the group agreed to a unanimous decision or that certain members (name them) continue to oppose the decision.

Summary

    State that the meeting leader recapped the activity, discussion, and decisions.

Next meeting

    State when and where the next meeting is scheduled and announce those who are scheduled to deliver presentations.

Adjournment

    State the time that the meeting was adjourned.

Mechanics of an Effective Meeting

When peace talks between warring nations are in the news, so are the mechanics of meetings—technical decisions about scheduling, location, table and seating arrangements, and on-time arrival. Before the Israelis and Arabs met in 1991, for example, they first had to agree on where to hold the meeting (Madrid, Spain), the shape of the table (T-shaped), and who would sit across from whom. Far from being trivial, these decisions were necessary for the meeting to take place. Although the mechanics of a meeting may not have the same urgency in business as they do in world politics, they are important because they set the tone for what is to come.

SCHEDULING   Although meetings can be scheduled at any time during the day, some times are preferable to others. The first thing in the morning, right after lunch, and an hour into the day are popular times to schedule meetings. As business becomes more hectic, many more businesspeople now hold working breakfasts, lunches, and dinners. These meetings are often conducted in offices with meals brought in.

Often, meetings are scheduled to accommodate personal working styles. While early risers hold 8:00 A.M. meetings, late workers hold meetings after hours. When scheduling your meeting, consider also the travel needs of meeting participants. An 8:00 A.M. meeting that forces people to get up at 5:30 may be counterproductive. Even if participants do arrive on time, they may be too tired to accomplish anything else during the day. Nevertheless, early-morning scheduling is not unusual. When Chemical Bank holds an 8:00 A.M. meeting in its downtown Manhattan offices instead of its midtown headquarters, participants who live in Connecticut must rise before 5:00 A.M. and catch trains before 6:00 A.M.

If you are having a series of meetings, set the time for the next meeting at the end of the current meeting. Because almost everyone is present, this procedure is the most efficient way to coordinate schedules. To schedule an initial meeting, write a meeting memo instead of using the phone. Trying to work out a schedule by phone can literally take two or three days as you call and recall participants with conflicting schedules.

LOCATION   Deciding where to hold a meeting—in your office, in the conference room, in someone else's office, at an outside location—depends on how much space you need and the kind of environment that is best for the group. For example, even if your office is large enough to seat five, you may need a table to spread out papers; perhaps the overhead projector is available only in the conference room.

Political considerations also affect meetings with clients. Agreeing to go to a client's office, for example, delivers the implicit message that you are committed to his or her needs. Think about the image you want to create and choose your location with that image in mind.

TABLE AND SEATING ARRANGEMENTS   Table and seating choices can either enhance a meeting or create communication barriers. Here are some considerations:

1. The natural place to sit during a meeting in your office is behind your own desk; your papers are there and so is the phone. However, the desk sends an implicit message of control—it says that you are in charge of the discussion. To remove the subtext of power, move to a separate seating area or to a conference room where people can sit across from one another as peers.

2. Position yourself at a conference table so that you can make easy eye contact with influential people—the meeting leader, for example, or a key ally. At a rectangular table, sitting across the table rather than side by side, makes eye contact possible. At a circular table, all positions are equal. With no "good" seats or "bad" ones, there is no obvious seat of control and the discussion can get intense. At a semicircular table, the leader maintains control by virtue of sitting in the center.

3. Even when seating is informal, certain people have traditional places at the table. The leader, for example, usually sits at the head of the table while a key ally or the department manager may sit directly across. To avoid mistakes, wait for key players to be seated before choosing your place.

4. Choose your seat with your own purposes in mind. If you intend to provide input, choose a controlling position (say, toward the head of the table). If you have little to say, choose a spot that allows you to remain relatively unnoticed.

5. Consider also where "troublemakers" will sit. When you expect dissension, orchestrate a seating arrangement that separates troublemakers from one another. Figure 15.3 shows two alternatives. In seating, as in war, "divide and conquer."

ARRIVING   When President François Mitterrand of France attended the 1991 summit of Western leaders, he repeatedly arrived late for official summit sessions. Diplomats suspected that he had planned his lateness. Indeed, many believed that he deliberately timed his arrivals to confer on himself the status of "senior among equals."[19] Such gamesmanship did not endear Mitterrand to the other heads of state, and purposefully arriving late at business meetings is equally a political error. Do your best to arrive on time, but if you cannot, take your seat without interrupting the progress of the meeting.

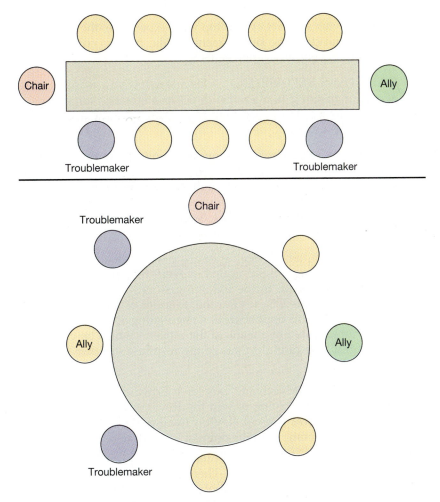

FIGURE 15.3   Seating Arrangements

THE ART OF NEGOTIATING

negotiation
Process of give and take in which both parties try to leave the bargaining table with what they perceives as a "good deal"

Many meetings are held for the specific purpose of making a deal. You negotiate with suppliers for more favorable prices, with prospective clients on contract terms, with your counterparts in other departments to divide the workload on important projects. In every case, the goal is mutual benefit. A **negotiation** is a process of give and take in which both parties try to leave the bargaining table with what they perceive as a "good deal."

Admittedly, negotiations often involve people who personally dislike one another and may even take place between bitter adversaries. When the atmosphere is professional, however, opposing positions and negative feelings are beside the point—ultimately, all participants are trying to achieve something that benefits them by finding a common ground that is acceptable to everyone.

Mutual benefit, for example, characterized negotiations in 1991 between a United Way fund raiser and a group of truckers. At a 6:00 A.M. meeting, the fund raiser handed out pledge cards and pencils to the truckers and asked for contributions. A particularly grumpy driver stood up and told the fund raiser what he could do with the pencil. Keeping his negotiating goal in mind (raising money), the fund raiser calmly replied, "I'll be happy to do whatever you like with that pencil *after* you sign the pledge card." The comment disarmed the group and convinced everyone—even the disgruntled driver—to make a pledge. In the end, both sides won.[20]

Negotiating Structure

Although negotiating styles and tactics develop with experience, there is a basic structure to most negotiations. The key elements in the process combine common sense with important communication skills.[21]

KNOW YOUR OBJECTIVES BEFOREHAND   Decide what you want to come away with when your meeting is over and develop a strategy for getting it. Think of your strategy as a kind of road map to get you from the beginning to the end of the negotiation process.

STATE YOUR POSITION   Be concise, direct, and unemotional as you tell people what you want (they cannot read your mind). When it will expedite the process, use team communication. For example, although Al Neuharth often negotiated with potential advertisers at *USA Today*, he refused to ask for orders. After pitching the potential customer's president or CEO, Neuharth turned over the negotiations to Cathie Black, the paper's publisher, to close the deal.[22]

LISTEN   As we saw in Chapter 2, listening means paying attention both to the facts and to nuances of meaning communicated in everything from tone to body language and what is left unsaid. In the following story, consultant Mark H. McCormack relates how the late Charles Revson, founder of the cosmetic giant Revlon, used his sensitivity to his opponents as a negotiating advantage. Revson, it seems, not only communicated by means of the office in which he conducted face-to-face meetings but was careful to gauge the response of other people to their mutual surroundings:

> Several years ago when advertising executive Edward McCabe of Scali, McCabe, Sloves, Inc., was trying to win the Revlon account, he went to meet Revson for the first time at Revlon headquarters. The cosmetic tycoon's office was ostentatious to the point of intimidation.
>
> According to McCabe, it "looked as if it had been built for Mussolini and shipped to New York piece by piece." There were marble columns, oversized nautical maps on the walls, a 25-foot conference table surrounded by black leather chairs dotted with gold studs. At Revson's place at the head of the table sat a solid gold phone.

When Revson entered the room, recalls McCabe, "I expected him to belch lava." But Revson's first words to McCabe were, "Do you think this room is ugly?"

McCabe wasn't ready for this, but he managed to mumble something about having different tastes in interiors.

"I know you think it's ugly," Revson insisted. "That's okay. But I'm looking for someone who also understands that many people would think it's beautiful."[23]

THINK   When no one is saying anything, be silent. For one thing, silence not only pressures the other person to talk but gives you time to think. In negotiations, remember that silence is a void that most people feel compelled to fill. Use that tendency to your advantage by waiting for people to speak—and perhaps say more than they intend.

DEFINE AREAS OF AGREEMENT AND DISAGREEMENT   Define the areas of both agreement and disagreement as you see them. Even when you agree on nothing but your negotiating goals, establish good will and common ground by accentuating the positive. As for areas of disagreement, don't try to debate them—just list them. Your goal is to reach a consensus on the points to be negotiated.

CONCEDE A POINT   Concede the point that is least important to your position. If, for example, you and a potential supplier disagree on a project deadline, on one party's responsibility for supplying a key component, and on quality standards, concede the deadline date if your schedule is flexible. Be positive but make it clear that you are making a sacrifice. Your concession sets the stage for the other side to respond in like manner.

SEEK CONCILIATORY RESPONSES   Negotiations can proceed only if the other side is as willing to compromise as you are (or should be). In your dealing with your potential supplier, for example, if your opponent counters your concession by saying, "Okay, I can supply the component without additional cost," you have made progress. If no concession is offered, try to learn more about the issues dividing you by asking questions. You may discover, for instance, that your quality expectations are the problem. In your opponent's view, you may be asking for so much that further negotiation is impossible. Ironically, just defining the key stumbling block may put the negotiation back on course—there may now be room for movement on both sides.

When no concessions are made and no explanations given, negotiations have broken down. Resist the temptation to concede too much just to get a deal—in the end you will probably be dissatisfied. Instead, suggest another meeting after both parties have had time to think.

Thus far, the main theme of this chapter has been the principle that successful communication during meetings means defining your personal communication style in each role that you play. Remember, however, that you will frequently be limited by corporate cultural expectations. Each company's unique personality determines which individuals attend meetings and what is expected of them, the setting and frequency for meetings, and even the shape of the table and where people sit. General Motors, for example, has long been notorious for holding endless meetings before making major decisions. While some companies require daily meetings, others meet once a month; while some companies encourage active involvement, others use meetings as slide theaters where everyone sits back and watches the show.[24]

The broad dimensions of corporate culture and its impact on communication are discussed in some detail in Chapter 1. In the next section, we will explore some of the specific affects of the corporate hierarchy on meeting behavior and outcomes.

Don't negotiate with yourself. Have the patience to wait for the other fellow to make a counter-offer after you've made one.

Richard Smith
Partner,
Smith, McWorter & Pachter

MEETINGS AND THE CORPORATE HIERARCHY

The way you communicate at meetings is influenced by the positions in the corporate hierarchy of the various people with whom you attend meetings. Interactions change depending on whether you are meeting with *supervisors*, *peers*, or *subordinates*.

Meeting with Supervisors

When you meet with your supervisors, they are in control. Even when you have been asked to take center stage and make a presentation, it is their meeting and your role is limited. Although most managers (as we observed earlier) appreciate honest differences of opinion, the *way* you disagree and *when* you speak are as crucial as what you say.

Meeting with Peers

When chairing a meeting of your peers, start by establishing control. At the same time, make it clear that although your manager has asked you to lead the group, you want to consult on the agenda. Ironically, consultation gives you more rather than less power. Even before the meeting begins, you can take the lead in hearing out and trying to reconcile divergent views. In addition, because you are probably the only participant with a total picture (or at least a more complete picture), you are at an advantage in maintaining control over the meeting.

Meeting with Subordinates

Having a more complete picture also enables you to control meetings with subordinates. That position, however, also makes it more likely that you will be responsible for any miscommunication. Knowing less than you do about the meeting's purpose, subordinates may misunderstand your objectives—unless you make them absolutely clear. Be as specific as possible, therefore, when you tell the group what you hope to accomplish. Naturally, you could get to the point by saying something like, "What we want is information on the health-insurance costs of various companies." You run the risk, however, of oversimplifying the purpose of your meeting. You are more likely to avoid subsequent miscommunication if you inform participants that "What we want here is information on what American Express, Motorola, and Caterpillar Tractor are asking employees to pay for health insurance and how premiums have changed in the last two years."

It is not unusual for employee teams to meet to discuss problems, suggest solutions, and make proposals to management. Nor is it unusual for firms to award prizes for successful teamwork. Motorola, however, has taken the idea of effective teamwork a step further by organizing an international event called the Total Customer Satisfaction Team Competition. Teams are evaluated on the basis of ideas for saving time and money and increasing overall productivity. Interestingly, some team members come from outside customers and suppliers, and all are judged on their ability to share their innovations with other units of the company.

INTERVIEW

Tessa Warschaw, Corporate Consultant on Negotiations

We asked Tessa Warschaw, best-selling author and corporate consultant, for her views on conducting successful negotiations. An advocate of the win–win negotiating style, Warschaw presents negotiating seminars in the United States, Canada, Asia, and Europe and has special expertise in the negotiating styles of women.

Question: How do you define a skilled negotiator?

Answer: Skilled negotiators try to get what they want while helping the other person come away with something, too. Their goal is to win the dollar on the table while leaving the loose change. I learned very early in life that this win–win strategy keeps options open. If you go for the jugular and try to destroy someone, you leave that person little choice but to try to destroy you, too.

Question: Is personal style important in negotiation?

Answer: Everyone has a different negotiating style, and successful negotiators are always aware of the style of the person with whom they are dealing. They realize that while a passive person is unlikely to attack, a hardball player will go for the gamewinner. Thus, when negotiating with a hardballer, it is a mistake to mention anything personal because it will be used against you. The key to successful negotiating, especially with a person like this, is being willing to walk away from an idea or even a job.

Question: Can a negotiating strategy be prepared in advance?

Answer: You can strategize your part of the negotiation, but you can't strategize what the other person will say. That's why it's important to develop contingency plans. If things go in a direction that you don't expect, you can abandon Plan A and go with Plan B or C.

Physical preparation is also necessary. Don't eat or drink heavily before a negotiation. It takes energy away at a time when you want to feel lean. And get enough rest. The Japanese realize this. They often fly to the United States a week in advance of a meeting. This gives them time to get acclimated, relax, and take care of last-minute details. By contrast, Americans are on the plane for twenty hours—eating and drinking all the way—get two hours sleep, and walk into the meeting. They think they are ready to negotiate, but they're not.

Question: Do women have a negotiating handicap?

Answer: A study measured the physiological responses of men and women during negotiating sessions. When men negotiate, their heart rates increase when they're winning. When women negotiate, their heart rates increase when they're losing. Many women expect to lose, so they fight just to stay alive. I don't believe that most women are hungry or passionate enough to negotiate for what they really want. Many will do anything to keep the status quo.

Question: If you were to give business students one piece of advice about negotiating, what would that advice be?

Answer: Recognize that negotiating is really about relationships and about people with different styles trying to make a deal. Start by looking at your own negotiating style. If you are the type who takes care of others at the expense of yourself, you may wind up forgetting your own agenda. You may have to fight against your inclinations in order to be successful. Then analyze your opponents. If they play hardball, be ready for the attack. You can't be shaken or forget your own bottom line.

Source: Interview with Tessa Albert Warschaw.

PROGRESS CHECK

1. What do we mean by "active participation" in a meeting?
2. What is negotiation?
3. How can corporate culture affect meetings?
4. Explain how interactions change depending on whether you're meeting with supervisors, peers, or subordinates.

INFORMAL BUSINESS CONVERSATIONS

informal business conversation
Unscheduled meeting between as few as two and as many as four people

If formal meetings occupy one end of the oral communication spectrum, brief, informal business conversations occupy the other. **Informal business conversations** are unscheduled meetings held on the spur of the moment, with as few as two and as many as four people. We will also include some phone calls in this category. Many observers believe that the real business of a company takes place during these conversations. They point out that when conversation time is limited and agendas narrow, communication must be focused and productive. Indeed, some companies design their buildings with these meetings in mind. Corning Glass, for example, designed an engineering building with escalators rather than elevators to encourage conversation.[25]

Like other forms of business communication, the most productive brief encounters benefit from preparation. In a basic sense, being prepared means having a personal agenda—a mental list of what you want to accomplish. It also means having at your disposal the questions and documents that you will need during conversation. Before you see a colleague in the hall and ask, "Do you have a minute to talk about the production problem?" you should know what you want when the conversation is over. Because unscheduled conversations are expected to be short and to the point, preparation is especially crucial.

The success of brief encounters also depends a great deal on your attitude: You must be as committed to getting something done in this setting as you are in a formal meeting. That means giving your conversation partner your undivided attention. If you divide your time between reading phone messages, flipping through journals, or giving instructions to a secretary, you are sending a clear message that you do not consider the conversation important.

Improving Informal Meetings

Here are some suggestions to maximize the effectiveness of brief, informal conversations. We will then examine some additional requirements for phone communication.

- *Keep a limited agenda.* You are squeezing important business into unscheduled time, so don't try to accomplish too much.
- *Be sensitive to other people's schedules.* Unless it is urgent, don't interrupt managers when they are facing deadlines. Wait for a more opportune time. And don't be put off if a colleague tells you to come back later. This is not a brush off, just good business.
- *Be sensitive to other people's feelings.* If a co-worker seems angry or upset (the reason why is unimportant), postpone your conversation. Your idea won't get a fair hearing.
- *Follow basic conversation etiquette.* Don't monopolize the conversation (people will stop listening); don't interrupt (let people finish before you begin speaking); stick to the topic (it's the only way you will get anything done); and keep your emotions in check (make your points through solid argument and support, not anger).
- *Send follow-up memos.* Some conversations require follow-up memos to summarize what was said and what actions will be taken. For example, if you agree during a brief meeting with a co-worker to perform a marketing survey as part of a larger project, forestall misconceptions by writing a memo stating what you will do.
- *Learn to deflect conversations.* There will be times when you do not want to divulge information—perhaps a co-worker asks you about a new project before you have presented it to your manager. In these cases, resist the pressure to respond to direct questions. Instead, deflect the question by saying something like, "I'm reporting to Bill about this next Tuesday. I'll be

glad to discuss it when I pass that stage." Deflection may be necessary if an issue is politically sensitive or a project is someone else's responsibility. For example, although copywriters are typically involved in creating new advertising campaigns, they often defer questions to account managers.

- *Listen for the subtext.* As we saw in Chapter 2, nonverbal cues often communicate more clearly than words. Here, for example, Mary Kay Ash recounts her reaction to the nonverbal language of a business associate: "I remember how offended I was when I was having lunch with my sales manager, and every time a pretty waitress walked by, his eyes would follow her across the room. I felt insulted and kept thinking to myself, 'The waitress's legs are more important to him than what I have to say. He's not listening to me. He doesn't care about me!'"[26] Nonverbal cues can also communicate such positive attitudes as attentiveness and interest.

Communicating by Phone

Conversations that take place on the phone are crucial to business success. Mary Kay Ash explains how two of her sales managers make the phone an integral part of business communication:

> I know one national sales manager who calls each of his thirty-five sales representatives at least once a week. Although he no longer personally makes customer calls, constant communication with his sales force keeps him abreast of what's going on in the field. Another sales manager with forty sales representatives makes about twenty-five random calls to his people each week. "How's it going?" he might say to them in a friendly way. "What can I do for you? If you have any questions, just ask." He makes it perfectly clear to each of them that he's never too busy to accept a call. When he's not available, he makes a point of returning every call from his salespeople before he goes to sleep each night.[27]

The following suggestions are designed to help you improve the effectiveness of your telephone communication:

- *Identify yourself.* When placing a call to someone who does not know you, clearly identify yourself and the organization you represent. When answering a call, identify yourself with your full name ("Hello. This is customer service. Emily Quinn speaking").

- *Leave clear messages.* When you cannot reach someone, leave your name, title, company name, and phone number as well as a specific time to return your call ("Don, you can call me back anytime after 3:00"). You may also want to leave a brief message ("I'm calling to find out when I can expect to receive my first payment"). Messages like this improve efficiency because the person you are calling can follow-up on the problem before returning your call.

- *Realize the subtext.* Each of the following behaviors sends a clear message of control: waiting a week to return a call (or not returning it at all), carrying on a conversation with someone in your office while on a call, or interrupting an important meeting to take calls. Explains Julius Fast, an expert on nonverbal communication: "When you meet with a client and the meeting is interrupted by frequent phone calls, the subtext can be, 'I'm an important person.' It's a dangerous ploy because it can easily end up annoying the client."[28] Similarly, when the restructuring of General Motors was announced recently, one Chevy dealer summed up complaints about the company's unresponsiveness by observing that his telephone calls to divisional headquarters were never returned.

- *Prioritize your phone calls.* If you have four phone calls to make in the next fifteen minutes, start with those that you can finish quickly. By getting

Employees must be with Heath at least three years before they can answer the phone. The policy ensures that customers are greeted by someone who knows the ropes. It's had a very positive effect.

Janice Heath
President, Heath Electronic Manufacturing Co.

your short calls out of the way, you will be able to devote full attention to your final—and most important—call.

■ *Return every phone call or redirect it elsewhere.* When you are away from your desk, either ask someone to pick up your calls or use an answering machine or voice mail. Because delays in responses imply that the caller is unimportant, try to return calls promptly. If you choose not to return a call, realize that you may be making a lasting impression.

■ *Handle interruptions properly.* When you are on one call and another comes in, put the first party on hold—but just long enough to get the name and number of the second caller. It is rude to carry on an extensive conversation with a second caller while a first is put on hold. In general, try to avoid putting people on hold for long periods. When you have to pause in order to look for information, offer to call the person back.

■ *Think about the impression you make.* It is easy to make a poor impression on the phone. Some cases in point:

> "I'm sorry. Mary isn't here. She's in the bathroom."
> "That's not my department. I can't help you."
> "Why are you calling me for this?"

Say instead:

> "Mary is not at her desk right now. May I take a message?"
> "Although I can't handle that problem, I will transfer you to Chris Anderson, who can."
> "I would like to help you get to the bottom of this, but I'm not sure how."

■ *Build goodwill with customers.* When a customer calls with a complaint, take down the facts, promise to follow through, and call back. And don't be defensive. Instead of saying, "We've never had a complaint before on that model," tell the customer that you will investigate the problem and get back with an answer.

■ *Make calls when others are likely to receive them.* When you call people on a regular basis, keep track of the most convenient times to reach them. Then call only during those times. For example, the best time to reach many busy executives is before 9:30 in the morning.

■ *Learn to end a conversation.* Ending a conversation when the other party wants to continue talking can be difficult. "Usually when I'm late for an appointment, it's because I don't know how to cut people off on the telephone," admits Michele Ateyeh, president of jewelry manufacturer Angela Cummings, Inc. "I'm afraid to be rude."[29]

How do you end a phone conversation that has gone on too long? Interrupting, summarizing, and promising to help often works. Say something like, "Let me restate what I think you're saying." Another way to end a conversation is to focus it on a solution rather than a problem: "I hear the problem. What do you think we should do to solve it?" This technique is especially helpful when people describe a problem in detail, forgetting that what they really need is a solution. When these techniques fail, be honest: "I'm swamped with work, so I'll have to speak with you next week."

PROGRESS CHECK

1. Suppose you stop in the hallway and talk with a co-worker for a few minutes. Why is it important to communicate effectively, even during this brief, informal chat?
2. When might you want to deflect a conversation?

WHAT'S AHEAD

Knowing how to communicate effectively in both speech and writing will help prepare you to meet the challenge of finding a job. We will turn next to the subject of employment communication as we explore, in Chapter 16, writing résumés and cover letters and, in Chapter 17, employment interviewing.

SUMMARY OF CHAPTER OBJECTIVES

1. **List the responsibilities of a *meeting leader*.**
   Meeting leaders define and limit the task of meetings, choose participants, set meeting times, and create agendas. The leader also convenes the meeting, focuses the group's progress on accomplishing its objectives, encourages active participation, and sets the tone for the meeting. In addition, leaders facilitate decision making and bring meetings to a close. Perhaps the leader's most stressful task is handling difficult people.

2. **Classify *formal meetings* according to seven general purposes.**
   Formal business meetings are usually convened to accomplish specific tasks. The primary purposes of meetings are (1) to give or exchange information, (2) to develop new ideas, (3) to make decisions, (4) to delegate work or authority, (5) to collaborate, (6) to persuade, and (7) to inspire and build enthusiasm. The leader has the primary responsibility for defining the meeting's purpose.

3. **Describe a *simple agenda* and a *formal agenda*.**
   The agenda is a written document that tells meeting participants what a meeting hopes to accomplish. Simple agendas are used for short meetings with relatively few participants. They inform participants about general goals without listing the sequence of events. Formal agendas, which are used in larger, longer meetings, list the order of business and the approximate time allotted to each agenda item.

4. **Identify the responsibilities of a *meeting participant*.**
   Effective participants work with the leader to accomplish the group's goals. The contributions of meeting participants can be improved if they are willing to take and change posi-

tions; to present ideas in simple, organized ways; to avoid arguments and personal confrontations; to commit themselves to fair interchanges with other group members; and to understand nonverbal cues.

5. **Explain the purpose and content of *meeting minutes*.**
   Meeting minutes provide a written record of what occurred at a meeting. Minutes record the positions of individual members on key issues, state the number and nature of decisions that were made, highlight individual participation, and summarize the proceedings and conclusions. Minutes, which are usually written by either the group leader or a secretary, follow a traditional format.

6. **Describe the *mechanics of a meeting* and their influence on a meeting's outcome.**
   The mechanics of a meeting involve technical decisions about scheduling, location, table and seating arrangements, and on-time arrival. These decisions set the subtext for the meeting and often establish who is in control—and who wants to be. Mechanics provide nonverbal cues that are often invaluable to achieving group and personal objectives.

7. **Explain the steps in the *negotiating process*.**
   Negotiation, which involves give and take between two or more parties at a bargaining table, reflects an identifiable process. As a negotiator, you must know what you want to accomplish before you begin. At the start of the session, state your position and then listen to the response. Remaining silent gives you time to think and pressures the other parties to talk. When positions are clear, define agreements and disagreements and be willing to concede a point that is not

critical to your position. Look for similar concessions from your negotiating partner, and if you do not find them, try to encourage conciliation.

8. **List ways to improve *informal business conversations*.**

Because business is often conducted in informal conversations, it is important to focus on improving such encounters. Helpful suggestions include limiting goals, being sensitive to the scheduling problems and feelings of others, learning the art of deflecting conversations, and being alert to nonverbal cues. In addition, conversations that adhere to the rules of etiquette and are followed up with summarizing memos are more likely to succeed.

9. **Describe methods for improving *telephone communication*.**

Although telephone conversations are crucial to business success, they are not always conducted effectively. To improve communication, identify yourself at the start of the conversation, be conscious of the impression that you make, and learn how to end conversations. Poor impressions are made when interruptions are handled badly, when phone calls are not returned, and when messages are unclear. Effective phone communication gives you the opportunity to establish goodwill with customers and co-workers. In every phone call, focus both on what is said and what is left unsaid.

REVIEW AND DISCUSSION QUESTIONS

1. Why is it important to communicate effectively at meetings? (*Ch. Obj. 1, 4*)

2. When you lead a meeting, what are your responsibilities? (*Ch. Obj. 1*)

3. What are seven general tasks that meetings can accomplish? (*Ch. Obj. 2*)

4. Distinguish between simple and formal agendas. (*Ch. Obj. 3*)

5. What are the responsibilities of a meeting participant? (*Ch. Obj. 4*)

6. What are meeting minutes, and what function(s) do they serve? (*Ch. Obj. 5*)

7. Summarize the "mechanics" that can affect the outcome of a meeting. (*Ch. Obj. 6*)

8. Describe the steps involved in effective negotiation. (*Ch. Obj. 7*)

9. How can you improve your communication effectiveness during brief, informal business conversations? (*Ch. Obj. 8*)

10. Summarize tips for improving telephone communication. (*Ch. Obj. 9*)

APPLICATION EXERCISES

1. Think of a meeting in which you participated that didn't seem to get very much done (perhaps a meeting at your present job, a former job, at school, or at a social group). Analyze the failure of the meeting: Why didn't it "work"? What might the leader have done differently to make it more effective? What could you have done? (*Ch. Obj. 1, 4*)

2. Now think of a meeting in which you participated that accomplished a great deal. Analyze the success of this meeting: Why was it more effective than the one you discussed for EXERCISE 1? What did the leader do differently, if anything? What did you do differently? (*Ch. Obj. 1, 4*)

3. EXERCISES 3 and 4 deal with an actual meeting in which you are a leader or participant. Classify this meeting according to its general purpose. What do you hope to accomplish? (*Ch. Obj. 2*)

4. Create a formal agenda for this meeting. Be as specific as you can regarding participants and the order of business. If you are a participant rather than the leader, create what you feel is a probable agenda. (*Ch. Obj. 3*)

5. During the meeting or immediately afterward, write out meeting minutes that record what happened. Make your minutes concise but thorough; if it's applicable, use the outline format discussed in this chapter. Make sure that your recorded minutes fulfill all the functions discussed for meeting minutes in this chapter. (*Ch. Obj. 5*)

6. During meetings, there are nearly always some people who dominate the conversation while others sit there and say very little. As a meeting leader, how can you deal with this situation? (*Ch. Obj. 1*)

7. Think of meetings that you've either attended or led in which there were one or more

blamers, boilers, or know-it-alls. Using the suggestions made in the chapter, list some specific statements that you might have made to help deal with these obstructionists. (*Ch. Obj. 1, 4*)

8. Cover the right-hand column in TABLE 15.2. Test yourself on common failures of meeting participants. Can you think of an example of each type of failure? (*Ch. Obj. 4*)

9. Keshia wants to hold a meeting of several key employees, suppliers, and customers. What factors does she need to keep in mind in order to make this meeting as effective as possible? (*Ch. Obj. 6*)

10. According to legend, King Arthur of Britain held regular meetings with his nobles at a circular table—whereby they became known as the "Knights of the Round Table." Why do you think Arthur chose a round table for his meetings? What are the advantages and disadvantages of this arrangement? (*Ch. Obj. 6*)

11. Suppose that you want to ask your boss (current or former) for a raise. You honestly feel that you deserve a raise, but you also realize that because money is tight, getting your raise will require good negotiation skills. Write a detailed description of each stage that you might encounter during this negotiation. What are your boss's objections likely to be? How might you counter those objections? What areas of similarity and difference are you likely to find during the course of negotiation? (*Ch. Obj. 7*)

12. Your instructor will ask for two volunteers to role-play a negotiation in front of the class. The participants may choose the subject about which they will negotiate; possibilities include a promotion, a new job, or a conflict over a work-related issue. If they wish, they can take a few minutes to prepare by thinking about their respective positions and objectives. Then they will conduct the negotiation while the class listens. (Unless one of the participants actually feels that the other has successfully negotiated a concession, it is not necessary to resolve the issue.)

After the participants have finished their negotiation (or your instructor has called it a tie), the class should give the two negotiators feedback about their techniques. Did they listen to each other well? Did they do an effective job of listing similarities and differences, conceding points, or seeking responses? What advice could you give to each? Be tactful. (*Ch. Obj. 7*)

13. Why is it important to communicate effectively even if you just happen to encounter a business colleague in a hallway? (*Ch. Obj. 8*)

14. Jack meets Antonia in the corridor as she's hurrying back to her office. "Hey, Antonia!" he says. "I'm glad I ran into you; how about going over the sales figures from last quarter?" Antonia looks at her watch quickly and says, "Perhaps we could make it some other time, Jack; the marketing meeting ran longer than I expected, and I have some important papers waiting on my desk."

"Great—let's talk about it right now," responds Jack, and proceeds to discuss sales statistics while Antonia shifts her weight from one foot to the other, nods impatiently, and steals periodic glances at her watch.

What do you think of Jack's communication style? What improvements could he make? (*Ch. Obj. 8*)

15. Phil calls Nancy because he wants to update her on a project that he's working on. Nancy's assistant takes a message because Nancy is in a meeting. Phil waits a week, gets no response, and dials Nancy again. This time, she answers the phone herself and seems a bit flustered when Phil identifies himself. "Oh, uh, I'm sorry I didn't call you back earlier," she mumbles. "But I knew we were late on sending those reports to you and I thought you were going to complain about it. I thought I'd let Sam [her boss] call you back instead; I don't get paid to listen to people yell about late orders."

What is your opinion of Nancy's telephone communication skills? How could she improve them? (*Ch. Obj. 9*)

*B*UILDING YOUR RESEARCH SKILLS

Set up an interview with a businessperson in your community to discuss the role(s) that meetings play in his or her organization. What types of meetings does this person attend most often (informational, brainstorming, etc.)? Do the meetings seem constructive? Why or why not? Ask this professional to recall especially effective meetings and

to explain why they seemed more worthwhile than others.

Write a one- to two-page summary of your discussion with this person. What conclusions can you reach regarding the ingredients of an effective meeting? Your instructor may ask you to present your conclusions to the class.

BUILDING YOUR TEAMWORK SKILLS

This chapter discusses the importance of paying attention to the "subtext" of a conversation. Subtext, for example, can include a wide variety of nonverbal cues, such as eye contact, gestures, posture, and tone of voice. This exercise will help you think about the ways in which subtext has influenced conversations that you yourself have had with others.

Your instructor will divide the class into small groups. Each team member should think of conversations in which he or she has participated and in which subtext has played a role, either in making the conversation more effective or less so. One member of each team should write down a list of everyone's experiences.

Now have someone from each team present the team's list to the class as a whole. Explain the role, whether positive or negative, played in each instance by subtext. What conclusions can the class draw about nonverbal cues that facilitate or block communication?

COMMUNICATING IN A WORLD OF DIVERSITY

Reuben Mark, chairman of Colgate-Palmolive Company, does something different with his Saturdays: He spends them in a community center in New York City's tough Lower East Side. There, Mark and his wife Arlene tutor, praise, scold, and in general mentor a group of teenagers from the ghetto. Their goal: persuade the teens to stay in school.

Since 1986, the Marks have spent their Saturdays hanging out with the group of twenty-three kids, all of whom have special educational or emotional needs. Group members do homework, play board games, discuss problems, or just horse around. The Marks circulate among the group, talking to the kids about their progress and their goals. Get-togethers are occasionally followed by trips to neighborhood restaurants.

Meetings, of course, were not always friendly; in the beginning, fights broke out frequently. Progress began when students realized that the conflicts were self-defeating and ultimately developed their own code of conduct. Among the rules: no weapons, no violence, and no insults (each insult incurs a twenty-five-cent fine).

Says Maritza Pineiro-Hernandez, one member of the group: "At first I didn't think the Marks would make a difference, but they did. I would have quit by the seventh grade." Instead, Maritza is enrolling at New York University next fall.

Why do you think the Marks's approach is successful?

Source: Peter Nulty, "I Have a Dream," *Fortune*, November 16, 1992, pp. 142–44. © 1992 Time Inc. All rights reserved.

CASE 15.1

The Timely Management of Seemingly Inefficient Behavior

Traditionally, time-management consultants have advised businesspeople to make the best use of their time by minimizing informal chats and meetings, phone calls, and other "interruptions." Lately, however, research has shown that such informal conversations can be a valuable asset. In fact, many of today's most successful executives rely on these interactions to help them manage better.

"The astonishing fact," reports consultant Stephanie Winston, "is that a CEO's days are taken up with little but interruptions.... They use a fluid time style to make abundant connections and draw in streams of information. The torrent of questions, comments, updates, requests, and expectations is a rich resource to be mined. There's a very high schmooze factor. People say, 'Isn't that wasting time?' No, because it provides lubrication and establishes ties."

A study by Harvard professor John Kotter bears out these conclusions. Kotter found that effective executives spend 76 percent of their time talking with other people; often these talks are unplanned conversations with a wide variety of people, both employees and individuals from outside their firms. Moreover, conversations frequently deal with non–work–related topics; many of them involve friendly, humorous banter. The executives in Kotter's study rarely gave direct orders; instead, they asked lots of questions and tried to influence people's work indirectly—an approach that Kotter terms "the efficiency of seemingly inefficient behavior."

Avis CEO Joseph Vittoria practices this approach. "My business," explains Vittoria, "requires a lot of personal contact, whether it's here in the office or getting on a chartered plane and hitting four or five offices in the field. The door is always open, and people are always stopping by. I like them to have the opportunity to talk about what's on their mind. It's important that everybody has access. All of us have outside appointments and meetings, but when I'm here it becomes access time."

Vittoria keeps his own calendar and leaves big blocks of time unscheduled to accommodate informal visits and spur-of-the- moment meetings. "I really don't believe it's my responsibility to 'run' this company," he says. "It's my responsibility to communicate with the people who run this company.... I can't remember once in years when I waved someone off if I wasn't tied up. Often I'll wave people in when I'm on the phone."

Questions and Applications

1. Traditionally, how have time-management consultants viewed unplanned, informal conversations?
2. In what ways is this view is changing? Why?
3. Explain the role of informal interactions in Joseph Vittoria's management style.

Source: Alan Deutschman, "The CEO's Secret of Managing Time," *Fortune*, June 1, 1992, pp. 135–46. © 1992 Time Inc. All rights reserved.

CASE 15.2

The Gift of Good Communication
Pays Off at Glassboro State College

When Phil Tumminia first called on Henry Rowan, he had no idea that this simple visit would end up breaking records.

Tumminia was the director of the Glassboro State College Development Fund; Rowan was the founder and head of Inductotherm Industries, an industrial-furnace maker with $468 million in annual sales. Tumminia's cold call was the beginning of a two-year series of visits and discussions between the two men. The ultimate result was that Glassboro State College, located in southern New Jersey, received the largest donation ever given to a public institution: $100 million.

To say the least, Tumminia's success demonstrates the importance of good communication. In fund raising as in many other sales-oriented jobs, success often results from a long, patient interchange between fund-raiser and client. According to Rick Nahm, head of fund raising at the University of Pennsylvania, "So many of the mega-gifts are the result of years of contact, where the initial discussion is for something smaller. As time goes on, the donor gets more interested."

After his first visit, Tumminia stayed in regular contact with Rowan. Much of their rapport resulted from the fact that Tumminia focused on Rowan's interests and needs. Says Tumminia: "We talked a lot about what we were doing and what [Mr. Rowan's] interests were. I would make

515

very specific suggestions about what we could do and try to address what he wanted."

Their discussions revealed, for example, that Rowan liked the idea of endowing a new engineering school. Although he could have donated money to an existing engineering department, "building one from scratch," says Rowan, was "much more exciting." When Tumminia realized the source and nature of Rowan's enthusiasm, they started planning the creation of a new school at Glassboro. Ultimately, Rowan agreed to provide the $100 million endowment.

Although Henry Rowan's gift makes him a star in fund-raising circles, Phil Tumminia is modest about his accomplishment: "You can only do what you're capable of doing. In this case, I listened to what he was saying."

Questions and Applications

1. Why do you think Tumminia was successful in obtaining this large donation?
2. What was Tumminia's personal agenda? What was Rowan's?
3. Explain this case in terms of the principles of person-to-person communication discussed in this chapter.

Source: Pamela Sebastian and Gary Putka, "Glassboro Gift: A Small Appeal Has Big Payoff," *The Wall Street Journal*, July 13, 1992, pp. B1, B10. Reprinted by permission of *The Wall Street Journal*, © 1992 Dow Jones & Company, Inc. All rights reserved worldwide.

EMPLOYMENT
COMMUNICATION

16

Targeting Your Career: Writing Résumés and Cover Letters

CHAPTER OBJECTIVES

After studying this chapter, you should be able to:

1 Describe the *job search* in terms of eight distinct stages.

2 Describe the process for defining your *interests, marketable skills, personal traits,* and *accomplishments* and linking these to career choice.

3 Explain how to *target* a field and a career by analyzing the *work environment* and the forces of supply and demand that affect the *job market.*

4 List the elements of an effective *résumé.*

5 Describe the differences among *chronological, functional,* and *targeted résumés.*

6 List the elements of an effective *cover letter.*

7 Describe specific *networking techniques.*

8 List three formal sources that can assist you in finding a job.

9 Explain the basic approach for answering *help-wanted ads.*

The best career advice given to the young is, "Find out what you like doing best and get someone to pay you for doing it."

Katherine Whitehorn
British columnist

THERE'S MORE THAN ONE WAY TO FIND A JOB

As the following examples show, finding a job is more complicated than it used to be.

■ Colgate University senior Bill Connell was a history major without a job—a situation that he was determined to change. Starting with a desire to work in advertising, Connell spent months researching job possibilities in the hope of finding something that few others had seen. His efforts paid off when he discovered that Leo Burnett, one of the country's largest advertising agencies, was signing new accounts at a time when other agencies were cutting back. He learned everything he could about Burnett and wrote the firm, requesting an interview. Burnett agreed—with the stipulation that Connell pay his own expenses to and from the interview. Connell's $700 investment turned into an offer. After graduation, Connell joined Burnett as a media buyer while many of his less aggressive classmates continued their job searches.[1]

■ Neal Stubblefield graduated from the Georgia Institute of Technology over ten years ago—too late, in the view of most graduates, to ask his alma mater for career help. When he was laid off, however, Stubblefield contacted Georgia Tech's alumni-placement service and learned about a school-sponsored job fair. He left the fair with two offers and a short while later was working at a full-time job.[2]

■ Sue Quinlivan of Fairfield University's Career Planning Center in Fairfield, Connecticut, believes that job hunting requires aggressive communication. She advises students to read business papers and journals for the names of people who have just been promoted, to write them congratulatory notes, and to follow up with phone calls asking for meetings. "It's gutsy to pick up the phone and call someone you don't know," she admits. "But they can be a great source of advice and information" and may even hire you, whether on a part-time or full-time basis.[3]

As these stories demonstrate, finding the right job in today's complex business environment involves initiative, flexibility, and a job-hunting strategy akin to a sophisticated marketing plan. It also involves mastering a distinctive set of employment-communication skills aimed at clarifying personal job goals and convincing employers to hire you.

CHAPTER OVERVIEW

With uncertainty and change as facts of business life today, flexible, responsive employment communication is critical—as is the ability to tailor your communication to the needs of both specific employers and the general job market. As you look for your first job, voluntarily change jobs—or careers—in search of opportunity, or leave a job for any one of a variety of reasons, your communication skills will develop over the course of your career.

The job search, however, will probably be your first business communication experience. It may also be your hardest. Through letters, résumés, and conversations, you will give prospective employers reason to hire you—or pass you by. Your communication skills may very likely mark you as distinctive or ordinary, as the best candidate for the job or as just another also-ran.

This chapter will explore the eight distinct stages of the *job-search process*, which are summarized in Figure 16.1. This process starts with *self-analysis* and moves quickly to *targeting* first a field and then a specific job through research. It involves creating both a *résumé*—a statement of your career objectives, experience, and education—and a *cover letter* to capture attention and interest. It requires that you cultivate a *network* of people who can help you find a job and identify sources of employment counseling and job leads. It also teaches you such basic skills as focusing on newspaper help-wanted ads and communicating via "cold" letters and calls.

Although we will present the components of the job-search process as sequential stages, it is important to remember that many of these "stages" usually occur simultaneously. Moreover, some that we present as "late" stages in the process may actually occur before others that are presented as "earlier" stages. For example, networking, which we have detailed at stage five, should occur throughout the job search. And stage six—identifying formal sources of employment help—may occur before a résumé is written.

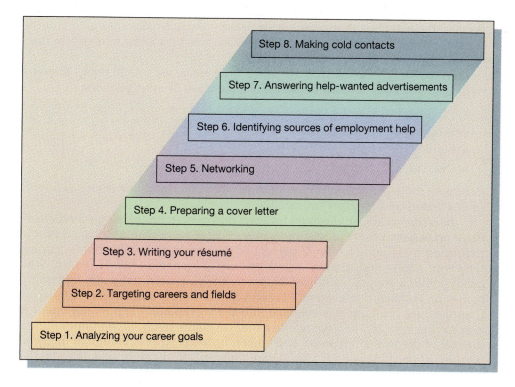

FIGURE 16.1   *Stages in the Job Search*

ANALYZING YOUR CAREER GOALS

self-analysis
Job-search process of defining your interests, skills, personal qualities, and accomplishments

If you do not know where you are going, every road will get you nowhere.

Henry Kissinger
Scholar and former
Secretary of State

The process of defining your interests, skills, personal qualities, and accomplishments is known as **self-analysis**. This process is the first step in building your résumé—the most important employment-communication tool in the job-search process.[4] In order to appreciate the likelihood of career mistakes and the need for early and careful self-analysis, consider the findings of a recent survey: Fewer than half the senior executives who were interviewed said that they would pursue the same career if they had a chance to start over.[5]

As a very practical matter, however, analyzing your career goals should begin early in your college career as you choose a major—the field that you intend to study in depth while you are a student. In many ways, deciding on a major is a prelude to deciding on a career and should involve the same process of defining your interests, skills, personal qualities, and accomplishments.

Start with Your Interests

Analyze what you like to do best so that you can look for a job that allows you to do it. Start by making a list of the things that give you personal satisfaction. For example:

- Write for the student newspaper
- Listen to opera music
- Do crossword puzzles
- Exercise an hour a day
- Play the piano

After creating your list, ask yourself one of the classic questions of career fulfillment. What would you do with your life if you were independently wealthy and did not have to work? You might answer, for example, that you would write novels, start your own company, or do fund raising for the American Cancer Society. You are looking for the same thing in both exercises: namely, the activities that reflect your *values*—the activities that give you the greatest personal satisfaction. Identifying these activities is the first step in finding a way to make them part of your work.

At the same time that you are listing your interests, list the things that you would rather *not* do. This list might include activities like the following:

- Working outdoors
- Working with your hands
- Managing people
- Dealing with budgets

In finding the right career, understanding what you don't like is just as important as understanding what you do like.

In recent years, studies have shown that people are placing considerable value on personal time. For example, in a study of more than a thousand people conducted by Hilton Hotels, 77 percent of the respondents said that "spending time with family and friends" was a priority—compared with 61 percent who cited "making money" and just 29 percent who placed value on "spending money on material possessions."[6] Employers like San Francisco's Levi Strauss & Company are bringing this message into the workplace: "Top management is now saying it's O.K. to have another life," explains Jenny Crowe-Innes, Levi's director of employee relations.[7] Remember, however, that in an age of mergers, restructuring, downsizing, and global competition, Levi Strauss may be the exception rather than the rule. With most companies asking employees to do more rather than less, personal time may be the first "benefit" to go.

Define Your Skills

Your next step is defining your skills—the abilities and talents that can give you an edge in the workplace. Make a list of your skills, just as you did your interests. Be as specific as possible, and ask yourself whether you would be willing to use each skill in your work. Here, for example, is one person's list of job-worthy skills:

- Selling products
- Managing a team of workers
- Working with customers
- Analyzing personnel requirements
- Public speaking

Another person's list reflects a quite different set of experiences and desirable job-related activities:

- Analyzing financial data
- Programming computers
- Budgeting and keeping financial records
- Writing financial proposals

To evaluate your own skills, ask yourself the following questions about each of them:

- Do I enjoy performing the skill?
- Am I able to perform the skill at a professional level?
- Do I have experience performing the skill, either at work or in other activities?
- Is this something that I would be willing to do in the future?

Define Your Personal Qualities

Next, compile a list of the qualities that define your personal character. As much as your skills and interests, these qualities influence the kind of job you should seek. Many of these traits, including those on the following list, may be obvious during job interviews:

creative	friendly
hard-working	funny
sensitive	responsible
aggressive	detail-oriented
analytic	intense
flexible	efficient
self-starting	intuitive
determined	visionary
warm	open to risk
open	artistic

Your résumé should also reflect these traits. For example, writing that you created a plan to raise advertising revenues for the campus newspaper shows creativity, analysis, vision, aggressiveness, and determination.

Analyze Your Accomplishments

In business, nothing impresses more than results—the tangible products or accomplishments that stem from your efforts. You may have already achieved results in a number of areas—from the experiences that you have had in school, in part-time and full-time jobs, in community and leisure activities, in the military, and at home. Results are the building blocks of your résumé. They are also the references that most impress employers during job interviews. For example, each of the following accomplishments tells an employer that you have achieved results:

If I had learned to type, I never would have made brigadier general.

Elizabeth P. Hoisington
Brigadier General,
U.S. Army

- Took a public speaking course and delivered five speeches
- Took a business-writing workshop while working at General Motors
- Organized the local chapter of Students Against Drunk Driving
- Ran the New York City Marathon in 4 hours and 10 minutes
- Supervised a group of seven tank mechanics while stationed with the U.S. Army in Saudi Arabia
- Used a personal computer to analyze four potential mortgage deals to find the most favorable option

Results like these tell employers what you have done in the past and the kind of work that you are capable of doing in the future. Note, too, that results can be obtained in a wide variety of activities.

Because results reveal skills, you also can work backward from your accomplishments to define marketable skills. For example, the accomplishment described above as using "a personal computer to analyze four potential mortgage deals" demonstrates the skills of analysis, computer competence, and problem solving.

Self-analysis is the process used by most vocational counselors to help people narrow options and choose careers. Counseling also includes *job targeting*, the next step in your personal job-search plan.

TARGETING CAREERS AND FIELDS

It is not enough to be busy, so are the ants. The question is: What are we busy about?

Henry David Thoreau
American naturalist
and writer

By combining the interests, skills, and personal qualities that you defined in the first stage of the job-search process, you can create tangible job possibilities. Targeting careers and fields is stage two of the job-search process. For example, a skill in sales, an interest in computer games, and an orientation to detail may make computer sales an ideal career. Similarly, good communication skills, an interest in people, and a warm, open personality may be the starting points for careers in public relations, employee relations, and convention planning.

To get a better sense of the kind of job possibilities that exist in today's market, you can begin by consulting the *Dictionary of Occupational Titles*. A publication of the U.S. Department of Labor, this guide offers a comprehensive list of job titles ranging from actuary to credit manager, media analyst to compensation and benefits administrator, customer-service representative to retail buyer.

Once you have sampled a catalog of contemporary job descriptions, remember that many careers apply to different industries. Your interests, therefore, can also be a guide to various industries from which to choose. Let's say, for example, that your career choice is compensation and benefits administration. If you are also interested in fashion, you could decide to apply your career choice to the field of retailing and, specifically, to job openings in organizations like The Limited and Macy's. If you are interested in sports, you may decide to apply your career choice as a systems analyst to the business of running a major league baseball team.

Once you have familiarized yourself with the general terrain of employment opportunities, you can begin narrowing the task of targeting the employment map by beginning a two-part process: analyzing the *work environment* and the *job market*.

Analyze the Work Environment

work environment
Physical, social, cultural, and economic conditions that define the work place and its surroundings

Targeting a career and an industry involves analyzing the **work environment**—the physical, social, cultural, and economic conditions that define the workplace and its surroundings. To get a better idea of how your environment can affect your choice of career and industry, ask yourself questions like the following:

- Do I want to work indoors or outdoors?
- Do I prefer a small business or a large corporation?
- Do I prefer a job with regular hours or one that involves evening and weekend work? (Shift work, for example, is often required in retailing and in the hotel and restaurant industries.)
- Do I prefer to work for a manufacturer or a service business (the difference between General Motors and Merrill Lynch)?
- Am I willing to relocate? (Similarly, do I want to work in a small town like Bentonville, Arkansas, or in a large city like Chicago? Do I want to work in the South, Northeast, Pacific Northwest, or Midwest or in a specific city like Cleveland, Milwaukee, or Seattle? Would I be willing to work wherever the company sent me?)
- Would I consider working in a foreign country?
- Do I want a job with constant deadline pressure (say, a printing plant manager for a newspaper) or pressure that varies by season (a tax accountant or retail buyer)?
- Do I want to work for a unionized company like Ford or a nonunionized company like Nissan?

Analyze the Job Market

Targeting a career also requires that you analyze the forces of supply and demand that affect the job marketplace. These forces are both short- and long-term. From a short-term perspective, our economy is currently saturated with too many executives who handle administrative and managerial functions—a surplus that reflects the mergers, downsizing, and global competition that intensified during the 1980s. From the long-term perspective, however, these same jobs will show employment growth. Figure 16.2, for example, suggests that prospects for executives will increase 27 percent between 1990 and 2005.

Such information also suggests the speed at which you are likely to climb a chosen career ladder. When a field is saturated, you will wait longer for promo-

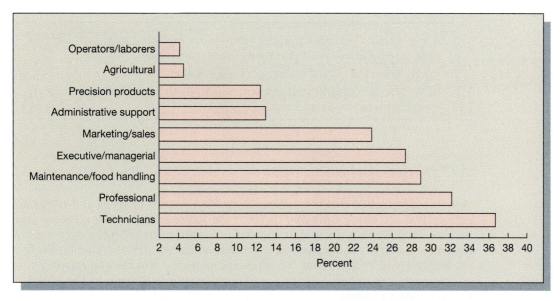

FIGURE 16.2   *Projected Employment Growth for Major Job Categories, 1990 to 2005*
Source: Bureau of Labor Statistics, as quoted in Sylvia Nasar, "Employment in the Service Industry, Engine Boom of 80's, Falters," *The New York Times*, January 2, 1992, p. D4.

INTERVIEW
Alan B. McNabb, Director, Career Development Center, Indiana University

Professor Alan B. McNabb, director of the Career Development Center at Indiana University, has helped thousands of students find jobs. Through workshops and job-search strategy courses, internships, and contact with alumni and on-campus recruiters, McNabb's department has given students the opportunity to present themselves to prospective employers and the skills to be effective. We asked Professor McNabb for his views on the job-search process.

Question: What characteristics define a successful job search?

Answer: There will always be a job market for students who are aggressive—who never say die—who put together quality résumés and cover letters; who take the time to interview with on-campus recruiters; who network their parents, their parents' friends, and school alumni; who pound the pavement during vacation breaks trying to meet people. Students who try this hard are almost always successful.

Campus recruiters notice people with a real hunger to go places, to be somebody, and do something. They look for students who, when closed out of the recruiter's interview schedule, will write a letter saying, "I couldn't get on your campus interview schedule, but I have strengths I would like to discuss. . . . I like what you do. . . . I like your corporate culture, and I would like you to consider me for a job." People like this are hard to ignore.

Question: What other qualities do recruiters look for in job candidates?

Answer: Strong written and oral communication skills are essential. They also look for adaptability and flexibility—for people who understand that they're going to be in many jobs over their careers and perhaps several careers over their lifetimes. Recruiters also

tions, and changing jobs will be harder than it is when opportunities abound. Naturally, supply and demand also affect salaries.

PROGRESS CHECK

1. A big part of getting the right job is knowing what's "right" for you. How do you know what you really want from a job?
2. What do we mean by the term *work environment*?
3. What questions could you ask yourself to determine the work environment that would be best for you?

WRITING YOUR RÉSUMÉ

With the information that you have collected in your self-analysis and career targeting, you are ready for stage three of the job-search process: creating your résumé—the written document that will be your primary job-search tool. A **résumé** is a personal advertisement through which you try to convince employers to grant you an interview. Your résumé performs this task by relating your education, work experience, and personal accomplishments to the needs of prospective employers.

Moreover, your résumé can actually create opportunity in the job market. Many employers will view your résumé both as tangible evidence of your ability to communicate in written form and as a statement of how you see yourself. As

résumé
Written document in which a job applicant relates his or her education, work experience, and personal accomplishments to the needs of prospective employers

your first work project, your résumé will be evaluated on its merit. You should also remember, then, that your résumé can erase job-market opportunities for the same reasons that it can create them.

We will begin our discussion of résumé writing by describing the various components from which effective résumés are built. We will then offer some specific advice on style and layout before proceeding to a discussion of different ways to organize a résumé, including descriptions of the different formats that are most effective under different circumstances.

As you read this section, try to think of your résumé as part of the employment-interviewing process. That is, if you are granted an interview, your résumé will be on the employer's desk during the interview session. Questions about your background that are not answered on your résumé will be addressed directly in the interview. Therefore, although you may decide to omit from your résumé an employment gap that lasted two years, you should be prepared to answer questions about that gap during the interview.

Building Your Résumé

When an employer receives a résumé, he or she expects to see specific blocks of information, including your name, address, phone number, education, and work experience. Some résumés also mention job objectives, community and professional activities, and employment references.

NAME, ADDRESS, AND PHONE NUMBER   Open your résumé with your name, address, and phone number. This information identifies you and gives employers a way to reach you if they are interested in your qualifications. You should

A résumé is a balance sheet without any liabilities.

Robert Half American personnel-agency executive

---

look for demonstrated leadership skills and the ability to work in groups. They want to see evidence of these traits in what students have done outside the classroom. They also want to see a tolerance toward diversity. With the workplace becoming more diverse every day, they can't afford to hire people with narrow, bigoted perspectives.

Question: What are the most common mistakes that students make in writing résumés and cover letters?

Answer: Many students undersell themselves. They don't realize that many of the things that they have done in life are transferable to the workplace. For example, many campus activities demonstrate leadership. While most employers consider grades important, they consider them to be only one of about ten key factors. Skills like leadership are often perceived as more important than straight A's.

Question: How should students handle background problems?

Answer: By taking a positive approach that builds on strengths and by never apologizing for weaknesses. Also, giving an employer a complete picture can help explain a difficult situation. For example, if your grade-point average is a B– but you supported yourself through school, you should let the employer know that you paid your own tuition. This information demonstrates that despite a relatively weak grade-point average, you can balance several balls at once, you are responsible, and you understand the pain it takes to get ahead.

Question: Is there a single thing that can give students the greatest advantage in the job search?

Answer: To know themselves and the job they want. They have to understand what they can offer. They have to understand what the organization is looking for. And they have to be able to relate their strengths and skills to the company's needs. That's really what it's all about.

Source: Interview with Alan B. McNabb.

also keep in mind that because accessibility will be critical during your job search, it is a good idea to have an answering machine receive calls when you cannot. If you are currently employed, listing your work number may be risky—a co-worker may pick up the phone. Instead, direct all messages to your home number or address or to another phone number at which messages can be received. For example:

Joanne Cleveland
1111 South Orange Street
Hollywood, FL 33021
(305) 555-1111—home
(305) 555-2222—message

Place this information at the top of the first page. There is no need to identify your résumé with a label like "Résumé," "Qualifications Brief," or "Background Sheet"—it will be clear at a glance what the document is.

JOB OBJECTIVE   The next heading is often "Objective," which should reflect the job target that you defined for yourself in step two of your search. For example:

- Objective—Administrative assistant
- Objective—Entry-level compensation and benefits administrator
- Objective—Credit manager in a mid-size women's specialty store

By including this information, you help prospective employers pinpoint a slot into which you might fit. However, you also run the risk—often unnecessarily—of restricting the prospective employer's view of you and your goals. If a job opening does not precisely match your stated objective, an employer may assume that you would not be interested or that you are not qualified. Nevertheless, a job-objective statement is often valuable and is necessary on a targeted résumé, which will be examined later in the chapter.

EDUCATION   Until now, your greatest accomplishments have probably occurred in school. Your course of study, the skills and abilities that you have acquired, major career-related projects and reports, grades and awards, and extracurricular activities all point to your ability to achieve results. The job of your résumé is to tie your accomplishments to your job objective. For example, if your objective is an editorial job in publishing, you can point to the fact that you majored in English with a minor in journalism, that you had a B+ average in your major, that you were the editor of your school's literary magazine, and that you were part of a course-related volunteer program to teach English as a second language to local high school students. Such activities will become less important over the years, but before you have accumulated a body of work experience, they will form the core of your résumé.

Include the names and locations of all the higher-education institutions that you have attended, including technical schools, community colleges, four-year colleges and universities, and graduate schools; the dates you attended; and the degrees you received. If they are job-related or show distinctive personal qualities, mention awards, special projects, and grades.

In recent years, more and more firms have been checking educational claims for accuracy. This check may be conducted prior to employment or in the first few months after hiring. If inaccuracies are found after you start working, you may be subject to immediate dismissal.

WORK EXPERIENCE   Your résumé also lists your previous work experience. At this point, of course, it is probably limited, but it will eventually comprise the bulk of your résumé. Be sure to include part-time and summer jobs, especially those that are related to the kind of work you want to do. For example, if your job target is to become a management trainee in a nationwide chain of child-care centers, note that you worked for three summers as a teacher's assistant in a nursery school.

Whether you use a chronological, functional, or targeted format, your résumé should list the names and locations of organizations, dates of employment (if you are still employed, write "19XX–Present"), and job titles. As we will see, formats for listing and explaining functions and accomplishments will vary according to different résumé forms.

COMMUNITY AND PROFESSIONAL ACTIVITIES   You may also decide to mention community and professional activities tied to your job target. For example, if you are applying for a job as a fund-raiser, mentioning that you recently raised $5,000 for the American Cancer Society is a significant credential. Even activities unrelated to your job target can show such qualifications as initiative, the ability to lead, or aptitude for working as a member of a team. For example, mentioning that you led the effort to organize a chapter of Students Against Drunk Driving at your college will impress managers looking for a self-starter.

REFERENCES   Your résumé may also include **references**—a list of people whom an employer may call to learn about your ability, character, and background. References may be previous employers, college professors, community leaders, or even well-known or influential friends. (Writing requests for personal references is discussed in Chapter 6.) Many résumés include a standard tag line like "References available upon request." Most employers, however, assume that you will provide a reference list when they ask. In a format like that of a résumé, where every word counts, the tag line adds nothing and may detract from more important items like your statement of achievements.

When a request for references is made, give employers the names, titles, organizations, addresses, and phone numbers of the people involved. Type the list neatly on a separate sheet of paper. Before including people on your personal-reference list, be sure to tell them about your intention and ask permission. If possible, explain your job objective for prospective references so that when they are called, they can focus on those aspects of your experience that are tied most closely to your employment objective. For example, if you are applying for a job as a market researcher and use your marketing instructor as a reference, remind her about your class project survey to assess student reaction to tuition increases. Because your goal is to highlight accurate information about your past, you may regard such nudges in the right direction as ethical.

> **references**
> In recruiting, a list of people that a prospective employer may contact to learn about a job applicant's abilities, character, and background

Mastering Résumé Writing Style

Résumé writing requires a clipped, action-oriented style that focuses on results. Rather than sentences that elaborate on sometimes unnecessary details, use phrases that start with action verbs. For example, instead of writing,

I was chosen by a committee to coordinate the college blood drive that resulted in the donation of 100 pints of blood

write,

Coordinated college blood drive. Increased donations by 50 percent

The subject of your résumé is what you have *done*, and action verbs—*coordinated, increased*—stress successful activities. So-called *personal power verbs*, including the following, will help you emphasize your activities and accomplishments:

wrote	managed
sold	taught
produced	tested
founded	translated
solved	programmed
collected	interviewed
prepared	devised
built	expanded
organized	planned

Try to limit your résumé to one page by eliminating repetitions and unnecessary personal data. For example, if you performed the same function for three different companies, describe your common responsibilities only once. Don't waste space mentioning your age, height, weight, marital status, number of children, religious affiliation, hobbies, or the names of high schools and college fraternities or sororities. Including this information makes you appear unfocused and detracts from your professionalism.

Choosing an Effective Layout

Résumés that contain "fat" paragraphs or require close reading to cull essential information will not get a reading at all. Nor will those that are too long. The following suggestions are designed to help you produce a résumé with eye appeal.

- *If possible, limit your résumé to one page.* Break this rule only if it is absolutely necessary. Keep in mind that most employers are too busy to read long documents. Similarly, limit the amount of space that you devote to each item in the résumé. As a rule, no paragraph or section should contain more than ten to twelve lines.

- *Use plenty of white space.* To produce a feeling of openness and easy readability, use margins at least one inch wide and double-space between major sections. Remember that many employers read résumé information in sections, starting first with what interests them. Coupled with headings, white space enables readers to find information quickly. At the same time, single space within sections.

- *Use upper-case letters.* Type headings and important titles in UPPER-CASE letters. Be consistent in using this and other effective techniques throughout your résumé.

- *Use underlining and bullets effectively.* Underline results or accomplishments that you want to emphasize. Because the reader's eye is normally drawn to underlined sections anyway, remember to use the technique sparingly and with your job target in mind. Punctuate specific accomplishments with bullets that look like ■ or •.

- *Use consistent indenting.* Arrange information in the body of the résumé in visible columns. For example, in a chronological résumé like the one in Figure 16.3, dates appear at the left margin while job descriptions are indented to the right. At the top of page one, of course, your name, address, and phone number should be centered in order to catch the reader's eye.

- *Produce a perfect final copy.* Crossing or whiting out mistakes is not acceptable on a résumé. To eliminate spelling, grammar, and punctuation errors, draft your résumé on a word processor and proofread the final copy several times. Make sure that all names and companies are spelled correctly. Take the same care in addressing envelopes.

- *Print your résumé on high-quality paper.* In order to get copies as good as your original, take your résumé to a printer for photo-offsetting. Use white, ivory, or off-white paper only.

MILES HENDERSON
322 Main Street
Allentown, PA 18103
(215) 555-4321

OBJECTIVE   To obtain a corporate public relations position

WORK EXPERIENCE
1992 - Present   BLACK & DECKER - Allentown, Pennsylvania
                               Public Relations Manager

                               • Managed staff of four public relations
                                 specialists.
                               • Handled media inquiries.
                               • Acted as public spokesperson for top
                                 executives.
                               • Planned and implemented in-house
                                 publications, including a monthly
                                 employee newsletter.

1989 - 1992   EASTMAN KODAK - Rochester, New York
                               Public Relations Specialist

                               • Wrote press releases for distribution to local
                                 and national media.
                               • Conducted interviews with top executives
                                 for use in employee publications.
                               • Handled routine media inquiries.

EDUCATION
1985 - 1989   Kent State University, Kent, Ohio

                               B.A. degree in journalism
                               Graduated cum laude
                               Editor in chief student newspaper

COMMUNITY ACTIVITIES
1992 - Present   Literacy Volunteer

FIGURE 16.3 *Sample Chronological Résumé*

Organizing Your Résumé

Organize your background into one of three résumé formats: *chronological*, *functional*, or *targeted*. Your choice depends on your previous experience and your job target.

CHRONOLOGICAL FORMAT   A **chronological résumé** arranges your work experience, education, and personal history in a *reverse* time sequence—that is, with the most recent experience in each category listed first. The chronological résumé has the advantage of highlighting your work experience and career growth as it focuses on names of employers, dates of employment, and specific job titles and responsibilities. It is the résumé of choice when you have an impressive job history that shows movement up the career ladder, especially in such traditional fields as education and government. The chronological résumé should not be used when your history shows major employment gaps, repeated job changes, or little or no career progress. Chronological résumés are also ineffective when you are applying for your first job. Follow these guidelines to organize a chronological résumé:

1. Devote the greatest space to your most recent work experience. *Working backward* from that point, detail each of the positions that you have held in the past. Include company names, locations, dates of employment, titles,

chronological résumé
Document in which the applicant's work experience, education, and personal history are arranged in a *reverse* time sequence—that is, with the most recent experience in each category listed first

and responsibilities. Make sure that there are no time gaps—account for all of your time from your first to most recent job.

2. If you are a recent graduate, vary the format by listing your education before your work history.

3. Do not describe your experience in neutral terms. Rather, describe your work history with your job objective in mind. Focus on the accomplishments and responsibilities that will impress prospective employers.

4. Describe only your major achievements and responsibilities. Don't mention the routine parts of your jobs.

5. If you have held the same job for several employers, describe it only as it applies to your most recent position.

Figure 16.3 is an example of a chronological résumé. Note how the consistent use of white space, capitalization, spacing, and underlining gives this résumé a clean, open appearance.

functional résumé
Résumé that highlights the applicant's accomplishments and abilities rather than his or her work history

FUNCTIONAL FORMAT   A **functional résumé** highlights your accomplishments and abilities rather than your work history. The flexibility of this format allows you to focus on your strengths in ways that support your job objective. Because you can emphasize functions rather than jobs, this format is excellent for recent college graduates with little or no work experience. Under various functional headings, school and community activities and volunteer and part-time work all can take on added importance.

A functional résumé is also useful to people with employment gaps, to job-hoppers, to those who have made little career progress, and to people seeking to change career directions. It is not suggested, however, when you want to emphasize steady job growth and promotions, when your work experience involves a limited number of functions, and when you are applying for work in such traditional fields as education and government. Follow these guidelines for constructing an effective functional résumé:

1. Choose three to five functional headings to highlight not only your accomplishments and responsibilities but also your job goal. Choose descriptive functional headings like these:

Management	Public Relations
Sales	Training
Writing	Fund Raising
Accounting	Purchasing

2. Prioritize these functions in terms of your job objective. For example, if you are trying to get a job in sales, list this function before all others—even if you have more experience doing other things.

3. Do not link functions to employment by stating where your accomplishments took place. This information will emerge in the job interview.

4. List employment and education at the bottom of the résumé and include relevant names, dates, locations, and titles. If you have little or no prior work experience (many recent graduates fall into this category), eliminate the employment section. The same advice holds for people with major employment gaps.

Figure 16.4 is a sample functional résumé. Note that the major functional headings have been created to categorize and highlight the nature of the candidate's accomplishments, and not the employers for whom she achieved results. "Work Experience" is thus reserved for a separate functional heading.

targeted résumé
Résumé that highlights abilities and achievements that relate to a specific job goal

TARGETED FORMAT   If you have a specific job objective, a **targeted résumé** highlights abilities and achievements that relate to a specific goal. However,

ROBERTA S. REVEZ
4567 WEST SALEM DRIVE
CHICAGO, IL 60622
(312) 555-9876 - Home
(312) 555-3694 - Message

PURCHASING/RETAIL:
- Selected merchandise for women's sportswear department.
- Traveled extensively on buying trips to Europe and the Pacific Rim.
- Developed merchandising strategies.
- Determined retail prices and store markups.
- Worked with designers to select catalog merchandise.

ADMINISTRATION:
- Processed merchandise orders.
- Enforced quality-control standards.
- Helped develop the firm's quick-response computer system.
- Handled supplier complaints.

MANAGEMENT:
- Trained and managed staff of three assistant buyers.

WORK EXPERIENCE:

1989 - Present   Sears, Roebuck and Company - Chicago, Illinois
                 Senior Buyer - Women's Apparel

                 Limited Stores - Chicago, Illinois
1984 - 1988   Buyer-Junior Sportswear
                 Assistant Buyer - Women's Apparel

1983 - 1984   Marshall Field - Chicago, Illinois
                 Floor Manager - Women's Apparel

EDUCATION:
1986 - 1988   Chicago University
                 Chicago, Illinois

                 Bachelor's degree in Marketing

1984 - 1986   University of Illinois, Chicago Circle
                 Chicago, Illinois

                 Associate of Arts degree

FIGURE 16.4   *Sample Functional Résumé*

because targeted résumés apply only to specific jobs or types of jobs, you will need a different résumé for each target. By the same token, this format is ideal when you have several distinctive job goals in different fields.

Targeted résumés emphasize capabilities over job history and are excellent for people who have accomplished a great deal outside the work setting (for example, unpaid fund-raisers). Generally, they are not very valuable when you are trying to start a career.

Follow these guidelines to write an effective targeted résumé:

1. State your specific field and job target at the top of the résumé.
2. Learn as much as you can about your job target and tie your capabilities and accomplishments to that target.
3. Your list of capabilities should emphasize the things that you can do to fulfill the responsibilities of your targeted career. Use the present tense to stress the fact that your capabilities apply to present and future work.
4. Your list of achievements should focus on the specific accomplishments that relate to your job target. Use the past tense to stress the fact that these are things you have in fact done.

SANDRA K. FITZGERALD
1322 Appletree Lane
Arlington, VA 22203
(703) 555-6678

JOB TARGET:	EDITOR, CONSUMER MAGAZINE
CAPABILITIES:	• Edit articles for publication. • Solicit articles from established authors. • Create page layouts and photo spreads. • Work with marketing staff to develop promotion ideas. • Write advertising copy.
ACHIEVEMENTS:	• Contributed eight articles to college literary magazine. • Worked as a consumer reporter for the college newspaper. • Sold advertising space for college paper. • Wrote senior thesis on the evolving consumer-protection movement.
EDUCATION: 1989 - 1993	SOUTHWEST MISSOURI STATE UNIVERSITY Springfield, Missouri B.A. degree, Communications Cited as newspaper reporter of the year.
WORK EXPERIENCE: 1989 - 1993	BURGER KING Worked my way through school as trainee, supervisor, and assistant manager.

FIGURE 16.5   *Sample Targeted Résumé*

5. Include work history and education at the bottom of your résumé. Include appropriate names, dates, titles, locations, and degrees.

Figure 16.5 is a sample targeted résumé. This candidate has worked from the general to the specific, describing her "capabilities" and then itemizing the "achievements" that enabled her to gain them through her work experience.

Table 16.1 compares the advantages and disadvantages of chronological, functional, and targeted résumés. As we have seen, deciding which format to use depends on your own background, job history, and career goals.

PREPARING A COVER LETTER

cover letter
Correspondence that accompanies a résumé in order to summarize an applicant's value to a prospective employer

Accompany each résumé with a **cover letter**—written correspondence to a prospective employer aimed at convincing the employer to grant an interview. Cover letters, in other words, are sales letters intended to sell your value. Writing an effective cover letter is stage four in the job-search process.

The best cover letters are written from the employer's perspective. When they have jobs to fill, employers are looking for signs people who will help them once they have been hired. To communicate this benefit, you should tailor each

TABLE 16.1	*Advantages and Disadvantages of Three Résumé Forms*		
	CHRONOLOGICAL	FUNCTIONAL	TARGETED
ADVANTAGES	Gives clear picture of work background Is useful for showing an impressive job history	Highlights accomplishments and abilities Focuses on strengths Excellent for recent graduates, job-hoppers, and career changers	Highlights abilities and achievements that relate to a specific goal Allows job hunter to target specific types of jobs
DISADVANTAGES	Shows employment gaps, job changes, and poor career progress Is ineffective when applying for first job	Does not show history of steady job growth and promotions Is not useful when experience involves limited number of job functions	Minimizes specific job history Forces job hunter to write different résumés for different job objectives

letter to the unique requirements of the job, the company, and the industry. Mass mailings (which are usually easy to spot) get few results.

Gathering the information that you need to write an effective cover letter often requires research into both industry trends and developments within your targeted company, such as personnel changes. We will talk about specific research techniques in Chapter 17. Here, we will focus on the components and format of the cover letter itself.

As you examine the components of an effective cover letter, adopt an audience-centered approach. Your value to a prospective employer exists only if the employer perceives it as he or she reads your cover letter and résumé. With this in mind, we suggest a visualization exercise before you begin writing: Picture a busy manager with dozens of résumés on his or her desk; the phone is ringing and piles of other work wait to be done. Now picture this manager as he or she throws out letters (and accompanying résumés) that ramble on for several pages in search of a point. Finally, picture this manager reading your letter, which is short and focused.

The moral: Write every cover letter with the idea that you have only a few seconds of reading time to capture and hold audience attention and no time to make a poor impression. According to Rick Kean, executive vice president of Dunhill Personnel Systems, it should take managers no more than forty-five seconds to scan a résumé and form an initial impression.[8]

The Elements of an Effective Cover Letter

Effective cover letters include no more than four or five paragraphs. Each paragraph has a purpose as a selling tool.

INTRODUCTORY PARAGRAPH   Open your letter with an attention getter—a statement that convinces the employer to read on. Create interest. You might begin by naming a person either within or outside the company whom the employer knows, by citing specific knowledge of the company's business, or by using a compliment. The last sentence of your introduction should state directly your interest in employment with your reader's company.

USE CONTACTS   The best way to stand out from the crowd is to mention a personal contact—a professional colleague, a friend, or a relative—whose name makes your letter unique by its very nature. Here are two examples:

APPLYING TECHNOLOGY

Filing Your Résumé in an Electronic Database

In an attempt to avoid costly employment agency fees, many companies are turning to computerized résumé data banks—electronic storage facilities that contain thousands of résumé files. With the stroke of a key, recruiters at AT&T, Avon, Citicorp, and other major companies scan these files for words and phrases that correspond to the specific skills and backgrounds that they want in job applicants. Not surprisingly, a successful electronic search often leads to a job interview.

When Hewlett-Packard's Atlanta office needed a computer engineer, the managers scanned an electronic résumé file for such key terms as *Unix, X Window,* and *Motif*—computer-operating systems that applicants would have to know. H-P managers then called up such secondary factors as previous job titles, educational degrees, and locations until they found people who most closely fit their desired qualifications.

With the number of companies using independent résumé databases growing every day, it makes good sense for job seekers to sign up with one or more services. Fees range from $20 to $50 for a six- to twelve-month period. Following are some of the most widely used résumé databases and their toll-free phone numbers:

- Job Bank USA (800-296-1872)
- SkillSearch (800-258-6641)
- KiNexus (800-828-9422)
- Peterson's Connexion (800-338-3282)

KiNexus and Peterson's Connexion operate through many college career centers and are free to students (nonstudents pay for the service). Some services set minimum application standards. For example, Job Bank USA requires a college degree and two years' work experience.

Instead of keyboarding every résumé into the computer, database companies use optical character readers to scan documents submitted

---

- Albert White, an employee in your accounting department, told me about an entry-level opening in accounts payable. I am interested in talking with you about this position.

- Andrea Swain, a close family friend, suggested that I contact you about a position in sales. As a recent graduate in business with several years experience in retail sales, I believe that my background is right for your company.

CITE KNOWLEDGE OF COMPANY BUSINESS   Another effective technique is to demonstrate knowledge of the company and, if possible, tie new business developments to your personal qualifications. Current knowledge comes from research—from reading local papers and national publications like *The Wall Street Journal, Business Week,* and *Fortune* and from reviewing annual reports and other corporate documents. Here are two examples:

- I read in yesterday's paper about The Coca-Cola Company's rapid expansion into markets overseas. With 25 percent of sales coming from Latin America, your firm has a need for qualified managers who know the soft-drink business and the Latin American culture. Because I am qualified in both areas, my background should interest you.

- An article I recently read about a cellular telephone joint venture between American Telephone and Telegraph and GTE Mobile Communications prompted me to write this letter. As a recent graduate specializing in communication technologies, I would like to apply for employment in this new joint venture.

COMPLIMENT THE COMPANY   In business as elsewhere, compliments never hurt—especially if they are sincere and reflect your knowledge about a company and its achievements. Use the compliment as a springboard to ask for an interview. For example:

- Ever since I began studying advertising in college, I have been impressed by the work Wieden & Kennedy has done, especially your campaigns for Nike

by job seekers. This information-entry method determines certain requirements for the look of submitted résumés. As you can see from the following requirements, résumé databases do not follow traditional résumé-writing guidelines. When submitting a résumé to an electronic database:

- Send originals, not copies, and avoid using dot-matrix printers that optical scanners find difficult to read.
- Do not fold the paper—optical scanners have trouble reading words that fall into the folds.
- Use technical jargon—computerized searches focus on key words that are specific to given fields.
- Use white paper—scanners read it best (avoid blue and gray paper).
- Avoid nonstandard typefaces, underlining, italics, and decorative graphics.
- Avoid double columns—scanners read from left to right.

To judge the quality of a résumé database, ask questions about the employers who subscribe. Find out the industries they represent, where they are located, and whether an entire company or only a division subscribes. Once you make the decision to sign on, continue your job search in traditional ways. After Curtis Northrup, a computer programmer, registered with an electronic résumé service, he sent résumés to companies in five states and, to give himself more career options, began studying accounting. Northrup studied and waited for four months until Computoservice Inc. of Mankato, Minnesota, discovered his résumé in the electronic database and offered him a job.

Source: Margaret Mannix, "Writing a Computer-Friendly Résumé: The Old Rules of Presenting Yourself Might Now Hurt," *U.S. News & World Report*, October 26, 1992, pp. 90,

---

and Subaru. As a copywriter, I would like to be part of such a creative, forward-looking organization, and I am enclosing my résumé for consideration.

- Having spent the last five years as a department-store buyer, I appreciate Saks' unsurpassed reputation as a fashion leader. I would like to explore the possibility of joining your buying staff.

MIDDLE PARAGRAPH #1: SELL YOUR VALUE   Turn next to answering the question on the mind of every prospective employer: "How will hiring this person help me do my work and improve company profits?" By describing your value, you can give employers an answer to that question—and a reason to invite you for an interview.

Sell your value through results—the achievements in school and the workplace that demonstrate a "track record." Remember, however, that although these results are indeed tangible evidence of your ability to perform, they will create interest only if they tap into company need. For example, telling a bank that has just closed its consumer-banking division about your expertise in handling retail customers is a waste of time. Despite the value of your genuine accomplishments, the need is just not there.

Writing this paragraph, therefore, means applying your research to your own background. For example, recall the excerpt that we quoted above from the cover letter to The Coca-Cola Company. The second paragraph of that letter might read as follows:

For the past five years, I have worked for Pepsico as a sales manager in Miami. Working in the midst of the city's large Hispanic population, I gained experience dealing with the cultural differences that can obstruct a deal. Half my sales force and three-quarters of my customers are Hispanic. My fluency in Spanish and my ability to close major deals with Hispanic customers are readily transferable to your operation.

Here is how another recent college graduate communicated personal value to a prospective employer:

> As you can see from my résumé, I am graduating with a degree in accounting. Because of financial need, I worked my way through school, maintaining a job throughout the school year. Despite this, I graduated with honors and participated in such extracurricular activities as the college band and chorus. I also created an advertising campaign for band concerts that raised attendance by 300 percent. I bring to you an enormous energy for work and an ability to organize my time to get things done.

Even without work experience, this person's competence, work ethic, and dedication would be attractive to most employers.

MIDDLE PARAGRAPH #2: SUMMARIZE YOUR BACKGROUND   Take the opportunity here to summarize additional aspects of your background that will help you get an interview. Focus attention on anything that the employer could find valuable. Remember, however, that because your résumé is attached, it is unnecessary to repeat everything that you have done. In fact, if you feel that the previous paragraph gave a complete picture of your background, you can omit this paragraph completely.

CLOSING PARAGRAPH: A CALL TO ACTION   Like other persuasive letters, a cover letter should close with a call to action. Your call to action can take two forms: It can ask employers to call you to arrange an interview or it can tell employers that you will call them to determine interest and arrange a meeting time. Here is an example of each closing form:

- I would like the opportunity to explain my background and qualifications to you in a personal interview. I look forward to hearing from you and to arranging a meeting in the near future.
- I will call you during the week of May 21 to learn if my background interests you and to arrange an interview time.

Figure 16.6 is a sample cover letter written by a recent college graduate. As you can see, this writer has emphasized her value and background into a single paragraph but otherwise adheres closely to the guidelines discussed above and, with the writer's résumé, is ready to be mailed. Before mailing a cover letter, however, make sure every name is spelled correctly and that job titles are up-to-date (you may have to call the company to gather certain information).

Following Up

If you have not received a reply after two to three weeks, consider calling the company. Your purpose is to ask if your letter and résumé have been received, not to restate your job qualifications (pushing may very well get you eliminated from consideration). If your employment application has in fact been lost, the employer will probably ask you for another copy.

You can also follow up in writing, asking about the status of your application and communicating any new information that might enhance your chance for an interview. If you just learned, for example, that you will be graduating cum laude, say so in the follow-up letter. Similarly, you would tell an advertising agency that a campaign you developed in your current job has just won an award. If you still hear nothing, assume that you are not being considered for the job or that it has been filled and go on to more fruitful possibilities.

At the same time that you are preparing your résumé and sharpening your letter-writing skills, you should begin looking for actual job openings. Start by building and refining your employment communication network.

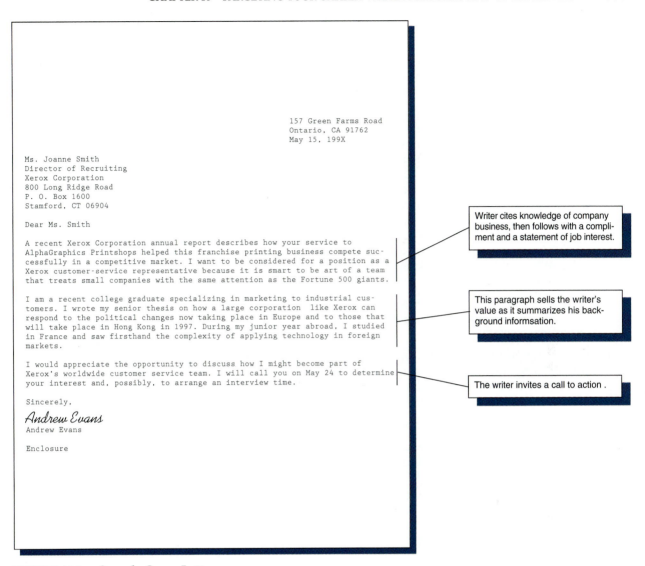

157 Green Farms Road
Ontario, CA 91762
May 15, 199X

Ms. Joanne Smith
Director of Recruiting
Xerox Corporation
800 Long Ridge Road
P. O. Box 1600
Stamford, CT 06904

Dear Ms. Smith

A recent Xerox Corporation annual report describes how your service to
AlphaGraphics Printshops helped this franchise printing business compete successfully in a competitive market. I want to be considered for a position as a
Xerox customer-service representative because it is smart to be art of a team
that treats small companies with the same attention as the Fortune 500 giants.

I am a recent college graduate specializing in marketing to industrial customers. I wrote my senior thesis on how a large corporation like Xerox can
respond to the political changes now taking place in Europe and to those that
will take place in Hong Kong in 1997. During my junior year abroad, I studied
in France and saw firsthand the complexity of applying technology in foreign
markets.

I would appreciate the opportunity to discuss how I might become part of
Xerox's worldwide customer service team. I will call you on May 24 to determine
your interest and, possibly, to arrange an interview time.

Sincerely,

Andrew Evans
Andrew Evans

Enclosure

Writer cites knowledge of company business, then follows with a compliment and a statement of job interest.

This paragraph sells the writer's value as it summarizes his background informsation.

The writer invites a call to action .

FIGURE 16.6   *Sample Cover Letter*

PROGRESS CHECK

1. Why is it important to have a good résumé when you apply for jobs?
2. Fill in the blank: The best cover letters are written from the perspective of the _____.
3. List some tips for getting an employer's attention in a cover letter.

If the house is on fire, forget the china, silver and wedding album—grab the Rolodex.

Harvey Mackay
American executive and business writer

NETWORKING

Studies have shown that networking, stage five in the job-search process, is the most effective way to find work. **Networking** involves talking and writing to people about your job search. When the Department of Labor asked job holders how they had found work, nearly half reported that they had relied on person-to-person contact. The Labor Department survey, which is summarized in Figure 16.7, compares networking, or "personal referrals," to six other job-finding methods. Other sources claim even better results for networking than those found in this survey. According to Lee J. Svete, college placement director at St.

networking
Process by which a job seeker talks and writes to people for assistance in his or her job search

PRACTICAL TIPS

Handling Background Problems

Because things left unsaid often raise questions, it is a good idea to address problems in your background in an open, honest way. Any of the following situations may require explanation in a cover letter.

Reason for Your Job Search. If you were one of the 6,000 people let go by Tenneco as a result of downsizing, chances are that your job loss had little or nothing to do with your competence. You must nevertheless anticipate the question "Why is this person looking for a job?" You can do so by writing:

> Due to the recent decision by Tenneco to cut its staff, I am now looking for a position as a sales representative.

There is no stigma attached to this type of layoff, and mentioning such circumstances in your cover letter will also eliminate any suspicion that you were dismissed for cause.

Similarly, if you are a recent college graduate, you can say simply that "I graduated from college last month and am now seeking full-time employment as an accountant."

Explanation of Gaps. If there is any way to explain a gap in employment or education, do it. If you explain nothing, employers may create their own worst-case scenarios ("Who needs people who spend a year after high school searching for themselves and then take six years to finish college?"). Ironically, the right explanation, as in the following excerpt, can actually make you a more attractive candidate:

> I spent a year between high school and college taking care of my sick mother, and these responsibilities also delayed my college graduation.

Many employers believe that this kind of dedication is transferable to the workplace.

Lawrence University in Canton, New York, "About 66 to 70 percent of those who do find jobs have been finding employment through contacts with alumni, parents, friends, and others. . . . If you cannot go in the front door you go through a side door."[9]

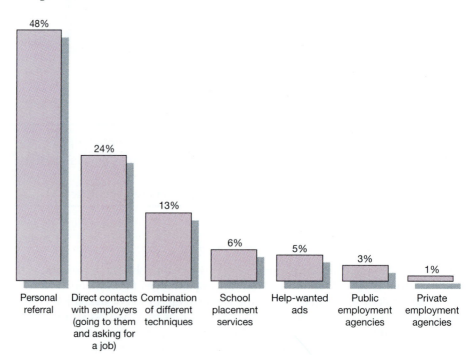

FIGURE 16.7   *How People Find Work*

Source: "Who's Hiring Who" by Richard Lathrop. Copyright © 1989 by Richard Lathrop. Excerpted by permission of Ten Speed Press, P.O. Box 7123, Berkeley, CA 94707.

There are times, of course, when the only explanation for a gap does not reflect well on a candidate's activities or experience. If such is the case, do not mention the explanation. If it is brought up in an interview, tell the truth and hope that your skills, qualifications, and attitude will overcome any negative impact.

Frequent Job Changes. Although it is common in many fields to change jobs frequently, it is generally not a good idea to highlight job changes in your cover letter or résumé. Focus on your job skills and past accomplishments and downplay job hopping by using a functional rather than a chronological résumé format.

Money. Salary requirements are one of the last things to discuss in a job interview, and unless the information is specifically requested, the subject of money should not come up in your cover letter. When a help-wanted ad asks your salary requirements, try to give a general range rather than a specific figure: "My salary requirement is in the low $30,000 range" is better than "I require a salary of $34,000." While the former implies flexibility, the latter does not.

Finally, remember that the first thing employers focus on when they receive your cover letter is what is *not* right—the obvious negatives that eliminate you from the running immediately. Only when they find no negatives are they likely to look for positive traits. Your writing challenge, then, is to anticipate negative reactions by taking a positive approach. For example, if you did not work during college because your parents paid your expenses, anticipate a negative reaction to your lack of job experience by indicating in your cover letter that you were able to devote all your four years exclusively to your studies.

Source: Richard H. Beatty, *The Perfect Cover Letter* (New York: John Wiley, 1989), pp. 87–97. Copyright © 1989 John Wiley & Sons. Reprinted by permission of John Wiley & Sons, Inc.

Making Your Contacts Work for You

Developing a network and using it effectively takes time and practice. It also means understanding that networking is yet another form of business communication. The following general suggestions are designed to help you communicate effectively in a network. We will also offer some more specific advice on preparing for and making the actual networking call.

- *Ask everyone you know for advice.* Discuss your job search with family, friends, former co-workers, teachers, and community businesspeople. If they can't help, ask for the names of other people whom you might contact. In networking, more is better. The more contacts you have, the more likely it is that you will find a source of help.

- *Be prepared and be specific.* Be ready with a short summary (no longer than two to three minutes) of your background and career objectives. And be specific about the type of help you want.

- *Don't ask for a job.* Asking directly for a job is one of the fastest ways to end a conversation—it puts your contact in a difficult position. Instead, ask for job-hunting advice. If a job is available, your contact can make the first move. This approach makes your intentions clear without creating an awkward situation.

- *Take notes.* Keep a file of meeting dates and conversations. Include the name, title, company, and phone number of the person you contacted, the person who introduced you, and the date and substance of your initial and follow-up contacts.

- *Become involved in activities that will enlarge your network.* Join clubs at school, become involved in community activities and charitable work, take part in such projects as political campaigns. Each activity will increase your number of potential contacts.

- *Send letters of introduction to new contacts.* The purpose of the letter is three-fold:

  1. To establish the source of the reference—for example:

     > Professor Abigail Andrews, of the University of Minnesota–Duluth, suggested that I contact you for information about entry-level career opportunities in accounting.

  2. To introduce yourself and your background.
  3. To make a request—for example:

     > I would like the opportunity to meet with you in your office to talk about the accounting field, my background, and career objectives. I will call you next week in the hope of setting up a time we can meet.

- *Call new contacts.* When you call a new contact, your primary goal is to make a favorable impression so that the contact will remember you when he or she hears of a job opening. A secondary goal is to come away with other networking contacts.
- *Make follow-up calls (but don't abuse people's time).* Keep in touch with your networking contacts on a regular basis—even after you have found work. A holiday card or an occasional phone call will ensure that your contacts will be there for you if you need them again. The best way to guarantee a continuing relationship is to become part of their professional network. Go out of your way to help when you receive a letter or call.

PREPARING TO MAKE THE CALL   Networking calls are difficult, even for seasoned executives who find themselves out of work. Yet most people are willing to listen and help—if they can. Career-management consultants William J. Morin and James C. Cabrera suggest the importance of anticipating the direction of a networking conversation and preparing questions and answers to keep it on track. Here is a scenario in which they demonstrate the application of their technique:

> You might begin by saying, "I'm calling at the suggestion of John Jones, an associate of mine who speaks very highly of your expertise in data processing."
>
> Your contact might reply, "It's nice of John to say that. Why did he refer you to me?"
>
> This is the time to ask for advice: "I'm looking for an objective viewpoint from someone with your background about the future of several segments of the data processing industry. I'd also like advice about opportunities you think are out there, since I'm in the process of making a career change. Let me make it clear that I'm not calling to ask for a job, just for information."
>
> Your new contact is likely to say, "I'd be happy to talk with you...."
>
> You might respond, "Before I start my job search in earnest, I'd appreciate some thoughts and comments about my résumé. I want to make sure my objectives come across clearly, and I'd like to be certain the personal accomplishments I mention are in line with the needs of the industry. Can we schedule a fifteen-minute meeting to talk in your office?"
>
> If the person agrees to the meeting, you've added another layer to your network. Or he or she may ask instead, "Do you have any questions I can answer over the phone?" Be ready with several, and give some thought to the order in which you ask them, regardless of whether you raise them in person or on the phone....
>
> Your final question should be, "Will you help me with introductions to some of the people we've discussed?"[10]

IDENTIFYING FORMAL SOURCES OF EMPLOYMENT

Your job search will bring you in contact with such sources of employment assistance as *college placement officers, on-campus recruiters*, and *employment agencies*. Learning to communicate with each source and understanding what each can and cannot do will help you to use these resources more efficiently. Acquainting yourself with available employment-assistance resources is stage six of the job-search process.

College Placement Officers

College placement officers are job-search professionals hired by colleges and universities to help students and alumni find jobs. They offer personal career counseling and testing as they help students analyze their career goals and guide them through the maze of the job market. College placement officers usually work closely with on-campus recruiters and so act as college-based employment agents who match students with jobs brought to them by employers.

> **college placement officer** Job-search professional hired by colleges and universities to help students and alumni find jobs

According to the College Placement Council in Bethlehem, Pennsylvania, more than eight out of ten placement centers offer career help to alumni, whether by giving them access to school-based job fairs (remember Neal Stubblefield's experience at the beginning of the chapter) or by offering personal career counseling. Note that many placement officers charge graduates an access fee for information.[11]

On-Campus Recruiters

When companies like Motorola, Aetna Life and Casualty, General Motors, and Intel Corporation have job openings, they often send representatives to college campuses. These representatives, known as **on-campus recruiters**, are highly trained professionals in the company's human resources department who interview students for jobs. Recruiters can generally tell very quickly whether student applicants have the background and qualifications to fill a specific position.

> **on-campus recruiter** Representative from a company's human resources department who interviews students for jobs

On-campus recruiting works well when recruiters arrive with an inventory of real possibilities. It does not work when jobs are scarce. According to Maury A. Hanigan, president of a firm that advises companies on recruiting activities, 32 percent of the companies surveyed during the recent recession conducted interviews at certain colleges even when they had no jobs to offer. Twelve out of 100 companies did no hiring although their recruiters visited dozens of colleges. When this happens, Hanigan adds, students are resentful: "It seems dishonest to them."[12]

Employment Agencies

There are, of course, employment-help choices outside the college campus. Private and public **employment agencies** match job candidates with specific jobs, often for a fee. Employment agencies fall into four categories: *private, public*, and *temporary agencies*, and *executive-search firms*. Each is geared to different populations with different employment needs.

> **employment agency** Organization that matches job candidates with specific jobs, often for a fee

PRIVATE EMPLOYMENT AGENCIES   Interviewers at private employment agencies sift through the applicant pool—reviewing résumés and references—to present a handful of qualified people for company interviews. With hundreds and often thousands of business contacts and with a large inventory of jobs on file, well-established agencies can shorten your search by matching you with

INTERNATIONAL ISSUES IN BUSINESS COMMUNICATION

Obtaining a Permit to Work Abroad

Working abroad is a dream for many Americans. Unfortunately, the dream is often derailed by the need to obtain foreign work permits. In countries as geographically diverse as Japan, France, and Australia, you cannot get a job without first obtaining the legal right to do so. Here are several examples of the restrictions placed on Americans who want to work abroad:

- In Scandinavia, work permits to non-natives are issued only when there is full employment in a job category. When permits are granted, they are valid for only three months.

- In France, employers must demonstrate that no French citizen can do the job for which the foreign worker is applying.

- In Holland, the government officially discourages applicants from non-European Community countries. When a work permit is granted, it is almost always in connection with a government-negotiated deal involving a major Dutch company.

With such restrictions blocking employment, Americans have only three ways to find work abroad. The following options may lead to legal employment:

1. Get a job with a U.S. company with offices overseas. Major corporations negotiate working arrangements for their American employees on a country-by-country basis. In exchange, the U.S. company often agrees to hire foreign nationals to work in the United States.

2. Find a foreign employer with the political clout to obtain a work permit for you. There are exceptions to every law, and

available jobs that meet personal career and financial needs. Working with an employment agency also allows you to fine-tune your interviewing skills as you answer the agency's screening questions.

Employment agencies earn money by charging fees for job placements. The fee is often based on a percentage of the applicant's first-year salary and may be paid by either the firm or the job candidate. In general, the simple economic principle of supply and demand dictates fee assignment.When applicants for a given position are in short supply, the company pays the fee; when there are too many qualified people applying for a position, the agency fee becomes the new job holder's responsibility.

Employment agencies often specialize in specific fields—accounting, banking, or computers, for example. To find a qualified agency, you can call the recruiter of a company for which you would like to work and ask for a referral to an agency that the company has used in the past. When you meet the agency representative, mentioning how you got there will also start the interview off on a positive note. The classified ads in your local newspaper will also point you to agencies that specialize in your field.

When no jobs are immediately available, call the agency once a week, both to get status reports and to express continuing interest. Remember that it is in the agency's best interest to find you a job—that is the only way it earns a fee. But also remember that it is to the advantage of the agent to steer you toward as many jobs as possible—some of which will be much further removed than others from your ideal employer.

PUBLIC EMPLOYMENT AGENCIES   State governments run public employment agencies to help residents find jobs. Because agencies are tax-supported, no fees are charged. Many offer computerized job banks that are updated daily and list openings found nowhere else. They also offer job counseling. For example, at the suggestion of a counselor at New York's Department of Labor, Phyllis

important foreign employers are able to find them. Your chances increase when you look for work in a high-need area, such as teaching English as a foreign language in Japan.

3. Find work through international-exchange and trainee programs that have already obtained permits for participants. Among these programs are:

■ Council on International Educational Exchange (CIEE)
205 East 42 Street
New York, NY 10017

■ International Agriculture Exchange Association (IAEA)
National Agricultural Centre
Kenilworth, Warwickshire CV8 2LG, England

■ International Association for the Exchange of Students for Technical Experience (IAESTE)
Seymour Mews, London W1, England

Often, the most productive route is to find a U.S. employer with offices overseas. These companies, located in every state, include Caterpillar Tractor Company; Westinghouse Electric Corporation; Sears, Roebuck & Company; Revlon, Inc.; and Arthur D. Little Inc.

When seeking a work permit, persistence pays off. So does preparing yourself with the skills that both U.S. and foreign companies find hard to resist.

Source: Arthur H. Bell, *International Careers: Everything You Need to Know to Land a Job Overseas, Including Employer Listings for Corporate Jobs, Government Jobs, and Non-Profit Jobs* (Holbrook, MA: Bob Adams, 1990), pp. 113–18.

Goldberg enrolled in a computer-training program that taught her WordPerfect, a word-processing program, and Lotus, a spreadsheet used in business planning.[13] Remember, however, that state agencies are most successful in finding jobs for people at the low end of the pay scale.

TEMPORARY EMPLOYMENT AGENCIES   When you work as a "temp," your employer is the temporary employment agency that provides your services, for a fee, to companies in need of short-term help. In tight job markets, the only work available may be temporary work. Such work, however, may also be a lucrative stopgap until you find a permanent position. Robert Half, founder of Robert Half International, a worldwide employment agency, believes that temporary work can also be a good stepping stone to a permanent job with the temporary employer:

> What better way for an employer to judge someone than to watch that person at work every day for a week or two, or even longer? Hiring someone represents a great unknown to employers, no matter how diligent they've been in evaluating a résumé, asking probing questions during an interview, and checking references. A temporary worker who has been on the job quickly becomes a known entity.[14]

Today, temporary agencies are becoming increasingly specialized. According to the National Association of Temporary Services, of the approximately 5 million workers who fill temporary positions, nearly 2 million work as specialized technical, industrial, and medical temporaries.[15]

EXECUTIVE-SEARCH FIRMS   Also known as "headhunters" and "body snatchers," **executive search firms** are specialized employment agencies that

executive search firm
Specialized employment agency that represents employers rather than individual job applicants, usually to identify, evaluate, and select high-level personnel

work for companies rather than individual job applicants. Used primarily to place high-level personnel, they earn more than 30 percent of the first year's salary for each job placement—a fee always paid by the company. Like private employment agencies, search consultants screen candidates with the right qualifications and arrange for the most qualified to interview for the job. Unlike employment agencies, however, they are often given exclusive listings—a particular service will be the only agency screening candidates for a particular position. Your chance of success, then, is much greater if you pass the screening stage.

Executive search consultants do not work for recent college graduates with limited job experience. As their name implies, they are geared to the executive job market and often contact employed executives with good reputations in the hope of enticing them with more attractive offers. The largest executive search firms in the country are Korn/Ferry, Russell Reynolds, and Heidrick & Struggles.

Table 16.2 compares formal sources of employment assistance. Included are the functions, advantages, and disadvantages of each.

ANSWERING HELP-WANTED ADVERTISEMENTS

Stage seven of the job-search process involves learning how to answer help-wanted advertisements. The classified-ad sections of such newspapers as the *Chicago Tribune*, the *Los Angeles Times*, the *Detroit News*, and the *Washington Post*, as well as such trade publications as *Advertising Age*, the *American Banker*, and *Chemical Week*, contain help-wanted ads for available jobs.

TABLE 16.2	*Comparing Sources of Employment Assistance*		
	FUNCTIONS	ADVANTAGES	DISADVANTAGES
COLLEGE PLACEMENT OFFICERS	Offer career counseling and testing Act as employment agents	Provide assistance to students and alumni	Have relatively limited number of job listings
ON-CAMPUS RECRUITERS	Are company interviewers	Can shorten the job search by matching students with actual jobs	May arrive with few, if any, jobs to offer
PRIVATE EMPLOYMENT AGENCIES	Match applicants with actual jobs	Have inventories of actual jobs that must be filled Can shorten the job search; gives applicants repeated opportunities to interview	Applicants may have to pay high fees May steer applicants to wrong jobs just to collect fees
PUBLIC EMPLOYMENT AGENCIES	Offer free placement service to state residents	Same as for private agencies	Deal primarily with jobs at the low end of the pay scale
TEMPORARY EMPLOYMENT AGENCIES	Place job candidates in temporary positions	Provide opportunities in tight job markets or where flexibility is required May lead to permanent positions	Offer short-lived jobs that do not include benefits
EXECUTIVE SEARCH FIRMS	Place high-level executives in relatively high-paying jobs	Work for companies and have exclusive listings Fees always paid by hiring companies	Do not work with recent college graduates

A company can choose to name itself in an ad or use a postal box number. You can assume that if a name is used, the ad describes a legitimate position. Companies also place ads with box numbers when they want to keep the search private. However, many of these ads do not describe real jobs. Often, they are placed by employment agencies and search firms trying to amass stockpiles of qualified candidates for particular kinds of jobs. Companies may also place ads to test the job market for certain positions. Responses not only tell them how many people would respond if a job were actually available, but also indicate the range of current salary requirements.

In most cases, responses to company-placed help-wanted ads are screened by assistants in human-resources departments. To make your application stand out, therefore, you will need a distinctive cover letter and résumé. One way to set yourself apart is to send your résumé via overnight mail or to fax it.

Answering an ad, however, is not the end of your effort. After a week or two, follow up with a phone call to express active interest. You can also send a second letter in response to an ad that does not mention the company's name, asking when you might hear from the company and requesting an interview. Include another copy of your résumé. According to consultants Morin and Cabrera, this type of persistence pays off:

> In one instance, a man we counseled answered a newspaper ad for a job he thought was totally in line with his career goals. Two weeks passed and no word came back to him. Even though he realized the ad could have been placed by someone stockpiling résumés, it interested him so greatly that he sent off another résumé and a second cover letter. He received a telephone call a few days later and learned that one of the screening criteria for the position was a test of persistence. Only people who responded twice were considered for the job.[16]

To use help-wanted ads, you need to learn the shorthand that saves companies advertising dollars (because newspapers charge advertisers by the line, brevity is a virtue). For example, "sal. $25K" means "salary $25,000"; "college grad w/excel . . ." means "college graduate with excellent . . ."; "strong wp, database mgmt & willingness to take on addit responsibility" means "strong word processing, database management and willingness to take on additional responsibility." In most cases, help-wanted shorthand is common sense, but sometimes knowledge of the field is needed to figure it out. For example, it would be difficult to translate "V-mail" into "voice mail" without a knowledge of this communication technology.

MAKING COLD CONTACTS

Because most job opportunities are never advertised, you may want to make a series of cold contacts after you have exhausted your networking ties. **Cold contacts**, stage eight of the job-search process, are unsolicited letters in which you introduce yourself and ask about job openings. Cold contacts are sales efforts in which you attempt to convince a firm that you are a valuable, although unknown, commodity deserving an interview.

Before writing a cold-contact letter, follow the same advice that we discussed for other cover letters. Research the company and, if possible, learn something about recent corporate developments. By reading the business section of a newspaper, you may find out, for example, that the American fashion designer Adrienne Vittadini is expanding its sales efforts abroad. With a major in marketing, an interest in international apparel sales, and fluency in

cold contacts
Unsolicited letters in which job seekers introduce themselves and ask about job openings

Italian, French, and German, you thus decide to write the letter in Figure 16.8 to the director of human resources. Even though it is a cold-contact letter, the letter's message may be convincing enough for the recipient to grant the writer an interview.

PROGRESS CHECK

1. What is networking, and why is it important?
2. Explain the potential advantages of taking a temporary job.
3. What are cold contacts? Why are they useful?

Writer ties information from a recent news article to her personal career goals.

Key job-related background information is provided.

The call to action states the writer's willingness to travel for an interview.

2222 Main Street
Piedmont, CA 94618
November 5, 199X

Ms. Erika Holmstead
Director of Human Resources
Adrienne Vittadini
1441 Broadway
New York, NY 10018

Dear Ms. Holmstead:

I noticed with interest an article in the November 3, 199X New York Times citing Adrienne Vittadini's business activities in Europe and Japan and the comment by your president, Richard Catalano, that, within five years, you expect to do half your business abroad. With a growing international presence, surely you will need an expanded sales staff. I would like to join Adrienne Vittadini in an entry-level international sales position.

My enclosed résumé sums up my academic experience in marketing and my interest in international apparel sales. Please note my fluency in Italian, French, and German. As the daughter of a U.S. diplomat, I was fortunate enough to spend fifteen years in Europe and to learn its culture as well as its languages.

Thank you for reviewing my qualifications and for considering my interest in working for Adrienne Vittadini. I look forward to hearing from you. Although I live in California, I would be willing to meet with you in New York for an interview.

Sincerely,

Caroline Becker

Caroline Becker

Enclosure

FIGURE 16.8   *Sample Cold-Contact Letter*

WHAT'S AHEAD

From all this effort, one or more interviews will emerge. Chapter 17 will examine how to communicate effectively during an interview so that you will improve your chances of receiving a job offer. We will also examine the various forms of written communication associated with the job-interviewing experience.

SUMMARY OF CHAPTER OBJECTIVES

1. **Describe the *job search* in terms of eight distinct stages.**

   Eight stages characterize an effective job search. These include analyzing your career goals, targeting a field and a specific career, writing a résumé, preparing a cover letter, networking, identifying formal sources of employment assistance, answering help-wanted ads, and making cold calls. Effective communication skills are essential at each stage.

2. **Describe the process of defining your *interests, marketable skills, personal traits,* and *accomplishments* and linking these to career choice.**

   Using the process of self-analysis, you can identify your interests by listing the things that give you personal satisfaction as well as the things that you would rather not do. Next, personal-skills assessment involves listing the abilities and talents that can give you an edge in the workplace. You can then define the personal qualities that influence your own job choice. Finally, list your accomplishments—the concrete results of your experience and activities that will impress prospective employers. The information that you compile in this process will lead you in one or more specific career directions.

3. **Explain how to *target* a field and a career by analyzing the *work environment* and the forces of supply and demand that affect the *job market*.**

   Analyzing the work environment is critical to making a smart job choice. This analysis requires decisions about such varied factors as working indoors or outdoors, working for a large corporation or a small business, working regular hours or adapting to shift work, and being willing or unwilling to relocate.

Targeting a field and a career also requires that you analyze the job market in terms of the need for workers and the salaries available in specific fields.

4. **List the elements of an effective *résumé*.**

   An effective résumé lists your name, address, and phone number; education; work experience; and community and professional activities. It may also include a job objective and references. Résumé style features abbreviated, action-oriented language and focuses on results. A clean, open layout invites prospective employers to focus on the résumé items to which you want to draw attention.

5. **Describe the differences among *chronological, functional,* and *targeted résumés*.**

   A chronological résumé lists work experience, education, and personal history in a reverse time sequence; it focuses on names of employers, dates of employment, and specific job titles and responsibilities. A functional résumé makes your specific work history secondary to your accomplishments and abilities. A targeted résumé ties your abilities and achievements to a clear and specific job objective, which is stated at the top of the résumé.

6. **List the elements of an effective *cover letter*.**

   An effective cover letter is made up of no more than four or five paragraphs. The introductory paragraph attempts to capture the reader's attention by mentioning a personal contact, citing knowledge of company business, or complimenting the company. The body of the letter describes your potential value to the business as it summarizes your background. The letter closes with a call to action that attempts to arrange an interview time.

7. **Describe specific *networking techniques*.**

   Networking involves talking and writing to people about your job search. It means asking everyone you know for advice, being prepared with a short summary of your background and career objectives, becoming involved in activities that will enlarge your network, writing to new contacts, and following up with phone calls and letters on a regular basis.

8. **List three formal sources that can assist you in finding a job.**

Formal sources of employment assistance include college placement officers, on-campus recruiters, and employment agencies. College placement officers are school employees who attempt to provide employment assistance for students and alumni. On-campus recruiters are company representatives who travel to campuses to interview students for jobs. Employment agencies link job hunters with jobs, usually for a fee. Employment agencies fall into four categories: private, public, and temporary agencies, and executive-search firms.

9. **Explain the basic approach to answering help-wanted ads.**

Because help-wanted ads often bring in hundreds of responses, you will need a strong cover letter and résumé to make your application distinctive. To communicate the importance that you place on an opportunity, you may decide to fax your résumé or send it by overnight mail. If you have not heard anything after several weeks, send a second letter expressing active interest. At this point you can also contact the company by phone.

REVIEW AND DISCUSSION QUESTIONS

1. Name the eight stages that comprise the job search process. (*Ch. Obj. 1*)
2. Explain the importance of self-analysis to your career. (*Ch. Obj. 2*)
3. How might you go about analyzing yourself to choose a career? (*Ch. Obj. 2*)
4. Describe how you could target a particular field and specific career. (*Ch. Obj. 3*)
5. What elements help to make an effective résumé? (*Ch. Obj. 4*)
6. Distinguish among chronological, functional, and targeted résumés. (*Ch. Obj. 5*)
7. Describe the characteristics of a good cover letter. (*Ch. Obj. 6*)
8. Summarize some important tips that can help you network effectively. (*Ch. Obj. 7*)
9. In addition to networking, what sources are available to help you find a job? (*Ch. Obj. 8*)
10. Describe the approach that you would take in responding to a help-wanted ad. (*Ch. Obj. 9*)

APPLICATION EXERCISES

1. Explain why good communication skills are important for finding the job you want and building a career. (*Ch. Obj. 2, 7*)
2. A major component of self-analysis involves understanding what your interests are. Make a written list of your own interests, whether job-related or not. Your list should include activities in which you're presently active as well as past activities that you enjoyed. Write a separate list of activities that do not interest you. (*Ch. Obj. 1, 2*)
3. Build on the list that you made for EXERCISE 2 to create a separate list of your skills. Write down all the skills and abilities that you feel you could bring to a job. (*Ch. Obj. 1, 2*)
4. Analyze your personal qualities. Compile a list of the characteristics and personality traits that make you the person you are. To remind yourself of additional items, you may wish to discuss this list—and the ones that you developed for EXERCISES 2 and 3—with a friend or relative. (*Ch. Obj. 1, 2*)
5. Analyze your accomplishments and experiences. Develop a list that describes your achievements, whether at work, at school, in athletics, in hobbies, or simply as personal goals that you have achieved in some tangible way. Be sure to use phrases and action verbs. (*Ch. Obj. 1, 2*)
6. Choose a field or an occupation that interests you. After consulting some reference sources, describe the ways in which the forces of supply and demand have affected that career path during the past decade. Is this occupation currently in demand? Why or why not? What is the outlook for jobs in this field for the next five years? Ten years? Write a brief report summarizing your findings. (*Ch. Obj. 3*)

7. The placement office at your school has asked you to write a concise guide for your fellow students on how to write effective résumés. In addition to presenting overall tips for writing a good résumé, your brief manual will explain when one should use chronological, functional, and targeted résumés. (*Ch. Obj. 4, 5*)

8. Working from the lists that you created for EXERCISES 2–5, write your résumé using a chronological format. Be sure to follow the guidelines described in the chapter for effective format, layout, and writing style. (*Ch. Obj. 4, 5*)

9. Now, write your résumé using a functional format. Follow the guidelines given in the chapter. Don't just copy what you wrote in your functional résumé; as you rewrite, evaluate your résumé to find ways of improving style and layout. (*Ch. Obj. 4, 5*)

10. Write your résumé using a targeted format. Target your résumé either to a job that you hold now or to a job that you would like to have. Which of the three résumé types do you find most appropriate for your needs? Why? (*Ch. Obj. 4, 5*)

11. From EXERCISES 8–10, select the résumé that you prefer and write a cover letter to accompany it. Address your letter to someone who is in a position to hire you for the job you targeted in EXERCISE 10. (*Ch. Obj. 6*)

12. Test yourself on the advantages and disadvantages of each type of résumé. Cover the information in TABLE 16.2 and test yourself on the pros and cons of chronological, functional, and targeted résumés. (*Ch. Obj. 4, 5*)

13. How good are you at networking? In the next week, try to develop three new contacts that you can add to your present network. Introduce yourself in person, call, or write a letter of introduction; follow the guidelines given in the chapter for communicating with these people. Write a brief description of the means by which you contacted each person, what you talked about, and how the conversation went. Do you feel that you handled each contact well? Can you think of ways to improve your networking skills? (*Ch. Obj. 7*)

14. Cover the information in TABLE 16.3. Test yourself on the functions, advantages, and disadvantages of each source of employment assistance. (*Ch. Obj. 8*)

15. Are you looking for a job? If so, scan the classified-ad section of your local newspaper or a trade publication in a field that interests you. Find two to three ads that sound interesting; send your résumé and a cover letter to each. The ads do not have to be in the same field. If you're seriously interested in these positions, you may wish to customize your résumé and/or the cover letter to suit each job.

   If you don't receive a response within two weeks, follow up with a phone call or another letter and résumé. Take notes on your experience with each ad. What can you learn from each experience? For instance, did you do a better job of customizing your résumé to one ad than another? Did you express yourself better in one follow-up phone call than in another? Use this information to help you in future job searches. (*Ch. Obj. 9*)

BUILDING YOUR RESEARCH SKILLS

Set up an appointment with someone with a great deal of experience in reading résumés from job applicants. This individual might be a human-resources professional, a manager who hires staff members for a company, or someone in academe who hires staff or faculty. Interview this person about what he or she looks for in résumés and cover letters. According to this individual, what characteristics make an effective résumé? Does this person prefer chronological, functional, or targeted résumés? What traits doom résumés and cover letters to the wastebasket? What advice does this person have for job applicants?

BUILDING YOUR TEAMWORK SKILLS

Your instructor will divide the class into small groups to work with résumés and cover letters that each member developed for EXERCISES 8–11 above. Make enough photocopies of your best résumé and cover letter to distribute one to each member of the group. Using the guidelines offered in the chapter, take turns evaluating each other's résumés and cover letters. Assess the format, layout, and writing style of each. What elements are effective? What elements seem less effective? Can the group members suggest changes or improvements?

COMMUNICATING IN A WORLD OF DIVERSITY

If you wanted to work for Sony, Japan's large consumer-electronics firm, you'd have to prove that you have *neyaka*.

Neyaka is a Japanese term meaning "optimistic, open-minded, and interested in many subjects." Sony executives believe that it is a vital personality trait in successful engineers and other technical employees. "There is a spiritual side of the world," says Sony founder and honorary chairman Masaru Ibuka, "that is very unpredictable, vague, and abstract, that is the source of human creativity. Creativity comes from looking for the unexpected and stepping outside your own experience." Senior managing director Minoru Morio agrees: "A good engineer is not necessarily young, but new in terms of his experience. We believe that having continuous success in the same area makes you believe too much in your own power, and harms your creativity."

The emphasis on *neyaka* guides project assignments at Sony. "If you want to lower the cost of an existing product or find a better way to manufacture it," explains one upper-level manager, "you assign it to experienced engineers who like what they are doing. If you are designing something new that is higher-priced, with lots of features, you give it to the rookies."

Suppose that you are interested in an engineering job with Sony. How might you write your résumé and cover letter to appeal to a hiring manager there?

Source: Brenton Schlender, "How Sony Keeps the Magic Going," *Fortune*, February 24, 1992, pp. 76–84. © 1992 Time Inc. All rights reserved.

CASE 16.1

Coming Soon from IBM to a Screen Near You

IBM plans to commit more than $100 million to create a new high-tech company that will electronically send videos, software, and other information into businesses and homes. Headed by IBM Vice President Lucie Fjeldstad, the new venture will start by offering services that would allow office workers to hold video conferences and work together simultaneously over their computer screens. Fjeldstad expects to expand these services into private homes within three years. Eventually, she plans to offer computer games, videos on demand, on-screen shopping, and interactive TV to both TV sets and computer screens in homes and businesses.

These technological advances are the result of improvements in cable-TV lines, which many experts feel can do a better job of transmitting video images than traditional phone systems. Three new IBM technologies—code-named *Planet*, *Orbit*, and *Comet*—will manage and distribute data along these huge networks. Says Michael Schwartz, vice president of a cable-industry research group: "Computer companies now see the cable pipeline as a means of getting multimedia to the home, whether it terminates in a computer or a TV set."

Fjeldstad acknowledges the risks involved in this new venture and admits that the new firm may not be profitable for at least four years. Ultimately, she wants about 75 percent of the company's employees to come from outside IBM.

Questions and Applications

1. Describe IBM's new venture.
2. What characteristics do you think IBM will look for when hiring employees for this new venture?
3. Suppose that you're applying to Lucie Fjeldstad for a job. How could you gear your résumé and cover letter to her concerns?

Source: Michael Miller, "IBM Commits More than $100 Million on Venture to Relay Video, Other Data," *The Wall Street Journal*, September 16, 1992, pp. B1, B5. Reprinted by permission of *The Wall Street Journal*, © 1992 Dow Jones & Company, Inc. All rights reserved worldwide.

From the Wastebasket at Accountemps

This chapter observes that because typographical errors and poor writing style will condemn it to the wastebasket, proofreading your résumé is crucial. The following excerpts are from actual résumés sent to the temporary employment agency Accountemps. Test your proofreading skills. Can you spot the mistakes? Revise each example so that it's correct (or at least makes sense).

1. Education: Curses in liberal arts, in computer science, in accounting.
2. My résumé shows my critical career developments. I'm also including other important parts of me.
3. Auditing for small manufacturing companies since 1877.
4. An obsession for detail; I like to make sure I cross my i's and dot my t's.
5. Self-Image: An octagon with smooth, radius angles versus a plain square with sharp corners.
6. Referees available on request.

Source: Catherine Friedman, "Proofreader Wanted," quoted in "Other Comments," *Forbes*, December 7, 1992, p. 30. First appeared in *Working Woman*, November 1992. Reprinted with permission of *Working Woman* Magazine. Copyright © 1992 by Working Woman, Inc.

Effective Employment
Interviewing

CHAPTER OBJECTIVES

After studying this chapter, you should be able to:

1 Describe the stages in the *interview sequence.*

2 Describe the different ways to prepare for a *job interview.*

3 Explain the importance of questioning the interviewer.

4 Outline the six stages of a *model interview.*

5 Identify specific techniques for *handling difficult and illegal questions.*

6 List strategies for *negotiating salary and benefits.*

7 Outline the different types of *pre-employment testing.*

8 Describe the nature of various *interview follow-up letters.*

The most difficult part of getting to the top of the ladder is getting through the crowd at the bottom.

Arch Ward
American sports editor

VICTORIA BROWN THINKS FOR HERSELF

When Victoria P. Brown, an MBA student at Columbia University, began interviewing for a job on Wall Street, she approached the process like a work assignment requiring the mastery of a new set of verbal and nonverbal skills. She bought an olive wool, man-tailored suit from F. R. Tripler & Company and hemmed it at midcalf to send the right nonverbal message. She learned the vocabulary of recruiting: "rounds" (as in boxing) are interview sessions; "call backs" are invitations for follow-up interviews; "ding" letters (after the sound of the bell in a prizefight) are letters of rejection; "stress tests" refer to a variety of psychological tactics used by difficult recruiters.

Brown also learned that interviewing is hard, often frustrating, work. She explains:

I walk into one man's office. He is interviewing me for a research-sales job. He greets me, points toward a chair across from his desk and then picks up his telephone. He talks into it for 20 minutes, all the while looking at me. Finally, he puts down the phone and places my résumé on the desktop near his computer screen so he can examine both at the same time. Now he never looks at me.

He starts out with the usual questions: "What would be your perfect job?" "What do you see yourself doing in 10 years?" Then he asks how I intend to market myself. I say he is looking at it. He asks how I deal with difficult people. I desperately want to give the same response, but reason prevails.

Although Brown has few regrets about her life so far, she quickly discovers that expressing self-satisfaction can be a mistake. Repeatedly, she is asked to talk about a time when she failed but can't think of anything to say. "There is no failed marriage in my past," she explains. "I have not colluded with [convicted insider traders] Ivan Boesky or Dennis Levine." 'Think again,' says the interviewer, and I want to say, I have not had the time to really fail. I am too young." When told by one interviewer that she is "just too well-rounded," Brown realizes that, at its worst, interviewing makes little sense.

After three months, dozens of interviews, and few job prospects, Brown finally comes to terms with the interviewing process. She realizes that she cannot become what recruiters want her to be. She can only be herself. Not surprisingly, it is at this point that offers begin to materialize. A Japanese bank, looking for a credit-research specialist, offers her a job after the fourth call back. The next day, a small securities house offers Brown a part-time job as an equity-research analyst, with the possibility of full-time employment. Pressed to make a decision, Brown puts off both companies for two weeks—the time she needs to think and choose.

I don't know the key to success, but the key to failure is trying to please everybody.

Bill Cosby
American actor and comedian

Brown turns to her friends for advice. One of them suggests calling a colleague at a financial-services company that might be hiring. After one interview, the man offers Brown yet another possibility: the chance to work on three research projects on a trial basis. Although this job intrigues her, she realizes that if she doesn't measure up, she will have to start interviewing all over again. It takes Brown five days to make up her mind. Risk or not, this is the position she wants. She calls the financial-services firm, says yes, and starts working the next week.[1]

CHAPTER OVERVIEW

Victoria Brown's experience features many of the elements that define employment interviewing: dressing the part, speaking the language, dealing with multiple interviews and difficult interviewers, experiencing self-doubt and self-realization, surviving periods of famine and periods of plenty, delaying decisions, networking with friends, having the chance encounter that leads to a job. These and other elements are the focus of this chapter, in which we will describe the employment-recruiting process in chronological order. The common thread that ties them together is the need for effective communication.

DEFINING THE JOB INTERVIEW

At the heart of this stage of the job-search process is the job interview. A **job interview** is generally a face-to-face encounter between a recruiter and a candidate in which the recruiter delves into the candidate's background, skills, job objectives, interests, and attitudes; in turn, the candidate asks questions about the position and the recruiting company. Typically, recruiters ask a series of probing questions to learn if the candidate is right for the job. Here are the ten most common qualities for which interviewers are looking when they question job candidates:

1. Intelligence and analytical ability
2. Creativity and flexibility
3. Communication skills
4. Work experience and required technical skills
5. Leadership qualities/team-playing ability
6. Initiative and entrepreneurship
7. Energy and stamina
8. Maturity
9. Interest in the position
10. Personal qualities and personality[2]

While the interviewer is assessing the candidate for these qualities, the candidate is conducting an assessment of his or her own to determine if the job is really desirable. If you think of the interview as a form of courting, you realize that the job choice is as much yours as the company's. It is a process in which job candidates and interviewers judge *each other* to decide whether they want to work *together*.

THE INTERVIEW SEQUENCE

Most companies—especially large ones—put candidates through more than one interview before deciding to hire them. Typically, this series, known as the **interview sequence**, consists of a *screening interview*, an *in-depth interview*, a *multiple interview*, and a *stress interview*.[3] Reading from top to bottom, Figure 17.1 depicts

job interview
Face-to-face encounter between a recruiter and a job candidate in which the recruiter assesses the candidate's background, skills, job objectives, interests, and attitudes; in turn, the candidate asks questions about the position and the organization

interview sequence
Series of interviews, constituting a multistage approach for evaluating job applicants

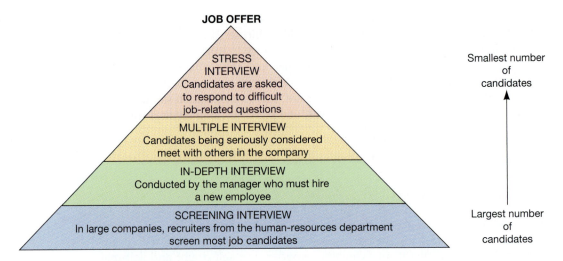

FIGURE 17.1   *The Interview Sequence*

the successive stages in the interview sequence. Realizing that interviewing is a multistage process is your first step in feeling comfortable with the process.

Keep in mind that you will not always encounter each stage and that the sequence varies from company to company. For example, at the Toronto-based Four Seasons Hotels, candidates pass through four to five rigorous interviews while recruiters look for friendly people who can work as part of a team. When a Four Seasons opened recently in Los Angeles, more than 14,000 people were interviewed for 350 jobs. Using a completely different interviewing style, Disney interviews candidates for jobs in its theme parks in groups of three so that interviewers can judge interpersonal qualities crucial to job success. Among the qualities analyzed are listening skills—interviewers want to know if candidates pay attention while others speak.[4]

The Screening Interview

screening interview
Normally the job candidate's first interview, which is usually conducted by a recruiter from the employer's human resources department

The **screening interview**, which is normally the candidate's first interview, is usually conducted by a recruiter from the human resources department. The site of the interview may be the recruiter's office, the placement office at the candidate's school, or perhaps a booth at a career fair attended by both recruiters and job hunters. Screening interviews are general interviews to determine whether you have the background, qualifications, and personality both to do the job and to fit comfortably in the organization. Although recruiters generally do not have authorization to hire from screening interviews, they can prevent candidates from moving to the next stage of the sequence. It is a good idea, therefore, to approach this stage fully prepared not only to answer questions but also to display an attitude that says you want the job. Your goal in a screening interview is to motivate the recruiter to pass your name on to the hiring manager for an in-depth interview.

The In-Depth Interview

in-depth interview
Extended interview between company official and a prospective job candidate

The **in-depth interview** brings together the manager who has a job to fill and prospective candidates who may fill it. At this stage, the manager will try to learn whether you can handle the job and whether your personality and interpersonal skills are right for the department and company.

Your goal during the in-depth interview is twofold: to answer questions and to get the manager to talk about his or her department, goals, problems, and needs. Audience analysis is crucial. To be successful, you must prove to the manager (your audience) that you can fill the position and help the company.

One of your goals, then, will be to shift the questioning from what you have done in the past (in school or on another job) to ways in which you can use your experience to help the company. Interestingly, even when managers ask, "So tell me what you did on your last job," they are really concerned with how your past experience relates to their current needs. It is up to you to make the connection between the past and the future by saying something like the following:

> While at Apple Computer, I conducted the same kind of marketing research that I think you need in your computer- software division. My work with Census Bureau databases revealed interesting population trends that are likely to affect computer purchases. Using the same techniques, I can find trends that will affect computer-software purchases—the kind of information that can help you better target your customers.

Getting managers to talk about their concerns, problems, and goals may require a gentle redirection of the interview. For example, if the manager only talks about the job in generalities, consider saying something like this:

> I really want to tell you how capable I am. But I can't unless you give me more specific details about the job. I have certain experience, and I want to be sure it applies to the kinds of things you are looking for.

As you proceed, try to put yourself in the manager's position. Try to imagine both the problems that he or she faces on a day-to-day basis and the approaches, solutions, and people that would help to solve them. When you convince a manager that you have the skills and personal qualities to help, you have transformed the power relationship in the interview from one in which the manager is in charge to one in which you both can help each other. Meanwhile, you are also building a sense of rapport, sharing, and chemistry with the interviewer. Your goal is to establish mutual comfort—the feeling that it would be acceptable to work together.

The Multiple Interview

Multiple interviews involve meeting with people at different levels of the organization. You may be asked to talk with potential subordinates, peers, division heads, and, in small firms, even company owners. At Hewlett-Packard, for example, candidates pass through at least a dozen long interviews after the initial screening.[5]

Because multiple interviews are usually shorter and less formal than in-depth interviews, and because they often take place with several people in such settings as lunches, candidates are often less vigilant about making a good impression. When your guard is down, you may make inappropriate comments that can eliminate you from the running. Even if you have already been told that your chances "look excellent," you can lose the opportunity by displaying poor social skills at lunch. "If there were nothing to be learned from the meal," says corporate recruiter and author Jeff Speck, "the firm wouldn't pay for it."[6]

People applying for jobs at Tandem Corporation, a computer company in California's Silicon Valley, are called back two or three times and must accept the position before discussing salary. The process, as one candidate recalls, is grueling but rewarding: "They had me here for four interviews. That's about four hours, for a position of stock clerk. It was clear that they were choosy about the people they hired. That said something about what they thought I was. They thought I was good."[7]

The Stress Interview

The purpose of **stress interviews** is to test the reactions of job candidates by asking them to respond to difficult situations. Although this technique can be used during screening, in-depth, or multiple interviews, it is most common during the in-depth interview. For example, if you are interviewing for a public relations job at Ford, the interviewer may describe a problematic business situation—say,

multiple interview
Interview at which a job candidate meets with people at different levels of the employer's organization

stress interview
Type of interview that tests the reaction of job candidates by asking them to respond to difficult situations

INTERVIEW

G. Frederick Reinhardt, III, International Private Banker

As the son of the American ambassador to Vietnam, Egypt, and Italy, G. Frederick Reinhardt, III, learned European languages and cultures by living and attending schools abroad. Reinhardt's knowledge was put to the test when he interviewed for an executive position with Merrill Lynch International Bank in London. We asked him about the series of interviews that led to a job offer and for advice to others seeking employment abroad.

Question: Why do you think you were offered the job?

Answer: There were three key factors. First, my experience with the international division of Chemical Bank in New York and Italy gave me a solid background in banking. Second, I knew the investment side of finance. And third, I spoke the languages and knew the cultures.

Question: Were you interviewed in languages other than English?

Answer: Although English was used most of the time, my American, German, and English interviewers would occasionally shift to French, Italian, and German. Because business requires a different vocabulary than conversational speech, they wanted to know whether I could use these languages in a business context. At the time, my Italian business vocabulary was the strongest because I had spent a number of years in Italy.

Question: Did the interviewers focus on your knowledge of European cultures?

Answer: They looked at my ability to adapt to the cultures of Italy, Switzerland, and Germany because I would be doing business in those countries. Specifically, they wanted to be sure that I understood the vast differences between the Italian

the recall of thousands of vehicles—and ask you how you would announce it to the media. If you are being interviewed for a job in corporate training, you might be asked to describe methods for improving the way service representatives respond to customer complaints.

A new type of stress interview asks candidates to act out on-the-job dilemmas, often in conjunction with actors playing preassigned parts. Management simulations of this kind are used at Purdue Frederick Co., a Norwalk, Connecticut, pharmaceuticals manufacturer, and at Colgate-Palmolive's plant in Cambridge, Ohio.

- At Purdue Frederick, would-be district sales managers are asked to respond to videotapes in which actors play salespeople interviewing for jobs. The task is to decide why the videotaped interviewees should or should not be hired. Test items are built into the exercise. For example, candidates who choose a handsome athlete with an impressive sales record were faulted because the athlete's well-connected father was responsible for his success.

- Before Cathy Waybright was hired recently as a team leader/production engineer at Colgate-Palmolive, she and three other candidates were told to find ways to get factory workers to wear hard hats in dangerous areas. Waybright recognized in her initial interview that Colgate employees would not respond favorably to a heavy-handed approach. "Anyone who suggested we dock the pay of people who didn't wear their hats or publicly humiliate them by posting their names was definitely on the wrong track," she recalls. Waybright thus suggested showing a video linking factory injuries to the failure to wear hard hats; she proposed using managers as role models.

Stress interviews are usually easy to spot. The interviewer, for example, may be abrupt, impolite, or even sarcastic. Frank Pacetta, Xerox Corp.'s district sales manager in Cleveland, starts by challenging prospective employees: "If you're so good, sell me my desk." Later, he asks how candidates financed their college educations, preferring those who paid their own way. "I want grinders," explains Pacetta.[8]

and German cultures, one being Latin-based and the other Germanic. They also focused on my knowledge of each country's business practices.

Question: Your family background gave you the opportunity to live all over the world and to learn different languages and cultures. Because few Americans have this opportunity, how can they prepare themselves to work abroad?

Answer: They can start sensitizing themselves at an early age to different languages and cultures. They can take part in exchange programs during high school and college. Spending a year in Asia, Europe, or South America is an invaluable learning experience.

For those already on the job market, it's a good idea to spend time traveling abroad and to join an international club run by a foreign chamber of commerce. These clubs, found in large U.S. cities, have programs for Americans who want to study foreign cultures.

To learn about the global marketplace, they should read publications like *The Economist* and the *International Herald Tribune* and study international business news in *The Wall Street Journal.* They should master geography and international current events. While many Americans can't identify the Prime Minister of England, every Englishman knows the President of the United States. They should raise their consciousness about international affairs well before the interview begins.

Finally, they should learn as much as they can about the interview process as practiced abroad. Many Americans don't realize that foreign interviewers are not governed by U.S. employment laws or practices. For example, while interviewers in the United States are not allowed to ask about marital status, age, or disability, interviewers in foreign countries can delve into these personal areas. As a result, interviews often center around your family as well as your ability to do a job.

Source: Interview with G. Frederick Reinhardt, III.

During stress interviews, try to answer questions directly and without getting flustered. Respond to the *content* of the question rather than the *tone.* For example, when you hear the question, "What makes you think I would ever hire you?" the interviewer is really asking about your strengths and the assets that you can bring to the organization. By keeping your composure, you can bypass the gruff phrasing, get to the underlying point, and demonstrate that you can handle the stress of business life.

Regardless of the interview type, you have the potential to create a lasting impression in the way you present yourself—through both verbal and nonverbal communication. In the next section, we will examine ways in which you can use careful preparation to build a positive impression and maintain it throughout an interview. Then we will conduct a step-by-step walkthrough of a *model interview.*

PROGRESS CHECK

1. What are job interviews?
2. Do all job interviews follow the same four-stage sequence?
3. Have you ever experienced a stress interview? How did you respond? Thinking back, what would you have done differently, if anything?

PREPARING FOR AN INTERVIEW

When Camille Lavington, an image consultant whose clients include American Express, General Electric, Mobil Oil, and Merrill Lynch, gives business seminars, she focuses on maximizing first impressions: "You give away your entire identity in the first three minutes," she contends. "People can read you like a book."[9]

Nowhere is this more true than in the job interview—a situation in which presenting an insecure or uncertain image may eliminate you as a candidate. According to a recent survey, more than six out of ten interviewers decide whether or not to hire a candidate within the first fifteen minutes.[10]

Following some basic rules, however, can help you build a positive impression from the start. These include doing your homework by finding out as much as you can about the company and the position before the interview begins, generating a list of questions, choosing an effective presentation style, being ready to handle difficult interviewers, dressing for business, arriving on time, using effective nonverbal communication, and coming prepared with your résumé and recommendations.

Remember that everything you say and do communicates a powerful subtext that can influence the interviewer's perception more strongly than your skills or education. Keep this subtext in mind as you prepare for the interview.

Research the Company

Researching the company before the interview has several advantages. First, it helps you equalize your relationship with the interviewer, giving you information to ask questions as well as answer them. Second, it allows you to formulate a list of specific questions that will influence your thinking and responses. Third, and most important, it allows you to judge whether or not you want to work for the organization.

Begin your research well before you schedule any specific job interview. As we saw in Chapter 16, learning as much as you can, both about a specific field and about specific companies, will help you target a career. There are various sources of research in terms of four major areas of inquiry: location, industries, companies, and employment organizations. Among other details, you can gather the following information:

- The goods and services that the organization sells
- The company's organizational structure, including the functions and locations of subsidiaries and divisions
- Employment trends (has the company been hiring or cutting staff?)
- Industry trends (are new products changing the field?)
- Earnings (in public companies, this number has a strong effect on stock price)
- External pressures affecting business operations (which may be exerted by government or by the general economic climate)

Your basic sources of information are:

- The company itself (for example, annual reports)
- Business and industry groups like the local chamber of commerce
- Specialized business publications and directories, such as Dun & Bradstreet's *Million Dollar Directory*

For information about both the general economic climate and specific companies, you can also consult business and trade publications like *American Banker* and *AdWeek* and business-oriented periodicals like *The Wall Street Journal*, *Business Week*, and *Fortune*.

Personal resources are also valuable. In your network of contacts, for example, you may find people who have worked or currently work for your target organization. In addition, the placement office at your college or alumni association may help you to locate people with firsthand knowledge about a company.

Most sources of employment research information are available at your library. Using computer-assisted research services like Nexis from Mead Data Central, Inc., you can tap into information databases to find business and trade information from hundreds of sources specializing in particular fields (for example, *Advertising Age* and *PC Magazine*); regional information from such local business publications as the *Nashville Business Journal*; company financial statements, including annual reports, press releases, and the reports of financial analysts; and current-events coverage of the business climate.

Upon request, virtually all companies provide not only annual reports but also sales and marketing brochures, which define company products and their potential in the marketplace. Another valuable source is a company's employee handbook, which explains both employees' obligations to the company and its commitment to them. You can ask to see a copy of the handbook at your interview.

Keep in mind that although your research will tell you a lot about a company and its industry, it will tell you very little about the specific job for which you are applying. You will, however, learn about job functions, managers and supervisors, career opportunities, salary and benefits, travel requirements, and relocation possibilities from the interviewer.

Generate a List of Questions

From your research, compile a list of questions that you want the interviewer to answer. Write these questions on a sheet of paper and bring them with you. As you formulate your questions, remember that most interviewers respond favorably when a candidate takes an active part in the interview. Naturally, they consider questions a sign of intelligence, assertiveness, and involvement. Appropriate questioning also demonstrates your ability not only to analyze the company's situation from your own perspective, but to use what you have learned to communicate your strengths and qualifications.

According to personnel agency owner Robert Half, attitudes toward candidate questions have changed over the years:

> Workers years ago felt [that asking questions] was inappropriate, and job interviews were very much a one-way street. The company asked questions about you and made a determination whether you were worthy of being employed there. Today, it is perfectly acceptable, even smart, to interview the company at the same time the company is interviewing you.[11]

Table 17.1 lists a number of questions that, as a job candidate, you might want to ask a prospective employer. As you can see, although some of the questions are straightforward requests for information ("What are the job responsibilities?"), others are attempts to analyze the job opportunity. Do not, however, waste time asking for detailed information that you can find in other sources. Questions like the following are a clear sign that you did not do your homework:

- What are your major products?
- How many people work for your company?
- How long have you been in business?

Work to Develop an Effective Presentation Style

How should you "present" yourself at an interview? In other words, how should you initiate and respond to questions? This is a crucial question. The first step in adopting an effective presentation style is to consider the interview yet another communication transaction involving a sender, a receiver, a message, a channel, a context, and feedback. The following guidelines should help you to implement this strategy.

- *Be a careful listener.* Listen carefully to all questions and give concise, direct answers.
- *Be organized and goal-directed.* Keep in mind that your purpose is twofold— to be offered the job and to evaluate the opportunity. Don't ramble or provide irrelevant background information. Ask questions that will help you make your decision.

TABLE 17.1	*Questions That You May Want to Ask an Interviewer*

OPENER

- Did my résumé raise any questions about my background or qualifications that I can answer?

JOB-CONTENT QUESTIONS

- What are the job responsibilities?
- To whom would I report and how many people would report to me?
- What do you consider ideal experience for this job?
- What personal qualities improve the likelihood of job success?
- What is the most serious problem facing this department?
- Are there any unusual job demands that I should know about?
- What have been some of the best results produced by people in this job?
- What would be my primary job challenge?
- Was the person who last held this job promoted? If so, can I speak with him or her about the position?
- I noticed in *Forbes* [name any appropriate business source] that you are expanding your _____ division. How will that affect my job responsibilities?
- Is there an untapped marketing opportunity for your product in _____?
- On my last job, we did _____. Would a similar approach increase efficiency in your department?
- Do you have a training program for this position?

JOB-OPPORTUNITY QUESTIONS

- Are you considering any layoffs in this division?
- Is your downsizing complete?
- What is the typical career path for someone who takes this position?
- Is opportunity more likely if I am willing to relocate?
- I noticed that your international division produces the same products in Europe and the Far East [name the appropriate parts of the world]. Does my background lend itself to working in those locations?
- What is the company's policy regarding in-house transfers?
- From which areas do your company's top executives come?

QUESTIONS ABOUT UNIQUE COMPANY CHARACTERISTICS

- What makes your company special?
- Can you describe the corporate culture?

Source: Adapted from Richard Lathrop, *Who's Hiring Who? How to Find That Job Fast!* (Berkeley, CA: Ten Speed Press, 1989), pp. 203-205. Excerpted by permission of Ten Speed Press, P.O. Box 7123, Berkeley, CA 94707.

- *Provide specific examples.* Concrete examples tell a story better than any generalization. Telling an interviewer that you have the skills to "increase sales" or "reduce production costs" is far less effective than supporting your claims with a descriptive anecdote. Paul Green, a management consultant with Memphis-based Behavioral Technology who developed Hewlett-Packard's interview system, tells the following story: "I was interviewing a plant manager and needed confirmation that the individual had a strong commitment to task completion. The candidate described a time when he had his appendix removed on a Thursday and was back in the office on Monday—to the shock of everyone at the plant. This story provided very strong evidence that he was a driven, hard-working person. He got the job."[12] To be effective, of course, the point of your anecdote must be your skills or personal characteristics.

- *Be conscious of your tone as well as your words.* Convey the feeling that you welcome the opportunity to talk about yourself and the position. Be enthusiastic and eager as you describe your background and ways that you can help the company. However, don't make the mistake of telling managers what their companies are doing wrong and then enumerating the changes you would make. Even if you have done considerable research, this approach is presumptuous—you don't really have inside information. Instead, focus on the employer's concerns and describe how your background qualifies you to deal with them.
- *Practice your delivery.* Annoying speech mannerisms—like repeating *you know*, *okay*, or *um* throughout your conversation—can compromise the impression that you make. Perfect your conversational delivery by becoming conscious of your habits. For example, it is often helpful to listen to yourself speak on a tape recorder.

Be Ready to Handle Difficult Interviewers

An interviewer's personal style can interfere with the normal exchange of information. At their worst, personal idiosyncrasies can actually obstruct communication. Interviewers who are extremely formal, disorganized, uninterested, arrogant, or obviously overworked may make your presentation difficult or give you less attention than you deserve. Obviously, interviewer styles and habits are as unpredictable as the personalities of people who conduct interviews; interviews themselves will be as unpredictable as the people who conduct them and the huge variety of circumstances in which they can take place. Regardless of the situation, however, certain good advice can remain constant. For example, focus on your communication objective. Try to maintain control of the interview, and be conscious of presenting yourself in a positive, forceful way.

Dress for Business

Although first impressions rarely win jobs, your appearance—your clothes, hair, shoes, makeup, and jewelry—can certainly cost you a job before you ever open your mouth. As the following guidelines suggest, your goal is to look the part by adopting the traditional "uniform" of business. Your appearance should make no "statement" other than the fact that you are part of the business world.

Appropriate interview clothing for men includes a two-piece dark suit, preferably in navy blue or gray, a conservative business shirt and silk tie (no lavender shirts or Hawaiian ties), patternless calf-length socks that match the suit, and matching leather shoes with no buckles. Conservative suits are also preferable for women, with skirt length at or below the knee. Frills and lace are inappropriate, as are plunging necklines, excessive jewelry, spike heels, mesh or patterned stockings, and heavy makeup.

Poor grooming choices communicate negative messages, including the following:

Pens in the shirt pocket	Tacky; nerdy
Extra-long fingernails	This person isn't serious.
Dark glasses	What is this person trying to hide?
Lasso ties	This guy knows nothing about business.
Mesh stockings	An unprofessional look

Dressing appropriately for an interview, or even for a series of interviews, does not require spending a lot of money. However, it does mean making good choices for the money that you do spend. Men can dress effectively with two to three business suits and a variety of shirts and ties for a week's wearing; women can vary a wardrobe of the same size with scarves and sweaters.

Be Punctual

Make it a point to arrive on time for job interviews. Keeping an interviewer waiting sets a negative tone that will be difficult to overcome.

How can you make sure that you will arrive on time if you are traveling to an unfamiliar location? Take a dry run to measure the length of the trip. And always give yourself a cushion—a half-hour or so of extra time that will enable you to get through the worst traffic jams.

Being "punctual," however, does not mean arriving too early. Announce yourself to the receptionist five minutes before the interview—no sooner. In business, where meetings are often held back to back, making a premature entrance may mark you as an amateur. Use the time between your arrival and your visit to the reception desk to get a cup of coffee or to sit somewhere—in your car or in a public area—and review your notes.

Shake Hands and Make Eye Contact

A handshake is an act of engagement—a gesture that says unmistakably that two people are connected. In a job interview, the handshake initiates the communication that will last throughout the meeting. At the same time, it says something about who you are. "As effectively as wearing overalls to your interview," says corporate recruiter Jeff Speck,

> a limp or clammy handshake can terminate your candidacy before you even get a chance to sit down. Not only is it just plain unpleasant, but it also says a lot of things about your personality that you'd rather not have revealed. Even if [you are] nervous...and insecure, there's no reason to betray that fact before you begin speaking.

> Likewise, the bear-grip or moray-eel handshake...can be equally offensive. I have actually had my hand injured by over enthusiastic candidates, and my pleasure at their sincerity was quickly quelled by the throbbing pain at the end of my wrist.[13]

As you enter the meeting room, give a clear signal that you are indeed initiating a handshake—extend your hand in the direction of the interviewer. Grasp the interviewer's hand in a relaxed, firm manner and shake hands for no longer than a second or two. Women use handshakes in the same way as men, although some women make the mistake of believing that a strong handshake marks them as too aggressive. On the contrary, a weak handshake marks them as unbusinesslike and ineffectual.

At the same time that you are shaking hands, make eye contact with the interviewer. Momentarily holding the interviewer's gaze communicates confidence. *Initiating* eye contact—rather than simply *responding* to it—is the most effective way to begin because it says that you are unafraid to make the first move.

Bring Your Résumé and Recommendations

Even though you sent a résumé to the company before your interview, it is wise to bring another copy in case the original has been misplaced. In addition, bring your recommendations, either in the form of the actual reference letters or as a list containing the names, titles, companies, company addresses, and phone numbers of your references. Type the list on a separate sheet of paper with your name, address, and phone number at the top. Tell the interviewer that you have your references with you if he or she wants to see them.

Table 17.2 summarizes the steps in preparing for an interview. It also highlights some of the problems that arise when these steps are mishandled.

TABLE 17.2	*Summary of the Steps in Interview Preparation*	

PREPARATION	VALUE	PROBLEMS WHEN POORLY HANDLED
Conduct thorough research	• Provides information to question the interviewer; • enables applicant to evaluate an organization; • equalizes relationship with interviewer	• Candidate may be perceived as uninterested, unmotivated, and unprepared
Prepare questions	• Demonstrates an active, assertive approach; • enables candidate to ask questions as well as answer them	• Inappropriate questions may influence the interviewer's perception of the applicant
Choose an effective presentation style, dress and body language	• Can provide a subtext of competence; • the *way* applicants talk is just as important as *what* they say	• Negative first impression is difficult to overcome
Handle difficult interviewers	• Enables applicant to salvage a difficult situation	• Inability places applicant at the mercy of the interviewer's idiosyncrasies
Prepare to be on time	• Communicates that applicants are serious about the opportunity and understand the importance of punctuality in business	• Lateness sets a negative tone that is difficult to overcome
Bring résumé and recommendations	• Demonstrates forethought and preparation; • can save the interview when interviewer misplaces critical documents	• Absence demonstrates lack of preparation and an unprofessional approach to the interview

A MODEL INTERVIEW

Most interviews follow a general pattern that includes six distinct parts: an *introduction, questions about work experience, questions about education,* a *discussion of current activities and interests,* an *analysis of strengths and weaknesses,* and *closing remarks.*[14] As we analyze each part of this pattern, remember that variations in this model are not only possible but likely. For example, an interviewer would probably ask recent graduates about education before work experience. In this section, we will describe the basic parts or stages of a "model" process by focusing on the nature and pattern of questions that are typically asked. In the next sections, we will focus more specifically on the content of some of these questions and ways of responding to them: namely, strategies for *handling difficult questions* (including illegal questions) and *negotiating salary and other compensation.*

As we mentioned earlier, your goal throughout the interview is to get the interviewer to talk about his or her department, needs, and problems so that you can demonstrate why you are the best candidate. When the manager is specific, you, too, can be specific in describing how something in your background applies to the present situation. If you are reluctant to probe, remember that most people—including businesspeople—love to talk about themselves and their problems. Your questions—and the active participation that results from them—should begin after the introductory phase of the interview.

```
              Ajax Property and Casualty Insurance Company
                              4 Ontario Way
                           Dearborn, MI 48128

                              JOB DESCRIPTION
                       ENTRY-LEVEL CLAIM REPRESENTATIVE

      General statement of duties
        Investigate claims, negotiate settlements, and authorize payment to
        claimants for losses covered under homeowner and automobile policies.

      Supervision received
        Report to a department manager who is responsible for 10 claim
        representatives.

      Supervisory responsibilities
        None.

      Typical duties
        (List includes only some of the duties required by the job.)
        1. Work with policyholders who file claims for damage or loss cov-
           ered under their homeowner or automobile policies.
        2. Contact claimants by letter or telephone to obtain information on
           repair costs or other records requested by the company.
        3. Input data into central computer.
        4. Keep written records of information obtained from claimants in
           order to process claims.
        5. Working with supervisors, negotiate a settlement with claimants
           and close cases.
        6. Analyze repair bills submitted by claimants according to stan-
           dards set by company.
        7. Work with accounting department to request payment checks.

      Minimum qualifications
        Education: BA/BS degree. Courses in insurance, economics, business,
        or accounting preferred.
        Experience: No prior claim representative experience necessary.
        Knowledge, skills, and abilities:
        1. Ability to communicate effectively with claimants in writing and
           over the phone.
        2. Strong analytic ability.
        3. Ability to understand and apply federal and state insurance laws
           and regulations.
        4. Ability to use a word processor.

      Desirable qualifications
        Good memory, observant, detail-oriented; knowledge of computer appli-
        cations; knowledge of home and automotive repair terminology helpful.

      On-the-job training
        Provided by company. Job holder must pass a written examination after
        completing an approved course in insurance adjusting. Licensing
        required by the state.
```

FIGURE 17.2   *Sample Job Description*

job description
Document specifying the objectives of a job, the work to be done, skill requirements, responsibilities involved, and working conditions

THE JOB DESCRIPTION   During the interview, the manager may refer to a **job description** which, like the one in Figure 17.2, outlines the requirements of the job. Included are the job title, general objectives, specific duties, the individual to whom the employee will report, supervisory responsibilities, and required education and skills. Because it describes in detail the job to be done and the qualifications of the ideal candidate, this document is especially important during screening interviews with company recruiters. It is less important during the in-depth interview, where the interviewing manager knows and can explain the requirements of the job in much better detail.

The Introduction

In the opening few minutes, a good interviewer has one overriding goal—to establish rapport and relax the candidate. Nonverbal language is important at this stage. A firm handshake, eye contact, and a smile all tell the interviewer that you welcome the opportunity to exchange information and demonstrate your worth.

Many interviewers engage in small talk to reduce tension. They may, for example, ask if you know a common acquaintance at a company listed on your résumé or about a community activity for which you volunteer. During this stage, an experienced interviewer lets you do most of the talking, realizing that the act of speaking will make you feel less self-conscious.

General job-related questions follow. The interviewer may ask, "Tell me about yourself," delve into how you learned about the job, or explore your job expectations. The following are a few popular introductory questions:

- Why are you interested in this job?
- What do you know about this company and this particular job?
- What do you see as the purpose of this interview?

These questions are important because they establish whether you and the interviewer share the same assumptions both about the interview's purpose and about the job.

Work Experience

Next, most interviewers turn to the body of the interview, expecting to learn about you and acknowledging that you will ask your own questions about the job and the organization. The first area of interest is usually work experience. The interviewer may begin by saying something like the following:

> Let's talk about your background and experience. If I get to know you well—both what you've done and what you hope to do—we can judge whether there are opportunities in our organization suited to your talents and interests. I'd like to hear about your jobs and schooling, your hobbies and interests, and anything else you'd like to tell or ask me. Perhaps the best place to start is with your work experience.[15]

A series of probing questions usually follows, often focusing on the specifics of one or more of your previous jobs. The primary purpose of these questions is to determine if your experience qualifies you for the present posi-

It is important to remember that, characteristically, interviewers draw early impressions and that these first impressions normally become rather firmly embedded. Indeed, some research has concluded that judgments formed during the first five minutes of an interview are unlikely to change. As a result, information offered or obtained early will probably count more heavily than information that comes out later.

tion. However, the questioning is also aimed at judging your adaptability, productivity, motivation, and leadership and assessing the development of your career over the years. You may be asked common work-related questions like the following:

- Describe the most difficult problem you faced in your last job and how you solved it.
- What were you best at? Give me specific examples.
- What things did you do less well?
- Tell me about your on-the-job people skills. Describe a situation in which you handled people effectively.
- Were there incidents when your people skills were less effective?
- Were deadlines a problem? How did you prioritize your responsibilities when working under pressure?
- When your job required you to shift tasks, describe how you organized your responsibilities.
- What is your career goal?
- How have the various jobs you've held in the past helped you pursue that goal?
- What work accomplishment are you most proud of?
- How much did you earn?
- What did you learn from the job?
- How did it disappoint you?
- Why did you leave your last job?
- I notice a pattern of job hopping—you stay in a job for a year and then move on. Why have you moved around so much?

Practice responding to these questions as you prepare for the interview. Later in the chapter, we will examine specific responses to difficult questions.

Education

Having explored your work history, interviewers usually turn next to education. Their interest lies not so much in your grades, major, or extracurricular activities as in the way your school accomplishments relate to your ability to do a job. Bear this fact in mind as you analyze the interviewer's questions and focus your answers accordingly. Provide the link between school and work by highlighting the specific knowledge and skills that will help you succeed. Demonstrate motivation by pointing to such items as extracurricular activities and volunteer work. Finally, be sure to describe all connections in a direct way—for example:

> When I was editor in chief of the student newspaper, I handled weekly deadlines as well as 18 credits. The paper won two awards that year, and I came away with a B+ average. Hearing the needs of your fast-paced office, I think this demonstrates my ability to juggle my responsibilities and do them all well.

During this stage of the interview, you may also be asked common education-related questions like the following:

- What was your major field and why did you choose it?
- What were your favorite subjects?
- What were the subjects you liked least?
- Why did you choose the college you attended?

- How did you pay for your education?
- Did you work at all while in school? How did you manage your time?
- Can you describe any turnarounds in your education? Did a course or teacher change your views of what you wanted to do in a career?
- Describe the toughest problem you faced while in school and how you solved it.
- Describe your extracurricular activities.
- What did you learn in school that will help you succeed on this job?

Be prepared to deal with these questions in the same way that you must deal with work-related questions. Be detailed in describing your activities and focus your responses—that is, tailor them to highlight the link between your past experience and the current needs of your potential employer.

Activities and Interests

In an attempt to learn what your leisure pursuits reveal about you, many interviewers turn next to your activities and interests. This discussion is often considered optional, especially if there is limited interview time. As you will see, many activities-and-interests questions are designed to explore not only the skills that give you the most satisfaction but, perhaps more importantly, your ability to deal with people, both as a leader and a team member. Follow the strategy of continually trying to tie your answers to the job opportunity and the employer's needs. Here are some typical activities-and-interests questions:

- Your résumé indicates that you are involved in various community activities. What do you do in these activities?
- Do your activities place you in a leadership role? Describe how you work with other people.
- With so many community ties, how would you feel about relocating?
- Do any of your community activities involve skills that you would also use on this job?

Strengths and Shortcomings

Everything that has transpired till now leads to the discussion of how *you* see your own strengths and weaknesses. As interviewers explore these issues, they ask themselves three key questions, each of which may be translated into a question directed at the candidate:

- Can this person do the job? (Do you have the right skills, knowledge, talents, and experience to work effectively?)
- Will this person do the job? (Will your interests and personal characteristics motivate you to do the work?)
- Will this person fit comfortably in the organization? (Are your personality, character, work ethic, and people skills compatible with the corporate culture?)

In order to tie the discussion to your ability to do the job, most interviewers start with your strengths. For example, they may start by turning the interview in the following direction:

> Now let's try to summarize our discussion. As you think about what we've covered, what would you say are some of your chief strengths? What are some of the assets that would make you a good prospect for an employer?[16]

At this point, you may be asked specific questions like the following:

■ What do you believe are your special qualifications for this job?
■ List three of your most outstanding qualities. How would your previous employers respond to this list?
■ What in your background makes you the ideal candidate for this job?

Moving on to your shortcomings, the interviewer may then lead with comments and questions like these:

> You've shown me some real strengths. Now, what about some of your qualities that aren't so strong? All of us have a few areas we'd like to improve. In the past you may have had constructive criticism from friends, supervisors, or other people who have come to know you well. Thinking of the future, what areas or what personal qualities need improvement for you to be fully effective in your job or career?[17]

Specific questions in this vein may include the following:

■ What additional training do you think you will need to do this job?
■ What limitations have been a problem for you over the years?
■ In performance appraisals, what weaknesses did your managers identify?
■ What skills are you still trying to develop?

Closing Remarks

In closing, the interviewer thanks the candidate for discussing his or her background and job qualifications and asks if there are any unanswered questions about the job or the company. When interviewers are extremely interested in the candidate, they may take this opportunity to try to "sell" the company by describing such inducements as its market strength and employee benefits. Finally, interviewers will usually tell you what will happen next—for example, "You can expect to hear from me within a week."

PROGRESS CHECK

1. Why are first impressions important during a job interview?
2. What are some questions that might be useful for you to ask an interviewer?
3. Describe some tips for presenting yourself effectively during an interview.

HOW TO HANDLE DIFFICULT QUESTIONS

Handle difficult questions by being positive. Positive responses give interviewers little reason to focus on the negative, and as a result, they are less likely to look for problems. According to Jean Marshall, manager of compensation and corporate human resources for Cyprus Minerals Co. in Englewood, Colorado, negativity often emerges when people say the first thing that comes to their minds. Such responses, says Marshall, "often open the door for further probing of negative behavioral patterns."[18] To avoid this tendency, develop a strategy based on the following guidelines:[19]

■ *Prepare for difficult questions.* Start by expecting that difficult or negative questions will be asked. Prepare for them by confronting them in advance. Make a list of all the questions that you would find difficult to answer. Then prepare the answers by focusing on positive outcomes—what you learned from a situation, how you grew, what you did to solve a problem.

Although the interview may be necessary as the only means of obtaining information about an applicant, differences in administration, situation, and interviewer skills often make them unreliable. Structured, or *patterned,* interviews rely on preselected questions which are based on job descriptions and which are asked of each applicant in the same sequence; interviewers record answers on written lists. On the whole, very little research has been devoted to the validity of the interview as a hiring tool.

■ *Learn to identify negative questions.* Often included in these questions are words like *weakness, problems, conflict, difficult, criticism,* and *least.* Remember, however, that experienced interviewers often couch negative questions in positive terms as they focus on a candidate's deficits—for example:

> If you had the opportunity to start your last job over again, what would you do differently?

or

> If you had the chance to go back to school to improve your job performance, what would you study?

■ *Turn negative questions into positive responses.* For example, you might describe what you learned from a difficult situation, how you grew professionally, or how you transformed a problem into an opportunity.

In response to the question, "If you had the opportunity to start your last job over again, what would you do differently?" you might say:

> I would have encouraged my manager to give me feedback about my work as soon as possible after I was hired. Pointing out the pluses and minuses of my work at this early stage would have helped me learn the company's expectations within a shorter period of time.

■ *Don't blame others for problems or rationalize negative situations.* Like most people, employers respond poorly when candidates minimize serious problems or shift responsibility for problems. For instance, don't blame your previous manager for the department's poor productivity or try to say that the problem was unimportant. Instead, describe problems in specific, concrete terms and offer suggestions for remedying them—for example:

> Our computer system couldn't handle the volume of work the department produced. As a result, we had weeks of orders backing up. After analyzing the problem, I wrote a report to my manager suggesting an upgraded system—one in line with the kind of system you have here.

■ *Don't reveal proprietary information about your previous employer. Proprietary information* is confidential information owned by a company. Revealing it in an interview marks you as untrustworthy and unethical. Rather than winning points for providing secrets, you lose credibility—

not surprisingly, interviewers will conclude that you would do the same thing to them.

Difficult Questions and Effective Answers

Remember that interviewers often use many of the same questions to elicit information and put job candidates off balance. Although there are thus many "right"—or at least standard—answers to the most common difficult questions, it is still valuable to analyze several successful approaches to some of them. Here, for example, is a series of typical difficult questions. Each is paired with a suggested approach for responding.[20]

- *Questions:* What do you like most about your current job? What do you like least?

- *Approach:* Focus on the things that you liked rather than those you disliked. If you paint a negative picture, the interviewer may wonder why you are still in the job or whether your negative comments reflect a poor attitude. Avoid talking about personal differences you had with co-workers.

- *Question:* What are your most serious weaknesses?

- *Approach:* Turn weaknesses into positive traits—for example: "I tend to get so wrapped up in what I'm doing that I can't think of anything else till it's done." Or, "I can't stand to see people waste time." Offer one or two weaknesses and then stop. If the interviewer presses for a third weakness, explain that nothing else comes to mind.

- *Question:* Does your grade-point average reflect your ability?

- *Approach:* If your grade-point average was mediocre, you can say something like, "I'm a results-oriented person. Schools test how well you show what you know, while work judges you on what you do with what you know. Although my grades were average, I was very successful in the jobs I held in college and I could contribute the same results here."

- *Question:* How much direct supervision do you need?

- *Approach:* Interviewers look for candidates who are self-starters and who motivate themselves throughout a project. An effective answer gives this impression while showing that you are nevertheless willing to ask for help. For example, you might respond by saying, "In most cases, my manager has to tell me something once, then I'm on my own. When a problem comes up, I try to be creative and consult with others involved in the project. When I encounter a problem I can't solve, I ask my manager for help. I try to come prepared with suggestions for handling the problem, so that the manager can see my thinking."

Illegal Questions

Federal law says that there are certain questions that employers cannot ask job applicants without threatening their equal opportunity for employment. Equal opportunity in the workplace is protected by several federal laws. For example, according to Title VII of the Civil Rights Act of 1964 and the Equal Employment Opportunity Act of 1972, candidates cannot be discriminated against on the basis of race, color, religion, sex, or national origin. The Age Discrimination in Employment Act of 1968 prohibits hiring discrimination against anyone aged forty or older, and the Americans with Disabilities Act of 1990 protects disabled individuals from discrimination. The protection of the Americans with Disabilities Act applies to any company with at least twenty-five employees. By 1996, the law will apply to companies with fifteen employees. As a result of these laws, any questions concerning race, color, religion, sex, national origin, age, disability, pregnancy, or health issues unrelated to work are illegal.

In general, questions are considered legal when they relate directly to the applicant's ability to perform job duties. They are illegal when they probe into areas unrelated to job performance. Questions like the following are generally considered illegal:

- Are you married or single?
- Do you plan to become pregnant soon?
- Are you HIV-positive? (Because AIDS is considered a handicap under the Vocational Rehabilitation Act of 1973, hiring discrimination based on this condition is illegal.)
- How much time do you spend with your family?
- How much does your spouse earn?
- You look forty pounds overweight. Do you think you have the stamina to do this work? (This question is illegal if there is no weight requirement for the job.)
- Has your driver's license ever been revoked? (This question is valid only if driving is part of your job.)
- How have you arranged your child care?
- What political party do you support?
- How old are you?

Although all of these questions are or can be regarded as illegal, a recent survey of job applications used by employers in Ohio showed that illegal questions were present on nearly three out of four applications.[21] In a particularly outrageous case, a recruiter for the Wall Street investment banking house Goldman Sachs asked a female applicant if she would "have an abortion to save her job." According to Gary Goldstein, president of an executive-search firm specializing in the financial-services industry, although most recruiters are more subtle, they still ask illegal questions. "Companies want to know," explains Goldstein, "why a woman isn't married, or if she is, why she'd want to spend so much time traveling."[22]

At the same time, however, the federal Equal Employment Opportunity Commission (EEOC) receives relatively few complaints about unfair hiring. While nearly 61 percent of the bias charges filed with the EEOC in a recent year involved advancement and discharge decisions, only 8.6 percent involved hiring.[23]

There are at least two ways to deal with illegal hiring questions. First, refuse to answer. Every applicant has the right to refuse to answer illegal questions. You must understand, of course, that refusal will probably eliminate you as a candidate. Second, you can choose to answer illegal questions that do not compromise your application. For example, if you are not HIV-positive or have no problem with child care, it is smart to answer these questions truthfully even though you know perfectly well that the interviewer is asking an illegal question.

HOW AND WHEN TO NEGOTIATE MONEY AND BENEFITS

Naturally, such employment conditions as salary, bonuses, vacation time, medical insurance, pension plans, and company savings plans are on every applicant's mind. However, bringing them up prematurely during an interview will weaken your bargaining position. As a rule, your strategy should be to wait until the company decides that it wants to hire you. Asking about money prematurely may also send the message that the job is less important than what you will earn. As a result, employers like Tom Melohn, co-owner of North American Tool & Die, are impressed by applicants whose initial questions concern approaches and procedures rather than pay.[24]

Pay your people the least possible and you'll get from them the same.

Malcolm Forbes
American publisher

This is not to say that you should go into the interview with no idea of the job's fair-market value. On the contrary, your sources may tell you a great deal. For example, newspaper ads often list salary ranges, and employment agencies have similar information. Members of your business network may also tell you what comparable jobs pay in the industry. In addition, the *Occupational Outlook Handbook*, a U.S. Department of Labor publication, provides a salary range for each listed occupation. Published salary schedules can also be helpful. Finally, once or twice a year, various popular publications, like *U.S. News & World Report*, track salaries for specific jobs according to region and position level (entry, senior, or managerial).

If an interviewer presses you for a salary figure at the start of the interview, try postponing the answer by saying something like the following:

> I really would prefer to make that determination after I've had a chance to explore the potential of working here and the opportunity for advancement.[25]

Or:

> The starting salary is not my most important consideration. As you know I'm earning $ _____ a year now. If you don't mind, let's postpone this discussion until you have a better idea of what I can do for you and I have a chance to know a little more about the job and the company.

When you finally start talking money, remember that you are involved in a high-stakes negotiation. While most of us no doubt feel that we are entitled to every penny we can get, the hiring manager has a responsibility to hire people for the least money possible. As a result, the negotiation may follow a pattern something like this:

> *Interviewer:* What starting salary would you accept?
>
> *Interviewee:* I was thinking of _____ [*you quote a figure 5-percent higher than you realistically think you can get*].
>
> *Interviewer:* We can't go that high. The position doesn't warrant it.
>
> *Interviewee:* Then what is your best offer?

At this point, the employer may decide to go higher than originally planned and offer you about what you expected in the first place. If the interviewer doesn't budge—and often he or she cannot because of budget restrictions on starting salaries—explain that although you are reluctant to go that low, you might compromise. You might reply, "Does $____ sound more realistic?" If the interviewer still refuses to change the original figure, do not feel forced to make a decision on the spot. Instead, say something like, "I would like to think about it overnight. May I call you tomorrow?"

Base your decision on opportunity as well as money. If you think there is a future in the company, consider accepting the job. It is often the only way to get ahead, especially during a recession.

Pricing yourself requires a healthy dose of reality testing—testing of the country's economic climate (is the country in recession or experiencing an economic boom?), of the specific marketplace for your skills (the industry and company), and of the way in which your past translates into today's dollars. In Figure 17.3, *The Wall Street Journal* analyzes the ways in which past experience, as expressed on the résumé of a fictitious senior executive, affects what that executive will be paid. Although the figures are different for entry-level candidates, the concept still applies. What you choose to include in your résumé—and what you choose to omit—will influence your market value, as will the phrasing in which you cast your accomplishments.

When talking about money, it is critical that you also consider **employee benefits**—the rewards that employers provide to individual employees to cover costs for such services as medical insurance and *perquisites* such as vacations and company savings plans. The importance of benefits cannot be understated.

In the business world, everyone is paid in two coins: cash and experience. Take the experience first, the cash will come later.

Harold S. Geneen
Former Chairman,
ITT Corporation

employee benefits
Programs provided by employers for individual employees to cover costs for such services as medical insurance, parental and sick leave, vacations, and company savings plans

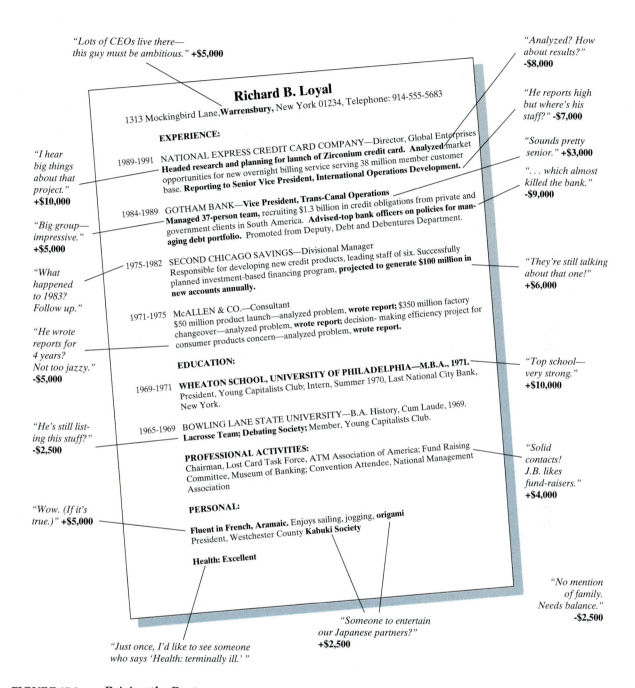

FIGURE 17.3   *Pricing the Past*

Source: Reprinted by permission of *The Wall Street Journal*, © 1991 Dow Jones & Company, Inc. All rights reserved worldwide.

According to recent figures from the U.S. Chamber of Commerce, employee benefits amount to 30.6 percent of total compensation paid to workers in the United States; payment for time worked amounts to 69.4 percent.[26]

An increasing number of employees now realize the importance of their benefits. According to a recent Employee Benefit Research Institute–Gallup Organization poll, 70 percent of the workers sampled said that benefits were "very important" when considering a job offer, up from 57 percent the previous year. Health insurance is especially critical, with 57 percent of the respondents seeing it as an absolute job requirement. Those who were already covered said that they would need an average pay increase of more than $4,000 to give it up.[27]

PRE-EMPLOYMENT TESTING

pre-employment testing
Process whereby employers evaluate job candidates through skills tests, lie detector tests, physical examinations, and reference checks

The decision to hire workers can be costly in terms of employment agency fees, job training, time spent interviewing, and time lost when new employees prove unfit. An increasing number of companies, therefore, use some form of pre-employment testing to screen workers. **Pre-employment testing** is a process of evaluating job candidates through the use of *skills tests, lie detector tests*, and *physical examinations; reference checks* are also considered part of the pre- employment screening process.

Skills Tests

skills tests
Testing used by employers to measure the aptitudes and abilities of job applicants

Skills tests measure the aptitudes and abilities of job applicants. These tests, like those we described earlier at Purdue Frederick and Colgate-Palmolive, may be part of a stress interview. Morris & McDaniel Inc., a management-consultant firm in Alexandria, Virginia, markets a multiple-choice "in basket" to test candidates for managerial positions. The materials enable companies to assess how applicants handle actual memos on subjects as varied as employee scheduling conflicts and sexual harassment complaints.[28]

Because the Civil Rights Act of 1964 prohibits the use of discriminatory hiring tests, the courts have ruled that all pre-employment skills tests must be limited to helping employers predict job success. Tests that are culturally biased or unrelated to job performance are considered discriminatory.

Lie Detector Tests

lie detector
(or polygraph)
Instrument for recording certain physical changes during a carefully controlled series of questions in order to establish an opinion about a person's honesty

Some companies administer specialized tests to uncover false statements made by job applicants. **Lie detectors**, or **polygraphs**, are instruments that record changes in cardiovascular, respiratory, and skin-response patterns; the results of changes in response to a carefully controlled series of questions are then used to establish an opinion about a person's honesty. Although such tests were at one time used extensively in pre-employment screenings, a 1989 federal law restricted their use. There are two main reasons for this restriction. First, polygraph tests are often inaccurate. According to the American Polygraph Association, incorrect or inconclusive results occur in about one out of ten cases; other studies contend that lie detectors are wrong about half the time. Second, a number of companies have abused the testing procedure by extending it to include inappropriate (and sometimes illegal) questions about such areas as an applicant's sex life and political beliefs.

The new law specifies that the refusal to hire cannot be based on test results alone and prohibits personal questions with no relevance to the job.[29] In addition, the new law states that lie detector tests can be administered only by the government; companies with sensitive Defense Department, FBI, and CIA contracts; companies providing security guards; and pharmaceutical companies handling controlled drugs. For example, because it handles controlled drugs, the Rite Aid drug chain still uses polygraph tests to screen job applicants and regards such testing an effective pre-employment screening tool.[30]

Physical Examinations

A physical examination may be given to determine whether an applicant can fulfill the duties required by a job. Under the Americans with Disabilities Act, however, it is unlawful to ask applicants if they are disabled, to inquire about the nature or severity of a disability, or to require an applicant to take a physical examination before a job offer is made. However, after you have received an offer and prior to your first day of work, your employer may require a physical examination.

Because the 1988 Employee Polygraph Protection Act prohibits the use of *physiological* instruments in the testing of employee honesty, some organizations have turned to more traditional paper-and-pencil tests. Are the results any more reliable? Many users say yes, but unfortunately most of the relevant studies have been performed by the companies who market the testing programs themselves. Moreover, even assuming the accuracy of available data, independent researchers place the validity of such tests somewhere below the "reasonable-doubt" standard of the U.S. justice system—and thus find such tests ethically questionable. Their use is already limited in a few states and is under study by federal lawmakers.

This requirement is legal as long as everyone working in a job category also takes the exam. If the examination shows the presence of a disability, the employer can choose not to hire you—if the disability prevents you from performing the job and if no reasonable accommodation is possible. For example, as long as such conditions do not interfere with job performance, the law protects a woman with a history of breast cancer, an office worker with a bad back, and people in wheelchairs. However, a candidate for the position of executive chauffeur could be refused employment if a physical exam revealed that glaucoma now limits peripheral vision.[31]

DRUG TESTING   The Americans with Disabilities Act does not prohibit pre-employment **drug testing**—screening for such illegal substances as cocaine and marijuana. An employer can test applicants for illegal drug use *before* making a job offer and choose not to make the offer if evidence of drugs is found.

drug testing
Pre-employment screening for such illegal substances as cocaine and marijuana

According to a recent survey, 63 percent of major U.S. corporations now administer drug tests to some or all job candidates; approximately 10 million drug tests are administered to job applicants and current employees in the United States. Chemical Bank, for example, uses urine testing to screen for drugs. When drugs are found on an initial screening, the urine is tested again, this time with a far more precise test, to make sure that the original findings were accurate. Each test series costs the bank approximately $78.[32] The management of Red Lion Hotels & Inns spent $40,000 on pre-employment drug tests at three of its hotels in Portland, Oregon. According to the firm, its drug-testing program has succeeded in attracting high-quality applicants, cut absenteeism and on-the-job injuries, and promoted a drug-free workplace.[33]

Reference Checks

reference check
Effort made by an employer during the screening process to verify a candidate's educational claims and work history

Finally, the screening process often includes a **reference check**—an effort to verify a candidate's educational claims and work history. Verification techniques range from a careful reading of reference letters that applicants bring with them to calling references to gather or confirm background information.

Employers are adamant about checking references because many candidates misrepresent or lie about their backgrounds. For example, of 773 doctors who applied for clinic jobs at Humana Inc. in a recent year, 5 percent gave false information about their medical credentials.[34] Among the information most frequently misrepresented are degrees and grades. You should expect all your references to be checked every time you apply for a job.

Table 17.3 summarizes various pre-employment tests. It also highlights some of the problems commonly associated with these tests.

FOLLOWING UP THE INTERVIEW

Your job-search task is not complete when the interview is over. To reinforce a positive impression, it is a good idea to follow up with a *letter of thanks*. Other letters may also be necessary, including *status inquiries* to check on the status of your application and *time-extension requests*.

Letters of Thanks

Use your thank-you letter to reinforce the employer's impression of both your value and your interest in the position. A thank-you letter may thus do any or all of the following:

- Thank the employer for the interview
- Say in no uncertain terms that you want the job
- Restate how you can help the company and why you are qualified
- Clear up any mistaken impressions that you may have made (optional)

TABLE 17.3	*Pre-Employment Testing: Purposes and Common Problems*	
TEST	PURPOSE	COMMON PROBLEMS
Skills Test	• Determines ability to function in a simulated job situation or in other situations requiring actual job skills	• Test may not reflect actual job situation • Candidate may respond poorly to pressured situation
Lie Detector Test	• When accurate, detects lies about applicants' backgrounds	• Test may give false or inconclusive readings • Test may be abused by companies that ask personal or inappropriate questions
Physical Examination and Drug Test	• Determines if candidate is physically able to perform a job • Identifies individuals who have recently taken drugs	• Exam may be used to discriminate illegally against applicants • Unless performed correctly, drug testing can yield false results
Reference Checks	• Verifies that applicant's claims are correct	• References provided by the candidate may be perceived as self-serving

ETHICS IN BUSINESS COMMUNICATIONS
When Reference Checks Go Too Far

Is an illegal hiring question still illegal if some-one other than the prospective employer asks it? Yes, says New York State attorney general Robert Abrams, who charged Equifax Inc., the giant Atlanta-based consumer-investigation firm, with asking illegal questions for client companies. As the nation's largest applicant-checking firm, Equifax conducts reference investigations for some 14,000 companies in all 50 states.

Reference checking is an important part of Equifax's business. Equifax convinces companies to buy its services with a marketing strategy that focuses on the hazards of hiring applicants without thorough background investigations. "What You Don't Know *Can* Hurt You," warns an Equifax brochure. "Facts the applicant doesn't reveal [such as] debt overload, medical problems....can come back to haunt an uninformed employer."

According to Attorney General Abrams, many of Equifax's questions—including those that are part of its "Reference Source Interview Guide"—are illegal. The following questions are those suggested by the Equifax guide: Are you aware of any physical problems or disabilities? If yes, provide details. Are you aware of any psychological problems or disabilities? Are you aware of any arrests? Is the person active in any community service organizations? If yes, describe activities.

By asking these questions, says Abrams, Equifax is invading applicants' right to privacy. In the process, it is also breaking tough human-rights and antidiscrimination laws that prohibit questions focusing on personal, non-job-related issues.

Among the companies accused of wrongdoing in its reference investigations was Delta Air Lines, an Equifax client. Delta hired Equifax to run reference checks on the Pan American World Airways employees that it was considering hiring after Pan Am's demise. According to Alina Bracciale, a former flight attendant for Pan Am, many of Equifax's questions were invasive. "They called a friend of mine and they asked him: 'Did he know me to have any financial difficulties, had I ever written any bad checks, had I ever filed for bankruptcy, did I belong to any clubs, did he know me to have any drug or alcohol problems, did I own or rent my own home?'...These things have absolutely no relation to your job."

Clearly, the arm of federal and state laws extends to reference-checking companies as well as to the companies who do the hiring. According to the New York State attorney general, it is as wrong to hire another company to ask illegal questions as it is to ask them yourself.

Source: Michael W. Miller, "Equifax Agrees to Alter Tactics in Job Inquiries," *The Wall Street Journal*, August 10, 1992, pp. B1 and B5. Reprinted by permission of *The Wall Street Journal*, © 1992 Dow Jones & Company, Inc. All rights reserved worldwide.

- Provide information that you did not have at the time of the interview (optional)
- Request action in the form of a decision.

As you can see from the sample letter in Figure 17.4, thank-you letters are brief and personal. Thank-you messages can also be communicated over the phone.

Status Inquiries

Many interviewers inform applicants when they will make a hiring decision. For example, if the interview is held on May 1, you may be promised a decision date of May 10. When the promised date has passed—or about two weeks after the interview if no date was mentioned—you may want to write a letter inquiring about the status of your application. If you have received another offer but would prefer the one in question, the letter of inquiry is essential. Your letter should refer to the following:

- The time lapse that created the need to write the letter

```
                                           158-12 83rd Street
                                           Detroit, MI 48202
                                           February 21, 199X

        Ms. Linda Alverez
        Director of Marketing Research
        General Motors Corporation
        3044 West Grand Boulevard
        Detroit, MI 48202

        Dear Ms. Alverez:

        I want to thank you for the opportunity to inteview with General
        Motors for a position as a marketing research assistant.
        Everything I learned about the position makes me interested in
        joining your company.

        I particularly enjoyed our discussion about how General Motors
        uses surveys to monitor the public's changing tastes in automo-
        biles. The three surveys I conducted for my college marketing
        courses convinced me of my strong interest in public-opinion
        research. Happily, I am also a car enthusiast. Ever since I was a
        kid, I remember looking forward each year to the day General
        Motors unveiled its new car models.

        During our meeting, I told you that I was applying to a night-
        school M.B.A. program. Today, I learned that I was accepted. I've
        already mailed my deposit and specified my plan to focus on mar-
        keting research.

        Thank you again for the opportunity to speak with you. I look for-
        ward to hearing from you shortly and to the possibility of working
        for America's premier automaker.

                                           Sincerely,

                                           Albert A Lee
                                           Albert A. Lee
```

FIGURE 17.4   *Sample Follow-Up Letter: Letter of Thanks*

- Your continued interest in the position
- The presence of another job offer (optional)
- Your potential value to the organization
- The request for a decision by a specific date

Figure 17.5 is an example of an effective letter of inquiry.

Requests for Additional Time

If you have interviewed with more than one company, the situation may arise in which one company offers you a job before the others. In that case, a letter or phone call requesting additional time may be necessary. If you want to consider all your options, you will want to ask the company that has made an offer for more time to decide. Your request should include the following elements:

- An acknowledgment of the company's job offer and a statement that you are interested in the position
- A statement that you are interviewing with another company and that you expect an offer within a short time
- A statement that you would appreciate the opportunity to let the company know by a certain date

```
                                    2222 Main Street
                                    Seattle, WA 98134
                                    September 30, 199X

Mr. Edward D'Angelo
Director of Operations
Monsanto Company
800 North Lindberg Boulevard
St. Louis, MO 63167

Dear Mr. D'Angelo:

At our September 14 meeting, you told me that you would make
your hiring decision for the position of purchasing manager no
later than September 29. Since I have not heard from you, I
would like to reiterate my interest in the position and ask that
you let me know whether I am still being considered.

I would appreciate your response by October 7, since I have been
offered another job and must let the company know by that date.

I would prefer the job with Monsanto because I see greater chal-
lenges and opportunities. I am especially interested in working
for a company that uses such a sophisticated just-in-time inven-
tory system to control the cost of raw materials. On a personal
basis, I felt very comfotrable with the people I met in your
organization.

If you would like to speak with me again before October 7,
please let me know. I look forward to your response.

                            Sincerely,

                            William Beer
                            William Beer
```

FIGURE 17.5 *Sample Follow-Up Letter: Status Inquiry*

- A restatement of your potential value to the company
- A request for an answer.

Remember: If the company to which you are writing is your first choice, communicate this fact so that no one mistakes your intent. If you are undecided, you can be more vague but still express genuine interest. The letter in Figure 17.6 is an example of a letter to a company that is not necessarily the candidate's first choice.

If you are a highly desirable candidate, an effective extension request may spur the company to improve its offer for fear of losing you. When this happens, you are in the enviable position of negotiating with two or more companies for the best offer. However, if the first company replies that it cannot wait while the second company is still deliberating, you will be forced to choose between the offer that you have and the offer that you may or may not have.

RESPONDING TO JOB OFFERS

In everything you have done up to this point, you have had a single goal—to get a job offer. Once you have received one or more offers, your next communication

*Ability is nothing
without opportunity.*

*Napoleon Bonaparte
Emperor of France*

301 Sunrise Highway
Dallas, TX 75221
March 15, 199X

Ms. Ellen Peterson
Vice President, Employee Benefits
Human Resources Department
TV Guide
250 King of Prussia Road
Radnor, PA 19088

Dear Ms. Peterson:

I received your offer to become an employee-benefits administrator for TV Guide, and I am very excited about the possibility.

However, since our meeting two weeks ago, I received a call from
another media company about a similar position, and I interviewed with that company last week. Because I am actively interested in both positions, I would appreciate an additional week
to make a decision.

The position you offer is both exciting and challenging, especially because you are about to redesign your entire benefits
program. With medical-insurance costs skyrocketing each year,
the opportunity to rethink your benefits plan is difficult to
pass up. My experience in redesigning J.C. Penney's medical plan
gives me the credentials to help you complete your work.

Please let me know as soon as possible if the additional week is
acceptable. I continue to look forward to the possibility of
working for TV Guide.

Sincerely,

Alicia Andrews

Alicia Andrews

FIGURE 17.6   *Sample Follow-Up Letter: Extension Request*

task is to respond in writing. Naturally, the nature of your response—what you say and the letters you write—depends on whether you accept or reject the job.

Accepting a Job Offer

You may receive an offer anytime from a day to six weeks after your final interview. Realistically, you can expect to wait about two weeks. Offers often come over the phone, with the manager repeating your salary, bonus potential, benefits, and starting date. When the conversation is over, you should understand fully the terms of the deal that you have made.

Do not feel pressured to respond right away: It is well within your rights to tell an employer that you want to think about the offer for a short time. Simply ask when the company needs a decision. Delaying your response may also give you a psychological advantage—you may well be perceived as an independent person who is not begging for the job. When you finally make your decision, communicate it with enthusiasm—let your employer know that your commitment is 100 percent. You can accept the offer on the phone or by letter. An acceptance letter has several important goals:

- Stating officially that you will take the job
- Repeating your enthusiasm for the offer
- Restating the basics of the offer, including your title, salary, and starting date
- Stating any miscellaneous details
- Looking forward to the future

Refusing a Job Offer

Every job offer is not an offer you should accept. Indeed, there are any number of realistic reasons to consider refusing an offer:

- *The job requires skills that would take too long to master.* Some jobs require so much learning that they put a great deal of stress on the skills and experiences you actually possess. If it looks as if it will take more than a year to master a job, consider turning it down.
- *You have negative feelings about your prospective manager.* If a manager is difficult or has a style that makes you uncomfortable, you may find working conditions similarly intolerable.
- *The employer is offering a "low-ball" salary.* If you should learn that others with similar experience and background are being paid more for the same job, your resentment may hinder performance; it may thus be wise to refuse the job before you experience trouble in performing it.
- *The offer is merely the best in a series of bad offers.* An offer may be the best you've received but still not what you want. Evaluate every job on its own merits, not by comparing it to other prospective jobs.
- *You are sick of job hunting and the company is eager to hire you.* Job hunting is stressful, even for those who take the process in stride. However, accepting a job that you really don't want because you are tired of the process is often a mistake. Focus on what you want, not on who wants you.[35]

Of course, refusing an offer is inevitable if you receive more than one offer at the same time. To decide between jobs, return to the objectives that you developed at the start of your job search. Before you consider money, benefits, or even job titles, focus on job duties, the people with whom you would work, and location. Ask yourself which job would be more challenging. Are you uncomfortable with any of the responsibilities entailed by a prospective job? When you make a decision, communicate your refusal in writing. Your letter should contain the following elements:

- Your decision not to take the job
- Your main reason for refusing the offer
- A statement that you will be taking another job (optional)
- A statement of appreciation for the offer and the time and effort made to consider your application
- A statement of thanks to all the people involved in the interview process
- A window left open to the future.

Address the letter to the person who officially offered you the job. In addition to communicating your refusal, your goal should be to build bridges to the future. Parting with friendly enthusiasm and grace makes it possible for you to contact the firm again in the future.

PROGRESS CHECK

1. What types of interview questions are illegal?
2. What are employee benefits? Why are they important?

PRACTICAL TIPS

A Futures Approach to Career Planning

The 1990s have convinced millions of American workers that many of their tried-and-true assumptions about job security are dead. A bad economy, corporate restructuring, and the crushing business debt accumulated during the high-flying 1980s have already brought an avalanche of pink slips. Many of the victims have been young careerists taught to believe that working hard and well would mean job security.

Learning that there are no guarantees, however, is only part of the lesson. Many of the newly unemployed have also learned to survive sequential layoffs as they jumped from one troubled company to another—from the frying pan into the fire. Patrick Ahearn, a senior human-resources manager, was one of these victims. He endured three downsizings in four years—Shearson Lehman Brothers, Grand Metropolitan, and Northern Telecom. The last came after his return from the Persian Gulf War. Instead of finding his job waiting, he learned that the company had cut its ranks and moved to Toronto.

With these harsh realities staring them in the face, jobholders are determined to give themselves more options. After taking a hard look at themselves and their careers, they have realized that surviving the job market of the 1990s may mean redefining the idea of the traditional career path. According to Charles Handy, a work-change authority, "Instead of climbing up the ladder, people now have to develop a portfolio of skills and products that they can sell directly to a series of customers. We are all becoming people with portfolio careers." As a result, a typical career that spans a period of decades may soon look very different than it does today. Here, for example, is a six-stage approach to career planning that, above all, is flexible and skills-oriented:

- Stage 1—Graduates may begin to work for large corporations, just as they do today. This experience provides critical job skills and initial contacts.

- Stage 2—After mastering their job responsibilities, careerists may begin moonlighting to broaden their skills and career networks. Working on a second job helps build a diversity of skills and also gives young workers the experience of selling themselves directly to customers. Self-confidence and flexibility inevitably grow.

- Stage 3—Equipped with a variety of skills, the careerists of tomorrow may then leave

WHAT'S AHEAD

The oral and written communication skills that we have analyzed so far in *Contemporary Business Communication* take place within the context of the communication challenges introduced in Chapter 1. Part VII of this text will take a closer look at these challenges. Specifically, Chapter 18 will focus on "COMMUNICATING IN A GLOBAL MARKETPLACE," Chapter 19 on "THE CHALLENGE OF DIVERSITY," and Chapter 20 on "MASTERING COMMUNICATION TECHNOLOGY."

*S*UMMARY OF CHAPTER OBJECTIVES

1. **Describe the stages in the *interview sequence*.** The interview sequence may include screening, in-depth, multiple, and stress interviews. The screening interview, which is usually conducted by a company recruiter, attempts to learn whether you are a viable job candidate. The in-depth interview, conducted by the potential supervisor, focuses more specifically on both the job and the candidate's qualifications to do it. Multiple interviews involve people at different levels of the organization who question the candidate from

the corporation. They may change industries, switch to smaller companies, or become entrepreneurs. During this period, they increasingly define themselves by skills rather than industry. With corporate downsizing a fact of life, the ability to move from computers to advertising to consumer-product manufacturing to banking is essential.

- Stage 4—By mid-career, it may be necessary to return to school for additional education (in computers, for example) or for credentials such as an MBA.

- Stage 5—Another corporate job may follow. The most successful careerists aim for high-visibility positions that make them more marketable and increases job security. Being buried for two or three years in a group assignment may mean that their work and careers are forgotten.

- Stage 6—As the new careerists close their careers, they may become professional itinerants, working on a project-by-project basis for a new breed of temporary-employment agencies. For example, after Linda Plevrites left Time Inc., where she was comptroller of the magazine division, a temporary agency found her interim work at an advertising agency. The fact that she could do the work gave her enormous satisfaction: "I found out that there is life after Time," she says. "I learned that I could walk in and work my way through the financials of any company in any industry. It's wonderful. I can't be chained up in the corporate world anymore."

Planning a career means charting it over a period of decades—from the time most people begin to work in their twenties to the time they retire in their sixties or seventies. As these six stages demonstrate, the task of preparing for a different kind of career future means learning flexible skills that can be transported from job to job and industry to industry. In the job market of the future, these skills may mean the difference between having a job and being unemployed.

Sources: Bruce Nussbaum, "I'm Worried about My Job!" *Business Week,* October 7, 1991, pp. 94–97; Bruce Nussbaum, "A Career Survival Kit," *Business Week,* October 7, 1991, pp. 98–104; John Schwartz, "How Safe is Your Job?" *Newsweek,* November 5, 1990, pp. 44–47.

their own perspectives. Stress interviews place candidates in difficult situations to determine how they respond.

2. **Describe the different ways to prepare for a** *job interview.*

Effective preparation begins with research about the company and its industry. Company and general business publications are useful sources. Research leads to a list of questions that a candidate can and should ask an interviewer about a company at different stages of the interview process. Preparation also includes thinking about presentation style, including such forms of nonverbal communication as dress and eye contact. Preparation also means developing techniques for handling difficult interviewers. To be properly prepared, you must also arrive on time and bring your résumé and recommendations.

3. **Explain the importance of questioning the interviewer.**

Questions indicate that you have spent the time and effort to analyze the company and that you are taking an active part in the interview. By indicating that you want to know as much about the company as the company wants to know about you, questions also help to place you on an equal footing with the interviewer.

4. **Outline the six stages of a** *model interview.*

During the introduction, the interviewer attempts to establish rapport with the job candidate. Work experience is examined in the second stage, in which the interviewer focuses on the specifics of previous employment. Interviewers generally turn next to education in order to determine whether school experience has provided applicable skills. Activities and interests are examined next to learn what leisure pursuits reveal about the applicant's personality, skills, and interests. Interviewers turn next to candidates' strengths and shortcomings in order to learn whether they can do the job, whether they would like to do it, and whether they would fit comfortably within the organization. Finally, closing remarks establish expectations for what will occur next.

5. **Identify specific techniques for** *handling difficult and illegal questions.*

   Make every attempt to answer negative or difficult questions in positive ways. Prepare for difficult questions by making a list of all the questions that you would rather not be asked; then design answers that focus on positive outcomes. Keep in mind that interviewers often ask difficult questions to put job candidates off balance. Handling illegal questions starts with a knowledge of both how to identify such questions and how the law protects job applicants from discrimination.

6. **List strategies for** *negotiating salary and benefits.*

   Always save the discussion of salary and benefits for the end of the interview process. You may be at a negotiating advantage if you wait until the company decides that it wants you. Before you begin talking about money, make every attempt to learn what comparable positions pay. Remember that during the negotiations, it is your goal to get as much money as possible, while it is the employer's goal to hold down salaries. Always consider the value of such employee benefits as health insurance and vacation time.

7. **Outline the different types of** *pre-employment testing.*

   Pre-employment testing may involve skills testing to measure the aptitudes and abilities of job applicants. Applicants may also be subjected to lie detector tests to determine whether all background information is truthful. While physical examinations may be required after a job offer has been made, drug testing may be given at any time in the interviewing process. Finally, reference checks are made to verify that educational claims and work histories are accurate.

8. **Describe the nature of various** *interview follow-up letters.*

   The purpose of thank-you letters is to thank the interviewer for the opportunity to interview with the company and to state interest in the job. Letters inquiring about the status of an application may be necessary if you have not heard from the company by a promised date (or after about two weeks if no date was mentioned during the interview). Requests for additional time may be needed when one company offers you a job before others with whom you have interviewed. Letters of acceptance inform the company that you will take the job; letters of refusal inform the company of your decision not to take the position.

*R*EVIEW AND DISCUSSION QUESTIONS

1. Name the ten most common qualities that employers seek in candidates during job interviews. (*Ch. Obj. 1*)

2. What are the four major stages of the interview sequence? (*Ch. Obj. 1*)

3. Describe the basic steps in preparing for a job interview. (*Ch. Obj. 2*)

4. Name several sources that you can use to research a company before a job interview. (*Ch. Obj. 2*)

5. During an interview, why is it important for you to ask questions of the interviewer? (*Ch. Obj. 3*)

6. What are the six stages of a model job interview? (*Ch. Obj. 4*)

7. During an interview, how might you handle questions that are difficult and/or illegal? (*Ch. Obj. 5*)

8. Describe effective strategies for discussing salary and benefits. (*Ch. Obj. 6*)

9. What types of pre-employment testing do companies use? (*Ch. Obj. 7*)

10. What possible steps might you take to follow up a job interview? (*Ch. Obj. 8*)

*A*PPLICATION EXERCISES

1. Your friend Tom sent his résumé to a large electronics firm and has been called in for an interview. "How are you going to prepare?" you ask. "Oh, I'm not going to do much for this interview," replies Tom. "The guy who's interviewing me is just someone with human resources—he's not the manager who'll actually hire people for the job. I'll read up on the company before my second interview." Do you agree with Tom's approach? Explain your answer. (*Ch. Obj. 2*)

2. Tom follows your advice, does his research, and does a good job during his screening interview. In fact, he gets called back for an in-depth interview. Because you were so helpful the first time, he comes to you for advice on how to dress and act for his in-depth interview. What do you tell him? (*Ch. Obj. 1, 2, 3*)

3. Your school's placement office has asked you to write a brief manual for your fellow students in which you describe the stages of the job-interview sequence and offer guidelines on how to prepare for each stage. Write this manual (one to two pages). (*Ch. Obj. 1, 2*)

4. The school's placement director likes the interview guide that you developed for EXERCISE 3 so much that she asks you to write a brief guide to negotiating salary and benefits. Write this guide (one to two pages). (*Ch. Obj. 6*)

5. This chapter notes that audience analysis is crucial to doing well in job interviews. Explain why. (*Ch. Obj. 1, 2*)

6. Choose a field or an occupation that interests you. Find out as much as you can about this field by doing research outside of class. Answer the following questions about the field you have selected:

   ■ What are the leading companies?

   ■ Where do they tend to be located?

   ■ What background and training are generally required for professionals who enter the field?

   ■ What are the salary levels?

   ■ What is the outlook for jobs in this field?

   Take notes on your research and keep track of which sources you find most useful. (*Ch. Obj. 2*)

7. Choose a company for which you would like to work (perhaps one of the firms that you read about in working on EXERCISE 6). Find out as much as you can about this firm by doing research outside of class. What types of jobs are available at this company, and what background and training do they require? What is the corporate culture? Is the company successful, and if so, why? Use sources mentioned in the chapter, and talk to anyone you know who is familiar with the company. You may also wish to check with a librarian to see if other research sources are available. Take notes on what you find out. (*Ch. Obj. 2*)

8. Use the information you gathered from working on EXERCISES 6 and 7 to write a report on the company you researched. Describe the firm, the role it plays in its industry, and its outlook (short- and long-term). Explain why you feel this company is or is not successful, and summarize the career path of company employees. Your instructor will determine the length of your report and may wish to have you present it to the class. (*Ch. Obj. 2*)

9. Based on your research and report for EXERCISES 7 and 8, draw up a list of questions you would like to ask if you were interviewing with that company. (*Ch. Obj. 2*)

10. Refer to the list of questions that interviewers frequently ask related to work experience and educational history (see the WORK EXPERIENCE and EDUCATION sections in this chapter). Suppose that you're being asked these questions during a job interview. Write an effective answer for each. If you wish, you may relate your answers to the industry and company that you researched for EXERCISES 7–9. (*Ch. Obj. 4*)

11. Refer to the questions itemized in the STRENGTHS and SHORTCOMINGS section of this chapter. Write effective answers for each. If you wish, you may relate your answers to the industry and company that you researched for EXERCISES 7–9. (*Ch. Obj. 4*)

12. We're all better at some things than at others. An important part of preparing for a job interview is anticipating any reservations which, based on your résumé or other information, interviewers may have about you. Look at your background from an interviewer's point of view, and think about what questions may come up. (If you wish, you may also refer to the questions listed in the section HOW TO HANDLE DIFFICULT QUESTIONS.) Draw up a list of questions or issues related to your own background, and then write effective responses that you could use during an interview in which any of those questions might be asked. (*Ch. Obj. 5*)

13. Suppose that you interview for a position with the company that you researched in EXERCISE 7. Write a follow-up letter thanking the interviewer and asking about the status of your application. (*Ch. Obj. 8*)

14. List the steps involved in preparing for a job interview. (*Ch. Obj. 5*)

15. Pre-employment testing, such as physical exams, lie detector tests, and mandatory drug screening, are a controversial issue. Some people feel that they're an invasion of job applicants' privacy; others feel that companies have a right to know if applicants take drugs. Do you feel that such pre-employment testing is ethical? Would your answer depend on the nature of the job involved? Explain. (*Ch. Obj. 7*)

BUILDING YOUR RESEARCH SKILLS

Research and locate two articles that discuss some aspect of the job search, the interview process, or both. (Both articles should come from sources outside class.) Did you find the articles useful? Why or why not? Write a brief report that summarizes their major points and suggestions and evaluates their usefulness to most job hunters.

BUILDING YOUR TEAMWORK SKILLS

Your instructor will divide the class into small groups. Meet with your group and take turns role-playing job interviews and salary negotiations. One volunteer should be the interviewer, another the applicant, and everyone should role-play the applicant at least once. The other team members should observe each interview and offer feedback to the participants. What did they do well? What might they do to improve? Try to offer constructive feedback regarding classmates' body language, tone of voice, posture, and other factors that can influence interviewers' decisions.

COMMUNICATING IN A WORLD OF DIVERSITY

The Americans with Disabilities Act will cause many companies to alter longstanding employment practices. Ricky Silberman, vice chairman of the U.S. Equal Employment Opportunity Commission, puts the matter rather bluntly: "It is a cataclysmic change," he believes, "when you tell employers of America that you have to look at a person's ability rather than their disability." The government recommends that all employers review their current job applications and interviewing policies, and that they eliminate any that may discriminate against applicants with mental or physical disabilities.

Suggestions for employers include the following:

■ Don't ask candidates or their references about applicants' disabilities.

■ Don't ask candidates or their references about their medical histories, prescription-drug use, or past workers' compensation or health-insurance claims.

■ Don't require that candidates "pass" medical exams before offering them jobs.

■ Don't refuse to hire disabled applicants because you fear their health-insurance premiums might be expensive.

Test your ability to apply the law. Are the following employment practices legal?

1. Asking a job applicant how he ended up in a wheelchair.

2. Requiring all new hires to report on their first day of work with a valid driver's license as identification.

3. Refusing, out of concern for the potential health-insurance costs, to hire a qualified applicant whose spouse is disabled.

4. Including this question on a job application: "Do you have any physical limitations that would prevent you from performing the job for which you are applying?"

5. Using an employment agency that discriminates against disabled applicants.

6. A hiring manager wonders about the health of one woman who's applying for a systems-programmer position. The manager asks the applicant about her medical history before offering her the job.

7. The hiring manager routinely asks all newly hired systems programmers about their medical histories.

Source: Joann Lublin, "Disabilities Act Will Compel Businesses to Change Many Employment Practices," *The Wall Street Journal*, July 7, 1992, pp. B1, B2. Reprinted by permission of *The Wall Street Journal*, © 1992 Dow Jones & Company, Inc. All rights reserved worldwide.

Truth and Consequences:
The Name of the Game in Résumé Writing

One newspaper called it "the résumé that ate San Francisco." It belonged to James Fang, who applied for—and was offered—the position of international trade director for the city of San Francisco. One reason the city government hired him was his legal background; after all, Fang's résumé resonated with phrases like *Hastings College of the Law (1987)* and *California Bar examination passage.* Naturally, his new employers assumed Fang was a lawyer.

He wasn't. "This is not a case," insisted Fang after the truth had come out, "of a person blatantly lying on a résumé to get a job." According to Fang, people wrongly assumed the reference to Hastings College meant that he had graduated from the school (he had attended Hastings but had not graduated). People also assumed, said Fang, that his reference to the "bar examination" meant he was a member of the California Bar (Bar members must also take *another* exam—one that Fang had not yet taken). Among those guilty of false assumption was the mayor of San Francisco, who thought Fang was an attorney when he hired him for the $65,000-a-year position.

Like the city of San Francisco, more and more employers today are finding that job applicants are willing to skirt the truth. One survey revealed that 11 percent of applicants lie about why they left previous jobs, 4 percent lie about former job titles, 3 percent list bogus employers, 3 percent concoct jobs, and 3 percent award themselves college degrees. The actual numbers, however, may be much higher. These statistics apply only to candidates who've actually been offered jobs, and most applicants never get past the screening stage.

It was thus that an executive recruiter for one firm thought that he had a winning candidate for a senior marketing-management slot—until he discovered that the man had lied during his job interview. The candidate claimed to have an M.B.A. from Harvard, which had "never heard of him," according to the recruiter. The candidate also claimed four years' experience with a previous employer (he had actually had two years) and said that he'd been a vice president of marketing (when his real position was several levels down from that).

Then there are the applicants who neglect to tell interviewers about felony convictions. Vericon Resources, Inc., a background-check company, has found new hires with criminal records including rape and child molestation. In one case, Vericon discovered that a new employee had a warrant out for his arrest on a theft charge. The employee's new job? Managing an apartment building, where he had keys to all the apartments.

In addition to being unethical, lying about your credentials can obviously cost you a job. Needless to say, applicants caught in lies don't get hired. Furthermore, even long-time employees who are caught in lies can be fired, no matter how long they've been with a company or how well they've performed there. Moreover, an employee who is fired for some other reason has no grounds for suing the company if it turns out there are lies on his or her résumé.

Mildred Johnson found this out the hard way. Honeywell Information Systems fired her after eight years as a manager; claiming that she'd been forced out for adhering to affirmative-action hiring goals, Johnson sued. While preparing the company's court defense, Honeywell's lawyer discovered that while Johnson had claimed on her résumé to possess a college degree and a year of management study, she had actually taken only six college courses. Johnson had also described herself as her own property manager during a time when she was unemployed and owned no property at all. In court, Honeywell claimed that Johnson had no right to sue because she had lied about her background. When the court agreed, Mildred Johnson lost both her case and her job.

Questions and Applications

1. In what ways do some job applicants misrepresent their credentials?
2. Your school's placement office asks you to write a memo to your fellow students about the issue of dishonesty in résumés, applications, and job interviews. Write this memo (one page), in which you discuss the ethical issues involved and the consequences to applicants and employees who are caught in lies.

Source: Joan Rigdon, "Deceptive Résumés Can Be Door-Openers but Can Become an Employee's Undoing," *The Wall Street Journal*, June 17, 1992, pp. B1, B11. Reprinted by permission of *The Wall Street Journal* © 1992 Dow Jones & Company, Inc. All rights reserved worldwide.

Wanted at Magna International: Employees Who Never Want to Go Hungry

Once it was just another tiny tool and die manufacturer. Today, however, Magna International is one of the top ten auto-parts makers in the United States. It is Chrysler's biggest components supplier, and Magna workers helped invent the fold-out child-safety seat for Chrysler's profitable minivans.

Magna's fast-charging growth reflects the gung-ho attitude of its founder and majority owner, Frank Stronach, who announces that "I never want to go hungry and I never want to crawl for anybody." Like its principal customers, the Big Three U.S. auto makers, Stronach's company is changing. While car makers once wanted their suppliers simply to make and deliver parts like door handles, today they're expected to design and produce entire "door systems," complete with armrests, interior trim, latches, and wiring. Explains Thomas Stallkamp, chief of procurement for Chrysler: "We want component makers to be the experts in technology—to keep us current in trim, motors, and stampings."

To stay competitive, Frank Stronach believes in motivating his employees with incentives. Nearly the entire pay of all Magna managers is tied to the success—or failure—of their factories. Each year, every production worker in those factories shares equally in 10 percent of the pre-tax profits. All Magna factories are kept small and feature the latest in manufacturing technologies.

Questions and Applications

1. Describe Magna's changing role in the auto industry.
2. Suppose that you're interviewing with Frank Stronach for a managerial position at Magna. What needs and concerns is Stronach likely to have? What qualities will he probably look for in you?

Source: Brian O'Reilly, "The Perils of Too Much Freedom," *Fortune*, January 11, 1993, p. 79. © 1993 Time Inc. All rights reserved.

COMMUNICATION
CHALLENGES

593

18

COMMUNICATING IN A GLOBAL MARKETPLACE

CHAPTER OBJECTIVES

After studying this chapter, you should be able to:

1 Explain the increasing importance of *cross-cultural communication* to United States business.

2 Identify and briefly describe the different audiences in the global marketplace.

3 Explain the connection between *culture* and communication, and describe the dangers of *ethnocentricism*.

4 Identify the problems encountered by people who can only speak English when they do business abroad. Explain the advantages of being *multilingual*.

5 Define and contrast the communication differences characteristic of *low-context* and *high-context cultures*.

6 List the key elements for successful written and oral communication across national boundaries.

DECODING CULTURE AT EURO DISNEY

Before the Walt Disney Company opened its theme park near Paris in 1992, it had become entangled in a cultural dispute that threatened to delay the opening. At the heart of the problem was the Disney image—and how it would be communicated halfway around the world from home.

Management of Euro Disney had demanded that 12,000 French employees at the new park adhere to a personal-appearance code that maintains Disney's clean, well-scrubbed, and (some would say) all-American image. So serious is Disney about this code that a violation can mean dismissal. As described in both a company video and a guidebook, the Disney code requires that:

- All beards and mustaches be removed.
- Men's hair be cut above the collar and ears.
- Women wear appropriate undergarments; mesh, lacy, or black pantyhose are expressly forbidden.
- Women's hair appear in one natural color, with no frosting or streaking.
- Women's makeup be limited; false eyelashes, eyeliner, and eyebrow pencil are prohibited.
- Fingernails be no longer than the ends of the fingers.
- Earrings be no larger than three-quarters of an inch in size and be limited to one in each ear.
- A daily bath is expected (though not required).

The French were somewhat taken aback by the imposition of these rules imported from America. Labor law professor Roger Blancpain considered the requirements a frontal assault on French and European cultures. "A certain kind of underwear? There's a limit, and that's going too far." According to Blancpain, Euro Disney management "should have been aware of the environment it was operating in and shown more sensitivity."

French union representatives handed out pamphlets in front of the Euro Disney employment office, warning job applicants that the appearance code represented "an attack on individual liberty." Other French critics went so far as to call Disney's rules a violation of "human dignity."

For its part, Disney based its position on nonverbal communication by associating employee appearance with corporate identity. Argued Thor Degelmann, a Euro Disney official: "Without an appearance code, we wouldn't be presenting the Disney product that people would be expecting. It would be like going to see a production of *Hamlet* in which everyone looked different than you expected. Would you ever go again?" Degelmann added that the wording used in Disney's American appearance code had in fact been "toned down" because of cultural differences.[1]

CHAPTER OVERVIEW

Disney's experience in France is not unlike the experience of many United States companies doing business abroad. In this case, a particular form of nonverbal communication—personal appearance—was the focus. In other cases, miscommunication may involve language differences, different definitions of personal space, variations in codes of proper etiquette, or even different concepts of the way in which time should be spent. Bridging the cultural gaps that create communication problems is the subject of this chapter. We will begin by examining the increasing importance—both to United States businesses and to individual American workers—of communication in a global marketplace.

THE IMPORTANCE OF GLOBAL BUSINESS

In the years ahead, a growing number of American business transactions will occur in an expanding world marketplace. Both as **importers**—companies that purchase raw materials and goods from foreign countries—and as **exporters**—companies that sell domestically produced goods and services abroad—American companies are already part of the global trading community. Today, in fact, the United States leads the world in both imports and exports. Leading United States exports include transportation equipment, electrical and electronic equipment, chemicals, computers, semiconductors, drugs, and food. For example, mail-order business in Europe accounts for 30 percent of Texas-based Dell Computer's total sales. Non-United States business contributes 80 percent of Coca-Cola's total operating profits. Service exporter Turner Broadcasting has created a worldwide presence in televised news with its Cable News Network (CNN).[2]

As even newer opportunities become apparent, the tendency—indeed, the need—to do business abroad is likely to increase even further. For example, with 700 million potential customers, Europe (including the Commonwealth of Independent States and East European countries) is the world's largest single market.[3] Both major corporations and entrepreneurs are closely watching the newly independent republics of the former Soviet Union and are preparing to establish and enter new markets. The People's Republic of China and the smaller Pacific Rim nations also present tremendous opportunities, especially in the manufacturing and textile industries. Most recently, Mexican trade agreements with the United States and Canada have opened doors to a multitude of opportunities. It seems clear today that virtually no facet of business will be left untouched by the trend toward globalization.

importer
Company that purchases raw materials and goods from foreign countries

exporter
Company that sells domestically produced goods and services abroad

In the old days, we used to say that when the United States economy sneezed the rest of the world went to bed with pneumonia. Now when the United States economy sneezes the other countries say "Gesundheit."

Walter Heller
American economist

GLOBAL AUDIENCES FROM THE BUSINESS PERSPECTIVE

Within the context of a global marketplace, there are a number of distinct audiences with whom communication takes place. Generally, these audiences and the differences between them can be defined by *culture*. In this section, we will examine these audiences from the perspective of the business situation—of individual businesspeople communicating via written and oral messages. We have cast each

Fly United to London, where history repeats itself every morning at 11:00.

Pageantry is part of every day, and every season, in London and throughout Britain.

The colorful ritual of the Changing of the Guard unfolds at Buckingham Palace every morning from mid-April to mid-August. Or, you can watch its cavalry equivalent at Horse Guards, off Whitehall, every morning at 11:00 (10:00 on Sundays).

But London isn't the only place you can witness such exciting spectacle: Scotland is renowned for its massed pipes and drums at the annual Edinburgh Military Tattoo. And, in Wales, you'll find Europe's most famous folk music festival, the Llangollen International Eisteddfod.

United Airlines can take you to Britain any time you want to go. United has non-stop service to London's Heathrow Airport from New York, Newark, Washington, D.C., Los Angeles, San Francisco, and Seattle on spacious 747's and 767's.

United Vacations also offers you a selection of specially priced fly-drive holidays, which include hotels, car rentals and extraordinarily flexible itineraries, plus theatre packages, independent tours and fully escorted tours. So call United Vacations at 1-800-328-6877 or your travel agent. And see history come to life this year, in Britain.

Britain. World Capital of Pageantry.

To the British, gasoline is *petrol;* a traffic circle is a *roundabout;* a cookie is a *biscuit;* and a biscuit is a *scone.* A movie titled *X, Y, and* Z made much less sense—and much less money—in the British Isles than it did in the U.S. After all, the British pronounce Z as *Zed.*
Source: © 1992 United Airlines; used by permission.

of these situations in cultural context—that is, within the context of cultures whose differences can directly influence the success or failure of business communication.

WORKING ABROAD   Companies like Caterpillar Tractor, Ford Motor Company, Exxon, and Dow Chemical are considered **multinational corporations**—firms which conduct significant business activities outside their home countries and which view the world as their marketplace. By the year 2000, multinationals are expected to control approximately half the world's assets. As a result, more and more Americans who work for such companies will be employed in locations outside the United States.[4] Today, more than 2 million Americans, many of whom work for multinational corporations or other foreign-based businesses, already reside in foreign countries.[5]

Of course, not all Americans who work abroad enjoy their stations or perform well at their jobs. According to some estimates, only 20 percent of transplanted American workers do well, while 40 percent to 60 percent either return home before the completion of their assignments or perform poorly.[6] Many of the problems associated with working abroad are directly tied to communication problems involving differences in language and culture. For example, when Susan Koscis, international program director for the American Management Association, ran a management-training program in Warsaw, she requested that a group photo be taken. "We asked the Polish consultant in charge of organizational details to arrange the photo session," she recalls,

> but when we asked about the photographer's arrival, we were told that no photographer had been hired. The explanation given by the consultant

multinational corporation
Firm which conducts significant business outside its home country and which views the world as its marketplace

Don't overlook the importance of worldwide thinking. A company that keeps its eye on Tom, Dick, and Harry is going to miss Pierre, Hans, and Yoshio.

*Al Ries
Chairman, Trout & Ries Inc.
advertising agency*

CURRENT ISSUES IN BUSINESS COMMUNICATION

American or Foreign?

A recent survey of United States consumers revealed that 85 of every 100 respondents would prefer to buy American products when given the choice. But how effective are marketers in communicating a product's country of origin to prospective buyers? As manufacturers purchase raw materials from global suppliers, assemble components in several countries, and complete the final assembly process in still another, it is becoming increasingly difficult to distinguish between "domestic" and "foreign-made" goods. The Ohio-assembled Honda Accord is a good example.

The following quiz is designed to test your awareness of this phenomenon. Match the product or service with the nationality of its maker.

PRODUCT	OWNER'S NATIONALITY
_c_ 1. Atari video game	a. Germany
___ 2. Holiday Inn	b. Great Britain
___ 3. Firestone tires	c. Japan
___ 4. Magnavox televisions	d. The Netherlands
___ 5. Videotape of *E.T.: The Extraterrestrial*	e. United States

Answers: 1. e; 2. b; 3. c; 4. d; 5. c. Atari is a California-based company; Holiday Inn is owned by London-based Bass PLC; Firestone is owned by Tokyo's Bridgestone Corp.; Magnavox is a brand name of the Dutch-owned Philips Electronics N.V.; the film library of Universal Studios is owned by Japan's Matsushita Corp.

was, "You said you wanted a photographer, but you didn't give me the authority to hire one." We had forgotten that the consultant was a product of the unmerciful Eastern [European] bureaucratic mindset. . . . What may seem like a straightforward issue to us can in fact have quite a different interpretation in another culture."[7]

Even though Koscis planned to attend to the smallest details to ensure her program's success, she underestimated the formality inherent in communication in this particular culture. Fortunately, her mistake cost Koscis only a photo, but it is easy to see how similar situations could create more serious problems for businesspeople in any number of foreign countries.

Not surprisingly, multinational companies expect their American employees to develop some level of understanding about the cultures of host countries. According to Kazuto Wakatsuki, a member of the international planning department at Japan's Saitama Bank, "Foreign employees are hired in part on their likelihood of 'fitting in' to the company and country. [Companies expect you to know] how the Japanese relate at work and in their social lives."[8]

WORKING FOR A FOREIGN-OWNED COMPANY   Many foreign multinationals also have active operations in the United States. In recent years, for example, Japanese companies have been making substantial investments in the United States. Michigan alone has some 300 Japanese companies—a number that has increased sixfold in eight years. Companies headquartered in such countries as Great Britain, Germany, and the Netherlands also have major holdings in the United States. These firms have turned to the American work force to fill their labor needs in United States facilities.[9]

Working for one of these companies typically requires learning to communicate within the context of the culture that foreign managers bring with them. Cultural differences may exist even though a company promises that its U.S. operation will be "all American." For example, when the German electronics giant Siemens acquired Computest, an automated computer test-equipment firm, a top Siemens executive flew in from Germany to assure the Cherry Hill, New Jersey, company that it would always remain "American." Turning to Computest's new managers, he asked, "Isn't that right, Fritz? Isn't that right, Hans? Isn't that right, Siegfried?"[10]

As more foreign industry moves into the United States, whether through mergers and acquisitions or through the establishment of foreign branches, American workers will be confronted more and more with foreign cultures. The employees who survive in their new environment will be those who adapt successfully to the culture and communication styles that parent-company managers bring with them.

At the same time, most foreign nationals who come to this country as managers of foreign-owned companies realize that they cannot impose their communication styles on U.S. workers. In turn, however, they expect an acknowledgment that business is conducted differently in their home countries. Jim Olson, Toyota Motor Company's Los Angeles-based vice president for external affairs, explains how his senior executive coordinator, a Japanese national, helps him make the right communication choices: "He tries to interface between two cultures," says Olson. "He warns me if I'm being too American, too pushy, in dealing with Japan."[11]

WORKING WHILE TRAVELING   Business communication often takes place during travel. American necktie manufacturer George Goldman, for example, travels regularly to Italy to purchase silk and other cloth. Joan Kennedy, a senior official at a fashion buying firm, travels to Paris, Milan, London, and Rome for the latest women's fashions. On a recent trip, Mike Bonsignore, president of International Honeywell, flew from his company's home base in Minneapolis to Hong Kong, Taipei, Tokyo, Alaska, and Calgary before returning home.[12] For all businesspeople involved in international travel, the ability to bridge cultural differences in written and oral communication is crucial.

Even employees of U.S. companies who never travel abroad may need to correspond with businesspeople in foreign countries. These correspondents may be fellow employees of the U.S. company, suppliers, wholesalers, retailers, or customers. Cigna Corp., a Connecticut-based insurer, recently hired 120 workers in Loughrea, Ireland, to process medical claims that are flown in daily from the United States. McGraw-Hill Data Services employs forty people in the same Irish town to maintain worldwide circulation files for the company's sixteen magazines.[13] Whether communication is done by letter or memo, whether it involves normal delivery channels or electronic mail, successful communicators must learn to consider the cultural contexts in which their communications will be received.

We have seen how cultural context can affect communication in a few increasingly common business situations, and we will turn next to a more detailed discussion of the relationship between culture and communication. Business situations like those that we have just described have spurred many multinational organizations to improve cross-cultural communication. As you can see in Table 18.1, for example, companies like American Express, Colgate-Palmolive, and General Electric have recognized the importance of cross-cultural training and have developed programs to expose both new and veteran management-level employees to the world of global business. Such companies have become convinced that effective cross-cultural communication requires a closer understanding of the nature of culture and the role of cultural differences as communication barriers.

CULTURE AND COMMUNICATION

culture
Shared products that make up a society, including languages, beliefs, rules, customs, myths, family patterns, and political systems

The shared products of human society make up a society's **culture**. Naturally, many of the components of culture—languages, beliefs, rules, customs, myths, family patterns, and political systems—determine the way people communicate.

Americans, like other national groups, communicate according to distinct cultural patterns that often do not coincide with the cultural patterns of other groups. Such patterns frequently inspire certain generalizations about a culture.

TABLE 18.1	*Examples of Corporate Cross-Cultural Training Programs*

COMPANY	PROGRAM
American Express Co.'s Travel-Related Services Unit	Gives American business school students summer jobs in which they work outside the U.S. for up to 10 weeks. Also transfers junior managers with at least two years experience to other countries.
Colgate-Palmolive Co.	Trains about 15 recent college graduates each year for 15 to 24 months prior to multiple overseas job appointments.
General Electric Co.'s aircraft-engine unit	Will expose selected mid-level engineers and managers to foreign language and cross-cultural training even though not all will live abroad.
Honda of America Manufacturing Inc.	Has sent about 42 U.S. supervisors and managers to the parent company in Tokyo for up to three years, after preparing them with six months of Japanese language lessons, cultural training, and life-style orientation during work hours.
PepsiCo Inc.'s international beverage division	Brings about 24 young foreign managers a year to the U.S. for one-year assignments in bottling plants.
Raychem Corp.	Assigns relatively inexperienced Asian employees (from clerks through middle managers) to the U.S. for six months to two years.

Source: These programs are described in Joann S. Lublin, "Younger Managers Learn Global Skills," *The Wall Street Journal*, March 31, 1992, p. B1.

Generalizations that apply to Americans, for example, include the following:

- Goal and achievement orientation
- Love of freedom
- Self-reliance
- Work orientation and efficiency
- Competitiveness and aggressiveness
- A high degree of organization
- Generosity[14]

Any one of these characteristics can get an American into communication difficulty when doing business abroad. For example, efficiency makes us time-conscious—we tend to get to the point immediately when we communicate. This tendency may be a mistake in Arab cultures, where getting to know someone is considered a prerequisite to talking business. Like many other cultural characteristics, our concept of time influences such communication strategies as word choice. For example, according to communication consultant Sana Reynolds,

> Americans communicate best with verbs. We like the feeling of adrenaline that communicating with verbs gives us. However, our style often offends cultures that use lengthy sentence lines. We're too brusque. We get to the point too quickly. . . . The Koran [the sacred book of Islam] states that Arabs should not do business with anyone until they know their business partner's father, his father's father, and his father's father's father. When we expect to conclude an agreement quickly solely on the basis of whether or not it is beneficial, we are perceived as rushing things along.[15]

In this section, we will examine two common barriers to successful cross-cultural communication in a variety of business situations: *ethnocentrism* and *culture shock*. Finally, we will survey some of the problems posed for the future of business communication by various *language limitations*.

Ethnocentrism

ethnocentrism
Tendency to judge other cultures by the standard of one's own culture

Successful global communication requires an awareness of the dangers of ethnocentricism and an effort to avoid them. **Ethnocentrism** is the tendency to judge other cultures by the standards of one's own culture. Ethnocentric communication often results from an insistence upon using one's own business values with little or no awareness of their differences from the values of other cultures.

Harry C. Triandis, an authority on cross-cultural communication patterns, provides the example in Figure 18.1 of an American and a Greek talking at cross purposes because of a basic failure to understand each other's cultural patterns. As you read, keep in mind that Greeks perceive supervisors as more authoritarian than do Americans; what is said by a boss—in this case, the American—is what a subordinate (the Greek) believes must be done. What the parties *say* appears on the left side of the diagram; what they are *thinking* appears on the right. Communication success (or failure) will be determined by the content that appears

VERBAL CONVERSATION	WHAT EACH IS REALLY THINKING
American: How long will it take you to finish this report?	I asked him to participate.
Greek:	His behavior makes no sense. He is the boss. Why doesn't he *tell* me?
Greek: I don't know. How long should it take?	I asked him for an order.
American:	He refuses to take responsibility.
American: You are in the best position to analyze time requirements.	I press him to take responsibility for his own actions.
Greek:	What nonsense! I'd better give him an answer.
Greek: Ten days.	
American:	He lacks the ability to estimate time; this time is totally inadequate.
American: Take fifteen. Is it agreed you will do it in fifteen days?	I offer a contract.
Greek:	These are my orders: fifteen days.

[In fact, the report needed thirty days of regular work. So the Greek worked day and night, but at the end of the fifteenth day, he still needed one more day's work.]

American: Where is the report?	I am making sure he fulfills his contract.
Greek:	He is asking for the report.
Greek: It will be ready tomorrow.	

[Both silently acknowledge that the report is not ready.]

American: But we had agreed it would be ready today.	I must teach him to fulfill a contract.
Greek:	The stupid, incompetent boss! Not only did he give me wrong orders, but he does not even appreciate that I did a thirty-day job in sixteen days.

[The Greek hands in his resignation. The American is surprised.]

Greek:	I can't work for such a man.

FIGURE 18.1   *Cross-Cultural Communications*

Source: Philip R. Harris and Robert T. Moran, *Managing Cultural Differences,* 3rd ed. (Houston: Gulf Publishing Co., 1991), p. 271.

in the right-hand column. Neither the American's response nor the Greek's response is "right" or "wrong." Differences exist that must be acknowledged, accepted, and understood in order for effective communication to take place.

ACCOMMODATION   In order to counter ethnocentric tendencies, *adaptation* must also occur. Although you naturally start with a certain sensitivity toward your own culture, you must be willing to accommodate communication differences that exist in other cultures. You must realize, for example, that it is considered inappropriate in Egypt to use first names unless invited to do so, or to address someone without including his or her rank or title. Similarly, in Hong Kong, aggressive communication is considered inappropriate—the Chinese are reserved and modest in conducting business. In Brazil, events—not hours and minutes—define time. When you meet with a Brazilian client, it is a mistake to launch immediately into business decisions.[16]

Consideration of cultural differences is called **accommodation.** Successful communication accommodates the customs, behaviors, and discussion topics of your foreign audience. The *degree* of accommodation is influenced by *cultural imperatives, cultural adiaphoras,* or *cultural exclusives.*[17]

accommodation
Consideration of cultural differences

A request for "french fries" will produce only perplexed stares in France. Even at the local McDonald's outlets in Paris, you should ask for *pommes frites*.

Source: © 1992 Chubb Group of Insurance Companies; used by permission.

cultural imperatives
Business customs and behaviors that must be recognized during communications

cultural adiaphoras
Customs and behaviors for which accommodation is optional

cultural exclusives
Customs, behaviors, and conversational topics from which foreigners are excluded

culture shock
Psychological disorientation that arises when people do not understand or misinterpret cues received from other cultural groups

CULTURAL IMPERATIVES   Business customs and behaviors that must be recognized during communication are known as **cultural imperatives.** The success of the interchange—often the entire business relationship—can depend on this recognition. In Asia and Latin America, for example, a level of trust must be developed before business discussions can begin. Time spent developing friendships may seem wasted to busy Americans, but only by spending this time will business be possible.

CULTURAL ADIAPHORAS   Customs for which accommodation is *optional* are known as **cultural adiaphoras.** You may decide either to participate in these customs or to follow United States cultural standards. For example, Americans are not expected to bow in Japan when meeting Japanese businesspeople. When they do, however, the bow is interpreted as a gesture of good will.

CULTURAL EXCLUSIVES   Customs, behaviors, and topics of conversation from which foreigners are excluded are known as **cultural exclusives.** For example, it is a mistake to use stationery depicting the symbolic Aztec eagle in communications with Mexican businesspeople. That symbolic eagle is considered a cultural exclusive for Mexican use only. Similarly, discussions of the emperor's role in Japanese society is off limits to non-Japanese.

Culture Shock

Understanding the *communication environment* helps Americans doing business with foreigners avoid **culture shock**—the psychological disorientation that arises when people misinterpret or do not understand the cues they receive from other cultural groups. Culture shock often leaves individuals feeling uprooted and unsure that they can communicate appropriately. An American businesswoman in Japan, for example, may find it difficult to work unless she is aware of the role typically filled by women in Japanese culture. The Japanese may be unwilling to speak to her directly, preferring instead to speak to a man. Culture shock can make people unhappy in their work and consequently reduce productivity.

Many companies are thus becoming increasingly aware of the importance of *intercultural competence*—an understanding of the roles that language and culture play in communication. Although language differences constitute the most obvious communication barrier separating Americans from their foreign business contacts, they are often the simplest obstacles to overcome. The problems associated with language limitations are equaled—and often surpassed—by a more subtle problem that we will discuss shortly at some length: the problem of learning to deal with the marked cultural dissimilarities found in *high-context* and *low-context cultures.*

If you speak three or more languages, you're multilingual. If you speak two languages, you're bilingual. If you speak one language, you're American.

Anonymous

Language Limitations

Not surprisingly, American businesspeople frequently find it a distinct disadvantage to use English to communicate in non–English-speaking countries. When oral and written translations move thoughts from one language to another, such nuances as tone of voice and emphasis can easily be lost. According to the bureau chief of a major United States news agency, language limitations also reduce business power. "Foreigners who cannot understand," he explains, "are spoon-fed what their hosts wish to spoon-feed them. . . . Many American executives become showroom managers sitting in well-decorated offices with a staff of secretaries, but have little control over operations. Business goes on around them and decisions are made without them."[18]

For example, even though they speak English in England, they speak *British* English—a language very much different from *American* English. Consequently, miscommunication can occur even when we deal with English-speaking people. A letter written by an American supplier to customers in London telling them to expect shipment on "10.2.95" would most likely be interpreted as a delivery date of February 10, 1995—eight months before the intended delivery date of October 2. The confusion is created by differences between European and American dating systems. While our system lists the month first, followed by the day and year, the European system lists the day, month, and year.

Although English is generally considered the international language of business, it is nevertheless a mistake to assume that every foreign businessperson either knows English or can understand American usage. In fact, only about half of the 750 million people who speak English learned it as their first language, and those who speak English as a second language are much more limited than native speakers.[19] According to a Bechtel executive stationed in a Japanese village outside Tokyo, while most of the village residents can read and write English, their frame of reference is the English they were taught in school. Most of them, therefore, have great difficulty in understanding American speech, which is by no means the same thing as the "English language."[20] Moreover, in some Arabic-speaking countries, including Tunisia and Lebanon, French—not English—is considered the language of international trade.

Americans must also learn to deal with the nonstandard English spoken by international business contacts in such diverse countries as Nigeria, India, Singapore, and the Philippines. Although English is the official business language in these countries, it is not the language of everyday speech and is therefore peppered with nonstandard variants. Here are several examples of the patterns and expressions common among non-natives:

- Ramesh said he will be coming here soon, isn't it?
- I can't got it, too.
- He suggested me to meet with you in Bombay.
- She hasn't had no idea, also.
- Don't you mind my smoking?
  Yes [="Please go ahead. I don't mind at all."]

England and America are two countries separated by the same language.

Attributed to Irish playwright George Bernard Shaw

Recognizing how they have mangled English, city officials in Tokyo are spending $75,000 to replace about 300 English nameplates that guide English-speaking businesspeople and tourists through Tokyo's city hall. For example, an office sign reading, "Powder and Electricity Regulation" will be changed to "Explosives and Electricity." An ungrammatical sign that announces the "Loaning Section" will also be corrected.[21]

For these and other reasons, lack of language *fluency* often makes it difficult for foreign managers, company representatives, and executives to compete globally. Being "fluent" in a language involves more than an ability to speak and write with grammatical correctness: It means understanding the meaning of what is being communicated. As we saw earlier, Susan Koscis of the American Management Association failed to get a photograph because she did not communicate effectively from one culture to another. Similarly, a language barrier between two linguistic cultures may extend well beyond mere letters and words.

At the same time, however, language fluency certainly begins with learning the correct way to speak and write a language. "Is it any wonder," asks Victor Hao Li, president of the East-West Center, "that American sellers have difficulty penetrating foreign markets?" Li points to the fact that while 20 million Japanese are studying English, only a few thousand Americans are studying Japanese. Americans, he suggests, "do not speak the most important language of all for their purpose—the language of the customer."[22] Moreover, language-related problems are likely to increase in the years ahead as foreign governments take the lead in insisting that government contracts and negotiations be conducted in the language of the contract-granting country. This is already the case in such nations as Belgium, Spain, and Thailand.[23]

TABLE 18.2	*Percentage of College Students Registered in Foreign Language Courses: 1986–1990*	
	1986	**1990**
Spanish	411,293	533,609 *up* 30%
French	275,328	272,555 *down* 1%
German	121,022	133,380 *up* 10%
Italian	40,945	49,726 *up* 21%
Japanese	23,454	45,717 *up* 95%
Russian	33,961	44,384 *up* 31%
Latin	25,038	28,178 *up* 13%
Chinese	16,891	19,490 *up* 15%
Other	55,302	56,353 *up* 2%

Source: Data from Modern Language Association. Reported in "Students in Language Are Found at New High," *The New York Times,* September 25, 1991, p. B6.

A recent study by Dunhill Personnel Systems revealed that only one out of four American managers is fluent in a foreign language. Japanese and German, considered important languages for the twenty-first century, are spoken by few. Moreover, only one in sixteen managers questioned considered foreign-language skills a must for his or her career.[24]

In recent years, more and more students have begun to study foreign languages—in large part because they understand the relationship between language fluency and personal career success. Although less than 8 percent of all American college students are now enrolled in foreign-language courses, the trend is toward greater interest. Table 18.2 shows that although Japanese and Russian language courses experienced the greatest enrollment increases during a recent four-year period, Spanish, French, and German maintained their positions as the most popular foreign languages. According to Helene Zimmer-Loew, president of the Joint National Committee for Languages, this trend probably reflects a growing interest in the global marketplace. "I think many [foreign language students] are majoring in business and they see a second language as an absolute necessity because of a shrinking global economy."[25] For example, being fluent in a foreign language may be critical if you work for a company with manufacturing plants overseas. Van Heusen manufactures many of its shirts in Thailand. Nike athletic clothing is made in Malaysia. Jones New York suits are made in Korea. American managers who deal with foreign counterparts in these manufacturing facilities are finding more and more that speaking the language is of great help in conducting successful relations.

PROGRESS CHECK

1. The chapter notes that many Americans who work abroad often perform poorly or return home before their assignments are completed. Why do you think this happens?
2. Can you give some examples of patterns of thought and behavior that characterize "American culture"? How might some of these patterns constitute barriers to communication on the part of foreigners?
3. What is *culture shock*? What causes it and how can we avoid it?
4. What does *language fluency* mean? Besides taking language courses in college, what can you do to improve your fluency in a foreign language?

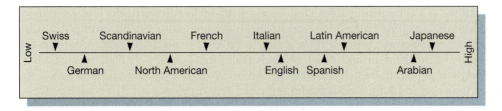

FIGURE 18.2   *High– and Low–Context Cultures*

LOW-CONTEXT VERSUS HIGH-CONTEXT CULTURES

Although the process of bridging the cultural communication gap begins with language, it does not end there. The process also requires that you understand the cultural context in which communication takes place.

Edward T. Hall, an anthropologist and authority on cross-cultural communication, divides cultures into two basic types: *low-context* and *high-context cultures.* Communication in **low-context cultures** depends on explicit written and verbal messages. Germany, Switzerland, the Scandinavian countries, and the United States are considered low-context cultures. By contrast, communication in **high-context cultures** depends not only on the message itself but also on everything that surrounds the explicit message, including nonverbal language. China, Korea, Japan, and the Arab countries are considered high-context cultures. Figure 18.2 places eleven world cultures on Hall's continuum.

Adding Context to International Communication

Communication context directly influences communication style. In low-context cultures, for example, written agreements and messages determine business deals, while in high-context cultures written correspondence and agreements are often far less important than interpersonal relationships, personal status and titles, and the social environment in which the business deal takes place. Several factors affect communication in low- and high-context cultures: *personal relationships; timing; level of formality; etiquette;* and *body language,* including *eye contact, gestures, touch, personal space,* and *clothing.*

PERSONAL RELATIONSHIPS   In high-context cultures, trust often precedes business. Trust is usually built on personal relationships established over a period of time. While Americans, for example, may try to cement a business relationship by getting straight to the point, members of high-context cultures frequently engage in a kind of "courting" behavior before business begins. In such countries as Guatemala, Japan, Saudi Arabia, and China, experienced businesspeople build relationships by engaging in small talk about such topics as their countries, families, and business associates. They allot time for relaxed dinners or lunches in which business is not discussed. Only when personal relationships are cemented does attention turn to business relationships.

This process may take hours and extend over several meetings—more time than most Americans are comfortable giving. Americans tend to be direct, wanting to get down to business immediately after shaking hands, beginning a presentation, or opening a letter. To be successful in high-context cultures, Americans must learn to approach partners and clients gradually until personal relationships are established.

In high-context communication, such relationships are based on information about you and your company. Before the start of a meeting or presentation in such high-context cultures as Latin America or Korea, send an annual report or other documents describing your company's products and history. Enclose a résumé or letter describing your personal background. When beginning a business relationship by mail, it is even more important to introduce yourself through such documents.

low-context culture
Culture in which communication depends on explicit written and verbal messages

high-context culture
Culture in which communication depends not only on the message itself but also on the context surrounding the explicit message, including nonverbal language

I traveled a good deal all over the world, and I got along pretty good in all those foreign countries, for I have a theory that it's their country and they got a right to run it like they want to.

Will Rogers
American actor and
humorist

TIMING   While promptness characterizes business culture in the United States, inattention to time characterizes many high-context cultures. For example, while an American may consider it an insult to be kept waiting, a Latin American or Arab businessperson may feel no such pressure. Edward T. Hall recounts the following episode, which involves an American agricultural attaché assigned to an embassy in Latin America who arrived a few minutes ahead of schedule for a meeting with his local counterpart (a government minister):

> The hour came and passed; five minutes—ten minutes—fifteen minutes. At this point, [the attaché] suggested to the secretary that perhaps the minister did not know he was waiting in the outer office. This gave him the feeling he had done something concrete and also helped to overcome the great anxiety that was stirring inside him. Twenty minutes—twenty-five minutes—thirty minutes—forty-five minutes (the insult period)!
>
> He jumped up and told the secretary that he had been "cooling his heels" in an outer office for forty-five minutes and he was "damned sick and tired" of this type of treatment. This message was relayed to the minister, who said, in effect, "Let him cool his heels."

Hall also provides some insightful analysis of this little anecdote. "What bothers people in situations of this sort," he explains,

> is that they don't realize they are being subjected to another form of communication, one that works part of the time with language and part of the time independently of it. The fact that the message conveyed is couched in no formal vocabulary makes things doubly difficult, because neither party can get very explicit about what is actually taking place. Each can only say what he thinks is happening and how he feels about it. The thought of what is being communicated is what hurts.[26]

M-TIME AND P-TIME   Whether low-context or high-context, different cultures tend to rely on different time systems. According to Hall, for example, most Westerners are on **M-time (monochronic time)**. M-time is a way of viewing time according to sequential activities that proceed in a linear way. Time is regarded as having a "tangible" quality in that it can be saved, spent, wasted, or lost. By contrast, people in high-context cultures are on what Hall terms **P-time, or poly-chronic time.** P-time is an attitude toward time that emphasizes building human relationships rather than meeting schedules. P-time is based on the twofold conviction that all human relationships, including business relationships, take time to build and that, in the long run, the process is time well spent.[27]

In Japan and other high-context cultures, P-time behavior is exhibited in some circumstances and M-time in others. When a meeting is called in Japan, for instance, everyone is expected to arrive on time. Once the meeting begins, however, P-time takes precedence, and the focus turns to developing interpersonal relationships.[28] It is during this time that credibility and rapport are established, both of which are essential to the success of future business.

LEVEL OF FORMALITY   High-context cultures generally demand formality and proper etiquette in both personal and written communication. Unless the culture requires otherwise, you should address foreign business associates by their surnames and use titles and formal forms of address.

Formality is such an entrenched part of the business culture in Japan that when the Dai-Ichi Kangyo Bank, the world's largest, ordered its employees to stop addressing one another according to rank, many employees resisted. Bank policy, for example, formerly required that a senior manager be addressed with a title like *kacho* (section chief) or *bucho* (department head) placed at the end of his name (as in *Tanaka-kacho*). The new policy now dictates that everyone be referred to by his or her last name, plus *san*—the Japanese version of *Mr., Mrs.,* or *Ms.* According to one senior manager who complained about the change, "I would hesitate to call the chairman Miyazaki-san." Among other companies that

_{*U.S.*} ✳ **M-time (monochronic time)**
Way of viewing time according to sequential activities that proceed in a linear way

_{*Japan*} ✳ **P-time (polychronic time)**
Attitude toward time that emphasizes building human relationships rather than meeting schedules

have adopted this less formal style are Sony Corp., Kao Corp., Shiseido Co., and the Bank of Tokyo.[29]

In most countries, including the United States, proper etiquette requires that meetings begin with a formal handshake. Indeed, in Europe and South America, people shake hands at every encounter, even if they have met, spoken, and shaken hands earlier in the day. In Japan and other Asian countries, people bow when they meet. In many cultures, handshakes less firm than those exchanged by Americans are the accepted norm. As the director of Atlanta's L' École des Exécutifs points out, "Do not presume to judge a person by his or her handshake. The rule to remember here is, 'Don't crush until you're crushed.'"[30]

BUSINESS CARDS   Generally speaking, the exchange of business cards is an important exercise in formal behavior. In Japan and other Asian countries, business cards are given to almost everyone you meet. They are presented in a formal way, using both hands, handled with care, and read slowly and carefully. Diana Rowland, author of *Japanese Business Etiquette,* tells how an overly casual reaction to a business card once cost a United States business executive an important deal. "Even though they liked his product, the Japanese reasoned that such inattention was representative of what they could expect from him later."[31] Other forms of expected behavior vary from country to country. In many countries, for example, turning the card over and writing on the back would be considered offensive.

As Figure 18.3 illustrates, the appropriate international business card should contain your name, title, and company information, all written in English on one side and in the local language on the other.

FORMALITY AND CULTURAL SENSITIVITY   Formality also requires sensitivity to other cultures. For example, attire that might be considered sophisticated in one culture might be regarded as garish in another. A Swiss client may be offended by an American's attempt to turn a joint meal into a "power breakfast." Cultures vary greatly on the appropriateness of gift giving, and because people in different cultures often laugh at different things, humor should always be used with care. When President Jimmy Carter went to Mexico, for instance, he made the following televised comment to Mexican President José Lopez Portillo: "We both run several kilometers every day. In fact, I first acquired my habit of running here in Mexico City. My first running course was from the Palace of Fine Arts to the Majestic Hotel where my family and I were staying. In the midst of the Folklorico performance, I discovered that I was afflicted with Montezuma's Revenge." His hosts considered Carter's reference—American slang for certain intestinal problems associated with the local water—inappropriate and insulting.[32]

BODY LANGUAGE   As we saw in Chapter 2, body language in virtually all forms communicates nonverbal messages. We have already examined the ways in which body language functions in United States culture, and in this chapter, we will consider briefly the ways in which it can affect cross-cultural communication. Because nonverbal communication patterns differ from country to country and culture to culture, an understanding of body language is essential to anyone who hopes to communicate successfully with members of other cultures. We will focus on *eye contact, gestures, touch,* and the use of *personal space;* finally, we will also say a few words about *clothing* as a means of nonverbal communication.

EYE CONTACT   Prolonged direct eye contact suggests an intimacy with which few American businesspeople are comfortable. Yet extended eye contact is common in many high-context cultures. Arabs, for example, believe that the eyes are the windows to the soul and that staring is permissible to discover what is in the other person's heart. From the Arab point of view, avoiding direct eye contact can thus communicate impoliteness, insincerity, and, at its extreme, dishonesty. Americans, on the other hand, may view Arab eye-contact behavior as intrusive and even threatening.

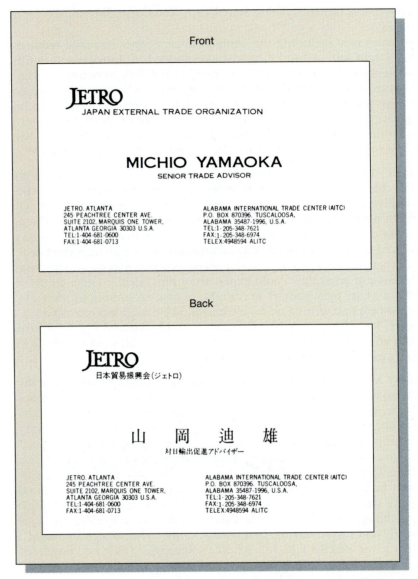

FIGURE 18.3   *Japanese Business Card for a U.S. Company Representative*

A different pattern exists in Japan, where children are taught never to look directly at someone who has superior status—a teacher, for example. This pattern persists into adulthood, with Japanese workers lowering their eyes, as a sign of respect, when speaking with supervisors.

GESTURES   Far from being universal, gestures have very different meanings in different cultures. For example, when President George Bush flashed a "V" sign with the back of his hand while on a visit in Australia, it was interpreted by Australians as an obscene gesture rather than the intended signal of victory.[33] Here are just a few examples of the ways in which different gestures can mean different—and often pointed—things in different cultures:

- In Hong Kong, winking or beckoning with one's index finger is considered rude.
- In Brazil, the American sign for OK—thumb and index finger touching to form a circle—is considered vulgar. In France, the same sign means zero; in Japan, it refers to money.
- In Yugoslavia, shaking the head from side to side means yes.

The frequency of gestures also differs from culture to culture. While the French and especially the Italians use many more gestures than Americans, the Japanese use far less.

Will the unification of Western Europe into a single common market, the demise of communism, and the proliferation of modern media bring about a single system of gesturing throughout Europe? According to Oxford University psychologist and body-language expert Peter Collett, culture-specific gestures are likely to be strengthened by the trend toward unification. "We've got everybody espousing European unity," observes Collett, "but at the same time there is this enormous rise of nationalism."[34] Figure 18.4 demonstrates how the meaning of certain gestures varies in different parts of Europe.

TOUCH   In general, it is a good rule of thumb to avoid physical contact. Don't slap backs or touch heads. In Malaysia and other Islamic countries, the head is believed to contain sacred spiritual and intellectual powers and should never be touched.

PERSONAL SPACE   Concepts of the appropriate personal space for conducting business differ markedly from culture to culture. Consider these two examples of how attitudes toward personal space vary around the world:

- Latin Americans insist on conducting business in the "intimate" and "personal" zones. Americans who feel uncomfortable with this behavior often back away and may be perceived as cold and unfriendly. To protect themselves from such a personal "threat," experienced Americans use desks or tables to separate themselves from their Latin American counterparts. "The result," explains Edward T. Hall, "is that the Latin American may even climb over the obstacles until he has achieved a distance at which he can comfortably talk."[35]

- Arabs follow a pattern similar to that of Latin Americans. Because Arabs consider smelling another person a sign of involvement, they sometimes stand so close to others that they can smell and be smelled. For Arabs, reports Hall, to smell another person "is not only nice, but desirable, for to deny him your breath is to act ashamed. Americans, on the other hand, trained as they are not to breathe in people's faces, automatically communicate shame in trying to be polite."[36]

FIGURE 18.4   *Gestures in Europe: Regional Differences Prevail*
Although Western Europe may be well on its way to its announced goal of economic unity, its tapestry of diverse cultures remains as intricate as ever. Gestures, for example, continue to reflect centuries of cultural differences. As in America, the thumb-and-index circle means "okay" in most of Europe; in Germany, it's an indelicate reference to the receiver's anatomy. In most of Great Britain—England and Scotland—the finger tapping the nose means, "You and I are in on the secret"; in nearby Wales, however, it means, "You're very nosy." If you tap your temple just about anywhere in Western Europe, you're suggesting that someone is "crazy"; in Holland, you'll be congratulating someone for being clever.

Not surprisingly, failing to understand differences like these can lead to serious miscommunication. Julius Fast, an authority on nonverbal communication, tells the following story about an American oil man and a Saudi prince:

> An American businessman [was] sent to Saudi Arabia to negotiate an oil deal with one of the four thousand Saudi princes. He was finally able to arrange an interview to fit into the prince's crowded schedule. It took place in a large ballroom just before a reception. Eager to make his point, the American started his pitch.
>
> The prince, interested in the project, moved within six inches of the American's face. But the American was uncomfortable at this close encounter, and moved back until there was what he considered a comfortable four feet between them.
>
> The prince moved into the distance at which he felt comfortable, six inches, and the American moved back again, unaware of what he was doing. In this way, the two men, in the next fifteen minutes, covered the entire floor of the ballroom while they talked, the American moving back, and the prince moving forward.
>
> The prince, however, became increasingly unhappy. The subtext he was receiving was clear to him. "I don't want to be close to you. You offend me. I dislike you." The businessman, too, began to feel uneasy. Why was this man getting so unpleasantly close, breathing in his face? He could actually smell the food the prince had eaten. He even felt a disturbing sexual subtext to this closeness, and he found himself stumbling, reddening, and looking away. In the end, the deal fell through. No matter how profitable the collaboration would have been to both men, the subtext of each annoyed the other.[37]

CLOTHING   One of the biggest mistakes that an American can make in a foreign country is to advertise citizenship through inappropriate clothing. A Texan wearing flashy boots and a ten-gallon hat, a Floridian sporting white shoes and an open shirt, and a California businesswoman wearing a high-fashion pants suit would all be considered out of place in Asia, where businessmen dress in traditional suits and businesswomen in tailored dresses. When traveling to Japan, choose socks without holes. Custom requires that shoes be removed when entering restaurants and homes.

By way of summary, many of the major differences in low-context and high-context cultures are encapsulated in Table 18.3.

PROGRESS CHECK

1. The chapter quotes one businessperson as saying, "Americans do not speak the most important language of all for their purpose—the language of the customer." Explain this statement. Do you agree? Why or why not?
2. Describe some basic differences in the communication patterns that you would use to do business with someone from Japan, as compared to someone from Denmark.
3. Are you on monochronic or polychronic time? Explain.

GUIDELINES FOR SUCCESSFUL CROSS-CULTURAL COMMUNICATION

The cultural differences that we have examined thus far have a direct impact on all forms of communication. We will explore this impact next as we suggest practical guidelines for both writing and speaking in cross-cultural contexts. We

TABLE 18.3	*Comparing High- and Low-Context Cultures*	
	LOW-CONTEXT CULTURES	HIGH-CONTEXT CULTURES
Personal Relationships	Relatively unimportant compared to the details of the deal.	Very important since business is built on personal trust.
Time	Business is conducted according to the clock; punctuality is valued. *M*-time organizes activities sequentially in a linear time frame.	Events rather than the clock determine schedules. *P*-time permits as much time as neccesary to build relationships.
Formality	A certain level of formality is expected including handshakes and identification by title and and company.	A high degree of formality is required during personal meetings and in correspondence.
Body Language		
• *Eye Contact*	Minimal direct eye contact.	Arabs: extended direct eye contact. Japanese: avert eyes to superiors as a sign of respect.
• *Gestures*	Meanings vary throughout the world.	Meanings vary throughout the world.
• *Touch*	Handshakes are acceptable; otherwise, avoid physical contact.	In general, the same customs apply.
• *Personal Space*	Americans conduct business within the social zone, standing or sitting four to twelve feet apart.	Arabs and Latins conduct business within the intimate zone, standing or sitting between eighteen inches and four feet apart.
• *Clothing*	Suits are expected attire for both men and women.	In general, the same customs apply.

will begin with a general survey of ways to improve written communication and then offer some guidelines for adapting to high- and low-context cultures, including some suggestions for accommodating certain gender differences that characterize different cultures. Finally, we will discuss some specific guidelines for directing foreign correspondence and conducting oral communications, both formal and informal, in cross-cultural contexts.

Improving Written Communication

The following guidelines for effective written communication will help you adapt your writing to the needs of foreign audiences. They focus on such critical factors as *translation, language usage, organization, level of formality,* and *tone.*[38]

TRANSLATION   When dealing with non–English-speaking people, or when you are not sure of your contact's ability to understand written English, have your document translated before it is sent. Translations make good business sense because an individual receiving an untranslated letter might choose to file it away rather than admit that he or she cannot read it. This response, for example, is fairly likely in Asian countries where "saving face" is critical. Because hiring a translator also costs money, recipients may forego the expense if they are uncertain of the document's value. When dealing with a translator, the following guidelines will help ensure acceptable results:

1. Choose a translator who is either native to the country where the item is to be read or who has lived or traveled there. If you are sending a proposal to Berlin, find a translator who has lived in Germany. You may also need a translator familiar with regionally correct spelling. In England,

Australia, India, and New Zealand, for example, *color* is spelled *colour,* *theater* is spelled *theatre,* and *organization* is spelled with an *s* not a *z.*

2. If you are translating technical or specialized documents, choose a translator familiar with the field. A report for a pharmaceutical company should be handled by someone familiar with medical terminology. Specify for your translator trade names or other words that should remain in English.

3. Take the time to explain your purpose and audience to your translator before he or she begins working. Point out where your actual words must be translated and where it is acceptable to translate the idea or mood. Explain the tone for which you are striving—friendly or formal—as well as the pace.

In recent years, translation services like Berlitz and Corporate Language Services have turned to computers and fax machines to send documents instantaneously to offices in foreign countries for native-country translations. All-Language Services, a company with ninety translators working in fifty-nine languages, has seen a fourfold increase in the volume of Japanese translations since

Westerners, especially Americans, typically feel comfortable in Australia. Australians, like Americans, are direct, like to be given a strong handshake, and usually prefer to be called by their first names. Language can sometimes be a problem, however. Americans have come to recognize the widespread use of—to them—mystifying slang expressions through such media as the popular *Crocodile Dundee* movies and travel advertisements such as this Qantas Airlines print ad. Asking an Australian to interpret the words and phrases in the well-known song *Waltzing Mathilda* is particularly educational. Driving around Australia (on the left side) will also prove revealing. Yield signs read "Give Way" and traffic circles are called *roundabouts.*

Source: © 1992 Qantas Airlines; used by permission.

Fair Dinkum* Australia.

*fair dinkum/—*Colloq.* —*adj.* 1: true, genuine, dinkum ‹are you fair dinkum?›—*interj.* 2: assertion of truth or genuineness ‹it's true, mate, fair dinkum› 3: Come have a fair dinkum great time in Australia.

1986. While large corporations have always used professional translation services, midsize and small businesses are now using them as well. "Translation is no longer an afterthought," cautions Thomas F. Seal, president of Alpnet, a language service with twenty-two offices in nine countries. He notes, for example, that growth in the demand for translators coincides with growth in new-product applications. "When companies are designing products upfront," he reports, "they are realizing the need to do translation. We've seen a large increase in contacts from the development phase."[39]

Despite the use of professional translators, however, mistakes are common—and even legendary. For example, a counter display for the Parker Pen Company's Quink brand of ink said in English, "Avoid Embarrassment—Use Quink." The Spanish version, "Evite Embarazos—Use Quink," translated as "Avoid Pregnancy—Use Quink." Similarly, when Coca-Cola introduced Coke into China during the 1920s, Chinese characters were used to translate the product name *phonetically*. Although the *sound* produced by the chosen characters was correct, their meaning was bizarre: "Bite the wax tadpole." Pepsi suffered a similar fate when the company translated its American slogan, "Come alive, you're in the Pepsi generation," into Thai. The translation told consumers that "Pepsi brings your ancestors back from the dead."[40]

LANGUAGE USAGE   Start with the assumption that most non-English speakers who have studied English possess a basic vocabulary of about 3,000 English words. It is important to rely on these words—which are the most common words in English—to communicate your thoughts. The following guidelines will help you to communicate through basic English:

1. When you have a choice, eliminate infrequently used words. Write *dishonesty* rather than *duplicity; send* rather than *disseminate; uncommon* rather than *esoteric;* and *hide* rather than *obfuscate.*

2. Avoid using slang words or phrases whose meaning is obvious only in the United States. For those unfamiliar with Bart Simpson, references to "having a cow" will be lost. Similarly, avoid using allusions to sports. In cultures unfamiliar with American football and baseball (most of the world), references to "scoring a touchdown" or "not being able to get to first base" will be confusing.

3. Choose specific-action rather than general-action verbs. For example, refer to "*purchasing* new equipment" rather than "*getting* new equipment." The verb *get* makes the action ambiguous. The reader is not sure whether you are going to borrow the equipment, lease it, or buy it.

4. Use correct grammar and punctuation. Be especially sensitive to sentence fragments, run-on sentences, and the need to have a clear link between pronouns and antecedents.

5. Eliminate redundant, unnecessary words—they will only obscure your intended meaning.

Adapting to High- and Low-Context Cultures

ADAPTING TO COMMUNICATION STYLES   When writing a business letter to low-context contacts in countries like Germany, Switzerland, or Sweden, state the point immediately, be direct, and then close your letter. Terse communication is expected in these cultures. However, using the same approach in high-context cultures is a mistake. As we explained earlier, these cultures often prefer more elaborate, personal communication that approaches the main point indirectly as a means of establishing individual trust and confidence. The type of communication described above for low-context cultures is acceptable in high-context cultures only when the parties already know one another and have built a relationship over a period of time.

INTERVIEW

George Simons, Consultant to Business on International Communication

Dr. George Simons has conducted seminars in over twenty-five countries on the issue of cross-cultural communications. He specializes in training people from diverse cultures and background to work together more effectively, and his clients include Apple, Colgate, Digital Equipment, Mobil, PepsiCo, Procter & Gamble, Shell, and Whirlpool, among many others.

Based in Santa Cruz, California, Dr. Simons was eager to provide his insights into successful cross-cultural communications. It is particularly interesting to note his thoughts about international business writing and the response that he gave to our final question, which not only addresses the importance of global communication but also sets the stage for our discussion of communicating in a diverse work force—the subject of Chapter 19.

Question: When writing to a business contact in another culture, what are some of the main issues to consider?

Answer: The first issue is whether writing is appropriate. In some cultures, a written letter or memo will simply be discarded. In others, written documents are essential before any meaningful discussion can begin. For example, the Germans usually want to see ideas on paper before they talk. In contrast, you can send letters to a Latin American until you are blue in the face and nothing will happen until you sit across a table and have a cup of coffee. This is a critical issue in international communication and probably the one people get into disasters with first— just not knowing whether oral or written communication is appropriate.

Question: When considering language barriers, do you think Americans can safely assume that others speak and understand the language?

Answer: Managers have to realize that non-Americans have trouble understanding American English. When dealing with people who speak English as a second language or who are from another English speaking culture like India or Great Britain, they have to be

Power and status differences between writer and reader in high-context cultures also affect the directness or indirectness of a message. A team of business instructors with experience in cross-cultural communication report as follows on the potential pitfalls of corresponding with government bureaucrats in Malaysia:

> Government bureaucrats [in Malaysia] bottom-line almost everything they write "down" to the citizenry. . . . But a businessperson writing "up," asking governmental permission for some action, is expected to be circuitous to the greatest possible extent. The longer the letter, the more "respect" it shows. Moreover, the businessperson is expected to include many long paragraphs praising the bureaucrat (or, more subtly, the bureaucrat's administration) in the most lavish terms. This "respect" is necessary because high-context cultures usually have definite social divisions, and there are appropriate sets of verbal behavior depending upon whether one is speaking to another who is higher or lower in the social order.[41]

BECOMING SENSITIVE TO CULTURAL PREFERENCES   Cultural preferences affect the level of formality and tone of all written communication. The following guidelines will help you in adapting your writing style to your reader's cultural preferences:

1. In high-context cultures, informal personal notes, often written at the bottom of documents, are commonly used once a business relationship has been established. Memos are rarely written to establish responsibility in case something goes wrong. When errors do occur in Middle

ready for a language gap. A Saudi talking to a Nigerian will have less trouble understanding each other's English than they will understanding an American. Both speak English as a second language and are more likely to be more readily aware of these limitations of vocabulary and grammar.

Because Americans assume that everyone speaks English as they do, they don't limit their vocabulary; they use dependent clauses and nuances that many non-Americans can't handle. To avoid these problems, Americans doing business abroad should discipline themselves to a vocabulary of 2,000 to 3,000 words and avoid nuances, except when they have the time and skill to work out an understanding face-to-face. They should expect the same limited vocabulary in written documents as well. One cannot easily peg a correspondent's level of sophistication by his or her writing.

Question: How do cultural differences affect the way people respond to written documents?

Answer: As Americans, we have to realize that what others expect in terms of a letter or a memo might be very different from what we expect. When I get a memo, I like it as clear as possible. I want the outline to jump out at me and the layout to make reading easy. I want bullets to focus my attention on key points.

The same approach can be offensive to someone who expects a nice greeting and an introduction. Instead of bulleting the information, they want it described in three different ways. The Japanese expect a less direct approach than we're used to, and miscommunication is possible when they don't get it.

Question: To what extent do communication patterns that exist in other countries become factors when people live and work here?

Answer: It depends on the degree of acculturation and assimilation. For example, on the surface, second-generation Hispanics or Asians may behave very much like North Americans but down deep, there is a different set of values that keeps reinforcing itself. When people group together in tightly knit communities and preserve the culture, as is often the case in Hispanic and Asian communities, old values continue to influence communication into the third and fourth generations.

Source: Interview with George Simons.

Eastern and Asian countries, the person in charge takes responsibility to the point of accepting a temporary salary reduction—or, if necessary, even resigning.

2. When writing to business associates in high-context cultures, use a polite, respectful tone—even when writing to subordinates. For example, ask if the reader will "consider" doing something; say that the completion of an assignment is "requested, if at all possible." Even when the recipient has no choice but to comply, this language communicates that there is an option to refuse—a way of saving face. Avoid putting Asians, including the Japanese, in the position of having to admit failure.

3. Find out the appropriate means for conveying specific types of information, including orders, refusals, requests, apologies, and thanks, and adapt your writing style accordingly. For example, instead of apologizing for a specific problem, you may need to write a generalized, unconditional apology—"I deeply apologize for any problems or misunderstandings my company may have caused." Similarly, instead of directly refusing a request, an indirect approach may be more appropriate—"Your catalog contains many interesting products that require further analysis."

4. Try to adapt your *language style* to the language style preferred in your reader's culture. For example, business communication in Arabic- and Spanish-speaking countries tends to be more colorful, often including exaggerations, flowery adjectives, and metaphors. The opposite is true in such low-context countries as Germany. Germans tend to avoid any suggestion

of flowery prose or exaggeration. They shun superlatives like *best* and *most* and minimize the use of such personal pronouns as *I* and *my*. For best results, use a passive, terse, impersonal style when writing to Germany.

UNDERSTANDING GENDER BIAS   Women are at a distinct disadvantage in many of the world's male-dominated societies such as Japan and Korea. In Pakistan, Yemen, and other Muslim countries, women may even be publicly rebuked for wearing Western clothing.[42] Asians may simply ignore women even when they are in a position of power. Ursula Gogel-Gorden, a director of product development at sportswear manufacturer Seattle-Pacific Industries, experienced this behavior when she was negotiating to buy yarn in Japan. Although she was in charge, all questions were addressed to a younger male colleague who was forced to keep repeating, "You have to talk to her."[43]

To minimize such problems, American businesswomen should be aware of customs regarding dress prior to visiting a host country. In many cases, Western

Diversified Investment Corporation
166 San Felipe
San Diego, CA   99222
USA

          Mr. Felix Adams, Deputy
          Merrill Lynch International Bank Ltd.
          25 Ropemaker Street
          London, EC2Y 9LY
          ENGLAND

Diversified Investment Corporation
166 San Felipe
San Diego, CA   99222
USA

          Mrs. Karla Isler
          20 Bunzstrasse
          Wohlen, Ag.
          5610 SWITZERLAND

FIGURE 18.5   *Letters Addressed to Foreign Correspondents*

dress for business meetings may be entirely acceptable while the same style is not appropriate for sightseeing. To minimize confusion over status, the American businesswoman should indicate her title and detail her responsibilities in writing for Asian contacts prior to meeting with them.

LEARNING TO DIRECT FOREIGN CORRESPONDENCE Foreign correspondence is addressed differently than correspondence in the United States. The examples in Figure 18.5 illustrate the correct format for addressing envelopes to foreign businesspeople in England, Switzerland, Italy, and Japan. As you can see, there are differences in the treatment of job titles and names; there are also differences in the ways you should handle the foreign correspondence that you receive.

Job Titles It is essential to use correct job titles in all addresses and to use these titles in correspondence. Do not use first names in a letter unless you are specifically invited to do so. In addition, learn the appropriate use of respectful titles. In Mexico, for example, refer to professionals by profession and name: *Architecto (architect) Hernandez* or *Licenciado (lawyer) Valdez*. Do not, however,

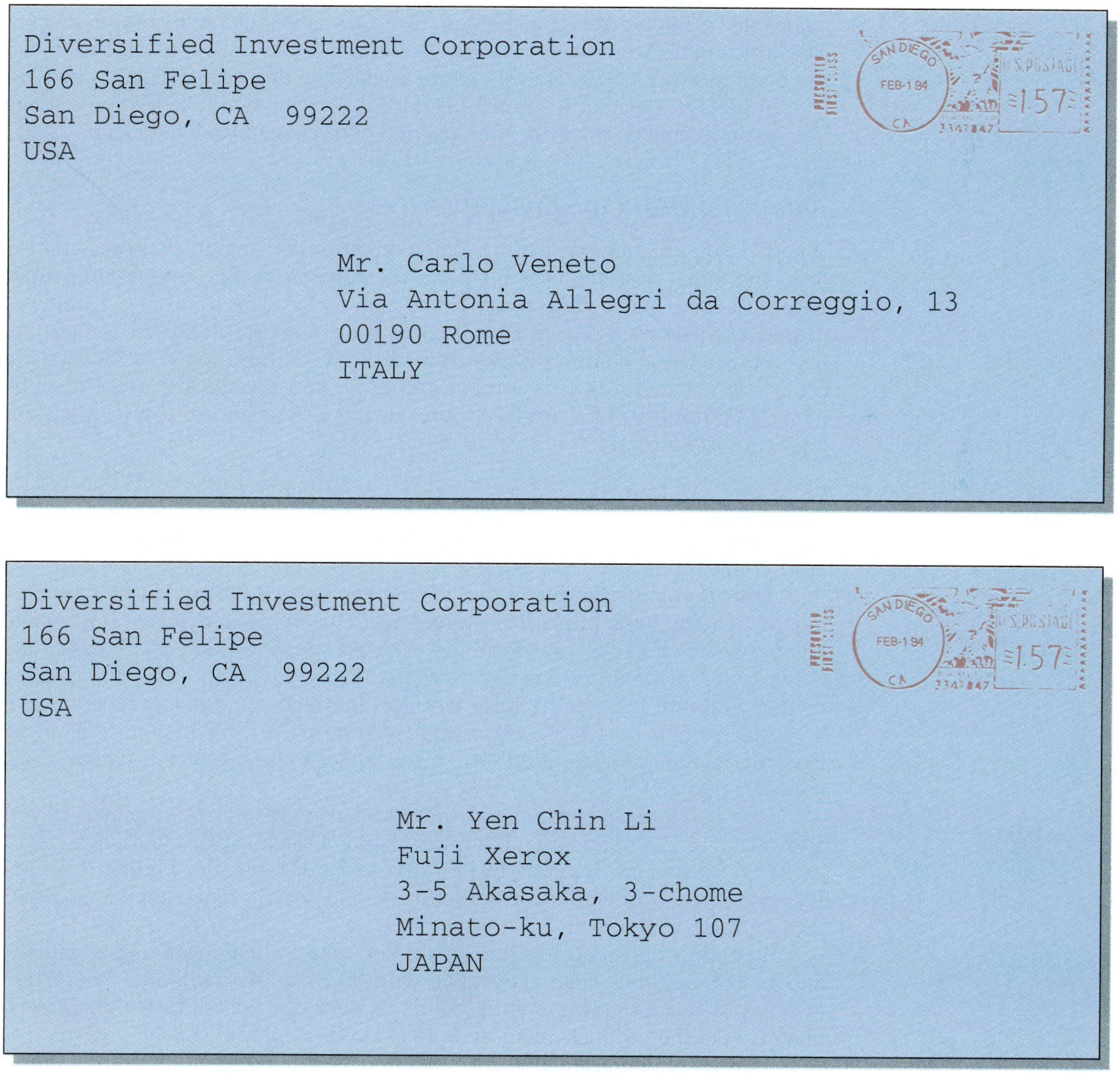
Diversified Investment Corporation
166 San Felipe
San Diego, CA 99222
USA
SAN DIEGO
FEB-1 94
CA
1.57
Mr. Carlo Veneto
Via Antonia Allegri da Correggio, 13
00190 Rome
ITALY
Diversified Investment Corporation
166 San Felipe
San Diego, CA 99222
USA
SAN DIEGO
FEB-1 94
CA
1.57
Mr. Yen Chin Li
Fuji Xerox
3-5 Akasaka, 3-chome
Minato-ku, Tokyo 107
JAPAN

FIGURE 18.5 *Letters Addressed to Foreign Correspondents (Continued)*

assume that titles always have the same meaning in other countries as they do in the United States. For example, the designation *deputy* in England is equivalent to our *vice president*, while *managing director* refers to the *chief executive officer* of a corporation.

FIRST AND LAST NAMES　　A potential problem in communicating with Asians of Chinese descent is the correct use of given name and surname. Assume, for example, that you are either about to write or be introduced to Song Wei, who happens to be the director of your company's Hong Kong office. His name is not *Mr. Wei*—that is tantamount to calling someone *Mr. Billy*. Because the Chinese surname is placed first and the given name last, this individual should be addressed as Mr. Song. Many Asians will assist their Western counterparts in this decision by underlining their last name on their business cards or in written correspondence.

RECEIVING FOREIGN CORRESPONDENCE　　The form in which documents are received may differ markedly from what is standard in the United States. For example, letters may be handwritten because of the shortage of word processors or even typewriters. In Germany, although an individual signs a letter, his or her name often is not typed below the signature. Germans prefer to de-emphasize personal contributions and to emphasize the company. Naturally, this practice makes responding difficult when the signature is illegible. Response reliability also differs. In India, for example, the mail service is so poor that letters are frequently lost. If you receive no response after a period of time, send the letter again.

Improving Oral Communication

Whether you are communicating in conversation, during an oral presentation, or in the midst of a business meeting, the cultural background of your audience influences what you say and how you say it. The following guidelines, geared to these three forms of oral communication, are designed to help you improve your oral-communication skills in cross-cultural contexts.[44] When you are preparing to speak to a foreign audience, you should also remember the general communication advice in our earlier discussion of low-context and high-context cultures.

CONVERSATION　　Simplify your speech as much as possible. When talking with people whose native language is not English, follow the same principles suggested for written communication. In general, use basic, simple vocabulary and avoid jargon.

Even if you are not fluent in the language of the country that you are visiting, learn a few basic phrases and greetings. The ability to express simple statements like "Hello," "Good Morning," "Excuse me," "Goodbye," "Please," and "Thank-you" will permit you to interact casually with people who do not speak English and will indicate to those who can that you are considerate enough to try to learn their language. According to Anne Oliver, director of L'École des Exécutifs, simple consideration "will bring smiles to faces—even if you don't say it exactly right."[45]

Try also to gear your *tone of voice* to what is culturally acceptable to your audience. For example, while loud, aggressive speech is expected when people exchange ideas and opinions in Latin America, Greece, the Middle East, and Italy, the same behavior is considered rude and socially unacceptable in Pacific Rim countries and Japan.

In high-context cultures like Japan, you may actually need vague, indirect, and even ambiguous language as you work to establish credibility. You should also avoid boasting about your goods or services. Instead, use descriptive brochures or the products themselves to tell your story.

Finally, remember that silence means different things in different cultures. While Americans, for example, interpret the refusal to talk to someone in the same room as a sign of anger, the English adopt this behavior when they do not

ETHICS IN BUSINESS COMMUNICATION
Honest Cultural Differences

Americans doing business abroad learn quickly that "truth" may be expressed in one way by Americans and in quite another way by non-Americans. Conversely, Americans who fail to learn this lesson may find themselves being open and overly candid to those who have no intention of reciprocating. These different behaviors do not imply that one group is more "ethical" than another, but rather that people communicate truth in different ways and that, to non-Americans, truth may have a lower priority than other values, such as saving face, loyalty, and sensitivity.

When Americans say "yes," for example, they usually mean "yes," and a whole set of expectations flows from that answer. If you ask an American business colleague for a memo by the end of the day and he agrees to write it, you can usually expect the memo on your desk before you leave work. This may not be the case in Asia, where saving face may be more important than giving an accurate answer. Thus, if an Asian colleague in the same circumstances realizes that he cannot finish the memo in time, he may still answer "yes." That "yes," however, could mean "Yes, I heard you," or "Yes, I understand how important this is to you," rather than "Yes, I will do what you ask."

By contrast, Europeans—and especially Germans—say "no" when they really mean "maybe." For example, when a contract containing two or three minor problems is presented to Germans, they may reject it immediately. Moreover, they may call the document unacceptable and say that they would never want their thoughts interrupted. Edward Hall reports that such differences in consider signing it. However, when the largely cosmetic changes are made—a process that may take no longer than a moment or two—they may embrace the document and sign it without hesitation.

Honesty is also influenced by the tendency of people in such high-context cultures as Mexico, Pakistan, and Japan to tell you what you want to hear in order to please or to avoid offending. Asking someone directions in these countries will guarantee an answer—but not necessarily proper directions. Koreans take this habit to an extreme. In Korea, the *kibun,* or sense of harmony that surrounds a person, is more important than objective truth. As a result, Koreans may change bad-news messages to make them less upsetting. Moreover, they are unlikely to deliver bad news in the morning. Even urgent messages are put off until afternoon so that the recipient can reconstitute his or her sense of *kibun* at home.

How do you deal with the varying shades of honesty that you will find around the world? Certainly, anger and disappointment are inappropriate responses. Rather, you are better advised to make every attempt to understand the link between honesty and culture and the context in which responses are made.

Sources: Lennie Copeland and Lewis Griggs, *Going International: How to Make Friends and Deal Effectively in the Global Marketplace* (New York: Random House, 1985), pp. 104-6. See also Ronald E. Dulek, John S. Fielden, and John S. Hill, "International Communication: An Executive Primer," *Business Horizons,* January–February 1991, pp. 20-25; and Philip R. Harris and Robert T. Moran, *Managing Cultural Differences,* 3rd ed. (Houston: Gulf Publishing, 1991).

want their thoughts interrupted. Edward Hall reports that such differences in *verbal cues* can greatly affect communication:

> When the American wants to be alone he goes into a room and shuts the door—he depends on architectural features for screening. For an American to refuse to talk to someone else present in the same room, to give them the "silent treatment," is the ultimate form of rejection and a sure sign of great displeasure. The English, on the other hand, lacking rooms of their own since childhood, never developed the practice of using space as a refuge from others. They have in effect internalized a set of barriers, which they erect and which others are supposed to recognize. Therefore, the more the Englishman shuts himself off when he is with an American, the more likely the American is to break in to assure himself that all is well. Tension lasts until the two get to know each other.[46]

The same internalized barriers often make the British resent the telephone. When they are preoccupied, they view it as an intrusion and are often reluctant to call others, afraid that their calls will be equally intrusive. Although business and emergency calls are acceptable, social calls are sometimes considered pushy and even rude. Instead of calling, the English prefer to write notes.[47]

ORAL PRESENTATIONS AND MEETINGS   Successful oral presentations and meetings allow for differences in *formality, tempo,* and *audience behavior;* they also consider the virtues and pitfalls of using an interpreter. The following guidelines will help you target these three critical factors.

FORMALITY   As you saw in Chapter 14, the United States business culture considers the best oral presentations to be those that are delivered extemporaneously. That is, using notes and visual aids, effective speakers deliver presentations in a natural, conversational style that appears spontaneous. We also interact with our visual aids, writing comments and instructions on chalkboards, flip charts, and overhead transparencies as we speak. However, this presentation style may be considered unacceptable in countries where more formal, rehearsed presentation styles are required. In countries as diverse as Germany and Japan, the American approach may be interpreted as a lack of preparation—even an insult. When we write on visual aids, for instance, we risk sending the message that we did not take the time to complete our work in advance.

In high-context cultures, formality also requires that the individuals involved in the presentation be similar in rank and age to members of their audience. Despite his or her competence, a presentation delivered by a thirty-year-old to a group of senior Japanese executives is considered inappropriate and is, in the end, bad business practice.

TEMPO   As a rule, deliver your presentation in a foreign host country at a slower pace than you would in the United States. In high-context cultures, always allow an extended period at the beginning for the exchange of greetings and other forms of socializing. In general, prove your personal integrity first, communicate your company's reputation next, and then present your proposal or product.

When delivering a presentation in English to an audience that speaks English as a second language, take your time in dealing with questions and comments. Rushing someone who is searching for a precise English word is considered disrespectful.

Expect interruptions in such high-context cultures as Saudi Arabia, Japan, and Latin America, where presentations are normally delivered in small segments, each followed by a question-and-answer period. Because such interruptions digress from the topic and allow people time to relax before returning to business, they are considered social as well as information-gathering activities.

AUDIENCE BEHAVIOR   In America, we are used to certain behavior on the part of listeners who may ask questions or communicate nonverbally. In Japan, however, audiences follow different patterns. For example, when they disagree with something that has been said, Japanese listeners may begin talking among themselves. If they become uncomfortable, such situations can be defused by turning immediately to another subject. Find out later what caused the problem and, if possible, develop an alternate strategy.

As we saw earlier, Asians frequently avoid direct eye contact. Instead of looking directly at the speaker, Chinese, Malaysian, and Japanese listeners often stare at the floor. Keep in mind that this behavior shows respect rather than inattention.

USING AN INTERPRETER   An experienced American journalist in the Far East recounts the following anecdote about a business conversation conducted at cross purposes. With the help of an interpreter, an interchange between an American businessman and his Chinese client was going smoothly until the American, responding to a Chinese proposal, said, "It's a great idea, Mr. Li, but who's going to put wheels on it?" Not wanting to admit ignorance, the interpreter informed the Chinese businessman that "the American has now made a proposal regarding the automobile industry."[48]

The moral of this story is twofold. First, if you do not speak a language or are not fluent enough to conduct business in it, use English or hire an interpreter. Second, when you do decide to use an interpreter, avoid difficulties by following some basic guidelines.

1. Choose an interpreter who knows something about your field, especially if it is technical or requires a specialized vocabulary. If necessary, give the interpreter a list of the technical words that you will use.
2. Before you begin, brief the interpreter about your remarks.
3. Speak clearly and keep sentences short; avoid unnecessary, specialized, or infrequently used words, as well as slang and figures of speech that cannot be translated easily.
4. Repeat key points in order to ensure that your message is communicated correctly.
5. Speak for a minute or two, then allow the interpreter to translate.
6. Do not interrupt while the interpreter translates even if he or she speaks for a long time.

Despite these precautions, of course, mistakes happen—even at the highest levels. When President Jimmy Carter went to Poland in 1977, the interpreter translated his arrival speech by telling the crowd, "The president says he is pleased to be here in Poland grasping your secret parts."

As we have seen throughout this chapter, doing business in the global marketplace requires a level of sensitivity to other cultures and communication styles. Communications consultant Sana Reynolds emphasizes the importance of this sensitivity by focusing on the link between communication and understanding. "I've always felt that speaking and writing facilitate thought," she says. "Speaking and writing also influence thought. Once you truly become sensitive to the needs of others, you will begin to *understand* why people are different. It is not just going to remain at the level of the way you write and speak."[49]

Doing business in the global marketplace also requires detailed information about foreign cultures. In this chapter, we examined some general principles for analyzing cultural differences and some specific examples of how these principles apply in different parts of the world.

Keep in mind, however, that no single chapter or book can give you the kind of in-depth information needed to actually conduct business abroad. Perhaps the best information is gained firsthand; perhaps the most desirable quality is the willingness to accept differences among cultures, societies, and individuals. Ethnic groups within your community can provide information on their cultures, customs, and countries. Most universities sponsor student organizations for different ethnic groups, and the foreign-language faculty at your school may be able to assist you with advice and information about doing business abroad.

PROGRESS CHECK

1. When communicating with a business colleague in another country, is it better to write a memo or to propose your ideas face-to-face?
2. Many people in other countries study English in school. Can American businesspeople assume that these people will understand American English? Explain your answer.

WHAT'S AHEAD

Culture shock can take place within our own society as well as in our contacts outside the United States. Just as we have the tendency toward ethnocentrism when communicating abroad, we also tend to judge the diverse groups within our society by our own cultural standards. As you will see in the next chapter, ethnocentrism affects the interplay between men and women and between racial and ethnic groups. Contemporary business is also witnessing the entry of new groups into the workplace. More and more elderly are returning to work, and we are also seeing mentally and physically challenged individuals in positions of responsibility. Because of the emergence of so many varied groups of people, it is more important than ever to recognize the need to communicate effectively in a diverse environment.

Realizing that different cultural patterns exist within our own society is the first step in overcoming the barriers that may stand in the way of communication. Chapter 19 will explore the communication differences that emerge from cultural diversity and offer suggestions for overcoming them through training and awareness.

*S*UMMARY OF CHAPTER OBJECTIVES

1. **Explain the increasing importance of *cross-cultural communication* to United States business.**

   With international trade essential to the survival of the United States economy, the ability to communicate across national boundaries is becoming a requirement for many United States workers. The opening of new markets in both Eastern and Western Europe will provide greater foreign-trade opportunities in the years ahead.

2. **Identify and briefly describe the different *audiences* in the global marketplace.**

   Working abroad for a United States company involves living and working in a foreign culture and makes effective cross-cultural communication a necessity. Similar cross-cultural communication skills are needed to work for foreign-owned companies based in the United States. Even workers based in the United States and working for United States companies are often involved in cross-cultural communication during travel and in written correspondence.

3. **Explain the connection between culture and communication, and describe the dangers of *ethnocentrism*.**

   Culture determines the way people communicate. Americans communicate according to distinct cultural patterns that may or may not coincide with the patterns followed by other national groups. *Ethnocentrism* refers to the judgment of other cultures by the standards

of one's own culture. Without some degree of accommodation, ethnocentricism will make effective communication impossible. The degree of accommodation necessary for effective communication is influenced by cultural imperatives, cultural adiaphoras, or cultural exclusives.

4. **Identify the problems encountered by people who can only speak English when they do business abroad. Explain the advantages of being *multilingual*.**

   American businesspeople working in non-English-speaking countries often encounter disadvantages when they do not speak the language. Nuances are lost as translations move thoughts from one language to another. In addition, businesspeople abroad are often forced to rely on the English-speaking members of foreign audiences to translate conversations and/or written documents. Even when dealing with foreigners who speak English, it is a mistake for Americans to assume that foreigners' understanding of English is good enough for complex business concepts. Realizing the importance of language competence, an increasing number of American students are studying foreign languages in colleges and universities.

5. **Define and contrast communication differences characteristic of *low-context* and *high-context cultures*.**

   In low-context cultures, communication depends on explicit written and verbal messages. By contrast, communication in high-context cultures is linked not only to explicit messages but also to the context in which communication occurs and to nonverbal language. Personal relationships, timing, level of formality, etiquette, and body language have different meanings in low- and high-context cultures. Understanding these differences affects communication success.

6. **List the key elements for successful written and oral communication across national boundaries.**
Effective written communication depends on the use of translators when necessary, proper language usage, adaptation to com-

munication styles, and sensitivity to cultural preferences. Because message transmission depends on the mail, you must also learn the correct format for directing foreign correspondence.

Oral communication follows many of the same guidelines as written communication. Language must be simple, direct, and jargon-free. During oral presentations and meetings, formality, tempo, and audience behavior differ in high- and low-context cultures; consequently, miscommunication is likely when attitudes are ethnocentric. When language barriers exist, interpreters are necessary to bridge the communication gap.

REVIEW AND DISCUSSION QUESTIONS

1. Why is it important for American business-people to be able to communicate cross-culturally? *(Ch. Obj. 1)*
2. Describe the various audiences found in the global marketplace. *(Ch. Obj. 2)*
3. Describe some key differences between American business practices and those of other countries. *(Ch. Obj. 2, 4)*
4. What do we mean by the word *culture*? Explain how cultural backgrounds can influence communication styles. *(Ch. Obj. 4)*
5. Distinguish among cultural imperatives, cultural adiaphoras, and cultural exclusives. *(Ch. Obj. 3, 4)*
6. Distinguish between low-context and high-

context cultures. Give an example of each. *(Ch. Obj. 5)*
7. Summarize key factors that affect communication in low- and high-context cultures. *(Ch. Obj. 5)*
8. Create a table that compares the preferences of low- and high-context cultures regarding personal relationships and body language. *(Ch. Obj. 5, 6)*
9. Describe steps that American businesspeople can take to adapt their writing to foreign audiences. *(Ch. Obj. 6)*
10. What can United States businesspeople do to improve oral communications and presentations made to foreign audiences? *(Ch. Obj. 6)*

APPLICATION EXERCISES

1. Choose a company—perhaps in your community—that has done business with another nation or is considering doing so. Interview a businessperson from this firm about the company's experiences in communicating with customers and colleagues in the foreign country. What lessons did the firm learn? What would it do differently next time? Take notes during the interview and write them up in a short report to give your instructor. *(Ch. Obj. 1, 6)*
2. How good are you at communicating cross-culturally? Describe several steps you can take to improve your ability to do business in a global marketplace. *(Ch. Obj. 1, 6)*
3. Refer to the chapter's discussion of audiences in the global marketplace. If possible, give an

example of someone from each audience with whom you yourself have communicated. Did you experience any difficulties in communicating? *(Ch. Obj. 2)*
4. Describe an occasion when you might have behaved ethnocentrically without meaning to. What cultural misunderstandings might have played a role in your behavior? *(Ch. Obj. 3)*
5. Jim Mason runs SmallCo Sweats, a small firm that manufactures athletic clothing decorated with the logos of American sports teams. He has been reading a lot lately about how the world is turning into a "global village," and he figures that there must be a market for his products outside the United States. As an experienced entrepreneur who's not afraid to take

risks, Mason decided to add exporting to his company's activities. He feels ready to take on this new challenge because he just finished two semesters of Spanish at a local community college. "One year of Spanish should be enough to get by," reasons Mason. "After all, Spanish is a pretty easy language. Besides, everybody down there knows English." What advice would you give Jim Mason? *(Ch. Obj. 3, 5)*

6. Your advice so impresses Jim Mason that he asks you to write a letter (in English) to the firm's first Latin American prospect, a Bolivian business owner. Your letter will be the firm's first contact with this customer. Keep in mind that although your Bolivian correspondent reads English, it is not his native tongue. *(Ch. Obj. 4, 5, 6)*

7. Your letter to the Bolivian customer worked so well that Jim Mason asks you to write a similar letter to another prospective customer, this time in Argentina. However, because this correspondent knows very little English, you decide to hire a translator to rewrite your letter in Spanish. Describe your approach to selecting and working with this translator. *(Ch. Obj. 6)*

8. After a few more letters have been exchanged, the Bolivian prospect invites Jim Mason down for a visit. Mason asks you to go along. During the flight to La Paz, he asks you for pointers about the best way to approach his prospective business deal. What would you tell him? *(Ch. Obj. 3, 5, 6)*

9. The athletic shirts that SmallCo Sweats sold to Argentina and Bolivia are worn by teams in major soccer games that are broadcast over international TV. A distributor in Basel, Switzerland, calls to suggest selling the shirts in Europe. You and Jim Mason decide to meet with the distributor personally to discuss possible business arrangements. As always, Mason asks you to handle the communication. Describe the oral presentation that you will make during your meeting with the Swiss distributor and four German colleagues. *(Ch. Obj. 4, 5, 6)*

10. Unfortunately, the first shipment of SmallCo Sweats to Basel mistakenly arrived in Brussels. Jim Mason is so upset that he sits down and writes a personal note of apology to Walther Zimmer, the Swiss distributor. Because you know Mason, you offer to look at the letter before it is sent. Here's the letter:

Dear Walther:

I feel really low about this whole business. Apparently we dropped the ball and sent the stuff to the wrong town. I just don't know how it happened. Of course, Brussels does sound a lot like Basel, but still, we goofed. We're sending another shipment and it should arrive momentarily. Sorry about the mix-up, but you're a cool dude and I know you won't have a cow. Keep in touch.

Sincerely,

Jim

Would you suggest any changes to this letter? If so, rewrite it. *(Ch. Obj. 1, 4, 6)*

11. Interview someone from another country who is now living or visiting in the United States. Ask about experiences encountered in living and working in America. How do customs, traditions, and communication patterns differ? Write a summary of your interview. *(Ch. Obj. 3, 5)*

12. *Business Week* has asked you to write a short article entitled "Communicating in a Global Marketplace." Choose a country that was discussed in this chapter and write an article summarizing the ways in which the nation's customs affect its business practices. Does this country have a high- or low-context culture? How do its business practices differ from those in the United States? What advice would you offer an American planning a business trip to that country? *(Ch. Obj. 1, 3, 5, 6)*

13. Several exporters in Mexico were impressed by your *Business Week* article. They have asked you to give a presentation in English at the annual meeting of their professional association in Mexico City. The topic they have requested is "Effective Business Communication in the United States." You know that these businesspeople are eager to increase their United States business and are looking to you for practical tips on how American businesspeople communicate. Write a draft of your speech. *(Ch. Obj. 3, 6)*

14. Marta Schultz was sent to Tokyo as a representative for her company to negotiate an important business deal with a new customer. You see her in the hall after she returns and eagerly ask how the trip went. "Terrible!" she says. "I've never been so frustrated in my life. When I handed Mr. Yakamoto my business card, he spent the next five minutes scrutinizing it. I felt like he wasn't listening to me at all because he never looked at me. I kept trying to establish eye contact, but he just kept his eyes lowered." Maria's assistant, Bob, chimes in, "Yeah, it was really strange. They kept asking me the questions even though I told them that Maria is my boss." The worst thing, Maria continues, is that she couldn't tell whether they liked her presentation. "I kept asking them to agree to our terms, but they kept avoiding the issue. Finally, I had to leave because I had an

appointment to keep with a supplier." What advice would you give Maria? *(Ch. Obj. 1, 5, 6)*

15. To save money, many companies are taking advantage of new technologies to communicate with foreign customers. Rather than meeting in person, businesspeople may "talk" via electronic mail or send letters via facsimile machines. Discuss the advantages and disadvantages of these media for international communication. *(Ch. Obj. 3, 5, 6)*

BUILDING YOUR RESEARCH SKILLS

Jim Mason is so thrilled with the success of SmallCo Sweats' overseas marketing that he decides to expand into other nations. Imagine that your communications class is the entire staff of SmallCo and that Mason has asked all of you to help develop international marketing plans. Your instructor will act as Mason's chief operating officer and will divide the class into small teams, each of which will target a particular nation, such as Saudi Arabia, China, Nigeria, England, Hungary, Mexico, and Australia.

Each team should research the customs and traditions of its designated country. Think about how these factors might influence the country's cultural and communication patterns. Take notes on what you read so that you can report back to the group.

BUILDING YOUR TEAMWORK SKILLS

Reassemble into the groups that you formed for the exercise in Building Your Research Skills. Team members should discuss what they learned from their research and then develop a set of communication guidelines appropriate for the country that your group targeted and researched. Can you think of any marketing ideas that might work for this nation? Are there any marketing ideas that work for United States consumers but should definitely be avoided in foreign marketing? Create a written report summarizing your team's conclusions. A team spokesperson can then present this report to the class.

COMMUNICATING IN A WORLD OF DIVERSITY

As more corporations go multinational, the ability to communicate globally is becoming more important than ever. Look, for example, at the experiences of airplane maker Airbus Industries, a consortium supported by the French, German, British, and Spanish governments. Airbus managers must remain alert to the communication challenges posed by its four-nation work force.

"There are times," says German chief operating officer Heribert Flosdorff, "when there seem to be massive conflicts because of the different educational backgrounds and different approaches. We Germans tend to be more fact-oriented, while the French are more intuitive. The British tend to play arbiter and get smashed from both sides." Meanwhile, English marketing director Adam Brown quickly did learn to tailor his communication style to a multinational sales force. "We British," he explains, "tend to sort of hint at what results we expect. I soon learned that the Germans sometimes didn't actually understand that I wanted them to do anything in particular."

Relate Airbus's experiences to the concepts discussed in this chapter.

Source: Quotes taken from Kenneth Labich, "Airbus Takes Off," *Fortune,* June 1, 1992, pp. 102-5.

DSP Group Takes it Slowly in Japan

Almost everyone would agree that when it comes to culture and communication patterns, the United States and Japan are a world apart. As we saw in this chapter, while United States culture is low-context, Japanese culture is high-context. When you further consider the barriers of very different languages, social customs, and histories, the result is two nations that often have trouble understanding each other. These differences help explain why United States firms frequently find it difficult to do business in Japan.

Lately, however, several small American companies have had a measure of good luck selling their products in Japan. Their experience offers some useful guidelines to other businesspeople who are interested in tapping Japanese markets.

One lesson they teach is to start slowly and build. Because it typically takes several years and a good deal of market research to start earning a profit, building a Japan-based business takes patience. "You need more than a pay-as-you-go mentality," notes one consultant. "It takes a lot of up-front work."

California-based DSP Group Inc., a semiconductor manufacturer, has total annual sales of $8 million—with nearly half its profits coming from sales in Japan. The firm's chief executive moved with his family to Tokyo and lived there for more than a year, cultivating Japanese customers and suppliers. Today, DSP Group operates a Tokyo office consisting of six desks wedged into a tiny building; modest though this office is, however, DSP execs see it as a good start. Says one, "To compete in the consumer [electronics] market, we have to be here."

Another lesson: Sweat the details. Japanese consumers are discriminating buyers, and small imperfections—small, that is, by American standards—loom large for Asian customers. Shoe manu-facturers, for instance, have found that Japanese customers pay close attention to the quality of stitching on footwear. Even a slight tilt in the seams can kill a sale if a Japanese consumer questions whether the whole shoe was made poorly. Because sloppy packaging signals careless manufacturing in general to Japanese consumers, other companies have learned to devote extra care to their packaging.

And a final tip: If you want to make money in Japan, watch your image. Firms that sell items through catalogs have found it prudent to remove some low-priced products from their Japanese catalogs even though the same items are big sellers in other countries. Why? Japanese consumers tend to judge products according to product lines and overall performance of their manufacturers. If some catalog items seem cheap, Japanese consumers may very well question the quality of all the merchandise in the catalog.

Questions and Applications

1. Discuss some key cultural differences between the United States and Japan.
2. Explain how these cultural differences can affect business communication patterns.
3. What have the firms discussed in this case learned about doing business in Japan?
4. How could SmallCo Sweats (see APPLICATION EXERCISES 5 through 10) apply these lessons to its own products?

The Ethics of Communication in Russia

In this chapter, you encountered many suggestions to help smooth communication between members of different cultures. But here's one communication tool you didn't read about: Danish butter cookies.

A box of butter cookies was just what Jonathan Daly needed to get his point across with post-Soviet Union businesspeople. For three months, the American graduate student had attempted to view several Soviet government documents. He tried to communicate his goal in a variety of ways: friendly, informal chats; quiet visits to different government offices; tactful hints about what he wanted; and outright requests for the information. Nothing worked until he heard about a Russian employee's weakness for Danish munchies. One tin of cookies—and the documents were his.

Daly is only one of many Western academics doing research in Russia these days. With the collapse of the Soviet Union, its government archives, once top secret, have been declassified. These archives represent a rich resource that illuminates a little-known period of Russian history. American, British, and German researchers are eagerly searching for documents that might provide valuable information about the Soviet past. To their dismay, however, they often find that the Russians who control the archives expect payment for their cooperation.

Mark Kramer, a professor at Brown University, tried for nine years to find out whether the Soviet Union had considered invading Yugoslavia in 1948. The government refused to let him examine the relevant documents; Kramer says he was always told that the papers were "off-limits to foreigners, classified or just didn't exist." Recently, however, when Russian archivists declassified holdings from the post-World War II period, Kramer eagerly applied for permission to do research. When he finally arrived in the archive reading room, a Russian employee demanded $100 in cash. The archivist hinted, says Kramer, that "I would be given access to more materials if I paid more." Kramer refused to pay and stormed out. He knows of other researchers, however, who coughed up $150 to view historical records.

Other Westerners report similar experiences. One professor was offered the opportunity to photocopy all the documents he wanted—if he bought the archive a photocopy machine. He refused.

Is this practice ethical? No, say some Westerners. Patricia Grimsted, a Harvard University professor and expert on Soviet archives, feels that the documents in question constitute a unique historical find that should not be commercialized. Graduate students complain that the "bribe-and-learn" approach puts them at a disadvantage—they can't compete with more prosperous professors in doing historical research. Russian scholars are angry, too—they have even less chance of coming up with the necessary dollars.

The attitude of Russian archivists, however, may simply be the logical result of their heritage. Their nation's Communist culture has long discouraged free communication and open discussion. As one American businessman notes, Russians don't share the American concept of "public domain"—the public's right to know. Indeed, while Russian deals would certainly be called "bribes" in the United States, they are not illegal in Russia; the new government has yet to develop laws that define the concept of such unprecedented access to information.

Sometimes, however, the oldest communication methods still work the best, no matter what countries are involved. As Jonathan Daly notes, "Anyone who takes the trouble to cultivate a friendship will have no problems."

Questions and Applications

1. How have Russian archivists responded to the opening of their nation's classified documents?
2. How do these archivists feel about information? Relate their attitudes to broader patterns of Soviet culture.
3. Do you feel that the archivists' behavior is ethical? Explain your answer.

Source: Andrea Rutherford, "Information Flow Is Freer in Russia, but It Is Not Free," *The Wall Street Journal*, July 10, 1992, pp. A1, A14.

The Challenge
of Diversity

CHAPTER OBJECTIVES

After studying this chapter, you should be able to:

1 List important *demographic changes* that are transforming the American workplace and marketplace.

2 Outline eight elements that define individual and group *communication patterns.*

3 Explain how such factors as *gender, age, physical disability,* and *racial/ethnic stereotypes* can contribute to miscommunication.

4 Identify three *communication patterns* common to many African Americans.

5 Explain how *gender differences* affect communication.

6 Describe the communication breakdown inherent in *sexual harassment.*

7 Describe the special communication needs of older and physically challenged people.

8 Explain the nature of *diversity training.*

America is not like a blanket—one piece of unbroken cloth, the same color, the same texture, the same size. America is more like a quilt—many pieces, many colors, many sizes, all woven and held together by a common thread.

Jesse Jackson
American civil rights leader

FROM MELTING POT TO SALAD BOWL

As we saw in Chapter 18, differences between national cultures are a constant threat to successful business communication. As the following examples demonstrate, cultural diversity can also be a major factor in miscommunication *within* a national culture.

- After presenting his report at a staff meeting, an Asian-American businessman was asked a series of questions. Instead of answering them, he either repeated what he had said in his report or appeared to ignore the questions put to him. Rather than being difficult, this man was operating on the common Asian assumption that public meetings are basically rituals to demonstrate consensus. Among Asian Americans, questions are typically asked and answered *before* a meeting begins. In this case, the speaker may well have perceived public questioning as a challenge to his competence.

- On his first day at work, a Hispanic junior accountant received what he thought was a warm, friendly welcome. Frank, his Anglo department manager, introduced Juan to the staff, showed him how to operate office equipment, and joined him for lunch in the company cafeteria. Having interpreted Frank's behavior as a sign of friendship, Juan was confused when the next day Frank acted as his supervisor rather than his friend. Initially believing that Frank had extended friendship, Juan assumed that his supervisor would act the same way every day. Consultant Jean Mavrelis explains that, to many Hispanics, "once a personal relationship has been established, maintaining the friendship becomes a duty, not an option." Reared in a different culture, however, Juan's boss regarded his behavior as perfectly appropriate in a business context. "He helped Juan feel welcome," says Mavrelis, "but the next day, it was back to business. He assumed that Juan would come to him if he had any questions or problems."[1]

These misunderstandings all are based on differences in communication style rather than substance. As both the American public and workforce become increasingly diverse, learning to overcome misunderstandings based on race, ethnicity, gender, age, or physical challenges will be vital to personal career as well as business growth.

CHAPTER OVERVIEW

In order to understand *diversity*, we might begin by replacing the concept of America as a "melting pot" with a concept that fits America as it moves into the twenty-first century. The "salad bowl," perhaps, should be our new model, and with it we might adopt a new golden rule: "Do unto others as others would *want* done unto them."[2]

Successful communication involves recognizing and accepting the great diversity among Americans (indeed, among people everywhere). Although people may be grouped together in classifications based on such factors as gender, age, race, or employment, tremendous diversity exists among the members of each group.

While Figure 19.1 identifies each element as a slice of the diversity pie, it is important to recognize the extent to which the slices in that pie overlap each other. For example, although some classification systems refer to "racial/ethnic" groups, a *racial* group is, technically speaking, a subgroup of an *ethnic* group. The broader term ethnic group encompasses such characteristics as race, religion, national origin, and culture.

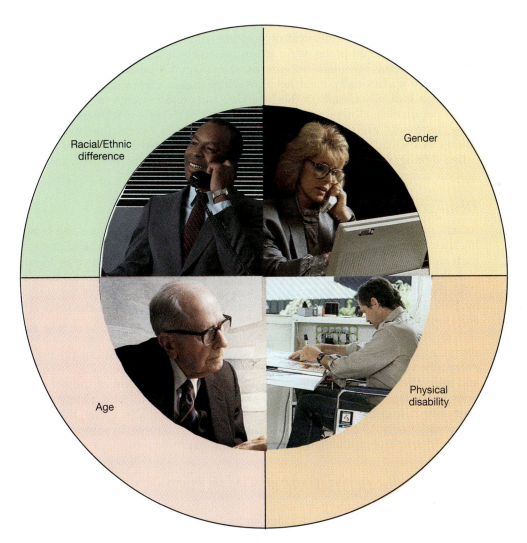

FIGURE 19.1   *The Major Elements of Diversity*

Moreover, the four major categories in Figure 19.1 do not constitute an exhaustive list of every element that may be used to identify the diversity that we encounter every day in both the workplace and the marketplace. The work and market environments, for example, may include individuals who are mentally challenged yet capable of performing a variety of jobs. Because many jobs, tools, and accompanying instructions are designed to communicate to the approximately 90 percent of the population composed of righthanders, even handedness can be considered a source of diversity. In this chapter, we will focus on the *major* elements of diversity.

Successful communication is based on the knowledge that many groups have different communication patterns and that understanding these patterns will help eliminate communication barriers. Learning to communicate successfully in a diverse workforce also means recognizing the nature of *stereotyping* and *prejudice* and their impact on communication. It means being aware of *gender* differences in communication styles. It means recognizing that *diversity* extends to the *elderly* and the *physically challenged*. Finally, it means defining what diversity means to each of us and then adapting preconceptions to improve our communication skills.

THE DEMOGRAPHY OF CHANGE

Until recently, the communication barriers that now characterize a diverse culture in the United States were given relatively little attention as a serious problem in doing business. Because most managerial positions in the United States have traditionally been held by white males, communication patterns have been typically based on the behavior and requirements of that segment of the population. However, the demographics of today's workforce and business customers are changing radically, and trends reveal that even more change lies ahead. These population trends are analyzed by the social science called **demography**, the statistical study of population size, density, and geographic distribution.

Demographics of the American Workforce

Increasingly, women and minorities are entering the U.S. workforce and bringing their own styles of communication with them. The following statistics highlight some of the dramatic changes in the U.S. workforce. For example, Figure 19.2 shows that while women comprised less than 30 percent of the workforce in 1950, their numbers had grown by 50 percent—to over 45 percent of the total—by 1990. By the year 2005, it is estimated that over 47 percent of the total U.S. workforce will be women.

In addition, experts estimate that by the year 2005, African Americans will comprise 12 percent of the U.S. workforce, Hispanics will account for one of every nine workers, and one worker in twenty will be Asian American.[3] Women and minorities, including immigrants, will comprise 85 percent of the net additions to the labor force between now and the year 2000. In 1985, nearly one of every two new entrants into the labor force were white males; today, this group accounts for only 15 percent of the growth in the workforce. In companies with 100 to 999 employees, males are actually a minority.[4]

DISTINCTIVE COMMUNICATION PATTERNS

Racial/ethnic differences, gender, age, and physical challenges often create communication barriers as strong as those that separate people in different countries. Different cultural patterns often produce distinctly different communication styles. As we analyze these patterns, keep in mind that we are describing general

Change is the law of life. And those who look only to the past or present are certain to miss the future.

John F. Kennedy
35th President
of the United States

demography
Statistical study of population size, density, and distribution that results in the collection of vital statistics

There is a new minority in the American workforce: white males. . . . Increasingly, the "average worker" is a woman.

John Naisbett
and Patricia Aburdene
American business writers
and social researchers

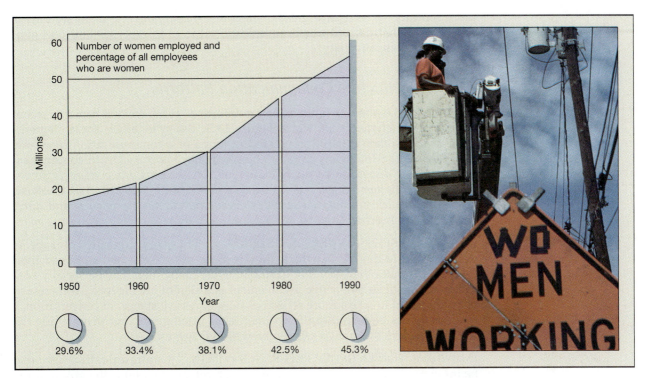

FIGURE 19.2   *Women in the Workforce*
Source: Bureau of Labor Statistics data reported in Tamer Levin, "Case Study of Sexual Harassment and the Law," *The New York Times*, October 11, 1991, p. A17.

communication patterns. Individual differences play a large part in any communication interaction, as does the degree to which an individual has been assimilated into the mainstream culture.

Stylistic differences form the foundation for the discussion of communication patterns of specific groups, including African Americans, Hispanics, Asian Americans, women, and men. Recognizing that different communication patterns exist is only the first step in learning how to adapt to them and to communicate with those people whose styles differ from our own.

A Word about Racial and Ethnic Identity

Before we discuss in detail communication patterns and some of the elements that affect them, we must clarify some important distinctions. For example, although it may sometimes be implied in this chapter that such groups as African Americans are monolithic in nature—that is, rigidly unified in identity and purpose—it is obviously erroneous to base judgments on such an assumption. Strong cultural variations exist between those who trace their roots hundreds of years in this country and first- or second-generation Jamaicans, Haitians, or persons from other Caribbean countries. The same is true, of course, for Hispanics (Cuban Americans, Mexican Americans, Honduran Americans, and so on) and Asians (Korean Americans, Japanese Americans, Chinese Americans, and so on).

We must therefore distinguish between *racial identity* and *ethnic diversity*. By **racial identity** we mean an identity given to a category of people who share similar physical characteristics; **ethnic diversity** refers to a range of identifying characteristics that includes shared values, communication patterns, and behaviors. It is important to remember, however, that racial and ethnic diversity are not mutually exclusive: It is possible, for example, that a black person from Mexico will have communication patterns similar to those of other Mexican Americans—and quite different from those of other African Americans. We

racial identity
Identity attributed to a category of people who share similar physical characteristics

ethnic diversity
Range of identifying characteristics that includes shared values, communication patterns, and behaviors

must continue to recognize these distinctions throughout the main sections of this chapter that discuss miscommunication due to stereotypes and prejudice and racial/ethnic diversity.

Elements Affecting Communication Patterns

To highlight the possible range in communication styles, we will begin by examining the key elements shown in Figure 19.3. Taken together, these elements form *communication patterns*. Expressed in terms of a communication spectrum, they include the following pairs of complementary approaches to communication: *initiating discussion versus listening, individual versus group reference points, facts versus intuition, personal versus impersonal disclosure, rational versus emotional expression, challenge versus agreement, confrontation versus compliance,* and *direct versus indirect assertion.*[5]

INITIATING DISCUSSION VERSUS LISTENING   The way people interact is defined by the degree to which they initiate discussion or listen and then respond to what others say. For example, while many men may be socially conditioned to believe that active involvement is a sign of intelligence, women may be conditioned to take a more reflective, nonaggressive stance. In conversation, a man may thus believe that the woman lacks intelligence and drive while the woman may see the man as self-centered or overaggressive.

INDIVIDUAL VERSUS GROUP REFERENCE POINTS   Communication can also be influenced by whether the communication reference point is the group or the individual. Is the individual speaking from his or her own point of view or from the perspective of a group? Different points of reference, for example, can frequently be seen in differences between Anglo and Asian-American communication styles. For example, while an Anglo business executive may decide to focus on his or her personal accomplishments as a way to impress others, the Asian American is more likely to point to the accomplishments of a work team.

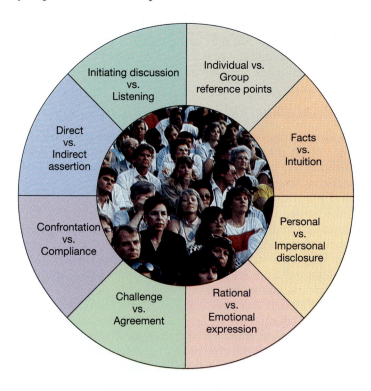

FIGURE 19.3   *Determinants of Individual Communication Patterns*

FACTS VERSUS INTUITION   While some people focus on facts as the basis for reasoning and persuasion, others are more likely to rely on intuition. This dichotomy is often used to contrast the typical communication styles of technical experts and laypeople. While experts usually try to persuade by presenting "facts," laypeople are more likely to rely on "intuition" to persuade others of their understanding of an issue. To avoid miscommunication, experts must be receptive to the nonanalytical communication styles of laypeople (and vice versa).

PERSONAL VERSUS IMPERSONAL DISCLOSURE   Degree of *self-disclosure* is also a crucial part of communication. On one end of the spectrum, for instance, are cultures in which people freely share personal information in order to build relationships as a preliminary step in communication. On the other end are cultures in which people prefer to focus almost immediately on the task at hand.

Du Pont's Diversity Brings Benefits

At Du Pont, men and women of many ages and cultures work together to meet the needs of the world marketplace. People are valued for the individual talents that they bring to the job.

Diversity of experience and perspective gives Du Pont a competitive edge, and creates a working environment in which women and minorities are moving into higher levels of management and into nontraditional jobs where they can develop their greatest potential.

Diversity results in increased productivity and profitability, and benefits our customers, our employees, and the entire minority community.

Diversity makes an important difference at Du Pont.

Better Things for Better Living

For giant firms that literally view the world as their marketplace, diversity has long been a fact of life. In addition to serving customers around the globe, Du Pont maintains production and marketing facilities in dozens of countries. The result is a highly diverse company workforce.

Source: © 1992 Du Pont; reprinted by permission.

For example, while a Greek American might begin a business meeting by talking about his family or personal activities, a British American is more likely to begin by focusing on the business at hand.

RATIONAL VERSUS EMOTIONAL EXPRESSION   While some groups tend to express themselves by referring to facts, others are more emotional. As we will see later in the chapter, many African Americans tend to have a more "heated" or emotional style of communication than Anglos or Asian Americans. Differences in communication patterns across generations also illustrate how these factors can influence communication styles. A newly hired young person, for example, might display more excitement over news about an across-the-board pay raise than the older worker whose experience and seniority allow him to regard the raise as deserved and expected.

CHALLENGE VERSUS AGREEMENT   Supporting another person's ideas is usually done through direct agreement ("I like the merchandising plan for the new store. Let's go with it"). But it also can be accomplished through challenge. Although you may basically agree with what someone says, you may sometimes encourage "debate" as the best way to test the value of an idea.

CONFRONTATION VERSUS COMPLIANCE   Communication is also influenced by tendencies toward confrontation or compliance during disagreements. Faced with a conflict, for example, a woman is more likely than a man to be conciliatory in an attempt to restore harmony. In the same situation, a man is likely to be more confrontational in expressing his disagreement. In such instances, misunderstanding is inevitable. While the female is likely to see only hostility and anger in the man's approach, the man tends to see only weakness and lack of conviction in that of the woman.

DIRECT VERSUS INDIRECT ASSERTION   Finally, communication styles differ in the degree to which people rely on either direct statements or indirect references. Asian Americans, for example, tend to be vague, passive, and indirect, whereas African Americans tend to argue positions in more direct, aggressive ways. The communication style of Hispanics lies somewhere in between these two.

STEREOTYPES AND PREJUDICES

stereotype
Distorting generalization based on the distinguishing characteristics of particular groups, including sex, race, physical appearance, occupation, and place of residence

Stereotypes are responsible for a great deal of the miscommunication that occurs among diverse groups of people. **Stereotypes** are distorting generalizations based on the distinguishing characteristics of particular groups. Such characteristics may range from sex, race, and physical appearance to occupation and place of residence. The stereotyped group, therefore, need not be a minority. Just as there are stereotypes of Hispanics, African Americans, Asians, older people, and the physically challenged, stereotypes also exist for so-called WASPs—White Anglo-Saxon Protestants, both male and female. Although each group may possess real differences in values, attitudes, and behaviors that distinguish it from other groups, these differences become stereotypes when they are simplified and distorted—that is, when they are used to ignore facts about a group that do not conform to our generalizations about the group.

prejudice
Combination of belief and behavior that results from preconceived judgments about other groups of people

Stereotypes, therefore, lead to faulty thinking about groups and their members, and faulty thinking may lead in turn to tendencies in behavior. Prejudice is one form of such behavior. **Prejudice**, then, is a combination of belief and behavior that results from the preconceived judgments that we sometimes make about other groups of people. A recent study by the National Opinion Research Center reveals that, not surprisingly, stereotypes and prejudices die hard. For example, a quarter century after the civil-rights movement heightened our awareness of stereotypes, a majority of respondents still view African Americans as more prone to violence and less intelligent than whites. According to the survey, sixty-two percent of nonblacks believe that African Americans are more likely than whites to "prefer to live off welfare." Fifty-six percent perceive African Americans as more violent than whites, and fifty-three percent believe that they are less intelligent.[6]

In the next sections, we will discuss some of the ways in which stereotypes can affect both individual and organizational attitudes and behavior. On the personal level, we will see how *confirmation bias* and *ethnocentrism* reflect learned attitudes toward both individuals and groups and our responses to their cultures. We will also examine the *entrenched organization* as an important embodiment of attitudes and behavior on the institutional level.

CONFIRMATION BIAS   Table 19.1 identifies many of the stereotypes found in our contemporary culture. As you review the table, keep in mind that once we form stereotypes, we become more likely to find specific examples that reinforce our beliefs and attitudes. This process is known as **confirmation bias.**

Stereotypes are based on an *ethnocentric* view of the world. The meaning that one group attaches to the communication style of another is often based on meanings derived from the culture of the judging group. This is just one important way in which stereotypes lead both to miscommunication and to poor judgment. An Anglo male manager, for example, may decide not to promote an Asian American to a managerial position because of the Asian's modesty, unwillingness to speak during meetings, and unwillingness to make eye contact. The Anglo manager may have decided that the Asian American lacks necessary leadership skills, while the Asian, steeped in a culture that marks aggressive behavior as inappropriate, is merely doing what, for him, is culturally correct.

THE ENTRENCHED ORGANIZATION   Stereotypes can also lead to so-called "entrenched organizations" like the one shown in Figure 19.4. According to

Sometimes it's like hair across your cheek. You can't see it. You can't find it with your fingers but you keep brushing at it. Because the feel of it is irritating.

Marian-Anderson
African American
opera singer

confirmation bias
Specific examples of cultural behaviors that reinforce beliefs and attitudes about members of a culture

The less secure a man is, the more likely he is to have extreme prejudice.

Clint Eastwood
American actor

TABLE 19.1 *Contemporary Cultural Stereotypes*

AFRICAN AMERICANS
good athletes
undisciplined
less intelligent than whites
violent and criminal

ASIAN AMERICANS
intelligent and industrious
clannish
arrogant
good technicians; poor managers

HISPANICS
macho men; subservient women
unmotivated
don't want to speak English
volatile tempers

ANGLO AMERICANS
arrogant
insensitive
abusers of power
oppressors

WOMEN
intuitive; nonanalytical
poor in math
emotional
not committed to career
poor leaders

MEN
insensitive
macho
treat women like objects
unemotional
threatened by women in power

ELDERLY
intolerant of change
prone to illness
hard to teach new ways
unmotivated
hard of hearing
set in their ways

PHYSICALLY CHALLENGED
physical impairment generalized to
    mental impairment
need constant care
expect others to drop everything to
    help them

Source: Adapted from Marilyn Loden and Judy B. Rosener, *Workforce 2000: Managing Employee Diversity as a Vital Resource* (Homewood, IL: Business One Irwin, 1991), pp. 65–67.

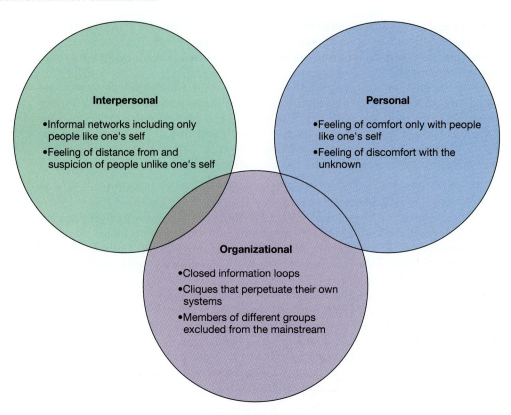

FIGURE 19.4   *Communication in the Entrenched Organization*

entrenched organization
Organization with three separate levels: (1) *personal*, in which people surround themselves with others who share the same background and values and who are uncomfortable when communicating with people who are different; (2) *interpersonal*, in which informal networks develop around similar people who generally avoid interaction with members of groups outside the network; and (3) *organizational*, in which diverse groups are excluded from closed information networks

LET'S DISCUSS
It will be more comfortable for students to analyze organizations with which they are no longer directly involved. Therefore, ask, "To what extent was your high school an entrenched organization? What steps did the administration take to reduce the

Price Cobbs, a diversity consultant with ODT, Inc., **entrenched organizations** have three separate levels. On a *personal* level, people surround themselves with others who share similar backgrounds and values and who are uncomfortable when communicating with people who are different. On the *interpersonal* level, this tendency often leads to the creation of informal networks made up of similar people who generally avoid interaction with members of groups outside the network. Finally, on an *organizational* level, diverse groups are excluded from closed information networks and isolated in organizations often dominated by cliques.

Recasting the entrenched organization requires open discussion of communication differences. Ironically, heightened awareness of racial, ethnic, and gender issues can make such discussions more rather than less difficult. Managers, for example, may be reluctant to take action for fear of being perceived as prejudiced. Not surprisingly, however, it is only through communication feedback that change will occur.

PROGRESS CHECK

1. Name the major components of diversity.
2. How is the American workforce expected to change by the year 2000?
3. Distinguish between stereotypes and prejudices. What do they have in common?

RACIAL/ETHNIC DIVERSITY

Reflecting trends in the general population, both consumers and members of the workforce are also becoming more multicultural in their group makeup. As a result, neither communication within a group nor communication between groups can be based on the belief in a homogeneous, Anglo-American audience. In this section, we will examine three major racial/ethnic groups: *African Americans, Hispanic Americans,* and *Asian Americans.* For all three groups, the nature of both external and internal communication has undergone profound change. We will also look at differences in communication styles that result from racial and ethnic diversity. These differences, too, can obstruct internal as well as external business communication.

Communicating with African Americans

While the total U.S. population increased 9.8 percent during the last decade, the African-American population grew by 13.2 percent. Currently, some 29.2 million African Americans live in the United States, accounting for more than one of every nine Americans. With an annual spending power estimated at about $260 billion, this group of consumers is increasingly being viewed as a major force in the American marketplace.

Figure 19.5 shows the distribution of African Americans by county. Growth in this segment of the population during the past decade has occurred not only in the central cities but also in metropolitan suburbs. For example, Gwinnett County, Georgia, a suburb of Atlanta, saw its African-American population increase 344 percent between 1980 and 1990.[7]

AFRICAN AMERICAN COMMUNICATION STYLES   In a book entitled *Black and White Styles in Conflict,* Thomas Kochman described a number of differences in the communication styles of African and white Americans. Among the communication patterns that Kochman identifies are *emotional intensity, the use of argument*

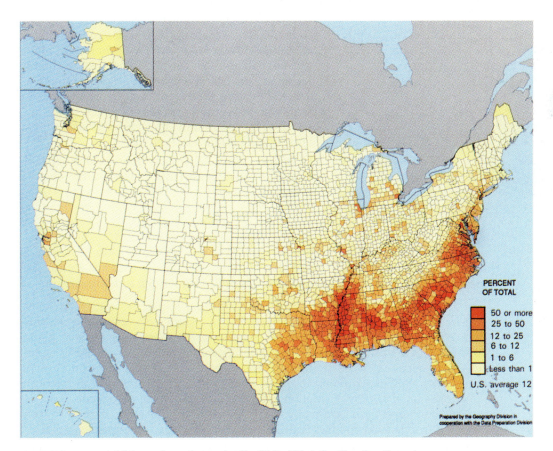

FIGURE 19.5   *African Americans in the U.S.: Distribution by County*
Source: The United States Census Bureau.

INTERVIEW

Helen Turnbull, Organizational Consultan in Workforce Diversity

Helen Turnbull, Principal Consultant at Florida-based Human Facets and a native of Scotland, designs and implements organizational-change and diversity-training seminars for such major corporations as Texas Instruments, IBM, Motorola, and National Westminster Bank. Her goal is to help organizations manage change and value rather than resist the diversity of the workforce as they learn concrete communication and coping skills. We asked Ms. Turnbull about the impact of diversity on written and oral communication.

Question: Can you identify common communication patterns that distinguish the way women and minorities express themselves in writing in comparison to white, native-born males?

Answer: Women choose more relationship-oriented words which imply a "let's do this together" consensus. For example, "I would like to  share my views with you" or "I would appreciate your input." White males, on the other hand, are more directive and bottom-line oriented. They may write, "I need to provide you with information" or "I require your feedback." Their approach is to ask for informa-

tion and move on. Both genders focus on getting the job done but come at the task from different orientations.

People with Hispanic or Middle Eastern backgrounds use more conversational and anecdotal writing styles than the mainstream business standard. Their approach is indirect in both writing and speaking. To the native-born American this may seem unnecessarily protracted, but conversely, to people from other cultures our style can sometimes seem too directive and intrusive.

Question: Do Hispanics, Asians, and ethnic blacks who have lived in this country for a long time or who are second- or third-generation Americans continue to embrace the communication patterns of their culture of origin or do they adopt mainstream American patterns?

Answer: Cultural identity and core values run deep. Ethnic traditions are our original roots, and they persist in our behavior. Often, even in second- or third-generation families, people continue to honor their original cultures, languages, and customs. However, as people assimilate, they learn to balance both cultures. Second-generation Japanese-American businesspeople, for example, are often comfortable getting down to business fairly quickly, but when they go back to their families and community, they unconsciously shift back to more traditional patterns.

Question: Many Americans now speak English as a second language. How does this affect communication?

during *persuasion,* and *distinct body language.*[8] We will look more closely at each of these patterns. It should be noted that although Kochman's analysis focuses on oral communication styles, it also has implications for written communication.

EMOTIONAL INTENSITY   Different emotional styles present in African-American and Anglo cultures can sometimes be a source of communication friction. While many African Americans tend to present themselves in what white Americans perceive as "intense," "dynamic," "demonstrative" ways, Anglos themselves are generally more restrained. Not surprisingly, miscommunication may occur when Anglos who tend to prefer emotional restraint interpret the African American's open display of emotion as aggressive, inappropriate, or rude. Wary of the "low-key" approach favored by many Anglos, African Americans may in turn suspect the underlying motives and sincerity of their white counterparts.

PERSUASION AND ARGUMENT   According to Kochman, when engaging in debate to air differences of opinion, African Americans may challenge oppo-

Answer: When people learn English as a second language, they tend to select a limited vocabulary and stick to it, especially in the early years of learning the language. As a result, they have a much smaller written and oral vocabulary than native-born Americans who have an enormous variety of English words at their disposal. When native speakers argue or debate a point, they can do so from many different directions. They can maneuver their way around the language more easily and persuade—through the power of words. People who speak English as a second language don't have this luxury, especially if they are recent immigrants. The longer people live and work in the country, the more their oral and written skills improve. But in the initial years, they are at a disadvantage because the thought processes involved in translation takes time. Because of this, they may take longer answering questions or writing letters or memos than native-born Americans. In fact, they will tend to avoid written communication when they can.

Question: What effect do racial and ethnic stereotypes have on our ability to communicate?

Answer: A significant effect. Stereotypes are generalizations about *groups* and are not true for *all individuals* in each group; however, let me give you some examples. When white males make spelling or grammatical errors, the mistakes are often laughed off. But when the same spelling and grammatical shortfalls are found in people of color, they are more likely to be viewed as an educational deficit.

Accents and speech patterns are also subject to stereotypes. The British accent is considered socially acceptable, and when I came to this country thirteen years ago from Scotland, I realized that my accent was perceived favorably. Hispanics, Koreans, Vietnamese, or even inner-city blacks don't have this advantage. Their accents or dialects are not socially acceptable and are often unfairly considered indicators of a lack of intelligence.

Articulation is another problem. For example, the Chinese use different facial muscles to pronounce words. While English comes from the front of the throat, Chinese comes from the back. As a result, Chinese people who speak English as a second language have a lot of trouble pronouncing certain of our letters. It is not just the *accent* that puts us off but the *articulation* of the words as well. We need to have more patience with each other.

Question: How do people who must work together overcome communication differences?

Answer: We must suspend our judgment. We should not judge others negatively because they are indirect, or their accents aren't clear, or their tone of voice is tentative, or they avoid eye contact. We must learn patience and suspend judgment long enough to realize these differences don't make one of us right and the other wrong. They simply mean that we approach communication from a different frame of reference and, many times, a different value system.

Source: Interview with Helen Turnbull, Human Facets.

nents with "rhetorical" displays that make use of "emotional" means of expression. For many Anglos, however, "argument" functions primarily as an expression of anger, not as an appeal to emotion for the purpose of persuasion. When confronted during debate with emotionally charged opposition, they may consider rhetorical outbursts as argumentative expressions of anger, even when the focus is on the topic being discussed and not on themselves. For whites, Kochman suggests, "struggle is viewed as negative. It means we are less likely to hear the validity of someone else's viewpoint if we're too intensely involved in our own. . . . They say: 'I can't talk to you now, you're too emotional.'"[9]

Both African Americans and Anglos who use emotion as an important component of debate tend to distrust the "low-key" debating style of others. Considering themselves committed advocates for their ideas, they are often confused by the detached stance that other people take to their ideas. Kochman argues that for blacks, "the refusal to contend is withholding and cheating, and it demonstrates an unwillingness to get at the truth."[10] Conversely, as spokespersons rather than advocates, people less likely to use emotion tend to believe that the merits of an idea will speak for themselves.

BODY LANGUAGE According to diversity consultant Bob Mezoff, when two whites are speaking, the listener tends to look directly at the speaker while the speaker usually looks away, glancing occasionally at the listener. By contrast, African-American speakers tend to maintain almost continuous eye contact with listeners who usually look away. The African-American listener may also pace the conversation by first looking toward the speaker after a block of information has been communicated and then looking away—a sign that the speaker can continue. Understanding may be indicated with no more than a slight nod of the head. The Anglo listener, on the other hand, is more likely to respond to the speaker with a series of verbal fillers like "uh-huh" or "I see" that indicate interest and involvement.

Integrating these two different styles in a business interaction is fraught with problems. Patti Watts, a writer for *Management Review,* explains:

> If a white employee is listening to a black boss, both are looking at each other. But the exchange of gaze feels uncomfortable because each expects the other to look away more often. Each may even feel as though the other is being threatening or intrusive.

> The communication breakdown can be even more severe when a white boss is talking to a black employee. Because the black employee is not looking at the white boss, the boss is likely to think the employee isn't listening. . . . White bosses also misinterpret the black listening style to mean that the employee doesn't understand what is being said. The white boss waits for the expected verbal fillers and when they are not forthcoming, the boss is likely to simplify what has just been said—assuming the employee hasn't understood. Most . . . whites are unaware the differing styles exist.[11]

Communicating with Hispanic Americans

The 22.4 million Hispanics living in the United States make up one of every eleven U.S. residents—a fact that highlights the importance of successful business communication with the country's growing minority population. Figure 19.6 shows the distribution of Hispanics by county throughout the United States. They are centered in California, Texas, New York, Florida, and Illinois. Southern Texas also has a large, rapidly growing Hispanic population that has become a clear demographic majority in some areas. More than 950,000 Hispanics live in Dade County, Florida; with nine out of ten residents of Laredo, Texas, being Hispanic, the clerk who rings up sales at the local supermarket may very well speak only Spanish.[12]

Vons, the largest supermarket chain in California, studied the state's Mexican culture for two years before opening Tianguis, a separate ethnic food chain that appeals to Hispanic cultural patterns. The nine stores in the Tianguis chain duplicate the feeling of an open-air marketplace and are designed to encourage the Mexican tradition of shopping as a form of family entertainment. To encourage conversation, for example, aisles are wider than those in traditional supermarkets—a design element that encourages people to stop and talk.[13] The company's marketing strategies reflect an awareness of the relationship between its communication practices and the cultural preferences of its customers. Vons has thus increased customer loyalty by successfully reaching a minority target market.

Communicating with Asian Americans

Totaling nearly 7 million people, Asian Americans represent less than 3 percent of the total U.S. population. However, they are the fastest-growing minority in the United States, and their influence often surpasses their number. In San Francisco,

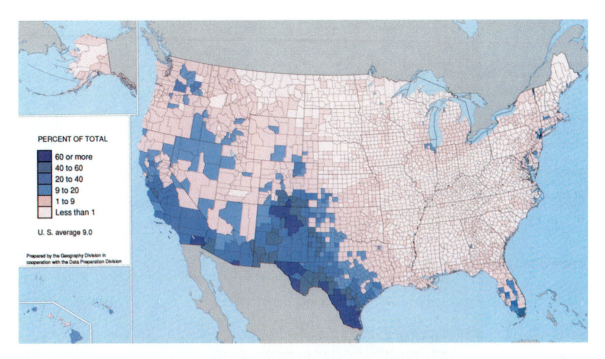

FIGURE 19.6   *Hispanics in the U.S.: Distribution by County*
Source: The United States Census Bureau.

for example, nearly three out of ten residents are Asian American, while the Los Angeles–Long Beach metropolitan area is home of the largest number of Asian Americans in the United States. Asian-American influence is related in part to income. According to the U.S. Census Bureau, the median household income for Asian Americans is $36,102, compared with $30,406 for non-Hispanic whites, $21,921 for Hispanics, and $18,083 for African Americans.[14] Figure 19.7 shows the population concentration of Asian Americans in the United States.

During the past decade, 140,000 Chinese and Korean immigrants have settled in the Flushing area of New York City. This immigration wave brought with it at least 35 banks, only a few of which are American. Citibank, Chase Manhattan, and Chemical Bank must now compete with the China Trust Bank, the Shanghai Banking Corporation, and the Amerasia Bank for deposits and other business. Not surprisingly, the ability of Chinese bankers to understand and communicate with customers has resulted in stiff competition for American bankers. According to Thomas Tai, president of the Flushing Chinese Business Association, "Chinese banks thrive because of their personal relationships. They pay attention to past records, reputations of friends and family from the original country." To bridge this communication gap, American banks now offer transactions in three languages. Citibank has opened an Asian Banking Center where Korean, Mandarin, and Cantonese are spoken and where personal relationships are strongly emphasized.[15]

When Southern California Edison discovered that five of its customer groups—Cambodians, Chinese, Hispanics, Koreans, and Vietnamese—needed special language attention, the utility turned to its workforce for a solution. Eleven bilingual workers were identified to serve as company spokespersons and ambassadors. They then received special training in communication, public speaking, and issues affecting the corporation.[16]

ETHNIC DIVERSITY AND COMMUNICATION STYLES   Consider this example of a human resources problem faced by a typical American manufacturing firm:

When a management slot in engineering opened up, an Asian American was among the candidates considered. Although the Asian candidate met

American business will not be able to survive if we do not have a large diverse work force, because those are the demographics—no choice! The company that gets out in front of managing diversity, in my opinion, will have a competitive edge.

*David Kearns
CEO, Xerox Corp.*

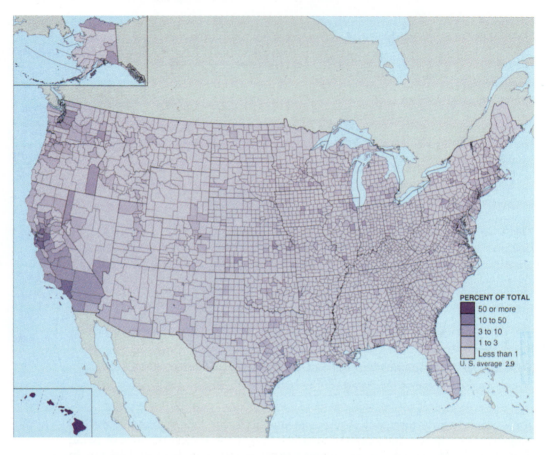

FIGURE 19.7 *Asian Americans in the U.S.: Distribution by County*
Source: The United States Census Bureau.

all the qualifications—in fact, no one in the department matched his credentials—he was perceived as passive, self-effacing, and lacking in the management skills needed to do the job. What managers failed to realize is that for many people of Asian heritage, self-effacement is consistent with an emphasis on organizational rather than individual achievement.

Or consider just one facet of a recent episode in the history of U.S. racial and ethnic relations:

In the summer of 1992, clashes between Anglos, Hispanics, and African-American customers and Korean small-business owners in Southern California were fueled, in part, by a lack of understanding of Asian communication styles. Traditionally open to family and community members but closed to outsiders, Korean shopkeepers are perceived as "clannish" and "uncommunicative." "There is consistent and persistent rude treatment," reports John W. Mack, president of the Los Angeles chapter of the Urban League.[17]

In both of these cases, it may be possible to overcome the communication problems by trying to understand the deep-seated cultural patterns that are at work. It may also be necessary to question assumptions. Making diversity work, says consultant Lennie Copeland, "means laying aside some assumptions and looking beyond style at results."[18] Obviously, abandoning assumptions about ethnic minorities means recognizing that, like African Americans, Hispanics and Asian Americans have distinct cultural values that influence communication style. Table 19.2 shows how some of the most important Hispanic and Asian-American values compare to those of Anglo Americans.

TABLE 19.2 *Comparing Cultural Values*		
HISPANICS	ASIAN AMERICANS	ANGLO AMERICANS
Authority is respected and seldom challenged.	Authority is obeyed and respected.	Authority is often questioned, sometimes circumvented.
Self-sacrifice is good.	Self-sacrifice is important and expected	Self-sacrifice is unhealthy and unnecessary.
Emotional expression is important.	Emotions downplayed for group cohesiveness.	Certain emotions downplayed for each gender (men shouldn't cry; women shouldn't yell).
Relationship-oriented rather than task-oriented.	Achieve for honor of family, company, class, or society.	Task-oriented for personal, emotional, or material rewards.
Time is vague/relative.	Time is not always specific.	Time is precise.
Music, family members, and food are preferred or welcome additions to the work environment.	Music, family members, and food are only part of the work environment under certain work circumstances.	Music, family members, and food are rarely part of the work environment, except in unusual circumstances.

Source: Adapted by permission from Carmen Colin and Diane Johns, ODT, Inc., Box 134, Amherst, MA 01004.

PROGRESS CHECK

1. Why might whites and African Americans sometimes have trouble understanding one another?
2. Cover the "Hispanics" and "Asian Americans" columns in Table 19.2. Test your understanding of what you just read by filling in the covered information.

GENDER AND COMMUNICATION

Men and women communicate and receive information from such contrasting vantage points that their conversations are often akin to cross-cultural communication. Deborah Tannen, a professor of linguistics at Georgetown University and an expert on gender differences in communication, believes that linguistic conflicts between men and women frequently stem from the fact that men tend to speak a language of status and independence while women speak a language of connection and intimacy. These patterns affect communication as strongly in the workplace as they do at home. We will discuss in some detail gender differences in communication style. In addition, we will examine one of the more extreme consequences of a breakdown in interactions between men and women in the workplace: *sexual harassment*.

Gender Differences in Style

In order to clarify Tannen's distinction between gender communication styles in an office situation, let's examine the following scenario. Suppose a decision must be made by a woman whose tendency is to consult with her colleagues. In many ways, the discussion is as important as the decision because it shows evidence of involvement, connection, and communication. Faced with a similar decision, a male colleague might tend to take matters into his own hands and act according-

Whether women are better than men I cannot say—but I can say they are certainly no worse.

Golda Meir
Former Prime Minister
of Israel

ly. If he can make the decision himself, he may feel that there is no need for conversation. In such a case, a woman trying to get input from a male colleague by asking "What do you think?" might find that her quest for information is interpreted as a directive to decide.

In this illustration, it is quite easy to detect the source of potential conflict in a difference in gender communication styles. According to Tannen, the conflict here could result from a very common task encountered in business interactions: *asking for information and offering help.* Men and women also differ in the way they interpret the purpose of conversation—a distinction that Tannen calls *report-talk* (male) versus *rapport-talk* (female); a similar difference in style affects the reaction of men and women to public speaking. Tannen also believes that patterns of speech follow two different styles: *powerful and powerless.* Finally, she observes distinct differences in *body language.*[19] In addition, Sally Helgesen, author of *The Female Advantage: Women's Ways of Leadership,* explains that women have a tendency to communicate via a *web of inclusion*—a communication style that stresses personal contact and information sharing. We will borrow Tannen's and Helgesen's categories to explore further the nature of gender differences in communication styles.

Being a woman is a terribly difficult task, since it consists principally in dealing with men.

Joseph Conrad
English novelist

metamessage
Communication that focuses on the relationships and attitudes between the people delivering and receiving the message

ASKING FOR INFORMATION AND OFFERING HELP   Although asking for information and help is a common business activity, the *act* of asking is frequently interpreted very differently by men and women. According to Tannen, the interpretation of the request message may be affected by an accompanying "metamessage" with broader implications. **Metamessages** are communications that focus on the relationships and attitudes between the people delivering and receiving the message. The request for help, for example, may send the metamessage "I am weaker and less knowledgeable than you"—and thus imply a status difference that many men find uncomfortable or inappropriate. On the other hand, offering help may send a metamessage implying higher status and competence. "I know the information and am therefore more competent than you."

Women, then, often tend to avoid asking men for help. When women ask, they are often made to feel incompetent. However, when women themselves are faced with requests for help, they tend to provide as much information as possible as clearly as possible. Unlike men, their goal is more often to create connections, and to do so, they try to minimize the perception of a difference in knowledge or expertise.

REPORT-TALK VERSUS RAPPORT-TALK   Regardless of the medium of the interchange, women generally seek to establish relationships while men are more likely to focus on information. Tannen terms this difference *report-talk versus rapport-talk.* Because men tend to view conversation as a mechanism to negotiate status, they also tend to see the interchange as an opportunity to exhibit their knowledge and skill—that is, to report to others. Consequently, men often take center stage and thus monopolize conversation. The same tendency to capture and keep attention tends to make such men more comfortable with public speaking.

Women, on the other hand, may tend to focus on similarities and connections as they seek to build rapport—that is, sympathetic relationships. Instead of emphasizing the status difference that comes with displaying knowledge and expertise, they tend to place less emphasis on these differences in an attempt to develop rapport.

The tendency to take center stage even in private conversation also tends to make many men more comfortable than women in delivering public speeches. Such men simply use the mechanism of report-talk to establish their expertise in a public setting. According to Tannen, when faced with public audiences, many women experience self-doubt, in part because they are not used to putting themselves on "display." Claiming attention by publicizing expertise and credibility is not the way these women prefer to communicate.

POWERFUL VERSUS POWERLESS LANGUAGE   By the very nature of their language choices, men and women communicate differently. For example, many women tend to build relationships through indirect, overtly "polite" language choices. While men, therefore, tend to ask directly for what they need ("Please get this memo back to me before lunch"), women often use an indirect approach that may be perceived as powerless ("I have a deadline to meet and don't know how I can do it and get the memo out, too. Can you help me by finishing this memo before lunch?"). According to Tannen, rather than actual powerlessness, indirect language may reflect women's preferences for making connections.

DIFFERENCES IN BODY LANGUAGE   Body language also reflects gender differences. Tannen notes that while many women attempt to establish intimacy by sitting close to one another and establishing eye contact, men are more likely to sit at angles and rarely look at one another directly. Indeed, our culture has given men reasons to avert their gazes. One man looking directly at another may be interpreted as a show of hostility—a nonverbal threat. The exchange of direct looks between men and women can also be interpreted as having sexual overtones that are certainly inappropriate for business.

WEB OF INCLUSION   In order to identify gender differences in managerial communication styles, researcher Sally Helgesen duplicated a study conducted by management scientist Henry Mintzberg, who followed five male executives through their workdays in 1968. More than twenty years later, Helgesen followed the same pattern, this time focusing on women. She identified three important differences in communication style—differences that create for women managers a *web of inclusion.* The relationships that develop from these preferences in communication style influence responses to such activities as managing interruptions and encounters and sharing information.[20]

HANDLING INTERRUPTIONS   The male executives in Mintzberg's study spent much of their time handling crises. Interrupted continually by subordinates seeking help, they quickly learned to use secretaries as "shields" to protect themselves. By contrast, although the female managers in Helgesen's study were also interrupted, they made greater efforts to be accessible to subordinates. For example, many of them maintained open-door policies.

PREFERRED ENCOUNTERS   The male executives preferred face-to-face meetings or phone calls to gather information. Most considered mail a burden unworthy of too much time or full attention. Although female managers also preferred face-to-face discussions, they considered mail extremely important, often scheduling up to an hour each day to handle it.

SHARING INFORMATION   Although both male and female managers collected enormous amounts of information, the women tended to be more willing to share it. Men tended to view information as an important source of power and sometimes seemed threatened by the idea of sharing it. By contrast, women welcomed the opportunity to share their thoughts and information. Said one woman in Helgesen's study: "I see myself as a transmitter—picking up signals from everywhere, then beeping them out to where they need to go." According to Helgesen, sharing seemed to be a natural extension of the women's concern for relationships.

Analysts like Tannen and Helgesen suggest that the flexible, people-oriented communication style of women managers may ultimately be better suited to the increasing diversity of the American workforce. Madelyn Jennings, a senior vice president for the Gannett newspaper chain, explains: "It's going to be increasingly important to understand the different cultural ground rules that employees are bringing to the workplace." The result, says Jennings, is a role reversal. "Rather than women having to adapt, men are going to have to learn from women."[21]

Sexual Harassment

During 1991 Senate Judiciary Committee hearings, Oklahoma University law professor Anita Hill charged that Judge Clarence Thomas, a nominee for the U.S. Supreme Court, had sexually harassed her when they worked together at the Equal Employment Opportunity Commission. Though never proven, her charges struck a chord among people—men and women—across the nation. Recent surveys go a long way toward explaining why. As Figure 19.8 shows, 38 percent of women polled by *The New York Times* in October 1991 claimed that they had experienced harassment in the workplace.[22]

sexual harassment
Illegal behaviors ranging from blatant to subtle sexually oriented hints, suggestions, and comments that contribute to a hostile working environment

GROUNDS FOR SEXUAL HARASSMENT   **Sexual harassment,** of course, is much more than a breakdown in communication. It consists of a range of behaviors from blatant physical contact to subtle sexually oriented hints, suggestions, and comments that contribute to a hostile working environment. Although victims of sexual harassment may be men or women, the overwhelming majority are women. The courts now recognize certain behavior not only as creating a hostile and unfair working environment but as constituting grounds for legal action. The standard for judgment is no longer what a "reasonable man" would do, but rather how various forms of behavior can be viewed through the eyes of a "reasonable woman."[23]

Sexual harassment charges are based on one or more of the following forms of behavior: improper physical conduct, unwelcome sexual advances, coercion, favoritism, and visual and indirect harassment. In many cases, however, both men and women remain confused about what is acceptable communication and what is not. According to Barbara Otto of 9to5, a working women's advocacy group, acceptable communication is marked by a high degree of com-

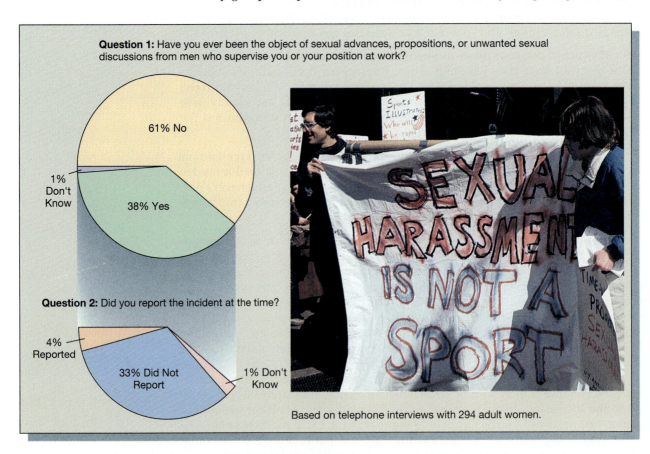

Question 1: Have you ever been the object of sexual advances, propositions, or unwanted sexual discussions from men who supervise you or your position at work?

61% No

1% Don't Know

38% Yes

Question 2: Did you report the incident at the time?

4% Reported

33% Did Not Report

1% Don't Know

Based on telephone interviews with 294 adult women.

FIGURE 19.8   *The Pervasiveness of Sexual Harassment*

Source: Elizabeth Kolbert, "Sexual Harassment at Work is Pervasive, Survey Suggests," *The New York Times*, October 11, 1991, P. A1.

munication respect. The following examples demonstrate how harassment differs from acceptable conversation.[24]

ACCEPTABLE	HARASSMENT
"You look very nice today"	"You have a great body"
A handshake, a pat on the shoulder, or casual eye contact	Patting or touching private body parts or staring lewdly at someone
Asking a co-worker for a date but not insisting or pestering	Repeatedly asking a co-worker for a date and refusing to take no for an answer.

Only through awareness, education, and mutual respect will sexual harassment disappear. Says Sheryl Handler, president of Thinking Machines, Inc.: "I don't think changing things in the corporate structure is enough. If people really learned to listen to another human and respect another human, that would level the field. I look forward to men and women learning to listen and respect and understand—to do that not because they should but because it gives them genuine pleasure."[25]

DEALING WITH HARASSMENT   Psychologists studying the ways in which people deal with sexual harassment have found a range of behaviors. As Table 19.3 shows, while some of these responses focus on confronting the harasser and seeking help, others not only do little to correct the problem but can actually be destructive to the victim's self-esteem. The most adaptive responses for both the harassment victim and the business organization involve clear channels of communication.

I've been sexually harassed every day I've spent on the trading floor. That's life in this business. That's life, period.

Sharon Kalin
Founder of Kalin Associates

TABLE 19.3 *Strategies for Dealing with Sexual Harassment*	
STRATEGIES	EXAMPLE
A. INTERNALLY FOCUSED STRATEGIES	
Detachment	Minimizing the situation, treating it as a joke or deciding that it is not really important
Denial	Pretending that nothing is happening; trying not to notice, hoping it will stop; trying to forget about it
Relabeling	Offering excuses for the harasser or interpreting the behavior as flattering
Illusory Control	Attributing harassment to one's own behavior or attire
Endurance	Suffering in silence, either through fear of retaliation, blame, or embarrassment or in the belief that no one will help
B. EXTERNALLY FOCUSED STRATEGIES	
Avoidance	Quitting a job; dropping a class; finding transportation alternatives; moving
Assertion/Confrontation	Confronting the harasser, making it clear that the behavior is unwelcome
Institutional Help	Asking for help; reporting the incident
Social Support	Seeking support and acknowledgment of the reality of the occurrence
Appeasement	Attempting to placate the harasser

Source: Table based on comments made by Dr. Louise Fitzgerald and reported in Daniel Goleman "Sexual Harassment: It's about Power, Not Lust," *The New York Times*, October 22, 1991, p. C12.

ETHICAL ISSUES IN BUSINESS COMMUNICATION

How Companies Eliminate Sexual Harassment in the Workplace

Responsible companies are serious about stopping sexual harassment in the workplace. They realize that inaction can lead to low morale, the loss of talented employees, and possible legal action. A recent study placed the annual cost of sexual harassment to a typical *Fortune* 500 company at $7 million. As a result, action has already begun at most large and medium-size firms in the form of strong policy statements and even stronger action. An estimated 90 percent of all *Fortune* 500 companies conduct employee training seminars on sexual harassment. Here is how three companies make the point in their written policy statements.

- AT&T No supervisor shall threaten to insinuate, either explicitly or implicitly, that an employee's submission or rejection of sexual advances will in any way influence any personnel decision regarding the employee's employment, wages, advancement, assigned duties, shifts, or any other condition of employment or career development.

- DOW [Managers should] encourage the complainant, where appropriate, to request the harassing employee to stop the offensive behavior.

- NEWSWEEK [A] supervisor who knows . . . an employee was being sexually harassed [faces] disciplinary action.

Programs with the most effective sexual harassment policies receive commitment from the very top of the organization. For example, during the sexual-harassment debate generated by the 1991 Senate confirmation hearings for Supreme Court nominee Clarence Thomas, AT&T chairman Robert E. Allen sent an electronic mail message to every employee, reiterating company policies and stating penalties for violating those policies.

Corning Inc., a company that has received high marks for its commitment to ridding the workplace of sexual harassment, advises employees to take a three-pronged communication approach:

1. Tell the harasser that the behavior is offensive, explaining how it made you feel and how it has affected your work and career.

2. If the problem continues despite your efforts, bring the situation to the attention of management.

3. Take part in any investigation. If you don't want the harasser or witnesses to know your name, then there may be no formal action.

Corning has convinced female employees that it takes gender issues very seriously. Partly as a result of the company's strong policies to combat sexual harassment, the attrition rate for salaried women has dropped from 16.2 percent in 1987 to slightly higher than 2.6 percent today—the same as its rate for men.

Sources: Joann S. Lublin, "Sexual Harassment Is Topping Agenda in Many Executive Education Programs," *The Wall Street Journal*, December 2, 1991, pp. B1, B6; George Smith, "Consciousness-Raising among 'Plain Old White Boys,'" *Business Week*, October 28, 1991, p. 32; and Stephanie Strom, "Harassment Rules Often Not Pushed," *The New York Times*, October 20, 1991, pp. 1, 22.

PROGRESS CHECK

1. What are *metamessages*?
2. What do we mean by a "web of inclusion"? Explain its significance.
3. How can good channels of organizational communication help both individuals and businesses resolve issues of sexual harassment?

THE ELDERLY AND THE PHYSICALLY CHALLENGED

Just as racial, ethnic, and gender differences affect communication, so do differences that result from age and physical ability. In examining the role of the eldery and the physically challenged as both workers and consumers, we will see that many of our habits in communicating with them result as much from our perceptions as from reality.

Age and Diversity

Older people are becoming an increasing presence in business, both as workers and consumers. As this segment of the population grows in number and importance, it is critical to understand the reasons why miscommunication exists and to suggest ways to minimize it.

As a whole, the U.S. population is aging. Between now and the year 2000, the number of people between the ages of 50 and 65 will grow twice as fast as the general population. While the elderly—those aged 65 and older—accounted for one of every nine residents of the United States in 1980, they are expected to number one of every five Americans by the year 2030. This trend, of course, will affect the workplace in a very significant way. While nearly half the current American workforce is 35 or younger, that percentage will drop to 39 percent by the turn of the century. That statistic translates into a graying workplace in both domestic and international corporations.

OLDER PEOPLE AS CO-WORKERS   The Age Discrimination in Employment Act of 1967 outlaws discrimination in the workplace against anyone aged 40 or older. Although most workers retire by age 65 and an increasing number take early retirement in their fifties, many older workers remain employed through their fifties, sixties, and into their seventies.

Many corporations encourage the employment and retention of older workers because of the value that they bring to the job. Often the most knowledgeable employees, older workers also tend to be more dependable, missing fewer days of work and changing jobs less frequently.

Companies like Days Inns, Corning Glass, Travelers Insurance, and Digital Equipment encourage the hiring of older workers. At Days Inns, for example, one out of three members of the 450-person reservation sales staff is 55 or older. With the turnover rates for this group averaging less than 1 percent—compared to 70 percent for younger workers—company management is convinced that hiring older workers has been the right decision.[26]

OLDER PEOPLE AS CONSUMERS   Realizing the demographic and economic power of older people, businesses are also trying to attract and keep this group as customers. Companies like AT&T aim advertising messages at the older market, and many companies have launched products specifically aimed at older consumers. For example, Doubleday & Company now prints books with larger-than-normal type faces that are marketed to older consumers through a book club.

COMMUNICATING WITH OLDER PEOPLE   Just as stereotypes affect the way we communicate with different racial, ethnic, and gender groups, they also influence communication across generational lines. A number of common communication fallacies can be avoided. One widely held stereotype is that age necessarily entails physical impairment. For example, many people shout at older people, assuming that because they are older, they cannot hear as well as younger people. Usually, this is not the case.

A second tendency is talking down to older people. Never assume that age has impaired a person's ability to understand concepts. Indeed, the older person's understanding may be greater than that of the speaker. Similarly, retailers, supervisors, and fellow workers should not be patronizing. Rather, they should assume that if an older person needs help, he or she will ask for it.

Managers and co-workers should also avoid equating *reluctance* to change with *inability* to change. Although older workers may have performed a task a certain way for years, they are just as likely as younger workers to change if given adequate reasons. For example, following a style that was common for many years, many older workers indent paragraphs in business letters. Today, indenting has been replaced with the full block paragraph style (see Appendix I). Explaining that block style is both easier to read and the current standard is usually reason enough for most traditionalists to accept the change.

Finally, many older people are more "formal" than younger people in their business interactions. When writing to any customer—and especially to an older customer—it thus is a good idea to refer to the person by his or her last name unless you are asked specifically to use the recipient's first name. For example, "Dear Mr. Abbott" would be more appropriate than "Dear Joe."

Disability and Diversity

The Americans with Disabilities Act of 1990 (ADA) was landmark legislation designed to protect the rights of people with disabilities. This law bans employment discrimination against individuals with disabilities that limit a major life activity. The law also makes discrimination against the disabled illegal in public accommodations, transportation, and telecommunications.

THE PHYSICALLY CHALLENGED AS CONSUMERS   Title III of ADA is intended to improve access to public facilities for physically challenged people. As a result, businesspeople are likely to interact with physically challenged people even more in

Many of the nation's 30 million hearing- and speech-impaired citizens can see immediately that these fingers are spelling out R-O-L-M—the name of the giant communications firm that has opened up many new communication channels for them. ROLM's Telecommunications Devices for the Deaf (TDDs) permit hearing- and speech-impaired employees and customers to communicate more easily via telephone and PhoneMail.

Source: © ROLM; reprinted by permission.

the future. These contacts are opportunities to establish good will and a continuing business relationship. Mishandled, they can be a source of continuing problems.

Many businesses have already made changes to accommodate the law. For example, operating instructions in most of the nation's automatic-teller machines are also displayed in Braille. The Red Lobster chain of seafood restaurants provides Braille menus for sight-impaired diners. Messanote, a Philadelphia restaurant, built a wooden ramp from its parking lot and printed several menus in Braille. Pilgrim State Bank in Cedar Grove, New Jersey, eased access to loan officers by moving offices to street level.[27]

THE PHYSICALLY CHALLENGED AS CO-WORKERS   Title I of ADA is designed to create equal employment opportunity for qualified individuals with disabilities. It ensures that people in wheelchairs, the vision- and hearing-impaired, and those with other disabilities limiting a major life activity have equal employment opportunity. According to the law, "reasonable accommodation" for the physically challenged includes providing readers and interpreters and adjusting or modifying training materials, examinations, or other company statements and documents. In addition, firms covered by the Act must make the workplace readily accessible and usable by the physically challenged and must, if necessary, provide these employees with part-time or modified work schedules.[28]

COMMUNICATING WITH THE PHYSICALLY CHALLENGED   No law, of course, can legislate away entrenched communication patterns that commonly put the physically challenged at a disadvantage. In the workplace, these changes generally result only through the concerted personal efforts of every employee. Management, however, can help improve communication by providing flexibility whenever possible. For example, when Scott Weed, who is deaf, started his food-industry career with Winn-Dixie in Theodore, Alabama, his managers had to find a way to get his attention. "When they want to call me," reports Weed, "they just blink the lights on and off. Sometimes the boss sends someone to get me." According to Weed, some co-workers have learned rudimentary sign language and many often simply write things down. Notes can also be sent through electronic mail.

Management can also assist physically challenged customers and workers by anticipating physical obstacles and finding ways to overcome them. For example, if you are the manager of an air-express company and your checkout counters are too high for people in wheelchairs, you might provide clipboards so that they can write comfortably.

One approach to interacting with the physically challenged is to think of such physical-ability differences as severe hearing impairment in the same way that you think of cultural differences. Explains Melanie Crawford, an Alabama rehabilitation counselor: "There are lots of misunderstandings about what deaf people can do. Instead of looking at it as a disability, look at it as a language barrier. A deaf person can be perceived as a non–English-speaking person rather than as someone who is handicapped. It's a cultural difference."[29]

An important fallacy to avoid is equating physical impairment with mental impairment. Neither wheelchair dependence nor hearing impairment has anything to with intellectual limitation. Indeed, problems faced by the disabled often have more to do with communication than ability. Crawford explains, for example, the problems that deaf people must cope with. Communication problems, she argues, "foster isolation. Sometimes things are misunderstood or misinterpreted. The deaf worker misses out on office gossip and is not able to provide input into the job." Managers, retailers, and fellow workers should also avoid any expression of pity. Self-sufficient people neither want nor deserve it. In most cases, when a physically challenged person needs help, he or she will ask for it.

Finally, managers should keep abreast of the latest technology to improve communication. For example, the Kurzweil Personal Reader, manufactured by Xerox, uses computer technology to read printed words to visually handicapped people at a rate of up to 350 words per minute.

Basic advice for communicating with any person with disabilities is summarized in Figure 19.9. These "ten commandments," developed by the Chicago-based National Center for Access Unlimited, are useful for any person who interacts with physically challenged friends, co-workers, or the general public.

DIVERSITY TRAINING

Realizing that traditional business communication is based on patterns established long before the dramatic demographic changes described earlier in this chapter, a growing number of firms are turning to formal training programs to

1. Speak directly rather than through a companion or sign language interpreter who may be present.

2. Offer to shake hands when introduced. People with limited hand use or an artificial limb can usually shake hands and offering the left hand is an acceptable greeting.

3. Always identify yourself and others who may be with you when meeting someone with a visual impairment. When conversing in a group, remember to identify the person to whom you are speaking.

4. If you offer assistance, wait until the offer is accepted. Then listen or ask for instructions.

5. Treat adults as adults. Address people who have disabilities by their first names only when extending that same familiarity to all others. Never patronize people in wheelchairs by patting them on the head or shoulder.

6. Do not lean against or hang on someone's wheelchair. Bear in mind that disabled people treat their chair as extensions of their body.

7. Listen attentively when talking with people who have difficulty speaking and wait for them to finish. If necessary, ask short questions that require short answers, a nod or shake of the head. Never pretend to understand if you are having difficulty doing so. Instead repeat what you have understood and allow the person to respond.

8. Place yourself at eye level when speaking with someone in a wheelchair or on crutches.

9. Tap a hearing-impaired person on the shoulder or wave your hand to get his or her attention. Look directly at the person and speak clearly, slowly, and expressively to establish if the person can read your lips. If so, try to face the light source and keep hands, cigarettes and food away from your mouth when speaking.

10. Relax. Don't be embarrassed if you happen to use common expressions such as "See you later" or "Did you hear about this?" that seem to relate to a person's disability.

FIGURE 19.9 *Communicating with the Physically Challenged*
Source: National Center for Access Unlimited, Chicago.

help improve communication in a changing environment. **Diversity training** focuses on improving awareness of the different attitudes, behaviors, and communication patterns that characterize different groups and aids in developing skills to deal with these differing patterns.

Diversity training benefits white male managers as well as other groups, all of whom must learn to adapt to the prevailing mainstream of business culture. For some companies, such training is absolutely essential—for example, at the regional Allstate Insurance center in Skokie, Illinois, where 525 employees speak no less than 17 languages.[30] Moreover, the importance of this type of training is also directly related to the increasing number and diversity of *customers* in the marketplace of the contemporary company.

diversity training
Process of improving awareness of different attitudes, behaviors, and communication patterns and developing skills to deal with these differences

The Importance of Diversity Training

Diversity affects both a company's internal and external relationships. For example, federal equal employment opportunity laws require the hiring of women and minorities, while other laws prohibit discrimination based on age, race, nationality, sex, or physical disability. At the same time, government at all levels, the private sector, and the general public all have recognized the need to manage diversity in order to promote understanding, efficiency, and, ultimately, productivity. A key challenge in business today, therefore, is to make diversity work for the company and its customers. Lennie Copeland, a diversity consultant at San Francisco-based Copeland Griggs, points out that productivity results not simply from the recognition of organizational diversity, but from its effective management. "Simply throwing different people together," he observes, "does not create a productive work environment—or even a genuinely diverse one. People tend to cluster with people like themselves, those with whom they feel comfortable and who confirm old stereotypes. . . Prejudice and cultural misunderstandings cause conflict, bad decisions, and poor results."[31]

Inevitably, a diverse workforce with poor communication will also create high turnover, increased absenteeism, and low productivity. Moreover, companies that fail to train and empower diverse groups will lose the problem-solving and creative perspectives that these groups bring with them. Gannett News Media President Nancy J. Woodhull credits organizational diversity with the success of the national newspaper *USA Today:* "Without women [and minorities]," she claims," *USA Today* would have been *USA Yesterday.* The reason we were interesting [from the start] is that there were a lot of ideas from different people with different points of view in our news meetings every day. There were women; there were minorities; there were young people; there were old people."[32] To best understand the needs of women, African Americans, Asian Americans, and Hispanics, Gannett and other forward-looking companies have turned to members of the groups they want to reach.

We didn't all come over on the same ship, but we're all in the same boat.

*Bernard Baruch
American financier
and statesman*

What Individual Companies Are Doing

Among the many companies that have instituted diversity training are Digital Equipment, Kinney Shoe, Avon, and Xerox. Although the nature of their programs varies, they all are aimed at improving multicultural communication.

DIGITAL EQUIPMENT   The Valuing Differences program at Digital Equipment helps people understand that miscommunication is often based on stereotypes and false assumptions about other groups. Aided by a facilitator, eight to ten employees come together in a Core Group to confront their prejudices. Digital's program is considered one of the leading diversity-training programs in the United States.

Digital is also a leader in programs designed to combat sexual harassment. Using role playing, videos, and group discussions of actual cases, Digital employees volunteer to spend hours in sexual-harassment seminars that are booked six months in advance.[33]

KINNEY SHOE   Kinney Shoe—a nationwide footwear chain with nearly 4,000 stores—stresses the importance of diversity in both its human-resources pool and its customer base. "We stress that talent is color- and gender-blind and culture-neutral," explains Kinney's Fair Employment Practices director Bob Jacinto, who heads a concerted effort to hire employees who reflect the chain's diverse customers. To improve communication within its 36,000 member multicultural workforce, the company conducts 8-hour seminars that stress the value of diversity in both hiring and day-to-day work situations. Jacinto blames stereotyping for many of the problems associated with communicating in a diverse workforce. He cites research evidence that negative hiring decisions are often based on an applicant's accent or poor English-speaking skills. "We assume [by people's accents] that they don't have the skills to sell shoes. But certainly they could," he explains.

Kinney's diversity-training program also shows employees how communication patterns affect different groups of people in different ways. In one situation, for example, a supervisor is shown praising a Native American worker, never realizing that, to many Native Americans, public praise is an embarrassment.[34]

AVON   Spurred by the mandate of affirmative action, Avon had an excellent track record in hiring minorities and women. But while women moved up in the company to positions of greater responsibility during the 1970s and 1980s, minorities did not. To correct the situation, Avon developed a diversity-training program. Working in conjunction with the American Institute for Managing Diversity, Avon sent groups of twenty-five managers, from different racial and ethnic backgrounds, to three-week stays at the institute's Atlanta headquarters to learn to speak—and listen—to one another.

XEROX   Taking a different route, Xerox is trying to overcome subtle roadblocks to women's upward mobility. In 1990, CEO Paul A. Allaire assembled an informal panel of six senior female executives to help eliminate ingrained and often unconscious patterns that are prejudicial to women. One of the suggested changes was the elimination of definitions interpreted as aggressive or male. For example, instead of defining *leadership* as "an intense desire to win," the panel suggested a more sex-neutral definition. Xerox now defines *leadership* as an "intense desire to succeed."[35]

Diversity and Commitment

Bridging the communication gap among diverse groups begins with a commitment based on a number of important principles. First, communication among diverse groups is *cross-cultural communication* that may require the same development of knowledge and positive attitudes as communicating across national boundaries.

Regardless of their intent, managers and fellow workers should realize that it is possible for both words and actions to have negative effects on other individuals or groups. For example, because humor is often culture-based, it can be misinterpreted.

Communicating successfully in a diverse workforce is as much a matter of comfort as competence. For example, if Anglos in positions of power are uncomfortable with diversity, they are likely to communicate that discomfort to others. Similarly, women, minorities, older people, and the physically challenged

In addition to incorporating diversity training into its program of continuing personnel training, communications giant Xerox has developed a number of products designed to assist the physically challenged. For 42 million reading-handicapped people who are blind, learning-disabled, or illiterate, Xerox's Kurzweil Personal Reader makes it possible to read most kinds of type and printed material at a speed of up to 350 words per minute.
Source: © Xerox; reprinted by permission.

should realize that the need to "fit into" an organization can be as important as hard work.

Perhaps the most important principle for managers and co-workers to recognize is that differences are assets with the potential to make the organization stronger, more creative, and more productive.[36] It is the duty of the organization to ensure that its assets are used to the fullest.

PROGRESS CHECK

1. Why is it important to communicate effectively with older employees and customers?
2. Summarize some tips for facilitating communication with physically challenged people.
3. Who benefits from diversity training?

WHAT'S AHEAD

The dual challenges of communicating in a global marketplace and communicating with diverse groups share a common thread. In both cases, success is linked to surmounting cultural barriers that obstruct communication.

In the following chapter, we address the challenge of understanding and harnessing communication technology. Although mastering this challenge does not require understanding a different culture or speaking a foreign language, it has everything to do with being comfortable when you are asked to learn something about a new and unfamiliar world. In addition to humans, this world—especially the region occupied by business—is peopled with machines, procedures, and enormous time-saving opportunities.

SUMMARY OF CHAPTER OBJECTIVES

1. **List important *demographic changes* that are transforming the American workplace and marketplace.**

   An increasing number of women, older workers, minorities, and physically challenged people are transforming the workforce. By the year 2005, 47 percent of the U.S. workforce will be women, 12 percent African Americans, 11 percent Hispanics, and nearly 5 percent Asians; native-born Anglo males will be a minority. During the remainder of this decade, women and minorities will make up 85 percent of the net additions to the workforce.

2. **Outline eight elements that define individual and group *communication patterns*.**

   The key elements that form communication patterns are expressed in terms of complementary pairs on a communication spectrum. Key pairs include initiating discussion versus listening, individual versus group reference points, relying on facts versus intuition, a personal versus impersonal approach, rational versus emotional expression, a style that challenges versus one that expresses agreement, an approach that uses confrontation versus compliance, and the use of direct versus indirect assertions.

3. **Explain how such factors as *racial/ethnic stereotypes, gender, age,* and *physical disability* can contribute to miscommunication.**

   Stereotypes are distorted, inflexible generalizations about members of a particular group. Often, they are the basis for miscommunication. Once stereotypes are formed, new information is placed within their context, thus creating communication barriers that are difficult to overcome.

4. **Identify three *communication patterns* common to many African Americans.**

   Thomas Kochman, an authority on African-American communication styles, believes that the communication patterns of many African Americans are likely to be characterized by emotional intensity, the use of argument during persuasion, and distinct body language.

5. **Explain how *gender differences* affect communication.**

   According to linguist Deborah Tannen, while men tend to speak a language of status and independence, women tend to focus on connection and intimacy. This fundamental difference expresses itself in the way men and women ask for information or offer help, in the way they relate to one another through "report-talk" or "rapport-talk," in their reaction to public speaking, in the power or powerlessness of their language, and in differences in nonverbal communication. Sally Helgesen, an expert on women's leadership styles, believes that, unlike men, women form a web of inclusion that involves frequent person-to-person contacts and the sharing of information.

6. **Describe the communication breakdown inherent in *sexual harassment*.**

   Sexual harassment consists of a range of behaviors from blatant grabbing and touching to subtle sexually oriented hints, suggestions, and comments that create a hostile working environment. Sexual harassment exists when respect for members of the opposite sex is absent and when members of one gender perceive persons of the opposite sex as a threat to their power.

7. **Describe the special communication needs of older and physically challenged people.**
   The passage of federal legislation and the aging population combine to ensure that older and physically challenged people will have a place of increased importance in the workforce. The elderly and the disabled are also important business customers. Because the average worker is younger and is likely to have no physical disability, miscommunication can occur. The communication differences that separate the disabled and older

people from others can be as profound as those between men and women and between racial and ethnic groups.

8. **Explain the nature of *diversity training*.**
   Diversity training focuses on improving awareness of the attitudes, behaviors, and communication patterns that characterize women, minorities, older workers, and physically challenged people; it is also directed at developing the skills to deal with these patterns. Diversity training is important because of the changing demographics of the workforce and because poor communication contributes to low productivity, high turnover, and increased absenteeism. The ability to communicate in a diverse workforce also brings the benefit of varied problem-solving and creative approaches.

REVIEW AND DISCUSSION QUESTIONS

1. Summarize key demographic trends in the American workforce. By the early twenty-first century, how much of the labor force will be African American, Hispanic, Asian-American, or female? *(Ch. Obj. 1)*
2. List eight important elements that contribute to the communication patterns of individuals and groups. *(Ch. Obj. 2)*
3. Describe the three levels found in an entrenched organization. *(Ch. Obj. 2, 3)*
4. Describe three differences between the "typical" communication patterns of Anglos and African Americans. *(Ch. Obj. 4)*
5. Identify some of the important cultural values that might tend to influence Hispanic and

Asian-American communication patterns. *(Ch. Obj. 5)*
6. Describe some key differences between "typical" communication styles of women and men. *(Ch. Obj. 6)*
7. What is sexual harassment? Why is it so difficult to define precisely? *(Ch. Obj. 7)*
8. Describe stereotypes about older people that can affect communication with older co-workers and customers. *(Ch. Obj. 8)*
9. What is diversity training? Why is it important? *(Ch. Obj. 9)*
10. What can businesses do to bring together diverse groups in the workplace? *(Ch. Obj. 9)*

APPLICATION EXERCISES

1. Why is it important for you to be able to communicate effectively with various American cultural groups? *(Ch. Obj. 1)*
2. Does a company have an ethical obligation to offer diversity training for its employees? Explain your answer. *(Ch. Obj. 1, 9)*
3. No matter how much we talk about cultural patterns, it's important to remember that we are all individuals. Refer to FIGURE 19.3 and the discussion of the eight determinants of individual communication patterns. Assess

your own communication style in terms of these eight elements. Make a written list of those that influence your style most heavily. How does your personal communication pattern compare to the chapter discussion of your particular cultural background, gender, age, and so forth? In what ways is your style similar to or different from the general description? *(Ch. Obj. 2)*
4. Jim Mason, the CEO of athletic clothing maker Smallco Sweats, has decided to explore

new markets inside the United States, starting with Asian Americans. Borrowing a Japanese-English dictionary from the library, he translates the company's slogan into Japanese, has it printed on company stationery, and asks you to spearhead a direct-mail campaign targeting Asian Americans. Do you agree with Jim's approach? Explain your answer. (Ch. Obj. 3, 5)

5. OK. You've talked Jim out of his direct-mail campaign to Asian Americans, but he decides nevertheless that a similar approach will work in the Hispanic market. He thus asks one of his managers, a New York woman whose family comes from Puerto Rico, to draft a letter in Spanish and do a mass mailing to Hispanics living in San Antonio, Texas. What is your opinion of this approach? (Ch. Obj. 3, 5)

6. Refer to the cultural stereotypes listed in TABLE 19.1. Now consider some individuals—either people you know personally or celebrities you have heard about. Make a list of those individuals who contradict the negative stereotypes given for each cultural group and gender. Include a sentence or two explaining why you feel that each individual on your list is an exception to the stereotype. Your instructor may want you to share your list with the class. (Ch. Obj. 3)

7. Think of an organization with which you're familiar—perhaps your workplace or a group to which you belong. Analyze this organization at three levels—personal, interpersonal, and organizational—to evaluate whether it is an entrenched organization. If so, in what way(s) is it entrenched? Who are the "mainstream" members and who are the outsiders? Explain your answer in a short written report. (Ch. Obj. 2, 3)

8. One evening you share a pizza with the leader of the organization in EXERCISE 7 and end up talking about the group's degree of entrenchment. The group leader is quite interested in your analysis of the organization and asks you to develop a diversity- training program to make the group less entrenched. Write a memo summarizing the key elements of your training program. (Ch. Obj. 2, 3, 9)

9. Discuss the ways in which differences in cultural communication patterns might lead to misunderstandings between Anglo and African Americans. How might these differences cause each group to stereotype the other? (Ch. Obj. 3, 4)

10. During the next week, listen carefully to conversations around you. See if you can find examples of "male" and "female" communication patterns as discussed in this chapter. Notice examples of report-talk/rapport-talk; asking for information/offering help; and powerful/powerless language. Write down your observations and explain how these conversations exemplify male and female communication patterns. Your instructor might want you to share your observations with the class. (Ch. Obj. 6)

11. What advantages and disadvantages do you see in the typical male patterns of communication? In the typical female patterns? Which approach might be more effective in the workplace of the 1990s? Explain your answer. (Ch. Obj. 1, 6)

12. The chapter notes that acceptable communication between people is marked by a high degree of "communication respect." What do you think this means? Explain why communication respect can reduce communication problems, whether between men and women or between people of different cultural groups. (Ch. Obj. 3, 7)

13. Interview a businessperson in your community about how his or her company meets the special needs of older and disabled customers and staff. What does the company do to make its physical facilities accessible? How does it meet the special communication needs of physically challenged people? Do you have any recommendations on how this company might improve its services to these people? Take notes during your interview; then write a report and turn it in to your instructor. (Ch. Obj. 8)

14. Refer to the discussion of diversity-training programs at Digital Equipment, Kinney Shoes, Avon, and Xerox. What features, if any, do they have in common? How do they differ? Which program sounds most promising to you? Explain your answer. (Ch. Obj. 9)

15. The chamber of commerce in your community has asked you to give a speech on "Diversity as a Business Strategy for the 1990s." Local businesspeople are interested in hearing your opinions on why diversity is an important issue. They'd like to know what makes a good diversity-training program and how such a program can affect their profitability. Write a one-page summary of your speech. (Ch. Obj. 1, 9)

BUILDING YOUR RESEARCH SKILLS

Suppose that your class is the entire staff of Smallco Sweats. CEO Jim Mason, who is a bit discouraged after you politely pointed out his mistakes in APPLICATION EXERCISES 4 and 5, has decided that market research is more important than he had realized. He has thus asked your class to split up into teams, each of which will focus on a potential customer segment. Possible customers include African Americans, Asian Americans, Hispanics, physically challenged people, the elderly, women, and Native Americans. Using sources other than this textbook, each group will read about the cultural values and communication patterns of its assigned customer segment. What factors are important in communicating with this segment? What should people do—and not do—when communicating with this customer base? Take notes on what you read so that you can report back to the group.

BUILDING YOUR TEAMWORK SKILLS

Reassemble into the groups you formed for the BUILDING YOUR RESEARCH SKILLS exercise. Working as a team, draft a memo to Jim Mason that summarizes the cultural values of your assigned customer segment and explains how these values influence communication patterns. Then appoint a group member to organize the group's notes into a finished draft of the memo. What guidelines can you suggest for communicating with the consumers in your assigned segment? Have your spokesperson present the memo to the class.

COMMUNICATING IN A WORLD OF DIVERSITY

The personal computer that you work on might well have come from Charlene Wang Chien's company. Born in Taiwan and educated in England and the United States, 42-year-old Chien worked for several years as a quality-control engineer in California. When her husband returned to Taiwan to teach at a university, Charlene started a computer-manufacturing firm there. Her reason, as she modestly puts it, was "to give me something to do." Within two years, First International Computer Company was turning such a profit that it also gave Charlene's husband something to do, too—he quit his teaching job and joined the firm to oversee technology.

Although Taiwan has a tight job market for skilled workers, First International has earned fierce loyalty from its employees. One reason is Charlene's talent for keeping in personal touch with her 800-person staff. She remembers their birthdays, visits them when they are ill, and loves to play matchmaker (so far she's fixed up fourteen couples who later married). Moreover, Charlene and her husband have given employees a 20-percent ownership share of the firm's stock.

Last year, First International doubled its annual sales to $115 million. But Charlene remains characteristically low-key about her success. "Any personal wealth we may have on paper," she maintains, "is secondary to the financial power we now have to expand the company."

Relate Charlene's management style to the chapter's discussion of communication patterns for Asians and women. In particular, how has Charlene's style—both as an Asian and a woman—contributed to her success?

Source: Louis Kraar, "Iron Butterflies," *Fortune*, October 7, 1991, pp. 143–154. © 1991 Time Inc. All rights reserved.

Saving Lives through Communication

In all too many U.S. cities, familiar social problems like drugs, poverty, and unemployment combine to make the lives of inner-city residents miserable. And of course violence can erupt, as it has happened in Miami, Los Angeles, and other urban areas with deadly results.

Can good communication help ease the hardships of inner-city life—indeed, help people stay alive? The Miami city government hopes so. After urban riots killed more than eighteen people in 1991, the city government began an innovative program that encourages frequent and focused communication among African-American, Anglo, and Hispanic community leaders. The Miami program includes a variety of initiatives. Minority leaders, top police officers, and government officials meet almost weekly to discuss ways to prevent urban violence. Several Miami police officers, for example, attended a course that taught them to apply the nonviolent principles of civil rights leader Martin Luther King, Jr., to potentially explosive conflicts.

Coordinators of the program also realize that when it comes to good communication, nothing succeeds like speaking the language of the people you're trying to reach. Toward this end, the Miami police have enlisted the help of rap artists to help them reach inner-city youths. According to Major Dan Flynn, the message that the department wants to convey is "take pride in your community. Don't burn your community."

The government has also called for help from more traditional media. On one occasion, for example, minority leaders and local media executives convened at a local community center to discuss ways of defusing urban tensions. One hot topic: the role played by the media in creating and perpetuating negative images of the inner city. Among other things, community leaders pointed out the need for increased attention to urban issues and more "good news" stories. Schools are getting involved, too. Tony Lesesne, a ninth-grade English teacher, has devoted several class periods to discussing urban violence with his students. "I tell them I don't want to see them on TV," says Lesesne. "One of the things I try to make them learn is that you can get killed out there."

So far, the city's efforts have prevented a deadly recap of riots in Miami and other cities. The police department's close working relationship with community groups, says Police Chief Calvin Ross, "went a long way when Los Angeles erupted." Miami, adds Assistant Police Chief Donald Marsh, "is prepared for the worst and hoping for the best."

Questions and Applications

1. Discuss the roles that may be played by prejudice and cultural misunderstanding in urban violence.
2. Summarize several steps that the Miami city government is taking to improve communication among cultural groups.
3. Can you think of any other steps the city government might take to promote good cross-cultural communication?

Source: Jose de Cordoba, "Long, Hot Summer?" *The Wall Street Journal*, July 7, 1992, pp. A1, A5. Reprinted by permission. © 1992, Dow Jones & Company, Inc. All rights reserved.

Sexual Harassment, Unfortunately, Is Alive and Well

Recently the Pentagon released its first major study of sexual harassment in the military—and the results are not encouraging. According to the study, 64 percent of women in the U.S. Armed Forces said they had been sexually harassed in some way. Sometimes the harassment was relatively subtle, involving leering, teasing, and name-calling. More than one-third of the women surveyed, however, had experienced more serious forms of harassment—touching, pressure for sexual favors, and even rape. (Do not assume, by the way, that sexual harassment is just a "woman's problem." Seventeen percent of the men in the Armed Forces admitted that they, too, had been harassed by military personnel, both male and female.)

The Pentagon report agrees with other studies of sexual harassment in the military. The U.S. Naval Academy, for instance, found that sexual harassment is widespread on the Annapolis campus. Many victims never complain, however, because they're afraid of reprisals from the harassers or their friends.

How do these statistics compare to those from private industry? Surveys reveal that 30 percent to 40 percent of businesswomen and 14 percent to 15 percent of businessmen have been sexually harassed. Why are the military's figures higher? Perhaps because there is a smaller percentage of women in the Armed Forces than in private business. Generally, the higher the percentage of minorities in a group, the lower the rate of harassment.

Over the past decade, the military has introduced new policies to help integrate women more equitably into the Armed Forces. Recent studies indicate, however, that policies are frequently unenforced or ineffective. Perhaps working against the success of official policy is what the women surveyed describe as a work atmosphere that simultaneously discourages men—subtly or not so subtly—from treating their female co-workers as equal colleagues.

"The results are sobering," admits Christopher Jehn, assistant secretary of defense for management and personnel. "These numbers are clearly too high . . . We've got to redouble our efforts to bring the numbers down. The policy is clear: Sexual harassment will not be tolerated." Jehn notes that the Pentagon plans to conduct another survey in two or three years to measure the military's progress.

Questions and Applications

1. Would you consider the Armed Forces an entrenched organization? Who are the mainstream members and who are the outsiders? Explain your answer.

2. Sexual harassment is clearly a problem for the people who experience it. Explain why it is also a problem for the Armed Forces in general or for any organization in which it occurs.

3. Suppose that you are an independent consultant specializing in organizational communication and sexual-harassment issues. The Pentagon asks you to assess the situation and develop a training program to reduce the rate of sexual harassment among current members of the military. Write a one-page report summarizing this program.

Source: Susan L. Webb, Pacific Resource Development Group, Inc. Seattle, WA.

Mastering Communication Technology

CHAPTER OBJECTIVES

After studying this chapter, you should be able to:

1 List the benefits of *communication technology.*

2 Identify the six *communication functions* performed by computers.

3 Explain the advantages of writing with a *word processor.*

4 Outline the ways in which computers are used as *telecommunications tools.*

5 Explain how databases, presentation graphics, desktop publishing, computer printers, photocopiers, and facsimile machines can improve communication.

6 Identify the features, advantages, and disadvantages of *voice mail.*

7 Explain how *electronic meetings* are conducted through *teleconferences* and *videoconferences.*

8 Explain the impact on business travel of cellular phones, pagers, and laptop and palmtop computers.

9 Describe the phenomenon of *telecommuting* and how to overcome its pitfalls.

THE MANAGER AS COMMUNICATION CENTER

Philippe Kahn, founder and CEO of Borland International, a $500-million Scotts Valley, California–based software company, is a communication-technology addict. It is not only his business but also his passion to make technology work for him wherever he happens to be.

Kahn manages Borland through a heavy reliance on electronic mail, a computer-to-computer message-transmission system that uses both cellular and ordinary telephone lines. He transmits regularly from Auckland, New Zealand, Paris, New York, or from a hilltop near his Scotts Valley office. Sitting under a tree in the California sun, Kahn connects his portable laptop computer to a cellular telephone and communicates with employees, suppliers, and current and potential clients.

Although Kahn believes that most face-to-face meetings waste time, he is in constant touch electronically with managers at Borland's eleven subsidiaries and three sales offices around the world. Indeed, he welcomes electronic communication and often allots three hours a day to answer as many as 150 messages from employees whom he rarely meets. A confessed insomniac, Kahn often keys in messages as late as 2 a.m. He also uses travel time to his advantage, preparing presentation slides on his laptop as he makes his way cross-country aboard late-night red-eye flights.

Kahn rarely lets anything stand in the way of getting messages where he wants them to go. He has been known to connect his laptop to hotel phone lines by disassembling permanent telephone connections in the wall. He routinely carries a soldering iron, screwdrivers, and pliers to make his work easier. While performing this task a few years ago in a Paris hotel located across the street from the U.S. embassy, a room service attendant reported Kahn's strange actions to hotel managers. Ten minutes later, eight French and American security officers barged into his room, demanding to know what he was doing with tools under the table. Kahn recalls that he was interrogated for half an hour before they realized he was not a spy.

Although Kahn usually reconnects hotel phone jacks, he sometimes leaves his handiwork in place, reasoning that the next time he registers, he may be able to request the same room and avoid the inconvenience of creating his own communication center from scratch.[1]

CHAPTER OVERVIEW

Although Philippe Kahn is a master at making communication technology work for him, the same equipment that allows him easy access to people all over the world is available to most businesspeople: As offices become increasingly computerized, paper messages are being replaced by messages created and transmitted via computers. Sophisticated computer printers then make copies that facsimile machines disseminate through data and phone lines.

Technology is also changing business conversation. Paging and voice-mail systems, cellular telephones, teleconferencing, and videoconferencing make it possible to keep in touch at any time of the day or night from anywhere in the world. These communication technologies give businesspeople the freedom to leave the office without fear of missing an important call or meeting.

This chapter examines ways in which technology is changing business communication. We will discuss the links between written and oral communication and technology and examine how technology is transforming the nature of business travel. We will also examine the phenomenon of *telecommuting*, which allows businesspeople to work from home and a variety of other non-office locations. We begin by identifying the benefits that communication technology has brought to the workplace.

BENEFITS OF COMMUNICATION TECHNOLOGY

Communication technology has revolutionized the workplace by allowing people to send messages faster and more efficiently than ever before. In the same way, technology has influenced today's global marketplace. As you can see in Table 20.1, hundreds of millions of messages—many of them traveling around the world—are sent and received via telephone, electronic mail, and voice mail by just one company—Eastman Kodak. Bruce Hoeffel, executive director of international human resources at 3M, sums up the impact of new technologies like faxes and electronic mail on global communication: "The speed of communications that we have today has greatly aided the ability of the manager to perform global work without working 24 hours a day."[2]

The process of creating, organizing, and distributing messages is also made more efficient through the use of technology. Here are just a few examples:

- Word processors allow business writers to insert and delete material and move blocks of text from one point to another with the stroke of a key. Revisions are easily inserted to produce clean, finished copy.

TABLE 20.1 *Telecommunication Needs at Eastman Kodak*	
TELECOMMUNICATION NEED	NUMBER
Monthly long-distance phone calls within the U.S.	1,100,000
Monthly long-distance international calls	50,000
Minutes spent annually on long-distance international calls	4,500,000
Minutes of customer calls annually to Kodak's 800 numbers	60,000,000
Telephones in Kodak's U.S. offices	50,000
Telephones in Kodak's foreign offices	10,000
Worldwide Kodak employees using electronic mail	59,987
Electronic messages sent in one year	103,000,000
Kodak voice-mail users	28,000
Messages received each year on voice mail	21,800,000

Source: Data reported in Joan E. Rigdon, "Crossed Wires: Phone Service Overseas Provides a Mixed Picture, Kodak Finds," *The Wall Street Journal*, October 6, 1991, p. R6.

- Facsimile machines reduce dead time to a bare minimum. Instead of writing a letter and waiting for the mail to deliver it—a process that can waste days—message delivery via fax machines or electronic mail is immediate. Responses to messages can then proceed without delay.
- Teleconferences and videoconferences allow meetings to take place without the expense or inconvenience of business travel.

Despite such advantages, however, the benefits of communication technology are not being fully realized at thousands of firms, both small owner-managed businesses and giant corporations. Instead of delivering a promised "paper free" business environment, the new technology still encounters resistance from people at all organizational levels, many of whom find equipment and applications intimidating. Electronic mail, for example, continues to be a problem for many would-be users at the ice cream headquarters of Ben & Jerry's Homemade in Waterbury, Vermont. Only 30 percent of the staff uses a system that was installed several years ago. "There are too many options," says inventory coordinator Christopher Lamotte, "and every option has suboptions. It's easier to just pick up the telephone."[3]

This chapter will familiarize you with the technology likely to be found in today's workplace and will explain how various systems can increase productivity. As you study this chapter, however, keep in mind that for all its advantages, there are times when communication technology is the wrong choice. Videoconferences, faxes, and electronic mail are frequently no substitute for personal visits to establish trust and personal ties. When a major manufacturing problem arose in Japan, for example, Xerox representative Brian Stern flew there to resolve the difficulty face-to-face—even though he could have held a videoconference from his offices in Stamford, Connecticut. Stern believes that when the stakes are high, personal contact is critical. Similarly, Xerox CEO Paul Allaire personally visits major potential clients to win contracts. His goal is to emphasize, through his presence, that Xerox stands behind its products.[4]

WRITTEN COMMUNICATION AND TECHNOLOGY

Communication technology has transformed the world of business writing. Word processing, computer networking, database management, presentation graphics, and desktop-publishing capabilities make creating and revising documents much faster and simpler. High-speed printers, facsimile machines, and copy machines have also become essential in today's workplace.

In the following sections, we will examine in detail the evolving relationship between technology and the written word, including the function of the computer as data manager and word processor and the range of options available in contemporary telecommunications. We will also describe the advent of *presentation graphics* and *desktop publishing* and survey developments in such technologies as photocopiers and fax machines.

Computers and the Written Word

There is a world market for about five computers.

Thomas J. Watson
Founder, IBM Corp.

IBM introduced the first personal computer in 1981, hoping to sell perhaps 250,000 machines over the life of the product. A decade later, more than 55 million personal computers had been purchased in the United States and another 55 million around the world.[5]

In today's business world, personal computers have six primary functions, all of which involve some aspect of communication: storing, retrieving, editing, displaying, printing, and transmitting data.

STORING DATA   Computers act like giant filing cabinets, storing letters, memos, reports, proposals, and other data on magnetic disks. The most obvious

Today's business professionals employ a dazzling array of communication tools to perform their jobs and serve their customers. This real estate agent uses a tiny Apple computer to match available homes with specifications provided by her clients. Instead of searching through volumes of printed listings covering an entire metropolitan area, she can supply her clients—almost instantly—with vivid descriptions of a variety of properties.
Source: © 1992 Apple Computer; used by permission.

advantage of storing data in a computer rather than on paper is that disks take up very little space.

RETRIEVING DATA   Because the data are kept in separate files on magnetic disks, data can also be easily and quickly retrieved. In addition, disk storage provides a lightweight, and usually cheaper, method of mailing data for retrieval on computers in different locations. A few keystrokes will yield needed data.

EDITING DATA   Once data is retrieved, it appears on the computer screen. Data can then be revised by rearranging it, adding or deleting material, changing the format, and so on. For example, you may decide that the last paragraph of a sales report is better suited to your introduction, that more current sales figures should be entered, or that reference to a problem that has been resolved should be deleted from the report. Again, correcting and polishing your document can be handled in a few keystrokes.

DISPLAYING DATA   The ability of computers to display data in different ways can be helpful both in analyzing it and in presenting it to an audience. For example, using a presentation-graphics program allows sales figures to be presented in the form of bar charts, pie charts, line charts, or other pictorial representations. These and other visual aids were examined more fully in Chapter 11.

PRINTING DATA   Computer instructions tell the printer to produce *hard copy* (a computer printout) with any number of different features. For example, you can

The newest computer can merely compound, at speed, the oldest problem in the relations between human beings, and in the end, the communicator will be confronted with the old problem of what to say and how to say it.

Edward R. Murrow
CBS news correspondent

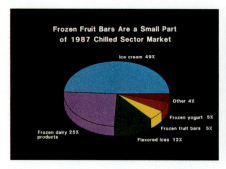

(a)

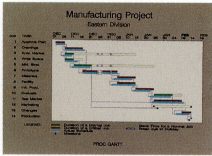

(b)

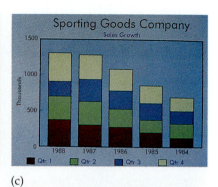

(c)

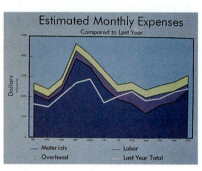

(d)

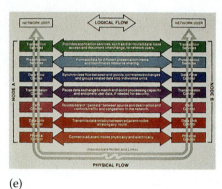

(e)

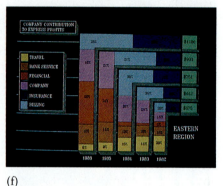

(f)

Today's user-friendly presentation-graphics software allows business people to create a wide array of attractive and informative visual aids. The computer-generated charts in this layout should all be recognizable from Chapter 11: (a) pie, (b) grouped bar, (c) subdivided column, (d) grouped line, (e) flow, and (f) subdivided column and bar. Dedicated presentation-graphics packages offer such additional features as three dimensions and tools for creative customizing (for example, embellishing charts with clip art). Another recent feature, dynamic show capability, permits such strategies as movie-like transitions between visual aids and even enhancing them with animation.

instruct the computer to use **boldface** type or *italics*, to print multiple copies of the same document, or to merge information from two different sources. This last function is helpful in "personalizing" form letters.

TRANSMITTING DATA   Information can be transmitted from one computer to another through **telecommunications**—the process by which information is converted into electrical impulses, transmitted through ordinary telephone or high-speed data lines, and reconverted by a receiving computer into usable information. As we will see, telecommunications is the basis for electronic mail, electronic bulletin boards, and on-line databases.[6]

We will focus next on several specific communication functions, including word processing and telecommunications. We will also survey options offered by databases, presentation graphics, desktop-publishing programs, and printing programs in producing more professional business documents.

Writing with a Word Processor

IBM coined the term **word processor** in 1964 to refer to a program that transforms a computer into a sophisticated electronic typewriter. While the earliest word processors were machines dedicated to this single task, today's word-processing software is typically used in general-purpose desktop computer systems.

Word processors serve a number of indispensable functions for business writers. They are typically used in note taking and in the organization, drafting and development, revising and editing, proofreading, and formatting of documents.[7]

telecommunications
Process by which information is converted into electrical impulses transmitted through ordinary telephone or high-speed data lines and then reconverted by a receiver into usable information

word processor
General-purpose desktop computer system used for a variety of sophisticated typewriter-like functions in creating, analyzing, and revising information documents

NOTE TAKING   Rather than relying on hand-written cards that can be easily lost, it is often more efficient to take notes on a computer as you gather research material for proposals or reports. Ideas and changes can be entered as they occur without limiting what or how you write.

DOCUMENT ORGANIZATION   Once data has been gathered and stored in your computer, it can be easily arranged by moving notes from one point to another. Many software programs automatically number footnotes and endnotes, so that rearranging information does not involve the task of renumbering your notes manually. The ability to reorganize your material is not only helpful in the creation of documents but invaluable in the later stages of document development, when changes are often necessary.

DRAFTING AND DEVELOPMENT   As a document-drafting tool, the computer provides enormous flexibility. For example, you can start to write at any point in your document—the beginning, middle, or end—and insert surrounding material later. Because the computer accomodates addition, deletion, and reorganization by moving sections around, your introduction can be coordinated with the body of your document and entered after everything else is complete.

REVISING AND EDITING   You can also make revising and editing documents fast and painless simply by using the function keys located on your computer keyboard. For example, assume that after drafting a letter to a new client, you decide that you would like the second paragraph to be included in every letter sent to new clients. Because your second paragraph can be stored and retrieved any number of times and moved to another specified document, you can simply retrieve it from one file and put it in another.

Stylistic and grammatical editing uses the same process. For example, using a "search-and-replace" feature allows you to locate specific words or phrases each time they appear so that you can automatically replace them with preferred words or phrases. If you want to change the term *underdeveloped countries* to *lesser-developed countries* in a document on international bank loans, you can simply instruct the computer to search and replace one term with the other every time the unwanted term appears. However, caution is advised if the replacement term can have more than one meaning. For example, instructing the computer to replace the term *black* with the term *African-American* may result in the sort of inadvertent error illustrated in these two sentences:

Sentence 1:   I suggest a new line of *black* velvet evening dresses for the fall season.

Sentence 2:   I suggest a new line of *African-American* velvet evening dresses for the fall season.

Word processors are also capable of producing foreign letters, accent marks, mathematical expressions, and graphical symbols. Here are several examples:

@   é   ñ   ß   ≤   ¥   £

PROOFREADING   Most word-processing programs include a "spell-check" feature that finds and corrects spelling mistakes. The program compares words used in your document against a built-in dictionary; questionable entries are highlighted for subsequent correction. Because spell-check features do not recognize proper names, abbreviations, and many technical terms, many programs allow the creation of "customer dictionaries" through the addition of specialized or frequently used words. A spell-check that has been modified in this manner will not, for example, reject as errors the names of Mr. Higgenbottom and Ms. Posner, two important clients with whom you correspond regularly.

FORMATTING   Here are just a few of the ways in which word processors enable you to control the appearance of your document:

- Setting left, right, top, and bottom margins
- Centering words or phrases
- Creating headers or footers (document identifications appearing at the top or bottom of the page)
- Automatically numbering pages at either the top or bottom of every page or every other page
- Aligning text on the right margin
- Indenting blocks of text
- Adding endnotes at the end of documents or footnotes at the bottom of appropriate pages
- Creating columns similar to those in newspapers or magazines
- Using a variety of typestyles (such as *italics* and **boldface**) and fonts (such as Helvetica or *script* in various sizes)

A computer does not substitute for judgment any more than a pencil substitutes for literacy. But writing without a pencil is no particular advantage.

Robert McNamara
American executive
and statesman

USING YOUR WORD PROCESSOR TO IMPROVE YOUR WRITING   The following suggestions will help improve the quality and speed of writing on a word processor:

1. During the drafting stage, practice "free writing," a process in which thoughts are entered into the computer as soon as they occur. Do not stop to correct spelling or grammatical errors, to make stylistic changes, or reorganize your ideas.

2. Consider printing out a paper copy of the document and making revisions on your hard copy. Incorporate final changes into the computer.

3. Make adequate revisions but limit the time spent fine-tuning your document. Spending too much time finding the right word or phrase is counterproductive.

4. Use the search command to locate and eliminate overused or wordy phrases like *the fact that* and *there are.*

5. Proofread your document twice—once on the computer screen and once on paper. Often, mistakes you miss on the screen will be obvious on your printout.

6. Learn to merge information from two or more files. For example, merging a form letter with a database of thousands of names and addresses produces personalized letters to everyone on the list.

7. Use consistent type styles for headings. For example, you may decide to use boldface each time a client's firm is mentioned.

Using the Computer as a Telecommunications Tool

The power of the personal computer lets you share ideas with others who are part of a communication network. Using a device known as a modem and special communication software, computers can send messages back and forth in the form of electronic mail and mail posted on electronic bulletin boards. A **modem** is a special device used to convert computer signals into signals that can travel by telephone lines to another computer. The same system can be used to tap into rich sources of information through such on-line databases as Dow Jones News/Retrieval or NEXIS.

modem
Special device used to convert computer signals to signals that can travel by telephone lines to another computer

electronic mail (E-mail)
Computerized mail service enabling users to transmit messages and documents instantaneously over telephone and data lines from one computer to another

ELECTRONIC MAIL   **Electronic mail,** or **E-mail,** is a computerized mail service that enables users to transmit messages and documents instantaneously over telephone and data lines from one computer to another anywhere in the world. In many companies today, all employees are connected to the same E-mail system.

The system works in the following way. Messages are sent using a modem to call up the computer's electronic-mail function. The sender is then given access to the system by inserting a special password. After the computer is instructed where to send the message, the text is entered and transmitted.

PRACTICAL TIPS
Avoiding Computer Viruses

Most people would probably identify Michelangelo as either a great Italian artist or, if they keep up with the popular culture, a Teenage Mutant Ninja Turtle. After March 6, 1992, however, the name Michelangelo took on new meaning when it became associated with a powerful computer virus with the potential to destroy years of reports, memos, letters, proposals, and other crucial business documents stored in computer memories around the world.

Computer viruses, including the Michelangelo virus, are computer programs that can destroy everything in a computer's memory bank. Created by talented but misguided computer programmers, they are passed from one computer to another through shared computer disks and over telephone lines. The Michelangelo virus, for example, was passed from one computer to another by disk but lay dormant in infected computers until March 6—the famous artist's birthday. Triggered to life when infected computers were turned on, the virus wiped out programs and files by writing over the hard disk, making data recovery virtually impossible. Those affected found entire word-processing and database files destroyed.

Although March 6, 1992, has come and gone, viruses remain a threat to everyone who uses a computer as a communication tool. For example, the *Friday the 13th* virus strikes every time that day appears on the calendar. *Stoned,* currently the most common computer virus, flashes this message on computer screens: "Your computer is now stoned. Legalize marijuana."

There are several ways to deal with computer viruses. The most drastic method is to isolate your computer by refusing to trade diskettes and avoiding communication networks. Because most businesspeople consider this solution impossible, many find it more feasible to copy computer files onto separate disks. If a virus destroys the computer's data, backups are at hand.

Many computer users periodically run "antivirus" programs that can detect the presence of a virus and destroy it before it causes damage. Once a week is usually sufficient for users who frequently trade diskettes or who subscribe to on-line telecommunications systems.

In the early spring of 1992, although reports of problems were received from countries as far away as South Africa, the Michelangelo virus ultimately produced little worldwide damage, destroying only a few dozen valuable files. Ironically, although its purpose was destruction, the results of the scare were positive in at least one sense. The episode alerted all computer users to the fact that data safety—without precautions—is an illusion.

Sources: Peter H. Lewis, "Safety in Virus Season," *The New York Times,* March 3, 1992, p. C8; Michael W. Miller, "High-Tech Hysteria Grips U.S.; Skylab? No, Michelangelo," *The Wall Street Journal,* March 6, 1992, p. A1; and Michael Rogers, "Not Too Much of a Headache," *Newsweek,* March 16, 1992, p. 60.

Messages are held in a recipient's electronic "mailbox" and can be viewed only with the proper identification. The same message can also be sent simultaneously to different people. Mailboxes can be checked for messages at any time, day or night.

A combination laptop computer and modem also increase mobility because messages can be transmitted via regular and cellular telephones from hotels, airports, homes, and other scattered sites. Systems can also be connected to fax machines that receive and print out electronic messages.

Electronic mail has become the backbone of many business communication systems. During a recent year, for example, some 15 billion electronic-mail messages were sent.[8] At Microsoft Corp., E-mail is considered "the lifeblood of the company." All employees are encouraged not only to pass ideas and information to one another via the computer but also to send messages directly to founder and CEO Bill Gates, who is himself a champion of constant electronic contact.[9] E-mail helps Apple Computer keep in touch with customers who can submit questions and comments over a system known as AppleLink. CEO John Sculley uses the same system to answer about a dozen messages a day, something he probably would not do if he had to use the phone.

USING ELECTRONIC MAIL   Although electronic mail should be viewed as another form of paper mail, users do not always approach it with the same professional standards or attention to detail. According to Sara Kiesler, a communications researcher at Carnegie Mellon University, E-mail etiquette has not been able to keep up with the fast pace of changing technology. By contrast, the printed word has long been governed by widely accepted rules of etiquette. Kiesler uses the following analogy to explain her point: "It's like all of a sudden there is this park in the middle of my company, and the park is open and there are no hours posted, so anybody can go into the park and cavort."[10]

Here are some suggestions for the more efficient companywide use of an E-mail system:

- Organize every letter and memo to be transmitted via E-mail according to the same format used in paper documents. The message displayed on the recipient's computer terminal should not contain any formatting surprises.
- Just as you would not send a printed document with spelling or grammatical errors, don't send E-mail with these mistakes either. Carefully proofread every document. If you find it difficult to catch errors on a computer screen, proofread a printout.

The threat to business communication from computer viruses is substantial enough to have created a small industry designed to combat them. Anti-virus software from Central Point is widely used in the prevention and detection of hundreds of viruses, including the Friday-the-13th Virus (top row, center) and the Stoned Virus (middle row, left).
Source: © 1992 Central Point Software, Inc.; used by permission.

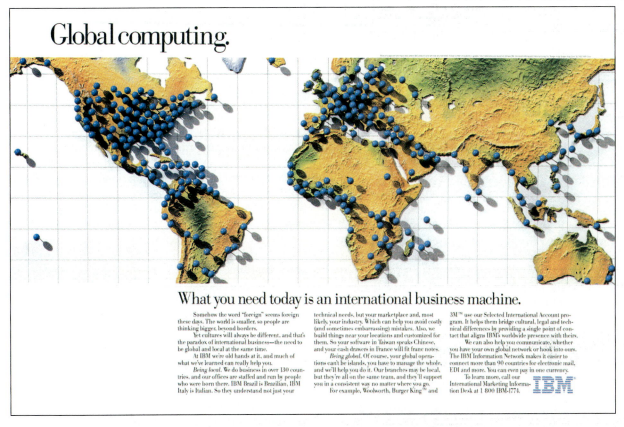

Multinational firms like computer giant IBM make it possible for other organizations to communicate through electronic mail on a global scale. IBM's Information Network can install E-mail networks that link employees, suppliers, and customers located across six continents and more than 90 countries
Source: © 1992 IBM Corp.; used by permission.

- Never use the system to vent your rage. One worker recently denounced 300 people at once over his company's E-mail system after discovering that someone had broken his motor scooter's kickstand in the company parking lot. According to Judith Martin, author of the syndicated "Miss Manners" newspaper column, profanities and anger are best left out of all business communication. "No electronic invention, whether in the present or the future, would make it prudent to scold someone. It's not like we have this new technology and suddenly there are no rules anymore."[11]
- Use E-mail for what it is intended—to transmit business communication in a fast, reliable way. Do not use it for gossip or small talk or personal business.

Implementing suggestions like these will be easier if you remind yourself that a person—not just a computer—is on the receiving end of your electronic message.

ELECTRONIC BULLETIN BOARDS   Much like their corkboard predecessors, **electronic bulletin boards** are public message centers that appear on computer networks. While electronic mail is intended for one recipient, electronic bulletin board messages are intended for anyone and everyone with access to the network. Companies like H&R Block, General Electric, IBM, and Sears operate commercial bulletin boards that serve millions of participants (H&R Block owns CompuServe, GE operates Genie, and IBM and Sears jointly own Prodigy). Currently, an estimated 45,000 bulletin boards connect computer users worldwide.[12]

Using a modem, the appropriate communication software, and a specially assigned password, computer users can connect their computers to the electronic

electronic bulletin board
Public message center that appears on computer networks

ETHICAL ISSUES IN BUSINESS COMMUNICATION

E-Mail and the Issue of Privacy

Alana Shoars arrived at work early one morning to find her supervisor at Epson America reading other employees' electronic mail. When she questioned the practice, she was fired for insubordination. "You don't read other people's mail," Shoars still maintains, "just as you don't listen to their phone conversations. Right is right, and wrong is wrong."

Or is it? The law is not clear. The Federal Electronic Communication Privacy Act of 1986 protects the privacy of electronic messages sent over such public networks as MCI Mail, SprintMail, and AT&T's EasyLink. But it does not protect messages sent through a company's internal communication system. Moreover, it is rare for a company's written code of ethics to address issues of communication technology.

Michael Simmons, chief information officer at the Bank of Boston, argues that it is in a company's best interest to review employees' electronic messages: "If the corporation owns the equipment and pays for the network, that asset belongs to the company, and it has a right to look and see if people are using it for purposes other than running the businesses." While monitoring the system at a previous job, Simmons discovered one employee using the computer to evaluate horses and place bets and another running his Amway business. Both were fired.

On the other hand, monitoring messages may still pose an ethical dilemma. According to Mitchell Kapor, former chairman of Lotus Development, the problem arises because E-mail falls somewhere between telephone calls and written correspondence. "Most business people," says Kapor, "feel comfortable with an employer's right to examine written material but wouldn't sanction listening in on phone conversations."

Companies like Federal Express, American Airlines, Pacific Bell, and United Parcel Service try to handle the problem by advising all employees that the company reserves the right to monitor messages. According to critics, however, this approach may satisfy lawyers but not those concerned with ethics. "Even if a company does post notice, is that something it should do?" asks Eugene Spafford, a computer science professor at Purdue University. "The legal question may be answered, but is it ethical? The company may say it is, but the employees say it isn't, and there's a conflict."

Source: Glenn Rifkin, "Do Employees Have a Right to Electronic Privacy?" *The New York Times,* December 8, 1991, p. F8.

network that contains the bulletin board. After entering the bulletin board, users are faced with a menu of options, including the ability to send and receive messages. This technology is also often used as a medium for sharing ideas within a business organization or government office.

Whether a bulletin board operates within a company or within a network containing several hundred thousand subscribers, all users face limitations on what they can and cannot say. These limitations were highlighted a few years ago after the Anti-Defamation League of the B'nai B'rith criticized Prodigy for carrying a series of anti-Semitic messages. Soon after, Prodigy announced a policy banning messages that are "grossly repugnant to community standards."[13]

database
Set of logically related computer files that can be accessed for different purposes

ON-LINE DATABASES   Many systems that offer electronic bulletin boards also offer on-line **databases:** commercially owned information sources that can be accessed through personal computers. As we saw in Chapter 10, on-line databases can be invaluable sources of business research. For example, you can get economic and business information through Dow Jones News/Retrieval, Dialog Information Service, and Nexus.

Although using an on-line database can be expensive (fees are based on time used), many firms subscribe because they feel that the available information is an essential business tool. Information can be accessed faster and more efficiently than through conventional means—a fact that makes employees more productive. Generally, on-line database computer searches are also more extensive than conventional compilations of data.

Computers are going to become as necessary to the business world as air.

Andrew Grove
President, Intel Corporation

Organizational Databases

Using database software, you can create your own information files that can be tapped in different ways. A **database** is a set of logically related computer files that can be accessed for different purposes. For example, a database may contain the names, addresses, phone numbers, and purchasing activity of all past and current customers. Databases help businesspeople write form letters and reports and generate mailing labels.

- *Form Letters.* A generic form letter like the one shown in Figure 20.1 (A) indicates where personal information is to be inserted. When the computer merges this letter with the database, it produces a customized final copy (B).

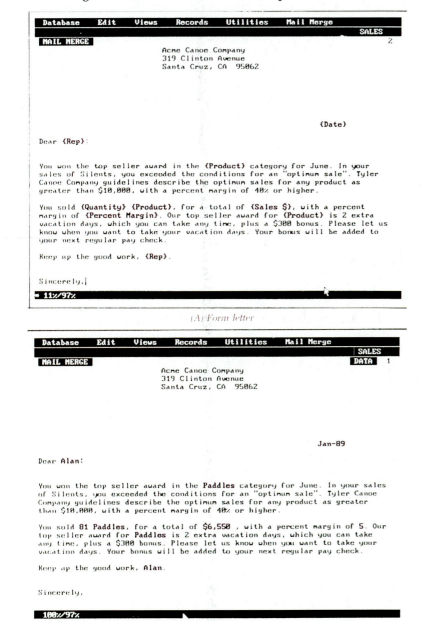

FIGURE 20.1   *Using a Database to Produce Customized Personal Letters*

- *Reports.* A database can also transfer critical information from a computer to a business report. For example, if you want to include a table showing the sales of each salesperson by type of product during a recent month, you can instruct the database to transfer this information to the table automatically.
- *Mailing labels.* The computer can be instructed to print out names and addresses on a roll of mailing labels. This function is especially valuable to businesses requiring bulk mailing and to individuals who correspond daily with dozens of people.

Presentation Graphics and Desktop Publishing

presentation-graphics software
Special computer programs used to create such visual aids as bar charts, line charts, pie charts, tables, drawings, and other graphics features by using data already in the computer

desktop publishing
Use of personal computers to design and lay out both text and accompanying graphics to produce camera-ready copies of a document

Presentation-graphics software allows sophisticated bar charts, line charts, pie charts, and other graphics features to be created by using data already in the computer. High-quality graphics are especially important in business reports and proposals. Graphics software also allows the transfer of color images to blank acetates via a computer printer. During an oral presentation, an overhead projector can then display the acetate cell on a larger screen.

Desktop-publishing systems make possible the production of professional-quality documents in the office. **Desktop publishing** refers to the use of personal computers to design and lay out both text and accompanying graphics to produce camera-ready copies of a document. This copy can then be duplicated by office copying machines or through commercial offset printing. Desktop publishing reduces both the time and cost of preparing camera-ready copy.

COMPUTER PRINTERS   Computer printers move words and images from the computer screen to the printed page. They are used in business offices to generate letters, memos, reports, proposals, and other documents. Printers can generate single or multiple copies of each page. Print quality depends to a large extent on the type of printer used. The most common type, the *dot-matrix printer*, forms each character by printing a pattern of dots. The higher the number of dots per inch, the higher the quality of the printed product.

Daisywheel printers produce characters that look as if they have been printed on a conventional typewriter—a personal touch that can be an advantage in certain correspondence. While daisywheel printers cannot produce sophisticated graphics, *inkjet printers* that spray ink onto the page at very high speeds are excellent for producing graphics programs. *Laser printers*, the most advanced printers available for personal computers, use the same process as copy machines to produce high-quality images on paper. Laser printers can produce text and sophisticated graphics, including drawings and photographs.

Printers differ in speed and in the ability to produce color reproductions. While laser printers can produce eight to ten pages per minute, other printers are much slower. Color is also becoming an important differentiating factor in the choice of computer printers. Although no desktop printer can compete with the pages that roll off a high-resolution printing press, the images produced by office machines are generally acceptable for business presentations. Figure 20.2 shows how images compare. While the images at the top of the figure are made with expensive machines that are not yet likely to be found in most business offices, the images at the bottom are made by machines that are becoming increasingly accessible.

Other Technologies

Both photocopiers and facsimile machines can duplicate original documents. The photocopier (or "Xerox machine") has been a staple in business offices for

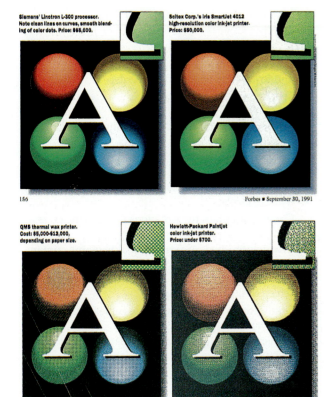

FIGURE 20.2 *Comparing Quality in Color Printers*

many years. Although the "fax" machine began appearing in offices only within the past decade, it has already revolutionized the work place.

PHOTOCOPIERS   Using a variety of processes that may include chemicals, lights, and lasers, **photocopiers** scan original documents to produce duplicates. Most office machines will accept originals and then collate copies in their proper order. The latest generation of copiers print in color as well as black-and-white. Some models, like the Xerox 5775 digital color copier, even allow users to create color copies from black-and-white originals. A small business personal copier, such as the models made by Canon, Mita, Sharp, and Xerox, can usually meet the document-duplication needs of smaller organizations.

FACSIMILE MACHINES   **Facsimile machines,** or **fax machines,** can be thought of in a broad sense as long-distance photocopiers. They are electronic devices that can copy and transmit original material, including text and graphics, to other machines in other locations.

Facsimile machines have changed the speed at which written communication is shared. Because documents can be transmitted by fax at the speed of a telephone call, it is no longer necessary to wait several days—or even overnight—for mail delivery. Instantaneous transmission is especially important in international business transactions—unreliable mail service can delay decisions or even cause proposed agreements to fail.

As we will see later in this chapter, fax machines are now being used in a number of innovative ways. Portable faxes, for example, give business travelers the ability to transmit documents from a variety of locations, including their cars. Fax machines are also becoming standard equipment in many video- and teleconferences to transmit documents to which participants at different locations must refer.

Table 20.2 summarizes the major communication technologies for business writers and identifies their most important uses.

Gutenberg made everybody a reader. Xerox makes everybody a publisher.

*Marshall McLuhan
Canadian communications
theorist*

facsimile (or **fax**) **machine**
Electronic device that can copy and transmit original material, including text and graphics, to other machines in other locations

TABLE 20.2	*Communication Technologies for Business Writers*
TECHNOLOGY	USES
Word-processing software	Developing, drafting, revising, proofreading, and formatting written documents
Electronic mail	Sending and receiving messages via computer networks
Electronic bulletin boards	Sharing information with other bulletin-board users
On-line databases	Providing excellent sources of current business research
Databases	Providing easy access to data in computer files needed to write letters and reports and create mailing labels
Presentation-graphics software	Creating graphics presentations that enhance written reports
Desktop publishing	Creating finished, profession-quality manuscript in the form of camera-ready copy
Computer printers	Transferring words and images from the computer screen to the printed page
Photocopiers	Duplicating single and multiple copies of original material
Facsimile machines	Transmitting original materials instantly over long distances

PROGRESS CHECK

1. What is a word processor? Explain its importance.
2. Define *telecommunications*. Name some technologies that involve telecommunications.
3. Cover up the "Uses" column in Table 20.2. Mentally fill in the information to test your understanding of what you have just read.

The computer revolution is the most advertised revolution in world history. Yet one of the funny things about it is that we probably still underestimate its impact.

Herman Kahn
American futurist

ORAL COMMUNICATIONS AND TECHNOLOGY

Just as technology is transforming the way in which words are written and delivered to receivers, it is also having a similar impact on oral communications. *Voice mail, cellular phones,* and *electronic meetings* like teleconferences and videoconferences all offer businesspeople new tools for conducting more productive conversations and meetings in the 1990s.

Voice Mail

voice mail
Computer-based call-processing system that handles both incoming and outgoing calls

Voice mail is quickly replacing the answering machine as a device for handling telephone messages. **Voice mail** is a computer-based call-processing system that handles both incoming and outgoing calls. Special computer chips and software convert the human voice into a digital code that can be stored on the computer's magnetic disks. The code can then be retrieved at any time for playback. Depending on the system, voice mail can help in the following ways:

- Voice mail allows messages to be recorded and coded for receivers with particular access codes. For example, if you are out of the office and want to inform a business client when a meeting is scheduled, you can give the client your code and leave a voicemail message.
- It allows messages to be recorded and saved in a "mailbox." A voice-mail

system can also forward messages to another location and/or to other individuals within the organization.

- Voice-mail messages can be distributed to a number of people simultaneously. For example, W. Thomas Stephens, CEO of Manville Corp., uses voice mail to send monthly messages to employees and to receive their responses.

- Voice-mail systems function as "secretaries" by allowing incoming calls to be screened. If you are waiting for a special call but do not want to take any others, you can program the system to answer calls with a message like "You have reached Rosie Berg-Bochner at Caterpillar Tractor. What is your name, please?" At this point, Ms. Berg-Bochner, who is listening to the caller's response, can either answer the phone or instruct the system to take a message.

- The system can function like a telephone bulletin board to supply general-interest information. For example, if you are a sales manager, you might leave a voice-mail message concerning the time and place of the next sales meeting, including special travel and hotel arrangements. Using a special access code, members of your sales staff can hear this information at any time. Similarly, salespeople can use the bulletin board to share information on such matters as competitors' products or price changes.

- In replacing the services of telephone operators, voice mail can also serve as an automated attendant. In this case, all calls are answered with a standard recording. For example: "You have reached the College Division of Prentice Hall. If you know the extension of the person you are calling, please dial it now. If you need assistance, please dial 0. An operator will be with you shortly. If you are dialing from a rotary phone, please hold."[14]

ADVANTAGES AND DISADVANTAGES OF VOICE MAIL   The most obvious advantage of voice mail is ensuring that no phone calls are missed. When Denver bank officer Crawford Cragun was temporarily unemployed, he purchased a voice-mail system that would answer all phone calls when his phone was busy. In this case, voice mail avoided the problem of missing calls from prospective employers. Says Cragun, "I'll never use my answering machine again."[15]

Voice mail also handles telephone messages quickly and efficiently because it eliminates the annoying practice of "telephone tag" (two people exchanging call after call because each is missing the other in turn). Third, it allows people like outside sales representatives, who are on the move throughout the day, to communicate efficiently with employees located in company offices. It also ensures that calls are handled correctly. For example, before Travelers Insurance switched to voice mail, it found that 75 percent of all incoming calls either never reached the correct party or resulted in incorrect information. In addition, nine out of ten written phone messages contained at least one error. Voice mail has eliminated these problems.[16]

However, voice mail also has disadvantages. Callers forced to listen to long messages, for example, can find the system annoying. Voice mail also delivers the implicit message that the caller's time is less valuable than the recipient's. Responding to customer complaints of depersonalization and to his own difficulty in reaching his staff, CEO Edward Crutchfield of First Union Corp. in Charlotte, North Carolina, finally banned voice mail from his organization.[17]

USING VOICE MAIL EFFECTIVELY   The following practices have helped many companies reap the benefits of voice-mail systems while minimizing problems.

- Consider your audience before deciding whether or not to use voice mail. Ask yourself whether your callers would be uncomfortable speaking to a computer (many people are), and keep in mind that people who still use rotary phones will be excluded.

■ Keep messages short and to the point. Remember that callers will hear the same message every time they call. It is also important to minimize the menu of choices to absolute essentials. For example, most systems allow callers to choose an option at any time without being forced to listen to the entire menu before making a selection.

■ When calling a voice-mail system, jot down notes so that you know what you want to say before you begin. Have an agenda.

■ Callers, too, should gear their messages to the recipient's voice-mail system. Talking to a computer makes it easy to forget that a person will eventually hear your voice.

Voice mail is also helping employers deal with diversity in the workforce. At Armatron International, Inc., a Melrose, Massachusetts, consumer-electronics manufacturer, an incoming trunk line includes Spanish-language voice-mail messages that permit the firm's Spanish-speaking workers and customers to call the company without encountering a language barrier.[18]

Electronic Meetings

Many companies use electronic meetings, including teleconferences and video-conferences, to reduce travel costs and losses in productivity that result from time spent away from the office. Both types of meeting require special communication skills.

Depending on the situation, teleconferences and videoconferences can be as effective as face-to-face meetings. In some circumstances, electronic meetings are more efficient than face-to-face meetings because they force people to be prepared. Realizing that every minute costs money motivates participants to be organized by having their facts correct and available. On the other hand, although electronic meetings are especially useful in communicating information, they are less valuable during brainstorming or creative sessions that require personal interactions.

teleconference
(or conference call)
Electronic meeting that uses ordinary telephone lines to bring together three or more people at various locations

TELECONFERENCES   **Teleconferences,** also known as **conference calls,** are electronic meetings that use ordinary telephone lines to bring together three or more people at various locations. Services offered by such commercial carriers as AT&T and MCI can connect dozens of people to the same call. Teleconferences can involve local, national, or international calls. If participants in such meetings have facsimile machines or electronic-mail systems, they can also share documents during the conference.

In many ways, a teleconference has more in common with a face-to-face meeting than with an ordinary telephone call. To communicate successfully, always remember that you are part of a conference involving many people. Here are some specific teleconferencing suggestions:

■ If possible, use a lightweight headset consisting of ear pieces and a built-in microphone. The headset allows you to move around the room with both hands free as you take notes, search through documents, or send or receive fax transmissions or electronic mail. If you are using a speakerphone, it is a good idea to mute the microphone when not speaking.

■ Identify yourself when speaking and direct your questions or comments to people by name. For example:

Ellen: Andy, this is Ellen. How many units can you have ready by the 25th?

Peter: Andy, this is Peter. Before you answer that, please consider the work you still have to do on the Simmons account.

Andy: Peter, Andy speaking. I'm well aware of that, and it isn't a problem. Ellen, I can have 2,000 units ready. How does that sound?

Remember that comments not specifically directed to an individual will be perceived as intended for the entire group.

A teleconference is a fast, cost-effective means of convening geographically dispersed people. A conference call can bring together anywhere from three to three hundred people and can be arranged for any time during the day or night.
Source: Courtesy MCI.

- If participants forget to identify themselves by name, you may interrupt the conversation by saying something like, "Please tell us who is speaking."
- Speak naturally as you would during any phone call but pause for others to comment.

If you are the teleconference leader, you have special responsibilities, including starting on time, setting the meeting tone (formal or informal), taking roll call so that everyone knows who is on the line, setting the agenda and focusing on the main issues, moderating the discussion, and summarizing key points. The leader is also responsible for handling the problem of people speaking over each other's voices.

Interestingly, the electronic medium makes handling some problems easier. For example, it is easy to detect leaders of different factions in a teleconference: Participants tend to defer to the leader, giving him or her the lion's share of speaking time.

VIDEOCONFERENCES   **Videoconferences** are electronic meetings that allow participants in scattered geographic locations to see one another on television monitors by way of images transmitted over telephone lines. As Rolm Co. CEO H. Mitchell Watson, Jr., explains, videoconferences can greatly improve productivity and lower travel costs: "We no longer lose two or three days of work when employees fly from New York City to Los Angeles for a two-hour meeting."[19]

Videoconferencing technology has improved in recent years as costs have decreased. In 1985, for example, Xerox spent $500,000 to equip each videoconfer-

videoconference
Electronic meeting that allows participants in scattered geographic locations to hear and see one another on television monitors by way of images transmitted over telephone lines

INTERVIEW

Gary Foley, Videoconferencing Manager for Xerox Corporation

In 1985, Xerox Corporation started Xerox Team Vision (XTV)—a videoconferencing network that now connects 13 corporate locations worldwide. XTV averages about 420 conference hours per month and saves Xerox millions of dollars each year in travel-related expenditures.

Via videoconference hookup, we asked Xerox Team Vision manager Gary Foley to talk about XTV, its business applications, and ways to maximize effective communication.

The videoconference rooms in which this interview took place were equipped with two monitors—one to show conference participants and the other to display graphics, including overhead transparencies, three-dimensional objects, and notes on a white board. In the following conversation, Foley describes Xerox Team Vision's technology.

Question: How are videoconferences used at Xerox?

Answer: They are used primarily for business meetings among geographically dispersed people. The development and manufacturing division uses about half of all network time to discuss the development of new products; plans for implementing new systems; project, design, and financial reviews; and staff meetings.

Question: How have people at Xerox responded to videoconferencing as a replacement for face-to-face meetings?

Answer: When people first walk into a room, they are somewhat intimidated by the camera, the microphone, the control table, and the monitors. However, once they sit down and begin discussing the issues, they forget about the technology and feel almost as if they are in a room together with the people on the screen. The majority of users view videoconferencing as an incredible time saver.

Question: What are the advantages of this technology?

Answer: Videoconferencing tends to be one of the most efficient meeting forms. Participants get more accomplished in a videoconference than they do in a regular meeting, mainly because they get right down to business. They know they have a certain planned time frame in which to get results. Regular meetings include a lot of conversation about nonbusiness issues.

Because there is a one-half-second audio delay, videoconferencing encourages people to sit back and listen instead of jumping into a conversation. People are forced to pause before speaking in order to avoid stepping on the last

ence room; today, comparably equipped rooms cost half that amount, and even less expensive modular rooms can be equipped for $50,000 to $100,000. The cost of holding meetings has also declined. Depending on the technology, an hour-long videoconference that once cost as much as $1,200 can now be held for between $30 and $400. Typically, the more expensive the operating cost of the system, the better the transmission quality.[20]

Metropolitan Life Insurance Company operates seven videoconferencing centers in six different U.S. cities. "We've identified 26 different types of meetings that we've conducted by videoconference," explains Arthur W. Yee, who helps direct MetLife's videoconferencing operations, "including vendor presentations, job interviews, award presentations, new product announcements, and personnel training. And we're always aggressively trying to find new applications." MetLife has been so satisfied with videoconferencing that it is adding six more centers, including facilities in London and Madrid.[21]

Liz Claiborne, the $2-billion women's clothing manufacturer, uses videoconference technology to keep in touch with its manufacturing operations in the Far East. A videoconferencing system links Claiborne's New York headquarters not only with its New Jersey production center but also with manufacturing operations in Hong Kong, Indonesia, and Sri Lanka. The system enables U.S.-based executives to view clothing samples without having to wait for shipments or having to pay costly air freight.

speaker's lines. Although this eliminates some of the spontaneity that is part of normal conversation, it results in a more orderly, more efficient meeting.

Question: Is it possible to link more than two sites?

Answer: Our network can link up to twelve sites. The person speaking during a multipoint meeting is the person who is shown on the screen. That person continues to see the person who spoke immediately before him or her. For example, if Carol in Texas starts talking, within a second everybody is watching her while Carol views the last person who spoke. The switching is voice-activated.

Question: Are videoconferences sometimes overused? Could teleconferences be used instead?

Answer: We're trying to help employees determine when it makes sense to use one medium over the other. When they actually need to look at equipment, when they need to draw something and make annotations, when they need to use the white board to brainstorm, videoconferencing makes a lot of sense. It also makes sense when they want to look people in the eye as they tell them, for example, that they have to make changes in their department, and

when they need to see a reaction. The phone doesn't provide any of this information.

Question: Can you give me an example of how videoconferencing has been instrumental in closing a deal?

Answer: I remember one situation where a customer in California was interested in purchasing Xerox products but needed a special application. The Xerox salesperson arranged for a series of videoconferences from the customer site in California to Leesburg, Virginia, where Xerox engineers, familiar with the product and application, worked. After each meeting, the customer would look at what the engineer did and ask, "Yes, but what if we did this?" The engineer would then fix the problem and bring it back for another look. After about six meetings, the Xerox team put together a multimillion dollar proposal and flew out to California to present the customized solution. The engineers in Leesburg told us that videoconferencing saved them about twenty-five worker days of time in the development of this deal.

Source: Videoconference with Gary Foley.

Businesses without either videoconferencing networks or network connections in a needed location can use special public facilities like those provided by Sprint. Xerox, for example, regularly uses Sprint facilities in Chicago and Toronto. Low-cost videoconference technology is also available to small businesses by way of videophone—a telephone that comes equipped with a baseball-card-sized color monitor that plugs into a regular wall jack. With a sale price of about $1,500, this technology is now affordable by many businesses.[22]

COMMUNICATION DURING A VIDEOCONFERENCE   Because videoconferences can connect participants in many different locations, special communication skills are needed to make the system work. As Wisconsin-based Parker Consulting president Lorne Parker points out, failure to adapt to the technology itself may result in communication problems: "People look at videoconferencing and see familiar components—a television screen and a telephone—and they don't think they need to learn anything new....That's a major barrier to effective use of the technology."[23]

The following practical suggestions are designed to help mprove communication during videoconferences. Keep in mind that videoconferences are most effective when participants have already established personal relationships with one another.

- If your company offers a training session, take advantage of it so that before your first meeting, you are familiar with the videoconference room and its technology.

- Videoconferences are transmitted over telephone lines with relatively limited capacity compared to that of the coaxial cables which transmit television images. The signal is compressed, and the result is in many cases not only a slight sound delay but images of participants who look as if they are swimming underwater. If participants are not careful listeners, the sound delay can make the communication more difficult. Being aware of the sound delay and the importance of listening is the best way to avoid interruptions—which is a general rule during teleconferences.

- Introduce yourself and your group at the start of a meeting. Introductions are especially important if the meeting includes a number of participants.

- To avoid confusion when addressing a participant in another location, address the individual by name.

- Be more deliberate or restrained in your gestures. Sudden arm and hand movements, for example, may seem exaggerated when transmitted. As a result, the picture is not as crisp and movements are more poorly defined than those that you see on television. On the other hand, body language that might go unnoticed in a face-to-face meeting is magnified in a videoconference.

- The videoscreen reproduces dark, contrasting colors with more clarity than pastel or light colors. Navy blue clothing thus is a frequently recommended color for videoconferences.

- Use a fax machine or a computer to send documents back and forth among meeting participants. Hard copies can be made of anything that appears on the monitor.

- If you are the conference leader, distribute an agenda at the start of the meeting.

- Keep in mind that, although the meeting may include many participants in various locations, the monitor displays only one location at a time.

- Be sensitive to the fact that the same microphone that carries your voice will also pick up sounds that you would rather not amplify. Because microphones will exaggerate the loudness and intensity of virtually all sounds, avoid such distractions as tapping your fingers on the table or laughing too loudly.

- Prepare visual aids using large print sizes with individual letters no smaller than one-fourth of an inch in height, a limited amount of print per page, and bold, simple drawings that contain only essential details.

Table 20.3 summarizes the primary communication technologies for business speakers and identifies their primary uses.

TABLE 20.3   *Communication Technologies for Business Speakers*

TECHNOLOGY	USES
Voice mail	Handling incoming and outgoing phone calls; recording and sending telephone messages
Teleconferences	Allowing business conferences by telephone with three or more people
Videoconferencing	Transmitting pictures and voices to create electronic meetings with two or more people in different locations
Cellular telephones	Allowing travelers to make and receive business calls at nearly any location

PROGRESS CHECK

1. Distinguish between electronic mail and voice mail. What do they have in common and how do they differ?
2. Summarize some etiquette tips for electronic meetings.
3. Cover up the "Uses" column in Table 20.3 and mentally fill in the information. How much can you remember?

TECHNOLOGY FOR BUSINESS TRAVELERS AND COMMUTERS

Despite the convenience of electronic meetings, business travel is often essential. Fortunately, technology can also help improve communication for business travelers. In fact, communication technology has changed the very nature of both business travel and daily commuting. No longer are travelers forced to be out of touch for long periods of time. Rather, they can be connected anytime and nearly anyplace through such devices as *cellular telephones, pagers,* and *portable computers.* Such electronic conveniences make communication possible when traveling across town or around the world, during business trips, or while commuting to and from the office.

Cellular Telephones

Portable cellular telephone technology is booming. In 1983, only 2,000 Americans had cellular phones. A decade later, that figure had grown to 7.7 million and is expected to rise to an astounding 33 million by 2001.[24] In response to the needs of today's business travelers, cellular telephones have been installed in many Avis, Budget, and Hertz rental cars and on airline flights.

Cellular telephones—wireless telephones that transmit voice and data in the form of radio signals—can turn travel time into productive time. Stuart F. Crump, Jr., a columnist for *Mobile Office* magazine, recommends that cellular-phone users take advantage of travel time to return the bulk of their phone messages and save only the most important messages for the office. He also suggests that users should "quit waiting around the office at the end of the day for the important phone call. Forward it to your car phone and head for home. Shift that waiting time to commuting time." Because the cost of cellular calls remains relatively high, Crump also recommends encouraging brevity by telling the call recipient that the call is being made on a cellular phone.

Pagers—battery-powered devices that signal telephone messages—allow you to stay in touch with your office and clients while on the road at far less cost than cellular phones. The latest generation of pagers is smaller and more efficient than its predecessors. While some models are features of digital wristwatches, others look like fountain pens. Instead of annoying beeps, many pagers feature message signaling by means of vibrations or tiny blinking lights.

If you want to be contacted while away from your office, give people your pager number. Callers may also enter phone numbers at which they can be reached. The caller's number is instantly transmitted to your pager's display screen. Some models, called *alphanumeric pagers,* allow callers to leave short messages, such as "Trip canceled" or "Kelly says yes." Some services combine paging and voice mail. SkyTalk, a service of SkyTel, connects callers to your voice-mail box and alerts you when the message is complete.

Some businesspeople who carry cellular phones also carry pagers to take advantage of lower combined operating costs. (Cellular phone calls can cost 90 cents for each minute of use whether or not you make or receive a call.) When your pager signals a call from a specific telephone number, you can thus decide whether to call back immediately from your cellular phone or wait to use a regular phone.[25]

cellular telephone
Wireless telephone that transmits voice and data in the form of radio signals

pager
Battery-powered device that signals telephone messages

PRACTICAL TIPS

Etiquette for the Cellular Phone

With cellular phones now weighing less than eight ounces and fitting in the palm of the hand, people are able to conduct business wherever they are—in restaurants, theaters, health clubs, and even on secluded beaches. Nothing stops them—not even the inkling that they may be intruding on others and displaying other forms of bad manners. Not surprisingly, then, the incredible pace at which cellular phones have become part of daily business has resulted in the need for a few new rules of phone etiquette.

"I heard one in church last week," reports Letitia Baldridge, a well-known authority on etiquette. Charlotte Ford, another analyst of manners, remembers spending a vacation at an expensive spa that was constantly disturbed by a business executive who insisted on using the hotel dining room as a private phone booth. Some people also feel strongly about pagers, finding them intrusive and often objecting to the unmistakable sound of a pager clamoring for attention.

Because etiquette usually trails far behind technology, we will offer some helpful advice on cellular phone usage.

- When in public, always speak in a low voice.
- Don't take calls if you are in the midst of a formal business meeting.
- Don't call from theaters.
- Let the ambiance of a restaurant determine whether calls are appropriate. While receiving calls is probably acceptable at McDonald's, it is an intrusion at a four-star French restaurant.
- If a call interrupts a face-to-face conversation, remember to excuse yourself before answering the phone. "Don't ignore those with you in favor of the disembodied voice," advises Judith Martin, author of *Miss Manners' Guide for the Turn-of-the-Millennium.*

Another problem peculiar to cellular phones is that they are a prime target for snoops. Because cellular messages are transmitted via radio signals, they are easily picked up by scanners as far as 100 miles away. According to Tom Kneitel, editor of *Popular Communications*, "Anybody who talks on a cellular phone and gives out personal information might as well get on TV and give the information out." Although the current generation of scanners is about to be foiled by a shift to digital transmission, chances are that hard-core eavesdroppers will find a way to translate data bits back into conversation and listen again.

Sources: William G. Flanagan and David Stix, "Telephone Voyeurs," *Forbes*, September 30, 1991, pp. 172-73; Charles Leerhsen, "If a Movie Usher Answers...Manners in the Age of the Cellular Phone," *Newsweek*, August 26, 1991, p. 62; and Molly O'Neill, "Where Silence Was Golden, Pocket Phones Now Shriek," *The New York Times*, September 25, 1991, p. A1.

Staying in immediate touch is essential to businesspeople like Donald Dodson, a La Mesa, California, medical-services consultant who subscribes to a nationwide paging service operating in about a hundred major U.S. cities. "My entire life," he explains, "depends upon clients and prospects being able to get hold of me."[26]

> *A computer isn't smart enough to make a mistake. Computers are dumb. Fast and efficient and dumb. No computer ever had an idea.*
>
> IBM advertisement

Laptop and Palmtop Computers

Generally weighing less than twelve pounds and operating on rechargeable batteries, laptop computers can serve as word processors, databases, or communication devices. With built-in power sources, both laptops and the smaller portable computers known as notebooks can be used while waiting in airline terminals, riding in cars or trains, or working in hotel rooms. For example, the NEC UltraLite III weighs a mere 4.8 pounds and measures just 1.5" by 9" by 11.5". It operates for up to five hours and includes an optional internal modem for E-mail and other messages.

Today's lightweight cellular telephones make it possible for businesspeople to communicate from previously inaccessible locations. Easily transportable, the cellular phone can be transported in a standard briefcase or tucked in a purse or a suit pocket.
Source: © 1992 Motorola, Inc.; used by permission.

Laptops have become increasingly sophisticated and now offer clear screens and adequate capacity to perform complex communication functions. Color monitors on some models now present crisper images, while others are even equipped with modems that allow transmission of computer documents to fax machines. Portable printers connected to laptops make it possible to produce finished products while away from the office.

Seth Reichlin, the director of marketing research for Prentice Hall's College Division, uses a laptop to record focusgroup meetings held outside his New Jersey office. During meetings, Reichlin can enter participants' ideas into the computer as they speak—a process that avoids the need to transcribe audiotapes.

AT&T is helping business travelers who use laptops by turning thousands of public phone booths into portable business offices. These booths come equipped with outlets that will accept laptop computers and portable fax machines as well as data screens for reading and revising text. Many of the new phones will also have keyboards on which travelers can enter and send text by way of phone lines to other computers. AT&T is currently placing these phones in airports across the country.[27]

As the name suggests, palmtops bring limited computer power to the palm of your hand. British computer maker Psion recently introduced an eight-ounce palmtop that includes a word-processing program. People using this software can shift documents from other word processors to their palmtops for reviewing or editing at their leisure. Wizard, another popular palmtop manufactured by Sharp, is used mainly as an electronic organizer to store phone numbers, schedules, and expenses.[28]

Manville Corp. CEO Thomas Stephens is a good example of a business traveler who makes portable technology work for him. Stephens carries a seven-pound notebook computer along with an adapter that converts the computer

INTERNATIONAL ISSUES IN BUSINESS COMMUNICATION

Technology and the Business Traveler

Many Americans probably would assume that the telecommunications technology used daily by U.S. businesspeople is available throughout the world. However, many international business travelers can testify to just how false such an assumption is. In the area of technology, the United States is far ahead of most of the rest of the world. For example:

- Only 124 telephone calls can be made simultaneously between the United States and the Commonwealth of Independent States. As a result, only about 10 percent of all calls to the former Soviet Union actually get through. AT&T estimates that an additional 2,300 lines are needed to connect these two nations. Ordinary Russians fare even worse. They are on a 32-year waiting list for a new phone.

- If a fax machine or other piece of electrical office equipment fails in Great Britain, its replacement may come without a plug. Manufacturers must sell plugless electrical products to accommodate Britain's great variety of sockets, and it is up to purchasers to install their own connections.

- Companies doing business in Brazil are prohibited from using E-mail to send data back and forth unless they disclose the purpose of the data and, more importantly, how its transmission will benefit Brazil. Kodak convinced Brazilian officials to waive the rule for the company only by explaining that $80 million worth of exports were at stake.

- Even basic office services are likely to be unavailable in China. Businesspeople cannot assume that they will find typewriters or copy machines, let alone more sophisticated office equipment like computers and faxes.

Man is still the most extraordinary computer of all.

John F. Kennedy
35th President
of the United States

telecommuter
Worker who "travels" to and from a job by way of such data-communications technology as electronic mail, voice mail, teleconferencing, answering machines, and telephone call-forwarding

into a fax receiver. Messages received via fax appear on the computer screen. When traveling overseas, he takes his 11-ounce Hewlett-Packard palmtop.[29]

TELECOMMUTING

In his classic work *Future Shock,* Alvin Toffler introduced the term *electronic cottages* to refer to homes wired to the company work place by an array of complex computer technologies. In Toffler's vision of the future, millions of workers would complete assignments and transmit material to and from the main office without ever leaving home. For some 5.5 million Americans, Toffler's vision of the future is today's reality. They are **telecommuters**—workers who "travel" to and from their jobs by way of such sophisticated data-communications technology as electronic mail, voice mail, teleconferencing, answering machines, and telephone call-forwarding. As telecommunications equipment becomes more sophisticated, more companies are turning to telecommuting as a viable working arrangement. Between 11 million and 25 million people are expected to be telecommuters by the year 2000.

At Los Angeles-based Pacific Bell, more than 1,400 of the firm's 16,000 management employees are regular telecommuters. Pacific Bell also rents space in a satellite center in nearby Riverside, from which workers can communicate with corporate headquarters, suppliers, and customers via computers, telephones, and fax machines. In the process, many hours of commuting time are now eliminated. Companies drawn to telecommuting to improve employee productivity have seen increases as high as 25 percent.[30]

Overcoming Telecommuting Problems

Despite the advantages of telecommuting for both workers and companies, personal communications and long-term career success may suffer when people

Frequently, U.S. businesspeople traveling abroad are frustrated by the lack of adequate telephone service. International business communication consultants Lennie Copeland and Lewis Griggs report that in South Africa, South America, and other places,

it can take over a year to get a phone, after an arduous application procedure. But even once you have a phone, or if you are working out of a hotel or office already set up with telephones, the going is not easy. . . In any country that is not technically developed, it may take hours of dialing to get through. The norm is one phone (if any) per office and very few private lines. . . If you are making long-distance calls from a hotel in China, a bellboy will arrive at your room after each phone call and present a bill to be paid at once.

Telecommunications links are poor in many countries because of an unwillingness to invest in the high-speed data lines that support the new technologies. Before Kodak started using these lines to connect its New York headquarters to Germany and England, it transferred crucial data via a modem and a voice line—a process that tied up the line for up to eight hours a day. Kodak's annual phone bills for this transfer reached $90,000. If there is a lesson to be learned from all this, it is to scale down your expectations when leaving the United States.

Sources: "Why Ivan Can't Place a Call," *Business Week,* December 14, 1992, pp. 92-93; Steven Prokesch, "Mere Plug at the Wire's End: In England That's Progress," *The New York Times,* January 31, 1992, p. A6; Joan E. Rigdon, "Crossed Wires: Phone Service Overseas Provides a Mixed Picture, Kodak Finds," *The Wall Street Journal,* October 4, 1991, p. R6; "Reach Out and Hold, Please," *U.S. News & World Report,* September 23, 1991, p. 15; and Lennie Copeland and Lewis Griggs, *Going International* (New York: Random House, 1985), pp. 180-81.

spend too much time out of the office. Chicago-based personnel consultant James E. Challenger explains:

Far from the center of power, telecommuters have the same problems as branch-office workers. They can't greet the boss personally each morning or converse casually over coffee during a coworker's birthday celebration. Personal relationships and personal growth also can't occur when all communication is electronic. This keeps telecommuters stalled at their present level, and professionals working at the office are more likely to win promotions.[31]

To overcome these problems, telecommuters must develop strategies to make themselves more visible. The following suggestions are designed to help workers outside the office participate more fully in office-based operations.

- Attend meetings whenever possible. Meetings give you a high profile in front of a large group of people. In addition, attend office parties and special functions. Some companies, including Pacific Bell, require attendance at staff meetings.
- Submit reports personally rather than through electronic mail. If you have been working on a major project for a month, don't use the computer to transmit it. Explain what you have accomplished in a person-to-person meeting.
- Put yourself on an electronic mailing list for office memos. Even the most routine memos allow you to stay in touch with changes in the company.
- Buy a telephone answering machine or become part of your firm's voice-mail system. This way you will not miss business calls if you step out.
- Use the telephone to stay in touch by calling in once or twice a day when you work at home.[32]

Taken together, such strategies also ease feelings of isolation, a major complaint among telecommuters.

"It's his first national story...so Dave goes up there to get away from it all. Got himself a first-class communications setup...all AT&T...interviews over the phone...he goes for a run...answering machine takes messages...his editor calls and he faxes rewrites... makes every deadline... series starts tomorrow."

With AT&T, on your own never means going it alone. 24 hours a day, we're there with the products, service and reliability you expect.

AT&T
The right choice.

The explosive growth of telecommuting in the 1990s has been made possible by communication technology. Today, it is possible to equip the home with such sophisticated communication tools as electronic mail, voice mail, fax machines, answering machines, teleconferencing services, and computer linkups between branch and main offices—all at reasonable costs.
Source: © 1992 AT&T; used by permission.

PROGRESS CHECK

1. What are cellular telephones, pagers, and laptop computers?
2. Do you think you would enjoy telecommuting to a job? Explain your answer.

WHAT'S AHEAD

This chapter marks the end of Part VII in *Contemporary Business Communication*. The goal of this section was to examine the challenges faced in business communications and how to convert them into opportunities. We have described the challenges of communicating across national boundaries, communicating with diverse customers and a diverse work force, and mastering communication technology. These concepts form the foundation for effective written communication.

SUMMARY OF CHAPTER OBJECTIVES

1. **List the benefits of *communication technology*.**

   Communication technology has dramatically improved message speed and efficiency. It has also facilitated access to the global marketplace. Efficiency is linked to the contributions of technology in creating, organizing, and distributing messages.

2. **Identify the six *communication functions* performed by computers.**

   Computers facilitate communication by storing data on magnetic disks rather than on paper. Data is easily retrieved from the computer's memory and projected on the computer screen so that it can be analyzed and edited. Because the computer can display information in different forms, various types of analysis and presentation are possible. Hard copies with different visual features are produced on the computer printer. Finally, the computer's telecommunication capability enables users to transmit messages back and forth among computers in the same network.

3. **Explain the advantages of writing with a *word processor*.**

   Writing with a word processor facilitates note taking, document organization, drafting and development, revising and editing, proofreading, and formatting. Using a word processor to your advantage requires learning a series of simple commands and using them consistently.

4. **Outline the ways in which computers are used as *telecommunication tools*.**

   Computers operate as telecommunication tools in three primary ways. They send and receive electronic-mail messages directed to specific individuals. They display public electronic bulletin-board messages, and they can transmit on-line databases that contain valuable sources of business information.

5. **Explain how databases, presentation graphics, desktop publishing, computer printers, photocopiers, and facsimile machines can improve communication.**

   Database software allows you to create individualized information files that can be used to create form letters, reports, and mailing labels. Presentation-graphics programs display data in a variety of visual forms, including bar charts, line charts, and pie charts. Desktop-publishing programs equip personal computers with the ability to design and lay out text and graphics programs and produce camera-ready copy. Computer printers move single and multiple copies of your work from the computer screen to the printed page. Photocopiers duplicate original documents and produce high-quality copies. Facsimile machines copy and transmit original printed material to other machines throughout the world.

6. **Identify the features, advantages, and disadvantages of *voice mail*.**

   Voice mail is a computer-based call-processing system that handles incoming and outgoing phone calls. Using voice mail, you can record messages for specific individuals or groups, save messages in your private "mailbox," and screen incoming calls. The system can also function as a telephone bulletin board and an automated attendant. Although voice mail eliminates the game of "telephone tag," it tends to depersonalize phone conversations and may annoy some callers.

7. **Explain how *electronic meetings* are conducted through *teleconferences* and *videoconferences*.**

   Teleconferences bring together three or more people at different locations by means of ordinary phone lines. Videoconferences transmit visual and voice images. Although electronic meetings share similarities with both ordinary phone calls and face-to-face meetings, they require special communication skills.

8. **Explain the impact on business travel of cellular phones, pagers, and laptop and palmtop computers.**

   Cellular phones, pagers, and laptop and palmtop computers enable business travelers to be in constant touch with their offices. Using these technologies, businesspeople can send and receive E-mail, voice mail, and facsimile copies and can use word-processing and database software.

9. **Describe the phenomenon of *telecommuting* and how to overcome its pitfalls.**

   Telecommuters work out of their homes or from satellite offices and communicate with headquarters via such sophisticated technologies as E-mail, voice mail, and teleconferencing. Although telecommuting generally improves productivity, it tends to place telecommuters out of the communication mainstream. To overcome this problem, telecommuters should attend scheduled office meetings, present completed assignments personally rather than electronically, and stay in close touch with managers and co-workers by phone.

REVIEW AND DISCUSSION QUESTIONS

1. What advantages does communication technology offer to business? *(Ch. Obj. 1)*
2. Name the major communication functions that computers serve in business. *(Ch. Obj. 2)*
3. Describe the benefits to be gained from writing with a word processor. *(Ch. Obj. 2)*
4. Describe how businesses and individuals can use computers for telecommunications. *(Ch. Obj. 4)*
5. Explain the benefits of using technolgies such as databases, presentation graphics, desktop publishing, computer printers, photocopiers, and facsimile machines. *(Ch. Obj. 5)*
6. What is voice mail? Explain its advantages and disadvantages. *(Ch. Obj. 6)*
7. Distinguish between teleconferences and videoconferences. What are their advantages and disadvantages? *(Ch. Obj. 7)*
8. How have communication technologies such as cellular phones, pagers, and portable computers changed business travel? *(Ch. Obj 8)*
9. What is telecommuting? Why is it a growing trend in business? *(Ch. Obj. 9)*
10. Which communication technologies make telecommuting possible? *(Ch. Obj. 1, 9)*

APPLICATION EXERCISES

1. For the next week, keep a written list of the types of communication technology that you use. Try to imagine what you would have done if that technology had not been available. How would it have changed the nature of your communication? Would you have communicated differently? Would you have been able to communicate at all? *(Ch. Obj. 1)*
2. Following tips in this chapter for free writing, editing, and revising a document, use a word processor to create a one-page, double-spaced document on any topic. Compare your experiences in writing this document to your previous experiences using a typewriter or composing a handwritten document. Did using the word processor affect your ability to write? If so, how? Did it make writing easier or harder? Explain your answer. *(Ch. Obj. 1, 3)*
3. Thanks to its international marketing and overseas sales of athletic clothing, Smallco Sweats, which began with two employees, now employs twenty-six. Like many growing companies, Smallco is discovering that growth makes it harder for staff members to communicate with each other. Due to space limitations, for example, Smallco employees occupy three separate floors of a downtown building, and many of them are gone two weeks at a time on business trips. You've noticed that employees who travel are forced to spend valuable time reading their mail and catching up on the latest developments when they return to the office. You've also observed that employees in one department don't always know what those in other departments are doing. You suggest to Jim Mason, Smallco's founder and CEO, that the firm needs to install an electronic-mail system. Jim is skeptical. "I've never even touched a computer," he says, "and I've gotten along just fine. Besides, look at how much the software costs!" Nonetheless, Jim respects your opinion; he asks you to write a proposal outlining the advantages and disadvantages of electronic mail and describing how Smallco would use an electronic-mail system. Write this proposal. *(Ch. Obj.4)*
4. John, an account executive at Smallco Sweats, is angry with Lauren, another account exec. Apparently, Lauren called on one of John's clients and gave him information that differed from what John had told the client. John found out what happened only because

the client happened to mention it to him during a phone call. Seething, John immediately called Lauren's office, only to find that she was gone on a two-week business trip. Lauren's secretary did not know if Lauren knew that the client in question was John's customer.

John was still furious, however, so he sat down at his comptuer and logged onto the electronic-mail system. He typed the following message:

LAUREN—WHAT DO YOU THINK YOU'RE DOING???!!! APPARENTLY YOU'RE TRYING TO STEAL MY CUSTOMERS AND MAKE ME LOOK BAD. WELL, IT'S NOT GOING TO WORK! I'VE TOLD THIS GUY THAT HE'S STILL MY CUSTOMER, NO MATTER WHAT YOU TOLD HIM. DON'T EVER GO BEHIND MY BACK AGAIN!!!

    JOHN

John sent this message to Lauren's mailbox for her to see the next time she used the computer. For good measure, he also sent the memo to all other Smallco employees, including Lauren's boss.

Is John using electronic mail appropriately? Explain your answer. How would you suggest he communicate with Lauren about this situation? *(Ch. Obj. 4)*

5. As you walk by his office one day, you hear Mack, one of Smallco's top sales representatives, grumbling to himself. You stop in and ask what's wrong. "I've had it with these computers!" snaps Mack. "I've been trying to call a government office to get information for a client, and all I get is a lousy voice-mail system. First, it asked me what I wanted and it listed a menu of ten different options. None of them really sounded like what I wanted, so I chose the option that said 'Further Information.' Then I got another computerized voice listing ten more options—telling me what buttons to press if I wanted government publications on this and that. I wasn't sure if any of them would be helpful, so I pressed a few more buttons. Each option just told me what address to write to—there was no information about what was in that publication. I've been on the phone for half an hour and I don't know any more than I did when I started!" "Couldn't you get an operator to help you?" you ask. "No," replies Mack. "That was never one of the options!"

Reassuring Mack, go back to your office and place a call a friend who works for this government agency. Describe some constructive suggestions that you would make for

improving the agency's voice-mail system. *(Ch. Obj. 6)*

6. Smallco decides to upgrade its phone lines to allow teleconferencing. At the same time, it adds videoconference equipment to its largest meeting room. You suggest to CEO Jim Mason that Smallco's staff might need some training in how to conduct effective teleconferences and videoconferences.

"Why?" asks Jim. "Isn't it just like talking on the phone?" You take a deep breath and decide that you'd better write a memo to all employees that summarizes instructions and guidelines for making the best use of the new teleconferencing equipment. Write this memo. *(Ch. Obj. 7)*

7. You've been assigned to an important new project at your company, and things are going well. Now your boss has asked you to make a twenty-minute presentation to the board of directors in which you will explain the importance of this project to the company, summarize your progress so far, and describe what still needs to be done. Because the project is fairly technical, you will have to make sure that your points get across even to board members who don't understand the technical details. You want to give a great presentation to impress the board. Describe how you could use the various technologies discussed in this chapter to prepare and present an effective presentation. *(Ch. Obj. 1–8)*

8. Recently, SmithKline Beecham's pharmaceutical division handed out laptop computers and portable computer printers to all of its 1,800 salespeople. Managers estimate that each salesperson now averages 1.5 more sales calls per week. Explain this result. Relate SmithKline Beecham's experience to the discussion in this chapter. *(Ch. Obj. 1, 8)*

9. Communication technologies have many positive uses. Take computerized pharmacy databases, for example. A nationwide database allows prescriptions to be filled quickly, day or night, even if you're not in your hometown. Many people, however, feel that these technologies can also have negative effects, such as a potential invasion of privacy. Write a one-page essay discussing the ethical questions raised by communication technologies. Describe the ways in which computers and communication technologies might affect privacy. Do you feel that the potential risks are worth the advantages? Explain your answer. *(Ch. Obj. 1–8)*

10. At last, you've decided to fulfill a lifelong dream: starting your own business. A local

bank has offered to lend money to help entrepreneurs buy and operate the communication equipment needed to run small companies. The bank's corporate loan officer has agreed to meet with you to discuss a possible loan. She asks you to bring to the meeting a written business proposal summarizing the equipment you would like to buy, how your company would use these various technologies, and why they would help you do business more effectively and efficiently. Think about how you would use the technologies discussed in this chapter to start, manage, and market your company— not to mention providing your product or service, billing customers for it, and managing your profits. Then write the proposal. *(Ch. Obj. 1–8)*

11. Three employees at Smallco Sweats have asked the company to let them telecommute to their jobs from home. Angela, who heads up the human-resources department, is intrigued by the idea but doesn't know much about it. She knows, however, that you're taking a business communications course in which you have discussed this trend, so she pays you a visit. "Is this telecommuting a good idea?" she asks. "I'm afraid we might lose touch with these employees and not know what they're really working on. What are the pros and cons of telecommuting for an employer?" What would you tell her? How can an employer stay informed about telecommuters' work? *(Ch. Obj. 9)*

12. Based on your recommendations, Smallco gives these employees the go-ahead for telecommuting. The employees come to you for advice about what communication technologies they should have in their home offices. What would you advise? *(Ch. Obj. 1, 9)*

13. Several months later you call one of these telecommuters, Bob, and ask him how the arrangement is working. "Well, it's both good and bad," he explains. "It's great to be able to work at home, and I do get a lot done. But lately I've noticed that I seem to be left out of things. My office held a birthday party the other day and people forgot to invite me. And I get the feeling that no one knows what I'm doing—I made that great sale to Japan last month and I don't think anyone at the office realizes it except my boss." After hanging up, you decide to write a memo to the telecommuters in which you discuss problems related to telecommuting and how to approach them. Write this memo. *(Ch. Obj. 9)*

14. Interview a businessperson about how his or her organization uses the various technologies discussed in this chapter. Which technologies does the company use and not use? Which seem most useful? Which employees have access to these tools? For instance, if the firm uses electronic mail, do all of its employees belong to the E-mail system? How did the firm decide which workers to include? Does the company use any of these tools to communicate internationally? What advantages and disadvantages does this person see in using communication technology? How have these technologies changed business procedures? Take notes during the interview and write a report summarizing what you learn. *(Ch. Obj. 1–8)*

15. For each of the following business situations, describe what type(s) of communication technology, if any, you would recommend as the most effective. Explain your recommendations. *(Ch. Obj.1-8)*

a. A company president wants to thank every one of her 1,072 employees for their hard work after the company winds up its most profitable year ever.

b. The company's president wants to send every employee instructions explaining the new and rather complicated procedures for accessing the company's customer database.

c. A marketing manager wants to discuss an important sale with a possible new client in Japan.

d. The vice president for human resources decides to hold a meeting that includes all eight of the company's vice presidents, who are geographically dispersed in North America, Asia, and Europe. The purpose of the meeting is to discuss plans for a new company-wide training program on cultural diversity.

BUILDING YOUR RESEARCH SKILLS

Selecting and buying the right computer can be a difficult—but very important—decision, both for businesses and for individuals. This is true for the other sophisticated tools discussed in this chapter as well, such as fax machines, software, and printers. Suppose that your employer put you in charge of purchasing new equipment. How would you decide what to buy? Let's find out.

Your instructor will divide the class into teams, each of which will research a particular type of communication technology discussed in this chapter, such as personal computers, word-processing software, database software, fax machines, cellular phones, desktop-publishing software, computer printers, and photocopiers. Each group will identify the most popular brands in its technology category and compare prices. Other factors to research include reliability, repair history, strengths and weaknesses, and common uses in business. Something else to find out: If the equipment malfunctioned or you couldn't understand the instructions, who would you call for help? Take notes on your research and be prepared to discuss your findings with the other members of your team.

BUILDING YOUR TEAMWORK SKILLS

Meet with your team members from the previous exercise and discuss what you learned about your particular communication technology. Working as a group, draft a report that summarizes what to look for in purchasing this equipment. What are the advantages and disadvantages of the major brands? Which brand(s) would you recommend and why? Appoint a spokesperson to present your report to the class.

COMMUNICATING IN A WORLD OF DIVERSITY

As we observed in this chapter, good telecommunications can make a business much more competitive. This is true for nations, too. Singapore, for instance, has replaced its old telephone system with a new telecommunications network. Germany, Switzerland, and France are upgrading their national telephone networks to add new services and equipment. Japan plans to include every Japanese home, school, and business on a single network by the year 2015.

These nations aren't taking these steps simply to improve domestic phone service. A good telecommunications system can make a big impact on a country's economic health. In particular, service industries like stock trading and banking depend on good telecommunications to perform. No matter what its industry, almost every company today relies on computer networks to collect information, distribute it, and process financial transactions. Moreover, a good network can lower a company's telephone, fax, and postal costs. For example, it costs just one cent to shoot an electronic memo across the United States. To compete successfully with foreign firms, U.S. companies thus need competitive telecommunications.

Some experts feel that America's current telecommunications systems aren't up to the task. All of the phone lines in Hong Kong and Singapore, for example, can carry different types of information (voice, data, graphics, and video) over a single phone line at the same time; only 19 percent of the phone lines in the United States can boast this capacity. America has a wide variety of telecommunications companies, services, and options. The question is whether all these companies can work together to build a competitive global network. Says one researcher, "Everybody's in charge, but nobody's in charge. . . . I'd like to see a bona fide information infrastructure rather than a fragmented world of different systems for everything."

1. Explain how a good national telecommunications system can make a country more competitive in the global marketplace.

2. How do America's current telecommunications systems compare to those in other nations?

3. What needs to be done to make U.S. telecommunications competitive on a global scale?

Andrew Kupfer, "How American Industry Stacks Up," *Fortune*, March 9, 1992, pp. 30-46; and Peter Coy, "How Do You Build an Information Highway?" *Business Week*, September 16, 1991, pp. 108-112.

Modern Résumé Management

Have you ever applied for a job, only to be told, "Thanks, we'll keep your résumé on file"? Most likely, you assumed that the only "file" your résumé would ever see was a wastebasket sitting next to someone's desk.

While this situation is no doubt frustrating for you the job candidate, it may also be frustrating for the company to which you applied. Many firms receive tens of thousands of résumés every year, and keeping track of the paper deluge can be a nightmare. Catherine King, manager of employment at Johnson & Johnson's Ethicon division, gets more than 1,000 résumés a month. "We know we have a gold mine of people," she admits, "but [finding one] has been darn near impossible."

Technology comes to the rescue! Recently, Johnson & Johnson installed a new computer system that reads résumés and stores the information in an electronic database called a *résumé bank.* Now King can search the database for applicants who fit specific job guidelines. She's already used the résumé bank to locate and hire several likely candidates.

LouAnn Miller, director of professional recruiting at Prudential Insurance Co. of America, is also sold on software. "If everyone was in résumé banks," she is convinced, "it would make things so much easier." After using a résumé bank to hire sales representatives in several cities, Bruce Anderson, president of a Minneapolis firm, agrees: "It eliminated going to different employment services and advertising in newspapers throughout the country," he explains. Computers are also moving into other aspects of job hunting. If you apply for a job with Banc One Corp. in Columbus, Ohio, you might never meet with a human interviewer; instead, you'll fill out an application directly on a computer screen.

Some people claim that such technologies take the human touch out of hiring. Can a computer, ask some critics, really judge whether you are the best-qualified candidate for a particular job? On the other hand, some analysts point out that computers can eliminate some of the human subjectivity found in even the best corporate recruiters. And you won't have to worry about whether you wore the right suit to the interview.

Promising though these developments may be, job-application and résumé-tracking technologies still leave something to be desired. The devices that "read" résumés into the computer, for example, often have trouble with colored paper. Fancy details like unusual typefaces and underlining can also confuse them.

Computers also require a new approach to writing résumés. Up to now, applicants were advised to use lots of "action words" to summarize their job experience. With computers, however, nouns become the key words because employers use nouns to search the databases for likely prospects. One executive jokes that a computerized search is apt to select the résumé that contains the most nouns automatically–even if all it says is, "I have never been president, I don't program in Basic, C, or Pascal."

However, perhaps the biggest advantage posed by technology is the promise of fair treatment for all applicants. "You can easily keep race and gender information," explains Edward Gagen, a recruiting manager at Johnson & Johnson, and companies can use such data to maintain culturally diverse workforces. There's even a résumé bank called HispanData that hooks employers up with Hispanic job seekers.

"Every time a search is done," says a Banc One employment manager, "everyone in the database is considered equally and consistently based on their qualifications. Even though you have to apply for a specific job, you might get considered for vice president strictly based on what you say your skills are. The government likes that, and that's the way it should be."

Questions and Applications

1. How are computerized technologies changing the job application process?
2. What are the advantages and disadvantages of this trend for job applicants?
3. What are the advantages and disadvantages of these technologies from an employer's perspective?
4. Using these technologies removes some of the "human" element from hiring; it also makes the hiring process more objective. Do you feel this trend is positive or negative? Explain your answer.

Source: William Bulkeley, "Employers Use Software to Track Résumés," *The Wall Street Journal,* June 23, 1992, p. B6. Reprinted by permission of *The Wall Street Journal,* © 1992 Dow Jones & Company, Inc. All rights reserved worldwide.

Nickelodeon: Commercialism and Quality in Kid's TV

One communication technology that plays a big role in our lives is television. Indeed, some people think it plays too big a role, especially for American children. It's no secret, for example, that while some children's shows are educational in intent and effect, others depict violence to a degree that many parents find alarming. And then there's the question of advertising: Do advertisers have the right to target products to kids? Where do we draw the line between commercialism and quality?

One company that must continually walk this thin line is Nickelodeon, a cable TV channel owned by Viacom, Inc. that specializes in children's programming. Make no mistake: Nickelodeon is a commercial channel that accepts advertising and offers only two series that are openly educational. Many parents and teachers, however, praise the channel for offering quality programming that kids love. Nickelodeon's shows are hip and irreverent: kooky game shows, cartoons, preschool shows, and comic soap operas starring teenagers. Guest stars who act stuck-up may find themselves pelted with green goo. The popular *Double Dare* show features kids sliding through slippery obstacle courses filled with mud and various other types of slime.

The person most responsible for Nickelodeon's distinctive look—and its remarkable success—is president Geraldine Laybourne. Laybourne, a former teacher, feels that the channel's tongue-in-cheek approach is actually good for children. When Nickelodeon researched its market, Laybourne recalls, "we found that kids weren't happy about being kids. Their lives were full of pressure and demands, and they were terrified about AIDS, drugs, becoming teenagers and growing up. So we created a home base for them." Originally, Nickelodeon offered strictly what Laybourne calls "green vegetables—children's shows that were supposed to be good for them. But she soon decided that "the voice that comes from somewhere saying, 'Drink your juice,' just isn't the way to communicate with kids."

The new non-vegetable recipe definitely works. Nickelodeon is watched in over 57 million homes. Youngsters ages two to eleven watch more Nickelodeon than the children's programming on the four major TV networks combined. Because it delivers a big audience that can sometimes be hard to target, the channel is also popular with advertisers. Says one advertising exec, "The [advertising] agencies couldn't figure out where all the kids had gone, then they looked at Nickelodeon's numbers and said, 'Whoops, there they are.'"

Nevertheless, Nickelodeon's success still worries some adults who fear that its programming glues children even more firmly to their TV sets. Asks Elizabeth Thoman, executive director of the Center for Media and Values in Los Angeles, "Is there any time when Nickelodeon encourages children just to turn off the TV and go outside and play?" George Gerbner, a professor at the University of Pennsylvania, points out that Nickelodeon is most popular with kids from upscale households in which the TV is not otherwise on very much—kids who, if they weren't watching Nickelodeon, might be reading, playing, or doing something else actively constructive. On the whole, Gerbner fears that the easy availability of cable TV actually shrinks the range of knowledge that reaches children. Kids, he suspects, "are ultimately getting their information not from parents or school or church or community, but from a handful of conglomerates that have something to sell."

Another concern is Nickelodeon's entry into other communication media. A magazine will appear soon, and Laybourne is also planning a book deal, home-video and record labels, and a motion-picture distribution arrangement. In addition, Nickelodeon-inspired toys will soon hit stores. Peggy Charren, president of Action for Children's Television, admires the channel's programming but feels ambivalent about its commercial spinoffs: "It's one thing," she argues "if the television viewing experience is Nickelodeon. But it's another if your books and slacks and toothpaste all come from the same point of view, the same editorial policy."

Despite such reservations, however, Nickelodeon's popularity continues. "It's like CNN," says one TV producer. "Ten years ago, everyone said Nick who? Now it's taken for granted as part of the American television landscape."

Questions and Applications

1. Describe the approach that Nickelodeon uses to communicate with children. Why do you think Nickelodeon's approach works?

2. Is it ethical for Nickelodeon to accept advertising targeted to kids and then expand into other profit-making ventures such as toys and movies? (Keep in mind that without this money, the channel would have to find other funding or go off the air.)

3. Is it ethical for the channel to encourage children to keep watching TV, no matter how good its programming? Write a one-page essay presenting your views and explaining why you feel this way.

Source: Richard Turner, "Can They Do That?" *The Wall Street Journal*, July 13, 1992, pp. A1, A6. Reprinted by permission of *The Wall Street Journal*, © 1992 Dow Jones & Company, Inc. All rights reserved worldwide.

Preparing Business Documents

Preparing business documents requires a knowledge of the *mechanics* of business writing:

- Using the parts of a letter correctly
- Addressing business envelopes
- Preparing memos, reports, and proposals
- Formatting letters
- Documenting sources

Mechanics, then, refer to the "technical" aspects of preparing a document, and they are designed to improve communication by setting up clear *standards* for written documents. These standards are used consistently throughout the business community.

Appendix I will describe the business writing mechanics that apply to the letters, memos, reports, and proposals examined in this text. We will begin by focusing on the importance of document appearance.

THE APPEARANCE OF BUSINESS DOCUMENTS

Before your reader reads a single word you have written, the appearance of your document has communicated a message. It has told your readers how much care and concern you have put into your document, and it has testified to the professionalism of your approach. First of all, the appearance of business documents is influenced by paper quality and the accuracy of your word processing.

Paper

Paper quality is usually taken for granted—unless it is substandard. Paper that is transparent, too light, colored, or oddly sized may not be acceptable for business purposes. Here are the basic standards that all business paper should meet:

- *Weight. Weight* refers to the weight of four 500-sheet reams of letter-size paper. Most businesses use 20-pound paper for correspondence, reports, and proposals. Stationery used for business letters may be heavier than 20 pounds; for example, 24-pound paper is not uncommon. Lighter paper, especially if it is transparent (onion skin falls into this category), is not acceptable for business use, although it may be used for file copies or overseas mail.
- *Color.* The standard color for business paper is white, although off-white stationery in ivory or gray tones is also acceptable. Unless there is a special reason to use them, pastels—including green, blue, yellow, and lavender—are generally not appropriate for business correspondence. Colored paper is sometimes used in mass mailings as a way of attracting attention.
- *Size.* The standard size for North American business stationery and paper is 8 1/2 by 11 inches.

Reports, proposals, and most business letters are written on paper this size. Stationery also comes in two other sizes:

- Baronial (used for notes, memos): 5 1/2 by 8 1/2 inches
- Monarch (used by some executives for personal business correspondence): 7 1/4 by 10 1/2 inches
- *Cotton Content.* The best stationery has 100-percent cotton content; inexpensive paper bond is used primarily for routine mailings and documents.

Manuscript Quality

Manuscript errors are red flags that identify documents as unprofessional. Guidelines here are in fact quite straightforward: Run every document through the spell-check of your word processor. When this procedure is complete, proofread your document as well.

PARTS OF BUSINESS LETTERS

Business letters may contain as many as seventeen individual elements. As you can see in Appendix Table I.1, while seven of these elements are included in all business letters, ten others may be considered optional. We have arranged these items in the order in which they appear in business letters.

Heading

The *heading* of the business letter, which often consists of the *business letterhead*, usually contains the following elements:

- The complete legal name of the business

TABLE I.1	*Parts of a Business Letter*
STANDARD PARTS	ADDITIONAL PARTS
Heading	Reference line
Dateline	Personal or confidential notation
Inside address	Attention line
Salutation	Subject line
Middle	Identification line
Complimentary close	Enclosure notation
Signature	Mail notation
	Copy notation
	Postscript
	Continuation-page heading

- Full street address and/or post office box number
- Telephone number

The letterhead may also contain a *business logo* and may specify the department or division to which the letter writer belongs. Letterheads may also be personalized to include the writer's name and title. Today, an increasing number of letterheads contain fax numbers.

Dateline

The *dateline* immediately follows the letterhead. It should appear two to four lines beneath the letterhead. Leave one line space after the dateline if a *reference line* (see below) is used. If the next element of the letter is the *inside address*, the dateline should be followed by between two and twelve line spaces. The varied spacing accommodates letters of different sizes.

As you will see later in this appendix, the positioning of the dateline in reference to the left margin depends on the *letter format* you are using. In full-block and simplified formats, the dateline appears flush against the left margin; in block and modified-block formats, it appears two to three character spaces to the right of the center of the page and is aligned with the complimentary close. Another option is to place the dateline flush against the right margin.

Reference Line

Reference lines are designations referring the receiver of a document to a relevant file number or code. If your stationery does not include a printed reference line, place the line two lines below the dateline; align it immediately under the first character of the dateline. Again, placement of the reference line depends on your letter format. Dual reference lines designate the reference codes of both writer and recipient. In this case, the sender's reference line should appear before the recipient's reference line. Appendix Figure I.1 features dual reference codes.

Personal or Confidential Notation

When a letter contains personal or confidential material intended only for the addressee, the writer may make a special notation. This notation should of course be made on the envelope but can also be made in the letter itself. In letters, the notation *Personal* or *Confidential* appears two lines below the reference line. Following the notation are about four line spaces and then the inside address. Notations always appear flush left and may be capitalized or underlined:

> PERSONAL or <u>Personal</u>
> CONFIDENTIAL or <u>Confidential</u>

Inside Address

The inside address—which identifies the person and/or company to whom the letter is being sent—is an obligatory part of all business letters. It appears between two and twelve lines after the last element—dateline, reference line, or personal or confidential notation—of the letter. The most common spacing allows four lines before beginning the inside address.

The inside address is always single-spaced and appears in uppercase and lowercase letters. It is positioned flush left against the left margin. As a rule, the inside address should be no longer than five lines. To maintain this length, the recipient's title may be omitted. Here are some additional guidelines for composing the inside address:

- No line in the address should cross over the center point of the page. Lines containing too many characters should be broken in half and continued on the next line after an indent of two spaces.
- The inside address should begin with the person's *courtesy title*, followed by his or her full name. If the recipient's *professional title* is short enough, it can be included on the same line as the name. For example:

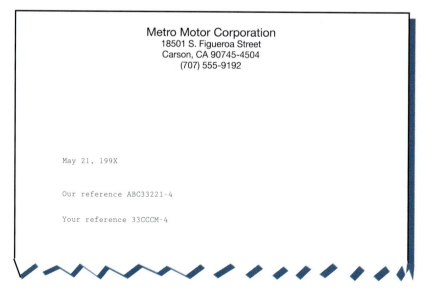

Metro Motor Corporation
18501 S. Figueroa Street
Carson, CA 90745-4504
(707) 555-9192

May 21, 199X

Our reference ABC33221-4

Your reference 33CCCM-4

FIGURE I.1   *Sample Letter—Dual Reference Codes*

Ms. Alexandra Bennington, Treasurer

Longer titles should appear on separate lines. For example:

Mr. Arthur Hawley
Vice President and Director of Human Resources

- The name of the recipient's company should precede the name of his or her department.
- Use the company's complete and official name. It is acceptable to abbreviate words like *Corporation (Corp.)* and *Incorporated (Inc.)*.
- When you are addressing a company rather than an individual, the inside address should include the name of the company, the department to which the letter is being sent, and the company's full address.
- When both a post office box and a street address appear on a company's letterhead, letters addressed to that company should use the post office box on both the envelope and inside address.
- Streets with numbers *one* through *twelve* should be spelled out, while streets numbered *13* and above should be written in Arabic numerals. For example:

3004 Tenth Avenue
127 42nd Street

- Use cardinal numbers (14, 15, 16...) when compass directions are included as part of the address. Use ordinal numbers (14th, 15th, 16th) when the numbered street makes no compass reference. For example:

333 East 30 Street
201 29th Street

Attention Line

The *attention line* is used when a letter is addressed to a company but directed to the attention of a specific individual. The purpose of the attention line is to prevent delays and ensure immediate attention: Even if the person named in the line is not available to receive the letter, it will be opened by someone else in the company.

The attention line should follow the inside address. It always appears flush left and should be set off from the other elements with line spaces before and after. In a simplified format, use two line spaces after the attention line:

McDonald's Corporation
McDonald's Plaza
Oak Brook, IL 60521

Attention Margaret O'Hara, Public Relations Department

Salutation

The official greeting that appears immediately before the body of the letter, the *salutation* follows either the inside address or the attention line. As you will see later in this appendix, salutations appear in all letters except those using the *simplified format.*

In most cases, the salutation is placed two lines below the preceding element (the inside address or attention line). A line space follows the salutation, separating it from the body of the letter.

Salutations usually begin with the word *Dear* followed by the proper form of address for the recipient. The specific salutation that you use will depend on three factors: whether the recipient of the letter is known or unknown to you, whether a title precedes the recipient's name, and whether you are writing to one or more than one person. Here are some examples. As you can see, the salutation in a business letter is always followed by a colon:

Dear Mr. Vanelli:

Dear Dr. Vanelli: (not Dear Dr. Vanelli, M.D.)

Dear Leslie Adams: (gender unknown)

Dear Customer Service Manager: (name unknown)

Dear Sir: (name unknown but gender known)

Dear Madam: (name unknown but gender known)

Ladies and Gentlemen: (a salutation to a company)

Dear Mr. Vanelli and Ms. Bloom:

Dear Mr. Vanelli and Mr. Deaver:

Dear Messrs. Vanelli and Deaver:

Dear Ms. Vanelli and Ms. Deaver:

Dear Mss. Vanelli and Deaver:

Dear Dr. and Mrs. Vanelli: (titled husband)

Dear Dr. Vanelli and Mr. Vanelli: (titled wife)

Dear Drs. Vanelli: (both spouses are titled)

Dear Friends: (group address)

Dear Stockholders: (group address)

Dear Employees: (group address)

Dear Neighbors: (group address)

Subject Line

The *subject line* summarizes the purpose of the letter. In most formats, it appears two lines after the salutation and two lines before the body of the letter. In a *simplified format* (which does not include a salutation), the subject line appears three lines below the inside address or attention line. The body of the letter begins three lines after the subject line.

The subject line begins flush against the left margin. It may begin with the word *SUBJECT* followed by a colon, or it may state the subject without introduction. To emphasize its importance, some writers capitalize all or part of the subject line. For example:

Dear Mr. Everhardt:
ANNUAL SALES MEETING

Here are preliminary plans for the annual sales meeting schedules next February 1. Included are . . .

OR:

Dear Mr. Everhardt:

SUBJECT: Annual Sales Meeting

Here are preliminary plans for the annual sales meeting scheduled next February 1. Included are . . .

Middle

The *middle* of the letter contains the letter's message. It follows the salutation or subject line and is separated from the previous element by a single line space. Line spaces also appear between each paragraph and between the middle and the complimentary close. Paragraph lines are almost always typed in single-spaced format.

In the full-block, block, and simplified formats, paragraphs begin flush left. In the modified-block format, they are indented five to ten character spaces.

Complimentary Close

The *complimentary close* appears one line space after the middle of the letter. It is used in all letter formats except the simplified format. It appears flush left in the full-block style; in block and modified-block styles, it appears two to three character spaces to the right of the center of the page. The complimentary close is always aligned directly beneath the inside address.

The first word of the complimentary close is capitalized and the last word of the close is followed by a comma. Depending upon your relationship with the reader, the close can be formal or informal. Here are some examples:

FORMAL

Very truly yours,

Respectfully,

Very sincerely yours,

LESS FORMAL

Sincerely,

Sincerely yours,

Cordially,

Cordially yours,

LEAST FORMAL

Best wishes,

Best regards,

Regards,

Kindest regards,

Signature

The letter writer's *signature* appears directly under the complimentary close. The writer's name is then typed below the signature—usually four line spaces after the complimentary close. When the letterhead does not include the writer's business title, a second line may also be added to include this information. In all letter styles, the typed name and title are aligned at the left, directly below the complimentary close. For example:

Sincerely,

Alice P. Fenton

Vice President, Recruiting

Most signature blocks do not include courtesy titles such as *Ms., Mrs., Mr.,* and *Miss.* An exception, however, can be made when the title is needed to clarify gender (*Mr. Fran Barron* or *Ms. Billy Diamond*). In business, the preferred title for women is *Ms.* That title is assumed unless the signer indicates *Miss* or *Mrs.*

If the writer's letterhead does not identify the name of his or her company, the company name should be typed, in all capital letters, two lines below the complimentary close. Four lines below this is the typed signature. For example:

Yours truly,

ELVIRA ELECTRONICS

Jonathan J. O'Brian

Jonathan J. O'Brian

Vice President

If someone signs the letter for the writer—secretaries often do this for their employers—that person should place his or her own initials just below and to the right of the signature.

Identification Line

The *identification line* indicates who wrote the letter and who typed it. This optional element is typed two lines below the signature block and flush against the left margin. When a personal signature is shown in the signature block, the writer's initials are optional.

The writer's initials usually appear in capital letters, the typist's initials in lowercase. The two sets of initials are separated by a colon. For example:

DAB:jw

JM:tb

Enclosure Notation

If an enclosure is included with the letter, its presence should be indicated immediately after the identification line or the signature line. It is acceptable to write this notation in any of the following ways:

Enclosure

Enc.

Encl.

enc.

encl.

The notation may also tell the reader something about the enclosed. For example:

Enclosures: two checks

OR:

Enclosures

1. contract

2. meeting agenda

Alternately, the notation may simply indicate the number of items enclosed:

> 3 enclosures

Mail Notation

A *mail notation* may appear after the enclosure notation. This entry indicates that the letter was mailed in a special way or in some way that is of interest to the recipient.
For example:

> BB:fhb
>
> Enclosures
>
> Certified

Here are some other commonly used mail notations:

> By messenger
>
> By Federal Express
>
> By United Parcel Service
>
> By fax

Mail notations are frequently omitted from original copies and added to file copies.

Copy Notation

Often, the person to whom a letter is addressed is not the only person receiving a copy of the letter. When copies are sent to individuals other than the addressee, a *copy notation* may be added at the end. This notation appears flush left after the enclosure and mail notations. When several people receive copies, the names are stacked on top of one another. Many writers place check marks after names on a list to indicate that copies will go to those particular individuals.

The copy notation can be made in several ways:

> Copy to
>
> Copies to:
>
> cc:

The following examples show various combinations of identification lines and enclosure, mail, and copy notations:

> BH:br
>
> Enclosures
> 1. check
> 2. contract
>
> By Federal Express
>
> cc: John McCoy

> AR:btt
>
> Copy to Ann Hastings

> WAA:ma
>
> Enc.

> Copies to: Carolyn Miller
>
> Ronald Yang

Sometimes, copies of a document are distributed to people whose names are not listed on the document itself. *Blind copies* are copies sent to individuals without the knowledge of the addressee. The initials *bc* should appear on both the copy of the letter sent to the blind-copy recipient and the file copy. The notation must *not* appear on the copy sent to the addressee.

Regardless of format, all notations, including the enclosure notation, mail notation, and copy notation, appear flush left. Double- or single-spacing may be used between notation items.

Postscript

Some letters end with *postscripts*—afterthoughts about subjects essentially unrelated to the main topic of the letters themselves. Postscripts should not contain comments directly related to the topic of the letter: Relegation of relevant material to a postscript may be perceived as an indication of a poorly organized document.

A single postscript begins with the initials *P.S.* If a second postscript is necessary, use the initials *P.P.S.* All postscripts should end with the typed initials of the writer. For example:

> P.S. The budget meeting has been rescheduled to May 1. MRB

> P.P.S. Call me next week to talk about the Anderson deal. MRB

Continuation-Page Heading

Long letters require *continuation sheets*—blank stationery—quality paper used for second and all subsequent pages of the letter. A heading is used on each continuation page. This heading should include the addressee's name, the date, and page number. This information is usually placed flush against the left margin, with each item starting a new line. It may also be spread out on a single line. For example:

> Edith Sakura
>
> April 14, 199X
>
> page 2

OR:

> Edith Sakura April 14, 199X page 2

OR:

Edith Sakura   April 14, 199X   page 2

The continuation-page heading should appear two to three lines from the top of the page and at least two line spaces should be allowed before resuming the body of the letter.

ADDRESSING BUSINESS ENVELOPES

First impressions are formed not when your recipient begins reading your letter, but when he or she receives the envelope containing it. To make the best impression, be sure that your envelope looks professional, with every element correctly formatted in its proper place.

The U.S. Postal Service recommends the following style for the various elements of the envelope. Unless otherwise indicated, all lines should be single-spaced.

- Place the address block, written in all capital letters, in the approximate vertical and horizontal center of the envelope.

- The addressee's name appears on the first line. If there is space, include the person's title on that line as well, using a comma to separate the name and title. Place long titles on the second address line.

- The company name comes next, followed by the complete street address or post office box number.

- The last line of the address block shows the city and the two-letter state abbreviation. Use a comma to separate the city and state. Allow two spaces after the state abbreviation, then add the ZIP code. As a general rule, the envelope should be addressed in the same manner as in the inside address.

- Follow the same pattern for the return address, which is placed in the upper-left corner of the envelope. Unlike the address block, the return address need not appear in all capitals. Most companies imprint the business name on their envelopes, and writers need only add their own names.

- Place delivery notations—for example, *SPECIAL DELIVERY* or *FIRST CLASS*—in all capital letters several lines below the postage area.

- Place forwarding and return-postage notations flush against the left margin of the envelope, about two or three lines below the return address.

These notations should be to the left of and above the address block.

- Place confidential and personal notations in the bottom-left corner of the envelope.

Appendix Figure I.2 shows how these elements are arranged on the envelope's face. The model shown is for a No. 10 business envelope.

PREPARING MEMOS

Just as companies print stationery for use in business letters, they print memos for internal use. Memos come in various sizes and may even include tear-off forms. In most cases, the company's return address is printed at the top of the memo. Just above or below the address may be the printed title *MEMO*.

Parts of a Memo

Memos are simpler than letters and include fewer elements. Unlike a letter, for example, a memo has no inside address, complimentary close, or signature line. In addition, many memos are not signed; instead, writers may simply initial them after the memo body.

Many memos begin with four fill-in-the-blank lines: *To, From, Date,* and *Subject*. These elements, known as *guide headings*, may be arranged on the page in different ways. Two examples are shown in Appendix Figure I.3.

While many companies include guide headings on printed memo forms, others simply expect writers to type in the headings themselves.

Allow two to three line spaces after the last guide heading before beginning the memo body, which consists of single-spaced paragraphs placed flush against the left margin. A line space appears between each para-

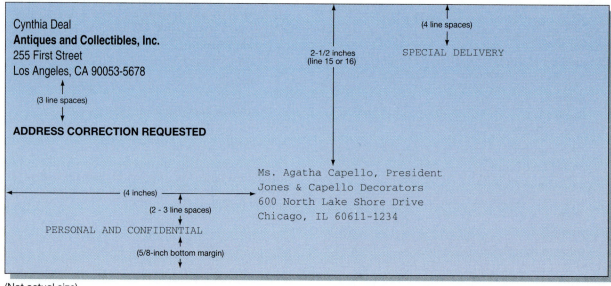

(Not actual size)

FIGURE I.2   *Elements on an Envelope*

Society of Manufacturing Engineers

One SME Drive • Dearborn, MI 48128
(313) 555-1695

To:

From:

Date:

Subject:

Society of Manufacturing Engineers

One SME Drive • Dearborn, MI 48128
(313) 555-1695

To: _____   Date: _____
_____
_____   Subject: _____
_____
From: _____   _____
_____   _____

FIGURE I.3   *Memo Guide Headings*

graph. Some memo forms include the word *MESSAGE* after the printed headings. In this case, begin the body of your memo about three lines below that. Two-part message forms may include the titles *MESSAGE* and *REPLY*. These headings should guide the placement of information in the document.

To help the readers scan documents for vital information, many writers incorporate headings into their memos. Although the style of your headings is largely a matter of preference, be consistent in creating headings throughout your document. Here, for example, is one way to style memo headings.

Primary-level headings. Capitalize and center; use upper- and lowercase letters.

Secondary-level headings. Underline and place flush against the left margin.

Third-level headings. Indent paragraph headings if your paragraphs are indented; otherwise, begin headings at the left margin. The heading is followed by a period and two spaces; the opening sentence of the paragraph begins on the same line as the heading.

Set off primary- and secondary-level headings from the body of your memo by allowing one line space above the heading and one line space below it. The same heading style can be used in reports and proposals.

If the body of your memo is more than a page long, use continuation sheets. *Continuation-page headings* in memos should follow the same style as that suggested

for business letters.

Many memos close with notations like those used in standard business letters. Notations should be placed at the end of the memo, flush against the left margin, consistently spaced, with or without line spaces between each item.

Because there is no signature block in a memo, notations begin either two lines after the last line of the memo body or two lines after the sender's handwritten initials. A distribution list may appear at the bottom of the notations, indicating who receives the memo in addition to the people listed at the head of the memo form. For example:

RAL:dh

Enclosure

Distribution

    Anna Serrell

    May Albright

    Betsy Alverez

PREPARING REPORTS AND PROPOSALS

A report or proposal that takes weeks or months to research and write can still make a bad impression if the appearance of the document is sloppy or inconsistent. A professional appearance comes from the consistent and correct use of margins, headings, line spacing, and page numbers.

Margins

All margins in the body of a report should be 1 inch wide. There is one exception: The first page of a chapter or a section requires a 2- to 2 1/2-inch margin. Although margin widths are fairly easy to determine for the right and bottom margins, the procedure may be more complicated for the top and left margins, especially if binding is used.

About 1/2 inch of paper is lost in the binding process, and margins must be adjusted for the loss. In top-bound manuscripts, leave a 1 1/2-inch margin at the top of each page *except* the first page of a chapter or section. After binding, the page will show 1 inch of margin space. To ensure that a 2- or 2 1/2-inch margin remains after the binding, allow a 2 1/2- to 3-inch margin for the first page of a chapter or a section. In left-bound manuscripts, use a 1 1/2-inch margin so that a 1-inch margin remains after binding.

Headings

Like those in letters and memos, the headings in reports and proposals must be planned in advance and must be deployed consistently. You can use any clear and reasonable heading system, but remember that you have one goal in mind: to make information easy to find.

Line Spacing

Depending upon either your personal preference or the chosen style of your organization, your report or proposal can be single- or double-spaced. In double-spaced documents, paragraphs are indented five spaces; in single-spaced documents, paragraphs usually begin flush left and are separated from one another by single line spaces.

Proper spacing around primary, secondary, and paragraph headings makes them more noticeable—and more effective. Here are some general guidelines for spacing around headings:

- Triple-space before and after primary-level headings.
- Triple-space before side headings; double-space after side headings.
- Do not add any extra line spacing before or after paragraph headings.

While quotations of fewer than four lines generally are incorporated into the text, quotations longer than four lines are typically set apart from the text. They appear below the regular text and are indented five to ten spaces from both the left and right margins. When the text is double-spaced, the excerpt is generally single-spaced. In addition, at least one blank space is added above and one blank space below the excerpt to separate it further from the regular text.

Page Numbers

Obviously, page numbers are crucial in long reports and proposals. Placement depends on whether your document is left-bound or top-bound.

- *Left-bound.* Page numbers are usually typed at the top right of the page, approximately 1/2 inch from the top edge and 1 inch from the right edge; alternately, they can be centered 1/2 inch from the top edge of the page.
- *Top-bound.* Because top binding makes numbers at the top right of the page difficult to read, they are usually centered at the bottom of the page, 1/2 inch from the bottom edge.

The front matter of reports and proposals is numbered with lowercase Roman numerals (*ii, iii, iv,* etc.) Although the title page is technically the first page of the front matter, it remains unnumbered. (It is included, however, in the page count.) Similarly, the letter of transmittal is considered *page ii,* but the page is often missing because it is considered a letter rather than text material. Thus, the actual page numbering may begin with the table of contents, which is often *page iii* of the front matter. Arabic numbers begin with the first page of report text.

Page numbers should stand alone and should not be set off by dashes, parentheses, or periods.

FORMATTING LETTERS

The *format* of a letter refers to the way in which the elements of a letter are placed on the page—for example, whether or not paragraphs are indented and where to place the date line, inside address, and salutation. Four different formats are used in business letters: the *full-block, block, modified-block,* and *simplified.* Your choice of format depends on personal preference and on the style adopted by your organization.

Full Block

Every line in a full-block format—from the dateline to the postscript—begins at the left margin. Paragraphs are single-spaced and a double space separates one paragraph from another. Appendix Figure I.4 depicts a letter in full-block format.

Block

The position of the dateline, reference line, complimentary close, and signature block differ in this format. Instead of flush left, they are usually typed two to three character spaces to the right of the center of the page. These elements may also be placed flush against the right margin or somewhere between the right margin and the center of the page. As you can see in Appendix Figure I.5, all the other letter elements are placed flush against the left margin. As in the full-block format, paragraphs are not indented.

Billows Real Estate
Commercial Real Estate Department
423 Bing Avenue
Irvine, CA 92733
(714) 555-7113

March 22, 199X

Mr. Samuel Jenkins
Western States Bank & Trust
1000 Michelson Drive
Irvine, CA 92730

Dear Sam:

Congratulations on your promotion to executive vice president in charge of real estate. I am delighted, but not surprised, by your success. Western States had the good sense to choose the most qualified person for the job.

Call me once you get settled. We'll have lunch and discuss several deals that look like opportunities for both our companies.

Cordially,

Jeanette Filippe
Jeanette Filippe
Executive President

JF:mm

> All the elements in a full-block format begin flush against the left margin. Allow at least two to four line spaces above and below the date. Exact spacing depends on the length of the letter. The writer limits the inside address to four lines by eliminating a separate line for the addressee's title.

FIGURE I.4   *Sample Letter—Full-Block Format*

Modified Block

The modified-block format follows the same pattern as the block format except that paragraphs are indented five to ten character spaces. Appendix Figure I.6 shows a sample letter in modified-block format.

Simplified

Letters using a simplified format look somewhat different than letters using any of the other three formats. There are three main differences:

- The absence of a salutation and complimentary close
- The inclusion of a subject line in every letter; typed in all capital letters, the subject line appears three lines below the inside address and three lines above the middle of the letter
- The signature line appears five lines below the middle of the letter because there is no complimentary close; often, the writer's name and title are typed in all capital letters.

All lines in this format are typed flush against the left margin; there are no paragraph indentations.

The simplified letter format enables you to address the reader when you don't know who the reader is. For example, when writing to a company rather than a specific individual, eliminating the salutation enables you to avoid stilted openings like "Dear Customer Service Representative." The sample letter in Appendix Figure I.7 is constructed in a simplified format.

DOCUMENTING SOURCES

When your report or proposal relies on secondary sources for information, you must acknowledge these

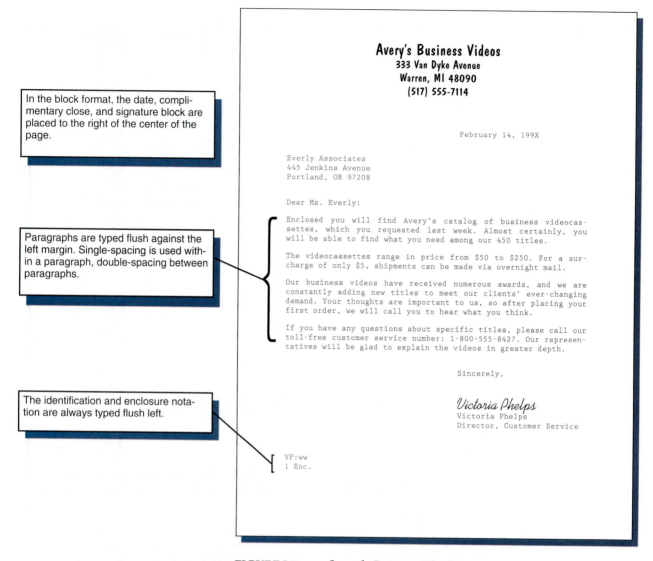

In the block format, the date, complimentary close, and signature block are placed to the right of the center of the page.

Paragraphs are typed flush against the left margin. Single-spacing is used within a paragraph, double-spacing between paragraphs.

The identification and enclosure notation are always typed flush left.

Avery's Business Videos
333 Van Dyke Avenue
Warren, MI 48090
(517) 555-7114

February 14, 199X

Everly Associates
445 Jenkins Avenue
Portland, OR 97208

Dear Ms. Everly:

Enclosed you will find Avery's catalog of business videocassettes, which you requested last week. Almost certainly, you will be able to find what you need among our 450 titles.

The videocassettes range in price from $50 to $250. For a surcharge of only $5, shipments can be made via overnight mail.

Our business videos have received numerous awards, and we are constantly adding new titles to meet our clients' ever-changing demand. Your thoughts are important to us, so after placing your first order, we will call you to hear what you think.

If you have any questions about specific titles, please call our toll-free customer service number: 1-800-555-8427. Our representatives will be glad to explain the videos in greater depth.

Sincerely,

Victoria Phelps
Victoria Phelps
Director, Customer Service

VP:ww
1 Enc.

FIGURE I.5   *Sample Letter—Block Format*

sources. You can make your acknowledgment either by inserting parenthetical references within your text or by footnoting or endnoting your reference material. Footnotes and endnotes can also add content. Complete source lists should appear at the end of your document.

Parenthetical References

Parenthetical references specify for readers the points in a document at which material has been quoted, paraphrased, or summarized. They also give readers enough information to find specific, fully cited sources at the end of your document.

Both parenthetical references and concluding source lists are usually written in one of two documentation styles: the *MLA style*, developed by the Modern Language Association; and the *APA style*, developed by the American Psychological Association. In MLA style, the end-of-document source list is called *Works Cited*; in APA style, it is called *References*.

MLA STYLE   In MLA style, parenthetical references include the author's name and page number after the material requiring documentation. In its simplest form, the parenthetical reference looks like this:

> Men and women often suffer from a form of cross-cultural communication (Tannen 14).

Notice that the author's name and the page number are enclosed in parentheses and that the reference includes no internal punctuation. Note also that the reference appears before the punctuation that ends the sentence.

When the author's name is used in the documented sentence, you need not repeat it in the parenthetical reference, which will include only the page number. For example:

> According to Deborah Tannen, men and women often suffer from a form of cross-cultural communication (14).

References to works written by *two authors* cite both names (joined by *and*) and the page number.

Lark and Lottish Corporation
56 Denville Road
Nashua, NH 03060
(603) 555-7115

April 11, 199X

American Cancer Society
4 Mandesta Street
Nashua, NH 03060

Dear Mr. Seligson:

There is no more worthwhile charitable organization in our community than the American Cancer Society. I am honored by your invitation to speak at your annual banquet next month.

My membership on several corporate boards places a great many demands on my time, and next month is my busiest travel period. Regrettably, because of previous commitments, I will not be able to accept your invitation.

Is there another American Cancer Society function at which I can speak? I have enclosed open dates in my schedule over the next three months.

Call me after you have looked at the schedule. I look forward to the opportunity to speak before an organization as worthwhile as your own.

Yours truly,

Martha Wilder
Martha Wilder
Chief Executive Officer

MW:jr
Enclosure

> The dateline, complimentary close, and signature block appear to the right of the center of the page, just as they do in block format. Here, however, paragraphs are indented five to ten character spaces. Notice that the lines in a paragraph are still single-spaced with double-spacing between paragraphs.

FIGURE I.6   *Sample Letter—Modified-Block Format*

When the source has *two or three authors*, all the names are cited in the reference. When a work has *more than three authors*, use the first author's name plus the abbreviation *et al.* For example:

> Cultural differences in the workplace must not be taken for granted; they must be managed (Harris and Moran 3).

> Adjustment letters should avoid emphasizing the negative situation described in the original complaint letter, but should focus on the actions being taken to correct the situation (Brusaw *et al.* 23).

If you must cite *two or more works by the same author*, your parenthetical references must differentiate between the works. Do this by providing the author's last name, a shortened title of the work, and page numbers. For example:

> (Tannen, *Understand* 111)

> (Tannen, *Conversational Style* 89)

Notice, by the way, that a comma separates the author's name and the title and that the title is underlined or italicized.

If the author of the work is a corporation or other organization, and if no individual author is cited, use the organization's name in your parenthetical reference. For example:

> (Xerox Corp. 57)

When no author, individual or corporate, is cited, your parenthetical reference should use the title of the work itself or an abbreviated version of that title. The abbreviated title should start with the word by which the work is alphabetized in the Works Cited list at the end of your document. For example:

> (*Statistical*, 345)

Here the title is underlined (italicized) because it is a book. When citing articles, use quotation marks.

There are times, of course, when more than one source will contribute to an idea cited in your document.

In this case, both sources (separated by a semicolon) should be included in your parenthetical reference:

(Tannen 167; Baron 64)

When your source cites another source, the names of both authors should be mentioned in your parenthetical reference. For example:

(Gilligan qtd. in Tannen 113)

In this citation, the abbreviation *qtd.* tells the reader that Deborah Tannen's book includes a *quote* by Carol Gilligan and that the source list at the back of the document includes an entry under Tannen's name.

Always place parenthetical references immediately after quoted material, even if the quote ends in the middle of a sentence. For example:

According to Deborah Tannen, "For most women, the language of conversation is primarily a language of rapport" (77) to establish connections and form relationships.

This format gives the reader enough information to locate the source of the quote in your Works Cited list.

APA STYLE   In APA style, parenthetical references also point the reader to the full citation at the end of your document. The purpose, then, is the same as that of MLA style; it is format that differs.

First, APA references distinguish between quoted material on the one hand and paraphrased or summarized material on the other. When citing *quoted material*, include the author's name, the year of the work's publication, and page number(s), which should be introduced with *p*, for one page and *pp*, for two or more pages. For example:

(Tannen, 1990, p. 101)

Notice that commas separate each element and that a period is used after *p*.

References to *paraphrased or summarized material* may or may not include page numbers; as a rule, the writer may decide whether or not the reader is likely to need the exact location of the cited material.

Although the same basic rules govern both MLA and APA citations, there are a few noteworthy requirements in APA style:

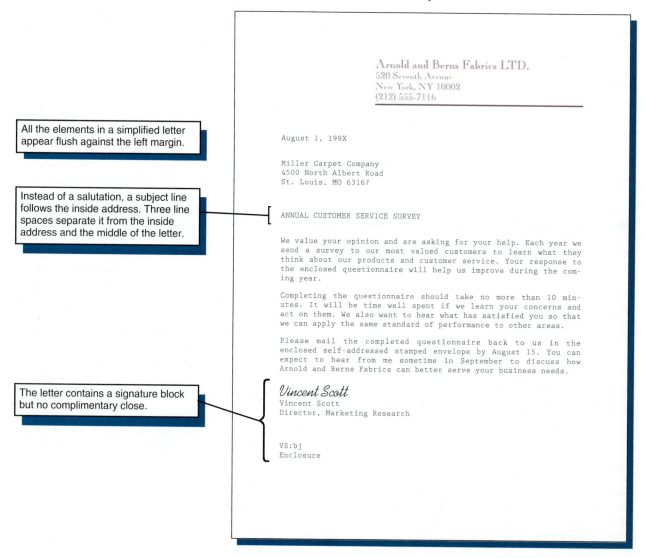

All the elements in a simplified letter appear flush against the left margin.

Instead of a salutation, a subject line follows the inside address. Three line spaces separate it from the inside address and the middle of the letter.

The letter contains a signature block but no complimentary close.

Arnold and Berns Fabrics LTD.
520 Seventh Avenue
New York, NY 10002
(212) 555-7116

August 1, 199X

Miller Carpet Company
4500 North Albert Road
St. Louis, MO 63167

ANNUAL CUSTOMER SERVICE SURVEY

We value your opinion and are asking for your help. Each year we send a survey to our most valued customers to learn what they think about our products and customer service. Your response to the enclosed questionnaire will help us improve during the coming year.

Completing the questionnaire should take no more than 10 minutes. It will be time well spent if we learn your concerns and act on them. We also want to hear what has satisfied you so that we can apply the same standard of performance to other areas.

Please mail the completed questionnaire back to us in the enclosed self-addressed stamped envelope by August 15. You can expect to hear from me sometime in September to discuss how Arnold and Berns Fabrics can better serve your business needs.

Vincent Scott
Vincent Scott
Director, Marketing Research

VS:bj
Enclosure

FIGURE I.7   *Sample Letter—Simplified Format*

- If you mention a work more than once, the full parenthetical reference is used the first time; all subsequent references include only author and page number.
- When citing works written in the same year by the same author, alphabetize the works in your References list and then assign a letter to each work (*a*, *b*, *c*, and so on); these same letters should then appear in your parenthetical references as a means of distinguishing among the author's various works. For example:

(Tannen, 1990a, p. 39)

Whether you choose MLA or APA style, it is important to use your chosen style consistently, both in your parenthetical references and in the source list at the end of your document. Do not mix citation styles.

Footnote and Endnote References

Footnotes and endnotes are alternatives to the parenthetical-reference method. In footnotes, complete sources appear at the bottom of the page on which cited material appears. A *superscript* in the form of a raised Arabic number coordinates the text reference to the footnote. Footnotes are numbered sequentially by page, chapter, or document. The same system is used in endnotes except that sources are found at the end of each chapter or the end of the work as a whole.

Both footnotes and endnotes may perform two different functions. *Explanatory notes* include commentary that supplements or explains the main point made in the text itself. Explanatory footnotes may also cross-reference other parts of the document or other sources. *Reference notes* establish the sources for quoted, paraphrased, or summarized material.

Use the following guidelines to include note numbers in your document:

1. The number should appear as superscript—that is, a little above the line of words.
2. The number should appear as close as possible to the text to which it refers, but after any accompanying punctuation.
3. One space should follow the number when it appears in the middle of a sentence; use two spaces when the number is followed by a new sentence.

Whether you use footnote numbers, endnote numbers, or parenthetical references, your citations must be coordinated with the *source list* in which you collect references to the material that you have used in your document. We will examine these source lists next.

Source Lists

Both parenthetical and endnote references are coordinated with a list of sources that appears at the end of your document; the sources for footnotes are found at the bottom of pages. As we noted earlier, MLA style refers to the source list as *Works Cited*; in APA style, it is called *References*. When you use endnotes, label your list *Notes*.

In each case, your list should contain *all* the sources actually cited in your document. If you consult a source but do not actually cite it in a quotation, paraphrase, or summary, you need not include it in your source list.

Your source list should begin on a new page, with entries arranged alphabetically according to authors' names. When an author is not named on a work, alphabetize the entry by the first significant word of the title (*The*, *A*, and *An* are not considered significant words).

We will turn next to the basic citation styles used to create lists of *Works Cited*, *References*, and *Notes*.

MLA DOCUMENTATION STYLE: WORKS CITED LIST

BOOKS   Citations for books include author, title, and publication information (place of publication, publisher, and date of publication). Each element is separated by a period and two spaces. All major words of the title are capitalized. When the source requires more than one line, the first line appears flush against the left margin and all following lines are indented five spaces. For example:

Harris, Philip R., and Robert T. Moran. *Managing Cultural Differences*. Houston: Gulf Publishing, 1991.

ARTICLES   Citations of articles from magazines, journals, and newspapers also contain three major parts: author, article title, and publication information. Publication information includes the title of the periodical, volume number, year of publication, and applicable page numbers. For example:

Sadker, Myra, and David Sadker. "Sexism in the Classroom: From Grade School to Graduate School." *Phi Delta Kappan* 67 (1986): 7.

Note that MLA styles reverses the order of the first and last names *for the first author only*. The title of the periodical is underlined (italicized), and the publication date is enclosed in parentheses.

When citing an article in a popular periodical or a newspaper, use the full date rather than a volume number. For example:

Sadker, Myra, and David Sadker. "Sexism in the Schoolroom of the '80s." *Psychology Today*, March 1985: 54–57.

When the date includes a specific day, the day should be written first, as in *14 March 1985*.

For the correct MLA form for all possible citations, consult Joseph Gibaldi and Walter S. Achtert, *MLA Handbook for Writers of Research Papers*, 3rd ed. (New York: MLA, 1988).

APA DOCUMENTATION STYLE: REFERENCES LIST

BOOKS   In APA style, book citations include four major parts: author, date, title, and publication information. For example:

Hall, E. T., and Hall, M. R. (1987). *Hidden differences: Doing business with the Japanese*. Garden City, NY: Doubleday.

In APA style, the last name of each author always appears first. The date of publication appears next in parentheses, followed by the title, which is underlined (italicized). Only the first word of the title is capitalized, as is any word following a colon. If the reader is likely to be unfamiliar with the city of publication (as with *Garden City, New York*), the U.S. Postal Service state abbreviation can be added.

ARTICLES   APA article citations also include four major parts: author, date, article title, and publication information. Publication information include the publication title, volume number, and applicable pages. For example:

> Cox, T., and Nkomo, S. M. (1990). Invisible men and women: A status report on race as a variable in organization behavior research. *Journal of Organizational Behavior*, 11, 1990. 238–256.

Note that quotation marks do *not* enclose the title of the article and that the inclusive page numbers are given in full. Page referencing contrasts with MLA style: MLA uses the full second number through 99 (for example, 26–37) but then only the last two digits (187–93) unless confusion could result (191–203).

In some journals, page numbers run continuously throughout an annual volume: That is, if the first issue of a volume ends on page 125, the second issue starts on page 126. In most journals, however, pagination is separate for each issue. To cite articles from journals in the latter group, include both the *volume number* and the *issue number*.

In APA style, the volume number is underlined (italicized) and the issue number follows immediately after within parentheses. For example:

> Droge, C., and Germain, R. (1990). A Note on marketing and the corporate annual report: 1930–1950. *Journal of the Academy of Marketing Science. 18*(4), 345–363.

For further information about citations using APA style, consult American Psychological Association, *Publication Manual of the American Psychological Association*, 3rd ed. (Washington, DC: APA, 1984).

FOOTNOTES AND ENDNOTES
When you use a note format, your source list can appear either at the bottom of separate pages or on separate pages at the end of the document. When you use endnotes, center the word *Notes* (no underlining or quotation marks) at the top of a separate page. Then skip four lines before starting the first note. Indent the first line of each note five character spaces; all other lines start at the left margin. Each note number is raised slightly above the entry and is written without a period.

The MLA style is frequently used to format footnotes and endnotes. MLA style is slightly different from that used in the Works Cited list that is usually coordinated with parenthetical references. For example, there is no reversal in the order of authors' names, and the publication information (place of publication, publisher, and date) is enclosed in parentheses.

FIRST REFERENCES   Here are some first-reference note forms for common types of sources. As you can see, subsequent references use a shortened form.

[1]Dennis Baron, *Grammar and Gender* (New Haven: Yale University Press, 1986) 134.

[2]Philip R. Harris and Robert T. Moran, *Managing Cultural Differences*, 3rd ed. (Houston: Gulf Publishing, 1991) 256.

[3]Dean Baquet and Martin Gottlieb, "Hospital Rewrote Reports in Failed Accreditation Bid," *The New York Times* 11 March 1992: A1.

[4]Kerry J. Rottenberger, "Can Anyone Become a More Effective Communicator?" *Sales & Marketing Management* August 1992: 60–63.

[5]Blair Johnson, personal interview, 25 May 1993.

[6]Tharon Howard, "Wide-Area Computer-Mediated Communication in Business Writing", *Bulletin of the Association for Business Communication* 55.4 (1992) 10–12.

SUBSEQUENT REFERENCES   To save time and avoid repetition, subsequent references appear in shortened form. Shortened source notes can use either a traditional style, which includes Latin abbreviations, or the MLA style, which does not.

In the traditional style, the following Latin abbreviations are commonly used:

- ibid. (Latin meaning "in the same place")
  This abbreviation is used when an entry is the same as the one immediately preceding it; when page numbers follow the abbreviation, the entry is the same but the page number is different.

- op. cit. (Latin meaning "in the work cited")
  This abbreviation is used when one or more references separate a reference from its original citation; to coordinate the reference with the original citation, include the last names of the authors as well as page numbers.

- loc. cit. (Latin meaning "in the place cited")
  This abbreviation is used in the same way as op. cit, except that it refers to exactly the same page number as the previous citation.

The following examples show how these abbreviations apply to actual sources:

> [1]Dennis Baron, *Grammar and Gender* (New Haven: Yale University Press, 1986) 134.
>
> [2]Ibid., 47.
>
> [3]Philip R. Harris and Robert T. Moran, *Managing Cultural Differences*, 3rd ed. (Houston: Gulf Publishing, 1991) 256.
>
> [4]Baron, op. cit., 67.
>
> [5]Dean Baquet and Martin Gottlieb, "Hospital Rewrote Reports in Failed Accreditation Bid," *The New York Times* 11 March 1992: A1.
>
> [6]Ibid.
>
> [7]Harris and Moran, loc. cit.

MLA style does not use Latin expressions to indicate subsequent references. Rather, MLA relies on shortened references to original sources. When footnotes or endnotes include only one work by an author, subsequent references need include only the author's last name and the page reference:

[8]O'Neill, 199.

To avoid confusion when you must cite more than one work by the same author, use a shortened form of each title, along with the author's name and page numbers:

[9]Smythe, *Communication* 234.

[10]Smythe, *Corporate Culture* 49–54.

A formal report may also include a bibliography whose purpose is to guide readers to additional sources. We will examine bibliographies next.

Bibliographies

A *bibliography* is an alphabetized list of the sources used to prepare a body of written material. A bibliography differs from lists of works cited, references, and notes in that it may include works not specifically referred to in the document. In addition, the bibliography uses inclusive page numbers for entire articles in periodicals, not just the pages specifically referred to as sources of cited information.

Each entry in the bibliography begins at the left margin, with the author's last name appearing first. Entries with no author are listed alphabetically by title (use the first significant word). All subsequent lines are indented five spaces. Entries are usually single-spaced, with a double line space between entries. As you can see from the following samples, the date in a bibliography appears later than it does in a source list:

Adler Nancy J. "Cultural Synergy: Managing the Impact of Cultural Diversity." In *The 1986 Annual: Developing Human Resources.* San Diego: University Associates, 1986, 229–38.

Copeland, Lennie. "Valuing Diversity: Making the Most of Cultural Differences at the Workplace," *Personnel*, 42 (June 1988): 52–60.

Hymowitz, Carol. "One Firm's Bid to Keep Blacks, Women: Corning Battles to Overcome Ingrained Biases." *The Wall Street Journal*, 16 February 1989, B1.

International Dimensions of Organizational Behavior. Boston: Kent Publishing, 1986.

Johnston, William B., and Arnold E. Packer. *Workforce 2000: Work and Workers for the Twenty-first Century.* Indianapolis: Hudson Institute, June 1987.

Leffler, Ann, Diane Gillespie, and Joan C. Conaty. "The Effects of Status Differentiation on Nonverbal Behavior," *Social Psychology* Quarterly 45:3 153–61.

Tannen, Deborah. *That's Not What I Meant! How Conversational Style Makes or Breaks Your Relations with Others.* New York: William Morrow, 1986.

In the bibliography, you can eliminate the need to repeat authors' names by using dashes instead of the same name several times.

To make an extensive bibliography more manageable, you can divide the entries into categories according to subject. For example, in a report on workforce diversity, the bibliography might be divided into the following headings: age, communication, cultural diversity, disability, gender, and race and ethnicity. It can also be divided by types of entries: books, journal articles, magazine and newspaper articles, and government publications.

To help readers evaluate the usefulness of sources, *annotated bibliographies* provide short comments on each entry. For example:

Hirsch, James S. "Older Workers Chafe under Young Managers." *The Wall Street Journal*, 26 February 1990, B1.

Discusses how the 3.4 million over-65 workers in the United States create unique problems and opportunities for themselves and their corporations.

If you decide to annotate your bibliography, remember that all entries must be annotated.

Basics of Grammar and Usage

For written communication to be successful, it must follow established rules for grammar and usage.[1] These rules allow both writers and readers to operate according to practices that communicate shared meaning. Appendix II will review the basics of grammar and usage rules, starting with the *parts of speech*—nouns, pronouns, verbs, adjectives, adverbs, prepositions, and conjunctions. We will then examine *sentence formation, punctuation, mechanics,* and *word usage.*

PARTS OF SPEECH

Nouns

A **noun** is a part of speech that names a person, a place, a thing, or an idea. Only proper nouns require capitalization. **Proper nouns** include names (*Albert Gore*), titles (*former President George Bush*), groups of humanity (*African Americans*), organizations (*Wal-Mart*), and places (*Mississippi River*). **Common nouns**, which refer to general classes of people, places, and things, are not capitalized. For example, while the company name *Avon* is capitalized, references to *the company* are not; while *Beverly Hills* is capitalized, *city* is not.

SINGULAR AND PLURAL NOUNS   When nouns refer to one person, place, thing, or idea, they are considered **singular**; when they refer to more than one person, place, thing, or idea, they are considered **plural**. To pluralize a regular noun, add an *-s* to the end of the noun. An *-es* is added to words that end in *ch, s, sh, x, or z* to make pronunciation possible. For example:

SINGULAR	PLURAL
desk	desks
book	books
flower	flowers
cross	crosses
match	matches
sash	sashes
tax	taxes

Irregular nouns are nouns that are pluralized by making changes other than adding final *-s* or *-es*. Here are some important rules that govern the spelling of irregular nouns:

1. In general, words ending in *-f* or *-fe* are pluralized by using a *v* in place of the *-f* or *-fe* and adding *-es*:

leaf	leaves
wife	wives
life	lives

2. In general, words ending in *-y* are pluralized by removing the *-y* and adding *-ies*:

party	parties
study	studies

3. Some nouns require internal changes to convert them from singular to plural. Here are just a few:

mouse	mice
man	men
woman	women
foot	feet
child	children

4. When the most important word in a compound word is the first word, pluralize that word to form the plural:

brother-in-law	brothers-in-law
mile per hour	miles per hour
editor in chief	editors in chief

If there is no difference in the importance of the words that make up the compound, place the *-s* or *-es* at the end of the entire compound:

tractor-trailer	tractor-trailers
nurse-practitioner	nurse-practitioners

5. Some nouns are spelled the same in the singular and plural forms. Words in this category include *deer, elk, fish, trout, salmon, rice,* and *wheat.*

POSSESSIVE NOUNS   **Possessive nouns** indicate ownership or a close relationship. Possession is generally shown by adding an -'s:

the writer's papers

the manager's office

the secretary's computer

the report's illustrations

When a singular noun ends in an *-s*, add an -'s to show possession—for example:

Charles Dickens's novel *David Copperfield*

the business's assets were considerable

When a plural noun ends in an *-s*, show possession by adding an apostrophe—for example:

Two years' neglect has left the building in disrepair.

Clients' problems must be dealt with before personnel problems.

Pronouns

A **pronoun** is a word that replaces or refers to a noun. The noun for which the pronoun stands is known as an **antecedent**. For example:

The CEO wants an immediate increase.

He wants it by the end of next week.

Here, the pronoun *he* replaces the noun *CEO* while the pronoun *it* replaces the noun *increase*.

MAKING PRONOUNS AND ANTECEDENTS AGREE

If different pronouns refer to different nouns in the same paragraph, clarity requires that the nouns sometimes be repeated. In the following paragraph, for example, the pronoun reference is unclear.

> Martha Feingold submitted the trip report three days after Elaine Wilky, her supervisor, asked for it. She analyzed her meetings in Baltimore and discussed how her insistence on the highest standards of customer service was making a positive impression on clients.

Who analyzed the Baltimore meetings? Who insisted on high standards of customer service? The following version clarifies the confusion:

> Martha Feingold submitted the trip report three days after Elaine Wilky asked for it. Feingold analyzed her meetings in Baltimore and discussed how Wilky's insistence on the highest standards of customer service was making a positive impression on clients.

To avoid confusion, pronouns should be placed as close as possible to their antecedents. In addition, many writers prefer to use a noun rather than a pronoun at the start of a new paragraph when the noun was used in the prior paragraph. Repetition of this type often improves clarity.

Pronouns can be either singular or plural, and they must match their antecedents in number. The following guidelines will help ensure accurate usage:

1. When two or more nouns are joined by the word *and*, the pronoun that refers to the nouns should be plural.

> Although Reebok and Nike are both in the athletic footwear business, they use different technology.

2. When singular nouns are preceded by *each* or *every* and are connected by the word *and*, use a singular pronoun:

> Every elected President and Vice President takes his oath of office on January 20 of the year following his election.

3. **Indefinite pronouns** do not refer to any specific person, thing, or idea: Rather, they depend on context for their meaning. Indefinite pronouns include such words as *anybody, anyone, each, every, everybody, nobody,* and *someone.* In most cases, a singular pronoun is used to refer to an indefinite pronoun:

> Anyone who has contributed to the project should submit his [or her] final draft by tomorrow.

CHOOSING GENDER-NEUTRAL PRONOUNS

Be sensitive to the gender implications of chosen pronouns. The conventions of grammar, like the conventions of society, have changed over the years. As a result, it is no longer wise to use masculine pronouns to refer to indefinite pronouns, to nouns, or to general categories that might include both men and women. This shift in acceptable form has occurred because the pronouns *he, his, him,* and *himself* are now seen as implicitly excluding women.

Sexist language can be avoided in three different ways:

1. By using a pronoun pair (*he and she, his or her*)
2. By making the antecedent plural
3. By rewriting the sentence to avoid the use of sexist language

Thus, this sentence—

> Every participant at the meeting championed his own personal agenda.

—becomes one of the following revised sentences:

> Every participant at the meeting championed his or her own personal agenda.

> The nine participants at the meeting championed their own personal agendas.

> Everyone came to the meeting with a personal agenda in mind.

SELECTING THE PROPER PRONOUN CASE   The

case of a pronoun refers to the relationship that word has to the other words in a sentence. Case shows changes in both person (first, second, and third person) and number (singular and plural). The **first person** refers to the speaker or writer; the **second person** to the person spoken or written to, and the **third person** to the person or thing that is spoken or written about.

Pronouns have three cases: subjective, objective, and possessive. Used in the **subjective case**, pronouns act as the subject of a sentence:

> We will review the report after lunch.

> You will be expected to complete the assignment by next week.

Used in the **objective case**, pronouns have three functions in the sentence: a **direct object**, an **indirect object**, or the **object of a preposition**:

> We watched *her* deliver the keynote speech. (*Her* is the direct object.)

> I gave them our estimate. (*Them* is the indirect object.)

> Please give the check to *him*. (*Him* is the object of the preposition *to*.)

Used in the **possessive case**, pronouns show possession or ownership:

> *Our* car was in an accident. Please bring the accident report to her office. (The possessive pronouns *our* and *her* show ownership.)

Although a compound construction should not affect the choice of pronoun, it often does when writers mistakenly use the wrong case for one or more of the pronouns. For example, if instead of writing,

> *Bill and I* plan to attend the conference

you were to write,

> Bill and me plan to attend the conference

you would have chosen the objective case (*me*) instead of the subjective case (*I*) to refer to one of the subjects of your sentence. Similarly, look at the following pair of sentences:

> The manager told *Karen and me* to start the new project.

> The manager told *Karen and I* to start the new project.

The first sentence is correct because the pronoun (*me*) is a direct object and thus takes the objective case; the second sentence, therefore, is incorrect because the *I* is in the subjective case, not the objective.

Confusion also frequently occurs after the use of linking verbs. A **linking verb** connects the subject of a sentence to a word that renames it. This confusion occurs most often with linking verbs that indicate a state of being (*am, is, are, was, were*). The pronoun that follows the linking verb renames the subject of that verb and must therefore be in the subjective case. For example:

> Last year, the top salesperson in the country was *I*.

It would be incorrect to write,

> Last year, the top salesperson in the country was *me*.

The linking verb (*was*) connects its subject (*salesperson*) with a pronoun (*I*) that must be in the subjective case.

Confusion also occurs quite often over the correct form of the possessive personal pronouns *its* and *whose*. Although these pronouns express ownership, they do not require the use of an apostrophe. Thus, while the first sentence in each of the following pairs is correct, the second sentence is incorrect.

> The mailroom has to revise *its* delivery schedule.

> The mailroom has to revise *it's* delivery schedule.

> The investors, *whose* stock skyrocketed after the merger announcement, were happy.

> The investors, *who's* stock skyrocketed after the merger announcement, were happy.

Remember: *It's* is a contraction for *it is* or *it has*, and *who's* is a contraction for *who is* or *who has*.

Verbs

Verbs describe an action (*write, think, deliver, scratch*), a state of being (*be, seem, exist*), or an occurrence (*become, happen*).

VERB TENSES   The **tense** of a verb tells you when an action, a state of being, or an occurrence took place. Tense tells you whether the action is current, happened in the past, or will happen in the future.

There are six verb tenses in the English language—three simple tenses and three perfect tenses. While both the simple and perfect tenses divide time into past, present, and future, the perfect tenses express more complex relationships.

The three **perfect tenses** show complex *time* relationships in the past, present, and future. These tenses combine an **auxiliary verb** (usually some form of the helping verb *have*) with the past participle form of the main verb.

It is extremely important to be able to recognize the **past participle** form of a verb. A typical dictionary, for example, shows the following forms of the verb *awake*:

awake   *awoke* or *awaked*
awaked or *awoken*   *awaking*

This entry means that either of the two forms *awoke* or *awaked* may be used as the past tense of the verb; either of the two forms *awaked* or *awoken* may be used as the past participle. However, the two different forms of *awaked* are not the same form of the verb any more than *awoke* and *awoken* are the same form. *Awaking* is the present participle.

It may also help to remember that a participle always has some of the characteristics of an adjective. For example, the past participle of the verb speak is spoken; the present participle is speaking. Thus, you can refer to the "the *spoken* word" as opposed to "the *written* word" or to "a *speaking* part" in a play.

Remember: The perfect tenses of a verb are formed with the past participle, not the past tense.

With this principle in mind, we can examine the formation of perfect verb tenses in English. The **present perfect tense** shows that action which started in the past continues into the present. The auxiliary verb *have* indicates the continuing action:

> I *have behaved* with integrity throughout this affair.

The **past perfect tense** describes a situation in which an action started in the past, continued for a period of time, and was completed in the past. It is usually formed by combining *had* with the past participle:

> I *had behaved* with integrity until the rumors began.

The **future perfect tense** indicates that an action will have been completed in relation to some specific future time. The auxiliary *will have* generally signals the future perfect tense:

> By the turn of the century, I *will have completed* my graduate education.

REGULAR AND IRREGULAR VERBS   Forming the simple and perfect tenses is straightforward for regular verbs. As a rule, these verbs add a *-d* or an *-ed* to form both the past tense and the past participle. In other words, the past participle is spelled and pronounced exactly like the past tense. However, anyone who has ever studied a foreign language knows that experience or memorization is required to use the principal parts of irregular verbs. A native speaker of English knows that the past tense of *take* is *took*, not *taked*. The non-native speaker must learn and remember that lesson.

THE VOICE OF VERBS   Through its **voice**, a verb indicates whether the subject of a sentence is performing or receiving the action named by the verb. Verbs using the **active voice** indicate that the subject is performing an action; verbs using the **passive voice** indicate that the subject is receiving the action. For example:

Active Voice   The manager *combined* two departments.

Passive Voice   Two departments *were combined* by the manager.

Sentences using the passive voice may or may not indicate who performed the action—for example:

> Two departments *were combined*.

Sometimes the performers are unknown, and sometimes they are relatively unimportant to the message. Sometimes the writer chooses not to mention them. Chapter 5, for example, includes guidelines for choosing the active and passive voices in business writing.

VERB MOOD   Verbs also communicate a writer's attitude toward a statement. This attitude is known as **mood**. English verbs have three moods: the indicative mood, the imperative mood, and the subjunctive mood.

The most common mood, the **indicative**, makes statements or asks questions:

> The consultant *sat down* at the head of the table.
>
> *Do* you *need* help completing the project?

The **imperative mood** is used to issue commands and direct orders:

> *Distribute* these pamphlets now.
>
> Please *take* this suit to the cleaners.

The **subjunctive mood** expresses conditions, including wishes, indirect requests, and speculation, and is often preceded by words like *if, unless,* or *that.* As you can see in the following example, verbs in the subjunctive mood are used in special ways:

> If the division *were run* correctly, profits would be higher.
>
> Unless profits *soar*, we'll have to declare bankruptcy.
>
> I wish [that] he *were* ten years younger.

Adjectives

Adjectives describe nouns and pronouns. For example:

> The *studious* boy walked to the library. (The adjective *studious* modifies the noun *boy.*)
>
> The *beautiful* vase graced the table. (The adjective *beautiful* modifies the noun *vase.*)

Adjectives can also communicate relative degrees of intensity by shifting from positive to comparative to superlative form. **Positive adjectives** are used in sentences that make no comparisons. **Comparative adjectives** compare two items; they usually end with an *-er* or are accompanied by the word *more* or *less.* **Superlative adjectives** compare three or more things and usually end with an *-est* or are accompanied by the word *most* or *least.* For example:

POSITIVE	COMPARATIVE	SUPERLATIVE
smart	smarter	smartest
fast	faster	fastest
strong	stronger	strongest
successful	more successful	most successful
verbal	less verbal	least verbal
busy	busier	busiest

The proper form of comparatives and superlatives—using the *-er* and *-est* endings or the helping words—is largely determined by the number of syllables in the adjective. As a general rule, use the *-er* and *-est* endings when an adjective has one syllable. Use *more, most, less,* and *least* when the adjective has three or more syllables. Remember, however, that adjectives with two syllables are sometimes treated one way and sometimes the other. When a two-syllable adjective ends in *-y*—for example, *busy*—the *-y* changes to an *-i* before the *-er* or *-est* is added.

The irregular adjectives in the following list do not follow these rules; comparative and superlative forms must simply be learned.

POSITIVE	COMPARATIVE	SUPERLATIVE
good	better	best
bad	worse	worst
many	more	most
some	more	most
little	less	least

Adverbs

Adverbs modify verbs, adjectives, other adverbs, and entire sentences. For example:

> The artist *carefully* painted the portrait. (The adverb *carefully* modifies the verb *painted.)*
>
> The manager made an *extremely* urgent phone call. (The adverb *extremely* modifies the adjective *urgent.)*
>
> Tom is *so* highly qualified for the job that we can stop interviewing other candidates. (The adverb *so* modifies the adverb *highly.)*
>
> *Unfortunately*, we cannot meet the production schedule. (The adverb *Unfortunately* modifies the entire sentence.)

Many adverbs are formed by adding *-ly* to adjectives—for example, *quick/quickly, slow/slowly, rapid/rapidly.*

Conjunctive adverbs are modifiers that logically connect ideas. They express addition (*also, furthermore, moreover, besides*), contrast (*still, nevertheless, conversely, however*), comparison (*similarly, likewise*), results (*therefore, consequently, thus*), time (*finally, next, then*), and emphasis (*indeed, certainly*).

Prepositions

Prepositions are part of **prepositional phrases**, which often state relationships in time or space. Prepositional phrases are composed of a preposition and a noun or pronoun that acts as an object—that is, it is governed by the preposition. For example:

Please give the report *to Joan*. (*To* is a preposition, *Joan* its object.)

We will eat lunch *after the sales meeting*. *After* is a preposition, and the noun phrase *the sales meeting* is its object.)

Some common prepositions are included in the following list. As you review them, keep in mind that some of these words may also function as other parts of speech.

about	concerning	on
above	despite	out
across	down	over
after	except	past
along	for	regarding
around	in	since
as	in addition to	through
at	into	till
because of	near	toward
before	next	under
between	of	upon
by	off	with

Conjunctions

Coordinating conjunctions connect two or more grammatically equivalent structures, including nouns, verbs, adjectives, and independent clauses. These common conjunctions include *and, but, nor, or, yet, for,* and *so*. In the following sentences, the conjunction *and* connects, respectively, two nouns, two verbs, two adjectives, and two independent clauses:

Please move the desk *and* chair.
We still have to type *and* collate the report.
The manuscript is correct *and* current.
He sent a copy to Smith, *and* he was sure to make four copies for Jones.

Correlative conjunctions also join equivalent grammatical structures, but they do so by functioning in pairs. Correlative conjunctions include:

both…and
either…or
neither…nor
not only…but also
whether…or

For example:

You can *either* have a draft now *or* a final report later.
Both Sam *and* I worked on it together.

WRITING CORRECT SENTENCES

Sentences are formed when the parts of speech are combined in grammatically correct ways. This combination produces *simple sentences, compound sentences*, and *complex sentences*.

Simple Sentences

A **simple sentence** contains a subject and a predicate. The **predicate** is the part of a sentence that contains the verb and its modifiers, as well as direct and indirect objects. A **direct object** receives the verb's action; an **indirect subject** refers to whom or for whom the action expressed by the verb was done. Consider the following examples of simple sentences:

The boy ran.

The subject of the sentence is *boy*, the predicate *ran*. This sentence has a simple predicate because it contains only a verb.

The boy ran quickly.

The predicate in this sentence is considered a complete predicate because it contains both the verb and its modifier (*quickly*).

The customer bought the car.

The complete predicate in this sentence includes an object (*car*) as well as a verb.

The recruiter gave the student an application.

This complete predicate includes a direct object (*application*) as well as an indirect object (*student*).

Compound Sentences

A **compound sentence** contains two or more independent clauses and may be connected by a coordinating conjunction (*and, but, for, or, nor, yet,* or *so*). An **independent clause** is a clause which contains a subject and a predicate and which can function on its own as an independent grammatical unit:

The recruiter liked the candidate, but she doubted that he would be willing to relocate to St. Louis.

Here the two independent clauses are connected by a comma and the coordinating conjunction *but*.

Complex Sentences

A **complex sentence** contains one independent clause and at least one dependent clause. A **dependent clause** cannot function as an independent sentence and must be joined to an independent clause.

Although consumers reacted positively to the new product during market tests, first-year sales were poor.

In this case, the dependent clause appears before the comma and is introduced by the subordinating conjunction *although*.

Constructing simple, compound, and complex sentences is not always straightforward. Consequently, writers sometimes make errors in sentence formation. In the next section, we will examine common types of errors by focusing on sentence fragments, comma splices and fused sentences, and sentences with internal flaws that affect communication.

Sentence Fragments

A **sentence fragment** is a part of a sentence that is treated as if it were a complete sentence. In most cases, sentence fragments are phrases or dependent clauses. For example:

> Although the market improved.
>
> The office with the panoramic view.
>
> After the proposal was presented.
>
> When the secretary learned the word processing program.

To determine whether a sentence is complete, check to see whether it contains a subject and a verb. If it does not contain both a subject and a verb, it is a **phrase** and cannot be a complete sentence. Does a subordinating word introduce the subject and verb and thus transform the clause into a dependent clause? For example:

> Wrote the report. (This fragment is a phrase that lacks a subject.)
>
> The report's cover. (This fragment is a phrase that lacks a verb.)
>
> Unless we receive a signed contract tomorrow. (This fragment is a dependent clause introduced by a subordinating conjunction.)

As in the last fragment above, a dependent clause often begins with a subordinating conjunction. Among the most common subordinating conjunctions are *after, although, as, because, before, even though, if, since, though, unless, until, when, whenever,* and *where.*

To correct sentence fragments that involve dependent clauses, you can either combine the dependent clause with an independent clause or drop the subordinating word that creates the dependent clause. For example, look at the following sentence fragment:

> The strike centered on wages and health-insurance benefits. Because these issues had the greatest economic impact on the average worker.

The fragment can be eliminated by combining the two sentences:

> The strike centered on wages and health-insurance benefits because these issues had the greatest economic impact on the average worker.

It can also be eliminated by dropping the subordinating conjunction (*because*) and creating an independent clause that functions as a complete sentence:

> The strike centered on wages and health-insurance benefits. These issues had the greatest economic impact on the average worker.

To correct sentence fragments that contain phrases, you can either rewrite the phrase so that it becomes an independent clause or combine the phrase with an adjoining independent clause to form a complex sentence. Here, for example, is a combination phrase and independent clause:

> Expecting a raise. He bought a new car.

This fragment can be transformed in the following ways:

> He expected a raise. He bought a new car.

The phrase is rewritten as an independent clause.

> Expecting a raise, he bought a new car.

The phrase is combined with the independent clause to form a complex sentence.

Comma Splices and Fused Sentences

Although a comma is used to *separate* parts of a sentence, it cannot *join*—that is, *splice* together—independent clauses without a coordinating conjunction following (*and, but, for, or, nor, yet* and *so*) to complete the connection. A **comma splice** (or **comma fault**) occurs when a writer tries to connect two independent clauses with nothing but a comma. For example:

> The auditor reviewed all the books, she focused on accounts receivable.

A **fused sentence** (also known as a **run-on sentence**) joins two independent clauses without the use of any punctuation or coordinating conjunction. For example:

> The letter attempted to establish good will between the customer and the company the customer responded positively.

Both comma splices and fused sentences can be corrected with periods or semicolons:

Comma Splice	The writer compiled the research, the first part of the project was complete.
Fused Sentence	The writer compiled the research the first part of the project was complete.
Correction with a Period	The writer compiled the research. The first part of the project was complete.
Correction with a Semicolon	The writer compiled the research; the first part of the project was complete.

Comma splices and fused sentences can also be corrected with coordinating conjunctions:

Correction with a coordinating conjunction	The writer compiled the research, and the first part of the project was complete.

Finally, comma splices and fused sentences can be corrected by turning one of the independent clauses into a dependent clause and, in the process, creating a complex sentence:

Correction by creating a complex sentence	Once the writer compiled the research, the first part of the project was complete.

Internal Sentence Flaws

Among the sentence flaws that can affect communication are *misplaced modifiers* and *dangling modifiers*.

MISPLACED MODIFIERS   A **modifier** is a word or a group of words that describes other words, phrases, or clauses. The position of a modifier in a sentence can affect the meaning of that sentence, sometimes significantly. A **misplaced modifier** is wrongly or awkwardly placed in the sentence so that the writer's intended meaning is obscured. For example:

> Women began entering the labor force in record number, although their opportunities for advancement were limited beginning in the 1970s.

What began in the 1970s—the entry of women into the labor force or the limitation of advancement opportunities? This error can usually be avoided by placing the modifier as close as possible to what is being described. In this case, because the modified event is the entry of women into the labor force, the meaning of the sentence is clarified when the modifier is placed at the beginning:

> Beginning in the 1970s, women began entering the labor force in record number, although their opportunities for advancement were limited.

DANGLING MODIFIERS   A **dangling modifier** describes something that is implied but not stated in the sentence. When such sentences are read carefully, they simply do not make sense:

> Hearing the whistle, the train pulled into the station.

The train, of course, cannot hear the whistle, and the reader must assume that appropriate listeners are implied—probably waiting passengers. With any luck, they will be waiting in the next sentence, where they can be brought into this sentence to eliminate the dangling modifier and clarify the subject of both sentences:

> Hearing the whistle, the passengers lined up on the platform to board the train when it pulled into the station.

PUNCTUATION

Punctuation marks occur within sentences (**internal punctuation**) and at the end of sentences (**end punctuation**). They separate thoughts into recognizable, digestible units that enable the reader to understand what is being said. First, we will examine end punctuation—the period, the question mark, and the exclamation point. Then we will discuss internal punctuation—the comma, the semicolon, the colon, the apostrophe, quotation marks, the dash, parentheses, brackets, and the ellipsis.

Period

A period is used to end sentences that are considered statements, mild commands, or indirect questions.

Statement	Here is the marketing plan for our new product line.
Mild command	Add more statistical data to the report.
Indirect question	The manager questioned why the department failed to meet its production schedule.

Periods are also used at the end of many abbreviations (*Dr., Ph.D., Ms., Mrs., Mr., a.m.*) and to separate dollars and cents in numerical expressions of money.

Question Mark

A question mark is used at the end of a direct question:

> Will your report tell me where to place the new distribution center?

In order to be polite, a request is sometimes phrased in the form of a question:

> Would you please send me five copies of the completed report?

The question mark is optional in this request, which is actually a mild command:

> Send me five copies of the completed report.

Exclamation Point

The exclamation point is used after a strong command or an emphatic declaration:

> Don't touch that!
> Watch out for the thin ice!

Comma

The comma is used within sentences and is the most common punctuation mark. It is used to separate and group words and phrases in order to make sentences more readable. The following guidelines will help you decide when a comma is necessary and when it is not.

1. Place a comma before a coordinating conjunction that connects independent clauses. Coordinating conjunctions include *and, but, or, nor, yet, so,* and *for.* When a comma is used in this way, the end result is a compound sentence. For example:

> The budget figures are due today, and I have seven other things on my desk.
> She will take the job, but she can't start until next month.
> You can move directly into the new office, or movers can place your belongings in storage.

2. Use a comma after an introductory word, phrase, or clause at the beginning of a sentence. For example:

> First, I would like to discuss the economy.
> On the other hand, our sales force is the best in the business.
> From its inception, the company has dominated the market.

After obtaining a mortgage, she bought a house.

Although I think we can get financing, I'm not sure.

3. Use a comma to separate items in a series. When items in a series, including words, phrases, and clauses, have the same grammatical form, commas are used to separate each item:

The ideal candidate should have experience, creativity, and judgment.

To move up the career ladder, you have to demonstrate a willingness to work, an ability to get the job done, and the common sense to take the advice of those who are willing to give it.

4. Use a comma to separate adjectives that equally modify the same noun. For example:

The luxurious, spacious conference room was the site for the board meeting.

However, a comma is not used to separate **noncoordinate adjectives**—that is, adjectives that do not equally modify a noun. For example:

Affluent American teenagers make up a large part of the consumer electronics market.

5. Use commas to set off nonessential elements in a sentence—that is, elements that can be removed from the sentence without changing the basic meaning of the independent clause. For example:

Mary Higgins, who joined the company last year, is handling the production problem.

An issue of concern to all employees, medical insurance benefits are being renegotiated this year.

By contrast, an essential element is *not* set off by commas because the basic meaning of the independent clause would change if the element were removed:

Packages marked "Fragile" generally arrive in good shape.

Because the phrase *marked "Fragile"* is an essential element of the sentence, it is not set off by commas.

6. Use commas to set off words of direct address:

I want to thank you, David, for helping the department meet its production goals.

7. Use commas to set off quotations that appear in a sentence from short explanations that appear in the same sentence. These short explanations often take the form of **speaker tags**—explanatory clauses like *he said, they answered*, and *she explained*. For example:

"Here are the disks with the final manuscript," said Peter, as he handed over the material.

However, a comma is not used when the word *that* separates the short explanation from the quoted material. For example:

As Peter handed over the material, he said that "the disks are in final form."

8. Follow the accepted rules in using commas in dates, names, and addresses:

May 21, 1996 **but** May 1996 **and** May 21

Michael Armstrong, Ph.D. **and** Michelle Peller, M.D.

McGrath, Angela (A comma is required when names are inverted.)

Los Angeles, California

When a city and state are used in a sentence, a comma is placed after the state as well:

The movie industry has been centered in Los Angeles, California, since its inception.

If an address appears as part of a sentence, use commas to separate the elements of the address. However, no comma is used to separate the state from the ZIP code:

You can reach me in care of Mr. Arthur Pond, Pond and Pluck Attorneys at Law, 1334 Main Street, Fayetteville, Arkansas 72701.

9. Use commas after the complimentary close in a letter:

Sincerely,

Best wishes,

Cordially,

Semicolon

Like a comma, the semicolon separates elements in a sentence, but it does so in a stronger way than the comma. Semicolons are used in three distinct ways.

1. Semicolons separate closely related independent clauses:

The copy machine produces color copies; it also collates.

You can also separate these clauses with a period, making each into a complete sentence. A semicolon, then, may be used where a period can be used; it signals less of a separation and indicates a closer connection between ideas.

2. Semicolons separate two independent clauses when the second clause begins with such words and phrases as *moreover, however, furthermore, nevertheless, consequently, on the one hand, as a result*, and *in short*:

Every employee receives two months of training; however, many require additional on-the-job instruction.

Remember: These words are *conjunctive adverbs*, not conjunctions, and cannot be used to connect two independent clauses. Without the semicolon, the result is a comma splice (fused sentence).

3. Semicolons separate lengthy items in a series or series items that already contain commas:

To prepare for this career, get a college degree; do extensive traveling in Germany, France, and Great Britain; and learn to speak German and French fluently.

Colon

The colon is used to introduce quotations:

> In the current annual report, the chairman writes: "The company achieved its best earnings in more than a decade."

It is also used to introduce lists:

> When you start the job, bring three things: a willingness to work hard, the ability to work smart, and old-fashioned common sense.

A colon is also used after the salutation of a business letter.

Apostrophe

Use the apostrophe to indicate the possessive form of a noun or an indefinite pronoun. **Indefinite pronouns** refer to nonspecific persons or things and include such words as *all, anyone, each*, and *everyone*:

> The manager's style was direct and abrupt.
>
> Ann's comments were directed at everyone's work.

When a singular noun ends in -s, show possession by adding an -'s. However, when a plural noun ends in -s, show possession by adding only an apostrophe. For example:

> The cleaning business's employee turnover is high.
> The retailing and wholesaling businesses' sales are down.
> Chris's injury is covered by the workers' compensation law.

When a sentence contains two or more consecutive nouns and you want to indicate *individual* possession, end each noun with an -'s. The following sentence says that Anita and Ron contributed separate comments:

> Anita's and Ron's comments are contained in this memo.

To indicate *joint* possession, add an -'s only to the last noun. The following sentence says that Joy and Mike are joint owners of the house:

> Joy and Mike's house is selling for $200,000.

Apostrophes are also used when one or more letters have been intentionally omitted from a word to form a **contraction**. Although contractions are common in both speech and informal writing, they should not be used in reports and other formal documents. Here are some of the most common contractions:

aren't (are not)	he's (he is)	isn't (is not)
can't (cannot)	I'm (I am)	let's (let us)
didn't (did not)	I've (I have)	there's (there is)
he'll (he will)	I'd (I would)	won't (will not)
		you're (you are)

Quotation Marks

Quotation marks tell the reader that you are citing the exact words spoken or written by someone else. For example:

> Page 12 of the report states that "no employee is entitled to more than four weeks' vacation a year."

Quotation marks always appear in pairs and are used to enclose short quotations of no more than four lines. Longer quoted passages are displayed on the page and are not surrounded by quotation marks. A **displayed quotation** begins on a new line and uses a block-indentation format.

Quotation marks are also used to enclose titles of short published works, including magazine and journal articles, essays, brochures, and pamphlets. They may also enclose words that are being used in a slightly different way than the reader might expect and often indicate irony:

> The CEO keeps talking about the company's "new spirit" but acts like nothing has changed.

Commas and periods are placed inside closing quotation marks, and colons and semicolons are placed outside. Quotations within quotations are enclosed within single quotation marks.

Dash

Dashes interrupt sentences to add information and, in the process, emphasize that same information. Dashes are also used to define or restate key concepts and thereby emphasize explanations and descriptions:

> Diversity training--practical lessons that help improve the way diverse groups communicate --has improved the interpersonal environment in many companies.

Dashes can also be used to add and emphasize new information:

> Consumer confidence has increased dramatically--by more than 50 percent--since last year.

Finally, dashes may be used to add an aside:

> With sales up, bonuses are likely to be large, but--if you believe the latest rumor--we may not see any bonus money for another month.

Dashes are formed by combining two hyphens, with no spaces left before, between, or after the hyphens.

Parentheses

Like dashes, parentheses set off information that interrupts the flow of a sentence. Unlike dashes, however, parentheses minimize and deemphasize the information they enclose. Parentheses are often used to enclose explanations, examples, and asides:

> Electronic mail (also known as E-mail) is revolutionizing the way people communicate in business.

> By moving the distribution center to another location (St. Louis, for example), we will save millions of dollars in transportation costs each year.

> Everyone is working twice as hard (and management would claim, twice as smart) as last year.

Parentheses also have some specialized uses. They are sometimes used to enclose the numbers in numbered lists:

> The meeting will cover three major issues: (1) current sales, (2) current expenses and ways to reduce them, and (3) projected profits for the next fiscal year.

Business and legal writing sometimes requires that numbers be spelled out first and then restated in numerical form. The restated numeral is enclosed in parentheses:

> The yearly rent for the Grove Street retail location is forty thousand dollars ($40,000).

Brackets

Brackets allow you to add words to a quotation that were not part of the original quote. Generally, these added words—or interpolations—enable you either to fit quoted material into the structure of your sentence or to clarify the quoted material:

> Jones made it clear that "[the company] is stronger now than it was a year ago."

> At the last meeting, Billings stated that "the dramatic increase in [consumer product] sales is responsible for at least half of the year's total profit."

Ellipsis

An ellipsis is a series of three dots that indicates that material has been omitted from a quotation. Consider, for example, the following quotation:

> "Every company faces a different marketing environment, depending on its products, competitors, customers, technologies, government influences, and so on, that helps define its corporate culture."

Now consider the same quotation with selected material left out:

> "Every company faces a different marketing environment . . . that helps define its corporate culture."

If the omission occurs at the end of a sentence, add a period to the three spaced periods of the ellipsis to produce a series of four spaced dots.

WRITING MECHANICS

Writing mechanics refers to the correct use of capital letters, italics (sometimes displayed as underlining in a typed manuscript), abbreviations, and numbers.

Capital Letters

The following guidelines will help you decide whether or not to capitalize a letter.

1. Begin the first word of every sentence with a capital letter.
2. Capitalize proper nouns, including the names of people, places, and things, and proper adjectives. **Proper adjectives** are formed from proper nouns. For example, starting with the proper noun *America*, we form the proper adjective *American*.
3. When an introduced quotation appears in the middle of a sentence, capitalize the first letter of the quoted words:

   > According to Thomas E. Deal and Allan A. Kennedy, "Companies that have cultivated their individual identities by shaping values, making heroes, spelling out rites and rituals, and acknowledging the cultural network have an edge."

   However, when the quote runs into the structure of your own sentence, the first word is *not* capitalized:

   > Thomas E. Deal and Allan A. Kennedy believe that "companies that have cultivated their individual identities by shaping values, making heroes, spelling out rites and rituals, and acknowledging the cultural network have an edge."

4. Use capital letters at the start of complete sentences that are part of run-in lists. A **run-in list** is a list of items that appears in normal sentence format. For example:

   > The poor selling season was caused by three factors: (1) The recession placed thousands of consumers out of work. (2) Consumer confidence is at a ten-year low. (3) Bad weather made it impossible for people to reach the stores.

Italics

Use **italics**, in the form of **underlining**, with titles of long written works such as books, reports, journals, magazines, and newspapers; the titles of television series; the titles of artworks and long musical compositions, such as operas; and the names of ships. Underlining is also used to differentiate foreign words from words written in English:

> There were only fourteen <u>summa cum laude</u> graduates in the entire university.

Finally, underlining can be used for special emphasis—that is, to focus the reader's attention on a key word or sentence:

<u>If we do not receive payment by January 30, your credit will be suspended.</u>

Abbreviations

Abbreviations are commonly used in business writing. While many abbreviations are unique to particular fields, others cut across different types of business disciplines. Here are some of the most common business abbreviations:

c. or ©	copyright	inc.	incorporated
cf.	compare	ltd.	limited
e.g.	for example	ms.	manuscript
et al.	and others	P&L or P/L	profit and loss
f., ff	and the following page, pages	sec.	section
		v. or vs.	versus (legal case)
		vol., vols.	volume, volumes
fax	facsimile	whsle.	wholesale
i.e.	that is		

Acronyms are also common in business. **Acronyms** are abbreviations formed by combining the first letter or letters of several words. They usually include no punctuation and are pronounced as words. For example:

random-access memory (RAM)

read-only memory (ROM)

radio detecting and ranging (radar)

The first time that an unfamiliar acronym or abbreviation appears in a work, write the complete term, followed by an abbreviated form in parentheses. Then use the abbreviated form throughout the rest of the document.

Numbers

The numbers *one* through *nine* should be spelled out, while numbers *10* and above should be written as figures.

If a sentence starts with a number, the number should be written out no matter how large it is. For example:

Five hundred and twelve people attended the stockholders' meeting.

To avoid this awkward construction, you can simply rewrite the sentence so that the number does not appear first:

The stockholders' meeting was attended by 512 people.

COMMONLY MISUSED WORDS

Words are misused for two major reasons: They are confused with other words or their meanings are misunderstood. Words are also considered misused when they are spelled incorrectly.

Homonyms and Other Commonly Confused Words

Homonyms are words that sound exactly alike but are spelled differently and have different meanings—for example, *hear* and *here*. These words are often misused in business writing. Other words that sound similar to one another are also subject to confusion. The following list contains some of the most commonly confused words:

WORD	MEANING
accept	to receive, to agree
except	with the exclusion of

We *accept* this check as payment in full.

We received all merchandise *except* one carton of books.

advice	opinion, recommendation
advise	to counsel, recommend

My *advice* is to delay the shipment for two weeks.

I *advise* you to hire Martha Peterson.

affect	to influence, change (verb); an emotional response (noun—rare)
effect	to cause (verb); result (noun)

Changing the price will *affect* consumer demand.

The *effect* of the new computer system will be improved productivity.

The creation of the European Community will *effect* a major change in the way business is conducted in Western Europe.

allot	to distribute
a lot	many, much

I plan to *allot* a new car to every district sales manager.

A 10-percent raise is *a lot* when inflation is only 4 percent.

allude	to refer to in an indirect way
elude	to avoid

He *alluded* to the merger during the meeting.

She *eluded* contact for over a week by having her secretary screen all her calls.

already	by this time
all ready	all prepared

The contract has *already* been sent to the lawyer.

We are *all ready* for the meeting.

assistance	help
assistants	helpers

I need *assistance* to finish the assignment on time.

You'll have three *assistants* on this project.

WORD	MEANING

brake — device for stopping
break — to destroy

I'm putting the *brakes* on this project because it is over budget.

The contents of this box can *break*, so wrap them with care.

canvas — heavy cloth
canvass — to poll

Have the painting crew cover the desk with a *canvas*.

The marketing department will *canvass* the neighborhood for consumer response.

capital — wealth; seat of government
capitol — government building

Our expansion plan depends on raising $100,000 in new *capital*.

Washington, D.C., is the *capital* of the United States.

Let's meet at the *capitol* building.

cite — to refer to
sight — vision, scene
site — location

She *cited* poor health as the reason for her resignation.

The store was quite a *sight* after the big sale.

The Jones Street *site* is likely to attract the greatest number of passersby.

complement — something that completes
compliment — a flattering remark

Gracious remarks that build goodwill are the perfect *complement* to many business letters.

Thank you for the *compliment*.

council — governing body
counsel — to advise
consul — foreign embassy official

We need the approval of the city *council* before we can build.

Counsel Ellen on the details of the contract before she talks to the client.

Bring your trade idea to the French *consul*.

defer — to postpone
differ — to be dissimilar

I plan to *defer* my bonus until retirement.

My plans *differ* from yours in three fundamental ways.

dissent — disagreement
descent — a decline or downward movement
descend — to come down

He cast the single vote in *dissent* of the purchase.

The stock price's steep *descent* was shocking.

Use the elevator to *descend* to the basement.

device — a mechanism
devise — to develop

This *device* may make us all millionaires.

I will *devise* a plan that can make us all rich.

elicit — to draw out
illicit — illegal

The survey questions will *elicit* the responses that we need.

Illicit merchandise was found on store shelves.

eminent — prominent, well-known
imminent — about to happen

The research was conducted by Alexandra Jones, who is an *eminent* scholar in her field.

Some major changes are *imminent*.

formally — officially, with tradition
formerly — previously

The CEO *formally* welcomed the new chairman.

She was *formerly* an account executive at a major advertising agency.

incidence — frequency
incidents — events

The *incidence* of shoplifting has decreased since we installed the new security system.

Four shoplifting *incidents* were reported last month.

interstate — between states
intrastate — within a state

The federal government regulates *interstate* trucking.

The federal government has no jurisdiction over *intrastate* trucking.

its — possessive form of *it*
it's — contraction for *it is* or *it has*

The computer is in good shape except for *its* keyboard.

It's been a long time since we talked business.

later — after a time
latter — the last-mentioned of two or more items

I will get back to you *later* with the details of the deal.

If there is a choice between an office with a northern or southern exposure, I prefer the *latter*.

lessen — to decrease
lesson — something learned

WORD	MEANING

Adding another person to the department will *lessen* the load on everyone.

Ann Morgan will provide *lessons* on business writing.

| *loose* | not tightly fastened |
| *lose* | to misplace |

Barbara's dress was *loose* after she lost twenty pounds.

Don't *lose* this file.

| *moral* | relating to the difference between right and wrong |
| *morale* | attitude; state of mind |

The only *moral* decision is to tell the truth.

After the merger, employee *morale* was at an all-time low.

| *passed* | past tense of *to pass* |
| *past* | at an earlier time |

Mike *passed* Mary in the hall.

In the *past*, the company offered dental insurance to all employees.

| *patience* | forbearance |
| *patients* | people receiving medical care |

After four postponements, my *patience* is wearing thin.

On an average day, the doctor sees ten *patients*.

| *personal* | private, intimate |
| *personnel* | employees |

Medical information is *personal* and confidential.

All *personnel* files are kept in the human resources department.

| *precede* | to come before |
| *proceed* | to start, to continue |

Research *precedes* writing.

With the research complete, you can *proceed* to write a first draft.

| *presence* | attendance at a place or event |
| *presents* | gifts |

Your *presence* is requested at the dinner honoring the chairman.

I will bring the *presents* with me when I come to the party.

| *principle* | standard, moral conviction |
| *principal* | main, foremost (adjective); administrator of a school (noun) |

Our company is built on the *principle* of treating the customer fairly.

One of the *principal* reasons for your promotion is your writing ability.

WORD	MEANING

The *principal* of the elementary school is active in community affairs.

| *respectfully* | with respect |
| *respectively* | in that order |

I *respectfully* request an appointment next Tuesday morning.

Third and fourth prizes went to John and Samantha, *respectively*.

| *stationary* | not moving |
| *stationery* | writing paper |

We are ordering eight *stationary* bikes for the company exercise unit.

Please write all letters on company *stationery*.

| *taught* | past tense of *to teach* |
| *taut* | tight |

I *taught* Bill how to use the computer.

The wrapping is *taut*, and the box is ready to be mailed.

| *than* | as compared to |
| *then* | at that time |

John has a larger office *than* Roger.

Until *then*, I have nothing to say.

their	possessive form of *they*
there	in a certain place
they're	contraction for *they are*

Place *their* files over *there*.

They're delivering the supplies tomorrow.

through	finished, done
threw	past tense of *to throw*
thorough	complete

When you are *through* with the memo, put it on my desk.

The boy *threw* the ball to his father.

The accounting department always does a *thorough* job.

to	toward
too	also
two	number following *one*

Give the original file *to* Mary and *two* copies to Sheila, *too*.

| *waive* | forgo |
| *wave* | flutter, move back and forth |

I *waive* my right of first refusal.

Wave to the president as he drives by.

| *weak* | not strong |
| *week* | seven days |

My *weak* back won't allow me to pick up the box.

You'll have the contract on your desk in a *week*.

WORD	MEANING
weather	climatic conditions
whether	if it is the fact that; in case

Bad *weather* may require us to postpone the meeting.

Tell me *whether* or not you are interested in the job.

whose	possessive form of *who*
who's	contraction for *who is* or *who has*

Whose property is this?

Who's here for the meeting?

your	possessive form of *you*
you're	contraction for *you are*

Hang *your* coat in the closet.

You're welcome to join us for lunch.

Words with Misunderstood Meanings

The following words are frequently used carelessly or incorrectly:

among	refers to two or more things or people
between	used when the referent is no more than two

Let's settle the matter *among* the three of us.

This is *between* you and me and no one else.

continual	indicates a series of successive actions
continuous	implies unbroken, uninterrupted movement

Continual rain implies a series of rain showers interrupted by short spells of sunny weather.

Continuous rain means that the rain has not stopped.

disinterested	unbiased
uninterested	without interest

Jack is a *disinterested* observer because he is not involved in the deal.

Jack is *uninterested* in real estate law, and he is currently studying theater.

imply	to suggest but not express
infer	to deduce from the evidence at hand

The manager *implied* that raises would be given in May.

The employees *inferred* that raises would be small.

loan	something lent (noun)
lend	to let another use (verb)

I need a $10,000 *loan*.

I'm willing to *lend* you $5,000.

practical	useful, sensible, or worthwhile
practicable	capable of being put into practice and functioning

Generally, she takes a realistic, *practical* approach.

Using solar energy as a primary energy source is not *practicable* in many regions of the world.

regardless	Although many writers use the word *irregardless* instead of *regardless*, adding the prefix is incorrect.

I want to buy the house *regardless* of the closing date.

REFERENCE

[1]This appendix is based on Lynn Quitman Troyka, *Simon & Schuster Handbook for Writers*, 2nd ed. (Englewood Cliffs, NJ: Prentice Hall, 1990).

Resources for Business Communicators

The most effective writers and speakers continue to study communication throughout their careers. They attempt to learn as much as they can about writing and speaking well by referring to the widest possible variety of sources—books, newspapers, newsletters, magazines and journals, and computer databases. They also gain knowledge through membership in professional associations.

The continuing study of business communication begins with identifying specific sources. We can start this process here. But because business communication is an ever-changing field, new and valuable sources are published every day, especially in such current fields as cross-cultural communication, diversity, and communication technology. It is your job to keep up with these changes, through reading and study, throughout your business career.

We will begin by listing books that are valuable business-communication resources. These books are keyed to the seven parts of *Contemporary Business Communication*. We will then examine other resources—including newspapers, magazines and journals, online databases, and professional associations—that apply to the entire business-communication field.

REFERENCE BOOKS FOR BUSINESS COMMUNICATORS

Part I—Fundamentals of Business Communication

Baldrige, Letitia. *Letitia Baldrige's Complete Guide to Executive Manners*. New York: Rawson Associates, 1985.

Burley-Allen, Madelyn. *Listening: The Forgotten Skill*. New York: John Wiley, 1982.

Deal, Terrence E., and Allen A. Kennedy. *Corporate Cultures: The Rites and Rituals of Corporate Life*. Reading, MA: Addison-Wesley, 1982.

DuBrin, Andrew. *Winning Office Politics*. Englewood Cliffs, NJ: Prentice Hall, 1990.

Fast, Julius. *Subtext: Making Body Language Work in the Workplace*. New York: Viking, 1991.

Iaconetti, Joan, and Patrick Ohara. *First-Time Manager*. New York: Collier Books, 1985.

Marsh, Peter. *Eye to Eye: How People Interact*. Topsfield, MA: Salem House Publishers, 1988.

Peters, Thomas J., and Robert H. Waterman, Jr. *In Search of Excellence: Lessons from America's Best-Run Companies*. New York: Harper & Row, 1982.

Walton, Donald. *Are You Communicating?* New York: McGraw-Hill, 1989.

Part II—Writing Basics

The Chicago Manual of Style, 13th ed. Chicago: University of Chicago Press, 1992.

Dumond, Val. *The Elements of Nonsexist Usage: A Guide to Inclusive Spoken and Written English*. New York: Prentice Hall Press, 1990.

Lutz, William. *Doublespeak: How Government, Business, Advertisers, and Others Use Language to Deceive You*. New York: HarperPerennial, 1989.

Maslow, Abraham. *Motivation and Personality*. New York: Harper & Row, 1954.

Strunk, Jr., William, and E. B. White. *The Elements of Style*, 3rd ed. New York: Macmillan, 1979.

Troyka, Lynn Quitman. *Simon & Schuster Handbook for Writers*, 2nd ed. Englewood Cliffs, NJ: Prentice Hall, 1990.

Part III—Organizational Letters and Memos

Baugh, L. Sue. *Handbook for Memo Writing*. Lincolnwood, IL: NTC Business Books, 1990.

Brock, Luther A. *Sales Lead-Getting Model Letter Book*. Englewood Cliffs, NJ: Prentice Hall, 1986.

Devries, Mary A. *Prentice Hall Style Manual: A Complete Guide with Model Formats for Every Business Writing Occasion*. Englewood Cliffs, NJ: Prentice Hall, 1992.

Fielden, John S., Ronald E. Dulek, and Jean D. Fielden. *Elements of Business Writing*. Englewood Cliffs, NJ: Prentice Hall, 1984.

Frailey, L. E. *Handbook of Business Letters*, 3rd ed. Englewood Cliffs, NJ: Prentice Hall, 1989.

Kennedy, Daniel S. *The Ultimate Sales Letter*. Holbrook, MA: Bob Adams, 1990.

Shurter, Robert L., and Donald J. Leonard. *Effective Letters in Business*, 3rd ed. New York: McGraw-Hill, 1984.

Part IV—Report and Proposal Writing

Brusaw, Charles T., Gerald J. Alfred, and Walter E. Oliu. *Handbook of Technical Writing*, 3rd ed. New York: St. Martin's Press, 1987.

Schumacher, Michael. *Creative Conversations: The Writer's Complete Guide to Conducting Interviews*. Cincinnati, OH: Writer's Digest Books, 1990.

Talman, Michael. *Understanding Presentation Graphics*. Alameda, CA: SYBEX, 1992.

Tepper, Ron. *How to Write Winning Proposals for Your Company or Client*. New York: John Wiley, 1990.

Thomsett, Michael C. *The Little Black Book of Business Reports*. New York: AMACOM, 1988.

Zelazny, Gene. *Say It with Charts: The Executive's Guide to Successful Presentations in the 1990s*. Homewood, IL: BusinessOne Irwin, 1991.

Part V—Forms of Oral Communication

Boone, Louis E. *Quotable Business*. New York: Random House, 1992.

Eigen, Lewis D., and Jonathan P. Siegel. *The Manager's Book of Quotations*. New York: AMACOM, 1989.

Hoff, Ron. *I Can See You Naked: A Fearless Guide to Making Great Presentations*. Kansas City, MO: Andrews and McMeel, 1992.

Kieffer, George David. *The Strategy of Meetings*. New York: Warner Books, 1988.

Leech, Thomas. *How to Prepare, Stage, and Deliver Winning Presentations*. New York: AMACOM, 1982.

Maggio, Rosalie. *The Beacon Book of Quotations by Women*. Boston: Beacon Press, 1992.

Nierenberg, Gerard I. *Fundamentals of Negotiating*. New York: Hawthorne, 1973.

Nierenberg, Juliet, and Irene S. Ross. *Women and the Art of Negotiating*. New York: Simon & Schuster, 1985.

Part VI—Employment Communication

Allen, Jeffrey G. *The Complete Q & A Job Interview Book*. New York: John Wiley, 1988.

Allen, Jeffrey G. *The Perfect Job Reference*. New York: John Wiley, 1990.

Beatty, Richard H. *The Perfect Cover Letter*. New York: John Wiley, 1989.

Bell, Arthur H. *International Careers*. Holbrook, MA: Bob Adams, 1990.

Bolles, Richard Nelson. *What Color Is Your Parachute?* Berkeley, CA: Ten Speed Press, 1993.

Jackson, Tom. *The Perfect Resume*. New York: Doubleday, 1990.

Kaponya, Paul. *How to Survive Your First 90 Days at a New Company*. Hawthorne, NJ: The Career Press, 1990.

Lathrop, Richard. *Who's Hiring Who? How to Find That Job Fast!* 12th ed. Berkeley, CA: Ten Speed Press, 1989.

Morin, William J., and James C. Cabrera. *Parting Company: How to Survive the Loss of a Job and Find Another Successfully*. San Diego, CA: Harcourt Brace Jovanovich, 1991.

Part VII—Communication Challenges

Copeland, Lennie, and Lewis Griggs. *Going International: How to Make Friends and Deal Effectively in the Global Marketplace*. New York: Random House, 1985.

Gilligan, Carol. *In a Different Voice*. Cambridge: Harvard University Press, 1982.

Harris, Philip R., and Robert T. Moran. *Managing Cultural Differences: High Performance Strategies for a New World of Business*, 3rd ed. Houston, TX: Gulf Publishing, 1991.

Helgesen, Sally. *The Female Advantage: Women's Ways of Leadership*. New York: Doubleday Currency, 1990.

Kochman, Thomas. *Black and White Styles in Conflict*. Chicago, IL: University of Chicago Press, 1981.

Loden, Marilyn, and Judy B. Rosener, *Workforce America: Managing Employee Diversity as a Vital Resource*. Homewood, IL: BusinessOne Irwin, 1991.

Tannen, Deborah. *That's Not What I Meant! How Conversational Style Makes or Breaks Your Relations with Others*. New York: William Morrow, 1986.

Tannen, Deborah. *You Just Don't Understand: Women and Men in Conversation*. New York: William Morrow, 1990.

GENERAL AND SPECIALIZED NEWPAPERS

Published every workday by Dow Jones & Company, *The Wall Street Journal* is the most complete business newspaper in the country. It is a valuable source for business research and includes many articles that focus on specific communication issues.

National Business Employment Weekly

Published weekly by Dow Jones, the *National Business Employment Weekly* lists current employment opportunities and contains helpful job-search articles.

Commerce Business Daily

Published every workday by the United States Department of Commerce, the *Commerce Business Daily* provides daily updates on the goods and services that the government is buying, the specific agencies that are buying, due dates for bids, and how to get complete specifications in the form of formal RFPs.

BUSINESS MAGAZINES AND JOURNALS

Among the leading business magazines with periodic features on business communication are:

> *Business Week*
> *Forbes*
> *Fortune*
> *Inc.*

In addition, the Association for Business Communication publishes two journals that focus on current business communication topics and research:

> *The Bulletin of the Association for Business Communication*
>
> *The Journal of Business Communication*

These publications can be obtained by writing to:

Association for Business Communication
Department of Management
College of Business Administration
University of North Texas
Denton, TX 76203

ONLINE DATABASES

Online databases are valuable sources of research data for reports and proposals, investment research, and job searches. With thousands of databases available to computer users, it is impossible to mention all of them here. Instead, we will highlight a cross section of databases to demonstrate their potential as information sources.[1] Each description includes the name, producer, and phone number of the database as well as the vendor through which it is accessible. Specialized databases, like those mentioned here, are available through such commercial database vendors as Dialog, Nexis, and Prodigy.

ABI/INFORM
> Producer: UMI/Data Courier
> 800 626-2823
> Vendors: BRS, Data-Star, Dialog, Info Globe, OCLC, HRIN, Orbit, and Thomson Financial Networks
> *Description*: ABI/INFORM is a leader in online indexes and abstracts of business articles. Included are more than 1,200 periodicals dating back to 1971.

American Banker
> Producer: American Banker-Bond Buyer
> 800 356-4763
> Vendors: Data-Star, Data Times, Dialog, Mead, and NewsNet
> *Description*: The American Banker contains the full texts of all major news stories on banking and financial services.

BioBusiness
> Producer: BIOSIS
> 800 523-4806
> Vendors: BRS, Data-Star, and Dialog
> *Description*: BioBusiness focuses on business opportunities in genetic engineering, pharmaceuticals, agriculture, and food technology.

Business Wire
> Producer: Business Wire
> 415 986-4422
> Vendors: Bridge, CompuServe, Delphi, Dialog, Dow Jones News/Retrieval, Mead-Nexis, NewsNet, and VU/TEXT
> *Description*: Business Wire contains the full text of press releases announcing new products, legal action, financial information, and personnel changes.

Financial Times Full Text
> Producer: Financial Times Business Information (Call vendors directly.)
> Vendors: Dialog, FT Profile, Mead–Lexis/Nexis, and Reuters
> *Description*: An online version of the United Kingdom and international editions of the Financial Times, the Financial Times Full Text provides business articles from the European perspective.

Japan Technology
> Producer: SCAN C2C
> 800 525-3865
> Vendors: Dialog, ORBIT
> *Description*: Included in Japan Technology are abstracts of articles from Japan's top 600 science and technical journals.

Project Access Computer Information Center
> Producer: Project Access
> 312 565-0815
> Vendor: Central Educational Network
> *Description*: This online database provides employers with information about compliance with the Americans with Disabilities Act.

Database Vendors

Listed here are five of the most popular database vendors.

CompuServe
> CompuServe, Inc.
> 5000 Arlington Centre Boulevard
> P.O. Box 20212
> Columbus, OH 43220
> 800 849-8199

Dialog
> Dialog Information Service, Inc.
> 3460 Hillview Avenue
> Palo Alto, CA 94303-0993
> 800 334-2564

Dow Jones News Retrieval
> Dow Jones & Company, Inc.
> Information Services Group
> P.O. Box 300
> Princeton, NJ 08543-0300
> 609 520-4629

GEnie
> GE Information Services
> 401 North Washington Street
> Rockville, MD 20850
> 800 638-9636

Nexis
> Mead Data Central, Inc.
> 9393 Springboro Pike
> P.O. Box 933
> Dayton, OH 45401
> 800 227-4908

PROFESSIONAL ASSOCIATIONS

Many professional associations focus on various aspects of business communication. In these associations, you will find a network of professional colleagues, continuing-education opportunities, conferences, and a host of learning materials. For more information about these associations, consult *The Encyclopedia of Associations*, available at most libraries.

American Society for Training and Development
> 1640 King Street
> Alexandria, VA 22313
> 713 683-8100

Association for Business Communication
> Department of Management
> College of Business Administration
> University of North Texas
> Denton, TX 76203
> 817 565-4423

Committee on Public Doublespeak
> c/o National Council of Teachers of English
> 1111 Kenyon Road
> Urbana, IL 61801
> 217 328-3870

International Association for Cross Cultural Communication
> 3840, rue Marcil
> Montreal, PQ, Canada
> 514 485-4788

International Communication Association
P.O. Box 9589
Austin, TX 78766
512 454-8299
International Listening Association
c/o Mary Wise
Center for Information and Communication
Science
Ball State University
Muncie, IN 47306
312 285-1889
International Training in Communication
2519 Woodland Drive
Anaheim, CA 92801
714 995-3660
Multicultural Network of the American Society for
Training and Development
c/o Eric King
80 Central Street
Foxborough, MA 01719
508 635-7127

National Association for Corporate Speaker Activities
1730 North Lynn Street, Suite 402
Arlington, VA 22209
703 525-1191
Society for Technical Communication
901 N. Stuart Street, Suite 304
Arlington, VA 22203
703 522-4114
Toastmasters International
P.O. Box 9052
Mission Viejo, CA 92690
714 858-8255

---

[1]Database information from "Databases," *Online Access*,
Fall 1992, pp. 54–78.

CHAPTER 1

1 Thomas A. Stewart, "GE Keeps Those Ideas Coming," *Fortune*, April 12, 1991, pp. 41–47.

2 Faye Rice,"Champions of Communication," *Fortune*, June 3, 1991, pp. 111–20.

3 Claudia H. Deutsch, "A Revival of the Quality Circle," *The New York Times*, May 26, 1991, p. F23.

4 Anne B. Fisher, "Morale Crisis," *Fortune*, November 18, 1991, pp. 69–80.

5 Thomas J. Peters and Robert H. Waterman, Jr., *In Search of Excellence: Lessons from America's Best-Run Companies* (New York: Harper & Row, 1982), pp. 64–65.

6 Sue Shellenbarger, "Cutting Losses When Partners Face a Breakup," *The Wall Street Journal*, May 21, 1991, p. B1.

7 James S. Hirsch, "To One Xerox Man, Selling Photocopiers Is a Gambler's Game," *The Wall Street Journal*, September 24, 1991, pp. A1, A12.

8 L. E. Frailey, *Handbook of Business Letters*, 3rd ed. (Englewood Cliffs, NJ: Prentice Hall, 1989), p. 9.

9 Tom Peters and Nancy Austin, *A Passion for Excellence: The Leadership Difference* (New York: Warner Books, 1985), p. 97.

10 Mary Jo Bitner, Bernard H. Booms, and Mary Stanfield Tetreault, "The Service Encounter: Diagnosing Favorable and Unfavorable Incidents," *Journal of Marketing*, January 1990, p. 71.

11 Larry Armstrong and William C. Symonds, "Beyond 'May I Help You?'" *Business Week: The Quality Imperative*, January 15, 1992, pp. 100–103.

12 Louis E. Boone, *Boone's Business Quotations: Wit and Wisdom of Our Time* (New York: McGraw-Hill), 1992.

13 Rice, "Champions of Communication," p. 116.

14 John Markoff, "IBM Chief Gives Staff Tough Talk," *The New York Times*, May 29, 1991, p. D1.

15 Dan Dellus, *DS Letter*, vol. 1, no. 3 (1971). Published by Didactic Systems, Inc., Box 457, Cranford, NJ 07016.

16 Claudia H. Deutsch, "Call It 'CEO Disease,' Then Listen," *The New York Times*, December 15, 1991, p. F23.

17 Fred Luthans and J. K. Larsen, "How Managers Really Communicate," *Human Relations*, 39 (1986), 181–88.

18 E. M. Rogers and A. Rogers, *Communicating in Organizations* (New York: Free Press, 1976).

19 Joseph B. White, Gregory A. Patterson, and Paul Ingrassia, "American Auto Makers Need Major Overhaul to Match the Japanese," *The Wall Street Journal*, January 10, 1992, p. A1.

20 This discussion of the grapevine is based largely on Davis, "Management Communication and the Grapevine," *Harvard Business Review*, September—October 1953, pp. 43–49.

21 The quote and examples in this section come from Daniel Goleman, "Anatomy of a Rumor: It Flies on Fear," *The New York Times*, June 4, pp. C1, C5.

22 This discussion of corporate culture is based largely on Terrence E. Deal and Allen A. Kennedy, *Corporate Cultures: The Rites and Rituals of Corporate Life* (Reading, MA: Addison-Wesley, 1982), pp. 3–28.

23 Personal interview with Sana Reynolds, November 6, 1991.

24 John Holusha, "A Softer 'Neutron Jack' at G.E.," *The New York Times*, March 4, 1992, p. D1.

25 Doron P. Levin, "Experts Doubt Cutbacks Alone Will Save G.M." *The New York Times*, December 23, 1991, pp. A1, D5.

26 Deal and Kennedy, *Corporate Cultures*, pp. 98–100.

27 Philip J. Hilts, "Maker of Implants Balked at Tests, Its Records Show," *The New York Times*, January 13, 1992, p. A1.

28 "Unbecoming an Officer," *Time*, September 30, 1991, p. 52.

29 Barbara Ley Toffler, "When the Signal Is 'Move It or Lose It,'" *The New York Times*, November 17, 1991, p. F13.

30 George C. Dillon, "The Prospect of Competitive Ethics: Good Ethics Is Good Business," speech delivered at the Racing for a Competitive Edge Conference, March 20, 1991. Reprinted in *Vital Speeches of the Day*, June 15, 1991, p. 527.

31 Barnaby J. Feder, "Helping Corporate America Hew to the Straight and Narrow," *The New York Times*, November 3, 1991, p. F5; and Chris Lee, "Who Gets Trained in What: 1991," *Training*, October 1991, p. 55.

32 Roger Cohen, "For Coke, World Is Its Oyster," *The New York Times*, November 21, 1991, p. D1.

33 Statistics cited in Marilyn Loden and Judy B. Rosener, *Workforce America: Managing Employee Diversity as a Vital Resource* (Homewood, IL: Business One Irwin, 1991), pp. 6–7.

34 Alan Deutschman, "The Trouble with MBAs," *Fortune*, July 29, 1991, p. 72.

35 Elizabeth M. Fowler, "Careers: Training 21st-Century Executives," *The New York Times*, June 20, 1989, p. D13.

36 Christopher Conte, "Labor Letter," *The Wall Street Journal*, September 3, 1991, p. A1.

37 Donald Walton, *Are You Communicating?* (New York: McGraw-Hill, 1989), p. 7.

38 Bart Ziegler, "Japanese Speakers Call America Lazy, Nearly 'Finished,'" *Arkansas Democrat- Gazette*, January 21, 1992, p. A7.

CHAPTER 2

1 Quoted in Donald Walton, *Are You Communicating?* (New York: McGraw-Hill, 1989).

2 Nancy Marx Better, "The New Office Order in Grooming Rituals," *The New York Times*, September 29, 1991, p. F23.

3 John Holusha, "Chemical Makers Identify a New Hazard: Their Image," *The New York Times*, August 12, 1991, pp. D1, D7.

4 Both Allaire and Sanchez are quoted in Gabriella Stern, "Chief Executives Are Increasingly Chief Salesmen," *The Wall Street Journal*, August 6, 1991, pp. B1, B7.

5 Walton, *Are You Communicating?* p. 24.

6 David J. Jefferson, "Amid Jitters over Solvency and Stability, Life Insurers, Agents Try to Calm Public," *The Wall Street Journal*, July 26, 1991, p. B1.

7 Kevin Goldman, "NBC Pitches Shopping Show to Affiliates," *The Wall Street Journal*, May 20, 1991, pp. B1, B7.

8 Dana Milbank, "Seeking New Members, Steel Union Now Woos White-Collar Workers," *The Wall Street Journal*, May 23, 1991, p. A1.

9 This pattern of questioning is suggested in Phillip L. Hunsaker and Anthony J. Alessandra, "Giving—and Getting—Feedback," *Working Woman*, April 1987, p. 35.

10 Walter Kiechel III, "When Management Regresses," *Fortune*, March 9, 1992, pp. 158, 162.

11 Joan E. Rigdon, "Managers Who Switch Coasts Must Adapt to Different Approaches to Use of Time," *The Wall Street Journal*, August 14, 1991, pp. B1, B5.

12 James S. Hirsch, "Flood of Information Swamps Managers, but Some Are Finding Ways to Bail Out," *The Wall Street Journal*, August 12, 1991, pp. B1, B5.

13 Michael W. Miller, "Credit-Report Firms Face Greater Pressure: Ask Norwich, Vermont, Why," *The Wall Street Journal*, September 23, 1991, pp. A1, A6.

14 Michael Lewis, *Liar's Poker: Rising through the Wreckage on Wall Street* (New York: Penguin Books, 1989), p. 13.

15 Julius Fast, *Subtext: Making Body Language Work in the Workplace* (New York: Viking, 1991).

16 Albert Mehrabian, *Nonverbal Communication* (Chicago: Aldine-Atherton, 1972).

17 Fast, *Subtext*, p. 5.

18 "Updating the Hot Line to Moscow," *Newsweek*, April 30, 1984, p. 19.

19 Fast, *Subtext*, p. 60.

20 Mehrabian, *Nonverbal Communication*.

21 James S. Hirsch, "To One Xerox Man, Selling Photocopiers Is a Gambler's Game," *The Wall Street Journal*, September 24, 1991, p. A12.

22 Mark H. McCormack, *What They Still Don't Teach You at Harvard Business School: Notes from a Street-Smart Executive* (New York: Bantam Books, 1984), p. 33.

23 Russell Mitchell, "The Gap," *Business Week*, March 9, 1992, p. 58.

24 K. L. Burns and E. G. Beier, "Significance of Vocal and Visual Channels for the Decoding of Emotional Meaning," *Journal of Communication*, vol. 23 (1973), 118–30; and Albert Mehrabian and M. Weiner, "Decoding of Inconsistent Communications," *Journal of Personality and Social Psychology*, vol. 6 (1967), 109–14.

25 Daniel Goleman, "Non-Verbal Cues Are Easy to Misinterpret," *The New York Times*, September 17, 1991, pp. C1, C9.

26 McCormack, *What They Still Don't Teach You at Harvard Business School*, pp. 241–42.

27 Barbara Prete, "Publishing for Literacy," *Publishers Weekly*, November 30, 1990, pp. 27–34.

28 Al Newharth, *Confessions of an S.O.B.* (New York: Penguin, 1989), p. 110.

29 Tom Peters, *Thriving on Chaos: Handbook for a Management Revolution* (New York: Alfred A. Knopf, 1987), p. 436.

30 Philip R. Harris and Robert T. Moran, *Managing Cultural Differences: High Performance Strategies for a New World of Business*, 3rd ed. (Houston Gulf, 1991), p. 36. For more information, see Lyman K. Steil, "Listen My Students...and You Shall Learn," *Toward Better Teaching*, Fall 1978.

31 Florence L. Wolff, Nadine C. Marsnik, William S. Tacey, and Ralph G. Nichols, *Perceptive Listening* (Englewood Cliffs, NJ: Prentice Hall, 1983), p. 154.

32 Ralph G. Nichols, "Do We Know How to Listen? Practical Helps in a Modern Age," *Speech Teacher*, March 1961, pp. 118–24; see also Lyman K. Steil, *Your Personal Listening Profile* (New York: Sperry Corporation, 1980).

33 Lyman K. Steil, *Effective Listening: Key to Your Success* (New York: Random House, 1983).

34 Dana Milbank, "No Glamour, No Glory, Being a Manufacturer Today Can Take Guts," *The Wall Street Journal*, June 3, 1991, pp. A1, A7.

35 Ibid.

36 Leon Festinger, *A Theory of Cognitive Dissonance* (Stanford, CA: Stanford University Press, 1957).

37 Milbank, "No Glamour, No Glory," p. A7.

38 Faye Rice, "Champions of Communication," *Fortune*, June 3, 1991, pp. 112, 116.

39 McCormack, *What They Still Don't Teach You at Harvard Business School*, pp. 109–10.
40 Daniel Pearl, "More Firms Pledge Guaranteed Service," *The Wall Street Journal*, July 17, 1991, p. B1.
41 Nichols, "Do We Know How to Listen?" pp. 118–24.
42 McCormack, *What They Still Don't Teach You at Harvard Business School*, p. 239.
43 Nichols, "Do We Know How to Listen?" pp. 118–24.

CHAPTER 3

1 William Lutz, *Doublespeak* (New York: HarperPerennial, 1989), p. 131.
2 John Fielden, "What Do You Mean I Can't Write?" *Harvard Business Review*, May–June 1964. Reprinted in *Harvard Business Review*, September–October 1990, p. 238.
3 Charles L. Brusaw, Gerlad J. Alred, and Walter E. Oliu, *Handbook of Technical Writing*, 3rd ed. (New York: St. Martin's Press, 1987).
4 William J. Cook, "Big Trouble for Big Blue," *U.S. News & World Report*, January 4, 1993, pp. 28–29; Thomas McCarroll, "How IBM Was Left Behind," *Time*, December 28, 1992, pp. 26–28; and John W. Verity, "Deconstructing the Computer Industry," *Business Week*, November 23, 1992, pp. 90–100.
5 Louis E. Boone and David L. Kurtz, *Management* (New York: McGraw-Hill, 1992), p. 150.
6 Ford Motor Co., *1993 Annual Report*.
7 Louis E. Boone, *Quotable Business* (New York: Random House, 1992), p. 155.
8 Cornelia Droge, Richard Germain, and Diane Halstead, "A Note on Marketing and the Corporate Annual Report: 1930–1950," *Journal of the Academy of Marketing Science*, vol. 18, no. 4 (Fall 1990), 359.
9 L. E. Frailey, *Handbook of Business Letters*, 3rd ed. (Englewood Cliffs, NJ: Prentice Hall, 1989), pp. 72–73.
10 Abraham H. Maslow, "A Theory of Human Motivation." *Psychological Review*, July 1943, pp. 370–96.
11 This section is based on L. Sue Baugh, *Handbook for Memo Writing* (Lincolnwood, IL: NTC Business Books, 1990), pp. 26–34; Fielden, "What Do You Mean I Can't Write?"; Marya W. Holcombe and Judith K. Stein, *Writing for Decision Makers: Memos and Reports with a Competitive Edge* (Belmont, CA: Lifetime Learning Publications, 1981), pp. 9–20; Thomas Leech, *How to Prepare, Stage, and Deliver Winning Presentations* (New York: Amacom, 1982), pp. 60–75; "Tax Report," *The Wall Street Journal*, January 29, 1992, p. A1; and Patricia H. Westheimer, *Power Writing for Executive Women* (Glenview, IL: Scott, Foresman, 1989), pp. 45–58.
12 Fielden, "What Do You Mean I Can't Write?"
13 Holcombe and Stein, *Writing for Decision Makers*, p. 12.
14 "Tax Report," *The Wall Street Journal*, January 29, 1992.
15 Information based on Karen DeWitt, "Using Credit Cards, Students Learn a Hard Lesson," *The New York Times*, August 26, 1991, pp. A1, A17.
16 Alex Osborn, *Applied Imagination* (New York: Charles Scribner's, 1958).
17 Information based on Joseph Pereira, "From Air to Pump to Puma's Disc System, Sneaker Gimmicks Bound to New Heights," *The Wall Street Journal*, October 31, 1991, p. B1.
18 "Mindmapping: A New Way to Think on Paper," *Fortune*, November 16, 1992, p. 12.

CHAPTER 4

1 Patrick M. Reilly, "Dear Competitor: Would You Be So Kind as to Share Your Ideas?..." *The Wall Street Journal*, July 30, 1992, p. B1.
2 William Strunk, Jr., and E. B. White, *The Elements of Style*, 3rd ed. (New York: Macmillan, 1979), pp. 15, 71.
3 Interview with Sana Reynolds, November 6, 1991.
4 Edward P. Bailey, Jr., *The Plain English Approach to Business Writing* (New York: Oxford University Press, 1990), pp. 47–53.
5 Bailey, *The Plain English Approach to Business Writing*, pp. 26–27.
6 Charles, T. Brusaw, Gerald J. Alred, and Walter E. Oliu, *Handbook of Technical Writing*, 3rd ed. (New York: St. Martin's Press, 1987), p. 469.
7 L. Sue Baugh, *Handbook for Memo Writing* (Lincolnwood, IL: NTC Business Books, 1990), p. 45.
8 Marya W. Holcombe and Judith K. Stein, *Writing for Decision Makers: Memos and Reports with a Competitive Edge* (Belmont, CA: Lifetime Learning Publications, 1981), p. 61.
9 Lynn Quitman Troyka, *Simon & Schuster Handbook for Writers*, 2nd ed. (Englewood Cliffs, NJ: Prentice Hall, 1990), pp. 141–42.
10 Information from Michael W. Miller, "AT&T Goes to Bat for Customers against Credit Firms," *The Wall Street Journal*, June 12, 1991, p. B1.
11 See Brusaw, Alred, and Oliu, *Handbook of Technical Writing*, pp. 256–57.
12 Document examples provided by Sana Reynolds.
13 Information for this section is from Bailey, *The Plain English Approach to Business Writing*, pp. 37–46, 72–84; Baugh, *Handbook for Memo Writing*, pp. 67–77; Holcombe and Stein, *Writing for Decision Makers*, pp. 117–24; Roy W. Poe, *The McGraw-Hill Guide to Effective Business Reports* (New York: McGraw-Hill, 1982), pp. 122–26; and John Tarrant, *Business Writing with Style: Strategies for Success* (New York: John Wiley, 1991), pp. 41, 134–36, 168–69.
14 Interview with Sana Reynolds.

CHAPTER 5

1 Alison Leigh Cowan, "Trying to Decode Proxies? Read Very, Very Carefully." *The New York Times*, April 13, 1992, pp. D1, D4.
2 Lynn Quitman Troyka, *Simon & Schuster Handbook for Writers*, 2nd ed. (Englewood Cliffs, NJ: Prentice Hall, 1990), p. 83.
3 William Zinsser, *Writing with a Word Processor* (New York: Harper & Row, 1983), p. 25.
4 The following section is based on suggestions made by Troyka, *Simon & Schuster Handbook for Writers*, pp. 57–59.
5 Cited in Sherry Sweetnam, *The Executive Memo: A Guide to Persuasive Business Communications* (New York: John Wiley, 1986), p. 155.
6 Sam Howe Verhovek, "Educators to Study Utilization (Use) of Plain English," *The New York Times*, October 4, 1991, pp. B1, B6.
7 Examples from William Lutz, *Doublespeak* (New York: HarperPerennial, 1989), pp. 104–29.
8 John Tarrant, *Business Writing with Style: Strategies for Success* (New York: John Wiley, 1991), p. 35.
9 Roy W. Poe, *The McGraw-Hill Guide to Effective Business Reports* (New York: McGraw-Hill, 1982), pp. 48–49.
10 "Business Briefs," *The Wall Street Journal*, June 18, 1991, p. A1.
11 "Wrong Punctuation Costs Banks a Privilege," *The New York Times*, February 9, 1992, p. 31.
12 "Business Briefs," *The Wall Street Journal*, June 18, 1991, p. A1.
13 Patricia H. Westheimer, *Power Writing for Executive Women* (Glenview, IL: Scott, Foresman, 1989), p. 18.
14 John S. Fielden, "What Do You Mean You Don't Like My Style?" *Harvard Business Review*, May–June 1982, p. 129.
15 See Sue A. Hershkowitz, "Improve Your Writing Skills: How to Write Material That Gets Results," *Business Credit*, December 1988, p. 33.
16 Sweetman, *The Executive Memo*, p. 100.
17 These strategies are suggested by Fielden, "What Do You Mean You Don't Like My Style?" pp. 135–38.
18 John S. Fielden, *The AMA Handbook of Business Letters* (New York: AMACOM, 1989), p. 11.
19 "How to Boost Sales: Pen a Better Letter," *The Wall Street Journal*, October 4, 1991, p. B1.
20 Interview with Sana Reynolds, November 6, 1991.

CHAPTER 6

1 Suein L. Hwang, "Customers May Face a Surcharge If They Don't Fold Their Napkins," *The Wall Street Journal*, March 13, 1992, p. B1.
2 Andrew Tobias, "Money Angles: 'Dear IRS...'" *Time*, April 8, 1991, p. 54.
3 "Strategic Communications," in *The Complete Book of Contemporary Business Letters*, ed. Stephen P. Elliot (Ridgefield, CT: Round Lake Publishing, 1989), p. 228.
4 See Robert L. Shurter and Donald J. Leonard, *Effective Letters in Business*, 3rd ed. (New York: McGraw- Hill, 1984), pp. 216–20; Andrea B. Geffner, *How to Write Better Business Letters* (New York: Barron's Educational Series, 1982), p. 103; and William C. Paxson, *The Business Writing Handbook* (New York: Bantam Books, 1981), p. 40.
5 John S. Fielden and Ronald E. Dulek, *Bottom-Line Business Writing* (Englewood Cliffs, NJ: Prentice Hall, 1984), pp. 17–18.
6 See Fielden and Dulek, *Bottom-Line Business Writing*, pp. 28–46; Geffner, *How to Write Better Business Letters*, pp. 25–26; and Ellen Roddick, *Writing That Means Business: How to Get Your Message Across Simply and Effectively* (New York: Collier Books, 1986), pp. 43–44.
7 Fielden and Dulek, *Bottom-Line Business Writing*, p. 31.
8 Geffner, *How to Write Better Business Letters*, p. 28.
9 Peter J. Leets, "Managing Your References," *National Business Employment Weekly*, November 1–November 7, 1991, p. 13.

CHAPTER 7

1 Werner's comments are cited in Robert L. Shurter and Donald J. Leonard, *Effective Letters in Business*, 3rd ed. (New York: McGraw-Hill, 1984), pp. 88, 89.
2 Ibid., p. 89.
3 Ibid., pp. 89–90.
4 Ibid., p. 130.
5 Suggestions in this section are from John Tarrant, *Business Writing with Style* (New York: John Wiley, 1991), pp. 115–16; L. E. Frailey, *Handbook of Business Letters*, 3rd ed. (Englewood Cliffs, NJ: Prentice Hall, 1989), pp. 668–70; and Charles T. Brusaw, Gerald J. Alred, and Walter E. Oliu, *Handbook of Technical Writing*, 3rd ed. (New York: St. Martin's Press, 1987), p. 23.
6 Information from Laurie McGinley, "Flight Attendants Complain Carry-Ons Include Everything But the Kitchen Sink," *The Wall Street Journal*, June 5, 1992, pp. B1, B12.
7 Michael Adams, "The Udder Delights of Stew U," *Successful Meetings*, March 1991; and Katharine Davis Fishman, "The Disney World of Supermarkets," *New York Magazine*, March 11, 1985, p. 22.
8 Frailey, *Handbook of Business Letters*, p. 681.
9 Ibid., p. 542.
10 Ibid., pp. 562–63.
11 John S. Fielden, Jean D. Fielden, and Ronald E. Dulek, *The Business Writing Style Book* (Englewood Cliffs, NJ: Prentice Hall, 1984), P. 62.

CHAPTER 8

1   Wayne King, "Auto Insurer Reaches Pact in New Jersey," *The New York Times*, December 15, 1992, p. B1; Robert Hanley, "In Allstate Offices, the Questions Fly," *The New York Times*, September 18, 1991, p. B4; and Wayne King, "The Risks in New Jersey," *The New York Times*, September 18, 1991, pp. B1, B4.
2   Ray E. Barfield and Sylvia S. Titus, *Business Communications* (Hauppauge, NY: Barron's Business Library, 1992), p. 121.
3   Ibid., p. 122.
4   Ed Gregory, "Dillard's Doubles Paperwork Penalty," *The Tennessean Business*, May 3, 1992, p. B1; Dana Milbank, "As Stores Scrimp More and Order Less, Suppliers Take on Greater Risks, Costs," *The Wall Street Journal*, December 10, 1991, p. B1.
5   The following discussion is based on Robert L. Shurter and Donald J. Leonard, *Effective Letters in Business*, 3rd ed. (New York: McGraw-Hill, 1984), pp. 131–40.
6   From "An Open Letter to Sears Customers," *The New York Times*, June 25, 1992, p. B2.
7   Richard W. Stevenson, "Sears's Crisis: How Did It Do?" *The New York Times*, June 17, 1992, p. D1.
8   The following discussion is based on John S. Fielden, Jean D. Fielden, and Ronald E. Dulek, *The Business Writing Style Book* (Englewood Cliffs, NJ: Prentice Hall, 1984), pp. 45–61, 92–94.
9   "Microsoft Founder Gates, in Memo, Warns of Attack and Defeat by Rivals," *The Wall Street Journal*, June 19, 1991, p. B8.
10   Joan O'C. Hamilton, "To: All Readers, Subject: Corner-Office Sound-Offs," *Business Week*, July 22, 1991, p. 30.
11   Brett Pulley, "Lost Horizons: A Grand Tradition Can Make a Fall That Much Harder," *The Wall Street Journal*, September 16, 1991, p. A1.
12   G. Pascal Zachary, "Tech Shop," *The Wall Street Journal*, May 28, 1992, A1, A14.

CHAPTER 9

1   Teri Lammers, "The Elements of Perfect Pitch," *Inc.*, March 1992, pp. 53–55.
2   Fara Warner, "Subaru Pitches 600,000 of Its Rivals' Customers," *Brandweek*, March 1, 1993, p. 4.
3   Ibid.
4   Daniel S. Kennedy, *The Ultimate Sales Letter* (Holbrook, MA: Bob Adams, 1990), pp. 30–31.
5   Lammers, "The Elements of Perfect Pitch," p. 54.
6   Quotes taken from *Eating Well* subscription letter.
7   "1990 Survey of Selling Costs," *Sales & Marketing Management*, February 26, 1990, p. 75.
8   From subscription letter for *Harvard Business Review*, dated May 8, 1992.
9   Kennedy, *The Ultimate Sales Letter*, p. 56.
10   "People," *U.S. News & World Report*, December 30, 1991/January 6, 1992, p. 32.
11   Techniques suggested by Kennedy, *The Ultimate Sales Letter*, pp. 66–80.
12   Letter from Luther A. Brock, *Sales Lead-Getting Model Letter Book* (Englewood Cliffs, NJ: Prentice Hall, 1986), p. 39.
13   "The Ideal Collection Letter," *Inc.*, February 1991, p. 59.
14   Ibid.
15   "Hands-on Manager's Tips: Making Them Pay," *Inc.*, April 1988, p. 128.
16   "The Ideal Collection Letter," p. 59.
17   Ibid., p. 60.
18   Ibid., p. 61.
19   The information on writing persuasive memos is based on a discussion in John S. Fielden, Ronald E. Dulek, and Jean D. Fielden, *Elements of Business Writing* (Englewood Cliffs, NJ: Prentice Hall, 1984), pp. 53–77.

CHAPTER 10

1   Annetta Miller and Karen Springen, "Egg Rolls for Peoria," *Newsweek*, October 12, 1992, pp. 59–60; Richard Gibson, "China Coast Restaurants May Mushroom," *The Wall Street Journal*, April 18, 1993, p. B1.
2   Miller and Springen, "Egg Rolls for Peoria," p. 60.
3   Ray E. Barfield and Sylvia S. Titus, *Business Communications* (Hauppage, NY: Barron's Educational Series, 1992), pp. 141–42.
4   Jeff Bailey, "Environment: Waste Hauler Goes under the Microscope," *The Wall Street Journal*, May 11, 1992, p. B1.
5   David Steinberger, "Growing New York: Simplify, Simplify," *The New York Times*, January 18, 1992, p. 23.
6   Studies cited in Terry R. Bacon, "Collaboration in a Pressure Cooker," *The Bulletin of the Association for Business Communication*, 53:2 (June 1990), p. 4. See also Janis Forman, "Collaborative Business Writing: A Burkean Perspective for Future Research," *The Journal of Business Communication* 28:3 (Summer 1991), 236.
7   Bacon, "Collaboration in a Pressure Cooker," p. 4.
8   Eben Shapiro, "Home Library on Disks to Be Offered by Sony," *The New York Times*, May 23, 1991, p. D9.
9   Pamela Sebastian, "Business Bulletin," *The Wall Street Journal*, January 23, 1992, p. A1.

10   Kenneth Eskey, "Census Figures Out Americans in 1990," *Birmingham Post-Herald*, November 3, 1992, p. A5.
11   Christopher Beard and Betsy Wiesendanger, "The Marketer's Guide to Online Databases," *Sales & Marketing Management*, January 1993, pp. 36–41, 86.
12   Martha E. Williams, "The Online Industry at a Glance," *Online Access*, Fall 1992, pp. 21–22.
13   Cynthia Crossen, "Studies Galore Support Products and Positions, but Are They Reliable?" *The Wall Street Journal*, November 4, 1991, p. A9.
14   "Privacy Is Chic in L.A.," *Adweek's Marketing Week*, February 13, 1989, p. 2.
15   Lourdes Lee Valeriano, "Western Firms Poll Eastern Europeans to Discern Tastes of Nascent Consumers," *The Wall Street Journal*, April 27, 1992, pp. B1, B2.

CHAPTER 11

1   Deirdre Carmody, "One More Time: Magazine Is Reborn," *The New York Times*, April 13, 1992, pp. D1, D7; Daniel Goleman, "How Viewers Grow Addicted to Television," *The New York Times*, October 15, 1990, pp. C1, C8; and Robert W. Pittman, "We're Talking the Wrong Language to TV Babies," *The New York Times*, January 24, 1990, p. A23.
2   Gene Zelazny, *Say It with Charts: The Executive's Guide to Successful Presentations* (Homewood, IL: Business One Irwin: 1991), p. 11.
3   This section is based on Zelazny, *Say It with Charts*, p. 19.
4   These guidelines are suggested by Charles T. Brusaw, Gerald J. Alred, and Walter E. Oliu, *Handbook of Technical Writing*, 3rd ed. (New York: St. Martin's Press, 1987), p. 207.

CHAPTER 12

1   Mary B. W. Tabor, "Panel Warned in 1985 of Vulnerability of Center's Parking to Bombing," *The New York Times*, March 1, 1993, p. B5.
2   Ray E. Barfield and Sylvia S. Titus, *Business Communication* (Hauppauge, NY: Barron's Business Library, 1992), p. 183.
3   John Schell and John Stratton, *Writing on the Job: A Handbook for Business & Government* (New York: New American Library, 1984), pp. 208–19; and Raymond V. Lesikar, *Report Writing for Business*, 6th ed. (Homewood, IL: Richard D. Irwin, 1981), pp. 109–12.
4   These types of reports are discussed in Herman A. Estrin and Norbert Elliot, *Technical Writing in the Corporate World* (Los Altos, CA: Crisp Publications, 1990), pp. 32–37; Charles T. Brusaw, Gerald J. Alred, and Walter E. Oliu, *Handbook of Technical Writing*, 3rd ed. (New York: St. Martin's Press, 1987), pp. 346–47, 686–93; and William C. Paxson, *Write It Now! A Timesaving Guide to Writing Better* (Reading, MA: Addison-Wesley, 1986), pp. 27–46.
5   Lawrence D. Brennan, personal interview, November 25, 1992.
6   Information from Brusaw, Alred, and Oliu, *Handbook of Technical Writing*, pp. 339–46; Paxson, *Write It Now!*, pp. 52–53; and Patricia C. Weaver and Robert G. Weaver, *Persuasive Writing: A Manager's Guide to Effective Letters and Reports* (New York: Free Press, 1977), pp. 76–79.
7   This sample report is based on Report of the Bus Safety Committee, a document issued in Westport, Connecticut, June 8, 1992.

CHAPTER 13

1   Jay Abraham's story is found in Ron Tepper, *How to Write Winning Proposals for Your Company or Client* (New York: John Wiley, 1990), pp. 31–32, 125–26.
2   William C. Paxson, *Write It Now: A Timesaving Guide to Writing Better* (Reading, MA: Addison-Wesley, 1985), p. 75.
3   John Schell and John Stratton, *Writing on the Job: A Handbook for Business and Government* (New York: New American Library, 1984), p. 148.
4   Paxson, *Write It Now*, p. 76.
5   Information for this section is based on Paxson, *Write It Now*, pp. 76–77; Paxson, *The Business Writing Handbook* (New York: Bantam Books, 1981), p. 82; and Schell and Stratton, *Writing on the Job*, pp. 154–55.
6   Tepper, *How to Write Winning Proposals for Your Company or Client*, p. 137.
7   Information for this proposal comes, in part, from Anthony P. Carnevale and Leila J. Gainer, *The Learning Enterprise*, published by The American Society for Training & Development and the U.S. Department of Labor, Employment & Training Administration, 1990, pp. 35–37.
8   Tepper, *How to Write Winning Proposals for Your Company or Client*, pp. 135–36.
9   Proposal provided by Dr. Beatrice Harris, partner in Harris, Rothenberg International, October 14, 1992.

CHAPTER 14

1   Randall Rothenberg, "Seducing These Men: How Ad Agencies Vied for Subaru's $70 Million," *The New York Times Magazine*, October 20, 1991, pp. 30–40, 65–66.
2   George V. Grune, "Challenges to the Magazine Industry: Some Plain Talk." Speech delivered to the Magazine Publishing Congress, New York, October 31, 1989. Reprinted in *Vital Speeches of the Day*, January 15, 1990, p. 202.
3   Gerald M. Phillips and J. Jerome Zolten, *Structuring Speech* (Indianapolis: Bobbs-Merrill, 1976), p. 76.
4   Thomas Leech, *How to Prepare, Stage, and Deliver Winning Presentations* (New York: Amacom, 1982), pp. 48–49.

5 John J. Makay, *Public Speaking: Theory into Practice* (Fort Worth, TX: Harcourt Brace Jovanovich College Publishers, 1992), p. 149.
6 Tom Peters, *Thriving on Chaos* (New York: Alfred A. Knopf, 1988), p. 149.
7 Ron Hoff, *I Can See You Naked: A Fearless Guide to Making Great Presentations* (Kansas City, MO: Andrews and McMeel, 1988), p. 9.
8 T. Boone Pickens, "Foreign Investment in Japan: Keiretsu Business Practices." Speech delivered to the Japan Society, Los Angeles and San Diego, October 23, 1990. Reprinted in *Vital Speeches of the Day*, January 1, 1991, p. 171.
9 Makay, *Public Speaking*, p. 262.
10 Elias Kusulas, "A Client's View of Real Estate Services: The Decade of the Customer." Speech delivered at Colliers International Property Consultants Sales Conference, Illinois, September 17, 1990. Reprinted in *Vital Speeches of the Day*, January 15, 1991, pp. 214–15.
11 George C. Dillon, "The Prospect of Competitive Ethics: Good Ethics Is Good Business." Speech delivered at the Racing for a Competitive Edge Conference, New York, March 20, 1991. Reprinted in *Vital Speeches of the Day*, June 15, 1991, p. 526.
12 Harvey B. Mackay, "How to Get a Job: How to Be Successful." Speech delivered as an MBA Commencement Address, Penn State University, University Park, Pennsylvania, May 11, 1991. Reprinted in *Vital Speeches of the Day*, August 15, 1991, p. 656.
13 John Cady, "The Food Industry's Role in Advancing Public Confidence: Strategies for Regaining Public Confidence." Speech delivered before the Food and Drug Law Institute, Palm Beach, Florida, April 24, 1991. Reprinted in *Vital Speeches of the Day*, July 1, 1991, p. 567.
14 Newton N. Minow, "Television: How Far Has It Come in 30 years." Speech delivered at the Gannett Foundation Media Center, Columbia University, New York, May 9, 1991. Reprinted in *Vital Speeches of the Day*, July 1, 1991, pp. 552–53.
15 Leech, *How to Prepare, Stage, and Deliver Winning Presentations*, p. 96.
16 Linda Winikow, "How Women and Minorities Are Reshaping Corporate America." Speech delivered to the Women's Bureau Conference, Washington, DC. October 23, 1990. Reprinted in *Vital Speeches of the Day*, February 1, 1991, p. 244.
17 Mackay, "How to Get a Job," p. 659.
18 Grune, "Challenges to the Magazine Industry," p. 204.
19 Claudia H. Deutch, "The Parables of Corporate Culture," *The New York Times*, October 13, 1991, p. F25.
20 Leech, *How to Prepare, Stage, and Deliver Winning Presentations*, p. 166.
21 Louis E. Boone, *Quotable Business* (New York: Random House, 1992), p. 63.
22 Dick Jansen, "Putting More Oomph in Your Oratory," *Business Week*, June 4, 1990, p. 165.
23 Ibid.
24 Deirdre Fanning, "The Public Equivalent of a Root Canal," *The New York Times*, December 2, 1990, p. F25.
25 Janssen, "Putting More Oomph in Your Oratory," p. 165.
26 Hoff, *I Can See You Naked*, pp. 67–68.
27 Interview with Sarah Weddington, March 19, 1990.
28 Hoff, *I Can See You Naked*, p. 216.

CHAPTER 15

1 Al Neuharth, *Confessions of an S.O.B.* (New York: Plume Books, 1989), pp. 114–16, 125.
2 George David Kieffer, *The Strategy of Meetings: How to Make Your Next Business Meeting a Win for Your Company and Your Career* (New York: Warner Books, 1988), p. 20.
3 Clyde W. Burleson, *Effective Meetings: The Complete Guide* (New York: John Wiley, 1990), p. 1.
4 Ibid., p. 32.
5 Terrence E. Deal and Allen A. Kennedy, *Corporate Cultures: The Rites and Rituals of Corporate Life* (Reading, MA: Addison-Wesley, 1982), p. 71.
6 Ibid., p. 18.
7 Kieffer, *The Strategy of Meetings*, p. 124.
8 Sue Shellenbarger, "Companies Team Up to Improve Quality of Their Employees' Child-Care Choices," *The Wall Street Journal*, October 17, 1991, p. B1.
9 Ibid.
10 Information from G. Pierre Goad, "Trying to Assimilate Roy Rogers Outlets, Hardee's Is Ambushed by Irate Clientele," *The Wall Street Journal*, August 28, 1991, p. B1.
11 Mary Kay Ash, *Mary Kay on People Management* (New York: Warner Books, 1984), p. 54.
12 Quote cited in Seth Godin and Chip Conley, *Business Rules of Thumb: Words to Live by and Learn from That Touch Every Aspect of Your Career* (New York: Warner Books, 1987), p. 105.
13 Ron Hoff, *I Can See You Naked: A Fearless Guide to Making Great Presentations* (Kansas City, MO: Andrews and McMeel, 1988), p. 138.
14 Factual information about advance ticketing is from Thomas R. King, "Tired of Lines? Theaters Take Orders by Phone," *The Wall Street Journal*, October 11, 1991, pp. B1, B8.
15 Keith Schneider, "In Exxon Deal, Transportation Chief Wins Another One for the President," *The New York Times*, March 21, 1991, p. A18.

16 Juliet Nierenberg and Irene S. Ross, *Women and the Art of Negotiating: Techniques for Achieving Success in Your Business and Personal Relationships* (New York: Simon & Schuster, 1985), p. 169.
17 Kieffer, *The Strategy of Meetings*, pp. 44–45.
18 Outline suggested by Burleson, *Effective Meetings*, pp. 85–86.
19 William E. Schmidt, "To Mitterrand, Lateness Is Still Très Fashionable," *The New York Times*, July 17, 1991, p. A10.
20 Mary Beth Grover, "Letting Both Sides Win," *Forbes*, September 30, 1991, p. 178.
21 These negotiating steps can be found in Burleson, *Effective Meetings*, pp. 46–49.
22 Neuharth, *Confessions of an S.O.B.*, pp. 151–52.
23 Mark H. McCormack, *What They Still Don't Teach You at the Harvard Business School* (New York: Bantam Books, 1989), p. 51.
24 Ibid., p. 70.
25 Thomas J. Peters and Robert H. Waterman, Jr., *In Search of Excellence: Lessons from America's Best-Run Companies* (New York: Harper & Row, 1982), p. 122.
26 Ash, *Mary Kay on People Management*, p. 31.
27 Ibid., pp. 35–36.
28 Julius Fast, *Subtext: Making Body Language Work in the Workplace* (New York: Viking, 1991), p. 141.
29 Enid Nemy, "New Yorkers, Etc.," *The New York Times*, November 3, 1991, Sec. 1, p. 50.

CHAPTER 16

1 Daniel P. Wiener, "A Road Map to That First Job," *U.S. News & World Report*, May 13, 1991, p. 88.
2 Tony Lee, "Alumni Go Back to School to Hunt for Jobs," *The Wall Street Journal*, June 11, 1991, p. B1.
3 Wiener, "A Road Map to That First Job," p. 88.
4 The following approach to self-analysis was suggested by Tom Jackson, *The Perfect Résumé* (New York: Doubleday, 1990), pp. 16–38.
5 Amy Saltzman, "The New Meaning of Success," *U.S. News & World Report*, September 17, 1990, p. 56.
6 Carol Hymowitz, "Trading Fat Paychecks for Free Time," *The Wall Street Journal*, August 5, 1991, p. B1.
7 Saltzman, "The New Meaning of Success," pp. 56–57.
8 Christopher Conte, "Labor Letter," *The Wall Street Journal*, December 3, 1991, p. A1.
9 Elizabeth M. Fowler, "When You Can't Get in the Front Door," *The New York Times*, August 20, 1991, p. D17.
10 William J. Morin and James C. Cabrera, *Parting Company: How to Survive the Loss of a Job and Find Another Successfully* (San Diego: Harcourt Brace Jovanovich, 1991), pp. 270–71.
11 Robert Half, *How to Get a Better Job in This Crazy World* (New York: Plume Books, 1990), p. 94.
12 Elizabeth M. Fowler, "Flaws Seen in Campus Recruiting," *The New York Times*, August 6, 1991, p. D7.
13 Charles Strum, "As Recession Tightens Its Grip, Hopes of Jobless Dwindle and Fears Mount," *The New York Times*, November 14, 1991, p. B8.
14 Half, *How to Get a Better Job in This Crazy World*, p. 94.
15 Ibid.
16 Morin and Cabrera, *Parting Company*, p. 250.

CHAPTER 17

1 Victoria P. Brown, "An M.B.A. Runs the Gauntlet," *The New York Times Magazine*, June 12, 1988, pp. 22, 42, 52.
2 Taken from Jeff B. Speck, *Hot Tips, Sneaky Tricks and Last-Ditch Tactics: An Insider's Guide to Getting Your First Corporate Job* (New York: John Wiley, 1989), p. 61.
3 See William J. Morin and James C. Cabrera, *Parting Company: How to Survive the Loss of a Job and Find Another Successfully* (San Diego: Harcourt Brace Jovanovich, 1991), pp. 286–90.
4 Larry Armstrong and William C. Symonds, "Beyond 'May I Help You?'" *Business Week: The Quality Imperative*, 1991, p. 100.
5 Tom Peters, *Thriving on Chaos: Handbook for a Management Revolution* (New York: Alfred A. Knopf, 1988), p. 315.
6 Speck, *Hot Tips, Sneaky Tricks and Last-Ditch Tactics*, p. 170.
7 Terrence E. Deal and Allen A. Kennedy, *Corporate Cultures: The Rites and Rituals of Corporate Life* (Reading, MA: Addison-Wesley, 1982), p. 12.
8 James S. Hirsch, "To One Xerox Man, Selling Photocopiers Is a Gambler's Game," *The Wall Street Journal*, September 24, 1991, p. A12.
9 Nancy Marx Better, "Image-Making, from Soup to Sales Pitch," *The New York Times*, December 8, 1991, p. F29.
10 Leonore Cervera, "First Impressions Count," *USA Today*, September 19, 1988, p. B1.
11 Robert Half, *How to Get a Better Job in This Crazy World* (New York: Plume Books, 1990), p. 167.
12 Tom Washington, "Why It Pays to Master the Art of Story-Telling," *National Business Employment Weekly*, August 18, 1991, p. 9.
13 Speck, *Hot Tips, Sneaky Tricks and Last-Ditch Tactics*, p. 148.
14 Model interview described in Morin and Cabrera, *Parting Company*, pp. 278–86. Information from Henry Morgan and John Cogger, *The Interviewer's Manual* (New York: Drake Beam Morin, 1980).
15 Morin and Cabrera, *Parting Company*, p. 280.

16 Ibid., p. 284.
17 Ibid., pp. 284–85.
18 Jory L. Laine, "How to Respond to Negative Questions," *National Business Employment Weekly*, November 1–November 8, 1991, p. 5.
19 These suggestions are contained in Laine, "How to Respond to Negative Questions," pp. 5–6.
20 Sources for this section are Jeffrey G. Allen, *The Complete Q&A Job Interview Book* (New York: John Wiley, 1988), pp. 38, 55, 84; and Morin and Cabrera, *Parting Company*, pp. 292–306.
21 Marisa Manley, "Employment Lines," *Inc.*, June 1988, p. 132.
22 Laurie P. Cohen, William Power, and Michael Siconolfi, "Financial Firms Act to Curb Office Sexism, with Mixed Results," *The Wall Street Journal*, November 5, 1991, pp. A1, A12.
23 Joann S. Lublin, "Rights Law to Spur Shifts in Promotion," *The Wall Street Journal*, December 30, 1991, p. B1.
24 Peters, *Thriving on Chaos*, p. 316.
25 Interviewee responses in this section suggested by Half, *How to Get a Better Job in This Crazy World*, pp. 186–87.
26 Data from U.S. Chamber of Commerce, *Employee Benefits: 1991*.
27 Albert R. Karr, "Labor Letter," *The Wall Street Journal*, August 13, 1991, p. A1.
28 Amy Saltzman, "To Get Ahead, You May Have to Put On an Act," *U.S. News & World Report*, May 13, 1991, p. 90.
29 Janell M. Kurtz, and Wayne R. Wells, "The Employee Polygraph Protection Act: The End of Lie Detector Use in Employment Decisions?" *Journal of Small Business Management*, October 1989, pp. 76–80; David E. Nagle, "The Polygraph Shield," *Personnel Administrator*, February 1989, pp. 18–23; "Ban on Lie Detector Use Now in Effect," *Mobile Register*, December 28, 1988, p. A7; and, Albert R. Karr, "Law Limiting Use of Lie Detectors Is Seen Having Widespread Effect," *The Wall Street Journal*, July 1, 1988, p. A19.
30 "Lie Detector Ban Impacts Retail Hiring," *Chain Store Age Executive*, October 1988, pp. 198–201.
31 U.S. Equal Employment Opportunity Commission, *The Americans with Disabilities Act: Your Responsibilities as an Employer* (Washington, DC, 1991), pp. 6–7.
32 Interview with Fred H. Block, M.D., Corporate Medical Director, Chemical Banking Corporation, January 6, 1993; Chris Lee, "Who Gets Trained in What: 1991," *Training*, October 1991, p. 58; Minda Zetlin, "Corporate American Declares War on Drugs," *Personnel*, August 1991, pp. 1, 8; and, Andrew Kupfer, "Is Drug Testing Good or Bad?" *Fortune*, December 19, 1988, pp. 133–40.
33 Leslee Jaquette, "Red Lion Pleased with Drug-Testing Program," *Hotel & Motel Management*, February 25, 1991, pp. 3, 36.
34 "Firm Says 5% of Doctors Lied in Recruiting Efforts," *The Wall Street Journal*, February 11, 1988, p. A39.
35 Stacey Slaughter Miller, "Employment Briefs: Reasons to Refuse an Offer," *National Business Employment Weekly*, November 1–November 7, 1991, p. 17.

CHAPTER 18

1 "A Dress Code Chafes in the Land of Haute Couture," *The New York Times*, December 25, 1991, pp. 1, 48; and Philip R. Harris and Robert T. Moran, *Managing Cultural Differences*, 3rd ed. (Houston: Gulf Publishing, 1991) pp. 464–71.
2 Patrick Oster, "Breaking into European Markets by Breaking the Rules," *Business Week*, January 20, 1992, pp. 88-89; Roger Cohen, "For Coke, World Is Its Oyster," *The New York Times*, November 21, 1991, p. D1; and Robert Neff, "Guess Who's Selling Barbies in Japan Now?" *Business Week*, December 9, 1991, pp. 72–76.
3 Jon C. Madonna, "If It's Markets You Need, Look Abroad," The New York Times, January 5, 1992, p. F13.
4 Ronald E. Dulek, John S. Fielden, and John S. Hill, "International Communications: An Executive Primer," *Business Horizons*, January–February 1991, p. 20.
5 "Reports from U.S. Service Posts," U.S. Department of State, August 1991.
6 Lennie Copeland and Lewis Griggs, *Going International: How to Make Friends and Deal Effectively in the Global Marketplace* (New York: Random House, 1985), p. xix.
7 Frank L. Acuff, "What It Takes to Succeed in an Overseas Assignment," *National Business Employment Weekly*, August 25, 1991, p. 17.
8 Arthur H. Bell, *International Careers* (Holbrook, MA: Bob Adams, 1990), pp. 72–73
9 Paul Ingrassia, "Japanese Firms Come to Detroit, and City Is Glad to Have Them," *The Wall Street Journal*, May 7, 1991, p. A1.
10 Jack Egan, "Business without Borders," *U.S. News & World Report*, July 16, 1990, p. 29.
11 Peter t. Kilborn, "Liasons Hired by Tokyo Act to Help or to Control," *The New York Times*, June 3, 1991, p. B6.
12 Clements P. Work, "If This Is Belgium, It Must Be Tuesday," *U.S. News & World Report*, July 16, 1990, pp. 31–32
13 Bernard Wysocki, Jr., "American Firms Send Office Work Abroad to Use Cheaper Labor," *The Wall Street Journal*, August 14, 1992, p. A1.
14 These generalizations were suggested by Harris and Moran, *Managing Cultural Differences*, pp. 347–48.

15 Interview with Sana Reynolds, November 6, 1991.
16 Jonathan R. Moller, "Guidelines for International Protocol: Egypt, Hong Kong, and Brazil," *Federal Express International Newsletter*, June 1991, pp.2–3.
17 Discussion of cultural imperatives, adiaphoras, and exclusives is based on Philip R. Cateora, *International Marketing* (Homewood, IL: Business One Irwin, 1990), pp. 103–5, 108.
18 Copeland and Griggs, *Going International*, pp. 113–14.
19 James F. Stoner and R. Edward Freeman, *Management*, 5th ed. (Englewood Cliffs, NJ: Prentice Hall, 1992), P. 531.
20 Copeland and Griggs, *Going International*, p. 100.
21 Jim Impoco, "Outlook: Let's Talking English," U.S. News & World Report, April 20, 1992, p. 14; Naoki Kameda, "'Englishes' in Cross-Cultural Business Communication," *The Bulletin of the Association for Business Communication*, March 1992, p. 5.
22 Quote cited in Harris and Moran, *Managing Cultural Differences*, p. 48.
23 Copeland and Griggs, *Going International*, p. 100.
24 Elizabeth M. Fowler, "Career: Managers Lack Fluency in Language," *The New York Times*, June 11, 1991, p. D6. See also Harris Collingwood, "Ready to Travel?" *Business Week*, March 2, 1992, p. 46
25 "Students in Language Are Found at New High," *The New York Times*, September 25, 1991, p. B6; and "U.S. Plans Scholarships to Push Foreign Studies," *The New York Times*, December 25, 1991, p. 11.
26 Edward T. Hall, *The Silent Language* (Garden City, NY: Doubleday, 1959), pp. 27–28.
27 Edward T. Hall and Mildred R. Hall, *Hidden Differences: Doing Business with the Japanese* (Garden City, NY: Anchor Press/Doubleday, 1987), pp. 16–18.
28 Cateora, *International Marketing*, p. 123.
29 Urban C. Lehner, "Just Wait until Young Teller-San Tells Old Chairman-San 'Get Lost,'" *The Wall Street Journal*, April 24, 1992, p. B1.
30 Perry W. Buffington, "Practical Protocol," *Sky*, November 1991, p. 80.
31 Frederick H. Katayama, "How to Act Once You Get There," *Fortune: Pacific Rim*, 1989, p. 87.
32 Comment cited in Robert T. Moran, "What's Funny to You May Not Be Funny to Other Cultures," *International Management*, July–August, 1987, p. 74.
33 "Bush Hands Out Wrong Sign," *USA Today*, January 3, 1992, p. A4
34 "In Athens, It's Palms In," *Newsweek*, December 10, 1990, p. 79.
35 Hall, *The Silent Language*, p. 209.
36 Edward T. Hall, *The Hidden Dimension* (Garden City, NY: Doubleday & Company, 1966), p. 149
37 Julius Fast, Subtext: *Making Body Language Work in the Workplace* (New York: Viking, 1991), pp. 204–5.
38 This section is based on information from Copeland and Griggs, *Going International*, pp.24–27. See also Dulek, Fieldsen, and Hill, "International Communication," pp. 20–25; and Harris and Moran, *Managing Cultural Differences*, pp. 45–47, 397.
39 Clifford J. Levy, "The Growing Gelt in Others' Words," *The New York Times*, October 20, 1991, p. F5.
40 Examples cited in Cateora, *International Marketing*, p. 489; and Harris and Moran, *Managing Cultural Differences*, p. 64.
41 Dulek, Fielden, and Hill, "International Communication," p. 24.
42 Tad Friend, "The Geography of Bare," *Condé Nast Traveler*, April 1992, p. 179.
43 Katayama, "How to Act Once You Get There," P. 88.
44 Sources for this section include Copeland and Griggs, *Going International*, pp. 116–17; Dulek, Fielden, and Hill, "International Communication," pp. 20–25; Hall, *The Hidden Dimension*, pp. 131–32; and Katayama, "How to Act Once You Get There," p. 88.
45 Buffington, "Practical Protocol," p. B1.
46 Hall, *The Hidden Dimension*, p. 131.
47 Ibid., p. 132
48 Francine C. Brevetti, "Hazards of Skimping on Skilled Chinese Interpreters," *Asian Wall Street Journal*, June 13, 1988, p. 16.
49 Interview with Sana Reynolds, November 6, 1991.

CHAPTER 19

1 Stephanie Simon, "Cultural Clash Can Sow Office Confusion," *Chicago Tribune*, August 21, 1990, p. 1; Christine Moore, "Experts Urge Harnessing Skills of Multicultural Work Force," *Employment Review*, June 28-August 1, 1990, p. 4; and David Treadwell, "Races Split by 'Cultural Divide,'" *Los Angeles Times*, January 13, 1989, Sec. 1, p. 21.
2 Susan Crabtree and Marg Hile, "Cultural Diversity Challenges the Workplace," *Resource*, April 1990, pp. 46-47.
3 Elizabeth Kolbert, "Sexual Harassment at Work is Pervasive, Survey Suggests," *The New York Times*, October 11, 1991, p. A17; Department of Labor, Bureau of Labor Statistics, *Monthly Labor Review*, p. 31; Marilyn Loden and Judy B. Rosener, *Workforce 2000: Managing Employee Diversity as a Vital Resource* (Homewood, Ill.: Business One Irwin, 1991), p. 6.
4 Dorothy J. Gaiter, "Equal Opportunities," *The Wall Street Journal*, November 22, 1991, p. R14; and William B. Johnston and Arnold E. Packer, *Workforce 2000* (Indianapolis: Hudson Institute, 1987), p. 95.
5 The following discussion is based on Loden and Rosener, *Workforce 2000*, pp. 87-99.
6 "Archie Bunker, Alive and Well," *Newsweek*, January 21, 1991, p. 57.

7   Kathy Bodovitz, "Black America," *American Demographics Desk Reference*, July 1991, p. 8.
8   Thomas Kochman, *Black and White Styles in Conflict* (Chicago: University of Chicago Press, 1981), p. 11.
9   Connie Lauerman, "Do You Hear What I Hear?" *Chicago Tribune*, November 5, 1985, Sec. 5, p. 1.
10 Lauerman, "Do You Hear What I Hear?"
11 Patti Watts, "Bias Busting: Diversity Training in the Workplace," *Management Review*, December 1987, pp. 53-54.
12 Kathy Bodovitz, "Hispanic America," *American Demographics Desk Reference*, July 1991, pp. 14-15.
13 Richard W. Stevenson, "Catering to Consumers' Ethnic Needs," *The New York Times*, January 23, 1992, pp. D1, D8.
14 Kathy Bodovitz and Brad Edmondson, "Asian America," *American Demographics Desk Reference*, July 1991, pp. 16, 18.
15 Donatella Lorch, "Banks Follow Immigrants to Flushing," *The New York Times*, August 7, 1991, pp. B1, B2.
16 PR News, 127 E. 80th St., New York, NY 10021 (no date).
17 Seth Mydans, "Shooting Puts Focus on Korean-Black Frictions in Los Angeles," *The New York Times*, October 6, 1991, p. L20.
18 Lennie Copeland, "Learning to Manage a Multicultural Work Force," *Training*, May 1988.
19 Deborah Tannen, *You Just Don't Understand: Women and Men in Conversation* (New York: William Morrow and Company, 1990).
20 Sally Helgesen, *The Female Advantage: Women's Ways of Leadership* (New York: Doubleday, 1990), pp. 8-29.
21 Barbara Rudolph, "Why Can't a Woman Manage More Like...a Woman?" *Time*, Fall 1990, p. 53.
22 Kolbert, "Sexual Harassment at Work is Pervasive, Survey Suggests," p. A1.
23 Joann S. Lublin, "Companies Try a Variety of Approaches to Halt Sexual Harassment on the Job," *The Wall Street Journal*, October 11, 1991, p. B1.
24 These examples are patterned after Barbara Kantrowitz, "Striking a Nerve," *Newsweek*, October 21, 1991, pp. 34-40.
25 Sue Shellenbarger, "Is a Dream Workplace Any Closer to Reality?" *The Wall Street Journal*, October 18, 1991, p. B4.
26 Jerry Goodbody, "Hooray for Older Workers," *Adweek's Marketing Week*, May 27, 1991, p. 26.
27 Udayan Gupta, "Disabilities Act Isn't as Burdensome as Many Feared," *The Wall Street Journal*, April 20, 1992, p. B2.
28 U.S. Equal Employment Opportunity Commission, *The Americans with Disabilities Act: Your Responsibilities as an Employer* (Washington, D.C.: Government Printing Office, 1991), p. 4.
29 Jean Lakeman, "Deaf Student Refuses to be Discouraged, Eventually Finds Work at Supermarket," *Mobile Press Register*, April 19, 1992, p. C1.
30 Timothy D. Schellhardt, "Managing," *The Wall Street Journal*, April 29, 1991, p. B1.
31 Copeland, "Learning to Manage a Multicultural Work Force."
32 Sharon Nelton, "Meet Your New Work Force," *Nation's Business*, July 1988, p. 3.
33 Joann S. Lublin, "Sexual Harassment Is Topping Agenda in Many Executive Education Programs," *The Wall Street Journal*, December 2, 1991, p. B1.
34 Joyce E. Santora, "Kinney Shoe Steps into Diversity," *Personnel Journal*, September 1991, pp. 72-77.
35 Joann S. Lublin, "Rights Law to Spur Shifts in Promotions," *The Wall Street Journal*, December 30, 1991, p. B1.
36 Personal correspondence with Dianne LaMountain, LaMountain and Associates, November 12,1991.

CHAPTER 20

1   Gene Bylinsky, "Saving Time with New Technology," *Fortune*, December 30, 1991, pp. 98-104.
2   Lourdes Lee Valeriano, "Executives Find They're Always on Call as Computer, Fax Supercede Time Zones," *The Wall Street Journal*, August 8, 1991, p. B1.
3   Thomas McCarroll, "What New Age?" *Time*, August 12, 1991,, p. 45.
4   Gabriella Stern, "Chief Executives Are Increasingly Chief Salesmen," The Wall Street Journal, August 6, 1991, pp. B1 and B7.
5   Andrew Pollack, "The Computer Age: Still a Work in Progress," *The New York Times*, August 11, 1991, Sec. 4, p. 1.

6   Information based on W. E. Wang and Joe Kraynak, *The First Book of Personal Computing* (Carmel, Indiana: SAMS, 1990), pp. 2-5 and 155.
7   Sources for this section include Lynn Quitman Troyka, *Simon & Schuster Handbook for Writers*, 2nd ed. (Englewood Cliffs, N.J.: Prentice Hall, 1990), pp. 763-768; W. E. Wang and Joe Kraynak, *The First Book of Personal Computing* (Carmel, Indiana: SAMS, 1990), pp. 57-71; and Charles T. Brusaw, Gerald J. Alred, and Walter E. Oliu, *Handbook of Technical Writing*, 3rd ed. (New York: St. Martin's Press, 1987), pp. 713-718.
8   McCarroll, "What New Age?" See also Joel P. Bowman, "The Influence of Electronic Transmission on Written Communication," *Mid-American Journal of Business*, Fall 1992, pp. 3-10.
9   Kathy Rebello and Evan I. Schwartz, "Microsoft: Bill Gates's Baby Is on Top of the World. Can It Stay There?" *Business Week*, February 24, 1992, pp. 63-64.
10 "Wanted: Miss Manners for E-Mail," *Northwest Arkansas Times*, February 23, 1992, p. 8C.
11 Ibid.
12 Michael W. Miller, "A New Medium: Bulletin Boards Become a Major Means of Communication," *The Wall Street Journal*. October 27, 1991, p. R8.
13 Barnaby J. Feder, "Toward Defining Free Speech in the Computer Age," *The New York Times*, November 3, 1991, p. E5; and Michael W. Miller, "Prodigy Computer Network Bans Bias Notes from Bulletin Board," *The Wall Street Journal*, October 24, 1991, p. B1.
14 These features are described in Cary Lu, "Hello? Hello?" *Inc.*, March 1989, pp. 135-136. See also Claudia H. Deutsch, "Call It `CEO Disease,' Then Listen," *The New York Times*, December 14, 1991, p. F23.
15 Chip Johnson, "Telephone Companies Hope `Voice Mail' Will Make Answering Machines Obsolete," *The Wall Street Journal*, July 23, 1991, pp. B1, B8.
16 Phillip Elmer-DeWitt, "Hello! This is Voice Mail Speaking," *Time*, May 22, 1989, p. 98.
17 Martha Brannigan, "Labor Letter," *The Wall Street Journal*, February 18, 1992, p. A1.
18 Andrew Mehlman, "Voice Mail: Pest or Progress," *USA Today*, November 1990, pp. 91-92.
19 Faye Rice, "Champions of Communication," *Fortune*, June 3, 1991, p. 120.
20 "Teleconferencing on a Budget," *Inc.*, April 1992, p. 131; and Anthony Ramirez, "Video Meetings Get Cheaper, and a Bit Better," *The New York Times*, February 5, 1992, p. D9.
21 Alex Kozlov, "Hello Out There in Witchita," *Management Digest*, special advertising section, 1991, p. 12. See also Andrew Kupfer, "Prime Time for Videoconferences," *Fortune*, December 28, 1992, pp. 90-95.
22 For more information on videophones, see William M. Bulkeley, "The Videophone Era May Finally Be Near, Bringing Big Changes," *The Wall Street Journal*, March 10, 1992, p. A1.
23 Kozlov, "Hello Out There in Wichita," p. 16.
24 "Not Just a Yuppie Toy," *Business Week*, February 24, 1992, p. 36; John Huey, "New Frontiers in Commuting," *Fortune*, January 13, 1992, p. 57; and Molly O'Neill, "Where Silence Was Golden, Pocket Phones Now Shriek," *The New York Times*, September 25, 1991, p. A1.
25 Don Dunn, "Pagers That Do More Than Beep," *Business Week*, February 4, 1991, p. 101.
26 Neal Santelmann, "Beepers Come of Age," *Forbes*, June 12, 1989, p. 170.
27 John J. Keller, "AT&T to Give Public Phones Office Skills," *The Wall Street Journal*, October 3, 1991, p. B1.
28 William M. Bulkeley, "Sophistication, Popularity Gain for Palmtops," *The Wall Street Journal*, September 16, 1991, pp. B1, B7.
29 Bylinsky, "Saving Time with New Technology," p. 99.
30 Richard Perez-Pena, "For Traffic-Weary Workers, an Office That's a Long Way from the Office," *The New York Times*, January 7, 1992, p. A12.
31 James E. Challenger, "The Potential Pitfalls of Telecommuting," *National Business Employment Weekly*, October 18-October 24, 1991, p. 13.
32 See Sue Shellenbarger, "Work & Family: Employers Set Rules for Doing Homework," *The Wall Street Journal*, August 16, 1991, p. B1; and "Doing their Home Work," *Monsanto Magazine*, October 1992, pp. 7-13.
33 "Laptop Computers Enhance Salespeople's Efficiency," *The Wall Street Journal*, June 23, 1992, p. A1.

accommodation (p. 603) Consideration of cultural differences

acknowledgment (p. 224) Informative letter telling the reader that information or materials have been received

action (p. 284) Final step in the AIDA concept; implies that readers must be convinced to take specific steps to purchase the product

active listening (p. 60) Listening that requires involvement with the information of a message and empathy with the sender

active voice (p. 149) Writing style in which the subject of a sentence performs the action

adjustment (p. 187) Company's response to a claim

adjustment letter (p. 210) Good-news letter written in response to a claim letter to inform the customer how a company intends to handle a specific problem

agenda (p. 491) Written document that defines a meeting by telling participants why is was called and what it should accomplish

aggressive collection notice (p. 288) Written correspondence in the form of a firm request that attempts to convince a debtor to pay a bill

AIDA concept (p. 278) Principle that an individual goes through four steps—*attention, interest, desire,* and *action*—before making a purchase decision

anecdote (p. 454) Short entertaining account of some event

appendix (p. 388) Back matter that supplements material persented in the text of a report or proposal

arithmetic mean (or average) (p.317) Measure of central tendency calculated by adding the sum of all researched observations and dividing by the number of observations

articulation (p. 474) Process of determining the clarity and distinctiveness of vocal sounds

attention (p. 278) In the AIDA concept, first step in capturing and holding an audience so it will continue to read a document or listen to an oral presentation

audience (p. 37) Receivers of verbal, nonverbal, and written messages

audience analysis (pp. 84, 450) Process by which business communicators analyze the needs and knowledge of their readers or listeners in order to improve the likelihood of communicating effectively through written documents and oral presentations

back matter (p. 388) Supplemental information included in the parts of the report that follow the report body

back order (p. 245) Order that the company promises to ship at some later date, which may or may not be specified

bar chart (p. 346) Diagram consisting of horizontal bars of varying lengths, each representing different items for comparison

bibliography (p. 388) Back-matter list identifying all references used in researching a report or proposal

bilateral bar chart (p. 347) Diagram starting from a central point to show positive or negative deviations from that point

blamers (p. 495) Meeting participants who focus on problems rather than solutions

boilers (p. 495) Meetings lparticipants who typically respond with anger when they do not get their way

border (p. 356) Any line that surrounds a visual aid to separate it from surrounding text

brainstorming (p. 90) Creative problem-solving technique in which ideas are listed as they come to mind and which encourages unrestrained participation in group discussion

brainstorming session (p. 489) Group process of generating new ideas in an open, nonjudgmental, nonauthoritarian atmosphere

buffer (p. 237) Protective barrier that helps cushion the shock of bad news

bullets (p. 125) Visual cues such as asterisks and dashes that indicate critical information by highlighting items contained in lists

business communication (p. 5) Communication required of an organization in both its internal and external environments

business report (p. 301) Compilation of organized information gathered on a specific topic and delivered to specific users

caption (p. 355) Brief narrative that supports the title and focuses on the most important point of a visual aid

cause-and-effect pattern (p. 112) Writing approach that focuses on events or consequences and the reasons for them

cellular telephone (p. 689) Wireless telephone that transmits voice and data in the form of radio signals

channel (p. 43) Medium through which message sender and audience communicate

chart (or graph) (p. 344) Diagram that presents numerical data in visual form to show trends, movements, distributions, and cycles

chronological pattern (p. 114) Writing approach used to describe a series of events chronologically, either in the order in which they occurred or in reverse sequence

chronological résumé (p. 531) Document in which the applicant's work experience, education, and personal history are arranged in a *reverse* time sequence—that is, with the most recent experience in each category listed first

claim (p. 187) Notice from a customer of a problem with a good or service

climactic-order pattern (p. 113) Writing approach that presents the material with which the reader is most likely to agree first

cognitive dissonance (p. 59) State of conflict arising from exposure to messages that contradict one's value system

cold contacts (p. 547) Unsolicited letters in which job seekers introduce themselves and ask about job openings

collaboration (p. 14) Process in which two or more people join together in a team to produce and deliver a message

collaborative meeting (p. 490) Formal meeting in which participants work together to prepare memos, letters, or reports or to develop projects

collaborative writing (p. 309) Process of creating finished reports and proposals by groups or individuals working together

collection letter (p. 286) Written correspondence seeking to persuade a debtor to pay an outstanding debt while encouraging continued business

collection series (p. 287) Written correspondence categorized according to the four types of increasingly persuasive appeals used to collect outstanding debts: *reminders, inquiries, aggressive notices,* and *last-resort letters*

college placement officer (p. 543) Job-search professional hired by colleges and universities to help students and alumni find jobs

column (or vertical-bar) chart (p. 348) Diagram consisting of vertical bars of different heights, each height representing a different quantity

communication (p. 5) Meaningful exchange of information through messages

communication barriers (p. 38) Problems that arise during the communication transaction and raise the possibility of misunderstanding and confusion

communication channels (p. 11) Formal and informal pathways that define the manner in which messages are sent within an organization's communication networks

communication flow (p. 11) Direction taken by communication within a formal communication channel

communication network (p. 13) Interaction pattern involving upward, downward, and horizontal communication

complaint (p. 8) Message indicating a problem with a good or service or the perception of such a problem

component comparison (p. 344) Data-presentation technique in which the size of each item is shown as a percentage of the total

composition (p. 74) Process of combining parts or elements into a coherent whole by following a writing plan to produce a rough draft and finally a finished draft

conclusions (pp. 318, 387) Logical result of the evidence presented in a report or proposal

confirmation bias (p. 639) Specific examples of cultural behaviors that reinforce beliefs and attitudes about members of a culture

connotation (p. 158) Implied meaning of a word or phrase

context (p. 46) Every factor surrounding and affecting the transmission of a message

core idea (pp. 82, 449) One-sentence statement of the central message of a written or oral presentation; sometimes called the *thesis statement*

corporate culture (p. 18) Patterns, traditions, and values that make one organization distinctly different from another

correlation analysis (p. 318) Statistical technique used to measure the positive, negative, or nonexistent relationship between two or more variables

cover letter (p. 534) Correspondence that accompanies a résumé in order to summarize an applicant's value to a prospective employer

credibility (p. 271) Degree to which a statement, a person, and/or a company is perceived to be ethical, believable, trustworthy, competent, responsible, and sincere

credit (p. 186) Arrangement whereby a business sells goods or services to another business or individual in exchange for a promise to repay the money

credit reference (p. 208) Good-news letter in which one company attests to the financial well-being of another

cultural adiaphoras (p. 604) Customs and behaviors for which accommodation is optional

cultural exclusives (p. 604) Customs, behaviors, and conversational topics from which foreigners are excluded

cultural imperatives (p. 604) Business customs and behaviors that must be recognized during communication

culture (p. 600) Shared products that make up a society, including languages, beliefs, rules, customs, myths, family patterns, and political systems

culture shock (p. 604) Psychological disorientation that arises when people do not understand or misinterpret cues received from other cultural groups

customer service (p. 8) Act of ensuring that customers feel valued and that their needs are met

cynical listening (p. 60) Defensive listening that occurs when receivers fear that a message will take advantage of them

database (p. 678) Set of logically related computer files that can be accessed for different purposes

decision-making meeting (p. 490) Formal meeting called to debate issues and make decisions

deductive organizational pattern (p. 111) Writing approach in which discussion moves from a *general* idea to a series of *specific* ideas

delegating meeting (p. 490) Formal meeting in which specific tasks are assigned to individuals or groups who are then responsible for their completion

delivery (p. 472) Method of giving any form of speech or oral presentation, including voice quality and body language

demography (p. 634) Statistical study of population size, density, and distribution that results in the collection of vital statistics

derived credibility (p. 39) Receiver's judgment of the sender while the message is being communicated

descriptive summary (p. 382) Synopsis which acts as an expanded table of contents to tell the reader what to expect and which states the purpose and scope of a report

design (pp. 74, 120) Process of planning, writing, illustrating, and structuring a document to make it inviting and easy to read

desire (p. 281) Third step in the AIDA concept; implies that a document can prompt an emotional reaction that propels people to action

desktop publishing (p. 680) Use of personal computers to design and lay out both text and accompanying graphics to produce camera-ready copies of a document

diplomacy (p. 238) Art of handling affairs in a tactful way to avoid arousing hostility

direct organizational pattern (p. 112) Writing approach that presents the main point in the beginning part of a message

direct request (p. 177) Straightforward written message that asks another individual for information, merchandise, or assistance

diversity training (p. 656) Process of improving awareness of different attitudes, behaviors, and communication patterns and developing skills to deal with these differences

downward communication (p. 11) Message flowing from a superior to a subordinate level of an organization

drug testing (p. 579) Pre-employment screening for such illegal substances as cocaine and marijuana

editing (p. 137) Correcting mistakes in grammar, spelling and punctuation and producing a document consistent in style for such elements as numbers, abbreviations, and capitalization

electronic bulletin board (p. 677) Public message center that appears on computer networks

electronic data interchange (EDI) (p. 245) Ability to transmit information about orders and other communications via computer linkups maintained by various companies in a supply chain

electronic mail (E-mail) (p. 674) Computerized mail service enabling users to transmit messages and documents instantaneously over telephone and data lines from one computer to another

empathy (p. 41) Ability to experience the world from another person's perspective

employee benefits (p. 576) Programs provided by employers for individual employees to cover costs for such services as medical insurance, parental and sick leave, vacations, and company savings plans

employment agency (p. 543) Organization that matches job candidates with specific jobs, often for a fee

employment-related letters (p. 216) Good-news letters presenting job offers, acknowledging candidates' applications, inviting applicants for interviews, or discussing additional details after an offer has been accepted

entrenched organization (p. 640) Organization with three separate levels: (1) *personal*, in which people surround themselves with others who share the same background and values and who are uncomfortable when communicating with people who are different; (2) *interpersonal*, in which informal networks develop around similar people who generally avoid interaction with members of groups outside the network; and (3) *organizational*, in which diverse groups are excluded from closed information networks

ethics (p. 21) Standards of conduct and moral judgment accepted by society

ethnic diversity (p. 635) Range of identifying characteristics that includes shared values, communication patterns, and behaviors

ethnocentrism (p. 602) Tendency to judge other cultures by the standards of one's own culture

evaluation (p. 59) Listening stage involving the decision to accept or reject, like or dislike, agree or disagree with a message

evidence (p. 114) Details that communicate information and support the core idea of a document

examples (p. 117) Descriptive stories and specific cases that make information real and memorable

executive summary (p. 382) Synopsis in the body of a report that condenses it into relatively few pages

executive-search firm (p. 545) Specialized employment agency that represents employers rather than individual job applicants, usually to identify, evaluate, and select high-level personnel

exporter (p. 597) Company that sells domestically produced goods and services abroad

extemporaneous speaking (p. 472) Delivery method in which the speaker relies on speaking notes rather than on a complete manuscript or memorization

external audience (p. 5) A company's customers and suppliers as well as the general public, other businesses, and government officials with whom it interacts

external communication (p. 6) Communication with the major audiences in a company's external environment

external data (p. 320) Data, primary or secondary, generated by sources outside an organization

external meeting (p. 487) Formal meeting that involves outsiders as well as company personnel

external proposal (p. 410) Proposal issued outside an organization to prospective clients in government or private industry

external report (p. 303) Report distributed to interested parties outside the writer's organization

facsimile (or fax) machine (p. 670) Electronic device that can copy and transmit original material, including text and graphics, to other machines in other locations

feedback (p. 45) Messages returned by the audience to the sender that may cause the sender to alter or cancel an original message

figure (p. 355) Any visual aid, other than tables, including charts, maps, drawings, photographs, and other illustrations

flow chart (p. 351) Diagram describing the stages in a process

follow-up letter (p. 222) Informative letter written to ensure that everyone's version of the verbal points made at a meeting is the same

footnote (p. 356) Mechanism for explaining specific details in a visual aid

form report (p. 303) Document, such as an inventory-control report, following a specific format and focusing on specific information

formal agenda (p. 492) Agenda that schedules the order of meeting business and the approximate time allotted to each scheduled item

formal communication channel (p. 11) Communication sanctioned by company management

formal meeting (p. 487) Prearranged meeting with stated goals and involving a leader and participants

formal outline (p. 108) Organizational device that shows the precise relationship among ideas by following prescribed rules concerning content and format

formal report (p. 302) Relatively long document based on extensive research and organized according to a prescribed pattern

forward (p. 382) Introductory statement written by a person who did not author the report to provide a context for the report by discussing its background information or broad, general applications

freewriting (p. 92) Unstructured writing process that allows writers to express their thoughts without worrying about spelling, grammatical mistakes, or organizational problems

frequency-distribution comparison (p. 345) Data-presentation technique showing how many items fall into defined, progressive numerical ranges

front matter (p. 380) Parts of a formal report that are included before the body

functional résumé (p. 532) Résumé that highlights the applicant's accomplishments and abilities rather than his or her work history

general purpose (p. 80, 448) Primary reason for which a document is written or an oral presentation is made; typically to inform, persuade, and/or initiate action

glossary (p. 388) Alphabetized back-matter list, accompanied by definitions, of words and phrases used in a report

goodwill (p. 8) Prestige, loyalty, and reputation acquired by a company beyond the value of its products

goodwill message (p. 217) Message written to create a bond of friendship or understanding—personal, professional, or both—between writer and recipient

grapevine (p. 16) Internal information channel conducting information through unofficial, independent sources

greeting (p. 220) Goodwill message commemorating either holidays or special events

grid lines (p. 356) Series of horizontal and vertical lines crossing at 90-degree angles to establish specific values in an illustration

grouped bar chart (p. 347) Diagram comparing various parts of the same item

grouped column chart (p. 348) Diagram consisting of grouped or overlapping columns that compare two different

items at a given time and demonstrate how the relationship between those items changes over time

grouped line chart (p. 350) Line chart that makes comparisons between two or more items

headings (p. 124) Visual markers that indicate the parts of a document and give clues to its organization

hierarchy of needs (p. 86) Grouping that arranges in hierarchical order the physical, safety, social, status, and self-actualization needs common to most humans

high-context culture (p. 607) Culture in which communication depends not only on the message itself but also on the context surrounding the explicit message, including nonverbal language

horizontal (or lateral) communication (p. 13) Message flowing from sender to receiver within the same organizational level

importer (p. 597) Company that purchases raw materials and goods from foreign countries

impromptu speaking (p. 473) Delivery method in which the speaker makes remarks without advance preparation

in-depth interview (p. 558) Extended interview between company official and a prospective job candidate

index (p. 389) Alphabetized back-matter list of report topics that includes references to the pages on which each topic appears

indirect organizational pattern (p. 112) Writing approach that presents the main point in the latter part of the message

indirect organizational plan (p. 237) Method of organizing documents by *delaying* bad news rather than announcing it immediately

inducement (p. 284) Gifts or other consideration that encourages readers to take immediate action

inductive organizational pattern (p. 112) Writing approach in which discussion begins with a *specific* idea and moves step by step to a *general* topic

informal business conversation (p. 508) Unscheduled meeting between as few as two and as many as four people

informal communication channel (p. 15) Communication pattern independent of formal channels sanctioned by management

informal outline (p. 108) More loosely connected organizational device that need not follow the strict structural rules of a formal outline

informal report (p. 302) Relatively short document typically written over a short period and based on a comparatively small research base

information overload (p. 47) Need to digest an expanding number of messages from a growing variety of sources

informational meeting (p. 489) Formal meeting in which information is delivered to participants by means of oral reports

informative speech or presentation (p. 448) Address that describes, demonstrates, or explains information

informative summary (p. 382) Abbreviated version of a report that includes conclusions and recommenda-

tions as well as descriptions of purpose, scope, and methods

initial audience (p. 84) First reader of a document

initial credibility (p. 39) Receiver's judgment of the sender prior to receiving the message

inquiry letter (p. 288) Written correspondence seeking to determine if a problem exists that is preventing a customer from making required payment; typically, the third step after a statement and reminder letter

inspirational meeting (p. 490) Formal meeting that attempts to build enthusiasm toward the company and its products, encourage teamwork, or generally improve organizational morale or interaction

interest (p. 280) Second step in the AIDA concept; implies that the message has tapped a need in the reader, either to solve a problem or to satisfy a desire

internal audience (p. 5) A company's employees and owners

internal communication (p. 6) Communication through channels within an organization

internal data (p. 319) Data generated within an organization

internal meeting (p. 487) Formal meeting that involves only personnel within an organization

internal preview (pp. 385, 461) Sentences and paragraphs that appear at the beginning of text-discussion sections to introduce the material that will be covered in them; verbal signpost that tells listeners what the speaker intends to say before he or she says it

internal proposal (pp. 306, 410) Persuasive document that attempts to convince top management to spend money on specific projects intended to change or improve the organization

internal report (p. 302) Report distributed to individuals within the writer's organization

internal summary (pp. 385, 461) In documents, sentences and paragraphs that appear at the close of text-discussion sections to restate key points and to link them both to other report sections and to the report's specific purpose; in oral communication, verbal signpost occurring at a key point within a speech, restating and emphasizing what was just stated, and connecting internal elements

interpretation (p. 59) Listening stage during which meaning is placed on a message

interview sequence (p. 557) Series of interviews, constituting a multistage approach for evaluating job applicants

introduction (p. 383) Preamble in the body of a report intended to gain readers' attention by providing them with the information they need to evaluate the report itself

investigative report (p. 377) Short report that examines and analyzes details of a particular topic and presents conclusions and recommendations based on that analysis

invitation (p. 191) Request for business associates, potential customers, or personal acquaintances to attend a business or social event

item comparison (p. 344) Data-presentation technique in which relative rankings of individuals, geographic areas, products, production facilities, or other variables are examined to determine similarities or differences

job description (p. 568) Document specifying the objectives of a job, the work to be done, skill requirements, responsibilities involved, and working conditions

job interview (p. 557) Face-to-face encounter between a recruiter and a job candidate in which the recruiter assesses the candidate's background, skills, job objectives, interests, and attitudes; in turn, the candidate asks questions about the position and the organization

journalists' questions (p. 93) Six questions (who, when, where, what, why and how) coined by journalists for use as guidelines to structure their thinking in interviewing and preparing stories

know-it-alls (p. 496) Meeting participants who try to control meetings, often by leading participants in directions that they prefer regardless of group goals

labels (p. 356) Headings and subheadings that define the parts of a visual aid, including all identifications of items being compared

last-resort letter (p. 288) Written correspondence expressing a reluctance to begin legal action but a determination to do so if a delinquent customer does not pay within a stated time limit

legend (p.356) Marginal explanation of symbols used in a chart

letter of condolence (p. 219) Goodwill message sent when a business associate or an associate's family member dies

letter of recommendation (p. 214) Good-news personnel letter which speaks positively about a candidate's background and performance and which may tie the candidate's knowledge, skills, and abilities to a specific job objective

letter of sympathy (p. 220) Goodwill message conveying personal concern on such occasions as illness, accident, or other misfortune

letter of transmittal (or cover letter) (p. 380) Front-matter page that officially conveys the report to the reader, identifying the specific report being sent, the person to whom it is directed, and the reason for sending it

lie detector (or polygraph) (p. 578) Instrument for recording certain physical changes during a carefully controlled series of questions in order to establish an opinion about a person's honesty

line chart (p. 349) Diagram showing the relationship between numbers on the intersection of horizontal and vertical axes

list of illustrations (p. 381) Front-matter list of the figures and tables included in a document

listening (p. 57) Act of sensing, interpreting, evaluating, and reacting to what is being said

low-context culture (p. 607) Culture in which communication depends on explicit written and verbal messages

M-time (monochronic time) (p. 608) Way of viewing time according to sequential activities that proceed in a linear way

management plan (p. 413) Component of a proposal that describes plans for managing a proposed change after it is approved

manuscript reading (p. 472) Delivery method in which the speaker reads to an audience from a detailed prepared text

mean (or average) (p. 116) Measure of central tendency calculated by adding the sum of all observations and dividing by the number of observations

measure of central tendency (p. 317) Method for producing a single representative score that can be viewed as a typical score for a group, object, or event under study

median (p. 317) Midpoint score in the distribution of quantified observations arranged in numerical order

meeting minutes (p. 500) Written record of what occurred at a meeting

message (p. 41) Written, oral, or nonverbal communication transmitted by a sender to an audience

message of adoption (p. 268) Document that seeks to persuade readers to *start* doing something

message of continuance (p. 268) Persuasive message that urges the continuation of a behavior

message of discontinuance (p. 269) Persuasive message that asks for a behavior change

metamessage (p. 648) Communication that focuses on the relationships and attitudes between the people delivering and receiving the message

mindmapping (or clustering) (p. 91) Visual technique for grouping information into categories

minutes *See meeting minutes*

mission (p. 77) Fundamental purpose for which a document is written

mode (p. 317) Most frequently occurring number in a series of quantified observations

modem (p. 674) Special device used to convert computer signals to signals that can travel by telephone lines to another computer

multinational corporation (p. 598) Firm which conducts significant business activities outside its home country and which views the world as its marketplace

multiple audiences (p. 84) Primary, secondary, and/or initial audiences who receive, use, and may provide feedback regarding a document

multiple interview (p. 559) Interview at which a job candidate meets with people at different levels of the employer's organization

narrative report (p. 303) Report whose format is largely determined by what the writer decides to say and how he or she chooses to say it

negotiation (p. 504) Process of give and take in which both parties try to leave the bargaining table with what each perceives as a "good deal"

networking (p. 539) Process by which a job seeker talks and writes to people for assistance in his or her job search

noise (p. 43) Anything that interferes with a message by distorting its meaning

nonverbal communication (p. 49) Form of communication, including nonvocal and nonverbal vocal communication, taking

place through such media as gestures, eye contact, clothing, and tone of voice

nonverbal vocal communication (p. 50) Form of nonverbal communication, including tone of voice and such voice qualities as loudness

nonvocal communication (p. 50) Form of nonverbal communication including gestures, eye contact, facial expressions, posture, touch, clothing, and the use of space

observational study (p. 323) Method of collecting primary data by actually viewing the actions of respondents

obstructionist (p. 495) Meeting participant whose personality or hidden agenda threatens group success

offensive listening (p. 60) Listening that tries to catch the sender in a mistake or contradiction

on-campus recruiter (p. 543) Representative from a company's human resources department who interviews students for jobs

online database (p. 322) Computerized information-retrieval system operated by commercial suppliers and made available to business users for a service fee

oral presentation (p. 447) Extemporaneous speeches, frequently participative and delivered using only notes and visual aids to guide the speaker's performance

order (p. 185) Direct request asking a seller to ship specified goods to the sender

order acknowledgement (p. 207) Formal letter of explanation concerning receipt of an order for merchandise

order fulfillment (p. 8) Process by which orders are received by company representatives to satisfy customer needs

organization (pp. 74, 105) Process of arranging information and connecting different ideas to produce a unified, coherent message

organization chart (pp. 11) Diagram indicating formal lines of communication and interrelationships among the positions, departments, and functions of an organization

P-time (polychronic time) (p. 608) Attitude toward time that emphasizes building human relationships rather than meeting schedules

pager (p. 690) Battery-powered device that signals telephone messages

paralanguage (p. 54) Nonverbal vocal messages embodied in tone, emphasis, volume, and pauses

partial delivery (p. 245) Seller's decision to deliver in-stock items while back-ordering all others

passive voice (p. 149) Writing style in which the subject of a sentence is acted upon

periodic report (p. 303) Report distributed according to an established schedule, such as weekly, quarterly, or annually

personal reference (p. 189) Recommendation stating that an applicant is qualified to perform the duties of the job for which he or she is applying, attesting to the applicant's character, or both

personal space (p. 53) Physical space between people engaged in communication

persuasion (p. 268) Process of influencing or changing attitudes, beliefs, values, or behaviors

persuasive meeting (p. 490) Formal meeting involving presentations designed to achieve group consensus or support for a course of action

persuasive memo (p. 289) Document seeking to change the recipient's attitudes, beliefs, values, or behaviors

persuasive speech or presentation (p. 448) Address in which a speaker tries to convince an audience to accept a point of view and/or take specific actions

pictorial chart (p. 348) Bar or column chart using graphic symbols instead of horizontal or vertical lines

pie chart (p. 346) Diagram presenting data as wedge-shaped sections of a circle; used for component comparisons, with the entire circle representing 100 percent of a given whole and each wedge a portion of the whole

plagiarism (p. 328) Act of using someone else's words or unique approach without crediting the source

planning (p. 73) Process by which document objectives are set, audience needs and responses assessed, and a course of action developed to accomplish established objectives

planning outline (p. 462) Full-content outline that includes every part of a speech or presentation—introduction, body (including main points and supporting materials, internal previews, and summaries), and conclusion

polite listening (p. 60) Mechanical listening characterized by inattention

pre-employment testing (p. 578) Process whereby employers evaluate job candidates through skills tests, lie detector tests, physical examinations and reference checks

prejudice (p. 638) Combination of belief and behavior that results from preconceived judgments about other groups of people

presentation visual (p. 342) Visual designed to support a message and requiring a directive title and interpretation by the writer or speaker

presentation-graphics software (pp. 362, 680) Special computer programs used to create such visual aids as bar charts, line charts, pie charts, tables, drawings, and other graphics features by using data already in the computer

prewriting strategies (p. 90) Techniques for gathering and organizing ideas, including such processes as *brainstorming*, *mindmapping*, and *asking journalists' questions*

primary audience (p. 84) Reader for whom a document is directly intended and who will actually use its information

primary data (p. 319) Data collected specifically for use in preparing a report or proposal

primary headings (p. 124) Visual markers indicating major organizational sections in a document

primary source (p. 89) Person or organization supplying firsthand information on a subject

problem/solution pattern (p. 112) Writing approach that focuses first on a particular problem and then on possible solutions

progress report (p. 373) Short report providing status information on current work, including what has happened on a project since the previous report

pronunciation (p. 474) Formation of the proper sounds to create words

proofreading (p. 159) Process of checking for obvious errors or inconsistencies in a document's content, grammar, and spelling

proposal (pp. 306, 407) In sales, written communication that tries to convince the reader that the writer or the writer's organization can solve a particular problem or meet a specific need; document presenting ideas and plans for consideration by others who may accept them and agree to invest funds in their development

public relations (p. 15) Communication conducted by an organization with such publics as stockholders and the general public

questionnaire (p. 325) Scientifically designed list of questions used to gather primary data

racial identity (p. 635) Identity attributed to a category of people who share similar physical characteristics

random sample (or probability sample) (p. 324) Sample chosen so that each member of a population has an equal chance of being selected

reaction (p. 59) Listening stage referring to the response generated by a message

reasoning (p. 271) Process of using available evidence to reach a conclusion

receiver (p. 43) Audience to whom a message is transmitted

recommendations (pp. 318, 388) Specific actions suggested as a result of conclusions presented in a report or proposal

reference check (p. 580) Effort made by an employer during the screening process to verify a candidate's educational claims and work history

reference table (p. 343) Table with title and number that usually does not appear immediately following the text reference; ordinarily contains highlighted data

references (pp. 388,529) In a report or proposal, the section in the document body that lists material from other sources actually cited in the text; in recruiting, a list of people that a prospective employer may contact to learn about a job applicant's abilities, character, and background

reliability (p. 316) Extent to which data collected in a research study is consistent, stable, and free from systematic sources of error

reminder letter (p. 288) Written correspondence informing a customer that payment has not been received

report visual (p. 342) Visual aid designed and presented to let its data convey the necessary information

request for proposals (RFP) (pp. 10, 306) Detailed, formal government document requesting proposals and bids on a specific project

research (p. 73) Systematic investigation of a subject in order to discover facts, opinions, or beliefs

résumé (p. 526) Written document in which a job applicant relates his or her education, work experience, and personal accomplishments to the needs of prospective employers

revision (pp. 74, 137) Process of transforming a rough draft into a finished document by adding, deleting, replacing, and reorganizing words, sentences, and paragraphs

rhetorical question (p. 455) Question designed to produce receiver involvement in a subject without requiring an answer

rule (p. 356) Internal line that separates the various elements of a chart or table

rumor (p. 17) Story about an organization which is in general circulation but which is unconfirmed by facts

sales letter (p. 275) Written communication channel used for locating prospective accounts or increasing sales to current customers

sales proposal (or private-industry proposal) (p. 306) Persuasive document seeking to convince potential buyers to purchase a firm's goods or services

sample (p. 324) Group selected as a representative of a larger, statistically significant group

scope (p. 382) Any limitations, such as time and geography, that define a document's coverage

screening interview (p. 558) Normally the job candidate's first interview, which is usually conducted by the recruiter from the employer's human resources department

search strategy (p. 319) Systematic method for locating research sources

secondary audience (p. 84) Readers, other than the primary reader, who will use the document in a variety of ways or who may be asked to comment on its content

secondary data (p. 319) Data that has been previously analyzed, evaluated, organized, and published

secondary headings (p. 124) Titles used to organize information into subsections within the context of primary headings

secondary source (p. 89) Person or organization compiling data and ideas supplied by others

self analysis (p. 522) Job-search process of defining your interests, skills, personal qualities, and accomplishments

sender credibility (p. 39) Extent to which a sender is perceived as believable, competent, authoritative, and so on

senders (p. 38) Participants in the transaction who communicate messages to an audience

sensation (p. 58) Physiological process by which sound waves are transmitted from the ear to the brain

service encounter (p. 8) Interaction between a customer and a company representative

sexual harassment (p. 000) Illegal behaviors ranging from blatant physical contact to subtle sexually oriented hints, suggestions, and comments that contribute to a hostile working environment

simple agenda (p. 491) Agenda that outlines meeting goals without describing the sequence of meeting events

singular report (p. 303) One-time report designed to deal with specific issues and to aid in making specific decisions

skills tests (p. 578) Testing used by employers to measure the aptitudes and abilities of job applicants

solicited proposal (p. 410) Proposal submitted in response to a formal or informal request

speaking notes (p. 463) Abbreviated keyword outline designed to guide a speaker's actual delivery

special-occasion speech (p. 449) Address of presentation, acceptance, or commemoration

specific purpose (pp. 82, 449) Brief summary of the reason for which a document is written or an oral presentation is made

speech (p. 447) Highly structured form of address in which a speaker addresses an audience gathered to hear a message

speech tension (or *stage fright*) (p. 475) The body's "fight-or-flight" reaction to the stress of delivering an oral presentation or otherwise performing before an audience

spot table (p. 343) Unnumbered, untitled table included in the text of a document; ordinarily contains incidental data

statistics (p. 116, 317) Mathematical expressions that describe findings in an objective, uniform way and provide standards for determining whether those findings are valid measurements or chance occurrences

stereotype (p. 638) Distorting generalization based on the distinguishing characteristics of particular groups, including sex, race, physical appearance, occupation, and place of residence

strategic planning (p. 76) Process by which managers determine the major objectives of an organization and choose courses of action to achieve those objectives

stress interview (p. 559) Type of interview that test the reactions of job candidates by asking them to respond to difficult situations

style (p. 154) Distinctive method of expressing thought in writing or speech; refers to the *way* something is said or written rather than *what* is said or written

subdivided bar chart (p. 347) Diagram dividing each bar of a figure or a chart into components of a single item

subdivided column chart (p. 348) Diagram showing how the individual parts of a whole change over time

substitute-delivery letter (p. 246) Letter informing a customer that one item can be sent in place of another that is either temporarily out of stock or permanently out of inventory

subtext (p. 50) Unspoken language with the power to communicate meaning

summary (p. 386) Closing section of a report that condenses its most important information

surface chart (p. 350) Line chart that is shaded between the baseline and trend lines which add up to the uppermost line

survey (p. 324) Method of collecting primary data in which respondents' knowledge, attitudes, and opinions are assessed through interviews and questionnaires

table (p. 342) Systematic arrangement of data and/or words in rows and columns to provide readers with a fixed reference and a method of comparison

table of contents (p. 381) Front-matter list of a report's primary and secondary headings to provide readers with an overview of the material that follows

tactical planning (p. 76) Process by which objectives are translated into specific, achievable plans

targeted résumé (p. 532) Résumé that highlights abilities and achievements that relate to a specific job goal

technical plan (or work statement) (p. 413) Part of the body of the proposal that describes in detail the work that will be completed

telecommunications (p. 672) Process by which information is converted into electrical impulses transmitted through ordinary telephone or high-speed data lines and then reconverted by a receiver into usable information

telecommuter (p. 693) Worker who "travels" to and from a job by way of such sophisticated data-communications technology as electronic mail, voice mail, teleconferencing, answering machines, and telephone call-forwarding

teleconference (or conference call) (p. 684) Electronic meeting that uses ordinary telephone lines to bring together three or more people at various locations

terminal credibility (p. 39) Receiver's judgment of the sender after the message has been delivered

testimonial (p. 274) Words of praise for a firm, for its products, or for an idea generated by someone whose name or reputation the reader respects

time-series comparison (p. 345) Data-presentation technique that shows how items change over a specific time period, usually weeks, months, quarters, or years

title fly (p. 380) Optional opening page of a formal report that includes only the report title

title page (p. 380) Front-matter page of a formal report that usually includes the title, the name of the intended recipient, the author's name, and the submission date

topic sentence (p. 153) Sentence that states the purpose of a paragraph

transactional communication (p. 37) Communication involving two or more participants who react to one another in order to create meaning

transition (pp. 153, 460) Word, phrase, or sentence used to connect ideas and produce coherent paragraphs

transmittal letter (or cover letter) (p. 223) Informative letter accompanying materials sent from one person to another and providing written records that the materials have indeed been sent

trip report (p. 376) Short report that summarizes the events of a business trip

trouble report (p. 377) Short report that attempts to determine the cause of a problem and presents recommendations for solving it and preventing its recurrence

unsolicited proposal (p. 410) Proposal that has not been invited by the potential customer who receives it

upward communication (p. 13) Message flowing from a subordinate to a superior level of an organization

validity (p. 316) Extent to which a research study accurately measures what it was intended to measure

verbal signpost (p. 460) Brief statement that gives listeners "clues" to the organization and structure of a speech

videoconference (p. 686) Electronic meeting that allows participants in scattered geographic locations to hear and see one another on television monitors by way of images transmitted over telephone lines

visual aids (p. 340) Tables, charts, and illustrations used to present data in visually appealing and understandable ways

voice mail (p. 683) Computer-based call-processing system that handles both incoming and outgoing calls

voice quality (or *paralanguage*) (p. 473) Distinctive nature of a variety of voice elements, including loudness, pitch, rate, pauses, articulation, and pronunciation

word processor (p. 672) General-purpose desktop computer system used for a variety of sophisticated typewriter-like functions in creating, analyzing, and revising information documents

work environment (p. 524) Physical, social, cultural, and economic conditions that define the work place and its surroundings

work plan (p. 309) Document specifying work to be accomplished, the individuals to perform it, and completion deadlines for each phase of the project

"you" attitude (p. 156) Writing style that focuses on the reader rather than the writer

PHOTO CREDITS

CHAPTER OPENING PHOTOS

PHOTOS AND ART IN CHAPTERS

INTERVIEW PHOTOS